THE ENCYCLOPEDIA
OF YACHT DESIGNERS

THE ENCYCLOPEDIA
OF YACHT DESIGNERS

Created and Edited by Lucia del Sol Knight and Daniel Bruce MacNaughton

Foreword by Llewellyn Howland III

W. W. NORTON & COMPANY, INC. · NEW YORK · LONDON

The Encyclopedia of Yacht Designers
Lucia del Sol Knight and Daniel Bruce MacNaughton

Copyright 2006 by Lucia del Sol Knight
and Daniel Bruce MacNaughton
Foreword copyright 2006 by Llewellyn Howland III
Encyclopedia entries copyright by the individual authors
and reprinted with permission

All rights reserved
Printed in Italy
First Edition

Composed in Renaissance Antiqua and Optima,
both designed by Hermann Zapf
Manufacturing by Mondadori Printing, Verona
Book design and composition by Robert L. Wiser

Library of Congress Cataloging-in-Publication Data
Knight, Lucia del Sol.
The encyclopedia of yacht designers / created and edited
by Lucia del Sol Knight and Daniel Bruce MacNaughton ;
foreword by Llewellyn Howland III. — 1st ed.
p.   cm.
Includes bibliographical references and index.
ISBN 0-393-04876-4 (hardcover)
1. Yacht designers—Biography—Dictionaries.
I. MacNaughton, Daniel Bruce. II. Title.
VM139.K57 2006
623.82′023—dc22
2005020773

W. W. Norton & Company
500 Fifth Avenue, New York, NY 10110
www.wwnorton.com

W. W. Norton & Company Ltd.
Castle House, 75/76 Wells Street, London, W1T 3QT

1   3   5   7   9   8   6   4   2

CONTENTS

Foreword by Llewellyn Howland III

vii

Preface

viii

Acknowledgments

ix

Introduction

x

Subscribers

xii

**THE ENCYCLOPEDIA
OF YACHT DESIGNERS**

1

About the Writers

499

Index

502

DEDICATIONS

For my best friend Bob,

who many years ago transformed my life by taking me sailing

among so many other things.

Lucia del Sol Knight

Brooksville, Maine · January 2005

For my parents,

Donald Wesley MacNaughton and Naida Sanders MacNaughton.

From their calm and sincere hearts

they taught me to love boats, people, and life.

There could be no greater gift.

Daniel MacNaughton

Eastport, Maine · November 2004

FOREWORD

In eighteenth-century France, when Denis Diderot and his confreres compiled the first modern encyclopedia, the world's useful knowledge could be contained in thirty-five folio volumes of text and copper-engraved plates. From architecture to zoology, from Abu Bakr to Zeno of Citium, it was all there on the printed page, finely bound in three-quarter morocco. What was not included was not knowledge.

Alas, knowledge seems to expand in inverse proportion to our ability to understand or make use of it. The more we know, the less. And the less we know, the more we struggle to overcome our ignorance.

There was a time when I thought I knew a great deal about yacht design. Well, maybe not about the mathematics or physics of yacht design, but at least about the art of it. I also thought I knew a great deal about yacht designers. Had I not bought and sold and read and edited books by and about them? Had I not written at length about such giants as Starling Burgess, Francis Herreshoff, Walter McInnis, A. Cary Smith? Did I not count several designers among my cherished friends? Just as important, had I not for more than half a century obsessively studied the design pages of every yachting and boating magazine I could lay my hands on, including the earliest issues of *Aquatic Monthly* and *Forest and Stream* (and not forgetting that rarest of all American yachting periodicals, *The American Yachtsman*, which first appeared in all its lavish splendor in February 1887 only to vanish without a trace the following June)? The answer in every instance: yes, yes, and yes again.

But then came the morning in 1997 when Mainers Lucia and Bob Knight and Dan MacNaughton paid me a visit in Jamaica Plain to discuss an idea that Lucia had for a book. Her idea, improbably enough, was to compile a biographical dictionary of yacht designers. An *encyclopedia* of yacht designers, if you can credit such a thing. Might such a venture be editorially and financially feasible, Lucia and Bob and Dan wanted to know? And, assuming that they could find a publisher for such an undertaking, might I be willing to contribute a brief biographical entry or two—and could I suggest others who also might be interested in contributing?

Advice, like the common cold, is easy to give, hazardous to receive, and generally hell to live with. Having never compiled an encyclopedia on any subject and having not the slightest ambition to do so, I assured Lucia and Bob and Dan that sure, I thought an encyclopedia of yacht designers might be, in the argot of the book trade, commercially viable. I also suggested that it might be, in the argot of the book trade, a challenging project.

As to which yacht designers rated a place in the encyclopedia, I saw no problem. I mean, how many American and English yacht designers of consequence have there ever been? A hundred and fifty? Two hundred? As to rating the designers and then commissioning biographies of appropriate length, again, where was the problem? Give the Herreshoffs, the Burgesses, the Fifes, Charles E. Nicholson, George Watson, and Olin J. Stephens the most space. Give lesser designers less space. The rest would just be filling orders and banking large royalty checks.

When I spoke of 150 to 200 entries, Lucia mentioned the likelihood that the book might include yacht designers currently practicing, as well as those retired or deceased. She also spoke of including designers from throughout the world. Designers who specialized in large motoryachts, as well as designers who seldom worked on boats larger than twenty or thirty feet. She and Bob and Dan began mentioning names I'd never heard of in countries where the largest body of water was no bigger than a bathtub. The prospect was dizzying. The time was late. I bade good-bye to the *encyclopédistes* from Maine and went out for a jog to clear my head.

An encyclopedia of yacht designers? Madame Knight, you must be sniffing glue.

Ten years, 87 of the world's finest yachting writers, 525 of the world's best yacht designers, 650 drawings and photos of representative yacht designs, and uncounted thousands of hours, letters, e-mails, faxes, phone calls, and driving, sailing, and flying miles later, Lucia del Sol Knight's idea has become a reality. Not just a reality, but also arguably the most useful, most comprehensive, most important one-volume work of yachting history ever published in any language. Truly, *The Encyclopedia of Yacht Designers* is a publishing miracle. All students and lovers of yacht design, all serious followers of the sport of yachting or recreational boating will need to own and to study it. Periodically revised and updated, it should remain a standard reference for decades to come.

Although I can take no credit for the creation of this wonderful book, I am honored to have a place in it. I am grateful to find in its pages so many of the great, the worthy, and the undeservedly forgotten men (and women, though too few) who have dedicated their lives to one of the most difficult, most demanding, and least remunerative of all professions. I only pray that in Valhalla yacht designers of earlier generations will take pleasure in browsing these pages, recalling old friendships and rivalries, revisiting old triumphs and controversies, and realizing just how much their art and example have contributed to the greatest sport in the world.

—Llewellyn Howland III

PREFACE

With the help of literally hundreds of people, we are proud to launch *The Encyclopedia of Yacht Designers.* The book recognizes 525 designers from around the world who have shaped the field of yacht design over the last two hundred years. It is drawn from the vast knowledge of people who have not only enthusiastically shared what they know but have done so for the pleasure of expanding all of our horizons.

My own horizons have been greatly expanded since 1994 when, as a consequence of buying our fourth boat, I tried to learn more about yacht designers. I could not find a book about designers, and so decided to fill the vacuum by creating it myself. By persuading my old friend and former colleague Dan MacNaughton to help, I knew we had a chance to write and publish the book I envisioned. Dan brought to this partnership a fine style of writing and lifelong knowledge of boats, and working together we've seen the vision evolve and mature.

In 1994, Dan and I devised a working plan. I would assemble a list of potential designers to include in the *EYD*, have the list vetted by Jon Wilson and Joel White, and research the chosen designers, and Dan would write the entries. This worked quite well for the first few years, but by the time we turned our attention to designers outside the United States, we had to face the reality that we lacked access to the research materials necessary for well-rounded and accurate entries. We needed foreign writers. Fortunately, we were able to enlist most writers to contribute to our book, for the good of the field of yacht design and a copy of the *EYD*.

Our most ardent supporter, Louie Howland, shared his worldwide contacts with us, and we enlisted writers and Editorial Board members from the United States, France, the Netherlands, Australia, and Great Britain. Since then our Editorial Board has grown to thirty-three, and the number of writers involved has grown from one to eighty-seven.

After the entries were written, editing each one proved time-consuming. Dan and I exchanged much back-and-forth with the writers, and when the entries seemed up to snuff, we sent them forth to the Editorial Board for review. Through the exceptional perseverance of the few and the authority of the many, we are now confident that the entries are as complete, solid, and comprehensive as they can be.

By 2001 we were ready to begin the search for illustrations for the entries, which was the second enormous challenge we faced. We estimated we would use between six and seven hundred photos and drawings to supplement the text, and that many would be copyrighted, requiring payments and permissions. Again Louie Howland provided a solution to the fairly monumental task of raising the money needed: we would sell "subscriptions." Our two hundred Subscribers have truly enabled this encyclopedia to demonstrate with images the achievements of the designers.

Of course Dan and I underestimated how long it would take to write an encyclopedia. In January of 1997, our W. W. Norton editor, Jim Mairs, asked how long we thought it would take. I remember shrugging my shoulders and saying, "Two years?" "Good," he said. How we struggled to meet this deadline, but it was not until the spring of 2004 that Dan and I were finally able to turn to each other and say with awe, "Hey, we did it—the encyclopedia is done!"
—Lucia del Sol Knight

When Lucia and I agreed to create *The Encyclopedia of Yacht Designers*, one of the biggest reasons was that we wanted to do something together utilizing the talents we had observed and respected in each other over many years of friendship. The payoff for that part of the idea has been handsome for both of us, and for our families. Sailing as we were into unknown waters, it has been a much longer voyage than we anticipated, in the great tradition of epic voyages. But as is often the case, the rewards from that voyage have been different, and deeper, than we could ever have known at the outset.

We started with the idea that we might make money with the *EYD*. When we realized how much larger the project was than we had first envisioned, we had to search our souls, take a deep breath, and renew our commitment to an endeavor that, barring some miracle, could not possibly compensate us financially for our investment of time. But that is what we did, and we've never regretted it.

Between the lines of this book lie countless evenings of wonderful conversation between us and our family members, friends, and associates, many days of exciting travel, many days of sailing, boat shopping and repair, many hours of tear-streaming laughter, and all the victories, defeats, conflicts, devastating losses, and personal growth that ten years of life bring, all shared. We are glad to be done, just as we are glad to pick up our moorings at the end of a long cruise, but as with a cruise, the trip has been its own reward, and I think we will sail together again.

My work on this book consisted of a good part of my spare time over an eventful decade during which I worked first in a boatyard I owned along with my family, then in a plastic fiber factory resembling something out of Steinbeck or Dickens, and now, in one of Maine's best wooden boatbuilding yards. My day-to-day life has of necessity been dominated more by those jobs and the many personal episodes of those years, than by this project. So despite the fact that my name appears on the cover of the *EYD* along with Lucia's, let there be no mistake—the initial idea, the vast majority of the hours, most of the planning, all of the expense, and virtually all of the blood, toil, tears, and sweat of producing this book are hers. In the history of yachting there have been a number of publishers and editors who, through their sincerity, natural ability, and bulldog determination, have helped to clarify, consolidate, and invigorate the "Art and Science of Yacht Design." Beside C. P. Kunhardt, W. P. Stephens, William Atkin, Maurice Griffiths, Thomas Fleming Day, Boris Lauer-Leonardi, Charles Mower, and Jonathan Wilson let history record, Lucia del Sol Knight. This is her book.
—Daniel B. MacNaughton

ACKNOWLEDGMENTS

A BOOK OF THIS MAGNITUDE could not have been written without the help of many people. Our thirty-three-member Editorial Board continuously guided our work; our eighty-seven writers completed their work with skill and good cheer; and our two hundred Subscribers made it possible for us to produce a book profusely illustrated.

Additionally, some very significant people were involved from the start and helped a great deal to shape the EYD. They include Rutger ten Broeke, Volker Christmann, Llewellyn Howland III, David Payne, Thomas G. Skahill, Jacques Taglang, and Bob Wallstrom.

Other influential people who were generous with their time and knowledge are Bent Aarre, Kurt Hasselbalch, Virginia Crowell Jones, Harold Kidd, Bette Kough Noble, Claas van der Linde, Iain McAllister, J. Scott Rohrer, John Rousmaniere, David Ryder-Turner, BG Thorpe, and Cynthia Voigt.

Along the way, we were fortunate to have the assistance of Mary Babcock, Peter Barlow, Maria Bernier, Barbara Bishop, Barney Boardman, Betsy Braunhut, Anne and Maynard Bray, Andre ten Broeke, Blanka ten Broeke, Philip Budlong, John S. Carter, Marcus Chevreux, Charles Chiodi, William Collier, Michael Collins and Bonnie Bird, Nic Compton, Chris Curioli, Helen and George Cuthbertson, Will Dallimore, Anne Davidson, Charles Dawson, Adrienne d'Entremont, Peter d'Entremont, Mike and Tony Dixon, Roger F. Duncan, Thomas R. Dyer, E. Weston Farmer Jr., Sturgis Haskins, Kennosuke Hayashi, Elma and Mike Henry, Arthur R. Herrick Jr., Anita Jacobson, James Jermain, Sir Peter Johnson, Bob Johnstone, Bruce and Pamela King, Jesse and Manami Knight, Tapani Koskela, Kristin and Udo Lammerting, John Lammerts van Bueren, Anthony L. Leggett, Harvey Loomis, Patricia J. Loun, Ruth Lowell, Gunilla and Ulf Lycke, Nancy Lynch, Tom MacNaughton, Ross MacTaggart, Olle Madebrink, James L. Mairs, Anita Mason, Cathy Matero, Duncan McIntosh, Ann and David Montgomery, Adrian Morgan, Marilyn Mower, Matt Murphy, Ian Nicolson, Chris Noble, Jeremy Noble, Tom Nye, Jay and Phyllis Paris, Robert Paulig, Rosemary Poole, Betsy Powell, Greg Pugh, Tom and Lucie Roach, Sydney Rockefeller, Chet Sawtelle, Monica Schroderus, Colin and Angela Shannon, Victoria Sharps, Kerstin Simberg, Margaret Tate Smith, Timothy K. Smith, Jack A. Somer, Peter Spectre, Elliott Speer, Sherry Streeter, Corinne Sucsy, Luce Taglang, Gene Trainor, Marifrances Trivelli, Jennifer Trowbridge, William and Miriam Truslow, Charles Van Patten III, Pat Wallstrom, John Walsted, Gabryella Wasowicz, Ann Wattson, Joel White, Brook Wilensky-Lanford, Jon Wilson, Robert L. Wiser, and Masumi Yamaoka.

And finally, our thanks to the Internet and to the fortunate fact that so many people from around the world speak such good English.

INTRODUCTION

THAT OFTEN-SEEN PHRASE "The Art and Science of Yacht Design" comes close to being a cliché, but it is hard to avoid because it is inherent in the peculiar nature of the field. Where possible in *The Encyclopedia of Yacht Designers* we have tried to identify the extent to which each designer is known as an artist or a technician, or more rarely, as both.

There has always been room in the field for artistry, and there always will. A person with experience of the kind of boat he or she wishes to design can, by following tradition, scantlings rules, and rules of thumb, produce a strong, seaworthy boat that can be made to sail or motor properly, without being any kind of engineer or technical innovator at all. If he has the gift for aesthetics, he might make a career of it and might well find a devoted following and a place in history. Nobody dislikes a beautiful boat, and there is always room for another one even if it explores often-visited ground. After all, art is often a subtle thing, and is not always about breakthroughs.

It is also remarkable how often a good-looking boat is, in fact, good at everything her visual personality suggests she would be. I believe this is because the lines of any hull and the proportions of a sailboat's rig speak to parts of the human mind that are older, deeper, and calmer than the parts of our mind that habitually deal with our modern, day-to-day lives. After all, the world we live in is largely a world we human beings have built. It is not the world we evolved to live in—that world is wilder and more primitive, and full of elemental forces. It is made up of fundamentally beautiful things. Our species evolved over millions of years to live and work in that world, and we are very, very good at it still, when we get the chance. That is the world in which we invented ships and then discovered the beauty that lay within them, like the pot that lives in the clay. Today the beauty of a ship is a thing almost anyone can understand. I hope that with the *EYD* we have honored the artists who have practiced yacht design, and I hope that yachtsmen and society as a whole will always honor them.

The history of yachting, however, is mostly written about those designers who innovated technically, and thereby won races. And this may not be unfair—the beauty of a given boat and the satisfaction she brings to her owners may be the achievement of a lifetime, but it is the type of achievement that lives only in the boat itself and a few people's hearts. It can be described and recorded, but it is not the stuff of newspaper headlines. So there is much broader discussion of the inventors—the victors on the battlefield of the yacht racing course.

The great virtue of racing as an influence on the field is its inherent emphasis on technical excellence. In a process resembling natural selection, boats that win are copied, while boats that lose are not. If a boat that wins is ugly, it is a minor problem and she may even achieve a sort of radicalistic panache as a result. Over the years technical innovations have come through both instinct and research, but the consistent winners have been those with the best science.

A review of yachting history reveals that most successful innovations in yacht design are rooted in superior structural engineering, and superior engineering often consists of the early and appropriate adoption of improved materials, whether the invention is steam-bent oak frames, bronze screws, welded steel, extruded aluminum, epoxy glue, or, perhaps soon, carbon nanotubes. In most cases improved yacht construction has been all about the search for a higher strength-to-weight ratio. In racing classes where the rules suggest a certain overall weight for the boat, a boat built of lighter materials can have more weight in ballast, which makes her faster. In classes where there is no weight restriction, lighter boats are usually faster boats. Since boats, first power and then sail, began to plane across the surface of the water, the emphasis on weight reduction has received even greater emphasis. A close look at what we now think of as heavy older yachts will often reveal consistent efforts to reduce weight, within the technological limitations of their day. In cruising boats, heavy displacement is often a desirable feature, but even then, construction that allows weight to be shifted from structure to ballast can make a better boat.

The influence of racing on yacht design has not been all positive. The ability to perceive the legitimacy of each innovation has always been clouded by the influence of the various handicapping rules under which most boats have been raced since the beginning. Handicapping rules are employed in an attempt to allow boats of disparate size and type to compete on an equal footing, placing the emphasis on the skill of the skippers and crews. From the moment boats began to be built to compete under an existing rule, their designers had to find and exploit the weak points of that rule: to make the boat fast without the rule detecting it or, describing the same effort in less appealing terms, to fool the rule into thinking the boat was slower than it was.

In almost every case each rule has eventually encouraged a distorted type of boat in which glaring faults are tolerated because they were necessary in order to win races. It has always been difficult for the general public to tell what is a legitimate speed-producing innovation and what is a rule-induced distortion, and before long "high performance cruising boats" begin to display both kinds of characteristics, evolving in some senses but heading down evolutionary dead-ends in others. Like a law of nature it has always been so and will remain so until someday, perhaps soon with the help of technology, a truly objective handicapping system is developed. The *EYD* is meant to clarify and celebrate excellence in technical design, whether it is in the always-necessary efforts to beat handicapping rules or in the more straightforward development of designs that are truly better for their intended purposes.

An important principle, well illustrated by the field of yacht design, is that within each new material or each new technical evolution there lies the potential for beauty, perhaps even a whole new aesthetic genre. Revolutionary yachts have brought such features as cutaway forefoots, multiple hulls, Marconi rigs, light displacement, reverse sheer, synthetic materials, and so on, and most have been condemned on aesthetic grounds when they first appeared, but within a few years there has always developed a sense of proportion, a standard of finish, and a modernistic aesthetic that expresses and fulfills the potential within the new.

When we look for the real giants of the field, we find those individuals who have done all of the above, producing technically superior yachts that were breathtakingly beautiful in both their modernity and in whatever of their lines descended from what had gone before.

We give more space to the giants, as one must, but we also mean to celebrate the work of those who made good yachts even if they did not make history. Many are the obscure designs that have something worth recapturing, and many are the boats afloat today which, like any works of art, may be valued all the more if something is known of their creators. We have tried to find and preserve this information.

The *EYD* is a reference book recording in one source much of the history of yachting. In the course of putting it together Lucia and I have gained a sense of historical perspective that is hard to acquire without having undertaken such a detailed study. One of the things that we have learned and that we hope the readers will perceive is that many inventions appear over and over again. Some, like extreme fin-and-bulb sailboat keels, seem to have been invented long ago but have been waiting for construction technology capable of making them strong. Others, like clever and functional forward-facing rowing devices, have been invented

in various forms numerous times but have achieved only limited popularity, perhaps because, despite the obvious drawback of facing aft while rowing, an oar is a superbly simple and logical device in the form it has known for centuries. Likewise there has always been a tendency for racing sailboat hulls to get wide, flat, and light in the search for speed, until the safety issues become so apparent that a rule is made pulling the acceptable limits back within logical bounds. With a new rule or a new generation of sailors the cycle begins again. As the saying goes, "Those who fail to study history are doomed to repeat it." We hope that the *EYD* will help to establish an historical context from which yacht design may progress in more of a straight line.

Like every field today, it seems, yacht design is going through a period of intense development as we come to grips with the changes resulting from revolutionary information-processing technology. As I write this, nearly everyone in the field is seeking the right balance between the proven and aesthetically pleasing traditional tools of yacht design, the splines and spline weights, the drafting pencils and inking pens, the ships curves, planimeters, drafting tables, drafting machines, vellum and the like, and the computers and remarkable new software that can do so much, so fast. We are at risk of losing the warmth and personality of both the drawings and the boats even as we are assured of increased accuracy and more rapid and reliable evolution. The balance between art and science is a dynamic one, and each designer must choose his tools and find his niche. Better tools can serve both art and science in the hands of a master, or they can simply produce bad work in more quantity. There is no substitute for care.

Those of us who grow up with boats often do so in relative isolation, and like any provincials we acquire prejudices, even if they are based on ignorance rather than ill will. I have found that exposure to other points of view has expanded my appreciation of yacht design in its many permutations, and my lifelong interest in the field has become much deeper and broader as a result. Things I thought I knew for sure, I now must say are theories. Things I have disliked, I now must say don't work "in my experience." But we never have to abandon our affection for anything we love, and with understanding comes the ability to love more things. Over the years I've come to believe that learning and loving are intertwined in every sense. Certainly writing the *EYD* has been all about both, and I hope that reading it will be, too.

—Daniel B. MacNaughton

SUBSCRIBERS

Douglas D. Adkins
John G. Alden, Naval Architects
Rex Alison
Dennis C. Amendola
Antique Boat Museum, Clayton, NY
John D. Atkin (1918–1999)
Australian National Maritime Museum

B. Devereux Barker III
Peter Barlow
Todd Bassett & Lee Taylor
Jay R. Benford
Pol Bergius
Bill Bickley
Martin Black
Jon & Susan Blake
Albert Barnes Boardman III
Phil Bolger & Susanne Altenburger
Kim & Susan Bottles
Anne & Maynard Bray
Rutger & Blanka ten Broeke
Roger A. Burke
Charles Butt

Roc & Helen Caivano
Stephen C. Calhoun
John S. Carter
Rand Castile
Harlen Chapman
Chesapeake Bay Maritime Museum
Volker Christmann
William E. Clapp
Classic Boat Magazine
Robert M. Clements
Henry A. Clews
Andrew Coffey
George W. Cole
Paolo Corzetto
D. Joshua Cutler

Charles A. Dana III
John R. Daverman
John David
Susan Nelson Davis
George P. Denny III
Peter & Ann Louise d'Entremont
Richard John Derby
David Dickmeyer
Sue Drew
Bartlett S. Dunbar

Eastern Yacht Club
Tim Eastland
Frank Eberhart
Tuck Elfman
Ben & Dianna Emory
John Engel

Tom Fexas
Fiberglass Specialties of Lake Tahoe
Flat Hammock Press
Terry Fong/AFA Photography
Germán Frers
Egmont Friedl
Ed Fry
JoAnne & Richard Fuerst
Benjamin A. G. Fuller

G. W. Blunt White Library,
    Mystic Seaport Museum
Martin Gellert & Jackie Michaud
Jessica M. Goodwin
Austin Goodyear
Meade Gougeon
Alan J. Granby
Uwe Greinert
Bernard H. Gustin

William A. Hall
R. Bruce Jr. & Alicia Hammatt
Tonia & Cy Hannon
Jack Harley
Hart Nautical Collections, MIT Museum
Charles L. Hatton
Kennosuke Hayashi
Joachim A. Heitmann
Robert M. Helsell
Jean & Don Higgins
Steve & Julie Hintz
Ron Holland
Frederick E. (Ted) Hood
Joseph C. Hoopes Jr.
Llewellyn Howland III
Hudson Fisheries Trust, Inc.
Jack E. Hunter Jr.

Independence Seaport Museum,
    Philadelphia
International Yacht Restoration School
    (IYRS)

O. Joan Jardine-Brown
Mr. & Mrs. Stephen B. Jeffries
Gary Jobson
Martin Joffe
Jon B. Johansen
Carol John
Malcolm Johnston
Peter & Hadley Johnstone
Robert L. Johnstone III
Douglas P. Jones
Gregory O. Jones
Gwyndaf M. Jones
Terrence Jones
Virginia Crowell Jones
Michael F. Joyce

Walter C. Keenan IV
Charles W. Knight (1911–1994)
Jesse Benton Knight

Kristin & Udo Lammerting
William W. Lamprell Jr.
William W. Lamprell Sr. (1922–1998)
Lawley Boat Owners Association
Legendary Yachts, Inc.
Steve K. LeLacheur
Claas van der Linde
Nicholas J. Lockyer
Beal Lowen & Carol Brayton
Walfun & Judy Luey

Julie Mackie
Maine Boats & Harbors
James L. Mairs
Mariners' Museum, Newport News
Patrick D. Matthiesen
John Mayer
Iain McAllister
Brian V. S. McKenna
Michael & Debbie McMenemy
Jacques Mégroz
Marinus Meijers
C. G. Mellevold
Benjamin Mendlowitz
Captain Richards T. Miller, USN (Ret.)
Stephen & Rebecca Milliken
Silvia Minas
Channing C. Moser

New York Yacht Club
George Nicholson
Peter Nitze
Chris & Bette Noble

Christopher I. Page
Frank & Katrina Parson
Laszlo Pataki
David Payne
William M. Peterson
Philadelphia Wooden Boat Factory
Frederico Pinheiro de Melo
Thomas S., Jr., & Nancy G. Post

John S. Rando Jr.
Lukas Reimbold
Jean-Marc Ritzenthaler
Kurt & Sally Rivard
Tom Roach & Lucie Edwards
Tad Roberts
John Rock
Thomas O. Rodes
J. Scott Rohrer
Lester Rosenblatt
Thomas A. Rothschild
Jake & Sally Roulstone
John Rousmaniere

Matteo Salamon
Scanship Maritime Archive
Frank & Axel Schattauer Sails
Nicholas Schaus
Seawanhaka Corinthian Yacht Club
John R. Sherwood III
ShowBoats International Magazine
Thomas G. Skahill
Philip, Dorsey & Stephen Smith
Theodore F. Smolen & Anne M. Billert
Brian R. Snow
South Street Seaport Museum
Sparkman & Stephens
J. T. (Tommy) Spinosa
Zlatko Stojanovic

Jacques Taglang
Taylor & Rhyneer Families
Richard S. Taylor
Walter Teller
Charles Tetro & Teeter Bibber
Alix Thorne
Liffey Thorpe & Peter Suber
Robert & Elizabeth Tiedemann
Donald Tofias
Gene Trepte
Alex Turner

David Urmston & Suzy Katsuda

Dr. Armand Versaci
Cynthia & Walter Voigt

H. E. Scott Welch
Joel White (1930–1997)
Pip & Judy Wick
David & Mary Jo Wilcox
Jon Wilson & Sherry Streeter
Allen Winston
Mrs. Estelle Wittholz
Walter O. & Audrey Wittholz
WoodenBoat Publications
Thomas Wylie

A. Yokoyama

BJARNE AAS

1886–1969 · Norway

The beautiful and competitive International One-Design class is Bjarne Aas's most famous creation, and it stems from his early success in the design of International Rule meter boats. His boats were beautiful and seaworthy, and they were fast, especially in heavy weather.

During the 1920's and 1930's, in Scandinavia as elsewhere in Europe, the 6- and 8-Meter classes dominated both regional and international yacht racing. From 1924 through 1936 both classes competed in the Olympic Games, and until the advent of the Star in 1932, they were the only Olympic keelboat classes. This domination of the racing arena nurtured intense competition not only among yachtsmen, some of whom purchased new boats almost annually in search of the slightest advantage, but also among the designers who created boats for this dynamic and lucrative market. In Bjarne Aas and his rival, Johan Anker, Norway contributed two of the most significant designers in the International Rule classes.

Having qualified as an engineer at the Horten Technical School in 1906, Aas entered employment as a mechanical engineer and designer for boatyards, first in Trondheim, then in Bergen. Ultimately he ended up at Fredrikstad in southern Norway, close to the Swedish border.

In 1917 Aas started a boatyard at Asgard, Krakeroy, a Fredrikstad island, and for the next forty years, until he retired in 1957, he designed a long series of boats, among them winners of Olympic medals, the Gold Cup, and the One-Ton Cup. Aas's international breakthrough came in 1922 at races in Copenhagen,

Bjarne Aas: *If* (opposite). The 8-Meter *If*, slipping upwind in light air, leaves almost no sign of her passage through the water. International Rule yachts are usually excellent performers in a wide range of conditions, and Aas was one of the masters of the genre. © *Beken of Cowes*

Denmark, where he won with *Askeladden* in the 6-Meter class. His 6-Meter *Elisabeth V* won a gold medal in the sailing Olympics held at Le Havre, France, in 1924.

For many years, Aas was the dominant designer and builder in the 5.5-Meter class as well as the 6-Meter class. He designed and built at least forty 6-Meters for Scandinavian customers, including several for Crown Prince Olav of Norway and five for the Danish yachtsman William Vett. Aas was also well known in other countries, including the United States. In 1936 Aas moved his yard to Isegran, an old naval base near the town of Fredrikstad.

The Internationals (as the International One-Designs are known) were the result of a commission given to Aas in 1936 by a group of yachtsmen from New York, led by Cornelius Shields Sr. A well-known American racing helmsman, Shields was quite taken with an Aas-designed 6-Meter named *Saga*, then racing in Bermuda. The syndicate asked Aas for a modified one-design version with a small cabin. In 1937 Shields's syndicate took delivery of twenty-five Internationals on Long Island Sound, and a group of yachtsmen in Bermuda ordered seven more. Soon there were fleets in Norway and in Northeast Harbor, Maine.

The International was specifically designed to be both beautiful and a good performer, while retaining the wholesome and seaworthy characteristics of the meter boats of the day. This combination surely explains her great popularity. Another key to her success is the strictness of the class rules, which govern even the cut of the sails. This has the effect of keeping older boats competitive, and holds the line on the cost of a successful campaign.

The original Internationals were impeccably constructed with full-length, glued Oregon pine planking at Aas's own yard at Isegran. Before the Nazis invaded Norway at the beginning of World War II, 85 identical Internationals had been built. To protect the building

molds during the war, Aas buried them in a salt marsh. After the war, the molds were salvaged and construction began again. In all, over 150 Internationals were built by Aas. In addition to the fleets in Bermuda, Norway, and the United States, the class spread to Sweden and Scotland, and the first World Championship was held in 1959.

As boatbuilding technologies of the late 1950's and early 1960's squeezed out wooden boat construction in favor of fiberglass, Aas steadfastly continued to build only wooden Internationals. Norway's fleet began to scatter and deteriorate. Following Aas's death in 1969, his son, Henrik, produced a fiberglass mold to the same specifications as the wooden boat, but production costs were too high for the venture to be successful. The fiberglass mold came to the United States in the 1970's, and despite a fire that destroyed the mold, the idea took root, new molds were made, and a whole new group of glass boats came into being. Today, the International One-Design World Class Association authorizes two builders for the class: C. W. Hood Yachts in Marblehead and Tjorns Yacht Service in Gothenburg, Sweden.

The World Championship, which had lapsed, was revived in 1982. Today there are ten active fleets in five countries, with wooden and fiberglass boats racing on an equal footing. Used Internationals rarely come on the market, and when they do, they command high prices, as befits a universally acknowledged classic.

Aas was also a keen designer of motorboats. His design for *Tjerne* started production in 1937. He was instrumental in improving the performance of the Chris-Craft gasoline engines that were being imported from the United States. As well, he designed fishing vessels and rescue craft, and took out many patents for his innovations. He was one of the brains behind the CR (Cruiser/Racer) Rule of 1950, which sought to encourage the production of yachts that were suitable for both cruising and ocean racing.

Bjarne Aas: International One-Design. The 1936 design for the International One-Design was inspired by that of *Saga*, one of the many 6-Meters Aas drew. While his 6-Meters were of necessity designed to exploit a rule, the International had only to combine beauty, speed, seaworthiness, and practicality. © *Mystic Seaport, Rosenfeld Collection, Mystic, CT, Image acquired in honor of Hudson H. Bubar*

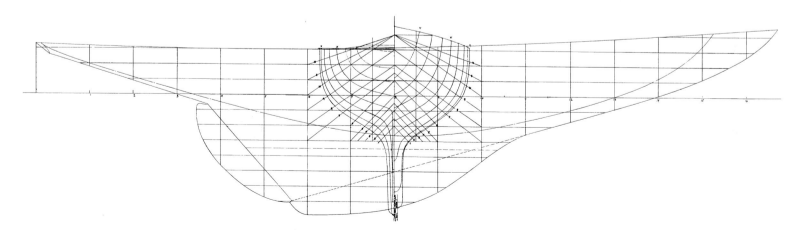

Bjarne Aas: International One-Design. The International One-Design performs well under a wide range of conditions. Her lines show a minimal wetted surface area for speed in light air, while her sections suggest power without pounding in a bay chop. A deep keel, narrow hull, and long, well-shaped ends make her fast upwind in a breeze. *Drawing courtesy International One-Design World Class Association*

In its coastal heritage center at Isegran, the Fredrikstad Museum features Aas's masterpieces, the 6-Meter *Askeladden* and the International One-Design *Huttetu*, both fully restored and actively raced as sailing ambassadors celebrating Isegran's heritage and the designing skills of Bjarne Aas.

—Bent Aarre, Chris Ennals, and Daniel B. MacNaughton

ABEKING AND RASMUSSEN

see Henry Rasmussen

JOE ADAMS

Born 1931 · Australia

This versatile Sydney-based designer has made his mark with a family of fast, easily sailed keelboats and offshore racers with a distinctive style that is instantly recognizable: light, narrow, easily driven hulls with fractional or double headsail rigs.

The meter series includes the popular Adams 8- and Adams 10-Meter boats, simple and fast day boats with the ability to make occasional passages. Adams's long waterline hulls ignore the IOR rating rules and have gained popularity among shorthanded and singlehanded racers, while his larger designs have campaigned in the Melbourne-Osaka two-hander and the BOC Singlehanded Around the World Race.

In Australia, Adams is known for "The Flying Footpath," a ferrocement boat named *Helsal*. Light despite her construction, she was entered in the 1973 Sydney-Hobart Race and broke the eleven-year-old elapsed time record. Among his more mainstream designs are family boats such as the Careel 22 and Mottle 33, both of which enjoyed long production runs, and the versatile steel Adams 40, aimed at the do-it-yourselfer. Well over 150 Adams 40's have been built.

—Jeffrey Mellefont

CARL A. ALBERG

1900–1986 · Sweden/United States

In his independent design work, Carl Alberg is remembered for a number of successful wooden ocean racers and cruising yachts, and for his many wholesome, moderate, and sensible fiberglass cruising sailboats such as the Cape Dory line and the Alberg 35. He is also known for his work in the John G. Alden design office in Boston.

Alberg was born in the city of Gothenburg on the west coast of the Swedish peninsula. There, he studied naval architecture at Chalmers Institute of Technology. At age twenty-five he emigrated to the United States, where he worked at several Massachusetts shipyards, such as George Lawley and Son in Neponset and Bethlehem Steel's Fore River plant in Quincy.

While a sparmaker at the Lawley yard, Alberg met John Alden, who hired him as a

Joe Adams: Adams 10-Meter. Light, narrow, and easily driven—that's the Joe Adams recipe, typified by the Adams 10-Meter class. Well supported from the start, it now has nearly three decades of strong competition behind it. *Photo courtesy David Payne*

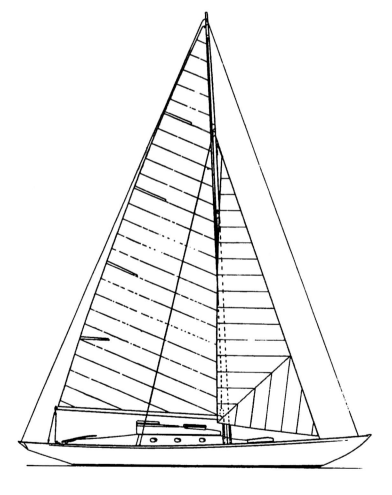

Carl Alberg: *Corinne III.* The handsome 34-foot *Corinne III* was the 1934 lottery boat of the Swedish Cruising Club. Sailing clubs raised money from these lotteries, and lucky winners might be someone who otherwise could not afford to buy such a vessel. © *Tony Dixon*

draftsman in 1929; he remained at the Alden office for twelve years. He drew the lines for many successful and well-remembered yachts such as the beautiful 53-foot yawl *Tioga Too* and the 39-foot ketch *Staghound*, two-time winner of the Transpacific Race in 1953 and 1955. His work at Alden's office stands out because of the clean, modern look of both the drawings and the boats, an overall moderation of proportion, and an inclination toward simple shapes that nonetheless convey personality.

Alberg served in the U.S. Navy during World War II, designing conversions of yachts and fishing vessels into mine sweepers and patrol boats. Following the war, he returned to the Alden office. He opened his own design office in Boston in 1946. Two years later, he formed a partnership with yacht broker and insurance agent Lawrence J. Brengle Jr.

The next few years saw a number of successful designs including the 52-foot yawl *Katuna* in 1948 and the 67-foot yawl *Sea Lion* in 1952. These were featured in *The Rudder* and *Yachting* magazines for a number of years. During the Korean War he worked at the Charleston Shipyard, after which he joined the U.S. Coast Guard as chief marine engineer and architect. For the next ten years he turned out many designs in his spare time.

Alberg's 28-foot fiberglass Triton began its production run in 1959 when it became the first boat offered by Pearson Yachts. By 1967, when production stopped, 707 Tritons had been built. The Alberg 30, based on Alberg's earlier wooden Odyssey design, proved popular on San Francisco Bay. Whitby Boat Works built more than 710 between 1962 and 1983.

The Alberg 35, built by Pearson, is another wholesome, early fiberglass cruiser that is much sought after today. Also well known is the Pearson Ensign, which came out in 1962 and grew to be the largest class of one-design full-keel racing boats in the United States, numbering 1,600. The Ensign (hull designed by Alberg, with the cockpit, cabin, and deck arrangement designed by Everett Pearson) originally appeared as the interesting but little-known Electra, which has a longer cabin trunk on the same hull.

Alberg retired from the Coast Guard in 1963 and began his work for Cape Dory Yachts. He began with the 19-foot full-keel Typhoon and the Cape Dory 28. The series eventually included ten designs up to 45 feet in length. The Cape Dory line quickly achieved a good reputation among experienced cruising sailors and was also popular with former wooden boat owners. The line became known for its "normal" good looks, comfort, and ease of handling, combined with good construction and quality hardware.

The term *classic* is seldom applied to boats of fiberglass construction, but it is often used to describe Alberg's fiberglass designs. Older fiberglass Albergs typically have few sharp angles in their deck structures. One surface blends into the next through a large radius curve, avoiding difficult lay-up work and stress concentrations and resulting in a somewhat old-fashioned streamlined look that is nonetheless highly appropriate to the construction. Alberg boats are usually of heavier-than-average displacement, creating a steadier, more comfortable motion underway, and they tend to be of full-keel, attached rudder configuration, which is easier on the helmsman and makes the boats more controllable in heavy weather. These features, which most people find desirable, are rare in fiberglass boats and may be another reason why Albergs are still in demand.

Alberg died in Marblehead, Massachusetts. He had drawn the designs for fifty-six yachts from which about ten thousand boats were built.

Carl Alberg: *Catspaw.* The 19-foot Cape Dory Typhoon is a strong, safe, well-proportioned family daysailer and weekender that has proved to be one of Alberg's most popular designs. Her traditional underbody, moderate ends, sweeping sheer, and fiberglass-appropriate cabin trunk typify his highly regarded production-built cruising boats. © *Peter Barlow*

A partial collection of Alberg's plans are at the Peabody Essex Museum in Salem, MA.

—Daniel B. MacNaughton with Thomas G. Skahill

John Alden. Considered the best offshore racer among designers of his time, Alden was the first skipper to win the Bermuda Race three times: in 1923 at the helm of *Malabar IV*, in 1926 with *Malabar VII*, and in 1932 with *Malabar X*. Beginning in 1921, he built one *Malabar* a year for himself, sailing them long enough to tweak as much speed out of them as possible, then moving on to the next. *Photo courtesy Chester M. Sawtelle*

John Alden: *Serena*. A fine-lined and long-ended racing machine of 1916, the 83-foot LOA *Serena* (ex-*Escapade II*, ex-*Amorilla*) was built by George Lawley and Son. She raced successfully in West Coast races, including three Transpac Races, before being sold back to the East Coast in 1982. *Photo courtesy Newport Harbor Nautical Museum, Newport Beach, CA*

JOHN GALE ALDEN

January 24, 1884–March 3, 1962 · United States

The name John Alden has become forever associated with graceful sailing craft of what is broadly called the traditional type, especially his schooners, which most would rank among the most beautiful offshore racing and cruising yachts ever built. However, he was also a competitive and broadly talented designer who created many successful one-design classes along with Q-Class boats, R-Class boats, 6-Meters, and 8-Meters, which in their day would hardly have been called traditional.

In his early career Alden became famous for his racing schooners, which represented a major part of the first generation of yachts truly suited to the emerging sport of offshore ocean racing in the United States. Over the years his racing yachts evolved in response to changing rating rules and technical development, but they continued to exhibit the refined good looks and graceful proportions that had been so much admired in his schooners.

Alden was not a yachting-cap-and-blue-blazer kind of yachtsman. He was a down-to-

earth New Englander and an offshore sailor of great experience and little pretense. Indeed, Alden's most famous schooner designs were often smaller adaptations of the Gloucester fisherman type. Today we admire their great beauty, and this along with their demonstrably excellent seakeeping ability is sufficient reason why we see more being built each year.

For much of Alden's career, these schooners were the most successful ocean racing yachts extant, and the sophistication of design and rig that they possess is partly due to the demand that they win races. They are not a product of sentimentality, although we might now be quite justified in some nostalgia for a time when one could take such a vessel to sea with the expectation of racing victories. With contemporary inshore racing tending more and more toward classic yacht regattas, and with many of the superb Alden yachts participating, some of his vessels may yet meet their old rivals under the conditions for which they were built.

Born in Troy, New York, Alden's family summer home was in Sakonnet, Rhode Island, and provided his early exposure to boats, first rowboats on fresh-water ponds, then cat-

boats on the open western end of Buzzards Bay. The family moved to the Boston area in 1900, beginning his exposure to the Gloucester fishing schooners that were berthed there and introducing him to hundreds of subjects for his many sketches of boats, a habit he was to pursue for the rest of his life and which would lead to his interest in designing.

Alden was largely self-educated in naval architecture, although he did take some courses at MIT. He spent a short time in the office of W. Starling Burgess, then spent a year apprenticing in the office of B. B. Crowninshield before being put on the payroll in 1903. Crowninshield was making a name for himself with the design of fishing schooners, among other racing and cruising sailboats. In 1909, Alden opened his own design practice in Boston. He struggled financially for years, but gradually commissions for schooners, motoryachts, catboats, runabouts, yawls, ketches, sloops, and launches began to flow into his office. In addition to design, the office also offered insurance and brokerage services.

Alden became famous for a series of yachts named Malabar that he owned and raced and

John Alden: *Malabar II.* Alden's early Malabar schooners were more cruisers than racers. The 41-foot 6-inch LOA 1922 *Malabar II* must be close to the ultimate in a gaff-rigged cruising boat of her size with her simple rigging, long keel, and wonderfully clear decks. She is still going strong along with many of her sisterships. © *Mystic Seaport, Mystic, CT*

which came out at roughly one-year intervals beginning in 1921. In the first ten boats, all schooners, he explored and refined the concept of the small racing schooner, and they largely dominated offshore racing during the 1920's and early 1930's, including first-place finishes with *Malabar IV* in the revived Bermuda Race of 1923, with *Malabar VII* in 1926, and then with *Malabar X* in 1932, when the first four places were taken by Alden designs. *Malabar XI* was a yawl; *Malabar XII* and *XIII* were ketch-rigged. In size, the Malabar series ranged from 41 feet 3 inches for *Malabar I* to 58 feet 3 inches in *Malabar X*.

The smaller schooners are masterpieces of simplicity and ease of handling, making them superb cruising boats. The larger schooners are magnificent yet seakindly racing machines,

with many possible sail combinations and an expectation of large crews to get the most out of them. All the boats could be sailed shorthanded, however, and all were perfectly beautiful.

The Alden schooners were influential in helping to generate enthusiasm for offshore racing and cruising. Their strong, deep, short-ended hulls, which offered security, easy motion, dry decks, and greater interior volume, stand in marked contrast to the coastwise racer/cruisers of the day and set a standard for healthy offshore boats that endured and evolved considerably for several decades.

Another popular Alden concept was his group of 43-foot schooner designs. Variations included a gaff or marconi main, a keel or centerboard underbody, and several interior arrangements,

but all were superb cruising boats with the typical Alden combination of graceful good looks, clear decks, and easy handling with good seakeeping ability. As with many of his other boats, Alden arranged construction of many of

John Alden: *Calypso* (opposite). Built in 1925 by Abeking and Rasmussen in Germany, this 39-foot 7-inch LOA sloop was one of twenty-five designed by Alden between 1913 and 1928 for the Universal Rule R-Class. Fierce competition developed between Alden and L. Francis Herreshoff, another prolific R-Class designer. Universal Rule classes declined when the United States agreed to use the International Rule in several classes starting in the late 1920's. *Photo courtesy John G. Alden Naval Architects*

John Alden: Malabar Junior. This 30-foot yawl of 1926 was a shapely and popular design with much of the appeal of Alden's larger schooners in a more affordable size. While she lacks their distinctive clipper bow, her hull lines closely resemble those of a working Friendship sloop. *Drawing courtesy John G. Alden Naval Architects.*

John Alden: *When and If.* Colonel George Patton ordered a boat that he could sail around the world "when and if he came back from the war." He didn't come back, but the 63-foot 5-inch LOA *When and If* was waiting to go. Launched by F. F. Pendleton in 1939, she is seakindly, comfortable, rugged, and beautiful, the quintessential fast and able Alden schooner. © *Benjamin Mendlowitz*

these schooners in small Maine boatyards, which could produce a boat at a lower price than yards closer to Boston and New York. Sometimes he had the boats built on speculation, but few waited very long for a buyer.

From 1925 into the 1950's, the Alden office produced over nine hundred different yacht designs as well as designs for fireboats, tugs, and trawlers. About 150 schooners between 37 and 131 feet were designed during these years, among them the famous Malabar series, the aforementioned 43-footers, and the widely admired and still-sailing 74-foot *Lelanta II* and the 103-foot *Puritan*. There were 323 sloops, including several versions of the popular 31-foot Malabar Junior, the series-built 36-foot Coastwise Cruiser, the custom-designed 50-foot *Cock Robin*, and the 57-foot *Zaida*. Among the 216 yawls and ketches were the Off Soundings yawl, the 53-foot *Malabar XIII*, the 71-foot *Royono* (ex-*Mandoo II*), and the 75-foot *Karenita*, the latter three of which are still sailing.

Twenty-Six Raters, Q-Class boats, and R-Class boats were designed, along with 106 one-designs, including the 18-foot 1-inch Biddeford Pool One-Design, the 18-foot 3-inch Alden O Class, the 28-foot 6-inch Triangle, the 21-foot 2-inch Indian Class/Nantucket One-Design, the 18-foot 4-inch Sakonnet, and the 37-foot 9-inch U.S. One-Design. Forty-four motorsailers, including the 62-foot *Trade Wind*, and 88 power yachts, including the 50-foot *Gosling* and the 60-foot *Mobjack*, came out of that period.

During World War II, Alden worked in partnership with the nearby office of Eldridge-McInnis, running a firm with ninety employees. During the Korean War the Alden office expanded to over a hundred people and designed a number of vessels for the U.S. government, including several specialized freighters, a harbor tug, and a 95-foot Coast Guard cutter.

After the war, the primary handicapping rule in the United States was the CCA Rule, which encouraged more aerodynamically efficient marconi-rigged sloops and yawls with mostly inboard rig. Hulls tended to have overhangs of moderate length and a somewhat cutaway underbody, and in general the whole racing scene moved strongly away from the schooners of the past. Despite Alden's success with the earlier type, he was a member of the Cruising Club of America, encouraged the new rule, and went on to produce some of the most successful examples of that style.

Some writers have taken pains to point out that a great many of Alden's designs, including some of his most famous ones, were actually drawn by other hands under his employ.

As many of these draftsmen went on to become famous designers under their own names, the implication is that Alden should receive less credit for these boats, and the draftsmen more. Better to say that John Alden found, focused, and refined these talents by giving them the opportunity to participate in his designs. In some cases the designs follow very closely Alden's personal style, and in others we can see clearly that when he liked what was evolving on one of his draftsman's boards, he let it find its own ultimate definition.

Probably no other design office has produced as many successful designers, and this must be greatly to John Alden's personal credit. At one time or another the following individuals all worked in the Alden office: Carl Alberg, S. S. Crocker, Clifford Swaine, William McNary, Charles MacGregor, Dwight S. Simpson, Winthrop L. Warner, Howard I. Chapelle, K. Aage Nielsen, Ralph Winslow, Fenwick Williams, Murray Peterson, Al Mason, Charles W. Wittholz, Charles Schock, and Phil Ross.

Upon retirement in 1955, Alden sold his business to his associates. He died at the age of seventy-eight in Winter Park, Florida. The Alden design office continues on Commercial Wharf in Boston, with Niels Helleberg as chief naval architect.
—Daniel B. MacNaughton

ANDRÉ ALLÈGRE

Born April 25, 1925 · France

André Allègre quotes the astronomer Sir Fred Hoyle: "To solve a problem, I never work in a conventional manner. If the truth lies along that path, others would have already found it." Then he adds, not without humor, "My intellectual guides? Archimedes and Leonardo da Vinci!" And when asked why, in 1968, Eric Tabarly chose him to design his giant trimaran *Pen Duick IV* (later renamed *Manureva*), Allègre drew his reasons from Tabarly himself: "Our viewpoints, our goals, our ideas and our conceptions were the same." Thus, it is hardly surprising that Allègre's main contribution to contemporary naval architecture has been the introduction of trimarans to offshore racing.

Allègre acquired a passion for multihulls in his teens, and it has never released its hold on him. He built his first canoe when he was fourteen, and his first catamaran a year later. At Algiers in 1953, he designed and built his first trimaran, Kito *Rani*, 11.5 meters in length with a displacement of 3.5 tons. From this period came his first professional drawings, the catamaran *Catalina* and the 6.5-meter trimaran *Samoa*. He started his own yard in Sète on the Mediterranean Sea in 1962. During the 1970's, he built the largest trimaran in the world at that time, the 29.40-meter *Jacques Borel*.

Allègre's father was an excellent cabinetmaker, and from him André inherited his desire for perfection. As a young child, he could sail any vessel that came into his hands. An early technical education in the French school system later helped him to educate himself as a naval architect.

Before his recent retirement, Allègre designed small and light sport multihulls such as the *Tristar 16* as well as creating a unique 25-meter trimaran, basically a giant laboratory that brings together many of his innovations. Among these inventions are a winged rudder, and a series of foils and adjustable fins mounted on the main hull and amas that control lift and prevent the hulls from diving into the water at high speeds—a desirable goal in a yacht meant to sail around the world at speeds exceeding 40 knots. —Jacques Taglang

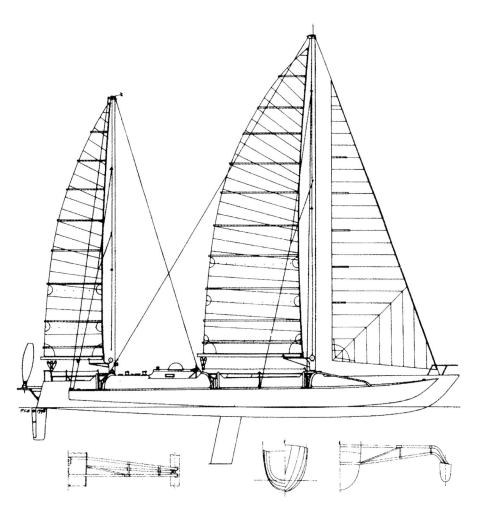

André Allègre: *Pen Duick IV*. The 20.8-meter *Pen Duick IV*, built in 1968 of Duralinox (aluminum), was the first modern trimaran. It was inspired by Eric Tabarly, for the third OSTAR (Observer Singlehanded Transatlantic Race). Tabarly withdrew some days after the start following a collision with a cargo ship. *Drawing courtesy Chevalier & Taglang*

JUAN MANUEL ALONSO ALLENDE

1918–1984 · Spain

Juan Manuel Alonso Allende was one of the most prominent figures in Spanish yachting after World War II, combining a successful designing career with top-level international dinghy racing campaigns and involvement in yachting administration.

His education in naval architecture at Madrid's Escuela Tecnica Superior de Ingenieros Navales was interrupted by Civil War action, including service as a fighter pilot in the celebrated Garcia Morato Squadron. From 1944 into the 1960's he designed a series of pleasure vessels, including ocean racers: the Galea Class was probably the most successful, with one of these 36-foot sloops, Juan Olabarri's *Mizar*, winning Class III in the 1968 RORC Channel Race. Many of his designs were built by the Udondo yard, founded by one hundred members of the Real Sporting Club in Bilbao.

Allende also became 1957 Snipe World Champion and competed in the Torquay (Firefly), Naples (Flying Dutchman), and Acapulco (Star) Olympics. For many years he was Spanish representative to the IYRU, and a member of the Technical, Small Boat, and Permanent Committees, and from 1954 to 1968 he was president of Real Federacion Española de Clubs Nauticos. —Juan Olabarri

HOBART L. "HOBIE" ALTER

Born October 31, 1933 · United States

A pioneering designer of small catamarans who mastered the new boatbuilding technology of synthetic materials, Hobie Alter started out as a young surfer and shaper of wooden surfboards in southern California. Dissatisfied with the board's weight and the difficulty of finding good balsa wood, he experimented with synthetic foams, then in their early stages of development and little used in any industry. Styrofoam dissolved when it came into contact with polyester resin, so he settled on high-density polyurethane foam. He developed ways to shape it in molds, and in 1958 introduced the first successful foam surfboards. Lighter and easier to make than wooden boards, they stimulated an international boom in surfing.

Alter moved on to improve other "toys," as he called the objects he enjoyed playing with. In 1963 he designed and built one of the first modern skateboards, with special recessed wheels. Attracted to sailing, especially in catamarans because of their potential for high speed, he found that most catamarans were too heavy to be launched off a beach and sailed by one person. "There was an opening there," he recalled. "I wanted something better and so I gave it a try."

To keep the boat light, Alter used foam-fiberglass sandwich construction (a process he pioneered in his surfboards), a trampoline for the deck, and asymmetric hulls—flat on the inboard side and curved on the outboard side—in place of centerboards to reduce leeway. The asymmetrical concept had originated in Micronesia and was used by the Hawaiian catamaran designers Woody Brown and Rudy Choy on their large catamarans.

The Hobie 14 was introduced in 1969. Weighing 215 pounds, with a single 115-square-foot, fully battened sail, it was initially priced at only $999. An important feature was its narrow 7-foot 8-inch beam, which met a crucial requirement then governing West Coast boat design, the "C.H.P. rule." This was the state law (enforced by the California Highway Patrol) requiring that trailers be no wider than 8 feet. Not requiring a special trailer, and with its swooping sheer and steeply raked mast, the Hobie 14 looked exciting, performed well, and quickly caught on among surfers.

The sailing establishment, historically wary of multihull designs, rediscovered them at *Yachting* magazine's One-of-a-Kind Regatta in 1969 in Chicago, where one boat from each class competed. In the last race, in a strong wind and rough sea, the Hobie (sailed by Alter) was second to finish in the multihull fleet, beating or outlasting much larger boats. In 1971 Alter produced the Hobie 16, a two-person, asymmetrically hulled, sloop-rigged catamaran that became even more popular than the 14, with more than 150,000 boats built. Hobie Cats were marketed cleverly by Alter's company, Coast Catamaran. It sold boats through its own dealer network, which consisted largely of Hobie sailors, and it sponsored proprietary learn-to-sail and racing programs that emphasized a pleasant lifestyle at the beach independent of yacht clubs. This informality had an important appeal at the time when, as Alter accurately put it, "sailing had a reputation for being a little uptight."

Alter continues to come up with new products. The successful ones reflect his personal interests and fascination with technology. These include several high-performance catamarans, a small powerboat called the Hobie Skiff, and an innovative radio-controlled model glider airplane. Less successful have been boats developed by marketing specialists to fit presumed niches.

As multihull sailing underwent explosive growth after 1970, Alter's key role was recognized in 1986 by the United States Yacht Racing Union, the national governing body of U.S. sailors, when it named the trophy for the national multihull championship the Hobie Alter Cup.   —John Rousmaniere

Hobie Alter: Hobie Cat 14. The Hobie Cat 14, surfboard-maker Hobie Alter's "beachable, high-speed, low-maintenance boat," is among the most successful designs ever. The prototype was named *April*, for the month of its launch in 1968. © *Peter Barlow*

EIVIND AMBLE

Born September 18, 1937 · Norway

A specialist in small craft and yacht design, Eivind Amble graduated from the Technical University of Trondheim in 1961 as a naval architect and marine engineer. Soon thereafter he became deeply involved in systematic research on sailboat performance using towing tanks, a new way of thinking for Norwegian designers.

In the late 1960's Amble assumed responsibility for design and development work at one of Norway's largest yacht companies, Fjord Boats, which became a leading small motoryacht builder in Europe during the 1970's. Over a period of twenty years Amble designed numerous motoryachts in various sizes for many yards, along with many one-offs and motorsailers.

With regard to sailboats, Amble once said, "I was fighting to earn my living by designing sailboats but that was impossible in Norway because there were not sailors enough to buy. You can live for it but not from it." Nevertheless, Amble designed the Admiral's Cup yacht *Liz of Hankö* in 1977 and the Mini-Ton boat *Whitchie*, which raced successfully. A Half-Tonner,

Eivind Amble: Norselander. Back in 1966 Eivind Amble designed a 24-foot motorsailer that gained a lot of admiration and interest. With gradually more emphasis put on performance under sail, several designs of the same breed were to follow. The Norselander is the latest example of Amble's much-refined version of the Norwegian double-ender concept. *Photo courtesy Eivind Amble*

Fram VIII, created for Crown Prince Harald in 1983, was also very competitive.

Amble continues to be an active member of several technical committees of the Offshore Racing Council (ORC), ICOMIA, and the Norwegian surveying group VERITAS. He is also a well-known columnist for leading Norwegian yacht magazines. He practices in Kristiansand, Norway. —Bent Aarre

ALBERT ANDERSSON

December 10, 1853–May 21, 1926 · Sweden

Albert Andersson was a pioneer in Swedish yacht design. Together with Colin Archer (1832–1921) from Norway and Carl Smith (1843–1920) and J. H. Seldén (1855–1921) from Sweden, Andersson created the modern, carvel-built, double-ended yacht.

Carvel construction was common in the 1880's in Sweden. A good example of the type is Andersson's design *Minerva,* the lottery boat of the GKSS (Gothenburg Royal Yacht Club)

Albert Andersson: Bianca. The 75-Square-Meter skerry cruiser *Bianca,* 13.45 meters in length, was built at Gamleby Boatyard by Knut Holm in 1913 for J. Lagerwall in Stockholm, Sweden. Her original name was *Blanka.* © *Per Thelander*

Alan Andrews: _Medicine Man._ One of the Andrews 56 class, _Medicine Man_ has been a consistent winner on the West Coast for over ten years. © _Geri Conser_

dance with the first of these rules, Andersson designed _Hermione_. He went on to design boats in keeping with the International Rule and the Skerry Cruiser Rule, the latter of which he took part in creating in 1908. Among the boats from these years are the 6-meter boat _Freja_ from 1908 and the 150-Square-Meter skerry cruiser _Meit_, designed for the Swedish artist Anders Zorn. For one of the first long-distance sailing enthusiasts, Sven Grenander, he designed the yacht _Naima_.

* This is a reference to the Lloyd's insurance standards of construction. The Register was different.

—Ulf Lycke

ALAN ANDREWS

Born 1955 · United States

California designer Alan Andrews has consistently explored the possibilities of newly developed materials and design innovations. After graduation from Stanford University with a degree in mechanical engineering, he worked first as a draftsman for designer Doug Peterson and then as house designer/engineer for Dencho Marine. In 1979, he established his own company, Alan Andrews Yacht Design, in Long Beach, California.

After one of his designs, _Details_, won the 1982 MORC International Championships, his main interest became designing successful offshore racing yachts. The impressive catalogue of competitions his boats have won includes, among others, the Transpac, SORC, the Chicago to Mackinac, and the Newport to Ensenada, many of them more than once.

His yachts are sleek, with very little overhang and often plumb stemmed; they range in size from 27 to 100 feet and are quite modern in appearance. Although his emphasis is on racing, Andrews has also designed several cruising yachts, which have shown themselves to be lively performers.   —Walter Voigt

DANIEL ANDRIEU

Born August 8, 1946 · France

His dream was to become an all-around naval architect, and surely Daniel Andrieu has succeeded. His sailboats have won many trophies, and his recent fast powerboats are highly regarded.

Born in Boulogne, near Paris, Andrieu used to spend all his holidays in Brittany and elsewhere on the French Atlantic coast. Drawn to creative pursuits, he studied architecture at Ecole des Beaux-Arts in Paris. He soon decided

in 1888. (Lotteries were common in Sweden from the end of the nineteenth century to the 1950's; yacht clubs sold lots to raise money and the prize was a yacht.)

Andersson was born in Gothenburg, Sweden. Since his father was employed at the Gamla varvet ("the old shipyard"), he was brought up with the sea and boats. After his education at the Shipbuilding Institute in Gothenburg and apprenticing at shipyards in England, Andersson returned to Gothenburg. Beside his work controlling the quality of the construction, he taught shipbuilding at the Chalmers Institute of Technology. Among his pupils were Carl O. Liljegren, Axel Nygren, and Hugo Schubert, who came to be some of the most important new modelers in the decades around 1900.

While others went on designing modern double-enders, beginning in the 1890's Andersson and Hugo Schubert, inspired by Nathanael

Herreshoff, introduced boats of the _Gloriana_ type. GKSS's lottery boat _Carmen_ in 1893 is one of the first boats designed according to the Seawanhaka Rule.

In the 1890's Andersson moved to Stockholm. Here he came to work with controlling construction quality and representing Nordiska Veritas, the equivalent of quality control by Lloyd's.* In Stockholm the Cube Rule (Sweden's name for the Length-and-Sail-Area Rule) was in practice, and Andersson designed several good yachts according to it. One of the most famous is _Saga_, the first Swedish boat to win the Sinebrychoff Trophy, given by the Nyland Yacht Club in Helsinki and open to boats from yacht clubs in the Baltic Sea and in Danish waters. Among the fin-keel designs, _Vikingen_, the winner of King Oskar II's Jubilee Cup, was the most prominent of several good boats.

In 1902 and 1904 the KSSS (Royal Swedish Yacht Club) created cruiser rules. In accor-

that construction was the most fascinating area of architecture, and chose to specialize in the computer applications just beginning to appear in this field. From 1974 to 1976 he was a consultant in computer science for the Paris University Architecture School.

When the French yachting magazine *Bateaux* was looking for a young designer to illustrate the lines of sailboats they were testing, Andrieu seized the opportunity to perfect his training and to turn himself toward naval architecture. For six years, he analyzed and redrew a hundred production sailboats, and read and re-read the Barnaby book, *Basic Naval Architecture*.

During this period, Andrieu became friends with a group of young La Rochelle yachtsmen who were campaigning in the new Mini-Ton class. He sailed with Bernard Nivelt and Philippe Pallu de la Barrière, both devotees of data-processing. Using the then-new programmable pocket calculators, they developed programs for IOR-related calculations and structural calculations (notably for rigging and for rudders), as well as programs for hull scantlings.

In La Rochelle, the group learned rapidly because young designers Jean Berret, Michel Joubert, and Philippe Briand didn't let them off lightly, and they pursued all kinds of design experiments. In 1981, Andrieu and François Chevalier teamed up to draw the lines of the Half-Tonner *EJP* for Jacques Phillipot, while Andrieu was designing for himself a Quarter-Tonner, *Cyfraline,* with the assistance of a spon-

sor. *Cyfraline* came in second in the World Championship of 1981 and immediately established him as a celebrity.

In the following two years, *EJP* and *Cyfraline,* with the Half-Tonner *Anthor,* enhanced Andrieu's reputation when they scored two first places in their World Championships, four second places, and one third. *Cyfraline 3,* a One-Tonner, won in the Southern Cross race in Australia in 1985. Henceforth Andrieu became a force to reckon with.

Andrieu received orders from Prince Felipe of Spain and from the Jeanneau yard (the Sun Light 30, of which a thousand were built), and designed *Elf Aquitaine* (which placed first three times in the Half-Tonner World Championships). He had famous customers such as G. Walker (*Indulgence V, VI,* and *VII,* placing first in the Three-Quarter-Tonner World Championship, and first and second in the Admiral's Cup) and the Australian Rick Stove, and he designed the French challenger for the 1987 America's Cup, *Challenge France.*

Since Andrieu became the Jeanneau yard's primary designer, the number of yachts produced with his designs has totaled around three thousand. This hasn't prevented him from continuing to gain recognition for other designs, especially his one-designs, the JOD 24 and 35. Since 1995, his *Iris* catamaran ferries, ranging from 25 to 40 meters in length, with hydrojet power and speeds of up to 38 knots, have opened new avenues of design, but he has

not forsaken the production of yachts or high-level racers. Andrieu was part of the design team of French challenges for the 2000 and 2003 America's Cup, and designed the International America's Cup Class yachts *6e Sens* (1999) and *Le Défi Areva* (2003).

Andrieu practices in La Rochelle, France.

—François Chevalier

HUGH MORGAN "BONES" ANGELMAN

March 7, 1886–January 31, 1967 · United States

Hugh Angelman had one of the most distinctive styles in naval architecture. While he also drew powerboats and sailboats of a contemporary style, his most widely known designs are strongly tradition-based sailboats, bringing a "big sailing ship" look to smaller yachts.

The most noticeable feature of a typical Angelman design is a short, well-executed clipper bow, with a high-steeved bowsprit of the type commonly seen on larger vessels. It makes for a dramatic look, probably Angelman's main reason for doing it.

In various combinations, Angelman used taffrails, pinrails, gaff rigs, square sails, false gun ports, great cabins, and ornamentation to add to this dramatic effect. Despite the old-time trappings, Angelman's boats sail well, and *Sea Witch,* the first of a long line of boats built to her plans, won the 1951 Honolulu Race. The

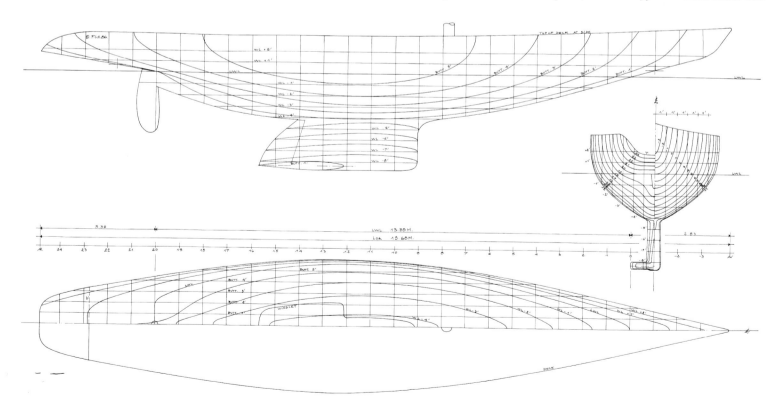

Daniel Andrieu: *Challenge France.* Built in 1986, this 64-foot 7-inch 12-Meter was the French challenger for the 1987 America's Cup, sailing under the banner of the Société Nautique de Marseilles. © *Chevalier & Taglang*

35-foot Sea Witch ketch is Angelman's best-known design, and has been built by many yards in the United States and overseas. There is a range of similar designs with lengths from around 23 feet up to around 45 feet.

Angelman also drew sleek schooners and other boats of more contemporary styling, many of which have been successful racers. The 63-foot schooner *Wetona* (later *Quest*), the 45-foot schooner *La Volpe*, and the 40-foot ketch *Resolute* are good examples, and the latter two are still in active service in 2000. He designed many fast and able power cruisers, some conventional and others of a lightweight, reverse-sheer, chine-hull type that was controversial but proved both functional and popular. His talent for these designs came entirely from some inner knowing, as he had no formal training.

Born Hugh Morgan in Bonham, Texas, Angelman moved to Los Angeles when he was six, taking the surname of his mother's new husband, Eugene Angelman, soon thereafter. Although the nautical magazines often referred to him as "Angleman," this was incorrect. As a boy, he was a chronic truant, but he educated himself by constantly reading, a habit he maintained throughout his life. At the same time, he crewed on racing boats and worked in local boatyards, receiving his training at the trade from some highly regarded local boatbuilders, such as Cookson and Callahan, where he was in close contact with designer C. D. Callahan and builder Charles Cookson.

In 1919, while Angelman was building a boat with his lifelong friend, Willard Buchanan, the two were approached by Tom Smith, who admired their work and commissioned them to build a boat for him to Angelman's design. By carefully purchasing materials, they were able to build two to the same design. Smith was so impressed that he proposed to financially back Angelman in a boatyard, and thus began Wilmington Boat Works (soon known as Wilbo) south of Los Angeles in Wilmington.

Smith and Angelman remained partners for the next ten years, and both built homes and lived on the property of the boatyard. Angelman developed Wilbo into a large business, building boats designed by many of the best designers of the day, including himself, until he retired from boatbuilding at Wilbo in 1945. Wilbo built its last Angelman design, the ketch *Golden Hind*, in 1959.

Angelman worked with a number of draftsmen and collaborators over the years, but his most notable partnership was with Charles G. Davis, who joined him as a young man in about 1938. After World War II, Davis was involved with the redesign of the Sea Witch ketch when so many were built around the world. Angelman sold Wilbo in about 1946, and in 1949 he became associated with the South Coast Company in Newport Beach. Davis followed shortly afterward.

Around 1950 Angelman and Davis left South Coast and went into business for themselves. For the next ten-plus years they turned out a number of designs under the name of Angelman and Davis, later Angelman, Davis, Ward (1960), and later yet Angelman and (Victor) Ward (1963).

Angelman and his wife lived and cruised aboard their Sea Witch ketch *Sea Rover* for many years, moving ashore in 1963. Under the sobriquet of "The Mudflat Philosopher," he commented on the events, customs, and conditions of the times. Often humorous, yet trenchant and topical, he opined on the mores of the boating community, society, business, and life in general. When the urge came, he enjoyed easy and welcome access to the boating press to vent his thoughts and observations.

—Daniel B. MacNaughton with Thomas G. Skahill

JOHAN AUGUST ANKER

1871–1940 · Norway

Johan Anker's international reputation is largely due to his extensive work in International Rule designs, his creation of the extremely popular Dragon One-Design class keelboat, and his development and use of the marconi rig. He was also a founding and extremely influential member of the IYRU. In Norway, he is considered one of the leading figures of the new Norway that arose after its formal separation from Sweden in 1905. Of all the famous designers of his era, Anker was perhaps the best helmsman, winning many regattas over nearly four decades.

Designing in a straightforward manner according to the purpose for which each yacht was ordered, Anker was usually commissioned to design boats to win races. He was considered an artist in yacht design and was greatly concerned with the beauty of the lines. He often continued to alter designs until the progress of the construction rendered this impractical.

Anker was born at Halden, in the southeastern part of what is now Norway, near the Swedish border. His interest in sailing was awakened during summer holidays spent on

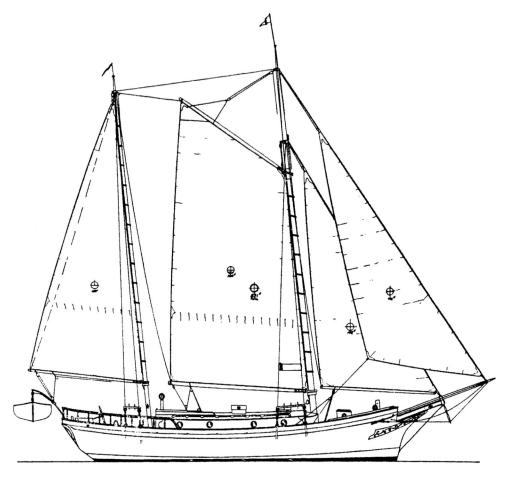

Hugh Angelman: Sea Witch. These 35-foot ketches, designed in 1937, were built at Angelman's Wilmington Boat Works before and after World War II, with others built elsewhere later. Despite their heavy scantlings, they did well in ocean racing, placing second in the Transpac Race in 1949 and first in 1951, among other major events. *Drawing reproduced from Yachting magazine*

the Hvaler Islands, an archipelago sheltering the western seaboard of the windy Skagerrak, the straits that separate Norway and Sweden from Denmark. There he sailed boats that his father, who in 1883 was a founding member of the Royal Norwegian Yacht Club, had designed as a hobby.

His father expected Anker to continue in the family forestry business but accepted his son's desire to study engineering, with the understanding that he would join the company at a later date. Anker began his education in Norway's relatively new capital of Kristiania (later called Oslo), and then continued on to the "Technische Hochschule" outside of Berlin-Charlottenburg, Germany. He chose yacht design and construction as the central focus of his studies. Despite this interest, he joined the family firm upon graduation.

It was in 1898 that the twenty-seven-year-old Anker, while bedridden with a broken leg, designed his first yacht, the *Brand*. This yacht had a fin keel with a separate spade rudder, a type common for a brief period prior to the Universal Rule. In 1905 Anker left the family business and bought himself a partnership in the established boatyard of Christian Jensen at Vollen, a small boatbuilding village to the southwest of Oslo. The Anker and Jensen partnership lasted until 1915, when Jensen left to design workboats. The yard's reputation endured.

Thanks to the wealth of his family, Anker was able to build several yachts at his yard to his own designs. These included *Brand II*, built to the 1898 Copenhagen Rule, a precursor to the International Rule of 1906. *Brand II* won Scandinavia's Kattegat Cup in 1906 and helped establish Anker's reputation as an up-and-coming designer.

In October of 1906 Anker represented Norway at the London Conference that saw the founding of the IYRU. He became the driving force for the European International Rule because of general dissatisfaction with the Copenhagen Rule. That same year he designed and built the 8-Meter *Brand III*, the first yacht he designed in accordance with the new International Rule. *Brand III* won the Kattegat Trophy in 1907. *Brand IV* was Anker's first 12-Meter design and was another successful racer that confirmed his reputation as Norway's leading yachtsman, designer, and yacht builder.

In the first two decades of the twentieth century Anker benefited from the surge of nationalism that began when Norway became fully independent and King Haakon VII was crowned. Anker's racing successes continued to be widely acclaimed by the Norwegian public.

In 1908 Anker helmed the 8-Meter *Fram* in the sailing Olympics held on the Solent. He

Johan Anker: *Rollo*. Anker's career got a boost in 1911 when his 12-Meter *Rollo* defeated boats by the day's top designers. While his designs were very successful on the race course, it is said that aesthetics were a top priority. *Rollo* would certainly tend to bear this out. © *Beken of Cowes*

came in third in two races and fourth overall, but it represented the start of an enduring relationship between Anker and yacht racing in the United Kingdom. It also represented the start of his relationship with Olympic yacht racing, which was cemented four years later when his 12-Meter *Magda IX* won the gold medal for its class in Stockholm, with him serving as sailing master.

Anker earned an important victory in 1911 at the Coronation Regatta, including during the first European Week, held at Cowes on the Isle of Wight, where his 12-Meter *Rollo* defeated three Fife designs and a Mylne design to win a gold medal.

From then until his retirement just before World War II, over four hundred yachts were built at Anker's yard. He designed, built, and often skippered a stream of highly successful

International Rule yachts. Ranging from 6- to 15-Meters, his boats dominated international class racing. During the fourth European Week, held in Norway a fortnight before the diplomatic chain-reaction that started World War I, Anker introduced the marconi rig to the otherwise entirely gaff-rigged 12-Meter on his yacht *Symra*, which won the class.

Anker was Crown Prince Olav's sailing tutor and mentor since the end of World War I. In 1928 he won the gold medal as helmsman on board Crown Prince Olav's *Norna* in the Amsterdam Olympics.

Then came the Dragon. In 1927 Anker won a design competition held by the Royal Gothenburg Yacht Club. The result was the Dragon One-Design class (Drake, in Norwegian). The design was first published in the Swedish magazine *Seglarbladet* in December 1928. Boats

Johan Anker: Dragons. The Dragons *Tyra*, *Scampi*, and *Whisper II* are shown at speed. First designed and built in 1927, the 29-foot 2-inch LOD Dragon One-Design class became immensely popular for racing and was selected as an Olympic class in 1948. Fast, sleek, stable, and seaworthy, they have been a cost-effective alternative to the meter classes. *Photo courtesy Iain McAllister*

built to Anker's winning design spread quickly through Norway, where it was most popular as a junior boat, as well as the rest of Scandinavia and Germany.

The first British-built Dragon was *Anita*, launched from a yard on the river Clyde in Scotland in 1938. By the end of that year, 25 Dragons were racing on the Clyde, and at the outbreak of World War II, 125 Dragons were registered in Britain. A cost-effective alternative to the 6-, 8-, and 12-Meter classes, the Dragon One-Design class grew to be one of the most popular in the world. After World War II, in a generous gesture, the heirs of Johan Anker waived all royalties on British-built boats, which further lowered the cost of production as well as increasing the popularity of the class.

The measure of the Dragon's success can be judged by its selection in 1948 as an Olympic class. Since then, the Dragon, which started life as a cruiser/racer, has taken on more of a racing boat appearance, with a shortened cabin trunk and a larger foretriangle. It has mostly been built of fiberglass since 1968, but wooden boats continue to be restored. Despite all the changes, they retain their good looks and seaworthy hull form. Today, Dragons are actively sailed in more than twenty-six countries on five continents. In the year 2000, a total of 1,619 boats were registered with the various national associations.

An active organizer, Anker held the chair of the Royal Norwegian Yacht Club and the Scandinavian Sailing Association, and he was a member of the IYRU's permanent committee. He was also a keen skier, hunter, and sports fisherman and found the time to be chairman of the Norwegian Hunting and Fishing Association.

Anker continued to design and sail in regattas until 1939. As late as the summer of that year, at the age of sixty-eight, he sailed to victory as helmsman on Crown Prince Olav's 8-Meter *Sira*, in the Kattegat Cup. When Johan Anker

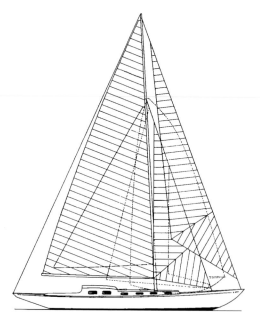

Johan Anker: *Noreine*. This 55-foot cutter shows the marconi rig that Anker championed. Its moderate proportions—luff about twice the length of the foot—were well suited for ocean work, sacrificing some efficiency to windward for better motion and drive in a seaway. © *Tony Dixon*

died in 1940, Norway mourned. Coming as it did at the start of the occupation of Norway and the loss of its freedom, Anker's passing represented the end of an era just as his early successes had represented its start. A film about Anker's life and career was made in 1998, and a book about him is forthcoming.

Anker's home, "Lillehaugen," contains photographs of his yacht designs and racing triumphs. A model of *Rollo* is suspended from the ceiling in the dining room. A monument to Johan Anker was unveiled by Crown Prince Olav in 1949. It stands on a rocky plateau near Hanko, the sailing mecca of Norway.

—Bent Aarre, Erdmann Braschos, and Chris Ennals

COLIN ARCHER

1832–1921 · Norway

Colin Archer was a Norwegian designer of Scottish descent. He became a national hero for his design of the Norwegian Redningskoite, or sailing rescue vessel, and the Arctic exploration vessel *Fram*.

The Redningskoite was designed in 1893 in response to a request from the newly formed Norwegian Society for the Rescue of the Shipwrecked, for a vessel to rescue the crews of endangered coastal vessels working in constant peril along Norway's long, rugged, and exposed lee shore. Redningskoites are beamy, heavy-displacement, double-ended, gaff-rigged ketches with very deep forefoots and some outside ballast. Their dimensions are 45 feet length on deck, with an impressive 15-foot 3-inch beam, 7-feet 3-inch draft, and 27-ton displacement. Sometimes referred to as "the best boat for the worst weather," their overall configuration, massive construction, and other details were all carefully thought out to match the severe demands of winter service in sea and weather conditions almost unimaginable to most yachtsmen. Before the days of radio and guided only by a telegraph and semaphore system on shore, they followed the fishing fleets and put to sea in bad weather so as to be where they were needed, when they were needed.

The Redningskoite was an overwhelming success, saving thousands of lives and countless vessels. Power-driven rescue vessels have now taken over their work, but many of the Redningskoites are still sailing thanks to their rugged, high-quality construction and the deep affection of the Norwegian people as well as other loving owners. Surviving examples, often converted to yacht service, are said to be as symbolically important to Norway as the Statue of Liberty is to the United States.

Many designers have adapted the Redningskoite model to yachting purposes, beginning with William Atkin in the United States. Atkin produced much smaller but fairly literal interpretations in the form of *Eric* (her drawings contain the credit "after Colin Archer"), *Thistle*, and *Dragon*, plus a host of more modified versions. W. I. B. Crealock modified *Eric* to create the popular fiberglass Westsail 32, bringing the direct influence of Archer into the modern era. Other designers influenced by the Redningskoite in some of their work include Albert Strange, Philip Rhodes, and Germán Frers Sr. Reproductions large and small continue to be built in significant numbers.

The Redningskoite model has become known as the "Colin Archer type," which is fair enough, but it is important to recognize that Archer's work was by no means limited to a narrow range. While he drew many other vessels that closely resembled the Redningskoite, such as his pilot cutters and some fishing vessels, his designs were always purpose-specific and included a wide variety of beautiful racing and cruising yachts, many of which are not outwardly Scandinavian in character.

Archer was born in Larvik, Norway, to Scottish parents who had emigrated there in 1825, when his father became a lobster merchant. He attended high school in Larvik and worked for a year and a half at a local boatyard. In his late teens he traveled to Hawaii and California and then Australia, where he worked on a sheep farm belonging to his four brothers. When his father fell ill in 1861, he returned to

Norway. The sheep farm provided an income that apparently lasted for the rest of his life, making it possible for him to pursue his interests without great financial pressure. He opened his small shipyard in Larvik in 1865.

At that time the pilot-boats and fishing craft of Norway were undecked, clinker-built double-enders with inside ballast. They had evolved more or less naturally among the local marine communities. As such "evolved" boats are apt to be, these were beautiful and functional up to a point, but Archer observed that there was much loss of life all along the coast due to their lack of decks or ultimate stability, and their poor windward performance.

Archer was able to make critical improvements to the design of the boats, including fully decked hulls, some outside ballast (an innovation at the time), more draft, less beam and flare, more weatherly rigs, and carvel construction. His designs retained as much of the original character as possible, probably in an effort to gain acceptance. These boats, the evolution of which ultimately led to the Redningskoite type, were very successful, but acceptance of the changes was slow among the local people. Eventually, however, the logic behind the improvements could not be denied, and the type was universally adopted. Probably more lives were spared as a result of these improvements than were ultimately saved by the later Colin Archer lifesaving vessels, and this is yet another reason why Archer is revered by the Norwegian people.

Until 1871, most of Archer's work concerned designs for practical purposes, but yachting was beginning to catch on in Norway, and in that year a yacht of his design, *Maggie*, won the Gothenburg International Regatta. From that time on, much of his work involved designs for yachts. Over the years his boats became the most successful racers in Scandinavia, and yachtsmen from many countries had to buy Archer boats if they wanted to be competitive in those waters.

The most famous single vessel that Archer designed must surely be the Arctic exploration vessel *Fram*, in which Dr. Fridtjof Nansen and Captain Otto Sverdrup made their voyage, and which also went to the Antarctic under Captain Roald Amundsen. *Fram*, an all-wooden vessel built in 1893, was designed to withstand the Arctic pack ice. Her plans show a ship of absolutely massive construction, with a shape that was intended to yield to crushing ice by rising bodily upward. This she did, and on her Arctic voyage she survived twenty-two months in the ice, far longer than originally anticipated. *Fram* is now a Norwegian national heroine, safely preserved in a museum in Oslo.

Another well-known Colin Archer vessel is *Asgard*, which was built for Erskine and Molly Childers. Childers was the author of the famous sailing novel *The Riddle of the Sands*. A big, handsome, counter-sterned ketch, *Asgard* is the vessel that Childers used to smuggle arms into Ireland in 1914, a deed that was to cost him

Colin Archer: *Christiania*. The 45-foot Redningskoite has a well-deserved reputation as one of the best heavy-weather vessels ever designed. Their dramatic role in Norway's first rescue service makes surviving examples national treasures. This is Redningskoite No. 10, *Christiania*. © *PPL Photo Agency*

his life before a firing squad. Today *Asgard* is preserved in Ireland.

During his lifetime and for a short time after his death, one of Archer's influences on naval architecture was his wave-form theory, an attempt to bring science into the hull design process, which up to that point was mostly a matter of educated guesswork and evolution. This theory influenced the work of many other designers, including Johan Anker of Norway and Edward Burgess and A. Cary Smith of the United States.

The theory considered the fore and aft distribution of the vessel's underwater volume, as illustrated by the curve of cross-sectional areas, to indicate how the water was actually parted and then rejoined as the boat passed. It produced an immediate improvement in performance over similar vessels in which the theory had not been employed, but over time it has come to be viewed as an oversimplification and is no longer utilized. The theory appeared to work probably because it resulted in very smooth and straight diagonals, hull lines that were (and still are) much neglected in favor of the more easily visualized waterlines and buttock lines. The diagonals had previously been used only as fairing lines to cross-check the accuracy of the other lines, but after the wave-form theory and the work of other designers, they have slowly become recognized as the lines that best show the path of water past the hull when a vessel is heeled. Many contemporary designers consider the diagonals the

most important hull lines, and this is the ultimate remaining legacy of the wave-form theory. Today most of Archer's influence is in the form of his beautiful and impressive double-ended designs, which continue to be the basis of much modern design and construction work.

In all Colin Archer personally designed and built sixty-nine yachts, fifty pilot-boats, and fourteen rescue boats. He retired in 1901 and died on February 8, 1921. In his book, *Colin Archer and the Seaworthy Double-Ender,* author John Leather quotes Norwegian designer Johan Anker: "As long as there are sailing craft on our waters, so long will his memory live."

—Daniel B. MacNaughton

DANIEL JOSEPH ARENA JR.

October 29, 1916–January 23, 1995
United States

A competitor in outboard and 151-class inboard racing on the West Coast while in his teens, Dan Arena and his partner Dan Foster came to Detroit in 1938 for a run at the Gold Cup in a boat they had built themselves and powered with a Hispano-Suiza V8 engine. The boat was outclassed, but everyone was impressed by the two twenty-one-year-olds from Oakland, California.

The next year Arena was asked by owner Herbert Mendelson to drive a new Gold Cup class boat named *Notre Dame,* which had won the 1937 Gold Cup. She soon proved troublesome, and

Arena recommended that a whole new boat be built around the *Notre Dame* engine, an extraordinary twenty-four-cylinder Duesenberg. Mendelson told the young racer to design it.

That second *Notre Dame,* with a single-step bottom inspired by the Jacoby outboard hydroplanes, was beaten by the Apel-designed *My Sin* at the Gold Cup in 1939, but she was the first Gold Cup boat to run at more than 100 mph and the first of more than a half-dozen Unlimited raceboats that Arena would design, three of them Gold Cup winners. In 1962 his *Miss U.S.* exceeded 200 mph, a longstanding record for piston-engine, propeller-driven boats.

From 1955 to 1971 the raceboat designer devoted his time to fiberglass, inboard-powered recreational boats, which he manufactured in the Bay area under the name Arena Craft. He also built custom boats to his own designs, including a boat for Howard Arneson, inventor of the Arneson surface-prop drive system, an idea Dan Arena helped to develop.

—Joseph Gribbins

DONALD ARONOW

March 1, 1927–February 3, 1987 · United States

An American speedboat builder, racer, and designer, Don Aronow singlehandedly transformed the sport of powerboat racing. After becoming a millionaire in real estate development in New Jersey in the 1950's, he moved to Miami Beach, Florida, and was drawn to powerboat racing. Raymond Hunt had recently developed his Deep-V hull shape, and Dick Bertram established the superiority of the new design by winning the 1960 Miami-Nassau Race. Basing his ideas on the deep-V shape, Aronow collaborated with other designers and within one decade started and sold four companies that became the core of the muscle boat industry.

In 1961 Aronow founded Formula Boat Company. In 1965 he started Donzi Marine. In 1966 he started Magnum, and by 1967 Aronow was designing boats completely on his own. During this time he developed breakthrough hull designs that served as the forerunners of powerboats to follow. In 1969 he founded Cigarette Boats and the Cigarette Racing Team.

Over the years Aronow's powerboats won more than eleven world and twenty-five U.S. championships and have held twenty-five world speed records. In 1987 he was shot to death on 188th Street in North Miami Beach, Florida, also known as "Gasoline Alley," the very street he made famous. The case involving his murder has not been closed.

—Robert McKenna

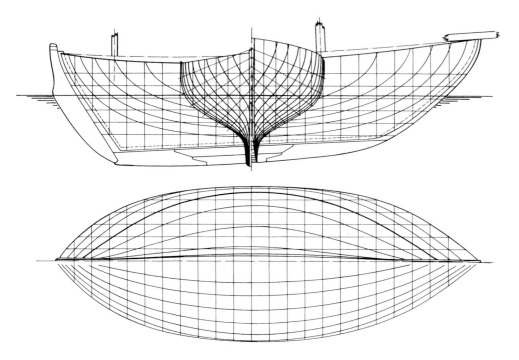

Colin Archer: Redningskoite. Redningskoites had to perform rescues close to shore on an exposed coastline in heavy weather. The lines emphasize buoyancy, lateral plane, stability, and motion dampening rather than speed. The result was tremendous power and control. The 1893 concept continues to influence cruising yacht design. *Drawing reproduced from Juan Baader's* The Sailing Yacht

JOHN DAVENPORT ATKIN

August 19, 1918–November 11, 1999
United States

The son of prolific designer/writer William Atkin, John Atkin began his design career at the end of World War II when he started working in his father's office. Until William's death in 1962, it is difficult to separate the work of the two men, as during this time they collaborated on many designs, and John created completely original work as well as designs that revisited themes begun in his father's earlier work. However, it is clear that John Atkin brought to the collaboration a superb eye and refined drafting talent. He did not attempt to continue his father's extremely high rate of productivity, but concentrated instead on detail, aesthetic refinement, and precise drafting so as to produce the highest quality of work possible.

Atkin produced designs that were notable for their extreme functionality, based on an enormous amount of personal experience and owner feedback. He continued the family tradition of designing a broad range of tradition-based boats, including rowing boats, small sailboats and motorboats and cruising power and sailboats of all sizes. His boats are also noted for their great beauty of line—again he was able to draw on experience from actual results in literally hundreds of designs.

Two of Atkin's best-known designs are *Island Princess*, a 36-foot 7-inch, chine-hulled schooner, and *Maid of Endor*, a 23-foot, gaff-rigged sloop of such exquisite beauty that its design has been published in nearly every major magazine's design section at one time or another, and continues to be built today.

John Atkin is also well known for his refinement of his father's popular Norwegian-style double-ended type into a faster and more distinctly "Atkin" type. Like William, John drew a number of highly refined and practical motorboats, suited to modern power plants, as well as many excellent plywood designs. Most of Atkin's designs contain references to traditional types and emphasize practicality over ostentation.

Born in Huntington, New York, John Atkin published his first design at age fifteen. He studied naval architecture at New York Technical School and attended Yale University. He worked for a while as a draftsman for Consolidated Shipbuilding Corporation, and in 1939

John Atkin: *Island Princess.* *Island Princess* combines the romance and handling characteristics of a traditional schooner with V-bottom construction intended to appeal to the amateur builder. Atkin's intimate familiarity with traditional design elements enabled him to retain an authentic look and feel, in what became one of his most popular designs. *Photo courtesy Pat Atkin*

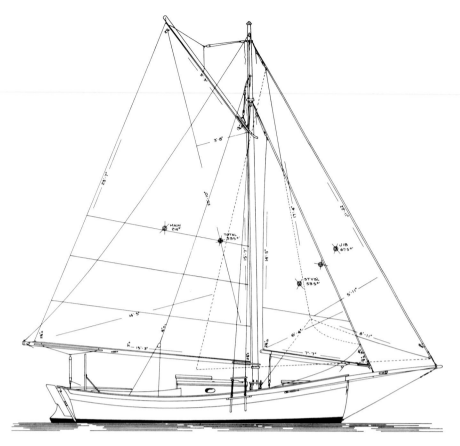

John Atkin: *Maid of Endor.* This tough, seaworthy, easy-to-handle pocket cruiser is good for gunkholing or even more ambitious cruising. She is also a perfect expression of John Atkin's aesthetic gift, with every line a study in exuberance and personality, and a strong sense of reliability. She was among Atkin's favorites. *Drawing courtesy WoodenBoat Publications*

moved to Luders Marine Construction Company in Stamford, Connecticut. During World War II he served as navigator and first mate on tugs and transport ships in the Pacific. He joined the Atkin design office in Darien, Connecticut, in 1946.

Like his father, John Atkin understood the importance of getting his work and his philosophy into print. He continued his father's long series of designs for *Motor Boating* magazine and wrote a column called "Around the Shop Fire" for *Boat* magazine, under the name "John Davenport." He also wrote for *Nautical Quarterly* and published a small collection of his work in his book *Practical Small Boat Designs.* He was an accomplished marine surveyor. John Atkin died in Connecticut.

—Daniel B. MacNaughton

WILLIAM ATKIN

October 14, 1882–August 1962 · United States

In a field whose history is largely dominated by racing boats and their designers, William Atkin stands out as one of the great designers of boats meant strictly for cruising, daysailing, fishing, living aboard, or any of the other noncompetitive activities that have always brought people into close communication with nature and with each other. This is what Atkin felt boats were for.

Atkin was one of the first designers to write at length about his designs, and large numbers of them appeared in print along with his comments, many in the famous *Motor Boating & Sailing* "Ideal" series. His writing was powerful and poetical, painting a picture of each boat's natural environment and how she might be best enjoyed. He designed and wrote about an extremely wide range of boats of all sizes and types. Some readers were confused by statements that seemed to conflict. He would portray first one type of boat as the best to own, and then another, though they might be quite different. In fact it is clear that he loved them all and was only hoping to match the right boat with the right person.

While he drew many wonderful large vessels, Atkin's first love was designing boats that average people could incorporate into their day-to-day lives. With many of his designs having been made available as stock plans, it is probable that there are still more Atkin-designed, home-built boats in the world than those of any other designer except, probably, today's Philip Bolger, in many ways Atkin's philosophical successor.

Atkin was born in Harlem, New York, the son of a successful printer. The family moved to Montclair, New Jersey, soon after his birth. For reasons unknown, Atkin only attended school until the seventh grade. He came into contact with boats and boatbuilding on the Jersey shore, where he spent as much time as possible. Eventually he fell in with Cottrell Wheeler, who became a lifelong friend, and the two built *Buddie II,* a small motorboat of Atkin's design.

Buddie II was a success, and encouraged by interest on the part of potential customers, the two decided to go into business together. Following the traditional pattern, Atkin began his career as a combination designer and builder, serving a local market out of a small shop in Huntington, Long Island, which he and Wheeler bought in 1906. It was always referred to as The Red Boat Shop. Due to intense local demand and good financial backing, it seems the business was successful from the very first, building about nineteen motorboats to Atkin's design, the largest of which was 40 feet in length.

Atkin married Dorcas Wilson in 1912. They had two sons, William Wilson Atkin and John Davenport Atkin.

By 1912 Atkin and Wheeler required a larger shop better suited to the use of power tools, so at that time they designed and constructed The New Shop, a much bigger building with a well-developed waterfront facility. There they produced thirty-one boats, ranging from an 18-foot hydroplane to the 115-foot express cruiser *Cabrilla.* Some of the spirit of the shop and of the times can be expressed by the fact that they also designed and built *Cabrilla's* twin 750-hp V-8 engines and their transmissions, a degree of confidence few boatyards would display today. The business Atkin and Wheeler lasted until World War I, but then ceased operations for reasons not explained, although it may be that the yard was never able to cope with the overhead of the larger facility; Atkin was an advocate of small boatbuilding shops for the rest of his career.

During the war Atkin, who had suffered partial paralysis of his left leg due to polio and was unable to serve in the military, became editor of *Yachting* magazine, quite a leap for a young boatbuilder and probably based on the quality of some earlier writing for *The Rudder.* Three years later he became technical editor of *Motor Boat,* beginning a close and productive association with Editor William Nutting.

One of the products of that association was Atkin's design for the 45-foot schooner *Typhoon,* a traditional-looking boat having a radical hull design with a broad transom and an

William Atkin: *Chantey*. *Chantey* has the charm that comes from a relatively small size for her type, somewhat huskier-than-average proportions, and some extra exuberance in all her major curves. She hearkens strongly to her working-class roots, and it is doubtful that she would be improved by any departure from her mostly paint finish. © *Peter Barlow*

extravagantly long and hollow entrance. She made a very fast transatlantic passage under the command of Nutting and survived a very rough return voyage (with the twenty-two-year-old, British yacht-designer-to-be Uffa Fox aboard). However, it is likely that the unbalanced hull form was not a total success, the best

evidence of which is that most of Atkin's subsequent work retained much more traditional similarity between the forward and aft shapes of the hull. Nonetheless, the publicity surrounding the voyage and the design served to make Atkin a nationally known designer.

Another product of Atkin's work with Nut-

ting was the popularization of Norwegian-style double-enders in America. In the early twentieth century, small yachts were beginning to make long offshore voyages, and interest in seaworthy cruising boats was high. During a trip to Scandinavia, Nutting became fascinated by the famous Norwegian Redningskoites and

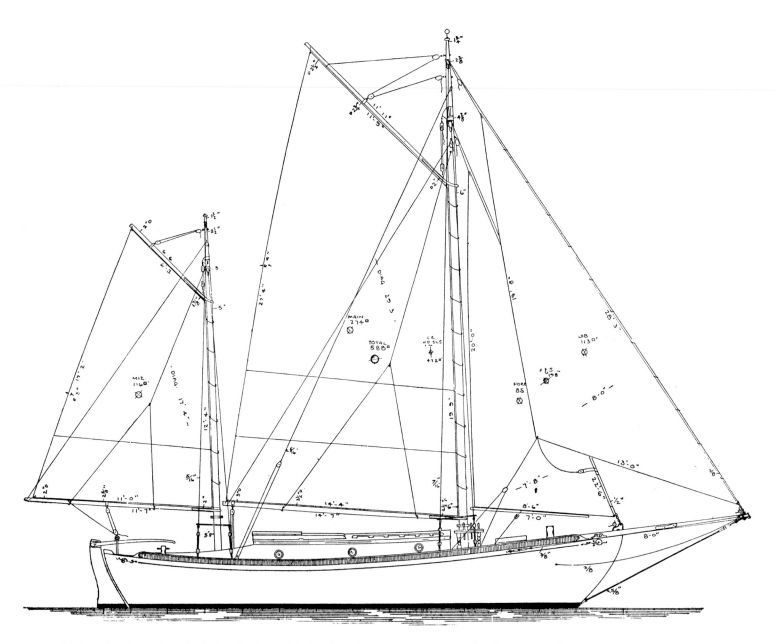

William Atkin: *Eric.* The 32-foot, double-ended ketch *Eric*, first built in 1925, served to introduce Norwegian design elements into American yacht design, and became the progenitor of a long line of similar yachts by William Atkin, his son John, and many others. The original *Eric* is still sailing virtually unmodified from the original plans. *Drawing courtesy Pat Atkin*

pilot cutters designed by Colin Archer. The broad-beamed, heavy-displacement type lent itself to miniaturization, so the 47-foot Redningskoite was scaled to 32 feet. The design, published as *Eric*, evolved somewhat before it was eventually built in 1925, but it ultimately became the progenitor of several generations of American double-ended designs. Eventually the design was modified and adapted to fiberglass construction by designer W. I. B. Crealock, resulting in the well-known Westsail 32. The original *Eric* is still sailing, owned by one of the editors of this encyclopedia.

After *Eric*, double-enders of Norwegian influence became a staple of Atkin's design output, with numerous examples produced during the rest of William Atkin's career as well as that of his son John. Adaptation of the type

to American recreational sailing resulted in a less beamy, more straight-sided boat that was faster.

Another type that was popularized by Atkin for pleasure use was the Seabright Skiff. Originally a round-bilged rowing skiff with a flat bottom and a boxlike skeg instead of the typical keel structure, the type was perfect for launching off the beaches of New Jersey, and served multiple purposes including fishing. Owing to the shape and structure of the Seabright hull, it lent itself to the installation of gasoline engines when they became practical, and the type quickly evolved to include powerboats of good speed and ability. Atkin was intrigued by the type and drew many variations for many purposes and in many sizes, including even large sail and power

yachts. Among the smaller skiffs were a number of boats with a tunnel drive, for use in extremely shoal waters.

Atkin was also fascinated by simple, lapstrake, flat-bottomed skiffs and drew almost every conceivable variation for a wide range of purposes. It was a type that few designers seemed to notice, perhaps due to its universal application to every mundane purpose, but Atkin turned to it whenever economy and simplicity were considerations. He was able to infuse it with more style and grace than practically anyone before or since.

Also among Atkin's designs are a host of powerboats in every size and type and for every purpose. Although some have become outdated owing to advances in hull design, and the designer is better known for his sailboats, many are unique and enduring classics well deserving of close examination. Atkin also designed houseboats, shanty boats, and working craft of many types.

Atkin worked at a very rapid pace, averaging twenty designs a year. At one time he is said to have had more boats in *Lloyd's Register* than any other designer. His drafting was not as meticulous as his son John's would be, but he understood the value of personality and uniqueness in every design. Most designs that saw print were referred to by a name, and each one was given some individual features, even quirks, that served to give it a certain personality. This seems to have contributed to the great popularity of the designs and to the affection with which Atkin boats are held by their owners. Bland mass-produced boats would have been incomprehensible to Atkin, and he became a strong critic of modern mass-marketing techniques in his later career.

In 1926 Atkin made a more direct entrance into the publishing field by introducing *Fore An' Aft,* "a cruising magazine conceived by cruising men and dedicated to cruising." The magazine restricted itself to covering yachts no more than 50 feet in length, with most much smaller. A handsome, appealing, and well-written magazine, it lasted until 1929, when it ceased publication, probably due to the national economic crisis beginning in that year.

Georges Auzépy-Brenneur: Akela 50. Designed in 1985, the Akela 50 class is one of Auzépy-Brenneur's best-known designs. Built of both wood-epoxy and aluminum, the class has seen many victories in offshore races. The 15.24-meter sloop reflects the designer's preference for long, light hulls and is capable of speeds greater than 24 knots. *Drawing courtesy Georges Auzépy-Brenneur*

In 1947 William and John Atkin began *The Book of Boats,* which was to be a quarterly publication. Only two issues ever came out, but they have continued to be reprinted. Other books by William Atkin include *Three Little Cruising Yachts, Motor Boats,* and *Of Yachts and Men.*

Never much of a businessman, Atkin is said to have been paid only $100 apiece for the designs published in *Motor Boating,* and much less than the going rate for his other designs. The cancellation of a boatbuilding project in which he was a middleman wiped him out financially at the onset of the Depression and cost him his home. It was only when his son John joined his office after World War II that more realistic business practices came into play.

The 1938 hurricane destroyed the Atkin family's home on Pratt's Island on Long Island Sound, along with many plans and models. The family had to swim for their lives at the height of the storm. Soon thereafter Atkin designed and built a new home and office named Anchordown, in Noroton, Connecticut. The building combined nautical elements with 1930's notions of modernity, and is still in use as a residence.

John Atkin joined the design office after World War II, and the two men worked together from then on. It is difficult to separate their work, especially as for one reason or another, some of it seems to be deliberately misattributed. What is clear is that the two men enjoyed working together, and continued to do so until William Atkin's death.

—Daniel B. MacNaughton

GEORGES AUZÉPY-BRENNEUR

Born May 30, 1935 · France

Almost no area of yachting is untouched by Georges Auzépy-Brenneur's talent. Besides his large sailing yachts and motorboats, he is the designer behind an armada of more than 250,000 Dufour Wing sailboards (1978) and 190,000 Tabur dinghies. In his racing designs he is known for his refusal to distort his hulls to accommodate the vagaries of the rating rules.

However, it is in his design of over sixty large sailing yachts that Auzépy-Brenneur has built his primary reputation. Among these is the remarkable 19-meter steel schooner *Wild Rockett* (1971). Designed for cruising, the vessel entered several OSTAR's (Observer Singlehanded Transatlantic Races). She put in a notable performance at the start of the 1972 race, driving to windward in heavy air. She remained in first place for twenty-four hours, ahead of *Pen Duick IV* and *Vendredi 13,* until she had to return to Plymouth owing to a damaged mainsail. She was the second-place monohull in the 1978

Route du Rhum and third in the 1982 Route du Rhum, only outstripped by pure racers longer than her. Her design was innovative for the time. Although Auzépy-Brenneur had applied to her, as always, Admiral Turner's metacentric theory, she had wide, flat sections carried well aft, and an underbody terminating in a strong bustle. Balance, stability, and power were central to her design concept.

Confident from this success, Auzépy-Brenneur revisited this concept in the cold-molded ketch *Kriter* (1973), which placed third in elapsed time in the first Whitbread around-the-world race in 1973–74, and this despite the handicaps of an excessively high rating and a very bad first leg. This performance brought many orders for big cruising sailboats, including a 24-meter ketch named *Nesea IV* (1976) and a 27-meter schooner, *Dame des Tropiques* (1990).

Auzépy-Brenneur learned design through three years of training under designer Eugène Cornu, from 1956 through 1958. His first independent design was the 7.97-meter sloop *Alerion* (1959), an early ULDB. Two years later at Algiers he executed his first professional commission, *Pacane,* in the same style as *Alerion.* Since then he has retained his interest in long, sharp, and light hulls, such as the Akela 50 class *Caisse d'Epargne du Pas de Calais,* which in 1992 won Class II in the Europe 1 Star competition, and the 50-foot BOC racer *Sicli* (1992), twice the winner of the Round Britain Race, in 1993 and 1998.

Not limiting his efforts to the design of custom yachts, Auzépy-Brenneur is also the creator of many lines of production sailboats ranging from the famous 5.80-meter Midjet, drawn in 1967 and a fixture at regattas for the next twenty years, through the 13.37-meter cruising sloop or ketch Rorqual of 1973. He also likes to draw classic yachts such as *Alcyon* (1993), and even traditional designs such as the 17-meter schooner *Acalyouli* (1968). Auzépy-Brenneur has also produced many motorboats for work and pleasure, including the 31-meter yacht *Timeless* (1992).

Originally from Brittany, Auzépy-Brenneur learned to sail with the marine scouts at Casablanca. Since then, his passion for yachting has led him to participate in many regattas and cruises, experiences that have served to display his talent and advance his career. A devotee of baroque music and a friend of wolves, his two other passions, he has an eternally inquiring mind, always looking for any new idea that can affect yachting. Residing near Paris since 1963 and always active, he has drawn more than 442 design studies and plans, of which more than 320 are for sailboats, and he has utilized almost all types of construction materials.

Auzépy-Brenneur's office is outside of Paris in St. Cloud.

—Jacques Taglang

VINCENZO VITTORIO BAGLIETTO

1891–1978 · Italy

In a career that spanned the most disrupted decades of the twentieth century, Vincenzo Baglietto first earned a degree in naval engineering at the University of Glasgow, then completed his military service in the Italian air force. After World War I, he joined the family shipyard in Varazze as the shop engineer. Among the sailboats he designed between the two world wars, Baglietto always fondly remembered the 8-meter *Bona*, originally built for Eugenio di Duke of Ancon, and launched in 1934. For her time and class, she represented a unique and exceptionally lucky racing vessel. From 1936 to 1938, in forty-nine races, she won twenty-five times and took second place fourteen times, including the Italian Cup in Genoa in 1937 and the French Cup at Cannes in 1938.

Bona's successes cannot be attributed solely to the strength of her design. Her construction plans displayed a new methodology in which great care was given to details that are usually overlooked. Baglietto applied this standard to all production in the shipyard, not only to racing vessels. Another of his notable designs was the 6-meter *Viky II*, built in 1932, which won many races both abroad and in Italy.

The designer also found success in the field of motorboats. Several became famous: *Baglietto I* won in 1923 in Monaco, and *Baglietto XXI* was victorious in 1924 in both Cannes and Barcelona, where she won the King Alfonso Cup, in each case setting speed records in the International 7.5-liter class. These fast speed boats gave a foretaste of the performances of *Cabac*, *Cabar*, *Ravanello*, and *Lia III*, which, with a 300-hp Isotta Fraschini motor, became the first Italian boat to exceed 100 kilometers per hour, capturing the world record for its class.

The very slender lines of the bow and the concentration of weight in the stern, together

Vincenzo Baglietto: Alagi. Baglietto's early career was marked by meteoric success in racing motorboat design. Among his numerous record breakers was the 500-hp Alagi, winner of the 1938 12-liter (engine displacement) class, with races held that year in Venice, Geneva, and Detroit. *Photo courtesy Franco Belloni*

with a careful study of the center of gravity, constituted the major innovations of the extremely fast racers *Alagi* and *Asso R.B.*

On November 24, 1938, in Arona on Lake Maggiore, Guido Cattaneo in the *Asso R.B.* captured the world speed prize for racing powerboats at speeds of 150.6 kilometers per hour. Among restricted boats, she was the fastest in the world. *Asso R.B.*, whose wood and light-alloy hull measured 5.3 meters, was powered with a 500-hp Isotta Fraschini Asso M 12 C. To deliver her power, she utilized two counter-rotating propellers on one shaft, designed and patented in 1936 by Giustino and Guido Cattaneo and a precursor to the modern assembly used in some recreational vessels.

In the years prior to World War II, Baglietto worked on a new hard-chine underbody shape that was revolutionary for its time, first using one chine, then two. There was great interest in this unusual design for both recreational and military boats. Indeed, it became the underbody

of the Italian MAS (Anti-Submersible Motorboat). In 1935–37, Baglietto designed the MAS 501–525 series, of which eight models were built and which, when fully equipped, could reach a speed of 44 knots. All the MAS boats built in the years prior to and during World War II were designed by Baglietto; his shipyard saw to their construction.

In the years following World War II, he again took up the design and construction of recreational and racing vessels. In that period, Baglietto was the first Italian to utilize laminated structures, adapting them to shipbuilding, and a new type of underbody that was especially suited for high speed on rough seas.

Pietro Baglietto: *Twins VII* (opposite). Few designers have achieved consistent victories in both sailing and powerboat competition. Baglietto was an exception. Among his many winners were a series of 5.5-Meter yachts named *Twins*. *Photo courtesy Franco Belloni*

Returning to the design of sailboats in 1948, he launched the yawl *Caroly*, measuring 23.66 meters, for Riccardo Preve, who took it on a Genoa–Buenos Aires–New York–Genoa cruise, something quite unusual for those years. Another sailboat, *Ea*, launched in 1953, was a Class I RORC sloop belonging to Guido Giovanelli and Filippo Cameli (one of the main characters in the 1950's open-ocean racing scene on the Mediterranean).

During this period, Baglietto joined forces with his nephew, Pietro. Born in Genoa in 1923, Pietro graduated with a degree in naval engineering from the University of Genoa and became the head of technical management for the shipyard from 1956 to 1979.

Pietro Baglietto is remembered for his original Class III RORC design for *Lanzerota*. Taking advantage of loopholes in the regulations, he created a fast boat that performed particularly well in races held on triangular courses. At the beginning of the 1950's, Pietro turned his attention to the 5.5-Meter class and designed a series of boats named *Twins*, owned by Max E. Oberti. In 1953, *Twins VI* won in Grahara (Helsinki) and in 1954, she won the Italian Cup in Genoa. *Twins VII* won the Scandinavian Gold Cup in 1955 and the French Cup in Geneva in 1956. In 1959, the Baglietto shipyard recommended the in-house design and construction of mass-produced motoryachts.

—Franco Belloni

CHARLES BAILEY SR.
1845–1923
CHARLES BAILEY JR.
1864–1952
WALTER BAILEY
1867–1927

New Zealand

The Baileys were key figures in New Zealand yacht design and construction for nearly seventy years, thirty of which involved a head-to-head rivalry with the Logan family, to the infinite benefit of both.

Charles Bailey Sr. took over the Beddoes yard at Devonport on Auckland's North Shore in 1872. Gradually, as the Auckland yacht fleet grew, he became a leading builder of the centerboard open sailing boats of various local classes and of keel yachts. He had no training as a designer and built from half models. Bailey was an excellent helmsman and promoted his business by building and sailing the best of the open sailing boats at regattas and match races in Auckland and nearby ports for large amounts of prize money. From 1879 on, he had a strong rival in boatbuilder Robert Logan Sr.

Charles Bailey Sr.: *Viking.* This big yawl, slashing along close-hauled in smooth water, shows the classic slender, clipper-bowed model typical of Bailey's larger designs. The yawl rig contributed much to its ease of handling, especially in the days before auxiliary engines simplified maneuvering in close quarters. *Photo courtesy Harold Kidd*

Charles Bailey Jr.: *Heartsease.* In 1897 the designer and his brother Walter launched the 48-foot *Heartsease*, built with design input from J. G. Trevithick for A. B. Donald, one of the Baileys' best customers for whom they had built a long line of beautiful Pacific trading schooners. She is now in Sydney. *Photo courtesy Harold Kidd*

BAGLIETTO · BAILEY

Bailey's large yachts, *Daphne* (30 tons, 1874), *Erin* (10 tons, 1877), and *Rita* (13 tons, 1881), his large fishing boats, and his trading cutters were all very successful in their fields of endeavor. He was also instrumental in crystallizing the form of the Auckland mullet boat (an indigenous ballasted centerboard type that is still racing) with his 24-footer *Manola* in 1885.

Charles Bailey Jr. began apprenticing under his father in 1878. He had formally trained in naval architecture, and had designed and built a number of important yachts before he and his brother Walter took over their father's yard in 1893.

From 1881 onward, like his father, Charles Jr. made a reputation for himself as the designer, builder, and helmsman of outstandingly successful open sailing boats that benefited from lightweight construction techniques, often using cedar.

Charles Jr. and Walter traded as "C. & W. Bailey" until 1898. During this period, they built a large number of yachts, many of them 2½- and 5-Raters for New Zealand and Australian owners. They often used kauri wood in a double- and triple-diagonal frameless method pioneered by Robert Logan Sr. in about 1878, an early ancestor of what is now cold-molded construction. The Bailey new raters were matched, often boat for boat, season after season, by Logan raters. Generally, the Logan yachts proved slightly superior, but the competition improved the breed enormously, providing Auckland (and Sydney, Australia) with a stock of craft that formed the backbone of yacht racing until 1940. The strength, materials, and craftsmanship that went into these yachts were so good that a large number still survive.

In 1897 the Bailey yard produced the 30-foot Linear Rater *Meteor*, which for the first time immediately had the legs of her Logan counterpart. She was sold to an owner in Sydney and helped to open a large export market to Australia that would occupy the Bailey and Logan yards well into the twentieth century.

After splitting with Walter in 1898, Charles Jr. carried on alone and became increasingly busy with commercial work, building some fine schooners and trading cutters for the Pacific Islands trade, plus ferry boats and coastal traders. He also developed stock motor launches for the many remaining roadless areas of the country.

Walter Bailey cofounded the firm of Bailey and Lowe in 1898 and was also very successful in the commercial field, especially in launch work. The firm also produced some yacht designs of merit, including some 24-foot Linear Raters and a number of the influential racing mullet boats of the turn of the century.

—Harold Kidd and Robin Elliott

John Bain: *Red Pirate*. The 80-foot *Red Pirate*, launched in 1948, is a development of the Westwind class, the first of which came out in 1930. In this series of designs, Bain advanced powerboat design by lightening the displacement, reducing the drag of the rudder, and experimenting with a flush-deck configuration. *Photo courtesy Piero Maria Gibellini*

JOHN BAIN

1889–1980 · Scotland

A pioneer of British motorboating, John Bain was the first in Britain to develop semiproduction boatbuilding and a line of stock boats, as well as his trademark "Bain stern."

The son of a Scottish designer and builder of model yachts, Bain learned the principles of yacht design first from his father and later at evening classes he attended while he was an apprentice at a joinery firm. In 1914 he was hired by the James A. Silver boatyard, which had been active on a peninsula near the mouth of the Clyde since the mid-1800's. Bain became yard manager in 1916, a difficult period for the yard owing to the onset of World War I. He designed small craft and utility craft for the war effort.

The first motoryacht designed by Bain at Silver's was launched in 1919. Built on speculation, the 23-foot 6-inch *Maple Leaf* served to establish a production run of these yachts, afterward known as the Maple Leaf class. Essentially a motoryacht in miniature, with low fuel consumption, the design proved successful, and between 1919 and 1921 six or seven more were built. Their success led to a number of custom-designed boats also built at Silver's.

In 1928 the yard launched the 42-foot *Brown Owl*, a twin-screw motoryacht with a canoe stern, which represented another stock Bain

design. The Brown Owl class was produced until the mid-1930's, in 42-, 47-, and 52-foot versions. Under Bain's direction, Silver's became the first yard in Britain to utilize something resembling a production line, successfully reducing labor costs and thereby broadening the marketability of the boats, even as the company acquired a reputation for its high quality and disciplined approach.

After the onset of the Great Depression in the 1930's, Bain introduced the Silverette, a new class of small powerboats built at low cost for a wider market. The 30-footer made a success of the yard and made John Bain famous. A 36-foot version was soon offered. The 60-foot *Westwind* was launched in June 1930 and incorporated many innovative features that appeared in future Bain designs.

Aiming for a seaworthy yacht capable of 14 knots, Bain lightened the displacement, created a new underwater shape, introduced a low-drag, unsupported spade rudder, and designed a distinctive elliptical stern that came to be known as the Bain stern. This design contributed elements to the popular Silver Leaf class, produced from 1932 to 1951 and ranging from 42 to 52 feet in length. By the mid-1930's Silver's had become the most productive and respected motoryacht builder in Britain. A few sailboats were also designed and built in the 1930's, and in 1939 the yard began producing a number of motorsailers.

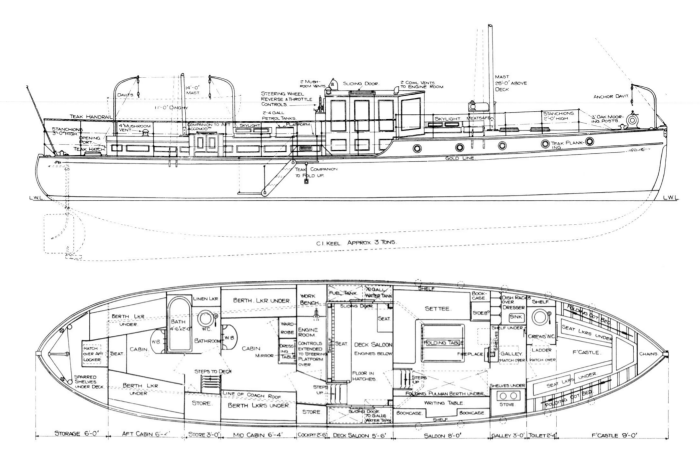

John Bain: *Brown Owl.* This 52-foot, twin-engine cruiser, launched in 1928, was the first of what became the Brown Owl class. She was among the first yachts in Britain to be built with some production line methods. *Drawing courtesy Piero Maria Gibellini*

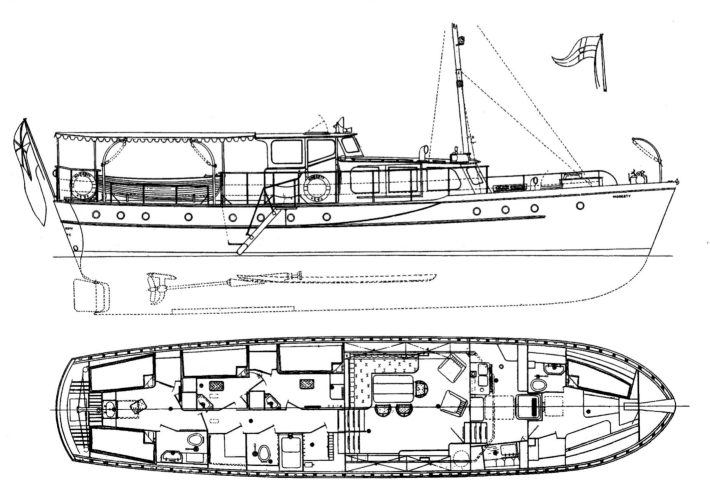

John Bain: *Modesti.* The Ormidale cruisers came in 55-, 57-, and 58-foot versions. *Modesti* was a 58-footer built in 1955. Note the high flush deck aft and the space it provides both on deck and below. *Drawing courtesy Piero Maria Gibellini*

During World War II Bain contributed to the war effort by building "Fairmile" gunboats and motor torpedo boats, ranging in length from 100 to 120 feet, along with harbor launches, dinghies, and naval cutters. Because of Bain's careful hoarding of leftover teak from these projects, Silver's was one of the few yards able to offer teak hulls immediately after the war.

Many of Bain's boats were involved in the Dunkirk evacuation, including the Brown Owls *Wairakei*, *Wairakei II*, and *Moiena*; the Silverette *White Orchid*; and the 80-foot custom-built *Conidaw*, which alone removed over nine hundred men from the beaches.

Besides *Conidaw*, Bain designed other large custom yachts, such as the 72-foot *Silver Fox*, built in 1937, and the 80-foot *Red Pirate*, of 1948. *Silver Fox*, like the Brown Owl class, had a canoe stern and heavy displacement, whereas *Red Pirate* was an evolution of the *Westwind* design, with a shallow hull and the Bain stern. *Red Pirate* was the first motoryacht he drew with a flush deck. It inspired the design of the Ormidale class,

which was produced in 55-, 57-, and 58-foot versions from 1948 to the mid-1960's. The first *Ormidale* won the Pavillon d'Or in 1948, beating ninety British, Dutch, and Belgian vessels.

John Bain left Silver's in 1957.

Bain also designed for other yards. He drew a 40-footer for Anderson in 1947 and designed the 62-foot *Joanne of Garth* for A. M. Dickie and Sons in 1953. His collaboration with Dickie and Sons continued for a number of years. Until the 1970's, his designs were also used by other important yards in the United Kingdom, such as R. A. Newman of Poole and James N. Miller and Sons of Saint Monas. From 1959 to 1963 Miller launched various yachts designed by Bain, ranging from the 58-foot *Sea Crest* to the 73-foot *Wild Venture*.

Over his long career, Bain produced more than five hundred designs, and in Britain is considered the father of the family-owned and -operated power yacht. With their elegant and timeless appearance, good seakeeping ability, high-quality materials, and precise construction, surviving examples are well re-

garded and much sought after. Many of his yachts are still in use around Britain, in the Mediterranean, and in U.S. waters.

Bain was also an excellent teacher. His evening classes in the Rosneath village school were attended by apprentices from many boatyards because of his reputation for preparing first-class workmen.

Such was the great respect people held for John Bain that following his death at the age of ninety-one, numerous representatives from many of the most important yards in Scotland attended his funeral. —Piero Maria Gibellini

JON BANNENBERG

July 8, 1929–May 26, 2002 · Australia/England

According to Jon Bannenberg, "People do not lose 30 percent of their volume when stepping aboard a yacht." There is no need, therefore, to scale down their space requirements compared to, say, their apartment or even their castle. This notion is not entirely practicable in a

Jon Bannenberg: *Sagitta*. With an aluminum hull and composite superstructure, the 57-meter *Sagitta* was the last of a long collaboration between Australia's Oceanfast yard and Bannenberg. The interior is typical of the clean, light, and meticulously laid-out Bannenberg style. *Photo courtesy Dickie Bannenberg*

40-footer but is clearly suited to the 400-foot motoryachts he designed. In addition, Bannenberg followed the compelling precept that in all his work he "at least attempts to make each design a work of art." He not only revolutionized the look of modern yacht design but also changed its methodology: once the province of naval architects alone, methodology under Bannenberg's influence sometimes involved a collaboration between a technician who knew the sea and an aesthetician who knew the client.

Born of Dutch and Australian parentage, Bannenberg was educated at the Sydney Conservatorium of Music. After graduating in 1951, he sailed by freighter to London, where he played piano in clubs and designed sets for the Old Vic theater. While a partner in a leading antiques gallery, he began designing rooms around the artwork he sold, so that by 1954 he and his wife Beaupré could open their own architecture and design firm.

Although an enthusiastic sailor, Bannenberg had no particular plans to design yachts—he worked mostly on offices, homes, museums,

and an occasional aircraft. He also helped redesign London's Ritz Hotel, and one-third of the suites and public spaces in the new ocean liner *Queen Elizabeth 2*.

But in 1963 a 40-foot powerboat with an exterior and interior designed by Bannenberg was shown at the London Boat Show, and other yacht assignments followed. Bannenberg took a giant leap, however, when asked by a German businessman to design the 72-meter yacht *Carinthia VI*. Bannenberg had already decided that the design of older motoryachts was based on nineteenth-century sailing yachts, but that Italian designers had broken with that tradition in what he called a "generic excess of fantasy." He was determined to expand on that notion. With no inflexible preconceptions, Bannenberg could freely discount common yacht-design limitations, and did so for *Carinthia VI*. With a fine bow, supple sheerline, wide decks, and a harmonious superstructure featuring wraparound, grille-covered windows, *Carinthia* was a harbinger of Bannenberg's nonconformity, if not his later more contentious style. Indeed, Bannenberg himself felt that *Carinthia* was an

"electrifying opportunity, revolutionary, even avant-garde for the time."

Carinthia was followed in 1972 by Bannenberg's 38-meter *Pegasus*, and then by various designs built at the world's leading shipyards. He was soon asked to design one of the most talked-about yachts of the era, Adnan Khashoggi's 86-meter, Benetti-built *Nabila*, recognized at her 1979 launch as original almost beyond imagination, an extravagance almost beyond measure.

Next, Bannenberg began collaborating on a series of revolutionary motoryachts ranging from 36 to 55 meters in length and built at Oceanfast, in Western Australia, including *Parts VI, Antipodean, Mystique, Opal C, Bolkiah, Sound of Pacific, Moecca, Oceana,* and in 1998 *Thunder*. During this time he had advanced his notion of carrying the superstructure to the rail. While this eliminated side decks, it increased the usable interior volume over that available in traditional island deckhouse yachts, and substantially altered the perceived balance between hull and superstructure.

In the 1980's Bannenberg designed a variety of yachts between 42 and 57 meters long including *Acajou,* built by Esterel; *My Gail III* and *Lady Ghislaine,* built by Amels; *Bengal, BBC Challenge,* and *Southern Cross III,* built by Sterling; and *Stefaren,* built by Brooke. Brooke also built Bannenberg's own 37-meter sailing yacht *Beaupré,* an evolution of *Acharné,* a 112-footer designed in collaboration with Ron Holland and built by the Royal Huisman Shipyard.

Through the early 1990's, several Bannenberg designs were built in Holland at the Van Lent and de Vries shipyards, the components of Feadship, perhaps the greatest name in twentieth-century motoryacht building. These included *Azteca, Paraiso, Cedar Sea II,* and *Siran,* ranging from 47 to 64 meters in length; and *The Highlander,* a 46-meter yacht built for Malcolm Forbes. In the 1990's Lürssen Werft, in Germany, also launched two award-winning Bannenberg yachts: the 72-meter *Coral Island,* in 1994, and the 96-meter *Limitless,* a stunning variation on the earlier *Carinthia,* launched in 1997.

Jon Bannenberg found a unique way to harmoniously integrate many elements, and in doing so introduced numerous signature touches including padded overheads and bulkheads, large round windows, the extensive use of glued-in exterior glass, tender and automobile garages, and composite superstructures. Bannenberg and his staff complemented the basic structures with the design of everyday details such as towels, stationery, china, glassware, decorative items, and crew uniforms.

Bannenberg completed more than two hundred important yachts, approximately fifty of

Jon Bannenberg: *Talitha G.* Built by Krupp in Germany in 1929, the 263-foot LOA *Talitha G* was completely rebuilt at the DML shipyard between 1992 and 1994. Bannenberg replaced her single funnel with two, one accommodating the satellite TV dome, and created an eclectic interior combining art nouveau and art deco styles. *Photo courtesy Dickie Bannenberg*

A. C. Barber: *Stormbird*. Built in 1933, *Stormbird* is pictured here in the early 1960's, when Fraser Johnston raced her in one of three consecutive seasons of division wins on Sydney Harbour. With her canoe stern and raised deck, Barber called the lightly built design "his honest little yacht." *Photo courtesy David Payne*

tury. He received an Order of the British Empire, and while he was relatively unknown elsewhere, in Sydney he was referred to as "our local designer."

Barber studied shipbuilding in England and was briefly a student of naval architecture at Durham University in County Durham. He began designing boats in Melbourne, Victoria, in 1912, before moving to Sydney in 1915. During World War I he was a designer at Kidman's Boat Builders. Once established on his own after the war, he became a success, as exemplified by the very desirable address of his offices, at 77 Pitt Street in Sydney. His plans were carefully drawn, well detailed, and considered works of art by many builders.

Among his early designs were the 14-foot Cadet dinghy, still an active class in the 1990's, and the 25-foot *Colleen*, the first of the Derwent class yachts, with which he won Australia's first-ever yacht design competition. Later he drew large yachts such as the 62-foot motor sailer *Lauriana* (these days a charter boat in Sydney Harbour), the 73-foot ketch-rigged motor sailer *Lady Ellen*, and the luxurious 75-foot motor cruiser *Miramar II*.

Rani, winner of the first Sydney-Hobart Race in 1945, is one of Barber's best-known yachts. With 34 feet LOA and canoe stern, she is typical of his yacht designs, a seaworthy, well-balanced, rugged boat. A later design, *Ripple*, also won the Hobart race. His last yacht commission was a 39-foot, raised-deck vessel drawn in 1958.

In his later years Barber owned a small ferry company, Hegartys, but after selling that business in 1960, when he was probably in his eighties, he left for the mountains.

—David Payne

GIORGIO BARILANI

Born February 1, 1933 · Italy

In 1943, the Barilani family moved to the estate of Benito Mussolini on Lake Garda, where Giorgio's father groomed and maintained Mussolini's automobiles. Barilani began to study at the Architecture University in Milan, but soon abandoned this pursuit and sought work as a draftsman. He took part in various competitions sponsored by U.S. magazines and won first prizes in both aeronautical and nautical subjects.

In November 1956 Barilani presented himself to Carlo Riva and began collaborating with the Riva boatyard, first as a part-timer, and also worked with some important European yards. From 1965, he worked under an exclusive contract with Riva. In 1970 he became a director and was responsible for Riva's

them over 36 meters in length, as well as several cruise ships. It has been said that you may love or disdain any of them, but you cannot be neutral about them. Still, Jon Bannenberg was the first yacht designer since Charles E. Nicholson in the 1930's to be inducted into the prestigious Royal Designers for Industry. Though he abandoned traditional ideas for daring personal ones, he once speculated modestly that he could have been even more daring—one wonders.   —Jack A. Somer

ARCHIBALD C. BARBER, OBE

ca. 1880's–ca. 1960's · Australia

The enigmatic A. C. Barber bridges the gap between Walter Reeks and Alan Payne in the history of Australian yacht design. He is thought to have designed more than four hundred vessels, from dinghies to 350-foot ships. His dates of birth and death remain a mystery, but he appears to have arrived in Australia from England toward the end of the nineteenth cen-

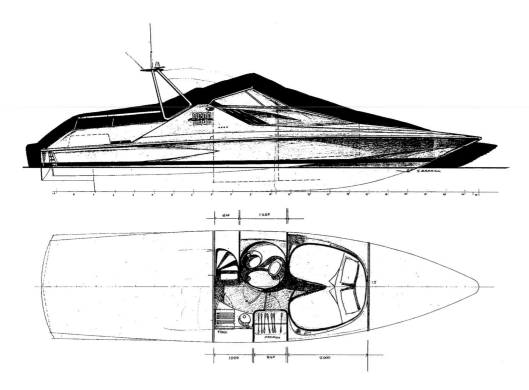

Giorgio Barilani: Riva 2000. Fifty-four of the Riva 2000 class were built between 1975 and 1980 and measure 11.28 meters long. Note the unusual but effective interior layout. *Drawing courtesy Piero Maria Gibellini*

Giorgio Barilani: Black Corsair. A total of eight of the Black Corsair class were built between 1985 and 1991. They ranged from 18.75 to 19.50 meters in length. *Photo courtesy Piero Maria Gibellini*

production until 1996. Having learned under the extremely fussy Carlo Riva, he resumed his studies at the Architecture University in Venice and graduated in 1976.

After Carlo Riva retired, Barilani became responsible for the most successful boats created by the yard. His 1972 redesign of the Aquarama, subsequently called the Special, represented the first motorboat with an integrated stern platform.

Among his most beautiful and successful designs were the runabout *Rudy*, introduced in 1971; the motoryacht *Super America*, of 1972, and its evolutionary progeny such as the Furama and Corsaro, plus the offshore Riva 2000, which came out in 1975; the Saint Tropez, of 1976; the fast commuter *Bravo*, of 1979; and the big, open, 60-foot *Black Corsair*, whose production began in 1985. All these boats represented milestones in Italian design, as certified by the title "Nautical Pioneer" Barilani received from UCINA (the union of Italian nautical builders) in 1990.

Today Barilani, a retiree living on Lake Garda, is still involved with pleasure craft as a member of the Board of Directors of the Association of Italian Nautical Designers (AS.PRO.NA.DI.), of which he has been president for many years. —Piero Maria Gibellini

JAMES RENNIE BARNETT, OBE

1864–1965 · Scotland

The successor to G. L. Watson as head of G. L. Watson and Company, J. R. Barnett continued that firm's notable activity in the design of large steam yachts. Born in Johnstone, Renfrewshire, Scotland, Barnett was the son of a cashier. In July 1881, at age sixteen, he joined G. L. Watson and Company. Between 1884 and 1887, during his apprenticeship there, he studied naval architecture at the University of Glasgow, where he received the first prize in the class of Buoyancy and Stability in Ships. He also won the South Kensington First Class Honours and Medal for Naval Architecture in 1886.

In 1888 he joined the Sutherland shipbuilders William Droxford and Son as a draftsman, but in July 1889 he returned to Watson's as chief draftsman. Among his other projects he was closely involved in the design of the America's Cup challengers *Thistle, Valkyrie II, Valkyrie III*, and *Shamrock II*.

By the time Barnett took over the firm after the death of Watson in 1904, it had become almost exclusively focused on the design of large steam yachts for American and British owners. In due course the order book would reflect a rise in the number of much smaller

Morgan Barney: *Ildico III.* Designed for the short high seas and strong tides of Vineyard and Nantucket Sounds, this 45-foot launch was built in 1906 by H. Manley Crosby in Osterville, Massachusetts. She featured a high freeboard forward, limited beam, a relatively deep underbody, and was heavily built. © *Mystic Seaport, Mystic, CT*

motoryachts. Other than three 6-Meter racing yachts, the International Rule passed the firm by. However, Barnett did design a number of successful ocean sailing yachts.

The economic uncertainties in the years leading up to World War I meant that of the thirty-one large steam yachts designed by Barnett, only fifteen were actually built. Those launched included *Vanadis*, at 1,233 tons; *Liberty*, at 1,571 tons; and *Sapphire*, at 1,421 tons. Immediately after World War I, a number of Watson steam yachts were designed with straight stems and what were known as cruiser sterns. Such immersed counters had a steadying effect and helped reduce vibration. Before long, however, owners' tastes moved back to the more graceful clipper bow and long overhanging stern. The interwar years produced further fine designs such as the steam yacht *Thalassa*, at 700 tons; the auxiliary schooners *Elk* and *Sunbeam II*; and the 1,582-ton steam yacht *Nahlin*, said to be the most beautiful of the steam yachts of that period and the last major steam yacht to be built in Britain. Barnett successfully maintained the firm's reputation for seaworthy, handsome, and finely crafted vessels.

Between 1904 and 1947 he was the consulting naval architect to the Royal National Lifeboat Institution (RNLI), in succession to G. L. Watson, and was responsible for the development of the motor lifeboat, work for which he was awarded the Order of the British Empire in 1918. On his retirement from the RNLI in 1947, he was awarded the institution's gold medal for his services to lifeboat design. Barnett retired from G. L. Watson and Company in 1957 at the age of eighty-three.

—Martin Black

MORGAN BARNEY

September 25, 1878–June 22, 1943
United States

Beginning his yacht design practice at about the time of the advent of the marine gasoline engine, Morgan Barney was instrumental in developing the first boats utilizing the new type of power plant. His primary interest was in sailing yachts, of which he designed many, but most of his design commissions were for the new types of powered vessels. He designed many notable large gasoline-powered yachts, among them four gas-powered yachts all named *Ildico*—a 35-footer in 1903, a 70-footer in 1904, a 45-footer in 1906, and a 75-footer in 1909—all for C. H. Davis. Contemporary accounts characterize his boats as being notably able, good looking, and economical to operate.

Barney was born in New Bedford, Massachusetts, and spent summers on Nashawena Island in Buzzards Bay and later at South Dartmouth. He developed an interest in racing small catboats and built several that were successful. He was long associated with the New Bedford Yacht Club. He graduated from MIT with a degree in naval architecture in 1900. In 1902 he went to work with designer H. C. Wintringham in New York City, followed by a stint with George Lawley and Son in South Boston in 1903. He then opened his own office in New York and designed such motoryachts as the 62-foot cruising launch *Vorant III*.

During World War I Barney specialized in converting ore-carrying barges into oil tankers through an innovative use of concrete, saving material costs as well as volume. Barney

worked with inventor Hudson Maxim on the design of a torpedo-proof ship, improved the design of torpedoes, and conducted secret work for the British government in an attempt to reduce the threat from submarines.

The Morgan Barney Collection of plans is at Mystic Seaport Museum, Mystic, CT.

—Daniel B. MacNaughton

ANTONIO BAVA

1858–1941 · Italy

One of the pioneers in the design and construction of recreational boats in Italy, Antonio Bava joined the Costaguta shipyard in Voltri (Genoa) in 1898. He collaborated on the construction of the 5-ton rig *Nella* for the Duke of Abruzzi, the 2-ton rigs *Lydia* and *Ilva*, and the one-ton *Gianduia*. In 1906, after the International Rule was adopted in Italy, Bava designed and built the 8-Meters *Nila II* (1908), *Gian-Maria* (1910), and *Doge* (1912), and the 6-Meters *Isa* (1908), *Viola* (1909), and *Dalgra* (1911).

After World War I, Bava continued the design and construction of International Rule vessels. Among these were *Aline III* (1919), *Enigma* (1920), *Primrose* (1920), and *Dilemma* (1935), the latter built after he joined the engineer De Marini in starting a shipyard in Sturla (Genoa). Two of Bava's boats, *Azio V* (1902) and *Catalina* (1905), won the Club Nautique Cup in Nice, France.

During his long career, Bava designed boats ranging from the 2-ton *Idea* (1890), whose rating formulas dated from the end of the nineteenth century, to those of the meter classes.

—Franco Belloni

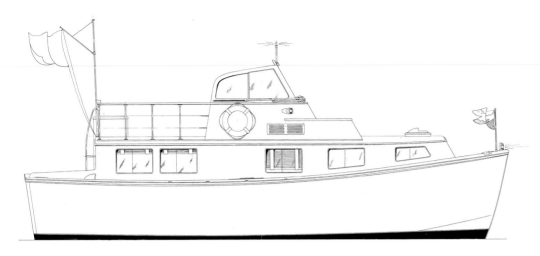

David Beach: *Deborah.* Along with his other achievements, Beach was an innovator in the arrangement of spaces. Here he has utilized almost the entire hull for interior space by placing the bridge on the cabin top, producing a gain in outside seating space as well, while retaining a relatively low profile. © *Mystic Seaport, Ships' Plans Division, Mystic, CT*

DAVID D. BEACH

Born May 1, 1918 · United States

David Beach began designing boats and yachts following World War II, a time when many Americans were flocking to more modernistic boats, cars, houses, and furniture. His broadly appreciated designs of small powerboats combined modest streamlining with appealing proportions and good performance. Many were intended for nonprofessional builders and helped to introduce a new generation of boat owners to the sport.

From 1935 to 1940 Beach attended the University of Michigan, studying marine engineering and naval architecture. Later he completed the course of the Westlawn School of Yacht Design. Before World War II he worked on submarines, both in the design office of the Electric Boat Company in Groton, Connecticut, and as a junior naval architect at the Cramp Shipbuilding Company in Philadelphia. At war's end he was with a design office associated with Dooley's Basin and Drydock in Fort Lauderdale, Florida, building air-sea rescue boats for the Pacific Theater.

After the war Beach became the assistant naval architect for Ventnor Boat Works in Atlantic City, New Jersey, building wooden runabouts and racing craft, including Guy Lombardo's *Tempo V.* Shortly thereafter he started a private practice in Maywood, New Jersey, designing small craft and sportfishermen for boatyards between Cape Cod and Cape May. His work was printed in various publications including *The Rudder's* How-to-Build series,

Mechanix Illustrated, and the *Sports Afield Boatbuilding Annual.*

Between 1954 and 1965, Beach worked as a naval architect for Higgins Boat Company in New Orleans, Louisiana; Outboard Marine Corporation in Waukegan, Illinois; and Owens Yacht Company in Baltimore, Maryland. From 1965 to 1997, he was on the technical staff of the National Marine Manufacturers Associations (NMMA) concerned with government agency standards. During 1970, on leave from the NMMA, he served as a consultant to the Food and Agricultural Organization of the United Nations in central and western Africa to help in the development of small fishing vessels.

He retired from the NMMA in 1994 to return to private practice, to concentrate on custom designs of small powered recreational craft, but is still a consultant to that organization. On his boards currently (2004) is the design for a 45-foot river cruiser.

The David D. Beach Collection is at Mystic Seaport Museum, Mystic, CT. —Lucia del Sol Knight

JOHN BEAVOR-WEBB

1849–1927 · Ireland/England/United States

John Beavor-Webb was born in Kinsale, Ireland. He is best known for designing *Genesta* and *Galatea,* challengers for the America's Cup in 1885 and 1886, respectively, and two of the four *Corsairs.*

After graduating from Trinity College in Dublin with a degree in structural engineer-

ing, Beavor-Webb moved to southern England in 1871 to work with the well-known boatbuilder Dan Hatcher. In 1876 Hatcher was commissioned to build the Five-Tonner *Freda.* Beavor-Webb supervised the work and subsequently skippered her with great success. In 1879 he designed a second *Freda* for the 20-ton class, and in 1880 he steered her to sixteen firsts and five seconds out of thirty-three starts.

In those days much of a yacht's ballast was inside the hull. When Beavor-Webb took the second *Freda's* design to Hatcher for a building estimate, Hatcher asked him, "How much lead will you put in the keel?" When Beavor-Webb replied, "All," Hatcher refused to build her. So Beavor-Webb hired some men and built her himself. After *Freda* proved successful, British designers followed Beavor-Webb's lead, cutting down the beam and increasing draft, displacement, and the ratio of ballast to displacement.

Freda's success led in 1884 to a commission to design the cutter *Genesta* (81 feet LWL) to compete in the 1885 America's Cup race. Thomas Lawson described her in his history of the America's Cup as "long, narrow, very deep, with low bilges and wall sides, a straight stem, a high overhang aft, long bowsprit, short mast, and tall topmast." She was, he wrote, "a most shipshape craft." Built of oak on a steel frame, *Genesta* was the first composite yacht to challenge for the America's Cup.

The following year Beavor-Webb designed the cutter *Galatea* (86 feet LWL). Built in steel, she was launched in May 1885. Although apparently specially constructed to challenge for the America's Cup of 1886, her lines were not so fine as *Genesta's* and she was never more than a cruising boat.

Beavor-Webb sailed aboard both challengers and steered *Galatea* in one race, and so could claim to be the first amateur to take the helm in an America's Cup series. However, *Genesta* was defeated by the Edward Burgess–designed *Puritan,* and *Galatea* suffered an even more comprehensive defeat at the hands of *Mayflower,* another Burgess design.

Beavor-Webb met his future wife in New York. After they were married, he moved there and continued his design career. He specialized in such spectacular steam yachts of the day as J. P. Morgan's second *Corsair,* at 560 tons (1890), and Morgan's third *Corsair,* at 1,396 tons (1899); the 443-ton *Intrepid;* and the 573-ton schooner *Utowana,* which won the Coronation Cup in 1902 and competed in the famous 1905 Transatlantic Race won by the William Gardner–designed schooner *Atlantic.*

—Ian Dear

John Beavor-Webb: *Utowana*. The 573-ton *Utowana*, photographed in Cowes Roads in 1904, was built in Philadelphia in 1891 and took part in the 1902 Coronation Cup. *Utowana*, the only fore-and-aft-rigged yacht in the race, won easily, becoming the first American vessel ever to win a British offshore race. *Photo by Kirk, courtesy Ian Dear*

John Beavor-Webb: *Galatea*. *Galatea*, seen here sailing past the spectator fleet, was the Royal Yacht Squadron's 1886 challenger for the America's Cup, but it lost 2 to 0 to the defender, the Edward Burgess–designed *Mayflower*. Beavor-Webb was at the helm in the second race, but missed the outer mark and would have been disqualified if the time limit had not expired. *Photo courtesy Ian Dear*

Harry Becker: *Cindy-Lou*. The 13.18-meter *Cindy-Lou* (ex-*Sioux II*) was a 22-Square-Meter skerry cruiser built in 1939 at Rödesund Boatyard, Karlsborg, by Becker for A. Åkesson of Motala, Sweden. © *Per Thelander*

HARRY BECKER

1905–1993 · Sweden

One of Sweden's most prolific designer/builders, Harry Becker learned his trade by working in boatyards. At the age of fifteen he showed the first signs of his talent for producing fast boats with a design for a skerry cruiser, which his father built for him at the family yard, Rödesund Boatyard, established in Karlsborg on Lake Vättern in 1911. The partnership between father and son continued until, in due course, Becker took the yard over from his father in 1920 and ran it until it closed in 1947.

Becker has been called the world champion of 22-Square-Meter skerry cruisers. *Flamingo* from 1955 won the Skerry Cruisers Trophy several times. His 30-Square-Meter *Tre Sang* stood out as being nearly unbeatable. Becker was the one who increased the length of the yachts. A good example is *Cindy-Lou* from 1939 and the 30-Square-Meter *Rapid* from 1938. He also designed for the 6-Meter class and the International 5-Meter class.

In 1950, three years after the yard closed, Becker opened Beckerboats in partnership with his son, this time on the Baltic coast in Lidingö. The partnership participated in the boating industry for the next thirty years, producing a steady stream of sailboats and motoryachts to Becker's own design. They include the Avanti, the Becker 27, and the Flamingo 40. In 1980, thirty years and 2,200 boats later, Harry Becker retired.

—Bent Aarre with Ulf Lycke

ROBERT PARK BEEBE

November 21, 1909–August 19, 1988
United States

Many decades after the advent of practical internal-combustion engines for yachts, virtually all transoceanic passages made for pleasure are made under sail. Owing to the handy trade winds, which offer generally downwind sailing along convenient routes, and the economical nature of sailing over long distances, this will probably always be true. But what of the person who would really rather be using a powerboat at either end of such a passage, or who wants to make voyages where the winds are more variable or contrary? And what about those sailors who, because of physical limitations, must have a power-driven vessel but can't see themselves with one of today's run-of-the-mill powerboats?

Robert Beebe is one of the few designers to tackle the question of small seagoing powerboats head-on. He felt that freeing the offshore voyager from the trade wind routes would encourage cruising in areas that were off the beaten path. By seeking areas of little wind instead of avoiding them, yachtsmen might enjoy safer, more economical, and more comfortable passages.

In his book, *Voyaging Under Power* (Seven Seas Press, 1975), Beebe lays out in detail his theories and formulas for analyzing the performance and fuel economy of powerboat designs. Settling for speeds at the upper end of what a displacement-hull sailboat could attain, he was able to design relatively fine-lined hulls that were both easily driven and capable of carrying sufficient fuel for transoceanic passages. His own boat, *Passagemaker*, traveled 3,200 nautical miles on 1,200 gallons of fuel, which is excellent for a hefty, 50-foot vessel.

Far from being high-tech freaks, Beebe's boats are a cross between a commercial fishing vessel and a voyaging sailboat. They have long, straight keels with a protected single screw and attached rudder, high freeboard, and largely flush decks except for the wheelhouse. A substantial chunk of ballast is carried on the keel for stability. A short sailing rig, primarily for steadying and auxiliary purposes, but also good for boosting the fuel economy under favorable conditions, is employed as well. Beebe was an authority on paravane roll dampers or "flopper stoppers," which are a key element in comfortable offshore voyaging under power.

Beebe was born in the Philippines, the son of an army officer. He graduated from the U.S.

Naval Academy in 1931 and served as navigational officer on the USS *Saratoga* during World War II. After the war he served at the Naval War College in Newport, Rhode Island, teaching strategy and tactics. Later he was superintendent of the Line School at the U.S. Naval Postgraduate School in Monterey, California.

An amateur designer during his thirty-year naval career, Beebe worked as a full-time designer after his retirement in 1961. While he is famous for his voyaging powerboats, he also drew sailboats and small craft, and wrote articles for *The Rudder* and *Yachting* magazines. He was well known for his enthusiasm for the sharpie type and designed a number of kayaks. He felt that a good boat was either small enough to carry or large enough to live aboard.

Beebe gave his boats a certain "something"

suggesting a joy in command, a feeling that is common to sailboats but often missing in powerboats in which dining and partying at dockside seem to be the primary activities. Not so with the Beebe boats—they are born to run, and this would be part of their appeal to sailors and ex-sailors. A Beebe powerboat sliding along efficiently and authoritatively is something to be taken seriously, and it would be more surprising to find one parked at a marina dock than anchored in some secluded cove far from the nearest fuel pump.

Beebe continued to design yachts up until his death in Carmel, California, at the age of seventy-eight.

The Capt. Robert P. Beebe Collection is at Mystic Seaport Museum, Mystic, CT.

—Daniel B. MacNaughton

Robert Beebe: *Passagemaker.* The 50-foot *Passagemaker* was something different in the world of powerboats, and among the very few designed for transoceanic travel. Emphasizing fuel economy, safety, and comfort, Beebe and his wife lived aboard her for many years, during which they traveled over 60,000 miles and made three ocean crossings. © *Peter Barlow*

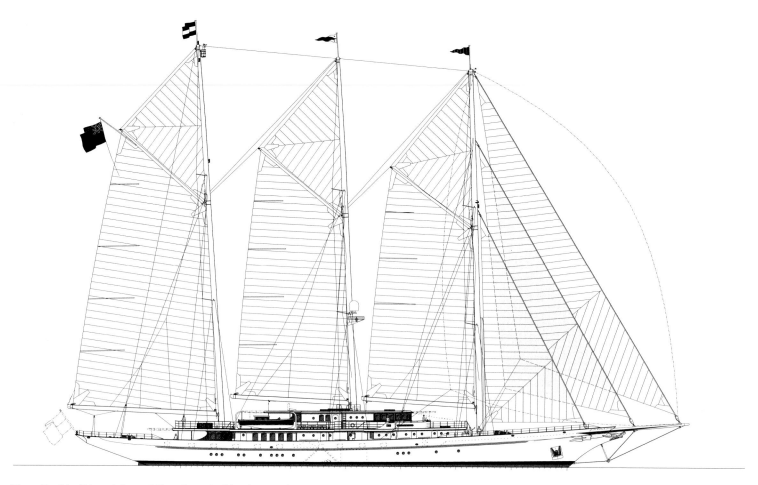

Pieter Beeldsnijder: *Athena.* When launched by the Royal Huisman Shipyard in autumn 2004, the three-masted schooner *Athena* became Pieter Beeldsnijder's undoubted masterpiece, the shipyard's greatest achievement, and the world's largest aluminum sailing yacht. *Drawing courtesy Pieter Beeldsnijder*

PIETER CORNELIS JOHANNES BEELDSNIJDER

Born October 8, 1937 · The Netherlands

Pieter Beeldsnijder is surely one of the most gifted and versatile naval architects of the contemporary period, equally at home shaping a classic schooner or modern ketch, a displacement motoryacht or high-speed sportfisherman, a long-range trawler or jewel-like tender. Moreover, Beeldsnijder is similarly adept at interior styling, a relatively new specialty born in the postwar boom years as yachts grew too large and complex for a single architect. With his dual capabilities, and a strong sense of organic design, Beeldsnijder has carved a unique niche in the field.

Born in Amsterdam, Beeldsnijder studied shipbuilding between 1951 and 1955, and furniture making and design from 1956 to 1958, both in Amsterdam's Fifth Technical School. He then attended Hendrik de Keizer School, graduating in naval architecture in 1962, and immediately joined the design office of G. de Vries Lentsch Jr., the noted Amsterdam shipyard. Beeldsnijder was assigned to the lofting floor, where one of his first tasks was to lay out the lines of the Dutch royal yacht *Groene Draeck.*

He assisted in the design and engineering of the motoryachts *Blue Jacket* (110 feet), *Blue Albacor* (105 feet), and the Greek royal yacht *Theseus* (90 feet). Beeldsnijder also participated in the construction and rig design of several sailing yachts built by the shipyard to the designs of Philip Rhodes and Olin Stephens.

In 1959, after working on Robert Clark's 176-foot, three-masted schooner *Carita* (later *Fleurtje*), Beeldsnijder joined the new Clark office in Amsterdam, where he designed large motoryachts and sailing vessels, including Sir Francis Chichester's *Gipsy Moth III.* Beeldsnijder briefly opened his own design office in 1963 and completed work on *Storm VI,* a 110-foot, twin-screw, steel-and-aluminum motoryacht. In 1964, he became chief designer and engineer for the Hakvoort Shipyard, in Monnickendam, where he drew a series of very handsome North Sea fish and shrimp trawlers for Dutch fishermen; purse seiners, stern trawlers, car ferries, and Stone Suckers for Denmark, Norway, Ireland, and Scotland; and a number of yachts between 50 and 150 feet long.

In 1972 Beeldsnijder opened Pieter Beeldsnijder Naval Architects in Edam. Now called PB Design, the firm has created a wide variety of work. Among production yachts, Beeldsni-

jder drew nine designs in the Gouwzee series of small sailboats and motorsailers, ranging from the 7.5-meter "Perky" to the 15.4-meter Clipper, and a series of 60- to 70-foot aluminum sportfishermen for Striker USA. There have also been several designs for the Dutch Striker (built at Hakvoort) including the 110-foot sportfisherman *Quaeso.* As well, he designed a 52-foot motorsailer for Taiwan's Cheoy Lee, and for Japan's Tayana Yachts he drew a fast trawler series, a 55-foot sailing yacht, and the Surprise 45 and 58 sailing yachts, of which about a hundred were built of fiberglass. The first Surprise 45 was built of aluminum, however, by the Royal Huisman Shipyard, which began a long and fruitful relationship for the designer.

Beeldsnijder's outstanding custom projects are his first masterpiece, the 110-foot staysail schooner *Gloria,* followed by a significant group of motoryachts, including *Tonga* (103 feet), *Luisamar* (143 feet), *Jefferson Beach* (162 feet), *Madeleine* (187 feet), and an exploration motoryacht with the oddest name of the century, $T_6Y_3T_9T_3I$ (151 feet). Beeldsnijder also created the basic design for the 200-foot motoryacht *Mylin IV.*

Among Beeldsnijder's more important sailing yacht projects for which he did both exterior styling and interior design are *Volador, Bell Fontaine, Huaso, Hetairos, Cyclos II, Happy Joss,* and *Metolius* (all in collaboration with Henry Scheel, Ron Holland, and Germán Frers, and all built at Huisman). In 1985 Beeldsnijder took a brief break from yachts to do industrial design, styling for aircraft, luxury homes, and stereo equipment.

Beeldsnijder has been honored for his work, including receipt of the 1989 Megayacht Award in Italy, the 1992 *ShowBoats International* Award for Best Interior of a Sailing Yacht Under 40 Meters (for *Shanakee*), the 1993 International Superyacht Award for Best Interior/Exterior, and the 1994 *ShowBoats International* Award for Best Sailing Yacht Over 35 Meters (the last two for the 143-foot *Juliet*). In 1998 the Superyacht Society Design Award for Best Sail Interior and the International Superyacht Design Award for Best Sail Over 36 Meters were given to Beeldsnijder for his 156-foot aluminum sloop *Hyperion*, built at Huisman for cyberstar Dr. Jim Clark.

Although his collaboration with Germán Frers might seem Beeldsnijder's crowning achievement, in 1999 Jim Clark assigned Beeldsnijder (in collaboration with Gerard Dijkstra, who did the naval architecture of the underbody and rig) to create the complete design of a new yacht to be named *Athena*. At 292 feet overall, her superlatives are beyond expression, except that she is truly a yacht for the new millennium—and a Beeldsnijder yacht at that.

—Jack A. Somer

KURT BEISTER

April 1, 1909–February 5, 1997 · Germany

One of Germany's most important designers of modern arc-welded yachts, Kurt Beister was noted for his remarkable manual and technical aptitude even as a young man working in his father's small machine factory in Düsseldorf. He grew up sailing on the nearby Rhine.

In 1931, at the age of twenty-two, Beister developed and built his first significant design, an 8.6-meter one-design keelboat. With the support of his sailing associates in the Rhineland, he developed this boat into the first "Einheits-Revierklasse" (Inland Water One-Design class) with a fleet of six boats. This class was followed by others, among them national racing dinghies that he built from his own design. Beister never sought formal training in boat design.

With the advent of World War II, Beister served in the navy, stationed on Norderney, a small North Sea island, where he created the harbor dinghy *Seeschwalbe* (Sea Swallow) during his off-duty time. Proper building materi-als being unobtainable in wartime, he built the early models out of driftwood from the naval war's abundant litter along the North Sea coast. Together with the aid of local youths, who later became his coworkers, he built a small fleet of hard-chined training dinghies, 3.75 meters in length with a 10-square-meter sail area. The uneven and unpredictable quality of the building materials demanded especially solid construction.

After the war, Beister established a yard on Norderney for the construction of steel-hulled yachts ranging from 9 to 18 meters in length. His first contracts and his raw materials came from his former sailing club members in Düsseldorf and the Ruhr, and their contacts in international business quickly broadened his reputation as an "artist with yachts."

Beister's rather conservative designs reveal his close study of his internationally famous colleagues: the longitudinal elevations of his hulls recall Philip Rhodes's designs, the entry lines of the bow sections recall those of Henry Gruber, and the tightening of the girths in careful deference to the measurer's tape echo Olin Stephens. The fullness of the lines of his bows, on the other hand, are a concession to the hard chop of the North Sea.

Kurt Beister favored long and slender yachts that did not sacrifice grace of line to extravagant demands for luxury and space below decks. His designs are notable for the harmonious and original relationship between the lines of the deckhouse profiles and the hull. One of his innovations was the use of teak gratings screwed over steel decks to allow the rapid drainage of any water taken on board. His yard closed in 1969, a victim of competition from the fiberglass stock boat industry.

—Robert Volmer

JAY R. BENFORD

Born January 9, 1943 · United States

Jay Benford is one of the few designers who have demonstrated an ability to be both completely faithful to traditional forms and innovative within those forms. He also produces appealing and functional boats in a modernist style. His boats represent a broad range of concepts, and refreshingly he does not have just one notion of what is best. His work displays a belief that there are many different reasons to own a boat, and many styles and types of boats, all of which have their applications.

Jay Benford: *Iota.* The 18-foot canoe yawl *Iota*, one of many traditional small cruising yachts created by Jay Benford, not only has a distinctly classical appearance but also is a practical cruiser for a couple wanting to spend considerable time aboard. *Photo courtesy Jay Benford*

Jay Benford: _Strumpet_. Ernest K. Gann, in an interview about his Benford-designed, 35-foot trawler yacht _Strumpet_, originated the quote that she will "drink six, eat four, and sleep two in perfect comfort." Styled after the Scottish fishing trawlers, she has a very pleasant and powerful motion at sea. _Photo courtesy Jay Benford_

One of Benford's biggest contributions to modern yacht design is the attention he has paid to very small cruising yachts, bucking the trend toward largeness that has caused cruising to be seen as an expensive pastime. Many of these small yachts are full of traditional detail and complexity. If the budget is restrictive, many owners will just make the boat smaller. Benford's 18-foot canoe yawl _Iota_ may be one of the best examples of such a boat.

Benford has also pursued economy through simplicity rather than smallness, keeping the size and living space while using unconventional forms and construction to keep costs down. His large plywood sailing dories, such as the 34-foot _Badger_, exemplify this approach.

Another unusual aspect of Benford's body of work is his willingness to seek new ways of arranging spaces in boats. The Benford 30 is one of the smallest boats ever to have a great cabin aft. To accomplish this, the cockpit is placed well forward in front of the wheelhouse, completely reversing the norm, an arrangement offering great space and good visibility from the cockpit.

Benford's series of powerboat designs began with the 50-foot Florida Bay Coaster, a multidecked, shoal-draft mini-freighter that features tremendous interior volume and a "big ship" feel. Sometimes Benford's less conventional boats are unnerving to traditionalists, who are not comfortable seeing, say, a Pinky schooner hull with a ketch rig, square topsails, and a nontraditional cabin trunk. Still, if a strictly traditional design is wanted, Benford can do it as well as anyone. His design palette is so broad that nobody could like all the boats, but all of the boats are exciting, unique, and fascinating in one way or another. Few could look through a Benford design catalogue without picking up some valuable new ideas.

Growing up in Rochester, New York, in a sailing family, Benford gained much of his early experience on Lake Ontario. He started drawing boats for fun at age twelve. He was in the naval architecture program at the University of Michigan for two years, leaving there for the opportunity to apprentice in the office of John Atkin in Connecticut in 1963 and 1964. A distinctive feature that he may have picked up in the Atkin office is his use of silhouette drawings, which somehow capture the overall form and character of a boat as it is actually experienced out on the water better than many other views.

Benford moved to Seattle, Washington, in 1966 where William Garden, whom he had met previously, advised him to find employment with the Foss Tug Company. Benford spent two years there as staff naval architect while designing yachts on the side. His drafting style is reminiscent of William Garden's work, especially in its great detail, its harmony between the various design elements, and the aesthetic touches designed to make the drawings themselves more emotionally appealing to the viewer.

In 1969 Benford opened his independent design office in Friday Harbor, Washington. He lived aboard the Leigh Coolidge–designed 50-foot, fantail motoryacht _Kiyi_ (1926), and the 34-foot topsail ketch _Sunrise_. He moved to the Chesapeake Bay region in 1984 and lived aboard the 1926 classic 75-foot houseboat _Odyssea_.

Presently Benford's office is in Saint Michaels, Maryland, where he designs yachts, sells plans, and operates Tiller Publishing. Tiller has published many handsome and informative booklets on yachts and yacht design, including among others Benford's own books _Small Ships_ (fifth edition, 2001), _Pocket Cruisers and Tabloid Yachts_ (revised edition, 2000), and _Small Craft Plans_ (revised edition, 2000).

—Daniel B. MacNaughton

Nathaniel Benjamin: *Rebecca*. The 60-foot LOD schooner *Rebecca* was launched in 2001. Designed for comfortable, safe cruising, she is seakindly, responsive, fast, and unusually weatherly. She was built using traditional carvel plank-on-frame construction fastened with bronze. *Rebecca* won the 2002 Antigua Classic Yacht Regatta, as well as races in the Caribbean and New England. © *Benjamin Mendlowitz*

NATHANIEL P. BENJAMIN

Born February 12, 1947 · United States

Nat Benjamin's career is founded in the kind of realities that were once the rule in the lives of coastal working people. He has seen plenty of bad weather offshore and knows the difference between the boats and gear you can rely on in such conditions and the ones that scare you to death. He has repaired plenty of old boats and knows what lasts over the years and what doesn't. And like most people who have taught themselves a trade out of such experiences, he has acquired a deep respect for things that are simple, strong, reliable, and long-lived, and that take their beauty from those same characteristics, artfully displayed.

Teaming up with Ross Gannon to form the Gannon and Benjamin Marine Railway in 1980, Benjamin designs many but not all of the wooden boats the yard builds and repairs. The yard is on the harbor in Vineyard Haven on Martha's Vineyard, Massachusetts. Born in New York City, Benjamin is self-taught and values simplicity of design and responsibly harvested, quality wood for his plank-on-frame vessels. His designs include the 60-foot schooner *Rebecca*; the 65-foot schooner *Juno*; the 25-foot

Canvasback, a plumb-stem centerboard sloop; *Meta*, a 20-foot catboat; *Swallows and Amazons*, a 23-foot sloop; the 40-foot gaff-rigged sloop *Liberty*; the 21-foot Bella class of gaff-rigged sloops; and a 32-foot lobsterboat-style powerboat. A 33-foot clipper-bowed ketch was destroyed while under construction in 1989 in a disastrous fire at the boatyard, whereupon her owner had her built again, but lengthened to 37 feet.

A typical Nat Benjamin design is gaff-rigged and intended to sail almost entirely under her working sails. She has wide, roomy decks uncluttered by needlessly wide cabin trunks, costly winches, or gear associated with countless special-purpose sails. The shapes of her hull and superstructure are strong, graceful, and nostalgic, but she is largely free of ornamentation. Her frank lack of "gear" on the decks and overall simplicity are stunning in today's boating context. She is connected to the past, but in both her design and construction represents the best of what is known today, according to Nat's priorities. Her strength, her resistance to neglect, and her enduring appeal also form a connection to a long-distant future; both the boats and the Gannon and Benjamin reputation have about them an air of immortality.

—Daniel B. MacNaughton

ALFRED BENZON

1855–1932 · Denmark

Alfred Benzon was the second and most influential designer in a family line that presided over the initial growth of yachting in Denmark. His life spanned an era during which small boat racing developed from purely local events into international regattas, and races once contested in workboats came to be sailed in yachts professionally designed according to scientific analyses of hull and material characteristics. His father, C. B. Benzon, helped found Denmark's first yacht club, and his uncle, Eggert C. Benzon, designed and built what was probably the first Danish yacht.

At the outset, the new sport of yacht racing demanded a rational and standardized means of handicapping, and Benson took a leading part in these discussions and debates. He wrote widely read articles, and his efforts were the driving force behind the Sejllaengde Rule (the Copenhagen Rule), used in Scandinavia and Germany from 1893 to 1905.

Benzon's most important contribution to handicapping, however, came in London in 1906 when, as a participant in the creation of the International Rule, he added to the final

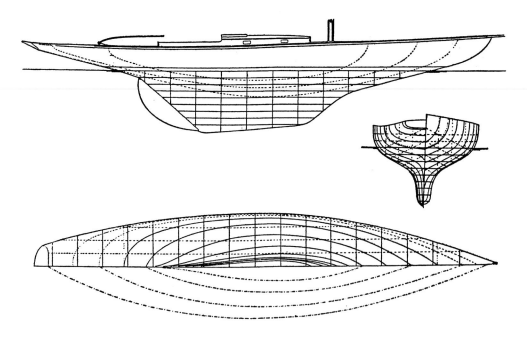

Alfred Benzon: *Fix*. The 8-Meter *Fix* was drawn in 1908 by Alfred Benzon, who helped create the International Rule under which she was created. Perhaps this is why she seems particularly moderate and appealing. Later designers would eventually create less lovely boats as the quirks of the rule were gradually found and exploited. *Drawing courtesy Bent Aarre*

Eggert Benzon: *Caroline*. The cutter *Caroline* was designed in 1866, when yachting in Denmark was in its infancy. She shows the influence of British yacht design more than that of Danish working craft. *Drawing courtesy Bent Aarre*

equation the *d* measurement (the difference between chain girth and skin girth). This encouraged the design of wholesome, deep-bodied hulls rather than the scow-like hulls that would otherwise have resulted.

Benzon never supported himself with his design work, although he drew a wide variety of both cruising and racing boats for his fellow yacht club members. His earliest design was probably the straight-stem cutter *Attila* (14.5 tons, 1883), a somewhat moderated version of the English type. However, after the 1890's, his boats reflected the American type as defined by Nathanael Herreshoff's *Gloriana*, with her overhanging bow and a cutaway forefoot contributing to a greater waterline length when heeling.

Two of Benzon's most successful racers prior to the introduction of the International Rule were *Enten-Eller* (1897), which won nearly every race she entered, and *Paradox* (1904), which won the Kattegat Cup in 1905 and the Sound Cup in both 1905 and 1906. After 1906 he designed a series of meter boats following the new International Rule he had helped create. They include the 6-Meters *Star* (1907) and *Tit Tit* (1912), the 7-Meter *Lux* (1909), and the 8-Meters *Fix* (1908) and *Fox* (1908).

For the Royal Danish Yacht Club, Benzon drew the first one-design classes in Denmark. These were the 24-foot Aelling (1898), of which thirteen were built; the 30-foot Terne (1899), of which six were built; and the 28-foot Maage (1910), of which thirty were built.

By any account, Alfred Benzon was an esteemed citizen, a cultural and civic leader in Danish society. He directed the family firm of A/S Alfred Benzon (established in 1863, then as now an important pharmaceutical company), acted as a council member for the city of Copenhagen, served on several boards, earned a reputation as a good painter, and sat as chairman of the Royal Danish Yacht Club.

—Bent Aarre

EGGERT C. BENZON

1823–1912 · Denmark

Yacht racing in Denmark began inauspiciously. In 1855, the first organized race in the country included a fleet of double-ended, clinker-built fishing boats and a single yacht, *Cosak*, a 26-foot vessel designed by Eggert Benzon in 1854. She was probably the first yacht designed purely for pleasure in Denmark. *Cosak* capsized during the race, and though the boat was retrieved, three of her crew drowned.

The tragedy was probably not the fault of *Cosak*'s designer. Benzon ran a shipyard in

Nykøbing Falster, in northwestern Denmark, where he started out as a designer and builder of commercial vessels. Prior to *Cosak*, he had already designed and built a host of commercial schooners with a reputation for seaworthiness (he would build forty-eight in all).

In spite of the *Cosak* episode, he was asked to build thirty more yachts, many of which competed safely and successfully. Indeed, one of his boats, *Echo*, survived a gale on the Baltic in which 350 larger vessels foundered. *Cosak* returned to race very successfully in 1858.

In Denmark, where the gap between rich and poor people was never as pronounced as it was in England, few large yachts existed, and although the aristocracy was represented, the middle class and professional people dominated the yachting scene. In the beginning, the focus was primarily on racing in the vicinity of Copenhagen, but the sport soon took hold in all the coastal cities. Despite the near-perfect coast of Denmark, cruising as it is known now didn't become common until after 1900.

After Denmark lost the southern part of the country in a war against Germany in 1864, English engineers arrived to design a countrywide rail system. Some of the engineers brought their own yachts with them. Consequently, English cutters supplied the pattern for many of Denmark's earliest yachts, with some moderation of their excessively narrow beam and deep draft. Later, American designer Nathanael Herreshoff's *Gloriana* (1891) offered a better model with her radical new bow shape and long overhangs.

Benzon's largest yacht was the schooner *Tumleren* (100-foot LWL), built approximately in 1890, and his last yacht was completed in 1896. His connection to the beginning of Danish yachting extends beyond his own achievements as a yacht designer and builder. His brother C. B. Benzon helped to found the first Danish yacht club, later to become the Danish Royal Yacht Club, and his nephew, Alfred Benzon (for whom Eggert built *Svanen*, Alfred's first boat), became one of the most influential men in Danish yachting history.

—Bent Aarre

OSWALD BERCKEMEYER

Born April 8, 1934 · Germany

After working as an engineer in South Africa for many years, Oswald Berckemeyer returned to his native Germany in 1977. Following retirement from a later job, he began designing yachts for the home boatbuilding market.

Berckemeyer began sailing at age ten, and by the time he was fourteen he had designed and built a 10-foot sailing dinghy. Later, working in his spare time in South Africa, he designed, built, and sailed the Flamenca 25. This led to a commission to design a larger version that resulted in Berckemeyer's favorite yacht, the Miura 31.

The Miura 31—her name comes from the most famous Spanish fighting-bull breed, which fit quite well with her pointed bow and big tumblehome belly—became the largest keelboat class in South Africa. There followed the Corrida 36 and the Gitana 43.

The stock plans for yachts that Berckemeyer now sells from his office in Probsteierhagen, Germany, are for either aluminum or Speed Strip sandwich construction. He offers modern-looking yachts, such as the updated Miura 32 MK2 and the Dash 39, and plans for more classic designs but with thoroughly modern underwater bodies, such as the Gitana 54 and the Classic 44.

—Tom Roach

GEORG BERG

1873–1962 · Denmark

Denmark's most productive designer of the well-known spidsgatter, Georg Berg helped to define the type. The spidsgatter (meaning simply "double-ender" in Danish) evolved from older working boats, retaining their shapely

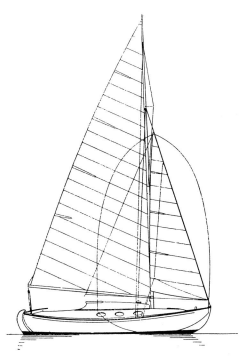

Georg Berg. This design is a typical Danish spidsgatter, with her shapely double-ended hull, firm bilges, and tall rig, but she features an unusual raised deck configuration that considerably increases the useful space both on deck and below, while simplifying the construction. *Drawing courtesy Bent Aarre*

double-ended character but changing from lapstrake construction to carvel and from traditional rigs to marconi, while reducing wetted surface area. Spidsgatters are widely respected for their combination of good looks, speed, comfort, and rough-water ability.

Berg's designs were much alike, with a strong sheer, hollow stern sections, and relatively large sail area. His work influenced that of other designers such as Aage Utzon of Denmark and K. Aage Nielsen of Denmark and the United States.

Berg grew up in the town of Fåborg on the island of Fyn, the son of a pharmacist. Around 1900 he became a ship designer in the German town of Flensburg, but soon after he moved to Copenhagen, where he took a job at the big shipyard of Burmeister and Wain. In his spare time he sailed and designed yachts. He lost his job in the Depression of the 1930's, but thereafter managed to make a modest living from his design work. Around 1938 the family moved to the small town of Skaelskør, where they were closer to the boatbuilders with whom Berg was working.

Later in his life Berg burned his drawings. Fortunately many of his spidsgatters are still sailing.

—Bent Aarre

JEAN BERRET

Born January 16, 1946 · France

Among prominent French naval architects, Jean Berret and Daniel Andrieu can be distinguished in part by their height—it's a rare sailboat that has enough headroom for either man. Nevertheless both proved themselves in small yachts and in them won their first yacht-racing laurels. Today they have largely yielded the joys of the cockpit to other helmsmen in order to devote their time to the drawing board and computer.

Berret was born in the French corn-growing region. He discovered yachting, as did many French yachtsmen, through the Touring Club of France. He studied in Paris and then entered the Boulle School, known for producing some of France's best cabinetmakers. In 1968, he transferred to L'Ecole des Arts Décoratif. Along with some friends, he built a Quarter-Tonner, *Bémol*, in 1969, which led the yachtsmen of La Rochelle to have to reckon with Berret.

With his Three-Quarter-Tonner, *Oesophage Boogie*, Berret earned himself a place in the international design world. His victories included two Mini-Ton Cups and four Half-Ton Cups, and his One-Tonner *Phénix* won the 1989 Admiral's Cup. His 5.5-Meters have also shown the diversity of his design capabilities, in a field often dominated by specialists.

Frank and Julian Bethwaite: 49er. Perhaps the culmination of the two Bethwaites' many years of designing, building, and racing planing skiffs for Sydney Harbour, the 49er brought this style of sailing to the international scene, where it was an immediate success. © *Robert Keeley*

On his own since 1977, Berret regularly works for France's greatest yards, such as Bénéteau, Dufour, Fountaine-Pajot, and CNB. His First 41.5 design, created in collaboration with designer Philippe Stark, is representative of his talent and has sold well around the world.

Since 1983, Berret has been collaborating with engineer Olivier Racoupeau. Their numerous creations, such as the Open 50-foot and Open 60-foot Class, an 82-foot Catamaran class, and a number of production and custom offshore cruisers, are achieving widespread recognition.

The Berret and Racoupeau office is in La Rochelle, France. —François Chevalier

Jean Berret: Alliage 48. The Alliage 48 is representative of contemporary French performance cruiser designs. A light hull and minimized underbody combine with somewhat higher freeboard than would be typical of a racing boat, while a long, low cabin trunk provides headroom and acts as part of the deck. *Drawing courtesy Chevalier & Taglang*

FRANK BETHWAITE, OAM
Born May 26, 1920
JULIAN BETHWAITE
Born July 14, 1959

New Zealand/Australia

Frank Bethwaite's most recent and notable work has been associated with his son, Julian, both of whom worked on developing the new Olympic class two-person skiff, the 16-foot 6-inch 49er, and its junior feeder class, the 14-foot 6-inch 29er. However, to most people in the world of yacht design, Frank Bethwaite is also well known for his pioneering work on the effects of wind and water on high-speed planing dinghies.

As a youngster in New Zealand, Frank Bethwaite displayed an early interest in boats, building models and designing a collapsible canoe. He also took up flying (both real aircraft and models) and studied aeronautical engineering. During World War II he worked as a test pilot and became a squadron leader in the Royal New Zealand Air Force, earning the Distinguished Flying Cross for valor. In 1954 he set the World Open Endurance Record for model aircraft, and in 1958 he moved to Australia to head field operations for the Commonwealth Scientific and Industrial Research Organization.

Frank Bethwaite became a member of the Northbridge Sailing Club on Sydney's Middle Harbour, where he developed a fast two-person dinghy. He drew the lines for the 14-foot NS14 restricted development class, and followed that up with the Northbridge Junior, a singlehander for children. His work on wooden wing masts refined the concept of streamlined mast sections, and during the 1960's he did further research on sailing rigs, focusing on the reduction of aerodynamic drag.

This work culminated in a new production class dinghy, the Tasar. The Tasar, strongly influenced by Australian 18-footers, was well ahead of her time, with a rotating mast and extremely lightweight. Frank Bethwaite drew the lines while Ian Bruce prepared the boat for industrial design. Frank was also a leading designer and builder of high-performance centerboards and rudders.

Bethwaite's continuing interest in high-performance dinghies also led to the development of the 49er, in conjunction with his son. Julian Bethwaite, a champion Australian 18-foot skiff sailor, ran a campaign in the early to mid-1980's based on a two-person Eighteen (the class usually has three crew). Rule changes ultimately prevented the Prime series of boats (named after the sponsoring company) from proceeding further, but the concept led the Bethwaites to develop the 49er at a time when the ISAF was looking for a more spectacular class that would be "TV friendly." At the Lake Garda Olympic class trials in September 1996, the 49er dominated its competition and was selected to compete in the 2000 Olympic Games on Sydney Harbour.

Frank Bethwaite has consistently aimed to reduce aerodynamic drag in all the boats he has developed. In 1993 he published his theories in a book, *High Performance Sailing*. Already in its third printing, it has become a standard reference within a very short time. In January 2000, Frank Bethwaite was awarded the Medal of the Order of Australia for his service to the sport of sailing as a designer and innovator.

—Robert Keeley

MICHEL BIGOIN

Born May 1, 1930 · France

Born in Tours on the Loire River, Michel Bigoin became interested in boatbuilding as a boy, and constructed his first boat when he was sixteen. After studies in Paris, he was awarded a diploma as a *modeleur mécanicien*. The step from scale models to full-scale hulls is only a small one, which Bigoin took as soon as he graduated.

Bigoin began work at Dornier, a yard that built Stars and other racing class boats. Success with his own racers in regattas, notably at the Cercle de la Voile de Paris, attracted many yachtsmen to his workshop.

When Bigoin was twenty-four, he built for his own use the first French 5O5 in cold-molded wood. The next year, he joined Gaubert's yard in Marseilles, where he was in charge of prototypes and production building. It was for

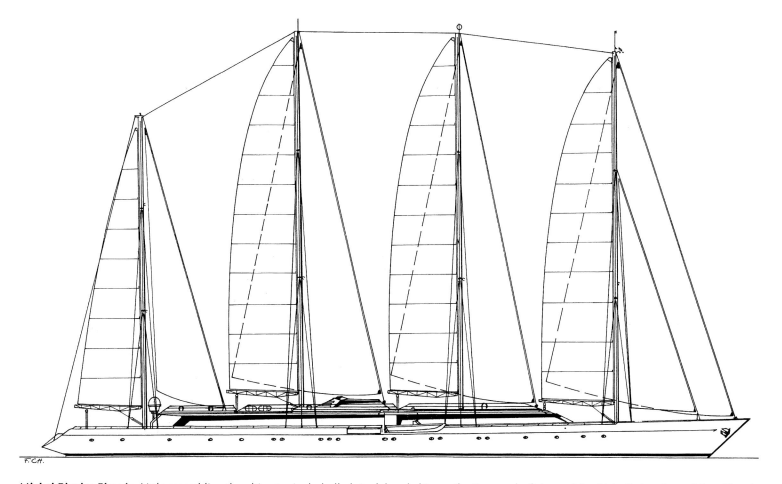

Michel Bigoin: *Phocéa*. Little resembling the ultimate single-hulled singlehanded transatlantic racer built in 1976 for Alain Colas, the 246-foot *Phocéa* (ex-*Club Méditerranée*) has been rebuilt as a luxurious charter vessel. In 1998 she set a transatlantic record from Sandy Hook to the Lizard in Cornwall, of 8 days, 3 hours, and 29 minutes. *Drawing courtesy Chevalier & Taglang*

Gaubert's that he designed his first yacht, the racer/cruiser *Flying Forty*. Bigoin went on to design numerous production fiberglass boats for the Société Marseillaise's Nautical Department and for the Air Liquide Company.

Bigoin's association with the Parisian architect Daniel Duvergie—working on racer prototypes and then on the series built from these prototypes—gave him many successes in the Mediterranean as well as in the Atlantic. A crowning achievement was the conception, with Duvergie and Eric Tabarly, of the famous *Pen Duick V*. She was said to be the first monohull fitted with water ballast tanks and a bulb keel, and she was the 1969 winner of the singlehanded Transpacific Race from San Francisco to Tokyo.

The spin-offs from this substantial victory weren't as fruitful as Bigoin and Duvergie might have hoped, but Bigoin's collaboration with Tabarly led to his most prestigious project. In 1974, Bigoin designed for Alain Colas the 72-meter schooner *Club Méditerranée* for the OSTAR (Observer Singlehanded Transatlantic Race).

Established in 1980 at the Pharo, cradle of boatbuilding in Marseilles, Bigouin's Naval Yard of Marseilles began building large yachts.

Two years later, French tycoon Bernard Tapie entrusted *Club Méditerranée* to Bigoin for refitting into one of the best-known French yachts, now named *Phocéa*. Bigoin has recently retired.

—François Chevalier

ARTHUR BINNEY

1865–1924 · United States

After graduating from MIT, Arthur Binney worked for a variety of employers including a machine company and an organ maker, all in the Boston area, before joining forces with Edward Burgess in 1888. Burgess's fame at that time was at its zenith; he had just designed three consecutive successful America's Cup defenders: *Puritan* in 1885, *Mayflower* in 1886, and *Volunteer* in 1887. When Burgess died in 1891, Binney took over the business and formed Stewart and Binney. Not long afterward, he further expanded his involvement in the industry by becoming one of the directors of George Lawley and Son.

Best known is Binney's design for the sloop *Pilgrim*, developed for the 1893 defense of the America's Cup. She lost to *Vigilant*, the first of Nathanael Herreshoff's Cup defenders that would dominate the series until the J-Class

competitions in the 1930's. Binney designed two boats for Edward Burgess's son W. Starling Burgess, the 22-foot LWL sloop *Helene* in 1899 and a second *Helene*, also 22 feet LWL but 34 feet LOA, in 1901. Binney was instrumental in encouraging and educating the younger Burgess in preparation for his own career as a yacht designer. He had a similar influence on the young Charles Mower, who worked in Binney's office from 1895 to 1899.

Along with Edward Burgess and B. B. Crowninshield, Binney's yacht design also influenced the design of fishing schooners. At least fifteen such schooners were built to Binney's plans, including the 99-foot *Arthur Binney* (1892), the 109-foot *Mary G Powers* (1892), and the 107-foot *Maggie Sullivan* (1893).

Binney became prolific and highly successful, being much in demand. Although he designed a broad range of yachts, he was best known for his steam and power launches, which were prized for their combination of seaworthiness, speed, and luxury, and for his role in the transition of the Massachusetts Bay Knockabout class from racing sloops with minimal accommodations to the nimble 30- to 45-foot cruiser/racers so popular after World War I.

—Walter Voigt

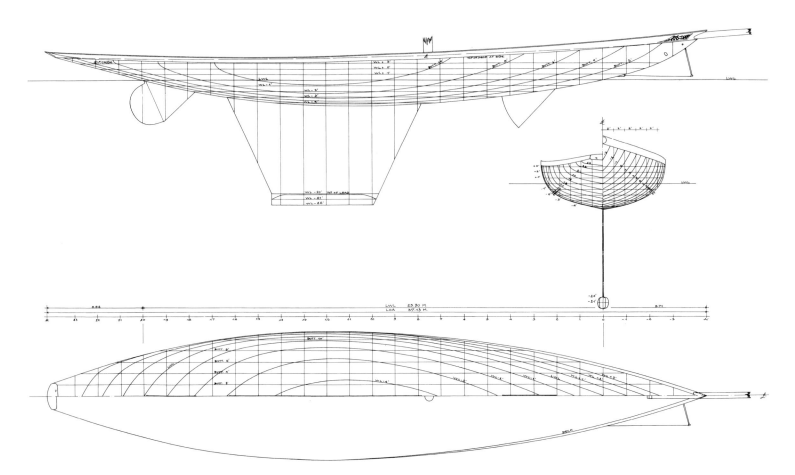

Arthur Binney: *Pilgrim*. The 121-foot 10-inch, fin-keel cutter *Pilgrim* was built for the 1893 America's Cup defense, but lost to the N. G. Herreshoff–designed *Vigilant* in the selection trials. In form and extremity, the design anticipated today's racing yachts, but she was too flexible to withstand the resulting strains, and the superior engineer won. © *Chevalier & Taglang*

WILLIAM MAXWELL BLAKE

June 9, 1874–1939 · Great Britain

When English yachtsmen call a 22-foot 5-inch cruising sloop "one of the prettiest small yachts ever designed," it is really saying something. When you find that yacht—the Deben Four-Tonner—to be one of the simplest and least pretentious boats you could imagine, you know you're looking at greatness. The designer of that sloop, W. Maxwell Blake, pursued yacht design mostly as a hobby after he retired from a career as a naval architect designing large ships in Singapore.

Blake designed only a few yachts, ranging up to 13 tons (Thames Measurement), but an unusually large number of boats were built from some of his plans, including many Deben Four-Tonners. Blake also designed Sir Francis Chichester's Eight-Tonner, *Gipsy Moth II*, which won sixteen RORC races in her career. Most of his designs were cruising boats suitable for rugged service and offshore voyages, but he also designed and raced dinghies.

Having a deep interest in the disappearing traditional working craft of England, Blake meticulously measured such boats and drew plans for them much as his counterpart Howard Chapelle did in America during the same time period. Blake's drawings were published in both *Yachting* and *Yachting Monthly* magazines in the late 1920's and early 1930's. He is said to have been the first to pursue such an interest so thoroughly, and the drawings are noted for their intricate detail.

Blake was born at Bramerton Hall, near Norwich, and attended Woodbridge School. He apprenticed first at Robertson's Boatyard in Woodbridge, then later at Forrest and Son's Shipyard at Wivenhoe. He moved to Singapore in 1901 to work as a naval architect at the United Engineers Shipyard. He stayed for twenty-eight years. During this period, Blake took an interest in the traditional working craft of Southeast Asia, publishing in *Yachting* articles such as one about the fishing vessels of Borneo. He was active in the maritime community of Singapore and became commodore of the yacht club. He designed at least one yacht, the 6-Meter *Monsoon*, which was shipped home to England upon his retirement in 1929 at age fifty-five.

After settling in Felixstowe on the East Coast of England, Blake concentrated on designing yachts. As a large ship designer, he had great respect for engineered scantlings and scientific design principles, but his study of traditional watercraft gave him a similar respect for evolved design characteristics serving both aesthetics and function.

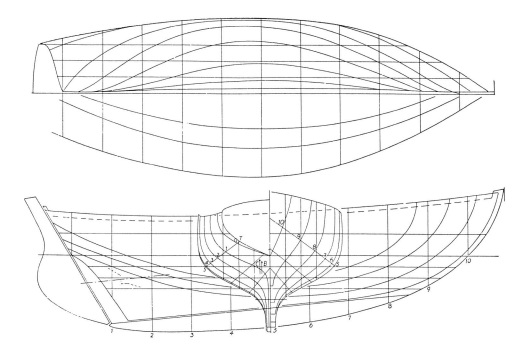

W. Maxwell Blake: Deben Four-Tonner. The 22-foot 5-inch Deben Four-Tonner is one of England's best-known small yacht designs, but she may have acquired some hybrid vigor from foreign influences. Her bow has a lot of Norway in it, while her broad beam, wide transom, and firm sections seem quite American. *Drawing courtesy* Yachting Monthly *magazine*

Blake felt that evolutionary forces in the design of traditional vessels tended to produce scientifically valid results. Hence, some believe his work represents a middle ground between the "scientific" light-displacement designers and the "rule-of-thumb" heavy-displacement designers of his day. He utilized the metacentric shelf theory (now regarded as an oversimplification) to help produce yachts that handled and balanced well under changing conditions, he calculated weights meticulously, and he drew easily understood construction drawings.

Blake emphasized ease of construction, making it possible to seek lower building costs by working with small yards having low overhead. Scantlings were relatively light but strong, meeting Lloyd's standards for the day, but with additional hanging and lodging knees.

Whisstock's Boatyard in Woodbridge built most of Blake's yachts, and the yard commissioned him to design the Deben Four-Tonner in 1936. The first of fifty was launched in 1937. One, *Leading Wind*, was sailed singlehanded around Britain by a woman in 1938. Several Four-Tonners made their way to North America as well. A larger version was launched in 1946. Measuring 25-feet 6 inches LOA, these Deben Six-Tonners were not as popular as the little Four-Tonners, which remain Blake's single most notable contribution to yacht design.

—Daniel B. MacNaughton

EDWIN AUGUSTUS BOARDMAN

1877–1943 · United States

A prominent designer of small racing sailboats in the early decades of the twentieth century, Edwin Boardman is well known for his skimming-dish scows and scow-like racers, which benefited from early measurement rules. Even his designs in other types tended to have U-shaped sections reminiscent of scows, making them quite fast in smooth water. Notable survivors include the 27-foot 6-inch LOA Northeast Harbor A Class sloop (originally called the Eastern Yacht Club One-Design), attractive gaff-rigged knockabouts with small cabins. George Lawley and Son built twenty-five of these boats for the 1912 racing season in Marblehead, Massachusetts. Several years later, six were sold and formed a fleet in Northeast Harbor, Maine; the rest of the Marblehead fleet followed them to Maine after World War I.

Boardman was born in Boston and graduated from Harvard University in 1899. He was a sportsman first, last, and always, and a yacht designer more by avocation than vocation. A prominent racing skipper, with victories in the 1905 and 1910 Seawanhaka Cup races (the Seawanhaka International Trophy for Small Yachts begun in 1896) sailing boats of his design, he crewed on T. O. M. Sopwith's *Endeavour* during a series of informal races after the America's Cup

Edwin Boardman: Northeast Harbor A Class. With their U-shaped forward sections the A Class sloops were notoriously wet in a chop, but they were also fast, powerful, safe, and attractive boats suitable for occasional short cruises. The class remained active from 1912 until 1971. © *Petér Barlow*

PHILIP CUNNINGHAM BOLGER

Born 1927 · United States

Perhaps more than any other contemporary designer, Phil Bolger has devoted a significant part of his career to the development of boats that are easily and rapidly constructed by amateur builders. A considerable amount of this work has been dedicated to getting the most out of sheet plywood as the construction material. The results, sometimes derided as "Bolger boxes," can be deceptively crude looking. While they often sacrifice traditional good looks in the interest of simplicity, closer examination discloses the designer's sophisticated grasp of modern marine carpentry and hydrodynamics.

Along with builder Harold "Dynamite" Payson, Bolger coined the phrase "instant boats" to describe certain designs that can be built in short periods of time. Among the early examples is the 15-foot 6-inch Gloucester Light Dory (also known as the Gloucester Gull), a graceful, popular, and able rowing boat that Bolger has said will get him into heaven if nothing else does. The majority of his work involves simplified plywood construction, but strip-plank and plank-on-frame construction techniques are sometimes specified, as well as the use of steel and other materials.

Significant work has also been done in the development of efficient and handy power-driven craft. In his early career Bolger designed the well-regarded Egg Harbor 31. Recently he has encouraged the production of long, light, moderately powered boats that behave well, use little fuel, and go fast without leaving an objectionable wake. One of his recent designs is the 39-foot Tahiti, a plywood passagemaker with a 5,000-nautical-mile range.

Bolger has considerable experience in the use of small sailing and rowing craft, with the result that his small craft designs are purpose-specific and sophisticated in detail, while they range from traditional to radical in appearance. Following the philosophical tradition of L. Francis Herreshoff, one of his mentors, Bolger has done a great deal to affirm the validity of very small craft, emphasizing their excellent cost-benefit ratio in the face of a boating world that has become obsessed with the high end of the market.

Bolger's recent work has continued to emphasize practicality of construction, the elimination of failure-prone features, integrated flotation in as many designs as possible, improvement of the rough-water behavior of instant-boat types, shoal-draft cruising, "field-repairability," simplicity of systems, and practical long-term living aboard in climates ranging from the tropics to the arctic.

competition of 1937. He was closely associated with the Manchester Yacht Club.

Boardman was the author of several well-read books including *The Small Yacht, Its Management and Handling for Racing and Sailing* (1909) and *Yacht Racing* (1931). He also wrote many influential articles providing advice on the design and use of small racing boats. In later years he was an insurance broker.

Some of Boardman's drawings are at Hart Nautical Collections, MIT Museum, Cambridge, MA.

—Daniel B. MacNaughton

PAUL BÖHLING

1906–1968 · Germany

One of the pioneers in German steel and aluminum boat construction, Paul Böhling studied naval engineering, then developed his shipbuilding skills in various Berlin yards. He later worked as plant manager at several Hamburg yards, founding his own yard at Hamburg-Harburg in 1949.

Before World War II, Böhling was a leading figure in the development of the 25-Square-Meter, steel-hulled centerboard cruiser, later adopted by the German Sailing Association as the national Blitz-Jollenkreuzer class boat.

The aluminum 12 KR boat *Kormoran* (a 17-meter oceangoing yawl that raced under the European KR Rule) brought Böhling the most recognition, with her second place in the 1955 Newport-Marstand Transatlantic Race. Other well-known yachts from his board were the 10 KR *Barbara*, the 9 KR *Inschallah*, 7 and 4 KR centerboarders, as well as 30-Square-Meter centerboard cruisers such as *Sünnschien* and *Trotzkopf*.

Although most of Böhling's work was in steel and aluminum sailing yachts, he also designed wooden boats built at other yards such as Matthiesen and Paulsen, as well as numerous motorboats. He always kept clear in his mind the distinction between racing and cruising boats, and routinely tested all his designs in towing tanks before construction.

Böhling died at age sixty-two, a victim of a traffic accident.

—Volker Christmann

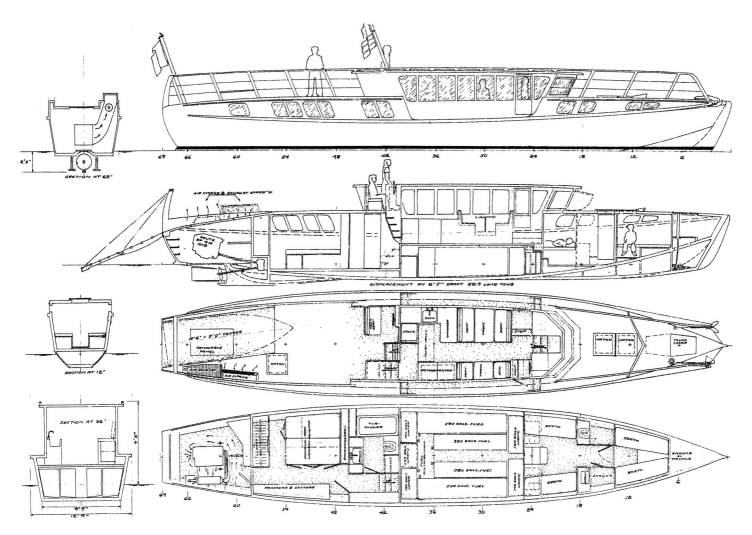

Phil Bolger: *White Eel.* *White Eel* is an economical and unsinkable 69-foot, diesel-powered passagemaker with a 5,000-mile range. The flat-bottomed plywood boat was designed for an American client to cross the Atlantic and cruise the canals of France. *Drawing courtesy Phil Bolger*

While Bolger has become famous for his nontraditional, even iconoclastic work, he is also a superb draftsman with a highly educated eye. When traditional beauty is one of the client's requirements, he demonstrates the breadth of his talent by supplying it in spades, producing a boat that looks better in the water than it does on paper—the mark of genius in three-dimensional design. His 115-foot replica of the frigate HMS *Rose* is a stunning example, and the 37-foot *Moccasin,* along with a host of her descendants, displays Bolger's ability to create a strong traditional feel and a satisfying appearance while actually charting new territory in her combination of features, if not in the individual features themselves.

A prominent writer on the subject of yacht design, Bolger embodies the spirit of innovation and illustrates the personal rewards of the design process. His writings serve to both educate us and increase our appreciation for the length and breadth of the field of yacht design. Most notable are his writings for the now-defunct *Small Boat Journal* (later *Boat Journal*) and his books *Small Boats, The Folding Schooner, Different Boats, 30 Odd Boats, 103 Sailing Rigs,* and

Phil Bolger: *Queen Mab.* Bolger's idea of a "personal watercraft" is *Queen Mab,* a 7-foot sailing catboat designed in 1996 and named after Percy Bysshe Shelley's poetical fairy queen. *Photo courtesy Phil Bolger*

Boats with an Open Mind. More books are on the way, along with a steady stream of articles, many of which appear in the magazine *Messing About in Boats.*

Bolger grew up in Gloucester, Massachusetts. He attended Bowdoin College in Maine and served in the army just after World War II. He worked in the offices of naval architects Lindsay Lord and John Hacker before beginning his own career. Bolger's first design was the outboard runabout *Hazard,* which he built in 1949 for his own use. He opened his design office in 1952. From 1985 to 1999 he lived and worked aboard the 48-foot, lug-rigged *Resolution,* which he still owns. In 1992 he married Susanne Altenburger, and the firm name became Phil Bolger and Friends. Designs after about No. 620 have been done in close partnership, and many of the most recent designs are Susanne's concepts. There is plenty of demand to keep them busy. The firm's telephone is unlisted and email is discouraged!

The office of Phil Bolger and Friends is in Gloucester, Massachusetts.

—Daniel B. MacNaughton

Dick Boon: *Skagerrak.* The classic styling and demonstrable seaworthiness of *Skagerrak*, a 1991 edition of Dick Boon's Doggersbank motoryacht series, caught the eyes and hearts of yachtsmen everywhere and made the line popular and enduring. *Photo courtesy Dick Boon*

DICK BOON

Born February 18, 1938 · The Netherlands

Dick Boon—inventor, theorist, and naval architect—has a searching mind and a lucid, elegant philosophy: to design safe, practical, timeless craft that keep their value; to draw hull forms with low resistance to minimize engine size and fuel consumption and to maximize range; and to refine scantlings to increase strength and re-duce weight, construction time, and cost. Many naval architects might share this philosophy, but few stick to it with greater tenacity than Dick Boon. He is also an unabashed and highly articulate evangelist for his rigorously reasoned, often controversial ideas, because he believes absolutely in what he says and does.

Born in Amsterdam, Boon went to work for a local drydock company in 1954, studying nights at the British Institute for Engineering Technology. After receiving his degree in 1959, he taught sailing for two years. In 1961, while living aboard a houseboat and waiting for a license to open his own sailing school, he be-

Dick Boon: Explorer. The concept model for a modern, globe-girdling, 85-meter Explorer Yacht, with its "shippy" good looks and powerful promise, point to the versatility, pragmatism, and lasting value of Dick Boon's many oceangoing designs. *Photo courtesy Dick Boon*

gan doodling designs for traditional Dutch round- and flat-bottom sailboats. In 1964, hooked on naval architecture, he formed Vripack Yachting in partnership with another designer, who died, however, within a year. Since then, Boon has produced hundreds of designs, from which more than seven thousand yachts and commercial vessels have been built to his immaculate specifications.

Boon's first major Vripack project was a line of sail and motor yachts to be built of steel, a material the Dutch understand masterfully. Eventually, some eight hundred Argonaut 7.5-meter sailing yachts and more than three thousand Aquanaut motoryachts ranging in length from 7.5 to 27.5 meters were built to Vripack designs.

In the late 1960's, Boon took a leap into a new area, starting a trend that continues today. Reasoning that sturdy workboats and deep-sea fishing trawlers were the safest and most comfortable, if not the fastest offshore hull forms, he modeled a 10.8-meter motoryacht and 10.8-meter motorsailer after them. The line was named Doggersbank, after a well-fished North Sea shoal. The Doggersbanks proved that a yacht could be seaworthy and handsome, yet inexpensive and easy to maintain; whether the client chose commercial or yacht-quality finish, it would still offer the pleasures of yachting. Some Doggersbanks were designed for clients who had fishing, canal passaging, or high-latitude cruising in mind. Several Doggersbanks under 20 meters have crossed the oceans on their own bottoms.

In 1971, a 19.3-meter trawler undertook a circumnavigation. This is an unusual performance for a small-displacement motoryacht, but it reflects the sort of client Dick Boon attracts—serious, practical yachtsmen. By the end of 1999, in a ringing endorsement of his original notion, more than five hundred Doggersbanks had been built, with the line ranging in length from 11 to 37 meters.

Boon is also an inveterate researcher. Most of his early boats were built of steel, though he occasionally prescribed aluminum scantlings. He became convinced in the 1980's, however, that aluminum was far superior, even for very large displacement motoryachts (an idea that many naval architects resist, and Boon brilliantly defends). In 1985, an aluminum Doggersbank crossed the Atlantic; in 1987, a 21.3-meter aluminum sportfisherman delivered a speed of 32 knots; and in 1992, Boon saw the launch of an aluminum Offshore 90 at the Palmer Johnson shipyard in Wisconsin, his first American-built yacht.

This was followed in 1996 by the 46-meter *Turmoil*, the first modern yacht modeled after an offshore research vessel. It won a *ShowBoats* award for most innovative motoryacht. In 1997 Palmer Johnson launched Boon's 38.1-meter aluminum *Our Way*. Boon's next research vessel yacht, the 36.9-meter *Freesia*, won the 1998 International Superyacht Society's Design Award.

From the outset, Boon has experimented with new propulsion methods, and now advocates diesel-electric systems with Schottel-type azimuthal propellers for yachts longer than 30.5 meters. Vripack also advances the use of computers in its own designs and subcontracts CAD/CAM services to shipyards for complete yacht building packages. The Vripack office has grown from two or three people in the 1960's to more than thirty computer-literate designers and engineers in its own building in the Dutch village of Sneek.

But success has not spoiled Dick Boon. He'd still love to teach sailing some day.

—Jack A. Somer

MARCELINO BOTÍN

Born 1962 · Spain

When Olympic gold medalist Luis Doreste steered the Botín and Carkeek–designed Sinergia 40 *Telepizza-Pepsi* to a substantial class victory at the IMS World Championship in Valencia in July 2001, Marcelino Botín's reputation as Spain's leading designer of IMS Rule racing yachts was cemented, and Botín and Carkeek's ranking along with the world's best was ensured.

Botín's friendship with South African Shaun Carkeek began in 1994 while both were studying at Southampton Institute in England. Since establishing their Santander, Spain, office in 1995, Botín has shared the design credits for some highly successful IMS racers, including the 1999 46-footer *Zurich*, fulfilling her design brief by winning the largest possible number of Spanish IMS circuit races, including victory in Copa del Rey. Further Copa del Rey victories followed in 2001 with *Telepizza-Pepsi*'s continued success in the 600 Group, and World 50-Foot Circuit Champion *Caixa Galicia* taking second in the 500 Group.

These successful designs are credited with particular harmony to local sea conditions, sporting high-aspect-ratio rigs influenced by the latest thinking with regard to America's Cup Class. Botín is a member of the design team working on the Team New Zealand 2007 America's Cup challenge.

—Iain McAllister with assistance from Botín and Carkeek and John Lynch

THOMAS DAVID BOWES

1884–1965 · United States

Thomas Bowes designed more than three hundred yachts, including express cruisers, traditional schooners, up-to-date cruising sloops, ketches, and yawls of all sizes, as well as diesel yachts, houseboats, some sportfishermen, and even a presidential yacht. He also established a solid reputation for designing commercial vessels, notably tugboats, fireboats, barges, and fishing vessels.

A lifelong resident of Philadelphia, Bowes set up his own practice after graduating from Cornell University in 1905, with a degree in both mechanical engineering and naval architecture.

Thomas Bowes: *L'Aiglon*. The 64-foot LOA, gasoline-powered cruiser *L'Aiglon* was launched in 1923 at the Robert Jacob yard on City Island, New York. Later Bowes would increasingly specify diesel engines for his numerous high-speed cruisers. *Photo courtesy Independence Seaport Museum, Philadelphia, PA*

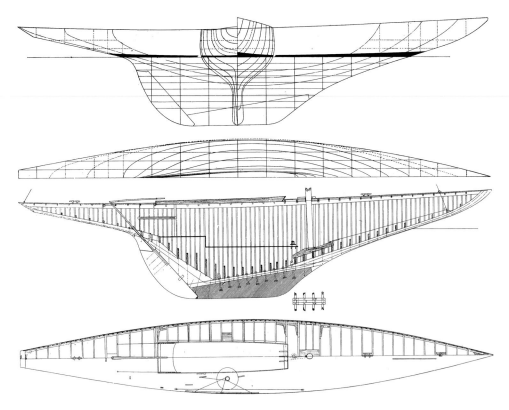

David Boyd: *Circe.* The outstandingly successful 6-Meter of the late 1930's in Europe, *Circe* defeated the Olin Stephens–designed *Goose* for the Seawanhaka Cup in 1938 and successfully defended against the Norwegian challenger in the following year. Boyd went on to design some good 6-Meters after World War II, but never regained the same prominence. © *Tony Dixon*

His first published design (in *The Rudder*, September 1905) was for a 54-foot auxiliary schooner. Briefly in 1909–10, he and J. Murray Watts worked together as Bowes and Watts. By 1911, he had teamed up with the older and more experienced designer Charles Mower to form the firm of Bowes and Mower. Until World War I, they turned out many sailboats and motoryachts. During the war, he was appointed to serve with the Council of National Defense.

The prosperous 1920's led to plenty of work in Bowes's office (he formed no more partnerships), with commissions from many prominent Philadelphia yachtsmen for large, high-speed diesel cruisers. Bowes not only designed the vessels but also meticulously supervised their construction. Despite the Depression of the 1930's, Bowes continued to get design commissions for major yachts. A large portion of his work for both sailing and power yachts emphasized shoal draft, even for yachts intended for offshore work.

Bowes's sailing yachts ranged from lovely traditional schooners to a wide variety of handy-looking, inboard, marconi-rigged cruiser/racers with moderately long ends and strong sheers, often with shoal draft. Power yachts intended for offshore often took their visual cues from his seagoing tugs, minesweepers, and pilot-boats, and as a result of his great experience with these types, have a look of great strength and authenticity. Bowes had a superb sense of proportion through the whole range of types in which he worked, and was an excellent draftsman.

During World War II, Bowes not only designed minesweepers and submarine chasers for the navy but also became the president of Penn Jersey Shipbuilding in Camden, New Jersey. There he designed and built one hundred 85-foot diesel tugs, fourteen 269-foot long cargo vessels, and twenty tankers known as TI-M-AI ships.

Following the war, his private practice turned mostly toward commercial vessels. He designed eighty diesel tugboats that were universally fast, rugged, and strikingly good looking. Although designed for use on the Delaware River, his tugs and fireboats could be found as far away as Israel and the Panama Canal as well as the major ports of the United States.

One exception to commercial work was his design for a 24-foot, round-bilge sloop, which became the Corinthian One-Design in 1952. Designed for the Corinthian Yacht Club of Philadelphia, these boats proved to be popular, fast, comfortable, dry, and easily handled.

Bowes actively designed until his death at age eighty-two.

A collection of Bowes's plans is at the Independence Seaport Museum in Philadelphia, PA.

—Lucia del Sol Knight

DAVID BOYD

1902–1989 · Scotland

It is a sad irony that David Boyd, the most successful designer of 6-Meter yachts in Europe during the post–World War II period, should be better remembered for the failure of his two America's Cup challengers. History suggests that neither *Sceptre* (1958), which lost to the Olin Stephens–designed *Columbia*, nor *Sovereign* (1964), losing to the Olin Stephens–designed *Constellation*, were as bad as contemporary commentators stated. In both cases Boyd was up against the combined skills and organizational excellence of designer Olin Stephens and the New York Yacht Club syndicates that masterminded the defense effort. It says much for Boyd the man that he received many letters of warm commiseration from fellow yacht designers in Britain and elsewhere after each of the America's Cup contests.

Boyd was born in Fairlie, Scotland, the elder son of David Boyd, who was a ship's joiner at the yard of William Fife, the renowned designer and builder. Young Boyd went to school locally until the age of fourteen, when he was apprenticed to a shipbuilder in Ardrossan, a town to which his family had moved.

In those days, night school—two nights a week, from 7 P.M. to 10 P.M.—was the rule for apprentices. For Boyd, this involved an hour's rail journey each way to and from Glasgow, where he studied at the Royal Technical College—this after a whole day's work in the yard, starting at 7 A.M.!

Upon completion of his apprenticeship, Boyd moved from job to job as work became available, but he eventually secured a draftsman's position with William Fife III. Thus, to his sound grounding in naval architecture and ship construction was added the influence of Fife in both standards of workmanship and design aesthetics. To these influences were added the high standards of Alexander Robertson and Sons, yacht builders at Sandbank in Argyll, when Boyd moved to that firm in 1931.

As Robertson's naval architect, Boyd was responsible for many of the fine yachts therefrom. Typical of his cruising-yacht designs is the yawl *Zigeuner*, at 34 tons, Boyd's favorite design, built in 1936 after he had taken over the management of the yard. The following year he produced the incomparable 6-Meter *Circe*, which won the Seawanhaka Cup in 1938 from the American *Goose* and went on to defend it successfully on the Clyde in 1939 against the Norwegian *Noreg III*.

After World War II, he was much in demand for the design of 6-Meter class yachts in both Britain and Europe, many of which were built under his direction at Robertson's. *Titia* gave him another Seawanhaka Cup victory and represented Britain at the Helsinki Olympics, and *Royal Thames* won the One-Ton Cup in 1958. He also produced some good 5.5-Meters, when that class came into being in the early 1950's.

As well as some excellent cruisers, of which *Greylag* (1962) is a good example, he designed the Piper, a 24-foot one-design, in 1966. Resembling a small meter boat, this class met a need for an up-to-date yacht that could be raced on the often choppy waters of the Clyde estuary. Of fiberglass construction, boats of this class still race in various venues of the estuary and provide exciting, if rather wet racing.

An outstanding craft designed by Boyd and built at Robertson's is the 8-Meter cruiser/racer *Sunburst*. Earlier, in 1950, the IYRU had introduced the Cruiser/Racer Rule for a number of classes ranging from 7-Meters upward. The idea was to produce boats that would be suitable for both inshore and offshore racing. The rule, like that producing the "pure" Meter boats, was formula-based, with various limits and restrictions. The 8-Meter class was the most popular, especially in Scottish waters, although some were found on the South Coast and in Scandinavia. More than twenty boats were built to the 8-Meter rule, but when *Sunburst* came on the scene, she quickly "cleaned up" the prizes for the class, so much so that interest in the class diminished very quickly

thereafter. It was, in effect, rather a fine end to a distinguished career, for David Boyd retired in 1967.

Had he not taken the direction he did in early life, Boyd would undoubtedly have made his name as a naturalist, such was his lifelong love of the natural world. A quiet, rather introverted man, he was as proficient as a wild fowler, game shooter, and fly fisherman as he was as a helmsman, especially of his 1930 Fife 6-Meter *Alana*.

Boyd's standing as a designer, not withstanding the America's Cup boats, is as high as any in the contemporary British scene, and boats of his design and construction command high prices to this day.

—David Ryder-Turner

PETER BRETT

1910–1983 · England

In recent years, Peter Brett has become well known for his Rival range of oceangoing fiberglass cruising yachts. He began designing as an amateur in northwest England before World War II, but the first design to bring him wide notice was his 25-foot LWL cruiser/racer *Fair Rover*, built in 1952. She was the first of many Brett designs sturdily built by Allanson and Sons of Freckleton. Even this early in his career, *Fair Rover* embodied the principle elements of his style, as listed

in *Yachting World*'s 1951 design review: "an able sea boat, capable of extended passages with a small crew [whilst] at the same time small and simple enough to be inexpensive to build . . . [additionally having] shallow draft . . . and suitable for off-shore racing, with a suitable rating."

Previously, Brett had steered his converted fishing boat *Merry Conceit* to victory in the inaugural 1931 Round the Isle of Wight Race, and in 1948 participated in the singlehanded Firefly class British Olympic selection trials. His successful eleven-season campaign with *Fair Rover* in RORC Class III events proved his skills as both a helmsman and a designer, and attracted increasing numbers of commissions for similarly eye-catching craft. A run of Dee 25 sloops (25 feet LWL, 30 feet LOA) was developed from *Fair Rover*. Michael Tomlinson's Dee 25 *Rondinella* created a stir when she was the only Class III finisher in the storm-wracked 1956 Channel Race.

Tomlinson later ordered the 37-foot LOA *Pellegrina*, and her type, together with the Dee 25, became much sought after by discerning offshore racing and cruising yachtsmen, such as future Irish Cruising Club commodore Rory O'Hanlon, who extensively cruised both sides of the Atlantic in his 37-foot, Brett-designed *Tjaldur*, built by Tyrrell of Arklow in 1964.

Brett's seaworthy sloops had sweet sheerlines leading to a bold bow and a cute stern, with practical and cozy seagoing interiors and a

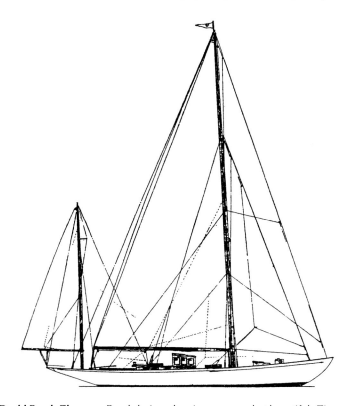

David Boyd: *Zigeuner.* Boyd-designed cruisers are rare but beautiful. *Zigeuner* is a prime example and reminds us of the influence of William Fife Jr. (III), for whom Boyd worked at one time. Semicomposite in construction, she is still racing. *Drawing courtesy David Ryder-Turner*

Peter Brett: Rival 41. The Rival 41 has a bold bow, sweet sheerline, and rugged good looks. Though no longer in production, the Rival's seakeeping abilities keep this series of more than five hundred boats popular with bluewater cruisers. *Photo courtesy George Martin*

reputation for willfully slogging it out in dirty weather. These attributes became broadly recognized by the owners of the more than five hundred Rival production yachts, ranging in overall length from 31 to 41 feet, that were built to a number of Brett's designs since 1965. Although they are no longer in production, their popularity and demand by blue-water cruisers ensure that the designer's name will be revered for many years to come.

—Iain McAllister

EDWARD SAMUEL "TED" BREWER

Born 1933 · Canada

Ted Brewer is one of the leading advocates of moderation in yacht design in a boating world that is often polarized between modern and traditional ideas, racing and cruising, wood and fiberglass. His boats follow a comfortable and pleasing middle ground, which has given them broad appeal.

Brewer designs typically have a very normal look above the waterline, with conventional sheer, moderate ends, conventional deck arrangement, and a masthead rig with a moderate-aspect-ratio mainsail. Below the waterline, they usually have a fin keel with a separated rudder on a strongly faired-in, full skeg. Often the underbody is basically a full-keel, attached rudder configuration with a "Brewer bite"; that is, the lower, aftmost portion of the keel has been cut away to reduce the amount of wetted surface area, producing a profile halfway between a full-keel and a separated rudder configuration. Topside height is somewhat higher than average, and cabin trunk height a little lower. The Whitby 42, perhaps Brewer's best-known design, exhibits all of these characteristics.

Brewer has also produced a number of interesting, ultra-shoal-draft sharpies and Downeast-style power yachts that have been very well received, but his most conventional boats are the most popular. Notable exceptions are the Rob Roy 23 and the Nimble 20, 24, and 30, Brewer's interpretations of the canoe yawl concept. More modern than the originals and deviating from the older designs, these yawl-rigged, shoal-draft cruisers emphasize comfort and safety.

Born in Ontario, Canada, Brewer enrolled in the Westlawn School of Yacht Design while a lieutenant in the Canadian army. In 1957 he resigned from the army and joined George Cuthbertson (cofounder in 1969 of C&C yachts) as a yacht broker. In 1960, Brewer graduated from Westlawn and moved to Connecticut to work at Luders Marine Construction as assistant designer. He worked closely with A. E. (Bill) Luders Jr., son of the firm's founder, and was involved in a diverse array of yachts, both sailing and power, including the 12-Meters *Weatherly* and *American Eagle*. He also worked on the design of nearly forty-five 5.5-meter sloops, among them Gold Cup and Olympic winners.

Brewer sailed aboard Bill Luders's *Storm* in races all over Long Island Sound and points north and on other Luders-designed boats in SORC and Annapolis-Newport Races. He sailed on his own design, the 60-foot auxiliary ketch *Mystic*, which placed second in Class B in the 1969 Transpac Race.

Following the closing of the Luders yard in 1967, Brewer moved to Brooklin, Maine, to establish his own practice. In early 1969, he and Jim Betts created Yacht Design Institute (YDI), a correspondence course in small craft design, with Brewer writing most of the texts. That spring, Bob Wallstrom joined Brewer as a partner and eventually bought out Betts's share of YDI as well.

During the next ten years the firm produced over a hundred custom and production designs, from a 25-foot catboat to the exquisite 62-foot charter ketch *Traveller III*. Better-known production designs include the Whitby 42, Aloha 28 and 34, Cabot 36, Jason 35, Lazyjack 32, Quickstep 24, Cape North 43, Morgan 38, and Olympic Adventure 47. In the early 1970's Brewer originated the radius-bilge method of building metal yachts with the design of the successful Goderich 35.

In 1979, Brewer moved to Washington State, producing 160 more designs ranging from a dinghy to the handsome 45-foot schooner *Sophia Christina*, the beautiful Whitby 55 ketch, and the powerful 70-foot schooner *Tree of Life*, named by *Sail* magazine as one of the "100 Greatest Yachts in America." He also designed the 60-foot singlehander *Wild Thing* (1993), which set a new course record in the 1996 Singlehanded Race to Hawaii.

Prolific and entertaining, Brewer has written three books: *Understanding Boat Design* (now in its fourth edition), *Cruising Yacht Design*, and *Ted Brewer Explains Sailboat Design*. His articles on design and cruising are countless and have been published in nearly all major North American yachting magazines.

In 1999, Brewer and his wife Betty moved to Gabriola Island in British Columbia, where he still writes for boating magazines, works on a few custom designs, lectures at the Silva Bay Shipyard School, and continues his hobby of model railroading.

—Daniel B. MacNaughton and Bob Wallstrom

Edward Brewer: *Han Solo. Han Solo* is a steel, 60-foot, three-masted schooner with the radius-bilge hull form that Brewer pioneered in the 1970's. She has twin bilge keels to keep her draft at a reasonable 6 feet and has proved to be very successful, cruising easily at 10 knots in moderate breezes. *Photo courtesy Ted Brewer*

Frederick Brewer: *Stormy Petrel.* The 43-foot *Stormy Petrel* was built at Walton Hubbard Jr.'s South Coast Company in 1937. She has carried this name under many owners as a successful racer and cruiser. Recently she has been sailing out of Newport Harbor, California, as she has for most of her sixty-eight years. *Photo courtesy Newport Harbor Nautical Museum, Newport Beach, CA*

FREDERICK C. BREWER

1870–1947 · United States

As the original designer involved in the creation of the Bird One-Design class of San Francisco, Fred Brewer made one of the most enduring contributions of his career. Refined to a degree by Sam Crocker in John Alden's Boston office, the 30-foot Bird is unique, with a raised deck forward and other features that make her an ideal small racer/cruiser for the heavy winds and chop of San Francisco Bay. Many of the original boats still race hard, eighty years after they were built.

Born in England, Brewer began racing with his father and brothers under the burgee of the Egremont Sailing Club. Around 1890 he began his apprenticeship in marine engineering and construction. At the turn of the twentieth century, he emigrated to British Columbia. There he formed the partnership of Brewer and McBryde, which was active in the design of both commercial and pleasure craft. He moved to San Francisco around 1919 and became the in-house designer at the Madden and Lewis yard in Sausalito, where he produced the design of the Bird, the first four built by that yard.

Moving to southern California in the early 1930's, Brewer became the designer for Walton Hubbard Jr.'s South Coast Company in Newport Beach. He designed for it a series of handsome sloops, ketches, yawls, cutters, and motorsailers in the 29- to 60-foot range, including the 49-foot yawl *Brilliant* (placing second in Class C in 1936 and third overall in the 1939 Honolulu Race), the 50-foot ketch *Wayfarer*, the 60-foot ketch-rigged motorsailer *Vagabundo*, and the 55-foot schooner *Samarang*. The 42-foot 11-inch sloop *Stormy Petrel* and *Samarang* still compete in southern Californian wooden boat races.

Fred Brewer is remembered by many old-timers as a true pioneer who left the imprint of his considerable talent on a wide area of the West Coast of the United States.   —Thomas G. Skahill

PHILIPPE BRIAND

Born June 14, 1956 · France

Philippe Briand–designed racers break records: In October 2003, the 42.6-meter *Mari Cha IV*, codesigned with Clay Oliver and Greg Elliott under the aegis of Jean-François d'Etiveaud, smashed the transatlantic monohull record on her maiden passage, crossing in 6 days, 17 hours, 52 minutes, and 39 seconds. Previously, in October 1998, the maxi boat *Mari Cha III* had passed Lizard Point in southwestern Cornwall, England, to set a new record for a transatlantic passage by a monohull, with a time of 8 days, 23 hours, 59 minutes and 43 seconds. *Mari Cha III*'s helmsman was also her designer, and no doubt Philippe Briand savored this culmination of his work, a four-year project to create a 44.7-meter hull (the largest boat ever built of carbon fiber at the time) with a $15 million budget. The resulting yacht trimmed 2 days, 13 hours, 22 minutes, and 22 seconds off the record previously set by *Nicorette* in 1997.

Philippe Briand: *Mari Cha III.* The ketch-rigged *Mari Cha III* broke the transatlantic record for a monohull under sail in 1998, covering the distance between New York's Ambrose Light and England's Lizard Point in 8 days, 23 hours, 59 minutes, and 43 seconds. Interior design was by John Munford. *Photo courtesy Jacques Taglang*

The real-life experience aboard *Mari Cha III* was beneficial to Briand. He was able, once again, to measure the gap between theory and practice: "When you are conceiving such a boat, you always have a vision of her ideal performance," he explains. "In your armchair, in front of the computer, it is easy to trim the sails in an optimum manner. But in practice, when it is necessary to set the spinnaker in 35 knots of wind, you realize it's another thing."

The son of Michel Briand, a successful racing yachtsman from La Rochelle, Philippe was eleven when he decided to become a designer. At nineteen, he began an internship for over a year with the Swedish designer Pelle Petterson, who was working on the 12-Meter *Sverige,* Sweden's 1977 America's Cup challenger. At the end of 1977 he worked on another 12-Meter, a very light displacement concept in which he tried to deepen the draft when the boat heeled through the use of winglets attached to the keel. The project was never completed. In 1978, he opened Philippe Briand Yacht Architecture (PBYA) in La Rochelle.

During the 1987 America's Cup races at Perth, Australia, Briand's 12-Meter *French Kiss* surprised everyone by winning the semifinals in the Louis Vuitton Challenge Cup. He repeated this feat in 1992 in San Diego with the America's Cup Class boat *Ville de Paris,* one of the first round of boats built for the new class.

Like many of his French design colleagues, Briand works mostly alone or assisted by a very small team. He encountered the limitations of this approach when two Briand-designed America's Cup Class boats, *France 2* and *France 3,* were routed in the French Cup challenge of 1995. (In recent America's Cup matches, no lone talent has so far been able to meet the barrage of challenges presented by large and diverse design teams overseen by a technical director.) The French press harshly criticized Briand for his individualism following the defeats. Perhaps with this in mind, he worked with his colleagues Peter Van Oossanen and Sébastien Schmidt on designs for the Swiss challenge for 2000 in Auckland; the ultimate winner was New Zealand's *Black Magic.*

Having raced constantly since his childhood, Briand has also become a fearsome skipper of his own designs. He won the Half-Ton World Champion aboard *Freelance* (1983) and the One-Ton World Champion with *Passion* (1984). He was skipper of the 34-foot IOR boat *Corum* (1987) in the 1987–88 season and of another 34-foot IOR boat named *Corum* (1989) in the 1989 season. Briand sailed the 36-foot *Sun Fast* to victory when she won the La Rochelle competition of 1993.

PBYA designs also were successful in the 1991 Admiral's Cup, the Swiss Bol d'Or of 1995, the 50-foot North American Championship, and the San Francisco Big Boat series of 1988, the 1985–86 Whitbread Round the World Race, the 1985 Fastnet Race, the Quarter-Ton World Championships of 1984 and 1986, and the 1981 Seahorse Maxi Series. In 1982 the catamaran *Elf Aquitaine II* was the winner of the 1982 Route du Rhum Race. She was the first catamaran to be built entirely of carbon fiber and was fitted with one of the first wing masts for an offshore multihull.

Thanks to this impressive list of successes, Briand is now managing one of the busiest European yacht design offices, with boats under construction in the best of French and foreign yards. Briand is a reserved man and an untiring observer. He has always adapted to the state of the art, utilizing tank tests, wind tunnel tests, one-half-scale sailing models, and computer simulations and specifying the most sophisticated construction materials. His indisputable talent has enabled him to design boats suited to various handicapping rules as well as custom yachts of other types, mostly monohulls but also some famous multihulls. To date nearly eight thousand boats designed by PBYA are sailing the world.

Mari Cha III's record-breaking transatlantic passage won Briand the 1998 Superyacht Society Design Award and inspired many more commissions for large yachts. The collaboratively designed *Mari Chas IV,* with masts towering 146 feet above the water and carrying two full-sized maxi rigs, lopped more than 2 hours off the transatlantic monohull record in 2003.

Philippe Briand continues to practice in La Rochelle, France.   —Jacques Taglang

FRED S. BRINTON
see Harold Lee

JOHN BALMAIN "JACK" BROOKE, OBE

July 28, 1907–1992 · New Zealand

Throughout his life, Jack Brooke produced approximately one hundred designs that kept him in the forefront of yacht and sailboat designers in New Zealand despite his strictly part-time involvement. He was born near Auckland and spent his childhood living close to Narrow Neck Beach, on Auckland's North Shore. Indeed, the rest of his life also centered around this pleasant beach on the Rangitoto Channel, open to the east but sheltered from the prevailing westerlies.

Brooke was a bright student and won scholarships enabling him to complete an engineering degree at Auckland and Canterbury Universities. In 1926 he designed the Brooke Canoe, which was the wellspring for the Wakatere ("Flying Canoe" in Maori) Canoe Club, later the Wakatere Boating Club. During the 1930's he designed a series of extremely fast centerboarders for Auckland's 14-, 16-, and 18-foot classes and some very basic hard-chine 14-footers for the Wakatere Boating Club. He also adapted the 11-foot 6-inch Frostbite to local conditions and for amateur construction, for the same club. This design proved hugely successful countrywide.

A landmark keel-yacht design in 1939, also with strong U.S. influence, was *Gleam*, a 34-foot LOA (26-foot LWL) light-displacement sloop. Several of his postwar designs stemmed from this successful yacht. By the outbreak of war in 1939, he was regarded as the premier designer of fast centerboarders in the coun-

try, specializing in hard-chine planing hulls.

During World War II, Brooke worked as an engineer at the Dominion Physical Laboratory on the design of advanced equipment for the manufacture of munitions and ranging gear. For this he received the Order of the British Empire in 1947. After the war he spent the rest of his working life as a prominent government scientist and administrator. He

was commodore of Auckland's prestigious Royal New Zealand Yacht Squadron in 1969.

His postwar designs included the keel yachts *Judith* and *Wakaya* (1947), *Chiquita* (1951), *Karangi* (1958), and *Kiariki* (1960); the enormously popular Sunburst centerboard class (1964); the 90-foot brigantine *Spirit of Adventure*; and the 110-foot brigantine *Ji Fung* for Outward Bound in Hong Kong in 1979.   —Harold Kidd

Jack Brooke: *Mania.* A Y-Class, square-bilge 14-footer, *Mania* was built in 1935 at Gordon Miller's yard in Auckland, New Zealand. The class was introduced in Auckland in 1914 and was quite heavily built until Brooke designed the much lighter *Muimai* in 1934, followed by *Mania*. Both carried a marconi rig and lots of sail. *Photo courtesy Harold Kidd*

JAMES W. BROWN

Born 1933 · United States

The case for multihulls—or any of the other innovations in which he has been involved,—could have no better advocate than Jim Brown. An engaging conversationalist and writer full of ideals, humor, and anecdote, devoid of didacticism, Brown has achieved broad acceptance of his theories and concepts partly by the sheer positive force of his personality.

Brown is best known for his line of Searunner cruising trimarans, which because of their simple plywood, glue, and fiberglass construction, and his excellent plans and instruction manuals, provided access to desirable cruising and liveaboard boats for many home boatbuilders. This was particularly the case in the 1960's and 1970's when there was considerable willingness to reject conventional design premises and to adopt a new, liveaboard lifestyle. The five sizes of Searunners range from 25 to 40 feet.

The Searunner trimarans, while possessed of an angular and modernist attractiveness rather than traditional beauty, are essentially conservative in design, settling for speeds well short of those achievable by multihulls even as they are significantly faster than most cruising monohulls. This conservatism combined with rugged construction, good buoyancy, and generally moderate proportions has resulted in practical boats with a good safety record. At last count, there were fifteen hundred Searunner owner/builders. Having little enthusiasm for racing, Brown designed only cruising multihulls.

Brown grew up in New York, went to school in Connecticut, and came into contact with sailing during summers on Long Island Sound. He attended Dartmouth, but soon moved to Miami. Adventure called, and he got a job working on one of the early windjammer cruise vessels in the Caribbean. While in Miami, he and a friend designed and built a catamaran, on which the two of them cruised the Caribbean, and Jim was first introduced to a third world culture.

In the late 1950's Brown moved to Sausalito, California, to learn about fiberglass boatbuilding technology. At this time he met Arthur Piver, a pioneering multihull designer who became his mentor. After a period of boatbuilding and experimentation, Brown began producing his own designs in 1963.

By the late 1960's, Brown had become a successful designer. He had not forgotten his earlier experiences in the Caribbean, and at that time made a three-year cruise to Mexico, the Caribbean islands, and South America with his young family. This experience gave him new respect for other cultures and their working watercraft, and diminished his interest in the American dream.

Beginning in the 1980's, Brown concentrated for many years on the development of working multihulls for third world countries. He became friends with Dick Newick, another prominent multihull designer best known for his racing trimarans. Their discussions about third world problems and needs led to a series of sailing multihull workboats, the first of which was SIB (for "small is beautiful"), a 32-foot "sailing pickup truck" trimaran prototype, the design for which was commissioned by noted multihull sailor Phil Weld. She was intended to be buildable by local people with modest skill levels and was the first boat to incorporate the Constant Camber cold-molding method, developed jointly by Brown and Newick.

Constant Camber is a method that employs a single master mold to create compound-curved, cold-molded panels that are then used to build the boat. The mold has the same constant curvature over its entire surface, so each piece of veneer has a consistent shape, simplifying the process by which they are produced. From 1983 to 1985, Brown taught a course on designing and building boats using the Constant Camber method at WoodenBoat School in Brooklin, Maine.

Jim Brown currently works with his longtime partner, designer John Marples. Recent projects have included a line of Searunner catamarans for cruising and charter work, and his only production design, the WindRider, a small roto-molded trimaran that allows sit-down-inside comfort not unlike a sea kayak.

—Daniel B. MacNaughton

Jim Brown: _Troika_. The trimaran _Troika_ is shown traveling fast, on an even keel, with her crew comfortably ensconced in her deep central cockpit. She is a good example of the solid cruising comfort that Brown has pursued in his work. © _Peter Barlow_

ALAN H. BUCHANAN

(Dates unknown) · England

In a career spanning more than fifty years, Alan Buchanan became one of Britain's most prolific designers, with more than two thousand designs to his credit.

Educated as an aeronautical engineer, skills that afforded him considerable success as a designer of racing sailboats, most of Buchanan's body of work was accomplished during the 1950's and early 1960's. With the introduction of the IOR in 1969, however, he stopped designing racing craft and continued to design cruising vessels along with powerboats and workboats.

Buchanan's racing boats were typically narrow, deep, moderately long-ended, and heavily ballasted—the antithesis of the type encouraged by the new rule, a type the designer felt would be unseaworthy. At the height of his career designing racing boats, almost half the ocean-racing fleet were his designs, one winning the Sydney-Hobart Race in 1961.

Buchanan designed many one-design classes, including the Yeoman Class (33-foot 1-inch LOA sloop, 1956), the Colleen Class (23-foot 2-inch LOA sloop, 1950), the Clipper Class (of which Buchanan's own sloop, the 30-foot 3-inch LOA *Taeping*, was the first in 1954), the East Anglian Class (27-foot 9-inch LOA sloop, 1956), and the Tuskar Class (34-foot LOA sloop or yawl rig, 1953).

Buchanan's small yachts, including a number of shoal-draft estuary cruisers, frequently employed raised decks, doghouse-style cabin trunks often with a characteristic streamlined window shape, and distinctly English character and charm. Larger yachts had fewer stylistic notions, stressing a clean and competent look and good seakeeping ability.

A number of Buchanan's designs featured reverse-sheer and modernistic cabin trunks, but these were usually placed on hulls that were otherwise quite conventional; the designer did not move far into light-displacement or cutaway underbodies.

Now retired on the Channel Island of Jersey, Alan Buchanan received the Small Craft Medal for 1996 awarded by the Royal Institution of Naval Architects.   —Daniel B. MacNaughton

GEORGE BUEHLER

Born June 17, 1948 · United States

On his Web site, George Buehler speaks of his affection for simple, strong, reliable, and economical boats and, like many designers, expresses frustration with the common definition of the word *performance* as a synonym for

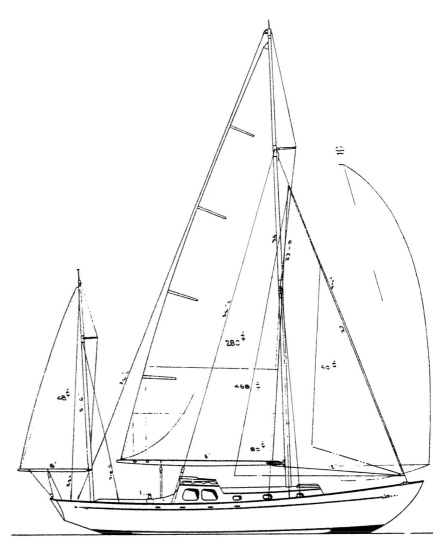

Alan Buchanan: Tuskar Class. The Tuskar Class of 1953 was a 34-foot LOA yawl suitable for racing and cruising and rigged as either a yawl or a sloop. As with much of Buchanan's work, she combines conservative proportions with dramatic styling in an appealing mixture. *Reproduced from* The Rudder

speed. The performance of a boat, Buehler says, is measured "by whether or not it does its designed goals well. A race boat that loses regularly and a cruising boat which is hard to handle are not performance boats."

Buehler says his appreciation of boats has broadened considerably since he first started designing around 1970, when he was full of fairly fixed ideas. He is willing to design for any goal, in any size, and while most of his work is strongly traditional in character, he also says he will work "in any style," with the sole provision that the boat must be safe to use as planned. However, it is clear that in his sailboat designs, Buehler prefers heavy-displacement, long-term cruising boats over race boats or weekend cruisers, and in his powerboat designs, the more seaworthy, traditionally styled cruising boats with excellent fuel economy are his favorites. He offers both custom designs and stock plans.

Many of Buehler's boats are planned for relatively easy amateur construction. They are often "long for their size," making for hulls

that are easy to plank or plate, and there is a noticeable absence of reversing curves.

While he began his design career using traditional methods, Buehler has gradually made the transition to fully computerized drafting and currently does no hand drafting at all. He feels that his work has become much more precise, partly due to the inherent accuracy of the machine but also due to the ease of making changes until the drawing can no longer be improved. In his steel designs, he is experimenting with numeric cutting machines, which will accept a disc from his computer and cut the steel to precise shapes, ready for assembly.

Buehler was born in Oregon, grew up around boatyards and fishing boats, and participated in other traditional activities of that area. After graduating from high school, he moved to Maine, where he worked in several yards as a carpenter, including on the replica of the schooner *America* built at Goudy and Stevens in 1967.

In 1970 he designed his first boat for his own use and spent several years aboard cruising to

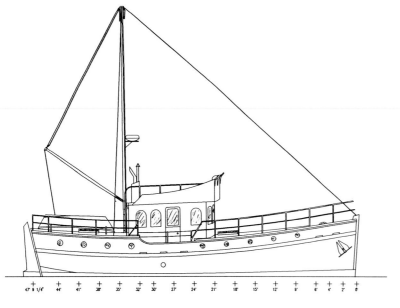

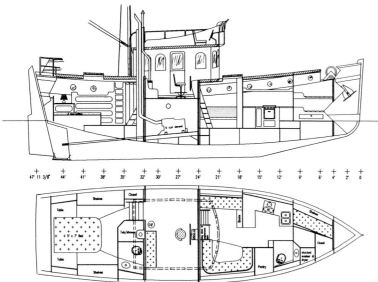

George Buehler: Diesel Duck 48. Buehler created the salty Diesel Duck 48 as a tribute to his Pacific Northwest heritage. As he puts it, "While the kite shops, the B&Bs and the No Smoking signs may have taken over where once lived boatyards and cluttered docks and working fleets, the sight of Diesel Duck heading out to sea will make old people pause and remember and young people wonder about the world now gone." *Drawing courtesy George Buehler*

Raymond Bunker: *Rambler.* Designed and built in 1958 by Bunker and Ellis, *Rambler* was a husky, 34-foot, no-nonsense cruiser. She shows the kind of Downeast sensibility that made Bunker's designs ideal for use on the often-challenging Maine coast. © *Peter Barlow*

Mexico and Hawaii. She resulted in requests for similar designs, thus launching his professional career. His involvement with computers began in 1988. He is the author of *The Troller Yacht Book*, *Buehler's Backyard Boatbuilding*, *How to Find Where You Are from the Sun*, and *George Buehler Yacht Designs*, his stock plans catalogue. He has just finished a new book, *Cruising on Land*, which is about RVs and the similarities between the RV and boating lifestyles.

Buehler currently lives and works on Whidbey Island in the state of Washington with his wife Gail, collecting "old boats, stray dogs, and interesting machines."

—Daniel B. MacNaughton

RAYMOND BUNKER
September 6, 1906–January 13, 1994
RALPH ELLIS
December 22, 1910–March 14, 1994

United States

Ray Bunker teamed up with Ralph Ellis to form the firm of Bunker and Ellis in Manset, Maine, following the end of World War II. They became well known for their Downeast cruisers, of which the wooden 42-foot *Jericho*, launched in 1957, is probably their best known. They designed and built fishing boats for the local market and beautifully detailed, high-quality yachts based on those designs for the summer people.

Bunker and Ellis would build these boats after work and on weekends. The designs were always based on hand-carved half models. They launched their first boat, a 32-footer, in 1946. One of their most popular hulls was the 42-footer, which first appeared in 1951. This boat became known to area residents as a picnic boat, because it was not used for commercial fishing.

The largest boat designed and built by Bunker and Ellis was their 44-footer, of which they built three, including *Waterbed* and *Sea Queen*. Many boats have been restored, such as the 1956 *Bellatrix* and the 1970 *Fancy*. The last boat produced by Bunker and Ellis was a 37-foot lobsterboat, in 1978. In total, they designed and built fifty-eight boats.

Bunker and Ellis then retired. In 1983 Ellis's son Don set up shop in the same facilities under the name Ellis Boat Company and began designing and building in fiberglass such successful boats as the Ellis 36. The business is still in Manset, producing work and pleasure yachts as well as being the first choice for the repair, maintenance, and restoration of Bunker and Ellis boats. —Jon Johansen

EDWARD "NED" BURGESS

June 30, 1848–July 31, 1891 · United States

The short but intense career of Edward Burgess left a lasting impression on American yachting history. The Burgess office in Boston, Massachusetts, produced a remarkable 137 designs in only seven years, among them *Puritan*, *Mayflower*, and *Volunteer*, defenders of the America's Cup in three successive matches. Burgess was largely responsible for the emergence of the compromise type of racing yacht, which found a healthy middle ground between the British "plank-on-edge" cutters and the American "skimming-dish" sloops.

Compared to N. G. Herreshoff and other emerging rivals, Burgess was less of an engineer and more of an artist. As his education was mostly devoted to natural sciences, he relied primarily on intelligence, common sense, and intuition in his design work. All of these faculties must have been good, because while it is recorded that his boats sometimes needed minor adjustments after they were built, ultimately they were highly successful. Burgess's designs have a reputation for unexcelled beauty, and his work greatly advanced the field of yacht design in terms of shape, proportion, and configuration.

Evolution in the construction of his designs progressed slowly, owing to Burgess's lack of an engineering education. At the time of his death at the pinnacle of his career, the yachting world was beginning to see engineering and construction breakthroughs that heralded lighter displacement, higher ballast ratios, and related important developments. These advances might have represented difficult challenges to Burgess's supremacy if he had lived longer.

Burgess's designs consisted primarily of hull lines and sail plans, and typically left the construction details and interior arrangements to the discretion of the builder. Because lines and sail plans are comparatively quick to create, Burgess was able to produce a large number of designs in rapid succession. He drew in ink on a paper-and-linen surface prepared by his wife (quite an involved process at the time) and, unlike most other contemporary designers, did all his designing on the drafting table rather than by making a model.

Ned Burgess was born in Sandwich, Massachusetts, to supportive and wealthy parents who had made a fortune in the sugar trade and owned an ever-increasing fleet of yachts designed by N. G. Herreshoff. Burgess and his brothers had access to small sloops and catboats from an early age, sailing out of Salem Harbor in Massachusetts. He sailed (and won) his first race in the family sandbagger *Cassie* around 1862 in Gloucester. Burgess and two of his brothers

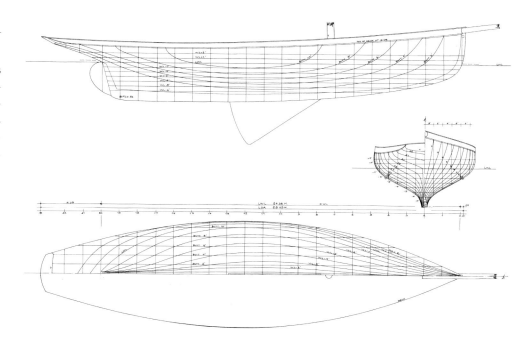

Edward Burgess: *Puritan.* *Puritan* was Burgess's first America's Cup defender, in 1885, and served to popularize the "compromise" type, being neither so deep and narrow as British yachts of the day, nor as wide and shallow as American yachts, and proving superior to both. *Puritan* beat the John Beavor-Webb–designed *Genesta* in the 1885 match. © *Chevalier & Taglang*

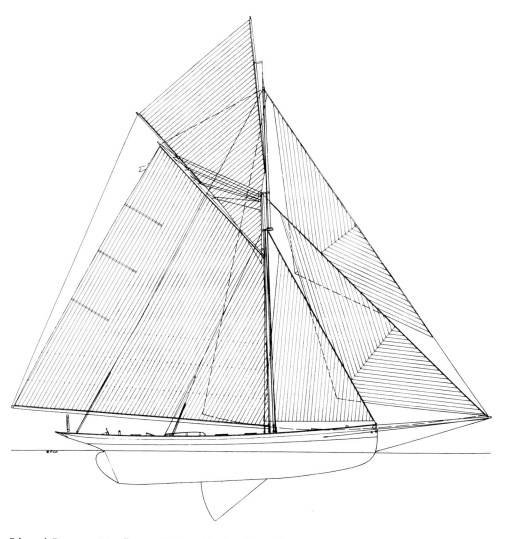

Edward Burgess: *Mayflower.* This profile drawing of Burgess's second America's Cup defender, *Mayflower*, is very similar to his design of *Puritan*, winner of the 1885 America's Cup. *Mayflower* defeated the John Beavor-Webb–designed *Galatea* in the 1886 race. © *Chevalier & Taglang*

Edward Burgess: *Papoose.* *Papoose* was the yacht that brought Burgess to prominence in the 40-Foot (LWL) class in 1887. She shows strong British cutter influence and helped to demonstrate some of the virtues of the type to American yachtsmen. *Photo by Nathaniel Stebbins. Courtesy Society for the Preservation of New England Antiquities*

Edward Burgess: *Volunteer.* In 1887 Burgess's third America's Cup defender *Volunteer* reflected some evolution of the "compromise" type. Above the waterline, the principal difference is a flaring clipper bow, but below there is a more salient keel and a smaller centerboard, trends that were to continue in the evolution of more modern types. *Photo by Nathaniel Stebbins. Courtesy Society for the Preservation of New England Antiquities*

helped to found the Eastern Yacht Club in 1870. As a young man he took a lot of ribbing from his brothers, who claimed he would rather work on perfecting his boats than sail them.

Burgess demonstrated great skill in mechanical matters and had a strong interest in natural history, especially entomology. He graduated with the Harvard class of 1871 and went on to teach entomology there for a year. He then worked for fifteen years as an instructor in entomology at the Bussey Institute and became secretary of the Boston Society of Natural History. He married Caroline Louisa Sullivant in 1877. They had two sons, William Starling Burgess in 1878 and Charles Paine Burgess in 1888.

In the summer of 1883, Burgess and his family traveled to England, where he studied the design of English yachts, which differed sharply from American practice and had many strong proponents on both sides of the Atlantic. The family fortune was lost that summer (sources do not reveal how), and Burgess returned home to much-reduced circumstances.

The work to which he turned in order to support himself and his family was yacht design and brokerage. He formed the Eastern Yacht Agency with his brother Sidney, but things were tough at first and Sidney gave up on the venture after a year. Sydney went on to design a number of successful yachts, but apparently not as a business venture.

Burgess first commissioned other designers to create boats for his clients. He selected A. Cary Smith to create *Moya*, a design based on the English type for *The Field* magazine, and he arranged for Dixon Kemp to design *Lapwing* for J. Malcolm Forbes. His stock in trade seems to have been English-influenced yachts for the American market. Burgess designed the small sloop *Columbine* and had her built for his own use in 1883. She was apparently his first design and was followed in 1884 by his first commissioned design, the 30-foot waterline cruising cutter *Rondina*, built by the Lawley yard in Neponset, Massachusetts, in 1884.

At the time there was considerable polarity between the design philosophies of the United States and Britain, which incidentally persists to some degree to this day. American yachts tended to be broad, shallow centerboarders referred to as "skimming-dish" types, typically sloops, while the British yachts were typically deep, narrow cutters. Both styles of yachts had evolved under the influence of local handicapping rules and natural conditions, but had developed to unhealthy extremes.

Cutters had become so narrow that they lacked buoyancy enough for safety at sea and had little space for accommodations. On the

Edward Burgess: *Constellation*. Shown here on Long Island Sound, *Constellation* spent most of her sixty-odd years sailing out of Marblehead, Massachusetts. She was built in 1889 for E. D. Morgan, who subsequently owned the Nathanael Herreshoff–designed *Gloriana*. The iron-hulled centerboard schooner was built on City Island, New York. *Photograph courtesy Peabody Essex Museum, Salem, MA*

other hand, they could not be capsized and showed great speed under the right conditions. Sloops became so wide and shallow that they had little ultimate stability in a knockdown, but they were also fast and allowed access to the many shallow bays and harbors on the East Coast of the United States. By bringing some British influence into American types, Burgess created a healthy hybrid—moderate in both draft and beam, sometimes having a centerboard and sometimes not—that surpassed both its immediate ancestors in speed, safety, and practicality.

The correctness of Burgess's design philosophy and his competence as a designer must have been immediately obvious to a number of influential yachtsmen, as he had completed only seven or eight designs and was only thirty-six years old when he was commis-

sioned by the Eastern Yacht Club of Marblehead, Massachusetts, to design an America's Cup defender. The commission had first been offered to N. G. Herreshoff, who declined it. Boston's desire to defend the Cup was partly political, as Boston-area yachtsmen had a strong desire to upset New York's domination of the sport, and apparently there was some feeling that the New York Yacht Club had too strongly adopted the skimming-dish type.

Burgess's *Puritan*, a compromise type with an 80-foot waterline length, beat the A. Cary Smith–designed skimming dish *Priscilla* for the right to defend the Cup and went on to beat the British cutter *Genesta*, designed by J. Beavor-Webb, in 1885. *Puritan* had a centerboard, but she was narrower, deeper, and heavier than typical American boats and had most of her ballast outside, on the keel. Her success amounted

to proof that an inherently more desirable new type of yacht was now available, and generated a flood of new design commissions.

At the time, the America's Cup races were closely followed by a large number of Americans from coast to coast, and Burgess's success as a young, innovative underdog propelled him to a degree of fame seldom seen by a yacht designer today. The Burgess design office grew into a prosperous business. The subsequent Cup defenders *Mayflower* and *Volunteer*, which achieved their successes in 1886 and 1887, respectively, against the English *Galatea*, designed by J. Beavor-Webb (a near duplicate of *Genesta* but built in steel), and the Scottish *Thistle*, an innovative design by G. L. Watson, served to confirm that Burgess was one of the master designers of his period. His book *American and English Yachts* was published in 1887.

Edward Burgess: *Wild Duck.* The 146-foot steam yacht *Wild Duck*, built around 1890, was one of thirty-five designed by Edward Burgess. Note her tall rig and lower sails, which are all bent on and, though covered, are ready to set. In later steam yachts, sailing rigs would become more vestigial in nature. © *New Bedford Whaling Museum-Old Dartmouth Historical Society*

Yachting society seemed to be aware that Burgess still faced financial limitations, for after the *Volunteer* win, the people of Boston built him a fine townhouse, and cash amounting to over twenty thousand dollars was raised in New York and Boston as a gift.

Besides his America's Cup defenders, Burgess's portfolio included racers in other contemporary racing classes, as well as schooner yachts, several innovative commercial fishing and cargo schooners, pilot-boats, steam yachts (thirty-five of them), catboats, cruising boats, and day-sailers. He worked for the U.S. government as a consultant, helping to select designs for naval vessels, including those to which the battleship *Maine* was constructed. In 1886 he modernized the famous schooner *America*, adding a bulb-shaped ballast keel and more sail area.

Burgess was much involved in the 30-, 40-, and 46-foot waterline racing classes of the day and used these relatively small, inexpensive classes for a degree of experimentation, straying outside of the compromise type on occa-

sion. He achieved particularly notable success in a series of yachts for the famous yachtsmen Charles Francis Adams III and his brother George Caspar Adams, named *Papoose, Babboon, Harpoon, Gossoon,* and *Raccoon.* The 40-foot class was the most active, and he began his involvement with it in 1887 with his design for *Papoose,* which ended an eleven-year winning streak on the part of *Shadow,* designed by N. G. Herreshoff. *Papoose* was the first of a series of Burgess-designed boats for that class, which between 1887 and 1890 amounted to fourteen of the twenty-one boats built.

Burgess boats dominated the 40-footers until the arrival in 1889 of *Minerva,* designed by William Fife of Scotland and a breakthrough in terms of her relatively light displacement and reduced wetted surface area. The 46-foot class largely replaced the 40-footers in 1891, and Burgess designed a number of boats for the new class with well-founded expectations of success.

But 1891 was the year in which N. G. Herreshoff returned to racing yacht design with

Gloriana, a breakthrough boat that, partly through an improved overall configuration and partly through superior engineering, defeated all the other yachts in her class and would have represented a serious blow to Burgess's career. Unfortunately the summer of 1891 was when Burgess, greatly overworked, fell ill with typhoid fever and soon died. The knowledge that his newest yachts had all been defeated was kept from him. Following his death, yachting circles raised thirty thousand dollars for his family. His wife died soon after, leaving W. Starling Burgess a young orphan.

Edward Burgess and N. G. Herreshoff were friendly rivals who viewed each other with great respect. Following Burgess's death, Herreshoff served as a mentor to Burgess's young son Starling, who with tremendous aptitude of his own and a background now dominated by two of the best yacht designers of the age, went on to become a designer of equally great accomplishment.   —Daniel B. MacNaughton

WILLIAM STARLING BURGESS

December 12, 1878–March 19, 1947
United States

"The ideal designer of sailing yachts," wrote Douglas Phillips-Birt, "is a magnificent creature who is at once a hydrodynamicist, an engineer, a practical boat-builder, an experienced seaman under sail, and an artist." The Boston-born yacht designer and aviation pioneer W. Starling Burgess was all these things and more. Only N. G. Herreshoff and Starling's own father, Edward, rank together with him among America's best yacht designers. As a dreamer of sea and air, he stands alone.

Except for a cleft palate (surgically repaired while he was still an infant), Burgess had a fortunate childhood. Even his wealthy grandfather's dramatic business failure in 1883, which disrupted the easy existence of Burgess's parents, had a positive result: it transformed Edward Burgess from a sailing dilettante into the foremost American yacht designer of his time. In 1891, however, at the height of his powers, the forty-three-year-old Ned Burgess died of typhoid fever. Just six months later, his wife Caroline (Kitty) also died. Starling Burgess, thirteen, and his brother, three, were on their own.

Sailing, steam engineering, naval ordnance, poetry, and manned flight were Burgess's passions at both Milton Academy and Harvard University (class of 1901), from which he took a leave of absence to serve in the navy during the Spanish-American War. By the time he was a college senior, this brilliant student had settled on a career in yacht design. He opened a design office in Boston in January 1901. He never did graduate from Harvard.

As a seventeen-year-old, Burgess had commissioned from longtime family friend "Uncle Nat" Herreshoff an ultra-light 22-foot sloop, *Sally II*. Now, six years later, Burgess began his own design practice with a succession of very fast, very light, jib-and-mainsail racers. His first major success was a celebrated monster and winner of the Quincy Cup, *Outlook* (1902), a cantilevered scow sloop that managed to support (just barely) an overall length of 52 feet 7 inches and 1,800 square feet of sail on a waterline of just 20 feet 10 inches. *Outlook* helped to hasten overdue rating and scantling reforms in America and to usher in the Universal Rule, which was one of N. G. Herreshoff's greatest contributions to the sport of yacht racing.

Among the more conventional of Burgess's early designs were the 18-foot knockabout *Comforter* and the 21-foot, cabin-class sloop *Little Haste*, winner of the East and West championship in 1902. Nonetheless, both *The Rudder* and *Sail and Sweep* condemned *Little Haste*

as a perversion of the rating rules. One can almost hear Burgess cheerfully agreeing, "True, quite true."

The sole proprietorship of W. Starling Burgess Company lasted two years. It was followed in December 1902 by a joint partnership between Burgess and the skilled and experienced designer and marine engineer A. A. Packard (1871–1948), which, as Burgess and Packard, opened its first boatshop in Salem in early 1904. By this time Burgess had designed for building elsewhere the 33-foot LWL cruising ketch *Peggy*; the 25-foot LWL open-class sloops *Venire, Dorothy May*, and *Chewink II*; three 21-footers; and four one-design 18-footers.

Between them, Packard and Burgess generated more business in their first year together than Burgess himself would enjoy as a designer until the 1920's. Among the boats were

two packet schooners, the 40-Rater *Pellegrina* and the 37-foot moderate-draft yawl *Teva*; three one-design classes (including the Cataumet 14-footers and Mattapoisett 15-footers); two 25-Raters; and the highly touted *Kolutoo* (successor to *Outlook*), which tried but failed to wrest the Seawanhaka Cup from the Canadian sloop *Thorello* in 1903.

First married in 1901 and soon thereafter a widower, Burgess became involved with the estranged wife of the owner of *Outlook* and *Kolutoo* in 1903. In part to stay clear of the divorce between Rosamond Tudor Higginson and her husband, Burgess traveled to London in November 1903, where he worked on a book titled *The Modern Yacht*, which he never completed, and briefly opened an office of Burgess and Packard. A book of his poems, *The Eternal Laughter*, was also published in 1903.

W. Starling Burgess: *Outlook.* Measuring 51 feet 7 inches on deck on a waterline of just 20 feet 10 inches, the scow sloop *Outlook* was one of the single-season racers competing in the Quincy Cup, which she won in 1902; she carried 1,800 square feet of sail. The Quincy Cup was a race uninhibited by limits on sail area; crew weight was limited to 850 pounds. *Photograph by N. L. Stebbins. Courtesy Society for the Preservation of New England Antiquities*

Burgess's first big victory after his return to Boston came with the scow sloop *Corinthian*, winner of the San Francisco Challenge Cup in both 1905 and 1906. An unapologetic rule-beater that owed nothing to the new Universal Rule, *Corinthian*, like *Outlook*, depended on a truss girder to carry her 56 feet of overall length on a 25-foot waterline. With a semi-balanced rudder, a deep centerboard plate, and 1,400 square feet of sail, *Corinthian* was a brutal machine that romped on San Francisco Bay.

The firm now turned its attention to the "autoboat" craze. With gasoline engines becoming more (or less) reliable at ever higher horsepowers, it was inevitable that a lover of absolute speed like Burgess would enter the field. On July 10, 1904, the 32-foot, Burgess-designed *Mercedes* managed to reach 24.7 mph, enough to break the existing world record in her class. *Mercedes USA* and the 32-foot *Macaroni*, with a Fiat engine, followed, as did a twin-screw 40-footer. But there were no further records for Burgess.

Meanwhile, Burgess had married Rosamond Tudor and Burgess and Packard had begun work on a new boat shed (and a house for the newlyweds) overlooking Marblehead Harbor. In 1905, too, the Salem shop turned out two gasoline-powered cruising launches, the 40-foot cabin-class racing sloop *Cricket* and the handsome 50-foot LOA sloop *Pontiac*. Another Burgess design of the time was the Essex-built *Elizabeth Silsbee*, the first commercial fishing schooner to be powered with an auxiliary gasoline engine. Like Edward Burgess before him, Starling Burgess had a special love and understanding of fast and able fishing and pilot schooners.

Burgess's first Universal Rule Q-boat, *Orestes*, defeated Clinton Crane's first Q-boat, *Soya*, in September 1906. Also in 1906 the great small boat builder W. P. Stephens joined the firm and inspired Burgess to try his hand at the design of a sailing canoe. Sailing canoes remained a special interest of Burgess's thereafter. In that same year, Burgess and Packard built the first seven boats in the famous Winter Harbor 21-foot class, which is still active today.

In 1907, A. A. Packard withdrew from the partnership. The newly formed (as of April 1908) W. Starling Burgess Company continued designing and building in Marblehead, but at a reduced rate.

The new firm's primary output in the final years of the decade were Sonderklasse sloops, a highly competitive international open class of flat-out racers whose nominal length could not exceed 32 feet (the total of waterline length, beam, and draft) and 550 square feet of sail. *Sally VII* was Burgess's first attempt in the class. His second, *Wolf*, made it to Kiel for the 1909 challenge against Germany. His third, *Beaver*, won the 1910 German-American championship and was runner up in the Spanish-American championship. His final boat in the class was *Ellen*, which beat Germany in 1913 but was prevented by war from defending her title in 1914. In all, Burgess designed nine Sonder boats in the period, along with two new Q-Class boats and two new P-Class boats, of which the second, *Onda III* (1913), was still sailing in 2001. The big motor-sailer *Sepoy* and the 50-foot cabin launch *Prilla* were also from Burgess's board. By the end of 1910, Burgess had, by his own account, designed "in all 223 yachts and commercial vessels ... also five one-design classes."

In 1910, too, Burgess wrote, "I have become interested in flying and built five aeroplanes. I encountered many difficulties and disappointments, but became completely fascinated with the work. In December [1910], the Burgess Company was offered by Wilbur Wright license under the Wright patents. We are the sole licensee for the Wright Company in America. In January, 1910, I became the Wright Company's first civilian pupil. Flying is the most wonderful sport in the world."

For his work in aviation Burgess was awarded the Collier Trophy in 1915. By February 1916, however, financial control of the Burgess firm had passed to Glenn L. Curtiss. Then, on November 8, 1918, the Marblehead factory and

W. Starling Burgess: *Nina*. The staysail-rigged, 58-foot 10-inch schooner *Nina* started her long, successful career with a bang, winning the Fastnet Race in 1928, the year she was launched. More than three decades later she won the 1963 Bermuda Race, at the time the oldest boat ever to do so. *Reproduced from a Burgess and Morgan Design Catalogue*

W. Starling Burgess: *Triple Threat*. The 30-foot 6-inch Atlantic class sloop is easily recognized, with its fractional rig, set-back forestay, and long but snubbed overhangs. Between 1928 and 1930, Abeking and Rasmussen in Germany built over one hundred. Class champions include Cornelius Shields, Robert "Bus" Mosbacher, and Briggs Cunningham. © *Benjamin Mendlowitz*

W. Starling Burgess: _Rainbow._ Harold "Mike" Vanderbilt skippered Starling Burgess's 126-foot _Rainbow_ (foreground) to victory in the 1934 America's Cup against the British challenger _Endeavour_, designed by Charles E. Nicholson. Here she is crossing tacks with the William Gardner–designed _Vanitie._ © Mystic Seaport, Rosenfeld Collection, Mystic CT. Image Acquired in Honor of Franz Schneider

offices (including all of Burgess's early business and design files) perished in a general-alarm fire. The marriage of Starling and Rosamond was also in flames, Burgess's long battle against stomach ulcers was underway, and World War I had brought yacht design work to a standstill.

Burgess's first significant peacetime commissions were the 6-Meter marconi sloops _Sheila_ and _Genie._ Both boats were highly innovative in design and rig, but neither were winners (although _Sheila_ had a long sailing career). In October 1921, Burgess and young Frank Paine formed a design partnership, with L. Francis Herreshoff and Norman Skene as associates. In 1923 the firm added the boat industry leader A. Loring Swasey, himself a pioneer designer

of powerboats and large yachts. It was a powerful team, albeit a short-lived one, from which resulted the Gloucester racing fishermen _Puritan, Mayflower,_ and _Columbia;_ the revolutionary staysail schooner _Advance;_ John Barrymore's big schooner _Mariner;_ and some excellent open-class racers built to both the Universal and International Rules.

In 1925 Burgess's marriage to Rosamond broke up, his Boston design partnership dissolved, and he formed a New York design and brokerage partnership with yachtsman/designer Jasper Morgan (and later with Linton K. Rigg). Between 1925 and its termination in 1930, the firm produced an astonishing range of important one-design and open-class racers, several motoryachts, the incomparable

ocean racing schooner _Nina,_ and some fine cruising boats.

Especially productive was the firm's relationship with German yacht builder Abeking and Rasmussen, which produced eighty-five Atlantic One-Design sloops, fourteen one-design 10-Meters, and three M-Class boats, not to mention several one-design 8- and 12-Meters. The 75-foot LWL K-Class cutter _Katoura_ (later yawl-rigged _Manxman_) and the 54-foot LWL M-Class boat _Prestige,_ both built by Herreshoff, were outstanding boats of their size and time. As for _Enterprise,_ the successful America's Cup defender in 1930, she was not Burgess's best J-Class boat. But she did the job.

The Burgess, Morgan and Rigg partnership did not survive the Great Depression. Neither

W. Starling Burgess: *Ranger.* For the 1937 America's Cup, Starling Burgess teamed with an up-and-coming Olin Stephens to design *Ranger*, last of the great America's Cup J-Class boats. She beat the Charles E. Nicholson–designed *Endeavour II*. *Ranger* once sailed the thirty-mile Cup course at an average speed of more than 11 knots. © *Mystic Seaport, Rosenfeld Collection, Mystic CT. Image Acquired in Honor of Franz Schneider*

did a third Burgess marriage. Burgess's brief association with yacht broker Boyd Donaldson was another casualty, but not before it produced the double-ended cutter *Christmas*, which is still sailing, and a second successful America's Cup defender, *Rainbow*. Again, *Rainbow* was not Burgess's best J-Class boat. Indeed she was his worst. But she did the job.

Very little went well for Burgess in the early years of the Depression. His physical and emotional health, his finances, his friendships, his family life (he had now married for a fourth time) were all under siege. Only a challenging new design venture with Bath Iron Works and Alcoa in Maine brought him back from the brink. Even in his darkest hours, however, Burgess never lost his mastery as a yacht designer. As for his J-Class boat *Ranger*, Harold Vanderbilt's triumphant America's Cup defender in 1937, she *was* Burgess's best J-Class boat, she was Olin Stephens's best J-Class boat, and Kenneth Davidson's and Gil Wyland's and Geerd Hendel's too. She did the job. And how.

The Yankee One-Design, the Small Point One-Design, the ultrafast aluminum powerboat *Tinavette*—Burgess never lost his touch. But after a successful recovery from stomach surgery and the lapsing of his contract with Alcoa for the development of a high-speed aluminum destroyer, Burgess turned his energies to other defense-related work and restricted his yachting to weekend cruises with his daughters and with protégé Marjorie Young. The defense work he did for Weaver Associates and then directly for the navy in World War II was important to the war effort and satisfying to him. Like his aviation work, it deserved far more attention than it has received.

In March 1947, Burgess was on assignment at the Stevens Institute in Hoboken, New Jersey, where he had spent many exciting hours tank-testing hulls before the war in company with Kenneth Davidson, Olin Stephens, and others. His health, it seemed, was sounder than it had been in years. His new marriage to Marjorie Young was a study in happiness. He was even able to report to Marjorie at breakfast on March 19 that he had just revisited the fantastical city of a childhood dream—a city with gold towers whose precise details had eluded him for more than sixty years. Now, suddenly, in a dream they had reappeared in all their glory.

Burgess died of a heart attack later that morning.

The W. Starling Burgess plans are at Mystic Seaport Museum, Mystic, CT and at Hart Nautical Collections, MIT Museum, Cambridge, MA.

—Llewellyn Howland III

BURGESS

E. FARNHAM BUTLER

see Cyrus Hanlin

THOMAS HARRISON BUTLER

1871–January 29, 1945 · England

For those who love small cruising yachts full of character, ability, and style, pre–World War II England was a golden era, when some of the best craftsmen and materials, a high degree of technical advancement, and a number of artistically gifted yacht designers came together at the same time. Moreover, prewar yachtsmen had a unique willingness to look at the smallest cruising yachts with the same respect and interest that others devoted to the largest yachts. Thus one sees a whole range of yachts of only 20 to 30 feet in length on deck designed with the worst weather conditions in mind, but still having charming interiors of the highest craftsmanship. Many were created by amateur designers, most notably Albert Strange, W. Maxwell Blake, and T. Harrison Butler.

Butler was a personal friend of Albert Strange and an admirer of his work, which influenced his own early designs. In Butler's canoe-sterned designs he refers to "the Albert Strange parabolic stern," apparently sharing most critics' opinion that nobody ever drew better sterns of that type. Butler's work seems a bit more "scientific" than Strange's, and his boats are generally beamier and more modern in shape and rig. He was happiest designing yachts in sizes with which he had personal, practical experience, and much of his work was directed toward the perfection of a type of small cutter or sloop.

Butler's boats were all heavy-displacement, long-keeled sloops, cutters, and ketches, mostly with marconi rigs having relatively small headsails. He usually adopted either a transom or canoe stern. Because he was a tall man, he paid particular attention to headroom sufficient for seating comfort in the smaller designs. He achieved standing headroom when it seemed practical, but kept deckhouses as small and narrow as possible so as to maximize deck space and keep their aesthetic and structural impacts to a minimum. He never employed doghouses or streamlining of any kind.

Cockpits were usually small, and always non-self-bailing, because it was Butler's opinion that being swept out of a shallow cockpit presented a greater danger than the water the cockpit could admit. Eventually some of Butler's yachts did make transoceanic voyages and three circumnavigations, but this would have been a surprise to him. In most such cases the cockpits were modified to the self-bailing type.

T. Harrison Butler: *Askadil.* Typical of small English cruising yachts from the first half of the twentieth century, *Askadil* is a tough and elegant seagoing yacht in a small package. Her great fore and aft symmetry, heavy displacement, moderately cutaway underwater profile, and near perfect aesthetics exemplify his work. *Photo courtesy O. Joan Jardine-Brown*

Beauty and charm are a great part of Butler's legacy. Apart from the sternpost there are no straight lines anywhere in a Butler hull. Pronounced sheers are characteristic, but all the curves in the hull are easy. He never used more than five weights to secure his battens on the drawing table, preventing distortions in the lines and producing boats that were easy to plank.

Butler owned a converted Plymouth Hooker for twenty-two years, but openly criticized the popular notion that the natural evolution of fishing boats inevitably produced good designs for cruising in local waters. He felt that comfort, ease of handling, and safety were seldom priorities in commercial vessels, thus making them a poor foundation for a yacht. Butler's next boat was *Vindilis,* one of his own designs.

A frequent lecturer and writer, Butler wrote two books, including *Cruising Yachts: Design and Performance;* the fourth edition was published in 1996. In his writing, Butler discusses at length his effort to eliminate strong weather helms and is equally concerned about the behavior of small yachts in bad conditions. Many of his designs are described as "metacentric," meaning they conformed to the metacentric shelf theory, which involved a set of calculations comparing the buoyancy of the forward and aft immersed

T. Harrison Butler: *Vindilis.* Built in 1935 by A. H. Moody and Son, the pretty 23-foot 6-inch LWL yawl *Vindilis* belonged to Butler, who cruised in her extensively. She predates his metacentric shelf studies and shows a long aft overhang and mizzen, both of which were rare in his later work. *Photo courtesy O. Joan Jardine-Brown*

Butler spent his childhood in Dorset. After studying for three years as an undergraduate at Oxford, he began his clinical work at St. Bartholomew's Hospital in London. He had been introduced to sailing by commercial boatmen from Weymouth, and he began doing research on yacht design while at Oxford. His first designs date from this time. In 1904 he had one of his designs published in *The Yachtsman,* possibly his first to see print.

It is believed that Butler drew over a hundred boats in his lifetime, but he had the habit of destroying his older drawings, and as a consequence many of the earlier designs can only be found in magazines (notably *Yachting Monthly* in the years between 1910 and 1945).

Butler continued designing until his death, putting many hours of the most meticulous work into each design and voicing his opinions about design-related matters quite forcefully, but he was extremely humble about his own designs and went out of his way to discuss their faults. Biographers always stress Butler's strong moral sense, generosity, simple tastes, and even temperament.

The Harrison Butler Association was formed in 1973 and has membership worldwide. Some designs—for wooden construction—are available through Butler's daughter, Joan Jardine-Brown.

—Daniel B. MacNaughton

portions of the hull as it heeled. The idea was that the relative buoyancies of the forebody and afterbody should not change much as the boat heels, so that fore and aft trim would stay the same and the steering qualities would remain the same. The theory is not much used today, but it is true that, with few exceptions, boats designed according to such considerations tended to exhibit the desired qualities.

To American eyes, Butler's designs are narrow, but he felt that beam was a virtue English designers had not explored sufficiently, and indeed his boats are beamier than most of their contemporaries. He noted that American boats were often far beamier than English ones, and while he expressed great reservations about their behavior, he suggested they deserved more study, for "if they make for good yachts then many of our notions require modification."

Like many designers and boatbuilders, experience led Butler toward simplicity. He seldom drew a separate compartment for the head, preferring to place the head (often a bucket) in the forward cabin. He was not a believer in sinks or any other fixtures that produced a hole in the hull. Typical of the time, his boats generally had small engines started

by hand and used kerosene for lighting. He disliked wasted space, and his interiors were very well detailed in beautifully executed drawings that show lamps, chain, and galleyware in their proper storage places. The particular mix of simplicity and sophistication is part of the strong appeal of Butler's designs.

Among Butler's credits is *Zyklon,* a 19-foot LWL sloop of great toughness, charm, and comfort that became the Z-4-Tonner, said to be the first series-built yacht. Some fifty-two were built in the late 1930's by Alfred Lockhart Ltd. The largest Butler design we know of is *Maid of Arden,* a handsome canoe-stern ketch of 44 feet LOD. She has the unusual feature of an asymmetrical deck layout in which the long narrow cabin trunk is considerably offset to port, allowing space for a large dinghy to be stored on the starboard deck. Butler writes that he began her lines plan by respacing little *Zyklon*'s sections and changing the scale, an approach he used quite often.

By profession, Butler was an ophthalmic surgeon, both successful and honored. When he sold a set of design drawings, he charged only one guinea, enough to cover the cost of reproduction. Purchasers were invited to make a donation to one of his favored charities.

ST. CLARE J. BYRNE

1831–December 13, 1915 · England

From about 1840, wealthy yachtsmen such as Thomas Assheton Smith of the Royal Yacht Club (later the Royal Yacht Squadron) began to take an interest in steam propulsion, despite the resistance of the yacht club, which refused to allow steam yacht owners to be members until 1844. However, by the last decades of the nineteenth century, steam yachts were fully accepted and being built in large numbers. St. Clare Byrne made a career out of designing yachts to meet the new fashion, with Thomas Brassey's world-girdling *Sunbeam* and W. K. Vanderbilt's *Valiant* among the most famous of his designs.

Byrne was born in Liverpool into a shipowning family with yachting connections. His elder brother, Andrew, owned the famous Fife-built *Corali,* and the younger Byrne sailed on her as a young man.

In 1852, he began a shipbuilding apprenticeship with Cairds of Greenock in Scotland, designing and building there his first yacht, a centerboarder called *Stranger.* She was the first of her type on the Clyde, was very successful in the hands of her young designer, and may have

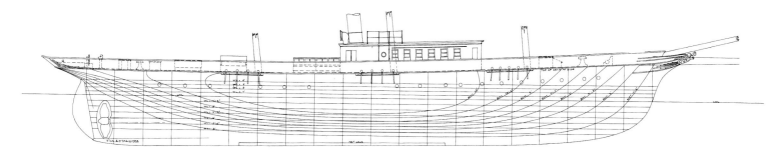

St. Clare Byrne: *Sunbeam*. Designed in 1874, *Sunbeam* typifies the fully rigged sailing auxiliary steam yacht. She cruised extensively, including a voyage around the world in 1876–77, and saw service in World War I, first as a hospital ship and later as an auxiliary in the Indian navy. © *Chevalier & Taglang*

reflected the influence of the American centerboard sloop *Truant*, which had been brought to the Mersey in 1852. About 1856 he joined the Canada Works of Thomas Brassey, the great nineteenth-century railway contractor, where he was in charge of shipbuilding and built a number of iron yachts including *Cecilia* and *Rosette*. From about 1860 to 1866 he managed the Birkenhead Ironworks of Laird Brothers, and presumably he oversaw the construction of the yard's most famous privateer, the CSS *Alabama*. Following her sinking by the USS *Kearsage*, after two successful years of commerce raiding on behalf of the Confederacy, the British Government paid 3.25 million pounds in compensation to the United States, and consequently, according to Herbert Reiach, who subsequently worked for Byrne, this subject was taboo.

In 1866, Byrne moved to Hull, where he owned the Humber Ironworks, and subsequently joined the firm of Humphreys, Byrne and Pearson. Owing to his wife's ill health, he returned to Liverpool in 1869 and set up in business as a consultant naval architect specializing in yacht design. As such he was among the first professional yacht designers (as opposed to designer/builder) in the world.

Other Byrne designs include the 7½-Tonner *Meta*, designed for his own use and built in 1858 to race against the American-style centerboard sloops of the Birkenhead Model Yacht Club. She was the first successful deep-keeled cutter in that club. She was followed in 1859 by *Vision*, 7½ tons, of the same type. It appears that Byrne was influenced by the theories of John Scott Russell at this time.

His first designs after 1869 were for the Ten-Ton class then in vogue, a class in which he raced himself. In 1870, he designed *Naiad* for Alexander Richardson, but possibly his most successful boat in this class was *Pastime*. In 1874 Thomas Brassey Jr. (later Lord Brassey) asked him to design the famous *Sunbeam*. She was the first of many auxiliary steam yachts with both sailing capability and full steam power.

Although Byrne began his career with sailing yachts, it is with the design of these sailing auxiliaries and the later large steam yachts that his name is chiefly associated. He approached the design of these large vessels from the point of view of the commercial naval architect, and as a result his designs may be described as little ships rather than large yachts. In this respect his work contrasts with that of his contemporary G. L. Watson. The difference can be easily seen in the ends of the vessels. Byrne desired to keep both bow and stern beyond the reach of big seas, so he kept them high and short although still graceful and pleasing to the eye. Watson, on the other hand, whose background is sailing yacht design, favored long and graceful ends that captivated the eye. Both approaches are instantly recognizable.

Upon his death in 1915, Byrne was described in *Yachting Monthly* as the doyen of British yacht designers.

—Brian Smith

St. Clare Byrne: *Alva*. With a greater emphasis on steam propulsion than in *Sunbeam*, *Alva* was built in 1885 for the railway magnate W. K. Vanderbilt. She was lost in 1892. © *Peabody Essex Museum, Salem, MA*

C

GUSTAVE CAILLEBOTTE

1848–February 22, 1894 · France

When he began his involvement with yachting in 1876, Gustave Caillebotte still was an impressionist painter. His father had recently died, leaving him a fortune important enough to give him financial security for the rest of his life. Following the deaths of his younger brother and mother, Caillebotte remained with another young brother, Martial. He shared with Martial his passions for yachting and philately, forsaking for a time his painting career.

The entry of the Caillebotte brothers in the Cercle de la Voile de Paris (CVP) Yacht Club corresponded with a major event in the history of yachting: the publication of Dixon Kemp's book *Yacht Designing*, subsequent editions of which appeared under the title *Yacht Architecture*.

The French yachting scene also found support in the pages of the new weekly *Le Yacht, Journal de la Marine*, beginning in 1878. Caillebotte participated in its development, convinced that the exchange of views was essential. In seven years, Caillebotte alone published some 2,500 lines in *Le Yacht*.

In 1886 Caillebotte founded the Luce Boat Yard with naval architect Maurice Chevreux. He tested every type or class he encountered, sailing Argenteuil clipper types (influenced by American sloops), English plank-on-edge cutters, imported sharpies, and the Chevreux cutter *Thomas*.

Convinced that the elegant new yacht designs from Great Britain would prove superior, Caillebotte proposed a restricted rule for the CVP in the late 1880's, under which sail area would be limited to 30 square meters. The Caillebotte-designed *Moucheron* and the Chevreux-designed *Buffalo* sailed against some Clippers d'Argenteuil in 1890, with *Moucheron* winning the first six regattas. Three additional 30-Square-Meters were launched that autumn, and *Moucheron*, *Sauterelle*, and *Fauvette* shared honors in the autumn regattas. More were launched the following year, including *Le Lézard*, a replica of which was recently built in Marseilles.

Caillebotte's design for *Roastbeef* (1892) proved to be more efficient than *Le Lézard*. She won all the races in which she sailed, with the exception of one against the Caillebotte-designed *Criquet*, which was in fact *Criquet*'s sole win. In July, some yachts of the class sailed for opening regattas at Duclair, near Rouen, then at Le Havre and Deauville in Normandy, where *Roastbeef* won again. In October, the 30-Square-Meter fleet grew with the arrival of *Araignée*. She carried a classic houari rigging and ran her elder sistership off the track. The two protagonists dominated the last races of the season.

But in October 1892, the CVP meeting rang the death toll for the 30-Square-Meter fleet. In December, the club adopted the Union des Yachts Français's new rule whereby the 1893 30-Square-Meter Cup became the One-Ton Cup (Coupe des Un Tonneau). The new rule led yachtsmen to order new yachts whose designs led to lighter and narrower hulls. The Five-Tonner *Dahut*, which Caillebotte codesigned with the designer Godinet, was built at Luce's yard. Three Half-Tonners—*Demi*, her sistership *Kilt*, and *Isis*—as well as the One-Tonners *Annette* and *Mignon*, designed for himself, were built at Luce's. *Mignon* was launched in autumn 1894, eight months after the death of her designer.

Of the twenty plans Caillebotte drew between 1890 and his death, more than half were published in *Le Yacht* and some were reproduced in foreign magazines. Because of the elegance of his designs and the impressive number of victories achieved by his yachts, Gustave Caillebotte had a great impact on French yachting.

—François Chevalier

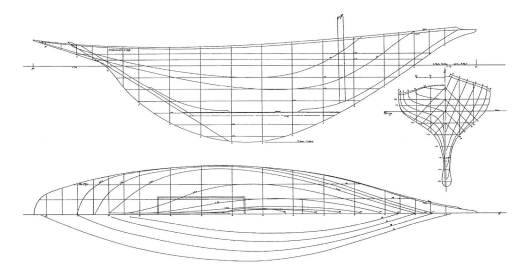

Gustave Caillebotte: *Mignon* (opposite). The Three-Tonner *Mignon* (1894) was Caillebott's last creation. She was designed under the 1892 national French Rule and was launched after her designer's death. *Photo courtesy Jacques Taglang*

Gustave Caillebotte: *Le Lézard*. The design for *Le Lézard* was the archteype of the 30-Square-Meter class Caillebotte proposed for the Cercle de la Voile de Paris (CVP) Yacht Club. All subsequent CVP 30-Square-Meter boats were a variant of her. *Courtesy Chevalier & Taglang*

WENDELL H. "SKIP" CALKINS

1912–1977 · United States

One of the early proponents of the light-displacement movement, Skip Calkins was born in Minneapolis, Minnesota, and moved to Los Angeles when he was nine years old. He graduated from MIT in 1938 with a degree in naval architecture and marine engineering.

Calkins's first job was with Bath Iron Works in Bath, Maine, which entailed work on the U.S. Navy's Destroyer program. In 1940, he returned to the West Coast and wartime employment, first with Douglas Aircraft and next as chief draftsman at L.A. Shipbuilding and Dry Dock (later Todd Shipyard). Next he was chief designer in charge of building wooden tugs, patrol boats, and picket boats for the navy at Ackerman Boat Works in Newport Beach, California.

After the war ended, Calkins owned and operated a small boatyard in Newport Harbor engaged in yacht and commercial construction and repair, while designing the popular P-14 sloop, the 17-foot Sharp-Shooter sloop, and some racing hydroplanes.

His first major design was the 50-foot *Legend*, a light-displacement sloop featuring a long waterline, short ends, low wetted surface area, and a foil-shaped keel, with moderate sail plan. This boat became an extremely successful ocean racer, winning many of the major West Coast racing events over the next ten years, including the 1957 Honolulu Race, and spawned a series of Calkins 50-foot sloops built first by Driscoll Boat Works of San Diego (five built) and later by American Marine (twenty built overseas). Other 50-foot and several 40-foot designs were built by different yards in and out of the United States; the largest of his boats was the 72-foot *Whistle Wing*. There were other designs, including some particularly good-looking 38- to 45-foot power cruisers, from his board, as well as commercial fishing craft.

During the Korean conflict, Calkins was supervisor of shipbuilding for the U.S. Navy at Long Beach Naval Yard. Later he became chief naval architect at National Steel and Shipbuilding Corporation in San Diego through 1959. In 1960 he returned to private practice in San Diego and became a mentor to the young designer Doug Peterson during the 1960's.

In 1970–71 Calkins was hired by the Trust Territory of Micronesia (Palau and Saipan) to develop local building of fishing vessels, and he designed and supervised construction of more than a hundred deep-sea craft. In 1972 Calkins returned to San Diego, where he worked for Doug Peterson until his death.

A modest yet extremely talented designer, a mathematical wizard, and something of a genius in his field, Calkins was not one to put himself forward without invitation, but his designs and their owners spoke for him, and he was unmistakably one of the fathers of light-displacement design. —Thomas G. Skahill

Wendell Calkins: *Legend*. Built in 1951, this 50-foot sloop was one of Calkins's earlier designs. It helped to establish his career within the new wave of post–World War II, light-displacement racer/cruisers. Her many wins include the 1957 Transpac Race to Honolulu in a fleet of thirty-four. *Photo courtesy Newport Harbor Nautical Museum, Newport Beach, CA*

CONSTANTINE D. CALLAHAN

ca. 1875–1940 · United States

C. D. Callahan's origins are obscure, but his boats are engraved in the annals of southern California yachting history. He practiced in San Pedro and was the first formally trained naval architect to design sail and power craft for the local boatmen. His boats were built by many local boatbuilders and later by his own firm, Cookson and Callahan, which he operated with master builder Charles Cookson until 1921, when Cookson became too ill to work.

One of Callahan's achievements was the program of naval architecture, boatbuilding, and steam and gas engineering that he taught at the Marine High School of San Pedro from 1912 to 1916. The program produced many craftsmen who filled the ranks of the local marine trades in later years.

His best-remembered boats are the 50-foot yawl *Winsome* (1909), the 38-foot sloop *Alert* (1910), the 74-foot motoryacht *Rainbow* (1920), the 48-foot cruiser *Mapuna* (1912), and the 47-foot yawl *Siwash* (1910). A surprisingly modern-looking yacht, *Siwash* is now owned and sailed by the fourth generation of the Howard Wright family, whom she has served for more than ninety years. All of Callahan's designs, both sail and power, had a yachtlike look to them and have enjoyed the ultimate compliment of great longevity.

—Thomas G. Skahill

DANIEL MILLARD CALLIS

October 26, 1881–February 14, 1964
United States

One of the principal yacht designers who practiced during the burgeoning southern California boating market of the early 1920's was D. M. Callis. His specialty was large motoryachts, but among the three hundred pleasure craft he designed between 1921 and 1940 were a number of sailboats and smaller launches and runabouts. Callis also designed commercial vessels of many different types.

Born in Baltimore, Maryland, Callis was educated at Baltimore Polytechnic Institute and served his four-year apprenticeship in the drafting room of the Marine Department of Maryland Steel Company, later Bethlehem Shipbuilding. He worked at some of the larger eastern shipyards, where he later held positions of increasing consequence. Ultimately he was appointed naval architect for Todd Shipyard's Seattle plant. Wartime activity led to his appointment as chief district supervisor for the U.S. Shipping Board during World War I, followed by private practice in Seattle after the Armistice.

When Callis struck off for southern California in about 1921, he was joining a rush of yacht designers and builders lured there by the good times, first locating in Wilmington. Within a few years he had developed a client base, which included motion-picture actors, directors, and producers, and produced a wide range of designs for power and sailboats for the business leaders of the time. By 1929, the largest of Callis's yachts were being built. *Hermana*, a handsome 68-foot motoryacht of progressive styling, is still in active service, as is the 62-foot schooner *Destiny*, and *Sobre Las Olas*, the 101-foot motoryacht also built in 1929. As YP 131, *Sobre Las Olas* did patrol and escort service in World War II. The 81-foot motoryacht *Portola* (ex-*Dolphin*), called a "sturdy cruiser" by *Pacific Motor Boat* magazine in June 1928, today cruises out of Long Beach Harbor.

Constantine Callahan: *Siwash*. Built by Fulton Marine Construction of San Pedro, California, in 1910, the 47-foot *Siwash* has been owned by the same family (now the fourth generation) since new. Always beautifully maintained, she has held many racing records during her long life. *Photo courtesy Tom Skahill*

Daniel M. Callis: *Portola*. Built in 1928 by the highly regarded Harbor Boat Building Company at San Pedro, California, the handsome 81-foot motoryacht *Portola* remains at her home port in Long Beach, California, and her original Winton Diesel still provides her power. © *Benjamin Mendlowitz*

François Camatte: *France.* The 8-Meter *France* won the Coupe de France in 1937 against a British challenger. Based in Cannes, she's still sailing the Mediterranean. *Photo courtesy Jacques Taglang*

Eventually the D. M. Callis Company settled in Long Beach, and Callis himself fared relatively well during the Depression. Design articles in *Pacific Coast Yachting, Sea,* and *Pacific Motor Boat* magazines attest to a practice reflecting the times. A 36-foot cutter came from his board in 1931, and in 1934 Callis took over the plans for a Nantucket-type fishing boat designed by Philadelphia designer Thomas Bowes, and turned it into an auxiliary schooner. The years 1935 and 1938 saw Callis completing designs for a 40-foot motorsailer and a 32-foot sloop that was to become a stock model for Ben Cope Boat Company of Newport Beach. During World War II he supervised naval construction at several yards on the West Coast.

Callis also maintained an active role in other maritime affairs. At the request of the California State Legislature, he created the Yacht Architects, Brokers and Surveyors Association and became its first president, maintaining this interest throughout his career. He also promoted the early Predicted Log Races on the West Coast. Predicted log racing is a system that continues to be popular today in which motoryachts of varying size and speed are able to compete on a level basis. He was the second commodore of the Long Beach Yacht Club as well as a member of the Society of Naval Architects and Marine Engineers.

D. M. Callis died at Long Beach, California.

—Thomas G. Skahill

FRANÇOIS CAMATTE

May 29, 1893–July 9, 1960 · France

In the history of French naval architecture, François Camatte was one of the few designers to have devoted his career almost exclusively to the design of International Rule yachts, and he became one of France's foremost specialists in that genre.

Aside from his passions for fishing, contact with the boats of Cannes Harbor, and a natural aptitude for drawing, nothing predisposed Camatte to become a naval architect. In 1920, a year after demobilization following World War I, he began work as a draftsman in Despujols's yards, first in Arcachon and then in Antibes. This brought him into contact with various designers who undoubtedly influenced his choice of a career in yacht design.

Soon Camatte set up a one-man office in Cannes. Self-taught, he had little knowledge of mathematics. All calculations were made with the assistance of a planimeter, a slide rule, and sometimes graph paper, but he achieved excellent results, and his boats floated perfectly on their lines.

Camatte's first designs were boats for the 5-meter MOCAT class. They were an immediate success, and some months later he designed his first 6-Meter, *Pampero II.* The 6-Meter class seems to have been Camatte's natural element; he designed nearly sixty. He also designed ten successful 8-Meters.

In 1932, Camatte's one-design *Cote d'Azur* won a design competition sponsored by the Union of French Nautical Societies. By 1961, two hundred boats were built to this design. He also designed English 18's, 6.5-meter SI's, and the 22.3-meter ketch *Odyssey* (1935). After World War II, he drew a number of 5.5-Meters, and more cruisers: the 14.5-meter cutter *Morwak* (1948), the 16.5-meter cutter *Nagaôna* (1950), and his last design, the 15-meter sloop *Vigor* (1960.)

One can place Camatte among those whom André Mauric called "purely intuitive creators, guided by their aesthetic senses rather than technical knowledge."

—Jacques Taglang

WILLIAM MACPHERSON CAMPBELL

1901–1980 · Scotland

William Campbell's designs exude unmistakable Scottish origins—as his name undoubtedly confirms—but much of this versatile architect's best work was done anonymously, as the in-house designer at A. M. Dickie and Sons of Bangor, Wales.

Campbell apprenticed with John A. McCallum and joined Dickie's in the early 1920's, soon after Peter Dickie arrived from his family's famous Tarbert yard to set up in Bangor.

The nature of a tendering yard—building sailboats and motoryachts up to 100 feet in LOA—demanded adaptability and practicality and no doubt offered an opportunity to study the

W. MacPherson Campbell: *Cruinneag III.* Better known for his motor cruisers and motorsailers, often drawn on fishing-boat lines, Campbell nevertheless was a most competent sailing yacht designer. *Cruinneag III,* built almost entirely of teak, is an outstanding example of his ability to draw a well-balanced and handsome cruising yacht. She is still sailing on the Scottish west coast. *Photo courtesy Iain McAllister*

Manuel Campos: *Gaucho*. A heavy-displacement, double-ended, 50-foot LOD ketch in the Colin Archer tradition, *Gaucho* was launched in Argentina in 1943. She has sailed extensively offshore, earning the CCA's Blue Water Cruising Medal for a 60,000-mile cruise in the 1940's. © *Mystic Seaport, Mystic, CT*

MANUEL MAXIMILIANO CAMPOS

ca. 1894–August 26, 1987 · Argentina

Outside of his native country, Manuel Campos is known primarily for his design of *Lehg II*, the 30-foot cutter in which the Argentine Vito Dumas made a nonstop circumnavigation of the world near the stormy fortieth parallel known as the "Roaring Forties." Another famous Campos design is *Gaucho*, a 50-foot ketch that made extensive offshore voyages and was apparently the first Argentine yacht to visit the United States. Both yachts won the Cruising Club of America's Blue Water Cruising Medal.

Campos worked in Buenos Aires and began his professional design career in 1921 as an apprentice designer for the Argentine navy. He eventually became chief architect and designed Corvettes and Frigates as well as smaller naval craft.

Lehg II, *Gaucho*, and other examples of Campos's work are heavy-displacement double-enders whose characters were influenced by the work of Norwegian designer Colin Archer. With Argentina close to some of the roughest sea conditions in the world, it is no surprise that Campos looked to Archer's famously seaworthy double-enders for inspiration. Some of Campos's early work was influenced by the local "Balleneras," 35- to 40-foot, double-ended, lapstrake open boats with inside ballast, strongly resembling the native Norwegian working boats that preceded Colin Archer, so there may have been a degree of parallel evolution.

In 1947 Campos demonstrated his versatility when he designed the yawl *Fortuna*, a countersterned ocean racer of conventional modern character that was highly successful, her wins including the first Cape Town to Rio race. Other work included smaller cruising boats, some of shoal draft and light displacement. Unfortunately, the sloop *Sirio*, in which Vito Dumas cruised prior to *Lehg II*, was recently scuttled in New Jersey.

Campos continued his navy work for many years, but even after retirement continued to design yachts. —Daniel B. MacNaughton

GIULIO CESARE CARCANO

Born 1910 · Italy

Inspired by enthusiasm for the sport of sailing and by racing in 6-Meter, Star, and Soling classes, Giulio Carcano became a designer. Based on his experience, his design concepts, and his understanding of functionality, and regardless of the fact that the latter was acquired in another field (motorcycle design), he was determined to design yachts. As an amateur, he

work of other designers. That, together with wartime torpedo boat design and construction work at Fairmile and Saunders Roe and postwar responsibility for the survey and disposal of requisitioned small craft, provided sure grounding for Campbell's subsequent, Glasgow-based career as an independent designer, consultant, and broker.

From his drawing board came a fleet of characterful yachts, motorsailers, and motoryachts, infused with varying amounts of Scottish fishing boat kinship and Campbell's signature: a shapely bow profile despite a short overhang. His largest design, the 110-foot motorsailer *Southern Cross II*, was built in steel by the Glasgow warship builder Yarrows in 1962 to replace the client's first Morris and Lorimer–built 75-footer, which as *Giralda* was subsequently owned by the Count of Barcelona, father of King Juan Carlos of Spain.

Other superbly preserved and cherished examples of his work include the 53-foot ketch *Vistona* (ex-*Nancy Rose*) of 1937—perhaps his finest set of lines—and the 58-foot motoryacht *Seaway*, both Bangor-built and now Mediterranean-based. The Dickie of Tarbert–built 64-foot ketch *Cruinneag III* of 1936 and the jaunty 40-foot MFV yacht *Sgarbh* of 1947 still grace home waters and blend with the scenery—as a Campbell boat should. —Iain McAllister designed racing boats both for himself and for his friends in the 5.5-Meter class and in the RORC and IOR classes.

Carcano was born in Milan and graduated from the University of Milan with a degree in mechanical engineering. From 1936 to 1966, he was director of design for Guzzi Motors in Mandello del Lario, a town on Lake Como. (He designed the famous motorcycles Guzzino and the innovative Galletto.

From 1960 to 1969, Carcano designed eight 5.5-Meter sloops: the five he owned were all named *Volpina*. *Manuela* was designed for the president of the IYRU, Beppe Croce, and one named *Violetta V* was for Gino Alquati. The last 5.5-Meter design by Carcano was never built because the class ceased to be included in the Olympics following the 1968 games.

Carcano's designs varied from those of other designers of the time because his had a V-shaped bow section of the hull, with the center sections being flat. The keel was formed like that on the Star, with a lower freeboard than on other boats in its class. The boat was designed and built at the minimum weight, at a time when the American designer C. Raymond Hunt and the Swedish designer Einar Ohlson were designing hulls close to the maximum weight of about 4,500 pounds. Among the boats Carcano designed for ocean racing was the 22-foot *Vampa*, which represented a unique example in the interpretation of RORC Rules.

With his five *Volpinas*, Carcano was one of the main contenders in his class and was chosen to be the Italian challenger after national trials for the French Cup (1961, 1963, and 1964), the Gold Cup (1961 and 1962), and the Italian Cup (1963). In 1966 in La Baule, he won the international championship in France, and in 1961 he placed third in the world in his class. With one of his boats, *Volpina VI*, Giuseppe Canessa won the Italian Cup in 1962.

—Franco Belloni

SHAUN CARKEEK

Born 1972 · South Africa/Spain

Shaun Carkeek brings a strong sailing background to the highly successful Spanish-based design office of Botín and Carkeek.

History shows that yacht design partnerships can succeed given a sensible division of labor. South African Shaun Carkeek's partnership with Spaniard Marcelino Botín has ensured full attention to the myriad of detail that goes into not just the designing, but also the building and campaigning of a successful, modern, Grand Prix racing yacht. The results prove it, with Botín and Carkeek designs rapidly moving to the forefront of IMS Rule Grand Prix racing, culminating in victory for their Sinergia 40 Racer/Cruiser design *Telepizza-Pepsi* at the IMS World Championship in 2001.

Born in Pretoria, Carkeek moved to Cape Town and took up sailing at age eight, representing South Africa in both dinghies and keelboats. During yacht design studies at Southampton Institute in England, he met Botín and the partnership that has been described by a leading boatbuilder as "the future of IMS" was formed.

The partners are immersed in most design aspects of their small, developing office. Botín has a particular interest in computational fluid dynamics, which he concentrates on in the testing stages, while Carkeek concentrates on all areas of design, as well as styling, new concept boat development, project management, and structural design, where his racing and cruising background helps with the technical solutions required with these types of boats.

Many successful Botín and Carkeek designs have been built under Carkeek's supervision in Cape Town by Harvey Yachts, including the IMS 46 cruiser/racer *Zurich* (1999), winner of Spain's prestigious Copa del Rey, and the IMS

Giulio Carcano: *Volpina*. The 5.5-Meter sloop *Volpina* (one of five of that name) is proof that an amateur designer can sometimes beat his professional rivals. Carcano's 5.5-Meters were consistent winners, often with their designer at the helm. *Photo courtesy Franco Belloni*

Richard Carter: *Blaze*. *Blaze* is a typical example of Dick Carter's work in IOR-influenced cruiser/racers. Her clean overall look and the harmony between the lines of the sheer and cabin trunk were a virtual trademark of the Carter design office. *Photo courtesy Dick Carter*

Richard Carter: *Tina*. *Tina* brought Carter considerable recognition when she came out in 1966, winning the One-Ton Cup that year. Anticipating the future direction of IOR-inspired design, her mast was stepped well aft, resulting in a large foretriangle and a small, high-aspect-ratio mainsail. *Photo courtesy J. Scott Rohrer*

racer *Banco Espirito Santo* (2001). With their hard turn at the bilge and slab topsides, these are designs with an instantly recognizable difference: that in their very purposefulness they have their own special beauty.

—Iain McAllister with Shaun Carkeek

ABDON CARTER

see George Melville "Mel" McLain

RICHARD ELIOT CARTER

Born June 10, 1928 · United States

Dick Carter was a racing sailor and a yacht designer. His reputation as the latter was set by the success of his first three designs: the 33-foot 8-inch LOA *Rabbit*, the One-Tonner *Tina*, and the 42-foot Admiral's Cup competitor *Rabbit II*. He sailed all three masthead-rigged sloops to a remarkable series of victories in European waters.

Born in Nashua, New Hampshire, Carter graduated from Yale University in 1950 with a BA in

art history. He is a self-taught designer. *Rabbit* was launched in 1965 in the Dutch yard of Frans Maas. She competed successfully on both sides of the English Channel and astounded the yachting world with an overall win in the Fastnet Race in her first year. Her shape was simple, with roundish sections rising from a V-shaped centerline, and easy, sweeping buttock lines. She had a larger-than-average sail area in a masthead rig, and considerable beam to help her carry it. Relatively shallow, *Rabbit* took no draft penalty and used a small trim tab to add some lift to her stubby fin keel.

The 37-foot LOA *Tina* was launched in 1966. Developed from *Rabbit*, she featured a deeper keel of much-reduced chord length. Her rig was unusual, as Carter had moved the mast well aft to create a much larger foretriangle. Like *Rabbit*, *Tina* was beamy and had enough freeboard to make her commodious below and dry in a sea.

Where *Rabbit II* (1967) was a larger development based on *Tina*, the 42-foot LOA *Red Rooster* (1969) was something very different.

Rooster's long waterline and flat-floored hull made her especially light and powerful. With virtually no overhang aft, her rudder hung on the transom and a small vertical skeg. She drew 9 feet with her 2-ton centerboard down, and 2 feet 9 inches with it and the retractable rudder in the up position. She carried considerable internal ballast.

Rooster's crew was still rigging her and learning how to make her go when they joined the 1969 U.S. Admiral's Cup team at Cowes. *Rooster* led the team to America's first Admiral's Cup victory. She was the individual high-point yacht for the series and overall winner of the Fastnet Race.

Much of the success of these boats was due to the designer's keen attention to detail. Halyards running inside the mast and under the deck, lifting keels, and twin wheel steering were innovations seen on Carter designs.

Carter took an active role in the development of the IOR through regular committee work at IYRU. As a New Englander experienced in both the CCA and the RORC measurement rules, he contributed an American point of view to the process.

In the 1970's, while continuing to design and race custom boats built according to the new IOR, his company Carter Offshore developed and marketed a line of production racer/cruisers. Over two hundred boats were built to a 33-foot design in 1969, and a 37-footer based on the successful One-Tonner *Ydra* came along in 1973. Following the Carter 37 came the 30, 39, and 42 built variously in the United States, Poland, Greece, and England.

In America, a group of midwestern yachtsmen commissioned and promoted Carter's North American 40 as a one-design class on the Great Lakes. Among his custom IOR designs of the period were the 42-foot Hong Kong Admiral's Cupper *White Rabbit* and the Three-Quarter-Tonner *Ariadne*, overall winner of the 1977 Plymouth–La Rochelle Race.

Perhaps the most imposing of Carter's works was the 128-foot three-masted schooner *Vendredi Treize* built for the 1972 OSTAR (Observer Singlehanded Transatlantic Race) from Plymouth to Newport. She featured a simple sail plan of three self-tacking, roller-furling jibs. She proved fast but was beaten to the finish line by a catamaran, an event that proved the advent of the modern offshore multihull.

Carter Offshore was based for years in Nahant, Massachusetts. Carter was assisted for many years by Clive Dent. Others who worked at the office in "The Tower" were Yves-Marie Tanton, Robert Perry, and Chuck Paine.

—J. Scott Rohrer

ANTONIO DE LANCASTRE DE MELLO E "TONY" CASTRO

Born 1962 · Portugal/England

Portuguese by birth, Tony Castro came to the United Kingdom in 1970 as a student, graduating with a full BSc in naval architecture at Strathclyde University and a masters in aero/hydrodynamics from Glasgow University, having written a thesis on variable-geometry appendages titled "The Search for Zero Leeway."

Castro spent several years at Ron Holland's office in Currabiney, Ireland, opposite the Royal Cork Yacht Club, before branching out on his own by designing a Mini-Tonner, *Billycan*, for noted Clyde racer Bill MacKay, an old friend from his student days. Castro moved his office to Hamble, the heartland of Britain's sailing community, in 1982 and a year later saw *Justine III* win the One-Ton Cup back in his old stomping ground of Cork. She remains the only yacht to win every race of a top Ton Cup competition.

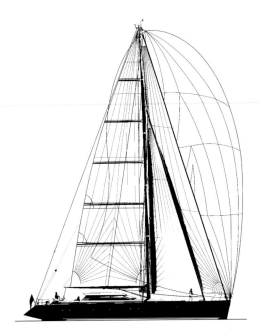

Tony Castro. At first glance the Bn-417 sloop looks like a medium-size, high-performance family cruiser, but in fact she is 29 meters in length and represents another example of how contemporary yacht design is being influenced by powered sail-handling equipment. *Drawing courtesy Tony Castro*

A live wire and avid innovator, Castro has been successful in virtually every arena to which yacht design has taken him. He produced the first IOR boat with a non-NACA (National Advisory Committee for Aeronautics) plan form keel, dreamt up Spinlock's tiller extension, created one of the most popular club racers in U.K. waters in the Cork 1720 class, drew performance cruisers for the Dutch shipyard Jongert, and designed the Jubilee Sailing Trust's barque, built to train the disabled to sail and the largest wooden ship built in Britain for a hundred years.

Castro practices in Hamble, Southampton, England.

—Tim Jeffery

JULES DE CATUS

1838–1910 · Belgium/Switzerland

An excellent example of the self-taught designer, Baron Jules de Catus was a generous and brilliant nineteenth-century amateur who did not charge for any of his designs. He lived comfortably on his annuities and devoted his life to his passions: writing, travel, the arts and sciences, and especially yacht designing.

Born in Tarbes, Belgium, de Catus spent part of his childhood in Brittany, until his family moved to Switzerland, where he began sailing on Lake Geneva in a small lateen-rigged dinghy. He lived in Switzerland for the rest of his life. His design work unfolded there

from 1859 until his death in 1910, in interesting parallel to the birth and growth of yachting on Lake Geneva. The Société Nautique de Genève (SNG) was not founded until 1871, and indeed, the first yachts to sail on the lake were imported from Great Britain. But soon local residents became involved in the design and construction of sailboats better adapted to the flukey local winds. Jules de Catus was one of the most prolific, designing sixty yachts of all types over the course of fifty years.

Frequent visits to England's Isle of Wight exposed de Catus to the techniques of mode making, drafting, and naval construction. A voracious reader and pursuing all innovations, he was inspired by both English and American yachts, though he always had to take into account his local conditions. His passion inspired him to publish numerous articles and plans in French yachting magazines, as well as publications in England, Switzerland, Germany, and Belgium.

His first design, a yachting and fishing *péniche* (barge), was probably completed in 1859, followed in the next quarter century by a number of other examples of the same type. His first yacht for the lake appears to have been the 8-meter LOA yawl *Espadon* (1885), supporting 50 square meters of sail. In 1888 he designed *Pétrel*, 6.5 meters LOA and carrying 70 square meters of canvas, and in 1890 he designed the 9-meter LOA yawl *Flirt*, which carried 72 square meters of sail. In 1888–89 de Catus designed five rescue boats. He took the lines off a number of historic vessels in recognition of yachting's roots in traditional workboats.

It was in 1892 that de Catus designed his first racers to the newly adopted Godinet's Rule, a handicapping system previously chosen by the Club Yacht de France. The 3-ton *Wanda*, 10.57 meters LOA, was launched that year, a design inspired by the Nathanael Herreshoff–designed bulb-keel cutter *Wasp*. The next year, *Wanda*, renamed *Gyptis*, won her first regattas.

Design commissions from Swiss yachtsmen swiftly followed, resulting in a series of 1-, 2-, and 3-ton racers, such as *Lucifer*, *Cigale*, and *Thaôs*. Subsequent designs such as *Charming* (1896) were influenced by Herreshoff's fin-bulb-keel *Dilemma*. Following the advent of the International Rule in 1906 (a development de Catus had criticized), the designer remained faithful to the light construction encouraged by Godinet's Rule.

A generous amateur, de Catus worked to put yachting within the reach of as many people as possible. He had already published in 1881 a work devoted to model building, *Petit traité de la construction et du gréement des modèles de bateaux* (*A Small Treatise on Model Building and Rig-*

ging). In 1890 he published *Construction pratique des bateaux de plaisance et yachts* (*Practical Building of Pleasure Boats and Yachts*). An excellent educational resource, this book was accompanied by a series of complementary articles. De Catus's enthusiasm for amateur construction never left him.   —Jacques Taglang

HOWARD IRVING CHAPELLE

February 1, 1901–June 30, 1975 · United States

Best remembered as a marine historian, Howard Chapelle did more than any other individual to record and preserve the nature of traditional American watercraft, ranging from the smallest dugouts and skiffs to clipper ships. What is most remarkable is that he did this, not in the context of the current nationwide revival of interest in traditional boats, but at the very hour when our national interest in such subjects was at its lowest ebb, beginning after World War I.

Chapelle sought out and measured countless wrecks and near-wrecks; talked to local boatbuilders, merchant sailors, and fishermen; and located long-forgotten plans and half models. He was able to produce drawings for boats that had never been drawn before, and re-create complete plans from fragments. Because he did what he did when he did, a vast treasure has been preserved in the form of detailed information. It is difficult to imagine today's revival of interest in traditional boats without his work.

Much of Chapelle's historical work can be seen in his books: *The Baltimore Clipper* (1930), *History of American Sailing Ships* (1935), *American Sailing Craft* (1936), *History of the American Sailing Navy* (1949), *American Small Sailing Craft* (1951), *The National Watercraft Collection* (1960), *Bark Canoes and Skin Boats of North America* (1964), *The Search for Speed Under Sail* (1967), *The American Fishing Schooners* (1973).

Chapelle also researched the details of traditional wooden boatbuilding, and wrote what was probably the first comprehensive text on the subject, entitled simply *Boatbuilding* (1941). It remains one of the best references on the subject.

While he is less well known for his own designs, Chapelle drew at least 120 original designs during his career, working in his tradition-based style. He wrote what for many years was the authoritative work on the subject, *Yacht Designing and Planning* (1936).

Many of his designs were adaptations of traditional watercraft for yacht purposes, typified by the widely known *Glad Tidings*, a

Howard Chapelle: *Privateer.* Typical of Chapelle's yacht designs is the Chesapeake bugeye ketch *Privateer*, which in hull and rig closely emulates her working ancestor, while a harmonious deckhouse and other details produce a comfortable and practical yacht with character far beyond the ordinary. © *Peter Barlow*

yacht version of the double-ended Pinky schooner. A traditional Downeast Maine fishing vessel famous for its offshore ability, the Pinky was a type that he patriotically defended against the popular Scandinavian double-ended types as a basis for American yachts. Other well-known designs include adaptations of the ultra-shoal-draft New Haven sharpie type for yacht use.

Born in Tolland, Massachusetts, Chapelle lived most of his early life in New Haven, Connecticut, where his father owned an oyster business. It was here where he acquired his interest in New Haven sharpies and probably historic watercraft in general.

Beginning around 1919, Chapelle held a variety of waterfront jobs, including work constructing small and large vessels, stints on a cargo schooner, and employment with a marine engine manufacturer. He studied naval architecture at the Webb Institute from 1919 to 1923, and worked in the offices of such well-known designers as Charles Mower, William Gardner, William H. Hand, Walter McInnis, and John Alden.

Chapelle opened his own design and surveying office in 1930. During the Depression a series of his articles appeared in *Yachting* magazine, stressing the economy of traditional boats with traditional standards of finish and their appropriateness for the local conditions for which they were designed. From this period forward, he continued to work in boatbuilding, design, and historical research.

During World War II Chapelle commanded the army's Marine Transportation Section of the Research and Development Division. In 1950 he was awarded a Guggenheim Fellowship, which enabled him to study naval architecture at the National Maritime Museum in Greenwich, England. In 1957 he became curator of transportation at the Smithsonian Institution in Washington, D.C. He was appointed the Smithsonian's Senior Historian in 1967 and became Historian Emeritus upon his retirement in 1971. —Daniel B. MacNaughton

IRWIN CHASE

Died 1974 · United States

From 1906 to 1923 Irwin Chase was chief designer at the Electric Launch Company (soon known as Elco) in Bayonne, New Jersey, and helped that business grow into the United States' first large-scale production builder of powerboats. In 1915 he designed the first Elco Cruisette, a simple, 32-foot powerboat assembled on a production line that brought boat ownership to many who could not previously

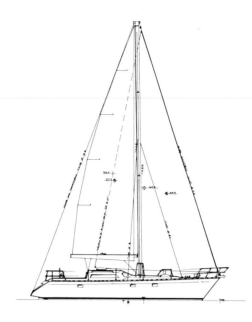

François Chevalier: *Croisière.* This 11.5-meter sloop doesn't look particularly unconventional above the waterline—a good example of a modern cruising boat design—but she has a secret below the waterline: a bulbous bow like that of a tiny supertanker, intended to reduce resistance. *Drawing courtesy François Chevalier*

afford it. Elco went on to make large numbers of their popular standardized powerboats and a series of custom-built boats for over thirty years. Many examples survive and are much admired by collectors and yachtsmen.

Chase studied naval architecture at the University of Michigan, graduating in 1905. He became Elco's chief designer in 1906, replacing Alfred "Bill" Luders. Besides the more routine aspects of his work, Chase experimented with stepped-planing hulls, varying the fore and aft and athwartships angles of the steps until he obtained a model that was fast and could maintain control in turns. The 20-foot Elcoplane was one of the world's first planing hulls, with *Bug*, the first of the line, launched in 1911.

During World War I the company built 550 torpedo launches for the British Admiralty in 488 working days. In 1923 Chase was named general manager and ceased doing design work.

With Chase at the helm during World War II, Elco became one of the primary developers and the largest builder of the famous PT boats, employing more than three thousand men and women and for a time producing an average of one PT boat every sixty hours. Although it made a ten-million-dollar profit during the war, Elco suffered financial losses while trying to downsize after the war, and was shut down by its parent company on the last day of 1949. Chase then went to work at Electric Boat in Groton, Connecticut, until his retirement.

—Daniel B. MacNaughton

FRANÇOIS CHEVALIER

Born August 29, 1944 · France

A yacht designer, author of many articles on contemporary yachting, coauthor of a number of books on the history of yachts and yacht design, and an accomplished artist in several mediums, François Chevalier has had a unique career.

Chevalier was born the day after Paris was liberated during World War II. As a boy he learned to sail on the Seine River in a Caneton Class dinghy and then in a 5O5, before he got into cruising. After training as an architect at the Paris School of Fine Arts (Ecole des Beaux-Arts), he enrolled in the Westlawn School of Yacht Design. The first boat built to his design, *Ratso* (1978), sailed in the OSTAR (Observer Singlehanded Transatlantic Race) and in the first BOC. In 1982 his gift for variety was displayed in a transatlantic hydrofoil, a 60-footer for the BOC, an 82-foot cruising trimaran, and even a light hydroplane.

Chevalier has been a professor of naval architecture at the University of Nantes, writes for French and foreign maritime magazines, is an illustrator for major French publishers, and continues to paint in watercolors.

In 1983, Chevalier coauthored with Jacques Taglang a major book on the history of the America's Cup entitled *America's Cup Yacht Designs, 1851–1986*, and then *American and British Yacht Designs*, a monumental two-volume reference with more than four hundred plans. Their *J-Class* book was published in 2002. Chevalier has written a number of other yachting-related books in both modern and historical veins, and has specialized in the re-creation of lines plans for classic yacht restorations. His office is in Paris. —Jacques Taglang

C. MAURICE CHEVREUX

1864–ca. 1916 · France

Maurice Chevreux's life was heavily influenced by the arts. A violinist and the child of two musicians, he was also affected by his friendship and partnership with the impressionist painter/yacht designer Gustave Caillebotte. He published his famous *Traité de la Construction des Yachts à Voiles* (*Treatise on the Construction of Sailing Yachts*) in 1898.

Born in Le Havre, Chevreux studied naval architecture with M. Le Laidier, the Lloyd's surveyor in that city, and then with the naval architect Gaston Grenier. Shortly thereafter he left for Scotland, where he became private assistant to the Clyde designers Robert Caird and George Eldridge. Returning home, he worked at the Forges et Chantiers de la Mediterranée at Granville. To complete his technical education, he entered Ecole d'Application du Génie Maritime, becoming an engineer of naval construction.

Chevreux managed the Argenteuil yard on the Seine River near Paris until it went bankrupt in 1885. Beginning in 1886 he supervised work at the Luce Boat Yard, also near Paris, on behalf of his partner, artist Gustave Caillebotte. Thus began a wonderful chapter of his life, as Chevreux designed for Caillebotte *Mouquette*, the first boat built by the yard, and in the process introduced the painter to naval architecture, which he would later practice professionally.

In 1885 Chevreux drew the lines for *Pioche*, a Five-Tonner that remained unbeaten until the advent of the Chevreux-designed *Freia*. His 3-Rater *Thomas* (1887) won seventy first prizes in her first three years. Chevreux designed the first example of the 30-Square-Meter class of the Cercle de la Voile de Paris (CVP) in 1890, a development class initiated by Caillebotte.

Chevreux then joined a yard belonging to Benjamin Normand, brother of designer Jacques-Augustin Normand, as a construction supervisor for a series of torpedo boats. He designed 267 boats of all types for the yard and at one time held a speed record for petroleum launches with *Météor*, which achieved 11 knots in 1891.

After opening his own practice, he designed *Bettina* (1895) for the Baron Edouard de Rothschild, and she won the second Coupe de France. *Honeymoon* (1896) was considered by many to be the fastest 5-Rater ever built.

In 1905, he designed *Paris*, a superb Sonderklasse, and then in 1908 he conceived *Punch*, his first 6-Meter. In 1909 came *Anemone II*, a 15-Meter, and in 1910 *Anemone III*, an 8-Meter that won seven first prizes in twenty-one regattas in the English season. —Jacques Taglang

ARTÙ CHIGGIATO

1902–1984 · Italy

Between the ages of twenty and twenty-five, Artù Chiggiato designed *Daila* and *Daila II*, both being casada-type motorboats—the style seen in the lagoons of Venice. After graduating with a degree in civil and industrial engineering from Padua in 1927, he continued to design boats for friends as well as club boats for the most important nautical club in Venice, Compagnia della Vela. He designed both sailboats and motorboats, the largest being the 22-meter motoryacht *Barbana* for Count Loredan, built in 1933–34. As manager of the

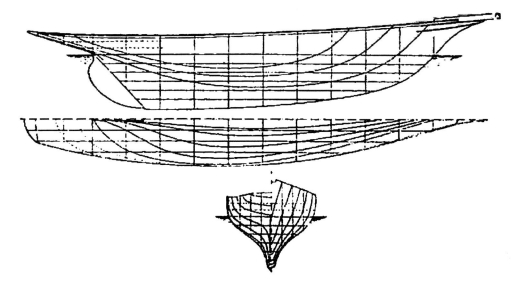

C. M. Chevreux: *Thomas.* Inspired by Gustave Caillebotte, in 1887 Chevreux designed *Thomas*, a cutter that resembles the narrow English cutters of the time, but with a wider beam. Chevreux designed her after the end of the Length-and-Sail-Area Rule of 1886, which killed the narrow cutters but produced skimming-dish types that were equally unsatisfactory. *Drawing courtesy Jacques Taglang*

Lagoon Navigation Firm, he also designed a passenger steamboat.

During World War II, Chiggiato designed comfortable, shoal-draft boats for Venetian sailors who could only navigate within the lagoons: boats of various lengths up to 8.5 meters. In 1946, he designed the *Vento Perso*, a beautiful 12-meter double-ender with harmonious lines and long overhangs that became famous in 1947 for making an Atlantic crossing, uncommon for its time, from Trieste to Rio de Janeiro.

In 1946 in Florence, at the Assembly of the Union of Italian Sailing Societies (currently known as the Italian Sailing Federation), Chiggiato was named president of the Technical Commission. He represented the federation in London on IYRU projects from 1947 to 1965.

Chiggiato's contacts with English designers influenced his work and led him to publish his designs in the English boating magazines. In 1950, he entered his 6.85-meter *Bas* in a *Yachting World* design contest calling for an inexpensive keelboat. Chiggiato's design, in spite of its extremely high technical sophistication, did not win because its price exceeded the required limit. However, in another design competition sponsored by the same journal held in 1956, he placed third.

At the end of the 1950's, Chiggiato designed the sloop *Sintesi*, measuring 5.92 meters and sleeping two, for sailors who wanted a small, economical cruising boat. Promoted in the magazine *Vela e Motore* (*Sail and Motor*), which introduced it at the first Milan Nautical Expo-

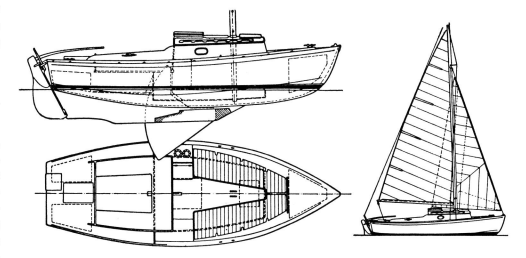

Artù Chiggiato: *Valetta.* Among other types, Chiggiato created a number of appealing small cruising sailboats. *Valetta* provides the essentials for a crew of two and manages to keep the centerboard trunk from intruding on the cabin space—quite a trick in a shoal-draft cruiser. *Reproduced from Juan Baader's* The Sailing Yacht

sition in 1961, one hundred were built. Chiggiato modified the *Sintesi* in 1962, replacing the centerboard with a fixed keel, and in 1967 he redesigned the sails so as to enable it to compete with the boats in "C"-Class with a rating of 14.73 feet LWL.

Chiggiato also designed vessels for the ocean racing classes (RORC and IOR), racing boats that must have comfortable living accommodations for cruising voyages. In the late 1950's and early 1960's, when the Celli-Pirelli boatyard decided to build fiberglass motorboats, Chiggiato was entrusted with the design of these boats. Among the most remarkable models were *Alligatore* (6.51 and 7.63 meters), which sleeps two; *Caimano* (6.51 meters); *Levriero* (4.27 meters); and *Giaguaro* (4.90 meters).

—Franco Belloni

RUDY CHOY

Born July 12, 1923 · United States

Rudy Choy's catamarans have dominated offshore multihull racing on the American West Coast for over thirty years. Well read, warm, emotional, extremely eloquent, and, as some have said, capable of selling ice to Eskimos, this designer has played a crucial role in communicating the benefits of the modern seagoing catamaran to the American sailing public.

Born in Hawaii, the son of a businessman and immigrant from Korea with little understanding of the ocean, Choy was first taught about the sea by his childhood friend, and later business partner, Alfred G. Kumalae (1922–1992). His first exposure to catamarans was in 1947 when as a Waikiki beachboy he assisted two friends in building what quickly became acknowledged as the most influential catamaran of the 1950's: *Manu Kai*. She was designed by Woodbridge Parker "Woody" Brown (born 1910) and Alfred Kumalae.

While Brown's background as a world-record glider pilot greatly influenced *Manu Kai*'s aircraft-like lightweight construction, knowledge of the cross-sections of ancient double canoes (which he and Kumalae had researched in Honolulu's Bishop Museum) contributed to her hull design. Other considerations were the need for shallow draft to allow for easy beaching, and suitability for building with sheet plywood. Instead of centerboards, she was thus designed with asymmetrical and deeply rockered hulls to provide for some grip while going upwind. The canoe-sterned *Manu Kai* proved to be a great success and sailed for decades off the beach in Hawaii's day-charter trade. She became the model for many other early catamarans in the United States, including those designed by Skip Creger, Victor Tchetchet, and Robert Harris, as well as the first catamarans designed and built by the Cunninghams in Australia. Even the Hobie catamarans owe their basic hull shape to *Manu Kai!*

Manu Kai was followed by *Alii Kai*, a 39-foot beach catamaran, and by *Waikiki Surf*, a 40-foot ocean racing catamaran, both designed by Brown with the assistance of Choy. Five days after her launching in 1955, *Waikiki Surf* sailed from Honolulu to Santa Monica, California, to participate in the 1955 transpacific regatta from Los Angeles to Hawaii. Being a catamaran, her entry was refused, but she sailed with the fleet and would have won on corrected time by many hours.

Sensing better business opportunities on the mainland, Choy and Kumalae subsequently moved to California, while Woody Brown stayed in Hawaii to further pursue catamaran sailing and surfing (forty-six years later, at age eighty-eight, he was still surfing the Hawaiian waves!). Choy was dismayed by the official yachting establishment's refusal to accept catamarans to transpacific racing, and initially intended to abandon catamaran design, but just two years later he was back with the completion of his breakthrough design, Aikane. An unofficial entry, this 46-foot catamaran nonetheless beat the entire fleet of monohulls in the 1957 and 1959 transpacific regattas and quickly cemented Choy's reputation as the foremost racing catamaran designer on the American West Coast.

Buoyed by the success of Aikane, Choy and Kumalae, together with Warren Seaman, formed C/S/K Catamarans in 1957. The firm was subsequently joined by Vince Bartolone. Kumalae left it in the late 1960's and moved back to Hawaii.

Choy never had any formal design or engineering training. Nonetheless, with the design of Aikane he had found his style, which would always make C/S/K-designed catamarans easily recognizable in the decades to come. They were characterized by asymmetrical, rounded, deep V-shaped hulls with the maximum curvature inboard and a hard-chine outboard; usually the absence of centerboards; a high freeboard; narrow, triangular transoms; and very full raking bows to prevent nose-diving in the strong winds around the Hawaiian islands. Important designs that followed were *Lani Kai* (46 feet, 1960), *Allez-Cat* (43 feet 6 inches, 1963), *Imi Loa* (42 feet 6 inches, 1963), *Pattycat II* (44 feet, 1964), *Seasmoke* (57 feet 9 inches, 1967), *Glass Slipper II* (50 feet, 1966, at the time of her launching, the world's largest foam-fiberglass sandwich catamaran), *World Cat* (44 feet, 1965, world's second catamaran to complete a circumnavigation), and *Polynesian Concept* (Polycon, 35 feet 10 inches, 1968, fitted with symmetrical hulls and daggerboards). Built very light and optimized for the prevailing downwind long-distance races on the American West Coast, many of these catamarans dominated local races for years. Unlike some

Rudy Choy. Here are five rakish-looking catamarans designed by Choy at the start of the 1968 Transpac Race. From left to right: *Polynesian Concept, Imi Loa, Lani Kai, Illusion,* and *Seasmoke. Reproduced from Buddy Ebsen's* Polynesian Concept

CHIGGIATO · CHOY

other pioneer designers of multihulls, C/S/K never really catered to the home boatbuilding market. The firm usually attracted a more affluent clientele and preferred to work only with a select few boatyards, keeping it apart from the "shoddy workmanship" image that multihulls often had then.

C/S/K was formally disbanded around 1973, three years after Choy moved back to his native Hawaii to start a catamaran charter business, but Choy continued to design some catamarans up until 1985, including *Aikane X5*, which Choy considers his masterpiece. In 1989 this 62-foot 6-inch catamaran set the transpacific sailing record at an average speed of 14.6 knots (and an average wind speed of 13.5 knots) with Choy on board. In 1990, Rudy Choy designed his last catamaran, the powerful 43-foot daysailing catamaran *Kiele VI*. Five years later he suffered a stroke, which robbed him of his speech. Rudy Choy has not designed any catamarans since then, but is still a partner in the firm of Choydesign, headed by his son Barry.

—Claas van der Linde

CHRIS-CRAFT

see Joseph Napoleon "Nap" Lisee, Arnold William Mackerer, and Christopher Columbus Smith

THOMAS CLAPHAM

July 30, 1839–July 19, 1915
England/United States

Occasionally a designer's contribution to the field becomes so fully assimilated that the originator is almost forgotten. In today's yachting world, we are apt to forget that the concepts of light displacement, shoal draft, and

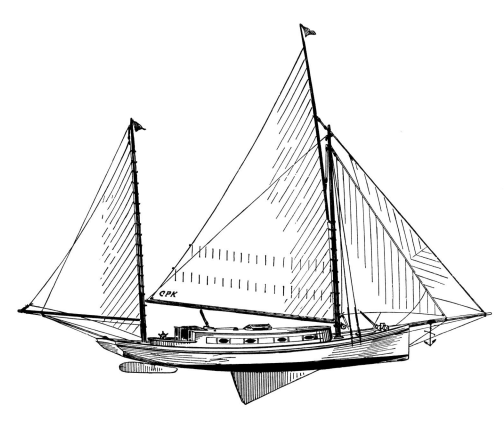

Thomas Clapham: Nonpareil or Roslyn sharpie. This sketch by C. P. Kunhardt shows the rig chosen to render Clapham's improved sharpie-yacht type more seaworthy and easily handled than her working ancestors. By combining a light, easily propelled hull with a small and efficient rig, Clapham planted the seed of the modern light-displacement yacht. *Reproduced from C. P. Kunhardt's* Small Yachts

chine hull forms, at least as they apply to yachts, had a point of origin: Thomas Clapham.

The British-born Clapham moved to the United States in his early thirties and lived on the income from his family's considerable estates in England. He was fascinated by the working sharpies of Long Island Sound, many of which sailed out of Roslyn, New York, where he lived. He had noticed that they combined speed, ease of handling, and very low cost with the advantages of shoal draft, and he felt they had good seakeeping potential.

Becoming one of the most effective voices arguing against the deep, narrow, heavy-displacement English cutter types that were then dominating the yachting scene, Clapham carried on a sharp and contentious correspondence with C. P. Kunhardt, a leading advocate of cutters and editor of *Forest and Stream* magazine, in which their exchanges were published. Kunhardt never backed down, but retained his sense of humor and frequently headed his letters with an illustration captioned, "Coffee and Pistols for Two."

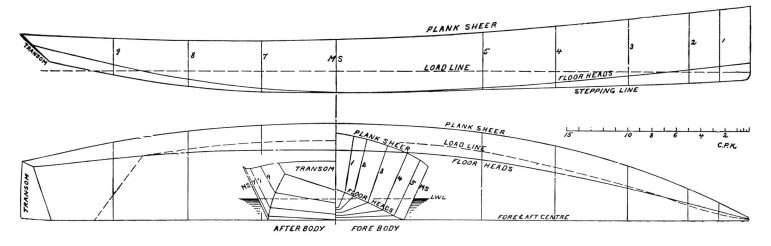

Thomas Clapham: Roslyn sharpie. The lines of a Roslyn sharpie show its differences from the traditional New Haven model. While her bottom is quite flat, amidships it is V-shaped both forward and aft, and there is considerable flare to the topsides, all improvements intended to eliminate pounding and increase seaworthiness. *Reproduced from C. P. Kunhardt's* Small Yachts

Finally Kunhardt told Clapham, "As you seem to know so much about boats, why don't you get to work and build them?" Facing a need to earn a living, after serious financial reversals, Clapham started to focus his life on yacht design and construction.

The first phase of Clapham's work was the creation of a yacht version of the working sharpies. The originals had flat, rockered bottoms, which were very economical to construct but pounded annoyingly at anchor and sometimes when sailing. Clapham eliminated this problem by deepening the profile forward and introducing deadrise both forward and aft while keeping the midship sections nearly flat. In many cases the ballast was moved to an external shoe and the topsides were given increased flare, changes that greatly improved the capsize resistance of the type.

They become known as Nonpareil sharpies, and sometimes simply as Roslyn sharpies. In the interest of seaworthiness and ease of handling, Clapham changed the original rig to one he called the Roslyn yawl, with a triangular mizzen having a sprit boom, a mainsail with a nearly vertical gaff (closely resembling a sliding gunter rig), and a large club-footed jib set on a long bowsprit; some even had double headsails. The rig combined a low center of effort and short masts for stability, with the ability to balance under jib and mizzen in strong winds or when the mainsail was being reefed.

Clapham built many variations on this theme, ranging up to 75 feet in length. They made many successful cruises and offshore passages, and against all predictions handled rough weather with complete success, remaining dry and comfortable in conditions that turned the heavy, narrow cutters into virtual submarines. They offered large amounts of living space at a fraction of the cost of a cutter with the same accommodations. Shoal draft made them well suited to cruising large areas of the American coastline. Lighter displacement meant smaller sails and lighter gear, which made them easier to sail. To the yachtsman of the day they were an utterly radical concept, but a lot of Clapham's boats were built and a lot of minds were changed.

Ironically, while Clapham's ideas were frequently criticized in the American yachting press, his boats were highly regarded in England, where the cutter type originated, and they were also popular in France and South America. A surprising number of boats were built in Roslyn for export.

Clapham also designed and built several round-bilged boats with otherwise sharpie-like characteristics, and these boats likely helped to inspire his acquaintance Ralph Munroe, creator of the famous Presto type of round-bilged sharpie.

Working entirely by eye and without formal training, Clapham achieved a further breakthrough in sailboat design. His rare body of experience probably clarified for him the fact that light-displacement boats often achieved higher speeds because they were to some extent sliding over the water instead of plowing through it. He experimented with sailing models in an effort to increase this tendency and eventually developed a new theory of hull design, which held that for minimum resistance, both the sections and the buttock lines of a hull should be segments of circles small or large. The result was a scow-like hull with little or no distinct centerline shape. His conclusion was an oversimplification, but it was close enough to the truth for his boats to achieve radically higher speeds than their rivals.

In 1889 the first of the new boats, the 20-foot *Bouncer*, walked away from her competitors, winning her first four races and collecting three special prizes for the outstanding nature of her performance. Similar boats of larger size followed with similar results. In what has to be one of the most satisfying phases in yachting history, the 40-foot sloop *Myth*, a Clapham design sailing on the West Coast, after several years was "withdrawn from racing, conceded to be unbeatable, for the general good of the sport."

Clapham didn't quite make it to the concept of planing, in which a hull breaks free of its wave pattern and skims across the water's surface. It was not until 1928 that Englishman Uffa Fox, inspired by planing motorboat hulls, produced the first true planing sailboat.

The success of Clapham's chine-hull yachts soon caused yacht racing rule makers to ban any yacht "with an angle of bilge," after which Clapham largely lost interest in racing boat design. He did propose a fin-keel, light-displacement, chine-hull America's Cup defender, and perhaps rightly claimed some credit when the design of Cup boats soon moved away from cutter types and toward his ideas, minus the chines.

Clapham may have been the first to employ reverse sheer, a characteristic now frequently utilized with light displacement to maximize interior space, and in 1898 he designed a form of double-hulled scow, which came close to being an early catamaran.

Thomas Clapham died at home in Roslyn, New York, at age seventy-five.

—Daniel B. MacNaughton

Despite a lack of formal training, by the time of his death at age seventy-nine, Robert Clark had long been known as one of the foremost yacht designers in Britain. In 1935 his first published design won fourth prize in a *Yachting Monthly* motorsailer design competition, and in 1936 he shared second prize in another *Yachting Monthly* competition for 30-foot LWL cruising boats.

A scaled-down version of this second boat, *Mystery II* (26-foot 3-inch LWL), was built the same year, and she caught the eye of Colonel C. F. King, who was keen to build an ocean racer at the cutting edge. Rather bravely he went to Clark, who was then still completely unknown. The result was *Ortac* (35 feet LWL). Now best remembered for being the first yacht to be fitted with a pulpit, she was also one of the first to sport a masthead cutter rig.

The naval architect Douglas Phillips-Birt commented that along with the Laurent Giles–designed *Maid of Malham*, *Ortac*'s generous overhangs and cut-away keel represented a new line of development which set the course for subsequent offshore design." By winning the RORC's Open Division points championship her first year (1937), *Ortac* immediately brought the young Clark to the forefront of ocean-racing design. Before World War II began, a number of successful Class I ocean racers and smaller boats came from Clark's board. In 1939 they included several Class I ocean racers, such as *Erivale* (38 feet 5 inches LWL), *Ben-*

Robert Clark: *Lara*. The 42-foot LWL centerboard yawl *Lara* was another successful Class I ocean racer before and after World War II. *Photo by Whorwell & Son*

Robert Clark: *Benbow.* Both *Benbow* (No. 151, 50-foot LWL) and *Erivale* (No. 236) were highly successful Class I ocean racers before and after World War II. They are shown here at the start of the 1950 Dover-Kristiansand Race. *Erivale* was "one of the first yachts built with bent timbers, multiple stringers, and bent hanging knees," according to *Yachting World* editor Bernard Hayman. *Photo by Whorwell & Son*

bow (50 feet 3 inches LWL), and *Lara* (42 feet 3 inches LWL) along with a number of smaller boats. "Size and proportions were different for all those yachts," commented Bernard Hayman, who worked for Clark in the late 1940's, "but Robert gave a very similar character to most of his designs and some—*Benbow*, for example—were slide-rule developments from earlier tables of offsets."

Clark spent most of World War II working for the Admiralty. Following it, he was one of the first, if not the first, to use cold-molded construction for a larger design when he produced the 30-foot LOA *Lilith* in 1949. She was built up with five plies of veneer over a more or less solid mold. With the war over, he was again in demand from the ocean-racing fraternity for whom he designed a whole line of flag-winning boats.

In 1950 Clark designed *Jocasta* (41 feet LWL) for Geoff Pattinson, one of the original donors of the Admiral's Cup. *Jocasta* proved phenomenally successful, winning the RORC's Class I championship four times, and was on the British team that won the first Admiral's Cup series in 1957. *Joliette* (28 feet 6 inches LWL) and her near-sistership, *Right Royal*, were two more competitive Clark designs, as were *Favona* (24 feet LWL), which in 1953 became the first Class III boat to win the Fastnet Race, and *Caprice of Huon* (32 feet LWL). Built in 1949, *Caprice* performed brilliantly as part of the Australian Admiral's Cup team in 1965 and contributed to their win in 1967.

After designing *Pym* (27 feet LWL), which topped the RORC's Class III championship in 1958 and 1960, Clark's interest in conventional ocean racing seemed to wane. One obituarist commented that Clark found the RORC rating rule, introduced in 1957, too much of a straitjacket for his artistic temperament.

Whatever the reason, Clark turned more and more to designing cruising boats and to record breakers for the new breed of ocean-racing yachtsman. The 39-foot sloop *Gipsy Moth III*, in which Francis Chichester won the first Singlehanded Transatlantic Race in 1960, and *Gipsy Moth V* (38 feet 5 inches LWL), were both Clark designs, as were the 58-foot ketch *Sir Thomas Lipton*, in which Geoffrey Williams won the 1968 Singlehanded Transatlantic Race, and the 59-foot ketch, *British Steel*, in which Chay Blyth made the first nonstop singlehanded circumnavigation against the prevailing winds in 1970–71.

Perhaps also Clark's lack of formal qualifications in an age that demanded more precision and less artistic flair had something to do with his shift in interest. Certainly when the largest yacht he ever designed, the 170-foot steel schooner *Carita*, was built in the late 1950's, there were problems with her construction. And typically, when Francis Chichester pointed out that *Gipsy Moth III* was 13 inches longer than designed, Clark retorted, "If that's the only difference from the plans, you ought to be grateful."

"He was at his best with the broad concepts of lines plans, sail plans, and general arrangement drawings," wrote Bernard Hayman in *The Times* when Clark died. "Detail was not his forte. . . . He was a good sailor himself, striking in his manner, and with great presence."

—Ian Dear

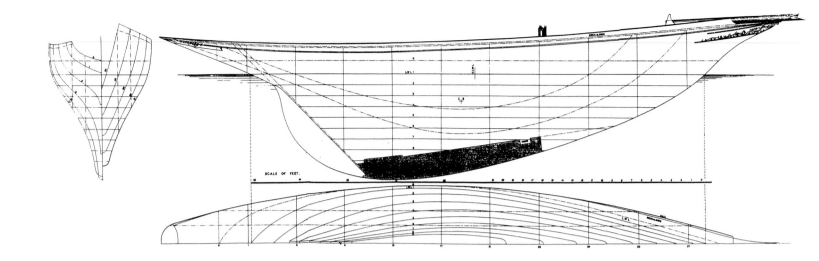

C. P. Clayton: *Ghost.* A 20-Rater under the Length-and-Sail-Area Rule, *Ghost* exemplifies the deep and narrow cutter type with which Clayton had great success. *Reproduced from Dixon Kemp's* Yacht Architecture

CHARLES POLE CLAYTON

1845–ca. 1912 · England

Following the success of the new breed of yacht designers in evading the restrictions of the old tonnage rules, the Yacht Racing Association introduced the Length-and-Sail-Area Rule in 1886. Yachts built under this rule became known as *raters*. C. P. Clayton produced a number of successful designs under this rule, particularly in the smaller yachts up to the 40 rating.

Clayton was born at Birkenhead, near Liverpool on England's west coast, the son of Mr. Ashley Clayton, owner of the Woodside Graving Dock. Following an education at Rossall School, he served a shipyard apprenticeship with his father's firm and also was employed by the Canada Works of Thomas Brassey and the Millwall Ironworks on the Thames. He worked at yards at Sunderland and Liverpool, where he was employed in the design of merchant vessels. He also traveled abroad as, according to Dixon Kemp, the lug rig which he introduced in the New Brighton Sailing Club boats was based on a rig he had seen in Callao, Peru, and Montevideo, Uruguay.

Clayton commenced his yacht-designing career while still living in Birkenhead, when he designed the Ten-Tonner *Kismet* in 1873 as well as the NBSC (National Boating Safety Council) 50-foot class *Jabberwock* at about the same time. Subsequently he designed further craft for the NBSC class, including *Elaine* (1876), the first of the class to be lug- rather than spritsail-rigged.

Following a move to Hythe, near Southampton, in about 1880, Clayton began his career proper as a yacht designer. He was not a prolific designer, producing about forty designs by the late 1890's, and it was remarked in the yachting press that he "really designs more for pleasure than profit." However, his designs ranged from small raters to 200-ton steam yachts such as *Peridot* for Mr. Cuthbert Quilter. He designed a number of successful craft in accordance with the earlier rules, but it is the graceful raters he produced to the 1886 rule such as *Mohawk* (40-Rater), winner of the Queen's Cup at the Royal Yacht Squadron regatta in 1896, and *Stephanie* (20-Rater) that constitute his main claim to fame. Several of these yachts were extremely successful for their owners.

Known as an expert on rules and rating, Clayton frequently contributed letters and articles on these subjects to the yachting press. He was a member of the committee that devised the Linear Rating Rule of 1896, based partly on the work of Professor William Froude.

Clayton was not only a theoretical yachtsman but also a practical one. While on the Mersey, he raced *Kismet* successfully and also sailed in the open boats of the New Brighton Sailing Club. His membership in the Cheshire Yacht Club in particular would have brought him into contact with other engineers and in particular the yacht designers Byrne and Richardson. After his move to Hythe, he continued his racing career in the small raters he designed.

—Brian Smith

JOAQUÍN COELLO

Born 1946 · Spain

In a very active and varied career, Joaquín Coello has been involved in the design of Whitbread and America's Cup challengers, submarine and surface warships, and marine and aeronautic gas turbines, and has skippered yachts in some of the major endurance races. As design team leader and skipper of the 1981–82 Spanish Whitbread entry *Licor 43*, he is credited with stirring a passion for the event in Spain that resulted in three further Spanish Maxi entries in later years.

After graduating from Madrid's Escuela Tecnica Superior de Ingenieros Navales, Coello joined the state-sponsored shipyard of Bazan, where he rose to become technical director. In 1979 he was elected Spanish Yachtsman of the Year for his participation in the 1978 Route du Rhum Singlehanded Transatlantic Race aboard a boat of his own design, *Gudrum IV*. He was then able to combine his practical and technical experience in a collaboration with Pedro Morales and Xavier Soler in the design of the fractionally rigged, 59-foot aluminum-hulled *Licor 43* and, remarkably, skippered her to finish each leg of the Whitbread race despite being twice dismasted.

Recent work on the leading edge of yacht racing has included his position as director of the design team for the Spanish America's Cup challengers *Rioja de España* (1995) and *Bravo España* (2000).

—Alfredo Lagos Sr. and Iain McAllister with assistance from Alfredo Lagos Jr.

COLLAMORE FAMILY

see George Melville "Mel" McLain

THOMAS EDWIN COLVIN

Born June 27, 1925 · United States

One of the few contemporary designers whose concepts spring more from a background in working sail than from yachting traditions or the influence of handicapping rules, Tom Colvin draws boats that serve well the practical needs of liveaboard and voyaging yachtsmen, plus an independent breed of coastwise cruisers. He is also an accomplished writer on marine subjects and is especially well known for his boatbuilding treatise, *Steel Boatbuilding* (Volumes One and Two), and his book *Cruising as a Way of Life*.

Colvin was born in Chicago and from the age of five displayed a total fascination for boatbuilding. He sold his first professional design the year he entered high school. At age fourteen he began crewing on working boats, some powered by sail and some by steam. By age twenty he had become a Master in Sail approved for any ocean and any tonnage, and by twenty-three was an unlimited Master in Steam. During World War II he twice served on convoys in the notorious Murmansk, Soviet Union, run. He also found time to study drafting and engineering.

In 1952 Colvin became the senior designer for the Newport News Shipbuilding and Dry Dock Company in Virginia and worked as a consultant for Kaiser Aluminum in Chicago. For many years he ran his own shipyard out of Hampton, and later Miles, Virginia, and now runs a design office in Alva, Florida. He has designed over three hundred vessels under his own name.

Colvin's work is distinguishable by its strong connection to working coasting schooners, pinkies, skipjacks, sharpies, and Chinese junks, among others, and places a strong emphasis on simplicity, strength, and durability throughout. Many Colvin designs have a chine hull and traditional gaff or Chinese rigs. All, including his marconi-rigged boats, are designed to handle well under working sail. Many have been built without engines. Most Colvin boats emphasize paint finishes rather than varnish, and durability rather than ornamentation.

Colvin has lived aboard and voyaged for years at a stretch, including sixteen years aboard his 48-foot aluminum Chinese junk *K'ung Fu-Tse*. While he designs boats with rigs of all types, he has done more than any other American designer to promote the Chinese lug rig, and is one of the few to perform comparative tests to determine its performance characteristics. He often specifies the rig for boats, emphasizing ease of handling. Colvin has also

produced many designs for sharpies and has been a leading advocate of that type for those seeking economy and shoal draft.

An experienced shipbuilder working in wood and metal, Colvin has done a great deal to explain and popularize steel and aluminum construction in the United States, and to encourage amateur builders. Perhaps his most popular design is that for *Gazelle*, 42-foot, V-shaped bottom, steel, Chinese lug-rigged schooner that he owned for many years and has been reproduced many times, often by owner/builders.

—Daniel B. MacNaughton

ALBERT E. CONDON

1887–July 15, 1963 · United States

Working in various yards in Maine and Massachusetts, Albert Condon was primarily known as a designer of commercial vessels with an unusually pleasing aesthetic character. He also drew a good number of sailing and power yachts, ranging from 16 to 100 feet, that are widely recognized for their sweet lines.

As a young man Condon interspersed his formal education with real-world experience in boatyards. He graduated from Hebron Academy in 1908 and learned naval architecture from an MIT-educated tutor, a two-year night-course program from Franklin Union in Boston, and his own studies.

Beginning in his teens, Condon worked for his uncle Rufus Condon at his yard in Friendship, Maine. In subsequent years he worked for Charles A. Morse of Thomaston, Maine, and the famous George Lawley and Son yard of Neponset, Massachusetts. Through the years surrounding World War I and up until 1921, he designed navy ships for Portsmouth Naval Shipyard and Bath Iron Works.

After 1921 Condon again worked for Rufus Condon, and then for Gray Boats in Thomaston, Maine, where he produced many of his power yacht designs. Later he worked at the I. L. Snow yard in Rockland, designing most of his sailing yachts. At the beginning of World War II he moved to the Pierce and Kilburn yard of Fairhaven, Massachusetts. Here he designed many of his famous eastern rigged (aft wheelhouse) draggers, and is credited with some of the best evolved plans of that type. In 1948 he retired to Thomaston, Maine, where, often in ill health, he designed a number of boats before his death. Throughout his career he worked almost entirely without draftsmen.

The Albert E. Condon Collection, representing designs produced from 1929 through 1951, are at Mystic Seaport, Mystic, CT.

—Daniel B. MacNaughton

Thomas Colvin: *Gazelle*. The 42-foot schooner *Gazelle* illustrates several of Colvin's favorite themes, with her easily handled Chinese lug rig, light displacement, moderate draft, and roomy interior, made all the more so by the absence of a cockpit footwell, a feature he avoids whenever possible. Over seven hundred yachts of this design have been built in steel, and a few have been built in aluminum and wood. *Drawing courtesy Thomas E. Colvin*

PASCAL CONQ

see Jean-Marie Finot

WILLIAM EWALD COOK

Born October 22, 1940 · United States

Bill Cook began his working life as an English professor, but a 1972 transatlantic voyage inspired him to become interested in a career as a yacht designer. His first widely recognized design was his own *Rogue's Roost,* the cold-molded, light-displacement One-Tonner. Launched in 1977, she came in second in the fleet in the 1978 SORC.

For the New York Yacht Club (NYYC), Cook designed the New York 36 class in 1980, which numbered over sixty boats, the largest one-design class in the club's history. Also for the NYYC he designed in 1994 the International Cup 18-Meter class, which allows restricted development of rig, keel, rudder, and deck layout, but not the hull shape, which is fixed. His largest design to date is the 85-foot *Matador²,* winner of the Maxi World Cup in three consecutive years: 1990, 1991, 1992.

Cook came into contact with boats during his summers on Cape Cod. He earned a doctorate in English from Harvard and went on to become a professor at Manhattanville College in New York. During his sabbatical in 1972, he and his wife, Toni made a two-way transatlantic voyage, which convinced him to become a yacht designer. He took the Westlawn School of Yacht Design correspondence course and graduate courses at Yale University and the Stevens Institute in Hoboken, New Jersey. In 1974 he went to work for designer Bruce Kirby, and in 1977 he opened his own office.

As a designer of boats racing under the IOR, he is credited with an ability to create competitive boats that are fast, good looking, and easy to handle under all conditions. In his IOR maxi-boat designs he has created larger, heavier boats for a given rating than did other designers, which proved to be a successful combination. Notable racing successes include three Maxi World Championships, overall wins in the Miami-Nassau Races, the Annapolis-Newport Races, the Chicago-Mackinac Races, and a One-Ton North American Championship.

One of his favorite custom designs is the cold-molded *Caroler,* a 58-foot yawl for a former Concordia yawl owner, designed to have the Concordia style and character in a much larger boat. Production boats include the Schock 41, the New York 36, the Ocean Cruising 52, the Great Harbor 26, and the Impulse 21 and 26.

Whizzbang, launched in 2000 at Lyman Morse in Thomaston, Maine, is a 52-foot 8-inch canoe-

William Cook. This 56-foot yawl-rigged motorsailer shows the nice balance of modern features, a timeless aesthetic, and serious passagemaking abilities, for which Cook's recent work is noted. *Drawing courtesy William Cook*

stern, keel/centerboard, cutter-rigged motorsailer with a pleasing blend of modern features and timeless aesthetics. Built of foam-cored fiberglass, she is a serious passagemaker, with two transatlantic voyages under her belt. Other recent projects include a design for a singlehanded Open Class racer. Cook was chair-

man of the Mystic Seaport Board of Trustees from 1995 to 2000 and is the vice president of the Cape Cod Maritime Museum. In 2003 he completed a 4,500-mile cruise to Greenland, for which he was awarded the Royal Cruising Club Trophy by the Cruising Club of America.

Cook's office is in Hyannis on Cape Cod, Massachusetts. —Daniel B. MacNaughton

LEIGH HILL COOLIDGE

March 8, 1870–January 9, 1959 · United States

Leigh Coolidge designed yachts and commercial vessels of all types on the West Coast of the United States from around the turn of the twentieth century until the early 1950's. From his board came lumber schooners, racing and cruising sailboats, tugboats, speedboats, government patrol boats, and rumrunners. His practice spanned the transition in yacht design from sail to power.

Born in Portland, Maine, Coolidge first worked as a shipwright in South Boston at William B. Smith Shipyard and at George Lawley and Son, the latter during the time when Lawley built the America's Cup boats *Puritan* and *Mayflower.*

Coolidge moved West in 1890 and briefly attended the University of Washington but was

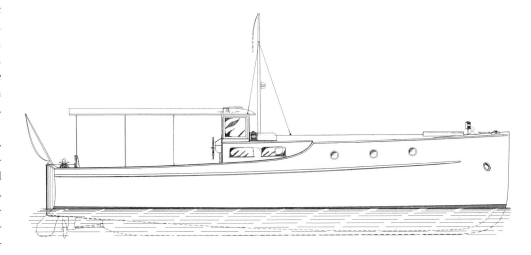

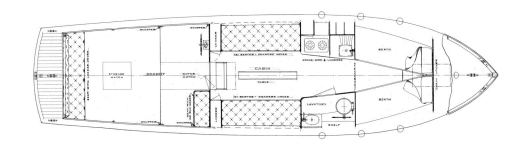

Leigh Coolidge. In the 1920's the N. J. Blanchard yard commissioned Coolidge to design this 36-foot cruising powerboat for standardized production. *Drawing courtesy Puget Sound Maritime Historical Society*

Leigh Coolidge: *Kiyi.* The wonderful pilothouse of the 50-foot *Kiyi* encourages cruising in the rainy weather of her native Pacific Northwest, while her roomy decks are ideal for better weather. With her economically propelled hull and excellent dinghy storage, it's hard to understand why more designs like hers are not built today. © *Benjamin Mendlowitz*

essentially a self-taught designer. He assisted in the design and construction of five very highly regarded four-masted schooners at a shipyard in Ballard, Washington. Their success allowed him to open his own office as a designer on the Grand Trunk dock in Seattle. In 1927, H. C. Hanson joined Coolidge in a partnership that lasted eighteen months. Coolidge returned to practicing alone until 1945, when he formed the firm Coolidge, Hart and Brinck.

Aside from the well-known 40-foot schooner *Sindbad* (1927) and the lovely 50-foot fantail motoryacht *Kiyi* (1926), both of which are still in active use, perhaps his greatest legacy to Puget Sound yachting is the Blanchard 36-foot Standardized Cruiser, of which twenty-eight were built between 1924 and 1930 at Norman J. Blanchard's yard on Lake Union. These were the first stock cruisers produced in meaningful numbers on Puget Sound. A year after the first Blanchard 36 was built, a highly similar design, called the Lake Union Dreamboat, was built by the Lake Union Dry Dock Company, which copyrighted the Dreamboat name.

Coolidge is also well known for his design of the 125-foot oceangoing *Mikimiki* tug, originally designed for Young Brothers Towing Company in Honolulu in 1929. She was originally designed with a single diesel installation, which by 1928 was changed to a twin-engine configuration. During World War II Coolidge, working for the Army Transport Services,

adapted this twin-screw design, which became known as the Miki-class tug. Some sixty-one were built for army service in both the Atlantic and the Pacific. A number survive and continue to work today, some as yachts.

Coolidge was an early pioneer in designing and making high-speed racing propellers. He founded the Coolidge Propeller Company in 1917 and sold it to partner Fred Dobbs in 1926. A company by that name operated in Seattle well into the 1990's. Coolidge's 10-meter hydroplane design, *Seattle Spirit*, was acknowledged as the fastest motorboat on the West Coast in 1910. Her successor to the title, the famous *Oregon Wolff II*, also used Coolidge propellers. Other Coolidge designs for stepped hydroplanes were published in *Pacific Motor Boat* magazine and built in Washington, Oregon, and California.

A self-confident, dapper, and aloof nature earned Coolidge the nickname "The Duke" among his associates. His attention to detail was legendary, and his reputation as a perfectionist was widespread among both boatyards and his clients. Coolidge's practice slowed in the 1950's and he died in 1959 at the age of eighty-eight.

The Coolidge drawings and notebooks are accessible from the Puget Sound Maritime Historical Society at Seattle's Museum of History and Industry.

—Daniel B. MacNaughton with J. Scott Rohrer

HENRI COPPONEX

1906–1970 · Switzerland

The landlocked country of Switzerland has acquired a reputation for excellence in yacht design and competition, partly through the achievements of yachtsmen and designers such as Henri Copponex, who was particularly well known for his work in the 5.5-Meter class.

Copponex was born on Lac Léman (Lake Geneva). At age thirteen, he was already distinguishing himself by building his own sailboat models, which often won regattas organized by the Model Club (Cercle des Modèles). He became a sought-after crewmember, racing aboard the 8.5-Meter (International Class) *Simbad* in 1922, and was helmsman of such 6.5-Meter (International Class) boats as *Tishé* and *Cigogne*. In 1930, he skippered the 6-Meter (International Rule) *Cigogne II* and also the successful 30-Square-Meter *Cigogne III* and *Cigogne V*. He won the Swiss championship in the 6-Meter and 15-Meter classes (SNS, or Société Nautique Suisse Class) and represented Switzerland sailing 6-Meters in the 1948 and 1952 Olympics.

Beginning work as a naval architect in 1934, Copponex designed his Lemanic One-Design class, then the 30-Square-Meter *Cigogne III*. In 1937 he designed the 6-Meter *Cigogne IV* and in 1939 launched the successful Lacustre Class, and went on to do excellent work in the 15-Meter SNS

Henri Copponex: Lacustre class. Typical of the one-design classes of Lake Geneva, the Lacustre class is still very active in Switzerland. Her sail plan is narrow like that of a Square-Meter yacht, and carries a large genoa. © *Klaus Kramer*

Attilio Costaguta: *Italia*. The 8-Meter *Italia* won the Olympic gold medal at Kiel, Germany, in 1936. Attilio Costaguta and his brother Ugo were among the first to create successful Italian-designed racing yachts under a variety of rules, and *Italia* certainly has the look of a winner. *Photo courtesy Franco Belloni*

class. In the years 1950 to 1960, he became famous for his 5.5-Meter designs. During the 1960 Napoli Olympic Games in Italy, five 5.5-Meters designed by Copponex were on the starting line, and in these same games he himself won the bronze medal. He was a member of the Société Nautique de Genève (SNG), a civil engineer, and a qualified measurer for handicapping rules.

A modest man, Henri Copponex was nonetheless generous with advice. He inspired many Swiss to become proficient yachtsmen, and he won international respect with the quality of both his design work and his sportsmanship.

—Jacques Taglang

EUGÈNE CORNU

November 5, 1903–1988 · France

More than a decade after his death and nearly thirty years since his last design, one can recognize Eugène Cornu's boats with little difficulty. They are characterized by their handsome period styling and sweeping sheerlines, but above all they are examples of exceptional boatbuilding. Cornu was a shipwright's son, and nearly every detail of his yachts was the object of a specific drawing.

At age sixteen and with little advance training, Cornu became an apprentice in a shipyard near Paris. In 1923, he joined the Jouët yard in Sartrouville as a draftsman. While he worked there, he drew ninety-three lines plans for navy launches, rescue boats, and motoryachts. After 1928 he drew sailing yachts. In 1943, at the request of the French Olympic champion Jacques Lebrun, he drew the lines of the famous *Bélouga*, a small, light, 6.5-meter centerboard cruiser of which several hundred were built, with many still sailing.

It was only in 1947, after a great deal of practical experience at Jouët's, that Cornu opened his own office. He drew 193 designs, among them 13 International Rule yachts. Many believe that he produced the best French yachts of the period, including a number of 12-Meters under the IYRU Cruiser/Racer Rule, and the yachts *Striana* (1955) and *Hallali* (1956), which took many honors in RORC races over the years. Cornu also saw great success in the 5.5-Meter class.

A spirited and courageous individual from the beginning, Cornu suffered from polio, and at age twenty chose to have his affected leg amputated. With the help of crutches, he chose the size of his boatbuilding projects by the strength available in his arms. His handicap did not prevent him from sailing, and while he rarely went to sea except to test his new yachts, he often sailed on rivers, singlehanded in a small dinghy. Said to be a touchy character, he

was jealous of his creations and systematically recovered his lines plans from boatyards once they were lofted. When Cornu retired after fifty-one years of work, he never took up a drawing pencil again. —Jacques Taglang

UGO A. COSTAGUTA
1869–1903
ATTILIO COSTAGUTA
1877–1942

Italy

Ugo Costaguta was the owner of a shipyard of the same name headquartered in Voltri, which is located 17 kilometers west of Genoa. Although he began to design boats at an early age, his professional career officially began in 1894 when he designed and built *Drafin*, measuring just over 8 meters in length, for the Marquis Ippolito Cattaneo of Belforte. The design showed little influence from English and American boats. Her fine performance in international races confirmed Costaguta's capabilities, and commissions began to come in.

The Duke of Abruzzi, who had previously been obliged to turn to foreign designers and builders, placed an order with Ugo for the 5-ton *Nella*. Having admired the results achieved with *Nella*, he then put Ugo in charge of designing and building *Artica,* a 10-ton yacht with which he challenged the French for the French Cup and won in Marseilles in 1902. This was the first big international success achieved by an Italian yacht. *Leda* was also built for the same owner. *Melisenda,* which won the Italian Cup in Nice in 1904, was built for Mario Dall'Orso.

One of Ugo's last designs dates from 1902: a 1-ton custom design measuring 6.4 meters with a sail area of 29 square meters, and built for the Cornigliano Sailing Club. In his short life of thirty-four years, Ugo Costaguta designed winning sailboats under three different tonnage rating formulas, one English and two French, all used in Italy.

Upon Ugo Costaguta's death, management of the shipyard passed to his brother Attilio, who had already been involved there in production. Among the boats designed and built by Attilio is the 8-Meter *Ondina* for Gian Franco Tosi, who brought the Italian Cup back to Italy in 1911. *Sirdhana* was built for Carlo Alberto Conelli de Prosperi the following year. *Orietta* won the Italian Cup for Count Gaddo della Gherardesca in 1935. The 6-Meter *Vega II* was built for the navy, and *Miranda II* was built for Carlo Ciampi. All of these boats, through their fine performances in all fields of racing, confirmed Attilio Costaguta's skill.

Attilio did not ignore the advent of motor-powered vessels in Italy. In 1907 at the Principality of Monaco Exposition, he introduced his motorboat *Anadiomede,* built for Costantino Tassara. This boat made an excellent impression and led to many other motorboats through the years.

Attilio also designed two one-designs: one in 1904, measuring 7.2 meters, for the Lariano Royal Racing Club on Lake Como, and the other in 1909, Voltri, measuring 7.5 meters, for the Verbano Royal Yacht Club of Stresa on Lake Maggiore.

Attilio won his most coveted commission in 1935, when the Italian Royal Sailing Federation asked him to design and build the 8-Meter *Italia,* which won the Olympic gold medal at Kiel, Germany, in 1936. It was on this yacht during the Olympics that the Genoa jib, conceived by the head sailmaker at the Costaguta shipyard, was first used.

—Franco Belloni

DANIEL H. COX

1872–1955 · United States

Throughout the first half of the twentieth century, the firm of Cox and Stevens designed yachts that reflected the technological advances of the era. Many of their large yacht designs, typified by *Winchester* and *Nourmahal,* were powerful but refined in both form and function.

The firm illustrated the degree to which yacht design is a continuum of artists and engineers who learn from one generation, adapt to the present, and train those who will rise to prominence in the next generation.

The firm of Cox and Stevens was formed in 1905 by Daniel Cox, his older brother Irving (formerly a partner in Gardner and Cox), and Colonel Edwin A. Stevens, whose father founded the Stevens Institute of Technology. They broadened the scope of their new firm to include not only yacht design, but also commercial vessel design, marine engineering, and yacht brokerage services. Their offices were in New York City.

Colonel Stevens (1858–1918) was an enthusiastic yachtsman but was not very active in the firm. Irving Cox's experience was enhanced by the partnership with Daniel, a U.S. Naval Academy graduate who specialized in ship construction until he resigned his commission in 1902 to do private design work. By the 1920's, when Irving became less active, Daniel was the major partner. Irving died in 1935, leaving Daniel to run the firm until his retirement in 1947.

Cox's smaller designs—sailboats, launches, and express cruisers—were often reviewed in *The Rudder,* yet the firm was especially well known for its seagoing yachts. Many of its large steam and diesel yacht designs resembled

commercial or military vessels with plumb bows and squared profiles, rather than sailing ships with their clipper bows and bowsprits. The 225-foot *Winchester* (4th) was fittingly referred to as "a private destroyer." She was built in Maine in 1915 by Bath Iron Works. Her two steam turbines could produce 7,000 hp and she became famous for her damaging wake in Long Island Sound. In fact, her owner, Peter Rouss, lent her to the navy during World War I, a practice followed by other owners of large yachts as well.

The 264-foot, 1,969-ton *Nourmahal* was built in 1929 at the Fried Krupp yard in Germany. Designed jointly by Cox and Stevens with Theodore Ferris, Vincent Astor's new yacht looked like a white steamship with high sides and a flared bow. With two six-cylinder diesel engines, the yacht went 16 knots and had a cruising radius of over 16,000 miles. A crew of over forty was required. Cox grew to favor diesel power because it allowed more space for accommodations, it required fewer crew, and the fuel needed to achieve the same cruising speed and range as an equivalent steam yacht cost less.

The largest private yacht of the era came from Cox's drawing boards in the early days of the Depression. The four-masted barque *Sea Cloud* was launched in 1931 as a wedding present from E. F. Hutton to Marjorie Merriweather

Daniel Cox: *Winchester.* The 225-foot *Winchester* (4th) was built by Bath Iron Works in 1915. Shown here at moderate speed, her 7,000-hp steam turbines could produce a speed of over 31 knots, creating legendary wakes in her home waters of Long Island Sound. *Photo courtesy the Mariner's Museum, Newport News, VA*

Daniel Cox: *Apache*. Originally *Diamond W*, *Apache* is a 58-foot Seawanhaka schooner designed by Cox and Stevens and built in 1925. While her original foresail carried a gaff, in this picture she is carrying an unusual marconi foresail. A total of twenty-five sisterships were built at Bath Iron Works in Bath, Maine. *Photo courtesy the Maine Maritime Museum, Bath, ME*

Post. This magnificent yacht (316 feet LOA, 2,323 tons, and 35,000 square feet of sail) is still in service seventy years later as a luxury passenger vessel with thirty-four cabins and sixty in her crew.

In 1929, Daniel Cox formed a partnership with Gibbs Brothers to take over the firm's commercial work, allowing Cox and Stevens to concentrate on their burgeoning yacht design and brokerage services. Gibbs and Cox were known for their design of the liner *United States*. The company continues today.

In 1932, Philip L. Rhodes associated himself with Cox and Stevens, which allowed the firm to expand and do design work for yachts less than 75 feet long. Under their contract, Rhodes received full credit for his designs. With the death of head designer Bruno Tornroth, Rhodes took over this responsibility along with the engineering. During World War II, Cox and Stevens did military work, and in 1947 when Daniel Cox retired, Rhodes took over the offices and continued designing under Philip L. Rhodes, Naval Architects and Marine Engineers.

The Cox and Stevens, Inc. Collection is at Mystic Seaport Museum, Mystic, CT.

—Sheila McCurdy

CLINTON HOADLEY CRANE

January 30, 1873–December 1, 1958
United States

Few designers had careers as broad in scope, or designed for as many years, as Clinton Crane. He designed some of the earliest gasoline-powered racing boats, racing sailboats ranging from small class boats to the J-Class boat *Weetamoe*, and some of the largest and most elegant steam- and sail-powered cruising yachts ever built. He was designing as early as 1896, and with his later work in the 12-Meter class laid the groundwork to bring the America's Cup into the modern era.

Born in Englewood, New Jersey, Crane was introduced to sailing at summer camp, where he enjoyed the sailing canoes that were popular at the time. He studied engineering at Harvard, graduating in 1894, and worked for two years as an apprentice machinist at William Cramp and Sons Shipyard in Philadelphia.

Involvement with the local sailboat racing scene caused Crane to abandon his original plan to become a designer of ocean liners. He designed a boat to compete for the Seawanhaka Cup and had it built in 1896, and then, while a complete unknown, went on to win the right to sail against a Canadian yacht club by beating twenty-eight crack American boats. He continued to win the right to sail against the Canadian club for the next three years, but was never able to defeat them due to his inability to outdo Canadian designer G. Herrick Duggan, who was innovating dramatically in very light, high-speed scow forms. The experience served to convince Crane of the importance of light, strong construction and increased his interest in racing boat design in general.

Crane continued his engineering studies at Columbia University and in 1897–98 attended Glasgow University. At Glasgow he encountered the torpedo boat plans of French designer Jacques Normand, his introduction to high-speed powerboats. In 1899 he went directly into an independent design career by associating himself with the brokerage firm of Tams and Lemoine in New York, which became Tams, Lemoine and Crane in 1900. Crane had been offered employment with designers A. Cary Smith and William Gardner, but preferred the independence offered by Tams and Lemoine. Crane maintained a summer residence in Islesboro, Maine, where he raced in the local Dark Harbor class.

Designing *Vingt-et-Un* and *Vingt-et-Un II* for a company wishing to demonstrate two of its new engines, Crane saw early success with his gas-powered speedboats. The second boat surprised Nathanael Herreshoff by beating his steam-powered *Swiftsure*, an event that helped to pique Herreshoff's interest in gasoline power. During this period Crane's chief draftsman was A. E. Luders Sr., who would later become a highly regarded yacht designer in his own right.

Challenger, a fast displacement-hull powerboat that Crane designed to win the Harmsworth Cup, failed to do so apparently due to mishandling, but was followed by the successful *Dixie* and *Dixie II*. After this it became clear to Crane that future powerboat races would be won by hydroplanes, such as his own *Dixie IV*. He did not approve this type of boat, feeling it had no practical purpose other than racing in smooth water, so he stopped designing in this niche after 1911.

Crane achieved spectacular success with *Lanai* in the popular small "raceabout" development class. She proved to be invincible in sailing races throughout New England, and her owner subsequently commissioned him to design *Aloha*, a 127-foot hermaphrodite brig built in 1899. In 1910 he designed another *Aloha* for the same owner, a 218-foot barque said to be one of the most beautiful yachts ever built. It circumnavigated after World War I.

Clinton Crane: *Endymion.* The beautiful 135-foot schooner *Endymion* set a transatlantic speed record that stood for five years until the famous passage made by the Gardner-designed schooner *Atlantic,* in 1905. *Photograph by Nathaniel Stebbins. Courtesy of the Society for the Preservation of New England Antiquities*

Clinton Crane: *Noma.* The 262-foot steam yacht *Noma,* launched in 1902, shows the beauty of line and aristocratic bearing that made Crane a popular designer of these floating palaces, the scale of which has not been equaled until the megayacht trend of recent years. *Photo courtesy the Mariners' Museum, Newport News, VA*

Clinton Crane: *Dixie II.* Reaching a speed of 36 mph, *Dixie II* won the British International Harmsworth Trophy in 1908. She won the American Power Boat Association (APBA) Gold Challenge Cup in both 1908 and 1909, but was among the last displacement-type boats to do so. After *Dixie II* the winners were all hydroplanes, and speeds quickly went far higher. *© Mystic Seaport, Rosenfeld Collection, Mystic, CT. James Burton, Photographer*

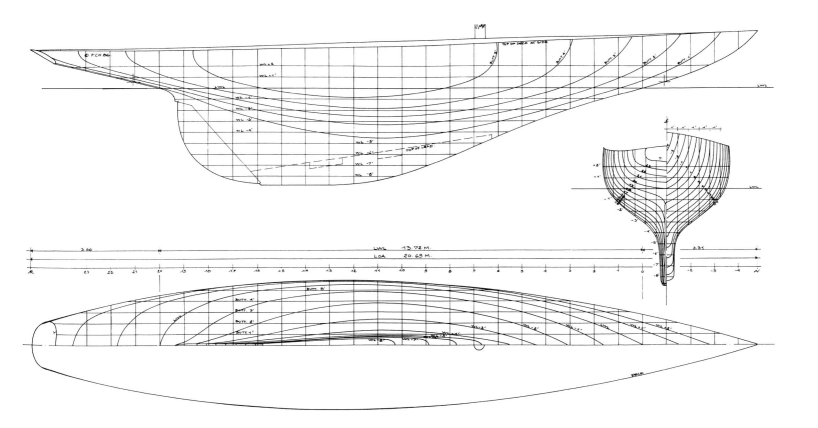

Clinton Crane: *Gleam*. The 12-Meter *Gleam* shows why the International Rule was so popular for so long. A competitive racer, she also served as a family coastal-cruising boat, and a look at her lines reveals moderation, common sense, speed, and beauty. © *Chevalier & Taglang*

In 1900 the Crane-designed schooner *Endymion* set a transatlantic speed record of 13 days, 8 hours from Sandy Hook, New Jersey, to the Needles off the Isle of Wight, a time that stood until the William Gardner–designed schooner *Atlantic* set her more enduring record in 1905. He also drew *Dervish*, a long-ended schooner of the extreme pre–Universal Rule form, which won the 1907 Bermuda Race. She had a 56-foot waterline length and measured 86 feet on deck! The 227-foot steam yacht *Vanadis* was built to Crane's design in Scotland. Besides being a large and beautiful yacht, she is remembered for the fact that, owing to a miscalculation of the amount of coal required for her delivery voyage to America, it was necessary to feed much of her fine interior joinerwork to the boilers for her to complete the trip.

Crane suddenly ended his dramatically successful design career in 1912 in order to rescue

Clinton Crane: *Weetamoe* (opposite). Uffa Fox described *Weetamoe*, launched in 1930, as "an excellent example of a yacht to the J class rule." Further, he noted that her "sail plan and her masting and rigging are a great advance and worthy of study." © *Mystic Seaport, Rosenfeld Collection, Mystic, CT*

his recently deceased father's lead mining company, which he restored to profitability and ran until his retirement in 1947. After 1922 he devoted more time to his yacht designs, but never again as a way to make a living. Instead he drew boats for friends and for fellow yacht club members, charging only his costs. During this period he began designing under the International Rule. At first his boats were beaten by the English in the 6-Meter class, but soon he hit his stride and became one of the best in the genre, with notable successes in the Seawanhaka Cup.

For the 1930 America's Cup defense Crane designed the J-Class boat *Weetamoe* in workspace he borrowed from designers Cox and Stevens because he did not have sufficient room. Most authorities agree that *Weetamoe* was the fastest of the spectacular fleet produced that year—the other three boats were *Enterprise*, *Whirlwind*, and *Yankee*, designed by Starling Burgess, L. Francis Herreshoff, and Frank Paine, respectively—but her consistent early success in the defender trials caused her owners to be conservative in their application of several potential improvements that were available to them, such as a lighter mast. The more aggressively campaigned *Enterprise* ultimately

won the right to defend the Cup with a spate of last-minute wins.

In the 1930's Crane's work helped to encourage the 12-Meter class in the United States. He designed *Gleam* for his own use, cruised extensively in her on the coast of Maine and elsewhere, and raced her at the highest levels. The class was eventually chosen to succeed the J-Class boats as the America's Cup Class, although at one time Crane suggested it was too small for that purpose. He said he would have preferred to use larger boats built to the CCA Rule—a path that, had it been taken, might have steered America's Cup competition in quite a different direction. *Gleam* is still sailing today.

Clinton Crane was president of the North American Yacht Racing Union and had a great deal to do with the formulation of the modern yacht racing rules. He is said to have been an advocate for old-fashioned sportsmanship rather than "the ends justify the means" approach. Crane loved designing racing yachts above all else, but during his professional design career it was the large cruising yachts that earned his living. He once said that he never created a racing boat that didn't cost him more to design than he was paid.   —Daniel B. MacNaughton

W. I. B. Crealock: Pacific Seacraft 37. The Pacific Seacraft 37 (previously the Crealock 37, introduced in 1974) helped to legitimize fiberglass construction and divided underbodies for offshore cruising. A considerable forward overhang, a versatile cutter rig, and a canoe stern set her apart from the crowd, but primarily she is a study in healthy moderation. *Photo courtesy Pacific Seacraft Corp.*

Francis Creger: Creger 32. Creger's catamarans of the 1950's and 1960's explored new ground and have distinctive streamlined shapes such as downward-curved sheers at the bows and a corresponding rapid rise at the sterns. The emphasis was on comfort, looks, and ease of handling. *Photo courtesy Claas van der Linde*

WILLIAM ION BELTON CREALOCK

Born August 23, 1920 · England/United States

Bill Crealock used his personal experiences sailing around the world to create a classic long-range cruising craft, the Crealock 37, in the early days of fiberglass boat production. Introduced in 1974, it's still in production (as the Pacific Seacraft 37) and in 2002 was inducted into the American Sailboat Hall of Fame at the Newport, Rhode Island–based Museum of Yachting. Writing for the Hall of Fame, author Greg Jones called the Crealock 37 "a classic American sailboat."

Born in England, Crealock developed an interest in sailing and design at an early age. He attended Glasgow University, studying naval architecture for two years before switching to studies in yacht design at a technical school in Glasgow. He served a five-year apprenticeship drawing freighters and other commercial craft, and spent some seven years bluewater sailing, crossing the Atlantic once and the Pacific three times, on vessels ranging up to 100 feet long.

Crealock ended up in southern California in the late 1950's, opening a small office in Newport Beach. In 1972, he moved to Carlsbad just north of San Diego, where he continues to practice.

In a career spanning more than four and one-half decades, Crealock has designed cruising sailboats for builders Pacific Seacraft (including the Dana series, Flicka, PSC-31, and Crealock 34 and 37), Excalibur, Columbia (including the Columbia 21 and 28), Clipper Marine, and Cabo Rico 45/47, 38, and 34/36. Custom designs included an 8-foot dinghy, a 90-foot brigantine, and a 100-foot catamaran. Crealock's early successes were the Westsail 42 and 43 and the famous Westsail 32, based on *Thistle*, a William Atkin design.

For the Crealock 37, Crealock focused on "design and control in the ultimate situation," as he put it. It featured a canoe stern for buoyancy and rough-water handling, a split underbody to reduce wetted surface area, and the cutter rig favored in the British Isles. It was an instant hit. *Fortune* magazine hailed it as one of one hundred American designs—not limited to yacht design—considered the best in the world.

Crealock is also the author of two books recording his youthful voyages, *Vagabonding Under Sail* and *Cloud of Islands.* —Steve Knauth

FRANCIS H. "SKIP" CREGER

February 2, 1920–December 5, 1999
United States

Skip Creger was an American catamaran pioneer who designed and built a large number of catamarans in Long Beach, California, during the 1950's and early 1960's. Building on his experience from many years of living in the Pacific, he constructed his first small catamaran in 1946, shortly before the Prout Brothers would do so in England and before Woody Brown and Manu Kai in Hawaii. His 16-foot Lear Cat, designed in 1950, and the 18-foot Sabre Cat, designed shortly after, were the first mass-produced beach catamarans in the United States and met with great success.

Creger's catamarans were easily constructed boats made of plywood sheets, with asymmetrical hulls and canoe sterns. Unusual for a multihull designer, speed was not an important consideration for Creger, who was more interested in ease of handling and seaworthiness. Thus, for his larger multihulls, such as the series-produced Creger 32 (before 1956), Creger 34, and Creger 40, he believed in the unusual theory of ballasting to improve seaworthiness and prevent capsizing.   —Claas van der Linde

SAMUEL STURGIS CROCKER

March 29, 1890–November 28, 1964
United States

Sam Crocker is best known for his small and medium-sized cruising sailboats, which were seldom radical in any way but often unique in character and easily distinguished from the work of other designers. Crocker boats tend to have a staunch, rugged look, based on a workboat heritage. Most seem comfortable, with a largely paint finish and simple, traditional hardware and details. Crocker seemed to know that part of the function of the appearance of a cruising boat is to reassure and bolster the confidence of her crew.

Many of Crocker's boats, such as the popular Amantha cutter, were beamy with plumb stems and wide transoms, showing some Cape Cod catboat influence, though they might be quite different in their other characteristics. Fourteen Amanthas were built by the Palmer Scott yard of New Bedford. Crocker was also very good with clipper-bowed yachts and was among the best designers of the raised-deck style of sailboats, with the popular Stone Horse, built by Edey and Duff, being one of the smallest and best examples and one of the few Crocker boats to be built of fiberglass.

Crocker was well liked by those who built his boats, not least of all because he had a thorough knowledge of boatbuilding methods and drew his plans with the builder in mind. One minor example of this is that he generally worked in ¾-inch = 1 scale (1:16), so that ¹⁄₁₆-inch on the drawings equaled 1 inch on the boat, making it easy to scale from the drawings with a standard ruler. The well-known builder and designer Bud McIntosh said Crocker was the best designer he ever worked with.

Study of the recent history of the Crocker family is complicated by the fact that all the first-born males are named Samuel Sturgis Crocker, with the generations alternating between the use of "Samuel" and "Sturgis" as a

first name. Born in Newton, Massachusetts, Sam Crocker studied naval architecture at MIT and graduated in 1911, after which he worked four years for naval architect George Owen of Newton. In the short period between 1916 and 1917 when the United States entered World War I, he designed, built, and repaired boats on his own at a small yard in Marion, Massachusetts.

During the war Crocker directed crews planking 110-foot subchasers being built at the Lawley yard in Neponset, Massachusetts. When the war ended, he helped to design and build flying boats with the firm of Murray and Tregurtha, including the NC-4, in 1919, the first seaplane to cross the Atlantic.

For the next five years, Crocker worked in the design office of John Alden in Boston, turning out many popular designs bearing a

distinct Crocker character, such as the Malabar Junior. In 1924 he opened his own office in Boston. Here his career began in earnest as he designed cruising and racing yachts and fishing craft. The fishing boats, trawlers, and seiners were known for their speed and carrying capacity.

While mostly a designer of sailboats, Crocker was also a successful powerboat designer. For many years he was an agent for several marine insurance firms.

Among Crocker's fast cruising yachts that were race winners was *Chantey*, winner of the New Bedford Race Week in 1930, 1931, and 1932; *Grey Gull II*, winner of the Bayside–Block Island Races in 1933 and 1934; and *Barbette*, winner of the Detroit-Mackinac Race in 1927 and 1929.

Crocker designed some larger cruising yachts, such as the 52-foot LOA cutter *Mercury*

Samuel S. Crocker: *Masconomo.* An example of Crocker's clipper-bowed designs, *Masconomo* is particularly interesting because he designed her for his own use. With a relatively slim hull, roomy decks resulting from a small cabin trunk, and a large cockpit, his emphasis seems to have been on daysailing. © *Peter Barlow*

Samuel S. Crocker: *Entre Nous.* The 30-foot Amantha cutter is one of Crocker's most popular designs, showing the influence of the Cape Cod catboat in her plumb stern and her beamy, wide-sterned hull, but combining it with a full keel, outside ballast, and a big cutter rig. *Photo courtesy Crocker's Boat Yard*

Samuel S. Crocker: Stone Horse. Crocker's design for the Stone Horse went through a series of evolutions before it became the popular raised-deck fiberglass boat so well known today, built by Edey and Duff. This wooden version shows a partial raised deck for comfort below, plus the large cockpit and good looks that combined to create broad appeal. *Photo courtesy Crocker's Boat Yard*

(1938) and the 48-foot 4-inch ketch *Sirius* (1936). A particularly successful design was for the 36-foot 8-inch LOA yawl *Milky Way* (1937). Crocker designed the schooner yacht *Mahdee*, which is said to be the first yacht with electric drive.

During both World War II and the Korean conflict, Crocker was resident designer at the Simms Brothers yard of Dorchester, Massachusetts, engaged in the construction of sub-chasers and aircraft rescue boats.

In 1956 Crocker moved to an office in his son S. Sturgis Crocker's boatyard in Manchester, Massachusetts, where he continued to work until he died in 1964, having designed 344 boats. The yard continues to be run by the Crocker family and specializes in building and repairing wooden boats.

The Crocker plans are at the Peabody Essex Museum in Salem, MA.

—Daniel B. MacNaughton

CROSBY FAMILY

Beginning in the mid-1770's · United States

H. Manley Crosby once told a reporter, "There's nothing like a good boat to make a man feel young again." To date, nine generations of the Crosby family, from 1760 through the present day, have participated in the family business. It has been estimated that more than twenty-five hundred boats have been built by the Crosbys over the course of two hundred years, and they are believed to be the longest-running boatbuilding family in the United States. The Crosbys began designing and building boats in the mid-1700's, when Jesse Crosby, a ship's carpenter in Centerville on Cape Cod, Massachusetts, trained his sons Nathan, Jesse Jr., and Daniel in the business. By 1798 all three sons had moved to two different locations in the neighboring village of Osterville, where they built schooners, packets, and workboats

for the local fishermen and sea captains.

According to a story handed down through the generations, around 1850 Andrew Crosby, Daniel's son, had a vision of a boat that would sail better than the narrow, unstable pinky types then being used by local fishermen. He began to design the new boat but died before it was completed. His sons, C. Worthington and Horace, struggled to complete the design and, through the help of their mother, Tirzah, were able to seek Andrew's advice through a séance.

The final result was a boat whose mast was placed far forward and carried one gaff-rigged sail, making for good speed in light air and easy handling in rough weather. Her beam was nearly half her length, providing good stability and plenty of room for a large fish well. The boys also included in the design a large "barn door" rudder for better steering, and a centerboard, for sailing in the Cape's shallow waters. When she was launched around 1850, a boatyard worker apparently exclaimed, "She comes about as quick as a cat," leading Horace and C. Worthington to name their design a catboat.

The Crosbys' design, called a Cape Cod catboat to distinguish it from narrower, sometimes deeper types that sprang up in other areas along the East Coast, became popular among the local fishermen. One of the designs, called the Chatham model, was ordered by over a hundred fishermen, for it proved ideal for working the local waters.

By the late 1800's, the Crosby brothers were joined by C. Worthington's sons, Daniel and Charles, and Horace's sons, Herbert F., Wilton, Joseph, and H. Manley. The family continued a trend toward larger catboats, which by that time were carrying summer sailing parties around the Cape Cod shoreline.

The late 1800's saw intense interest in catboat racing, and the Crosbys, now occupying six boatyards along the Osterville shoreline, began to design cats with a different look. *The Rudder* magazine stated in 1909 that "Daniel Crosby was the first to alter the accepted dimensions of the cat by increasing the proportion of the beam, building a boat 25 feet long and 11 feet 3 inches wide; before this the breadth of a boat that length had not exceeded 10 feet. This craft proved very successful and was at once copied."

Daniel's alterations to the former working catboat created enthusiasm for the virtues of Crosby designs far beyond the New England area, and orders started to come in from as far away as Canada, Cuba, and England. Collectively, the yards began to build up to seventy-five boats a year, and to accommodate the late-night hours, Wilton and H. Manley Crosby's shops were the first businesses on the Cape to be wired for electricity.

In 1914, after returning from a five-year stint designing and building boats in Brooklyn, New York, H. Manley Crosby designed and built the 25-foot Wianno Senior, a gaff-rigged

Crosby family: *Tang.* With her single large mainsail, plumb bow, wide beam, shoal draft, and an oval-front cabin trunk merging into an oval-backed coaming surrounding the deep and wide cockpit, *Tang* displays all the characteristics typical of a Cape Cod catboat, a type that the Crosby family of designers and builders helped originate. © *Peter Barlow*

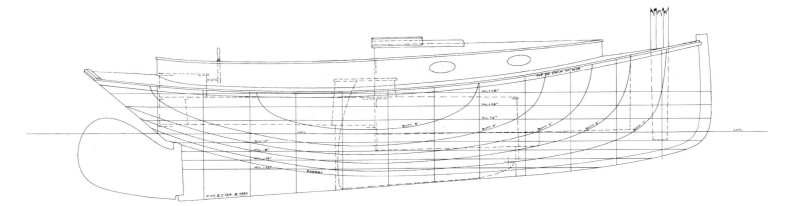

Herbert Crosby: *Gracie.* *Gracie* is believed to be the first catboat to sail in New York waters. Her success as a pleasure boat is said to have inspired her builder, Herbert Crosby, to begin building catboat yachts. Her inboard rudder and sloping transom are not especially typical. © *Chevalier & Taglang*

knockabout sloop using steam-bent oak frames instead of the sawn pitch pine customarily used at that time.

The Wianno Senior proved popular among racers on the Cape. One hundred and fifty-eight were built from 1914 to 1987, and the Wianno is now one of the few wooden one-design class boats still actively racing in the United States.

The Wianno Junior, a 16-foot open-cockpit sailboat, was commissioned by the local Wianno Yacht Club members for the junior racing crowd, and designer H. Manley and his family members built sixty-seven between 1922 and 1940.

Although the Crosbys are best known for their catboat and Wianno designs, they also designed and built powerboats, including the Striper, a chine-built 24-foot fishing boat, and the 34-foot Tuna. Several Crosby-designed boats, the Wianno Senior, the Striper, and the Fast Cat, originally built in wood, were later redesigned in fiberglass versions.

Presently, the only Crosby-run boatyard remaining is E. M. Crosby Boat Works in West Barnstable, Cape Cod, Massachusetts.

The Crosby designs were created by the half-model method. Any drafted plans that exist today were completed either by delineators outside the family or by Ralph Crosby, who received a degree in marine architecture from MIT and created plans after the fact.

Twenty-eight drawings representing sixteen designs are in the Crosby Yacht Building and Storage Company Collection at Mystic Seaport Museum, Mystic, CT. Four designs are also available through the Ship Plans List/Maritime Collection at the National Museum of American History, Smithsonian Institution, Washington, D.C.
—Carol Crosby

WILLIAM FLOWER CROSBY

1890–August 17, 1953 · United States

Widely known as the designer of the hugely popular Snipe One-Design, as editor of *The Rudder* and later *Motor Boat* magazine, and as a prolific writer, Bill Crosby achieved his goal of making sailing accessible to large numbers of people, many of whom were amateur builders.

Crosby was born in the Hudson River town of Newburgh, New York, and raised downriver in Nyack in a family fascinated by catboat rac-

William Crosby: *Phffft* (Opposite). The Snipe class helped prove to a wide range of yachtsmen that top-flight racing competition could be had in a practical small boat affordable by the average family. Its success helped to usher in a wide variety of other one-design classes. © *Peter Barlow*

ing. His influence on the field became tremendous when he was named editor of *The Rudder* in October 1928. Through *The Rudder* he supplied his readers with not only the inspiring larger yacht designs of the day but also designs for small boats suitable for amateur construction. His 1931 plan for the Snipe was one such design.

At 15 feet 6 inches LOA the Snipe is a hard-chine sloop raced by a crew of two. In 1959 the IYRU granted the Snipe recognition as an international class. By then, many thousands had been built worldwide, making it one of the most popular one-design classes of the time. The class is still popular and active.

Crosby also designed numerous other class boats, including the 17-foot National One-Design centerboard sloop, many designs intended for the do-it-yourself builder, and a number of powerboats, plus racing and cruising sailboats.

When the United States entered World War II in 1941, Crosby left *The Rudder* to work with Pembroke Huckins designing PT boats, and at the Gibbs Gas Engine Company, both in Jacksonville, Florida. Following the war and until his death at age sixty-two, Crosby was the editor of *Motor Boat* magazine.

Crosby will also be remembered for the books he wrote, including *Small Boat Racing* (1934), *Boat Sailing* (1935), and *Amateur Boat Building* (1938).

The William F. Crosby Collection is at Mystic Seaport Museum, Mystic, CT.
—Lucia del Sol Knight

NORMAN A. CROSS

July 13, 1915–August 14, 1990 · United States

A pioneer American West Coast designer of trimarans, Norm Cross was born in Toronto, Canada, but moved with his family to Detroit, Michigan, when he was a child. He worked for fifteen years as an aircraft engineer, gaining expertise in areas such as wind-tunnel model designs as well as structural analysis. Experience with Arthur Piver's trimarans led him to open a multihull design firm named Cross Trimarans in San Francisco. Eventually it sold more than seventeen hundred multihull plans, mostly for cruising trimarans, but also a few catamarans.

Cross's best-known designs were the Cross 36 (catamaran, 36 feet, 1961) and the following trimarans: Cross 30 (30 feet, before 1964), Cross 24 (24 feet, 1964), Cross 26 (26 feet, before 1966), Cross 42 (42 feet, 1966), Cross 37 (37 feet 2 inches, before 1967), Cross 18 (18 feet, before 1974), and Cross 32R (31 feet 9 inches, before 1975).

Norman Cross: Cross 36. Cross sailed on Arthur Piver–designed trimarans in the San Francisco Bay area before launching his own multihull design office. The Cross 36, designed in 1961, was the first trimaran designed by Cross. *Photo Courtesy Amateur Yacht Research Society*

Almost always his trimarans emphasized spacious accommodations over performance and elegance. They were typified by long, shallow fin keels, ketch rigs, and covered center cockpits. Following the example set by Piver, most of his designs were suitable for home boatbuilding in plywood, often with hull sections consisting of a right-angled V-shape with chines above the waterline, although some were designed with rounded sections to be built from curved sheet plywood. Cross also designed a few large racing trimarans, with *Crusader*, a Cross 52R (52 feet, 1979), being his best known.
—Claas van der Linde

GEORGE F. CROUCH

December 30, 1878–June 4, 1959
United States

George Crouch, a prominent designer of high-speed powerboats, was instrumental in the development of planing-hull forms. His *Peter Pan IV* of 1911 was apparently the first to utilize a concave V-bottom configuration in a high-speed runabout. Some of his most famous work was in stepped hydroplanes; he and his brother, the designer Albert Crouch, are credited with the invention of the "three-point" hydroplane in 1915. George Crouch's work included a number of fast and comfortable commuter yachts, and he also designed fast runabouts of displacement form.

Today his best-known boat is *Baby Bootlegger*, a magnificent, streamlined, varnished mahogany racing hydroplane that won the Gold Cup in 1924 and 1925 and was recently fully restored. Other well-known trophy winners were *Miss Columbia*, *Delphines*, *Miss Syndicate*, *Sister Syn*, and several boats named *Peter Pan*.

Born in Iowa, Crouch attended the University of Wisconsin and graduated from Webb Academy (now the Webb Institute) in 1901 with a degree in naval architecture. From 1901 to 1902 he was employed as a draftsman at the William Cramp and Sons Ship and Engine Building Company in Philadelphia. From 1902 to 1905, he was a draftsman at Tams, Lemoine, and Crane in New York. He then taught naval architecture at Webb and became its president in 1920. From 1923 to 1924 he ran his own design and consulting business. In 1924 his boats won first, second, and third places in the Gold Cup race. This was just the beginning of a long series of wins for Crouch's racing powerboats, on both short- and long-distance courses.

From 1924 to 1928, Crouch became vice president and chief designer of the Dodge Boat and Plane Company, first in Detroit, later in Newport News, Virginia, where he created many highly regarded runabouts and racing powerboats. He then worked for himself until becoming the resident naval architect at the Henry B. Nevins Shipyard of City Island,

New York, in 1932. He joined Saint Johns River Shipbuilding Company and was in charge of all naval architecture for the war effort between 1943 and 1945, designing the YMS class of minesweepers and contributing to the design of the famous PT boats.

Known for his articles on propellers and high-speed motorboats, Crouch was the technical editor of *Motor Boat* magazine for thirteen years and also wrote many articles for *Yachting* magazine, among others.

George Crouch retired in 1950 and died at age eighty in Connecticut.

Designs produced while Crouch was at Nevins are in the Henry B. Nevins, Inc., Shipyard Collection at Mystic Seaport Museum, Mystic, CT.

—Daniel B. MacNaughton

BOWDOIN BRADLEE CROWNINSHIELD

1867–August 12, 1948 · United States

One of America's preeminent designers of racing and cruising sailboats during the early part of the twentieth century, B. B. Crowninshield was also one of the strongest influences on the development of the Gloucester fishing schooner. He is best remembered for two one-design classes: the Dark Harbor 17½ (LWL), of which over two hundred were built between 1909 and the mid-1930's, and the Dark Harbor

12½ (LWL), a cabin-less version built beginning in 1915.

Crowninshield was born in New York to a wealthy family with strong seafaring roots. *Cleopatra's Barge*, said to be the first yacht in the United States, belonged to one of his ancestors. The family moved to Boston in 1868 and then to Marblehead in 1874, where young Crowninshield started sailing and racing, quickly achieving recognition for his skill, especially in "tuning up" a racing boat to her best speed potential.

After entering MIT in 1885, Crowninshield transferred to Harvard the next year and graduated in 1890. He spent some time in the western states, but returned to work at John R. Purdon's yacht design firm in 1896 and opened his own office in 1897 in Boston. He saw success with his earliest racing designs, especially *Mongoose*, a 21-foot knockabout whose good reputation resulted in a steady stream of orders from the beginning.

Crowninshield was one of the earliest designers to vigorously pursue the hull characteristics that fully separated the yacht hull form from its working-class ancestors. While cargo carriers, fishing vessels, and the yachts that evolved from them tended to have short ends, deep forefoots, long straight keels, heavy displacement, and V-shaped sections, Crowninshield's style generally tended toward long ends, dramatically cutaway underbodies, short finlike keels with all outside ballast, quite

George Crouch: *Baby Bootlegger.* Shown here at speed on flat water, you can see the concave V-bottom hull form that gave *Baby Bootlegger* her great speed. She won the Gold Cup in 1924 and 1925, achieving speeds of 48.4 mph. © Benjamin Mendlowitz

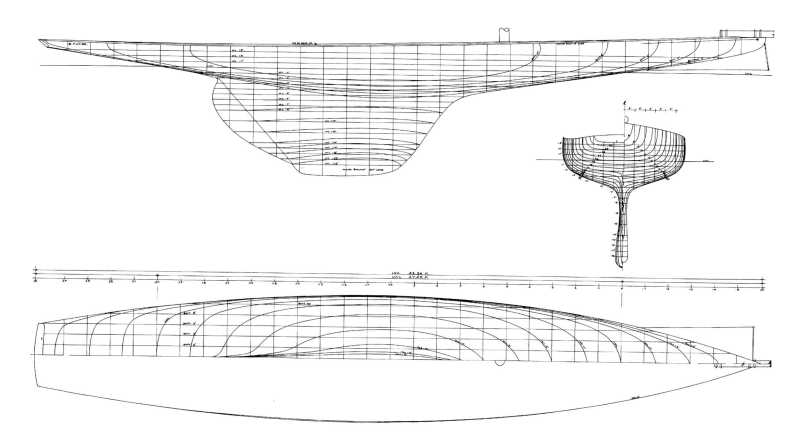

B. B. Crowninshield: *Independence.* A contender in the America's Cup defense trial of 1901, *Independence* shows the extreme, light, long-ended, flat-floored, deep-keeled, and heavily ballasted form that had become mandatory for success prior to the introduction of the Universal Rule. *Independence* lost to the N. G. Herreshoff–designed *Columbia.* © *Chevalier & Taglang*

light displacement, and U-shaped sections.

While there was nothing unseaworthy about the type, there is no question that the boats were optimized for inshore racing and cruising, with an emphasis on speed in smooth water and in light air. In those days of engineless coastal cruising, this "ghosting" ability contributed to both safety and convenience. In stronger winds it was a fast, wet, and exciting ride—maybe not a bad thing in those days before offshore voyaging and living aboard were common activities for yachts.

While yachts have always borrowed ideas from working vessels, Crowninshield was instrumental in passing some important concepts in the other direction. Prior to 1900, the Gloucester fishing schooners were of the clipper model, meaning that they sought the speed they needed to get to market by opting for shallow, beamy centerboard models (partly dictated by the shallow water of Gloucester Harbor) with a large sail area. This was exactly the wrong combination for the severe offshore weather they frequently encountered; they easily capsized and were hard to control, and there was great loss of life.

Crowninshield, his contemporary Thomas McManus, and others realized that while they weren't good workboats, the deep, narrow, outside-ballasted yachts of the day were

B. B. Crowninshield: *Quill II.* A rare survivor from the days before auxiliary engines, the 38-foot LOA *Quill II* displays the long-ended hull form typical of her era, along with her gaff yawl sail plan, a study in ease of handling for the engineless sailor. Launched in 1905, today *Quill II* sails out of Deer Isle, Maine. *Courtesy of Hart Nautical Collections, MIT Museum, Cambridge, MA*

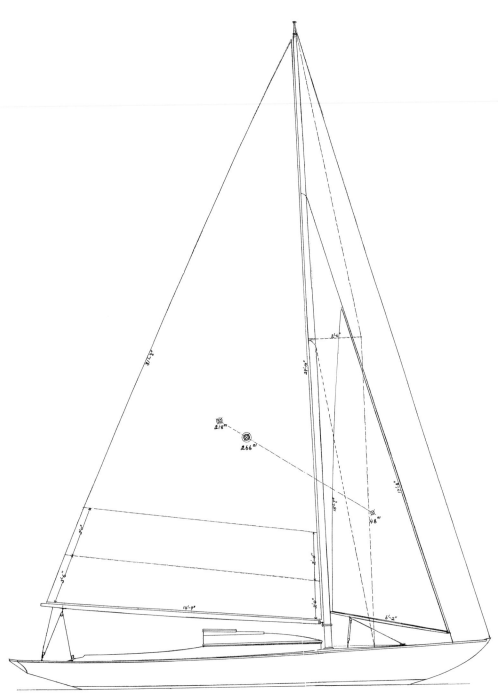

B.B. Crowninshield: Manchester 17½. This design differs from the better known Dark Harbor 17½ only in her marconi rig. One of the oldest surviving one-design classes in the United States, the gaff-rigged Dark Harbor is, like her near-sister, beautiful, fast, seaworthy, and wet. Dark Harbors are still sailing, largely in Maine waters. *Drawing courtesy Peabody Essex Museum, Salem, MA*

accepted norm. Crowninshield produced seventeen designs for fishing schooners, from which thirty vessels were built. The Crowninshield schooners had a particular exuberance to their lines which still contributes to their appeal.

Later designers such as William Hand and John G. Alden, both of whom began their careers in the Crowninshield office, recognized that the Gloucester form was easily adaptable to the newly popular sport of offshore yacht racing, and a whole generation of successful small schooner yachts resulted. Thus Crowninshield was involved in passing yacht ideas to commercial use, and then back again, in an example of vigorous and healthy evolution in design.

Few Crowninshield boats survive. The commercial sailing vessels suffered their inevitable fate when inboard engines changed their economic environment, changes in handicapping rules made the racing boats similarly obsolete, and a new emphasis on offshore comfort combined with the influence of auxiliary power created wholly different types of cruising boats.

While many of the Crowninshield boats were very carefully constructed, the engineering of lightweight hulls was not well understood at the time. The resulting flexibility accelerated the aging process, and this was undoubtedly exacerbated by the frequent, well-meaning replacement of the old gaff rigs with marconi sail plans generating new and unanticipated stresses on the hulls. However, enough boats do survive to demonstrate that few have ever drawn a prettier boat in the old-style, long-ended form than B. B. Crowninshield.

Besides the types already mentioned, Crowninshield designed vessels as disparate as racing canoes and cargo schooners, including the *Thomas W Lawson*, the only seven-masted schooner ever built. Thomas Lawson himself was a wealthy New York speculator who despite the fact that his namesake schooner was not an economic success, financed the design and construction of *Independence*, Crowninshield's attempt at an America's Cup defender in 1901. Unfortunately *Independence* was not a success, partly due to structural problems.

Among well-known surviving Crowninshield boats are the small schooner *Heron*, believed to sail in New Jersey, the yawl *Quill II*, the Dark Harbor 17½-foot (LWL) class, and the Dark Harbor 12½-foot (LWL) class, all located in Maine.

The Crowninshield plans are at the Peabody Essex Museum in Salem, MA.

—Daniel B. MacNaughton

uncapsizeable, and no matter how much they might punish their crews, they could maintain control and reach high speeds in heavy weather. Application of these yacht-based ideas to schooner design produced vessels of what is now known as the Gloucester schooner type, vessels that have been called "the finest and fastest fore and afters that ever sailed the seas."

Like a yacht, the Gloucester schooners had a cutaway forward and a deep, abbreviated finlike keel with strong drag and a raked rudder post. Unlike the inshore yachts, they were very V-shaped forward for driving

through heavy seas, and they were heavy so as to accommodate the catch they were bringing home. Crowninshield also introduced a straight line to the base of the keel, in profile, which made it safer and easier to haul the schooners, compared to the rounded profile common in yachts.

It would have been easy to design a more comfortable offshore vessel, but probably not one that would get to and from the distant Grand Banks and other fishing grounds with such a combination of safety and speed. Gloucester Harbor was dredged to permit the new type's deeper draft, and it became the

LOCK CROWTHER

September 9, 1940–September 28, 1993
Australia

Born in Melbourne, Victoria, Lock Crowther was one of a number of Australian designers who showed early signs of prowess through a passion for model aircraft design. He studied electrical engineering but soon turned his attentions to multihull yacht design, influenced by his father, Jack, who had lived in the Caribbean and been impressed with the speed of native outriggers.

To the area of multihull design, Crowther applied innovations such as foam sandwich construction and drag-reducing bulbous bows. He produced a string of racing boats, but he also had an interest in cruisers. Despite his extensive theoretical knowledge, he applied a strong practical slant to his work. With all his work he always relied heavily on testing, which took place on the water.

When Crowther was nineteen, he designed and constructed his first trimaran, the 20-foot *Bunyip*, which won a regatta in his home state of Victoria. It was the start of a career in which he would become one of Australia's pioneering multihull experts and in which he would eventually design a line of racing and cruising multihulls over a thirty-year period.

After graduating with a degree in electrical engineering, Crowther drew the Kraken 25 *Jabberwock*, which went on to win almost all of her two hundred races, proving a great early boost to his career. Soon after, he designed the racing trimaran *Bandersnatch*, which won the inaugural Sydney-to-Hobart multihull event in 1966.

In 1969 Crowther designed the Kraken 40 and sailed it to an easy win in the Newport to Bermuda multihull race. Then in 1972 he made a significant contribution to the overall perception of multihull sailing in the eyes of the Australian public when he comfortably won the Brisbane-Gladstone Race in another Kraken 40, *Captain Bligh*, through Cyclone Emily.

An attempt to move into boatbuilding was unsuccessful, though even here Crowther made a contribution of note, developing the first trimaran to use a gull-wing crossbeam shape. Other boats of note included *Bagatelle* (the first cat to use a massive beam-length ratio), *D Flawless*, and *Shotover*, which was the Brisbane (New South Wales)-Gladstone (Queensland) Race record holder from 1982 until 1993. Then the record went to another Crowther multihull, the 39-foot XL2, which averaged 14.8 knots over the 310-nautical-mile course.

Crowther also designed the trimaran *Bullfrog/Verbatim*, initially sailed by experienced

Lock Crowther: *Deguello*. *Deguello* was the Crowther family's own cruising yacht, pictured here off Balls Pyramid near Lord Howe Island, in the middle of the Tasman Sea. Good oceangoing capabilities were an integral part of Crowther's design philosophy. *Photo courtesy Crowther Family*

Australian offshore sailors Cathy Hawkins and Ian Johnston. This multihull competed in the Transpac, the Trans-Tasman, and the 1988 Round Australia shorthanded race, among others.

Cruising multihulls to Crowther's designs included the Catana 40 and the Spindrift series (of which over 150 were built). In 1989 he launched his own 46-foot cat *Deguello*. It was aboard this craft that he died of a heart attack while sailing north from Sydney towards the Great Barrier Reef, a fitting end for a man of great humor who enjoyed all his moments on the water. After his death, his son Brett took over the Crowther design office in Newport, New South Wales, and Brett remains active in the field.

—Robert Keeley

ROBERT D. "PETE" CULLER

1909–1978 · United States

During his fifty-year career, Captain Pete Culler designed and built scores of traditional wooden vessels, ranging from skiffs and dories to a 91-foot coasting schooner. His commonsense approach, self-effacing style, and simple philosophy earned him a place in the wooden boat movement that began in the 1960's, a reaction to the advent of fiberglass boat production. Known as "Pete" or "Cap'n Pete," he also authored three books.

Born in upstate New York, Culler started his career early, learning the trade from commercial sailors and boatbuilders in the waning days of sail. In 1929, he served as apprentice to a Maryland master shipwright in the construction of his own boat, a replica of Joshua Slocum's *Spray*. Culler used her for many years, calling her a testimony to "simple, honest materials and good workmanship."

The 52-foot schooner *Integrity*, based on a nineteenth-century packet, is another notable Culler design, built in 1962 while he worked for the Concordia Company. *Integrity* was company founder Waldo Howland's family boat for many years.

Culler also designed the ill-fated *John F. Leavitt*, a 91-foot coasting schooner launched in Maine in 1979, as the first commercial freight carrier built in that region in forty years. She was abandoned at sea in a winter gale during her maiden voyage.

Among Culler's favorite boats were the small craft of the harbor—flat- and file-bottom skiffs, and carvel and lapstrake rowing and sailing craft—which inspired him as a guiding force behind the creation of the Traditional Small Craft Association. Through the organization, he encouraged others to follow in his footsteps. "It's only a boat: go ahead and build it," he would say.

When Culler died in 1978, *WoodenBoat* magazine editor Jon Wilson acknowledged Culler's "commitment to beauty and simplicity on the water." Culler leaves behind his books, which are known for their clarity, common sense, and old-fashioned philosophy ("Experience starts when you begin" is a Culler favorite). They include *Skiffs and Schooners, Spray: Building and Sailing a Replica of Joshua Slocum's Famous Vessel*, and *Boats, Oars and Rowing*. In his introduction to *Skiffs and Schooners*, he wrote, "If I have produced anything, however small, of further use to the World of Boats, it will make my efforts worthwhile."

—Steve Knauth

Pete Culler: *Joseph W. Russell.* Culler's small schooner designs, based on coasting schooners rather than fishermen, are easily distinguished. Mainsail booms don't extend very far over the transom and the foresail is not a great deal smaller than the main. Hulls are voluminous, with large and dramatic bows and sterns. © *Peter Barlow*

CHARLES CUNNINGHAM
Died 1986
LINDSAY CUNNINGHAM, OAM
Born 1934

Australia

As the designer of the world's fastest sailboat, *Yellow Pages Endeavour*, Lindsay Cunningham is notable for that feat alone, but the achievement is all the more remarkable because he has had no formal training in yacht design. Cunningham was introduced to yachting by his father, Charles. Together they designed twenty-five catamarans in different classes and raced them on Port Phillip Bay in Victoria.

In the early 1950's, Lindsay and Charles Cunningham were catamaran-design pioneers in Australia. The 20-foot cat Yvonne of 1953,

All subsequent designs were codesigned by father and son, including X.Y. 16, a 16-foot cat designed before 1963; Astral 20 cat, before 1963; Allouette 35-foot cat, before 1971; and the famous C-Class catamarans.

The greatest of catamaran classes is the massive International C-Class, the fastest around-the-buoys sailboats in the world. As codesigner and helmsman, Lindsay won the C-Class world championship in 1966 sailing his *Quest II*, and the design for this high-tech class helped Australia lead the world in the International Catamaran Challenge Trophy (or "Little America's Cup"). *Quest III, Victoria 150,* and *Edge I, II,* and *III* all regained or defended the trophy for Australia between 1970 and 1996, employing various wing-sail and part-wing-sail rigs. All these boats were designed in Lindsay's spare time, while he worked for the national telephone company (Cunningham was educated as an electrical engineer). Following Charles's death in 1986, and Lindsay's retirement in 1989, Lindsay continued to design catamarans.

The pinnacle of Lindsay's design career came when he created the extraordinary sailing machine *Yellow Pages Endeavour,* current holder of the World Outright B- and C-Class sailing speed records. The 12-meter-long vessel is essentially just three small planing hulls joined by carbon fiber and Nomex cored beams, supporting a 12-meter-high asymmetrical wing-sail. It set a record of 46.52 knots in 1993.

In 1999 Lindsay Cunningham was made a Member of the Order of Australia for his services to yachting.

—David Payne with Claas van der Linde

PHILIP EDWARD CURRAN

Born November 23, 1946 · Australia

Like many other designers, Phil Curran is self-taught. He came to naval architecture on a whim and has since relied on a natural eye and aptitude to create a wide range of power vessels from 5 to 55 meters in length, in collaboration with others and through his own company, Computer Design Marine.

Curran's family operated commercial fishing trawlers off Albany in Western Australia, and he soon became involved in yacht racing at Perth. Although an electrician by trade, he started designing boats with a commission from "a friend of a friend" for a 49-foot (14.94-meter) steel cruising yacht.

In 1978, Curran designed a production powerboat, the Deepwater 28, of which some forty were built. There then followed a succession of

Lindsay Cunningham: *Yellow Pages Edge.* Designed in Cunningham's spare time, the Class C catamaran *Yellow Pages Edge* was a successful candidate for the Little America's Cup. Note the wing sails that are standard fare for the Class C cats. © *Robert Keeley*

designed by Charles, was truly a groundbreaking beach catamaran, earlier than the equally groundbreaking Shearwater in Europe (1964) and Hobie Alter of the United States in 1968. Over five hundred Yvonnes were built. Another design by Charles was the 16-foot cat Quick Cat of 1955; over twenty-five hundred Quick Cats were built. Even today you can still see Yvonnes and Quick Cats sailing in Australia.

gamefishing cruisers for Western Australia–based builder Precision Marine, ranging from 37 feet (11.28 meters) to 65 feet (19.81 meters). The 17-meter model was named Australian Powerboat of the Year by *Modern Boating* magazine in 1986, as was the Precision 40 in 1988.

Internationally, Curran is best known for his motoryacht designs created in concert with Jon Bannenberg for Oceanfast Marine—Curran provides the hull envelope, Bannenberg styles the superstructure and interior. Their first collaboration, *Never Say Never*, was considered the world's first genuine high-speed motoryacht in the luxury class.

Curran credits his ocean racing experience for giving him a fresh approach to powerboat hull design. Indeed, he says that another of his renowned motoryachts, *Oceania*, resembles the classic Alan Gurney–designed racing maxi *Windward Passage* in its underwater form.

Through Computer Design Marine in Henderson, Western Australia, Curran has developed a wide range of aluminum powerboat designs available as kits for both professional and amateur builders. The kits provide either all of the precut components or solely the software.

Curran is recognized by the Australian Chapter of the Royal Institute of Naval Architects and is also a member of the Society of Naval Architects and Marine Engineers and the Institute of Marine Engineers. He is a recipient of the Prince Philip Duke of Edinburgh design award, four separate Australian Design Awards, and a *ShowBoat International* award.
—Mark Rothfield

ALEXANDER CUTHBERT

(Dates unknown) · Canada

Both the fourth and fifth challenges for the America's Cup came from Canada in 1876 and 1881, and both yachts were designed and built by Alexander Cuthbert, of Cobourg, Ontario.

Cuthbert was a skilled racing skipper and builder who designed by evolved "rule-of-thumb" methods rather than the more scientific processes that would soon dominate the field. He was an advocate of the shoal-draft American centerboard type. His first Cup challenger was the schooner *Countess of Dufferin*, which he skippered in the unsuccessful 1876 match sailing against the Joseph van Deusen–designed *Columbia. Atalanta*, his second challenger, was the first sloop to challenge for the Cup. She was defeated in the 1881 races by *Mischief*, a sloop designed by David Kirby.
—Daniel B. MacNaughton

GEORGE CUTHBERTSON

Born 1929 · Canada

Cofounder of famed C&C Yachts, George Cuthbertson was born in Ontario, Canada, and moved to Toronto at the age of thirteen. He joined the Royal Canadian Yacht Club (RCYC) as a junior member, learned to sail, and acquired an interest in boats, which became his life's work. After graduating as an engineer from the University of Toronto in 1950, and at the behest of some RCYC members, he worked on the Club's 8-Meter fleet, modifying and redesigning a class that dated back to the early years of the twentieth century. His task was to produce a yacht that would return the Canada's Cup to Toronto after forty-five years in American hands. In 1954, success was achieved with the 8-Meter *Venture II*, one of the boats that he had redesigned. His yacht brokerage and design company stood on firm ground.

With this success, Cuthbertson was commissioned to design the 54-foot yawl *Inishfree*, which won the Freeman Cup four times between 1959 and 1963. George Cassian (1933–1980) bought into the fledgling business in 1961 and the firm of Cuthbertson and Cassian was formed. Other commissions followed in the United States and Canada, culminating in the masthead sloop *Red Jacket*, "the meanest, hungriest 40-footer afloat."

George Cuthbertson: *Red Jacket*. Launched in 1966, *Red Jacket* won eleven of thirteen starts in her first year, including the Freeman Cup and the Lake Ontario International. The first ever balsa-cored racer then became the first Canadian boat to win the SORC in 1967. *Photo courtesy George Cuthbertson*

George Cuthbertson: *Signor Rizzoli.* The largest yachts in series production at the time, eight C&C 61's were built by Erik Bruckmann for American and European owners. Their "first-to-finish" performances included the 1972 heavy-weather upwind Bermuda Race (won by *Robob*), Marblehead-Halifax and Annapolis-Newport Races (won by *Sorcery*), both Mackinacs, and many corrected time wins, particularly on the Great Lakes, in the SORC, and overseas. *Photo courtesy George Cuthbertson*

In 1965, *Red Jacket* was a highly innovative design with a balsa wood core to lighten her weight. Her fin keel and underbody were especially designed to reduce drag and her tall sail plan made her very fast in light winds. Success came with her first season (1966) when she won eleven of the thirteen races in which she entered, including the Freeman Cup, the Lake Ontario International, and the Prince of Wales Cup. In the following year, she spent a season with the SORC off Florida. Against a ninety-five-boat field, she won three first places and a second, and in 1968 was the first non-U.S. yacht to win the overall championship in the SORC. The success of *Red Jacket* made Cuthbertson famous in North American yachting circles. This achievement was crowned by lively sales of two production yachts that he had also designed.

By 1969, a venture combining Cuthbertson and Cassian with three Ontario boatbuilders (Ian Morch of Belleville Marine Yard, George Hinterhoeller of Hinterhoeller Ltd., and Eric Bruckman of Bruckmann Manufacturing) created C&C Yachts. The production company was listed on the Toronto Stock Exchange in 1969, the "big year" for Cuthbertson. Besides the company listing, all three of the Canada Cup contenders in that year came from the drawing boards of C&C Yachts, including the winner, the 39-foot sloop *Manitou*.

Led by Cuthbertson, C&C did exceptionally well during the 1970's and 1980's. Its design team built an enviable reputation for fast, innovative yachts that were aesthetically pleasing and comfortable cruisers. By 1972, about a third of the boats taking part in the SORC races were built by C&C, and some seven thousand hulls

were sold in the United States alone (about 20 percent of the annual U.S. market for several years). These included half a dozen "61's," then the largest yacht available from a fiberglass mold. All the 61's performed impressively; one was even impounded for drug running.

For Cuthbertson, racing success was surpassed by the business success of C&C Yachts and the many thousands of its yachts sailing worldwide. His one regret was that he never had the opportunity to design a 12-Meter yacht to compete in the America's Cup.

C&C was sold in 1982, and Cuthbertson moved on to other activities. In 1974, he was elected an academician of the Royal Canadian Academy of Art. He is a member of the Toronto-based Antique and Classic Boat Society. He lives and works in southern Ontario.

—Tom Roach

D

OSCAR WILHELM DAHLSTRÖM

1876–1962 · Finland/Denmark

Practicing as both a yacht designer and a building architect, the first yacht Oscar Dahlström drew was the 22-Square-Meter *Singlan*, in 1916 at the age of forty. He was born in Vaasa, Finland, on the Gulf of Bothnia, and studied at a technical school. At Helsinki University, he studied to be a teacher.

Instead of teaching in Finland, Dahlström moved to Denmark in 1903. By 1908 he had been educated as an architect, and applied for and was granted Danish citizenship. In the 1920's, self-educated in yacht design, he drew eight 6-Meters, as well as other boat types, including the large schooner *Ragna* and the ketch *Akela*. —Bent Aarre

NORMAN EDWARD DALLIMORE

1883–1959 · England

Norman Dallimore spent his working life at Burnham-on-Crouch on the east coast of England, where he produced a range of designs for cruising yachts and daysailers. He was born and brought up in London and was introduced to sailing by his half-brother on an 18-foot cutter kept in Burnham.

Dallimore worked at the Burnham Yachtbuilding Company under the guidance of designers Harry C. Smith and Gilbert U. Laws before commencing his independent design career in about 1905. Burnham acquired a reputation for 6-Meter racers; Dallimore's contribution in 1909 was a gunter-rigged sloop. Later in his career he was influential in converting sail plans to the modern Bermudian rig. Dallimore also contributed entries to design competitions, and in 1913 won the *Yachting Monthly* prize for a 22-foot LOA, gunter-rigged daysailer.

During World War I Dallimore served as Royal Naval Volunteer Reserve Lieutenant. He moved to back Burnham in 1918 and com-

Norman Dallimore: *Bandor.* Built by William King and Sons at Burnham-on-Crouch in 1938, *Bandor* has the pretty sheer and graceful ends that typify her designer's work. *Photo courtesy Will Dallimore*

bined the designing of yachts with an insurance career in London.

The majority of Dallimore's designs were produced in the period between 1919 and 1939, during which he was an avid sailor and gifted helmsman. He developed a distinctive style encompassing both deep-draft and shoal-draft centerboard cruising yachts, motorsailers, and motor cruisers. He also designed several racing craft, including a one-design in 1932 for the Royal Burnham Yacht Club, where he was the official handicapper from 1928 until 1955. He was also in demand as a yacht surveyor.

Among his cruising designs were the 50-foot *Daffodil* of 1928 (the first Bermudian-rigged staysail schooner built in the United Kingdom), the 37-foot *Bandor* (1938), and the Brankiet Class (22-foot sloops built by Stebbings at Burnham). The largest vessel built to his design

was the 60-foot *Blue Trout*, built by Kings of Burnham in 1937, and the smallest, a canoe, *Mascot*, in 1910.

The Dallimore Owners Association is headquartered in Burnham. —Brian Smith

KENNETH S. M. DAVIDSON

February 8, 1898–March 19, 1958
United States

Probably the most important nondesigner in the field of yacht design during the twentieth century, Kenneth Davidson took the lead role in advancing the profession from a state of mostly art to one of mostly science, in which systematic experiment replaced guesswork.

The son of musicians, Davidson as a boy learned to play the piano and to sail, and he enjoyed making models of boats and airplanes. After his freshman year at MIT, he joined the army and became a pilot in World War I. Returning to MIT, he graduated with a degree in mechanical engineering and in his spare time built model boats and raced them on the Charles River. He worked in engineering firms for several years before joining the faculty of the Stevens Institute of Technology in Hoboken, New Jersey. (Stevens was founded by Edwin Stevens, a member of the *America* syndicate in 1851.)

Interested in understanding scientifically how sailboats worked, Davidson hooked 3-foot models of hulls to a spring scale and towed them in swimming pools. According to his daughter, Anne, this work reflected his fascination with music, sailing, and flight. "My father had a passionate interest in movement. He cared about how things moved. He had that kind of musical-scientific mind."

Since the late eighteenth century, large models had been towed in water tanks in an attempt to measure the design's resistance and to predict the finished boat's performance. In the 1870's, William Froude, an Englishman, came up with new methods and identified two distinct types of drag: frictional and wavemaking. While subsequent work with models of naval and commercial ships was successful, model testing of the 1901 America's Cup challenger *Shamrock II* by the English yacht designer George L. Watson had a disappointing result. In 1932 Davidson approached twenty-four-year-old Olin Stephens for assistance. With Rod Stephens, they tested a 34-foot Sparkman and Stephens sloop, *Gimcrack,* and her model. From the data they acquired, they developed mathematical coefficients that allowed reliable comparisons between models and finished boats.

Because Davidson's models were much smaller than those used in other tanks (about 4 feet long and displacing less than 80 pounds, rather than 20 feet long and displacing tons), model testing at Stevens Institute was inexpensive enough to be used for many pleasure boats. With the design of a $10,000 6-meter yacht capable of being tested for about five hun-dred dollars, many successful hulls built to this competitive international racing class were first tried out in the tank. A 6-meter sailor, Seward Johnson, funded the construction of a dedicated towing tank at Stevens Institute. Other designers who used the tank included men as experienced as Clinton Crane and as new to the game as A. E. Luders Jr. Davidson described his breakthrough work in an influential article, "Some Experimental Studies of Sailing Yachts," published in *Transactions of the Society of Naval Architects and Marine Engineers* (November 1936).

Olin Stephens would later say that his success was due in large part to Davidson's work. He credited Davidson with three major contributions to sailing yacht design: "He made very small models useful. He also was the first to understand the effect of leeway as it resulted in induced drag (i.e., the need to measure side force and its effect) and, lastly, he undertook the quantitative, scientific measurement and logical treatment of sail forces. Putting these things together, he could compute the estimated windward speed of any boat for which he had a model." Such an estimate is now known as a velocity prediction program (VPP) and is done by computer and sometimes by model testing.

The role of model testing was often misunderstood. "*Ranger* has been incorrectly called a tank project," claimed Harold Vanderbilt, the owner/skipper of the outstanding 1937 America's Cup defender designed by Starling Burgess with contributions by Olin Stephens. "Actually she was produced by her designer and selected by the tank. The tank was of inestimable value to us, for it told us what not to do, what not to build. Above all, it pointed to a beautiful creation—'Build this,' it said, 'and build it intact. Do not change it in any respect, lest you spoil it.' " *Ranger*'s success firmly established model testing at Stevens

Kenneth S. Davidson: Towing tank dynamometer. In this photograph taken in the mid-1930's at the towing tank at the Stevens Institute of Technology, Hoboken, N.J., Kenneth Davidson (center), the developer of small model testing, describes the dynamometer that, by measuring longitudinal and side forces as the model is towed down the tank, allowed the performance of a full-scale yacht to be predicted. Standing behind Davidson is Drake S. Sparkman, partner of the yacht designer Olin J. Stephens II, who worked closely with Davidson on model testing. *Photo courtesy Anne S. Davidson*

Institute as a design tool for many racing boats and for cruising boats intended to sail well, especially upwind.

Davidson, an enthusiastic sailor who kept a wooden boat off the house he built on Isle au Haut, Maine, raced in some boats that his tank tested. In World War II his scientific interests spread to other areas as the Stevens tank (later renamed the Davidson Laboratory) was used for warships, including aircraft carriers. He subsequently served as a science advisor to the government in a number of areas. At the time of his death in Paris, France, he was chief science advisor to the North Atlantic Treaty Organization. A major award of the Society of Naval Architects and Marine Engineers is named for him. —John Rousmaniere

LAURIE DAVIDSON, OM

Born 1928 · New Zealand

Laurie Davidson is one of the international "Big Three" of New Zealand yacht design (the others being Bruce Farr and Ron Holland). He has the distinction of having seen the IOR modified several times in direct response to the success of his designs, and with Doug Peterson he headed the design team that produced America's Cup winners for New Zealand in 1995 and 2000. For the 2002–03 America's Cup, he teamed up with Bruce Nelson and Phil Kaiko for the OneWorld Challenge by the Seattle (Washington) Yacht Club. The Swiss boat *Alinghi* won that year.

Davidson was born in Dargaville, northwest of Auckland on New Zealand's North Island. When the family moved to Auckland, the first boat Davidson crewed on at age thirteen was in the Arch Logan–designed, 12-foot Silver Fern class. He moved into the traditional, clinker-built, 18-foot M-Class, and at the start of the 1947–48 season created mayhem within the class when he designed and launched the radical *Myth*. So successful was this first in a new generation of M-Class boats that one group of owners tried to buy *Myth* from Davidson with the intention of burning her.

While working as an accountant, Davidson continued to design M-Class boats and was dominating the class by the time he abandoned accountancy in 1969 to join an Auckland-based ferrocement boatbuilding operation. A year later he was commissioned to design the Half-Tonner *Blitzkrieg*. Davidson himself took the helm to win the inaugural New Zealand Half-Ton championship, and the die was cast: he would become a full-time designer. He became the first New Zealand yacht designer to hold the IOR on computer.

Laurie Davidson: *Shockwave*. Freed from any rule considerations, in 2001 Davidson drew an elegant lightweight hull for this inshore racer. *Photo courtesy Bob Ross*

IOR designs began to push Davidson into the international spotlight, including the Half-Tonner *Tramp*, the 1972 Sydney-Hobart class winner *Unicorn*, and the Admiral's Cup team candidate *Snow White*. Nonrating boats were also boosting his reputation. In 1973 came the popular M20 fiberglass production trailer yacht. The Davidson 28 followed, and in 1974 when a Davidson 31 went into production, the builders already had orders for twenty.

In 1976 Davidson returned to the Ton classes with *Fun*, a radical trailable Quarter-Tonner. The offshore season of 1978 was to finally establish him as one of the best rule-boat designers in the world. *Pendragon* won the

Three-Quarter-Ton Cup in Victoria, British Columbia, and *Waverider* won the Half-Ton Cup off Poole, England.

Waverider's success topped a year of victories for Davidson designs throughout the world, but it was too much for the rule makers. An amendment to the IOR followed, *Waverider* was modified to meet the changes, and a year later off Scheveningen, Holland, it became the first yacht ever to win the Half-Ton cup twice. *Pendragon* was also modified—and won the One-Ton Cup off Newport, Rhode Island. Again the rule makers acted against what they deemed "an unhealthy trend towards ultra-light displacement." *Pendragon*'s rating was increased and the revision was quickly dubbed "the anti-Davidson rule."

Meanwhile, *Stormrider*, a trailer yacht based on the design of *Pendragon*, won the New Zealand 780 class championship in 1979, 1980, and 1981. A 44-footer for Los Angeles and the immensely popular Cavalier 37 production cruiser for Australia boosted Davidson's reputation even further, and the 46-foot aluminum *Shockwave* (1980) won all five of her races in D-Class of the Clipper Cup series in 1980. Once more the rule makers reacted with a change to increase *Shockwave*'s rating.

Davidson's 50-foot *Outward Bound* competed in the 1985–86 Whitbread Round the World Race and took Small Boat honors. Other designs have included the 50-foot San Francisco Big Boat series winner *Great Fun* (1981); the stock Davidson 35 (1981); a 36-foot and a 34-foot sports racer, plus the 51-foot *Jumping Jack Flash* (all 1982); the Davidson 40 and Cavalier 45 production yachts; the 46-foot *Samasan*; and 34-, 37-, and 40-foot production cruising yachts for an Australian company.

Davidson joined Bruce Farr, Russell Bowler, and Ron Holland on the first New Zealand America's Cup challenge (the 1987 series off Fremantle, Australia), but he never quite saw eye-to-eye with syndicate boss Michael Fay. He had nothing to do with the 1988 "Big Boat" challenge or the 1992 series, which were Farr efforts.

For the 1995 campaign that was to bring the America's Cup to New Zealand, Davidson headed a design team that included Doug Peterson and David Alan-Williams, with Tom Schnackenberg as design coordinator. Although the syndicate always stressed teamwork, it was no secret that the overall design concept and characteristic "canoe" shape of *Black Magic* was the work of Laurie Davidson. *Black Magic* beat Dennis Connors's *Young America* 5 to 0.

He then headed the design team for the successful 2000 defense of the Cup, and at the end of the series *Black Magic* had not been beaten around a mark in ten consecutive Cup races. Just prior to this victory Davidson was named a Companion of the New Zealand Order of Merit for his services to yachting.

A few months after the successful defense, Davidson left Team New Zealand to lead the Seattle Yacht Club syndicate One World in the 2003 America's Cup. While not succeeding to win the Louis Vuitton Challenger Cup race, Davidson sets his sights on the next Cup race in 2005–06.   —David Pardon

CHARLES GERARD DAVIS

1870–January 25, 1959 · United States

Charles Davis was a highly regarded itinerant yacht designer, an influential author of How-to-Build magazine articles that greatly contributed to the first boom in homebuilt boats early in the twentieth century, and a gifted artist. He worked from roughly 1889 until about 1931, when the Great Depression put him—and many others—out of the yacht design business.

Born in Poughkeepsie, New York, Davis gained early cruising and racing experience first on the Hudson River and then on Long Island Sound. In 1889, at age nineteen, he began an apprenticeship in the office of designer William Gardner, a position that he held until 1892, when his eyes became strained from drafting. He then shipped out as a seaman for voyages on two sailing vessels. His many sketches from this period appear in his book *Ways of the Sea*, published in 1930.

Editor Thomas Fleming Day of *The Rudder* hired Davis in 1895 as a technical writer and design editor. Davis introduced the long-running series of How-to-Build articles, which added much to *The Rudder*'s popularity by

Laurie Davidson: *NZL 61.* Davidson mastered the America's Cup Class rule better than anyone when defending the cup in 2000. *NZL 61* dominated Italy's *Prada*, being ahead at all marks and having an edge in speed that was apparent from the first leg of Race 1. © *Terry Fong, AFA Photography*

making a variety of small craft both understandable and available to average people. During this period Davis designed the famous *Lark,* a light, fast, simplified, 16-foot cat-rigged scow aimed at *The Rudder'*s home boatbuilding audience and very much an ancestor of today's small craft such as Lasers and Sunfish.

Davis worked for the C. C. Hanley boatyard in Quincy, Massachusetts, in 1899 and 1900, and for the Electric Launch Company (Elco) of Bayonne, New Jersey, from 1901 to 1905. In 1903 Forest and Stream Publishing Company published Davis's book, *How to Build a Launch from Plans.* The book was influential in the early motorboating scene and served to explain basic principles of boatbuilding, yacht design, and gasoline engines to the general public. From 1908 to 1913 (according to the magazine, though a Davis resume says 1905 to 1910), he joined the new magazine *Motor Boat,* continuing his How-to-Build articles and maintaining his great popularity.

In 1906, *The Rudder* published Davis's book, *How to Design a Yacht,* an appealing and easily understood treatment full of his wonderful pen-and-ink sketches. The original edition was entirely hand-lettered throughout. Along with Norman Skene's *Elements of Yacht Design,* published in 1904, the two books were the first efforts to explain the technical side of yacht design to the reading public.

After *Motor Boat* was sold in 1913, Davis worked at the L. D. Huntington Shipyard in New Rochelle, New York. Then he worked for a year in Panama and for another year at a Canadian division of Elco, overseeing the production of 550 eighty-foot patrol boats. During World War I he was the superintendent of the Traylor Shipbuilding Company in Cornwells, Pennsylvania.

From the end of the war until the Depression, Davis held a variety of design-related jobs, including a period from 1925 to 1929 when he wrote books on historic sailing vessels and ship modeling that were published by the Marine Research Society of Salem, Massachusetts. Three books about ship modeling written by Davis during this period, and one written in 1933, are still in print.

In 1929 Davis took a short-lived job at the design firm of Tams and King; it went out of business in 1931. The next few years saw little demand for yacht designers. Davis turned to his interest in ship modeling, a skill he had developed as a young man, finding work restoring a collection of models for a wealthy client. From 1933 to about 1940 he was set up on the estate of another client, building ship models and teaching the client how to do the same. During World War II he was an inspector for the U.S. Navy. He continued to build ship models in the last period of his life, writing his final book on the subject in 1946.

Davis was known for his commonsense approach to yacht design, and many designers of the mid-twentieth century list him as a major influence. Designer Weston Farmer referred to him as "The Oracle," and said he "brought a driving wind of reality into early design thinking." Designer and columnist John G. Hanna called him "one of the greatest influences for good in the history of American yachting."

Some of Davis's models are in collections at Mystic Seaport Museum, Mystic, CT, and at Mariner's Museum, Newport News, VA.

—Daniel B. MacNaughton

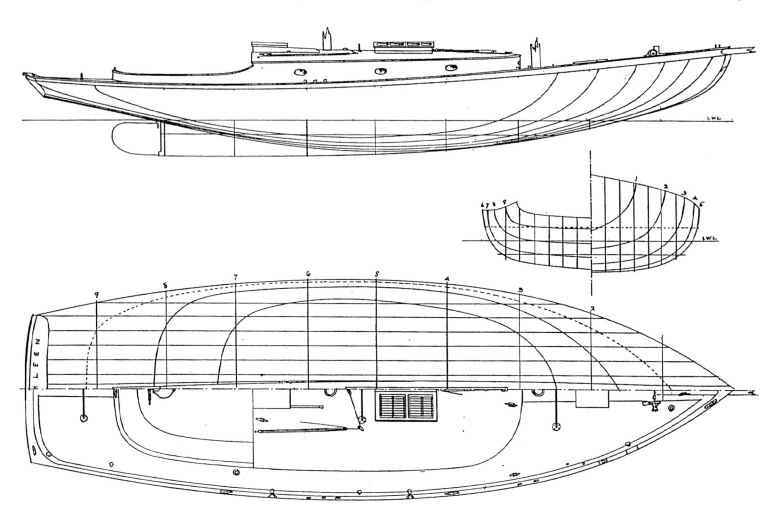

Charles G. Davis: *Kathleen.* The beautiful schooner *Kathleen,* launched in 1902, was designed for cruising, hunting, and fishing in the Everglades on the west coast of Florida, hence, her extremely shoal draft. To gain stability, Davis gave her a beamy, flat, and full-ended, scow-like hull. She was nonetheless eminently capsizeable. *Reproduced from Charles G. Davis's* How to Design a Yacht

Merle Davis: *Conejo.* Commissioned by their builders, Fellow and Stewart, in 1939, over twenty of the 44-foot 3-inch LOA Island Clippers were built. Their popularity was immediate, and each became successful in both class events and offshore racing. *Conejo* was the first winner of the San Diego to Acapulco, Mexico, race in 1953. *Photo courtesy Los Angeles Maritime Museum*

MERLE J. DAVIS

1910–1947 · United States

Boats were the consuming interest of Merle Davis's life, and he was equally good at designing, building, and sailing them. His successful designs for the 44-foot Island Clipper sloops, for the 26-foot sloop commissioned by *Sea* magazine, and for the design of a 52-foot cutter for the Honolulu Race promised a bright future. The West Coast boating community was therefore stunned by the sudden and untimely death of this talented and popular designer at the age of thirty-seven.

Davis was born in southern California. He came to the profession of yacht design by way of his talent for boatbuilding at his small yard in San Pedro. Early on he became recognized for the quality of construction of some 22-Square-Meter and 26-foot PIC (Pacific Interclub) sloops. Both classes were designed by Edson B. Schock in the early 1930's. It is perceived that Schock had discerned Davis's talent for design and fostered his early work.

For a time Davis worked at Wilmington Boats Works, where he learned design under Hugh Angelman while working at various jobs in the yard. By 1939, he was on his own in Los Angeles. His practice was augmented by his engineering competence, and a considerable amount of business came from the designs of modern rigs for some older but famous racing yachts. They included the 50-foot Edson B. Schock cutter (formerly schooner) *Jorie*, the 66-foot William Gardner sloop *Westward*, the 40-foot Abeking and Rasmussen yawl *Carola*, the 81-foot W. Starling Burgess M-Class cutter *Patolita*, and the 45-foot Edson B. Schock yawl *Flying Cloud*. All were brought to newly competitive form and successful second lives.

Eighteen of Davis's Island Clipper sloops were built by the premier San Pedro yard of Fellows and Stewart just prior to World War II and later during the early postwar period. They sold well and became a popular racing and cruising boat, usually competing as a class in regattas but with a number also participating in offshore ocean races. One of the class, *Conejo*, won the inaugural San Diego to Acapulco, Mexico, race in 1953.

During the war Davis served in the navy as a lieutenant in naval construction, and he met and worked with the young C. W. (Bill) Lapworth. At the end of the war, Davis opened a

R. O. Davis: *Burma*. The 58-foot *Burma* is shown reaching under storm trysail and jib. One of the best known of her designer's highly regarded motorsailers, she is also one of the few to have appeared under his own name. *Burma* far exceeds the ability of most powerboats while offering greater comfort than most sailboats. © *Mystic Seaport, Rosenfeld Collection, Mystic, CT*

design office in Long Beach, California—Merle J. Davis and Associates—with Bill Lapworth and David Hammill joining him after they were discharged from the navy.

In 1946, Davis drew the plans for Sea Islander, a 26-foot sloop, at the request of *Sea* magazine, which wanted to promote an affordable boat that could be built by an amateur owner. This design gained great popularity, and boats were still being built to it by both individuals and boatyards into the next decade.

The 52-foot cutter for the 1947 Honolulu Race—designed but never built—was the largest yacht Davis created and appears to have whipped up interest within the racing community. It was his final yacht design.

—Thomas G. Skahill

RICHARD ORDWAY DAVIS

June 30, 1899–December 1969 · United States

R. O. Davis is best known for his refinement of the motorsailer concept, first at the office of designer William Hand, later on his own as in-house designer for builder Henry B. Nevins, and finally with the Philip Rhodes office. He is particularly remembered for his motorsailers *Burma, Holiday,* and *Seer.*

The Davis/Hand motorsailers have business-like, no-nonsense good looks. At times some were rigged with long bowsprits and pulpits, enabling them to be used for hunting swordfish, which were caught with a harpoon thrown from the end of the bowsprit. Most were primarily motor-driven vessels but carried func-

tional sailing rigs that were useful for auxiliary as well as steadying purposes. Superstructures were moderate, and while the emphasis was on comfort, the designs come across as sensible seagoing vessels in a way that most powerboats and some sailboats do not.

Davis was born in Haverhill, Massachusetts. He had a limited formal education but nonetheless developed a natural talent for freehand and technical drawing. His first drafting work was done in the office of B. B. Crowninshield and was followed by nonnautical drafting jobs until he was hired by William Hand in 1926. The two men evolved the well-known Hand motorsailers over the next fourteen years. In 1936 Davis became associate designer. During his time at the Hand office, Davis was vested with the responsibility of running the office when Hand went fishing around Martha's Vineyard, Massachusetts.

With the threat of another world war in 1940, the Nevins yard in City Island, New York, was one of many boatyards awarded contracts to design minesweepers and aircraft rescue boats. Davis was recruited by Nevins in-house designer George Crouch, starting there in 1940 on a temporary basis as a designer/drafter and then becoming a permanent employee when the United States entered the war.

Following World War II, Davis rose to the position of in-house designer after Crouch's retirement. He produced some exceptional designs, including motorsailers incorporating the beautiful elliptical stern that graces some of his best-known work. Eleven motorsailers were designed but only three were built: the 82-foot ketch-rigged *Holiday* (1947), the *Seer,* and the 58-foot *Burma* (1950). After the Nevins yard closed in 1954, Davis moved to Maine, where he worked at the Frank L. Sample and Son Shipyard in Boothbay Harbor and later went to work for Philip Rhodes in New York City, although he did much of his work for Rhodes out of his home office in Waldoboro, Maine.

Davis was a superb draftsman with a talent for mechanical drafting and systems design, producing drawings that were highly detailed and packed with information not normally provided by a naval architect's office. This degree of detailing was of great benefit to the builders, who did not have to figure all these things out for themselves, and also to the owners, who were assured of a complete, properly functioning, and harmoniously outfitted vessel.

The Davis/Hand Collection is at the Hart Nautical Collections, MIT Museum, Cambridge, MA.

—Daniel B. MacNaughton with Michael and Debbie McMenemy and Bob Wallstrom

ARTHUR DeFEVER

Born June 6, 1918 · United States

While his early work was in fast, planing power craft such as his Hollywood Cruisers, Arthur DeFever is better known as one of the foremost developers of the modern yachtsman's trawler. He also designed commercial seining vessels. When he was approached for a yacht design that would embody the rough-water ability of the seiners along with good fuel economy, he designed the DeFever 50, now regarded by many as a classic.

These displacement-hull cruisers had deep forefoots, a relatively large beam, and long keels. For improved speed and motion, their hull shapes featured a finer entrance and run and more deadrise than the heavier commercial vessels. They were comfortable offshore and were capable of transoceanic passages owing to their great fuel economy and range. His Offshore 52, sponsored by the Offshore Cruising Society, was introduced in 1960, and the 58-foot Offshore Cruiser came the following year.

Commissions for very large vessels, such as *LAC 1* and *LAC 2* at 131 feet, transformed his practice into an international one in the early 1980's. In recent years DeFever has continued to work in this type and has also designed planing-hull powerboats and a few sailboats.

DeFever was born in San Pedro, California. His father was a prominent local mariner and hard-hat diver. As a boy DeFever restored a salvaged 18-foot sloop, thereby beginning his lifelong interest in boats. He studied engineering at the University of Southern California and naval architecture at the University of California. He had a summer job on the frigate USS *Constitution* while she was visiting the West Coast in 1933.

During World War II DeFever worked at a shipyard designing fishing vessels, seagoing tugs, and small freighters. After the war he continued to design fishing vessels and other commercial craft, as well as the Hollywood stock sportfishermen and cruisers.

DeFever moved his practice to San Diego in 1950, where he produced the largest body of his work over the next forty years. He retired briefly in about 1995; however, following the death of his wife, Dulcie, he returned to design the 60-foot Grand Alaskan, with other designs pending, for Oviatt Marine.

—Daniel B. MacNaughton

ROBERT E. DERECKTOR

September 12, 1921–October 10, 2001
United States

Throughout Bob Derecktor's life, he extolled the virtues of traditional craftsmanship and devoted much of his career to training and promoting craftsmen in the yacht building industry. While primarily a boatbuilder, Derecktor also designed approximately forty-two yachts, mostly sailboats. Among his better-known boats were the sloops *Charisma* (49 feet), *Boomerang* (64 feet), and *Vamoose* (40 feet); the ketch *Gray Goose* (36 feet); and the yawls *Figaro IV* (51 feet) and *Salty Tiger* (47 feet). These and others were successful in SORC, Bermuda, transatlantic, and Admiral's Cup racing.

Born in Meriden, Connecticut, Derecktor designed and built a 24-foot sloop at age thirteen, pouring the lead keel himself. He and a friend sailed it to Nova Scotia and back. When he was fourteen, he requested and got a meeting with Olin Stephens II, then twenty-six, at his home in Scarsdale, New York. Stephens recalled being impressed with sketches of Derecktor's boats and by his energy and self-assurance. But the desire to own a boatyard and build boats seemed to be Derecktor's first preference. He entered Swarthmore College in Pennsylvania to study mechanical engineering, but left after two years.

Derecktor built a 30-foot schooner when he was eighteen, which he sailed to the Chesapeake. While working at Owens Shipyard near Baltimore as a ship's carpenter, he mastered calculus, a subject he had failed in college. Deciding that calculus was important to his life's work, he returned to college and took the final exam, scoring 100 percent.

In 1940 the Owens yard was building navy patrol boats and Derecktor became a foreman; eighteen months later he was working at Julius Peterson's yard in Nyack, New York. With a recommendation from Olin Stephens, Derecktor moved to the Minneford yard on City Island, New York, where he continued to hone his skills. When he was barely twenty-one, he joined the navy and served in the Pacific for the next twenty-six months on PT boats, eventually working to repair them.

Returning home in 1946, Derecktor acquired waterfront property in Mamaroneck, New York, and began building wooden boats. The business did well, but his own ideas were often in conflict with those of his projects' designers, which led him into designing his own. (When Derecktor died, Olin Stephens said, "He built many S&S [Sparkman & Stephens] designs and because I felt responsibility to the owner, this was sort of an adventure with my confidence in his quality somewhat offset by Bob's cavalier attitude toward the plans he was supposed to follow. . . . He added both quality and color to the world of sailing.")

By 1956 Derecktor was building boats according to his own designs as well as those of Sparkman and Stephens, John Alden, Phil Rhodes, and others. The last boats he built of wood were the 12-Meter *Valiant* and his own *Mother Goose*, a 45-foot yawl, in 1971. He built a few boats in fiberglass but he and his workmen disliked working with the material, so he switched to aluminum construction in 1976.

Derecktor was demanding, direct, and uncompromising in what he believed was right. In the words of one of his repeat clients, Avard Fuller, "Tact and diplomacy cannot be counted

Arthur DeFever: *Tiempo 2.* This 49-foot design provides comfort and security that are remarkable for her size. With a flying bridge and roomy upper deck, high solid rails surrounding the aft decks and pilothouse, and an airy deckhouse with large windows protected from sun and rain, she is an ideal liveaboard cruiser for any climate. *Photo courtesy DeFever Cruising.com*

Robert Derecktor: *Salty Goose.* The 54-foot aluminum sloop *Salty Goose* was designed and built by Derecktor in 1973, just in time for the SORC, and gained a series second in Class A plus a berth on the U.S. Admiral's Cup Team. She remained in the front ranks of ocean racing for many years. *Photo courtesy Thomas G. Skahill*

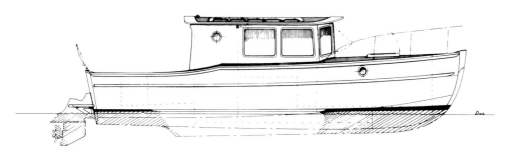

Sam Devlin: Surf Scoter 24. This practical powerboat features easy and economical stitch-and-glue plywood construction, and an outdrive motor that is relatively simple for the amateur builder to install. An interesting spatial arrangement combines the main cabin, galley, and steering area to form a roomy and practical open interior. *Drawing courtesy Sam Devlin*

among his greater virtues." Derecktor had other interests too. He designed and built award-winning furniture and collaborated with Buckminster Fuller on a geodesic house for the Philippines.

Derecktor built six America's Cup defenders or challengers: *Valiant, Marine, Stars & Stripes* (1985, 1986, and 1987), and *USA II.* He died in 2001, critical and uncompromising in his work ethic to the end.

—Thomas G. Skahill

SAMUEL DEVLIN

Born 1953 · United States

Sam Devlin runs one of the more productive woodenboat building operations in the United States, working with sheet plywood in the stitch-and-glue method to produce wood-epoxy composite boats aimed at mainstream boat buyers. He is one of the few wooden boat designer/builders who competes directly with fiberglass production shops.

Devlin has demonstrated that even the smallest sail and power boats can be sophisticated in design, strong and weather resistant in construction, and modest in cost. Devlin's boats are neither re-creations of the boats of the past nor an attempt to surprise or shock with their modernity, but a graceful combination of tradition-based proportions and unabashedly modern detailing.

Born in Eugene, Oregon, Devlin grew up around boats, enjoying deep-sea fishing and water skiing on the lakes. His father built plywood runabouts and owned a marine store. Devlin and his wife Elizabeth started building boats in 1977, moving to their present location in Olympia, Washington, in 1982.

Stitch-and-glue is a method of assembling plywood hulls without building jigs. Using plywood obliges many of Devlin's designs to be hard-chine, V-bottomed craft. After the panels have been cut to shape, holes are drilled along the edges, and wire is "stitched" through the holes to hold the curved edges of the panels in contact with each other until enough thickened epoxy is applied to do the job, whereupon the projecting ends of the wires are cut off flush, and the joint is reinforced with fiberglass tape. The method is not new, but under Devlin's influence it has seen a resurgence.

Devlin has a number of plans for sale, ranging from dinghies, skiffs, duck boats, and sneakboxes, to trawlers, powerboats, motorsailers, and pocket cruisers. He is the author of *Devlin's Boat Building, How to Build Any Boat the Stitch-and-Glue Way.*

—Daniel B. MacNaughton

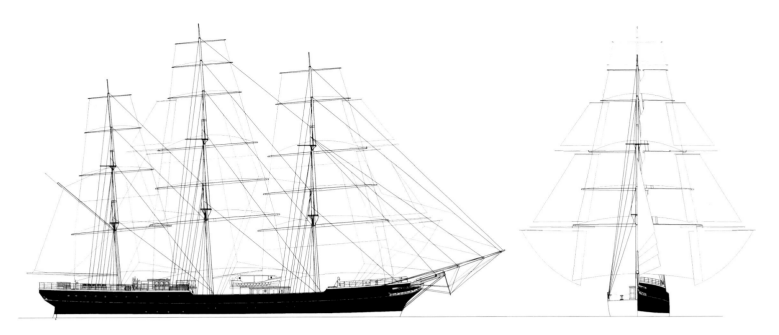

Gerard Dijkstra: *Stad Amsterdam.* This 250-foot full-rigged clipper ship was launched in 1999 and represents the Netherlands around the world. She is engaged in charter service and has won major Tall Ship race events. *Drawing courtesy Gerard Dijkstra*

GERARD DIJKSTRA

Born 1944 · The Netherlands

Few lives in boatbuilding and design show a sense of direction and purpose comparable to that of Dutch naval architect Gerard Dijkstra. From redesigns of such classic yachts as Charles E. Nicholson's *Endeavour* as well as his *Shamrock V*, to the design of the full-rigged clipper *Stad Amsterdam*, to one-offs like *Windrose* and *Lazy Jack*, Dijkstra has established a reputation for designing yachts that look traditional and at the same time are technically advanced.

Dijkstra was born in Amsterdam and studied aeronautical engineering at the prestigious University of Delft. He did not graduate, owing to a head injury sustained on the rugby fields, but went sailing instead. He apprenticed at places as different as The Society Shop (a chain of men's wear shops) in Amsterdam during 1966–67, after obtaining a minor degree in fashion design, and for sailmakers Ratsey and Lapthorn in New York, in 1969–70. Dijkstra considers himself self-taught as a naval architect, even though his knowledge as an aeronautical engineer surely serves him well.

Dijkstra began his seagoing career in 1967. Several short outings with friends on the IJsselmeer and North Sea nourished his desire to make longer voyages. In the same year he was hired as a crewmember for the maiden voyage of a large charter yacht, *Sol Quest*, making a passage from Poole, England, to Antigua in the West Indies. This first deep-sea experience was the beginning of a long career as crewmember, skipper, and solo sailor that would form the practical basis for his success as a designer and engineer.

In 1969, Dijkstra founded Ocean Sailing Development Holland BV, a company mainly involved with shorthanded ocean racing during its first ten years. Gradually its activities expanded to include yacht design as well as supervision of the construction of oceangoing sailboats and fast shorthanded racers.

During the 1970's Dijkstra became a celebrity in the Netherlands, first as a solo sailor and then as navigator and watchleader on the first Dutch-built *Flyer*, winner of the Whitbread Round the World Race in 1977–78. He later skippered the same yacht to victory in the Spice Race, nonstop from Jakarta to Rotterdam in 1980.

Bestevaer, a 16-meter LOA solo racer, was Dijkstra's first complete design to see the water. Dijkstra sailed the boat in the 1976 OSTAR (Observer Singlehanded Transatlantic Race). For the next six years, the yacht participated in all shorthanded racing events, ultimately under the name of *Kriter VI*.

From 1978 on, the company's projects included laminated-wood commercial vessels for third world countries. Between 1985 and 1993 Dijkstra focused on projects in Indonesia and Mauritania, among others. These projects took advantage of cold-molded wood's ability to provide longer-lasting boats built with a much smaller quantity of wood. During his time in Indonesia, computer-aided design (CAD) software became available, and Dijkstra and his assistants were among the earliest to adapt it to yacht design.

In 1995 a group of young Dutch designers joined the Dijkstra firm, leading to Lutra Design Group, a joint development between Dijkstra and Ad Konijnendijk. It is responsible for the high-tech racers designed by the office for IMS/IRM and Open Class racing. In 1999 Dijkstra's company became Gerard Dijkstra and Partners when designer Thijs Nikkels became a partner.

The redesign of large classic sailing yachts has become another specialty of the firm. The parameters of these designs have been as varied as the owners. Some yachts were rebuilt using modern techniques for longevity and economy, but with minimal changes to the original design. In others the original atmosphere was retained, but the redesign provided for more space and improved performance. In some cases the hull specifications were drastically modified.

Gerard Dijkstra: *Windrose.* The 46-meter *Windrose* is a unique Big Class schooner. Combining classic styling with a modern hull form and lightweight materials, she participates in Spirit of Tradition races. In May 2002 *Windrose* broke the schooner *Atlantic*'s record for a transatlantic passage. *Drawing courtesy Gerard Dijkstra*

Gerard Dijkstra: *Christoffel's Lighthouse*. The 90-foot plumb-bowed cutter *Christoffel's Lighthouse* is a modern reinterpretation of the pilot-cutter designs of the late nineteenth century, showing good performance owing to a long waterline and tall rig. *Drawing courtesy Gerard Dijkstra*

Dijkstra has drawn two lines of semicustom cruisers, the Bestevaer and Glen Daisy. These clipper-bow yachts, ranging from 33 to 144 feet, are traditional looking and deceptively modern.

Racing success for the designs in 2001 included an overall win in the Fastnet Race for the 52-foot *Tonnere* (by Lutra Design Group), a second and first place for *Stad Amsterdam* in her first Sail Training Association (STA) event, and the win of *Endeavour,* beating the later restorations *Shamrock V* and *Velsheda*. In 2004 the Royal Huisman Shipyard launched the 89-meter three-masted schooner *Athena,* a collaboration with Pieter Beeldsnijder, to which Dijkstra and Partners contributed hull form and rig architecture.   —Rutger ten Broeke

LUDWIG DINKLAGE

1892–1966 · Germany

The son of a Hamburg ship captain, Ludwig Dinklage sailed as a child on the Elbe and Alster Rivers. He began an apprenticeship at Blohm and Voss Shipyard before serving in the Imperial Navy during World War I. He resumed his study of shipbuilding after the war, working at various yards before opening his own boatyard in the mid-1920's. There he designed and built tenders, speedboats, launches, dinghies, and Canadian canoes, for which he introduced new construction practices.

Before the decade was out, Dinklage discovered a gift for writing, and over the rest of his career produced many books on sailing, such as *Lustkutter und dicke Damper, Seemannsdeutch und Seemannslatein* (*Graceful Yachts and Tubby Steamers, Sailor's German and Sailor's Latin*), and *Ozean-Wettfahrten, 70 Jahren Transatlantik-Regatten* (*Ocean Races, 70 Years of Transatlantic Regattas*). He served as publisher and managing editor for several sailing periodicals, and was a welcome reporter at all important regattas, above all at Kiel Week.   —Volker Christmann

DUDLEY DIX

Born May 7, 1949 · South Africa/United States

Born in Cape Town, the son of a South African champion racer in the Flying Dutchman class, Dudley Dix trained as a quantity surveyor. He designed and built his first yacht in 1973 and, while building an offshore boat in 1976 (using a design by Ericus van de Stadt), he became interested in designing and enrolled in the Westlawn School of Yacht Design. Success in the 1979 Cruising World Design Competition led him to move to full-time yacht designing as a profession.

The most notable of Dijkstra's redesigns is the Charles E. Nicholson–designed J-Class America's Cup challenger, the *Endeavour* of 1934. Sir T. O. M. Sopwith's unfortunate "should have won" yacht was found rusting away in an English mud berth, and rebuilt from scratch under ownership of the American Elizabeth Meyer. Dijkstra redesigned two other Nicholson-designed J-Class boats: *Shamrock V* and *Velsheda*. Other Big Class redesigns include the Arthur Holgate–designed *Adix,* the W. C. Storey–designed *Adela,* and a replica of *Harlequin* (based

on the lines of the George Watson–designed *Britannia*).

A major step forward for the office was the design of the clipper ship *Stad Amsterdam* and her sistership *Cisne Branco* launched in 1999 and 2000, respectively. The 250-foot LOA *Stad Amsterdam* was the product of an enormous community effort to create a Dutch tall ship, and she is an able representative of the Netherlands. Presently in the charter boat trade, she appears at many parades of tall ships and various races around the world.

As a designer, Dix has a strong reputation for practical concepts derived from his own experience as a boatbuilder. This has taught him the importance of strength, clarity, and detailing. As a result, his work is very popular with amateur builders, especially in the United States.

Dix prefers fast and light boats that are fun to sail. His Didi 38 design is an expression of this concept. The success of the Didi 38 has led to an expansion of designs of plywood racers and racer/cruisers. He is also designing a range of fiberglass power catamarans.

One of Dix's strong points is his ability to marry a traditional look above the waterline with a modern underbody, of which Shearwater 39 and 45 are the best-known examples. To Dix's delight, other yachtsmen expect his traditional-looking design to be slow, and are suitably impressed when his schooners overtake their more modern-looking yachts. In January 2001, Shearwater 45 was named the *Cruising World* Boat of the Year and also awarded the prize for Best Traditional Voyageur. Because he has designed a large number of schooner-rigged hulls, not all with a traditional style for the bow and stern, he has been nicknamed the "Schooner King."

Dix's emphasis on modern, fast hull designs with fin keels has led him to work with a variety of media: plywood, steel, and fiberglass. He uses swing keels and movable ballast, though these complications increase the cost and complexity of construction. He prefers to use other, simpler solutions whenever possible, reflecting the importance Dix places on the needs and resources of his clients—to him, the most important people on the design team.

Dudley Dix Yacht Design relocated from Hout Bay, Cape Town, South Africa, to Virginia Beach, Virginia, in 2004.   —Tom Roach

BENJAMIN T. DOBSON

1890–1959 · United States

His output was relatively small. His name was little known outside his profession. Yet B. T. Dobson was a naval architect and yacht designer of great skill and versatility who successfully practiced his craft in New Bedford, Massachusetts, for some forty-five years.

Born in Boston and raised in Gloucester, Dobson graduated from the Webb Institute, then started his design career under William H. Hand Jr. in New Bedford. He established his own design office in 1921. One of Dobson's earliest triumphs was the 49-foot gaff schooner *Rumpus,* built in 1925. *Rumpus* was a frequent winner in southern New England racing competitions during her first few seasons.

Dudley Dix: *Black Cat.* Dix designed and built *Black Cat* as his personal boat for long-distance racing. An experiment in low-cost, high-performance boats, the successful concept has resulted in an expanding range of radius-chine plywood designs. *Photo by Neil Rusch, courtesy Dudley Dix*

B. T. Dobson: *Cassiar.* Originally designed with crow's nests and a long bowsprit for swordfishing, the 64-foot *Cassiar* retains her aristocratic bearing and a delicate balance between some enlivening streamlining and seamanlike traditional detailing. © *Benjamin Mendlowitz*

In 1926 Pussey and Jones of Wilmington, Delaware, built the handsome 124-foot steel motoryacht *Siele* to Dobson's designs. She was followed by the 150-foot *Colleen* in 1928 and the 130-foot *Galaxy* in 1930. He also drew the plans for the 124-foot motoryacht *Bidou*, which Bath Iron Works launched in 1930. A sistership to *Bidou* became a casualty of the Great Depression and was never completed. All these substantial yachts had a distinctive bow shape and sheer that were Dobson's trademarks.

Dobson designed various powerboats and auxiliary sailboats in the 1930's. By far his best-known yacht was the experimental high-speed cabin cruiser *Revere*, of 1941, a streamlined fantasy built of a special copper-nickel alloy and with advanced communication and navigation features.

Many small craft were built to Dobson's designs for naval and military use in World War II. He also produced plans for a series of popular small cruisers and utility boats to be built in fiberglass by Palmer Scott of New Bedford after the war.

Perhaps the most admired of all Dobson's yachts was the 64-foot sportfisherman *Cassiar* that he created for Richard K. Mellon in 1949. Fast, able, elegantly understated in formal terms, *Cassiar* was among the handsomest round-bottom powerboats of her day.

The Dobson Collection is at the New Bedford Whaling Museum, New Bedford, MA.

—Llewellyn Howland III

WILFRED HEINRICH "HEINIE" DOLE II

July 21, 1910–April 9, 2003 · United States

While the majority of W. Heinrich Dole's work was in the design and construction of commercial vessels, his adaptation of the more successful of these forms into graceful and efficient pleasure boats earned him the highest regard among his contemporary yacht designers and builders in the Pacific Northwest.

Heinie Dole was a Washington State native descended from the Doles of Hawaii, early missionaries and planters in those islands. As a boy he designed and built a small open boat to sail the waters of Quinault Lake on the Olympic Peninsula in Washington. He worked

W. Heinrich Dole: *Katie Ford* (opposite). Perhaps the most popular of Dole's designs, *Katie Ford* still turns heads as she plies Northwest waters. Her tall sloop rig was considered slightly daring at the time she was launched, but she sails smartly even in the typically light summer winds of Puget Sound. *Photo courtesy J. Scott Rohrer*

as a machinist's apprentice while in high school and already had a solid understanding of mechanics when he entered Stanford University. When he graduated with a degree in mechanical engineering, jobs for engineers were scarce but he found work as a fireman aboard the seagoing dredge *Culebra*.

This early sea time pointed Dole in the direction of the marine trades. He spent much of his early career working in logging camps in the Northwest, which took him to Olympia, where he designed the handsome 31-foot cutter *Chantey* for his own use.

Chantey's long waterline (29 feet) and large sail plan made her one of the fastest boats on Astoria Bay in northern Oregon, where Dole had moved to take a job at Astoria Marine Construction Company in the late 1930's. Sharing design and engineering duties with Astoria Marine president Joseph Dyer, Dole stayed with the company for two decades. Aside from his commercial and military work at Astoria, Dole was able to draw a number of notable pleasure boats, both power and sail. He gladly acknowledged the influences of existing designs on his work, but the boats he produced were uniquely his own creations.

During World War II, Dole drew up a handsome new 44-foot cutter to build at the end of hostilities. This boat, *Katie Ford*, was a departure from the more compact *Chantey*. Her longer ends, large wheelhouse, and sweeping sheerline caught the attention of yachtsmen up and down the coast when the design appeared in *Pacific Motor Boat* in 1944. When asked about the longer overhangs of this design, Dole replied, "Having been to sea in both long and short ended boats, I can't see any difference in the discomfort of the two types."

Launched in 1946, *Katie Ford* proved to be one of the most successful and well-known auxiliary yachts in the Northwest. The next year, Dole produced *Janie*, a smart 40-foot "half-sister" of *Katie Ford*, for a Portland owner. Given the relatively shallow waters of the Columbia River, however, she was a centerboarder reminiscent of Phil Rhodes's work in the same type.

The ketch *Ebb Tide*, launched in 1957, resembled no previous Dole design. Heavy and short ended, her lines and rig were based on the Thursday Island pearling luggers of the South Pacific. Dole frequently let successful commercial types influence his work on yachts. That his power cruiser designs reflect familiar features of Pacific Northwest trollers and seiners is no accident.

Possibly Dole's finest centerboarder was the 47-foot *Patronilla*, built in the late 1950's for another Portland yachtsman. Despite being tailored for cruising on the Columbia,

Patronilla finished in the money three times on the Los Angeles–Honolulu (Transpac) Race. In the 1959 Transpac, *Patronilla*, *Ebb Tide*, and *Janie* all competed.

Heinie Dole's designs were all good looking, efficient, and well planned. That they are still around, active, and admired after fifty years is no surprise.

—J. Scott Rohrer

ROBERT STAYTON DORRIS

January 21, 1921–July 3, 1999 · United States

Robert Dorris was born in Phoenix, Arizona; his family moved to southern California in the 1930's and he spent his summers on the waters of Newport Harbor. He served in the U.S. Merchant Marine during World War II, after which he opened his own shop and began building boats in Newport Beach.

Dorris's early work included the design and construction of commercial fishing craft, many of the type used in the abalone fishery located around the offshore islands. These boats had to be both fast and strongly built, and Dorris boats were unrivaled in this matter.

A love of sailing produced the design and construction of a variety of sailboats for local clients, as well as custom sportfisherman, lifeguard craft, fireboats, and patrol craft for the city of Newport Beach. An avid sailor, Dorris regularly participated in ocean racing events as a valued crew, and was one of the regulars on actor Humphrey Bogart's 55-foot, Sparkman and Stephens yawl *Santana* until the actor's death in 1957.

A graduate of the Westlawn School of Yacht Design, Dorris was inducted into the Society of Naval Architects and Marine Engineers in 1961. His reputation continued to grow, and he produced several designs for Robert Newton's American Marine of Hong Kong. These included the Alaskan series of trawler yachts, 46-, 55-, and 65-foot models of wood construction, and the Laguna series of fast, twin-screw fiberglass cruisers (10, 11.5, 13, and 15.2 meters).

One of Dorris's larger designs was the 62-foot trawler yacht *Lands End* for the well-known yachtsman and three-time Bermuda Race winner Carlton Mitchell (*Finisterre*). *Lands End* was built by American Marine in 1972. Dorris's portfolio of designs at Mystic Seaport contains plans for a 104-foot 9-inch motoryacht (design No. 131, dated December 19, 1967). In his later years after retirement, Dorris frequently cruised his 41-foot, Howard Chapelle–designed schooner *Faith*, which he owned until his death.

The Robert S. Dorris Collection is presently being catalogued at Mystic Seaport Museum, Mystic, CT.

—Thomas G. Skahill

GORDON K. "SANDY" DOUGLASS

1905–1994 · United States

Sandy Douglass is best known for having designed the 17-foot Thistle (1945), 20-foot Highlander (1949), and 19-foot Flying Scot (1957) one-design classes, some of the earliest planing sailboat plans to achieve great popularity. He was a self-taught designer, gaining most of his experience on the race course, beginning with sailing canoes in the late 1910's and 1920's and continuing into the International 14 class in the 1930's. He won numerous class championships.

Through his racing, Douglass came into contact with English designer Uffa Fox, who inspired him to pursue the newly invented planing-hull types in both sailing canoes and racing dinghies. In an effort to find lighter means of construction he was the first to create molded-plywood sailboats, beginning with the 17-foot Thistle class just after World War II.

—Daniel B. MacNaughton

WIEBE DRAIJER

Born 1924 · The Netherlands

While he may not have been the most prolific of designers, Wiebe Draijer's originality and his capacity to rethink old problems have made him a unique figure among Holland's yacht designers.

Born in Haarlem as the eldest son of an officer in the Dutch merchant marine, Draijer saw his own nautical aspirations nipped in the bud by the German occupation. The only way to go to sea during World War II was to be trained to ship out for Nazi Germany, an unacceptable option for young Wiebe. So in 1942, instead of the naval academy, Draijer enrolled at Delft University, Holland's oldest and most prestigious. Initially he studied naval architecture, but he soon developed a more general interest and after the war switched to mechanical engineering, graduating in 1953. In 1964 Draijer became a full professor at Twente University, where he was Rector Magnificus from 1982 until 1985.

Draijer has had many deeply felt interests besides his scientific career. His sincere love of painting and sculpture led to a position as chair of the board of AKI, the Academy for the Visual Arts in Enschede. With his wife Nel, he sailed and raced *Goodwin*, a sturdy and stable steel One-Tonner from his own drawing board.

Much of the credit for the establishment of the Denk Tank (Think Tank) is shared by Draijer and his long-time friend, Professor Jelle Gerritsma from Delft University. In 1962, desiring to perform scientific research on hull shape for yacht design, they assembled a group of prominent Dutch yacht architects to explore the possibilities. In spite of some initial mistrust (after all, they were all direct competitors), they submitted their designs for tests at the up-to-date Delft Laboratories as a subject for general studies. Baron van Höevell was the first chair of this group, which has included designers such as Ericus van de Stadt, Dirk Koopmans, Jacques de Ridder, Gerard Dijkstra, Andre Hoek, Dick Zaal, Gerard de Vries Lentsch II, and Frans Maas.

Draijer's activities as a designer were not limited to a single type of boat. In 1964, he designed a 19-footer as a project for the student sailing club, resulting in *Euros*, a Class V RORC pocket cruiser that has subsequently been produced in quantity. His own *Goodwin*, a 37-foot steel yacht designed in 1965, was successful in the One-Ton Cup Races round Denmark and was also made available as a production boat. *Noah*, Draijer's favorite design, was drawn and built by Draijer in 1975. She was a fiberglass sloop of 32 feet with a transom-hung rudder, incorporating many of Draijer's ideas about rigging and outfitting.

Draijer's last yacht design, drawn in 1989, was a heavy steel-keel centerboarder named *Styx*, based on the Sixaern, a traditional and seaworthy fishing boat from the Shetlands. In *Styx* he and Nel extensively cruised the North Sea coast until the mid-1990's, when they ceased their ocean sailing.

By 1993 Draijer had retired, but he was invited by his long-time friend, boatbuilder Gait Kroes, to meet a new challenge. Draijer made the calculations for strength, ballast-weight ratio, spars, sails, and rigging for the reconstruction of a fourteenth-century Kampen cog, which was launched in 1998.

—Rutger ten Broeke

REINHARD DREWITZ

December 7, 1881–1955 · Germany

Both a designer and a keen racing yachtsman, Reinhard Drewitz had a major impact on the German jolly boats and jolly cruisers, racing dinghies and small yachts based on the dinghy type. His nickname, "Uncle Reinhard," given to him by the yachting community, expressed the high regard in which he was held.

The son of a publisher, Drewitz grew up in the family's country house at Lake Mueggelsee in Berlin. He sewed his first sail by himself from a sheet.

The unballasted jolly cruiser classes originated on the river Alster and on the eastern lakes of Berlin. The jolly boats of the Berlin Jollyboats Yachtsmen's Racing Union were built beginning in 1908. Drewitz had a decisive influence on their initial and subsequent development and on the rules of construc-

Wiebe Draijer: *Draijertje* (Little Draijer). *Draijertje* was conceived as a construction project for students of the Enschede Polytechnicum, where her designer was a professor. Intended as a one-design for series construction in fiberglass or cold-molded wood, the 19-footer saw considerable success in Holland, where more than thirty have been constructed. *Photo courtesy Rutger ten Broeke*

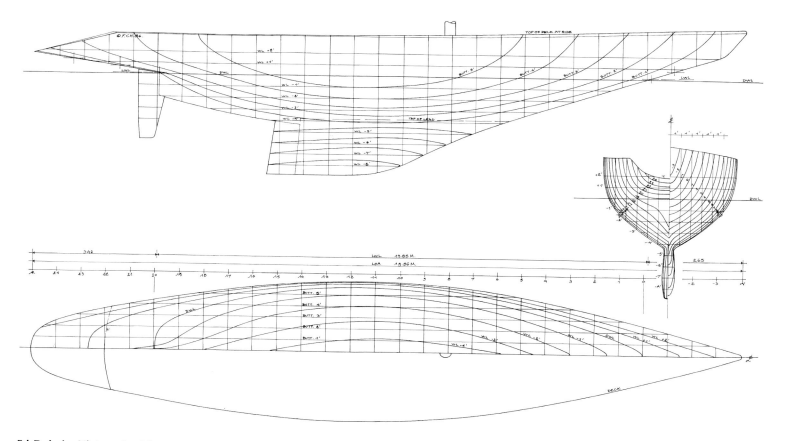

Ed Dubois: *Victory 82. Victory 82*, a 12-Meter, was built in 1982 for the 1983 America's Cup challenge. The series was won by the Ben Lexcen–designed *Australia II*. © *Chevalier & Taglang*

tion for both jolly boats and jolly cruisers.

The German Yachtsman's Association introduced the National Inland yawl within the context of this development. Even today old boats are restored and sailed, especially in South Germany and on Lake Bodensee. Drewitz's successful designs in the jolly boat class led to a good reputation in the yachting community, and many famous yachtsmen, such as Manfred Curry, raced in the class. The development culminated in the 15-Square-Meter jolly cruiser in 1920–21.

Drewitz's talents not only related to this class of boat, but also extended to larger racing yachts. He won many championships in these boats, as well as in boats of smaller classes.

In 1913 he designed a Sonder yacht for a client. After a while he bought the yacht because the client was dissatisfied with its performance. Drewitz was convinced that the boat could be made to perform. At the Kiel Week regattas, he proved the outstanding quality of the yacht and was chosen to represent Germany in a series of races in America. Another new and fascinating project was his extreme design for a 6-Meter, which was built at the shipyard in Buchholz.

A technical challenge was the design of a 30-Square-Meter jolly cruiser class (the designation being a measure of sail area), which was proposed at the twenty-sixth ordinary German

yachtsmen day in 1923. The class rules were worked out under the leadership of Drewitz.

The development of jolly cruisers continued. In Berlin the yachtsmen still remember the 45-Square-Meter jolly cruisers, which were often sailed by the Allies after 1945.

Reinhard Drewitz was extraordinarily successful as a yachtsman too. He took part in all the important sailing regattas, and won over six hundred awards, including championships in jolly boat classes at age fifty-nine and seventy. He died at the age of seventy-three. In his memory, the author was authorized to continue the yacht design office under the name Drewitz/Rührdanz.   —Hartmut Rührdanz

EDWARD GEORGE DUBOIS

Born April 18, 1952 · England

The 42-foot aluminum Two-Tonner *Police Car* is the yacht that put British designer Ed Dubois on the chart in 1979 after winning that year's Admiral's Cup. You couldn't miss her gaudy hull graphics, the "crew bus" with its blue flashing light, or the way her Australian crew drove the boat during a very windy summer season in the United Kingdom. In the big winds that preceded the tragic 1979 Fastnet Race, *Police Car* scorched around the Solent for the Admiral's Cup, with spray flying from her

low-freeboard hull and the boat firmly on her feet under a fractional rig.

After three years at Southampton College of Technology, Dubois graduated as a naval architect and went to work in Alan Buchanan's office on Jersey in the Channel Islands, where he had spent his summer vacations. But he soon felt it was too far from the action. Work permit problems prevented a move to New York, costing him an opportunity to join Sparkman and Stephens, so he briefly wrote for the Offshore column at the British fortnightly *Yachts and Yachting*.

Racing on the Bob Miller/Ben Lexcen–designed *Ceil V*, Dubois met skipper John Oakley, who offered him the chance to branch his company, Miller and Whitworth, away from its sailmaking roots. (Miller and Whitworth was the sailmaking company that Bob Miller–later known as Ben Lexcen–and Craig Whitworth operated until Miller left.) Dubois opened a design office within Miller and Whitworth.

Dubois's first commission, for an IOR Three-Quarter-Tonner, came from an old sailing friend from the Channel Islands. In the design for *Borsalino Trois*, Dubois used a lot of the ideas he had developed during his Three-Quarter-Ton studies at college. The boat was noteworthy for her big rig, moderate beam and displacement, and low prismatic hull form with an especially tight pintail stern.

George Herrick Duggan: *Glencairn.* In 1896 *Glencairn* was unusual for her long-ended, light-displacement, flat-floored hull. The combination of features proved to be successful and influenced Duggan and others to evolve and explore what eventually became the inland lake scow type. *Courtesy the Library of Congress*

Launched in 1976, *Borsalino Trois* was the RORC's champion boat for her class, also winning the Solent Points Championship. It was a year that also saw the launch of the much larger *Vanguard,* and *Enigma,* a little Quarter-Tonner from Northern Ireland. All three yachts were undeniably pretty, something that cannot always be said of IOR-influenced shapes. Dubois's sure aesthetic touch paid huge dividends twenty years later, in the superyacht market.

After the 1977 Admiral's Cup, Dubois left Miller and Whitworth, establishing his own office, Dubois Naval Architects, in Lymington. When the Australian team won the windy 1979 Admiral's Cup, due in no small part to *Police Car*'s contribution, his business blossomed. Westerly Yachts near Portsmouth, Yamaha in Japan, and the French yard Henri Wauquiez were among the first production boatbuilders to commission Dubois designs.

By any measure 1987 was a pivotal year for Dubois. In that year the 106-foot sloop *Aquel II* was launched in New Zealand. Previously

100-foot-plus sloops had not really been practical, owing to limitations in rigs and sail-handling systems such as the maximum size for rod rigging. Dubois was one of the first designers to be there at the outset of the new supersloop phenomenon, with *Aquel II* having particularly eye-catching, streamlined styling coupled with good sailing performance.

Since then, Dubois has launched a number of superyachts, including the 132-foot sloop *Kokomo,* winner of the Big Boat Cup in 2001; the 114-foot ketch *Beagle V*; the 147-foot *Timoneer*; and the 126-foot motoryacht *SQN.*

—Tim Jeffery

GEORGE HERRICK DUGGAN

September 6, 1862–October 8, 1946 · Canada

Imaginative, decisive, and a master of construction, George Herrick Duggan was an amateur designer of 142 yachts. Called "Herrick" by his sailing friends, he was only eighteen

when his first design hit the water, a 32-foot centerboard yawl built by Alexander Cuthbert, who would challenge for the America's Cup in 1881. After the officers of the Royal Canadian Yacht Club scolded Duggan for bringing ten soaking-wet men into its clubhouse—sailors he had rescued from a capsized boat in Lake Ontario—he cofounded the Toronto Yacht Club (the two clubs soon merged). He later helped found the Lake Yacht Racing Association, the first association of yacht clubs in North America, and the North American Yacht Racing Union, the ancestor of today's United States Sailing Association and Canadian Yachting Association.

After earning an engineering degree in 1883 from the University of Toronto, Duggan moved to Montreal to work for the Dominion Bridge Company. He helped found the Royal Saint Lawrence Yacht Club on the shores of Lake Saint Louis (a shallow bay at the junction of the Saint Lawrence and Ottawa Rivers) and served as its commodore from 1889 to 1890.

In 1896 the Royal Saint Lawrence challenged for the Seawanhaka Cup, a trophy put up for competition in 1895 by the Seawanhaka Corinthian Yacht Club in Oyster Bay, on the north shore of Long Island, New York. The cup was (and remains) the winning prize in an international challenge race run much like the America's Cup except that it is for small boats. Amateur small boat racing was then in its springtime. This was its first major competition, and the boats, built to a simple rule that balanced measured length and sail area, were relatively inexpensive. About twenty-five defense candidates (accounts vary) were built to plans by designers such as Nat Herreshoff, William Gardner, and the young Clinton Crane. In Montreal, fifteen (or eighteen) challenger candidates were built, five to Duggan's plans. In the finals off Oyster Bay, he sailed his design *Glencairn* against Crane's *El Heirie*. Thomas Fleming Day reported the results in *The Rudder*: "A more decisive victory than that achieved by *Glencairn* has seldom been registered in the annals of yacht racing."

Herreshoff, G. L. Watson, and a few other designers had recently discovered how to lengthen a heavy keelboat's sailing length beyond her measured length with a long overhang. Now Duggan did it in a lightweight centerboarder that depended on her crew for ballast. Glencairn's measured LWL of 12 feet 6 inches, determined when she was upright and at rest, allowed her a sail-area bonus. But when sailing close-hauled, Duggan intentionally heeled her well over at an angle of 20 degrees so her sailing LWL stretched to the same 15 feet of her competitors, with her hard bilge providing a long, powerful, yet slim low-resistance shape. Off the wind, he sailed her nearly upright on her wide, flat bottom, which planed easily.

From 1897 to 1904, the Royal Saint Lawrence Club successfully defended the Seawanhaka Cup in annual matches in Lake Saint Louis against challengers from Oyster Bay, Minnesota, England, Connecticut, and Massachusetts. As the boats increased in waterline length to 25 feet, Duggan's boats were always original.

Built in 1898, *Dominion* was a catamaran with a slightly tunneled hull. Sailing as he did in shallow water, Duggan also experimented with underwater appendages, and the 1902 defender, *Trident*, had three centerboards: a traditional one on the centerline plus a bilge board on each side, angled outboard about 20 degrees. This allowed the leeward bilge board to be vertical when the boat heeled, thereby providing an effective surface while the windward board was retracted.

The 1903 *Thorella II* had only the two bilge boards plus another new feature, double rudders. The leeward rudder worked deep in the water while the windward one waved in the air. These innovative features, which maximized performance while trimming the area of wetted surface, were promptly copied by small-lake sailors in Minnesota and Wisconsin who had adapted the *Glencairn*-type hull for their local classes, which became known as inland lake scows.

In 1902 Duggan moved to Nova Scotia to run a steel mill (where, characteristically, he founded the Royal Cape Breton Yacht Club). His protégé, F. P. Shearwood, did the detail work on these yacht club boats under Duggan's supervision and also sailed them. The Seawanhaka Cup was finally lifted from the Royal Saint Lawrence in 1905 by a scow-type boat from Manchester, Massachusetts.

As an engineer Duggan was known internationally for his work with bridges. The Alexandria Bridge across the Ottawa River was the world's fourth-longest cantilever span when it opened in 1901. He later designed the Saint Lawrence Bridge, whose cantilever span, at one mile, was the longest in the world. He headed the Dominion Bridge Company from 1919 to 1936. Duggan somehow found time to design scows and cruising boats for himself, other Canadians, Americans, and three owners in Finland.

Duggan's success, like Herreshoff's, was built on his engineering skills, experimental nature, and deep understanding of boats. As Clinton Crane observed in his autobiography *Yachting Memories*, "Duggan was a wonderful

George Herrick Duggan: *Cibou.* *Cibou* was a 45-foot tunnel-hull scow built in 1900 by a syndicate of Royal Cape Breton Yacht Club members. Duggan was a pioneer in the development and design of the scow type. *Photo courtesy Neil Libbey*

engineer and a past master of light construction, which means putting material in the places where it is needed and omitting all material from the places where it is not needed." While Duggan exploited the rating rule as ruthlessly as Herreshoff did with contemporary America's Cup defenders, his Seawanhaka Cuppers and the boats they inspired left behind something permanent and constructive in the inland lake scow, which has provided decades of fine, fast sailing in protected waters from Barnegat Bay to the Great Plains.

—John Rousmaniere

FRANCIS SPAULDING DUNBAR

1905–1991 · United States

Anyone interested in comfortable yachts for inshore and offshore cruising will enjoy a look at Spaulding Dunbar's series of handsome, shoal-draft, cruising ketch designs. Most employed tandem centerboards, a little-known option that Dunbar did a great deal to promote. Tandem centerboards offer tremendous control of helm balance, allowing it to be achieved under virtually any combination of sails. In fact, a tandem-board boat can be steered with considerable accuracy solely by adjusting the centerboards.

A number of these shoal-draft ketches were intended for offshore use, despite the fact that they were too shoal to allow quick self-righting if they capsize. While this might rule them out for some yachtsmen, the tandem centerboards do increase safety by offering outstanding steering control when running off in heavy seas (when the aft board would be lowered to encourage tracking, while the forward board would be raised to encourage the bow to head downwind).

An unexpected benefit of tandem centerboards was discovered in the Intracoastal Waterway, where it was found that the boat, running under power with only the aft board down, naturally tended to turn away from shoal water at the sides of the dredged channels. Apparently this occurred because of an increase in water pressure between the oncoming bow of the boat and the shoal, combined with the ease with which the bow could be pushed aside by that pressure, since the pivot point of the boat was brought so far aft by the aft centerboard.

Dunbar's portfolio also included more conventional sailing yachts, powerboats, and a number of one-designs. His boats have a unique and exciting appearance and achieve a timeless look through the incorporation of traditional forms and details into tastefully innovative concepts.

F. Spaulding Dunbar: *Lucy.* The 42-foot 4-inch yawl *Lucy* displays her designer's ability to use traditional forms like the clipper bow, sweeping sheer-line, and shapely transom in harmony with more up-to-date features such as a modern rig and doghouse-style cabin trunk, to produce a timeless yacht of universal appeal. © *Mystic Seaport, Rosenfeld Collection, Mystic, CT*

Dunbar was a big, tall man, and perhaps as a result his boats are known for their headroom, "floorspace," comfortable seating, and deck-space. Many of his boats are very luxurious in nature, but they achieve this luxury through comfort and quality of materials rather than gadgetry or ostentation.

Raised in Mansfield, Massachusetts, Dunbar's family summered in Chatham on Cape Cod, where prevailing southwest winds across Nantucket Sound produce a short steep chop and waters are shallow. Due to either his intelligence or perhaps the willpower of his very supportive mother, Dunbar excelled in school and skipped several grades, graduating from high school at age fifteen. He went on to study naval architecture at MIT. After graduating in 1926, he went to sea as a stoker in a steamship, rising rapidly in the ranks to second engineer. In 1929 he made a voyage in

a Portuguese square-rigger as an able seaman.

Dunbar's first design after college was a 52-foot ketch, a collaborative effort with designer Gordon Munro, for whom Dunbar worked beginning in 1928. Munro's firm failed in 1929, so Dunbar started his company, the Mill Pond Boat Yard, on his father's waterfront property in Chatham in 1932. He retained the yard for the rest of his life, sometimes renting it out to other proprietors.

The Stage Harbor Yacht Club, which Dunbar helped found, commissioned Dunbar to design a fleet of racing sloops that became the 20-foot Corsairs. This was followed by the 15-foot 6-inch Catabouts, a design that was lengthened to the 17-foot Whistlers following World War I. As the Depression affected the demand for boats, Dunbar spent two years at the Cape Cod Shipbuilding Company in Wareham. Here he designed several boats to be built

in series, including the 23-foot Cape Cod Senior Knockabout sloops. Back in Chatham in 1937, he designed a similar boat at 24 feet called the Monomoy.

During World War II Dunbar helped design PT boats at the Elco Company, which exposed him to plywood construction.

After the war, the Quimby Veneer Company of Bingham, Maine, commissioned Dunbar to design a series of fast powerboats built of mahogany plywood and mahogany lumber. Thus began the Bristols, which came to be highly regarded for their seaworthiness, performance, and utility. The line ranged from 13 to 51 feet long but the smaller runabouts—those between 13 and 19 feet—were particularly popular. Included in the line were Dunbar's handsome double-ended bassboats.

The 43-foot 4-inch LOA *Sea Goose* was Dunbar's first shoal-draft ketch with tandem centerboards. Launched in 1950, she had a draft of 3 feet and proved seaworthy, a natural concern. The 63-foot *Ocean Pearl*, another tandem-centerboard ketch with a draft of 5 feet 6 inches with the boards up, stands out as one of Dunbar's best-remembered creations. She was the second and larger of that type designed for Seward Johnson, and has made many coastwise and offshore voyages since her launch in 1958. The 58-foot *Nabob II* with a draft of 4 feet was launched in 1967.

Dunbar's own boat was the 26-foot *Little Dipper*, a ketch-rigged bateau. Dunbar died in Chatham at the age of eighty-five.

—Daniel B. MacNaughton

DANIEL DUVERGIE

Born November 1, 1928 · France

Daniel Duvergie created a number of France's most successful yachts. Born in Chartres, he studied in Paris and received an ETACA School Engineer diploma.

From the early 1940's, Duvergie's family was associated with the Sartrouville Yacht Club on the Seine River. There he met designer Jean-Jacques Herbulot, skipper Pierre Toureau, and Michel Bigoin, who, though very young, was building his own sailboats. At age sixteen, Duvergie began to learn how to draw lines plans.

While vacationing in La Rochelle following the end of World War II, Duvergie discovered shipbuilding at the Hervé yard, and made

friends with naval architect François Sergent. He participated in several races in England and delivered yachts from the Hervé yard. When Michel Bigoin moved to Agen to build fiberglass sailboats, he approached his childhood friend to help him interpret the RORC rule. Thus the two men designed the Samouraï class (5.8 meters LWL), which won many races. Then they prepared a prototype that resulted in the famous *Karate* (24 feet LWL). Orders followed, and Eric Tabarly asked the pair to concoct for him a real meteor for the singlehanded Transpacific Race of 1969. *Pen Duick V*, built in 1968 at the La Perrière yard in Lorient, foreshadowed the unrestricted modern transoceanic racing yacht type, twenty years ahead of its time. She finished ten days ahead of her competitors. Her LOA is 10.67 meters, beam is 3.5 meters, and draft is 2.2 meters.

Duvergie has stopped designing sailboats and has been involved with M-Class (Metric-Class) models, and more recently the Mini America's Cup Class. He recently retired.

—François Chevalier

JOSEPH MELVILLE DYER

August 22, 1898–December 23, 1974
United States

Joe Dyer spent his career in Astoria, Oregon, where he owned and operated the Astoria Marine Construction Company (AMCCO), a preeminent builder of wooden yachts, workboats,

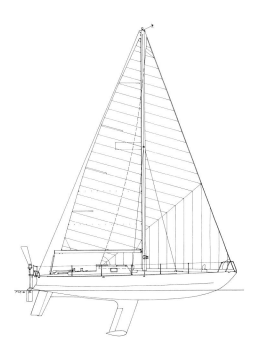

Daniel Duvergie: *Pen Duick V.* The 10.67-meter *Pen Duick V* (1968) is the ancestor of modern water-ballasted racers. Eric Tabarly commissioned her from Duvergie and Michel Bigoin for the Singlehanded Transpacific Race of 1969. She came in ten days ahead of the competition after 6,000 nautical miles. Recently refitted, she is now the property of the French Naval Museum. *Drawing courtesy Chevalier & Taglang*

and military vessels. Starting out designing fishing vessels and tugs, he sought commissions for yachts and began to see such work after he designed and built the much-admired sportfishing boat *Kingfisher* for his own use.

On the banks of the Columbia River, Dyer grew up building and sailing small boats, fishing for salmon, and crewing on tugboats. After navy service in World War I, he earned a degree in mechanical engineering from Oregon Agricultural College (now Oregon State University).

Dyer started AMCCO in 1924 with a contract to build ten Bristol Bay gillnet boats. His first-commissioned yacht design in 1927 was for the heavy-duty, 65-foot power cruiser *Ruth E.* He went on to design a number of handsome and fast power yachts, some with contemporary styling and some based on his workboat designs.

One of Dyer's most popular designs was the 28-foot Columbia River One-Design (CROD), created in 1933 for the Columbia River Yachting Association. Dyer raced his own boat of that design, *Tom Tom*, for many years. In 1952 he acquired the 45-foot power cruiser *Marymack*, which he had built in the late 1930's, renaming her *Merrimac*.

Many of the boats designed and built by Joe Dyer are still prominent in the classic yacht circles of the Pacific Northwest. —J. Scott Rohrer

Joseph Dyer: *Evening Star.* One of the early designers of cruising powerboats for the Pacific Northwest, Dyer helped to establish the characteristics of what became a local type. A comfortable enclosed wheelhouse, primarily "indoor" living space, seaworthy displacement hulls, and rugged workboat-inspired looks produced a yacht just right for her home waters. *Photo courtesy Robert Dyer*

E

IÑIGO ECHENIQUE

Born 1957 · Spain

Iñigo Echenique is one of the best-known names in Spanish yacht design, with his work ranging from the appendages of Olympic medal-winning dinghies to the America's Cup Class and a number of superyachts.

After graduating from Madrid's Escuela Superior de Ingenieros Navales, Echenique began his career in 1982 designing steel ocean-going cutters from 40 to 50 feet LOA for amateur construction. Around twenty were built, some completing circumnavigations. During the 1980's his work also included fiberglass production boat designs like the Dina and Brisa series, and the 92-foot LOA, steel sailing training schooner *Tirán*.

In 1991 Echenique became the chief designer of the Spanish entry for the America's Cup, *España 92 Quinto Centenario*, still arguably the best performing of the Spanish challengers. During this period he researched the hydrodynamics of dolphins, developing high-performance two-dimensional profiles that later influenced most of his designs, ranging from the appendages of the 470, in which Theresa Zabell won the women's Olympic gold medal and World Championships for Spain in 1996, to the rudder of the 384-foot tall-ship cruise liner *Sea Cloud II*.

During the final chapter of the IOR in 1993, Echenique designed the transformation of the Jeppesen Three-Quarter-Tonner *Xargo VI*, incorporating new deck, appendages, mast, rigging, sails, and layout. As *Galicia Calidade* in 1993 and *Xacobeo* in 1994, she twice won the Three-Quarter-Ton Cup and was nominated best Spanish racing yacht of 1994.

From 1992 to 1995 Echenique was technical manager at the northern Spanish boatyard Astilleros Mefasa during the construction of some well-known superyachts, including the Bruce King 41-meter ketch *Alejandra* and the 35-meter motoryacht *Xargo VII*.

Since 1995, along with the staff at his Acubens design office in Madrid, Echenique has continued to work on a diverse group of projects ranging from the 747 One-Design, which is very popular on the Atlantic French coast, to fast motoryachts, cruisers, and megayachts, and even a rowing boat. In 1996 his carbon fiber and foam 12-meter LOA Trainera seagoing rowing boat won the Spanish championships for her fourteen-strong crew from the small seaside village of Tirán.

Between 1996 and 2001, part of Echenique's work focused on the partial design and project management of *Sea Cloud II*, the largest sailing vessel built in Spain. Currently he is involved in the project management of yacht building throughout Europe.

Despite the high-tech nature of his profession, Echenique has never forgotten his basic love affair with all things related to the sea. In 2000 he published the book *Madeira do Mar* (*Wood of the Sea*), written in his native Galician, about his passion for the small, traditional, open Gamela fishing boats of south Galicia.

—Alfredo Lagos Sr., with Iain McAllister, John Lynch, and Alfredo Lagos Jr.

CURT WALTER EICHLER

1899–April 23, 1970 · Germany

Curt Eichler was born in Berlin into a family that sailed its 9-meter keel yacht on the Havel River. After earning an engineering degree in 1924 from the University of Berlin's shipbuilding department, he moved to Königsberg on the Baltic. There Eichler took a position at the Schichau Shipbuilding yard and also joined the local sailing club, Segelclub RHE (established in 1855 in Koenigsberg, Prussia, the oldest yacht club in Germany). He soon received his first big design commission, the 12-meter ketch *Baldur*. Other yachts of different kinds and sizes followed. Common to all was a unique balance of expedience, seaworthiness, and good looks. Accordingly, and fitting to the time he was living in, he always preferred cruising over racing yachts.

Because good wood for boatbuilding was rare or not affordable (and possibly also because of his experience in commercial shipbuilding), Eichler usually advocated steel for building yachts. He designed cruisers of 2.5- to 8-ton displacement, preferring round bilges with his typical rounded transom sterns or counter sterns with short overhangs. His own *Landsort* of 1951, an "8 KR" cruiser with a 6-ton displacement, was remarkable for its unique divided lateral plane, combined with a "durchlaufende Ballastschiene [long shallow keel]."

Eichler's design work includes about two hundred studies and projects that were detailed on about a thousand sheets, most of which still exist. His designs encompass a broad spectrum, from 3-meter dinghies to 24-meter fishery patrol boats, and sailing yachts of all types and lengths between 5 and 15 meters.

Eichler later became a lecturer at the School of Engineering in Hamburg, where he became best known for his nautical handbook *Vom Bug zum Heck* and particularly for his two-volume treatise on yacht building, *Yacht- und Bootsbau*.

—Volker Christmann

ELCO
see Irwin Chase and Glenville Sinclair Tremane

ELDREDGE-MCINNIS
see Walter J. McInnis

GREG ELLIOTT

Born February 2, 1956 · New Zealand

Greg Elliott acquired his interest in boat design while building dinghies with his father at their home in Auckland. In 1977 he produced his first design, the 25-foot 6-inch *Outsider*, for his brother, but it was the 1985 launch of *Party*

Greg Elliott: *Barter Card.* Never one to be influenced by the intricacies of a rule, Elliott designed this light-displacement flyer solely for speed. *Barter Card* has been racing in New Zealand and Australia with great success, at the head of any fleet. *Photo courtesy Bob Ross*

Pro—a plumb-stemmed, gray and yellow, light-displacement 40-footer with an extravagant reverse sheer—that notice turned his way. *Party Pro* rocketed to twelve wins in thirteen events in Auckland and introducing Elliott to the world market when she was wrecked on a reef during the 1987 Auckland Suva Race. Uninsured, *Party Pro* appeared to have sunk Elliott's career as well, but the Auckland yachting community

rallied behind him and raised $20,000 just to put him back in business. In 1989 the 17-meter *Future Shock* put to rest the ghost of *Party Pro* with a race record in the Auckland Suva event.

Two popular trailer sailer designs also helped Elliott's career. The 25-footer Elliott 770 has been a most successful racer, winning such races as the Australian Trailer Yacht Nationals and the Long Distance Night Race (Fleet A). Built of solid

foam-core construction, it has a retractable lead bulb keel and overnight accommodations. Another production yacht, the Elliott 96 (9.6 meters), is intended for bluewater racing.

Recent work has included a 52-foot racing schooner, a 17-meter ocean racing yacht, and a 9.6-meter performance cruiser. Elliott Marine is located in Auckland, New Zealand.

—David Payne

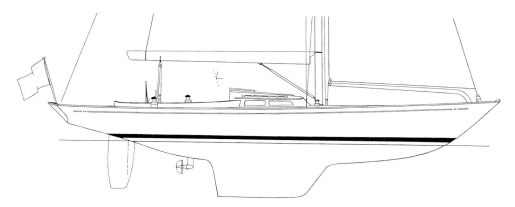

Mark Ellis: *Volunteer.* In 1996 Ellis received from a knowledgeable owner an unusual commission for a large daysailer of classic appearance with modern performance and construction. The resulting 47-footer is primarily for fast, comfortable daysailing and for looking at, but she does contain two berths, a small galley, and a navigation table. *Drawing courtesy Mark Ellis*

MARK ELLIS

Born February 4, 1945 · United States/Canada

Classic good looks, comfort, and excellent performance combined with a knowledgeable use of materials and meticulous functionality characterize the designs of Mark Ellis. The Nonsuch line of production wishbone-rigged catboats is his most widely recognized contribution to the field.

Born in Watertown, New York, Ellis began to teach himself yacht design from books while in high school. He realized that university-level naval architectural programs then available were aimed at the design of ships rather than

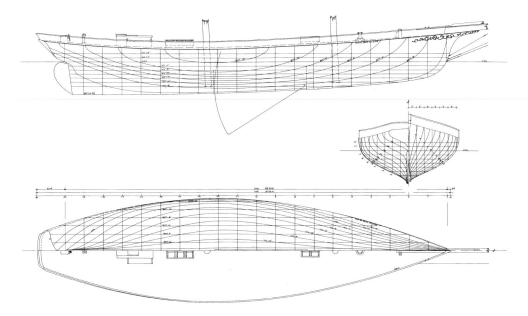

Philip Elsworth: *Montauk. Montauk*, a unique 102-foot schooner, was a radical departure from designs of the 1800's. Her beamy (25-foot) hull had a 22-foot-long centerboard and 48 tons of lead ballast molded to fit her frames. The long centerboard caused the mainmast to be stepped quite far aft. © *Chevalier & Taglang*

yachts. He opted for business school at Boston University, graduating in 1968. While at the university, he worked summers at C. Raymond Hunt Associates of Boston. After graduation, he moved to New York and joined Philip L. Rhodes, continuing to learn yacht design on the job.

In 1970, Ellis moved to Canada, joining newly founded C&C Yachts as a designer and manager of custom yacht sales. He left C&C in 1975 to found his own company, Mark Ellis Designs, based in Oakville, Ontario, Canada. Subsequently, in 1977 he joined with David Harris to found Harris and Ellis Yachts, a company specializing in retail sales and yacht brokerage.

Ellis has produced a wide range of vessels, both sail and power. The extremely successful Nonsuch 22, 26, 30, 33, and 36 catboats are wishbone-rigged and built by Hinterhoeller Yachts, as were the Niagara 35 and 42 cruising sloops. In addition to the series-built yachts, Ellis has produced custom designs for one-off construction. His most recent custom work is the 47-foot sloop *Volunteer*.

The first powerboats designed by Ellis were the Limestone series. They too reflect a respect for traditional lines but coupled with a deep-V planing hull and a midengine configuration. As a result, this boat offers outstanding smoothness, comfort, and safety in the most demanding sea conditions, as well as good looks. In the mid-1990's, Ellis designed the Downeast–style Legacy 40, Legacy 34, and Legacy 40 Express. Originally a joint project between a Canadian investor, Bruckmann Manufacturing, and Ellis, the boatbuilding firm of Freedom Yachts of Middletown, Rhode

Island, builds the Legacy series for the domestic market while Bruckmann retains a license to produce the boat for the Canadian market.

It is no surprise that Mark Ellis–designed powerboats are used by the Canadian Coast Guard, the Royal Canadian Mounted Police, the Ontario Provincial Police, and other government agencies.

Ellis feels that he takes a traditional view toward yacht design. He has a gift for designing boats that are extremely popular, long lasting, and exceptionally comfortable. His Nonsuch line, for example, is well known for its excellent windward performance, luxurious accommodations, and unparalleled ease of sail handling. When production ceased in the late 1980's, over a thousand hulls had been made. Production of this extremely popular design has resumed.

—Tom Roach

PHILIP R. "PHIP" ELSWORTH

1828–July 9, 1909 · United States

Two elements set Phip Elsworth apart from the American yacht designers of the 1880's: the unusual collaboration between a yacht designer/modeler and a professional architect, and his brief transition from the design of midsize sloops to experimental designs of centerboard schooners late in his designing career. Although only a few of his schooner yachts were built, it is in this category that he is most remembered in yacht history.

Elsworth was born in West Creek, New Jersey. The family moved to Pamrapo (Bayonne),

New Jersey, around 1841. He grew up on the waters about New York in vessels owned and sailed by his father, who was in command of a fleet of coasting schooners.

Through their passion for racing near their home, the Elsworth brothers' secondary careers evolved, Phip as a designer and his brother Joe as a highly regarded racing skipper. Phip Elsworth had no formal training in yacht designing. He made no pretensions to have a knowledge of naval architecture, yet he possessed in the highest degree a sense of form— the shape essential to speed in a vessel.

Broad, shoal, centerboard sloops and schooners were popular with the yachtsmen of New York who moored their boats in the shallow waters of Brooklyn and Staten Island. The majority of the boats Elsworth designed were safe, comfortable, family-type centerboard sloops in the 25- to 50-foot waterline range. Generally they had plumb stems and very short aft overhangs; a beautifully modeled, long and easy forebody, with an easy entrance; a point of maximum beam typically 55 to 58 percent aft of the forward end of the waterline; and full, convex buttock lines. As a class, they were deeper in body and more able than the average sloop and had a good reputation for speed.

Elsworth was an intuitive designer who cut his half models to the inside of the planking, thus making them more useful to the builder. It was the fairness of his hulls that was a great part of his success, producing curves with a "look-at-me-again" quality that an eye finds irresistible. His ability to calculate displacement curves or the center of gravity was limited. His lines were frequently taken off the models and drawn by the professional architect and yacht interior designer John G. Prague, an enthusiastic yachtsman and member of the Atlantic Yacht Club. Many of Elsworth's designs were built at the various Brooklyn shipyards of C. and R. Poillon.

In 1882, Elsworth was contracted to design the 102-foot *Montauk* for use as both a cruiser and a racer. She was, in several respects, a radical departure from the established type of 1882. First, her great depth of 10 feet and extreme beam of 25 feet were two dimensions "scientific" designers had insisted could not be joined if one desired speed—yet she was speedy. The experiment with depth essentially made her an early step toward a "compromise" design. Second, she had a 22-foot centerboard in place of the keel, and 48 tons of lead ballast molded to fit her frames. The extreme length of the centerboard caused the mainmast to be stepped far aft; thus the distance between the masts was greater than usual, allowing a wide-open area for the interior cabin design.

The capsize of Elsworth's *Grayling* on her trial sail rekindled venomous attacks on extreme centerboard designs; Elsworth was a protagonist of the great design debate, the two extremes being narrow-beam, deep-keel hulls, such as the British cutters, versus American beamy, shoal-draft, centerboard designs. Within a short period, the extreme centerboard type—which had accommodated the yachtsmen of New York, had allowed for spaciously elegant interior cabins, and produced optimal speed in light weather—was replaced completely by the compromise hulls exemplified by A. Cary Smith's *Fortuna*. For many years, *Montauk* and *Grayling* monopolized the majority of the prominent races on the East Coast, despite the fact that they were among the few large schooners he modeled.

It is believed that after designing the 1886 America's Cup contender, the big sloop *Atlantic*, Elsworth and his brother, Captain Joe, moved their oyster fishery to Greenport on Long Island, New York, where a substantial number of Elsworth's working models have been preserved.   —Nannette Poillon

OLLE ENDERLEIN

1917–1993 · Sweden

A beautiful boat was apt to be a good sailer, according to Olle Enderlein. This belief was reflected in Enderlein's many beautiful, fast-sailing, functional yachts in a wide range of sizes. From the early 1950's, he was one of

Sweden's most prominent yacht designers, known for his finely developed feeling for lines, proportions, and details.

In 1944 Enderlein won the Swedish Cruiser Club's design competition with *Gudingen*, a 9.15-meter family cruising boat. In 1947 he won the English *Yachting World* magazine's competition over forty-eight other designers with a 35-foot offshore cruiser. With this success, he was able to leave his job and work full-time on what had been his hobby of designing boats.

Enderlein was born in Norrköping, southwest of Stockholm. He was educated as an engineer and worked at Saab in Linköping, the Ship-Testing Institution at Chalmers Technical University in Gothenburg, and Archimedes in Stockholm, before starting his own yacht design firm at the end of the 1940's.

The very beautiful, Enderlein-designed coastal cruiser *Ballerina* (10.3 meters LOA) was launched in 1952 and began to win Baltic races. Later, in the 1960's, his boats won Baltic races in nearly all RORC classes. But boats built to race under the RORC rule and the later IOR were quickly victims of obsolescence, so he decided to design for the growing fiberglass industry. In the 1960's Enderlein had a very good and inspiring cooperation designing interiors with Sparkman and Stephens.

In his wooden boat period, Enderlein designed about three hundred, from small inshore boats to big one-offs (for instance, *Vagabonde* and *Dione*, about 16 meters LOA), and also motoryachts for Storebro Works. Enderlein's OE 29, 32, 33, and 36, built at Sund-

Olle Enderlein: Hallberg-Rassy 35. The HR 35 was an early series-built fiberglass cruiser. She was designed in 1968 and built by Christoffer Rassy at Kungsviken Boatyard in Orust, Sweden. During a period of ten years, about seven hundred yachts were built to the design. *Photo courtesy Hallberg-Rassy*

sor Shipyard, are still beauties sought after by yachtsmen. The boat Enderlein himself liked best was *Hambo*, a Half-Tonner designed in 1967, which won the Baltic Race and placed fifth in the One-Ton Cup in France in 1968. This design was soon put into fiberglass production under the name Mistress 32.

Best known, however, are the results of Enderlein's long cooperation with the Hallberg-

Olle Enderlein: *Sara Moraea*. *Sara Moraea* is one of two sisterships (the other is *Delight*) that exemplify the quality and beauty of Swedish design and construction. With an 8-meter waterline and graceful overhangs, she is typical of Enderlein's fast cruiser/racers, which are seen mostly on the Baltic. *Sara Moraea* lives on Scotland's Clyde estuary. *Photo courtesy James Houston*

Rassy Yachtyard on the island of Orust on the west coast of Sweden. During the 1970's, Enderlein designed a large range of motorsailers between 26 and 49 feet, which have been built in large numbers and exported to many countries. While many think of a motorsailer as a clumsy boat, Enderlein drew the type with beautiful lines and superstructures. One of his best-selling motorsailers has been the long-keeled and comfortable Monsun 31, of which 904 have been built. He also designed a range of motorsailers for the Orust-based boatyard Najad. Other well-known production-built sailboats include the Misil, Havsörnen, Mistral, and Shipman 28.

Enderlein's last design, never built, was a small centerboarder he drew in 1987. Enderlein spent the last seventeen years of his life with his wife in southern France, where the warm climate was of assistance to his health. He went home to Norrköping, his birthplace, in 1993, where he died the same year at the age of seventy-five.

Nine hundred of Olle Enderlein's drawings were given to the Swedish "Sjöhistoriska Museet" by his wife, and the museum has written a book about his life and work.

—Bent Aarre

MARTIN CORYELL ERISMANN

1877–1921 · United States

While he practiced early in the twentieth century, Martin Erismann's legacy endures into the twenty-first century by virtue of the quality of his work and his unique talents and pursuits. His body of work included nearly every type of design from small racing yachts and power cruisers, through large seagoing vessels and fishing craft, to floating dry docks and dredges. His designs for sailing craft and motoryachts appeared in *The Rudder, Forest and Stream,* and *Motor Boating* magazines from 1904 to 1921 and reflect a high degree of engineering skill and drafting ability.

Erismann was born in Lambertville, New Jersey. His mother came from a local family, the Coryells, and his father was of Swiss ancestry. He received his early education in Switzerland and was given the opportunity to travel about Europe and study many types of working and pleasure craft. He recorded their lines, construction details, and characteristics for future historical reference. His schooling provided access to early writing about naval architecture, imbuing him with a reverence for the traditions and customs of boat design and construction. Although progressive and even somewhat radical in his everyday practice, he would never-

Martin Erismann: *Queen Mab.* Erismann designed the 54-foot LOA *Queen Mab* while he was on the staff of the Fore River Shipbuilding Company. She was built by Robert Jacob of City Island, New York, in 1909. *Motor Boating*'s July 1911 issue commented, "Mr. Erismann was a pioneer in adopting the raised side and bow flare now commonly recognized as features of a good motor vessel." *Photo courtesy Tom Nye*

theless turn to these influences for inspiration throughout his career.

Upon returning to the United States, Erismann attended Webb Academy (later the Webb Institute) in New York for two years and then joined the William B. Sterns yacht yard in Marblehead, Massachusetts. In 1899 he went to work at Gas Engine and Power–Charles Seabury Company (later Consolidated Shipbuilding), in Morris Heights, New York; his designs included the 117-foot, twin-screw steam yacht *Akila* and other fast steam yachts and torpedo boats.

He then enrolled in the University of Glasgow to study under Professor J. Harvard Biles and earned a special degree in theoretical naval architecture. This also provided the opportunity to spend time around the famous Clyde shipyards.

Erismann next worked for two years at Maryland Steel Company, followed by three years as chief draftsman for Marine Construction and Dry Dock Company, on Shooter's Island just off Staten Island in New York. From 1906 to 1909 he maintained his own offices at Mariners Harbor, Staten Island, New York,

producing such major designs as the 85-foot *Milicete,* the 75-foot *Nokomis,* and the 54-foot *Queen Mab.* It was during this period that the Model Committee of the New York Yacht Club commissioned him to produce complete drawings for full-rigged models, which they wished to have in their famous collection. At the time, *The Rudder* magazine commented, "His selection was quite an honor and their confidence in him was fully justified."

After a brief sojourn in editorial work, Erismann worked at the Fore River Shipbuilding Company in Quincy, Massachusetts, on battleships and other military craft, cargo ships, and yachts.

In 1910 he joined the Boston office of Bowdoin B. Crowninshield and during this time renewed his efforts to collect the lines of local craft indigenous to New England, such as Pinkies, Isle of Shoals boats, Friendship sloops, and Hampton boats. He created great interest when he located one of the last of the now-extinct Block Island "Cowhorn" boats. Finding this vessel in unrestorable condition, he took off the lines and in 1911 commissioned the Lawley yard to build a replica, with carvel planking rather than the original lapstrake. He named her *Roaring Bessie* and sailed her as a yacht for the next few years, causing great interest.

Erismann relocated to Seattle in 1913, where he designed a number of yachts and commercial vessels and took an active interest in the development of local yachting and yacht racing.

When the United States entered World War I, Erismann was placed in charge of design at Craig Shipbuilding Company in Long Beach, California. After the war he returned East, where he became associated with Eads Johnson in New York.

An inheritance from his father left Erismann in a position to withdraw from commercial practice and to devote himself to assembling the data and information he had long been collecting for a book to be titled *Boats*. While fully engaged in working up the material acquired through exhaustive study over many years, and apparently in the prime of life and the best of health, he succumbed to a sudden attack of pneumonia, ending a career of high achievement and the promise of a work that would have been a most valuable addition to yachting history.

Among the projects he did complete was a twelve-page dissertation titled "The Effect of the Universal Rule in Recent Yachts," which was presented in 1906 at the 14th General Meeting of the Society of Naval Architects and Marine Engineers, of which he was a member. Although technical in nature, it is well grounded and clearly understandable, with comments that can be taken at face value today.

The above-mentioned paper closes with a quotation from John Ruskin, the influential

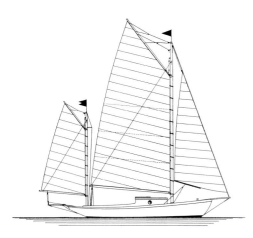

Martin Erismann. During his short life Erismann studied the many small craft indigenous to the various countries of England and Europe as well as those of the United States. He designed many smaller sailboats during his time spent on both coasts, including this 24-foot LOA yawl. *Reproduced from* The Rudder

writer, critic, and artist who had died just six years before: "With those in whose eyes the perfection of a boat is swift fragility, I have no sympathy. The glory of a boat is first its steadiness of poise, its assured standing on the clear softness of the abyss, and, after that, so much capacity of progress by oar or sail as shall be consistent with this defiance of the treachery of the sea." —Thomas G. Skahill

GUSTAF ADOLF ESTLANDER

September 18, 1876–December 1, 1930
Finland/Sweden

Gustaf Estlander first achieved fame in 1894 when, at age eighteen, his voyage alone in a canoe from Finland across the Baltic Sea to Stockholm was featured on the front pages of several newspapers. This energetic beginning was to set the tone for the rest of his relatively short life, which included creating approximately 350 yacht designs.

Born in Helsingfors (Helsinki), Finland, Estlander graduated as an architect in 1898. Until 1914, his firm designed and built many houses. During this same period he became a successful helmsman and yacht designer.

Estlander made his debut as a yacht designer in 1898 with the fin-keel racer *Singoalla*. She was followed by more extreme designs such as *Flamingo* and *Aldebaran*. Following the advent of the Square-Meter Rule in 1908, he produced a great deal of successful work in the various classes falling under its jurisdiction. His breakthrough came in the skerry cruiser classes with the 22-Square-Meter *Collibri II* (1917). From 1916 to his death in 1930, Estlander designed fast skerry cruisers in all classes from 15- to 150-Square-Meters, including the 75-Square-Meter *Trumph* and the 150-Square-Meter *Singoalla* from 1919.

The Square-Meter Rule was the favorite of many designers because there were few restrictions other than the sail area and sensible scantlings provisions. The rule tended to produce very attractive, long, light, narrow boats of wholesome form and with at least some cruising accommodations, and were considered by many to be the ultimate in beautiful, high-performance sailing yachts.

Square-Meter boats were also referred to as skerry cruisers because they had been originally conceived as ideal racer/cruisers for the sheltered inland waters and archipelagos common in Scandinavia (*skerry* means a small rocky island). They remained popular in those waters long after they were replaced elsewhere by boats designed in accordance with the International Rule.

Gustaf Estlander: *Trumph.* The 75-Square-Meter skerry cruiser *Trumph*, 17.4 meters in length, was built at the Pabst-Werft yard in Berlin in 1921. Estlander was accomplished in all the Square-Meter classes, which some consider the ultimate wooden sailing machine. © *Per Thelander*

After World War I, Estlander was attracted by a growing interest in Square-Meter boats in Germany, so he moved to Berlin where he became co-owner of the Pabst-Werke yacht yard. Unfortunately, just a few years later the yard burned down, whereupon he moved to Stockholm and opened a design office there. In 1927 he was granted Swedish citizenship.

During the 1920's Estlander continued designing Square-Meter yachts, among them boats for the new Nordic 22-Square-Meter class, but the growing domination of European competition by the International Rule of 1919 led him to try his hand in this new arena. Although he did design a 10- and a 12-Meter yacht, his real concentration was on the smaller 8-Meter and especially the popular 6-Meter class, designing a total of about twenty-five, including the 6-Meter *May Be* that won the Gold Cup in 1927. He also created the Mällar 22 class.

Estlander died suddenly in 1930. His death was mourned throughout the Scandinavian sailing world, and his trophies were enshrined at the Royal Swedish Yacht Club. One eulogist said of him, "Estlander was an artist both with the drawing board and with the tiller."

—Bent Aarre with Ulf Lycke

F

EARLE WESTON "WESTY" FARMER

November 17, 1903–May 16, 1981
United States

Weston Farmer was a prolific writer of stories about the lore, the black art, and techniques of boat design. A beautiful draftsman and designer as well, he is probably best remembered for his Tahitiana steel-ketch design, but his diverse work included a person-carrying, 13-foot 6-inch, model wood tug called the *Lady Mary* and the 85-foot aluminum yacht *Misty*, built by Palmer Johnson. His 1979 book, *From My Old Boat Shop*, was written with great humor and filled with words of wisdom and examples of good design.

Farmer spent his boyhood years in Minneapolis and his summers on Lake Superior at Isle Royale, where he got his first exposure to boating. His mother operated Rock Harbor Lodge, and his first boat was a 16-foot lapstrake launch named *Haywire*, powered by a 2-hp Caille gasoline engine. According to Farmer's son, the craft was literally held together by haywire. The family also owned the steam launch *Atalanta* to carry passengers to and from the lodge.

During his high school years Farmer earned credits working at Shepard's Boatworks in the winter, and later, during his late teens and early twenties, he served an apprenticeship at the Ramaley Boatworks in Wayzata, where he eventually designed and built runabouts. He spent one year at the University of Minnesota and then transferred to the naval architecture program at the University of Michigan. He returned to the mechanical engineering program at the University of Minnesota but dropped out in 1924 when he married Mary Murray, known as Bylo.

The publication in 1919 of an article Farmer wrote on propellers at the age of sixteen was his introduction to being a paid writer. The piece in *Everyday Engineering* earned him the magnificent sum of thirty-five dollars, and with that, by his own admission, came an in-

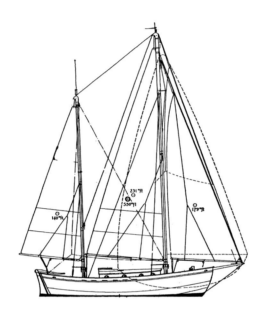

Weston Farmer: *Tahitiana*. *Tahitiana* was a redesign of Jack Hanna's famous ketch *Tahiti*. Designed for construction in steel, it gained a close approximation of *Tahiti*'s lines by the use of multiple chines. Thereby, the plates can be formed by merely clamping to the frames, precluding the necessity of large forming machinery. *Drawing courtesy Weston Farmer Associates*

satiable appetite to write.

With a growing family, things were tough for the young naval architect, so Farmer spent a year as a traveling insurance salesman. In 1925 he moved to New York City, where he teamed up with Philip L. Rhodes and shared a tiny, almost hole-in-the-wall-sized office. They each had their own outside, non-naval architecture ventures and so would spend half a day tending to them and the other half in the office developing yacht designs—one would be in the office in the morning and the other in the afternoon. So small was the office, crowded with drawing boards and files, visitors were said to have stood in the doorway.

By the winter of 1929, Farmer was working for the fledgling Fawcett Publishing Company in Robbinsdale, Minnesota, and revived an earlier involvement with aircraft. He became

the editor of *Modern Mechanics and Inventions Magazine* and was responsible for plans for homebuilders of airplanes that included engineering, drawings, and expositions. During this time he also wrote many articles, some occasionally published under the nom de plume F. Weston Earle (to keep from being too prominent, says his son Wes).

After four years of publishing and a few airplane crackups, Farmer decided it was time to move on to California, with his boatbuilding and drafting tools and family. But it was still the Depression era and business was slow, so he again became an itinerant naval architect. His time and travels found him working for Fellows and Stewart, South Coast, and Ackerman on the West Coast; Gibbs Gas Engine of Jacksonville, Florida; and Newport News Shipbuilding in Virginia.

While in Jacksonville, Farmer bought a small restaurant that he planned to open as a fast-food operation, perhaps some twenty years before anyone had heard of McDonald's, but it failed. That propelled the family up to Bayonne, New Jersey. There he worked at Elco Works on the designs of yachts and the fledgling PT boat. In 1941 Farmer was lured to the Annapolis Yacht Yard in Annapolis, Maryland, where British Vosper Victory PT Boats were being converted to American engines and armaments.

Farmer was an inveterate tinkerer and inventor, and after the conclusion of World War II, the family moved back to Minneapolis and Farmer developed an aluminum toy much like the later Erector sets made by the A. C. Gilbert Company. After several good years, the Gilbert Company began producing their own sets of steel, and Farmer saw the writing on the wall and sold out.

When television came along to the Minneapolis area, Farmer created, produced, and was host of the live TV show *The Idea Jackpot*, which attracted local inventors and venture capitalists. Eventually he returned to naval architecture. Farmer then became a consultant and designer for the well-known yards of Palmer Johnson and Burger, and designed several aluminum 85-footers such as *Misty* in 1969.

Following his love of designing small boats, Farmer designed well over two hundred plans for all sorts of vessels; the most popular might be one of the best-selling stock designs ever produced, the rugged 32-foot ketch called *Tahitiana* for which over two thousand sets of plans have been sold. *Tahitiana* was a redesign of Jack Hanna's ketch *Tahiti*, but it was built of steel. Farmer's list of plans—still being sold by Farmer's son—includes, among others, inboard- and outboard-powered cruisers, runabouts, shoal-draft garveys, canoe yawls, and a 25-foot fantail steam launch.

Farmer's dedication to keeping the art and science of yacht design pure included being critical of designers who would draw what he called "zip-zap" propellers (straight lines that gave only a bare indication that they represented propellers) or who didn't have a clue about how to develop a transom. He collected and commented on the works of naval architects or their writings, often flavoring their drawings or pages with salient and pithy comments.

Farmer's book *From My Old Boat Shop, One Lung Engines, Fantail Launches, & Other Marine Delights* was compiled of articles originally published in *National Fisherman* magazine and published in 1979 by the International Marine Publishing Company of Camden, Maine. A second edition was published in 1996 by Boat House Press. Farmer had a long and vigorous relationship with *National Fisherman* and contributed many opinionated articles and criticism.

Westy Farmer's son Wes said of his father, "A very varied career by a brilliant man. He never got rich, but left a great legacy."

—Bob Wallstrom

BRUCE K. FARR, OBE

Born 1949 · New Zealand/United States

Bruce Farr has achieved an international reputation for the design of racing sailboats, as well as cruisers of the modern, racing boat–based form. An early advocate of the light-displacement concept, Farr established his reputation in his native New Zealand, where boats of this type had found early and consistent acceptance as cruising boats and then began to see overwhelming success on the race course. He was one of the first designers to create large, light racing boats with wide transoms, dinghy-like sections, and minimized keels, capable of higher speeds than their more traditional predecessors under the right conditions.

From the beginning Farr and his design partners have emphasized superior high-tech engineering and increasingly sophisticated research and development as their route to success. Today the firm employs advanced computer modeling and analysis as well as tank and wind-tunnel testing to optimize its results. In their racing boats they have also found good success in the science of obtaining a favorable rating—a big part of the game throughout the long history of racing under handicapping rules.

Born into New Zealand's large post–World War II community of do-it-yourself boatbuilders, Farr and his family joined many others in building in their backyards simple and inexpensive boats to be raced against fellow yacht club juniors and in interclub regattas. New technologies such as epoxy glues, molded veneer, and plywood together with new performance dinghy classes whose only restrictions were hull length and sail area, led to dramatic innovation by designers and builders. Farr was in the thick of it.

Farr designed and built his first boat, a 10-foot 6-inch dinghy named *Resolution*, at age eleven. Two years later *Resolution* won a regatta in the Pennant Class against boats up to 14 feet long. Next he designed and built several examples of the 11-foot Moth restricted class. *Mammoth* took Farr, at age fifteen, to victory in the North Island Restricted Moth Championships. By 1968, he had won his fourth successive title.

Through trial and error, Farr learned how to squeeze every advantage from his designs, specifically concentrating on reducing their weight. After a series of successes there was sufficient demand for Farr's boats for him to cut his college career short and begin making his living designing and building boats.

Soon Farr recognized the limitations of being young, self-employed, and self-trained, and the eighteen-year-old found employment with designer/builder Jim Young in Auckland. Three years later Farr resumed working for himself, building yachts to his designs in the basement of his parent's home in Devonport.

Titus Canby was Farr's first keelboat, launched in 1971. Along with other innovations, the 27-foot LOA plywood sloop was light, displacing only 4,820 pounds, and she was fast, particularly upwind. In her first season she won the South Pacific Half-Ton Trophy in a fleet of twenty. She won it again in 1974.

More commissions followed. Farr's 18-footers won an unprecedented four world championships in a row. There were further successes in the Quarter-Ton, Admiral's Cup, and other events. Victories in the One-Ton Cup and Three-Quarter-Ton Cup continued despite IOR changes aimed at features typical of Farr's yachts, such as a penalty for wide sterns.

Most of the greatest designers have exploited the link between improved engineering and innovative yacht design, and from the begin-

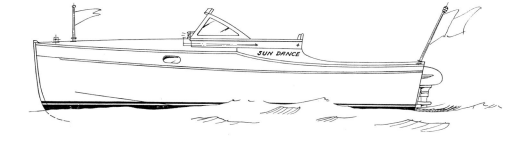

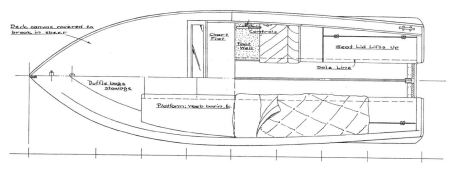

Weston Farmer: Sun Dance. The 17½-foot Sun Dance is a small outboard cruiser designed for the outdoorsman who doesn't need all the amenities of a larger cruiser. The arrangement plan shows that sleeping is done under a spray hood canopy, leaving the fore cabin dry for duffel. *Drawing courtesy Weston Farmer Associates*

Bruce Farr: Farr 40. A strict one-design class launched in 1997, the Farr 40 has also proved to be competitive under the IMS, CHS (Channel Handicap System), and PHRF (Performance Handicap Racing Fleet) handicapping systems. Featuring a clean deck layout, a carbon fiber rig with a non-overlapping jib, and no running backstays, she's a relatively simple and easily handled boat. © *Onne van der Wal*

38, the Noelex 30, and Sea Nymph's trailer sailer were developed to cushion the business from the fallout over the IOR.

Increasingly Farr's work was international, and in 1981 a decision was made to locate the practice more centrally, in Annapolis, Maryland, where it became known as Bruce Farr and Associates. Farr and Bowler scraped through the first few years, but Farr's decision to resume designing IOR boats propelled the firm to renewed success and by 1985 his designs again dominated IOR regattas worldwide.

New Zealand's first challenger for the 1987 America's Cup race was the product of a team of designers: Laurie Davidson, Ron Holland, Russell Bowler, and Bruce Farr. The team succeeded in obtaining Lloyd's* approval of the first fiberglass 12-Meter, which became *Kiwi Magic* (KZ-7). Ultimately she failed to win the challenger trials, but many felt she was the fastest boat, and she did go on to win the 12-Meter Worlds in Sardinia, Italy, in June of 1987.

In 1988, Farr designed the 90-foot waterline length New Zealand challenger that lost to the only catamaran ever sailed in an America's Cup match—Dennis Conner's *Stars & Stripes*—in the lawsuit-dominated series that eventually led to the creation of the new America's Cup Rule.

Another achievement was the success of the maxi ketch *Steinlager 2*, which won all six legs of the 1989–90 Whitbread Round the World Race. Since then Farr yachts have gone on to dominate the top spots in the Whitbread/Volvo races.

The IMS racing rule began to replace the IOR in the 1980's. The Farr 44-footer *Gaucho*, Farr's first IMS design, was a throwback to his designs from the early 1970's. She was ultralight and had a high sail area–displacement ratio, and she won her first five races. Protesters said she flaunted the spirit of the rule, and compromises within the Offshore Racing Council (ORC) resulted in the creation of two divisions within the IMS, one for cruiser/racers and one for racers.

The year 1992 marked a huge number of racing successes for Farr as boats to his designs won five of the international regattas. In the 1992 America's Cup race, the Farr-designed *New Zealand Challenge* (NZL-20) was a finalist in the much-protested Louis Vuitton Cup, losing to Italian challenger *Il Moro*, whose design team was led by Germán Frers.

For all his successes, Farr did not win an America's Cup match in six tries from 1987 through 2003. In 1995 he designed a boat for New Zealander Chris Dickson that was fast but underfunded. For the 2000 Cup in Auckland, he designed the New York Yacht Club's *Young America*, which after exhibiting superior speed almost broke in half on a wave and

ning Farr understood that his era was all about rapid evolution in construction materials. In 1976 he brought engineer/designer/sailor Russell Bowler into the fledgling office of Bruce Farr Yacht Design, first as a structural consultant, then as a full-time associate in 1980. Bowler's early innovation in lightweight sandwich construction was just the begin-

ning of his ongoing development of composite building techniques.

Farr's decision to diversify the business into cruiser/racers followed the IOR's Mark IIIa rating changes in 1979, which effectively favored the heavy-displacement majority at the expense of the winning light-displacement minority typified by Farr's work. The Farr

Bruce Farr: Carroll Marine 60. While the Carroll Marine 60 is one of Farr's latest creations, she displays the dinghy-like hull, efficient rig, and crisp aesthetic approach that has been typical of his work from the beginning. © *Onne van der Wal*

Bruce Farr: Volvo Ocean 70. Designed for the Volvo Ocean 70 class, this yacht represents a new extreme in ultralight round-the-world racers. The rule allows canting keels, multiple underwater appendages, water-trimming ballast, and carbon fiber hulls. A red button turns cameras on during dramatic moments, which should be many. *Drawing courtesy Farr Yacht Design, Ltd.*

never recovered. He returned three years later with San Francisco–based *Oracle BMW*. The most unusual boat at that year's Cup, she was narrowly beaten in the challengers' finals by the eventual winner, *Alinghi*.

Among Farr's successes were several one-design classes like the Farr 40, which became an international standard for class racing at the highest levels. To date Farr-designed yachts can claim forty world championships and numerous victories in series such as the Admiral's Cup, Commodore's Cup, Kenwood Cup, Sardinia Cup, and the Southern Cross Cup.

Farr is also well known for his cruising boats, which, freed from the direct influence of the rating rules, show similarity to the racers but in a cleaner and more moderate form. Both the racing and the cruising designs tend to have a pleasing appearance—a clean, functional look based on harmony between the major lines rather than trendy features or arbitrary styling.

Production builders of Farr designs include Beneteau, Boat Sales International, McDell Marine, Southern Wind Shipyard, Wally Yachts, DK Yachts, Nauta Yachts, Ovington, James Betts Enterprises, and Cookson boatbuilders.

In June 1999, the name of Farr's design firm was changed from Bruce Farr and Associates to Farr Yacht Design, as a reflection of the diversified approach of the design team, which numbered seventeen members as of 2004.

Bruce Farr and his company have received numerous awards ranging from New Zealand Yachtsman of the Year in 1976, to numerous Boat of the Year citations, to Farr's entrance into the Annapolis Maritime Hall of Fame in 2003. In 1990 Farr was awarded the Order of the British Empire for his services to yachting. He also holds the Science and Technology Silver Medal from the Royal Society of New Zealand, and served on the International Technical Committee of the Offshore Racing Council for many years. To date Bruce Farr and his firm have designed several hundred racing and cruising yachts ranging from 15 to 132 feet.

The Lloyd's insurance company created construction standards and monitored quality during building. As well, they published the book Lloyd's Register.

—Daniel B. MacNaughton

IAN FARRIER

Born February 15, 1947 · New Zealand

If there is one designer who has defined the concept of a folding trailerable trimaran, it is Ian Farrier. His multihull career began almost by accident in 1969 in his native New Zealand with the launch of his first 30-foot trimaran, a boat he had acquired unfinished two years previously only because he had been unable to find a suitable monohull for offshore cruising.

In 1972, Farrier moved to Brisbane, Australia, where he noted the growing popularity of monohull trailer sailers. Sensing a similar market opportunity for a trailerable trimaran, Farrier set out to develop a folding mechanism that allowed a person to quickly narrow the trimaran on the water to fit in a narrow marina berth or to provide a street-legal width for trailering. The first Trailertri incorporating Farrier's patented, double-strut folding mechanism was built in 1974 and proved to be a great success. It was followed by five more Trailertris of various sizes that were built to refine the folding concept and to test various configurations. During the following years, hundreds of Trailertris were built of plywood by amateur builders, and folding trimarans began to be a mass phenomenon. The Trailertri was followed in 1980 by the 19-foot Tramp, a daysailer trimaran that was first produced in Australia and later, as the Eagle, in the United States.

In 1984 Farrier moved to Chula Vista near San Diego, California, where he had found investors willing to back the development and production of a 27-foot, foam sandwich folding trimaran. The first F-27 was launched in 1985 and soon a hundred F-27s a year were produced by Corsair Marine. Provided with low-rocker, medium-volume floats and a round-bilge, planing center hull, the F-27 proved to be a versatile boat that was roomy, rugged and safe, easy to launch from a trailer, and still capable of winning races. The breakthrough design quickly set the world standard for a folding trimaran. Some 450 F-27s were eventually built until 1996, when it was superseded by the slightly larger and updated F-28. Corsair also built other Farrier trimarans, including more than 300 F-24s (24 feet, 1992) and the F-31 (31 feet, 1991, called F-9A for one-off builders). Other builders began construction of the performance-oriented F-25 (25 feet, 1992), which later became the F-82.

Farrier began to design larger multihulls. In 1994 he developed his first offshore trimaran, the F-36. The 36-foot, liveaboard cruiser was also his first nonfolding design, although it continued to be demountable for occasional transport. The year 1998 saw the development of Farrier's first catamaran, the F-41, a 41-foot cruiser with an emphasis on comfort and space rather than performance. In 2002, the maxi trailerable F-33, the oceangoing performance cruising trimaran F-39, as well as the F-22, a 22-foot economical hard-chine update of the original Trailertri series, were developed. That year, over two thousand Farrier-designed trimarans were sailing in many countries all over the world.

Ian Farrier has always designed with a view toward series production. He never was interested in one-off racing multihulls. Over the years Farrier's folding mechanism continued to be refined, and in keeping with global trends,

Ian Farrier: F-27. The F-27, Ian Farrier's most successful design, defined the concept of the trailerable folding trimaran. *Photo courtesy Ian Farrier*

Thomas Fearon: *Jessie.* The 40-foot catamaran *Jessie*, designed and built by Fearon in 1882, was one of the fastest of the small but competitive fleet of catamarans then racing in New York waters. Fitted with a cabin, she cruised to Florida and back to New York in the winter of 1882–83. *Photo by Edwin Hale Lincoln, courtesy Claas van der Linde*

his trimarans became longer and wider and the floats more voluminous in order to increase sail-carrying power. For boats up to 33 feet in length, his basic design philosophy, however, has remained the same: to provide easily trail-erable, safe, roomy, well-engineered multihull cruisers with performance provided by de-sign efficiency and good engineering.

—Claas van der Linde

THOMAS FEARON

May 15, 1842–after 1909 · United States

Thomas Fearon's catamarans were the fastest sailboats in the United States (and probably the world) in the 1880's, a role that had been played in the 1870's by N. G. Herreshoff's cata-marans. From 1876 until the late 1880's, there had been a brief but very intense period of in-terest in racing catamarans in the United States, particularly on the eastern seaboard and cen-tered in New York waters.

Triggered by the success of Herreshoff's *Amaryllis* at the Second International Regatta on New York Bay on June 23, 1876, catamarans were the focus of intense debate in the press, making front-page headlines in the daily news-papers and in a few cases attracting literally thousands of spectators to their races. This interest was due to their speed. With docu-mented average speeds over a race course of more than 14 knots (against the current) and top speeds said to have exceeded 25 knots, these boats were very fast—faster in fact than almost all available means of private individ-ual transportation on land or water: the auto-mobile had not been invented yet, horses and horse carriages required frequent stops and feeding, and even large steam yachts seldom achieved averages of more than 12 knots.

An excellent oarsman and already a re-nowned builder of lightweight rowing shells at his boatshop on the Hudson River in Yon-kers, New York, Fearon apparently built his first catamaran in 1878. Only fourteen or fifteen

Fearon-designed catamarans are documented (compared to just ten or eleven by Herreshoff), but these boats raced frequently and dominated the races in which they participated.

Like Herreshoff, Fearon fitted his catamarans with an elaborate system of universal joints and springs that provided for independent pitch-ing movement of the two hulls. With lengths of up to 42 feet, his boats were larger than those built by Herreshoff, who never built a cata-maran longer than 35 feet.

It is reasonable to assume that Fearon's cata-marans were also faster, if only because they were longer, but also because the leading cata-maran racer of the times discarded his Her-reshoff design for a Fearon boat once it became available. However, we know of only one sin-gle race when a Herreshoff catamaran met a Fearon catamaran head-on, and this was not representative, as it degenerated into a drift-ing race of a well-tuned Herreshoff boat against a Fearon-prototype with teething problems. Herreshoff generally relied on centerboards to

Joseph Fellows: Fellowscraft Thirty-Two. This standardized, raised-deck cruiser, the Fellowscraft Thirty-Two, was designed and built by Fellows and Stewart from 1922 to 1930. With full headroom, a complete galley, enclosed head, ample cockpit, and 10-foot beam, she slept four and got many families out on the water, becoming one of the most successful designs in company history. *Photo courtesy Newport Harbor Nautical Museum, Newport Beach, CA*

Joseph Fellows: *Vite.* *Vite,* a 39-foot Q-Class sloop designed and built by Fellows in 1914, was acknowledged as one of the finest and most successful racing yachts turned out on the West Coast before World War I, a Fellows masterpiece. *Fellows and Stewart Collection, Los Angeles Maritime Museum*

provide lateral resistance, but Fearon later also experimented with keels. (It is unclear whether these really improved performance.)

Like the Herreshoff boats, Fearon's catamarans had slender hulls and were very wide. With beam-length ratios of up to 0.69, they had very-high-righting moments, allowing them to carry enormous spreads of canvas and making them much more powerful and thus potentially faster than almost all the catamarans built until the 1960's, when new building materials finally made further advances possible.

Interest in catamarans waned in the late 1880's as their novelty wore off and other faster means of transportation became available, but Fearon remained obsessed with speed. In 1887 he experimented with a fast steam launch intended to beat Herreshoff's famous *Stiletto* (it was never heard of again). In 1903, Fearon built the "autoboat" *Vingt-et-Un*, following a design by Clinton Crane. *Vingt-et-Un* was the first really fast autoboat in the United States and triggered widespread interest in racing motorboats fitted with automobile engines. It was the last time that Thomas Fearon could claim to have built what was acknowledged to have been the fastest boat of her length in American waters.

—Claas van der Linde

JOSEPH FELLOWS
May 30, 1865–May 2, 1942
JOSEPH "RUSTY" FELLOWS JR.
October 14, 1906–July 6, 1962

United States

As a child in 1871, Joe Fellows emigrated with his family from England to America. He built his first boat at age ten and by 1889 at the age of twenty-four was considered a first-rate artisan, having worked in shipyards in Oregon and Washington. While in Seattle, he designed and built a 32-foot sloop named *Comet*, which he successfully raced and lived aboard for two years.

In Seattle, Fellows associated for a time with the young naval architect Leigh Coolidge, who taught him drafting. Next he moved to San Francisco, where he and a partner began building vessels for the Yukon gold rush. These were mostly large and small commercial vessels, but they also built some yachts to his design.

In 1896, with a contract to build "just one boat," Fellows moved south to San Pedro, California, locating his shop on Rattlesnake (now Terminal) Island. Far from stopping after one boat, he experienced immediate success building yachts and commercial craft for the growing southern California community. His extensive earlier experience was a sound base, and he was well liked, having a wonderful,

genial personality and a good sense of humor, factors that undoubtedly helped his business.

Fellows seemed to prefer building from a carved model, but he was also a capable draftsman, which helped to sell boats. Beginning with the 30-foot *Myth*, followed by *Venus, Mischief, Katrina, Sea Bird, Zarapico,* and *Shadow,* all successful sloops, the schooner *Aloha,* and his favorite, the 44-foot yawl *Minerva,* his reputation as a designer and builder of sailing yachts grew steadily.

In the early years of gasoline-powered boats, most designers tried to obtain high speeds by building long, narrow, relatively heavy hulls. Fellows's approach to powerboat design was to create a shorter, wider, and lighter boat, a type well served by the development of lighter gas engines that turned at higher rotations per minute. Soon his powerboats were widely recognized for their performance.

In 1908 Fellows sold a half interest in the business to Victor B. Stewart, a successful businessman and yachtsman. The business was moved across the channel to newly infilled Mormon Island near Wilmington, where it remained until 1929. This association allowed Fellows to concentrate on design, and the business flourished. The company name was changed to Fellows and Stewart in 1917.

Fellows and Stewart became the first West Coast company to come out with a line of stock cabin cruisers in 1923. These 26- and 32-footers were built in quantity over the next eight years and very well received. A few still exist, including *Madeline O,* based in San Diego and still in the hands of her original owner.

After years of experience at his father's boatyard, Rusty Fellows graduated from the University of Michigan in 1929 with a degree in naval architecture. His specialty was high-speed planing craft and fast cruisers, but he was also involved in the design of sailboats and was a fine sailor himself.

As his father grew older, Rusty Fellows began to act as principal designer as well as assume the responsibility of running the yard. The yard also built many boats designed by prominent outside architects, such as John Alden, Bill Luders, Nicholas Potter, I. Judson Kelly, George Wayland, Merle Davis, William Garden, and Dair Long. In 1929 the company moved back to Terminal Island at Berth 206, where more space was available for growth. They operated there until 1951, when land subsidence caused by successful underground oil drilling forced the move to Berth 213, their final and largest facility.

Although Rusty Fellows died of a heart attack in 1962, the business continued to operate until its sale in 1967.

—Thomas G. Skahill

FREDERIC A. "FRITS" FENGER
1882–June 1970 · United States

One of Frits Fenger's most notable achievements was his invention of the main trysail ketch rig, sometimes known as the staysail ketch rig. In this rig, the mizzen is somewhat larger and farther forward than usual. Instead of the usual mainsail, there are two sails completely filling the space between the masts, one of which is a mizzen staysail, which, unlike the usual sail of that name, has no overlap and is meant to be carried on all points of sail. The remainder of the space between the masts is filled by the main trysail, a triangular sail that comes to a point at the bottom and is wide near the top, stretched by a wishbone boom sheeted to the top of the mizzenmast.

The rig is said to be an aerodynamic improvement over the usual ketch rig, partly because it spreads a greater amount of sail for the length of the masts. It balances under many useful combinations of sails, including the mizzen staysail only, an ideal rig for very heavy weather. All the sails are of roughly the same manageable size and self-tending, reducing the strain on the crew. The shapes of the sails, especially the main trysail, and the wishbone booms, combine to produce a rig of great beauty. Fenger developed items of rigging and hardware that helped the rig to reach its potential.

Fenger made an extensive study of helm balance, which was one factor leading to the development of the new rig. He was one of the few designers to apply the "Arab dhow" underbody shape to yachts, in which the keel shows reverse drag, being deeper at the forward end than it is aft. This underbody shape provided good balance when teamed with the main trysail ketch rig, and was felt to help prevent the bow from being set off to leeward in squalls or in heavy seas. Having the deepest draft forward made it easier to free a vessel that had gone aground. Neither the underbody shape nor the main trysail ketch rig ever became popular, although they did prove effective in practice.

The 38-foot main trysail ketch *Diablesse* was Fenger's best-known design, of which fourteen examples were built, including Alexander Forbes's well-known *Stormsvala. Diablesse,* built in 1937 for Fenger's use, is still sailing on the coast of Maine almost completely unmodified from the original, having proved satisfactory in all respects to several owners.

Fenger was also instrumental in developing twin spinnakers for self-steering offshore, an innovation that was widely used by voyagers for many years, although it has now been rendered largely obsolete by the advent of effective self-steering gears and autopilots.

Fenger was a particularly good writer, and his book *Alone in the Caribbean,* describing an extensive cruise in his rudderless 17-foot sailing canoe *Yakaboo,* is a classic story of small-boat cruising and the pre–World War I Caribbean. Another was titled *Cruise of the Diablesse,* describing his experiences cruising the Caribbean in a 52-foot schooner (not the later ketch of the same name).

The Frederic A. Fenger Collection is at Mystic Seaport Museum, Mystic, CT. Yakaboo is in the Bruce Mines Museum near Sault Sainte Marie, Ontario, Canada.

—Daniel B. MacNaughton

THOMAS ELI FEXAS

Born January 26, 1941 · United States

Few designers have done more to revitalize modern powerboat design than Tom Fexas. By the 1970's powerboat design had become predictable, almost standardized. Ruler-straight lines had combined with fiberglass to produce many boats that at best had a kind of "lunar lander" look and at worst appeared to be the work of trailer and RV designers.

Tom Fexas dared to draw boats featuring exuberant streamlining that left behind the vehicular references of the 1940's and 1950's, and achieved a degree of excitement and individualism that, when it finally saw widespread exposure, was enthusiastically received by the public. Since Fexas began practicing, similar expression has been seen in megayacht design, but Fexas remains one of the few to bring such style to smaller yachts.

His boats seem to follow the idea that if one is going to choose a boat that is fast, fun, powerful, and impressive, why shouldn't it look that way? The designs of all the shapes, including those that have little to do with wind resistance, are strongly aerodynamic. Flat planes and straight lines are not part of the idea. Trawlers and tugboats are often described as "sailor's" powerboats, and there is some truth to that, but for those who love the sweeping sheers, curvaceous sections and ends, and harmonious superstructures of good sailboats, a Fexas powerboat has similar appeal.

The son of a doctor living in New York, Fexas began sketching boats as a young child and never stopped. He graduated from the State University of New York Maritime College

Frits Fenger: *Stormsvala* (opposite). The 48-foot 6-inch main trysail ketch *Stormsvala* clearly shows the details of her rig, which was the most notable innovation for which Fenger was known. © *Peter Barlow*

Tom Fexas: *Midnight Lace.* The 52-foot *Midnight Lace,* originally designed solely to suit her designer, was something new when she was first drawn in 1973. Fast and dramatically styled, she also featured unusually low fuel consumption. Along with her various descendants she opened a whole new niche in powerboat design. *Photo courtesy Tom Fexas*

with a degree in marine engineering and a minor in naval architecture, and in 1962 went to sea on the liner *Independence* as an engineer. After graduating from the Westlawn School of Yacht Design, he worked at General Dynamics designing submarines. He later worked as a marine surveyor.

Fexas's first commission in 1969 was for a 50-foot trawler yacht. Two more boats followed over the next two years, but during this time he was already working in a different direction. Having had a summer job as a teenager on a sleek Long Island Sound commuter yacht, he came to realize that he wanted to design boats with a similarly exciting look. On his own, he designed his first boat in the new style, a 52-footer that he named *Midnight Lace.* He took the design to various boating-magazine editors and was told he was on the wrong track. In 1974, a client came to the office wanting just such a boat. He was shown the plans, commissioned a design for a 44-foot version, had it built, showed it at the 1978 Fort Lauderdale Boat Show, and the public loved it. Fexas's career took off.

Since then Tom Fexas has done many custom designs, plus stock boats for Cheoy Lee, Burger, Palmer Johnson, Southern Cross, Derecktor, and American Marine. He has also written widely in numerous nautical magazines and is the power yacht consultant for American Bureau of Shipping. Recently he has drawn a number of large yachts, including the 141-foot *La Baroness* and the 126-foot *Time.* Tom Fexas Yacht Design is located in Stuart, Florida.

—Daniel B. MacNaughton

WILLIAM FIFE

1785–1865 · Scotland

The son of a wheelwright, William Fife founded one the greatest family dynasties ever in yacht design and construction. The Earl of Glasgow is said to have helped the Fifes (probably William's older brother, John Fife Jr.) to establish their boatyard on the beach at Fairlie on the river Clyde in Scotland in 1790. The early yard was little more than a section of open shoreline with a sawpit, near an existing iron smithy. But it was the beginning of a new life's work for William Fife.

Little is known for certain of Fife's early boats, except that he built fishing smacks and small coastal trading vessels that became known for their speed, looks, and structural quality. The early yard built a number of yachts at a time, in 1800, when it is estimated that only fifty yachts were intended for racing in Great Britain. Fife built a number of them. His first yacht to be recorded for posterity was *Comet,* a 6-ton (Thames Measurement) cutter built in 1807.

Fife made a strong impression with his second historically documented yacht, the yawl *Lamlash,* built in 1812. At 50 tons she was the largest yacht in the Clyde region and became the first flagship of the Royal Northern Yacht Club (which merged with the Royal Clyde Yacht Club in 1978 to form the Royal Northern and Clyde Yacht Club). She was a successful racer and the first Scottish yacht to cruise the Mediterranean. Under subsequent owners, *Lamlash* sailed as far as Tasmania and

Hawaii, among the earliest long-distance voyages by a yacht.

In 1813 Fife was chosen to build the 66-foot cargo vessel *Industry*, the second commercially viable steam-powered vessel in Europe. She was not only a success but also very well built, for she lasted until 1882. It is interesting to note that despite a demand for more steam vessels, Fife immediately returned to yacht building.

Also in 1813, Fife married Janet Jamieson. They had ten children, their eldest son being William Fife II. (All the children received the new spelling of the family name—prior to Fife, their family name was Fyfe.) William Fife II would eventually take over the yard and employ his brothers Alexander, Allan, and James.

William Fife designed all his boats using half models, but had a strong interest in the scientific aspects of yacht design. His friend James Smith, a yachtsman and scientist, made him aware of David Steel's book, *Naval Architecture*. With what he learned from the book, Fife was able to move to a more scientific approach, a significant leap that allowed his designs to evolve more rapidly with a reduced risk of failure. Fife valued the book so highly that he recorded the birth dates of his children inside, as others might do with a family bible.

The most famous of the fine yachts built by Fife is probably *Gleam*, a 30-ton cutter launched in 1832. She reportedly was the best boat of her time for windward work and the fastest yacht on the Clyde.

In the early 1830's, Fife was one of several designers and builders to advise a local experimenter, George Parker, on how to develop a practical proa or outrigger canoe. In 1832, Fife built Parker's 60-foot lateen-rigged *Ruby Queen*, which could sail at 10 knots, or even faster after she had been lightened. This project represented some of the very earliest experimentation with multihulls by Western yachtsmen and boatbuilders.

William Fife's good reputation as a designer and builder did not result in financial success. In 1839, he left the yacht building to his eighteen-year-old son, William Fife II, who had been apprenticed to him since the age of thirteen. Fife produced only workboats for the rest of his working life.

—Daniel B. MacNaughton

WILLIAM FIFE II

1821—January 13, 1902 · Scotland

During William Fife II's lifetime, the sport of yachting grew worldwide, supported by wealthy sportsmen whose intense rivalry ensured work for designers and builders. Fife II (also known as Fife Sr.) began his involvement with his

William Fife II (Sr.): *Cythera.* Here is *Cythera*, ghosting along in 1886. Originally cutter-rigged, at this point she has been lengthened slightly and made heavier and carries a yawl rig. Two years later she was lost off New Jersey in a hurricane. *Photo courtesy Hart Nautical Collections, MIT Museum, Cambridge, MA*

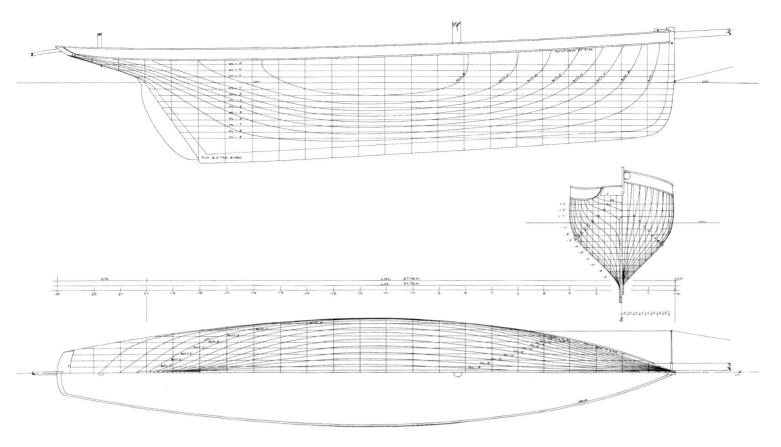

William Fife II (Sr.): *Cythera*. Designed and built by William Fife II in 1874, the 104-foot 2½-inch cutter *Cythera* has a beam of only 17 feet 9 inches, but is not as extreme as later yachts. She was a consistent race winner, sometimes carried a yawl rig, and was at one point lengthened. © *Chevalier & Taglang*

father's yacht design and construction yard at the age of thirteen as an apprentice. By the time he was eighteen, his father had resumed designing and building workboats, turning the yacht work over to his son.

After years of struggle, Fife II made the yard at Fairlie, on the Firth of Clyde in Scotland, an economically viable business. This enabled him to indulge his talent and aesthetic sense to the fullest, and his success laid the groundwork for his own son's even more spectacular accomplishments. Fife II became known as an innovator, developing lightweight, hollow spars for lightness and expanding sail plans for extra speed. Ultimately he and his son, William Fife III, cooperated in the management of the yard, working together for many years until Fife II's death.

The yacht-building portion of the yard remained in financial difficulty until 1848, when a friend loaned Fife the money to design and build *Stella*, a 40-ton cruising schooner (some sources call her a cutter) that was sold and launched in 1851. In 1852 she was lengthened by 6 feet and revamped for racing, at which she proved very successful. It was aboard *Stella* that Fife first encountered yachts from other locales, as he raced with the owner at the Irish regattas.

The 43-ton cutter *Aquila* was launched in 1851 and displayed some Fife innovations in the form of a sharp entrance and relatively deep draft.

Considered dangerously radical by some, her features were soon to become standard. She too was later lengthened by 6 feet.

Fife was probably a better businessman than his father and enjoyed an improving economy that aided the business. With *Stella*, the yard turned a decent profit on a yacht for the first time. With her and with the 50-ton cutter *Cymba*, built in 1852, Fife began a tradition of occasionally building boats on speculation, that is, without a buyer. This strategy is usually employed by yards that wish to avoid laying off their crew owing to lack of work, but the resulting increase in debt and the possible difficulty in attracting a buyer in a timely manner make it risky for a small operation. However, it consistently worked for the Fifes, who were not highly capitalized, probably because of the appeal of the finished product and their reputation, both of which were second to none.

It was a later spec boat that gave rise to William Fife II's most famous quote. A prospective buyer wanted him to greatly increase the height of her bulwarks, a notion that offended Fife's strong aesthetic sensibilities. He replied, "Na, I canna do it. I hae kept her a long time, but I'll keep her a while yet raither than make a common cairt [a cart] of her at the finish." The man bought the boat anyway, unmodified.

After *Stella*, Fife II designed and built a series of yachts that saw considerable success racing

in local waters, among them *Cinderella*, which was the first yacht on the Clyde with hollow spars and a jackyard topsail. By 1858 the yard's lean times were over and there was steady demand for Fife-designed yachts, which were produced at the rate of up to eight a year. The yard also continued to build fishing boats and coastal traders. Fife maintained a business interest in some of these commercial vessels.

In 1865 the Fairlie yard launched *Fiona*, which is thought to be Fife's masterpiece. She was a plumb-stem, counter-stern cutter, 75 feet in length, with a 15-foot 8-inch beam and an 11-foot 10-inch draft, setting 3,750 square feet of sail. Known as the Fawn o' Fairlie, she was virtually unbeatable and was believed to be the fastest yacht of her size anywhere for some eight or nine years. After her initial racing career, she was converted to a cruising boat, but in 1898 she was purchased by a yachtsman who began racing her again under handicapping rules. She continued to win prizes, including at the age of forty a major trophy donated by Kaiser Wilhelm II of Germany. Her owner died in 1906, and she was broken up in 1909. It was *Fiona's* spectacular success that gave the Fife yard an international reputation. From then on the yard was considered to be as good as any in Britain.

Another spectacular performer was the 60-ton cutter *Neva*, built in 1874. In four seasons she won fifty-seven prizes in ninety-five races.

The 59-foot LWL *Bloodhound* was another Fife yacht that had a very long life. Also built in 1874, she competed in the Fighting Forties, a 40-ton class, and when she became outdated was converted to a cruising boat. In 1907 she was on her way to being broken up when she was bought back by her original owner, the Marquis of Ailsa, who had William Fife III redesign and heavily modify her over a two-year period. Her underbody was cut away forward to reduce the wetted surface area, and she was given outside ballast and a new rig. She went on to win 143 prizes in 217 races prior to the start of World War I.

The first Fife-designed yacht to be built at another yard came in 1875. Too large to launch at Fairlie at the time, the 165-ton *Latona* was built at the Cowes yard of J. S. White.

Fellow Scotsman George Lennox Watson emerged in 1876 to challenge the dominance of the Fifes with his Five-Tonner, *Vril*, becoming a major but friendly rival of the Fifes.

By the mid-1880's, Fife's personal output had started to decline and his son took on an increasing role in the work of the yard. The year 1889 can be considered one of transition during which William Fife III took over the management of the company from his father. Until the end of his life, Fife II had the satisfaction of seeing his yard continue to expand, and watching his son become one of the most highly regarded yacht designers in the world.

—Daniel B. MacNaughton

WILLIAM FIFE III, OBE

1857—August 11, 1944 · Scotland

Rarely in the history of commerce does a successful family business last multiple generations without losing steam. Looking at the career of William Fife III (also known as William Fife Jr.), we can only wonder what happy chance of genetics or circumstances produced a universally acknowledged artistic and technological genius after a father and grandfather who were likewise yacht designers and builders of the highest caliber.

During a sixty-year career, Fife III designed over eight hundred yachts. He experienced spectacular successes and very few failures in designs ranging from small day-racers to the largest cruisers and racers of yachting's Golden Age. He saw yachts of his design built as far away as Australia and New Zealand, and yachts of his construction exported to these and many other countries. His designs show distinctive sheerlines, long ends, spoon bows, and counter sterns with dainty transoms, and the boats were built of the finest materials.

Interiors were particularly elegant. The name "Fife of Fairlie" was respected everywhere.

Fife is often compared to Nathanael Herreshoff of the United States. Their careers overlapped, they were sometimes competitors, and they occupied similar niches in the yachting circles of their respective countries. But while Herreshoff was primarily a brilliant technological innovator (whose boats often beat Fife's on the race course), Fife was an artist of form and proportion probably unrivaled in the history of yachting. Herreshoff would depart from any convention to make a boat fast, her beauty being a secondary (though still important) goal. If Fife ever designed a boat that was not a work of art, there is no record of it. Both designers headed what may have been the best boatbuilding yards of their respective countries.

Fife was educated at Brisbane Academy and then apprenticed to his father's yard. Unlike his father or grandfather, he placed a much stronger emphasis on developing his design skills than he did on becoming a carpenter. Continuing a family tradition of youthful achievement, he participated in the design and construction

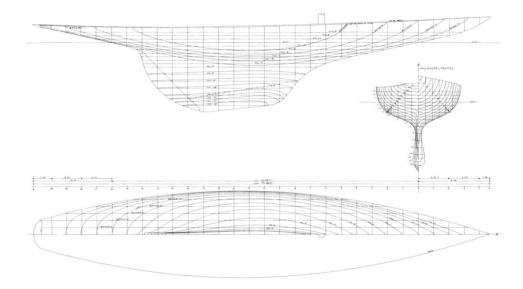

William Fife III (Jr.): *Shamrock III*. Fife designed two America's Cup challengers: *Shamrock* for the 1899 race and *Shamrock III* for the 1903 race. Shown here, *Shamrock III* is typical of the huge cutters that strove for that Holy Grail of yachting—a skimming-dish hull with a deep, heavily ballasted keel. © *Chevalier & Taglang*

William Fife III (Jr.): *Clio*. Designers often raced their own products. Fife designed and built *Clio* in 1921 to race in the newly established Clyde 30-Foot class. After a life of mixed fortunes, she has been restored to her original beauty. © *Benjamin Mendlowitz*

William Fife III (Jr.): *Susanne*. Reported to be William Fife III's favorite design, *Susanne* was an outstanding example of the great schooners that raced at the turn of the twentieth century. The picture captures better than any words the power and glory of these yachts. © *Beken of Cowes*

of the 28-foot cutter *Clio* in 1875 when he was nineteen. In 1876, he did the same with a yacht named *Camellia*. Later he designed *Cyprus*, which won virtually every trophy she raced for in her first year.

At the end of his apprenticeship in 1878, and seeking to broaden his knowledge and experience into the use of metal in boatbuilding, Fife signed on at the Fullerton and Company Shipbuilders at Paisley, Scotland, where he worked in the drafting office. This prepared him for the steel-and-wood composite construction that was then coming to the fore in yacht building.

In 1881, Fife became the manager of Culzean Ship Building and Engineering, a new yard in Maidens belonging to his client, the Marquis of Ailsa. Insufficient depth of water at the Fairlie yard had prevented the Fifes from building very large vessels, but at Culzean Fife could tackle such large steel-and-wood vessels as the 150-foot barquentine-rigged *Black Pearl* and the 110-foot steam yacht *Cassandra*. Here he also built *Clara*, a plank-on-edge cutter of 63 feet

LOA, 53 feet LWL, 8-foot 6-inch draft, and only 9 feet of beam. While not a practical type of boat, owing to her proportions, she became a great success in America, lending credence to the American "cutter cranks" by beating the beamy and shoal-draft American-style sloops. Fife's international reputation had begun.

Built nearly in the shadow of *Clara*, and at the same time, was the tiny plank-on-edge cutter *Vagrant*, a 22-footer that still sails today and is apparently the oldest surviving Fife-designed yacht. There was cooperation between the two boatyards at Fairlie and Culzean, especially in years when the Fairlie yard needed a bit more work. *Black Pearl*, for instance, was built at Maidens but was completed at Fairlie. Fife left Culzean in 1886 and turned his full attention back to Fairlie.

George L. Watson included Fife in the entourage accompanying *Thistle*, which failed to reclaim the America's Cup in 1887 against the Edward Burgess–designed *Volunteer*. During this effort Fife met people who would become future friends and clients.

In 1888 Fife received a commission from Charles Tweed of New York to build a 40-footer (LWL) that became the cutter *Minerva*. Tweed had no intention of racing her. With his eye for form, Fife chafed under the restrictions of the handicapping rules of his day, which put designers under pressure to distort the proportions of their hulls, so he was undoubtedly pleased by the nature of the design commission. *Minerva* was to be a fast cruiser, qualified for the 40-Foot (LWL) class but essentially designed without regard to rating rules. As a result, Fife was able to give her more beam, lighter displacement, and a clipper bow.

In *Minerva*'s first year, she was sailed across the Atlantic and then laid up. The next year she was borrowed by a 40-Foot class racing syndicate when their chosen boat lost her mast. Once *Minerva* began to race, she chalked up an unprecedented winning streak that brought fame to her designer/builder and to her Scottish racing skipper Charles Barr, who went on to become the most successful professional yacht captain of his day. *Minerva* beat every

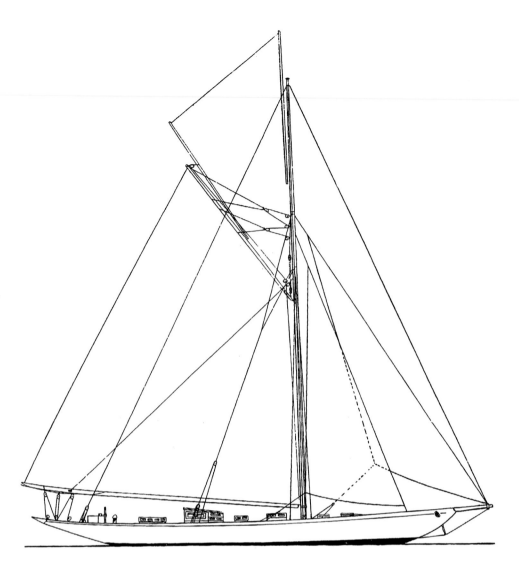

William Fife III (Jr.): *Moonbeam.* The 95-foot jackyard topsail cutter *Moonbeam* was designed and built by William Fife III in 1920 as a cruiser/racer. In this final evolution of the gaff topsail rig, note that there is no separate topmast. Soon all such yachts would carry the marconi rig. © *Tony Dixon*

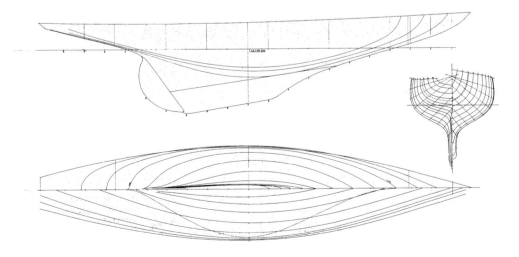

William Fife III (Jr.): *Zenith.* Fife helped write the International Rule, creating classes that evolved within certain guidelines. The drama of such rules is in the way each generation of yachts seems to reveal with ever-increasing clarity the "perfect" boat implied by the rule, until that point is passed and distortions come into play. Fife drew a generation of winners, like the 6-Meter *Zenith*, that illustrated their rule at its best. *Drawing courtesy David Ryder-Turner*

American boat for two years running and only began to share the prizes in her third year, racing against the Edward Burgess–designed *Gossoon.* While the plank-on-edge cutters continued to be popular for some time, *Minerva's* successes suggested there were advantages to a more moderate form. She was the beginning of a series of winning Fife-designed yachts.

It is believed that Fife took over the management of the Fairlie yard from his father in 1888, a time when there were just over two thousand racing yachts registered in the United Kingdom. Launchings doubled to sixteen in that year, increased to twenty-three the next year and then to twenty-nine in 1890 as Fife's work gradually became recognized. In 1889, the 1.5-Rater *Seagull* was built for Sydney R. Herman. This design has the distinction of being the first Fife design to be used for a replica in modern materials.

The 20-Rater *Dragon*, also built in 1889, became the first Fife yacht to carry the famous Dragon cove stripe that would become the Fife trademark. It was subsequently carved into every Fife yacht except *Solway Maid*, the very last yacht the yard launched, in 1940.

The yard got a major upgrade in 1890, when covered building sheds were constructed along with new offices and drafting areas. From that time forward, all of Fife's designs were created or recorded on paper. Sometime after 1894, a floating drydock was added, providing the capability to launch deep-draft yachts farther from the shore than the gently shelving beach at Fairlie allowed.

The largest class of cutters built to race in the 1893 season included the Watson-designed *Valkyrie II* for the Earl of Dunraven and *Britannia* for the Prince of Wales, the Joseph Soper–designed *Satanita*, and *Calluna* designed by Fife III. Although not a successful racer, *Calluna* led the way for other winners such as *Ailsa*, built two years later.

Fife designed the America's Cup challenger *Shamrock* for Sir Thomas Lipton in 1899. Lipton is said to have told him, "Now, Fife, I haven't money to burn; but, if it will make her a second faster, shovel on the notes." She was built by Thornycroft on the Thames, with a bronze bottom, aluminum topsides, and steel spars, and was straight-sheered and beamy with a deep fin keel and 13,492 square feet of sail. It is thought that she might have done better in her match against the Nathanael Herreshoff–designed *Columbia,* but during the races Fife fell ill and was unable to assist in her campaign.

Lipton turned to George Watson in 1901 to design the America's Cup challenger *Shamrock II* (which lost to the Herreshoff-designed *Columbia*), but he came back to Fife III for *Sham-*

rock III. Though she has been said to be one of the most beautiful America's Cup boats, she raced unsuccessfully against the Herreshoff-designed *Reliance* in the Cup races of 1903.

Growing discontent with the rating rules of the day led to the development of a new rule in 1906, developed by Fife, designer Charles E. Nicholson, and others. The International Rule was intended to produce more useful, practical, and good-looking yachts, which it surely did. It ushered in all the Meter classes, such as the 23-, 19-, 15-, 12-, 10-, 8-, and 6-Meters. Today the 6-, 8-, and 12-Meter classes are still racing. Unlike many designers who found particular success within the bounds of only one handicapping rule, Fife was adaptable enough to excel under all of them, and was a voice urging their continued improvement.

Lipton tried to convince the New York Yacht Club to accept a challenge for the America's Cup under the new International Rule, but the challenge was declined owing to a decision to sail future matches under the American Universal Rule. Nonetheless, in 1908 Lipton had another *Shamrock* built to the new International Rule, as a 23-Meter. (She was referred to as "*Shamrock* 23-Meter" to distinguish her from Lipton's five other *Shamrock*s.) She was considered by many to be one of Fife's most successful racing yachts, sailing in handicap events and against the only other 23-Meters ever built, namely, the Fife-designed *White Heather II* and *Cambria*, and the Charles E. Nicholson–designed *Brynhild II*. *Shamrock* continued to do well in competition until she began encountering marconi-rigged rivals in 1929. Lipton kept her until his death in 1930.

The introduction of the International Rule ushered in a productive period for Fife. He designed and built for all the popular classes, and less than two years after the advent of the rule, he was said to be capable of producing a 6- or 8-Meter yacht in a month's time. By 1913, almost all of the yard's output was in the form of International Rule yachts. Nicholson had become a serious rival in the Meter classes after about 1910, but even he wryly referred to the 6-Meters as "the Fife Class." Eight years after the advent of the new rule, various designers had created over eight hundred yachts within its parameters.

Not everything went so well. The big schooner *Waterwitch*, built in 1911 to beat the United States' *Westward* and Germany's *Meteor* and *Germania*, was a failure. Modified under Fife's direction to correct her faults, she became even worse. Her unhappy owner had her broken up when she was only fifteen months old, transferring her rig and equipment to a new Nicholson-designed schooner, *Margherita*, that beat the German boats under the same captain and crew. This highly publicized failure hurt Fife's business, especially in the big classes, but the effect was temporary.

During World War I, the Fife yard built small craft and seaplanes for the British navy.

William Fife III (Jr.): Fife Regatta. This photograph was taken at the 2003 Fife Regatta, a living memorial of which any designer would be proud, and shows, from left to right, the ketch *Belle Aventure* with the cutter *Moonbeam* behind, the 6-Meter *Sunshine*, and the cutters *Viola* and *Lady Anne*. *Photo courtesy David Ryder-Turner*

Fife received the Order of the British Empire for his contribution, and was also honored for employing men disabled in the war.

The postwar economy placed an emphasis on smaller boats, and Fife's domination of the popular 6-Meter class continued. Among these was *Celina*, said by some to be the prettiest 6-Meter ever designed.

Fife was a bachelor all his life and must have been concerned that he would leave no successor. In the early 1920's he made his nephew, Robert Balderston, a partner in the business. Balderston took Fife as his last name. Remarkably, the fourth Fife also proved to have great aptitude for yacht design, and as the years went on, he contributed more and more to all aspects of the business, designing many boats on his own. Moreover, much of the work from then on must have been a collaborative effort, and as no one who was there chose to record a history, it is difficult to say for sure where the work of one man ends and the other begins.

The 1920's saw increasing interest in ocean racing with relatively small yachts and amateur crews. Fife's principal rivals were Charles E. Nicholson and Alfred Mylne, particularly in the 8- and 12-Meter yachts. Fife was enthusiastic about the newer handicapping rules, which encouraged a far more wholesome and seaworthy cruiser/racer type than he had been asked to create in the past.

In 1926, Fife designed *Hallowe'en*, a marconi-rigged cutter of relatively modern proportions that is said to have had almost as much impact in Britain as the Olin Stephens–designed *Dorade* did in America around the same time. *Hallowe'en* set a course record in the Fastnet Race in 1926 (which held until the course was changed) but did not win on handicap. She sailed in the United States as *Magda* and *Cotton Blossom IV*, was rebuilt at the Museum of Yachting in Newport, Rhode Island, and returned to Europe under her original name, where she participates in classic yacht regattas today.

During the Depression of the 1930's, there was not much big-boat construction in Britain. Fife did better than most, however, building the magnificent 107-foot schooner *Altair* in 1931 and the 64-foot *Frea* in 1934. Many beautiful and successful 8-Meters were built during this period, as well as some fine ocean racers such as the 60-foot *Eileen*, built in 1935. The last boat built at Fairlie prior to World War II, when the British Admiralty took over the yard, was *Solway Maid*, a 52-foot 6-inch cruiser/racer that is still sailing in classic regattas in Europe.

William Fife III's design career ended at that time, and he died five years later. After the war, the yard was returned to Robert Balderston Fife, whereupon it was sold. It continued as the Fairlie Yacht Slip Company until 1985, when it was torn down to make room for a housing development.

The principal repository for the Fife design archives is Fairlie Restorations. A smaller collection is at the Scottish Maritime Museum at Irvine. The Royal Northern and Clyde Yacht Club, RHU Helensburgh, Scotland, has a very good representation of original Fife half models.

—Daniel B. MacNaughton

JEAN-MARIE FINOT
Born 1941
PASCAL CONQ
Born 1963

France

Among French designers, Jean-Marie Finot is a good example of the individualism that is a virtual obligation of traditional French culture. At the beginning of his career, he resisted working within a team to develop his design concepts, and the demands of advanced technology. However, demand for his work requires a large office. His diverse Groupe Finot is doing much to define the French design field, following the multidisciplinary team approach that is becoming popular with his Anglo-Saxon colleagues.

Since 1985 Finot has had at his side Pascal Conq, who specializes in racing boats, and since 1997 they have worked with Guillaume Verdier, who does structural calculations and drafting. Recently they were joined by Pierre Forgia, who creates presentation plans, interior arrangements, and deck plans as well as three-dimensional images, and Gérard Chenus, who has been specializing in the firm's computer-aided design.

Groupe Finot devotes approximately 30 percent of its time to new research, exploring new techniques and materials while remaining attentive to all possibilities that might improve their racing boat concepts. The result has been a series of successful boats spanning more than thirty years, with recent wins including those in the 60-foot Open Class, a win in the 1992–93 Vendée Globe Challenge by *Bagages Supérior*, and another in 1996–97 by *Geodis*, a 1991 BOC win by *Groupe Sceta*, a 1995 BOC victory by *Sceta Calberson*, and a success in the first 1998–99 Around Alone race with *Fila* (1997).

Although a residential architect by training, Finot was never fascinated by that line of work. He acquired an interest in the sea early on and became a permanent representative of the Glénans Nautical Center (CNG), where he made friends with designer Philippe Harlé. His first design was *Rebel* (1967). *Ecume de Mer* (1968) resulted in a number of orders after she won both the 1970 and the 1972 Quarter-Ton Cup.

In 1972 Finot began to pioneer in computer-assisted design. He set up his own office in 1973, at Jouy-en-Josas, close to Paris. Three years later, his yacht *Révolution* created something of a fervor in Cowes. The red-hulled yacht had most unusual lines and was certainly one of the first designed by computer. A colleague summarized the novelty: "From a theoretical curve starting from infinity and ending in infinity, Finot has only retained the part which touched the water without being preoccupied with either convention or aesthetics." *Révolution* won the 1976 RORC Championship, a victory she repeated in 1977, 1978, and 1979. She also won the Morgan Cup, the Channel Race, and the Cowes-Dinard competition.

A positive spirit beneath a gruff exterior, Finot sometimes joins forces with colleagues such as Jean Berret and Jacques Fauroux, working on behalf of the Bénéteau yard to create boats such as the famous First Class One-Design, among others. He has also designed a number of production yachts. Today there are more than twenty-seven thousand Finot-designed racers and cruisers, built in France, Italy, Japan, the United States, Canada, and Brazil and sailing throughout the world.

Pascal Conq was born in Brittany and grew up sailing. He was always fascinated by boatbuilding. At architecture school in Rennes (Brittany), he organized a naval architecture course with friends, and further educated himself by taking some U.S.-based correspondence courses. His studies did not prevent him from racing at the highest level, and he designed his own Quarter-Tonner, *Urgent*, with which he distinguished himself in the 1984 Micro-Cup regatta. Soon after he ended his architectural studies, Conq joined Jean-Marie Finot, where he worked on the designs for a 6.5-meter Mini-Transat boat and boats in the 50- and the 60-foot Open Classes, which have brought the group much of its recent fame.

The team distinguishes itself in its long-term research, aimed at the refinement of hull shapes, ballasting and weight reduction, rigging, and underwater appendages. Finot's 50- and 60-foot Open Class boats increasingly resemble sailboards, and some employ water ballast, swinging keels, and radically light structures to minimize displacement while retaining the ability to carry sail.

Finot carries on with his project "Objectif 100" (the design of the first sailboat to exceed 100 kilometers per hour), on which his Groupe Finot has been working since 1998. Successes in the 1992 Transat, then the 1996 Transat, and

Jean-Marie Finot and Pascal Conq: *Fila.* Designed in 1997 for Giovanni Soldini (Vendée Globe Challenge), *Fila* is a 60-foot Open Class racer fitted with a pendular keel and a wing mast. With Soldini at the helm, *Fila* broke the Around Alone race record in 1998–99 by crossing the finishing line in 116 days, 20 hours, and 8 minutes. *Drawing courtesy of Jacques Taglang*

the 1994 Route du Rhum are creating for the group a strong demand for yachts of up to 30 meters in length. Thus, Jean-Marie Finot and his team have become indisputable leaders in their sector of the design field. Current projects include many fast racers for the 40-foot Open Class and the 60-foot Open Class, and many cruisers of all sizes for production builders.

The Groupe Finot office is in Jouy-en-Josas, near Paris, France.   —Jacques Taglang

ROBERT "CAPTAIN BOB" FISH

ca. 1812–January 17, 1883 · United States

Today, Bob Fish is primarily remembered as the design mentor and racing partner of renowned designer A. Cary Smith, working out of what is now Bayonne, New Jersey. He was, however, a respected modeler/builder in his own right, working in traditional model and rule-of-thumb methods and without a formal education. An innovative designer, he experimented with new hull forms and rig details with some success, despite the difficulty of doing so within traditional methods.

Fish's work included both sailing and steam yachts of all sizes and boats for practical service. Notable were yachts built for the Duke of Wellington, the Prince of Wales Club, and Sir Francis Sykes of England. *Meteor*, a sailing yacht built to his design, once set a record for the run from Cowes to Lisbon, averaging 17 mph.

A highly skilled sailing master, Fish sailed yachts of all sizes in both American and European waters. In 1869 he made successful modifications to the William Townsend–designed schooner *Sappho*, which he raced successfully for her owner for several years.

Fish became well known for his racing catboats, and in 1852 introduced this American type to England, France, and Germany in the form of his famous 16-foot *Una*. In England the type was known for many years as an "Una," while in Germany it became known as a "Bubfisch Boat."   —Daniel B. MacNaughton

UFFA FOX, OBE

1898–October 1972 · England

Uffa Fox's accomplishments are numerous: he invented the world's first planing dinghy; he was an especially active dinghy and offshore racer and voyager; and he wrote books, first published in the 1930's, that continue to be influential. He was known for his love of life and willingness to joyfully depart from convention in both the design and the use of boats. He achieved revolutionary success in small development classes of dinghies and canoes and created numerous small one-designs that are still popular today.

Born on the Isle of Wight, Uffa spent his youth immersed in the harborside culture of Cowes, England's most famous yachting center. He was a member of the Cowes Sea Scouts and ultimately became the local scout master. While he served in that capacity, his scouts successfully sailed a 32-foot open whaleboat across the English Channel and back (this without parental permission and to their great chagrin).

Uffa's first apprenticeship was with S. E. Saunders, a boatbuilder working in high-speed powerboats and flying boats. During World War I, despite being part of a reserved occupation, he received his calling-up papers and joined the Royal Naval Air Service with dreams of becoming a pilot. Instead, he serviced and repaired flying boats, including some he had helped to build at Saunders.

At the age of twenty-one, seven years after he started his apprenticeship, Uffa became a professional small-craft builder. His shop and residence were in an old, iron river ferry, which at one point he had to move through several localities to escape taxation by proving that the vessel, normally tied to a riverbank, was indeed mobile.

Because he worked for himself, Uffa was able to turn the day-to-day operation of the yard over to his chief draftsman on occasion and take extended cruises. His first Atlantic crossing was on *Typhoon*, the 35-foot LWL ketch designed by William Atkin and owned by Bill Nutting of *Motor Boat* magazine that made her well-publicized voyages in 1922.

The early experience with Saunders led Uffa to speculate about the possibility of planing-hull sailboats. He believed that with the right hull shape and with her crew holding her bolt upright, a light sailboat could be made to plane over the water instead of through it. The perfect outlet for this idea was the International 14 dinghy, a development class in which certain design parameters were re-stricted to establish a specific size and type of boat, while others were left open to experimentation. He brought the idea to reality in an International 14 he built in 1928 and named *Avenger*. She was the first planing sailboat.

The concept worked so well that *Avenger* took first place in fifty-two of fifty-seven races. Uffa later sailed her across the English Channel to participate in two races in France, both of which he won, and then sailed back to England. Today *Avenger* is exhibited at the Cowes Maritime Museum. A succession of Uffa's 14's such as *Darina*, *Thunder*, *Thunder & Lightning*, and *Alarm* went on to dominate the class from 1928 to 1939. Following World War II, he continued producing winning boats, the final one *Hamble Bay* in 1959. After his success with the International 14's, Uffa became involved in a number of other development classes, such as the National 12's and 18's.

Among other ideas, Uffa was interested in the new concept of light displacement, in which state-of-the-art construction techniques and careful design enabled large amounts of weight to be eliminated from some boats, resulting in improvements in economy and function for certain purposes. *Vigilant*, a 22-Square-Meter class sloop of his design, was of such extremely light displacement that the racing authorities banned her from racing, even in the protected waters of the Solent, on the assumption that she was structurally unsound. This did not stop Uffa from taking her on an extended and successful cruise to Scandinavia, which not incidentally served to vindicate the design. Uffa's 30-Square-Meter *Sea Swallow* of 1938 was similarly a light-weather hull and joined eighteen other 30-Square-Meters racing against each other for the first time on the Solent and the Clyde.

Another high-performance development class with which Uffa had considerable involvement was the decked, sliding-seat sailing canoe. With the canoes *Valiant* and *East Anglian*, Uffa and Roger De Quincey ended forty-eight years of American dominance of the International Canoe Trophy. In 1934 he designed and built the twin sliding-seat canoe *Brynhild* to cross the English Channel and cruise the French coast.

During World War II, Uffa designed the Airborne Lifeboats in the same style as the International 14's but with an extra (third) skin. These laminated wooden boats, equipped with supplies, sails, motors, and a book describing how to sail, were dropped with parachutes from airplanes to enable downed airmen to rescue themselves. The concept was a success and many lives were saved. For the Pacific war, Uffa designed a 50-foot version that would

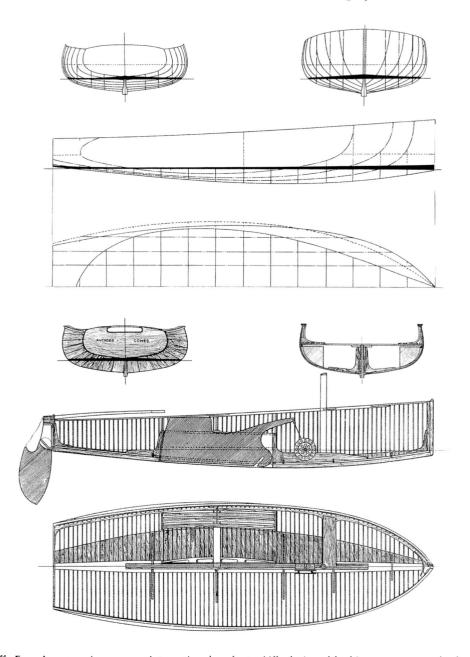

Uffa Fox: *Avenger.* *Avenger*, an International 14-footer Uffa designed for his own use, was the first planing dinghy. During the season of 1928 he and the boat performed brilliantly. In fifty-seven starts he collected an amazing fifty-two firsts, two seconds, and three thirds, including winning the Prince of Wales Cup, the blue ribbon of dinghy racing. © *Tony Dixon*

have carried over two hundred men, but the war ended before it was built.

After the war Uffa designed a series of dinghies for Fairey Marine, including the 9-foot Fairey Duckling, a highly regarded small dinghy; the 15-foot Swordfish (which was re-designed as the Albacore class); the 12-foot Firefly; and the 18-foot Jolly Boat. Fairey Marine also built his cruiser class Atalanta, an unusual, 26-foot, center-cockpit cruising sloop with rounded upper topsides resembling those of a submarine and twin ballasted drop keels, among other features. While too atypical to find universal acceptance, the Atalanta did prove to be a notable functional success as one of the earliest attempts at a small, light-displacement trailerable yacht with seagoing ability.

In 1948 Uffa designed the Flying Fifteen, a 20-foot LOA sloop that was the first planing keelboat. More than 3,700 Flying Fifteens have been built, along with 25-, 30-, 35-, and 50-foot versions (all waterline lengths). Of the 35-footer, Uffa said she "has the ability to plane, but since she is a cruiser this only happens occasionally and is rather terrifying." Other one-designs created by Uffa include the 14-foot Redwing, 14-foot Javelin, the Pegasus, Flying 10 and Flying 12, and the 16-foot O'Day Daysailer.

Uffa may have made his major mark in small racing boats, but he also participated in ocean racing and voyaging in large vessels, and was a highly regarded authority on all aspects of the design and construction of yachts of all sizes and purposes.

At Cowes Week in 1949, Uffa met Prince Philip and began a friendship that lasted throughout Uffa's life. Uffa designed the 24-foot *Fairey Fox* for use by the royal family on board HMY *Britannia*. In 1951, the people of Cowes gave the queen (then Princess Elizabeth) and Prince Philip the Flying Fifteen *Coweslip* as a wedding present. With the prince at the helm and Uffa as crew and tactician, the two won many races in *Coweslip* and in the Johan Anker–designed Dragon *Bluebottle*. Along with *Avenger*, *Coweslip* has retired to the public library in Cowes.

Uffa Fox wrote a dozen books, most notably his annuals *Sailing, Seamanship and Yacht Construction* (1934), *Uffa Fox's Second Book* (1935), *Sail and Power* (1936), *Racing, Cruising and Design* (1937), and *Thoughts on Yachts and Yachting* (1938). These books, featuring the work of many designers, are a remarkable record of the time. Assisting him with these books was his first wife Alma. Under Uffa's supervision, his draftsmen redrew all the plans in Uffa's exceptionally appealing drafting style to achieve a beautiful and unified look that has never been equaled in marine publishing.

Additionally, Uffa recorded sea chanteys, loved cricket, was an excellent horseman, and was seldom without a dog. He married three times and, at the end of his life, lived at the Commodore's House overlooking Cowes Harbor. He was made a Commander of the Order of the British Empire in 1959.

Uffa's plans that survived bombings and floods are in the possession of his nephew and former draftsman, Tony Dixon of Cowes.
—Daniel B. MacNaughton

MARTIN FRANCIS

Born January 14, 1942 · England/France

The Pyramid at the Louvre Museum, the Sciences and Techniques of Industry Museum at la Villette (Paris), the great sloops built by Trehard's shipyard near Cannes, and the superyacht *Eco* share common ground: they owe their technical excellence and futuristic vision to the English naval architect Martin Francis, who adopted France as his homeland for many years.

Francis studied at the Central School of Arts and Design of London and then pursued work as a cabinetmaker before becoming a professor of architecture and design. A devotee of classical music, he also became interested in structural materials and technology. In 1967, a construction engineer named Anthony Hunt introduced him to Norman Foster, with whom he worked on a modular house concept. This was the start of a long collaboration.

Uffa Fox: *East Anglia*. In *East Anglia*, Uffa won the final race of the 1933 International Canoe Championship of America. She and *Valiant* (sailed by Roger De Quincey), the two challengers, were designed and built by Uffa specifically for these races. © *Mystic Seaport, Rosenfeld Collection, Mystic, CT*

Martin Francis: *Eco.* Only recently has a 72-meter yacht been able to attain a speed of 30 knots while enjoying a transatlantic range. Here *Eco* is traveling fast. Her large, convex, wraparound windows provide a minimum of isolation from the passing view and hearken to the designer's experience with building architecture. *Photo courtesy Jacques Taglang*

In the early 1970's, Francis left England to participate in a Rolling Stones tour. It was also the opportunity for him to discover yachting, which he did when he sailed a Folkboat-like yacht designed by Ericus van de Stadt. Eventually he came to manage the Contessa dealership for France. He and his family then moved to the French Riviera near Antibes, where Francis worked for a mast builder.

Many who are drawn to the sea hope to design their own boat someday. In 1979, Francis was able to do this with *Prototype*, a 14-meter sloop built in the Biot yards. His goal was to sail around the world, but events dictated otherwise. A yachtsman ordered a 74-foot design, and another ordered the 82-footer *Deva.* A year later, Christian Trehard decided to launch his own yard by building two 80-foot sloops designed by Francis, *Chrismi II* and *La Concorde.*

From then on things went well for Francis. Among his more famous creations are *Samba Si* (17 meters), *Maximus Austriaticus* (22.55 meters), *Swagman* (18.15 meters), *Must* (28.2 meters), *Thriller* (16 meters), *Speedy Gonzales* (23.75 meters), *109* (33 meters), and the motoryacht *Golden Shadow* built in the United States. He also managed many refits. At the same time, his Parisian engineering company RFR participated in the creation of several famous futuristic buildings in France, Francis declaring that "problems are often common between buildings and boats."

In the late 1980's Martin Francis created his masterpiece, the superyacht *Eco.* George Nicholson introduced him to a customer who wanted to replace his two Feadships. The concept was for a water jet–powered yacht with a speed of 25 knots and a transatlantic range, equipped with the lastest technologies. In October 1988, after two years of studies, the contract was signed. The yacht's statistics were impressive: 72 meters LOA, propulsion by three Ka-Me-Wa water jets coupled to two MWN-Deutz diesel engines of 5,300 hp and to a 18,500-hp General Electric gas turbine. The yacht's speed exceeded 30 knots, and in her hull design and composite construction, she was very futuristic.

Francis's vision continued to be expressed in the project *Senses*, constructed at the Schweers Yard in Germany, and he looked forward to the realization of his dream: a 50-meter, single-engine monohull designed to complete a round-the-world cruise without refueling.

Francis Design is located in London.

—Dominique Gabirault

PAUL FRANCKE

January 10, 1858–ca. 1944 · Germany

For Paul Francke, a prominent designer of racing boats, life got off to a bad start when he lost both of his parents while he was quite young, but he became fortunate as a young man when he was befriended by one of Germany's most important early yachtsmen. Under Georg Belitz's guidance he became a highly successful racing sailor, competing in more than seven hundred regattas and rarely coming home without some sort of trophy.

Belitz also encouraged Francke to try his skill as a yacht designer. Francke never received formal training in naval architecture, relying instead on an intuitive design sense developed and refined through his experience as a helmsman and competitor. His breakthrough came with *Irrlicht I* and *Irrlicht II*, which he designed for a friend and in which he twice won the Kaiser's Prize.

Francke designed mostly racing boats, including one-designs and others that raced under handicap ratings. Early in his career he designed very successful Sonder boats and later produced 35-, 45-, 60-, and 75-Square-Meter boats in the National Cruiser classes. He also drew boats in the 30-Square-Meter Binnenklasse (boats intended for inland and sheltered waters). He was the first to introduce the spoon bow in Germany and was among the first in that country to design and sail ice boats.

All of Francke's designs show a harmonious beauty of line combined with meticulous detail, but without extravagance. He has been described as "correctness personified."

The exact date of Francke's death is unknown, lost in the confusion of the war years. It is known that he was publicly honored in 1943 on his eighty-fifth birthday.

—Volker Christmann

FRANK FREDETTE

1894–1986 · Canada

Frank Fredette designed more than fifty small vessels, from 14-foot open utility craft to 45-foot auxiliary sailboats. He was especially impressed with the seaworthiness of the able little tenders of sealing schooners and captured their look and feel wonderfully in his 20-foot Pelagic Sealing Skiff design. Several of these have been built on Vancouver Island and are in use today.

Living his entire life in Victoria, Fredette built his first boat as a boy and joined a sealing crew at age sixteen. He came to his career in design from the sealing industry of British Columbia. Self-taught as a designer, his work clearly showed the sailor's aesthetic in form and function. All of his pleasure boat designs included healthy characteristics of the small working craft of Vancouver Island. He worked by eye, ably assisted by his wife Irene, who did the necessary calculations on every design to check his instincts.

In 1950 Fredette designed and built the lively 21-foot, double-ended *Speedwell* for Captain Robert Thompson of the S/S *Maquinna.* Patterned after a Shetland Islands type, she was renowned as a club racer around Sidney, British Columbia, and is still in the family.

—J. Scott Rohrer

GERMÁN FRERS SR.

1898–1986 · Argentina

Germán Frers Sr. was one of the most prolific of pre– and post–World War II yacht designers. He began a design dynasty in South America that continues through to a third generation of respected yacht designers, all carrying the name Germán Frers.

Frers was a wealthy farm owner based in Argentina. His early interest in racing motorcycles and cars turned to sailing in the mid-1920's when he set out to design and build his own yacht, a 30-foot, Colin Archer–inspired double-ender named *Fjord*. She was greeted with some scorn by local yachtsmen, who preferred the sleek International Rule yachts imported from England and the United States for racing and day sailing. The double-ender offended their sense of what constituted a proper yacht.

Recalling those days, Frers wrote, "By 1925, I was dreaming of ocean voyages. The Norwegian type pilot-boats with their old rigging represented a return to the past. Something romantic. We were the Club's young members and wanted to be seamen, not yachtsmen. The older members, looking down on us, thought that what we called yachts were fishing boats."

It was not until *Fjord* came through a fifteen-hour South Atlantic storm unscathed that local attitudes changed, and the publicity surrounding the little yacht's seaworthiness did wonders for Frers's reputation. Soon, he had a number of orders for similar designs, establishing a trend toward simpler, less expensive sailboats.

In 1936, Frers was numbered among the crew of Julio Sieburguer's Argentine 6-Meter *Viking* at the Olympic Games, where they finished fourth. It was during the long transatlantic flight in the airship *Graff Zeppelin* that he drew the preliminary sketches for a racing and cruising keelboat later known as the Grumete. Boats of this 23-foot 6-inch, single-chine, classic, light-displacement design proved faster than more conventional boats, and set a trend for a series of similar designs that continue to provide keen class racing six decades later. The Grumete, of which more than three hundred were built during the 1940's and 1950's, led to the Cadete, a similar design 6 feet longer. It remains as a one hundred–strong class raced on the river Plate. Later came the Yachting World Light Crest, a 24-foot 10-inch design inspired by a competition organized by the British magazine.

Frers carried this low-budget, single-chine, light-displacement concept through into offshore racing. His first big break came with the

1954 Bermuda Race. *Trucha II*, a 38-foot, light-displacement, downwind flier drawn with a reverse transom and almost vertical stem, finished second overall.

The design, which proved to be well ahead of its time, was drawn to utilize the conventional wooden boatbuilding materials that were at hand, because modern lightweight materials such as plywood and the latest resins were simply not available in South America so soon after World War II. Frers compensated for the weight of her construction by reducing the ballast in order to keep the displacement light. She was very fast reaching and running, though not so competitive upwind, but since that year's Bermuda Race was predominantly downwind, *Trucha II* finished very much in the money.

Her truncated lines shocked many observers, including writer Alfred Loomis, who covered the event for the American magazine *Yachting*. He wrote of her, "*Trucha II* is a light-displacement box, 38 feet LOA. In overall length, only four boats in the entire fleet were shorter, but like an unsuccessful candidate for a beauty prize, *Trucha* was big in all the wrong places and rated sixth from the top of D-Class. Be that as it may, this Argentine sloop placed second in class and fleet."

Trucha II was one of three Frers designs to win an award that year, helping to set another record,

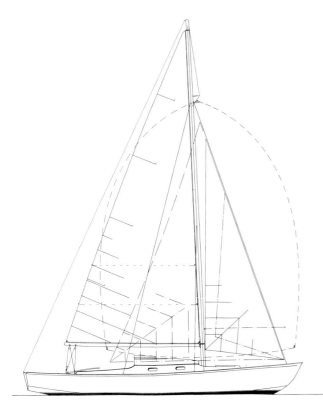 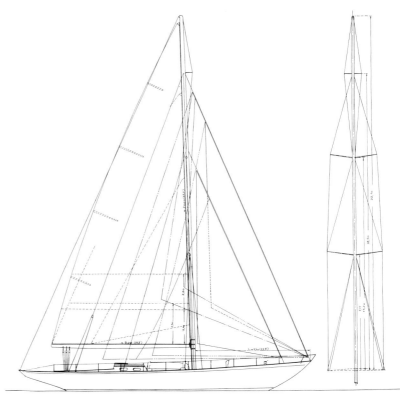

Germán Frers Sr.: Cadete. The Cadete, a 30-foot one-design, demonstrated fresh thinking that drew widespread notice. Her roomy, buoyant, fast, light-displacement hull performed better than traditional designs in local conditions, and displayed her designer's talent for creating good looks in what was, in 1946, a new type. *Drawing courtesy Germán Frers*

Germán Frers Sr.: Juana. In 1949, Germán Frers Sr. received a commission for "the most beautiful yacht possible." The result was the 63-feet *Juana*, a flush-decked cutter that won major races over several decades. She was recently fully restored and sails out of the French Riviera. *Drawing courtesy Germán Frers*

for no designer, let alone a non-American architect, had counted three prizes in the Bermuda Race before. Frers proved to be just as adept at designing yachts along classic lines, such as *Alfard*, a 16-Meter yawl fitted with a centerboard to cope with the shallow waters of the Plate estuary. She won the first 1,200-mile Buenos Aires–Rio Race.

The big breakthrough was *Fjord III*, a 50-foot classic designed in 1946. This one proved pivotal in establishing Frers's international reputation. She was built in something of a rush, for Frers set himself a three-month launch deadline in order to compete in that year's Buenos Aires–Rio Race. He missed the start by three days, but setting off anyway, *Fjord III* went on to set the fastest elapsed time to Rio. Two years later, she won the race outright.

Far from working in isolation, Frers made several trips to the United States and Europe, where he raced his own designs and rubbed shoulders with the likes of Olin and Rod Stephens, John Illingworth, and Uffa Fox. Frers returned home filled with fresh ideas to advance his own brand of design thinking. He turned his hand to designing a wide range of boats, from the *Batitu* junior trainer, through a succession of powerboats ranging up to 50 meters in length, to a number of small coasters.

The Bermuda Race continued to provide a happy hunting ground for Frers's own yachts. *Fjord V*, a 40-foot yawl, finished second overall and first in its class in the 1964 race. *Fjord VI*, a 43-foot sloop and one of the first offshore racers designed with a flush deck and with separate afterguard and crew cockpits, took third in its class in the 1972 classic. These forays abroad not only gave Frers the opportunity to extend his client base outside of South America, where he was already the leading architect,

but also introduced his two sons, Germán and Pepe, to the cut and thrust of international offshore racing.

Frers's eldest son Germán, who established his own reputation in the 1970's and 1980's with a succession of successful IOR and maxi race yachts, took over his father's design company in Buenos Aires. He now shares responsibility for all their racing, cruising, and superyacht designs with his son, Germán Jr., based at the Frers Studio in Milan, Italy.

—Barry Pickthall

GERMÁN FRERS

Born 1941 · Argentina

Germán Frers has been involved in yacht design since his schooldays, when he filled his notebooks with sketches of boats of all types, many of which were later completed and built as sailing models.

Frers also raced small dinghies at the Club Náutico San Isidro, starting at the age of eight and winning the local championship several times. Later he raced on his father's boats both in Argentina and overseas, competing in the Buenos Aires–Rio, Bermuda, Onion Patch, Admiral's Cup, Transatlantic, and SORC races.

During those years he developed a strong interest in yacht design and worked as a draftsman at his father's office after school. The first yacht built to his plans was *Mirage*, a CCA Rule–beating 33-foot yawl which he designed in 1958 at the age of seventeen. Frers was studying naval engineering at the University of Buenos Aires when Rod Stephens heard of the budding young designer from Buenos Aires. Always on the lookout for fresh talent, he sent Frers an invitation to join the famed

design firm of Sparkman and Stephens. It was an opportunity too good to miss. Frers went to New York in 1965 expecting to stay for a year, but remained there for five. "It was a marvelous experience for me—to get away and be independent, away from being my father's boy," says Frers now. The experience also proved quite a culture shock.

The young designer found himself thrown in at the deep end. No sooner had he been shown to a drawing board than he was given the task of designing a yacht to Britain's RORC Rule. He was not helped by the fact that he knew nothing about the rule or how to work out the scantlings, nor had he any drafting tools with which to draw the lines. "At home, I had always borrowed my father's instruments. I had brought none with me. So I went out and bought some triangles and curves and borrowed the rest. I was still borrowing tools the day I left."

Recalling his apprentice, Rod Stephens said of Frers, "He was above average—a nice fellow to have in the group—attractive, pleasant, intelligent. His father was not only a good man technically, but a fine man and I think some of this rubbed off on his sons. He was fortunate to have such a father, and likewise, his father was fortunate to have a son interested in carrying on in a very competent, clever and admirable fashion."

After three years the appeal of earning $4 an hour as a draftsman began to pale, especially with marriage on the horizon, so Frers chose to start an independent practice, setting up a design studio in a one-room apartment in Manhattan. His first commissions were for the sistership One-Tonners *Quest* and *Wizard of Paget*. Two further designs followed, but four boats in two years was hardly enough to feed a growing family. With no sign of an end to this

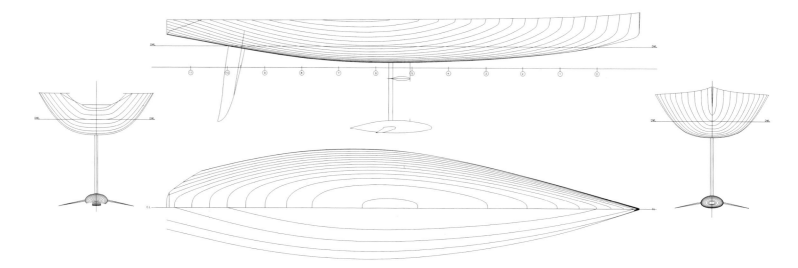

Germán Frers: *Il Moro V*. The lines of the 75-foot 4-inch America's Cup Class yacht *Il Moro di Venezia V* sum up the nature of the class: a lean, light, long-ended hull with the ultimate in high-tech appendages. *Il Moro* lost the finals of the 1992 America's Cup series to *America³*. *Drawing courtesy Germán Frers*

famine, Frers's wife Susana decided to take their two children home to her parents in Buenos Aires, and Frers followed soon after to take charge of the design office founded in 1928 by his father.

Frers's racing yachts are believed by many to be among the best designed and best looking in the world. In 1971 *Matrero*, the first design he did after returning from New York, did well sailing in England for the Argentine Admiral's Cup team and stirred international interest in his work. The next Admiral's Cup races saw *Recluta*, also from Argentina, finishing second overall against the best international competition. Soon after, the 55-foot *Scaramouche* was having a similar effect on the western shores of the Atlantic, confirming Germán Frers as the Man of the Hour, as *Yachting* magazine was to dub him. *Scaramouche* won the 1973 Port Huron–Mackinac Race, scored a class win at the 1974 SORC, and won every race in the Onion Patch series, including that year's Bermuda Race. Suddenly, at the age of thirty-three, Frers was at the top of his profession.

To date, Frers has drawn approximately seven hundred designs for the most famous names in offshore yachting from Europe, Britain, America, Japan, the Far East, Australia, New Zealand, and, of course, South America. Frers-designed yachts have won all the major trophies in the world, including the Admiral's Cup, Onion Patch, Bermuda Race, Transpacific, Whitbread Round the World Race, Sardinia Cup, Buenos Aires–Rio Race, Settimana delle Bocche, Two-Ton Cup World Championship, Middle Sea Race, and the Maxi World Championship. Frers is the exclusive designer for Nautor's line of Swan yachts, having created twenty new models since he started his involvement in 1979. He is also the exclusive designer for the Hallberg-Rassy line of cruising yachts.

In 1989 Frers moved to Italy to lead the *Moro di Venezia* design team in its 1992 America's Cup challenge. A considerable amount of research and development resulted in five boats, built from four designs. The third boat won the first World Championship for the new America's Cup Class in May 1991 and set the trend for all the challengers and defenders. *Il Moro di Venezia V* was the winner of the Louis Vuitton Cup in the final races against *New Zealand*, giving her the right to challenge for the America's Cup—the first European to do so.

Eight years later, Frers convinced fashion mogul Patrizio Bertelli to challenge for the America's Cup of 2000, then held by New Zealand. The Frers–Doug Peterson team produced *Luna Rossa*, the winner of the Louis Vuitton Cup after a highly contested series in which the U.S. representatives were eliminated from

Germán Frers: Swan 112. At 112.27-feet LOA, the Swan 112 is the largest yacht in the Nautor line. These sloops have standardized composite hulls, but otherwise are custom built. The wake gives an idea of the speed this yacht is traveling. With all-power-assisted sail handling it looks like a relaxed and effortless form of transportation. © *Nautor/PPL*

Germán Frers: *Luna Rossa*. Prada-sponsored *Luna Rossa* (right), designed by Germán Frers, Germán Frers Jr., and Doug Peterson, is shown competing in the 2000 America's Cup. The Italian America's Cup challenger *Luna Rossa* splits tacks with the eventual winner *Team New Zealand* in the 2000 finals. © *Photo by Guy Gurney/PPL*

the competition for the first time in the history of the Cup.

Speed and good seakeeping abilities are qualities of all Frers designs, but they have been taken to an extreme in the 95-foot *Stealth*, a pure sailing machine designed for Fiat chief Gianni Agnelli. This all-carbon fiber yacht is one of the fastest and most remarkable superyachts to be built since the great J-Class monoliths of the 1930's, and she set new benchmarks by which other maxi yachts are now judged. *Stealth* can average 12 knots in just 6 knots of breeze, sails effortlessly to windward at up to 18 knots in apparent windspeeds of between 15 and 20 knots, and is capable of daily runs exceeding 500 miles when crossing oceans.

Superyachts have become something of a specialty for the Frers and their design team, producing a series of yachts that continue to push the limits of size and performance. At one time during the early 1990's, a length of 100 feet was a boundary. The year 1999 saw the launch of Dr. Jim Clark's 155-foot megasloop *Hyperion*, a performance superyacht with such sophisticated electronics that she could be programmed to sail herself. This winner of the Millenium Cup will soon be surpassed by a number of yachts more than 200 feet long, fitted with push button–controlled rigs and advanced keel designs that allow the draft to vary from 10 to 25 feet.

—Barry Pickthall

GERMÁN FRERS JR.

Born 1969 · Argentina

It is unusual enough for both a father and son to make the grade as internationally known designers. For these genes to follow through to a third generation is even more rare.

The name of Germán Frers has been synonymous with yacht design since the mid-1920's. The late Germán Frers Sr. developed a reputation in South America for designing classic race-winning yachts. His eldest son Germán developed this into an art form. Now, his eldest grandson, Germán Jr. (nicknamed Mani) has brought high science to the blending of form with function. Working together, the two Frers now operate on a global stage, with work including America's Cup contenders, IMS designs, and record-breaking maxi yachts.

The America's Cup drew father and son together. During the 1992 campaign in San Diego, Germán Jr., then a twenty-two-year-old student completing his design studies at the Southampton Institute in England (home of the famous Wolfson tank-testing unit), spent the summer months working in the *Il Moro di Venezia* design office, helping to disseminate tank-test data and

Germán Frers Jr.: *Red, Red Wine*. *Red, Red Wine*, the first commissioned design by Germán Frers Jr., is a 35-foot light-displacement, water-ballasted flier that has been winning two-man distance races since her launch in 1992. © PPL Agency

develop the team's own velocity prediction program (VPP).

Back at Southampton, Frers made full use of the Institute's tank-testing facilities to win top marks for a Whitbread 60 design that he developed as his final-year project, proving his grasp of the high science that now carries yacht design forward into the twenty-first century. This technical background in the test tank and in computerized performance analysis is the perfect foil to his father's flair for producing great-looking yachts, and the two now share responsibility for all the new designs that carry the Frers design insignia.

Mani manages the Frers design studio in Milan, Italy, concentrating his technical skills on the computerized wind tunnel and tank-testing that aid in the perfection of keels, rigs, and hulls on all Frers designs. One of these projects was to make a thorough study of the IMS racing rule, which led directly to the development of the 40-foot racer *Yah Man*, winner of the IMS World Championship in 1999 and 2000. Other boats in which he has had a telling input include small, highly competitive one-design racers like the Este 24 and 10PF.

Frers Jr. also has a keen interest in Volvo 60 and Open Class racing, and has developed a series of designs to meet the 30-, 40-, and 60-Foot classes. His first 60-Foot design is in marked contrast to the wide "aircraft carrier" type 60's that have a poor safety record and limited abil-

ity to sail to windward. He came up with the novel idea of fitting wing ballast tanks onto a narrow hull with a low wetted surface area and low structural weight. The result was *Shining*, a boat that exhibits good seakeeping qualities both upwind and down and that won the Barcelona Race in 1999.   —Barry Pickthall

WILLIAM FROST

1872–1965 · United States

One of the strongest influences in the evolution of the Maine lobsterboat type was William Frost. He was born at Whale Cove, Digby Neck in Nova Scotia to a family that built schooners. As a young man, he built several sailboats, but then in the early 1900's became fascinated by the new marine "make-and-break" gas engines. He started designing boats that would optimize the effectiveness of the new engines.

In a memoir written more than seventy years later, Frost's daughter Wilhelmina Lowell said, "When I was about five years old, I can remember him building his first powerboat, which was a wonder then–to see a boat moving through the water with no sail!" She added, "After that, he went all out, as every man far and near wanted one."

Frost's early boats were made famous for their many victories in the races held around Digby and Annapolis Royal. Soon, it was his boats racing one another.

Frost visited back and forth quite a bit with a cousin in Beals Island, Maine. In 1909 his house in Nova Scotia burned, and three years later he moved to the Beals Island/Jonesport area. There

he continued to build his fast motor-powered boats. In later years, many referred to him as "the Wizard of Beals." Customers came from all over New England and beyond for fishing boats, commuter boats, cruisers, and yachts. During Prohibition he became famous for building a series of successful rumrunners and then the U.S. Coast Guard boats that chased them.

During the Great Depression, Frost moved to Somerville, Massachusetts, and then to Tiverton, Rhode Island. He later worked in the design office of Eldridge-McInnis and John G. Alden, during the partnership they formed for the duration of World War II. Following the war, Frost returned to the Portland, Maine, area and continued designing and building commercial and pleasure boats, including the well-known *Merganser* and her sistership, the *Leonard W*. Frost retired in the 1950's.

There is probably no one who has influenced the design of the Maine lobsterboat more than Frost. He brought with him from Nova Scotia the plumb bow, strong sheer, flat skeg-built bottom, and the cutoff stern that in combination became known as the Jonesporter or "razor-case" type. Many of his early boats in Nova Scotia also featured the torpedo stern.

Later the type was influenced by the increasing horsepower of the engines. The hulls stayed long and thin, but the underbody became wider and flatter on the run back to the stern. Frost utilized a reverse curve in the bottom, making the boat faster and steadier, and stopping the hull from pounding. His boats are still known and loved today for their speed, seaworthiness, smooth ride, and overall grace in the water.   —Jon B. Johansen and Ruth Lowell

William, Frost: *Alouette*. A 35-foot wooden sportfishing boat, *Alouette* was one of Frost's last boats, designed and built by him in the 1950's. Today, she can be found in South Freeport Harbor, Maine. *Photo courtesy Lowell Brothers, Even Keel Marine Specialities*

G

EGIDIO GALLINARI

(Dates unknown) · Italy

The first decade of the twentieth century was Egidio Gallinari's most productive period. Working in his shipyard in the port of Livorna, he produced designs for recreational and racing sailboats not only for Tuscan sailors but also for those from Genoa, Naples, and the lake region.

Italy's first challenge for the 1901 Coupe du Cercle de la Voile de Paris (the Paris Sailing Circle Cup, now known as the One-Ton Cup) was attempted by the Lariano Royal Racing Club and the Verbano Royal Yacht Club. For this Gallinari created two vessels, each displacing 1 ton: *Dai-Dai III*, measuring 6.6 meters, and *Dai-Dai IV*, measuring 7.5 meters.

Notable among Gallinari's boats are the cutter *Nautilus*, built in 1879; the 10-ton *Nada*, built in 1903; the 5-ton *Sfinge*, built in 1904; and the 6.5-meter National Class *Doritis*, built in 1911.

Gallinari also designed and built competitive motorboats both for private individuals and for Fiat, which at the beginning of the century was involved in motorboat racing. In 1905, his

Fiat X, skippered by Gallinari himself, won the Algeri–Port Mahon (Balearic Islands) Race in 12 hours, averaging 27 kilometers per hour, coming in 3 hours ahead of the second-place winner.

—Franco Belloni

DENIS HARCOURT GANLEY

September 3, 1943–May 24, 1997
New Zealand

Denis Ganley was one of New Zealand's best-known designers of steel yachts. He was born in Hamilton, New Zealand. His early involvement in the sport of yachting included helping his father build a Frostbite dinghy and sailing local P- and Q-Class sailboats on Hamilton Lake. Throughout his school career, sailing took priority over study. He excelled at other sports as well, including long-distance running.

At the age of sixteen, the lure of marine engineering took him to Listers, the famous diesel-engine makers in England. On returning to New Zealand he designed and built his first yacht, the 24-foot timber *Lone Gull*, in

1968. Ganley and his Irish wife, Philomena, spent "one glorious year" on the boat after the birth of their only child, Denise, in 1970. In 1974 Ganley established Denis Ganley Yacht Design with the slogan "Steel away with a Denis Ganley yacht design."

Despite his ambition, his family was unusually close. His practicality and down-to-earth humor were appreciated by his clients. His designs such as *Snowbird, Tara,* and *S130* were well-balanced, easy-to-build cruising yachts. His workboat and powerboat designs also gained popularity. Stock plans were sold to amateur and professional builders worldwide.

When the New Zealand government imposed a crippling sales tax on locally built boats in 1979, Ganley made a public vow that he could build a 26-foot yacht in ten weeks for less than $750. The result, the plywood *Caique*, became his most successful design.

Ganley's career high point was winning the 1986 Steel Award for Excellence for his *Pacemaker 40* yacht design, the only boat to ever win the award.

Ganley was always heavily involved in motor sport. Denis and Philomena Ganley died on May 24, 1997, when a truck and their Scimitar sports car collided while they were touring in the South Island of New Zealand. His designs are still much sought after worldwide.

—Rebecca Hayter

GANNON AND BENJAMIN

see Nathaniel P. Benjamin

WILLIAM GARDEN

Born November 5, 1918 · Canada/United States

Seldom does a designer display the versatility of William Garden. With the exception of racing boats designed to beat handicapping rules, he has worked on virtually every type and size of yacht for power or sail, as well as a wide

Egidio Gallinari: *Fiat X.* *Fiat X* was winning races in 1905 with a speed of 27 kilometers per hour. *Photo courtesy Franco Belloni*

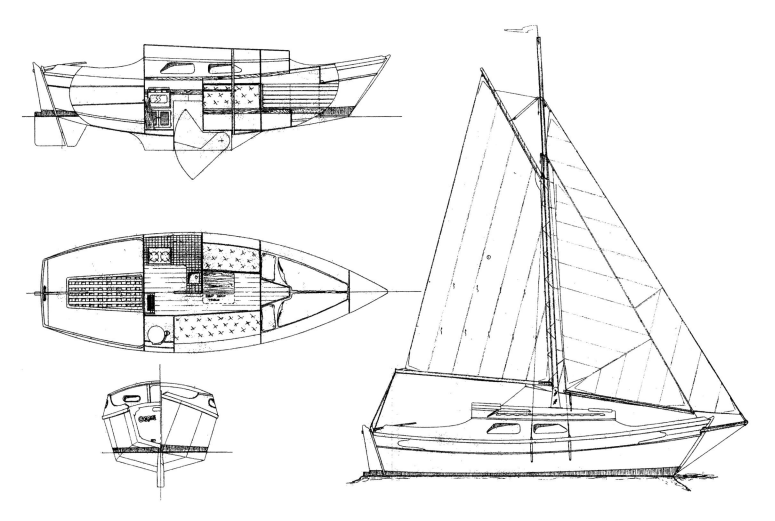

Denis Ganley: *Caique.* The 26-foot, plywood *Caique* was designed and built by Ganley in 1979 in ten weeks for under $750. Subsequently it became a very popular design. *Drawing courtesy Harold Kidd*

variety of military, commercial fishing, towing, and cargo vessels. His designs range from small dinghies and skiffs to yachts and commercial craft over 200 feet long. With over a thousand designs to his credit, Garden is also an unusually productive designer. The diversity of his work is not just a technicality—the whole range of types in which he has worked is refined over and over again.

Many consider Garden to be one of the best draftsmen ever to practice yacht design. His drawings are highly detailed, with close attention paid to the weight of each line. There is often a human figure to show scale, and many of his published designs include appealing perspective drawings of the boats in workaday situations, often grounded out against a wharf to have their bottoms painted. Lines defining the boats are precise. Lines showing background are casual. As a result the drawings have unusual warmth and appeal while efficiently communicating technical information and the character of each boat to eyes that may or may not be educated in yacht design. Many of his designs appeared in *The Rudder* over the years, which expanded public recognition of his work.

The breadth of Garden's aesthetic talent is unquestionable. His traditional vessels show a thorough understanding of older forms, proportions, and details, with "feel" ranging from dead serious to openly romantic according to each owner's requirements, but always with a distinct William Garden personality. He clearly prefers the rugged construction and detailing typical of Pacific Northwest commercial vessels.

In many of Garden's designs, the distinction between commercial and yacht uses is blurred; these boats offer both financial and spiritual rewards, a whole way of life created by the boat itself. His strictly commercial vessels are often so beautiful that they have directly inspired yacht versions of themselves. No wonder the line between the two uses is hard to define.

But Garden cannot by any means be pigeonholed as a traditionalist. His light-displacement cruising boats of both power and sail, ranging from conservative to ultramodern in appearance, are devoid of rating rule–inspired racing conventions and serve to illustrate the otherwise largely untapped potential of the type. And there are plenty of boats that fall everywhere on a continuum between traditional and contemporary, mixing elements of both.

It is significant that Garden, who has been practicing since 1936, has recently been designing a number of very large, ultramodern power and sailing yachts, such as the 97-foot power yacht *Czarina* and the motorsailer *Mikado,* commissions one might expect to go to younger designers. It just goes to show that Garden can do it all.

Garden's work has served to extend the limits of convention in yacht design. No one has done more to explore and develop the trawler yacht type of powerboat in all its potential variations, and his light-displacement sailboats, such as his own 60-foot LOA *Oceanus,* were among the earliest to show the many possibilities of that type in cruising boats. In his fast powerboats, Garden has done a great deal to counter the regrettable tendency of such boats to become short, fat, high, heavy, and overpowered. A long, low, light Garden powerboat, such as the 62-foot *Tlingit,* exemplifies his mastery of the type.

Garden was born in Calgary, in the province of Alberta, Canada. He and his family moved to the United States in 1924, and he started school in Portland, Oregon. His family then moved to Seattle in 1928, and his sailing experience began

William Garden: *Oceanus*. The 60-foot Sloop *Oceanus*, built of cold-molded wood in 1954, is a rare example of a light-displacement boat intended strictly for cruising and uninfluenced by any handicapping rule. She was owned and sailed by her designer for twelve years and proved comfortable, fast, and easy to handle. *Photo by Ray Krantz, courtesy William Garden*

in 1930. Garden enrolled in the Edison Boatbuilding School in 1936. During the period from 1937 to 1940, he worked as a part-time draftsman in the Seattle offices of H. C. Hanson and Ed Monk.

From 1940 to 1942 Garden was a partner in the Seattle boatbuilding firm of Le Clercq and Garden. During World War II he worked first at a yard building Coast Guard cutters, then at the Blanchard Boat Company building 65-foot army freight boats and 45-foot crash boats for the navy, and later for the Army Transportation Corps supervising construction of harbor tugs at the North Pacific Shipbuilding Corporation. He was then drafted and sent to work at an army ship repair company in the Aleutian Islands. "Only man in the Army to be employed in what he liked doing," he says. He was discharged in 1946 as a master sergeant.

In 1946 Garden opened his own design office in Seattle. While he had designed mostly workboats up to that time, as his office became busier he branched out into more yacht work. He was licensed as a naval architect and marine engineer in 1947, and continued to design both yachts and commercial vessels, part of the time with his most-noted marine engineers, Phil Brinck and Brinton Sprague.

Garden moved his office in 1969 to Toad's Landing, a tiny island off Sidney, British Columbia, that serves as his residence, design office, and boatbuilding shop. Garden is pretty much retired now, but takes on occasional design projects that interest him. He sails the small clipper-bowed schooner *Toadstool* that

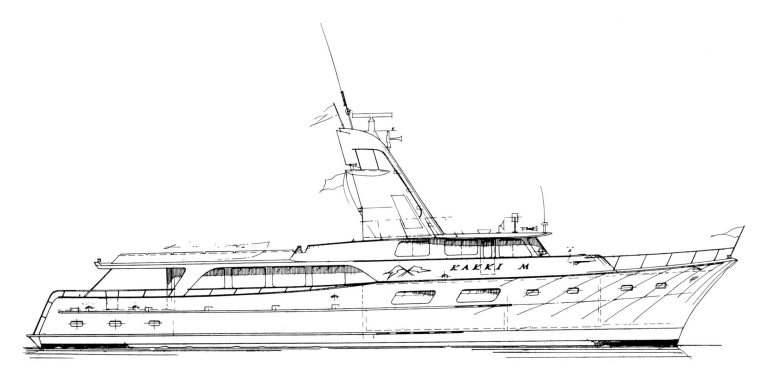

William Garden: *Kakki M.* This 104-foot motoryacht was built of wood, by Vic Franck in Seattle. Garden's eye for character is such that while every line of this vessel is modernistic, the overall effect is of strength, competence, integrity, and ability. *Drawing courtesy William Garden*

William Garden: *Maccoboy III*. It looks like a busy day aboard the motorsailer *Maccoboy III*. With her salty short sailing rig, rugged construction, and fishing boat–inspired looks, she is illustrative of a theme to which Garden often returned over the course of a very long career. © *Peter Barlow*

was built on the island. William Garden was presented with the W. P. Stephens Award by Mystic Seaport Museum's Yachting Committee in 1989, and the State of Washington Maritime Heritage Award in 1990. A well-rounded collection of Garden's designs is contained in his books *Yacht Designs* and *Yacht Designs II*, and an expanded edition of *Yacht Designs*.

The William Garden Collection of plans is at Mystic Seaport Museum, Mystic, CT.

—Daniel B. MacNaughton

WILLIAM GARDNER

May 10, 1859–May 7, 1934 · United States

From 1888 until his retirement in 1925, William Gardner was one of the United States' most prominent designers, producing racing sailboats of all sizes, elegant steam yachts, and commercial vessels. He was immortalized in 1905 when his 185-foot, three-masted schooner *Atlantic* set the transatlantic speed record for a monohull in a scheduled race, a record she continues to hold.

Gardner was the designer of the 1920 America's Cup contender *Vanitie*, which won many races over a long career but was not selected to defend the Cup. He designed many fine racing boats under the waterline-and-sail-area handicapping rule, the New York Yacht Club Rule, the Universal Rule, and the International Rule, along with many popular one-designs and cruising boats. He is regarded as one of the earliest U.S. designers to have a thorough scientific foundation to his work.

Born in Oswego, New York, Gardner made a voyage around Cape Horn in his early teens. At fifteen he enrolled in Cornell University, from which he graduated in 1880. After graduation he worked at John Roach's shipyard, later known as the Delaware River Iron Works. Here he acquired broad practical experience in all aspects of drafting and ship construction. During this period he met the highly regarded shipbuilding team of Gatewood and Bowles, who inspired him to study abroad, as they had done.

Through great persistence Gardner was able to gain admittance to the Royal Naval College at Greenwich, England, a rare privilege for a foreigner. He made the most of this unusual opportunity, studying advanced mathematics and naval architecture and getting private instruction from Reid and Jenkins, who were Lloyd's of London's chief consultants with regard to scantlings in commercial ships. In the process he drew complete plans for a battleship and cruiser, and spent as much time as possible sailing and visiting shipyards.

Gardner became personally acquainted with designers William Fife III and George Watson, as well as other British designers and yachtsmen of the day. After this period of education he spent two years working in shipyards on the Clyde and Tyne Rivers in Britain.

William Gardner: *Aztec.* One of the few steam yachts Gardner designed, the handsome 263-foot *Aztec* was built in 1902 by Lewis Nixon. The twin-screw vessel cruised at 15.9 knots. *Photo courtesy Mariner's Museum, Newport News, VA*

William Gardner: *Atlantic.* This lovely, 185-foot, steel-hulled schooner was launched in 1904. Under the command of hard-driving skipper Charlie Barr, she set a transatlantic record in 1905 that stood until 2005 (others had sailed the same course faster but not in a scheduled race). © *Mystic Seaport, Rosenfeld Collection, Mystic, CT*

In 1888, Gardner began his design practice in New York City, setting up shop at 1 Broadway, which would remain his working address for the remainder of his career. His first two commissions, received in his first year, were for the cutters *Kathleen* and *Liris.* Distinguished by their beauty and by their light but strong construction, both boats were very successful. *Liris* went on to beat the famous William Fife III cutter *Minerva,* and *Kathleen* was almost unbeaten in her first two seasons. These victories served to launch Gardner's winning reputation, and led to a number of commissions including *Alcea,* a 90-foot schooner that as *Nord Quest* had a successful racing career in Germany.

Gardner's career got another boost when in 1896 he designed the schooner *Quissetta.* She beat *Amorita,* designed by A. Cary Smith, one of America's most-respected designers. This victory was followed in 1897 by the victory of his 45-foot LWL cutter *Syce* over the William Fife III–designed *Kestrel.*

The bronze cutters *Weetamoe* and *Neola* came out in 1902. Both 85 feet in LOA, they raced together in tight competition, and in 1905 were given new, less flat-sectioned bows to take advantage of improvements in the handicapping rule (which had just changed from the old waterline-and-sail-area rule to a precursor of the Universal Rule).

The year 1905 also saw the famous victory of the Gardner-designed, 185-foot, three-masted steel schooner *Atlantic* (launched in 1904) in a transatlantic race sponsored by Kaiser Wilhelm II of Germany. Under the command of the famous yacht captain Charles Barr, she set a transatlantic record that has never been beaten by a nonplaning monohull: 12 days, 4 hours, and 1 minute from Sandy Hook, New Jersey, to Lizard Head in England. *Atlantic's* victory and record represented an actual and a symbolic accomplishment that permanently installed Gardner among the best of the world's yacht designers.

Success was not limited to large yachts. In 1906 the Sonder, a German development class, was introduced to the Eastern Yacht Club of Marblehead, Massachusetts, at the urging of Kaiser Wilhelm II. Originating at the Kiel Yacht Club in 1898, Sonder boats were ultralight, low-sided, very long-ended, deep-keel sloops with a maximum overall length of 40 feet. They were exotic, light, and fast and held the promise of regular international competition, with a championship series that alternated yearly between Germany and the United States. The initial German challenge generated many boats in the first year, including Sonders by noted designers Boardman, Burgess, Crane, Crowninshield, and Herreshoff. Unlike many of the other designers, Gardner drew only one boat (a condition imposed by the client), the result of which was *Vim*. She was selected for the challenge team and finished first of the six boats in the final series.

Vim undoubtedly helped to boost Gardner's small-boat design business, and was followed by winning Q-, P-, and M-Class yachts designed under the Universal Rule, successful 6-Meters under the International Rule, and a number of one-designs such as the Bayside Bird, Devon, Islip, Larchmont-Interclub, Larchmont O-Boat, Shrewsbury, Southampton, Southport, and Victory classes. Designer Francis Sweisguth is often credited with the design of the famous Star class, but he was working for Gardner at the time and the Star was a product of the Gardner office. Sweisguth refers to her as a Gardner design in his biography of the elder designer.

Gardner's involvement with the America's Cup began with what was to have been the 1914 match, in which Sir Thomas Lipton made his fourth challenge on behalf of England, to be sailed in 75-foot LWL sloops. One defense syndicate ordered a yacht from N. G. Herreshoff, which became *Resolute*, and yachtsman Alexander Cochrane commissioned *Vanitie* to be designed by Gardner and built by Lawley. The series was delayed by the onset of World War I, and was not sailed until 1920. After a closely fought contest, *Resolute* was selected to defend, which she did, beating Lipton's *Shamrock IV*.

After the America's Cup both *Resolute* and *Vanitie* were converted to the more practical and easily handled schooner rig, and continued to race against each other and the other yachts of the day. It is said that *Vanitie* eventually proved to be faster than *Resolute* under the new rig. At the time she was referred to as the fastest yacht in the world, and was considered to be one of the most beautiful as well.

Gardner's education and early experience positioned him as one of the United States' finest

William Gardner: *Vanitie*. *Vanitie* competed unsuccessfully against the N. G. Herreshoff–designed *Resolute* for the right to defend the America's Cup against Charles E. Nicholson's *Shamrock IV* in the match of 1914 (postponed until 1920). Under her later schooner rig, *Vanitie* was said to be the fastest yacht in the world. © *Chevalier & Taglang*

William Gardner: *Westward*. The 66-foot 6-inch LOA *Westward* was built in 1915 at the famed W. F. Stone yard in Oakland, California. Known for her exquisite lines and racing prowess, she continued to be a winner into the mid-1950's, and some of her racing records still stand. She was lost off the coast of El Salvador in 1958. *Photo courtesy Thomas G. Skahill*

and most popular designers of steam yachts. He designed the engines and other machinery of such yachts, along with the vessel itself.

While he employed assistants such as designer Francis Sweisguth, who began working with him in 1901, it is said that Gardner himself drew the hull lines of every yacht his office produced, and directly supervised all other aspects of every design. Gardner retired due to illness in 1925, but his firm continued on. He died at age seventy-four.

—Daniel B. MacNaughton

PAUL GARTSIDE

Born 1953 · Wales/Canada

Paul Gartside's emphasis is on practical, seaworthy designs for people who really use their boats. While his chief interest lies in the design of custom one-off boats intended for specific purposes, he designed the Oysterman production series and sells stock plans for a wide range of boats from dinghies and tenders to motor cruisers and sailboats. His work shows a strong traditional aesthetic influence combined with modern interiors and details.

Gartside was born in Prestatyn, Wales, and grew up on the river Fal in Cornwall in southwestern England, where his family established a boatbuilding and repair yard. His interest in yachts led him to the Southampton College of Technology and a diploma in yacht and boat design in 1974. He has been an associate member of the Royal Institute of Yacht Designers since 1979.

After graduation Gartside returned to the family business and, between 1974 and 1983, designed and built a range of boats, including both commercial and pleasure craft. Among these was the first of the Oysterman series of yachts. In 1983, he leased the rights to the molds, moved to Sidney, British Columbia, Canada, and founded the design and boatbuilding firm of Paul Gartside Ltd.

In British Columbia, he is known for his fine-quality wooden boatbuilding, his teaching in the marine industry, his infrequent trips to the barber, his sense of humor, his fashion sense, his rusty truck, his incredibly long rowing trips down the Yukon River and north up the Alaska coast to Barrow, and his almost-as-long trips in the 21-foot motor cruiser *Jennifer*.

Gartside considers himself a boatbuilder as much as a designer. His designs combine classic lines and sensibility with both modern and traditional construction materials. He has recently designed a series of steam launches and a number of motorsailers designed for Pacific Northwest conditions.

Gartside continues to practice in Sidney, British Columbia. —Tom Roach

Paul Gartside: *Surprise II.* The 22-foot 4-inch cutter *Surprise II* is a good example of neo-classic design, in that she reflects a perfect understanding of and respect for her traditional antecedents, while taking advantage of improvements in construction technology and displaying her designer's competence with the many details of a good cruising boat. *Photo courtesy Paul Gartside*

LESLIE EDWARD "TED" GEARY

June 1, 1885–May 19, 1960 · United States

Ted Geary grew up in Seattle. He was so well liked and showed so much promise as a designer and racing helmsman that a group of local businessmen paid his tuition to MIT so he could formally study naval architecture. Geary designed his first highly successful, 24-foot racing sloop at age fourteen, and at age twenty designed an improved version that was never defeated. Another of these early designs was the 42-foot sloop *Spirit*. Geary was at the helm when he successfully challenged the 46-foot William Fife III–designed *Alexandra* for the Dunsmuir Cup of Canada in a three-race series in 1907. At that time he was an engineering student at the University of Washington.

Graduating from MIT in 1910, Geary swiftly repaid his benefactors, designing commercial vessels of all types for local service. To satisfy a high demand for fast waterborne transportation in the Puget Sound area, he created many large and elegant commuter yachts for local businessmen.

With the design of the Universal Rule R-Class yacht *Sir Tom*, commissioned in 1913, Geary's reputation for fast sailboats continued to grow. He raced *Sir Tom* in the years from 1914 to 1930 from Canada to southern California, experiencing only two series defeats in that entire period, this in a class where new boats designed by the most famous designers of the day were being turned out every year. With *Sir Tom*, Geary held the Pacific Northwest title for fourteen years. In 1928 he quietly sent her plans to his Canadian rivals in the Lipton Cup series, whereupon she was beaten by *Lady Van*, a boat that strongly resembled the Geary design, but *Sir Tom* won again the next year. Another Geary-designed R-Class boat, *Pirate*, saw spectacular success and underwent a major restoration in Seattle, rechristened in 2005.

A long-time proponent of maritime safety in both recreational and commercial spheres, Geary made significant contributions to this important issue throughout his career.

Partly because the local taste was mostly for power craft, Geary is best known for an impressive series of beautiful, fast, efficient, and long-lived motoryachts roughly 80 to 150 feet in length. The years 1928 and 1930 saw the launching of four 96-foot near-sisterships that serve to define Geary's work in this genre. *Principia*, *Blue Peter*, *Canim*, and *Electra* were rugged but slender yachts displaying a workboat heritage and emphasizing seagoing ability and fuel economy. All are still in service. In 1931 the 147-foot *Samona II* was launched. She went on to make a circumnavigation of

Ted Geary: *Sir Tom.* Launched in 1914, *Sir Tom* was named for the British-Irish tea merchant and yachtsman Sir Thomas Lipton, who provided a cup for competition between Canada and the United States. *Sir Tom* dominated R-Class racing on the West Coast, winning against boats specifically designed to beat her. Geary was her helmsman for the entire period up to 1930. *Photo courtesy Puget Sound Maritime Historical Society*

Ted Geary: *Red Jacket.* Shown with her staysail schooner rig, *Red Jacket* originally had a gaff foresail. She is pictured racing in the north end of Lake Washington, with the Kirkland ferry just visible off her bow. Still extant and healthy, *Red Jacket* is based in Tacoma. *Photo by Ray Krantz, courtesy Seattle Yacht Club*

Ted Geary: *Malibu.* *Malibu,* a 100-foot motoryacht built by Seattle's Blanchard Boat Company, was Geary's 1926 design for a comfortable, go-anywhere yacht. Based on his successful commercial boats, but with elegant features and accommodations, she began the yard's trend away from long, narrow, yachtlike beauties with their excess of brightwork. *Photo courtesy Newport Harbor Nautical Museum, Newport Beach, CA*

Ted Geary: _Principia_. _Principia_ is one of four 96-foot motoryachts built to similar Geary designs between 1928 and 1931, the others being _Blue Peter_, _Canim_, and _Electra_. All are still in service today. Now back on the East Coast, _Principia_ recently underwent a complete restoration at the Billings yard in Stonington, Maine. _Photo courtesy Thomas G. Skahill_

South America via the Straits of Magellan and other voyages in the Pacific.

A strong supporter of local sailing programs for young people, Geary designed for training purposes the 18-foot Flattie class, now known as the Geary 18, in 1928. He sailed in the class and promoted it for many years, and over 1,500 Geary 18's are sailing today, with an active class association and new boats built each year from both wood and fiberglass.

During World War I, Geary designed many wooden cargo vessels. In the 1920's he created a series of handsome racing and cruising schooners, some of which are still sailing on the coast of Washington, including the 60-foot _Red Jacket_ (ex-_Katedna_) and the 57-foot _Suva_.

Geary opened a second office in southern California in 1930 and sought more business, which was in short supply during the Depression. While the number of commissions declined during that difficult period, he was able to continue work by concentrating on smaller designs, including the famous 45-foot Lake Union Dreamboat. This roomy, shapely, and practical cruising powerboat created for the Lake Union Dry Dock Company was the first of a number of similar designs for that yard and others.

Stranger, a 135-foot yacht equipped for oceanographic research, was designed in 1938, making her the largest private yacht to be built in the United States since 1931. She went on to long and varied service as both a yacht and government vessel, and among other exploits secretly updated charts of some areas in the Pacific in preparation for U.S. involvement in World War II.

Geary performed design work at the Craig Shipbuilding Company in Long Beach during World War II, and after the war remained there helping to convert yachts that had been commandeered by the government back into yachts. Geary eased into retirement in his sixties and passed away at his home when he was seventy-four.

—Daniel B. MacNaughton with Thomas G. Skahill

FREDERICK C. GEIGER

December 23, 1910–1982 · United States

A versatile talent, Fred Geiger produced many designs for sail and power yachts, large and small, under his own name and, as head designer at John Trumpy and Sons, designed a long series of large luxury motoryachts. He was highly regarded for his aesthetic sense and drafting skills, and was able to combine Trumpy's traditionally elegant detailing with a modest amount of postwar streamlining, with outstanding results.

Born in Overbrook, Pennsylvania, Geiger grew up around boats while summering at Eastern Point in Connecticut. In 1935 he completed the Westlawn School of Yacht Design correspondence course. He and partner Frank Harris then set up a design and brokerage business in Philadelphia called Yacht Sales and Service, through which Geiger produced a good number of designs, some of which were built by John Trumpy and Sons. The partnership lasted until Harris's death in 1955. During World War II and the Korean War, Geiger designed military vessels for the Philadelphia Naval Shipyard.

After 1955 Geiger went to work for Trumpy and headed their design department until his retirement in 1972, producing the large and comfortable wooden power yachts for which the yard was famous. Like John Trumpy before him, he was known for his very precise weight calculations, which took into account the weight of people and their gear, most of the other objects normally carried aboard, and even the weight of water that would be absorbed by the planking. As a result there were few surprises when his designs were launched.

Geiger's drawings are in the Frederick C. Geiger Collection at Mystic Seaport Museum, Mystic, CT.

—Daniel B. MacNaughton

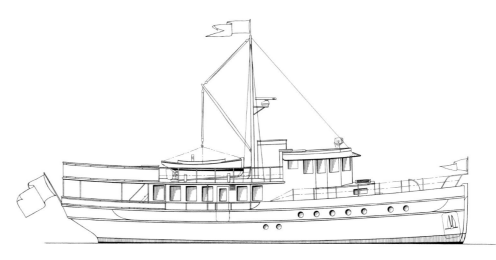

Dave Gerr: *Kestrel*. The 76-foot *Kestrel* is the largest to date of the unique ultrashoal, tunnel-drive, single-screw motorcruisers that Gerr Marine has reintroduced. Built of either wood-epoxy, fiberglass, or aluminum, these yachts are fully beachable. Drafts range from a mere 23 inches for the 42-foot Summer Kyle class to just 38 inches for *Kestrel. Drawing courtesy Dave Gerr*

DAVID GERR

Born May 19, 1953 · United States

A noted New York City yacht designer, David Gerr also made a mark in the marine world with his book *Propeller Handbook*, which is widely considered the definitive guide to propellers.

Born in New York City, Gerr studied physics at New York University, transferred to the Pratt Institute in Brooklyn, then graduated from the Westlawn School of Yacht Design in Stamford, Connecticut. He pursued naval architecture because it melded his interest in physics and art with his passion for boats. He landed his first job in 1979 at the New York office of MacLear and Harris, a firm widely known as pioneers of the multihull design and for monohull megayachts. It was there that Gerr developed his philosophy that no project was too big or too small to tackle.

In 1983 Gerr opened his own office, Gerr Marine, in New York City. He has designed more than a hundred boats, both custom and production, ranging from motorboats and sailboats to commercial vessels. Gerr strives to create rugged designs with a timeless quality. With Santa Cruz Yachts, Gerr created the Coastal Flyer, a jet-powered boat with an emphasis on seakindliness, maneuverability, and versatility.

Gerr also is known for his regular contributions to yachting publications, which then led to several book projects. In the mid-1980's, he was approached by International Marine, a division of publishing giant McGraw-Hill, to write his first book, *Pocket Cruisers for the Backyard Builder*.

That project led to his second book, *Propeller Handbook*. Gerr would say the propeller is a crucial element in yacht designs, yet there was lit-

tle information available for designers and backyard boatbuilders alike. The book describes in detail how propellers work and how to choose the correct one for a powerboat or sailboat. Other books to follow included *The Nature of Boats* and *The Elements of Boat Strength*.

Gerr remains in practice in New York City.

—JoAnn Goddard

HENRY J. GIELOW

1855–June 24, 1925 · United States

When Henry Gielow died, the *New York Times* eulogized him as "one of the nation's foremost naval architects" and *Motor Boating* magazine called him "one of the most noted marine designers and engineers." The designer of some of the most opulent and successful yachts ever built, Gielow produced a body of work whose hallmarks were, according to contemporary accounts, "economy of space, beauty, seaworthiness" and the "artistic arrangement of details."

Gielow also helped to create handicapping rules for powerboats and sailing yachts, and was an early advocate of gasoline and diesel engines (as opposed to steam) in large yachts. Although he was unquestionably a preeminent figure of the gilded age of American yachting, Gielow's name, like the vessels he designed, has virtually disappeared from memory.

Gielow achieved much of his celebrity as the designer of giant steam yachts such as the 258-foot, 1,255-gross-ton *Delphine*, launched in 1921 for Mrs. Horace E. Dodge at a cost of more than $1.5 million. At the time of Gielow's death, *Delphine* was the largest steam yacht, in tonnage, to have been built in the United States.

Born in Manitowoc, Wisconsin, a small village located some 180 miles north of Chicago

Frederick Geiger: *Ruth*. The 28-foot 6-inch ketch *Ruth* is representative of a number of Geiger's designs for cruising sailboats. Relatively high freeboard and short ends combine with a moderate sheer and a plain and simple house to create an air of no-nonsense strength and confidence. *Photo courtesy Robert Yorke*

on the western shore of Lake Michigan, Gielow was the son of early German settlers to that region. As a boy, he built and sailed model yachts as a hobby. As a student he excelled in mathematics and the applied sciences. He was a member of the American Society of Naval Engineers, a fellow of the American Geographical Society, and a member of the New York and Atlantic Yacht Clubs.

Beginning his professional life at age eighteen, Gielow started work for the U.S. Army Corps of Engineers in 1873. During his thirteen years there, Gielow designed several large dredges that significantly improved on existing machines, and supervised construction of the Muscle Shoals Canal on the Tennessee River.

In addition, Gielow continued what would be his lifelong study of steam engineering and hydrodynamics. He developed a theory of streamlines—which he later confirmed by testing a glass model—based on his belief that the then-current idea that water was displaced laterally at the bow of a vessel and replaced vertically in the run was wrong. Gielow reasoned that as pressure on a liquid is perpendicular to a surface immersed in it, water passing around a vessel would move as nearly as pos-

sible in a straight line along a path perpendicular to the surface of the hull—essentially along its diagonals. A devotion to meticulous and innovative engineering was an enduring characteristic of Gielow's work.

In 1886, Gielow resigned from government service and moved to New York City to set himself up as a naval architect, engineer, and yacht broker. One of his earliest published designs was for the steam survey launch *Lucerne*, apparently drawn by Gielow while he still worked for the army and built under his supervision in the Baltimore yard of E. J. Codd. The 75-foot *Lucerne* displaced 40 tons and, equipped with a 10 times 10 Westinghouse steam engine with two single-acting cylinders producing 50 hp, achieved a top speed of 13.5 mph during its trials, remarkable for its time.

For much of the next decade or so, Gielow's practice was devoted largely to the design of commercial vessels and machinery such as ferries, floating derricks, and a patented underwater rock cutter. Gielow's first large yacht, the flush-decked *Nydia*, was launched in 1890. Powered by a two-cylinder compound steam engine of Gielow's design, *Nydia* had an overall length of 122 feet 6 inches on a 106-foot wa-

terline, a beam of 16 feet 4 inches, and a draft of 6 feet. A number of important design commissions soon followed.

In 1897, the John N. Robins yard of Brooklyn, New York, builder of many of Gielow's designs, launched the 172-foot 6-inch steam screw schooner *Marietta*, the first of three progressively larger yachts Gielow designed that would carry that name. A year later, Merrill Stevens Engineering Company of Jacksonville, Florida, launched the 91-foot twin-screw houseboat *Whim Wham*. With a pair of 30-hp, two-cylinder White and Middleton engines, *Whim Wham* was among the first yachts of this size to be powered by gasoline engines rather than steam.

By 1904, about a dozen large steam yachts ranging from 99 to 211 feet, among them the 210-foot *Hauoli*—described as the fastest single-screw steam yacht in the world—had been built to Gielow's designs. He had also seen about a dozen of his motorboats built, many of them extremely fast for their time. The 60-foot *Rush*, built in 1900, reached a speed of 14 mph. *Onontio*, designed in 1904, reached a top speed of 27.72 mph, and just a year later, *Veritas* attained a speed of 29.1 mph. Also in 1904, Gielow completed his work of formulating

Henry Gielow: *Llewellyn.* The lovely steam yacht *Llewellyn* shows the low, lean hull form that is necessary to get the most speed out of engines with a low power-weight ratio. Like other steam-powered vessels, she would have been nearly silent underway. *Photograph by Nathaniel Stebbins. Courtesy of the Society for the Preservation of New England Antiquities*

the first comprehensive racing and measurement rule, table of time allowances, and rules of the road adopted by the fledgling American Power Boat Association.

While he is remembered primarily for his steamboats and motorboats, Gielow also designed a number of sailing yachts during the early years of the twentieth century. He was actively involved in the creation of the Universal Rule for sailing yachts, and designed the winning Q-Class yacht *Saetta* shortly after the rule's adoption. In 1905, he designed his first and most famous sailing yacht, *Effort*, for *Hauoli*'s owner, yachtsman F. M. Smith. Built of bronze by the Robert Jacob shipyard in City Island, New York (which built many of Gielow's early designs), *Effort* was launched in the spring of 1906 and achieved remarkable success.

With an overall length of 93 feet 3 inches and a waterline length of 65 feet, *Effort* was rated a 68-footer. Racing against such yachts as *Weetamoe*, *Neola*, and *Irolita* in her class, and the larger New York 70-footers *Yankee* and *Rainbow*, both of which she beat on several occasions, *Effort* started in twenty-four races in 1906 and compiled a record of fourteen first-place finishes, six seconds, and two thirds.

She won the first King's Cup, presented to the New York Yacht Club in 1906 by King Edward VII of England. During her career, *Effort* started fifty-four races and took prizes in forty-six of them. Unlike most of her competitors, *Effort* was often raced by her owner rather than by her professional sailing master.

Gielow's sailboat designs were not limited to racing craft. In the century's first decade he designed the 110-foot ocean cruising yacht *Agawam*, and in 1908 he designed the brigantine *Carnegie* as a magnetic survey vessel for the Carnegie Institution. Launched in 1909, the vessel was built of yellow pine on oak and fastened with locust treenails. All the vessel's metal fittings and machinery were bronze or copper, including the engine (excepting only its cast-iron pistons and steel valves) and the onboard producer-gas plant designed by Gielow. Gielow also designed several smaller boats, including a one-design, 20-foot 6-inch catboat for the Riverside Yacht Club.

Gielow designed some of the most luxurious yachts built in the United States. In 1914, the 203-foot steam yacht *Sialia* was launched at the Pusey and Jones shipyard and purchased by Henry Ford. He also designed the oceangoing

steam yachts *Nokomis I* and *Nokomis II* for automobile magnate Horace E. Dodge; the spectacular 125-foot diesel-powered houseboat *Zalophus*, launched in 1922 by the Consolidated Shipbuilding Corporation for circus entrepreneur John Ringling North; and *Goodwill*, a world-voyaging diesel auxiliary schooner yacht that twice sailed in the Transpac Race to Honolulu from California.

Despite his obvious success with designing what would now be called megayachts for the extremely wealthy, Gielow maintained a diverse practice. During World War I he designed a class of 190-foot, four-masted lumber schooners, as well as eighty-eight other commercial vessels between 1917 and 1924. In the latter year he also designed a class of shells for Yale University. In their new boats, Yale's oarsman were undefeated during the 1925 intercollegiate season. Gielow's firm lived on after his death, designing most of the lovely steam and motor yachts built by Bath Iron Works in Bath, Maine.

The Henry J. Gielow, Inc. Collection is at Mystic Seaport Museum, Mystic, CT, and some of his drawings are at the Maine Maritime Museum in Bath, ME.

—Stephen Rappaport

Henry Gielow: *Maria Delores.* The yacht *Maria Delores*, powered by an internal-combustion engine, shows how things had changed a few years after *Llewellyn* was built. A more efficient engine encouraged a larger boat for a given length. Like many yachts of her era, her design is influenced by the fast naval destroyers of the day. *Photo courtesy Newport Harbor Nautical Museum, Newport Beach, CA*

JACK LAURENT GILES

1901–1969 · England

J. Laurent Giles was one of the Great Britain's most innovative yacht designers, in both technical and aesthetic aspects of the field. He pioneered in lightweight construction and light-displacement hull designs and made many other innovations that have since become standard practice. His work left a seamless join between traditional and modern styling, and he produced pleasing yachts representing a whole spectrum of aesthetic types.

Giles was educated at Winchester College, Magdalene College in Cambridge, England, where he studied engineering, and at Durham University, where he qualified as a naval architect. He then started an apprenticeship designing merchant ships for Vickers-Armstrong, a naval construction yard at Newcastle-upon-Tyne, but he was a keen sailor and in his spare time he began designing sailing yachts.

After winning first prize in a design competition, Giles joined Camper and Nicholson's Southampton yard, where he came under the wing of Charles E. Nicholson. Nicholson and William Fife were the outstanding British yacht designers of the period. In 1927 he formed Laurent Giles and Partners with George R. Gill, setting up an office at Lymington, Hampshire. They were soon joined by the ocean voyager Humphrey Barton. From the start, the firm was a team effort, with Gill and Barton keeping a rein on Giles's more radical ideas.

Giles was among the first to put his designs through tank and wind-tunnel tests. As with the most successful designers of earlier times,

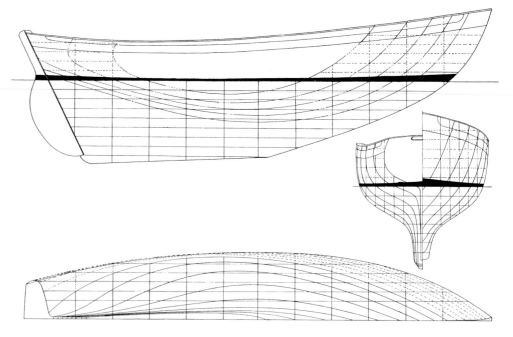

J. Laurent Giles: *Andrillot*. The famous Vertue class, originating with *Andrillot*, came to be seen as the ultimate expression of all that was good in British small yacht design. Strong, fast, comfortable, handsome, and supremely seaworthy, the popular 25-foot world-voyaging yacht has been updated several times and served as the basis of many designs by Giles and others. © *Tony Dixon*

he achieved much of his success by improving the structural engineering of the yachts themselves, as well as their rigs and equipment. He commented that while yacht designing was said to be an art, for him it was "a combination of calculations and controlled guessing with art." It was this inspired blend of technical know-how with great aesthetic taste and a lively, innovative mind that produced a number of firsts in the yacht-designing world.

Indeed, with only his second design, *Etain* (31 feet LWL), built in 1930, Giles showed his

willingness to break with tradition by giving her the first doghouse to be fitted to a small yacht, so beginning a revolution in below-deck accommodations. Other prewar designs included *Andrillot* (21 feet 6 inches LWL), the forerunner of the evergreen Vertue class; *Wanderer II* (21 feet LWL) for the globe-trotting Eric and Susan Hiscock; the much-admired modernized cutter *Dyarchy* (35 feet LWL); and two centerboard cruising boats, *Wapipi* (28 feet LWL) and her sistership, *Whooper*, which were the first yachts to have their masts stepped

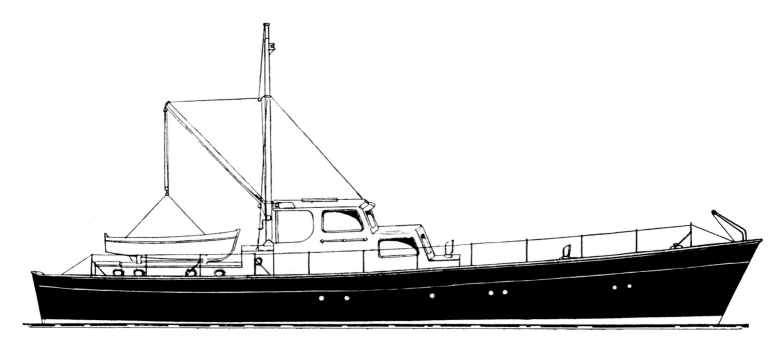

J. Laurent Giles: *Woodpecker*. Llewelyn Howland III has always upheld the 70-foot *Woodpecker* as his "beau ideal" among medium-sized, fast motor cruisers. Giles's treatment of the upperworks, together with an efficient seakindly hull, ensured a yacht of lasting appeal. *Drawing courtesy Jay Paris*

J. Laurent Giles: *Myth of Malham.* Designed by Giles in conjunction with the famous ocean racer and later designer John Illingworth, *Myth of Malham* was a radical departure from the norm in 1947. This photograph shows off her straight sheer, rounded bow, and cutoff counter, the most visible of the yacht's then-radical features. *Photo courtesy Sandy Illingworth and Jean Dupuy*

J. Laurent Giles: *Gulvain.* One of Giles's achievements was his introduction of the reverse-sheer configuration. *Gulvain*, a typical example of the genre, is also notable for her aluminum construction, something of an innovation in 1949. Moderately successful as an ocean racer in British waters, she is now in the United States. © *Peter Barlow*

on the coachroof, another radical innovation that helped make the interiors of small yachts more spacious. All these boats had the transom stern, which was a Giles trademark, and handsome conventional sheers, which he would continue to draw throughout his career when appropriate, usually on designs for cruising yachts.

The Vertue class has ended up being Giles's most widely beloved design. Numerous examples have made transoceanic voyages and circumnavigations, often singlehanded, and they might be one of the world's most well-proven small yachts for offshore voyaging. At the bottom of the size range in which most people would want to go to sea (25 feet LOA), Vertues proved to be strong, fast, weatherly, and comfortable. With plucky English good looks and a great design name (taken from a trophy won by one of the early boats), the Vertue class quickly became widely admired. The design was updated several times to accommodate changes in the rigging—from gaff

cutter to a deck-stepped Bermudian cutter rig, to a masthead rig—and the cabin trunk was lengthened and given a doghouse in at least four styles. The sheer was slightly raised and straightened to allow a bit more room under the side decks. Recently a new fiberglass version was introduced, and wooden custom-built versions still appear from time to time. Over two hundred Vertues have been built.

In 1930 Giles joined the RORC—he served for many years on its Technical Committee—and in 1936 John Illingworth, one of the club's top ocean-racing skippers, commissioned him to design *Maid of Malham* (35 feet LWL). *Maid* was a test bed for both Illingworth and her designer, and the experiments, in deck gear especially, were to pay dividends after the war. Probably the first British ocean racer to be tank-tested at the Stevens Institute of Technology in New Jersey, *Maid* had a masthead cutter rig and a short aft overhang, which saved weight and improved her rating. She also had

a style of bow overhang that characterized many subsequent Giles's designs, including the famous ocean racer *Lutine* (41-foot 6-inch LWL), built in 1952 to the CCA Rule.

Before the war intervened, Giles also designed the 12-meter *Flica II*. She took years to show her potential, as her original Devon crew refused to have winches—"winksies"—aboard her. During the war Giles worked for the Admiralty, designing the MFV (Motor Fishing Vessel), which was a versatile small naval craft meant to be converted to fishing after the war, and the "sleeping beauty," a submersible electric canoe for attacking enemy vessels while they were in harbor. He also worked in aircraft design in the United States, becoming exposed to new forms of lightweight construction that might have applications in racing yachts, something Illingworth was also keen to develop. Between the two of them they produced in 1947 a revolutionary light-displacement ocean racer, *Myth of Malham*

(33 feet 6 inches LWL). She was, in the words of naval architect Douglas Phillips-Birt, "about the heartiest slap in the face that conventional yacht architecture had ever received, but in fact her eccentric appearance tended to obscure the fact that she was a most brilliant and logical interpretation of sound principles."

Developed from *Maid of Malham*, *Myth* was of then radically light displacement and had a straight sheer, chopped-off ends, and—another first—double sliding companionway hatches. Some of the deck gear was made of aluminum alloy—the high-tech material of the day—designed by Giles to save weight. Much of this gear is now so accepted that it is hard to think of it as innovative. For example, the traditional sheet horse was replaced by a main-sheet track, and there were also tracks for the headsail sheet blocks fitted along both sides of the deck. She was immediately successful, winning both the Channel and Fastnet Races in 1947 and winning the Fastnet again in 1949.

Other successful light-displacement designs by Giles followed, including *Gulvain* (43 feet LWL), the first all-aluminum ocean racer, and *Fandango* (33 feet LWL). With these yachts Giles introduced a retroussé (forward-sloping) transom and a reverse-sheer configuration, which further improved the accommodations of smaller yachts and soon found popular acceptance. *Gulvain*, built in 1949, is claimed to be the first ocean racer to have rod rigging and halyards running inside the mast. She was one of the first ocean racers to have an aluminum mast—the very first were apparently the RNSA 24's, which Giles had designed two years previously. Built to the RORC Class III minimum length of 24 feet LWL, they were a highly successful one-design boat built for the Royal Naval Sailing Association.

Another trend-setting design was *Sopranino*, which at under 20 feet LOA was the first midget ocean racer. Among her long voyages was a transatlantic passage. The design prompted the foundation of the Junior Offshore Group in Britain and the Midget Ocean Racing Club (MORC) in the United States. Giles gave her a fin-and-bulb keel, with the rudder hung separately on a skeg, an idea he apparently copied from model-yacht design. He employed a similar underbody on the Italian-owned *Miranda IV* (39-foot LWL), which was highly success-

J. Laurent Giles: *Lutine* (opposite). While he was more usually associated with the RORC Rule, Giles designed *Lutine* to the CCA Rule. Built by Camper and Nicholson in 1952, she was campaigned by Sandy Haworth. She was always sailed to her maximum and was a beautiful sight. © *Mystic Seaport, Rosenfeld Collection, Mystic, CT*

Gerhard Gilgenast: *Margaux Rose*. Though remembered for his famously dynamic, turbine-driven, planing designs, plus such unique creations as *Izanami*, and his aerodynamic styling of the record-breaking *Octopussy* and *Moonraker*, Gilgenast could also produce displacement-hull classics such as the 152-foot *Margaux Rose*. Photo courtesy Jack A. Somer

ful in Mediterranean ocean races. She was the first ocean racer of any size to have such an underwater configuration, and though Illingworth found that it did not catch on with his own customers when he used it on his designs, Richard Carter and Olin Stephens reintroduced it in the 1960's with great success.

Although Giles will probably be best remembered for his ocean racers, he also designed a large number of cruising boats after the war, some of which struck such a popular note that they were then built in series. Three were *Rose of York* (27 feet LWL) and the New Channel class, *Trekka* and the Columbia class, and *Peter Duck* (25 feet LWL) and the Peter Duck class.

Giles was also one of the most notable designers of light-displacement motorsailers that were able to achieve high cruising speeds with good fuel economy and to sail brilliantly as well. His best-known design of this type was *Blue Leopard* (75 feet LWL), built in 1962, which was capable of sailing at 15 knots off the wind in force 5 and motoring at the same speed under her two 380-hp Rolls Royce engines.

When fiberglass entered the British boatbuilding scene in the early 1960's, Giles was quick to adapt to this method of construction. He designed production boats for both Moody and Westerly. His bilge-keeled Westerly Centaur, one of his last designs, had many innovations and proved especially popular, with about 2,500 being built.

The firm of Laurent Giles remains in Lymington.

—Ian Dear

GERHARD GILGENAST

June 6, 1938–August 1, 1991 · Germany

The sources of Gerhard Gilgenast's unique strengths as a naval architect may well be found in his decidedly artistic, often opinionated temperament, and his famous, well-worn toolbox. The teenage Gilgenast had to buy that toolbox and its contents in the early 1950's, when he began a three-year boatbuilding apprenticeship at the Abeking and Rasmussen shipyard in Lemwerder, near Bremen, Germany. That experience ultimately led him toward a career designing some of the twentieth century's most intriguingly styled, high-performance motoryachts.

Gilgenast was born in the East Prussian city of Elbing (now Elblag, Poland), near what is now Gdańsk. Toward the end of World War II, he escaped the Red Army with his family, who settled in Lingen, near the Ems River close by the Dutch border, in what soon became the Federal Republic of Germany.

Following his apprenticeship at Abeking and Rasmussen, Gilgenast bought a cheap ticket, took his toolbox, and jumped aboard a freighter bound for New York, where he found work at two great American shipyards—Minneford, on City Island, and Derecktor, in Mamaroneck. Ever a restless soul, in the late 1950's Gilgenast bought a jalopy for $50, packed his toolbox, and, like an itinerant artisan, made the rounds in search of more carpentry work.

After this hands-on experience, Gilgenast returned to Germany, and from August 1960 to

June 1963 he studied naval architecture at the renowned Bremen Technikum, returning during summer holidays to work at Minneford to earn his tuition. As an original, somewhat aesthetic thinker, Gilgenast was undeniably a rather lazy student, but he completed his courses successfully and, with his certificate (and toolbox), returned to America's shores.

For a time Gilgenast apprenticed with Bill Tripp, Phil Rhodes, and Sparkman and Stephens (with fellow apprentices Germán Frers and Gary Mull at his side). In 1969 Gilgenast returned to Abeking and Rasmussen as chief technical designer, and with his boatbuilding experience coupled with his innate gift for style, he began formulating a new motoryacht type ultimately to be characterized by its fluid lines, efficient propulsion, thoroughly analyzed structure, high speed, low noise, and long range.

In 1973 Abeking and Rasmussen launched the Aga Khan's Gilgenast-designed, 29-meter *Kalamoun*, a planing boat built of thin aluminum to keep it ultralight and fast. Though she later proved noisy and uncomfortable (and eventually was rebuilt), the Aga Khan was impressed enough to take Gilgenast to his private enclave for the superwealthy, in Porto Cervo, Sardinia, where Gilgenast helped design the new marina. Later the Aga Khan set him up as head of Maritime Promotion Service (MPS) to create "sophisticated yachts." Gilgenast established MPS design offices near his home in Lemwerder, Germany, and in Fort Lauderdale, Florida.

From then on Gilgenast produced a series of motoryachts of surpassing beauty and potency, many of them with seakindly semiplaning hulls. His next project was the Aga Khan's *Shergar*, a 46.6-meter semiplaning motoryacht built by Lürssen. She was powerfully propelled to 45.5 knots by two diesel engines and two gas turbine engines driving three water jets—typical of the dynamic propulsion of a very speed-competitive period in yacht design. Gilgenast's fame rose when he collaborated with the younger Dutch naval architect Frank Mulder in styling the Dutch-built *Octopussy*, the first large powerboat to break the 50-knot barrier. Gilgenast then styled her successor, the 66.7-knot *Moonraker*.

Next Gilgenast designed two rather conservative character boats: the 100-foot *F-100* and the 152-foot *Margaux Rose*. These were followed by a group of handsomely styled motoryachts, including *Azzurro, Falco I, Falco II, Alcor, Whirlwind, L'Aquasition,* and Gilgenast's own favorite, *TM Blue One.*

Gilgenast's affection for curves, large windows, and aggressive bow-rake came to define his style. In 1991 he did the hull architecture

and supervised tank tests in the Vienna Model Basin for a 191-foot motoryacht to be named *Izanami*. The project was in collaboration with Sir Norman Foster, England's noted cosmopolitan (nonnaval) architect.

Unfortunately, while the design was being refined, Gilgenast died at the age of fifty-three of cancer. He had been designing a sleek 92-foot motoryacht programmed to exceed 70 knots. The project clearly demonstrated Gilgenast's mature hand; unfortunately it has never been built. At his death Gilgenast also still owned a hundred-year-old wooden boat that he occasionally worked on himself—using, of course, the precious contents of his own decades-old toolbox.

—Jack A. Somer

THOMAS CHARLES GILLMER

Born 1911 · United States

Few yacht designers have approached their work with a more solid combination of education, experience, knowledge, and good taste than Thomas Gillmer. He graduated with a bachelor of science degree in engineering from the U.S. Naval Academy and did graduate work at Johns Hopkins University. He spent several years as an officer on naval destroyers and cruisers.

Gillmer apprenticed at the yard of a Nova Scotia boatbuilder, and for over thirty years served at the Naval Academy as a professor of naval architecture, chairman of Naval Engineering, and director of the Ship Hydro-

Thomas Gillmer: *Onatru.* The 30-foot Seawind ketch, built by Allied, was a successful early effort to produce a fiberglass yacht well suited to offshore voyaging as well as coastal cruising. Here *Onatru* displays her cabin trunk, which has an attractive, heavily rounded shape ideal for fiberglass construction. © *Peter Barlow*

Thomas Gillmer. This 42-foot 2-inch LOA, raised-deck cutter was built in 1981 as a high-performance offshore cruiser. With her centerboard up, she only draws 4 feet 6 inches, allowing her to navigate the shallow waters of the Bahamas and the Intercoastal Waterway. *Drawing courtesy Thomas Gillmer*

dynamics Laboratory. He has done extensive historical research on the entire history of watercraft. He has been designing boats for over fifty years, part-time, until his retirement from the Naval Academy and then full-time.

Small wonder that with the fortunate additional attribute of a "good eye," he has produced a number of vessels that unarguably deserve the much-abused adjective *classic*. One of his earliest and best-known designs is *Blue Moon*, a 23-foot, gaff-rigged yawl based on the historic English Falmouth Quay Punt (not a punt in the American sense of the word), but considerably interpreted. The boat was so universally beloved that more than one authority has dubbed it "perfect," a word one seldom hears in the jealous and competitive world of yacht design. But perfect she is, in the author's opinion. Like any true classic, we might be tempted to change this or that for one purpose or another, but then we wouldn't have a *Blue Moon*, and having one is a goal good enough all by itself—maybe one definition of a classic.

Many of us are a bit nervous hearing the word *classic* used to describe a fiberglass boat, but Gillmer's 30-foot Seawind, built by Allied Yachts as either a ketch or a sloop, surely qualifies. Unlike many "glass" boats that are made deliberately bland for broad market appeal, the Seawind had a strong sheer, a curvaceous bow, and a distinctive, heavily cambered transom that made her instantly recognizable. She was not an exercise in modernism, but a short evolutionary step across the threshold into fiberglass construction. Nor was she meant to be mistaken for a wooden boat, which might have risked the kind of ersatz detailing that spoils many a good job of production boatbuilding today. Her cabin trunk was unadorned with trim and heavily rounded—an obviously fiberglass structure with its own "look," avoiding the hard edges that are so popular on today's fiberglass boats and to which fiberglass is structurally unsuited. One Seawind, named *Apogee*, was the first fiberglass boat to sail around the world. Numerous other fiberglass and wooden boats bear the distinctive, enthusiastic looks so characteristic of Gillmer's work.

Gillmer is also well known for his extensive work as a marine historian, studying historical records and artifacts from the whole five-thousand-year history of seafaring, and writing on the subject in his book *A History of Working Watercraft of the Western World* (1994). He is famous for designing three significant historic replicas. *Lady Maryland* is based on an 1875 pungy schooner. The Baltimore Clipper *Pride of Baltimore* was very close to a fully authentic replica originally conceived and designed as a dockside exhibit. She was, however, taken to sea and eventually lost in a sudden squall, just as vessels of this extreme type occasionally were back in the days when blockade running and warfare under sail were more immediate risks than the weather. Her replacement is the incomparable *Pride of Baltimore II*, for which the Baltimore Clipper model was modified by Gillmer to produce a true offshore passenger carrier while retaining as much authenticity as possible.

Gillmer has written several other books and textbooks, including *Pride of Baltimore: The Story of the Baltimore Clippers 1800–1990* (1992) and *Old Ironsides: The Rise, Decline, and Resurrection of the USS Constitution* (1993).

—Daniel B. MacNaughton

FRANCESCO GIOVANELLI

1871–1945 · Italy

A skilled yachtsman who began designing 6- and 8-Meter racing boats when he became dissatisfied with those he was sailing, Francesco Giovanelli wanted to express and test new concepts, many of which proved to be successful, as the records of his yachts in Italy and France attest.

The Giovanelli-designed 6-Meter International Rule boats *Bamba*, *Nele*, *Petra*, *Ea*, *Grazia*, *Mebi*, *Maène*, and *Bambetta*, spanning the years 1912 to 1937, were built by the Baglietto shipyard in Varazze, outside of Savona on the

Gulf of Genoa. Baglietto also built Giovanelli's 8-Meter International Rule boats *Cheta* and *Bamba*, in 1925 and 1927, respectively. Four times Giovanelli-designed yachts won the Italy Cup—one of the major European trophies for the Meter classes—in Genoa in 1924, 1925, and 1932 and in Le Havre in 1930.

Aside from numerous technical articles, Giovanelli wrote two books: *Racing and Its Rules*, a manual in which he explained the racing rules with advice for those of less experience, and *Sailboats Go by Their Sails*, a collection of often controversial articles on technical problems, which had been published in nautical journals.

—Franco Belloni

JACOB KLAAS GIPON

1910–1999 · The Netherlands

Jacob Gipon may have limited international acclaim, but he was very significant in the Netherlands as a designer of traditional shoal-draft yachts.

The worldwide depression of the 1930's affected ordinary people's ability to build boats for pleasure in the Netherlands (as it did elsewhere). To make do, many Dutch yachtsmen converted small commercial and fishing boats, often old and in bad condition, to yachts. This is when Gipon's talent emerged.

Studying engineering for a short time at the Nautical Academy in Amsterdam, Gipon

Francesco Giovanelli: *Bamba.* The 8-Meter *Bamba* was built in 1927 by the Baglietto shipyard in Italy. *Photo courtesy Franco Belloni*

especially liked drawing. In April 1936 he published his first design, a small catboat, inspired by American examples. In these first drawings, typical Gipon elements were already apparent: simplicity in small yachts that could be built by amateurs. To achieve this he converted the original, round-bottomed Cape Cod catboat to a hard-chine design, enabling builders to use steel or plywood.

In 1937 Gipon drew his first traditional Dutch design, the 20-foot *Zeeschouw* (Sea Scow), a hard-chine, flat-bottomed fishing boat developed as a cheaper option to the more complicated and expensive "Aak." The design was published in Dutch yachting magazines. Unfortunately, when World War II broke out in 1940, there was no work for a young designer, and yachting as well as publishing came to a halt.

The period after the war saw a growing interest in the typical, traditional Dutch sailing craft. The building and launching of Princess Beatrix's Lemster Aak *De Groene Draeck* (The Green Dragon) by Gerard de Vries Lentsch Jr. gave a fresh impetus to public demand for new, small sailing yachts of this type.

Gipon's role in this development was significant because he managed to translate many old working-boat types into yachts. His connections with old fishermen and skippers were prime

sources of information. He developed a very distinctive style, based on designs of working craft that closely incorporated the typical properties of these old Dutch boat types.

—Rutger ten Broeke

PEPÍN GONZÁLEZ

1954–1989 · Spain

If any confirmation was needed that, at age thirty-five, self-taught designer and builder Pepín González had become one of Spain's leading yacht designers on the international Grand Prix racing circuit, it came when he was chosen as part of the design team for the 1992 Spanish America's Cup challenge. Tragically, within weeks he was killed by a car while cycling to work on his native island of Mallorca in the Mediterranean.

His brother and business partner, Amadeo, recalls that Pepín was a restless youngster but always competitive. He became interested in model-airplane competitions, which led to studies in aerodynamics and a subsequent interest in sailing.

In the mid-1970's the brothers completed a modified, kit-built Ron Holland Egythene IOR Quarter-Tonner. She was followed in 1983 by González's first design, the Bruce Farr–

influenced Quarter-Tonner *Barracuda*. The brother's complete control of the project—from Pepín's gifted work at the drawing board, through construction of the boat in their garage with Amadeo, to having the sails made by respected local sailmaker José Matheu—played a part in winning the prestigious Copa del Rey in Palma de Mallorca and kick-starting a career at the top end of yacht racing.

The year 1987 was a vintage one. The One-Tonner *Mallurca* took form under similar circumstances, winning the Copa de España and competing for Spain in that season's Admiral's Cup. One of many racing yachts designed and built by Pepín for the Spanish navy (Regatta Division), *Cote* placed second at the Quarter-Ton World races and *Sirius III* came in second in the Three-Quarter-Ton World races at Kiel.

Such success would only have led to greater things, but sadly it was not to be. González's name lives on in a trophy presented annually to the most successful yacht designed and built in Spain.   —John Lynch with Amadeo González and Iain McAllister

HAROLD GOWER

1899–1972 · Canada/United States

An influential designer of Maine lobsterboats, Harold Gower began his life in Westport, Nova Scotia. He left school at the age of thirteen to help his father run his fishing boat, and later joined the Canadian army until they found he was under age and discharged him. His first boatbuilding job was to install a new cabin on his father's boat.

When Gower was doing repair work on Grand Manan Island, Will Frost—whose designs fathered the Maine lobsterboat—asked him to come and help him in his shop on Beals Island, Maine. There they built lobsterboats and some rumrunners, working together for seven years before Gower went out on his own.

Gower began in 1933 by building small boats, but in 1936 he built a shop on Beals Island and soon designed and produced his first large boat. All the boats that Gower built over the years were of his own design, but with a lot of influence from Will Frost, such as the reverse curve in the bottom.

Like all lobsterboat builders, Gower's designs became longer and wider as time passed and engines increased in horsepower. From 1936 to 1972 Gower designed and built 111 boats, mostly traditional Maine lobsterboats, but with a few pleasure boats and one sailboat included. Over the years numerous other designers and builders have used the lines from his boats, a testimony to his abilities.   —Jon B. Johansen

Jacob Gipon: Lemster Aak. Prior to Gipon's design for this modest, steel 36-footer, built in 1964, the Lemster Aak type was not built less than 44 feet in length. By adjusting the proportions of the traditional design, Gipon created a pocket version combining excellent sailing properties with standing headroom. *Drawing courtesy Rutger ten Broeke*

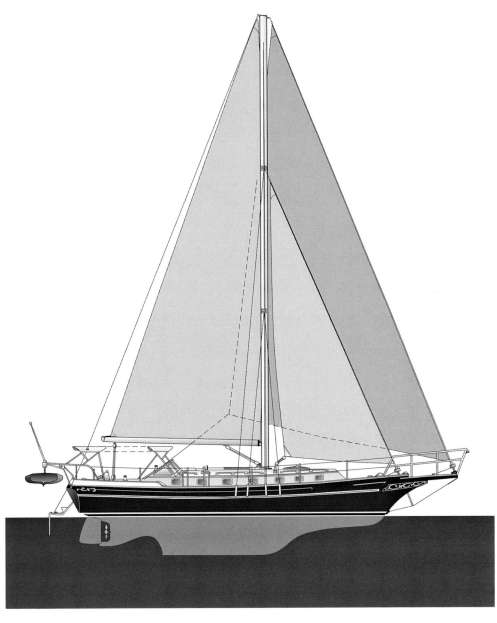

Ted Gozzard: Gozzard 44. The Gozzard 44 is a production fiberglass boat of conservative design, following proven design principles rather than pushing the envelope, and incorporating traditional ornamentation. She and other boats drawn by Gozzard have proved popular with cruising yachtsmen. *Drawing courtesy Ted Gozzard*

HEDLEY "TED" GOZZARD

Born June 13, 1933 · England/Canada

Ted Gozzard has the ability to design and build yachts that not only suit his particular circumstances, likes, and dislikes, but also have proved popular with large numbers of yacht buyers. Born in England, he immigrated to Ontario, Canada, in 1957 after serving an apprenticeship as a carpenter/boatbuilder and completing his national service in the Royal Air Force.

In Canada, Gozzard first became involved in designing and building houses, which led to work in subdivision development and management. Then in 1968, he "escaped the rat race" with his wife and two sons by becoming a "professional beachbum" in the

Caribbean. This experience led to a change in career and the design and construction of a 45-foot trimaran. In 1970 he returned to Canada and founded Bayfield Boat Yard in Bayfield, Ontario.

Bayfield was a success for Gozzard and his partners. Within a year, the company employed over fifty people and was producing two boats a week to Gozzard's designs, and his two sons were working with him. Production included the Bayfield 23, 25, 29, 32, and 40 fiberglass yachts as well as 35- to 40-foot designs made in steel by Bayfield and other manufacturers. The types of rigs included schooners, ketches, and cutters.

In 1982 Gozzard decided he wanted a family firm in which his sons could have a real role, so he sold his interest to his partners and

started North Castle Marine/Gozzard Yachts. He soon demonstrated that he and his sons had the ability to design and build high-quality yachts that sold well. These include the Pilgrim 40, a tug-style motoryacht, the Gozzard 31, the G37, the G41, and the G44. The G54 is underway.

For Gozzard, "yacht design is not rocket science, the guidelines are clearly set." He adds, "For the boat to perform safely in its intended element, its numbers must fit within proven and well-established formula." Within these rules, Gozzard and his sons design boats that suit them and their customers. He likes to give his yachts a traditional look. "I choose to extend the rig by using a bowsprit and lower the center of effort and yet stir the soul and quicken the heart," he states. Gilding and trailboards combined with a sweeping sheer help establish an emotional bond between boat and owner and, indeed, between owner and designer. It is this element of bonding that gives the designer feedback and allows him to develop his work, which Gozzard believes is important in his success.

Gozzard Yachts, located in Goderich, Ontario, is run by Ted, his sons Michael and Wesley, and daughter Jan. —Tom Roach

WALTER GREENE

Born 1944 · United States

One of New England's most highly regarded multihull designers and builders, Walter Greene was born in Connecticut on Long Island Sound. He went to the University of Vermont and graduated with a degree in history. In the early 1970's he began learning about boatbuilding when he went to work for Allan Vaitses of Mattapoisett, Massachusetts. When Vaitses sold the business, Greene went to work for Ted Hood in Marblehead.

Greene became interested in multihulls when he encountered Phil Weld's *Gulfsteamer* in the early 1970's. At about this time he also took the Westlawn School of Yacht Design's home-study course on yacht design.

Greene began sailing aboard multihulls in 1972 and built one at the Hood yard in 1976. He left Hood in 1977 and went to work for Handy Boat in Falmouth, Maine. There he built Phil Weld's *Moxie* and a trimaran of his own design, *Gauloises IV*. During the 1980 OSTAR (Observer Singlehanded Transatlantic Race), *Gauloises IV* was leading the race when it broke its wing deck, and *Moxie* went on for the win. When one of Greene's designs won the Route de Rhum Race in 1978, he began selling designs in Europe.

In 1980 Greene left Handy Boat and opened Greene Marine in Yarmouth, Maine. Here he has continued to build multihulls to his designs and those of other naval architects.

In 1983–84 he designed and built the 45-foot catamaran *Sebago*, featuring an innovative rerighting system that he invented. Greene continues to design multihulls for racing, cruising, and day charters. —Jon B. Johansen

MAURICE GRIFFITHS

May 22, 1902–October 11, 1997 · England

One of England's finest designers of sensible cruising boats, as well as a prolific yachting author and respected editor, Maurice Griffiths made his name from popularizing coastwise cruising in small, shoal-draft yachts rather than any spectacular racing or technological accomplishments.

At an early age, Griffiths fell in love with what Americans call gunkhole cruising, in which the discovery and enjoyment of small waterways, the unspoiled natural world, and out-of-the-way places offer simple but deeply felt pleasures. Early in his sailing years he realized that as a rule, English yachts were too deep for this type of cruising, and borrowing from both English working craft and American centerboard yacht types, he created a range of small, charming, and inexpensive, shoal-draft cruising boats that were ideal for the purpose.

Griffiths bought his first boat on a shoestring in 1921. A 6-ton cutter, she was followed by a succession of twenty other boats of diverse types, some of which were sold after a single season, partly to avoid yard bills and partly to allow the purchase of the next boat. This strategy provided a good education in the design of small yachts, and a lot of yachting at minimal cost.

At age twenty-four, Griffiths published his first book, *Yachting on a Small Income* (1925). The book and its author came to the attention of the owner of *Yachting Monthly* magazine, and he was soon made its editor, a position he held for the next forty years. Prior to his editorship, *Yachting Monthly* had been a failing publication serving mostly the interests of well-to-do yachtsmen. Griffiths completely reversed this slant and made the magazine into a practical, down-to-earth aid to the person of modest means. It eventually became one of the most influential and popular boating magazines in Great Britain.

Other books written by Griffiths include *Magic of the Swatchways* (1932), *Little Ships and Shoal Waters* (1937), *Dream Ships* (1949), *Swatchways and Little Ships* (1971), and *60 Years a Yacht*

Maurice Griffiths: *Moonlight*. *Moonlight* is one of Griffiths's popular Golden Hind 31's. Husky, chine-hulled sloops with both a raised deck and a cabin trunk, most have bilge keels for upright grounding. They emphasize comfort and versatility over aesthetics, and while they excel at inshore cruising, they have also made many offshore voyages. © *David Harding/PPL Photo Agency*

Designer (1988). Some of his writing concerns design considerations, while the rest evokes the actual experience of cruising. The quality of the designs, the writing, and Griffiths's beautiful pen-and-ink drawings made him one of the world's most beloved advocates of simple and healthy values in boats and their use.

Being particularly interested in shoal-draft boats that could take the ground upright, Griffiths developed improved centerboard configurations, and also experimented with leeboards and twin bilge keels. Many of his de-

signs incorporate the raised-deck configuration, which increases interior volume and reserve stability in a strong and simple structure. His first design commission, for a small centerboard cruiser, came in 1928. The boat is still sailing.

Griffiths went on to create about 140 designs, including the well-known Eventide 24 and 26, the Waterwitch 30, and the popular Golden Hind 31, which was built in both plywood and fiberglass. The Eventide became very popular after one owner sailed his homebuilt boat from Singapore to England. About a thousand have been built to date. Griffiths's work encompassed all building materials and a wide range of types. Although his reputation was founded in his small-yacht designs, his sturdy, offshore designs have made many long passages. The Golden Hind 31 is said to have made more Atlantic crossings, Far East cruises, and Pacific crossings than any other single design. About sixteen hundred Maurice Griffiths–designed boats are sailing today.

Griffiths was brought up in Ipswich on the river Orwell in the area of England known as East Anglia. The area is famous for its low and complex shoreline, and for the ever-shifting sandy shoals that make navigation challenging. The channels in between, called swatchways locally, captured Griffiths's imagination and that of many a reader. He had little formal education after the age of sixteen, and learned naval architecture largely through advice and instruction he received from an older designer, Frederick Shepherd.

Serving in the Royal Navy Reserve during World War II, Griffiths was given command of a fleet of steam drifters keeping the east coast of England free of mines. For his service he was awarded the George Medal. He saw similar service later in Suez. After the war he resumed the editorship of *Yachting Monthly*. Maurice Griffiths retired in 1967 and died in 1997.

—Daniel B. MacNaughton

JEAN GROBETY

Born May 25, 1922 · Switzerland

Hydrodynamic theory long fascinated Jean Grobety, a dentist by profession and a designer by passion. His father distinguished himself with his fast motorboats before World War II, and in 1953 Jean Grobety, who by then was spending all of his leisure time designing yachts, set a world record in the E-Class with *Runabout*.

Grobety's designs began to have an impact in 1972 when *Amethyst I* was victorious in numerous regattas. Her V-shaped hull was built from four plates of aluminum, thus greatly reducing the number of welds. In 1977 he designed *Amethyst II*, which led the lemanic fleet of the 1979 and 1981 Bol d'Or—Europe's largest lake sailing race—on Lake Geneva. In the next year Grobety's 5.5-Meter *Sapphire*, conceived according to the same principle, won the world championship.

In 1984, when several Swiss yachtsmen launched a challenge for the 1987 America's Cup, Grobety was involved in their plan for an aluminum 12-Meter. Unfortunately, Switzerland eventually withdrew their challenge. Grobety is now retired. —Jacques Taglang

HANS GROOP

Born 1932 · Finland

The skerry islands outside Vasa on Finland's west coast are in Hans Groop's home waters in the Gulf of Bothnia, and as he once said, "Here have always lived independent people who are also good boatbuilders." That the famous Swan yachts are built in this area is not a coincidence.

Groop had planned to be a flight engineer, but the job market was very poor. Instead he became a marine engineer and was employed at the big Wartsila shipyard. His work was to design small boats to serve big ships, along with lifeboats and commercial vessels.

Groop's start in yacht design came in 1967 when he designed the H-Boat for himself (the *H* stands for *Hans*) to be built in fiberglass. His intent was to create a classic-looking boat that would be well suited to the narrow sounds between the islands. This small, three-person, one-design keelboat made him suddenly famous, as the type soon spread out in large numbers in Scandinavia and Europe. It is still a strong racing class today.

From that time on, Groop was well known and got many design orders. His best-known production boats are the H35, Artina, Targa, Lohi-Joemarin, and the Finnsailor 30 and 34. Hans Groop also has the pleasure of designing wooden "church" rowing boats with twelve oars, for the Finnish lakes. It is an old tradition, and in some cases a necessity, to row to church on the other side of many of Finland's thousands of lakes.

—Bent Aarre

Hans Groop: H-Boat. The popular 27-foot H-Boat gave Groop his first big success story. A slender fiberglass keelboat, she was fast and maneuverable and had a pleasing character as well as a small amount of accommodations. H-Boats are actively raced under a class association. *Photo courtesy Bent Aarre*

HEINRICH A. "HENRY" GRUBER

1899–1959 · Germany/United States

Henry Gruber has earned a place among the great designers of racing yachts in the late 1930's. Looking beyond those boats, however, one finds incredible versatility. He could design everything from a square-rigger to a 12-meter and always produced yachts of beautiful, harmonious lines and strong, thoroughly calculated construction. He had careers designing yachts in both the United States and Germany from the mid-1920's until 1956.

Born in the tiny village of Steinberghaff on the shores of the Baltic Sea, Gruber was called Henry from early on, a result no doubt of the considerable Anglo-Saxon and Danish influence in that part of Germany, especially in maritime language and local dialect. His father was a marine engineer whose skills served the family well during this time of rapid technical progress.

During his childhood by the sea and among seamen, Gruber's imagination was captured by boats and ships, and he decided they should make up his professional career. He finished his secondary education in 1919 after spending two years in the coastal artillery of the navy at the end of World War I.

Gruber's first job was at a local shipyard in Flensburg, where he gained practical experi-ence before attending Technical University in Berlin. He received his diploma in shipbuild-ing in 1924 and worked in Kiel building small boats and yachts.

Renewed business relations between the United States and Germany made it feasible for Gruber to consider designing yachts in the for-mer. He moved to New York City in 1925.

American boatyards, fueled by a booming economy, were turning out racing and cruis-ing yachts in great numbers. Gruber spent the next ten years working for such well-known designers as W. Starling Burgess, where he assisted in the design of *Niña* (1928), and the J-Class America's Cup defender *Enterprise* (1930). Later, in 1933, he worked on the design of *Rainbow*, the 1934 America's Cup defender, again with Burgess. He also worked with New York designers Cox and Stevens. Next came the partnership of Megargel and Gruber, soon followed by the merged firms of Burgess and Donaldson, Megargel and Gruber.

Two notable yachts Gruber designed in this period are the 65-foot schooner *Barlovento* and the 39-foot 10-inch cutter *Binker*. *Barlovento*, de-signed by Gruber while at Cox and Stevens, was built in 1932 by the F. F. Pendleton Yard in Maine. She enjoyed a stellar career and at the time of this writing still raced successfully in the Pacific Northwest under the same name. *Binker* was included in *Uffa Fox's Second Book* (1935) and is one of fifty covered in *Best of Uffa*. *Binker*'s design is mistakenly credited to Burgess and Donaldson in Uffa's book as well as in Roger C. Taylor's *Still More Good Boats*. This error was corrected by Taylor in a letter to *WoodenBoat* magazine in July 1997.

While living in America, Gruber never gave up thoughts of returning to Germany, and in 1935 he and his family did so for good. Hitler had been in power for two years, and eco-nomically Germany seemed to be recovering. Yachts were being built, and the 1936 Olympic Games were held in Berlin. Gruber became known as the "German genius from America." Even a job offer from Sparkman and Stephens to become the chief draftsman on the W. Star-ling Burgess/Sparkman and Stephens *Ranger* design for the America's Cup of 1936 did not lure him back to the United States.

Gruber first lived in Flensburg, where he had his own office, Gruber Yachts. He worked closely with the Burmester Shipyard of Bremen, which became a major competitor of Abeking and Rasmussen in yacht construction. His first big success was his 1936 design of the composite-built, 59-foot-LOA yawl *Roland von Bremen*. She was shipped to Boston, fitted out at the Her-reshoff Manufacturing Company in Bristol, Rhode Island, and, with Gruber's friend Sher-

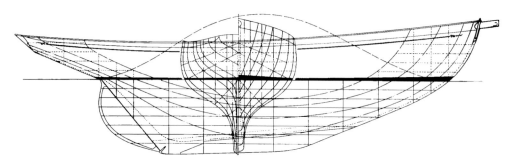

Henry Gruber: *Binker*. The 39-foot 10-inch LOA *Binker* was launched in 1934 at the Nyack, New York, yard of Julius Petersen during the period when Gruber was a partner in the firm of Burgess and Donaldson, Megargel and Gruber. For many years yachting writers attributed the design to W. Starling Burgess. It wasn't until 1997 that the error was discovered and the credit given to Gruber. © *Tony Dixon*

Henry Gruber: *Barlovento*. This handsome and able 64-foot schooner was designed in 1931 while Gruber was at Cox and Stevens Inc. She was built by the F. F. Pendleton yard in Wiscasset, Maine, in 1932, and had a stellar racing career on the East Coast. Today, *Barlovento* sails and occasionally races in the Pacific Northwest. *Photo courtesy Craig Downey.*

Henry Gruber: *Roland von Bremen*. Built at the Burmester Shipyard in Bremen, the 59-foot LOA *Roland von Bremen* was Gruber's big success after his return to Germany from the United States in 1935. The yacht's similarity to the Olin Stephens–designed *Stormy Weather* demonstrates Gruber's understanding of what made a successful ocean racer under the CCA Rule. © *Mystic Seaport, Rosenfeld Collection, Mystic, CT*

man Hoyt among the crew, finished eighth out of twenty-seven in her class in the 1936 Bermuda Race. After additional work was done on the yacht in Bermuda, she went on to win the Bermuda-Cuxhaven (Germany) Race on both elapsed and corrected time. Twenty-five years later, *Roland von Bremen* took part in the biannual Los Angeles–Honolulu Transpac Race in 1961, placing third in Class B and sixth overall in a fleet of forty-one. Today she is back in Germany in good sailing condition.

In 1939 Gruber designed a second yacht named *Roland von Bremen*, which has created some confusion over the years. This 49-foot cutter, *Roland von Bremen II*, placed third in the 1939 Fastnet Race (in which another Gruber design, *Nordwind*, fought a dramatic and famous duel with William Fife III's *Latifa*).

The pre–World War II years were the most productive for Gruber as ocean yacht racing grew in popularity. He designed *Helgoland*, another 59-foot LOA yawl very similar to *Roland von Bremen* except for her keel, followed by the 43-foot LOA sloop *Norderney* and the 42-foot LOA sloop *Borkum*. The German navy had a strong interest in competing with American and English yachts in the major sailing races and in 1938 ordered two identical 85-foot LOA ketches, *Nordwind* and *Ostwind*. Their design followed the RORC rating rule, and they

too were built of composite construction at Burmester. Extensive tank-testing was conducted on this design, including at different angles of heel and leeway at various speeds. Their final lines are narrow and deep and hint at an English influence.

Next Gruber designed the 12-meter yacht *Aschanti III* for shipyard owner Ernst Burmester. Until August 1939, the yard worked on various yacht orders, but everything changed on September 1 with Germany's invasion of Poland and the start of World War II.

During the war, Gruber was assigned to serve at the Burmester yard, which then became integrated in the shipbuilding program of Abeking and Rasmussen. By 1941 he was involved with the organization of two new branch yards in Swinemünde, designing naval vessels and organizing the supply of materials to these yards. He helped in the design of the KFK (Kriegsfischkutter) cutter, a 79-foot multipurpose vessel of which more than six hundred were built. Gruber, who is always associated with these sturdy vessels, also drew a sailing rig for the KFK, but only a very few were so equipped.

After Germany's surrender, Bremen became an American enclave within the British occupation zone. Gruber had not been a member of the Nazi Party, and this plus his language skills made him an ideal middleman in the postwar reconstruction period. But his work was mostly limited to repairs. His family had survived the war in Flensburg, and his American friends, including Sherman Hoyt and the Haffenreffer family, sent care packages and helped them through the postwar time. Only in 1950 was the family reunited and living together in Bremen, where Gruber continued to work for the Burmester yard.

The remarkable success of the European Recovery Program and the Marshall Plan made it possible for some Germans to think of ordering new but smaller pleasure craft as early as 1948. Gruber continued his work as one of Germany's leading designers. Between 1948 and 1956 the following yachts, among others, were built in accordance to his designs and the German KR rating, a handicap system for cruising sailing yachts: the 4.5 KR *Libelle*, 5.5 KR *Bagatelle*, 6.5 KR *Moije Bris*, the 24 KR staysail schooner *Aschanti IV*, the 11 KR *Heike*, and the 12 KR *Hamburg VI*.

Gruber retired about 1956 and died three years later at age sixty. His designs were included in four of Uffa Fox's five "yachting annuals." Uffa Fox says of Gruber in *Racing, Cruising and Design* (1937), "Every book of mine so far has had a design in it by Henry Gruber, and because Henry combines a great mathematical

Ferdinand Grünhagen. These rugged Weser-Jolle dinghies were designed for economical level racing in rough water. Note the rotating, tapered wooden luff spars, allowing roller furling of the jibs while nearly eliminating headstay sag, and the low and broad fully battened mainsails that maximize power and minimize heeling pressure. *Photo courtesy Volker Christmann*

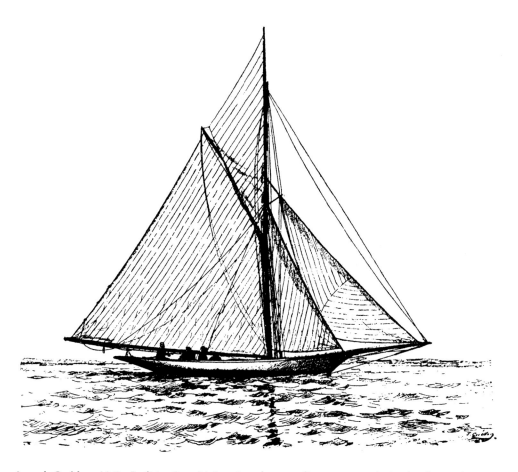

Joseph Guédon: Maïa. Built in 1892, *Maïa* enjoyed extraordinary success during her first racing season on the Mediterranean. *Drawing courtesy Jacques Taglang*

brain with his artistic ability, I hope that he will always be kind enough to let me include his best plans in my books throughout the years to come, for besides being plans of fast weatherly hulls they are a great joy to look upon and study."

—Egmont Friedl and Thomas G. Skahill

FERDINAND GRÜNHAGEN

1881–1953 · Germany

A self-taught amateur yacht designer and a machinist by trade working in Bremen, Ferdinand Grünhagen set down design guidelines for the class boat movement on Germany's Weser River basin. This movement produced boats, the so-called Weser-Jolles, that raced on an equal footing without handicaps. The rough local waters of the Weser required a runabout type, and Grünhagen's designs represented an unmistakable local type of half-decked centerboarders.

Four classes made up the Weser-Jolles, with subclasses for inshore, touring, and keel/centerboarders. The Grünhagen designs were extremely sharp under water and had full lines over the waterline and extremely full lines at the deck edge.

The Weser-Jolles evolved considerably under Grünhagen's hands, beginning in 1912 with a 5-meter centerboarder and ending in 1941 with a keel/centerboarder known as the "six and a half." Between the dates of these two examples lies the entire development of the dinghy/centerboarders that Grünhagen's work defined, such as a 6-meter cruising centerboarder, two heavy-weather dinghies, a 5.5-meter catboat, the 5.5- and 6-meter dinghies, the Weser kayak, 3- and 4-meter aluminum dinghies, a 7.5-meter keelboat, a racer/cruiser, and two aluminum centerboard double-enders of 3 and 4 meters. —Eberhard Wetjen

JOSEPH GUÉDON

1862–1947 · France

The Arcachon One-Design class is Joseph Guédon's most important contribution to yacht design in France. First designed in 1912, more than five hundred of these 4-meter, cat yawl-rigged dinghies have been built, with more every year. However, Guédon's long career is interesting for more reasons than this one success.

Born in Bordeaux, Guédon was an artist of considerable talent, working in ink, oils, and watercolors. He began working as a naval architect in the Aquitaine region in southwestern France, at that time an important center of French yachting where innovative developments were taking place in design, construction, and the manner in which yachts were sailed.

Guédon published his first work in the French magazine *Le Yacht* on the sharpie *Tou Ta Ra* in 1884. *Le Yacht* continued to publish his lines plans until his death.

In 1892, he designed the 5-Ton *Maïa*, which had a triumphal season in the Mediterranean and firmly established his reputation. *Maïa* was built at Bonnin's yard in Lormont, near Bordeaux. A close friend of the Bonnin family, Guédon worked with the yard until the end of his career. The 1910 *Lloyd's Register of Yachts* lists sixty-three of his eighty-nine designs as being built at Bonnin's. Additionally, Guédon's boats were built in Spain, Italy, and Switzerland.

Guédon directed some of his attention to the creation of one-design classes. In 1893 he published his first one-design class project for Arcachon, with others in 1898 and 1901, before designing the 1912 class that would prove so successful. He enjoyed drawing a wide range of boats, including pinnaces for Arcachon, fishing boats, motorboats, and torpedo boats for the navy. His racing boats were always noted for the fineness of their overhangs and the fairness of their lines.

In 1902 and 1903, Guédon drew the 13-Ton *Suzette*, which brought back to France the Coupe de France, and *Titave*, a seven-tonner that won the Italy Cup in San Remo. In 1907, he became an associate of A. Delannoy, which allowed him to enlarge the maritime and metallurgic workshops that he owned in Lormont. By 1910, only four years after the introduction of the International Rule, he had designed the 15-Meter *Encarnita*; the 10-Meters *Carmen* and *Corzo*; the 8-Meters *Ponchette* and *Principe Alfonso*; and the 6-Meters *El Machuca*, *Enia*, *Guyoni* and *Guyoni II*, *Mari-Pepa*, *Mignonne*, *Nougatine*, *Pilila*, *Pitusa*, and *Ranita*.

Guédon also designed many 6.5-Meters including *Phi-Phi* and *Bilitis*, which were highly successful, winning many trophies in Arcachon, Le Havre, and Meulan. In 1930 *Bilitis* won the first Bol d'Or, in Meulan.

The victory of Baron Philippe de Rothschild's 8-Meter *Cupidon III* at the 1926 Coupe de France in Norway confirmed the international stature of this highly productive designer.

—Noël Gruet

ALAN P. GURNEY

Born 1937 · England

Alan Gurney's most famous design is *Windward Passage*, the maxi boat that set course records for a number of major ocean races, most notably the ones for the Transpac and the MoBay Race (from Miami, Florida, to Montego Bay, Jamaica), which stood until 2003. His first widespread exposure as an independent designer was in 1958, when he won a design competition run by *Yachting World* magazine with his design for *Theme*, a 35-foot 6-inch sloop.

Gurney was born in Birmingham, England. At age fourteen he read Alain Gerbault's book *Flight of the Firecrest*, which captured his imagination and led him to a lifelong interest in boats. At seventeen he became an apprentice to naval architect J. Francis Jones, and at the same time took up dinghy racing. He then entered the army for two years, after which he took another apprenticeship with Kim Holman at Holman and Pye.

In 1960 Gurney moved to the United States and went to work for Bill Tripp. After a year Gurney opened his own office in Manhattan, and soon thereafter designed a double-chine sloop named *Wolverine*, which won *Yachting* magazine's 1963 One-of-a-Kind Regatta. In 1965 he designed *Kittiwake*, a 47-foot yawl that was a successful ocean racer, followed in 1966 by the 49-foot *Guinevere*, which won the 1967 SORC and other events. Both boats were fairly conventional, but meanwhile Gurney was paying attention to the work of Laurent Giles, Bill Lapworth, and Ericus van de Stadt in the emerging light-displacement type.

Gurney's next boat was *Hotfoot*, the prototype of the Nantucket 38 class and Gurney's first effort at a light-displacement, spade-rudder type. She was extremely successful, leading Gurney toward more work, notably the 44-foot *Baroda* and 73-foot *Windward Passage*.

Windward Passage was designed and built in 1968 for Bob Johnson to replace the famous record-setting L. Francis Herreshoff–designed *Ticonderoga*, a tough act to follow. She was shaped like a big planing dinghy, and her cold-molded wood construction enabled very light displacement and a high ballast-displacement ratio. She was 20,000 pounds lighter than the Tripp-designed *Ondine*, one of her main competitors at the time. An instant success, she continued to race for many years, undergoing several updates along the way, including modification from a ketch to a sloop rig. With these changes the boat remained competitive against newer designs well into the 1980's.

Gurney went on to design numerous other ocean racers, such as *Great Britain II*, for the 1973 Whitbread Round the World Race, plus stock boats for Islander Yachts, the O'Day Company, and others. Today Alan Gurney lives in Surrey, England, and has turned to writing about Antarctic exploration in books such as *Below the Convergence* and *The Race to the White Continent*. His latest book is *Compass*.

—Daniel B. MacNaughton

Alan Gurney: *Windward Passage*. Nowadays we expect big, offshore racing boats to be shaped like planing dinghies, but Gurney's 73-foot *Windward Passage* was something new when she appeared in 1968. In a pattern that has held throughout the history of yacht design, lighter, stiffer construction (in this case cold-molded wood) allowed the breakthrough. © *Photo by Bob Fisher/ PPL*

H

WILLI VON HACHT

1870–April 1931 · Germany

Along with Henry Rasmussen and Gustaf Est-lander, Willi von Hacht was one of the pre-eminent German racing-sailboat designers during the first two decades of the twentieth century. Fueled by the traditional rivalry between the trading ports and Hansetowns (Hanse was an association of trading ports) of Bremen and Hamburg, the boatbuilder and designer von Hacht supplied Hamburg's clientele with fast and well-built boats, while Rasmussen served Bremen.

Educated as a boatbuilder from 1884 until 1888—the year in which the Deutscher Segler Verband (the German Sailing Federation) was founded—von Hacht continued on as a journeyman and built his first boat to his own design in 1895. *Butt* was a skimming dish–type dinghy, short, wide, and flat (6.7 meters long with a beam of 2.7 meters), carrying an impressive 34-square meters of sail in a sloop rig. *Butt*'s successes on Hamburg's Lake Alster made the yachting scene aware of Willi von Hacht. In 1895, the year he took over his own yard, the Nord-Ostsee Kanal was opened. This channel linked the Baltic Sea and the North Sea for the first time, bringing together the two previously separate German coasts and sailing areas.

Thanks to his recent success on the race course, von Hacht was in a position to cease building and repairing workboats for Hamburg's river, port, and canals, and to focus instead on pleasure craft. *Butt* was followed by *Bussard* and *Beowulf*. Talented sailors like Friedrich Kirsten ordered *Windspiels* from von Hacht, and Richard C. Krogmann had a total of eighteen boats named *Tilly* designed and built, among them the winners of the 1906, 1911, and 1912 Samoa Cups, raced in Sonder class yachts.

Both royal and untitled but wealthy yachts-men ordered One-Ton Cup boats, Sonder yachts, Square-Meter boats, and 6-Meter yachts. The German One-Ton Cup winners of 1907, 1908, 1909, and 1911 all showcased von Hacht's ability. In 1930 his 30-Square-Meter boat *Michl V* was successful in Kiel and Sweden.

Since Willi von Hacht's death at the age of sixty-one, the Bajazzo prize, named after one of his designs that sailed on Hamburg's local lake (whose steadily shifting wind conditions produce amazingly random race results), is a reminder of this nearly forgotten naval architect and boatbuilder. —Erdmann Braschos

JOHN LUDWIG HACKER

1877–1961 · United States

John Hacker was a pioneer in the development of racing and recreational planing powerboats in the first half of the twentieth century. His boats featured flat planing sections aft on a hard-chine, a V-bottom hull, and speed combined with aesthetics. Author Robert Speltz dubbed Hacker's craft "the Steinway of runabouts."

Hacker worked in an era dominated by horsepower. Beginning in the 1910's, gas engines designed for the burgeoning automobile and airplane markets were adapted for marine use, propelling boats at an ever-increasing pace. While working for his father as a clerk, Hacker studied powerboat design as a sideline at night school and by correspondence. In 1911, he designed and built a stepped hydroplane, *Kitty Hawk II*, which reached a record speed of 50 mph. The speedboat *Gretchen*

Willi von Hacht: *Woge.* The 22-Square-Meter *Woge* has had a long and successful life. Built in 1922 to a restricted-sail-area rule, her long, light, short-ended hull anticipated the planing dinghies soon to come. She has won a lot of races over eight decades and continues to sail today. *Photo courtesy Manfred Jacob*

John Hacker: *Tinker.* Rapid development of powered vehicles, especially automobiles and boats, was one of the most exciting trends during the years just before the Great Depression. Many boats sported automotive-inspired details such as on the deckhouse of *Tinker*, a small but elegant commuter. © *Peter Barlow*

had a bow rudder, another Hacker innovation.

Three years later, he founded Hacker Boat Company in his native Detroit, Michigan, and built performance runabouts for Edsel Ford, J. W. Packard, and other wealthy, competitive clients. A friend of Henry Ford, Hacker got into production building with a low-priced, 21-foot 5-inch model that would be sold at Ford auto dealerships. The recession of 1921–22 killed that market, and Hacker went into custom powerboat design, eventually based in Mount Clemens, Michigan.

By 1928, Hacker was well established as a builder of fast, handcrafted mahogany boats, from 20-foot runabouts to commuter boats for a world clientele. A 40-foot commuter, designed and built for the King of Siam in 1930, was said to travel up to 60 mph. Around the same time, Hacker produced several champions of the prestigious international Gold Cup regatta, including *El Lagarto*, which won the national event three years in a row.

Hacker lost control of the business in the Depression year of 1934 (the Hacker Boat Company continued on without him into the mid-1950's). However, he continued designing and among his later work is *Thunderbird*, launched in 1940 when Hacker was sixty-three. The 55-foot commuter is capable of 60 mph and is still active on the West Coast. With her rounded polished metal superstructure designed to resemble the fuselage of an airliner, she is thought by many to be the ultimate expression of art deco styling in an existing yacht.

Hacker, known for his signature Panama hat, passed away in 1961. Original Hacker boats are sought after today, and the Hacker Boat Company in Silver Bay, New York, run by Bill Morgan, builds replica Hacker designs by hand.

Some of Hacker's plans are at the Mariners' Museum in Newport News, VA.

—Steve Knauth

HALVORSEN FAMILY

LARS HALVORSEN
1887–1936
HAROLD HALVORSEN
Born 1910
MAGNUS HALVORSEN
Born 1918
TRYGVE HALVORSEN
Born 1920

Norway/Australia

Three generations of the Norwegian Halvorsen family have been active as boat designers and builders, especially in Australia. Born in Norway, Lars Halvorsen learned much of his trade during the five years he spent working in boatyards around New York. He returned to Norway and set up a business there, but the accidental loss of a partially insured vessel ruined him. He then moved to South Africa, where there was an opportunity to be a boatbuilder. After two years

Halvorsen: *Silver Cloud II.* The Halvorsen motor cruiser *Silver Cloud II* displays the elegant styling, craftsmanship, and solid construction that have made the older Halvorsen cruisers collectors' items in Australia. *Photo courtesy Dr. Derek Freeman*

in Cape Town, he followed the suggestion that he and his sons could do better as boatbuilders in Australia, and they emigrated there in late 1924.

Setting up a business in Sydney, the self-taught Lars built many boats, including some to his own design. Several of his five sons gradually joined the growing business. His son Harold did all of the design work on the motor vessels, both pleasure and commercial, from 1932 on. Lars died in 1936, but by then the yards were known for their fine work and they continued to prosper. World War II brought considerable design and construction work for the armed forces, including a series of 38-foot, high-speed launches used to patrol the waters around New Guinea.

After the war, Harold continued to design motor vessels, but the growing sport of ocean racing in sailing yachts attracted his two brothers, Magnus and Trygve. Together they designed a series of sturdy ocean racing yachts, which were built by the family company. They bear the seaworthy characteristics and fine looks of the vessels designed by their Norwegian countryman Colin Archer from the late 1880's.

The Halvorsen racers were competitive too, and influenced other local designers as the

sport expanded during the 1950's and 1960's. Their finest achievement was the historic string of handicap victories won in the Sydney-Hobart Race by the magnificent 39-foot, canoe-stern *Freya*, in 1963, 1964, and 1965.

Harold Halvorsen's motor launches, which include designs up to 60 feet in length, are in the classic style of the period from 1930 to the 1960's and are showcases for the fine Australian timbers used in their construction and joinery. Many examples of these craft remain active and in excellent condition in Australia, where they are sought after by enthusiasts, as well as in other countries to which they were exported.

Harold's son Harvey, now living in California, has continued the family design tradition since 1970. Like his father, uncles, and grandfather, he has no formal training or qualifications in yacht design. The practical experience gained in their boatbuilding trade and family boating background is what has enabled the Halvorsens to design and build outstanding vessels that have a significant place in the development of Australian yacht design and construction.

—David Payne

CYRUS HAMLIN

Born 1918 · United States

Cy Hamlin is one of the most highly regarded designers of his generation. At the advent of mass-marketed fiberglass boats, Hamlin preferred to focus his yacht designing on custom cruising boats while modernizing and inno-

vating in wooden boat construction and design. He also turned much of his attention to designing commercial fishing vessels, planning ports (Portland and Eastport, Maine), and serving as a fishing vessel specialist in the third world through the United Nations and other international agencies.

One of the first in the United States to work in modern light-displacement hull types, Hamlin pioneered in glued strip-plank construction with structural interiors, reverse sheer, and efficient interior designs, all of which helped to propel light-displacement types into widespread public acceptance. It is widely agreed that much of Hamlin's work remains the best of the type, though some of the designs are now fifty years old. With the current increase in the popularity of wooden boats and the continuing evolution in modern wooden construction has come renewed interest in Hamlin's achievements.

Of particular note is Hamlin's glued strip-plank construction method developed in the 1950's, in which the bulkheads can form the building jig, the major interior components are structural, there are only a few frames, and all joints are glued. It closely resembles the most advanced wooden construction of today.

Hamlin is perhaps best known for his work on the Controversy series, created in the early 1950's in partnership with E. Farnham Butler at the Mount Desert Yacht Yard in Maine. These and subsequent designs in the same genre are masterpieces of ergonomic efficiency, with interiors that are carefully proportioned around the comfort and movement of the human body.

Halvorsen: *Freya* (opposite). The Nordic ancestry of *Freya* is obvious, with her canoe stern, deep hull, and seaworthy characteristics. Her three consecutive victories in the Sydney-Hobart Race remain unique—a credit to the design, construction, and sailing abilities of the Halvorsens. *Photo courtesy of* The Mercury (*Hobart, Tasmania, Australia*)

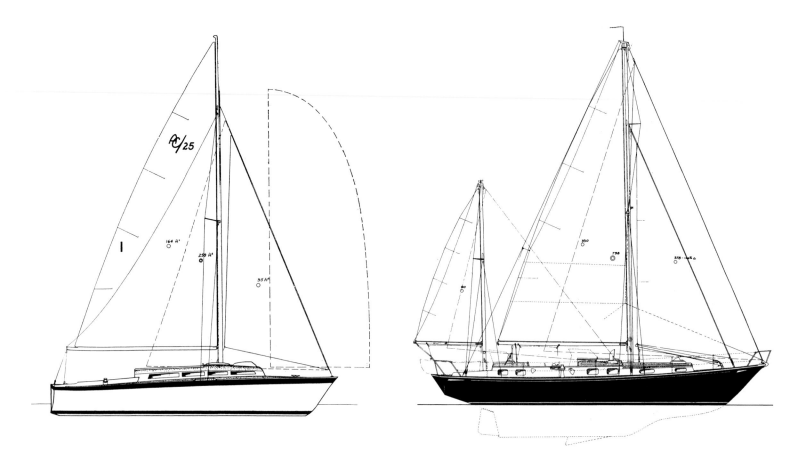

Cy Hamlin: Amphibi-Con. In the 25-foot 6-inch Amphibi-Con, Cy Hamlin and Farnham Butler created one of the classic cruising boats of her era. Her combination of light displacement, reverse sheer, simple, all-glued wooden construction, and shoal draft was new in the 1950's, and produced a roomy, practical, trailerable boat for average people. *Reproduced from* The Rudder

Cy Hamlin. Hamlin discovered many ways of achieving beauty in higher-freeboard, light-displacement types. Reverse sheer was the direct approach, but a sweet sheer and interesting, carefully shaped ends proved to be another, as in this comfortable 45-foot yawl. Today her freeboard no longer seems unusual. *Drawing courtesy Cy Hamlin*

The structures that enclosed these precisely defined spaces were ruthlessly efficient in their economy of material, construction labor, and weight. Instead of compromising all these economies in order to follow conventional aesthetic dictates, the sheer, hull shape, and shapes of the bow and stern were styled for maximum utility, resulting in reverse sheer to create more space in the middle of the boat where it was needed, and short ends.

Traditionalists were offended (hence, the choice of the "Controversy" designation), but the boats were a great success and are cherished by their many owners to this day. However unusual this styling may have been in its day, contemporary boats have gone so far beyond it that what were once considered to be Hamlin's most radical designs appear decidedly sleek to the modern eye—an example of the fact that while convention may change, good design endures.

Hamlin's trademark efficiency is typified by one of his most recent designs, the Elder-yacht, a 30-foot, glued strip and plywood cutter with many innovative features intended to make it easier for the not-so-young to sail comfortably and safely.

However, Hamlin's innovations should not obscure his ability to work within traditional forms. He is the designer of the 75-foot Hudson River sloop replica *Clearwater*, an authentic vessel of inspiring beauty that has sailed the Hudson since 1969. He also designed the famous Outward Bound 30-foot, glued strip pulling boats, which for nearly forty years have been a frequent sight along Maine's midcoast region and have a well-deserved reputation for seaworthiness and safety.

Hamlin grew up on Long Island, New York, and spent his summers in Cape Porpoise, Maine, where his fascination for boats took root. He began his design career in 1936 in a small Long Island boatyard. Moving to Maine in 1939, he worked until 1944 as a designer at the Hinckley yard in Southwest Harbor and also designed commercial vessels. He entered the army in World War II and served in a mapping battalion in the Philippines.

After the war Hamlin had a fellowship at the Stevens Institute in Hoboken, New Jersey. Returning to Southwest Harbor in 1947, he designed and built for his father the 23-foot sloop *Spicy Isles;* she served to illustrate his glued strip-planking technique and attracted considerable attention

on her fall delivery trip from Maine to Long Island. He then worked at the Mount Desert Yacht Yard for five years, developing with Butler the Controversy designs. From 1964 to 1985 Hamlin ran the Ocean Research Corporation, a firm concentrating on both naval architecture and worldwide commercial fishing.

Having designed several rating rules, Hamlin served as a consultant to the Cruising Club of America in redrafting its handicapping rules. He has taught boat design at the Landing School of Boatbuilding and Design in Arundel, Maine, since its founding in 1978, and is the author of *Preliminary Design of Boats and Ships.* Hamlin is famous for having once said, "You can make a small fortune as a naval architect, but only if you start out with a big fortune."

Hamlin is semiretired but maintains his office in Arundel, where he does some consulting, writes on boat design subjects, and prepares his lessons for the Landing School. His professional papers are at Mystic Seaport and his library will go to the Landing School, leaving Hamlin with nothing to do but start all over again.

The Cyrus Hamlin Collection is at Mystic Seaport Museum, Mystic, CT.
—Daniel B. MacNaughton

WILLIAM H. HAND JR.

1875–May 23, 1946 · United States

Today William Hand is associated primarily with his handsome motorsailer designs, generally considered to be the best of the type drawn to date, but he was also among the first to recognize the virtues of the V-bottom in powerboat design, and he designed numerous dramatic and beautiful schooners, including the famous Arctic exploration vessel *Bowdoin*.

Born in Portland, Maine, Hand lived in several different coastal communities on the East Coast, owing to his father's assignments with the U.S. Navy and Coast Guard. He attended Brown University for a short time, but was largely self-taught as a designer. For most of his career, his office was on the Fairhaven side of the New Bedford, Massachusetts, waterfront. He was also closely associated with the Hodgdon Brothers yard in East Boothbay, Maine.

Hand began his career designing small racing sailboats—mostly knockabout sloops—around 1900. The 16-foot *Little Nell* (1905) took nine firsts and one second place in ten starts at the Royal Canadian Yacht Club races in Toronto. He also drew designs for cruising boats rigged as catboats, yawls, and ketches, many of which were published in such yachting magazines as *The Rudder*. The gasoline engine, however, lured Hand away from sail.

Prior to World War I, Hand was one of the first to work in high-speed, V-bottom powerboat-types, designs he evolved from the deadrise workboats of the Chesapeake. He held a patent for one such configuration, and his boats were well known for speed, looks, and good behavior. Many of these "Hand V-Bottoms" held speed records. *Squke*, an 18-footer built in 1908, was Hand's first notable V-bottom powerboat; her 10-hp motor pushed her along at over 16 mph. His most famous was *Countess*, which won the 1916 New York Athletic Club Race from New York to Block Island with an average speed of over 27 mph.

After the war, Hand did some of his best work on a series of excellent offshore Gloucester-style schooner yachts, including the famous Arctic voyager *Bowdoin* (1921), which is still sailing on the coast of Maine and more northern waters. Compared to other schooners of the 1920's, Hand's were more reminiscent of their commercial ancestors, with stronger sheers and a more rugged appearance. A total of twenty-three were built.

In the resurrected Bermuda Race of 1923, five of the seventeen schooners entered were designed by Hand. There were four yawls and

William Hand: *Countess.* Prior to World War I, Hand recognized the construction and performance advantages to be found in V-bottom hulls. His V-bottom powerboats were fast, dry, and popular. The 40-footer *Countess* was his most successful racer and was built by Lawley in 1916. © *Mystic Seaport, Rosenfeld Collection, Mystic, CT*

William Hand: *Maramel.* Among the many schooners Hand designed in the 1920's was the 45-footer *Maramel*. In the 1959 Transpac Race, she came in seventh in Class E. *Maramel* was built by Rankin and Richard in Seattle, Washington, in 1929. *Photo courtesy Newport Harbor Nautical Museum, Newport Beach, CA*

Aesthetically, the Hand motorsailers were (along with the subsequent Davis designs) in a class by themselves. Their closest ancestors were the Maine sardine carriers and other fishing vessels, which is another way of saying that they were a totally fresh concept based on a proven idea. Their success represents a spectacular achievement in a field where concepts generally evolve in small increments from similar ancestors.

Hand motorsailers had long and husky displacement hulls, with superstructures midway in bulk between that of a sailboat and a powerboat, and always included a substantial wheelhouse. The look was refined but not delicate, graceful but serious. Although they were fundamentally yachts, some were used to fish commercially for swordfish, requiring only a crow's nest and an extended forward pulpit.

During World War II, large numbers of Hand motorsailers were drafted into the naval service as patrol craft or small antisubmarine coastal craft. Their seakeeping abilities made the boats prime candidates for this service.

One of the first Hand motorsailers, the 59-foot *Nor'easter* (1927), originally built for the Dupont family, is still sailing and in top condition. She was reacquired and restored by the Duponts and is often seen in Maine and Caribbean waters.

Much of Hand's design work was destroyed in the 1938 hurricane. Surviving designs are at Hart Nautical Collections, MIT Museum, Cambridge, MA, which also published The Guide to the Davis-Hand Collections, written by Kurt Hasselbalch.

—Daniel B. MacNaughton

William Hand: *Bluebill II*. The 60-foot 6-inch *Bluebill II* was built in 1933 by Hodgdon Brothers in East Boothbay, Maine. Hand's motorsailers were unique, combining rugged construction and workboat-inspired looks with functional sailing rigs in an appealing and practical mix. Between 1927 and 1940, forty-two were designed and built. © *Mystic Seaport, Rosenfeld Collection, Mystic, CT. Image Acquired in Honor of Franz Schneider*

CHARLES C. HANLEY

1851–1934 · United States

Born in Warren, Maine, Charles C. Hanley grew up in midcoast Maine and then around Boston after his family moved there when he was eight. As a boy, he apprenticed to a pianocase maker; then, at age twenty-four, "CC," as he was known, moved to Monument Beach on Cape Cod and began working as a blacksmith. Within a year he married Deborah Stevens, from an old and well-to-do family, and began designing and building racing catboats for wealthy clients, many of whom belonged to the Beverly Yacht Club, which, at the time, raced near where Hanley lived.

Hanley's rather exquisite boats succeeded locally, and so did his reputation. But when one of them, the 26-foot 6-inch catboat *Mucilage*, won handily against a fleet of Newport, Rhode Island, catboats in 1888 and then

ketches, including the 32-foot Hand-designed ketch *Sea Call*. Hand's schooners, such as *Black Hawk*, *Yankee Girl II*, and *Flying Cloud III*, continued to do well in subsequent races. Though not so numerous as the schooners of other designers, such as John Alden, Hand's remain some of the most appealing examples of the type.

As a successful swordfisherman, Hand experimented with his schooner designs to provide a seakindly type favorable to fishing at slow speeds under power. He concluded that the deep-bodied schooner hull was usable, but that large sail areas and a deep draft weren't necessary. By 1926 he started using more powerful engines, which had become increasingly reliable, and using sails only for auxiliary

power and steadying. He also changed from schooner rig to ketch. These yachts became known as Hand motorsailers.

Hand's motorsailers were clearly motor-driven vessels, designed to be fuel efficient, seaworthy, and comfortable. Their fuel capacity was very large (a 60-footer might carry 1,200 gallons, giving the vessel over 1,500 miles in range). However, the sailing rigs were large enough to serve as auxiliary power, to increase comfort and fuel economy by steadying the vessel and adding a boost to speed, and under some conditions to propel the boat on their own. The worse the weather was, the better they sailed, and in breezes above 18 to 20 knots, they performed very respectably on sail alone.

C. C. Hanley: *Harbinger.* *Harbinger* illustrates the difficulty in defining nautical terms. Going by her hull form and mast placement she is clearly a cat-boat, yet she sports a jib on a long bowsprit, making her a sloop by most definitions. *Photograph by Nathaniel Stebbins. Courtesy of the Society for the Preservation of New England Antiquities*

came into the hands of New York Yacht Club members, Hanley's fame soon became widespread. In 1889, his *Harbinger* beat the cutters of Edward Burgess and William Gardner in a race sponsored by Marblehead's Eastern Yacht Club.

His business prospered, considerably helped no doubt by his wife's connections and finances. By 1898 he had reached the peak of his career with a good busy shop, a nine-man crew, a fine big house, a daughter ready for college, and about forty-five boats to his credit. He was the acknowledged master of racing catboats.

Designing by carving half models of his hulls, Hanley then measured them in somewhat the same manner as N. G. Herreshoff. But unlike Herreshoff, Hanley was without a solid technical background or drafting skills. He was said to have a genius for proportion and by his own ac-

count admitted, "It was all guesswork, but somehow I usually guessed right." His boats were elegantly built with nonferrous fastenings and exceptional joinery, and were said to cost twice what comparable-sized working catboats sold for. Slippery hulls that were light but strong, with huge spreads of sail, accounted in large measure for their speed and racing prowess. Hanley was an accomplished sailor and delivered a number of his boats, one as far as Detroit.

Life began to change for the worse when Hanley's shop burned down in 1897. For reasons not now clear, he moved to Quincy, Massachusetts, after the fire and built a good-sized shop there, leaving his wife back in Monument Beach. (They never again lived together.)

Hanley's 45-foot sloop *Genesee* won all three races when competing for the prestigious Cana-

da's Cup in 1899, but times were changing and yachts designed on paper were gaining favor. Measurement rules such as those adopted by the Massachusetts Bay Yacht Racing Association (MYRA) made rule-of-thumb designing exceedingly shaky. When four of Hanley's catboats destined for Hull Yacht Club members and sporting the sail insignia HO (for Hull One-Design) failed to meet the letter of the MYRA rules, they were nicknamed "Hanley's Orphans."

Hanley nearly got a crack at designing an America's Cup candidate for the 1901 contest—it would have been a 90-foot LWL × 36-foot centerboarder—but Thomas W. Lawson decided to build the Crowninshield-designed (by drawn plans) *Independence* instead.

The Hanley Construction Company of Quincy, Massachusetts, backed by United Fruit mag-

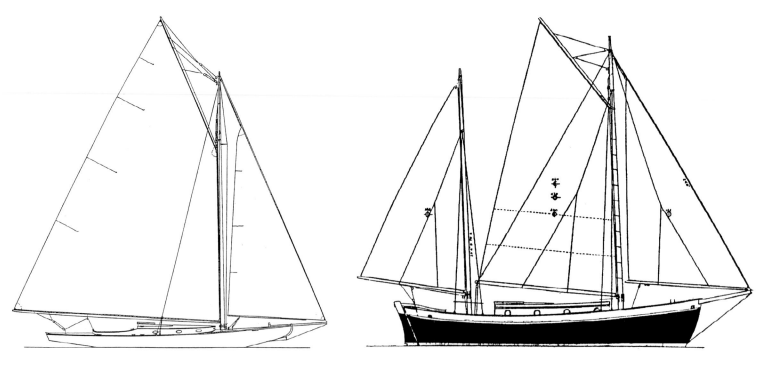

C. C. Hanley: *Genesee.* Hanley's 1899 Canada's Cup winner *Genesee* was designed by eye rather than calculation, but she was unbeatable in her time and locale. Only the rise of her run, her pointed bow, and her pretty cabin trunk differentiate her from the even-faster planing lake scows that were to come. *Reproduced from Charles G. Davis's* How to Design a Yacht

John Hanna: *Tahiti.* Few yachts have made a more successful appeal to romanticism than Hanna's *Tahiti* ketch. With her husky double-ended hull, high bulwarks, wide decks, gaff rig, bowsprit, and other salty details, she was everything fragile racing yachts were not. Countless examples were built, many of them in backyards. *Reproduced from* How to Build a Tahiti Ketch

nate Lorenzo Baker, occupied Hanley from the time of its founding in 1901 until 1903, when he quit, nearly penniless, and slowly set up a new shop on the opposite shore. With his designing days pretty much behind him—and building too, for that matter—he ultimately created a big storage yard with covered storage for 150 boats. This yard burned in 1920, after which he sold it to Fred Lawley, another talented designer. The facility later became Quincy Adams Yacht Yard.

Despite the setbacks noted, Hanley remained productive, in his later years teaming up with draftsman Erland Debes to create, on paper, several new designs. His doctor, George Sheahan, commissioned his best known of the era—and his final design—a cat-yawl named *Two Sisters*, now in Maine and renamed *Mollie B.* Ironically, this boat was built at Baker Yacht Basin, the old Hanley Construction Company yard that Hanley had stomped out of some twenty-five years before.

Hanley designed and built about seventy-five racing catboats and sloops during his career, many of which were equally distributed between Massachusetts Bay (twenty-two) and Buzzards Bay (nineteen). Although his reputation came from catboats, he built almost as many sloops (thirty-seven vs. thirty-one, with seven rigs unaccounted for). He generally built what he designed, ranging from the 17½-foot catboat *Kitten* in 1889 to the 53-foot sloop *Atricilla* in 1904. The records show thirty-two

boats between 20 and 30 feet LOA, with about an equal number of larger ones. His peak production occurred in the 1890's, with eight boats in each of the years 1892 and 1895.

The talented and ever-exuberant Hanley died in 1934, at age eighty-four.

Three of C. C. Hanley's half models, for the famous racers Genesee, Mucilage, and Cleopatra, are preserved at the MIT Museum in Cambridge, MA. There are old photographs of Hanley boats in various museum collections, but because he didn't make drawings (except for his brief time with Debes), none survive.

—Maynard Bray

JOHN GRIFFIN "JACK" HANNA

October 14, 1889–February 1, 1948
United States

Jack Hanna was a self-taught designer and columnist best known for his double-ended, heavy-displacement cruising boats. Designed in the Colin Archer tradition, they stressed romantic good looks and comfort at sea. The *Tahiti* ketch is widely considered to be the best example and is Hanna's most famous design.

Hanna recognized that while yachting headlines were always dominated by racing results and broken records, many cruising yachtsmen preferred comfort, ease of handling, safety, and strength over speed, and derived special satisfaction from boats that looked

like serious offshore voyagers of longstanding tradition.

Hanna's designs were often underrigged and seldom performed well in light air. Likewise, they were rarely shaped for efficient windward performance. He gave boats of this type large auxiliary engines, assuming that they would be powered under these conditions. Despite the lack of the large deckhouses we usually associate with the type, it may be best to think of his boats as early motorsailers. Hanna's designs may have been criticized for their deficiencies in sailing performance, but many contemporary yachtsmen indeed do power to windward and in light air, so perhaps the concept was more appropriate than most will admit. *Tahiti* must have been very close to the mark, for several designers have since openly interpreted her concept, with improved sailing performance the goal.

Gulfweed, another well-known design that is more of an all-around sailboat, is a chine-hulled vessel meant for the home boatbuilder, and was drawn in several versions.

Born in Galveston, Texas, Hanna lost his hearing at a young age. He achieved early success as a writer and was much admired by his peers for his sharp wit and conversational ability. As a boy, he demonstrated remarkable mechanical aptitude, and he built himself a number of small boats. He attended the University of Texas beginning in 1908, studying electrical engineering, but left after two years. He worked for a while designing propellers for the Glenn Curtis aircraft company. He and his wife moved to Dunedin, Florida, in 1921, where they lived for the rest of their lives.

In subsequent years, Hanna designed a number of oceangoing yachts, including *Golden Gain* in 1922, *Orca* (later *Tahiti*) in 1923, *Gulfweed* in 1923, and *Tahiti*'s larger steel sister, *Carol*, in 1924. While he designed cutters, schooners, and motorsailers, his double-ended ketches were what people wanted most, and he created them in various sizes. It was as part of the 1935 book, *How to Build 20 Boats* (by the editors of *Mechanix Illustrated*) that the *Tahiti* ketch first caught the imagination of backyard builders and bluewater cruisers.

Hanna's writing style is said to have been influenced by his need to communicate with most people in the form of short, terse, handwritten comments, owing to his deafness,

which had diminished his ability to speak clearly. His columns "Heaving the Lead," in *Motor Boat* magazine, and "The Watch Below," in *The Rudder*, were popular, incisive, and opinionated. While he sometimes got into trouble for not backing down when he had made a mistake, the columns had the same salt and sensibility of his boats, leading to his nickname "The Sage of Dunedin."

The *Tahiti* ketch remains a popular design and continues to be built and enjoyed by dedicated cruising people all around the world.

Hanna's drawings are at the Calvert Marine Museum in Solomons, MD.

—Daniel B. MacNaughton

WERNER HANSEN

1877–1932 · Denmark

Werner Hansen designed the bulb-keeler *Kismet* in 1904 when he was twenty-seven years old, but little is known about him prior to that. In 1906, when the International Rule was introduced, he submitted the winning drawing of a 6-Meter in a competition sponsored by a French magazine. With this first success, recognition and contracts followed immediately.

During his subsequent brief career, Hansen designed only 6-, 7-, and 8-Meters, but in

large numbers. They were much admired, not only for their performance in competition but also for their excellent sailing qualities and beauty. Within the limited scope of his work, Hansen ranked among the premier designers of his day. Of all his boats, the 6-Meters *Nurdug I, II* (which won the Olympic silver medal in 1912 for Denmark), *III*, and *IV* are probably the best known. Rigs evolved from gaff to gunter and then to marconi.

In 1919, the year before the International Rule underwent its first revision, Hansen was obliged to retire because of illness. He died at the age of fifty-five.

—Bent Aarre

HAROLD CORNELIUS HANSON

1892–1975 · United States

In the Pacific Northwest H. C. Hanson left a shipbuilding legacy dominated by commercial work but also including a significant number of pleasure boats. Among the best known of his sailboat designs is the 26-foot *Los Baat*, based on the famed Norwegian pilot-boat originally developed by designer Colin Archer. Hanson was also a major contributor to the evolved Northwest troller from that begat today's "trawler yacht."

Hanson apprenticed at the Pacific American Fisheries Company in Bellingham, Washington, where his father was the marine superintendent. The younger Hanson not only absorbed all the shipbuilding trades but also received an education in management by interpreting for his father, who had a serious speech impediment. He began drafting the yard's vessels and then designing them.

Increasingly drawn to design, Hanson gained further experience at such major yards as Heath's and Sloan's in the Northwest. During World War I, he oversaw work at shipyards with government contracts for the Emergency Fleet Corporation. After the war, middle-class people began taking advantage of the plentiful boatyards, and a booming economy created a strong pleasure boat market.

Hanson was employed in the Seattle office of Ted Geary for several productive years in the early 1920's, followed by a short partnership with Leigh Coolidge. By 1928, he had hung out his own shingle. His drafting skills were legendary: he could produce a set of plans very rapidly, drawing in ink on linen without even preliminary sketches.

Commissions for pleasure yachts intermingled with commercial work. The 70-foot *Anna Helen II* was designed as a traveling office and home for a dentist. A 50-foot motorsailer, which held a remarkable record for speed

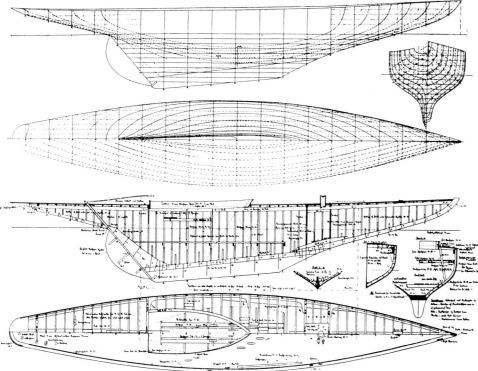

Werner Hansen: *Nurdig II.* *Nurdig II*, winner of the silver medal in the 1912 Olympics, is a glimpse of the state of the art in early 6-Meters. Her low gaff rig and long, shallow underbody would soon be things of the past, but the basic shape of the hull would remain typical for decades. *Drawing courtesy Bent Aarre*

with a low-power gasoline engine, was followed by a 50-foot motor cruiser in 1930. Fleets of fishing boats have been built to his designs for the governments of Chile, Peru, Mexico, Indonesia, Philippines, New Zealand, Australia, and the Soviet Union.

The Redningskoite-inspired sailboat design Los Baat was featured in *Pacific Motor Boat* magazine in January of 1931 as a commercial vessel. Deluged for a yacht version, the magazine ran a second article three months later. The magazine sold hundreds of plans for this double-ended, inside-ballasted sloop. A fleet of Los Baats developed and raced successfully in southern California, and the design was built all up and down the West Coast. Additional designs were featured for many years in the *Maine Coast Fisherman* and later *National Fisherman*.

Other notable designs included the 37-foot ketch *Mon Reve* for photographer Walter Miller in 1936, and the 88-foot *Lester E Jones* for the U.S. Coast and Geodetic Survey. Renamed *Summerwind*, she sailed out of Lake Union in Seattle as recently as 1997.

During World War II, Hanson designed several new shipyard facilities along with minesweepers, freighters, tugs, and patrol boats. He was again the government's representative, working with yards in Washington, Oregon, and California.

Hanson's commercial innovations include the development of new ways to weld steel boats.

Vulcan was the first welded-steel cannery tender in Alaska, and *Ruby II* was the first welded-steel tug on the West Coast. His utility fishing boats, including his tuna clippers, were highly prized by fishermen. He also spoke for the United States at numerous international maritime meetings and wrote extensive technical papers. His final design, in 1970, was *Acheron*.

Hanson died in his boat shop at home in 1975.

A large collection of his drawings, photographs, and papers was donated to the Whatcom Museum in Bellingham, WA.

—Lucia del Sol Knight

JACK BERTRAND HARGRAVE

June 10, 1922–February 26, 1996
United States

Jack Hargrave was one of the most successful designers of sportfishing boats as well as trawler yachts and larger luxury motoryachts. Beginning with his first boat in 1959, he designed almost the entire range of Hatteras fiberglass motoryachts. These included the Hatteras 41, of which 743 have been built, making it one of the most popular designs of its kind as well as the first large production boat constructed of fiberglass when it was introduced.

Hargrave's first yacht, designed while he was working at Rybovich and Sons, renowned builders of sportfishing boats in West Palm Beach, Florida, was *Seven Seas*, a 90-foot steel

motoryacht built by Burger in 1958. She was one of the largest yachts built in the United States during the postwar period and served to launch his career as an independent designer. In 1964 he designed *TX-41*, a twin-screw, four-engine screamer capable of speeds 60 mph and faster that traveled from Miami to New York City in 31 hours and 27 minutes, a record that stood for ten years.

The largest design to come from Hargrave's board was the 184-foot luxury yacht *Katamarino*, built in 1992 by Amels in Holland. He drew stock boats for Burger, Halmatic, Carver, Daytona, Atlantic, Prairie, Trumpy, and the Lazy Days Houseboat Company among others. Hargrave also drew commercial designs for fast ferries, dinner cruise boats, tour boats, and the unique, patented, integrated tug-and-barge system for offshore cargo carrying called the CATUG. At times Hargrave's design staff comprised up to twelve individuals.

Hargrave was born in Michigan, the son of a boat broker, and grew up in Duluth, Minnesota, on Lake Superior. There he spent summers working on and around boats. He attended St. Olaf's College, studying art and music, and would continue to draw and paint for the rest of his life. Unable to join the navy because he had lost sight in one eye in a childhood accident, he served on merchant vessels during World War II.

After the war he worked as a captain on a variety of charter vessels and private yachts.

H. C. Hanson: *Lewella.* The 45-foot cruiser *Lewella* was built in Tacoma, Washington, in 1930. Hanson produced a number of graceful pleasure yachts that possessed the same no-nonsense approach and "get-it-done" quality for which his famous workboats were known. *Photo courtesy Newport Harbor Nautical Museum, Newport Beach, CA*

Jack Hargrave: ***Katamarino.*** *Katamarino* is the ultimate expression of Hargrave's design talent. The hull design was extensively tested for efficiency and seakeeping ability, with particular emphasis on the underwater bulb, which is part of the bow, and the shape of the stern. She has a steel hull and an aluminum superstructure. *Photo courtesy Hargrave Yacht Design*

In 1955 he took the Westlawn School of Yacht Design correspondence course while helping to build a large yacht in South America. He later opened a small boatbuilding and repair shop in West Palm Beach, Florida, and went to work at the Rybovich yard before beginning his design career. Hargrave designed more than 250 yachts. The firm of Hargrave Yacht Design carries on in Fort Lauderdale under the direction of Michael F. Joyce.

—Daniel B. MacNaughton

designed his first sailboat, *Muscadet* (1963), a small 6.5-meter plywood cruiser that participated in several Mini-Transat Races, when he left the Center.

In 1979 Harlé raced in the Mini-Transat for his own pleasure, placing fourth, and this plus his cruising experience constituted his training. He saw particular success with his fast and easily handled cruising sailboats. His Sangria design was the first production-built cruiser to exceed a thousand copies. In the early 1980's he joined

forces with Alain Mortain, who specialized in general aesthetics and internal accommodations. Getting together with the CNG managers who wished to develop for their trainees a new small cruising boat capable of racing in the Mini-Transat, Harlé designed the 6.5-meter Coco Class (1984), one of which won the 1987 event.

The activity of the Harlé-Mortain office in La Rochelle grew rapidly, and among their successes were the Feeling 1090 (1984), the Punch 850, a light cruiser catamaran built of plywood,

PHILIPPE HARLÉ

1932–1991 · France

One of those who popularized yachting in France in the years 1950 to 1960, Philippe Harlé seemed destined for the sea at the age of fourteen, when he first began experimenting with his father's canoe, converting her into a sailboat. He was seventeen years old when he discovered the Centre Nautique des Glénans or CNG (Nautical Center of the Glénans), which had trained generations of young yachtsmen from France as well as the rest of Europe. He spent ten years there as an instructor, working with Philippe Viannay, founder of the center. Harlé cowrote in 1961 the famous *Cours de Navigation des Glénans* (*Course of Navigation of the Glénans*), which was translated into several languages and distributed around the world.

Influenced by the spirit of austerity that made the Glénans reputation, and drawing his inspiration from two pioneer CNG sailboats, the dinghy *Vaurien* and the small centerboard cruiser *Corsair*, Harlé began to design simple boats that were very easy to sail. He had just

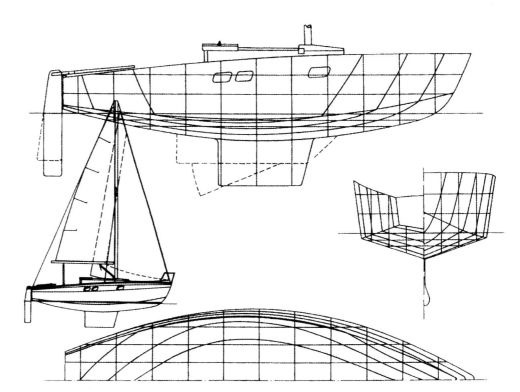

Philippe Harlé: Muscadet class. Built in plywood, the Muscadet class was launched in 1963 and is still popular in France. Length overall is 6.48 meters. *Drawing courtesy Jacques Taglang*

two 16-meter catamarans for chartering, cruisers such as the Etap 38 and the Dufour 54, and Harlé's pride, Jean-Luc Van Den Heede's 3615 Met, which finished third in the 1989 Vendée Globe Challenge. Harlé created a hundred designs representing a fleet of 14,000 units sailing throughout the world in all types and materials, some of which (such as 2,500 Sangrias and 1,500 Fantasias) set sales records.

An epicurean and well-informed enologist, he christened all his boats with good brands of liquor or wine. He was designing a new sailboat when he took ill and died, after many years devoted to yachting.　　　　　—Jacques Taglang

ADOLF HARMS

1879–December 20, 1955 · Germany

Between 1905 and 1934 Adolf Harms was one of the best-known yacht designers in Berlin. His most important contribution to yacht design is the influence of his work on the development of centerboard cruisers.

In his early life Harms worked in the great shipbuilding yards of Kiel, Hamburg, and Stettin. Only at the turn of the century did the twenty-year-old Harms begin to specialize in yacht building. His designs were well known far beyond the borders of Germany, especially in Austria, Switzerland, Russia, Holland, and Hungary.

Harms created 965 designs during his career. From his drawing board came such famous boats as the Sonder-class *Passat* and the 22-Square-Meter *Irmi*. He designed outboard boats, motorboats, motor cruisers, and racing rowboats, but above all he designed sailboats, from small racing dinghies and centerboard boats to large cruising yachts up to "125-er" Schäerenkruezer (inshore cruiser/racers).

Adolf Harms remained an active sailor throughout his life, for the most part cruising the waters of the Baltic Sea. He died in Kiel.

—Volker Christmann

FRANCO HARRAUER

Born 1927 · Italy

A prominent designer of high-speed powerboats, Franco Harrauer also designed trawler yachts and high-speed motorsailers, and he was the first in Europe to design large motorized catamarans.

Born in Genoa, Harrauer began his designing career at STIAN (the Italian Technical Society for Architecture and Naval Equipment), an organization based in Turin that attracted experts from various sectors of the marine construction industry. In 1966, he introduced Genoa to the first high-speed Italian sportfishing boat. Dubbed *Perseu*, she was designed for fishing offshore or onshore. Built by the Cozzani ship-

yard in La Spezia, she measured 10 meters and was equipped with two 300-hp Chrysler engines.

Other sportfishing boats followed. Among them was the *Tiger Shark*, measuring 17 meters and powered by two Caterpillar diesel engines and built in aluminum by SAI Ambrosini of Passignano sul Trasimen. *Tiger Shark* was selected for EXPO 70 in Osaka, Japan, as an example of Italian naval architecture.

Harrauer also collaborated with Renato "Sonny" Levi in the design of such prestigious large boats as the unique IAG V5 planing motorsailer built in 1978 by IAG Nautica of Mestre in Venice. She was 12 meters in length, and with her two 240-hp Aifo diesel motors, she was capable of traveling at a speed of 27 to 28 knots, and even close-hauled she performed well while sailing.

—Franco Belloni

ROBERT B. HARRIS

Born 1922 · United States/Canada

Bob Harris has enjoyed a long and varied career designing a wide variety of yachts, powerboats, and small commercial craft. Best known for his pioneering development work on multihulls, Harris's designs have ranged from small plywood sloops through large steel-hulled yachts. In addition, he assisted with Sparkman and Stephens designs such as for the America's Cup winner *Columbia* and the Swan 65 *Sayula* (winner of the 1973 Whitbread Round the World Race), and with the Frank MacLear–designed, 60-foot steel cutter *Angantyr*.

Harris was appointed a cadet at the U.S. Merchant Marine Academy in the spring of 1942 and saw wartime service in the Merchant Marine. In 1945, with a chief mate's certificate, Harris switched to sailing the *Atlantis*, a large ketch belonging to the Woods Hole Oceanographic Society. He soon realized his real interest lay in designing yachts. To help achieve this ambition, he apprenticed himself for four years to the Crosby Yacht Building and Storage Company of Osterville, Massachusetts.

For Harris, his real training in yacht design occurred during the seven years from 1950 to 1957 that he spent with Sparkman and Stephens, where he worked under the direction of designer Al Mason. There he researched and designed a number of small multihull racers. In 1959, his cold-molded *Tiger Cat* won *Yachting* magazine's One of a Kind race. This experience led him to write his first book, *Modern Sailing Catamarans*.

For the next ten years, Harris worked for Grumman Aircraft Corporation and for designer/builder Robert Derecktor, before becoming a partner in the firm of MacLear and

Franco Harrauer: *Planante Progettato.* Typically, fast sailboats are given auxiliary engines, but it is also possible to make a fast motorboat that sails when desired. The challenge is to design a hull that is easy to push in two radically different speed ranges. *Photo courtesy Franco Belloni*

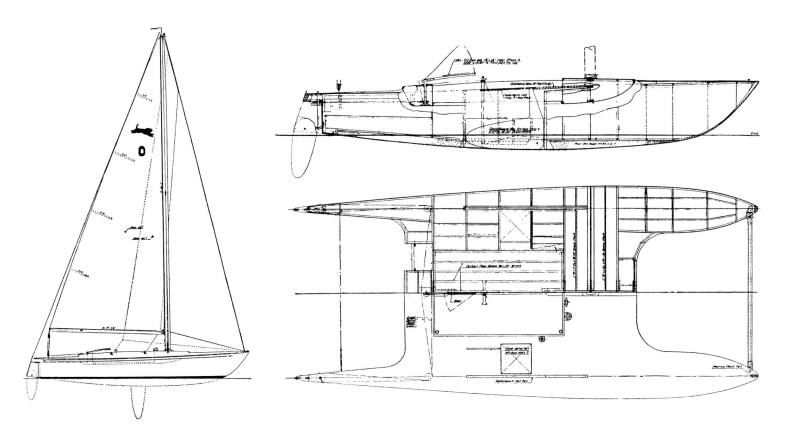

Robert Harris: *Ocelot.* The 21-foot 11-inch catamaran *Ocelot*, of 1956, shows an interesting phase in multihull development, to which *Harris* contributed a great deal. In profile she resembles a conventional sloop. When viewed from above, she displays her foil-shaped hulls and a shapely and rigidifying solid deck. *Reproduced from* The Rudder

Harris, Naval Architects and Marine Engineers, New York, specializing in multihull designs. The firm operated from 1961 to 1967. His 33-foot, ocean racing trimaran *Eclipse* won the 1973 Multihull Bermuda Race. He rejoined Sparkman and Stephens in 1967. In 1970, his second book on multihulls, *Racing and Cruising Trimarans,* was published. In the same year, he wrote a course of study on multihull yacht design for the Westlawn School of Yacht Design.

Late in 1972 Harris moved from New York to Vancouver, British Columbia, Canada, where he opened an independent design office. He designed several of the Jefferson series of motoryachts ranging from 37 to 65 feet long, and a series of auxiliary sailing yachts from 32 to 65 feet. A recent design was the Tayana/Vancouver 460 pilothouse sloop for Passagemaker Offshore Yachts of Toronto, Canada. His Vancouver series of oceangoing monohull yachts 25 to 65 feet in LOA have been built by a number of companies in Canada, Taiwan, and the United Kingdom.

Harris takes a practical approach to yacht design. He is dedicated to providing the best compromise of size and type of yacht to suit his client's requirements, within a budget, while maintaining high standards of performance, stability, strength, and seaworthiness. His office is still in Vancouver, British Columbia.

—Tom Roach

WILDER BRALEY "BILL" HARRIS

(Dates unknown) · United States

Bill Harris is best known for a series of designs he did for the Concordia Company, which were known as the Concordia 28, 31, and 33. Unlike the better-known Concordia yawls (which were primarily drawn by Ray Hunt although Harris did some of the work), Harris's Concordias were beamy, short-ended boats with outboard rudders, bowsprits, and boomkins—classic cruising boats with no concessions to racing or rating rules. Harris was known as a highly accomplished and meticulous draftsman.

The son of a professional draftsman, Harris grew up in Melrose, Massachusetts. He attended the University of Maine and was then associated with the Morse yard in Thomaston, Maine. In 1928 he took a job as a draftsman for John Alden in Boston. He also did design work for Eldredge-McInnis and Boston Yacht Sales.

Harris moved to Fairhaven in 1933. He worked at Furnham's Yacht Agency and did some design work for Major Casey along with designer Walter Cross. Through Cross, Harris came to the attention of Waldo Howland and the fledgling Concordia Company. He became their in-house designer, providing plans for such yachts as the sloop *Shawnee II, Prospector*

in 1937 (built again in 1940 after a fire destroyed the first one just prior to launching), and the 40-foot motorsailer *Hurricane* in 1939, and assisting as well on the Concordia yawl arrangements, details, and engineering.

—Daniel B. MacNaughton

RICHARD HARTLEY

1920–October 1996 · New Zealand

Richard Hartley was one of the first successful stock plan designers. He is particularly known for his trailerable sailers, the plywood Hartley 16 and 18 being the outstanding examples. In New Zealand he can take credit for allowing many "do-it-yourself Kiwis" to build their own boats and get out on the water.

Born in New Zealand, Hartley's family moved to Cornwall, England, where he was surrounded by the sea. The family returned to Auckland in the late 1920's. Hartley was tutored in naval architecture by Jack Brooks at a technical college before starting a boatbuilding apprenticeship. During World War II, Hartley was "manpowered" for the war effort, working at the Naval Dockyard.

Just after World War II, Hartley moved to Whangerai, outside of Auckland, where a local firm asked him to design a small powerboat to take advantage of the newly reliable marine glues

Richard Hartley: *We're Away.* The Hartley TS 16 was an early and subsequently huge success for Hartley. It epitomized his designs for simple, good boats that amateurs could build. The TS 16 must be ageless, as people are still building and racing them today. *Photo by David Boult*

John Harvey: *Oriva.* The 50-foot LWL cutter *Oriva* was designed in 1881 and built by Henry Piepgrass. Though harshly criticized at the time of her launch, she was a handsome vessel and performed well in local regattas. © *Chevalier & Taglang*

and plywood. This was the modest beginning of his career. He began designing boats in his spare time. In the mid-1950's he published the first of many editions of his book of plans. He was a full-time designer during the 1960's and 1970's before retiring and selling his business.

Hartley's range of designs was broad and included dinghies, kayaks, runabouts, cruisers, daysailers, and larger yachts. While he could not claim to have originated any style of boat, his plans are so well detailed and so considerate of the amateur builder's abilities that his simple and affordable designs have been built in great numbers. —David Payne

JOHN HARVEY

ca. 1825–1901 · England

W. P. Stephens considered John Harvey a "connecting link between the old and new." His career spanned the years between the era of ballast-shifting designs, which ended in the mid-1850's, and the compromise cutters of the late 1880's and 1890's. While many of his schooners and yawls were successful, he is remembered for his cutters and his involvement in the often strident competition be-

tween the advocates of British cutters and American sloops.

Harvey grew up in the shipbuilding town of Wivenhoe in Essex on England's east coast. His father was a partner in the yard of John Philip Sainty. Harvey modeled and built the 60-ton *Volante* in 1851, a typical and not extreme cutter. She very nearly beat the U.S. schooner *America* in the race for the 100 Guinea Cup sailed around the Isle of Wight in 1851, later known as the America's Cup.

The 20-ton cutter *Kitten* was built the following year. Considered a moderate cutter, her length was 4¼ times her beam. In modeling *Kitten*, Harvey was pressing to reduce the wetted surface area, a development he hoped would increase her speed. She was sailed by Harvey for five or six years and held her own in the 10-Ton Class. In 1870, eighteen years after her construction, *Kitten* would show up in Boston, the first British cutter in those waters.

After his father's retirement in 1862, Harvey took over the Wivenhoe yard. Designers of the time were making use of steel and iron framing to increase rigidity and strength while reducing weight. Doubting the longevity of such structures, Harvey sought rigidity through double planking combined with wooden frames

somewhat reduced in size. There was also a developing trend toward outside ballast, but Harvey was convinced that it was impossible to compensate for the strains imposed on the hull by that configuration. He went to elaborate lengths to place ever-increasing amounts of ballast as low as possible in the bilge, and to distribute the strains involved.

Along with a number of working schooners, Harvey built many narrow and heavily ballasted racing cutters and schooner yachts. They included the schooner *Rose of Devon* (1869), later converted to a yawl; *Sea Belle* (1874); the two-masted cutter *Miranda* (1876); and the radical yawl *Jullanar* (1878), codesigned with her owner. The proportion of ballast to displacement was progressively greater in each yacht, but very little of it was placed outside. In rejecting both composite wood-and-steel construction and outside ballast, Harvey ultimately made it difficult for his designs to compete.

In 1876, Harvey and a few others, including Dixon Kemp, began to lobby for *Lloyd's Register of Shipping* to expand and create a similar register for yachts. A "yachting Lloyd's" would develop formula rules for the regulation of construction and publish a register of yachts.

They succeeded: the rules were agreed to in 1877 and the first *Lloyd's Register of Yachts* came out in 1878 and provided copious data on the majority of prominent yachts. *Lloyd's* rules for construction have been a benchmark for quality ever since.

The schooner class had declined in popularity by about 1880, and was replaced with large cutters with outside ballast on the keel. The Harvey and Pryer yard, a partnership that began in 1875, failed to adapt to the new trends and closed in 1881.

Later that year Harvey moved to New York, where his cutters, the 50-foot *Oriva* (1881), the 70-foot *Bedouin* (1882), and the 60-foot *Wenonah* (1882), were under construction. He was hoping to capitalize on the success of his earlier cutters, which had been built in the United States during the 1870's, but he was unlucky enough to arrive in the midst of the great cutter-versus-sloop controversy.

British yachts of the time were narrow-beamed, deep-draft cutters. The Americans were designing broad-beamed, centerboard sloops. While some in the U.S. nautical press mocked the British boats as being totally unfit for local sailing conditions, others defended them with equal ferocity. There were strengths and weaknesses in both design camps, and ultimately a blending of the best features took form in a compromise type. Harvey's designs were savagely criticized in the press, and his New York cutters began faring poorly in races. His later cutters, the 65-foot *Ileen* (1883) and the 35-foot *Surf* (1883), completed his output for the period.

Harvey refused to design compromise cutters, and soon his commissions all but dried up. While *Bedouin* was a defense candidate in the America's Cup of 1885, she was never a serious threat to the Edward Burgess–designed *Puritan*, which successfully defended the America's Cup against the John Beavor-Webb–designed *Genesta*. Harvey was barely sustained by design commissions for a few steam yachts.

For a short time, Harvey worked in the office of William Gardner. Not much is heard about him after that, until 1898 when he returned to England with his finances in ruin. Designer George Watson organized a testimonial fund to sustain him during his retirement, in recognition of his contributions to the yachting community.

—Bette Noble and Lucia del Sol Knight

John Harvey: *Bedouin*. The 70-foot LWL cutter *Bedouin*, designed in 1882, was built with double planking on alternating sawn and steam-bent frames in the New York yard I of Henry Piepgrass. A purse winner in regattas organized by the Atlantic, Eastern, New York, and Seawanhaka Corinthian Yacht Clubs, she also competed in the 1885 America's Cup trials. *Photo by Nathaniel Stebbins. Courtesy of the Society for the Preservation of New England Antiquities*

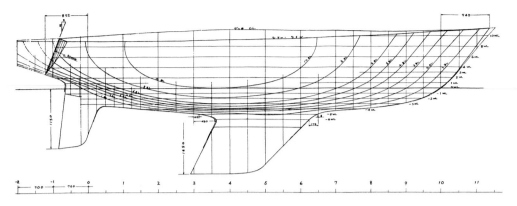

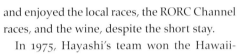

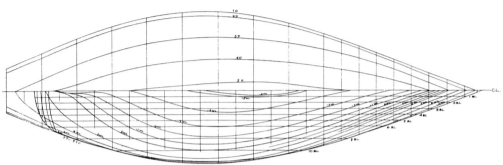

Kennosuke Hayashi: *Mermaid III.* Solo-sailor Kenichi Horie completed a nonstop circumnavigation aboard *Mermaid III*, taking 277 days in 1974. This is an outstanding record given her size: 28 feet 1 inch. *Drawing courtesy Kennosuke Hayashi*

KENNOSUKE "KEN" HAYASHI

Born 1939 · Japan

Born in coastal Japan, Kennosuke Hayashi has been interested in yachts since his youth, but only started sailing in his late teens. In his early twenties he sailed aboard designer Shuji Watanabe's *Dongame* and experienced the wonder of the ocean and its winds—as well as serious seasickness, which did not stop him from loving sailing.

After graduating from the Department of Physics at Rikkyo University, Hayashi joined the Yokoyama Naval Architecture Office as an apprentice. In 1969, he designed a wooden

sloop of 7.5 meters as his design No. 1, which entered various races with good results.

In 1973, Hayashi and Nobuwo Muramoto jointly designed *Mermaid III*, an 8.8-meter, cold-molded sloop in which Kenichi Horie completed a westbound nonstop circumnavigation taking 277 days. Ever since, Hayashi has been designing the boats for Horie's adventures: one for a circumnavigation of the globe, a solar-powered boat for the passage from Hawaii to Ogasawara, and even a stainless-steel, beer-barrel catamaran for the Transpacific Race from San Francisco to Kobe.

Hayashi worked in the office of Philippe Harlé in La Rochelle, France, for four months in 1974

and enjoyed the local races, the RORC Channel races, and the wine, despite the short stay.

In 1975, Hayashi's team won the Hawaii-Okinawa Race commemorating the Okinawa Marine Expo 1975. In 1978, the Quarter-Ton Cup World Races were held in Japan; however, Hayashi's team was dissolved and did not enter. He stopped racing then and concentrated on designing cruising boats, motorsailers, and charter catamarans.

In 1992, Japan first challenged for the America's Cup under the new International America's Cup Class Rule. Hayashi had been chief designer when Japan was contemplating entry in the 1987 challenge and stayed on to help with the new boat.

Long a member of the Nippon Ocean Racing Club, Hayashi was chairman of the Measurement Committee and director, contributing to the introduction of the IOR and IMS rule to Japan. At present, he is chairman of the Technical Committee of the Japan Sailing Federation (JSAF). He has designed well over a hundred different boats.

Kennosuke Hayashi practices south of Tokyo in Yokosuka, Japan.   —Kennosuke Hayashi

HEINRICH HEIDTMANN

1849–1911 · Germany

From the age of thirteen, Heinrich Heidtmann worked in his father's boatyard, so it is not surprising that the young and passionate oarsman soon began designing the boats being built by the family-owned workshop. Heidtmann's rowing boats were known for their racing performance.

Germania, launched in 1872, was considered unbeatable for many years and was followed by the equally successful *Methisto* and *Rabe*. In 1876 Heidtmann took over his father's yard, but while he is said to have been a prolific designer, little is known today about his work. Heinrich Heidtmann was also respected as a talented sailing helmsman. The yard continued on for many years after his death.

—Erdmann Braschos

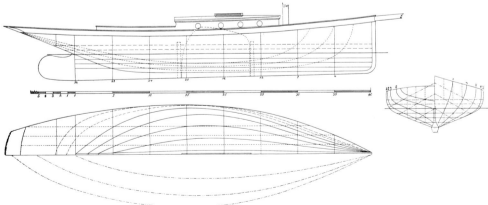

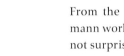

Heinrich Heidtmann. Little is known of this centerboard sloop or her designer. The yacht's sections may well have been influenced by American Cape Cod catboat designs, but in her rather severe-looking profile she is styled more like a deep-draft cutter. *Reproduced from C. P. Kunhardt's* Small Yachts

Richard Hein: *Constellation*. The 80-meter *Constellation*, designed by Hein of Oceanco, is typical of the firm's output of big, modern, fast, luxurious motoryachts. With a steel hull and aluminum superstructure, she carries 350 tons of fuel driving two 8,160-hp diesel engines, for a speed of 23.5 knots. *Photo courtesy Richard Hein*

RICHARD HEIN

Born 1958 · Monaco

Until the 1980's, one might well have believed that the era of large yachts had disappeared forever, swept away by two world wars. Its spectacular revival is partly due to the work of Richard Hein of the Oceanco group.

Hein abandoned his early studies in law, moved to England, and studied land-based architecture, earning his degree in 1979. In France, he joined the Guy Couach boatbuilders group, where he made his debut at Beaulieu-sur-Mer on the Côte d'Azur, subsequently moving to Cannes La Bocca. In the early 1980's, he moved to Fort Lauderdale, Florida, where he created a small Couach division.

Returning to France in 1986, Hein founded his own company, the A Group. He and two associates became technical consultants for yards such as Broward (United States) and VersilCraft (Italy), as well as for private customers. He participated in designing *Starlite* (1987), A Group's first yacht, built by Broward, and *Double Heaven*, built by Feadship.

In the late 1980's, a group of South African businessmen purchased the Dorbyl boatyard in Durban, renaming it SAS (South African Shipyards). They soon merged with Hein's Monaco-based A Group, and in 1992 Oceanco was created, with Hein as president.

Originally Oceanco's specialty was the construction of yachts longer than 100 feet on speculation rather than to order, which allowed customers to buy without the usual two or three years' wait for completion. The firm handled the entire process from design through delivery, constructing the hulls and primary mechanical systems in Durban, South Africa, and then transporting them to either of two Dutch yards, one at Dreumel and the other near Rotterdam, for completion.

From its first yacht, the 163-foot 4-inch *Indian Achiever* (1992), to later launches, such as the 80-meter *Constellation* and the 95-meter *Al Mirqab*, Oceanco enhanced the reputation it forged with *Caprice* (123 feet), *Applause* (149 feet 4 inches), *Ultimate* (143 feet 4 inches), *Lady's* (165 feet 8 inches), *Aspiration* (139 feet 1 inch), and *Sunrise* (170 feet 2 inches). *Avalon*, built in 1999, was the last boat done on speculation—all the other vessels being built are on order, a strategy different from that which characterized Oceanco at its beginnings.

The Oceanco office is in Monaco.

—Dominique Gabirault

NIELS CHRISTIAN HELLEBERG

Born January 22, 1940 · Denmark/United States

The head designer at today's John G. Alden and Company, Niels Helleberg is responsible for some of that firm's most-enduring designs. Most notable is the Alden 44, a centerboard cutter originally designed for a New York Yacht Club competition in 1975. The design didn't win the competition, but the boat has seen a long production run and is known for its good looks, ease of handling, and high owner satisfaction. Helleberg's *Sceptre d'Isle*, a 62-foot composite cutter, is known for having recorded a remarkable twenty-four-hour run of 324 nautical miles in the 2000 Bermuda Race. He has produced twenty-seven complete designs of boats ranging from 15 to 164 feet in length, with approximately 121 built as of this writing.

Helleberg is the inventor of the "Interkeel," an interchangeable keel-attachment system patented in 1993, and has also innovated centerboard control systems for offshore yachts.

Born in Gentofte, Denmark, Helleberg attended the Danish military academy in 1961–62 and earned a master shipwright certificate in yacht construction in 1965. In the same year, he acquired a master certificate for vessels up to 500 tons. He graduated from the Elsinore Institute of Naval Architecture with a bachelor's degree in naval architecture in 1969. He grew

up cruising with his family, and went on to serve a four-year apprenticeship under Poul Molich, before embarking on his design career.

Helleberg moved to the United States and started work in the Alden office in 1971.

—Daniel B. MacNaughton

JULIANE HEMPEL

Born 1964 · Germany

One of the few female naval architects designing yachts, Hempel has a wide portfolio from ultralight dinghies to straightforward contemporary cruiser/racers and is known for her R-Yacht designs in the 6- and 8-Meter classes according to the International Rule, still a hothouse for eager talents.

Born in southern Germany, Hempel traveled with her parents to Lake Constance for relaxation. At this lake, bordering Austria, Switzerland, and Germany, she developed her passion for sailing.

The woodenboat builder and refit expert Josef Martin, a respected supplier of cold-molded or traditionally planked yachts, encouraged her to rebuild, build, and design. In 1989, at the age of twenty-five, Hempel laminated a carbon-epoxy International Moth, whose camber inducers behind the mast improved the aerodynamics in the critical forward

area of the sail. Special lightweight carbon ears instead of the common rack for hiking out the tender dinghy provided much-appreciated buoyancy prior to capsizing.

In 1992 Hempel finished her academic education as shipbuilding engineer in Kiel with a study of an extensively tank-tested 8-Meter yacht. That boat became *Spazzo* four years later. It was the first new German 8-Meter design since Henry Rasmussen's prewar designs, which were featured at the Olympic Games in 1936. Hempel's goal was to keep the prismatic coefficient low and the canoe body shallow, and to gain keel wing span while distributing the volume smartly into the ship's ends. Nevertheless *Spazzo* is a remarkably canvassed (7 percent above average) 8-Meter boat, although the International Rule severely punishes the difference between chain and girth measurements with reduced sail area. Hempel's recent 6-Meter *Kontrapunkt* follows the *Spazzo* pattern.

Apart from consulting on R-Yacht refits like the 8-Meters *Angelita*, *Germania*, and *Mariebel*, and taking care of a *Hollandia* replica, Hempel designs contempory yachts. For example, a lightweight 9-meter/30-foot daysailer was a recent design, featuring little equipment, a canting keel with the option to lift it for berthing in shallow water, and a lot of fun. Hempel's office is in Kiel, Germany.

—Erdmann Braschos

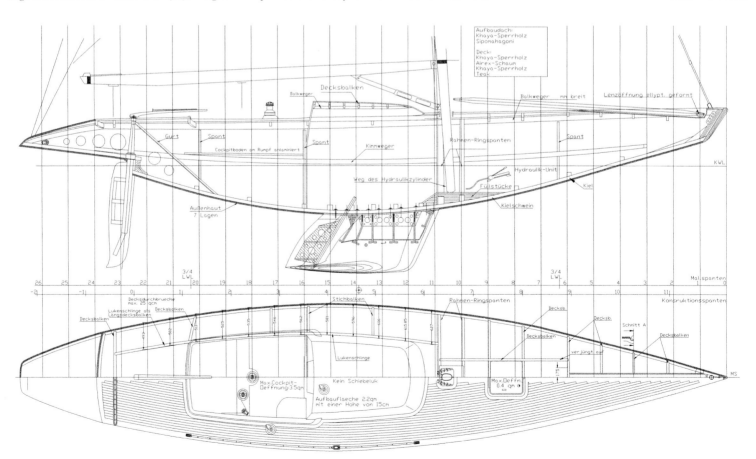

Juliane Hempel: *Spazzo*. *Spazzo* is the first new German 8-Meter design since the 1930's. *Drawing courtesy Juliane Hempel*

Geerd Hendel: *Salamar. Salamar* has a relatively small superstructure for her long, lean hull, plus modest streamlining and a timeless quality, all common themes in the designer's work. © *Peter Barlow*

GEERD NILZ HENDEL

January 14, 1903–March 30, 1998
Germany/United States

In a career lasting over fifty years, Geerd Hendel designed power yachts of all sizes, working vessels, military vessels, one-designs, and sailing yachts ranging from traditional schooners and many variations on contemporary yacht design themes to the first aluminum sailing yacht built in the United States. While his work was generally conservative in nature, he had a gift for the harmony of lines in hull form, sheer, and deckhouses, which enabled him to depart from traditional strictures and to create unusual designs of stunning individualistic beauty. Like many great designers he knew how to draw boats that, good as they might look on paper, looked their best in the water.

Born in Hamburg, Germany, Hendel was educated in public schools and then served a two-year apprenticeship at the Deutsche Werft shipyard in Hamburg. He then studied naval architecture at the Higher Technical Institute in Bremen and graduated in 1925.

After two years working in the design office of a shipyard in northern Germany, Hendel emigrated to the United States, in 1928. He worked for seven months in the office of naval architect Theodore Wells in New York City, and in 1929 was accepted as a draftsman at the Bath Iron Works shipyard in Bath, Maine, a position he held for several years. During the Depression he worked at the Bethlehem Shipbuilding Corporation in Quincy, Massachusetts, and the Rice Brothers Corporation in East Boothbay, Maine. He became a U.S. citizen in 1936.

From 1935 to 1939 he worked in the Bath and Wiscasset, Maine, offices of designer W. Starling Burgess, designing yachts and commercial vessels as well as producing working drawings for the 1937 America's Cup defender, the breakthrough J-Class sloop *Ranger*, which was built at Bath Iron Works.

In 1939, with aluminum provided by the Aluminum Company of America (later Alcoa), he had Rice Brothers build a 26-foot sloop of his design, entirely of aluminum. *Whistler* was the first aluminum sailing yacht built in Amer-

ica. Hendel owned her for over thirty years, and she is still sailing today.

Hendel worked for several months at Sparkman and Stephens in 1940 before taking a previously arranged job at the William Robinson Shipyard of Ipswich, Massachusetts, where he did design work for 110-foot subchasers and landing barges.

During his years working in Maine, Hendel developed a strong affection for the Maine coast, its people, and its boatyards. In 1942 he took work at the Camden Shipbuilding Company in Camden, Maine, taking charge of the hull building department and producing 165-foot rescue tugs, continuing in that capacity until the end of the war.

After the war Hendel opened his own design office in Camden. He lived and worked there for the rest of his life, retaining a close association with Camden Shipbuilding and its master builder Malcolm Brewer, local one-man builder Elmer Collemer, and many others, producing commercial tugs and fishing vessels, power yachts, and sailing yachts of all descriptions. Several of his larger designs were built by Abeking and Rasmussen in Germany. Geerd Hendel continued to actively design until just a few months before his death in Camden at the age of ninety-five.

Geerd Hendel's plans are at the Maine Maritime Museum in Bath, ME.

—Daniel B. MacNaughton

ROBERT GOLDSBOROUGH HENRY JR.

1908–1970 · United States

Bob Henry was a well-trained, highly capable, and unusually versatile naval architect best known for designing the Oxford 400 sloop. He designed winches and rigging gear for ocean racing yachts, managed wartime production in a boatyard, designed postwar production cruising yachts, and coordinated small craft design for the navy in World War II.

After graduating from MIT in 1934 with a BS in naval architecture and marine engineering, Henry joined Sparkman and Stephens in New York, where he produced designs for new rigging parts for ocean racing yachts, including pedestal coffee-grinder winches for prewar 12-Meter yachts.

In 1940, Henry became vice president and general manager of Oxford Boatyard in his native Talbot County, Maryland. There he modernized the facilities and managed wartime building of more than seventy wooden small craft for the Bureau of Ships, earning the yard two Army-Navy "E" production awards.

Before the war's end, he planned for the company's postwar production of yachts, publishing sailing yacht designs in *Yachting* magazine and advertising a stock auxiliary sloop dubbed the Oxford 400. Named for the 400 square feet of sail in its main and working jib, this 29-foot cruiser had full headroom in the cabin and a removable booby hatch forward that became a hallmark of Henry's designs. In addition to providing light and air forward, it could be turned around to act as a wind scoop. Oxford Boatyard built at least nineteen Oxford 400's.

Henry developed other stock designs for Oxford Boatyard, including a 24-foot cabin launch and a 14-foot dinghy dubbed the Oxford Sailer, but few of these were built before he left to join the navy's Bureau of Ships, first in mine and service craft, then as head of the Boats and Small Craft Design Section. Before his retirement in 1970, Henry worked on more than thirty-five contract designs, including riverboats for use in Vietnam, such as the armored LCM (landing craft, medium).

Continuing to freelance, Henry produced a series of sloops and ketches, notably the International 500 sloop or yawl, International 600 yawl, and International 800 yawl, all of which were built in Dutch and German yards. After more than two dozen were built of wood, Henry's International 500 was introduced in fiberglass in 1965.

Skipper magazine published a monthly design commentary column by Henry from 1961 until the magazine's disappearance in 1970. In 1965 he coauthored *Sailing Yacht Design* with Captain Richards T. Miller, a book originally written as a technical paper for the Society of Naval Architects and Marine Engineers (SNAME) that provided a wealth of technical data balanced with aesthetic considerations.

Henry's yacht designs are in the collections of the Chesapeake Bay Maritime Museum, Saint Michaels, MD.

—Pete Lesher

JEAN-JACQUES HERBULOT

1909—1997 · France

Although he never became a full-time professional naval architect, Jean-Jacques Herbulot occupies a special place in the French yachting landscape. A building architect employed by the city of Paris from 1947 until his retirement, he was also a distinguished and famous yachtsman with an impressive record: several French championship titles between 1932 and 1947 as well as notable participation in four Olympic Games (1932, 1936, 1948, and 1956).

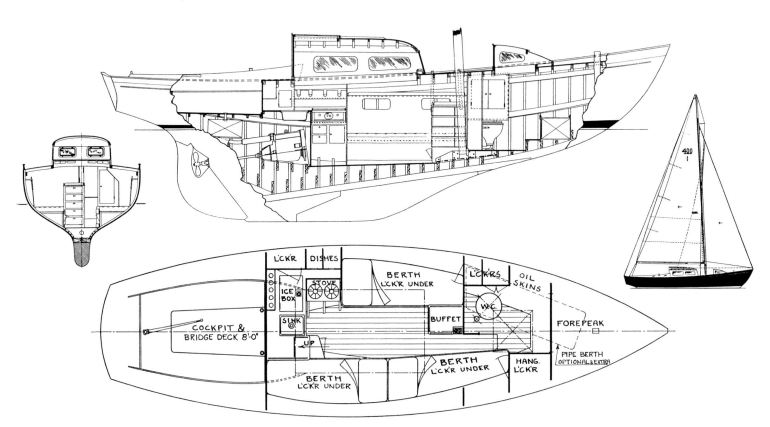

Robert Henry: Oxford 400. The Oxford 400 was Henry's best-known design. Her abbreviated cabin trunk creates a clear deck by providing headroom only where it is really needed, and complements her good proportions with a touch of distinction. *Drawing courtesy Chesapeake Bay Maritime Museum, Saint Michaels, MD*

A. Sydney DeWolf Herreshoff: *Arion.* One of the earliest fiberglass boats, *Arion* was built in 1951 by the Anchorage in Warren, Rhode Island. Slippery and pretty, this 42-foot ketch has a clean deck, roomy center cockpit, and easily handled rig. Builder Damian McLaughlin recently produced a close sistership. *Photo courtesy Lucia del Sol Knight*

ALGERNON SIDNEY DeWOLF HERRESHOFF

1886–May 7, 1977 · United States

Had Sidney Herreshoff been born with a different surname, his long and fruitful career might have achieved the recognition it deserves. However, he was born into the famous Herreshoff family of the Herreshoff Manufacturing Company, widely recognized as the premier American yacht designers and builders of the four decades spanning the turn of the twentieth century. Sidney's work was overshadowed by that of his father, the legendary Nathanael G. Herreshoff, and later his outspoken and flamboyant brother, L. Francis Herreshoff.

Sidney Herreshoff naturally gravitated to work as a draftsman at the family yard in Bristol, Rhode Island, and became chief designer in 1924 after the Haffenreffer family acquired Herreshoff Manufacturing. Nathanael decided to step back from full-time work in the yard he and his brother John had created. Continuing the design and construction philosophies of the elder Herreshoff, Sidney held to his father's proven methods of working from half models for hull lines, relying heavily on modifying existing models to fill new roles in the marketplace.

An example of the viability of this method was the particularly successful Fishers Island 31 class, a third-generation descendant of Nathanael's 26-foot *Alerion III* of 1912, whose offsets were expanded to create the Newport 29 in 1914; in 1930 Sidney extended the overhangs and adjusted the sheer on the loft floor. The result of this tinkering was a 44-foot sailing yacht of striking beauty and excellent sailing qualities, eminently suited to the highly refined and efficient Herreshoff building style.

Sidney's advancement to chief designer coincided with serious financial and management difficulties at the Herreshoff yard. The uncontrolled economy of the 1920's led to huge fluctuations in demand. The yard's production ranged from affordable daysailers like the 12½-footers and S-Class boats in the lean years, to J-Class racers and 160-foot powerboats in the boom times. The Great Depression of the 1930's brought a different set of challenges, as demand all but dried up except during America's Cup years. World War II pushed the yard back to full production overnight, building torpedo boats and coastal transport vessels.

Through these turbulent times, Sidney was responsible for overseeing the engineering, construction, and sea trials of boats from his own board as well as those of other designers. Of particular note are several elegant power craft of the commuter type, the sleek H-23 and Northeast Harbor 30 classes, modeled after the Square-

Herbulot designed his first boat, a 4.5-meter dinghy, in 1942; it was selected to race in the Free Zone France championship of 1943 and again in 1945. The following year, he designed the *Argonaute*, a small 3.8-meter centerboard yacht for the first French nautical training center. A number of Argonautes were built.

During the Depression of the 1930's Herbulot opened his house-architecture practice in Paris in 1932, with his wife Hélène, also an architect. To save money, they cut their own sails for their Star boat. The sails were of such good quality that they resulted in orders from other crews and created a supplemental income that allowed the Herbulots to sail and race each weekend. After the Libération, Herbulot pursued both his primary occupation as an architect and his part-time work as a sailmaker, specializing in spinnakers that were excellent in close reaching. The Herbulot spinnaker emerged as the only one likely to be set in Dragon One-Design and 5.5-Meter fleets.

Commissioned by the founder of the Centre Nautique des Glénans (CNG), Herbulot designed an 8.2-meter cutter, the "cotre des Glénans" in 1950. Then in 1952 he designed a 4.8-meter plywood dinghy, without frames and with self-supporting planking, the Vau-

rien. To date, more than 36,000 Vauriens have been built throughout the world. Next came the Corsaire, a light centerboard cruiser built of plywood; the Cap Corse, also of plywood; and the Cap Horn, one of which was sailed by Jean Lacombe in the first Singlehanded Transatlantic Race of 1960. Herbulot became the champion of the small, economical boats that enabled so many to participate in the development of yachting in France. The number of boats built from Herbulot's approximately ninety designs appear to be between 60,000 and 65,000, ranging from 3.8 to 20 meters in length.

Herbulot's sailmaking reputation led the English America's Cup challenger of 1958 to order all of *Evaine*'s and *Sceptre*'s spinnakers from him. During the races, *Sceptre* was soundly beaten by the Olin Stephens–designed Cup defender *Columbia*, but she did appear to be the faster when reaching. Although Olin Stephens urged him to open a sail loft in the United States, Herbulot preferred to carry on his parallel activity as a yacht designer in France.

Jean-Jacques Herbulot will be remembered as one of the most important figures of French yachting in the 1960's and 1970's.

—Jacques Taglang

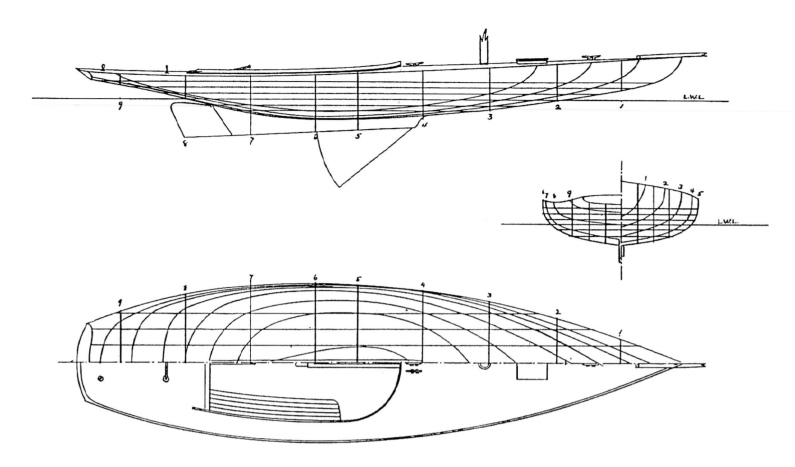

Charles Herreshoff: Red Bank Yacht Club One-Design. Long and low, with beautifully balanced ends, Herreshoff's 18-foot Red Bank Yacht Club One-Design shows the fast "wet" look of gentlemen's racing boats of the early twentieth century. *Reproduced from C. G. Davis's* How to Design a Yacht

Meter classes of Europe, and the Seafarer pocket cruiser, offering four berths and standing headroom within its attractive and able 26 feet. Sidney was also responsible for systems and machinery design, such as the Herreshoff sheet winches found aboard several of the J-Class boats vying for the America's Cup.

Upon the closing of the Herreshoff yard in 1946, Sidney Herreshoff continued designing yachts under his own shingle, often working in concert with his son, Halsey Herreshoff. In 1971, he and his wife, Rebecca Chase Herreshoff, founded the Herreshoff Marine Museum on the grounds of the old Herreshoff yard to commemorate the accomplishments of a remarkable family and a remarkable group of craftsmen.

Boats from Sidney Herreshoff's board display the hallmarks of his father's work: appropriate proportion in hull shape as well as scantlings, elegance of line and economy of material, and often, the signature Herreshoff hollow bow. His work shows, as did his father's, an eagerness to experiment and innovate, without losing sight of the successes of earlier boats. Sidney Herreshoff's importance to the legacy of Herreshoff Manufacturing Company has been largely unrecognized, lost beneath the legend of his father's accomplishments.

—Robert W. Stephens

CHARLES FREDERICK HERRESHOFF

1876–1954 · United States

Because he chose to apply his inventive mind mostly to the fledgling automobile industry, he's a little-known member of the famous Bristol, Rhode Island, family. Nevertheless, during the first decade of the twentieth century, Charles Frederick Herreshoff drew a small number of significant racing yachts, and was an important designer during powerboat racing's earliest, prehydrofoil years.

In 1900 and 1901 Herreshoff studied marine engineering and naval architecture at Glasgow University, Scotland, under the influential and charismatic Professor John Harvard Biles. It is interesting to note that this nephew of Nathanael Herreshoff was studying in Glasgow and living in the fashionable Clyde coast resort and yachting center of Helensburgh, a short train ride from Denny's of Dumbarton, builders of the G. L. Watson–designed 1901 America's Cup challenger *Shamrock II*. We can safely assume he was reporting back to his uncle. Certainly he went public with a technically detailed assessment of the yacht in a letter to the *New York Herald* soon after her launching. While based in Scotland, he advertised in the yachting press and in 1901 designed the moderately successful, light-displacement 65-Linear-

Rater *Nevada*, for Clyde shipbuilder P. M. Inglis.

By 1905 Herreshoff had moved back to the United States. His Lawley-built Canada's Cup defender *Iroquois*, designed for a Rochester Yacht Club syndicate, fought out a closely contested victory against the Royal Canadian Yacht Club's challenger *Temeraire*, designed by William Fife III.

By this time Herreshoff was already seriously involved in the design and manufacture of internal combustion engines and their application to automobiles and fast powerboats, first with the American and British Manufacturing Company of Bridgeport and later with the Herreshoff Motor Company in Detroit.

Herreshoff developed the power units and designed and sometimes constructed the hulls for some very successful, early endurance racing powerboats, including *Alabama* and *Vim*, the winners of the cruising boat and speedboat divisions of the 1908 and 1909 New York–Poughkeepsie Races. His *Vision* of 1905 held the world record for the mile championship in 1907. But in flat-out "drag" racing, such as the famous Harmsworth Trophy races, he wasn't unique in having his genius eventually eclipsed by that of the Crane brothers. Like Clinton Crane, Herreshoff seemed to lose interest following the arrival of the hydroplane type in 1910 and thereafter concentrated his energies on automobiles.

—Iain McAllister

HALSEY C. HERRESHOFF

Born September 6, 1933 · United States

A native of Bristol, Rhode Island, Halsey Herreshoff is a member of the eminent Herreshoff family. Captain Nathanael Herreshoff, cofounder with his brother John of the famed Herreshoff Manufacturing Company, was his grandfather, L. Francis Herreshoff was his uncle, and A. Sidney DeWolf Herreshoff was his father.

Herreshoff earned a degree in naval architecture at Webb Institute and a master's degree in mechanical engineering at MIT. He opened his design practice on the site of the defunct Herreshoff yard, later also the site of the Herreshoff Marine Museum. His designs have often incorporated shapes and elements of the best of the earlier vessels designed by his father and grandfather. Most notable among these are a 56-footer designed for Garry Hoyt and *Duende*, drawn for James Clark. More than ten thousand vessels have been built to his designs. Many of these were small and popular production sailboats built by Chrysler and Bristol Yachts. He also provides restoration services for Herreshoff yachts.

As president of the Herreshoff Marine Museum, which was founded by his parents in 1971, Herreshoff oversees the sixty-some vintage Herreshoffs in various stages of restoration. In 1992, his longtime interest in the America's Cup led to the founding of the America's Cup Hall of Fame at the museum. Over a period of twenty-five years he probably sailed more miles in 12-Meters off nearby Newport than anyone. He was a crewmember on *Columbia* in 1958, on *Courageous* in 1974, on *Freedom* in 1980, and on *Liberty* in 1983.

—B. Devereux Barker III

LEWIS FRANCIS HERRESHOFF

November 11, 1890–December 3, 1972
United States

L. Francis Herreshoff was perhaps the United States' finest designer/writer. Both of his talents were so notable that he undoubtedly could have become famous on the strength of either one alone. While times, technology, and tastes have changed in many ways since he was practicing, his designs are still being built in

significant numbers, and his books are eagerly devoured by each new generation of sailors that comes along.

As a son of Nathanael Herreshoff, L. Francis had a tough act to follow. He neither emulated his father nor distanced himself from him, but instead seems to have deliberately designed not just his boats, but also the nature of his career.

Unlike Nathanael, he did not become a boatbuilder even though his background made him one of the best-qualified people of his generation to do so. Nor did he attempt the incredible productivity of his father. Instead he concentrated on the production of beautiful and highly detailed plans intended to be viewed not just by boatbuilders, but by the less knowledgeable general public.

Apparently it took him a great deal longer to prepare a design than it did his father, but the plans were far more detailed. Many of his boats were more artistic conceptions than Nathanael's, many of whose designs were technologically excellent first and aesthetically pleasing second (though a close second). The most profound difference, however, is

L. Francis Herreshoff: *Live Yankee.* The 39-foot 6-inch LOA *Live Yankee* was among the designer's more radical yachts and was often described as the boat that killed the Universal Rule R Class because of her racing successes. She was built by Britt Brothers in West Lynn, Massachusetts, in 1927. *Photo courtesy Newport Harbor Nautical Museum, Newport Beach, CA*

L. Francis Herreshoff: *Fleetwing.* Herreshoff was an advocate of the Square-Meter classes. The relatively straightforward rule restricted sail area to fixed maximums according to the size of yacht desired, and encouraged a long and light hull of pleasing proportions and with useful accommodations. *Fleetwing*, a 30-Square-Meter, was built in 1932. *Photo courtesy Peabody Essex Museum, Salem, MA*

L. Francis Herreshoff: *Whirlwind.* Herreshoff's J-Class yacht *Whirlwind* failed to win the right to defend the America's Cup in 1934, but she is believed to have had great unrealized potential. She had the largest headsails of any J-Class boat, and with her canoe stern is thought by many to have been the most beautiful of her class. © *Mystic Seaport, Rosenfeld Collection, Mystic, CT*

how the younger Herreshoff wrote about many of the designs, describing the thinking behind them and the way they should be built. He became a virtual mentor to much of the boating world, whereas Nathanael wrote hardly a word on the subject.

Herreshoff paid particular attention to each yacht's hardware, which is as classically beautiful and functional as the rest of the boat, and he had an instinctive understanding of the engineering involved. It is said that if a Herreshoff turnbuckle is stressed to the breaking point, it shows simultaneous failure in all its parts, indicating remarkable balance in its proportions. Small wonder that ads for Herreshoff boats sometimes emphasize "Herreshoff-designed hardware."

Herreshoff designed some big, famous boats, such as the J-Class *Whirlwind*, the M-Class *Istalena*, and the spectacular 71-foot ocean racing ketch *Landfall*. His 72-foot *Ticonderoga* (launched as *Tioga* in 1936) is one of the most successful and beloved "maxi" ocean racers ever designed, with many record-breaking passages to her

credit and with a host of reproductions, near-reproductions, and larger derivative designs having been built in recent years. Still it is breathtaking to see how casually the designer refers to these accomplishments, which are obviously in one sense the pinnacle of his career, and it is revealing to note the love and fascination that he expresses when writing about some of his smallest designs.

At heart Herreshoff, heir to America's foremost yachting dynasty, was a minimalist. In his writing he reveals himself to be the sailing equivalent of Henry David Thoreau, stressing simplicity, wholesome singlehanded and family cruising, economy, an intense appreciation of nature, and the physical and psychological benefits of coastal cruising in sensible boats with ordinary people.

Modern readers—who are better acquainted with the economies of production-built boats and the minimalism of Herreshoff's philosophical successor, Phil Bolger, than with the world in which Herreshoff was writing—are apt to look at his designs and find them to be at

odds with the writing. Compared to some of our modern equivalents, Herreshoff boats are actually expensive, complicated, and difficult to build. But set in their time they were indeed artistically pleasing, often simple, and functional, and many (but not all) could be produced economically by any of the local boat-building shops.

Today many of the boats continue to be built, but it is mostly for the art in them, even though they are still excellent investments as boats go, particularly if they are built as called for in the plans and outfitted as simply as suggested in the specifications. Of course the true cost of a vessel is not known until she is eventually sold—Herreshoff strongly believed that beautiful boats were the most apt to be well maintained and to hold their value.

As with any creation that comes to be called a classic, Herreshoff's designs must be viewed as a whole to be understood. A good example is Rozinante, a canoe yawl that the designer suggested was the ultimate in simplicity and economy in her size. In fact she is a fairly expensive boat—other designers have produced functionally similar designs that cost much less. But few go so far as to suggest that it is possible to improve on Rozinante.

Once we move beyond initial cost, Rozinante continues to exhibit all the other virtues Herreshoff attributed to her: a comfortable means of getting up close and personal with nature, soothing the mind through simple activities and really good sailing. Most of the changes that have been tried—different rigs, more intricate interiors, inboard motors, complicated equipment—haven't worked out well. Like any true classic she has proved to be one of the most change-resistant and beloved boats ever designed, suggesting that there will be Rozinantes under construction as long as there are boats and nature and books.

While Rozinante is probably the most famous of Herreshoff's small yachts, he is also well known for the H-28, another ketch-rigged cruising boat that was conceived as a simple, economical yacht. The How-to-Build articles on the H-28, that appeared in *The Rudder* magazine in the early 1940's, and later in the book *Sensible Cruising Designs*, are possibly the best example of writing about yacht design ever produced. Again, to modern viewers the H-28 does not appear that simple in her fundamentals, but if she is built as drawn, she is still dramatically economical in her interior, rig, and equipment, which constitute a larger portion of initial cost and maintenance than is often supposed.

Herreshoff is also well known for his 36-foot, clipper-bowed ketch *Nereia*; the unusual double-ended, three-masted motorsailor *Marco Polo*; the ultra-shoal-draft *Meadow Lark*; and a host of small sailing craft and wholesome motorboats. He was one of the first to point out in print the advantages of the double-paddle canoe as the most economical and minimalistic cruising boat, and drew several canoes and kayaks. He drew his last complete design, a 38-foot leeboard ketch, in 1963.

Born in Bristol, Rhode Island, Herreshoff attended Rhode Island State College, graduating in 1910. Remarkably, his "certificate" was in agriculture, and he was a practicing farmer for several years. He served his apprenticeship at the Herreshoff Manufacturing Company, learning all aspects of the business under his father's tutelage. He did design work for the U.S. Navy from 1917 until 1921, when he went to work for the family's friendly rival Starling Burgess at the design firm of Burgess and Paine (later Burgess, Swasey and Paine), remaining there until 1925, when he went out on his own.

Herreshoff's fame was assured when in 1925 while still one of the designers at Burgess,

L. Francis Herreshoff: *Ticonderoga*. One of the most successful "maxi" ocean racers in yachting history, Herreshoff's *Ticonderoga* was still winning major races and setting records three decades after she was built in 1936, and continues to win classic yacht regattas today. Her influence on the design of large sailing yachts is still strongly felt. © *Mystic Seaport, Rosenfeld Collection, Mystic, CT*

L. Francis Herreshoff: *Swallow*. Half a century after its introduction, Herreshoff's Rozinante design, represented here by *Swallow*, continues to be reproduced year after year. An American interpretation of the British canoe-yawl type, she was meant to be an economical engineless cruiser for those who loved the natural beauty of the coast. © *Benjamin Mendlowitz*

Swasey and Paine, he designed *Yankee* for the R-Class under the Universal Rule. She was radical in terms of her rigid and lightweight, diagonally planked, longitudinally framed construction; her sail plan (which featured a larger-than-normal jib and spinnaker made possible by advances in staying technology); her high ballast-displacement ratio; and her box section spars. The boat quickly came to dominate her class.

Two years later, working under his own name, Herreshoff designed *Live Yankee*, an even more radical R-Class boat that was virtually unbeatable. By foretelling the unwholesome direction in which designs for future Universal Rule boats would have to progress in order to compete, this boat eventually helped spell the end of the rule in classes smaller than the J-Class boats used for the America's Cup.

Herreshoff went on to design a number of racing boats including some for the 22- and 30-Square-Meter classes, which he helped to promote in the United States; the 87-foot M-Class *Istalena*; Q-Class boats including *Questa* and *Nor'Easter V*; the J-Class *Whirlwind*; the 12-Meter *Mitena*; and the ocean racer *Persephone*. Most were successful, but some were not, partly from problems getting owners and rulemakers to adapt to the radical ideas embodied in some of the designs, and partly because Herreshoff himself was not particularly helpful in tuning the boats and training their crews once they were launched. It is thought that some boats had the potential for greatness that was never realized. *Ticonderoga* alone should be proof of the designer's capacity for producing the best racing boats of his time.

But Herreshoff was not the type of designer who enjoyed adapting his ideas to handicapping systems or submitting to rules he thought were ill-founded, and eventually he stopped designing racing boats and concentrated on cruising boat design. While at first he maintained a busy office that employed draftsmen such as Samuel Brown, Fred Goeller, Norman Skene, Aage Nielsen, and Fenwick Williams, he soon decided to be a one-man operation, and shortly after *Ticonderoga* he sought smaller commissions and worked alone. He is said to have worked very slowly, and produced only 107 designs during his independent career.

Beginning in 1942, Herreshoff designed and wrote extensively for *The Rudder* magazine, with the strong encouragement of editor Boris Laurer-Leonardi, and became one of the most widely admired authorities on all aspects of yachting. He was author of *Captain Nat Herreshoff, the Wizard of Bristol* (1953, published by Sheridan House); *An Introduction to Yachting* (1963, published by Sheridan House); the classic two-volume set, *The*

Common Sense of Yacht Design (1946 and 1948, published by *The Rudder*); and the immortal (and unfortunately abridged) compilation of a series of *Rudder* articles called *The Compleat Cruiser* (1956, published by Sheridan House).

At the time of his death in 1972, Herreshoff was assisting with a book of his designs subsequently published as *Sensible Cruising Designs* (1973, published by International Marine), and later another book was published, *An L. Francis Herreshoff Reader* (1978, published by International Marine), incorporating the earlier *Writings of L. Francis Herreshoff* (1946, published by *The Rudder*).

The L. Francis Herreshoff Collection is at Mystic Seaport Museum, Mystic, CT.

—Daniel B. MacNaughton

NATHANAEL GREENE HERRESHOFF

1848–June 2, 1938 · United States

By almost any reckoning, Nathanael Herreshoff, the "Wizard of Bristol," was the greatest American yacht designer and builder who has yet lived. Beginning just after the American Civil War, his career of more than seventy years spanned an era of exuberant industrialization. His work was infused with its spirit. He dominated the America's Cup races from 1893 to 1920, designing and building all of

that period's five successful defenders. He was responsible for a series of significant improvements in the design of steam engines, and invented numerous items of yacht hardware and rigging that are in common use today.

The seeming modernity of the surviving N. G. Herreshoff boats, their quantity, and the apparent youthfulness of adequately maintained examples make it somewhat startling to realize that the midpoint of his career was approximately a hundred years ago. Herreshoff has been the standard against which other designers and builders have been judged throughout the modern yachting era, and parts of this standard are timeless good design and the potential longevity of good construction.

Considering the affection with which Herreshoff yachts are cherished today, it seems strange to note that in their day some of his designs were criticized for their looks. Herreshoff's work was at the cutting edge of technology at the time, and probably offended a certain number of people simply because it was nontraditional. And while many designers have evolved their boats from working craft, partly so as not to have to start from scratch and partly to evoke the romantic association such types carry with them, clearly Herreshoff was in another league. Whether intended as racers or cruisers, Herreshoff boats were efficient machines first and objects of beauty second, though to our modern eyes almost all are beautiful.

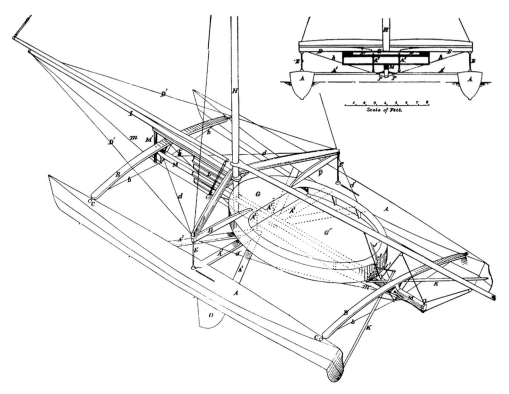

Nathanael Herreshoff: *John Gilpin.* Herreshoff's first foray into commercial boatbuilding on his own came with his patented concept for a practical sailing catamaran. Following the success of his original *Amaryllis*, he began a brief production run, of which the 32-foot *John Gilpin*, shown here, was the first. She was built in 1877. © *Chevalier & Taglang*

Nathanael Herreshoff: *Stiletto*. The 94-foot × 11-foot *Stiletto* was designed and built by Herreshoff in 1885 for his own use. With her lightweight construction and advanced steam engine, she was then the fastest steam yacht in existence, and went 26 mph in virtual silence. *Photo by Nathaniel Stebbins. Courtesy of the Society for the Preservation of New England Antiquities*

Herreshoff applied an education in engineering to the problems of yacht construction, and pioneered in light, rigid, durable structures and efficient building methods. He was among the first to recognize the advantages of reduced displacement, and was able to use his improved construction methods to achieve it along with increased ballast ratios, while also innovating in the reduction of wetted surface area. He was among the first to enthusiastically promote the multihull concept, and patented the first successful sailing catamaran in the United States. Not the least of Herreshoff's achievements was a host of one-design classes, many examples of which are still sailing.

Herreshoff grew up on the harbor at Bristol, Rhode Island, in an intellectually stimulating family of avid sailors. His father was an active yachtsman who designed and built himself a series of yachts, and his brothers were also active in boatbuilding and racing. His brother John Brown Herreshoff (1841–1915), seven years older than Nathanael, entered the boatbuilding business in 1863, despite the fact that he had been blind since age fourteen (blindness was a family trait that struck a number of Herreshoff's siblings). While a teenager,

Herreshoff designed several family-built-and-owned yachts.

In 1869, after graduating from MIT, Herreshoff went to work as a draftsman at the Corliss Steam Engine Company in Providence, Rhode Island, remaining there for nine years and gaining valuable experience in the design and construction of steam boilers and power delivery systems. During this period he designed several yachts, including the 120-foot steam yacht *Estelle*.

In 1874 he and his brother Lewis (who was blind) built a 17-foot sloop named *Riviera* and another boat named *l'Onda* on the shores of the Mediterranean. In *Riviera* they cruised on the inland waters and canals of France, Switzerland, Germany, and Holland, and on the Thames in England. They brought her back to New York on a steamer, from which she was relaunched on arrival and sailed by the brothers back to Bristol.

The young Herreshoff is believed to have been the first American to develop a practical sailing catamaran, a concept he patented in 1877. Starting with the 25-foot *Amaryllis* in 1876, Herreshoff catamarans stunned the yachting establishment. His 30-foot *Tarantella*, built

the following year, was capable of going upwind at 8 knots and close reaching at nearly 20 knots, speeds previously unheard of in so small a sailboat. Herreshoff concentrated on the design and production of catamarans for a few years, but while they attracted plenty of attention, not many were sold, probably in part because of the high price tag. Soon the rulemakers banned multihulls from competition, and Herreshoff moved on to more profitable ventures such as the development of improved steam yachts.

At age thirty-five, he married Clara DeWolf. They had six children, among whom were yacht designers L. Francis Herreshoff and A. Sydney DeWolf Herreshoff.

In 1878, Nathanael and John Herreshoff founded the Herreshoff Manufacturing Company. John Herreshoff handled the financial side of the business, benefiting from a thorough understanding of the yard's operations and the use of boats. While he had built many boats, John had not been very financially successful when working on his own. When the brothers went into business together, they resolved never to borrow money, and from that point forward the business remained on a sound

Nathanael Herreshoff: *Polly.* In the days before gasoline engines and planing hulls, length and lightness were the keys to speed. Herreshoff's steam yachts were popular partly because of his technical expertise, but also because he was able to create practical boats with gracious accommodations, like the simple and charming *Polly*. *Photo by Nathaniel Stebbins. Courtesy Lucia del Sol Knight*

footing. Nathanael was free to concentrate on creating masterpieces of the yacht-building craft and following through on their tuning and refinement. The yard found ample business without much paid advertising.

During the Herreshoff era, manufacturing in general was quickly moving from one-at-a-time, craftsman-built items to series-built standardized products made in factories. Herreshoff pioneered in semi-production-line boatbuilding methods, allowing rapid and accurate construction of any number of boats to identical specifications. By working from unprocessed raw materials such as timber, sail cloth, lead, steel, and bronze, keeping large amounts of that raw material on hand, and doing virtually all manufacturing on the premises, the entire production process was under Herreshoff control and maximum value was added to the materials.

Over three hundred people worked at Herreshoff's during its heyday, building boats with wooden, steel, and bronze hulls, in twenty-one buildings including three large hull-construction and final-assembly bays, a sail loft, foundry, machine shop, and sawmill. All of Herreshoff's designs were built at the Herreshoff yard, and he designed most of the yard's output.

Herreshoff carved half models to create his hull shapes, but he was an accomplished draftsman and produced thousands of drawings during his career. For his hulls he would draw only a profile, half breadth, and midsection before carving a model. He developed a machine for taking the lines off the models, so the offsets, which represented the full-size hull shape, could be provided for the lofting floor. While his influence in the field was to propel it toward a "scientific" approach to design, Herreshoff himself used both scientific and rule-of-thumb methods.

From 1868 to about 1891, the Herreshoffs' primary output was 169 steam-powered vessels, all designed by Nathanael Herreshoff. His quadruple-expansion engines were marvels of their time, and he was apparently the first to flatten the run of power-driven vessels to prevent them from squatting at high speeds. *Lightning*, the U.S. Navy's first torpedo boat, was designed and built by Herreshoff in 1875, and reached a then-remarkable speed of 21 knots. Two 175-foot torpedo boats (*Porter* and *DuPont*) were the longest vessels built by the Herreshoff Manufacturing Company.

The largest of Herreshoff's steam yachts were small compared to those of designers like Scotland's George L. Watson, but they were practical family cruising yachts in a way that the big yachts were not. John and Nathanael each owned steam yachts of roughly 100 feet LOA, and Nathanael used his for cruising with his family. While Herreshoff made a successful adjust-

ment to internal combustion engines, he never enjoyed being shipmates with the noisy new motors as much as he did with steam engines, which while they consumed a great deal of space were nearly silent in operation. The largest steam yacht Herreshoff built was the steel-hulled *Ballymena*, at 145 feet LOA.

This experience with steam-powered vessels honed Herreshoff's skills in the design of lightweight structures in both wood and steel. He was able to apply this expertise to sailboat design, increasing ballast ratios and often lightening displacement. He also invented lighter and more efficient hardware such as sail track and slides, and improved winches, anchors, cleats, and many other items, through careful engineering. While he did not invent them, Herreshoff was among the first to work with fin keels, bulb keels, separated rudders, folding propellers, and hollow wood and metal spars. The largest sailing yacht built by Herreshoff was the steel schooner yacht *Katoura* (1914), 162 feet LOD.

Herreshoff's dominance of sailboat racing began in 1891 when a new class of 46-foot LWL sloops was formed. This class included several boats designed by Edward Burgess, the most highly regarded designer of racing boats of his day. Relatively unknown as a designer of sailing yachts. Herreshoff designed and built the revolutionary *Gloriana* for the new class's first season. She won first place in every race that season, after which she was withdrawn for the good of the class.

Gloriana's most obvious innovation was a then-radical new bow shape. Prior to *Gloriana,* most yachts had short, sharp bows and deep forefoots. The new yacht was given a relatively long, flared, overhanging bow with a cutaway forefoot, and in one jump propelled yacht design strongly in the direction of the modern type. *Gloriana's* long overhangs gave greater waterline length when heeled under sail than at rest, fooling the rating rule into predicting a slower hull. Her flared topsides forward provided reserve buoyancy, making for a drier and more secure foredeck. The cutaway forefoot significantly reduced the wetted surface area.

Less remarked on were other innovations that probably contributed as much to her success. Herreshoff's understanding of scientific engineering enabled him to reduce weight throughout the rig and hull structure, using the weight savings to both reduce displacement and increase the percentage of the boat's displacement that was carried in the form of ballast, allowing more sail area. These innovations produced a faster and more powerful vessel.

Also in 1891, Herreshoff introduced *Dilemma,* another influential yacht. Her primary innovations were lighter-than-usual displacement, a bolted-on iron fin keel with ballast in the form of a lead bulb along its lower edge, and an abbreviated underwater profile featuring a separated spade rudder. Dull in light air due to a high ratio of wetted surface area to sail area, she was fast under other conditions and was economical to construct. *Dilemma* was the first of a long line of such boats and was a forerunner of the modern light-displacement type.

Many of Herreshoff's later designs were of a semi-fin-keel type, in which the keel was a bolted-on fin in a structural sense, but was made of wood and shaped at the top like a fair extension of the hull, providing a nearly optimum combination of simplified construction, reduced displacement and wetted surface area, and good hydrodynamic form. Herreshoff's work has continued to be viewed as one of the best all-around approaches to abbreviated underbodies and reduced displacement.

In the 46-footers, *Gloriana* was followed by the similar but even more highly developed and successful *Wasp.* The revolutionary character of these yachts led directly to the construction of the 84-foot waterline *Navahoe,* a steel cutter

with similar features, and then to the 124-foot LOA *Vigilant,* the America's Cup defender of 1893

Gloriana and *Wasp* earned Herreshoff a chance at the America's Cup defense, but he was also fortunate in his timing in that these promising successes occurred after competitor A. Cary Smith's heyday and before the rise of designer William Gardner. Herreshoff's close friend and competitor Edward Burgess had died in 1891. Thus Herreshoff was the obvious choice to design a Cup defender despite his brief experience in designing large sailing yachts. He went on to dominate the America's Cup for the next twenty-seven years, beginning with *Vigilant* (which he personally sailed in the 1893 series and which was the first large yacht to be built of bronze), *Defender* (1895), *Columbia* (1899 and 1901—the only yacht to defend the Cup twice until *Intrepid* in 1967 and 1970), *Reliance* (1903), and *Resolute* (built for the 1914 series, which was postponed until 1920 by the onset of World War I).

Herreshoff's Cup defenders showed progressive development in hull form, rig, construction and equipment, reduced weight aloft, reduced displacement, higher ballast ratios, and advantageous ratings. Things reached an extreme in *Reliance,* which had over 16,000

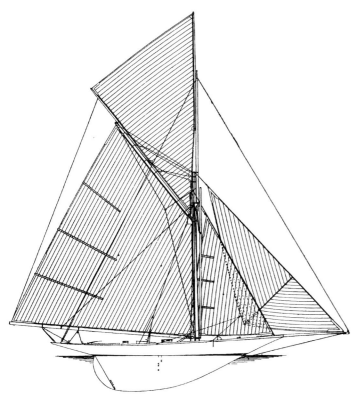

Nathanael Herreshoff: *Gloriana.* The boat that in 1891 launched Herreshoff's career as a designer of major sailing yachts, *Gloriana* was a breakthrough in part because of her then-radical overhanging bow and cutaway underbody, but also for less visible reasons such as a high ballast-displacement ratio. She was built for the 46-Foot class and was unbeatable. In one season she propelled the field of yacht design into a new era. *Reproduced from W. P. Stephens's* Supplement to Small Yachts

Nathanael Herreshoff: *Talayha.* The 102-foot marconi-rigged cutter *Talayha* was one of the Herreshoff yachts that made her mark on the West Coast of the United States. Built in 1899, she was first overall in the Honolulu Race of 1928, among other successes. She later was renamed *Athene. Photo courtesy Newport Harbor Nautical Museum, Newport Beach, CA*

Nathanael Herreshoff: *Reliance.* The boat that effectively killed the Seawanhaka rating rule, *Reliance* was the most extreme and perhaps the fastest of all the America's Cup defenders. She had the largest mainsail ever constructed, 54 feet of overhangs in 144 feet of length, and a scow-like hull. She was probably quite terrifying in a breeze. © *Mystic Seaport, Rosenfeld Collection, Mystic, CT. James Burton Photographer*

square feet of sail, more than 53 feet of hull overhangs in an LOD of 144 feet, a deep semifin keel with a huge amount of outside ballast, and a shallow, flat-floored, scow-like hull. Her many innovations included a hollow rudder that could be filled with seawater to ease her steering when heeled, twin steering wheels with foot brakes, and advanced winch designs.

It was widely agreed that in her extreme hull shape, *Reliance* had proved the faults of the old Length-and-Sail-Area handicapping rule, and by her success had made it necessary for future yachts built under that rule to emulate her, so a group was formed to consider a new rule. In 1904 they adopted Herreshoff's suggestion for what was to become known as the Universal Rule. The new rule took account of displacement for the first time, an important factor in limiting the development of extreme types.

The 106-foot LOA *Resolute*, the first Cup defender to be designed under the Universal Rule, was regarded as a much healthier design than her predecessor *Reliance*, with a deeper, less scow-like hull, and shorter, more seakindly V-shaped overhangs.

The Universal Rule was a handicapping system that allowed differing yachts to compete with each other on a somewhat equal basis, or to compete on a level basis without handicap in classes defined by a specific rating. Such classes were designated by a letter, as in the J-, M-, P-, Q-, R-, and S-Class boats. Boats built to suit the rule are considered by many to have been among the fastest under a wide range of conditions, most practical, and most beautiful of any rule-influenced designs before or since. The Universal Rule was in popular use until around 1928, when the

International Rule came into ascendancy for development classes, with the CCA Rule coming into use soon after to serve the emerging offshore cruiser/racer type.

Among Herreshoff's most popular and enduring work was a long series of one-design classes, beginning with the Newport 30 (one of the earliest one-designs in America) and ranging through such classes (designated by LWL) as the New York 30, 40, 50, 65, and 70, the Bar Harbor 31, the Buzzards Bay 15 and 25, the Newport 29, the Fish class, and the Herreshoff 12½ (also known as a Bullseye, with nearly four hundred built).

Belisarius, a 54-foot LOA yawl designed in 1935, was Herreshoff's last design, and it is interesting to note that again she is not simply a revisitation of established themes. A marconi-rigged keel/centerboard yawl, she is an early

Nathanael Herreshoff: *Chinook.* The New York 40's (40-foot LWL, 59-foot LOD), such as *Chinook*, were prized for their toughness, seaworthiness, and interior volume more than their looks, but they were driven very hard and were very competitive, earning the nickname "the Fighting Forties." They were knockabout sloops, meaning they carried no bowsprit. © *Mystic Seaport, Rosenfeld Collection, Mystic, CT*

example of what would become a typical CCA type. She also displays a radical bow with a strongly concave profile and long, narrow, V-shaped overhang serving all the functions of a bowsprit while being strictly a continuation of the hull.

Herreshoff is said to have been a man of few words, blunt, and a very hard worker. He was well respected by his workers and had a number of warm, lifelong friendships. His writing has a cool, calm, professional, and personable tone, which may be a good indication of his personality.

John B. Herreshoff died in 1915, and both Nathanael and the business suffered from the loss of his skills. John's heirs sold his stock in the company, and Nathanael sold most of his soon thereafter, though he continued to help manage the yard.

In 1924 the majority of the company's assets were acquired by the Haffenreffer family at auction; Herreshoff continued on as an advisor. He died in Bristol at age ninety, just a few months prior to the 1938 hurricane that destroyed much of the plant and many of the boats he had created.

The Herreshoff Manufacturing Company continued on until just after World War II, when the business was liquidated. The last boat built was a Fishers Island 31 (designed by Sydney DeWolf Herreshoff), hull No. 1521. Today the Herreshoff Marine Museum is located on the site of the Herreshoff yard.

The Herreshoff drawings are at Hart Nautical Collection, MIT Museum, Cambridge, MA, as well as the Herreshoff Marine Museum, Bristol, RI.

—Daniel B. MacNaughton

LYLE HESS

1912–July 12, 2002 · United States

The careful reader of this book may note that while some designers achieve great prominence and financial success, many others fail to make a living at the trade or struggle all their lives for recognition. Very often the difference seems to have as much to do with luck and good clients as with the quality of the work, and in no case is this more clearly illustrated than in the career of Lyle Hess.

Hess was one of the world's most respected designers of offshore cruising boats, but in the 1950's his tradition-based boatbuilding and design career was running contrary to the trend, so he left the business for fifteen years. Only when the now-famous liveaboard voyagers Larry and Lin Pardey spotted the

Lyle Hess: *Renegade*. This handsome and traditional 25-foot cutter was built at Hess's yard in Harbor City near San Pedro, California, in 1950. Her amazing success in both racing and long-distance cruising spurred additional designs for such well-known world cruisers as Larry and Lin Pardey's *Seraffyn* and *Taleisin. Photo courtesy Thomas G. Skahill*

Hess-designed cutter *Renegade,* tracked Hess down, and convinced him to design them a similar boat, did his career pick up again. The result was *Seraffyn,* one of the best and most thoroughly publicized liveaboard cruising boats of a generation.

Seraffyn's successful circumnavigation and other voyages, and the books and articles produced by the Pardeys, found an enthusiastic audience all over the world. Her traditional design and carefully selected gear and construction contributed to a revival of interest in quality wooden boats and in Lyle Hess's design work.

Hess turned out other unique and varied cruising boats. The *Renegade/Seraffyn* theme,

in which the appearance and characteristics of the traditional English cutter type were combined with American proportions and a more modern rig, has been revisited in several designs including *Taleisin,* a larger version for the Pardeys. The type has seen several meticulous executions in wood, under the strict control of the designer, and has also been built of fiberglass as the 28-foot Bristol Channel Cutter and the 22-foot Falmouth Cutter, some of which were offered as bare hulls for the owner to complete.

Other well-known Hess designs include the utterly untraditional but successful Balboa 20 and 26; the highly regarded Nor'sea 27, a trail-

erable traditionally styled double-ender; and the wildly popular Fatty Knees dinghy, of which over two thousand have been sold.

Hess's designs serve to point out the error in the assumption that traditional types are only good as character boats. When turning one's attention to modern types, it is easy to miss the difference between older ideas that are useful and those that are truly obsolete. For instance, the Hess boats have heavy-displacement, full-keel hulls, but their construction is carefully conceived to avoid excess weight, and all the weight not needed in the construction or contents of the boat is put into outside ballast, not the inside/outside combination that used to be seen. With firmer bilges and wider beam than the older cutter types, the result is a boat that really carries sail.

Unlike many traditional designs, which were created back when auxiliary power first became practical and were deliberately configured with short rigs, the Hess boats aren't just capable of carrying sail—they carry it. The long bowsprit and boomkin are used to form the base of a really substantial sail plan, usually of the marconi form. And again, unlike the older types, this sail plan is stayed so as to allow big, long-luffed headsails to stand to the weather as well as they would on a more typical modern boat.

All this adds up to a boat with tremendous available power—a Hess cutter can sail at her maximum speed for longer than just about any other type—as well as a broad range of stability, in a type that is comfortable for her crew, easily controlled, and utterly seaworthy. In the real world of offshore voyaging, that is the best-possible definition of the much-abused phrase *high performance.*

Lyle Hess grew up on the waterfront in Long Beach, California. There he taught himself to build boats, his earliest efforts being pieced together from scrap wood with the advice of local boatbuilders. He educated himself in the subject of yacht design largely by poring over back issues of boating magazines, especially British magazines, from which he acquired his lifelong fascination with the small, tough, liveable boats for which the British have always had a knack. English designer/writer Maurice Griffiths was one of his most important influences.

Unfortunately Hess entered his working life at the onset of the Depression, so he was unable to pursue his interests until World War II, when he obtained work building boats for the war effort. After the war he opened a boatbuilding shop and built several successful boats, including *Renegade,* which despite her tradition-based design twice won the Ensenada Race.

But Hess's interest in traditional design and construction was out of sync with the times, and he soon had to turn to bridge design and construction work to get by. The combination of his fortuitous meeting with Larry and Lin Pardey and the worldwide revival of interest in boats of the type Hess loved relaunched his career. —Daniel B. MacNaughton

HENRY R. HINCKLEY

1907–June 6, 1980 · United States

Although Henry Hinckley is better known as a boatbuilder than a designer, several designs can be attributed to him, including his yard's early powerboats, several early sailboats, and a couple of sailboat designs in the 1970's. More typically his yard built products following other designers' plans, notably stock wooden boats by Sparkman and Stephens and John Alden in the early years, and production fiberglass yachts designed by William Tripp, McCurdy and Rhodes, Bruce King, and Sparkman and Stephens in later years.

Hinckley was born in Northampton, Massachusetts. His family summered in Southwest Harbor, Maine. He graduated from Cornell University in 1932 with a degree in aeronautical engineering, and that summer, with help from his father, founded the Henry R. Hinckley firm. The Hinckley boatyard in Southwest Harbor, Maine,

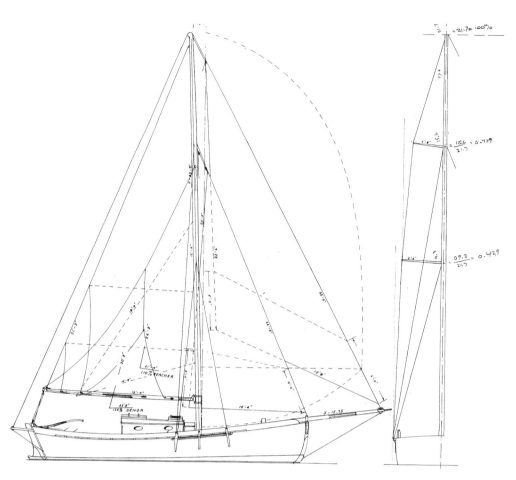

Lyle Hess: *Seraffyn*. The 24-foot 4-inch *Seraffyn* was the world cruiser that Hess designed for Larry and Lin Pardey. It was built in 1968. With their twelve-year odyssey on *Seraffyn* without an engine and only a sweep oar for power, the Pardeys started something of a revolution in world cruising for small sailboats. Today *Seraffyn*'s home port is in Beaufort, North Carolina. *Drawing courtesy Thomas G. Skahill*

Henry Hinckley: *Marmac*. In later years Hinckley would concentrate on boatbuilding, hiring others to do the design work, but he was educated as an aeronautical engineer and personally produced a number of successful designs himself. This crisp-looking, 42-foot powerboat, built by Hinckley in 1939, is a good example. It runs fast and level without much impression of effort. *Photograph by Nathaniel Stebbins. Courtesy Lucia del Sol Knight*

Andre Hoek: Truly Classic 65. Were it not for her modern spars and hardware, the Truly Classic 65 might pass for a yacht from any decade of the twentieth century, until she is hauled, at least. Below the waterline she is all modern, with great emphasis on reduced wetted surface area, allowing remarkable speed. *Photo courtesy Andre Hoek*

Andre Hoek: *Adèle*. This photo of the 180-foot aluminum ketch *Adèle* under construction conveys both the extraordinary size of the yacht and the successful combination of classic aesthetics and modern underbody that has made Hoek a major player in the large-yacht field. *Photo courtesy Andre Hoek*

got its start when young Henry was told to tear down the old boatyard on a piece of property his father had recently bought. Instead he began to fix it up and work on boats—it was too fascinating to resist.

Initially the Hinckley yard concentrated on producing cruising sailboats at a modest cost, and at one time it was believed to be the largest builder of stock auxiliaries in the country. The yard made the switch to fiberglass in 1960, being among the first in the world to do so, and soon began to aim at the top of the market, where quality and reputation were more important than cost. The yard is now recognized for building some of the best fiberglass boats in the world.

Henry Hinckley died in a car accident in 1980.

—Lucia del Sol Knight

EDMUND HINDENBERG

1818–1907 · Germany

As a young man, Edmund Hindenburg went to sea in his own merchant ship. The venture was sufficiently profitable to allow him a relatively carefree life thereafter, so he was able to play an active role in the development of yachting for over fifty years. Ultimately he became known as the Nestor of Berlin yachting. He often stayed in Hamburg but lived in Berlin and was one of the first members of the Mitgliedern der Berliner Segler-Vereinigung, der Tavernen-Gesellschaft (Berlin Sailing Club), a group of like-minded spirits.

He was a very successful sailor, but was also well known as a "boat doctor," rerigging, repairing, and modifying boats to improve their performance. From his drawing board came a whole fleet of successful pleasure boats, with an emphasis on centerboard cruisers.

—Volker Christmann

ANDRE HOEK

Born May 2, 1955 · The Netherlands

As young boys, Andre Hoek and his brother actively raced a traditional Dutch yacht called a Lemster Aak, and the young designer-to-be soon began modifying this traditional leeboard type so it would win more races against its peers. This move was not calculated to please his traditionalist opponents, but it gave Hoek a reputation for successful innovation within the bounds of traditional aesthetics. The reputation has served him well ever since, in a career that now includes the design of very large, high-performance cruising yachts.

Born in Amsterdam, Hoek grew up in a sailing family and raced Flying Juniors and 470's as well as traditional leeboard yachts. He studied marine engineering at the Polytechnicum in Haarlem, graduating in 1977 and adding a degree in naval architecture in 1980. He concluded his studies with a master's degree in economics from Websters University.

Hoek apprenticed at C&C Yachts in Canada, where he was involved in the design of various one-offs and series-built boats. Returning to the Netherlands, he took a job as salvage inspector and chief ship's engineer at ITC, a company employing submersible ships and barges in the transport of offshore drilling rigs. His racing career came to include successes in the One-Ton Class and in IMS 40's.

In 1986 Hoek opened a small design office in Amsterdam. The firm prospered and in 1988 relocated to Edam, where it is presently situated, in offices converted from a beautiful former orphanage dating from 1567.

Having acquired an understanding of fluid-flow dynamics, Hoek started his activities as a designer with a continuation of controversial modifications: he developed for traditional Dutch yachts leeboards with a dynamic wing profile providing hydrodynamic lift. His earliest successes were his modifications to several barges, making them more successful in the racing matches—"Skutsjes"—between sailing barges that are traditional to villages in the northern part of the Netherlands.

After these first successes, Hoek totally redesigned the traditional Lemster Aak type, using computerized speed prediction and design methods, a breach of tradition in a world where rules of thumb had been the guidelines for centuries.

Several of these Hoek designs were built in the 1980's and immediately began to win races. This presented members of the traditional establishment in Holland with a problem. They could accept the new boats and face having them win any race in which they participated, or they could take action. They chose action: a committee was formed to judge whether Hoek's designs should be barred from competition.

After intense discussions, the committee concluded that Hoek's designs were well within the parameters of the established Lemster Aak type, and that type amounted to a restricted development class, not a one-design. This decision in Hoek's favor was a tremendous success for the young designer and paved the way for an unprecedented number of new Lemster Aaks.

In 1988 Hoek received a commission for the 70-foot steel ketch *Kim.* This new design was a breakthrough in Hoek's career. Above the waterline *Kim* has a sweeping sheer, rather

long ends, classic deck structures, and other details reminiscent of the most beautiful designs of the past, while the underbody is very modern and abbreviated, making her a formidably fast boat. Hoek's rare ability to pull off this combination with total success in both the performance and the aesthetic aspects of the design positioned him perfectly to serve a generation of well-informed and well-to-do clients looking for just such a boat.

Kim was the first in a line of modern classics that continues to grow to this day. The "Truly Classic" series of boats 56, 64, 75, and 85 feet in length established an international name for Hoek's firm. Further work has included similar yachts ranging in size up to a 262-foot schooner. There have also been a number of motoryachts following the same design philosophy of classic good looks combined with modern amenities and performance. Hoek Design has also studied and optimized the famous Anker-designed Dragon One-Design, staying within the class rules but using the tolerances specified in those rules to produce a particularly fast boat.

The firm extensively uses computer velocity prediction programs, plus towing tank and wind-tunnel data to achieve optimum performance even in its most traditional designs.

In 1990, together with his wife Ineke, Hoek started Dutch Built, a virtual boatyard, having a permanent office with ten employees but contracting out the actual construction of the yachts. The firm succeeded and was bought out by Holland Jachtbouw in 1998. Hoek has also done refits, such as the Sparkman and Stephens *Tempest* for a Swedish owner.

In spite of plentiful and tough competition in the field, Hoek is regarded by many as the foremost expert when it comes to designing and optimizing traditional Dutch yachts, and a formidable designer of classic racing yachts.

—Rutger ten Broeke

BARON G. W. W. C. VAN HÖEVELL

1910–1994 · The Netherlands

Baron van Höevell received formal training in engineering and started his career as a designer with the aid of a small inheritance. He participated in design competitions in Holland and the United Kingdom, and in 1936 won a contest sponsored by the Dutch association of yachting clubs with his design for *Sea Horse.* After several of his plans were published in international yachting magazines (including *Yachting World, Yachting Monthly,* and *Die Yacht*), van Höevell achieved international recognition, resulting in an increasing number of design commissions.

Baron G. W. W. C. van Höevell: *Witte Raaf* (White Raven). The 53-foot keel/centerboard ketch *Witte Raaf II* was designed as an RORC racer. She was built of steel. *Photo courtesy Rutger ten Broeke*

Baron G. W. W. C. van Höevell: *Oranjebloesem* (Orange Blossom). *Oranjebloesem* was a highly successful design, of which both steel and fiberglass versions were built. While the 29-foot yacht brought the pleasures of coastwise cruising to numerous Dutch families, it was also employed for more adventurous offshore voyages. *Photo courtesy Rutger ten Broeke*

Höevell's credo was "A yacht should accommodate the entire crew." This was an unusual point of view at a time when the owner would reside in relative comfort in his own berth, while the crew had to be satisfied with improvised pipe cots in the fo'c'sle, which they shared with each other and perhaps with wet sails.

In the Netherlands during World War II, there was relatively little for a young, aspiring yacht designer to do. Most boatbuilding, except for the German forces of occupation, came to a standstill. Yet van Höevell kept himself busy. He designed for himself *Kortjakje* (Little Red Riding Hood), a 24-foot RORC yawl in which he incorporated many of his ideas on boatbuilding and yacht design. She had an outboard rudder like the Scandinavian Folkboat and was elegant, fast, and well balanced. About six yachts were built to this design in yards such as the van de Stadt yard in Zaandam, and they proved successful in North Sea and Atlantic races.

Immediately after *Kortjakje*, van Höevell created a very successful design, *Witte Raaf* (White Raven), a 44-foot ketch that did very well in races after the war. After *Witte Raaf*, the client ordered *Witte Raaf II*, which made her mark in various international races. She was one of the participants in the infamous Fastnet Race of 1961 that was canceled in midcourse due to gales. *Witte Raaf II*, with her designer on board, managed to reach Falmouth safely.

Van Höevell was the cofounder and first chairman of the Nederlandse Vereeniging van Kustzeilers (the Dutch Association of Coastal Yachtsmen) in 1946, an organization that promoted offshore sailing. It allowed full membership only after the candidate had sailed more than a thousand miles offshore. The organization was still prospering in the year 2000, with about three hundred members.

In 1962 van Höevell was instrumental, together with Professor Wiebe Draijer and Professor Gerritsma at the Polytechnicum in Delft,

in founding the Delft Denk Tank (Think Tank), a group of prominent yacht designers. The goal was to do scientific research on the physics of yacht construction and make the results accessible to the broader community of designers. Many outstanding Dutch designers, including Ericus van de Stadt, Willem de Vries Lentsch, Dick Zaal, Jacques de Ridder, and Dirk Koopmans, participated in the experiments, which have contributed greatly to the quality and development of Dutch yacht design.

Van Höevell designed *Oranjebloesem* (Orange Blossom) in 1960, a 30-foot sloop with a small doghouse and a raised foredeck. *Oranjebloesem* was his first fiberglass production boat and became a significant success. Of twenty-nine that were built, twenty-eight are still sailing.

Besides his work as a practicing yacht designer, van Höevell was a cofounder in 1968 of the Association of Dutch Naval Architects and played an active role in it. He was the only

Dutch member of the RORC, a British club, and in that function introduced the International Rule to Dutch boat design, which enabled the Dutch yachting community to participate in international races.

Van Höevell's career is typified by modesty and openness. He did not favor designing for the upper class and had only a modest role in designs for larger production yachts. He rarely worked with others, but had a few successful assistants, one of whom, Dirk Koopmans, became a great designer in his own right.

—Rutger ten Broeke

ARTHUR HOLGATE

Born 1930 · South Africa

At the age of fourteen, Arthur Holgate ran away to sea, spending the next three years on the barque *Lawhill,* after which he tried his hand at whaling. Marriage turned him toward a career on shore and he soon made his fortune with his A. C. Holgate Transport Company.

The sea continued to call, however, and after the death of his wife in 1959, he sailed with a friend to Australia. On his return, he de-

signed and built the steel-hulled schooner *Tich,* launched in 1961. Holgate sailed *Tich* as a charter boat for two years and then sold her in New York.

In the following years, Holgate designed, built, and sailed as charter boats a series of 75- to 95-foot steel-hulled schooners. Sold in the United States, the *Lorraine, Antares,* and *Jessica* are the best known. He still lives in the Cape of Good Hope and sails the waters of its bays.

—Tom Roach

RONALD JOHN HOLLAND

Born January 29, 1947 · New Zealand/Ireland

"O.E."—Overseas experience—is so ingrained in Kiwi culture that many New Zealanders take "the big trip" to see the rest of the world before settling down. Not only did Ron Holland see how the other hemisphere lived, but he also became a world-beater, a Kiwi who took on the best of the European and American race-boat designers. Holland became the "establishment" in IOR design in the 1970's and early 1980's before shrewdly and successfully changing tacks into the design of large yachts.

Lately he has become a pioneer in the 200-foot-plus market.

For a man who in his own words "failed miserably academically," the sea offered a whole store of wisdom. The Holland family lived in Torbay, one of Auckland's north-shore suburbs. His father gave Ron a 7-foot 6-inch P-Class dinghy for his seventh birthday. No matter that he capsized on his first outing or that he only sailed it in ankle-deep water for the next twelve months, the little Optimist-like pram propelled Holland into a sailing life, just like many other great Kiwi sailors.

Moving into the Flying Ant class, Holland became involved with a design from John Spencer, a designer who, if perhaps not sufficiently recognized outside his own shores, nonetheless helped set the light-displacement agenda there, so keenly embraced by the likes of Holland, Jim Young, Bruce Farr, and Paul Whiting.

By age twelve Holland had moved into bigger boats and three years later completed a 1,000-mile Auckland-Sydney passage on the 38-foot Alden ketch *Aloha.* "That was fulfilling a pretty big ambition," recalls Holland. "I had my fifteenth birthday in Sydney and went back to school for another year where I just didn't do

Ron Holland: *Imp.* Like many designers of large sailing yachts combining sophisticated sail-handling gear with high-performance hulls, Holland got started in IOR ocean racing. The 40-foot *Imp* was a breakthrough boat that won the 1977 Admiral's Cup as well as the SORC and the St. Francis Yacht Club Big Boat Series. © *Alastair Black/PPL*

anything. All I really wanted to do was go cruising in the Pacific."

In place of school, Holland started a boat-building apprenticeship with Brown's Bay sailor Keith Atkinson. One of the first yachts he worked on was a development of the Sparkman and Stephens–designed *Clarion of Wight*. But the five-year apprenticeship was poorly suited to a young man with Holland's wanderlust. "The guy I was working for wouldn't let me go ocean racing and there were a couple of races that came up that I really wanted to do," so he left.

John Spencer introduced Holland to American businessman George Kiskaddon, who had just commissioned a design for a 70-foot, plywood, light-displacement schooner. "This guy's just your cup of tea," Holland remembers Spencer telling him. "Because the design was so radical in its light displacement and beam to length ratio, they decided to build a 24-foot model. When Kiskaddon came down to go sailing in it in Auckland, I was one of the guys who went out with him and Spencer."

The 70-footer was called *New World* and for Holland, it was. When the scale model was completed, he went to San Francisco with the boat to feed information back to Spencer. There he met Warwick "Commodore" Tomkins and started ocean racing in the United States. The young man who could hold his own on the deck of an offshore racer and who drew boats in his schoolbooks and not much else had found his calling.

Among Tomkins's sailing circle were Gary Mull and Tom Wylie. Holland showed Mull his drawings for a 26-footer some friends of his had built back in Auckland and got his first proper job in a design office. Soon afterward, Mull was commissioned to design the light-displacement, 42-foot *Improbable*. "If you're building in wood, there's only one place and that's New Zealand," urged Holland. So *Improbable* ended up being built in the yard in which he'd served his apprenticeship, and Holland became the yacht's captain. He delivered her across the Atlantic for the Admiral's Cup of 1971.

Wanting to get back into designing, Holland joined Charlie Morgan's office for a year but ultimately preferred to create his own yachts. He started building the Quarter-Tonner *Egythene* in his spare time. Holland gave the boat a symmetrical water plane so she remained balanced when heeled, moderate displacement to ensure a decent-sized sail plan, and plenty of beam on deck to boost crew-induced stability. She won the North American championships and took the 1973 Quarter-Ton Cup in Weymouth, England. "It got me to Europe with a reputation for my own work," recalls Holland.

A commission from an Irish client for the One-Tonner *Golden Apple* brought Holland to County Cork, Ireland, where he set up shop in Curabinny, just opposite the Royal Cork Yacht Club.

Holland's career blossomed in the 1970's. Among his IOR winners were *Silver Shamrock*, which won the 1976 Half-Ton Cup; *Manzanita*, which won the 1977 Quarter-Ton Cup; and *Tilsag*, winner of the 1978 One-Ton Cup. He and friendly rival Doug Peterson dominated the decade, effectively drawing to a close Sparkman and Stephens's hegemony of offshore racing. In the 1979 Admiral's Cup, twenty of the fifty-seven-boat fleet had been drawn by Peterson and sixteen, by Holland. He also propelled the maxi class into a new era with the first large fiberglass composite yachts *Kialoa IV* and *Condor*.

If there was one definitive Holland racing boat, it was the 40-foot *Imp*, built in 1977. She featured a novel aluminum internal-space frame Holland had developed with innovative Swedish engineer Lars Bergstrom. *Imp* was top point scorer in the 1977 Admiral's Cup and remained good enough to be the runner-up two years later.

Racing success translated into production work. In the early 1980's France's Jeanneau was the world's biggest boatbuilder, and it, along with Finland's Nautor, were excellent clients. Holland's team, which among others included Butch Dalrymple-Smith, Pat Lynch, Rob Ja-

Ron Holland: *Mirabella V.* At 245 feet, *Mirabella V* is the largest sloop ever built—328 feet from the bottom of her keel to the top of her mast. Most fittings are custom made to withstand sailing strains on an entirely new scale. Industry jargon now includes the phrase "M5 technology." *Drawing by Nevil Swinchatt, courtesy Ron Holland*

cob, and, briefly, Tony Castro, pioneered the use of computer-aided design in yacht work.

Some of Holland's early very large performance cruising yachts, such as the 90-foot *Thalassi* in 1984, the 102-foot *Gleam* in 1987, and the 100-foot *Royal Eagle II* in 1989, were for existing racing boat clients. The 102-foot *Garuda*, built in 1986, was a significant project because it brought Holland into contact with the influential designer Jon Bannenberg and escalated the trend toward collaboration between naval architects, stylists, and other designers. Another key yacht was *Whirlwind XII*, built in 1987 at Royal Huisman in the Netherlands. At the time, her sloop rig pushed the absolute upper limits of available rod rigging and furling gear, and hastened the development of captive reel winches, technology that permitted even larger sailing superyachts.

In the summer of 1993 Holland relocated his office from Currabinny to nearby Kinsale following a complete reorganization of his business. His production work continues with yards such as Discovery Yachts and Trintella in the United Kingdom. The 151-foot motoryacht *Affinity*, launched in time for the 2000 America's Cup, shows that Holland has as sure a touch for three-deck, diesel-powered yachts as for his extensive list of large sailing vessels.

Ron Holland has continued to push the limits in the realm of superyacht design. The 210-foot *Felicita West* was his first collaboration with Perini Navi, a relationship that has continued to be successful in developing a series of yachts ranging in length from 141 to 223 feet. In November 2003 Holland celebrated thirty years in Ireland with the launch of the pioneering 245-foot *Mirabella V.* At the time of her launch she was the world's largest single-masted composite sailing yacht, with a rig towering to almost 300 feet. The creation of this extraordinary yacht resulted in all involved having to rethink and redesign previously tried and tested techniques.

—Tim Jeffery

EVA-MARIA HOLLMANN

Born 1947 · Germany/United States

A designer of high-performance offshore cruising and racing boats with modern styling, Eva Hollmann has the distinction of being one of very few female yacht designers practicing. Most of Hollmann's boats are of the light-displacement type, and she has been a strong advocate of positive foam flotation. The combination of high-speed potential, full self-righting capability, and virtual unsinkability makes her designs attractive to offshore voyagers, and stakes out a middle position between multihulls, which are capsizeable but

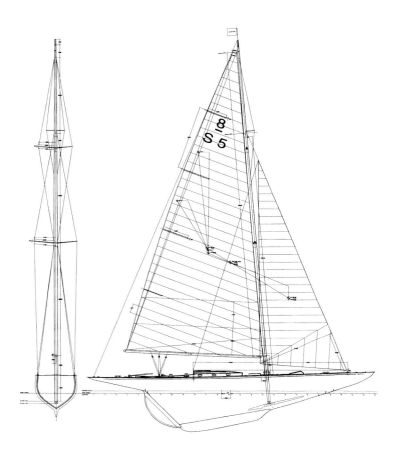

Tore Holm: *Cagg.* The 8-Meter *Cagg* was designed for the 1930 Kattegattpokalen (Kattegatt Cup). While she won the first of the three-race series, she ultimately lost to the Norwegian yacht *Silja*. Note the rounded forward end of the cabin top, a virtual signature of the designer in his 8-Meter designs. *Drawing courtesy John Lammerts van Bueren*

Tore Holm: *Gazell.* The 40-Square-Meter skerry cruiser *Gazell* was built in 1935 by Oscar Schelin at Kungsör Boatyard for A. Rydin of Norrköping, Sweden. During her first season she won both the Schubert's Cup and the W. Hellman's Memorial Prize. Her length overall was 15.35 meters, with a beam of 2.37 meters. © *Per Thelander*

often unsinkable, and heavy-displacement boats, which are often self-righting but too heavily ballasted to carry flotation.

Fantasy Two, Hollmann's proposal for a BOC Round-the-World racer, was designed to settle only 18 inches down on her lines, if holed.

Born near Hanover, Germany, Hollmann attended a technical high school and studied at Hanover Technical University and later at the Sorbonne in Paris. She was certified as a journeyman boatbuilder and naval architect at age twenty-four. She went to sea as a seaman on freighters for a few years, and then worked at the Abeking and Rasmussen yard in Bremen.

In 1971 Hollmann emigrated to the United States, working first as an apprentice for designer Britton Chance and later for Gary Mull. Her first independent design to be built in the United States was the 52-foot *Sunset Boulevard*, which took first place for Class A in the Transpac Race in 1975 and again in 1985. Hollmann's designs range in size from 8-foot dinghies to a 78-footer. The 50-foot FD-12, a fiberglass double-ender for offshore cruising, is her best-known production design. Eva Hollmann works out of an office in her home in Vista, California.

—Daniel B. MacNaughton

TORE HOLM

1896–1977 · Sweden

The most important of Tore Holm's boats were those built to the International Rule. He designed more than sixty, ranging from the 5-Meter class to the 10-Meter class, with the most numerous and successful boats being his 6- and 8-Meters.

Holm was born in Gamleby, Sweden, a small village on the Baltic coast less than a hundred miles south of Stockholm where his father, Knut Holm, owned and operated Holm's Yacht Yard. He was educated as a civil engineer at the KTH (Royal Technical High School) in Stockholm. Like many designers of his generation, he learned his trade under the eye of his designer/builder father. Tore and his brother Yngve took over the yard when their father died in 1938.

Holm's Yacht Yard served mostly Swedish and Finnish yachtsmen, few of whom had the extravagant wealth required to build and maintain the grand schooner yachts so popular among the international yachting elite. Accordingly, Holm's father concentrated on the more economical Square-Meter classes and later the International Rule classes.

The development of fast yachts in this size range became Tore Holm's abiding passion. It is impossible to be certain about his earliest work, as he is believed to have assisted his father in the design of Square-Meter boats while still in his teens. However, in 1919, four years before he completed his formal schooling, he did design a 55-Square-Meter and a 40-Square-Meter under his own name. In the following year his 40-Square-Meter *Sif*, with him at the helm, won a gold medal at the 1920 Olympic Games in Antwerp, Belgium. The fast *Britt-Marie* was built in 1921.

Conspicuous among Holm's International Rule yachts were the 8-Meters *Sylvia* and *Ilderim*. *Sylvia* won a bronze medal in the 1928 Olympics, and *Ilderim* would have won a medal at the 1936 Games had she not been disqualified in one of her races.

Of his 6-Meters, *Bissbi II* won the One-Ton Cup in 1930 and 1931 and a gold medal at the 1932 Olympics, and *Alibaba II* took two bronze medals, the first for Sweden in 1948 and the second for Finland in 1952. *Dulli* won the Gold Cup in 1933, and a series of boats, *May Be II, III, IV, VI, VIII,* and *IX*, distinguished themselves in Swedish regattas, often with Tore Holm at the helm.

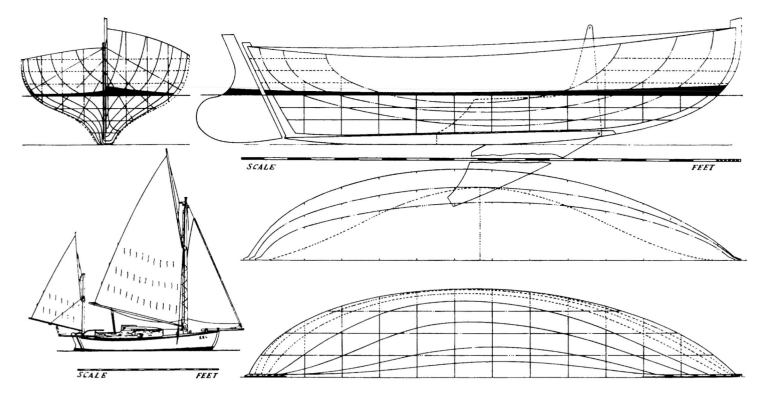

George Holmes: *Eel.* Designed and built in 1897 for her designer's own use, *Eel* illustrates the fascinating development of the small canoe yawl from Rob Roy–type cruising canoes, and was kept by Holmes for fifteen years. © *Tony Dixon*

Holm produced some offshore cruisers as well, of which the 53-foot *Havsornen,* winner of the 1937 Around Gotland race, deserves particular mention. After 1950, he produced a few more 5.5- and 6-Meters, but over the years gradually entered retirement.

—Bent Aarre with Ulf Lycke

GEORGE F. HOLMES

1861–1940 · England

George Holmes is best known for his contribution to the development of the canoe yawl type of small sailing cruiser. In one of yacht design's most fascinating vignettes, canoe yawls evolved in an unbroken progression from lightweight sailing canoes into charming and husky, small, double-ended cruising yachts with cabins. Holmes's work spans the whole period and includes examples from throughout the range of types.

Born at Hornsea on the Yorkshire coast, Holmes was the son of a prosperous local tannery owner. He started sailing in cobles while at school, but like many others following in the wake of the early canoe cruiser, John MacGregor, he became interested in canoes in the 1870's because of their low cost and portability. In 1883 he was one of the four founding members of the Humber Yawl Club (HYC) and appears to have started his design career at about the same time. He produced a succession of canoes, canoe yawls, and dinghies.

After Albert Strange joined the HYC in 1892 with his cabined canoe yawl *Cherub,* Holmes produced *Eel,* his first canoe yawl with a cabin.

At 21 feet LOA with a 7-foot beam and weighing about 1½ tons, *Eel* was designed and built for his own use. She was small enough to be transported by rail or ship but large enough to have Spartan accommodations. He kept her until 1911, when he designed and built the slightly larger *Snippet,* which he kept until his death. He continued to design small craft including canoe yawls and small motor cruisers for the rest of his life.

—Brian Smith

CARL HOLMSTRÖM

March 19, 1876–April 24, 1957 · Sweden

Carl Holmström designed about two hundred sailboats, including beautiful skerry cruisers, one-designs, and yachts under both the International Rule and the Copenhagen Rule. He was born in Malmö in southern Sweden. In 1901 he studied at the Chalmers Institute of Technology in Gothenburg, graduating as an engineer.

After apprenticing at shipyards in Malmö and Kiel, Holmström began work as a ship engineer at the big shipyards in Gothenburg. At the same time, he was a surveyor for Bureau Veritas. He started designing sailing yachts, at first fairly small boats of the popular Särklass A and Särklass B (*särklass* means a design rule that is locally accepted) as well as yachts designed to the Copenhagen Rule.

In turn-of-the-century Sweden, there was a wish for yacht racing with identical boats without the need for handicap calculations. For this purpose, Holmström designed the one-design boat Tärnor (Terns), which became very popular in the Gothenburg region. In the year 1908, when the Skerry Cruiser Rule was instituted, Holmström started to design in the classes up to 55 square meters. Beginning in the 1910's, he designed several fast 30-Square-Meter skerry cruisers to compete for the skerry cruiser trophy. One good example is *Aje,* which won the trophy in 1917.

Carl Holmström: *Toja.* The 12.50-meter *Toja* was a 40-Square-Meter skerry cruiser built at Abrahamssons and Mobergs Boatyard in 1920 in Gothenburg, Sweden, for S. Thoren. © *Per Thelander*

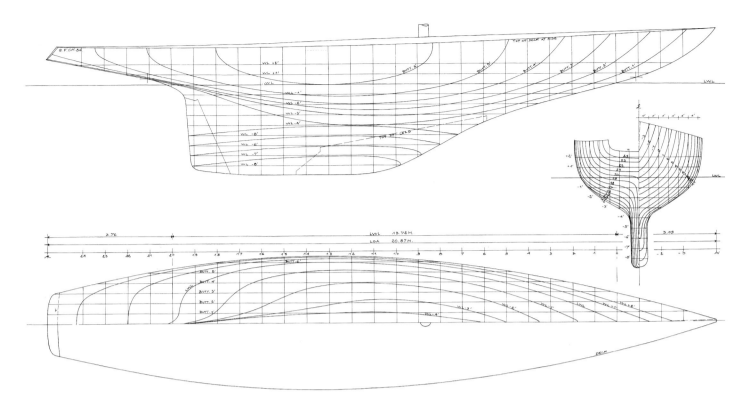

Frederick Hood: *Nefertiti*. Boston Yacht Club's entry for the 1962 America's Cup defender series, *Nefertiti* was designed and coskippered by Hood (with Don McNamera); she was only his fourth boat design. She was also a semifinalist in the 1964 series, skippered by Bill Ficker. © *Chevalier & Taglang*

Another development can be seen in the numerous 40-Square-Meter skerry cruisers around 1920. He designed lovely, long-voyage yachts. They didn't have as extreme lines as Estlander's and Westin's but had a length of about 12 meters. According to the conditions of the time, they were spacious inside, since the cabin was allowed to reach before the mast.

Within the International Rule, Holmström designed a series of successful yachts in the 6-, 8-, and 10-Meter classes. Most famous are his 6-Meter boats for the Gold Cup from the beginning of the 1920's: *Idol, Satana,* and *Konkret.* With Gustav Löfmark as helmsman, *Konkret* brought home the cup to Sweden from Hankö, Norway, in 1924.

During the first decades of the twentieth century, Carl Holmström was a frequent writer on questions of design and rules in the sailing magazines of the day. He died at the age of eighty-one.
—Ulf Lycke

FREDERICK EMMART "TED" HOOD

Born May 5, 1927 · United States

Few individuals have approached the kind of "renaissance yachtsman" status associated with Nathanael Herreshoff, but Ted Hood could well be one of them. Hood has designed and built a long list of fast, elegant, top-of-the-line cruising and racing sailboats, notably the Little Harbor and Black Watch series.

Hood is also one of the United States' most successful racing skippers. He designed, partly built, and sailed the 12-Meter *Nefertiti* for the 1962 America's Cup defender trials (at the time she was only the fourth boat he had ever designed), as well as *Independence* in 1977. He is well known as the founder of the Hood sail lofts, which dramatically innovated in sail design and construction. More recently Hood Yacht Systems, a company producing a line of roller-furling systems and other gear, has done a great deal to change the way yachtsmen look at sail handling and, indeed, the whole approach to designing rigs for cruising boats.

As a designer, Ted Hood is a master of timeless styling, which while full of traditional notions of beauty and harmony is certainly not traditional, and while thoroughly up-to-date is not at all "modernistic." A typical Hood design has a wide beam, moderately long well-shaped ends, low-to-moderate topside height, an unbroken and gracefully curved sheerline, low superstructures, deep centerboards, conventional modern rigging, and conventional interior and deck arrangements. While in many ways the boats are an exercise in moderation, they go quite a bit beyond moderate in terms of construction, equipment, and finish, and have high levels of sophistication and polish.

Below the waterline Hood designs are often much less moderate. Hood is one of the few designers who has consistently designed racing boats of rather heavy displacement, bucking the trend toward ultralight boats. At the same time the underbodies are greatly cut away, often

with a centerboard and sometimes no salient keel at all, just a whalelike hull and a rudder. The result is an extremely low wetted surface area combined with a good ability to carry sail—the recipe for excellent light-air speed—and shoal draft, which is very useful in a cruising boat.

Born in Beverly, Massachusetts, Hood grew up in a sailing family in Marblehead. At age twenty-one he began racing the family Bjarne Aas–designed International One-Design *Princess*, winning the first season's class championship using sails he had made himself. As a result, other owners began requesting that he make sails for them, and soon he was in the sailmaking business. Over the years the Hood sail lofts produced innovations in cloth technology and sail design, and at one time they were the largest manufacturer of spinnakers in the world. In the 1962 America's Cup campaign, all the 12-Meter boats, including the Australian challenger, the Alan Payne–designed *Gretel*, used Hood sails.

Hood purchased the Little Harbor Boatyard in Marblehead in 1954 and the Ted Hood Design Group was founded in 1959. The launching that year of the first Little Harbor *Robin* heralded the beginning of what was to become a series of fast, safe, and handsome yachts. *Robin* was a beamy, 40-foot LOA, shallow-draft centerboard sloop that won ten of her first fourteen races. That began a long series of Robins, some sloop-rigged, some yawl-rigged, and a long series of winning seasons.

Along with a large number of custom yachts, Hood designed such production boats as Little

Harbors ranging up to 60 feet in length, the Hinckley 43, Gulfstar 40, Hatteras 65 Sail Yacht, Tartan Black Watch 37, and five designs for Bristol Yachts. The WhisperJet 33 and 40 compete with the "picnic" type of powerboats. Hood also designed *American Promise*, a rugged offshore passagemaker in which Dodge Morgan set the speed record for a singlehanded round-the-world voyage.

The Ted Hood Company, comprising the Ted Hood Design Group, Little Harbor Custom Yachts, the Little Harbor Marine, and Little Harbor Yacht Brokers, located in Portsmouth, Rhode Island, was purchased in 1999 by the Talaria Company, which had previously purchased the Hinckley Company in Southwest Harbor, Maine. —Daniel B. MacNaughton

WARWICK JOHN HOOD, AO

Born July 1, 1932 · Australia

Australia's 1967 America's Cup challenger, the 12-Meter sloop *Dame Pattie*, is Warwick Hood's most widely known design. He was born in Westmead, New South Wales, and introduced to sailing during family holidays. At age thirteen he built his first boat, a VJ, in his backyard.

In 1950 Hood began an apprenticeship as a draftsman at Cockatoo Island Dockyard in Sydney. Concurrently he attended the five-year diploma course in naval architecture at Sydney Technical College, graduating at the end of 1954. He then worked as a draftsman at Garden Island Dockyard, Sydney. Having worked with Alan Payne at Cockatoo, Hood joined his design firm in 1956 and remained as Payne's principal assistant until 1963, when the practice closed temporarily and Hood went out on his own.

During his first year of practice, Hood designed two welded-aluminum-alloy vessels, a 13-meter power catamaran and *Yampi* (later renamed *Narranda*), an 11-meter ocean racing yacht, both representing the first use of this material in Australia. In 1963 Hood started the Hood Boat Company, which built and sold stock yachts to his design in the 1960's and early 1970's. The most popular among the designs is the Hood 23; many hundreds have been built, and it is still raced on Sydney Harbour and elsewhere.

Frederick Hood: *American Promise* (opposite). *American Promise* was the 60-foot cutter designed by Hood and built by Little Harbor Yachts for Dodge Morgan in 1985. She was designed specifically for a fast singlehanded circumnavigation. Her time of 150 days, 1 hour, and 6 minutes broke every previous singlehanded record. © *Benjamin Mendlowitz*

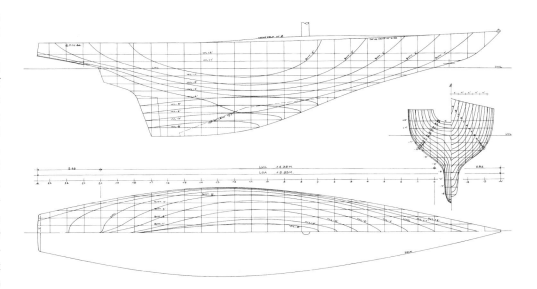

Warwick Hood: *Dame Pattie*. The 12-Meter *Dame Pattie* was Hood's 1967 America's Cup challenger, but she was no match for the Olin Stephens–designed *Intrepid*. Like *Intrepid*, she differs from the previous generation of 12's in her underwater profile, featuring a pronounced bustle aft. © *Chevalier & Taglang*

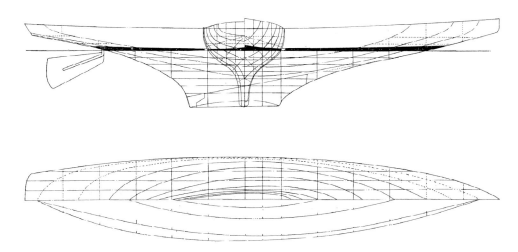

Linton Hope: *Bonito II*. The 18-foot LWL gaff sloop *Bonito II* was owned by Uffa Fox, one of his earliest boats. Fox described her as "slim and swift" and said she "taught me that a short-keeled boat with overhangs would steer herself and be easy on the helm and a very able sea boat." © *Tony Dixon*

Having worked with Alan Payne on the 12-Meter sloop *Gretel*, the 1962 America's Cup Challenger, Hood was selected to design and supervise the construction of the 1967 challenger, *Dame Pattie*. While she easily beat the much-modified *Gretel* in Australia, *Dame Pattie* lost to *Intrepid* in Newport.

Hood has designed many other yachts for both racing and cruising, in wood, steel, aluminum, and fiberglass. In 1981 he designed a 12-meter yacht to be the fastest on Lake Macquarie, New South Wales. This yacht named *Styx* easily achieved its purpose for a decade and now races on Sydney Harbour in the No. 1 Division.

In 1995 Hood was awarded the Office of the Order of Australia (AO) for services to the maritime industry of Australia as a naval architect. —Penny Cuthbert

LINTON CHORLEY HOPE

1863–December 20, 1920 · England

Linton Hope devoted much of his life to the study of hull shape and structure, whether in dinghies, yachts, racing motorboats, launches, or flying boats. His interest was always the same: to produce strength with light weight and the best shape for the purpose at hand. It is for his contribution to the evolution of the smaller, open-cockpit racing yacht that he will be best remembered. Some of his boats are still being sailed today, including the Belfast Fairies and the Broads One-Designs.

Educated at the Brighton School of Art and Science, Hope went on to found a similar establishment in Worthing, also on England's southern coast. During this period he designed three boats. One utilized an existing hull.

The next was a 13-foot dinghy built in 1884 for the Brighton Sailing Club, and in 1886 he produced *Haze*, a Three-Tonner.

Hope soon grew tired of his career in education, sold his interests, and in 1888 went to South Africa to seek wealth in the gold fields. His varying good fortune was cut short by malaria and he was forced to return to England in 1891.

While recovering from his illness, Hope joined various Thames sailing clubs and soon gained a reputation as a skilled helmsman. In 1893 he started the Thames Yacht Building Company. By 1896 he is said to have designed over forty yachts of 60 tons and over. His success with racing craft built to conform to that era's Yacht Racing Association (YRA) rules proved good for business, and his personal success with the 25-foot LOA *Kismet* contributed to his election to the YRA rating committee in 1897. This extremely light skimming dish, with her ⅛-inch-thick planking and a hull held in shape with piano wire stays, won forty firsts and fifteen of forty-five starts.

In 1900, Hope not only found time to design the Olympic Games winner *Scotia*, but also crewed in her when she won both the Half-Ton and Half- to One-Ton Class events. After this double win, the rules were changed to prevent this from ever happening again.

Hope was never afraid of innovation and was much concerned with the improvement of his era's balanced lug and gaff rigs. In 1902 he designed *Scamp*, winner of the Queen's Cup in 1903, with hollow spars and a sliding gunter rig. He also experimented with the marconi rig, which at one time he used on *Kismet*. In 1904 the Thames Yacht Building Company was closed, and a new company, primarily concerned with the design of motorboats, was set up under the name Linton Hope and Company. During this period he designed seagoing launches such as the 25-foot *Cornubia*, high-speed racing motor launches for the Harmsworth Cup like *Napier I*, and auxiliary yachts, including the 53-ton schooner *Mollihawk II*.

Lloyd's Register of Yachts for 1914 shows 168 boats designed by Linton Hope, and most of this work concerned smaller yachts under 10 tons, with just a few going up to 90 tons.

Hope's reputation earned him many commissions from abroad, with Half-Raters designed for the Naini Tal Yacht Club in the foothills of the Indian Himalayas; various Raters for the Sandgate Sailing Club of Queensland, Australia; a 14-foot dinghy for the Royal Cape Yacht Club, South Africa; and orders for motor launches for South America.

The 1913 edition of Dixon Kemp's *Manual of Yacht and Boat Sailing* lists Linton Hope as joint

C. Sherman Hoyt: *Mistress*. The 60-foot schooner *Mistress* raced successfully not only in the United States but also in Europe. She was built by Eastern Shipbuilding of Shelburne, Nova Scotia, in 1930. © *Peter Barlow*

editor, and several of his designs are to be found in this work.

World War I brought another change in Hope's career: as a member of the Royal Naval Volunteer Reserve working at the Air Board of the Admiralty, he designed seaplane floats and flying boat hulls for British aircraft manufacturers such as Supermarine and the company that became English Electric. After the war he worked as a consultant for Fairey Aviation, specializing in the design and construction of flying-boat hulls.

A number of Hope-designed yachts and one-design classes survive today, such as the Broads One-Designs and the Belfast Fairies, and many are benefiting from the current resurgence of interest in classic yachts. —Peter Daniels

CHARLES SHERMAN HOYT

1880–1961 · United States

Sherman Hoyt was born in Ohio, the son of a wealthy and established family (his grand uncle was Civil War General William Tecumseh Sherman); the Hoyt family soon moved to the Hudson River valley. They summered at Oyster Bay, Long Island, where Hoyt took to sailing at an early age, achieving considerable proficiency as a helmsman and competitor during his youth and college days. In 1901, he graduated Phi Beta Kappa from Brown University in Providence, Rhode Island, and decided to become a naval architect.

After early positions in shipbuilding and drafting, Hoyt enrolled and completed the naval architecture course at the University of Glasgow, Scotland, under Professor John Harvard Biles, the only available degree course in naval architecture in the world at the time. Here he began to make friendships and contacts that were to last throughout his life while working at the famed John Brown Shipyard at Clydebank and at Denny's in Dumbarton.

Returning to the United States at age twenty-six, Hoyt formed a partnership, Hoyt and Clark, with his longtime friend Montgomery Clark. This was based on the success of his design *Capsicum*, a Q-Class sloop that proved a winner over the racers of Clinton Crane, George Owen, William Gardner, and N. G. Herreshoff. Orders were received for additional designs, but due to a financial depression in 1908, they were never built, and the partnership was dissolved.

Hoyt obtained engineering employment with the Panama Canal Commission and then worked with Bethlehem Steel Company at the Wilmington, Delaware, plant, the former Harlan and Hollingsworth Shipyard. The year 1916 brought a commission for the U.S. Naval Reserve as senior assistant to A. Loring Swasey in the Bureau of Construction and Repair. (A similar situation pertained in 1939 at the now-named Bureau of Ships when at age sixty, Hoyt was appointed superintending constructor for the U.S. Navy with contracts with Luders, Elco, American Car Foundry, and other yacht yards during World War II.)

In 1919 Hoyt became affiliated with the firm of Gielow and Orr, and when Alec Orr retired, he became a partner in the newly formed Henry J. Gielow, Inc. Besides his 6-meter designs *Saleema, Lea, Paumonok,* and the Q-Class *Capsicum*, Hoyt's best-remembered design is the 60-foot schooner *Mistress,* designed and built in 1930. She competed very successfully in the 1932 Transatlantic Race to Plymouth and Fastnet Race, the 1934 Transatlantic Race to Bergen, Norway, and numerous offshore races on the U.S. side.

But naval architecture was a matter of choice with Hoyt, not necessity. He practiced it on and off for much of his active life, and it seems that when a decision was to be made between designing and sailing, he nearly always went sailing. He enjoyed this arrangement with the Gielow firm throughout their association from 1919 to 1932, and continued to participate in and enjoy many sailing adventures.

Hoyt's designs with Gielow were mostly sailing craft, and he often served as supervising architect at yacht yards building to Gielow designs. The 258-foot steam yacht *Delphine,* launched in 1921, is an example.

Hoyt was a legendary sailor, and there was hardly a race he didn't participate in. He was eagerly sought as a guest skipper, helmsman, or shipmate in America's Cup races, the Fastnet, the Bermuda Race, various Transatlantic Races, and virtually every other major race.

Hoyt's last years were spent in residence at the New York Yacht Club on Forty-fourth Street, where, sitting in his private chair (the only one ever so designated), he regaled fellow members and friends with stories of his experiences until his death. His book, *Sherman Hoyt's Memoirs, The best known yachtsman in the world tells the interesting story of his unique experiences at home and abroad,* published in 1950, does just that, and expertly.   —Thomas G. Skahill

GARRY HOYT

Born 1931 · United States

Garry Hoyt is known for his unusual designs and inventive mind. A former advertising executive, he turned to naval architecture in his midforties and designed the pioneering Freedom 40, a cat-ketch with an unstayed rig that was inducted by the Museum of Yachting into its American Sailboat Hall of Fame in 2000.

Growing up sailing small boats on New Jersey's Barnegat Bay, Hoyt parlayed that experience into a successful amateur sail racing record. While working for a prominent ad-

Garry Hoyt: *Blue Swanny.* For the Freedom 40 *Blue Swanny,* Hoyt designed the rig and concept and Halsey Herreshoff designed the hull. Seeking performance while retaining simplicity and ease of handling, the boat features bendy unstayed masts, a self-tending rig with a total absence of headsails, and a roomy flush deck. © *Peter Barlow*

vertising agency during the 1960's, he won world and North American titles in Snipes, Finns, and Sunfish. Hoyt was a member of the U.S. Olympic sailing team in 1968, racing in the Finn class at the Mexico City games.

Hoyt moved from small boat racing into yacht design in 1976 under the tutelage of Halsey Herreshoff, grandson of Nathanael Herreshoff. He immediately established a reputation for the unusual with the Freedom 40, a then-radical boat that was an instant success, winning several Caribbean regattas, including Antigua Race Week. Based on its success, Hoyt founded Freedom Yachts and designed five more models, ranging in length from 21 to 44 feet.

In order to concentrate his efforts on small sailboats of the type he grew up with, Hoyt sold the company in 1985. Those small boats include the Escape sailing dinghies, roto-molded craft intended for beginning sailors. Hoyt's other work includes models in the line of Herreshoff-inspired sailboats, most notably the Alerion Express Cat, a 19-footer that uses an unstayed rig.

Hoyt is the holder of several patents for sailing hardware, including a self-vanging boom, a single-line reefing system, and a spinnaker "gun-mount." He is the author of two books, *Go for the Gold* and *Ready About*.

Garry Hoyt's office is in Portsmouth, Rhode Island.

—Steve Knauth

FRANK PEMBROKE HUCKINS

1886–May 30, 1951 · United States

One of the most innovative designer/builders of fast powerboats, Frank Huckins established a boatbuilding company that continues to closely adhere to his original design concepts more than fifty years after his death.

Huckins was among the first to design planing powerboats, introducing the first of his planing designs in 1925. She featured the "quadraconic" hull form that is still in use today.

Huckins was born in East Boston. His father was a lumber dealer and his mother, a talented finish carpenter. His education complemented his natural engineering skills, and he began building boats for himself at an early age. When his father died, he inherited the lumber business.

A business connection in Florida led to Huckins's eventual migration to Jacksonville, where he became part owner of a successful millwork business. It quickly evolved into a boatbuilding operation, taking full advantage of the millwork factory's well-established production capability and proximity to the water. The Huckins Yacht Corporation built hull No. 1, the Fairform Flyer 42-foot Express Cruiser, in 1928. From the beginning Huckins's

designs were referred to as Fairform Flyers.

Huckins had strong ideas about how his boats should be designed, built, and finished. Working for much of his career with engines that had power-weight ratios barely sufficient for his purposes, and recognizing the importance of minimum overall weight in high-speed powerboats, he acquired a reputation for fanaticism concerning weight, patenting some aspects of his laminated construction methods, designing many fittings of aluminum, using curtains instead of doors in many parts of his yachts' interiors, holding water and fuel tank capacities to a minimum, and seeking simplicity in all aspects of design and construction. He abhorred flying bridges due to their weight and windage.

On the one hand, Huckins was willing to fight with owners to hold their boats to his detailed design specifications, right down to the paint colors (almost all the boats had minimum brightwork and were painted light gray on the exterior), while on the other hand, a client ordering a boat was presented with a vast array of Huckins-approved options and every boat came with an owner's manual designed to help with every detail on the use, maintenance, and repair of the boat. No two boats were alike, but all had the approval of Frank Huckins or they were not built.

Safety was an important consideration, and Huckins's boats kept the fuel tanks and engines in separate compartments, featured elaborate

drain systems to quickly channel away any fuel leaks, and had a range of innovative warning lights as well as carefully laid-out watertight compartments.

Huckins played an important role in the development of the PT boat design for World War II, and while his company built only eighteen and none of these saw action with the enemy, they were widely regarded as a superior boat.

The designer cruised extensively on the East Coast between Florida and Canada, serving as a charismatic salesman for his product. He competed often and successfully in predicted log contests, and was one of the founding members of the U.S. Power Squadron. He wrote all his own ad copy and had a popular regular column in *Motor Boating* magazine called "Huck says," which for years paid him exactly what his advertising in that magazine cost.

The Grand Manan 45 was Huckins's last design. To this day, Huckins motoryachts are considered to be among the best-performing powerboats, featuring a smooth ride, good fuel economy, and level running, the bows rising only about 2 to 3 degrees at speed without the help (and drag) of trim tabs.

The Huckins Yacht Corporation continues to build fiberglass boats very similar to those designed by Frank Huckins, and also restores and maintains the wooden originals.

—Daniel B. MacNaughton

Frank Huckins: Fairform Flyer. Huckins's design for his yard's Hull No. 1 displayed many of the characteristics that define a Huckins yacht today. A long, light, easily-driven, V-bottom hull that planes easily with little change in trim, she was comfortable, practical, and twice as fast as conventional yachts of her day. © *Mystic Seaport, Rosenfeld Collection, Mystic, CT*

ROBERT DAVID "ROB" HUMPHREYS

Born 1950 · England

"I still believe in the principle that if it looks right, it is right," says Rob Humphreys, who is Welsh to the core and has lost none of his accent despite living for more than twenty years in Lymington on England's south coast. Humphreys also believes that a designer "should cut his teeth on racing yachts," though he admits that some of his out-and-out race boat designs might have had a shade more seaworthiness, aesthetic appeal, and easy handling than were necessarily good for them on the race course. Not that the American owners of *Jade*, Larry and Debbie Woodell, complained when their small, light, clean-lined 40-footer won the 1985 One-Ton Cup in Poole against one of the biggest fleets ever assembled.

An industrial design graduate by training, Humphreys was never able to resist the lure of boats. His first design, the IOR Quarter-Tonner *Midnight Special*, was a "modest success" in 1973. He spent a few years in yachting journalism before the 31-foot Half-Tonner *Roller Coaster 4* made her mark as a runner-up in the 1979 Half-Ton Cup and the winner of the Aegean Rally the next summer.

Glafki III and *Flash* got tantalizingly close to Half-Ton Cup wins in 1981 and 1984, and then *Jade* delivered the big win in 1985. By this time a central figure in racing, Humphreys served on the Offshore Racing Council's International Technical Committee from 1987 to 1995. He drew the plans for the Whitbread maxi *Rothmans* for the 1989–90 race and was one of the designers of the radical 65-foot hydrofoiler *Blue Arrow*, which tried to muscle in on the acrimonious Big Boat v. Catamaran America's Cup Series of 1988.

From these racing roots, a widely diverse design business has prospered. His first really big sloop, the 128-foot Camper and Nicholson–built *Cyrano de Bergerac*, launched in 1991, was *ShowBoats International*'s Most Innovative Yacht of 1993.

Humphreys has enjoyed excellent success with the Gib Sea production yard in France: the Gib Sea Master 48 won the Easter Spi Ouest regatta in 1993, and the Gib Sea 414 was Le Bateau L'Année 1995. This habit of winning awards has continued with the British Oyster marque, as Humphreys succeeded Holman and Pye as designer of choice. His first Oyster, the 56, sold a company record of eleven at her 1997 introduction, with one example winning her class in the ARC Transatlantic Rally for Cruisers and Antigua Sailing Week. Humphreys has developed three additional Oysters, the 53 (U.K. Yacht of the Year in 2000), the 62, and the 66.

Rob Humphreys: Oyster 66. One of Humphreys's Oyster 66's shows just how fast a big performance cruising yacht can travel when driven hard. The postures of the crew suggest this is an exciting ride, but the boat seems to find it all in a day's work. © *Oyster/PPL Photo Agency*

Humphreys's diverse portfolio includes the British challenger for the 2002–3 America's Cup races, GBR Challenge (along with Simon Rogers), and a new fleet of 72-foot steel cutters for Sir Chay Blyth's Global Challenge race, built by the very clever Prefix building method in which frames and skins self-jig to cut labor time and increase accuracy. In addition, he has designed an Open Class 60 for young Briton Ellen MacArthur, filled numerous orders for 100-foot-plus sail and power yachts, and designed the Espace stackaway RIB (Rigid Inflatable Boat) whose lightness, efficiency, and compact stowed dimensions brought the Welshman back to his roots in industrial design.

Rob Humphreys Yacht Design is located in Lymington, England. —Tim Jeffery

CHARLES RAYMOND HUNT

1908–August 30, 1978 · United States

Though not a prolific yacht designer, C. Raymond Hunt was one of the field's most versatile and original thinkers. One of his first designs (the result of a collaboration between himself, Llewellyn and Waldo Howland, and designer William Harris) was the famous Concordia yawl, a 39-footer designed in 1938 as a beautiful, seaworthy, and comfortable cruising boat for Llewellyn Howland, the founder of the Concordia Company. The design later went on to be built in quantity and to see great success on the racing circuit.

Today, the Concordia yawl is the very definition of the word *classic*. While she represented the most modern thinking when she was created, she can also be considered a study in moderation, with few characteristics that could offend the sensibilities of any yachtsman from many decades of yachting history. Few would dispute that aesthetically she is one of the most successful designs ever drawn, with every line full of personality and "spring" and harmonious with every other line. And she was no fluke—Hunt designed a number of other boats larger and smaller that have similar character and met with similar success. It is hard to believe that in the same year, 1938, the same designer turned out the 110 design, an equally successful but radically untraditional one-design racer. The 110 is a 24-foot, double-ended, fin-keel sloop that was one of the earliest plywood boats. She had a flat, rockered bottom, vertical topsides and plumb ends, and absolutely rectangular sections. Narrow and light, she is a real performer that has seen great success as a club racer. Hunt revisited the 110 theme in the larger 210, 410, and 510. The 210 is a comfortable and successful one-design day racer, while the later two boats are one-of-a-kind cruiser/racers.

During World War II, Hunt worked in the design department of the U.S. Navy Bureau of Ships. There he developed a design for a higher-speed destroyer hull form that, while it appeared to work in the test tank, was never put to use in the war effort. After the war, Hunt utilized the hull form in a lobsterboat, creating what was then known as the "Huntform" hull. The hull had a single chine, and sections below the chine that formed the shape of an inverted bell, forward, flattening out toward the stern. It proved to be an improvement over earlier high-speed displacement and planing-hull forms, and among other things provided a beamier, more stable, and less rolly boat for a given speed. The lobsterboat was a success, and a number of commercial and pleasure boats were built using the concept.

C. Ray Hunt: *Starlight*. *Starlight* is one of the famous 39-foot 10-inch Concordia yawls, designed by Hunt in collaboration with others at the Concordia Company. Unique in countless details, harmonious in every line, she would rest easily on the eye of a yachtsman from any era, the very definition of timelessness. © *Benjamin Mendlowitz*

In 1956, Hunt was approached by businessmen Dick Fisher and Bob Pierce, who had developed a foam-filled fiberglass construction technique that they wanted to incorporate into a sailboat of his design. Hunt talked them into an outboard-powered boat instead, because he felt that was where the market was, and proceeded to create the prototype of a boat that combined the overall scow shape and sponsons of the older Hickman Sea Sled with a centerline shape like his Huntform powerboats. The result was the Boston Whaler, a fast, stable, strong, and safe multipurpose boat that has become the most popular production outboard boat ever built.

Hunt didn't stop there. Convinced that further breakthroughs in powerboat design were possible, he paid particular attention to the thinking of naval architect Lindsay Lord. In 1958 he produced the first Deep-V powerboat, which served as a tender for his America's Cup challenger *Easterner* in 1958. Witnesses were amazed at the boat's ability to maintain high speeds in rough water, and she caught the eye of a man named Dick Bertram.

Bertram immediately commissioned Hunt to design the 30-foot *Moppie* for the 1960 Miami-Nassau powerboat race. It proved to be rough-weather race, and *Moppie* won it handily, followed by another Hunt Deep-V. The rest of the fleet didn't finish until the next day. Bertram then went into the boatbuilding business, with *Moppie* serving as the plug for the famous Bertram 31, a highly successful production fiberglass cruiser of which 1,860 were built in sixteen years. The hull form has since become an industry standard, largely without further modification—which is remarkable in itself—and has proved successful in all sizes of fast powerboats. Hunt is said to be the only designer of the century whose boats won world championships in both power and sailing competitions.

In the Deep-V form, a deadrise angle of approximately 24 degrees is maintained throughout the underbody after the somewhat sharper entrance, with little or no flattening out aft. "Lifting strakes," much like inverted clinker planking or carefully shaped spray rails, run longitudinally. The result is a hull that planes without significant change of fore and aft trim, and because of its ability to disperse the energy of wave impacts, it gives the softest possible ride when encountering head seas at speed. Hunt patented the Deep-V but a competitor succeeded in invalidating the patent after it was discovered that Hunt had mentioned the concept in print more than a year before the patent was applied for, a violation of patent office rules.

Hunt also saw success in sailing development classes, such as the 5.5-Meter, which was an Olympic sailing class. His *Minotaur* won the 1960 gold medal, and *Chaje II*, sailed by the designer, proved so fast that she won the 1963 World Championship without even having to sail the last two races of the seven-race series.

The designer had a run at one of yachting's Holy Grails with his 12-Meter *Easterner*. Although she competed unsuccessfully to defend the America's Cup in 1958, with her varnished topsides, springy sheer, and well-shaped ends, *Easterner* has always been considered one of the best looking of all the 12-Meters. During the trials she showed bursts of speed which suggested that she had the potential to be a winner. But in many ways her campaign was a last-minute affair, and it is probable that she was never tuned up or sailed to her best potential. In a rare disappointment to her designer, she was not selected to defend the Cup. She went on, as *Newsboy*, to be a highly successful ocean racer on the West Coast. She has now been renamed *Easterner* and returned to her home waters around Newport, Rhode Island.

Born into a family with a strong background in sailing, Hunt was another of America's successful self-taught designers. He had no degree, and his formal education ceased after two years of prep school at Andover. At age fifteen he won the Sears Cup, a sailing championship for young people, and he repeated the win two

C. Ray Hunt: 210 One-Design. The 210 has a classic light-displacement form. Hunt used it for bigger yachts, but it didn't rate well enough for ocean racing under prevalent rules. Maximizing waterline length while minimizing weight, it is very fast under typical conditions. © *Mystic Seaport, Rosenfeld Collection, Mystic, CT*

years later. His early sailing experience in waters around Duxbury, Massachusetts, which are dominated by currents and shifting wind patterns, proved to be an ideal training ground for a racing skipper, and throughout his life he was admired as a first-class, "seat-of-the-pants" sailor. He had an uncanny ability to make a boat go and to sense changes in the weather and current, but he did it by instinct and was never able to explain how to anyone else. Those who sailed with him said he was one of the calmest people they had ever seen on a boat.

Hunt's early jobs were in the textile field and he later worked as a stockbroker. It is commonly assumed that the stock market provided his primary source of income for the rest of his life, as he was unlikely to have made a living on the relatively small number of designs he produced, even though some of them were produced in considerable numbers.

After he left school, Hunt began racing a supposedly outmoded R-Class sloop, in which he regularly won races, including some against the boat's designer, Frank C. Paine. Eventually Paine asked Hunt to come work in his office, though it is not clear whether this was in a paid capacity or as an unpaid apprentice. It was in the Paine office that he met Norman L. Skene and Llewellyn Howland, who presumably contributed much to his knowledge of yacht design. He campaigned the Paine-designed 8-Meter *Gypsy* in the 1929 Seawanhaka Cup competition, and raced aboard the Paine-designed J-Class boat *Yankee* in 1934.

In 1932 Hunt formed a loose partnership with Waldo Howland in the Concordia Company, which began designing and building frostbite dinghies and soon moved into the creation of larger cruising and racing boats, including the 39-foot Concordia yawl. In 1954 the Concordia yawl *Malay* became the smallest boat ever to win the Bermuda Race, and another won again in 1978 under the MHS (Measurement Handicap System) Rule.

Later Hunt designed the very similar Concordia 41, and it was in *Harrier*, his own 41, that Hunt, with his wife and children as crew, charmed and amazed British yachting circles by making a six-race sweep at the famous Cowes Week of 1955. *Harrier* probably would also have won the Fastnet Race of that year, had a broken turnbuckle not cost her a tremendous corrected-time lead, giving the win to the Rhodes-designed *Carina*. In 1957, *Harrier* won the Annapolis-Newport Race and the Cygnet Cup. She also won the New London–Marblehead Race three times.

Other successful offshore racers included the English *Drumbeat*, a heavy-displacement, keel-less-underbody sloop with a ballasted centerboard. Hunt gave credit for much of the technical work on that and other designs to his associate, the well-known designer Fenwick Williams. Designer Arthur Martin also worked in Hunt's design office.

Hunt did considerable research into spinnaker design and sailcloth improvements with both natural and synthetic fibers, and was one of the influences on the young Ted Hood, who went on to become famous as a designer and sailmaker. Some of Hood's designs are similar in concept to *Drumbeat*.

After World War II, Hunt saw considerable financial success as a lobster fisherman, and later worked out of the Graves Yacht Yard, designing, building, brokering, and chartering boats. Late in life, Hunt formed C. Raymond Hunt Associates, a design firm still practicing in Boston. Toward the end of his life he was continuing to design and experiment in technical matters, working with water ballast systems, multihull designs, and new sailing-rig concepts.

—Daniel B. MacNaughton

LAWRENCE D. HUNTINGTON JR.

January 12, 1867–December 18, 1946
United States

An innovative designer and boatbuilder, Larry Huntington owned a shipyard in New Rochelle, New York, from the 1890's until World War I. He was known for his willingness to experiment. Starting with the Half-Rater *Question*, he was an early innovator in light displacement, helping to create the high-speed scow type of sailboat, a probable forerunner of the Inland Lake scow. Built in 1895, *Question* was a contender for the first defense of the Seawanhaka Cup with Huntington at the helm. He also designed more conventional one-designs and a good number of cruising and ocean racing sailboats.

Many of Huntington's designs were entered in the earliest ocean races for small yachts. In the first Bermuda Race in 1906, two of the three boats entered (including the winner, the 39-foot 9-inch yawl *Tamerlane*) were his designs. In the 1907 Bermuda Race, another of his designs, the yawl *Hyperion*, placed second.

C. Ray Hunt: Hunter 23. This Hunter 23 displays Hunt's early Deep-V underbody. Strong lifting shapes including the ski-like protruding strakes encourage the hull to plane, and the deep, V-shaped sections running all the way aft disperse impacts with waves, allowing her to run faster in bigger seas than previous designs could. © *Peter Barlow*

Larry Huntington: *Tamerlane.* While the scene seems more like one from an idyllic cruise, note the racing number displayed in the rigging. This handsome 39-foot 9-inch yawl was immortalized when she won the first Bermuda Race in 1906. © *Peter Barlow*

wave-form theory obsolete, but the enthusiasm for science applicable to yacht design, boosted by Scott Russell, Archer, and Hyslop, continues to this day.

Hyslop was born in the town of Wigan in Lancashire, England. He went to sea at age thirteen. Beginning in 1858, he became involved in model-yacht racing, always a hotbed of development owing to the low cost of experimentation and competition. Hyslop moved to New York in 1862 and worked as a ventilation engineer. He became an early member of the Manhattan Yacht Club and took up cruising and racing in small yachts. The first full-size yacht built to his design was his 18-foot LOA sandbagger, *Boz,* in 1870.

Working as an amateur, Hyslop designed yachts for himself and his friends, including his 32-foot cutter *Petrel* in 1875; the 42-foot yawl *Audax,* designed for a friend in 1882; and the 48-foot yawl *Tern,* built in 1901, which he owned and sailed until he reached the age of eighty-five. Hyslop was official measurer for the Seawanhaka Corinthian Yacht Club in 1883, the New York Yacht Club in 1886, and the Larchmont Yacht Club in 1890. Besides his own designs, he drew as a record the plans for a number of successful racing yachts of the day.

Some of Hyslop's plans are found in two collections at Mystic Seaport Museum in Mystic, CT: the W.P. Stephens Collection and the Seawanhaka Corinthian Yacht Club Collection.
—Daniel B. MacNaughton

After ceasing to run the shipyard, Huntington lived and worked on Long Island, New York, in Florida, and finally on Harbor Island in the Bahamas. He spent the last years of his life there, continuing to design pleasure and commercial vessels until he was overtaken by blindness.
—Daniel B. MacNaughton

JOHN HYSLOP

1834–1919 · England/United States

Among the earliest designers to apply scientific theory to yacht design, as opposed to following an evolutionary style of development, John Hyslop studied the theories of hydrodynamics developed by Scotsman John Scott Russell and was instrumental in promoting Colin Archer's wave-form theory. Working as an amateur, he designed many yachts, all in accordance with Archer's theory.

Hyslop's experience with naval architecture began with an intense involvement in model-yacht racing in 1858. He soon became fascinated by Scott Russell's wave-line theory of design, which Scott Russell had studied from 1833. Scott Russell had performed a large

number of experiments relating to the waves created by hulls as they travel through water, leading him to the conclusion that if the waterlines of a vessel were formed in the shape of a versed sine in the forebody and a trochoid in the aft body (a "wave line" in Scott Russell's parlance), resistance would be minimized.

An admirer of Scott Russell's, Hyslop performed his own extensive tests with models and suggested that Scott Russells' wave-line curve was better applied to the curve of areas representing the longitudinal distribution of the immersed volume of the hull, than to any of the actual hull lines per se.

In this Hyslop was correct, and he soon became a regular correspondent with Norwegian designer Colin Archer, who had come to the identical conclusions a few years earlier. Hyslop supported Archer's wave-form theory in the United States, and it was adopted by designers such as A. Cary Smith and Edward Burgess.

While the wave-form theory resulted in faster hulls of improved form, it did so largely by its positive influence on the shapes of the diagonals, lines that up until that time had received little emphasis. Later research produced more advanced data that rendered the

John Hyslop: *Petrel.* Hyslop designed the 32-foot cutter *Petrel* for his own use in 1875. He was an early proponent of hydrodynamic theory and used the wave-line theory for longitudinal distribution of volume in her hull. The theory (later abandoned) led to improvements in speed because of its positive influence on the shapes of the diagonals. *Reproduced from C. P. Kunhardt's* Small Yachts

I–J

PETER A. IBOLD

Born August 1, 1936 · United States/France

At the end of the last century, naval architecture saw the traditional look come back in force. Peter Ibold is one of the founders of this trend, with one of the earliest examples being his 1970 design for the Endurance 35, drawn the year he founded his naval architecture office in Paris.

Born in Cincinnati, Ohio, Ibold grew up in Connecticut. His study of civil engineering, town planning, and economics took him successively to the University of Maine (BSc), University of California at Berkeley, and Stanford University (MSc). An around-the-world trip in 1964–65 aboard a 12-meter trimaran, a first for that time period, was an adventure and a revelation for Ibold. It led to a contract with National Geographic.

Starting out as a hobby, naval architecture became a passion for Ibold. In 1970, his design for the Endurance 35 won competition. Encouraged by an enthusiastic press, he put together his own design office. The office moved to Monaco in 1977 and then to the French Riviera in 1990 before he finally settled back in Paris in 1993.

Over the years, Ibold has designed more than fifty vessels, including powerboats, sailboats, yachts, and workboats. They have been built in a number of yards, such as Belliure in Spain, Statimer in France, and Colvic Craft in Great Britain. His collaboration with Belliure has been most fruitful. His greatest successes continue to be the Endurance series, with

Peter Ibold: Endurance 35. In 1970 the Endurance 35 won the International Amateur Boat Building Society (IABBS) International Yacht Design Competition from among thirty-four entries. Since then thousands have been built worldwide. The photo shows Spain's King Juan Carlos at the helm in a race off Palma de Mallorca. *Photo courtesy Peter Ibold*

more than one hundred and fifty 35-footers, forty 40-footers, twenty-five 50-footers, and about thirty 30-footers launched to date by Belliure alone.

For several years, Ibold lived on a Dagless Fleur de Lys, an English motoryacht. He has designed the motoryacht Albacore series (7 to 10 meters) as well as many other motoryachts.

Peter Ibold retains a love for all things concerning the sea, including his involvement with several foundations and maritime associations—a happy legacy of his round-the-world trip.

The Ibold office is in Paris, France.

—Dominique Gabirault

JOHN H. ILLINGWORTH

1903–March 1980 · England

Often called the founding father of modern ocean racing, Illingworth specialized in design of rigs and deck plans, as well as maximizing a yacht's interior. An outstanding ocean-racing skipper, he was an early experimenter with the masthead cutter rig and a strong advocate for building ocean racers smaller, lighter, and less expensively. Jack Laurent Giles drew the hull lines for two of his most successful boats, *Maid of Malham* (35-foot LWL), built in 1936, and *Myth of Malham* (33-foot 6-inch LWL), built in 1947, while Illingworth supervised their sail and deck plans and interiors. *Myth*, especially, was his concept. She exploited weaknesses in the RORC Rule and won both the 1947 and 1949 Fastnet Races.

Illingworth instituted the first Sydney-Hobart Race in 1945 and was a leading figure in the Royal Yachting Association, the RORC, and the Junior Offshore Group. He had no formal qualifications as a naval architect, but his professional background as an officer in the Royal navy's engineering branch undoubtedly helped in 1955, when he was based at Aero Marine, Emsworth, and turned to full-time yacht designing. Angus Primrose joined him in 1957, and when Aero Marine was sold in 1959, they formed the design firm of Illingworth and Primrose.

Illingworth was involved in more than five hundred designs. They include the minimum-displacement *Mouse of Malham* (24-foot LWL), which crept through every hole in the RORC Rule; the highly successful Class III French ocean racer *Maica* (24-foot LWL), which spawned several sisterships; the conversion and re-rigging of *Bloodhound* after the royal family purchased her in 1962; the revised rig of Chichester's *Gipsy Moth III*; and the designs of the 53-foot *Gipsy Moth IV*, now preserved at Green-

John Illingworth: *Oryx*. Illingworth designed the 38-foot LWL, Class I *Oryx* with Angus Primrose. Illingworth co-owned her and campaigned her as a member of the French Admiral's Cup team in 1969, his last season of competitive sailing. *Photo courtesy Sandy Illingworth and Jean Dupuis*

wich, and Max Aitken's Class I ocean racer, *Outlaw* (38-foot LWL).

In 1966 Illingworth's partnership with Angus Primrose was dissolved. He continued on his own as Illingworth and Associates before retiring to France, where he had a high reputation, in 1970.

—Ian Dear

DR. JOHN INGLIS

1842–1919 · Scotland

When George Lennox Watson arrived to serve the second half of his shipbuilding apprenticeship at the Pointhouse, the Glasgow, Scotland, yard of A. and J. Inglis, he couldn't have found a better mentor than the yard's young leader, John Inglis. At the time Inglis was still in his twenties. He had just completed an education at Glasgow University, which included studies in engineering under William Thomson (later Lord Kelvin), and the new science of hydrodynamics under one of its fathers, Macquorn Rankine. Inglis was already the designer of some innovative yachts. His part in the evolution of yacht design, both directly and through his influence on Watson, was notable.

Inglis took over the reins of the family business in 1867 at age twenty-five, when shipbuilding was a relatively new arm of the successful marine engine-building business started by his father thirty years before. *Erl King*, one of their earliest powered vessels, was the first ship to steam nonstop from London to Shanghai, and the clipper *Norman Court* of 1869 was

one of the fastest and most famous of her day. Inglis became the leading exponent on the Clyde for the forceful but sympathetic marrying of scientific principles to accepted practice.

Even before the company started shipbuilding, Inglis had been building small yachts in the engine shop, experimenting more freely than he could on ship contracts, particularly with ballast. His Five-Tonner *Hilda* of 1872 was allegedly the first yacht in Britain to carry all of her lead ballast outside, below a broadened wood keel—the last step before adoption of a true molded lead keel. For this reason Watson described her as "the grandmother . . . of our racers," and refined Inglis's ideas in Watson's own first effort, *Peg Woffington*, built when he was still engaged at Inglis's yard.

During the 1870's and 1880's the Five-Ton Class was the hotbed of small boat racing at Solent, Clyde, and Irish Sea ports. It was the arena for emerging young, scientifically trained designers to challenge not only each other but also the established old guard of designer/builders, particularly represented in the early 1870's by William Fife II's *Pearl*. Inglis designed and built *Hilda* and her 1874 development, *Viola*, with *Pearl* in his sights, but it was his pupil Watson who finally cracked the nut with his first racing yacht design, *Clothilde*, of 1875.

Inglis continued to design interesting cruiser/racers for himself, friends, and family, including the beautiful small schooners *Cordelia* and *Sheila* (1875) and the iron 20-ton cutter *Moira* (1876). These three yachts appeared under the pseudonyms *Concordia*, *Princess*, and *Mermaid* (along with *Hilda*, as *Ilma*) in his delightful 1879 book, *A Yachtsman's Holidays*. This lighthearted and entertaining treatise on the joys and vagaries of cruising his beloved west coast of Scotland was interspersed with comments on the red-hot yacht design issues of the day, for which he too took a pseudonym: "The Governor."

For the rest of his life, Inglis concentrated on the profitable design and construction of steam yachts and running his highly successful shipbuilding yard.

—Iain McAllister

NIGEL ANTHONY IRENS

Born October 13, 1946 · England

Could Nigel Irens have designed for a broader audience? It seems unlikely. He has created traditional gaff cutters with a modern twist, record-breaking multihulls, and a whole new idiom of powerboats with narrow hulls and outriggers. It must remain a source of slight bafflement to him that after twenty immensely productive years he is better recognized in France than he is in Great Britain.

It is easy to point out the contrasts in Irens's work, but perhaps *balance* would be a better word. In 1969 he began studying boatbuilding and boatyard management at Southampton College of Technology—his student digs were the 22-foot gaff yawl *Piskie*. More than twenty years later, after his reputation as a multihull designer was well established, Irens drew a series of traditional-looking craft: the 30-foot gaff cutter *Zinnia*, a small Western Skiff inspired by a visit to Shetland in his student days, and the lug-sailed *Romily* and *Roxanne* series built with unstayed carbon fiber spars.

But speed has been the central focus of Irens's work. He was the designer of *Clifton Flasher*, an extraordinary 27-footer carrying a five-element wing sail rig revolving around a single pivot. The rig developed enormous power, probably too much for the hull and its control systems, but *Flasher* managed to set a Class C record of 22.14 knots at the 1974 Portland Speed Trials.

Irens's first design was *Promenade*, a 60-foot trimaran drawn in 1977 for the Caribbean charter trade. In 1978 he and his friend Mark Pridie got hold of a salvaged Dick Newick–designed trimaran, which they rebuilt and entered in the Round Britain Race, winning their class.

But it was a Newick-style 40-foot trimaran of Irens's own design, *Gordano Goose*, that prompted the French to take heed by winning a twenty-four-hour race there in 1980. Her successor, Tony Bullimore's *IT '82*, won her class in the Round Britain Race of that year.

Nigel Irens: *Enza*. The catamaran *Enza* has been lengthened twice, first by 5 feet and then by 7 feet, ending up at 97 feet LOA. Skippered by Sir Peter Blake, she won the Jules Verne Trophy for the round-the-world race in 1994, circumnavigating in less than 75 days. *Enza* stands for "Eat New Zealand Apples." © *Mark Pepper/PPL*

In 1984, Mike Birch commissioned the 80-foot cat *Formula TAG*, which set a record of 518 miles in twenty-four hours, and as *Enza*, became the second Jules Verne Trophy holder ten years later. This evergreen boat was subsequently lengthened and altered for Tony Bullimore as his entry for The Race. One reason for the boat's enduring success was her pioneering composite construction.

There followed a series of multihulls that became progressively faster, lighter, and more powerful. Victories were racked up in the

Route du Rhum Race (*Fluery Michon VIII* in 1986), the Round Europe Race (*Apricot* in 1984 and *Fujicolor II* in 1997), and the singlehanded transatlantic race (*Fleury Michon IX* in 1988 and *Fujicolor II* in 1992 & 1996).

Seeing a narrow dugout canoe in Senegal started Irens down another path, that of low-resistance, narrow-hulled powerboats that slice through the waves rather than slamming over them, to produce the benefits of longer-range, lower-power requirements, and a less tiring ride. Together with Mark Pridie, Irens produced the 70-foot *iLAN Voyager* in 1988, a distinctive vessel thanks to her tiny vestigial floats, sprouting out like training wheels on a child's bike. She rattled off 1,455 miles around Britain at an average speed of 21 knots and with no fuel stops.

In 1998, a 115-foot development of the same concept, *Cable & Wireless Adventurer*, set a new 74-day round-the-world record, bettering the time previously set by USS *Triton*, a nuclear submarine. Irens's latest iLAN concept is for a 500-foot, 30-knot commercial ferry.

Urbane, charming, and generous of spirit, Irens has created fantastic boats without ever being fanciful. His common sense and the boatbuilder in him would not have permitted it.

Nigel Irens Design is located in La Trinité-sur-Mer, France.   —Tim Jeffery

JACOB M. "JAC" IVERSEN

1884–1974 · Norway/Sweden

Best known as one of the fathers of the Nordic Folkboat, Jac Iversen was born in Moss, Norway. He grew up around H. M. Iversen and Son, his father's boatyard, close by in Son, a little town on the east side of the Oslo Fjord. In 1902 Iversen started to design small rowing and sailing boats.

Iversen moved to the United States in 1905 and worked at the George Lawley and Son yard at City Point in South Boston, Massachusetts. He returned to his father's yard in 1907 and successfully designed several different Norwegian double-ender classes as well as International Rule Meter boats. In 1926 Iversen emigrated to Gothenburg, Sweden, and five years later moved to Stockholm, where he was invited to work at the Neglinge Yard by the owner Carl Plym.

After Plym's death in an airplane crash in 1931, Iversen started his own design office. His designs ranged over many hull forms and sizes, from model boats to 22-Square-Meter skerry cruisers and 6-Meters, to big offshore cruisers. He drew about a thousand designs in his lifetime.

When in 1941 a Scandinavian competition was offered for a Nordic Folkboat, Iversen's plan as well as Danish designer Knud Olsen's, were awarded second prize out of fifty-eight proposals. A first prize was not actually awarded, so there was no winner, but Iversen's drawing was very close to the final design. That design was drawn by Tord Sundén of Sweden, who put together the best elements from the best designs as requested by the committee.

The Folkboat became the most successful design ever for a one-design keelboat in Scandinavia. It spread worldwide. The Folkboat officially has no single designer and the drawing belongs to the Scandinavian Yacht Union, but if there had been one, it probably should have been both Tord Sundén and Jacob M. Iversen.

—Bent Aarre

FRED "POP" JACOBY SR.

1869–1958 · United States

Fred Jacoby Sr. began to build mahogany dinghies in a workshop behind his house in North Bergen, New Jersey, after he retired from civilian employment with the U.S. Navy in 1929. He had been a boatbuilder in his spare time since emigrating from Bavaria at the age of fourteen, and had studied design at Cooper Union in New York City.

When his son, Freddy, began to race outboards, Fred Senior along with his other son, Emile Jacoby, developed the Jacoby Flyaway Hydroplane for racing in outboard Classes A, B, and C. In the early 1930's these were lightweight, single-step hydroplanes; by the later 1930's they were three-point hydroplanes designed with the sanction of Adolf Apel, who held the patent.

All their boats were winners, especially when driven by Fred Jacoby Jr. Among the triumphs of their greatest racing year—1935—were seven firsts in eight races in a regatta at

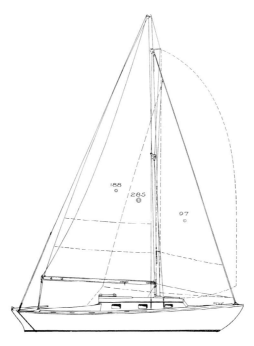

Jacob Iversen: International 25. One of Iversen's designs was an immediate ancestor to the famous Folkboat, and it looks like there is a lot of the same thinking in this International 25, which was offered for import to the United States in the 1950's. Her longer cabin trunk and higher freeboard make her a roomier boat. *Drawing courtesy Bent Aarre*

Savannah, Georgia; thirteen firsts in a weekend of racing at the Shrine Regatta in Washington, D.C.; first in the Delaware River Marathon; first in the Hudson River Marathon (finishing 20 minutes ahead of the fleet); and the American Power Boat Association's Outboard High Point Trophy for that year.

Fred Senior—always known as "Pop" to the outboard-racing fraternity—built these boats for nearly thirty years until 1958 (when he was eighty-nine), and they were shipped to outboard competitors all over the world. Altogether more than a thousand were built in the Jacoby's 20 by 50-foot boatshop. Fred Jacoby Sr., Fred Jacoby Jr., and Emile Jacoby were all elected to the American Power Boat Association's Honor Squadron in 1951.

—Joseph Gribbins

CHRISTIAN JENSEN

1870–1949 · Norway

Christian Jensen is best known outside Norway for his partnership with Johan Anker and as a quality yacht builder, but he was also a keen yacht designer. He was born in Vollen just outside Kristiania (now Oslo) to a family with deep nautical roots.

Jensen served his apprenticeship as a boatbuilder at Gudmundsen's yard in Vollen. He was educated as ship designer at the Kristiania Technical School under the old ship and yacht designer G. A. Sinding. He took over the Gudmundsen yard in 1897. In 1904 he spent time at both William Fife III's yard in Scotland and at Max Oertz's yard in Germany.

Johan Anker bought into Christian's boatyard in 1905, creating the partnership of Anker and Jensen that was to last ten years. Jensen had a great influence over many of the designs that were to be built at their boatyard. The 6-Meters *Rigolo* and *Sonja III* from 1909 and 1911 were his own design.

In 1915 the partnership dissolved and Jensen began to design and build workboats. The highlight was his design and building of *Maud* in 1916–17 for polar scientist Roald Amundsen. The ship was called the best Arctic ship in the world.

In the 1930's Jensen began to design yachts again, mostly for the following classes: 19½-Square-Meter, Nordic 22-Square-Meter, and both 6- and 10-Meter yachts. In 1937 alone, he designed four 10-Meters and one 12-Meter. The 6-Meters *Vinnia* (1935), *Tarzan* (1938), and *Flapper* (1939) provided close competition to the meter boats designed by Johan Anker and Bjarne Aas. After World War II, five Jensen-designed 8-meter yachts were designed and built and all are still sailing.

As a person, Christian Jensen was a gentle man of impeccable honesty who disdained the public spotlight. Without compensation, he generously helped many people with advice about difficult yacht design and construction questions. —Bent Aarre

NIELS JEPPESEN

Born 1956 · Denmark

Currently Denmark's largest production boat yard, X-Yachts was formed in 1979 by designer Niels Jeppesen; his brother, the builder Lars Jeppesen; and composite laminate specialist Birger Hansen. Offering performance cruisers and one-design yachts from their headquarters in Haderslev in southern Denmark, the company has produced ten world championship winners in the fiercely competitive One-Ton and Three-Quarter-Ton fleets, and classes of X-yachts are strong worldwide.

Jeppesen was born in Stubbekøbing, a small village on the Grønsund where sailing came naturally. He studied at the Shiptechnical School in Helsingor (Elsinore), where he de-cided the ships were too big for him. A new career as a schoolteacher took him to Haderslev, in southeastern Jutland, where, at the age of twenty-three, Jeppesen began X-Yachts with the introduction of the X-79 (7.9-meter LOA), a small, flat-bottomed racing boat. Within four years, the X-79 grew to become one of the largest one-design classes in Europe, with more than 350 boats built.

The X-102 followed and brought Jeppesen into the international spotlight. It won the Three-Quarter-Ton World Championship in Finland in 1981, and again in Spain the following year. The conspicuous success of the two yachts was such that when the partners announced the one-design class X-99, over a hundred boats were sold before the first boat was launched.

Since then, Jeppesen has designed thirty-one X-Yachts ranging in size from 30 to 73 feet (X-Yachts 73). These boats differ from one another in the accommodations and comfort level they offer, according to their designation as racers or cruiser/racers, but they are alike in their use of high-tech materials, their sound workmanship, their sleek modern look, and their emphasis on performance under sail. Jeppesen's boats have established enviable racing records, including three European IMS championships, and ten One-Ton and Three-Quarter-Ton World Championships.

The latest design in the Performance Cruising Line is the X-Yacht 73, with the central viewing/command platform inside the pilothouse and sailing and maneuvering accomplished just by push button via three captive winches. The Racing Line now also includes the IMX 40 and the IMX 45, felt by some to be the world's fastest IMS production models.

Jeppesen continues to practice in Haderslev, Denmark. —Bent Aarre

JOHN O. JOHNSON

1875–unknown
Norway/United States

Born in Norway, John Johnson immigrated to White Bear Lake, Minnesota, in 1893, working as a boatbuilder in partnership with fellow Norwegian immigrant Gus Amundson. He began Johnson Boat Works in 1896 in order to develop a new hull design based on his observations of

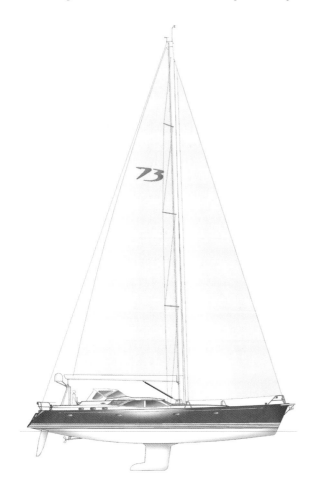

Niels Jeppesen: X-73. The largest model offered by X-Yachts of Denmark, the 73-foot X-73 explores a popular contemporary theme with her light, high-performance hull and abbreviated underbody combined with luxurious accommodations and a powerful sloop rig, which is rendered easy to handle by powered winches and furlers. *Drawing courtesy Niels Jeppesen*

John O. Johnson: Class E scow. This prototype for the Class E scow was built in 1896. Later boats would have a squared-off bow. Lake scows featured wide, flat-floored, ultralight hulls, and later examples were among the first sailboats to plane over the surface of the water. *Photo courtesy Tom Hodgson*

Rod Johnstone: J/24. Flush deck, good looks, light displacement, snappy performance, a degree of comfort, and strict one-design specifications combined to make the J/24 one of the most popular small keelboats on the water. Here Johnstone is at the helm of *Ragtime*. © *Onne van der Wal*

small craft in Norway, and evolved a skimming hull shape first expressed in his 38-foot *Wierdling*, built in the shop's first year. This boat was a crucial step in the evolution of the scow hull and is the first scow to have been built with bilge boards, although *Wierdling*'s bilge boards were replaced with a conventional centerboard by her first owner.

Johnson's bilge-board innovation was later used successfully in his 32-foot *Pluto*, a Class B scow built in 1903 that won the White Bear Lake Yacht Club championship. His design work was aided considerably by his association with C. Milton Griggs, a successful businessman from Saint Paul. Johnson modified the stern of Griggs's boat *Akela* (designed by Andrew Peterson), enabling her to win the White Bear Lake Yacht Club championship, the Interlake Regatta for the 23-foot sloop class in 1897, and the 1898 Centennial Races in Milwaukee.

He then designed and built *Minnezitka*, 38 feet long, for Griggs. The gaff-rigged *Minnezitka* was built over the winter of 1899–1900, with lines and a hull shape very much like later scows such as the Class E and especially the Class A, which shared much from Johnson's work. *Minnezitka* (the name means "water bird" in the language

of the local Indian tribe) went on to finish her first race a mile ahead of the second-place boat, on a 4-mile course. She was also the winner of the lake championship that year.

Johnson's influences included Nathanael Herreshoff, whose scow-like *Alfrida*, commissioned by Griggs, appeared on the inland lake racing circuit in 1896. In 1932 Johnson designed the Class X boat (also referred to as a Cub), a 16-foot hard-chine sloop intended as a learning boat for children. Over the winter of 1945–46 Johnson's 20-foot scow, featuring twin rudders, was accepted by the Inland Lake Yachting Association (ILYA) as a new class, designated Class D. The first boat of this class was built for a client from South Africa and initially called the "South African Racer." Class X and D scows continue as active classes, raced throughout the Midwest. In 1948, Johnson designed a 19-foot version of the Class X boat, called at first the Super X and later Class Y. The Y was the first ILYA-approved class to feature an overlapping jib. Still racing, the Class Y has shrunk to a few fleets after several years of great popularity.

Under Johnson's leadership, Johnson Boat Works produced the Class E scow prototype

(another prototype was built by the Palmer Boat Company of Fontana, Wisconsin), which set the style for the class, although the first ones produced had a pointed bow rather than the more familiar squared-off bow of today's Class E scows.

—Gregory O. Jones

RODNEY S. JOHNSTONE

Born January 15, 1937 · United States

Every once in a while in every field of endeavor, a concept comes along that is so clean, so simple, and so appropriate that those who see it say, "Why didn't I think of that?" Surely the J/24 is such a concept, and she would guarantee the enduring fame of her designer, Rod Johnstone, even if she had not been followed by race- and award-winning designs of more boats, from 22 to 53 feet long.

The J/24 is a small, light, beamy, flush-deck fiberglass sloop with modest accommodations for four and broad appeal for club racing, family outings, weekend cruising, and coastal racing. Fast, maneuverable, and easy to sail, she is seaworthy enough to venture out into rough water.

Rod and his brother Bob (the seasoned marketer who parlayed Rod's designs into one of the industry's most notable financial success stories) had the wisdom to present the J/24 internationally as a well-regulated one-design class. They ignored the influence of any handicapping rule, thus avoiding distortions in the design and any immediate threat of obsolescence while ushering in the return of the fractional rig sloop among IOR racing boats. In so doing, they created a boat for thousands of sailors, many of them former dinghy racers. The J/24 is the world's most popular one-design keelboat, with over 5,300 sailing and more being built every year.

Rod Johnstone grew up in Glen Ridge, New Jersey, and beginning in the late 1940's learned to sail with his parents on the Olin Stephens–designed Lightning Class sloop his father built in their garage. He became an Eastern Connecticut junior sailing champion and a finalist in the North American Junior Championships of 1953 and 1954. Johnstone sailed for Princeton University during his undergraduate years from 1954 to 1958, and during the 1960's he raced in a variety of one-designs, as well as some offshore racers. In 1967 he took a yacht design course from the Westlawn School of Yacht Design, and in 1970 he resigned from his job at General Dynamics in Groton, Connecticut, to start a sailing school in Essex, Connecticut. Later he went to work as a writer and ad salesman for *Soundings* magazine.

With help from family and friends, Johnstone built the J/24 prototype, *Ragtime*, in his garage in 1974. She was the biggest boat he could build in the space available. In her first season's racing, she won all but two of her twenty races. In 1976 Johnstone contracted with Everett Pearson of TPI Composites to build J/24's in quantity. In 1977 Bob became his partner, founding J/Boats Incorporated. J/Boats currently offers thirty designs, and more than ten thousand of them sail around the world.

Only two of Johnstone's designs have abandoned the one-design concept and made concessions to the IOR. Most designs are versions of the cruiser/racer concept, with stress on the racer end. The J/32, J/42, and J/46 deliberately address the cruiser market, with a more conservative look and proportions reminiscent of older designs. Sailing performance is not sacrificed.

Rod Johnstone: J/105 (opposite). While they come in a variety of sizes and range from out-and-out racers to performance cruising boats, all the J-Class boats were designed with the idea that high performance and ease of handling could be had in the same boat. © *Onne van der Wal*

The J/24, J/23, and J/80 have been designated International Classes by the International Sailing Federation. Along with the J/35, the J/24 has been inducted into America's Sailboat Hall of Fame. Johnstone's designs have won nearly every major race in the world and, with few exceptions, account for the largest number of entries in numerous race weeks in the United States. The J/44 class is the only offshore cruiser/racer design to ever merit a one-design division in the Newport-Bermuda Race.

The more recent designs, the J/90, J/125, J/133, and J/145, reach for very high performance with both race and luxury interiors, carbon fiber hulls, and asymmetrical spinnakers on retractable bowsprits reminiscent of those ultimate speed machines, the Australian 18's. However, they do not reach so far as to stray into the experimental realm, and they have managed to combine extreme speeds with relatively easy handling, consistent with the designer's philosophy that to sell well the boats must not only be fast but also be fun to sail.

The next generation of the Johnstone family has emerged to run the company as Rod and Bob Johnstone turn over day-to-day operations to them. J/Boats is located in Newport, Rhode Island.   —Daniel B. MacNaughton

MICHEL JOUBERT
Born May 14, 1944
BERNARD NIVELT
Born September 26, 1948

France

Top naval architects in the contemporary French yachting scene, Michel Joubert and Bernard Nivelt have personalities as forceful as they are original. They are leaving a strong and diverse mark in international racing and cruising boats.

Michel Joubert was born in Meudon. His father, Pierre Joubert, inspired young French Sea Scouts' dreams of the pure and the absolute with his illustrations for books of the *Signes de Piste* collection. Going to sea often allows an escape from the more or less oppressive world, and Joubert chose to join the French merchant marine. His strong liking for things mechanical led to his training as a first-class engineering officer.

Fascinated by yacht design, Joubert sketched all possible projects within his reach, and built a sailboat embodying his ideas. He soon made a name for himself among La Rochelle yachtsmen, particularly with his racer *Sing-Sing*. With his very first winning designs, he developed his favored long and light approach to sailboats, firmed up in 1972 with *Subversion*, which was an interesting surprise to competitors in Chan-

nel regattas. The following year the Jeanneau Company ordered from him the 11.3-meter *Gin-Fizz*, and Joubert became the favorite designer of the Gib Sea yard, for which he is still working regularly.

Bernard Nivelt was born in Deauville, Normandy, and found in his childhood that sailing was his universe. After studying mathematics, he joined INSA in Lyon, an engineering school specializing in physics. After he left INSA, he worked on three-dimensional drawing programs in the sciences faculty of Paris.

Nivelt was following almost the same path as Joubert by building in plywood his chine-hulled Quarter-Tonner *Pinor Major*. With *Pinor*, he sailed against the best of La Rochelle's young designers, builders, yachtsmen, and sailmakers. By this time the IOR had become so complicated that the sole way to analyze it was with programmable pocket calculators, and Nivelt was becoming a programming and rule expert.

It was during Nivelt's national service in the Bataillon de Joinville that he met Joubert. They sailed a Soling together and spent many hours talking about yacht design. Soon they joined forces, and for some time were so successful at penetrating the secrets of the rule, that Half-Tonner production became a La Rochelle specialty.

For this team, aesthetics has no place in racers—victories alone create demand. Nevertheless, Joubert likes to distinguish precisely between racing and cruising needs. His numerous designs for production-built family cruisers and offshore cruising sailboats, often built in steel or aluminum, are marked by his concern for course-keeping as well as the comfort of life aboard. He doesn't much appreciate advertising that talks about production yachts based on winning prototypes; he feels it is often misleading and inappropriate. He never misses an opportunity to proclaim what he thinks, and he enjoys bringing forth the opposite of what one is expecting from him.

In 1973, yachtsmen Gérard Janichon and Jérôme Poncet ordered from Joubert the design of their *Damien II*, a 46-foot, steel centerboard schooner, while singer Antoine bought a sistership, named *Om*. In 1976, he designed for the Archambault yard the sailboat that still remains his signature: the Surprise. She was an economical, simple, and pleasant sailboat that was nonetheless fearsome when racing. The Surprise Owners' Association remains one of the most active in France. Victories in the 1980 and 1982 Half-Tonner World Championship, followed by *Diva*'s fantastic success in the 1983 Admiral's Cup, gave Joubert and Nivelt international recognition, to such a point that in that year Nivelt opened an office in the United States.

The eclecticism that characterizes Joubert and Nivelt's systematic approach is bringing very diverse commissions. In 1982, the 65-foot catamaran *Charente-Maritime* won the big classics of several transoceanic races, and gave the two designers standing as multihull specialists. Fountaine-Pajot's yard approached them for their line of cruising multihulls, including the Louisiane, Fidji, and Venezia 42. This wave of orders culminated with Nivelt's participation in the 1988 America's Cup defender project, resulting in the catamaran *Stars & Stripes*, winner of the Cup against the Bruce Farr–designed *New Zealand (KZ-1)*.

The office also had a special knack for motoryachts, and as early as 1977, the Ange de Mer was a standard among French production powerboats. From open day-boats to cargo ships, and including the motorsailers of which Joubert is fond to the point of having just designed one for his own use, the success of their creations has remained constant.

Unsurprisingly, their monohull success has allowed the two associates to create all kinds of racing and cruising boats. In 1985, they designed Eric Tabarly's 82-foot maxi *Côte d'Or* for the Whitbread race. For the next two years their designs won the SORC Championship. In 1988, they designed another Whitbread yacht, *Union Bank of Finland*, an 84-foot maxi that was His Majesty Juan Carlos, the King of Spain's racer prototype. During this period, they drew the Dynamic Company's entire range of big sailboats, ranging from 47 to 80 feet, plus the Jeanneau yard's Selection, which was designed for the Tour de France à la Voile race in 1986.

Since then, with Jean-Yves Terlain's 60-foot sailboat *UAP*, renamed *Pour Médecins du Monde*,

Joubert and Nivelt have developed to the extreme the concept of the sailing sled for singlehanded races around the world. The yacht won the C-Star in 1988. In 1989, Pierre Follenfant, skipper of the catamaran *Charente-Maritime*, a dinghy racer and Ton Cup champion, ordered his 60-foot *TBS-Charente-Maritime* for the first Vendée Globe Challenge. These orders were followed by many others for the 60-foot Open Ville de Cherbourg, in 1993.

Nivelt was involved with the design team working on the French America's Cup effort for the year 2000. He already had designed an America's Cup Class yacht in 1995 for the French Yacht Club de Cannes. She never raced, but she was the yardstick for Fast 2000, the new Swiss Challenge.

The Joubert and Nivelt office is located in Agay, near La Rochelle, France.

—François Chevalier

JUDEL/VROLIJK AND COMPANY

TORSTEN CONRADI
Born 1956
FRIEDRICH JUDEL
Born 1948
ROLF VROLIJK
Born December 25, 1946

Germany

Known throughout the international offshore racing circuit, Friedrich "Fietje" Judel, Rolf Vrolijk, and their later partner Torsten Conradi constitute one of Europe's preeminent naval architecture practices. Admiral's Cup racers, one-offs, series production yachts, cruisers well

into the megayacht range, and repeated and finally successful America's Cup design work (Switzerland's *Alinghi*, which won the 2003 America's Cup race against Team New Zealand) mark the wide range of this versatile design team.

Judel and Vrolijk founded the company in 1978 in Hamburg. That year they designed the successful Quarter-Ton Cup yacht *Quadriga*. Another milestone was the Admiral's Cup yacht *Duesselboot* for Michael Schmidt, nowadays owner of the yard that builds the successful range of Hanse Yachts, all designed by Judel/Vrolijk and Company. *Duesselboot* showed many innovative design features, today common in modern racing yachts. These features established the young team in the world of ocean racing yacht designers. In 1986 naval architect Torsten Conradi joined as a third partner.

Soon *Container*, *Rubin*, *Pinta*, *Saudad*, and others won the Admiral's Cup, One-Ton Cup, Sardinia's Cup, and other trophies and championships in the 1980's and 1990's.

Beside these glamorous racing successes, innovative and demanding cruising yachts were designed: *Pinta Smeralda*, a 60-foot, high-performance cruiser, to be singlehanded; the 165-foot schooner *Lamu*, which was the largest fiberglass sailing yacht, when built; *Anny*, an 85-foot sloop with a drop keel, a stern dinghy bay/garage, and many more features like a "James Bond car"; and many other yachts ranging from 18 to 150 feet and from an ultramodern to "retro-classic" style.

Since the mid-1990's motoryachts and commercial projects have been added to the company's design portfolio. Fast catamaran ferries, small commuter powerboats, fishing boats, and river cruisers have also been designed.

In the days of IMS and IRC racing, Judel/ Vrolijk-designed boats were regular winners, with boats like the IMS 50's *Innovision* and *Banco Espirito Santo*, the successful Rodman 42 and Grand Soleil 44, or the beautifully finished, 66-foot, dark blue multirule racer *Sotto Voce* or the recent *UCA*, an 86-foot offshore racer for the 2003 Daimler Chrysler North Atlantic Challenge.

Yacht racing history was written with Rolf Vrolijk's involvement in the America's Cup, being the principal designer of the Swiss *Alinghi* team that finally succeeded in winning the thirty-first America's Cup in 2003. *Alinghi* was faster than the competitors, showed the best all-round capabilities, and brought the Cup back to Europe after 152 years.

Besides the necessary creative spirit and the competence and technical knowledge that make a yacht design office successful, it is also necessary to work with the most advanced tools available. From the beginning, computers became an essential part of the design

Judel/Vrolijk: *Alinghi*. Judel and Vrolijk were head designers of the team that produced the America's Cup Class yacht *Alinghi*. She won the 2003 finals against *Team New Zealand*, and brought the Cup home to Switzerland for the first time. © *Terry Fong, AFA Photography*

process. When the office moved to Bremerhaven in 1991, the decision was made to "abandon pencils" completely and to start a new era of progress by designing only with the computer. Although this is no surprise today, it was a progressive and farseeing step at that time, requiring big investments in hardware and software plus time. A recent move was to go completely to three-dimensional design and back this up with FE (finite element analysis) and CFD (computational fluid dynamics) calculation programs. It is always quite an experience for customers to see how their boat will look from various perspectives, even before the yard has bent the first frame.

Judel/Vrolijk and Company continues to practice in Bremerhaven, Germany.

—Erdmann Braschos

SCOTT JUTSON

Born July 9, 1956 · Australia

A designer with a strong belief in the value of modern technology, Scott Jutson has been at the forefront of yacht design in Australia since he moved there in 1985. Born in the United States, he sailed dinghies throughout his teenage years before attending the University of California. After graduating in film studies and political science, he became a regular on the U.S. maxi yacht circuit through the early 1980's, when he became interested in yacht design. He studied at the Landing School of Boatbuilding and Design in Kennebunkport, Maine.

Jutson's first major design, the Australian 18-foot Skiff *Colorbond*, was a graduation project. She reflected an all-out effort to apply up-to-the-minute use of composite construction and aerodynamic design to this development class, and at the time represented the peak of design in these lightweight three-crew dinghies. *Colorbond* is now on permanent display at the Australian National Maritime Museum.

Other projects have included the design of the only Formula 40 class catamaran built in Australia and the development of the Australian maxi yacht *Brindabella*. A wide range of power and sailing catamarans and racing and cruising monohulls have been designed in recent years.

Jutson has also made a name for himself through "optimization," a process of applying appropriate new technology to improve the performance of older boats by redesigning rigs and keels, saving the owners' money while he improves their boat's speed.

Jutson Yacht Design is located in Balgowlah, New South Wales, Australia.

—Robert Keeley

Scott Jutson: *Brindabella*. *Brindabella* was the second boat of this name and was intended to be a dominant line-honors boat for east coast Australian racing, including the Sydney-Hobart Race. Launched in 1993 she realized this desire, breaking records in all three major events as well as representing Australia in the Kenwood Cup in 1994. © *Bob Ross*

I. Judson Kelly: *Odyssey* and *Jada*. *Odyssey*, 58-foot 2-inch LOD, and *Jada*, 56-foot 2-inch LOD, are two almost identical designs built in 1938. *Odyssey* was a yawl, and *Jada* began as a schooner but became a yawl in 1955, after which they were intense rivals throughout their careers. Both boats remain in service. *Photo courtesy Newport Harbor Nautical Museum, Newport Beach, CA*

I. JUDSON KELLY

1891/2–1947 · United States

Although little biographical detail is known on this talented designer, the volume of work he produced and the reputation he achieved in his professional career established him as one of the most well-regarded yacht designers on the West Coast from the early 1920's up to World War II.

His talent for design was first recognized by S. Clyde Kyle, an entrepreneurial manufac-turer's representative, who took Kelly's de-sign for a 45-foot power cruiser and obtained orders from five customers. These he took to the well-known Stephens Brothers Boat Yard at Stockton, California, where the boats were built and proved quite successful.

Executives of American Car and Foundry (ACF) came to San Francisco and saw these boats. They were looking for a cruiser design that would fit their plans to make use of their Wilmington, Delaware, facility, which had been set up to build wooden railway coaches but was losing business to steel.

Kyle went east to handle sales in 1924 and Kelly joined him to design and supervise con-struction of their new line of quality cabin cruisers. This was in 1924, and during the next five years they designed and sold more than $5 million worth of boats.

The Depression put a temporary end to this market, so Kelly returned west and became affiliated with one of the premier western boatbuilders, the venerable Fellows and Stewart at San Pedro, California, founded in 1896. He produced some attractive stock cruisers for this firm in the early 1930's, including the Fellowscraft 38- and 47-foot models, which brought high compliments from that company. They publicly stated that Kelly's work had been so painstaking and complete that they did not find it necessary to make a single change in the details of either design.

Next Kelly reestablished his affiliation with Stephens Brothers in Stockton, long known for their high-quality cabin cruisers, sailboats, and commercial craft found on both coasts. "Thode" Stephens, who had been the designing member of the firm, had recently died, and Roy Stephens needed an "in-house" naval architect. The next generation, Theo, Dick, and Barre Stephens, were not yet of the age and experience to take over the business, and Judson Kelly was a known and appreciated quantity.

He designed several boats quickly, including the custom, 62-foot, twin-screw *Manana II* and the all-teak, 64-foot *Folly II*, and six 38-foot patrol boats for the U.S. Coast Guard. He was also responsible for the design of three sailing yachts that achieved great success in West Coast ocean-racing history: the 44-foot cutter *Pajara* (1937), the 58-foot yawl *Odyssey* (1938), and *Jada*, a 56-foot staysail schooner (1938), later yawl-rigged. All are still in service today and enjoy continued celebrity.

During World War II, Kelly was absorbed into the war effort at a large aircraft subcontracting firm in Los Angeles controlled by the owner of *Jada*. He was not heard from again. His boat designs still speak for him and remain well remembered in the annals of West Coast yachting.

—Thomas G. Skahill

DEREK KELSALL

Born June 15, 1933 · England

Just as the Prout brothers and Roderick MacAlpine-Downie must be considered the fathers of British catamarans, Derek Kelsall can rightly be called the father of British trimarans. In the late 1960's and 1970's Kelsall's trimarans dominated European multihull racing.

Kelsall's multihull career began in 1964, when he participated in the second singlehanded transatlantic race with *Folatre*, a self-built 35-foot Lodestar Piver trimaran. Kelsall's first trimaran design was *Toria* (42 feet 6 inches), which became the first trimaran to win a major offshore race when she won the 1966 Round Britain Race with Kelsall at the helm. Her design—round bilges, rather than the then-prevalent V-shaped

or hard-chine hulls, and high-buoyancy floats set high to always keep one float flying—set a standard for racing trimaran design. Kelsall also pioneered modern foam-sandwich construction at a time when multihull design was still focused on wood, plywood, or alloy.

Toria was followed by *Trifle* (42 feet, 1966), *Trumpeter* (44 feet, 1969), *FT* (35 feet, 1974), *Three Legs of Man*, and *Great Britain IV* (52 feet, 1976, with John Shuttleworth, then working for Kelsall). Both *Great Britain III* (80 feet, 1975) and *William Saurin* (93 feet, 1982) were among the world's largest trimarans at the time of their construction.

Most of Kelsall's designs during the 1960's and 1970's were racing trimarans, although there were also proas (*Sidewinder*, 51 feet 6 inches, 1970, and *Lillian*, 55 feet, 1972), the occasional racing catamaran (*V.S.D.*, 63 feet, 1977, with Shuttleworth), and even monohulls. Later, however, his focus shifted toward cruising and power boats, for which he preferred the catamaran over the trimaran for multihull seaworthiness. He also kept experimenting with innovations such as a variable-beam catamaran to facilitate trailering or a true amphibious catamaran that could

be trailered on its own permanent wheels. By 1999, Kelsall was based in Waihi, New Zealand, where he promoted his KSS, a foam-laminate construction method, which by first making all parts of a catamaran on a mold table facilitated the cost-efficient building of round-bilged catamaran hulls by professionals and amateurs, and where Kelsall Catamarans offers a large range of catamaran designs.

—Claas van der Linde

DIXON KEMP

1839–1899 · England

An influential yachting journalist and leading authority on yacht measurement, Dixon Kemp was instrumental in founding the Yacht Racing Association in 1875, acting as its secretary until 1898, and in inducing Lloyd's to extend its classification and surveying of shipping to yachts. This resulted in the first *Lloyd's Register of Yachts* in 1877. In addition, he devised the famous Length-and-Sail-Area Rule adopted by the Seawanhaka Corinthian Yacht Club in 1882 and by the Yacht Racing Association in 1887.

Dixon Kemp: *Lapwing.* *Lapwing*, a 35-foot LWL Itchen cutter commissioned by Edward Burgess and built by George Lawley in 1882, is shown ghosting along under her giant spread of canvas. She was the probable inspiration for Burgess's first commission in 1884, the 30-foot LWL cutter *Rondina*. *Photo by Nathaniel Stebbins. Courtesy of the Society for the Preservation of New England Antiquities*

George Kettenburg: PC class. The 31-foot P.C. (Pacific Coast) class, numbering seventy-nine, was designed and built by Kettenburg's yard in San Diego in 1929 to provide an all-around boat adaptable to a wide range of sailing conditions. Fleets were chartered in San Diego, Hawaii, Newport Beach, San Francisco, and Seattle. About twenty-seven boats sail out of the San Diego Yacht Club. *Photo courtesy Newport Harbor Nautical Museum, Newport Beach, CA*

Kemp started designing yachts in 1870 and learned his art "mainly by taking off the lines of every yacht I could get permission so to treat, and subjected the lines to every process of examination I could think of."

The 1900 edition of *Lloyd's Register of Yachts* credits him with forty-three designs, though earlier editions list others. Descriptions of them are hard to come by, but they included the 120-ton yawl *Freda*, built in 1885, which won the German Emperor's Cup in the 1897 Dover-Heligoland Race, and the 10-ton cutter *Firecrest*, in which Alain Gerbault completed a solo circumnavigation in the 1920's. According to Gerbault, Kemp knew how to design a long-lasting and dependable boat, and one of his designs, *Zoraida*, is still afloat as a houseboat.

Kemp's first book, *Yacht Designing*, published in 1876, introduced Edward Burgess to the subject, and in 1881 Burgess commissioned the design of two 27-foot sloops from Kemp. He had one built for himself and the other for one of his customers. Then in 1882 he commissioned from Kemp the design of a modified Itchen boat, *Lapwing* (35-foot LWL), supervising the sloop's construction before selling it.

Yacht Designing—subsequently published in several editions as *Yacht Architecture*—became the standard work on the subject for many years, as did Kemp's second book, *The Manual of Yacht and Boat Sailing* (1878). According to the American yachting journalist William P. Stephens, in writing *Yacht Designing* Kemp was among the first to give the term *yacht designer* common currency.   —Ian Dear

GEORGE KETTENBURG JR.
1904–1952
PAUL KETTENBURG
Born 1913

United States

The Kettenburg brothers were self-taught designers who achieved great success by virtue of their natural talent, an awareness of what their customers wanted, a proper interpretation of the handicapping rules, and a devotion to hull forms completely devoid of unwholesome or unappealing lines.

While still in high school, George Kettenburg Jr. began designing speedboat hulls for his father, a retired engineer who in 1911 had moved his family from Pennsylvania to San Diego, California. The younger Kettenburg

George Kettenburg: *Eulalie*. *Eulalie*, the first of the 46-foot 4-inch P.C.C. Pacific Cruising Class, was designed in 1946 and belonged to Kettenburg. Some twenty-six were built by Kettenburg Boat Works over the next seven years. P.C.C. boats claimed victories in all of the major events on the West Coast and several on the East Coast. *Photo courtesy Newport Harbor Nautical Museum, Newport Beach, CA*

showed a natural aptitude for both design and construction. Soon larger boats, first power and then sail, were being built to his designs and sold from a shop next to the family home on the water in residential Point Loma.

By 1929 their success necessitated a move to a waterfront location in the commercial area of Point Loma, where George's first great design, the 32-foot P.C. (for Pacific Coast) One-Design sloop, was produced and sold to buyers ranging from San Diego to Seattle and Hawaii. In major competition, the boat beat Herreshoff S-Class sloops along with R-Class and 6-Meter sloops from many designers, giving great impetus to the class. Thirty-one were built prior to World War II, and ultimately the total reached eighty-one.

That same year—1929—was also the year

Kettenburg brought out the 16-foot Starlet for junior sailors at the San Diego Yacht Club. Initially thirty boats were built, with more coming later. The class became the training vehicle for the many world and national champion sailors produced by that club, holding that position for over thirty years.

George's younger brother Paul Kettenburg, who had worked at the family business during high school, sought engineering employment in the East with a large manufacturing company, but rejoined the family business in 1943 to assist with the considerable amount of high-priority military work underway at the boatyard.

Near the end of World War II, the brothers foresaw an impending demand for new and larger boats. In 1946 George brought out the

P.C.C. (Pacific Cruising Class), a 46-foot 6-inch sloop, which was immediately ordered by many customers and saw many subsequent racing successes. A total of twenty-four boats were built over the next seven years and several went on to win the Transpac, Bermuda, Southern Circuit, and Swiftsure Races in as many years.

After George's untimely death from cancer in 1952, the reins of Kettenburg Boat Works fell to Paul. He brought forth a series of designs, both smaller and larger, based on the original design concepts of his brother, but incorporated changes to accommodate the requirements imposed by revisions to the CCA Rule.

First came the K-38 (thirty-six delivered) followed by the K-40 (forty built), the K-50 (twenty-four built), and the K-43 (seventeen built by Kettenburg plus two constructed of aluminum by another builder), and finally the fiberglass K-41 (thirty built). Paul remained at the head of the company until it was sold to a conglomerate in 1969.

George and Paul Kettenburg exemplify the type of intelligent, self-taught, disciplined, and inventive designers who are sometimes able to create a solid and enviable reputation in a field often dominated by more formally trained individuals. —Thomas G. Skahill

STEVEN KILLING

Born September 27, 1950 · Canada

Versatility has long been one of Steve Killing's strengths. In addition to designing a wide variety of craft, ranging from a replica of the War of 1812 schooner *Bee* to America's Cup yachts, he has played a significant role in advancing the technology employed in yacht design and the underlying theoretical knowledge.

Killing graduated from the University of Western Ontario in 1972 with a bachelor of engineering science (civil engineering). From 1972 to 1979 he was a member of the fabled C&C Design Group, during which time he spent a year aiding in the development of a unique yacht test-tank procedure at the National Research Council (NRC) in Ottawa. When the NRC test-tank facility relocated to

Bruce King: *Bemfujjo*. King's powerboat designs combine traditional styling references and finish with composite construction and jet-drive propulsion. Strong curves throughout the design make for a dramatic look, while careful allotment of space creates comfort and utility. Note how wide decks add safety while reducing the bulk of the cabin trunk. *Photo courtesy Bruce King*

St. John's, Newfoundland, in 1987, Killing helped develop a procedure and apparatus for yacht testing there as well.

Killing is best remembered from his C&C days as the project manager for the radical 40-foot daggerboard design *Evergreen* (on which he also sailed as bow man), which won the 1978 Canada's Cup match racing series for the Royal Hamilton Yacht Club against the Ron Holland–designed *Agape* of the Bayview Yacht Club of Detroit.

Since 1979, Killing has been president of Steve Killing Yacht Design, designing racing and cruising sailboats, classic racing powerboats, historic sailing vessels, and small craft in his office in rural Ontario near the Georgian Bay town of Midland. His services also include hull design, fairing, and computer lofting for other designers. He is a consultant to Design Systems and codeveloper of Fast Yacht, a computer-aided yacht design system, which in 1983 was the first integrated package of software for yacht designers.

Killing has participated in four America's Cup campaigns: as assistant designer on the Bruce Kirby–designed *Canada One* in 1983, as head designer for the *True North Challenge* in 1987, and as a consultant to the New Zealand challenges in 1988 and 1992. In 1982, he received the L. S. Lauchland Engineering Award for developments in the marine industry. In 1998, W. W. Norton published his book *Yacht Design Explained* (with coauthor Douglas Hunter), which John Rousmaniere pronounced "the new 'Bible' of yacht design." —Douglas Hunter

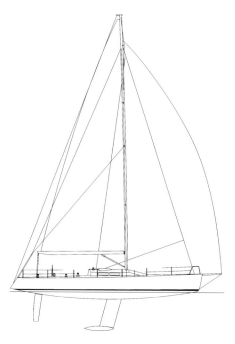

Steven Killing: Daniells 50. Killing's Daniells 50 design shows the contemporary racer/cruiser type in sharp focus. Her ultralight hull has a moderate beam, with a ballast bulb held very deep on a minimized fin. Large downwind sails are set from a bowsprit rather than a pole. A very deep rudder keeps her under control. *Drawing courtesy Steve Killing*

BRUCE P. KING

Born May 7, 1939 · United States

Those who believe that the golden age of yachting is behind us cannot be familiar with the work of contemporary neoclassic designers such as Bruce King. King has devoted much of his recent career to the creation of large wood-epoxy composite sailing yachts, which in size and quality of finish rival the most impressive yachts of years past, and in terms of sailing performance, ease of handling, comfort, and structural integrity probably exceed them.

In yachts such as the ketches *Whitehawk* (1978, 105-foot LOA), *Signe* (1989, 112-foot LOA), and *Hetairos* (1993, 125-foot LOA), and the sloops *Whitefin* (1983, 90-foot LOA), *Sophie* (1994, 91-foot LOA), and *Antonisa* (1999, 124-foot LOA), King has escaped the influence of handicapping rules, the limitations of conventional construction, and even the pressure of economics, to explore the state of the art in large sailing yachts. These yachts are designed and built to be as beautiful, fast, and strong as the generation that created them can produce.

Some of King's designs take their aesthetic departure from the work of L. Francis Herreshoff, especially the legendary clipper-bowed ketch *Ticonderoga* (ex-*Tioga*) of 1936. At 72 feet LOA, *Ticonderoga* was considered a large yacht during the 1930's, but while Herreshoff sketched larger boats following her type, he was never commissioned to complete their designs.

That good fortune fell to Bruce King, after he demonstrated with the design of his own boat, the 41-foot ketch *Unicorn*, that he has a particular gift for the clipper bows and other traditional aesthetic details often used by Herreshoff. At the same time, and again like L. Francis, he is not a traditionalist. Indeed, King had a solid background in racing-boat design and fiberglass production boats before he began designing in his current genre, and perhaps for this reason has been able to bring to the new work a certain flexibility of outlook. Tradition is just one of the colors on his palette.

An early advocate of cold-molded construction, King has placed special emphasis on engineering. A clean, aesthetically pleasing, and impressively strong visible structure is a hallmark of his large sailing yachts. With its great rigidity, its suitability for "one-off" construction, and its high strength-weight ratio, wood-epoxy composite construction is integral to both the function and the soul of these yachts. Most of them are, in fact, a celebration of fine craftsmanship in wood throughout both their structural and their aesthetic aspects, although one of the recent large yachts, the ketch *Alejandra* (1999, 134-foot 6-inch LOA), was built with an aluminum hull.

While best known for his sailing yachts, King has also turned out powerboats of similar caliber. The 1996 *Liberty*, a wooden, 80-foot interpretation of the high-speed commuter yacht concept popular in the 1920's, reflects the same aesthetic consideration and engineering expertise that have gone into the sailing yachts. In 1994 King attracted considerable attention with his design for the Hinckley Company's 36-foot Picnic Boat, an ultra-shoal-draft, water jet–powered day cruiser reminiscent of Maine lobsterboats of the past, but reinterpreted in a streamlined modern concept. Larger and smaller versions are currently in production. Another design for a 31-foot 6-inch, torpedo-stern wooden runabout, powered by twin 450-hp engines and capable of 70 mph, may well be seen as the ultimate expression of that type.

Born in Torrance, California, King was interested in boats as a teenager, and after a short time in college he became intrigued by the profession of yacht design. He received early guidance from West Coast designer/builder Hugh Angelman, and completed courses at the Westlawn School of Yacht Design. He apprenticed himself to a boatbuilder and built a 36-foot, ketch-rigged sharpie of his own design.

Bruce King: *Alejandra.* One can tell from her rigging and hardware that the 134-foot 6-inch *Alejandra* is a contemporary yacht, but by creating a hull with dramatic but elegant curves, minimizing superstructure, and emphasizing finish and craftsmanship, King has created a design that would be appreciated by yachtsmen of any era. *Photo courtesy Bruce King*

In 1964, King began to produce stock designs for the Ericson and Islander fiberglass boatbuilding companies, thus getting involved in the early stages of that rapidly expanding field. His two Ericson 35 designs were especially popular and successful. Soon thereafter he opened his own design office and since then has continued to design for Ericson Yachts, with twenty-four models created to date. Most of the Ericson boats are frankly modern in styling, but one, the Ericson Cruising 36, revealed some of the thinking that would shape King's future designs. The 36 was modern in her rig and underbody and in the basic proportions of her hull, but she had a clipper bow, a raised-deck configuration amidships with bulwarks forward and aft, and a traditional-looking transom, all blended together in an aesthetically sensitive manner.

During the early years of the IOR, King created a stir with a series of fast bilge board racers such as *Terrorist*, *Aggressive II*, and *Hawkeye*. In the mid-1970's he designed and built the 41-foot ketch *Unicorn* for his own use. This design caused a great deal of excitement owing to her particularly harmonious combination of modern and traditional design elements and her cold-molded construction. She was featured in *WoodenBoat* magazine (issue no. 20), and attracted the attention of the man who commissioned the design for *Whitehawk*, King's first large custom sailboat design.

In 1981, King moved to East Boothbay, Maine, and opened his office, Bruce King Yacht Design, in Newcastle. Recent work includes *Scheherazade*, a 154-foot ketch built by Hodgdon Yachts and launched in 2003, and *Avatar*, first of the new Hinckley 70's.

—Daniel B. MacNaughton

FRANCIS SHERWOOD KINNEY

Died ca. 1995
United States

One of Francis Kinney's most important contributions to the field was his major rewrite of *Skene's Elements of Yacht Design*, originally written by designer Norman L. Skene. Kinney's version expanded the scope of the original book, and while it is currently (and we hope temporarily) out of print, it is widely regarded as the most useful text available covering the basics of yacht design.

An important designer in his own right, Kinney carried on an independent career while he also worked in the office of Philip L. Rhodes and, for many years, that of Sparkman and Stephens.

Kinney preferred to design cruising boats rather than racers and had a particular gift for aesthetics, well illustrated by his famous design for the sloop *Pipe Dream*, which serves as an example in *Skene's* and is a masterpiece of long and strong curves without dead spots, in a hull that is lovely from every angle.

Growing up sailing in Edgartown, Massachusetts, Kinney raced successfully in local one-design classes. He attended Saint George's School and skippered in the Interscholastic racing series. In 1936 he crewed on the 6-Meter *Jill* when she won the British-American Cup. Kinney graduated from Princeton with a major in architecture. He then worked in a shipyard for five years before going to work in the Rhodes office and later at Sparkman and Stephens. He enjoyed cruising with his wife aboard a number of his own boats, the last of which was the 43-foot 6-inch yawl *Santa Maria*, built to his design.

Besides *Skene's*, Kinney wrote *You Are First*, a history of Sparkman and Stephens, and with Russell Bourne, *The Best of the Best*, a collection of Sparkman and Stephens designs.

—Daniel B. MacNaughton

BRUCE KIRBY

Born January 2, 1929 · Canada

A journalist who became first a self-taught amateur and later a wide-ranging professional yacht designer, Bruce Kirby was brought up sailing on a widening of the Ottawa River,

Francis Kinney: *Waupi*. One can easily argue that Kinney found in his work the ultimate aesthetic expression of the CCA type. A strong sheer, ample freeboard, dramatic ends, and a well-shaped cabin trunk with large elliptical ports combine with moderate displacement and a cutaway underbody to make *Waupi* a typical Kinney design. © *Peter Barlow*

where he raced gaff-rigged, 16-foot skiffs designed by George Owen. "I always sailed as long as I can remember," he has said. "When the ice broke in the spring, I'd have things floating down the gutter, racing one thing against another. My mother used to say that if they cut off my head, there'd be a sailboat inside."

During the long Canadian winters, Kirby absorbed the history of the pastime by studying old issues of *Yachting* magazine. In school he did poorly in math but much better in English and history. He was about to enroll in college when he contracted pleurisy. Recovering too late in the year to register for classes, he joined the Ottawa *Journal* as a reporter. He remained there for six years until he transferred to the Montreal *Star*, another daily newspaper.

When he was twenty-three, Kirby took a leave of absence to go to England and help a friend buy and prepare a boat for ocean cruising. They selected a G. L. Watson Company–designed, 73-foot ketch, built in 1909, and with friends sailed her into the Mediterranean, where they experienced winter gales. After the owner's wife became pregnant, the cruise ended—luckily for Kirby, for his appendix ruptured soon afterward and he might have died had he been at sea. He returned to Canada, resumed his journalism career, and, sailing on weekends, became one of his country's leading racing sailors. He represented Canada in the Olympics three times—in 1956 and 1964 in the Finn dinghy and in 1968 in the Star class.

Kirby's main class was the International 14, a restricted (rather than one-design) two-person dinghy, meaning that variations in shape and rig were permitted within tolerances. Sailing on the Canadian team that won the class world championship in 1958, Kirby was intrigued that the New Zealand boats were superior upwind in a strong wind. He decided to design his own 14. With little understanding of theory and technique, he drew the lines on shelf paper, but the shape looked right and his boat built from that design was fast and helped Canada win the 1961 world championship. What guidance he had was an old edition of Norman L. Skene's *Elements of Yacht Design*, first published in 1904. Not until later did he discover such crucial skills as calculating prismatic coefficients and wetted surface area.

Kirby produced three subsequent International 14 designs (called the Kirby Mark II, III, and IV) that also were extremely successful under him and other skippers. Other International 14 designers have included the Englishman Uffa Fox, the American Gordon "Sandy" Douglass (designer of the Thistle and Highlander), and two Canadians, Charles Bourke and

Roger Hewson (who later designed many cruising boats for Sabre Yachts, which he headed).

As a journalist, Kirby covered the 1962 and 1964 America's Cup matches in Newport, Rhode Island, where he met some leading American and Australian sailors. Rod Stephens recognized his name and took Kirby on a personal tour of a 12-Meter. "I've just been shown through Heaven by God," Kirby wrote his wife, Margo.

In 1965 Kirby became editor of *One-Design Yachtsman*, a Chicago-based monthly sailing magazine specializing in racing. Besides writing news and instructional articles in a style both precise and lively, Kirby encouraged a number of young boating journalists to the field. In 1969 he moved the editorial offices and his family to Rowayton, Connecticut. He remained the magazine's editor until 1975, when he became a full-time designer. (The magazine later evolved into the present-day *Sailing World*.)

In the fall of 1969, Ian Bruce, a Montreal industrial designer who had sailed Kirby-designed 14's, asked Kirby to design a dinghy small enough to be carried on the top of a car. As they talked, Kirby sketched the design on a legal pad. It had high-performance features not previously seen on small boats, including aerodynamically sophisticated appendages (the centerboard and rudder). Kirby's prospective client backed out, but the next year a prototype did well in the America's Teacup Regatta that *One-Design Yachtsman* sponsored for dinghy classes costing less than a thousand dollars. The 13-foot 10-inch, 130-pound singlehander, with 76 square feet of sail area in a cat rig, was first called the Weekender and then renamed the Laser. It has become an extremely popular international racing dinghy and was chosen as an Olympic class. By 1999, almost 170,000 Lasers had been built.

In 1972 Kirby designed a keel racer/cruiser, the San Juan 24, to the Quarter-Ton rating under the IOR. It has been one of the most popular boats of this size, with 1,300 launched. It was followed by other successful Kirby-designed IOR boats, including *Runaway*, a 39-footer that he co-owned and sailed as a member of the 1981 Canadian team at the Admiral's Cup in England, the major international ocean racing championship. At the same time that he was designing these deep-keel ocean racers, he also drew several cruiser/racers, including a shallow-draft centerboarder, the Nightwind 35, and a 23-foot one-design day racer, the Sonar, which became a popular club racer and the standard boat for competition by disabled sailors.

Kirby designed the 12-Meter *Canada One* in 1983 for his country's first challenge for the America's Cup since 1881. She qualified for the challengers' semifinals and was rebuilt

Bruce Kirby: Laser. The apparent simplicity of the Laser shows Kirby's intuitive design approach. High-performance features that had not been seen on small boats before gave the Laser the speed and handling that have made it one of the most popular classes in the world and earned it an Olympic berth. © *Peter Barlow*

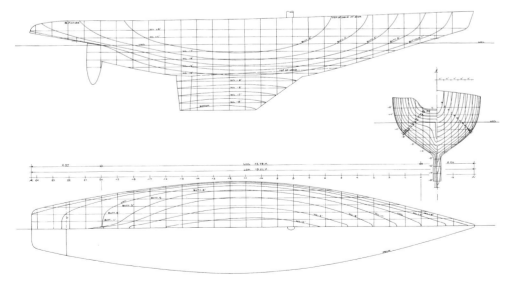

Bruce Kirby: *Canada One.* Designed for Canada's first America's Cup challenge since 1881, *Canada One* made it to the challenger semifinals before being eliminated. She was refitted with a winged keel and competed again in 1987 in Australia. © *Chevalier & Taglang*

Jan Kjaerulff: *Skylark*. The Aphrodite 101 class was designed in 1977 by Elvström and Kjaerulff as an up-to-date one-design with exciting looks and cruising accommodations. Featuring a simplified fractional rig and slender hull free of influence from the IOR, it found an appreciative market for more than five hundred boats. *Photo by Henrik Hansen, courtesy Bent Aarre*

with a winged keel for the 1986–87 Cup trials in Australia. In the 1980's Kirby also designed the first 8-Meters and 6-Meters with winged keels. In 1989 he was a member of the international committee of yacht designers that drew up the rules for the new America's Cup Class, which first raced in 1992.

In 1986 Kirby decided to build a shoal-draft boat for himself to moor off his house in the shallow upper part of the Five Mile River in Rowayton. He was drawn to the sharpie type—a narrow, flat-bottomed, wooden centerboarder long associated with the name of the Florida designer "Commodore" Ralph M. Munroe. He has designed five different sharpies between 18 and 31 feet long, built two of them for his own use, and sold more than six hundred sharpie plans to home boatbuilders through advertisements in *WoodenBoat* magazine. Built with modern materials, they are faster and more stable than traditional sharpies.

By 1999 Kirby had sixty-five designs to his credit in a very broad range of genres. His output during the 1990's included a 42-foot sharpie, a radio-controlled model boat, the Ideal 18 keelboat (popular as a club-owned trainer and racer), and a 23-foot pedal boat in which Dwight Collins completed a transatlantic

passage, unofficially breaking the record for a 2,000-mile passage by a self-propelled vessel. Kirby has occasionally written articles about yacht design and the America's Cup for boating magazines. In 1999 he returned to the news beat to write daily reports on the 1999–2000 America's Cup competition for an Internet magazine.

—John Rousmaniere

JAN KJAERULFF

Born 1943 · Denmark

Currently one of the most productive yacht designers in Denmark, Jan Kjaerulff has so many boats being built from his designs that he himself has lost count. After earning a degree in ship engineering in 1966, he went directly from school to work at the famous Knud E. Hansen design office in Copenhagen. However, he found that his interest in design did not extend to large vessels and he left Copenhagen for the United States to work in New York with Sparkman and Stephens, one of the preeminent yacht design firms in the world.

In 1971 Kjaerulff returned to Denmark and crewed for Paul Elvström when they won the European Championship the same year in the Sol-

ing class. Following their victory, the two formed a partnership, Elvström and Kjaerulff Yacht Design, with the intention of designing and racing a new boat for the Half-Ton Cup the following year. Elvström said to Kjaerulff, "If the boat isn't fast, I will forget that I have known you." With Elvström at the tiller, they won the Cup, which brought the new firm a flood of orders.

Elvström and Kjaerulff followed up with a host of family cruiser/racers for fiberglass production lines—Dynamic, Granada, Bianca, Nordship—each firm producing models of different sizes. Of course, with Elvström, one of the best helmsmen in the world, to show off their sailing qualities, these boats enjoyed an unbeatable presentation.

Kjaerulff's designs avoided the beamy hull forms the IOR encouraged, by preferring more slender elegant shapes. In 1977 he designed Aphrodite 101, a one-design racing boat marketed under the slogan "slim is in." It proved very popular, with more than five hundred built and joining fleets in Scandinavia and Central Europe.

Kjaerulff also made two exploratory ventures designing to the International Rule, neither successful. In the first, he designed a 12-Meter at the request of France's Baron Bich to compete for the America's Cup; however, the project was canceled before construction began. In the second, he experimented with fitting a 6-Meter hull with a stem bulb, as is common on commercial vessels; although the boat proved very fast on reaches, it sailed poorly to windward. Still, the experiment inspired the design of the very successful *Elvström–Coronet 38* motorsailer, where the bulb has worked well.

In 1984, the partnership split into two separate firms: Elvström Yacht Design and Kjaerulff Yacht Design in Copenhagen. —Bent Aarre

JEAN KNOCKER

1901–1998 · France

"Solid, simple, sure and fast on every point of sailing." This was Bernard Moitessier's characterization in the early 1960's of the boat he wanted, in response to Jean Knocker's generous offer to draw his future boat. "Free of charge, of course." But the two men disagreed on the concept. According to Knocker, the 9-meter-long hull had to be of molded plywood, whereas Moitessier wished it to be 12 meters. Built in steel, at 12.07 meters LWL, by Joseph Fricaud, the legendary *Joshua* was launched in February 1962. Jean Knocker renounced his role in the design, but ironically she has become his most famous creation.

English by birth and French by marriage, this Arts et Métiers engineer began to work at Michelin, at that time located in Clermont-Ferrand. Only after World War II did Knocker start to draw yachts, always without charge. His first design, *Peter Pan* (1954), was a narrow

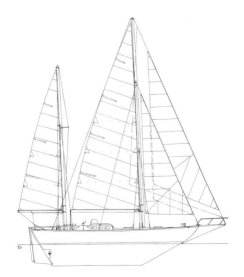

Jean Knocker: *Joshua*. The 14.12-meter LOA *Joshua* is a renowned yacht of which many young and not-so-young yachtsmen have dreamt. Launched in 1961, she has been refitted by the Maritime Museum of La Rochelle and remains an active sailer. *Drawing courtesy Chevalier & Taglang*

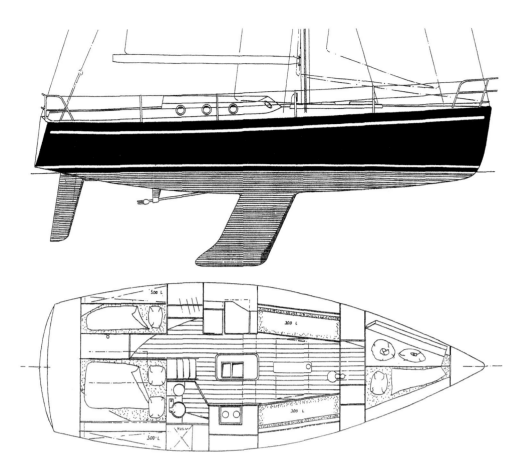

Dirk Koopmans Sr. With her beamy hull, Koopmans's popular 35-foot design No. 369 offers ample space for a small family. Like many of his recent designs she has a short doghouse at the companionway, creating standing headroom and allowing a view of the foredeck from below. He also designed a centerboard version. *Drawing courtesy Rutger ten Broeke*

sloop of 7.9 meters. He continued with the Carsaca series (1963–64) of ketch-rigged centerboard cruisers, of which about eight were built ranging from 9 to 11 meters. He then designed *Pierre Louis*, a ketch of 15 meters, *Rodéo* (1967), and *Karak* (1970), as well as several other boats from 12 to 15 meters long.

True to his English origins, Jean Knocker was a gentleman of character with a good sense of humor and an appreciation of culture.

—Jacques Taglang

DIRK KOOPMANS SR.
Born 1935
DIRK KOOPMANS JR.
Born 1962

The Netherlands

In the Netherlands during the 1980's, the name *Koopmans* became synonymous with sturdy centerboard yachts suited to shorthanded offshore cruising.

Dirk Koopmans Sr. studied ship engineering at the Polytechnicum Haarlem, from which he graduated in 1960. He opened his own design office in 1963. Initially motoryachts were his major focus, culminating in *Bylgia II*, a motor-

yacht with which Eelco Kasemier circumnavigated the world in less than two hundred days, a record that held for several years. Kasemier was also the first Dutch yachtsman to pass Cape Horn from east to west, in the sailing yacht *Bylgia I*, also from Dirk Koopmans's hand.

Although Koopmans became well known as a passionate offshore racer, as a one-man operation his business didn't permit more than brief participation in international events. Still, the publicity his designs received shifted his primary focus to oceangoing sailing yachts.

Initially Koopmans designed traditional, carvel-planked wooden boats, but he soon started to work with hot- and cold-molded construction. The Victoire 22 became Koopmans's first production fiberglass boat, of which hundreds have been built. His most recent designs are built of aluminum because of the advantageous ballast-displacement ratio it allows.

In 1986 Dirk Koopmans Jr. entered the design office after completing the same education as his father. He soon became a valuable partner, and since 1989 Dirk Koopmans Sr. has finally found the time and peace of mind to spend the bulk of his time sailing. He and his wife Elly sailed *Janine 5* over 120,000 miles in voyages that took them to the Arctic, Antarctica,

Alaska, Africa, and Australia. The articles written by Elly for the Dutch magazine *Waterkampioen*, illustrated with Dirk's photographs, made them national celebrities. Their example did much to promote the typical "Koopmans line" as a Dutch national type of yacht, born like the traditional Dutch leeboarders from the conflicting desires to sail in rough seas as well as shallow Dutch waters.

During the 1990's Dirk Jr. became more and more the manager of the design office, while his father worked at putting the experience gained on his long passages into new designs.

—Rutger ten Broeke

JAAP KRAAIER

Born 1913 · The Netherlands

In a career that straddled the years of World War II, Jaap Kraaier helped to bring a family boatbuilding yard into the modern era and designed a number of the Netherlands's well-known yachts, from the small Piraat dinghy to coasters, sturdy motorboats, and elegant deep-keel ocean yachts. There is an overtone of quality and competence in his designs.

As the son of a boatbuilder, Kraaier was exposed to boats and boating from the beginning, and he witnessed firsthand the construction of numerous dories, dinghies, and other small wooden working craft. In 1925, Kraaier became the first in his family to begin a secondary education, during which one of his teachers brought him into contact with the scientific principles of naval architecture.

Kraaier then worked at his father's yard, where his design work brought changes that were not always appreciated, since his father was rather a traditionalist, building by rule of thumb rather than from drawings. Because young Kraaier was an accomplished canoe racer who won a bronze medal at the 1936 Olympics in Berlin, he gradually introduced canoe and yacht building into the firm.

During World War II commissions were scarce, but they picked up after the war. New orders began coming in from U.S. customers. The yard began to prosper and expand, with Kraaier working full-time in the design department. His father retired in 1946. In 1948 Kraaier drew the plans for his most successful yacht, the 25-foot *Kemphaan*, a fast, slim cruiser/racer that was built in series. Orders for various larger yachts of both sail and power followed, partly owing to the exposure Kraaier received as the winner of several design contests sponsored by the Dutch magazine *Waterkampioen*.

Of his prize-winning designs, Kraaier's smallest was the Piraat, an 8-foot hard-chine dinghy designed for home boatbuilders. The whole boat consumed only one full sheet of waterproof plywood. Over the years some eight thousand Piraats have been built, and because of their excellent sailing and rowing properties they remain popular as a trainer for young sailors.

From the mid-1940's until the early 1950's, Kraaier had an interesting working relationship with the Indonesian government, resulting in the design and construction of twenty-four motor pilot-boats for the Indonesian navy, followed by six fast wooden motorboats for its coast

guard. His last commission for Indonesia was for a three-masted schooner, but the vessel was never built because the relationship between that country and the Netherlands deteriorated as the former colony declared and achieved its independence.

In the 1950's the yard expanded to the point where it was building large steel coastal freighters, all from Kraaier's own design. In 1961 Kraaier sold his shares to a fellow director of the firm and started his own design firm, which he operated successfully until the mid-1970's.

Jaap Kraaier can boast of having designed the largest and smallest vessels in Dutch waters. When we interviewed him about his career, he was eighty-six years old and told us that he still played tennis on a daily basis.

—Rutger ten Broeke

GAIT KROES

1920–February 9, 2001 · The Netherlands

"Holland's best kept secret" was the title used by Anglo/Dutch author Ron Valent in his November 1992 article for *Yachtsman* magazine about the Kroes brothers' yard in Kampen. In fact, for more than half a century the Kroes yard has been associated with beautiful, seaworthy yachts of clinker construction.

The Kroes name did not gain an international reputation for the simple reason that Gait Kroes, the designer, was reluctant to publish or sell his designs internationally. He preferred, he said, to keep the whole building process in his own hands.

Gerrit Kroes, father of Gait and Siem, and himself the son of a boatbuilder, started the yard in 1910 in Kampen, specializing in building masts, wooden blocks, and pumps. Later they built and repaired traditional working craft, building yachts as a sideline. However, in the late 1920's, the separation of the Zuider Zee from the North Sea by construction of a huge dike/nineteen mile-long dam, caused fishing in this area to decline, and the fishermen moved their work offshore.

The Kroes yard then focused more on yacht building and steadily established a name, creating traditional flat-bottomed leeboard yachts, canoes, and open day-boats. Gerrit began as a boatbuilder in the age-old Dutch tradition—by eye and rule of thumb. In a late stage of his career he was mentored by designer and boatbuilder J. P. G. Thiebout, who, after the closure of his yard in Amsterdam during the 1920's, had moved to nearby Zwolle.

Gerrit's sons took over the yard in 1955. Gait, who with the help of Thiebout had learned designing and lofting, was well primed

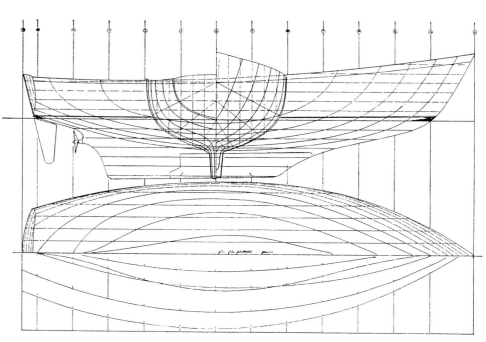

Jaap Kraaier: *Den Swarten Arent* (Black Eagle). The 37-foot *Den Swarten Arent* was unusual for her lapstrake construction. With it, Kraaier managed to create a motorsailer that combined sturdiness and seaworthiness with elegance and good sailing characteristics. *Drawing courtesy Rutger ten Broeke*

Gait Kroes: *Blauwe Reiger.* This 1953 design for the 30-foot lapstrake Scyth class was a slightly enlarged version of the Jupiter, a design that brought Kroes fame and commissions during the postwar period. The Scyth offered better headroom and enough extra space to be more suitable for family cruising. *Photo courtesy Rutger ten Broeke*

to be the designer. His younger brother Siem, trained as a ship's engineer, took responsibility for the technical aspects of their boatbuilding. Their working relationship was to last for almost fifty years.

In 1941 the Dutch magazine *Waterkampioen* published Gait Kroe's first design for *Stormvogel*, a small family cruiser for the Zuider Zee. This design already reflected most of the features that establish a Kroes boat: clinker construction, harmonious lines, a pronounced but sensitive sheer, outboard rudder, a long keel, and a ⅞ marconi rig.

Kroes designed *Jupiter*, a yacht in which he and his brother sailed many successful races offshore and on the Zuider Zee, in 1942. At first glance the design seems to bear a close resemblance to the Scandinavian Folkboat. *Jupiter* is larger and of heavier displacement and has far greater accommodations. In spite of her low freeboard, the designer included distinct tumblehome, giving the hull a rugged and solid appearance. The success of *Jupiter* spawned a series of new commissions.

In 1944 Gait Kroes won a design competition with *Jan Haring*, a cruiser/racer with accommodations for three and a waterline length of 21 feet. In a break with typical Kroes features, *Jan Haring* had an elegant counter stern and was designed for carvel construction. Unfortunately only one was built, by another yard, and according to the designer, "not too well."

For a contest sponsored by *Waterkampioen* in 1947, Gait Kroes designed *Boemerang*, a 24-foot cruiser with good seagoing abilities. *Boemerang* became a success and quite a few were built by various yards, mostly in Kampen. From the 1950's on, Gait Kroes published less and less because of his concerns about the tendency by some individuals to "borrow" yacht designs in Holland and abroad.

The 1960's were a prosperous period for the small yard. The Kroes name became synonymous with uncompromising quality. Yachts like the Scandinavian Folkboat and other non-Kroes designs were built at the yard, but the cornerstone of their production was always yachts designed by Kroes.

In the mid-1970's a new type of yacht came off Gait's drawing board in the form of *Alcedo*, combining spaciousness and shoal draft with a ketch rig. Several early clients owning Jupiters, Boemerangs, and Scyths opted for one of these comfortable boats to complete a long sailing career.

Gait Kroes finished and built his last two designs in the 1990's, the beautiful 32-foot 9-inch sloop *Sardijn*, and *Biesfarnt*, a half-open daysailer of 25 feet. In 1999 Gait and Siem, both without sons to succeed them, decided to retire and leave the yard in the hands of Nico Bakker, their long-time foreman.

The success of the yard was due in part to the superb quality of its products, but even more so to the Kroes brothers' rare talent for maintaining a personal relationship with their clients, based on mutual experience in yachting. From 1942 on, the small harbor in front of the yard on the Yssel River seemed more like a yacht club than a boatyard, and many races and other events organized by the brothers and their friends started from there. Today the harbor is filled with boats built by Gait and Siem Kroes, which have always had their berths at the same location and since their launching, have been maintained by the yard that built them.

—Rutger ten Broeke

JAMES KROGEN

1928–1994 · United States

James Krogen's first love was sailing, yet he left his mark on the world of boating with a series of burly, long-distance, diesel-powered trawlers. Born in Michigan, Krogen grew up sailing on Lake Michigan, became a schooner captain in his youth, crossed the Atlantic, and cruised extensively in the Bahamas.

Following a stint in the navy during the Korean War, Krogen established himself as a designer in Florida, drawing commercial craft for the navy as well as custom motoryachts for the recreational boating market.

In the 1970's, the long-range, liveaboard trawler we know today was in its infancy, nurtured by designers such as Ed Monk and William Garden. Arthur Kady, a sailor, pilot, and race-car driver, came to Krogen with the idea of developing a displacement vessel that could cruise long distances in safety and comfort. With his big-ship design background and practical on-water experience, Krogen went to work on what became a pioneering vessel.

Krogen based his subsequent design on the North Sea fishing boats of Europe, giving the boat the characteristic high bow, bulwarks, big superstructure, and diesel power. The result was the Kady-Krogen 42, which came out in 1976. At 42 feet, with a 15-foot beam and weighing in at nearly 40,000 pounds, the Kady-Krogen 42 had a range of more than 2,000 miles with a 700-gallon fuel supply, traveling at 7 to 8 knots. "Might, done right" was the company slogan, and the Kady-Krogen 42 was both an instant and enduring hit; more than two hundred boats were sold over the next twenty years.

Other designs followed as the trawler market grew through the 1980's. Among them was the Kady-Krogen 36 Manatee, which debuted in 1984. Nearly a hundred of these boats were sold in an eight-year production run. Krogen also designed several sail-oriented vessels, the Krogen 54 motorsailer and the Krogen 38 Cutter (which sold eighty-five boats in eight years).

James Krogen died at age sixty-seven. His son, Kurt, is carrying on the Krogen name, and recent designs include express boats, led by a 52-footer, to go along with its traditional trawlers. In 2002, the company celebrated twenty-five years in business. —Steve Knauth

LOUIS L. KROMHOLZ

1890–1965 · United States

While he was an excellent draftsman with a gift for powerboat aesthetics, little else is known about Louis Kromholz's career. In a practice that ranged from 1909 to 1961, Kromholz designed recreational motoryachts, motorsailers, and sailboats plus commercial and military vessels. He was largely a self-taught designer whose first published design was a 100-foot motoryacht, appearing in *Yachting* magazine in 1911.

Kromholz was a master of pre-streamlining deck structures and the subtle hull lines of pre–World War II powerboats. He later worked with streamlined forms, some of them quite exuberant and futuristic.

The Louis L. Kromholz Collection at Mystic Seaport Museum, Mystic, CT, contains many of his plans.

—Lucia del Sol Knight

TOKIHIRO KUMAZAWA

Born 1922 · Japan

Tokihiro Kumazawa has designed and built dinghies and offshore boats, including K20, which Yo Aoki sailed in his solo circumnavigation; Aoki was honored as the first Japanese Cape Horner. Designed in 1959, K20 uses plywood construction and more than 130 have been built.

The K16 racing dinghy that Kumazawa designed in 1963 has proved very popular, with 1,140 registered. There is also a K28, designed in 1970 with a round bottom, in which Masato Sako completed a round-the-world voyage. K28's have also made a round-trip of the Pacific and a circumnavigation via the Panama and Suez Canals.

After graduating from the Department of Naval Architecture at Kogakuin (now Kogakuin University) and from the Department of Economics at Senshu University, Kumazawa joined the Nihon Yusen Kaisha Company (NYK Line), which prospered prior to World War II but was devastated during the war. After the war he worked for the Japan Lifeboat Company and joined the Okamoto and Son Boat Yard as a designer and manager. Later he founded Yokohama Boat as a cooperating factory for the Okamoto Boat Company, and has been its president for many years.

Kumazawa has been involved in teaching boatbuilding at his alma mater and is associated with the Kumazawa Boat Research Laboratory, where sailboats are designed and built. Among his students are owners, or the children

of the owners, of the small and medium-sized shipyards throughout Japan, whose grassroots activities have greatly contributed to the promotion of sailing in that nation.

—Kennosuke Hayashi

CHARLES P. KUNHARDT

1848 or 1849–1889 · United States

As yachting editor of *Forest and Stream* magazine, a popular marine writer, and a yacht designer in his own right, C. P. Kunhardt was also notable for advocating on behalf of several technical "causes." Chief among these was his promotion of the British cutter type in the great cutter-versus-sloop debate of the 1870's and 1880's.

As leader of the "cutter-cranks," Kunhardt was convinced that the shallow centerboard sloops popular in America had become too delicate and extreme to be safe cruising yachts. He preferred the heavy, deep, and narrow British cutter and was famous for the severity of his argument. He continued this advocacy even as the British boats became extremely narrow and impractical owing to the pressure of the rating rule under which they sailed, and lost some of his following in the process, but his argument was bolstered by several notable capsizes among the centerboarders. Eventually a compromise type better than either of its predecessors held the day.

Kunhardt also advocated scientific yacht design as opposed to rule-of-thumb approaches and, particularly through the 1885 publication of his book, *Small Yachts, Their Design and Construction*, helped to demonstrate that a broad range of boat types was worthy of consideration for varying purposes, as opposed to a one-size-fits-all approach. He later published another book entitled *Steam Yachts and Launches*.

Among Kunhardt's other crusades were his promotion of the yawl rig for cruising, small yachts in general, strong and seamanlike rigs, long-distance cruising, singlehanding, and amateur rather than professional racing crews. While he acquired some enemies in the process, eventually most of his ideas were widely adopted. In *Forest and Stream* he allowed his opponents plenty of space, and as he was well liked by his acquaintances, it seems likely that much of his extremism in print was calculated to popularize his magazine, which it did.

Apparently Kunhardt had a sense of humor. In his long, ongoing argument with designer Thomas Clapham (a strong advocate of shoal draft and light displacement) he would write at the top of his letters "Coffee and Pistols for Two."

As a draftsman, Kunhardt's work was very strong on shading and appealing artistic detail, which made the drawings come alive for the average person.

Kunhardt was born on Staten Island, New York, the son of a shipping magnate. He graduated from the U.S. Naval Academy in 1870. He entered the navy, but resigned in 1873 after becoming ill while stationed in Panama. He went on to design, build, and deliver two gunboats for the government of Haiti. After a stint at Philadelphia's William Cramp and Sons Ship and Engine Building Company, he began writing, often under the pen name of "Big Topmast."

Kunhardt became yachting editor of *Forest and Stream* in 1878, and was succeeded in that position by designer and historian W. P. Stephens in May 1884. His book *Small Yachts* (recently reprinted) appeared in 1885. In 1885–86 he made a lengthy cruise (serialized in the magazine) from New York to North Carolina and back again in *Coot*, a small centerboard sloop.

Always on the lookout for a way to make his fortune, Kunhardt was involved with several mining concerns, most of them unsuccessful. In 1888 he purchased an old cargo ship and converted her into a man-of-war for a revolutionary faction in San Domingo. On her delivery trip in 1889, this vessel, with Kunhardt aboard, was apparently involved in a collision that sunk both vessels, killing all hands.

—Daniel B. MacNaughton

GUSTAV JULIUS "GÖSTA" KYNTZELL

July 12, 1882–July 16, 1961 · Finland

Gösta Kyntzell designed numerous yachts in many different classes. His boats were very beautiful and successful no matter which class they belonged to. He designed several 6-Meter yachts to the International Rule, a class that still has high prestige in Finland.

Kyntzell was born in Gamlakarleby in Finland. He came from an old family of sailors, so it was natural for him to get an education as a shipbuilder. After studying in Vasa he went to Neustadt in Germany, and his education was completed at Chalmers Institute of Technology in Gothenburg, Sweden. After some temporary engagements, Kyntzell became technical manager of Klippan's shipyard in Gothenburg in 1909. During his time in Gothenburg, he started designing sailing yachts. The first boat of his own, *Inga Lill I*, a Särklass A-type 30-Square-Meter, was built in 1907. He designed forty-three more yachts of his own, all called *Inga Lill* followed by Roman numerals. The last was built in 1959.

Because Kyntzell was one of the designers in the team that constructed the Nordic Folkboat, he named the first Folkboat built in Fin-

Gustav Kyntzell: *Femfemman*. In 1959 Kyntzell built his last personal racing yacht, the 5.5-meter L-20 class *Femfemman*. Here she is test-sailing in the 1960 Olympics off Naples. In 1961 she narrowly won the Gold Cup in Helsinki, with two victories, when her designer peacefully passed away, knowing she was doing well. *Photo courtesy Robert Paulig*

land, in 1942, *Lill Inga* without a numeral. He lost the race to launch the first Folkboat built in Scandinavia, owing to the strong Finnish winter conditions.

Moving home to Finland in 1911, Kyntzell became manager of the shipyard in Borgå. Up to 1917 he designed and constructed a number of skerry cruisers as well as other vessels. The first 6-Meter yacht he designed, *Weenonah II*, was built there in 1913. During his later years, up to the end of the 1950's, Kyntzell worked as a tradesman and designer and raced his own designs extensively.

In the years 1925 to 1935, Kyntzell diligently designed boats for the popular Nordic 22-Square-Meter class. During the next decade several good 6-Meter yachts came from Kyntzell's drawing board. The yacht *Inga Lill XXVI* from 1936, *Anitra II* from 1938, *Wire* from 1939, and *Violet*

from 1947 represented Finland in the One-Tonner and Gold Cup races. In 1939, Kyntzell designed *Katrina* for the 8-Meter class.

During the period from 1937 to 1947, Kyntzell designed boats in the international 5-Meter class. *Inga Lill XXVIII*, designed in 1939, won the International 5-Meter Trophy in the same year, with the designer as helmsman. He was not interested in ocean racing, which became popular at the time. Nevertheless, he designed a number of cruisers and crossed the Baltic with his open boats from race to race in different countries.

When the Gold Cup was moved to the 5-Meter class in the early 1950's, Kyntzell designed the yachts that came to represent Finland in the Gold Cup and Olympic Games, yachts like *Nina* and Kyntzell's own *Inga Lill XXXXIV* (Rome/Naples 1960).

—Ulf Lycke

L

FERNANDO LAGOS

1889–1976 · Spain

In 1915 Fernando Lagos began a design and construction tradition that is continued today by his descendants. His reputation as a highly technical, perfectionistic creator of safe, efficient, and beautifully designed yachts, where every detail was carefully analyzed, ensured a steady flow of work for his yard in Spain's northwestern town of Vigo.

After a sound education in mechanical and electrical engineering at the University of London, and in naval architecture at Glasgow's Royal Technical College, Lagos worked in the design office of John Brown on the Clyde in Scotland when they were building the Cunarder *Aquitania*. He returned to Vigo just before World War I.

Lagos designed a succession of seagoing cruising and ocean-racing yachts ranging in length from 20 to 45 feet, and many inshore runabouts, cabin cruisers, sportsfishermen (one being General Franco's *Marola*), sailing dinghies, and catamarans, all built by Astilleros Lagos. In addition, he regularly drew the plans for fishing vessels of around 32 meters LOA, built in wood by other yards.

During the 1950's Lagos was joined by his three sons, who introduced fast powerboat models such as the Lagos 7.5, and racing yachts such as the 10.3-meter LOA Delfin Class sloop for Real Club Nautico de Vigo.

Almost ninety years after its founding, the Lagos family continues to operate the yard, "devoted to wooden boats." —Alfredo Lagos Jr.

CARL LANE
1899–1996
ROBERT LANE
Born 1926

United States

Although only about thirty Penbo cruising powerboats were ever built, their continued popularity can be measured by how many of them have been restored. Father and son Carl and Bob Lane designed these trawler-inspired yachts at Penobscot Boat Works, their Rockport, Maine, boatyard, beginning in 1961.

The 1953 prototype Penbo, *Appalachia*, was a 36-foot round-bottom powerboat with a roomy, two-person layout powered by a single engine, and with workboat lines. Designed as Carl Lane's own boat, eight years later it would serve as a model for a line of cruisers that the family would produce until the last boat came down the ways in 1975.

There was a growing market for cruising powerboats at the time, spurred by Grand Banks, Marine Trader, and other production builders. Demand for the Lanes' previous staple, the Sea-O-Ramic 17- and 19-foot line of lapstrake runabouts, was drying up. The Lanes settled on three distinct molds for hulls from 36 to 44 feet long that were then adapted to accommodate indi-

Carl and Robert Lane: *Penchant.* The 42-foot *Penchant* (launched in 1967 as *Penobscot*) began as Carl Lane's own boat. Built by the Lanes' Penobscot Boat Works, she was the first of the Fifty Fathom Trawlers that were the largest and best-appointed Penbos. The great cabin that completely encloses the aft deck gives the boat a more modern appearance than the typical Penbo's open afterdeck. © *Peter Barlow*

vidual owner's needs for length and interior spaces. Always built in wood, these boats were given salty names: the Offshore Cruiser (similar to today's sedan), the Cruiser Carrier (with midship waist deck), and the Cruising Houseboat (with aft cabin and wing decks).

The Penbos invariably had just a single stateroom, with minimal guest accommodations. That often left room for an unusually large saloon and galley, a signature Penbo characteristic. The Penbo's roomy interiors were designed by Carl Lane and his wife Marie, who together had years of cruising experience. Bob Lane designed the hulls and was heavily influenced by New England's commercial fishing boat traditions. Most of the Penbos, he once said, were a combination of a Stonington (Connecticut) dragger and a Maine lobsterboat.

With a displacement hull, plumb stem, round bilge, and shallow, full-length keel, the average Penbo cruised at about 8 knots; its single—usually diesel—engine sipped an economic gallon-and-a-half of fuel per hour.

Penbos are prized as character boats by their owners. The 38-foot Offshore Cruiser *Scarlet*, built in 1963, has been restored, as has the 42-foot *Penchant* (1967), the 38-foot *Maddie Joe* (ex-*Acadia*) (1969), and the 40-foot *Salty* (1964), among others.   —Steve Knauth

SYLVESTRE LANGEVIN

Born September 23, 1934 · France

Although born far from the sea, by the time he was eleven, Sylvestre Langevin had learned to sail on crawfishing boats in north Brittany. At fourteen, he built his own Moth One-Design dinghy. In 1961, after obtaining an electro-mechanical engineering degree from ESME (High School of Mechanics and Electronics), he went to work at the naval yard Maine et l'Ancien, a metal boatyard at Concarneau.

After a period at SECMI, a large shipyard in Normandy, Langevin became the manager of the yachting department at CNAM at Château-du-Loire in 1966. He then worked for one year for Sud-Aviation, an airplane builder; it was at this time that he designed, with François Sergean, his first yacht, the centerboarder *Arpège*. In the same year, he also drew the steel cruising boats *Troll* (13.5 meters) and *Atlas* (10.5 meters).

Langevin has designed many cruising yachts, first in steel and then in aluminum, such as the Ftot and the Diam 40. In 1980, Marc Pajot ordered from him an 18-meter aluminum transatlantic racing catamaran. She became *Elf-Aquitaine I*. After victories with this yacht, including the Atlantic record, Langevin re-

Sylvestre Langevin: Diam 40. French designers have done a great deal in recent years to develop practical, modern cruising boats that utilize the particular advantages of steel and aluminum construction. Langevin's Diam 40 design combines modern aesthetics with shoal draft, and includes a small staysail that will be much appreciated in heavy weather. *Drawing courtesy Jacques Taglang*

ceived commissions for several transatlantic multihulls such as *Roger & Gallet*, *Meccarillos*, and *Ker Cadelac*, the latter two being trimarans fitted with foils.

Langevin has also designed the production trimaran classes Triagoz 25 and the Edel-Cat 33. However, it is primarily through custom orders that this designer has best expressed himself, while continuing to design customs and pilot-boats, lifeboats, trawlers, and workboats. With designer Ron Holland, Langevin participated in the development of a 40-meter yacht, *Beautemps-Beaupré*.

A founding member of IFAN (French Institution of Naval Architects), Langevin is the author of the popular book on metal construction, *Sailboats and Launches in Metal*, published in 1976.

Sylvestre Langevin's office is in Paris.

—François Chevalier

CHARLES WILLIAM "BILL" LAPWORTH

Born December 12, 1919 · United States

Bill Lapworth is among those who revolutionized ocean racing through the introduction of light-displacement hull forms in the 1950's and 1960's. He is best known for having designed the Cal 40, a light-displacement sloop

featuring a spade rudder and the ability to plane or surf downwind. Not only did his 1963 design become the most successful stock boat in racing history, it also served to introduce stock fiberglass sailboats to the winner's circle.

Born in Detroit, Michigan, Lapworth grew up racing catboats on the Detroit River and then larger boats in Mackinac races. Later he sailed on the famed Sparkman and Stephens–designed, 56-foot cutter *Blitzen* in major long-distance races on the Great Lakes. He graduated from the University of Michigan in 1941 with a degree in naval architecture and marine engineering. During World War II, Lapworth served as a naval officer in the Bureau of Ships at Quincy, Massachusetts, and later at the Naval Repair Base in San Diego, California.

After the war Lapworth became an associate with designer Merle Davis in Los Angeles; Davis died shortly thereafter in 1947. Lapworth bought out the business and from then on ran his own design office. He came into contact with the ideas behind light displacement from his experience racing International 14 dinghies and through the early successes of designers such as Laurent Giles in England. Lapworth had won the International 14 One-Design championships two years running, at Rochester, New York, in 1948 and at Montreal in 1949.

While light-displacement hulls became important contenders in ocean racing, Lapworth initially pursued the type with a view toward economy, recognizing the relationship between displacement and construction cost. His early design for *Flying Scotchman* utilized a dinghy-like hull, glued strip-plank construction, a flush-deck configuration, and simple interior elements, most of which served as structural members. As a result she was unusually inexpensive. A radical boat for 1950, she was moderately successful as an ocean racer and paved the way for Lapworth's future work.

Next came Lapworth's success in 1954 with his Class L series, beginning with the L 36, a one-design, light-displacement, ocean-racing class that included over seventy boats, the biggest class of its type at the time. His 46-foot, reverse-sheer sloop *Nalu II*, built in early 1954, was shipped east for that year's Bermuda Race and placed second in Class C and eighth overall in a fleet of seventy-seven boats. This boat went on to win Class C in the Transpac Race four times, finishing third overall in 1955, second in 1957, and first overall in 1959. A custom yacht whose owner was very tall and specified the reverse sheer, *Nalu II* was the only reverse-sheer design Lapworth ever drew. Another design, the L 50 *Ichiban*, placed second overall and first in Class B in the 1961 Transpac, and several others were built to this design.

In 1958 Lapworth met Jack Jensen, an engineer who saw a future in building stock fiberglass boats. Their first yacht was the well-received Cal 24, a conventional centerboard sloop. Next came the Cal 20, the first of the raised-deck Cals, which went on to become the most popular class of small ocean racers in the world at the time. They were followed by the Cal 30 and the Cal 28, the latter being the first of the series with a spade rudder.

The Cal 40 came out in 1963. Hull No. 2, *Conquistador*, won the SORC the next year. Cal 40's went on to win the Transpac Race for three years running starting in 1965, as well as the 1966 SORC, and took five of the first six places in Class D in the 1966 Bermuda Race, including the win. The Cal 40 was designed with little consideration for the CCA Rule under which she raced at the time, and in fact had quite a high rating for her size. No great performer in light air, she was powerful in medium winds and unbeatable in heavy air downwind, owing to her ability to surf for extended periods of time.

Lapworth, who did much to encourage the light-displacement revolution in the United States, was no fan of modern racing boats. He argued strongly against the switch from the CCA to the IOR handicapping rule and felt that the IOR was a negative influence on hull shape. He particularly objected to delicate modern rigs and the necessity for athletic crews willing to put up with extreme discomfort to go racing, unlike the more family-oriented and seamanlike ocean racing of the past. Lapworth never did design a boat for the IOR. He felt the newer IMS handicapping system may have a healthier influence, but remained concerned that modern boats were inadequately structured for offshore sailing.

Besides his talent as a naval architect, Lapworth was a consummate helmsman and was welcomed aboard ocean racers, many not of his design. He kept his hand in racing his own Cal boats, and in frostbiting dinghies in the off-season.

Bill Lapworth: *Nalu II.* *Nalu II* was one of Lapworth's early successes. Just out of builder Carl Chapman's yard in Costa Mesa, California, she was shipped east for the 1954 Bermuda Race and placed second in Class C in her first race. She went on to become a Transpac perennial, always placing well and winning overall in 1959. *Photo courtesy Newport Harbor Nautical Museum, Newport Beach, CA*

Bill Lapworth: *Melee.* The Cal 40 *Melee* is shown finishing the rough 1969 Miami-Nassau Race. She placed first in her class in that year's SORC and second overall in the series. *Photo courtesy Thomas G. Skahill*

Arvid Laurin: *Uddevalla.* A modernized, 7-meter, carvel-built Swedish double-ender, *Uddevalla* was built in 1934 for the Ågir Yacht Club in Uddevalla, Sweden, as the yacht club's lottery boat. She was raffled off to benefit the club. *Drawing courtesy Bent Aarre*

Lapworth retired in 1986, moved to Maryland, and bought the Cruising Cal 46 *Merrydown*, which he still owns. In 2001, Lapworth and his wife Peggy returned to California, settling in San Juan Capistrano.

—Daniel B. MacNaughton and Thomas G. Skahill

ARVID LAURIN

1901–1998 · Sweden

It is said of Arvid Laurin that "he could read a formula like a poem." Square-Meters and 5-, 5.5-, and 6-Meters came streaming off his drawing board. Within this limited sphere he produced a large number of designs through which he explored, experimented, and proved, again and again, his clear mastery of the class rules. The success of his boats, especially his 5.5-Meters, brought him to international attention, and his designs have won many world championships and Olympic medals for clients from all over the world.

Born in Lysekil on the west coast of Sweden, Laurin trained as an engineer at the Chalmers Institute of Technology in Gothenburg, intending to follow his father into the family-owned firm, Skandia, a manufacturer of heavy engines. In the period between the two world wars, he spent his free time sailing and became such a good helmsman that he won the silver medal in Star boats at the 1936 Olympics in Germany.

Although it was not until the 1950's that he became a professional yacht designer, he began drawing boats in the late 1920's. Despite his enthusiasm for racing, Laurin did design a number of offshore cruisers. Yachtsmen from the Koster Islands traditionally favored seaworthy double-enders, but wanting a similar type in a more modern interpretation, they approached Laurin. He responded with a line of cruising yachts, some of which later went into fiberglass construction. Typically, these yachts had flush decks with self-draining cockpits, and like the older double-enders, they

proved fine cruising boats. One of them, *Casella*, participated in the Transatlantic Race in the late 1950's.

Arvid Laurin died at the age of ninety-seven.

—Bent Aarre

VINCENT LAURIOT PRÉVOST

see Marc Van Peteghem

ANGELO LAVRANOS

Born June 8, 1945 · South Africa/New Zealand

Angelo Lavranos, who became designer of every type of yacht from one-designs to superyachts, was born in South Africa to Greek parents. The family sailed, and in his younger days Lavranos was no stranger to dinghy racing. After high school he attended the University of Cape Town, where he obtained a degree in philosophy. He planned an academic career, but the "designing bug" bit him.

Angelo Lavranos: *Wizard.* Few specifications for 15-meter LOA yachts list economy of construction among the requirements, but those for *Wizard* did, resulting in a chine-hull yacht of plywood construction. Intended for family cruising in New Zealand and occasional ocean voyages and fun races, she's a big, roomy, unique boat. *Photo courtesy Angelo Lavranos*

Lavranos's One-Tonners, Half-Tonners, and Quarter-Tonners are seen regularly at the Ton Cup competitions in Europe. *Royal Flush,* a Quarter-Tonner, won the Worlds.

While most marinas in South Africa contain a number of Lavranos's boats, he is probably best known for the L26 and L34 One-Designs. Ninety of each have been built. The L26, now in its twentieth year, still races for the prestigious Lipton Cup. The L34 has proved to be almost bullet proof and in addition to her round-the-buoy successes has won many long-distance races, including the Mauritius to Durban and Vasco da Gama (Durban to East London) Races.

Lavranos is a very versatile designer, drawing not only race boats but also a large number of cruising yachts up to the largest superyachts, such as the 30-meter *Snowgoose* and the 40-meter *Corster V.* About 30 percent of his work has been light commercial vessels, passenger launches, fishing boats, and sportfishermen. He also is credited with a number of very successful catamarans, some for racing and some for cruising, several of which are in production in South Africa.

In 1996 Lavranos immigrated with his family to New Zealand. He is now established in Auckland in partnership with Alan Wright, designing large power catamarans, sailing catamarans, and monohull sailboats, mostly for custom building. —Dave Cox

GEORGE F. LAWLEY JR.
1848–1928 · England/United States
FREDERIC D. LAWLEY
1878–1953 · United States

George Lawley and Son Corporation (founded in 1866 by British immigrant George Lawley) flourished under the guidance of three generations to become one of the premier yacht yards in America between the years 1874 and 1945. Always more famous as builders than designers, they nevertheless played an important role in yacht design in America.

Information about the design work of the first George Lawley is sketchy and uncertain. The yard made its initial impact in the Boston area by building racing cutters after the English model, and it is assumed that George Lawley designed them, drawing on knowledge he acquired during his apprenticeship in England. Furthermore, the close affiliation between the yard and the Boston Yacht Club, in an era when builders typically designed much of what they built, suggests that he achieved at least a local reputation with boats of his own design. George Lawley Jr. took over the design

On the strength of his amateur portfolio, Lavranos found work with yacht designer Angus Primrose in England for four years, and later worked for two years with Sparkman and Stephens in New York. Lavranos returned to South Africa in 1975 and opened his office in Cape Town. He designed a very successful series-built Quarter-Tonner named *Sweet Pea,* a One-Tonner for Jock Campbell, and a Three-Quarter Tonner for Dave Cox. All were very successful on the race course.

Over the years a large number of boats followed: *Voortrekker II* (holder of two BOC records) for the South African navy, One-Tonners such as *Assegai* and *Arkangel,* and some Two-Tonners. One very good commission was the BOC singlehander *Allied Bank.* She was leading in her race when she collided with an iceberg in the Southern Ocean. Her skipper, John Martin, was rescued by fellow South African Bertie Reed. *Allied Bank* was one of the very first of the wide, flat variety of Open 60's so favored today.

George Lawley Jr.: *Aspenet.* This 1896 drawing of the 31-foot knockabout sloop *Aspenet* is one of the few existing that can be attributed to the hand of George Lawley Jr. After many years sailing on the coast of Maine, the yacht is now undergoing restoration at the International Yacht Restoration School in Newport, Rhode Island. *Drawing courtesy Hart Nautical Collections, MIT Museum, Cambridge, MA*

work from his father. The Lawley yard started out in Scituate, Massachusetts, in 1866 and moved to City Point in South Boston in 1874. In 1910 the yard settled for good in Neponset.

In 1890, the firm incorporated and expanded the yard so that even the largest steel-hulled yachts could be built and maintained. At this time the founder George Lawley retired and his son, George F. Lawley Jr., became president of the newly formed corporation. The yard in Neponset grew into a vast enterprise encompassing more than twenty separate workshops, including facilities for riggers, sailmakers, and machinists, and even a shop for manufacturing engines, employing at its height more than five hundred workers. George F. Lawley and Son built some of the most luxurious, durable, and famous yachts of the age and became the yard of choice for many of the most important contemporary yacht designers.

In addition, the company continued to provide in-house design services for its clients, with George F. Lawley Jr. frequently doing the design work himself. The company's policy of crediting the design department rather than the designer makes it difficult, however, to estimate the degree or importance of his involvement with boat design. Lawley's 38-foot *Elf* was built in 1888, has undergone substantial restoration, and now sails in Maryland waters. In 1896, Lawley designed and built *Gosling,* the winning boat of the Boston knockabout class in the following year.

Among the designers employed at Lawley and Son was Walter McInnis, who worked there from 1912 until 1924 and went on to become a highly regarded designer under the name Eldredge-McInnis.

Fred Lawley, the only member of the family to receive a formal education in yacht design (MIT, class of 1900), began working in his father's firm upon graduation. After a thorough apprenticeship, he became superintendent of the works and head of the design department in 1902. From that date, most of the in-house designs, though not all, came from Fred's board. His yachts combined the thorough understanding of current design practice and theory with careful attention to sound construction practices and selection of the best materials for which Lawley and Son was famous.

Although few of Fred Lawley's yachts achieved a great reputation as racing boats, their owners and contemporary journals found much to admire in their beauty of line, their comfort under way, and the excellence of their finish, especially below decks. Motor cruisers to his design still extant include *Aloma* (1927), *Pot o' Gold* (1929), *Maebelle* (1929), *Old Glory* (1918), and *Welcome* (1910), according to the Lawley Boat Owners Association. Surviving sailboats include *Leilani* (1903), *Seminol* (1916), *Vega* (1905), and *Venture* (1910). He drew all manner of boats from small tenders to 100-foot-plus schooners, but the majority of his approximately 250 designs were for launches and motor cruisers. In the final years of his career, when he had formed his own yard under his own name, he seems to have left the design of sailboats almost

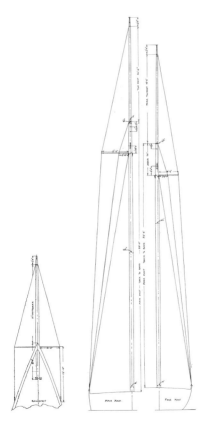

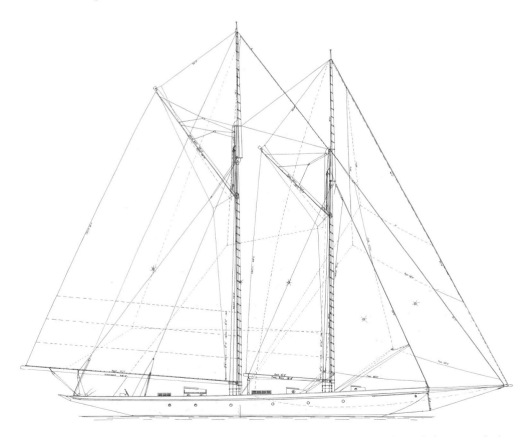

Fred Lawley: *Zurrah.* The 55-foot LWL schooner *Zurrah* was designed in 1901. Her rather flat sheer, typical of the time, probably made her seem sleeker and more sophisticated than would a stronger curve, which might have seemed more reminiscent of the commercial sailing vessels still quite active then. *Drawing courtesy Hart Nautical Collections, MIT Museum, Cambridge, MA*

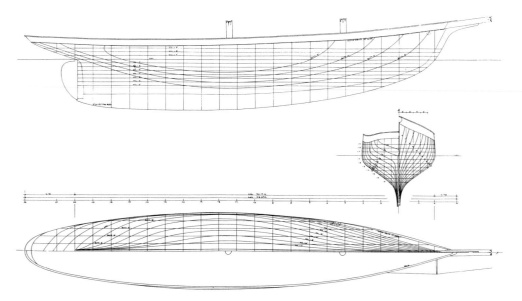

Dennison Lawlor: *Gitana*. While her designer was known to have advocated the cutter type in the great cutter-versus-sloop debates of his time, the 118-foot schooner *Gitana* is more of a compromise between the two. With moderate beam and draft and firm bilges, she was a highly successful racer, and later a well-traveled cruising yacht. © *Chevalier & Taglang*

entirely to others while he continued to design motor cruisers.

With one exception, Fred Lawley neither broke new ground nor pushed design boundaries. That exception came early in his career in the knockabout classes. These came in various sizes, defined by the waterline length (15, 18, and 25 feet were popular), but otherwise placed few restrictions on the designer. Fred Lawley had already designed and raced several of these while attending MIT, and his designs once he joined the firm, notably *Tabasco* (1902) and *Sally VI* (1903), met with frequent success. In 1904, he produced *Sally VII*. On a water line of 25 feet, she measured 50 feet overall, with an extremely flat bottom and a transom almost as wide as her beam—in form rather like a scow. She swept her class. *The Rudder* magazine called her a "freak," but also "by far the best-looking as well as the fastest boat of her class." However, although a fleet of knockabouts is still active in Nantucket, the class began to lose importance with the development of the new Universal Rule in 1904. Soon after, Fred Lawley appears to have stopped designing racing boats.

In 1925, the family sold its interest in G. Lawley and Son. Fred Lawley set up his own yard in nearby Quincy as F. D. Lawley, with himself as president and his father as a sort of president emeritus. The move began auspiciously. The yard's facilities, featuring the newest in tools and equipment, drew enthusiastic notice in the press, and orders for new boats promised a successful venture. But with the stock market crash of 1929 and the economic catastrophes that followed, the yacht market largely evaporated, and only the most established and conserva-

tively managed yards survived. George Lawley Jr. died in 1928, celebrated as the "dean of yacht builders," one year before the crash. In 1933, Fred Lawley sold F. D. Lawley and undertook a career in government service.

Some two thousand drawings of yachts built by Lawley and Son from 1910 to 1940 are at Hart Nautical Collections of the MIT Museum, Cambridge, MA, and a collection of twenty-seven drawings, representing thirteen designs, is at Mystic Seaport Museum, Mystic, CT.

—Walter Voigt

DENNISON J. LAWLOR

1824–January 1, 1892 · United States

Dennison Lawlor was a prominent designer of large steam- and sail-powered yachts in the mid- to late 1800's. He had one of the best eyes for hull form in the business. His pilot schooners are considered particularly handsome.

A self-made man, Lawlor was born in St. John, New Brunswick, Canada, and moved to Boston as a teenager. He served an apprenticeship with shipbuilders Whitmore and Holbrook and later engaged in boatbuilding in Gloucester before returning to Boston and opening his own yard, beginning forty years as a designer and builder under his own name.

In the early 1850's, Lawlor designed the merchant brigantine *News Boy*, which was radical in a number of features and also very successful, gaining the young designer worldwide recognition and launching his career. By the time of his death, he had designed nearly 500 vessels, including over 150 merchant ves-

sels, numerous fishing boats, many towboats, 15 pilot schooners, and 179 steam yachts, many of which were built at his yard in East Boston. His design work was said to have greatly benefited from his very broad experience in all aspects of construction.

As a member of the "cutter-crank" advocates of the early 1880's, Lawlor favored the British deep-draft, heavily ballasted cutters over the shallow American centerboard sloops.

Lawlor's best-remembered yacht is probably the 118-foot LOA, keel schooner *Gitana* of 1882. She enjoyed success in such races as the French Prix de la Ville de Nice and regattas of the New York Yacht Club and Eastern Yacht Club. Other remembered boats are his pilot-boats, the vessels *Hesper*, *D. J. Lawlor*, and *Phantom*, as well as the fishing vessels *Sarah Pryor*, *Sylvester Whaler*, and *Susan R. Stone*.

Lawlor was responsible for a number of inventions, including a double topsail used on square-riggers and a new cut for headsails. He was a major influence on the young Edward Burgess, who often visited with Lawlor during the period when the soon-to-be-famous designer was preparing for his career.

—Daniel B. MacNaughton

HAROLD LEE
1876–1963
FRED S. BRINTON
1872–1938

United States

The names of the Seattle naval architects Harold Lee and Fred Brinton are intertwined by virtue of their twenty-five-year partnership dating from 1907. Their particular focus was on large motoryachts, many of which are well remembered even today.

Harold Lee graduated from Yale University's Sheffield Scientific School, after which he spent two years at Cornell University studying under W. F. Durand, prominent marine engineer and propeller expert. Following his college years, Lee was engaged in practical shipyard work along the Atlantic seaboard, working in some of the leading yacht-building yards there. In 1906 he visited Puget Sound and, impressed by the business opportunities, decided to open an office in Seattle as a naval architect. Within a year he had more business than he could handle alone, so he contacted Frederick S. Brinton, whom he knew through Marine Construction Company in the East, and the firm Lee and Brinton came into being in 1907.

Fred Brinton, a graduate of the engineering department at the University of Pennsylvania, had twelve years of shipyard work as su-

Lee and Brinton: *Aurora.* The 104-foot *Aurora* had a long career under various names as a yacht, an oceanographic research vessel (as the *E.W. Scripps*), and a South Seas trading vessel. She was built in 1924 by J. H. Madden of Sausalito, California. *Photo courtesy Newport Harbor Nautical Museum, Newport Beach, CA*

Lee and Brinton: *K'Thanga.* *K'Thanga* was one of many large wooden power yachts designed on the West Coast in pre-Depression days. Her several owners cruised her extensively and always maintained her impeccably. *K'Thanga* was built in 1926 by John Twigg and Sons of San Francisco. *Photo courtesy Newport Harbor Nautical Museum, Newport Beach, CA*

perintendent at two of the leading shipbuilding plants in the East.

Lee and Brinton soon became one of the more prominent and enduring firms on the West Coast, working in both commercial vessel and yacht design. Shortly before they opened a branch office in San Francisco in 1920, the two owners took on as a partner George H. Wayland, who had been with the firm for some time, and the name was changed to Lee, Brinton and Wayland, with Brinton remaining in Seattle. Wayland went on his own in 1926, making a name for himself as a designer of many successful sailboats in San Francisco.

The volume of work produced from 1908 to 1932 was significant and includes such well-known boats as the 48-foot yawl *Marymount* (1908); 93-foot motoryacht *Lotus* (1909); 67-foot motoryacht *Missawit* (1917); 65-foot *Moby Dick* (1917); 63-foot *Felicia* (1922); 104-foot schooner *Aurora* (1924), later the Scripps Institute of Oceanography research vessel *E. W. Scripps*; 92-foot motoryacht *K'Thanga* (1926); 59-foot *Simba* (1927); and 65-foot motoryacht *Arequipa* (1927).

After Brinton retired in 1932, Lee returned to Seattle and continued on through World War II primarily engaged in government work, and then focused on the design of working craft and fishing vessels under the name Harold Lee and Associates. —Thomas G. Skahill

WILLIAM SHIELDS LEE JR.

Born June 26, 1942 · United States

Bill Lee began sailing on Sabots and Snowbirds in Newport Beach, California, at the age of thirteen when Dacron sails, alloy spars, and fiberglass boats were all new and suspect. He was influenced by the light-displacement designs of George Kettenburg and Bill Lapworth. By exploiting new building methods and materials, his 30-foot MORC boat *Magic* and his 35-foot *Chutzpah* took light displacement to a new level and influenced all of the next generation of West Coast yacht designers.

Born in Idaho, Lee eventually settled in Newport Beach. He attended California Polytechnic State University and graduated with a degree in mechanical engineering. He designed submarines for a year and then moved to Santa Cruz to work for the Sylvania Company. The 30-footer *Magic* was his first design; displacing 2,500 pounds, she promptly won the Monterey Bay race series. He began building the Santa Cruz line in 1974.

Lee's greatest and favorite design, *Merlin*, a narrow-beamed, 68-foot LOA sloop, set the modern standard for ultralight design, and in fact the term *ULDB* (ultralight displacement boat) was coined for her. ULDBs obtain extremely high speeds downwind and, if designed with all-around performance in mind, can achieve excellent average speeds in a wide range of conditions. Displacing only 24,000 pounds, *Merlin* set a course record in 1977 for the San Pedro–Honolulu Transpac Race. She knocked almost twenty-four hours off the old course record by completing the 2,225-mile course in 8 days, 11 hours, a record that lasted for twenty years years until beaten in 1997 by the 73-foot Reichel/Pugh-designed maxi ultralight racer *Pyewacket*.

Paying little regard to rating rules, Lee insisted "fast is fun," and stressed speed, ease of handling, and seaworthiness in his designs. They were intended for downwind racing in the Pacific, although they are now found on the East Coast and on the Great Lakes. His Santa Cruz 27 (145 were built) has introduced thousands of boaters to ultralight sailing and got Lee named to the *Sailing World* Hall of Fame. Also in the Santa Cruz line of boats have been the 33, 40, 50, 52, 68, and 70 models. In 1986, the Santa Cruz 52 was named Boat of the Year by *Sailing World* and in 1989 Saint Francis Yacht Club honored Lee as their Yachtsman of the Year.

Bill Lee Yachts filed for bankruptcy in 1994. Formed anew as Santa Cruz Yachts, the company continues to build the Santa Cruz line and counts Lee as a consultant. In 1998 Lee began Wizard Yachts, a yacht brokerage firm in Santa Cruz, California.

—J. Scott Rohrer and Daniel B. MacNaughton

ERNST LEHFELD

1900–1969 · Germany

The affordable, easy-to-build, lightweight dinghies and cabin cruisers designed by Ernst Lehfeld had considerable success from the 1920's through the 1960's. He is said to have invented the concept of the lightweight, self-bailing racing dinghy.

Lehfeld's interest in sailing started in school when he owned a boat, often homebuilt, an International 14-foot class dinghy named *Olympia Jolle*. This interest in a sport concerned his father, who thought it might detract from his son's future. Nevertheless, his father was able to persuade the owner of a steel-processing factory to hire the young man, who by then had obtained a degree in chemistry. This enabled Lehfeld to continue his hobby of designing racing dinghies. He was, however, reluctant to admit to his interest in design and rarely showed his efforts to others.

In 1923 Lehfeld had his first popular success when he designed a small 5-meter, hard-chined cabin cruiser for himself, the first of his Heintüüt series. There were nine models, culminating in a 1952 design of a 5 KR measured keelboat with a centerboard that is often homebuilt by sailors. Built of plywood, this lightweight cruiser introduced many people to sailing when circumstances and money in Germany were not supportive of the activity. Lehfeld's next popular design was the round-chined cabin cruiser, Sigrun, introduced in 1924.

Lehfeld produced his favorite design in 1952. This was Föhrjolle, the first self-bailing lightweight dinghy. It established his reputation as a popular designer into the 1960's.

When in 1959 the Bavarian Sailing Association started searching for a suitable dinghy to fulfill the desire of youth to sail the lakes of southern Germany, they chose a 1958, 5-meter Lehfeld design called Korsar. The boat's buoyancy in the forward sections helped it to climb its own bow wave and plane. With considerable built-in form stability, Korsar was well matched to the conditions of lakes, which had little or no chop, and the boat was surprisingly fast. Constructed in Lehfeld's preferred cold-molded technique, the laminations and glue were compressed together pneumatically, a revolutionary boatbuilding method for the time. Later this method was refined and became the now-popular vacuum bagging.

In 1960 Germany's leading sailing magazine *Yacht* advertised a contest to develop a contemporary lightweight dinghy capable of coastal cruising using a boom-tent for the night. Lehfeld's 5.80-meter answer became the one-design plywood Zugvogel (Wandering Bird). In Lehfeld's winning entry, the centerboard is replaceable by a 90-kg (190-pound) keel. The centerboard and keel versions have developed into two separate, actively raced and cruised classes. They serve as popular training boats, have completed remarkable voyages, and are currently available in fiberglass or wood.

—Erdmann Braschos

BRYAN LELLO

1910–1989 · South Africa

Born in Cape Town and raised an orphan, Bryan Lello became best known to South Africans as a journalist for the *Cape Times* newspaper. Just before the start of World War II, he joined the crew of the yacht *Driac* on a voyage from Durban to the Caribbean, and this started an interest in yachting that lasted for the remainder of his life.

After teaching himself how to design a yacht, Lello soon was able to support a semiprofessional status as a designer, and when he founded

Abel Le Marchand: *Luciolle*. Winner of the first Coupe de France, beating *Saint-Yves*, the 19.5-meter LOA *Luciolle* was a 20-ton yacht launched in 1891. *Drawing courtesy Jacques Taglang*

the magazine *S. A. Yachting* in 1957, he left the *Cape Times*. Lello became known for developing the use of fiberglass in yacht building with local producers. He developed two successful classes, the Speedwell (*Speedwell of Good Hope*) and the Lello 34. Most active from the mid 1950's to 1980, he died in 1989. —Tom Roach

ABEL LE MARCHAND

1840–1905 · France

Having inherited a small shipyard at Le Havre in 1865, Abel Le Marchand benefited greatly in his early career from the help and advice of his neighbors, the Normand shipyard. He was soon building up his own family yard, and made his speciality the design and construction of yachts.

His relevant analyses of the various clubs' handicapping rules quickly put Le Marchand in great demand. In 1891 his 19.54-meter LOA

cutter *Luciolle* won the first Coupe de France. His 16.40-meter LOA, bulb-keeled *Luciolle II*, built in 1895, and 22-meter LOA *Luciolle III*, built in 1987, won all the races in which they sailed.

Due to high demand Le Marchand founded a second yard in Cannes on the French Riviera in 1895. He was also interested in motoryachts, and in 1888 was the first builder to install a gas engine aboard a yacht, *Djezyrelys*. Several of his motor launches, including *Aya*, *Paquerette*, *Suzette*, and *Ninon*, won honors at the 1903 Paris Automotive Exhibition.

—Jacques Taglang

BEN LEXCEN, AM

March 19, 1936–May 1988 · Australia

The much-loved larrikin of Australian yachting and yacht design, Ben Lexcen was born Robert Clyde Miller in Boggabri, New South Wales. He endured a harsh childhood in the

bush and was eventually abandoned by his parents, ending up in the care of his grandfather. He received his only formal schooling between the ages of nine and fourteen.

Arriving in coastal Newcastle, Miller met the sea, model boats, and then skiffs. This combination had a profound influence on the young boy looking for an outlet for his enormous energy. At sixteen he built his first boat, a lightweight racing yacht, while apprenticing as a fitter and turner. By his early twenties, boats and sailing were his life. He learned sailmaking and opened a loft with partner Craig Whitworth, which eventually became a financial success.

Miller did some of his early racing in the exciting 20-foot Flying Dutchman, an international and Olympic class. It was a comparatively light, two-man planing dinghy, and it clearly had a significant impact on the future direction of his design work. His two radical designs for the local 18-foot skiff class in the early 1960's, *Taipan* and then *Venom*, were lightly built and

Ben Lexcen: *Anticipation*. *Anticipation* is a high-profile yacht in New Zealand, with many wins in her column. Her eighty-eight-year-old owner is said to never miss a race day. © *Terry Fong/AFA Photography*

partially decked, carried genoas, and had three crew. This was a different approach and the boats won races, changing the direction of the class's development.

Miller's first ocean racer, *Mercedes III* (designed in collaboration with owner Ted Kaufman), featured light displacement, with cold-molded construction and dinghy-like sections. At the 1967 Admiral's Cup she was the champion ocean racer. In 1968 the Miller-designed, round-bilged Contender class was chosen by the IYRU as a new trapeze-rigged singlehander. It is still a popular class.

Meanwhile, a boat that could probably be described as an overgrown Flying Dutchman, the 58-foot *Apollo* (designed for financier Alan Bond) was launched in 1969. *Apollo*'s exploits became a legend in Australian ocean racing. Years later when news spread to Sydney that she had been accidentally wrecked on a coral reef in a Queensland race, an informal wake was held in her honor at her home yacht club.

Miller was by now an internationally known designer. His next yacht designs, the near-sisters *Gingko* and *Apollo II*, were clean-lined, efficient-looking 45-footers at odds with the direction of other IOR designs. They were successful, but subsequent developments of the same design concept in various sizes generally did not fare well, and many were designs he would have liked to forget.

It was the first *Apollo* and Alan Bond that led Miller to the America's Cup. In Newport for the Bermuda Race, they chanced upon the 12-Meter *Valiant*, and after an altercation with her sailing master, Bond declared he would challenge for and win the America's Cup. He was serious, and in 1974 the Miller-designed *Southern Cross*, a big boat by 12-Meter standards, carried Australia's hopes again. She was soundly beaten by the Sparkman and Stephens–designed *Courageous*.

Undeterred, Bond challenged again for the 1980 Cup. This time Miller teamed with ex-Sparkman and Stephens designer Johan Valentjin to produce the mainstream 12-Meter design *Australia*. A much better design than *Southern Cross*, she suffered from bad sails in 1977, but rerigged in 1980 she was as good as or better than the defender. By now known as Ben Lexcen (he changed his name to disassociate himself from previous businesses with the Miller name tag), the designer blamed himself as a key crewman for tactical mistakes that might have cost *Australia* a real chance for the Cup.

Giving it one last go, Bond gave Lexcen free rein to design a new boat. Working at the Netherlands Ship Model Basin (an arrangement sanctioned by the America's Cup authorities), he bounced his ideas off two of their naval architects, Peter Van Oossanen and Joop Sloof. With the aid of their advanced tank-testing and early computer-aided drafting, he produced *Challenge 12* and then the brilliant *Australia II*. Her winged keel was a breakthrough in keel design under the International Rule, and *Australia II* overcame fitting failures to come from behind and win the Cup in 1983, after 132 years of U.S. domination. Lexcen, the superb crew, the backup team, and the boat became deserving national heroes. Lexcen was awarded the Member of the Order of Australia, an AM, in 1984.

Australia II's success allowed Lexcen to set up a design office, and a variety of work flowed in. However, as part of the Australian 1987 Amer-

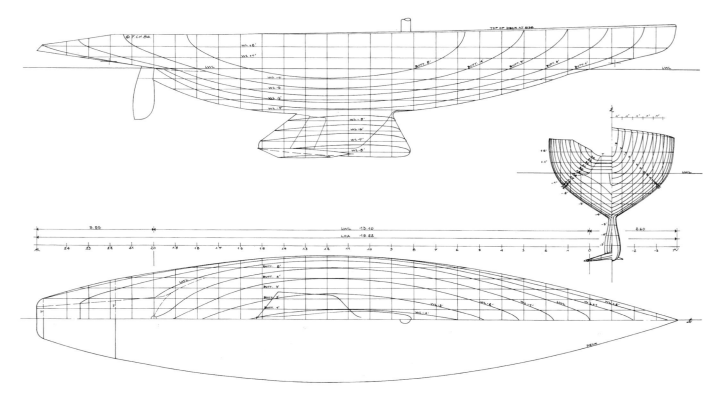

Ben Lexcen: *Australia II*. Lexcen's genius shone in the concept and detailing of *Australia II*, the boat that in 1983 finally took the America's Cup from the New York Yacht Club, putting yachting center stage in the world, with drama and heroics on all sides. © *Chevalier & Taglang*

ica's Cup effort, Lexcen's *Australia III* and *Australia IV* were beaten by the Kookaburra syndicate's boats for the right to be the defender.

Making light of his lack of education, Lexcen was a lateral thinker and something of a genius, able to grasp the essentials of numerous subjects in a short time. He was colorful, good for a joke, eccentric, moody, and impatient, with a constant feeling of tension about him. His sailing abilities were of championship quality; he won many titles and represented Australia at international events. His design method has been described as inspired guesswork, and often it was right too. But without the help of those with whom he collaborated, or who acted as draftsmen/codesigners (such as John King, Peter Lowe, and others already mentioned), it is likely that many of the boats would not have become reality.

Ben Lexcen died of a heart attack at age fifty-two, a rare, flamboyant, creative character who still had much to offer.

—Daniel B. MacNaughton and David Payne

ERNEST LIBBY JR.

Born 1935 · United States

Seven of Ernest Libby's Downeast boat–style designs are being built in fiberglass by Young Brothers of Corea, Maine, for both cruising and fishing, with many competing successfully in Maine lobsterboat races. Many are customized and finished off as fine, traditional yachts.

Libby learned to build boats with Riley and Adrian Beal on Beal's Island, when they were building a sardine carrier in the mid-1950's. However, he credits his uncle, Clinton Beal, with teaching him the most about designing and building boats when he worked for him from 1957 until 1963. Libby then left Clinton's shop and began building boats on his own on Beal's Island.

Over the years Libby has built over seventy wooden boats, all to his own design. While he was building his wooden boats, he became the designer for Young Brothers of Corea in 1978. The seven boats offered by Young Brothers range from 33 to 45 feet.   —Jon Johansen

CARL O. LILJEGREN

1865–1944 · Sweden

C. O. Liljegren, together with Albert Andersson, Hugo Schubert, and Axel Nygren, introduced the modern yacht design in Sweden in the 1890's. He was also one of the foremost innovators of the 1906 International Rule.

Liljegren was born in Gothenburg and studied at the Chalmers Institute of Technology to be a shipbuilding engineer. One of the teachers was Albert Andersson, and among the pupils were Schubert and Nygren. Liljegren began designing around 1890. His breakthrough came with *Puck*, the KSSS (Royal Swedish Yacht Club) lottery boat in 1893. In the middle of the 1890's Liljegren worked for the Herreshoff Manufacturing Company in Bristol, Rhode Island. He probably took part in the designing of the yacht *Defender*, winner of the 1895 America's Cup race.

After some years Liljegren returned to Gothenburg. During his absence and later when he was visiting the United States, he continued designing yachts for Swedish customers. A number of lottery boats for the GKSS (Royal Gothenburg Yacht Club) and other sailing clubs on the west coast of Sweden came from his drawing board.

With *Prisca* (1899), which Liljegren considered to be the foremost of his designs, he created a racing yacht that could compete with the best of Gunnar Mellgren's (1877–1929) designs.

Liljegren was a frequent and polemic debater of sailing rules. He appreciated Alfred Benzon and his Copenhagen Rule and later on the International Rule. On the other hand, he was doubtful about earlier rules and the Skerry Cruiser Rule. To the Copenhagen Rule he designed *Skagerak*, the lottery boat for the GKSS, in 1904. She was the challenger for the Kattegatt Cup the same year. In the beginning of the 1900's Liljegren designed a series of Särklass A and Särklass B yachts.

When the International Rule was instituted in 1906, Liljegren was one of the most diligent designers that first year. In 1907 he designed the 6-meter yacht *Anna* for the NSS (Norrköping Yacht Club), the 7-meter *Storm*, the 8-meter *Roxane*, and the GKSS lottery boat *Vanja*. He also designed several successful yachts up to the 10-meter class. The most famous of these were the 6-meter *Agnes II* (built by G. Kynzell) that won the One-Tonner Cup in 1910 and *Kerstin*, which took the bronze in 1912 in Stockholm.

During the 1910's, despite his criticism Liljegren came to design quite a lot to the Skerry Cruiser Rule. These were small 15-Square-Meter yachts up to the 75-Square-Meter yacht *Varunna II*. After 1907, many of Liljegren's designs were built at his brother's, G. R. Liljegren (1868–1932), shipyard in Färjenäs outside Gothenburg. During the 1910's and the beginning of the 1920's he also designed some cruisers and experimental hydroplane yachts.

In the 1920's Liljegren emigrated to the United States because he saw himself as misunderstood. He died there in 1944.

—Bent Aarre and Ulf Lycke

JAN HERMAN LINGE

Born January 28, 1922 · Norway

Using the suffix-*ling* as a trademark, Jan Herman Linge's body of work is easy to identify: the Olympic class Soling; the smaller Yngling; the motoryachts *Fjordling*, *Wesling*, and *Sagaling*; the sailing yachts *Gambling*, *Willing*, and *Laerning*. The well-known Soling, a three-person keelboat, replaced the now-venerable Johan Anker–designed Dragon at the 1972 Olympics at Kiel, Germany, and it has competed in every Olympics since 1972, with the addition of a cockpit sole as the only modification to the original design.

Linge was born in Trondheim on the Norwegian coast. He went to sea on a tanker at the age of fifteen and began correspondence courses to learn about shipbuilding. He became involved in the underground resistance against the Germans during World War II, and by 1942 his activities had drawn such notice that he was forced to escape, sailing to Sweden on a small boat of his own design. He resumed his studies in Sweden and, following the end of the war, traveled to England and the United States to study naval architecture (at the Stevens Institute of Technology in New Jersey) between the years 1946 and 1949.

Returning to Oslo, Linge found the market weak for sailing yacht design. For a short time around 1950 he developed fast torpedo boats for the Norwegian navy before moving into the civilian market to produce motorboat designs for the firm Båtservice-Gruppen. He opened his own design firm in 1957.

Linge introduced an experimental 5.5-Meter with a shortened reverse transom in order to concentrate weight toward the center. King Olav of Norway, a keen 5.5-Meter sailor, pronounced it the ugliest boat he had ever seen, but truncated his own boat in the same way when he saw that the "ugly" boat won races.

In 1964 Linge designed the Soling, the boat that would make him internationally known, although fame would have to wait until the 1972 Olympics. The Soling prototype was built of wood and was intended as a training boat for the then Olympic class 5.5-Meter. By 1966 it was built of fiberglass and in 1967 competed in trials to replace the Olympic class Dragons. The Soling was not the fastest of the contenders for Olympic class one-design status, but its good looks, fine sailing qualities, and reasonable construction cost made it the most suitable candidate.

In 1967, Linge followed the Soling with the Yngling (meaning "youngster"), a smaller adaptation of the Soling fitted with a cuddy and intended primarily as a trainer for young

sailors. The Yngling also found a warm welcome among sailors and clubs, especially in central and northern Europe, and has become an important international class.

—Bent Aarre

JOSEPH NAPOLEON "NAP" LISEE

1871–1946 · United States

One of the pioneer speedboat designers of the twentieth century, Nap Lisee worked first for what was to become Chris-Craft and later for Gar Wood.

Lisee was born in Troy, New York, and grew up there and in Marine City, Michigan. By his teens he had a local reputation as a woodworker, but his career as boat builder and designer began in earnest when in 1905 he went to work in nearby Algonac for Chris Smith, who would be the patriarch of Chris-Craft. At that time the Smith boat shop was building rowing skiffs, and gasoline-powered boats of increasing speed and local renown.

The rapid improvement of gasoline engines helped fuel the enthusiasm of the owners and the creativity of the builder/designers in those years, when development of racing speedboats was intense. By 1910 the Smith shop had ten employees and ten years of experience building boats and matching them with engines.

It is now difficult to sort out who designed the Smith speedboats before 1915. Among the shop's builder/designers between 1905 and 1915 were Nap Lisee, Jack and Martin Beebe, and Chris Smith himself. All of them were astute, self-taught "mechanics," as the word was used in 1910. The Smith shop was most likely a collaboration.

Be that as it may, their raceboats began to conquer the world. The series of boats named *Reliance* were small, light boats powered by Joe Van Blerck's small and relatively light engines and by the Sterling racing engines that became available after 1911. *Baby Reliance III*, greatest of them all, was a 26-foot hull with a 250-hp Van Blerck 12-cylinder engine, and set a record of 53.73 mph in 1912.

If Nap Lisee was only a member of the team that designed the *Reliances* and others, he was

---

Jan Herman Linge: Soling (opposite). Reaching in a stiff breeze, this Soling shows her characteristic stiffness, speed, and beauty. In 1969 her sailing qualities, looks, and heavy-weather handling abilities made her the unanimous choice of the IYRU for a three-person keelboat in the Olympics, finally replacing the venerable Johan Anker–designed Dragon One-Design class in 1972. © *Peter Barlow*

---

the sole designer of the raceboats Gar Wood campaigned from 1920 to 1933 as *Miss America I* through *X*. The first *Miss America* had two V-12 Liberty aircraft engines and shot through a measured mile at 76.66 mph after winning the Harmsworth Trophy and the Gold Cup for Gar Wood in 1920. The tenth *Miss America* had four V-12 Packard aircraft engines of 1600 hp each and set a world water speed record of 124.9 mph in 1932.

Lisee designed the first two *Miss Americas* in Chris Smith's shop, the final eight as Gar Wood's employee, having defected from Smith in 1923. Although in photographs they look like big wooden boxes full of engines—which they were—the *Miss Americas* had to have many components that were just right: engine beds, gearboxes, exhausts, steering apparatus, rudders and mounts, props and shafts, heights and angles of the hull's steps, and more. Nap Lisee got these things right. —Joseph Gribbins

CHARLES LIVINGSTON

1857–1937 · Scotland/England

During the nineteenth century, many yachtsmen had an interest in naval architecture, and some yacht clubs listed the advancement of the science among their objectives. As a result, there were many amateur designers. Charles Livingston was one of the most successful of these, particularly in the design of small raters (designed to the Yacht Racing Association's Length-and-Sail-Area Rule of 1886).

Livingston was born in Govan on the Clyde in Scotland, coming to Liverpool, England, as a boy with his parents. A man of boundless energy, he built an outstanding career in shipping while also devoting himself to yachting and

serving as owner at various times of over forty different yachts and as an officer of many clubs.

He designed over sixty boats, ranging from paddling and sailing canoes to the 33-ton cruiser *Alruda*, including open boats, canoe yawls, one-raters, Windermere yachts, the fast steam launch *Tetera*, and a number of fast cruising yachts such as *Molita*, still sailing on the west coast of Scotland. Possibly his most successful racing yacht was the 2½ Rater *Modwen*, one of the few boats to beat the famous Herreshoff *Wenonah* on the Clyde.

Five of Livingston's designs are at Mystic Seaport Museum, Mystic, CT. —Brian Smith

FREDRIK LJUNGSTRÖM

June 16, 1875–February 18, 1964 · Sweden

Fredrik Ljungström is best remembered as the creator of the Ljungström rig, featuring a revolving unstayed mast around which the sail was rolled. In the 1930's, this was new thinking. While the Ljungström rig had supporters and detractors, it has continued to influence subsequent designs, such as the Dick Newick–designed trimaran *Spark*.

Ljungström lived his entire life at Lidingö just outside of Stockholm. He was educated as an engineer and soon became well known in Sweden for his mechanically ingenius inventions, including turbine locomotives. In his free time he sailed, but it was not until 1933 that he began to design boats. He had an idea that every line should be a part of a circle, and he loved negative sheers, which gave some of his boats a radical look.

The 22-Square-Meter *Vingen* of 1921 was Ljungström's first boat. It had a high slim

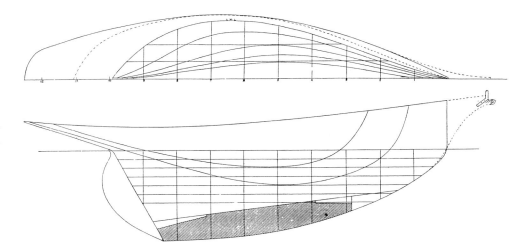

Charles Livingston. Little is known of this 20-foot LWL racing yacht except that she was designed in 1889 for use on Lake Windemere in England. Note the extreme fineness of the bow and the dotted lines, hinting at a modified and perhaps more visually balanced profile. *Reproduced from* Forest and Stream

Fredrik Ljungström: *Twin Wing*. With her many unusual features, it is hard to say what is most radical about *Twin Wings*, but the rig has continued to be used over the years by designers who seek the ultimate in simplicity and ease of handling. © *Mystic Seaport, Rosenfeld Collection, Mystic, CT*

Fredrik Ljungström: *Elly*. *Elly*, another Ljungström design, must have looked like the wave of the future in the 1930's—or perhaps the end of the world. While her hull form never took hold, her rig might have done so, were it not for the natural conservatism of yachtsmen and the influence of handicapping rules. © *Mystic Seaport, Rosenfeld Collection, Mystic, CT*

mainsail without a jib. His next boat, in 1931, was the 120-Square-Meter *Ebella*. The family was out sailing that boat in a gale in 1932 when his son got hit by the boom and nearly fell overboard. Thereafter Ljungström strove for a new rig that would prevent such a thing from ever happening again.

In 1934 Ljungström patented the Ljungström rig. The cantilevered mast rotated for reefing and furling of the sail, facilitated by ball bearings in the maststep and partners. His first versions had a backstay so the mast could bend to suit the wind and weather conditions. The loose-footed double sail could be split into two parts and spread out like a spinnaker when sailing downwind.

Besides designing yachts, Ljungström experimented with the application of the so-called circular hull for fishing boats and cargo ships. He made a visionary drawing in 1952 of a 2,000-ton freighter with both engines and a 1,000-square-meter Ljungström rig. In 1982, long after his death, a freighter was built in the United States with a Ljungström rig to save on fuel.

—Bent Aarre

LOGAN FAMILY

FAMILY PATRIARCH ROBERT LOGAN
1837–1919

New Zealand

In New Zealand, the Logan name is still synonymous with the very highest quality in yacht design and construction, even though Logan Brothers, as a business entity, closed down over ninety years ago. Their famous rivalry with the Baileys, another prominent family involved in yacht design and construction, pushed both families to design and build faster racers, creating a significant and colorful racing history in Auckland.

Patriarch Robert Logan immigrated to New Zealand in 1874. He had been a foreman with Robert Steele and Company on the Clyde River in Greenock, Scotland, where they built yachts to designs by William Fife II and G. L. Watson, and many famous clipper ships, such as *Taeping and Ariel*. After a brief period of employment by George Niccol in Auckland, he set up his own business at Devonport on the

north shore of Auckland's Waitemata Harbour in about 1878. Four of Robert's sons, John (1862–1929), Robert Jr. (1864–1932) Archibald (1865–1940), and William (1875–1956), worked for him and became skilled tradesmen and helmsmen. John and Arch were talented designers as well.

Quickly Logan obtained considerable yacht work because of his advanced designs and building techniques. Back in Scotland, Logan had been involved in building diagonal-planked lifeboats for the liner trade. He adapted this technique to yacht construction, introducing and perfecting the classic New Zealand double- and triple-diagonal frameless construction—an early ancestor of today's cold-molded technique—working with the long-lived, extraordinarily strong local kauri timber. This method used no glue, relying on rivets to hold the layers together, with oiled or painted cloth between the layers, and a system of longitudinal stringers and widely spaced floor timbers providing additional reinforcement. It was a relatively rigid and watertight building method, and is said to have been easy too.

Robert Logan: *Akarana* (above). *Akarana*, designed and built in 1888 by New Zealander Robert Logan, is one of a long string of successful and able cruiser/racers. *Photo courtesy Australian National Maritime Museum*

Robert Logan: *Waitangi* (right). The 10-Rater *Waitangi*, designed and built in 1894, is still sailing today, in part because of her triple-skin, diagonally planked, frameless hull construction, a light, rigid, and watertight ancestor of today's cold-molded method, and in part because of the nearly indestructible kauri wood used to build her. © *Robert Keeley*

Robert Logan: *Yvonne.* The 5-Rater *Yvonne* of 1893 survived the 1909 Rudder Ocean Race with only scratches after being driven over the rock mole at Port Chalmers when the fleet was struck by a sudden violent gale, a tribute to her Logan three-skin diagonal construction. *Photo courtesy Harold Kidd*

The yard's first significant yacht was the 28-foot centerboard cutter *Jessie Logan* in 1880, followed by a long run of varied and able keel yachts such as *Muritai* (1882, 13 tons), *Matangi* (1886, 16 tons), *Akarana* (1888, 7 tons), *Aorere* (1892, 7-Rater), and *Waitangi* (1894, 10-Rater). After 1895 he concentrated more on building wooden steamers.

In 1891 John, Robert Jr., and Arch set up in business as the Logan Brothers on the south shore of the Waitemata. They very quickly became the premier yacht designers and builders in the country, spurred on by competition with the Baileys. Arch's designs came to predominate, starting with his 5-Rater *Moana* in 1895, which was influenced by the big Watson-designed cutter *Britannia*, and progressing through a series of brilliantly successful larger raters, such as *Thelma* (1897), *Rainbow* (1898), *Iorangi* (1901), *Ariki* (1904), and *Rawhiti* (1905). Arch also produced outstanding designs for the short-lived Half-Rater "patiki" class around 1898 and for the 22- and 26-foot racing mullet boat classes in the early 1900's.

Logan Brothers wound up their business in 1910. John and Robert Jr. entered the house-

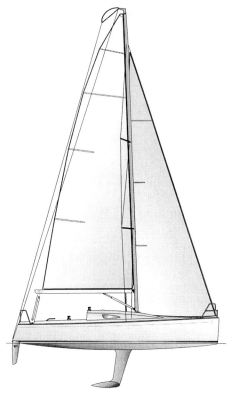

Marc Lombard: Figaro 2 One-Design. The Figaro 2 One-Design resembles larger, unrestricted offshore racing class yachts. She achieves spectacular speed, especially downwind, from a combination of ultralight construction, large sail area, minimum wetted surface area, and wide beam carried all the way aft. She features twin rudders to keep her under control. *Drawing courtesy Chevalier & Taglang*

building trade, while Arch continued designing and building boats from his harborside property in Ngataringa Bay. His yachts were typified by their beauty of line. He placed a great deal of importance on the hull profile and would start with that, often putting a draft in a drawer and pulling it out after several days to check that it was "right." Aesthetics came first, even with his working boats. Arch continued to be in demand for racing mullet boats, designing and building a number of champion boats in the 22- and 26-foot classes, the closest thing Auckland had to one-design racing.

With an upsurge in deep-keel, racing yacht construction in the 1930's, Arch Logan spent the rest of his working life producing a series of such designs, from *Little Jim* in 1934 to *Aramoana* in 1938, and supervising their construction. He also designed two successful dinghy classes, the marconi-rigged, 18-foot clinker patiki M-Class dinghy of 1922 and the similar 12-foot Silver Fern dinghy in 1933.

Arch Logan's younger son, Jack (1910–1984), was also a superb yachtsman and dinghy designer. In the 1940's and 1950's his personal yachts dominated the popular unrestricted 18-footer fleet on the Waitemata, beginning with Arch's last boat, *Matara* (1939), and later with his own designs: *Komutu*, *Tarua*, and *Te Kana*.

—Harold Kidd and Robin Elliott

MARC LOMBARD

Born February 12, 1959 · France

One's first ideas are often the best, and many are the naval architects who have asserted themselves quite young. Marc Lombard grew up with a hydrofoil in his mind and has not ceased to demonstrate the utility of this device.

Born near Paris at Antony, Lombard was lucky enough to have parents who were fond of yachting. From early childhood, he sailed aboard dinghies and cruisers. He enrolled in the Paris School of Sail at age fifteen and rapidly became an accomplished skipper, spending all of his leisure time on the water.

After high school, Lombard studied yacht design at the University of Southampton from 1977 to 1980. He worked briefly with Philippe Harlé and then designed his first 40-foot hydrofoil for Dominique Montessinos. The Formula 40 class was still young, and this hydrofoil trimaran was widely noticed. With his 45-foot catamaran *Bénéton*, Lombard raced in the La Baule–Dakar Race, and followed this with the design of the two hydrofoil trimarans *Lejaby* and *Ker Kadelac*, both achieving victories in 1987 and 1989.

Lombard's predilection for multihulls found an outlet with the mass production of the

Jeantot-Marine yards' Privileges series; two hundred boats have been built. He also has a liking for cruising monohulls, of which his 107-foot maxi *Notika-Tecknic* and *RM 10.50* (this last having received the 1999 Boat of the Year Award) are the proof. Also well known are *Run 50*, a fast sailing cruiser born from the latest offshore race developments; the 60-foot Open Class *Whirlpool-Europe 2*, launched for the 1998 Route du Rhum Race; and Roland Jourdain's 60-foot Open Class *Sil Enterprise*.

By 2000, Lombard had become a major force in the French Open 60 trimaran racing circuit. He designed *Banque Populaire II* in 2000 as well as *Banque Populaire III* and *Sopra Consulting* in 2001.

Lombard is working on developing designs other than the Open 60 class, such as the Beneteau Figaro II and the Opium 39. His office is in La Rochelle, France.

—François Chevalier

DAIR N. LONG

1916–1971 · United States

Dair Long was a name that flashed across the horizon in the days leading up to World War II. His first designs were sailboats, and as a virtually unknown twenty-one-year-old UCLA student, he won first prize in a design contest with the 9-foot I.C. (interclub) dinghy, which became a popular racing class. His next design was the 20-foot Viking class, a deep-keel sloop with a small cabin that grew into a fleet of twenty boats, some of which still sail out of Newport Harbor sixty-one years later.

Long went on to the University of Michigan to complete his degree in naval architecture and marine engineering. He soon focused on high-speed powerboats, which evolved into fast patrol and rescue craft, 45-foot picket boats and an 82-foot PT type, which figured prominently in World War II. Many of his high speed 63- and 85-foot AVRs (aviation rescue boats) were successfully converted to fast motoryachts by postwar yachtsmen.

When hostilities ceased, he concentrated on fast, rugged sportfishermen and cabin cruisers that were refinements of the ideas he had developed for military craft. In 1945 Long had designed the famous Harco 40 and the equally popular 26-foot Western Fairliner for the postwar boating boom. Both had long production runs and achieved an excellent reputation. Next followed a series of custom sportfishermen, which became the first choice for West Coast sportsmen who fished from Mexico to the offshore California islands and demanded boats that were fast, strong, soft riding, and fuel efficient.

A deep forefoot and "shockless" sections distinguished Dair Long's powerboat designs, with deadrise carried well aft to eliminate pounding in a seaway. A thorough knowledge of propeller design brought him additional recognition and undoubtedly ensured that his designs performed up to their full potential.

—Thomas G. Skahill

FREDERICK KISSAN LORD

1878–1968 · United States

In a career running through 1947, Frederick Lord designed a wide range of boats, including sailing yachts, runabouts, and naval vessels, but he is primarily known for his fast power yachts. He preferred V-bottomed hull forms and believed that a proper powerboat should be long and light so as to be easily driven and to ride level at all speeds.

Lord's best-known design was *Foto*, the 33-foot 6-inch chase boat he designed in 1929 as a working platform for photographer Morris Rosenfeld. The third and final boat to carry the name, *Foto* was everything Lord believed in, being long, lean, very light, and V-bottomed. He gave her generous flare all around to help keep spray off the cameras, and took pains to see that she was also very good looking. Morris Rosenfeld and his son Stanley used *Foto* for over fifty years, taking over a million photos considered to be among the best in the history of yachting. *Foto* has been restored and is in frequent use as a yacht.

The designer was an enthusiastic ship modeler and became interested in handicap racing of powerboats. He served as the official measurer for the Huntington Yacht Club and New Jersey Yacht Club for many years. He became a member of the Society of Naval Architects and Marine Engineers in 1905.

The Frederick K. Lord Collection is at Mystic Seaport Museum, Mystic, CT.

—Daniel B. MacNaughton

LINDSAY A. LORD

1902–1991 · United States

Lindsay Lord is best known for his work with planing powerboat hull shapes during the latter part of the twentieth century. Working from his office in Maine, Lord developed what he termed the *monohedron*, a literally "one-sided," planing-hull form where the aft portion of the chine runs largely parallel to the keel, creating a constant deadrise angle from around the middle of the hull to the transom. The hull shape is still in common usage, and paved

Dair Long: *Antiope.* Designing for the Harbor Boat Building Company, Long put his wartime experience with fast air/sea rescue boats into this post–World War II production model. It filled a niche for a fast family cruiser and sportfisherman. Fast, seaworthy, comfortable, efficient, and strong, these boats captured a large segment of the market. © *Peter Barlow*

Frederick Lord: *Foto.* The 33-foot 6-inch *Foto* was built for marine photographer Morris Rosenfeld, many of whose photographs illustrate this book. Light displacement and a relatively long, narrow, V-bottomed hull form make her fast and economical to operate. *Foto* is still going strong under new ownership. © *Mystic Seaport, Rosenfeld Collection, Mystic, CT*

Lindsay Lord. This 60-footer must have been quite a sight, with her exuberant streamlining and all-polished-aluminum exterior. With high freeboard and 18 feet of beam, she had remarkable accommodations and planed comfortably at a 17-knot cruising speed. *Drawing reproduced from* The Rudder

the way for other forms such as the Deep-V developed later by Ray Hunt. Lord's ideas were described in his 1963 book, *Naval Architecture of Planing Hulls*.

Working in an era when the performance limits of known planing-hull shapes were being extended by improved marine engines, Lord believed the science that had been used to design displacement hulls should be applied to planing shapes. In his book, which began as a doctoral thesis, Lord laid a foundation for "the intelligent approach to the problems of planing hull design and to the potential improvements to come.... Many a glorious vessel has been designed by rule of thumb, yet, in this scientific day, [it's important that] the rule of thumb be brewed from mathematics."

Born in Puerto Rico, Lord first gained experience while an undergraduate student of naval architecture at MIT in the 1920's and 1930's, designing fast powerboats for wealthy rum-running syndicates. He went on to earn a doctorate of science in naval architecture from George Washington University. He then taught naval architecture to students at George Washington and later oversaw naval architecture instruction for the U.S. Army, Navy, Coast Guard, and the Maritime Commission.

Lord was a lieutenant commander in World War II, assigned to the maintenance and development of PT boats and other high-speed patrol craft in the Pacific, "an ideal situation for the study of fast boats in hard service," he later wrote.

After the war, Lord established his own design office near Portland, Maine, and produced large U.S. Coast Guard patrol boats, oilfield supply boats, and luxury motoryachts. He was proud of his part in the establishment of the United States Power Squadron, for which he wrote courses and taught classes.

Lord never ceased his research. At age eighty-four, he was developing a new fast hull configuration to minimize "ridiculous wakes stirred up by planing hulls loaded beyond efficient capacity and overpowered to regain their intended speed."

—Steve Knauth

ROYAL LOWELL
November 23, 1926–November 11, 1983
CARROLL LOWELL
October 16, 1937–July 29, 1997

United States

Brothers Carroll and Royal Lowell became two of the best-known designers of lobsterboats and lobsterboat-style yachts on the Maine coast. They were among the first to popularize the lobsterboat hull as a luxury vessel, or "lobsteryacht," and added many refinements to the style throughout their designing and boatbuilding careers.

The Lowells' grandfather, William "Pappy" Frost (1874–1967), was one of the foremost developers of the Jonesport–Beals Island lobsterboat. He originated the so-called razor-case boat as a young man in Nova Scotia, and brought the style with him when he moved to Beals Island around 1912. The Lowell brothers took their departure from this well-known and much-admired workboat design.

Royal was born on Beals Island, Maine, and was a constant visitor to his grandfather's boatshop, where Frost taught him to design and build boats. The first boat he built was a kayak at age ten. He then began to build peapods with his father Riley Lowell (1905–1963), who was also the head man in Frost's shop. After a time in the Merchant Marine during World War II, Royal returned to Maine, designing and building wooden boats alongside his grandfather, father, and brothers in the Portland area. He also enrolled in a home study course through the Westlawn School of Yacht Design.

Carroll Lowell was born in Medford, Massachusetts, where the family had moved to find work during the Depression. He too grew up working side by side with Will Frost. He later did some rebuilding and redesigning of Frost's boats, most notably *Merganser* and his subsequent *Osprey*.

After Will Frost retired and his Portland shop closed, Royal and his father and brothers opened a yard inland, in Gray, Maine. Soon after, they moved to Yarmouth, nearer the coast.

Carroll, striking out on his own, had incorporated Even Keel Marine in Yarmouth in 1961 with partner Archie Ross. There Carroll built boats designed by his brother. After their father's death in 1963, Royal joined Carroll at Even Keel. The Lowells are credited with the first lobsterboat designed with a split wheelhouse, which was on the *Tam O'Shanter* in 1976 (designed by Royal and built by Carroll).

Royal started his own naval architecture firm in 1977 with partner Eliot Spalding, a sailboat designer. Over the years Royal designed numerous boats for prominent fiberglass companies, including Jarvis Newman, Sisu, JC, Bruno Stillman, Harris, Blue Seas, and Runaway. He also is credited with introducing the semi-built-down hull style.

When Royal died in 1983, Carroll began building more boats based on his own design work. One of his most popular lobsteryacht designs was the 38-foot wooden sportfisherman *Sea Scribe*, which he built in 1985. Carroll's boats are thought to add even more refinement and grace to the lobsteryacht style.

Carroll drew a number of designs for the Johns Bay Boat Company of South Bristol,

Carroll Lowell: *Sea Scribe*. *Sea Scribe* is a 38-foot wooden lobsteryacht designed and built by Lowell in 1985. A no-holds-barred luxury project, the *Sea Scribe* is considered Lowell's masterpiece. In this vessel, beautiful hull design is married with exquisite woodworking to create a lobsteryacht celebrated in books and magazines throughout the boating world. *Courtesy of Lowell Brothers— Even Keel Marine Specialties, Inc.*

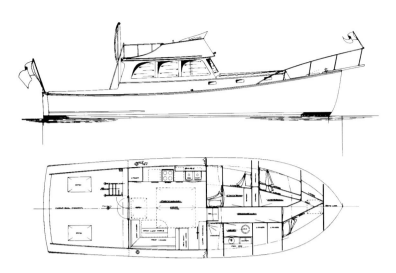

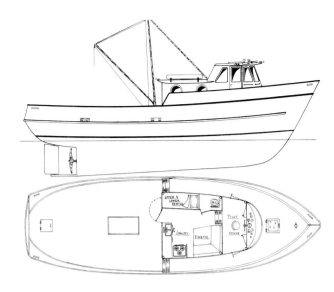

Royal Lowell: Newman 46. The Newman 46, built in fiberglass by Jarvis New-man, was among the first to popularize the use of the Maine lobster hull as a pleasure vessel. Some of the lobsteryachts created from this hull include *Annalokin*, *Cobber*, and *Concert*. *Drawing courtesy of William Lowell*

Nils Lucander: Empress. The 50-foot 3-inch Empress Fisherman design is a stock plan the designer recommended for either commercial or pleasure use. Lucander claimed it had superior speed and fuel economy, owing to his subtle manipulation of the hull shape. *Drawing courtesy Bob Wallstrom*

Maine, ranging from 28 to 42 feet in length. The 41-foot *Timber* was one of the best-known pleasure craft produced from this partnership. Carroll preferred to work in wood, but he also designed for some fiberglass builders, including a 29-footer for Bruno and Stillman. At the time of his death in 1997, he had just completed the design of a 42-footer for Webber's Cove Boat Yard in East Blue Hill, Maine.

Some of the Lowell brothers' most famous lobsterboats were of the "built-down" type, with heavily radiused garboards forming a deep, hollow skeg. They also designed an equal number of skeg and semi-built-down boats, including *Sea Scribe* and *Timber*, which feature a fair amount of deadrise and reverse curve without the hollow skeg area. The boats all have a reputation for seakindliness, and tend to run with their whole length immersed at speed, rather than rearing back onto a short planing surface.

Today Even Keel Marine is run by Carroll's sons, Jamie and Joseph Lowell, who continue to design and build pleasure and commercial craft in the family tradition.

—Jon Johansen with Ruth Lowell

NILS KARL JOHAN LUCANDER

1924–1998 · Finland/United States

Nils Lucander was ever inquiring of the veritas of the accepted precepts of naval architecture. His well-known quote was, "Before I design any boat or vessel, I try to learn the secrets of the sea. . . . Then I can do it much better."

Born in Brando-Villastad, Finland, Lucander enlisted in the Finnish army at the age of fourteen, eventually earning the rank of sargeant.

He was a veteran of the Russian War, or as the Finns know it, "*the Winter War*," during World War II and was wounded in action. He received the Disabled Veterans Badge (akin to the U.S. Purple Heart) and was awarded the Order of the Cross of Liberty, which is the second-highest Finnish award for valor.

At the conclusion of the war, Lucander emigrated westward through Sweden, first to South America, then through Florida to Toronto, Canada, until the 1950's when he arrived in Detroit, Michigan. There he began his design career working for the John Hacker firm.

Lucander had a great curiosity. He was a voracious reader with a huge library that enabled him to become a self-taught designer and a prolific writer. He designed over 250 yachts and commercial craft, according to Lucander's own writing; in 1973, in Brownsville, Texas, he designed the first truly "seagoing" oil spill retention boom, capable of withstanding both high seas and fast currents. It was known as the "LUCAN" Bottom Tension Oil Spill Control Boom. In 1972 he designed a new stabilizing system known as the Lucan stabilizer.

The three-keel concept Lucander used on tugs and fishing vessels embraced a foreshortened center keel with twin side keels from near amidship to aft. The keels are large enough to partially accommodate the engines. The shafts then are shorter and parallel to the load waterline, producing, as Lucander wrote, "maximum thrust with minimum alignment and vibration problems." The Lucander three-keel concept can still be seen on new designs created by others.

Lucander was fondly and respectfully known as the "Mad Finn, the Designer, the Inventor,

the Author, the Philosopher, the Soldier, and the Model Citizen" from the obituary of the 1999 Swedish Finn Historical Society quarterly.

—Bob Wallstrom

ALFRED EDWARD LUDERS SR.

June 26, 1878–April 7, 1964

ALFRED EDWARD "BILL" LUDERS JR.

December 31, 1909–January 31, 1999

United States

The Luders were among the United States' great designer/builders and were highly regarded in both fields. Alfred E. Luders Sr., founder of the Luders Marine Construction Company, designed almost every boat built by the firm until his son, known as Bill, came aboard. Alfred was primarily a designer of large and fast powerboats, many of them commuters, whereas Bill concentrated mainly on sailboats, from daysailers to 12-Meter America's Cup contenders.

The son of a shipping agent, Alfred Luders was born in New York and spent much of his early childhood at sea with his parents. When he was nine, however, his father was lost at sea and the family settled in New York City. Alfred entered the Webb Academy (now the Webb Institute) in 1895, where he studied naval architecture and marine engineering. He then apprenticed at the Nixon Shipyard in New Jersey and later at a Clydebank yard in Scotland. He graduated from Webb in 1899 and did postgraduate work in naval architecture at the University of Glasgow. Back in the United States, Alfred joined the Society of Naval Architects and Marine Engineers in 1902 and began working

A. E. Luders Sr.: *Robador.* The 107-foot motoryacht *Robador* was a fast commuter designed in 1929 for Commodore Robert Law of Greenwich, Connecticut. She had two, 12-cylinder, 700-hp Winton engines and was capable of 25 mph. She was the fifth of six vessels, all named for Commodore Law's two children. *Photo courtesy T. N. Law*

Luders: Luders 16 One-Design (above). The pretty and fast, 26-foot 4-inch L-16, designed by A. E. Luders Sr. and A. E. Luders Jr., is still an active one-design class. It popularized hot-molded plywood construction in the period between the end of World War II and the introduction of fiberglass; 186 were built. © *Benjamin Mendlowitz*

A. E. Luders Jr.: *Storm* (opposite). Here the lovely 40-foot LOA L-27 *Storm*, designed, built, owned, and sailed by her designer, is racing under one of several odd rigs designed to point out loopholes in the CCA Rule. She was a consistent winner under these rigs as well as her usual masthead-sloop rig. A number of sisterships were built, with a somewhat higher freeboard. © *Mystic Seaport, Rosenfeld Collection, Mystic, CT*

as a draftsman in the office of Tams, Lemoine and Crane in 1903. Working closely with Clinton Crane, Alfred was exposed to the design of early high-speed powerboats.

Alfred Luders's first published design was an 18-foot launch, in the August 1904 issue of *The Rudder*. His hydroplane of 1907 was one of the first to feature both a single stepped hull and a dip propeller (now known as a *surface piercing propeller*). After working at the Elco plant in Bayonne, New Jersey, from about 1906 until 1908, he founded the Luders Marine Construction Company in East Port Chester (Greenwich), Connecticut. In 1912 the yard moved to Stamford's south end district.

Alfred Luders was an astute observer of what worked, and much of his new yard was patterned after features he had seen at the Herreshoff yard in Bristol, Rhode Island. Large Douglas fir shear legs for lifting heavy engines into the commercial craft and stepping masts in large sailing yachts can be seen in photographs of both yards. The building shed's wider-at-the-base and narrower-at-the-eaves configuration was also a feature of both yards. In its heyday, Luders Marine Construction Company also had a sail loft, an upholstery shop, and a machine shop capable of building transmissions, large winches, and almost any other machinery. Alfred may have invented, and certainly was among the earliest to use, flexible engine mounts in 1926. Over the years the yard built everything from small daysailers (the Redwing class) to speedy commuters, from large luxury yachts to commercial vessels and military craft, from tugs to 110-foot subchasers and U.S. Coast Guard cutters.

Alfred Luders won several design competitions, such as a 1916 naval competition for the design of a vessel, not less than 66 feet long, that would appeal to yachtsmen for private use but if necessary could be taken into a voluntary U.S. Navy squadron of patrol boats. Luders's hard-chine patrol boat, YP-66, served in both world wars as patrol vessels.

Many of Bill Luders's early years were spent in the Stamford yard. He was also born in New York. In 1928 he enrolled at the Webb Institute, but soon dropped out because of illness. When he recovered, instead of re-enrolling, he went to apprentice at his father's yard. There he learned boatbuilding from the craftsmen and design from the Webb-trained naval architects who worked at the facility, including Paul G. Tomalin and G. Gilbert Wyland, as well as his father. Other designers who worked at Luders Marine Construction at one time or another include George Crouch, William Tripp, Stanley Potter, Paul Coble, Edward S. Brewer, and Bob Wallstrom.

Bill was a successful racing skipper throughout his life, beginning first in the 14-foot Redwing class designed by his father, later in 6-Meters, winning the Long Island Sound championship in 1928, and again in 1930 with *Totem*, one of his first designs. Another early design for a small power launch featured an unusual hooked stern designed to reduce squatting at speed. The design was later adapted to produce a 45-foot navy crash boat designed by his father.

The success of *Totem* helped to promote Bill's career even though at that time the industry was slowing down owing to the onset of the Depression. His subsequent design for the Fishers Island sloop, which after World War II became the Luders 16, helped the yard stay in business. In 1938 he designed the 44-foot Naval Academy Yawls, which were built first of wood and later in the 1960's from fiberglass to teach sailing and seamanship to midshipmen.

With the approach of World War II, the Luders yard was successful again with the winning design of a 110-foot subchaser. After the war, it pioneered in laminated-wood and hot-molded plywood construction, which produced economical, strong, and long-lived boats, such as the L-16, L-24, and L-27 sloops. In the early 1950's Luders was the lead yard for a new ocean class of minesweepers (MSO), building eight for the navy.

In the late 1950's, the yard was one of the first to use epoxy resin in hull and structural laminations, even employing a chemist on staff. In the early 1960's, Luders and the Regatta Paint Company collaborated to develop Luders Epoxy Bronze, a hard, racing-finish, antifouling paint that was ultimately used on all the 12-Meter sloops of the era and many of the other competitive sailing racers.

The Bill Luders–designed *American Eagle*, an unsuccessful 12-Meter candidate for the America's Cup defense in 1964, has gone on to become a formidable ocean racer. Bill drew fifty-three International 5.5-Meter designs over the years, which won both World and Olympic championships. His own auxiliary, the 40-foot LOA L-27 *Storm* (1955), was a highly successful ocean racer and served as a platform for several unusual rigs.

Bill Luders's sailboats had a distinctive and easily identifiable style. They were often somewhat longer-ended than their contemporaries and the ends were high, with V-shaped sections forward and small transoms well out of the water aft. Their sheers were unusually strong for a boat with fairly long ends, the freeboard was moderately high, and the overall effect was an appealing blend of delicacy, buoyancy, and modernity.

Sometimes Luders employed a distinctive type of cabin trunk, as on the L-16 and L-24, with vertical sides and a molded plywood top that rounded down to the deck at the forward end, so there was no flat forward end to the trunk. This gave a streamlined modern look while preserving the advantages of vertical cabin sides and simplifying the structure. It is probably unfortunate that more designers have not used the form since.

Handicapping rules were especially interesting to Bill; he amused himself and others by pointing out glaring loopholes in the CCA Rule by rigging his *Storm* as a ketch with a big mizzen and genoa; at other times *Storm* was rigged as a sloop with a nearly nonexistent mainsail for a big rating advantage. He also exploited the rules more subtly, as with the Rhodes-designed, Luders-built 12-Meter *Weatherly*, and with his own *American Eagle* design, the latter featuring a flat deck with a mound, referred to as Mount Luders, around the mast for measuring advantages.

Bill Luders was a believer in tank-testing big projects, such as the 12-Meter designs and many of his 5.5-Meter designs. One of his later cruising designs, the fiberglass Luders 33, which was built in the mid-1960's by Allied Boat Company, was also tank-tested, with the result that she is a surprising performer despite her very conventional overall configuration. Luders's last designs, drawn from 1980 to 1983, for the C. E. Ryder Corporation, were for three production cruising sailboat designs called "Sea Sprite."

All original Luders designs and drawings prior to 1962 were destroyed in a major fire at the yard in that year, but some prints and photos are in the Ships Plans collection at Mystic Seaport Museum, Mystic, CT.

—Daniel B. MacNaughton with Bob Wallstrom

HENK LUNSTROO

Born 1936 · The Netherlands

Few designers' work manifests more love and respect for Dutch boatbuilding traditions than that of Henk Lunstroo. His legacy is a small fleet of remarkable yachts, each a triumph of individual beauty and all sharing a visible reverence for the past.

Lunstroo received formal training as a shipbuilding engineer from 1952 until 1957. He started his career as a designer and draftsman at the Amsterdamse Scheepswerf working for G. de Vries Lentsch. During that period he helped to design a small fleet of shallow-draft wooden minesweepers for the Dutch Royal Navy. In 1961 he founded his own design office in Castricum.

Henk Lunstroo: *Borkumriff III*. *Borkumriff III* is the third Lunstroo-designed megayacht to be based on the proven traditional schooner concept. She was built to sail with a crew of only five and has accommodations for six to eight guests. The 103-foot aluminum-hulled yacht was built in 1982. *Photo courtesy Rutger ten Broeke*

Lunstroo's early work consisted mainly of a series of traditional leeboard sailing yachts, sturdy motorsailers, and a number of motoryachts. In 1970 his career took a decisive turn with a commission to design a 56-foot steel schooner yacht for a Finnish client. This beautiful, traditional boat was exhibited during the international Amsterdam Boat Show in 1971 and firmly established her designer's name in the market for larger luxury cruisers.

Commissions during this time included a beautiful 40-foot fiberglass ketch for a Swiss owner and the 85-foot schooner *Christina* for another Finnish client. Between 1978 and 1982 Lunstroo was engaged in the formidable task of designing the 90-foot schooner *Tina V* (later *Borkumriff II*). This yacht, built by the prestigious Royal Huisman Shipyard, earned him worldwide fame.

As a longtime member of the Dutch Society of Yacht Architects, Lunstroo was an ardent defender of the legal rights of designers, speaking as an expert in civil lawsuits on behalf of designers whose work had been used without permission.

Each of Lunstroo's designs is worked out in the most minute detail, including the styling and detailing of the interior, leaving little room for guesswork by the builders. Lunstroo did almost all of his design and drafting work himself, with very little assistance.

—Rutger ten Broeke

OTTO LÜRSSEN

May 25, 1880–May 17, 1932 · Germany

Otto Lürssen was born in the quiet Bremen suburb of Aumund, where in 1875 his father had founded Friedrich Lürssen Werft, a humble boatyard that built rowboats, small sloops, and other sporting craft. In 1886 his father teamed up with the automotive pioneer Gottlieb Daimler to produce the first craft driven by a gasoline-powered, internal-combustion engine, and from then on Otto Lürssen's fate became entwined in the yard.

At age fifteen Lürssen was apprenticed to a noted German shipyard at Tecklenborg; then he studied naval architecture and shipbuilding at the Bremen Technikum. Working first as an engineer, he joined his father at Lürssen Werft in about 1905.

Young Lürssen took a disciplined approach to boat design, introducing hydrodynamic theory and model testing to complement his father's old-world concern for craftsmanship. And while other designers explored the speed potential of the chined "V"-form planing hull, Lürssen rationalized that with powerful enough engines, a round-bilge hull form could be coaxed to plane just as fast, but would be more seakindly. He was right. In 1906, with Lürssen at the helm and a 40-hp Daimler engine growling under him, his first significant design, *Donnerwetter*, tested close to 35 knots,

Otto Lürssen: *Donnerwetter*. Active at a time when naval architecture was in thrall to the new internal-combustion gasoline engine, Lürssen broke into the limelight with a series of race-winning offshore powerboats, beginning with *Donnerwetter* (Thunderstorm). *Photo courtesy Lürssen Yachts*

won a series of European races, and placed the name *Lürssen* squarely in the international arena. In 1907 Friedrich Lürssen rewarded his son with a joint proprietorship in the yard.

By 1912 Friedrich Lürssen retired and turned the yard over to his son, who continued to develop racing boats with Daimler and other engine makers such as Siemens and Saurer, winning more prizes and setting speed records. He also applied his round-bilge concept to some noted cruising yachts, including *Maria-Augusta*, *Verteidigen*, and *Aloha-Oe*.

The demands of the German navy during World War I enabled Lürssen to further refine the performance of his hulls, and by war's

end he had built a few torpedo boats, dozens of remote-controlled explosive drones, and patrol boats powered by lightweight Maybach Zeppelin airship engines.

After the war, Lürssen continued designing motoryachts for European clients. But through a New York agent he began designing fast commuter yachts popular with American tycoons, including the 23-meter *Charming Polly* for Colonel H. H. Rogers, and the 22-meter *Oheka II* for the financier Otto H. Kahn. To build *Oheka II*, Lürssen devised a composite system of diagonal shell planking over Duralumin frames; the yacht reached a speed of 34 knots and was the fastest cruiser of her day. Until the Depression

struck hard in 1931, Otto Lürssen and his team designed some twenty-five motoryachts up to 30 meters long for wealthy Americans.

During Germany's illicit military buildup in the late 1920's and early 1930's, the navy again called on Lürssen for larger, better-armed attack craft. The yard launched the first of what would be a fleet of more than three hundred torpedo boats built before and during World War II.

In 1932, Lürssen died suddenly of a heart attack at age fifty-three. His concept for fast attack craft is still applied by modern navies. Making use of theoretical calculations, towing tank tests, and real-life performance tests, Otto Lürssen had an equally lasting impact on modern motoryacht design.—Jack A. Somer

WILLIAM E. LYMAN

1883–June 16, 1952 · United States

Lyman Boat Works, first of Cleveland and later of Sandusky, Ohio, was an innovative production wooden boatbuilding factory that became famous for its practical and appealing lapstrake plywood motorboats. It was founded as a one-man shop by Bernard E. Lyman in Cleveland, Ohio, a cabinetmaker from Berlin, Germany, at the beginning of the U.S. Civil War. Lyman was building rowboats to his own design, but the shop quickly expanded and he was soon designing and building sailboats up to around 65 feet in length.

When the gasoline engine showed up, Lyman quickly understood that it would result in a large new market—a prescience that seems to have been a family trait. He was soon specializing in gasoline-powered boats. Large, custom-built powerboats up to 75 feet in length, along with a steady stream of small craft, became the yard's primary output. Bernard's son, William E. Lyman, joined the Boat Works in 1901, learning the business from the bottom up.

With the advent of the outboard motor, the Lymans again saw the future more clearly than most, and concentrated on the development of boats that were well suited to it. They were among the first to broaden the transom and flatten the run of small boats in response to outboard motors.

After a stint of government work during World War I, the shop was retooled for efficient production building, with a major emphasis on outboard-powered boats. The company grew rapidly and moved to Sandusky after the elder Lyman's retirement in 1928.

Lyman Boat Works managed to prosper during the Great Depression owing to its ability to produce boats at reasonable cost and its willingness to quickly adapt its product line to

Otto Lürssen: *Oheka II*. Lürssen eventually applied the principles he developed in his many racers—in particular, powerful engines and round-bilged planing forms—to a group of handsome and grand commuter yachts built for export particularly to America, as exemplified by Otto Kahn's *Oheka II*. *Photo courtesy Lürssen Yachts*

William Lyman: Mariner. Lyman oversaw the transition of his family yard from boatbuilding using traditional methods to production line boatbuilding with wood (and later fiberglass). Lyman became one of the most recognized powerboat lines in the United States. Most Lymans were marketed to consumers with average means. The Mariner was one of the larger models. © *Peter Barlow*

changing circumstances. During the Depression the company produced the first "utility," a fast, open launch with a walk-around central engine box. It was to become a standard type for many builders.

Experience in rapid production for the government during World War II made Lyman Boat Works even more efficient, such that the company was well prepared for the postwar boatbuilding boom. Under Bill Lyman's management, Boat Works hit an extraordinary production peak of five thousand boats in the year 1958. The boats were sold all over the country through hundreds of dealers.

Lyman boats have a reputation for quality materials and construction, good handling characteristics, and tasteful, restrained good looks—all were designed by Bernard or Bill Lyman. Lyman Boat Works has changed hands several times but still exists and produces fiberglass boats. It will custom build using the old patterns and will restore the old boats, which are regaining great popularity with collectors and wooden boat enthusiasts.

—Daniel B. MacNaughton

DAVID LYONS

Born April 25, 1964 · Australia

David Lyons's design philosophy centers on safety and structural integrity, with an emphasis on IMS racers and high-performance cruising designs. Originally from the Tasmanian state capital of Hobart, he now practices in Sydney. Lyons began sailing early in life, cruising with his father and later racing dinghies. He graduated with honors from the University of New South Wales with a degree in engineering.

In 1988, Lyons designed the 25-foot JOG (Junior Offshore Group) racer *Box Office*, which won the Australian championship. She was very much an "offshore dinghy," with a vertical stem and a stern that flared out to about the same beam as amidships, much like an Australian racing skiff. The yacht was built using "exotic" epoxy, foam-sandwich, Kevlar, and carbon fiber construction. She was the first of the skiff-style design and construction in Australian JOG racing and went on to win three consecutive national titles.

The success of *Box Office* led to a commission to design the Robertson 950, a 31-foot production yacht for boatbuilder Bob Robertson, one of Lyons's mentors who influenced his approach to sailing and yacht construction. The boat was named the 1991 Australian Boat of the Year, and Lyons says it was one of the first IMS dual-purpose (racer/cruiser) yachts in Australia. Eleven have been built to date.

In the JOG, Lyons went on to design the NSW Grand Prix champion *Critical Path* and the 1994 Australian champion *Buck*, both radical boats developing further the same approach as *Box Office* and helping to establish him as an innovator. Larger designs such as the IMS 40 *Cuckoo's Nest* and the IMS 43 *Atara* saw success in stormy offshore events and helped boost his reputation for designing structurally sound boats. Recent designs include the 65-foot aluminum cruiser/racer *Valtair*, the 47-foot racer *Vanguard*, and the disabled-sailor-friendly *Aspect Computing*.

—Robert Keeley

David Lyons: *Atara*. The advent of the IMS Rule saw Lyons rise to the top group of Australian ocean racing designers, with a series of well-conceived racing yachts. *Atara* is seen racing here at Hamilton Island. *Photo courtesy David Payne*

FRANS MAAS

Born 1937 · The Netherlands

Frans Maas, an ardent ocean racer, was quick to seize the opportunities presented by the many technical transitions that were the hallmark of the second half of the twentieth century.

The son of a building contractor in Breskens, Zeeland, Maas started to build open daysailers as a young man before World War II. During the war, however, boatbuilding and sailing were prohibited by the Germans in the province. Once the war ended, there was so much reconstruction work to be done by his father's business that it was the late 1940's before young Maas could indulge his real love: boatbuilding and design.

As a designer, Maas was self-taught; magazines, contests, and books were his prime sources of information. He designed his first complete boat at the age of fifteen. His early designs followed the traditional path, with long

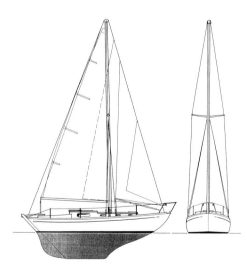

Frans Maas: Scheldejager. The 28-foot Scheldejager had a reputation for the strength and seaworthiness that were so necessary in the harsh conditions of the North Sea. Beginning in 1959, six were built, with iroko planking over steel frames. *Drawing courtesy Rutger ten Broeke*

Frans Maas: *Tonnerre de Breskens.* The 36-foot *Tonnerre de Breskens* was built in 1965 for renowned Dutch ocean racer Piet Vroon. Vroon had a lengthy list of successes with *Tonnerre*, even though her robust lines did not exactly please everyone's eye. *Photo courtesy Frans Maas*

keels, elegant hulls, and attached rudders. A few of these designs such as the Scheldejager, Breeon, and Sabine were quite successful in the Netherlands. A Sabine named *Santa Maria* completed the first circumnavigation by a Dutch yacht in 1969.

In the 1950's, the firm of Frans Maas was able to expand its operations. Boats were built of wood, composite wood over steel frames, or steel. With the low labor cost in postwar Holland, exports to Germany, the United Kingdom, and the United States became more and more important. International contacts proved vital and the yard acquired commissions to build boats by highly respected designers such as Olin Stephens, Robert Clark, Laurent Giles, and Ted Hood.

In the meantime, Maas went on developing and modernizing his own designs. Having observed the recent work of designer Ericus van de Stadt, Maas began to create designs with a separated keel-and-rudder configuration. *Ton-*

nerre de Breskens, the first boat of this type, was not exactly a beauty-contest winner when she came out in 1965, but Maas managed to stay just within the parameters set by the RORC and built a very fast boat. In her first year, out of sixteen races (among them Cowes Week) she won nine firsts, two seconds, two thirds, and two fifth places. *Tonnerre* was a turning point in Maas's career.

After the separation of keels and rudders proved so successful, the designs began a period of rapid development. New ideas were tested, and new materials such as fiberglass and aluminum began to impact the construction of hulls and rigs. Maas was one of the first builders to use a fiberglass hull (with wooden deck structures) in his Zeezot.

From its beginning in 1968, Maas was a member of the Denk Tank (Think Tank) initiated by Professor Gerritsma at Delft University, where the most important Dutch yacht designers had their designs tested. Maas drafted three versions of the Standfast 43. Models of all three versions were tank-tested at Delft, and the Standfast became Maas's first all-fiberglass boat.

As typical as his up-to-date thinking may be, however, Maas may also be credited for his devotion to other goals. As this entry was being written, his firm was involved in the restoration of *Ilderim*, a Belgian 8-meter from the 1930's.

The Maas office is in Breskens, the Netherlands.

—Rutger ten Broeke

JAMES RODERICK "ROD" MacALPINE-DOWNIE

May 9, 1933–January 9, 1986 · Scotland

Together with the Prout brothers, James Roderick MacAlpine-Downie must be considered the father of modern English catamarans. Coming from a long line of Scottish aristocracy and totally self-taught in the art of yacht design, MacAlpine-Downie drifted into his profession after his father died in a sailing accident, leaving a huge inheritance tax bill that forced the family to sell most of its Scottish estate.

Always more performance oriented than the Prouts, MacAlpine-Downie's career started with a series of successful beach catamarans, including the Thai series (17 feet 6 inches, 1959, two hundred built) and the Shark-B-class series (19 feet, 1962, more than a thousand built). They were constructed by Reg White's Sail Craft yard, which built most of the MacAlpine-Downie catamarans from then on. By that time, his symmetrical and round hull had already assumed their distinctive shape, which was characterized by spray-deflecting knuckles or spray rails in the hull's forward section and rather full aft quarters. These characteristics would not change and made his catamarans easily recognizable for many years to come.

By the early 1960's MacAlpine-Downie also became well known for his 25-foot Class C catamarans. In 1961 *Hellcat II* captured the very first International Catamaran Challenge Trophy, better known as the Little America's Cup because it is competed for in a similar format as the America's Cup and carries similar prestige in the catamaran world. For the next eight years MacAlpine-Downie's *Hellcat III* (1963), *Emma Hamilton* (1964), and the famous *Lady Helmsman* (1966, 1967, and 1968 defenses) successfully defended the Cup against American and Australian challengers.

In 1972 MacAlpine-Downie's focus turned toward outright speed records. His 60-foot proa *Crossbow* raised the absolute world speed sailing record from 26.3 knots in 1972 to 31.1 knots in 1975. This was followed by the biplane catamaran *Crossbow II*, which raised the world

speed sailing record to 36.0 knots in 1980, a record that would stand for a decade.

MacAlpine-Downie also designed a series of very successful cruiser/racer catamarans, including the Iroquois (30 feet 6 inches, 1965, more than 350 built), Apache (40 feet, 1970), and Comanche (32 feet, 1979), as well as a few powerful offshore catamarans: the 1974 Round Britain Race winner *British Oxygen* (70 feet, 1974), which at the time of her building was the world's largest offshore racing catamaran; *Sea Falcon* (70 feet, 1980); and *British Airways* (60 feet, 1984). Most were built by Sail Craft.

MacAlpine-Downie will always be remembered for his speed-oriented catamarans and proas. It is little known that his "bread-and-butter" designs were actually small cruising monohulls, almost all of them built in the United States by his partner Dick Gibbs, a sailmaker, boatbuilder, and racing yachtsman from LaSalle, Michigan. For twenty-two years, beginning in the mid-1960's, some thirty-five-thousand boats were built by several yards, including Gibbs, MFG, Monark, Chrysler, and Marine Starcraft, from sixteen designs from the design company MacAlpine-Downie/Gibbs. Most successful of these designs are two little daysailers, the Chrysler Mutineer (15 feet, 1968, seven thousand built) and the Chrysler Buccaneer (18 feet, 1966, four thousand built).

In 1984, two years before his death, an illness caused MacAlpine-Downie to give up sailing. It is perhaps fitting that his last design was the Challenger, a small but fast trimaran with a center cockpit and the option of steering by pedal to facilitate its sailing by a paraplegic; more than two hundred of these have been built.

—Claas van der Linde

ARNOLD WILLIAM MacKERER

1895–November 26, 1973 · United States

It can be accurately said that Bill MacKerer found Chris Smith, and Chris Smith found Bill MacKerer, at exactly the right time. In February of 1922 Chris Smith and three of his sons established the C. C. Smith and Sons Boat Company in Algonac, Michigan, a formalization of their world-beating racing-boat shop of the 1910's and the beginning of a stock speedboat business the world would come to know as Chris-Craft. Builder and designer Bill MacKerer—A. W. in his Chris-Craft correspondence—was hired a month later, and went on to design one of the most efficiently produced lines of boats in yachting history.

MacKerer was born in New York City and attended Stuyvesant High School before working as crew on one of his uncle's boats in New York Harbor. He was determined to be a boatbuilder, and he learned the trade at Ruddock's in New York in 1913 and at American Launch in 1914. In 1915 he worked with John Hacker, Niagara Boat Company, and Matthews.

MacKerer worked at Elco in 1917, just before serving in the U.S. Army during World War I. In 1919 he worked with Curtiss Aircraft's Seaplane Division for a time while taking night-school classes in naval architecture taught by Gerald Taylor White at Cooper Union. He returned to Hacker in 1920, and in early 1921 worked both there and at Ed Gregory's Belle Isle stock speedboat company. In the summer of 1921 he went to work with the Purdy brothers and finally joined the Smiths in the spring of 1922.

This restless, peripatetic employment history is not unusual in the world of boatbuilding and

James MacAlpine-Downie: *Crossbow*. The proa *Crossbow* held the absolute world record for speed sailing from 1972 to 1975. *Reproduced from an unknown source*

Arnold MacKerer: *Loon.* MacKerer designed the whole range of mahogany speedboats that made Chris-Craft famous. *Loon*, built in 1930, is near the bottom of the range in size, but has all of the elegance and utility of the larger boats. © *Peter Barlow*

Arnold MacKerer: *Cyn-Mar.* This Chris-Craft Catalina is a classic product of the company that built her and the decade in which she was built. MacKerer's 1950's streamlining was among the best—exuberant but with a natural feel. The interesting arrangement of spaces can be inferred from the photograph and deserves study. © *Peter Barlow*

design. But MacKerer's restlessness seems to have been the result of a creative drive to find the right place to do the work he wanted to do.

What MacKerer wanted was not just to build boats but to do so with a system, as an industry, at a time when the "standardized runabout" was an idea in the wind and in the boating magazines. He and the Smiths had the same idea, and they went on to develop boatbuilding on the model of Detroit's automobile plants. Raw material came in one end of the building and finished boats went into the Saint Clair River for water testing at the other end. In between, separate shops prepared engines, upholstery, hardware, and other components, and work was organized in teams, with farm hands and factory workers led and taught by craftsmen. It was MacKerer's idea to have a moving assembly line with each of these teams responsible for only one portion of production.

The Smiths built a new 50-foot × 150-foot plant in Algonac in 1922; four years later they added a 150-foot × 275-foot building; by the summer of 1926 the complex covered eleven acres. By the summer of 1927 *Motor Boating* magazine reported that "nowhere else in this country, and when we say that we can well include the world, has the present tremendous production of boats ever been thought feasible or practical." In 1927 Chris-Craft shipped 447 boats.

MacKerer left the Smiths for less than three years between 1925 and 1927 to be general man-

ager at Rochester Boat Works, but returned to become head of production and engineering for Chris-Craft. This meant that he ran the plant, calculated the costs of every item that went into the boats, and—despite his short fuse and self-description as a prima donna—worked easily with the Smiths for the next thirty-eight years with the exception of some Depression years. He respected them. They respected him.

MacKerer also designed every runabout, utility, cruiser, and motoryacht produced by Chris-Craft, from the upswept-deck runabouts of the 1920's to the crisp fiberglass cruisers of the 1960's. He was the designer of the Chris-Craft commuters of 1929–31—big runabouts with cabins and comforts; the affordable Chris-Craft overnighters of the 1930's; the 16-foot bottom-of-the-depression inboard utility boats available at prices as low as $495; the cruisers of the late 1930's (some of the handsomest cruiser designs ever produced); the streamlined barrel-back and otherwise up-to-the-minute boats of the 1940's and 1950's; the Chris-Craft Cobras; the big motoryachts and cruisers of the mid-1950's through the mid-1960's; and the fiberglass runabouts, skiboats, and family cruisers of the first half of the 1960's.

The Smiths let Bill MacKerer be who he was and do what he knew how to do, to their benefit and credit, and MacKerer seems to have been able to do the same with other professionals. Chris-Craft dealers always found

him to be interested in their ideas, and industrial designers on the Chris-Craft staff in the 1950's and 1960's were welcome to help make more attractive products out of the boats whose hulls and other components MacKerer designed.

When MacKerer retired in the summer of 1965 he was the longest-serving original employee of Chris-Craft, and a leader of an inspired team that had brought Chris-Craft from Michigan to the world in forty-three years—a patriarch of the boating industry.

Chris-Craft was family owned and managed until it was sold in 1960.   —Joseph Gribbins

FRANK REYNOLDS MacLEAR

February 26, 1920–July 11, 2004 · United States

In recent years the design of large sailing yachts has been revolutionized by a trend toward single-masted rigs that was largely set in motion by Frank MacLear. While the design of luxury cruising sailboats was his specialty, he also created a host of fast, clean-lined power yachts and was one of the earliest designers of popular multihulls.

Born in Denver, Colorado, MacLear graduated from the University of Michigan in 1943 with a bachelor of science degree in engineering, naval architecture and marine engineering. He went to work at Ingalls Shipbuilding Corporation before receiving a commission in the

U.S. Navy, which put him to work at the Norfolk navy yard. He was later stationed in Great Britain, overseeing the construction and repair of naval vessels, and during the occupation of Germany he was in charge of a number of shipyards.

Following World War II, MacLear undertook graduate studies in Switzerland at the University of Geneva. In 1948 he worked at Sparkman and Stephens for a short time, then embarked on an extended period of racing and passagemaking as a crew member in a wide variety of yachts; this lasted until the late 1950's. He regarded this period of his life as one of the best educational experiences possible in his chosen field, and thereafter remained a strong advocate of frequent real-life experience for all naval architects. In 1972 he was able to say that he had cruised and raced over 300,000 miles on more than fifty yachts.

When the time came to go back to work, MacLear worked at several aircraft companies. He went into partnership with designer Bob Harris in 1959, opening the office of MacLear and Harris in New York City. They worked together until 1967, when Harris went to work for Sparkman and Stephens.

One of MacLear and Harris's early emphases was on the brand new field of multihull design. At the 1963 Yachting One-of-a-Kind Regatta they introduced *Beverly*, a catamaran designed for the 300-Square-Foot class. At the time, she was considered the fastest sailboat in the world, reaching speeds of 25 knots. For years thereafter MacLear and Harris were the foremost multi-hull designers in the world, adapting the concept to many different purposes, including small recreational craft, cruising sailboats, power craft, and commercial vessels of a wide range of sizes.

MacLear's extensive sailing experience gave him a strong interest in easier sail handling and improved comfort levels, especially in larger, luxurious cruising boats. One of his first innovative designs to achieve wide recognition was *Angantyr*, a husky 60-foot 8-inch double-ender that was specifically designed for ease of handling by a very small crew. Her inboard cutter rig, with the mast stepped amidships, was described by her owner as a "one-masted schooner" because of the small mainsail set well aft, and the large forestaysail located well inboard. Tandem centerboards provided total control of balance and improved steering under a wide range of conditions. Designed in 1961, *Angantyr* was a total success and began MacLear and Harris's involvement with large, single-masted luxury cruising boats.

As large roller-furling gears began to appear on the market, MacLear realized their implications and adapted them for electric power. One of his designs was the first to cross an ocean with electric furling gear. He created roller-furling mainsails that wound up on a jack stay just aft of the mast, and eliminated the boom, cutting the sail with a high clew so it would reef and furl better, and sheeting it to the standing backstays. The headsail was also roller-furled, and there were often two, one an all-purpose genoa and the other, set farther forward, an enormous light-air drifter.

The powered furlers combined with powered sheet winches meant that even enormous sails could be controlled safely by one person. Placing the jack stay outside the mast allowed a smaller and lighter mast section and less friction, and avoided the loud wind noise sometimes associated with in-the-mast furling. At that point the only limits to the sizes of sails, spars, and single-masted yachts were those imposed by available technology, and the size of the big sloops has increased steadily ever since. MacLear also designed many divided rigs utilizing the same technology.

MacLear yachts were always conservative in construction and carried redundant systems, to ensure that the sail-handling gear always works, as well as manual backups. He concentrated primarily on cruising boats, partly because his designs were often larger than those allowed for racing and partly because the rules discourage the kind of innovative rigs he favored. One exception was *Jubilee III*, a 73-foot yawl designed to the CCA Rule that met with good success and was raced for part of her career by the Naval Academy. MacLear adapted his philosophy to traditional rigs as well, producing a number of square-riggers with electric furling sails.

MacLear's powerboat designs were also innovative, with a large number of catamarans and boats incorporating ideas like naturally- and power-ventilated steps in the underbodies, introducing air bubbles to help the hull break free of the drag of the water. MacLear's larger power yachts often were intended for serious transoceanic cruising.

Following his retirement, Frank MacLear divided his time in Watch Hill, Rhode Island, and New York City. He died on July 11, 2004.

—Daniel B. MacNaughton

THOMAS ANDREW MacNAUGHTON

Born March 1, 1948 · United States

A third-generation yachtsman with long experience in living aboard, Thomas MacNaughton has created a body of work that in some respects is a logical continuation of well-established evolutionary trends and in other respects is revolutionary. He is best known for his series of Chinese lug-rigged, heavy-displacement, liveaboard voyaging yachts, which range in length from 15 to 36 feet.

These boats represent MacNaughton's modern approach to heavy-displacement design in which hulls are not reproductions of historic types, nor are they simply light-displacement yachts made heavy. Instead, they emphasize a reduction in wetted surface area by virtue of moderately cutaway forebodies and carefully shaped sections, and they always feature very smooth diagonals. In addition, the yachts achieve great stability, partly through significant beam, but also by using advanced wood-epoxy construction to create high ballast-displacement ratios.

The result is a great ability to carry sail, making for speed in heavy weather, and a very high ratio of sail area to wetted surface area (as opposed to the ratio of sail area to displacement, which is a measure of acceleration only), resulting in speed in light air as well. Chinese lug is MacNaughton's usual first choice for cruising rigs, owing to its extreme ease of handling, economical construction, and technological simplicity. While the rig does not have a widespread reputation for speed, it seems to combine well with his modern heavy-displacement hulls. MacNaughton-designed boats have surprised many a more conventional competitor.

MacNaughton has also brought the "instant boat" concept to larger cruising boats, with his series of Silver Gull plywood cruising boats. In these boats there is no lofting or mold making.

Frank MacLear. This husky 53-footer shows the rig that her designer developed to take advantage of the then-new electric roller-furling and sheet-winch technology. The boomless mainsail, sheeting to the backstays and rolling up just aft of the mast, works in conjunction with a large roller-furling genoa for easy handling. *Drawing courtesy Frank MacLear*

Lines (most of them straight) are laid out directly on scarphed-to-length plywood panels, which are then cut to the line and bent and glued together just like a smaller "instant boat," creating large, shapely hulls in minimal time.

A broader and perhaps more dramatic contribution to the field has been MacNaughton's research and development of scantlings rules for several traditional and modern wooden construction methods as well as fiberglass construction. For round-bilged designs he favors sheathed strip construction, in which epoxy-glued wooden strip planking is covered inside and out with a thin layer of fiberglass or carbon fiber in epoxy. His scantlings rule results in a radically simple, easily built, and easily maintained structure that is unusually light for its strength. It has enabled designers and builders around the world to utilize the method.

MacNaughton's most popular designs have been a series of small chine-hull tugboat yachts, also featuring simplified construction in plywood, steel, or aluminum.

MacNaughton was born in Bangor, Maine, and grew up in a sailing family who lived aboard boats in the summer. He was exposed to one-design and ocean racing from an early age. He graduated from Hebron Academy and studied anthropology at the University of Maine in Orono. In the early 1970's, MacNaughton enrolled in the Yacht Design Institute run by designers Edward S. Brewer and Bob Wallstrom. Partway through the course he was hired by Brewer and Wallstrom as a draftsman, and he completed his education through hands-on work. Soon thereafter MacNaughton opened his own design office, and later he and his wife and daughter moved aboard a 25-foot Laurent Giles sloop, continuing to live and work aboard her, and then a 48-foot schooner, for the next sixteen years.

Since 1989 MacNaughton has resided in Eastport, Maine, where he and his wife Nannette run a busy design office producing a wide range of designs for both sail and power. Recent projects include a 60-foot, Colin Archer–style cutter, a 90-foot Maine coasting schooner, and a 134-foot schooner yacht designed to be crewed by handicapped individuals. MacNaughton also runs a popular correspondence course in yacht design, and markets drafting supplies through his Web site.

—Daniel B. MacNaughton

BRECKENRIDGE MARSHALL

1921–September 23, 1976 · United States

The line of Marshall fiberglass catboats is Breckenridge Marshall's chief claim to fame. Built by the Marshall Marine Corporation, the cats come in several sizes and were among the first traditional designs to be built in fiberglass. They have remained one of the most popular lines of small cruising boats owing to their roominess, stability, shoal draft, and easy trailerability, combined with the charm and character of the type.

Marshall raced in Rhode Island's Narragansett Bay during the 1950's and 1960's. He worked in 1958 for Beetle Cat–creator John Beetle at his shop in New Bedford, Massachusetts. In 1962 Marshall developed his first catboat design for what became the 18-foot 2-inch LOA Sanderling series, and opened his own yard in 1963.

The Marshall 22 was designed in 1965 and was just bigger enough than the Sanderling to offer greater cruising accommodations and an inboard motor. The daysailing 15-foot 6-inch LOA Sandpiper came out in 1972.

Tom MacNaughton: *Crown Jewel.* The 36-foot *Crown Jewel* is the largest of MacNaughton's Coin Collection range of comfortable, easily constructed, flush-deck, heavy-displacement, Chinese-rigged, liveaboard voyaging yachts, the smallest of which is only 15 feet LOA. The economical and low-tech rig can be completely controlled from the sheltered steering station. *Drawing courtesy Tom MacNaughton*

Breckenridge Marshall: *Grimalkin.* When designing production boats, one aims for broad appeal. Marshall hit the nail on the head when he created his popular line of fiberglass catboats, closely following the traditional Cape Cod type that had been a favorite for generations of yachtsmen of modest means. © *Peter Barlow*

Evan Marshall: *Moonlight III.* The ever-changing field of yacht design has recently made a place for stylists who create a look for yachts, inside and out, establishing a visual theme and décor rather than a structure or hydrodynamics. Marshall now specializes in stylistic work. *Drawing courtesy Evan Marshall*

A founding member of the Catboat Association and a member of many sailing clubs and organizations, Marshall was a great racing skipper. He sailed in thirteen Bermuda Races. He also wrote extensively on the subject of catboats built out of fiberglass.

Marshall Marine continues to build the catboats he designed on Padanaram Harbor in South Dartmouth, Massachusetts.

The Breck Marshall Collection representing eleven designs for catboats by other designers is at Mystic Seaport Museum, Mystic, CT.

—Daniel B. MacNaughton

EVAN KEITH MARSHALL

Born October 15, 1959 · United States/England

Evan Marshall has all the love of the sea and sailing that would be expected of someone born and bred on an island. Marshall's island, however, was Manhattan, New York City. His father was a passionate boater—indeed, he lost his life in a boating accident when Marshall was very young—and the family spent all its spare time afloat. Marshall has carried the family passion much farther than anyone expected and today appears on the major yacht design scene as a designer and stylist who has become remarkably successful in a very short time. His "sudden" popularity, however, is the result of an extremely painstaking apprenticeship in the industry.

Marshall worked for a short time at Shannon Boats in Bristol, Rhode Island, in the summer of 1983 doing project tooling, and received his bachelor's degree in architecture from Hampton University late that same year. He entered Yacht Design Institute's residential program in Maine, graduating in 1985 with an associate's degree in naval architecture. Landing a job at Sparkman and Stephens in Manhattan, Marshall's initial work was on detail: rudders and rudderposts, engine room layouts, and so on. Under the watchful eye of such in-house designers as the late Mario Tarabocchia, Marshall was soon drawing complete sets of lines for sailing yachts. In 1986 he made a decision to focus on the styling aspect of yacht design.

By January 1988 Marshall had resigned from Sparkman and Stephens to pursue his ambitions in Europe. Andrew Winch was then just starting to make a name for himself, mainly in sailing yachts, and seemed to offer the best learning experience. Marshall joined him, staying for four years.

In the summer of 1993 Marshall started his own studio in London, named Usonia III. His yacht projects range from handsome but subtle Italianate styling for *Posillipo* through an outrageous interior for *Opus*, the world's largest motoryacht, to innovative space planning for the 114-foot *Golden Eye*. The *Midnight Sun* project is for a small cruise ship for 350 passengers.

Marshall's latest work includes the exterior and interior styling of all the models—88 to 135 feet—for Destiny Yachts; the exterior and interior styling of the new Hatteras Yacht Company's 80-footer; the exterior and interior styling of the new Sensation 147- and 150-footers built in New Zealand; and the interior and exterior design of the new Luxus Cruise Lines 703-foot cruise ship, now under contract with a shipyard in southern Europe.

—Bob Wallstrom

ROGER MARSHALL

Born August 9, 1994 · England/United States

Roger Marshall specializes in good, all-around, comfortable, performance cruising sailboats and powerboats. He is an energetic designer as well as one of the most published. He has sailed thousands of miles and has a good feel for what makes a boat perform well in the deep ocean.

Born and raised near Plymouth, England, Marshall was educated at Southampton College of Technology (later the Southampton Institute), the school of boatbuilders and design in Southampton, England. He moved to the United States to work for Sparkman and Stephens in New York City in 1972, where he was on the design staff until 1977. Since that time he has operated his own office, Roger Marshall, Inc., in Jamestown, Rhode Island.

Marshall's sailboat designs tend to be more mainstream, comfortable cruisers with a nice easy motion and good handling. However, innovative designs are also part of his offerings. For example, the aluminum-hulled *Ocean Voyager* has a lifting keel and lifting centerboard to give this 47-footer 4 feet of draft for when it is alongside the owner's shallow-water property. Other sailboat designs utilize a range of materials from steel, aluminum, and composite fiberglass to carbon fiber.

Roger Marshall: *Ocean Voyager.* The 47-foot LOA *Ocean Voyager* was designed to be moored at the owner's dock in 4 feet of water and to sail fast and comfortably in the deep ocean. Launched in 1999, the accommodations reflect the owner's desire for the boat to be both a marine laboratory and a home during long research trips at sea. *Drawing courtesy Roger Marshall*

Arthur Martin: Energy 48. A sleek and able cruiser, the Energy 48 was one of the few powerboats able to boast fuel mileage of 13 miles per gallon or better. An auxiliary sailing rig and centerboard were available options. *Photo courtesy Marjorie Martin Burgard*

Marshall's powerboat designs, like his sailboats, tend to be comfortable, performance-oriented, purpose-designed cruisers; they range from sportfishing boats built in fiberglass to a replica 1920's steel tugboat with cruising amenities. He has designed powerboats for wood-epoxy custom construction to alloy-hulled trawler-style yachts.

The author of twelve books on yacht design, Marshall has two more books in the pipeline as well as being the technical editor for *Soundings* magazine.

—Bob Wallstrom

ARTHUR E. MARTIN

February 28, 1917–August 7, 1990
United States

The designer of the Energy 48 and the Alden Ocean Shell, among others, Arthur Martin trained as a naval architect at the Webb Institute in Glen Cove, New York. He worked in Bethlehem Steel's shipbuilding division during World War II and then for designer Ray Hunt and later the John Alden office before starting Martin Marine in Kittery Point, Maine, in 1971.

Martin designed the Energy 48 in 1979. A narrow, light-displacement cruising powerboat with an optional auxiliary sailing rig, she was conceived during the energy crisis of that decade. She is capable of 10 knots over a wide range of conditions while consuming only 1 gallon of diesel fuel per hour—less at lower speeds. Seventy gallons of fuel yielded a range of 1,000 miles. She has proved to be a comfortable, quiet, and economical boat to run.

The Alden Ocean Shell was the first sliding-seat shell built for recreational rowing using

Martin's Oarmaster drop-in rowing rig. She and the other seaworthy, high-performance, sliding-seat rowing boats designed by Martin are available in fiberglass, carbon fiber, and wood. Together they have been responsible for large numbers of people rediscovering the pleasures of recreational rowing.

—Daniel B. MacNaughton

DAVID P. MARTIN

Born May 12, 1930 · United States

David Martin primarily designs cruising and sportfishing powerboats. Significant designs include the line of Pacemaker wooden powerboats in the 1950's and 1960's, and the Alglas fiberglass powerboats that followed. The Pacemakers are perhaps the high-water mark of sensible streamlined styling, with every curve of the deckhouses and windows seeming to be just right, and the overall design a study in wholesome and appealing proportions. Since then Martin has adapted his designs to more contemporary notions of styling, but if the newer boats stress straighter lines and angles, they retain a sensibility that reveals the designer's extensive experience in powerboat design.

Continuous study of powerboat forms has led Martin to significant improvements in speed, comfort, and fuel efficiency throughout the field of powerboat design. Some of his early chine-hulled boats utilized the inverted bell–shaped underwater sections that were a precursor of the Hunt Deep-V configuration, but Martin also utilized round-bilge forms. In recent years he has worked mostly with warped-V forms, which he has helped to refine con-

siderably. In the early days, Martin was one of the first to eliminate intrusive engine boxes in his designs, and he has always been an innovator in the arrangement of interiors.

Martin's father was a racing powerboat builder and marine engine dealer who raised his family in Atlantic City, New Jersey. While still in his teens, Martin met the young Russell Post, who had just started the Egg Harbor Boat Company. He became an apprentice at Egg Harbor in 1948. In the same year, Martin began the Westlawn School of Yacht Design program in yacht design, working it in around his various jobs and completing the program in 1953.

In 1949 boatbuilder John Leek left Egg Harbor to start the Pacemaker Company, and Martin went with him. He landed a job at Sparkman and Stephens in 1952, eventually moving into the design department.

Martin set up an independent office in Brigantine, New Jersey, in 1954. His first important commission was for a 30-foot, twin-screw, V-bottom powerboat named *Jim-Ken*. The boat attracted considerable attention, and from that point forward Martin produced many custom designs for fishing boats and yachts, some of them for amateur construction, as well as stock models for Maycraft, Eastern Sea Skiffs, Egg Harbor, Hubert Johnson, and Ocean Yachts.

David Martin: Pacemaker (opposite). One of Martin's notable accomplishments was a wide range of designs for the Pacemaker Company. Shown is one of Pacemaker's most popular models at speed, displaying Martin's knack for putting tastefully streamlined superstructures on fast hulls. © *Peter Barlow*

The first design Martin drew for Pacemaker was a 40-foot Jersey Sea Skiff in 1959. This was only the first of his designs to sell over a thousand units. Over the years Martin has designed the rest of the line. He has also designed sailboats, houseboats, and small craft, and is the author of many magazine articles and *The Naval Architect's Handbook*.

David Martin continues to practice in Brigantine, New Jersey. —Daniel B. MacNaughton

ALVIN "AL" MASON

September 11, 1911–December 20, 1995
United States

In a sixty-year career, Al Mason produced only about 150 designs under his own name, but he had a leadership role in the design offices of Sparkman and Stephens, John Alden, and Philip Rhodes, and his unmistakable touch can be seen in many of the most successful designs of his time.

Mason was one of the field's best draftsmen. His drawings are beautifully crafted and detailed, with careful selection of line weights, shading, and many little touches such as fully detailed sails and berth cushions, horizon lines, and subtle indications of the water's surface. These were not strictly needed by the builder, but served to reveal the character of his boats in a way that few dimensioned drawings do.

Mason was a master of what might be called the CCA classic type, that wonderful form in which the grace and harmony of early racing boats were combined with scientific knowledge to produce what many agree were the only really good offshore cruising/racing boats ever to be encouraged by a handicapping rule.

While Mason designed a wide variety of types, including more traditional vessels, a typical Mason sailboat has wide beam, often a keel/centerboard underbody, moderate displacement, an attached rudder, well-shaped ends of moderate length, cabin trunks artfully designed to minimize their apparent height, and a masthead marconi rig all or mostly inboard. Virtually all of his boats feature sturdy scantlings and are, in relative terms, heavy.

To the consternation of the handicappers who had always viewed beam as a speed-inhibiting factor, Mason was one of the first to figure out how to use wide beam in a fast offshore sailboat. The most famous example of this type was the revolutionary *Finisterre*, a 38-foot 6-inch, keel/centerboard Sparkman and Stephens–designed yawl built in 1954. Her hull lines, at least, were drawn by Mason, and she was one of the most successful racing and cruising yachts in history. Her basic concept was re-

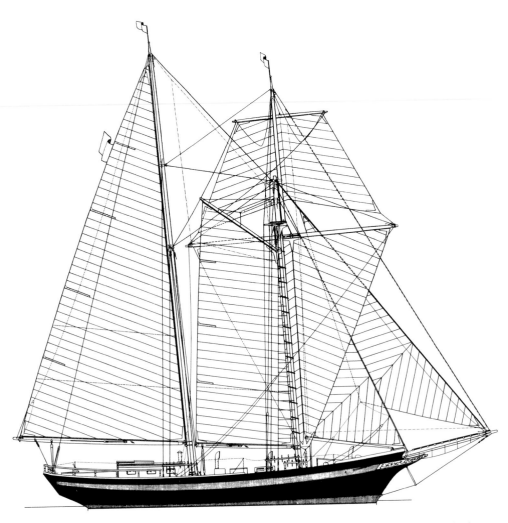

Al Mason. This 50-footer looks bigger than she is, with her classic proportions and square-topsail schooner rig, but she is no toy. Mason has carefully interpreted the square rig for ease of handling, and has combined it with a marconi main without the slightest incongruity. There is a distinct lack of clutter, and a well-tuned balance between traditional and modern features. *Drawing courtesy Anita Mason*

Al Mason. Mason's trawler yachts are strong, handsome, efficient, and capable of real offshore service as well as long-term living aboard. This 46-footer, with her low open-air bridge behind the wheelhouse, and the protected hurricane bridge in front of it, would be a joy to operate. The round stern is particularly attractive, and her full-width deckhouse maximizes the living space below. *Drawing courtesy Anita Mason*

visited again and again in Mason's own designs and those drawn by him under other names.

Beginning with the December 1930 issue of *The Yachtsman and Associated Sportsman,* Mason designed and published a total of twenty-eight how-to-build plans during his career, showcasing some of his designs that were not created for just one client, but for broad appeal. One of these boats, the popular 24-foot 1-inch Ostkust, is considered a virtually unimproveable classic and might be considered America's answer to the famous Folkboat, which she somewhat resembles.

A number of large and luxurious motorsailers were drawn by Mason, often with the unique combination of a graceful, long-ended "pure sailboat" hull and a large but well-proportioned superstructure. In these boats it is really the superstructure that puts them in the motorsailer category—it might otherwise be proper to call them "full-powered auxiliaries."

Mason's powerboats were fewer in number but no less notable. They are usually what might be called sailor's powerboats, where toughness, looks, fuel economy, and seakeeping ability are placed ahead of speed in priority.

Mason was born in Salinas, California. As young as age seven, he was drawing profiles of boats. By high school he was already a boat fiend and held a summer job in a Monterey Bay boatyard. After graduating in 1929, he went to work at the Wilmington Boat Works in southern California, doing drafting and design-related work under designer and builder Hugh Angelman, notably on the Nick Potter–designed, 76-foot schooner *Endymion.* He eventually went to work for the design firm of Lambie and Mabry.

Mason lost his job at Lambie and Mabry because he knew nothing about designing for steel. That is when he decided he needed more extensive broad-based training. He chose the Webb Institute of Naval Architecture and Marine Engineering in New York because he was desperately poor and could not afford college unless everything was paid for. He was twenty when he entered Webb, the oldest student in his class and the only one who had already established himself as a designer.

Mason's first independent design (and the ninth boat he had designed) was for a 62-foot, three-masted, composite-built schooner named *California,* designed in 1928 and built in 1933. She made one circumnavigation in 1949–53 and spent the majority of her life in the charter/cruise business. Mason's first design to see print in a national magazine was a 50-foot offshore racing and cruising cutter published in *Yachting* magazine in 1933.

After his graduation from Webb in 1936, Mason worked for the design firm of Gibbs and Cox in New York City, and soon thereafter in the John G. Alden office in Boston, producing work under his own name in his spare time. Back in New York he worked at Tams, and then began an on-again, off-again association with Sparkman and Stephens, which would ultimately add up to eighteen years.

Mason was recruited to Sparkman and Stephens by Gil Wyland when they were beefing up their staff in anticipation of the United States' involvement in World War II. Mason trained and supervised less-skilled draftsmen and checked their plans. As was true his entire life, he chafed under the paperwork. In his spare time after hours, he designed the Mason 31 and stock designs for Oceania.

Never one to stay at one job too long, Mason at times worked independently and also for Steelcraft and for Feadship (both companies went bankrupt), taught briefly at the U.S. Naval Academy, and then worked at Philip Rhodes office in New York City in 1956. Here he did some of his best large yacht work and assisted in the design of *Weatherly,* the 12-Meter yacht that successfully defended the America's Cup against the Alan Payne–designed *Gretel* in 1962. Mason also drew stock plans for Joel Johnson, Norge Boats, and Pacific Asian Enterprises.

In 1966 Mason went to work at the Naval Ship Engineering Center in Washington, D.C., where he stayed until his retirement in 1977. At various times he was a measurer for the CCA, the Storm Trysail Club, and the City Island Yacht Club.

Al Mason retired to Salinas, California, where he died at age eighty-four, less than ten blocks from where he had been born.

Mason's drawings are held by his daughter, Anita Mason.

—Daniel B. MacNaughton

SCOTT J. MATTHEWS

1869–April 8, 1956 · United States

The founder of the long-lived Matthews Company of Port Clinton, Ohio, Scott Matthews was a major participant in the development of roomy, handsome, and seaworthy power cruisers from their earliest days in the 1890's until his death in 1956.

Matthews built his first boat in 1890 for his own use, and then moved promptly into the series construction of naphtha launches, achieving the remarkable production rate of one boat per day by 1895. Initially located in Bascom, Ohio, where Matthews was born, the company moved to Port Clinton in 1906 with the help of a group of local businessmen, creating a large facility at which custom cruisers up to 120 feet in length were constructed.

Retaining his interest in series production, in 1924 Matthews introduced the first version of the Matthews 38, which proved to be one of the most popular stock power cruisers ever built, steadily evolving but remaining in production for over thirty years. Among her other features, the 38 helped to introduce hull forms with wider, flatter aft sections, increasing initial stability and interior space and reducing squatting of the hull so as to permit higher speeds. A number of other models of various sizes were marketed as well.

Matthews powerboats had a strong, seaworthy appearance compared to their competitors. Streamlining influences were kept moderate and tasteful. Many larger models were noticeably simple in line and arrangement for their size, giving them extra elbow room and a clean appearance. Auxiliary sailing rigs were an option for many of the earlier boats, and added to their functional appearance.

In 1912 the Matthews Company produced the 38-foot, double-ended cruiser *Detroit,* which *The Rudder* magazine editor Thomas Fleming Day navigated from Detroit, Michigan, to Saint Petersburg, Russia, making her the first gasoline-powered vessel to cross the Atlantic.

During World War I and World War II, the Matthews Company produced subchasers and

Al Mason: Ostkust. One of Mason's most popular designs, the 24-foot Ostkust is also widely believed to be one of the most appealing boats of her size ever designed. She combines the short ends, outboard rudder, and heft of an offshore cruiser with the delicacy of line and cleanliness of rig of a classic bay boat. The many boats built to this design are rarely altered in any significant detail. *Drawing courtesy Anita Mason*

Scott Matthews: *Galatea.* The Matthews 38 was designed in 1925. The tank-tested model was developed with a wider, flatter run than was typical at the time, providing greater stability and a level semiplaning ride at relatively high speeds. The 38 continued to be built, with only styling upgrades, until 1949, and hundreds were produced. *Galatea* was built in 1941. © *Benjamin Mendlowitz*

other vessels for the U.S. government, each time reverting to yacht production upon the advent of peace. Until the end of Prohibition in 1933, the high demand for fast motorboats for both smugglers and law enforcement officials was profitably served by the Matthews Company.

Scott Matthews died in 1956. His heirs continued to operate the company for ten years, but sold it in 1966. It then made the transition to fiberglass construction, continuing until 1975, when it ceased production. In 1977 a Matthews Owners Association was formed and continues to serve owners and enthusiasts.

—Daniel B. MacNaughton

ANDRÉ MAURIC

1909–2003 · France

Tradition and modernity, classicism and a fascination with the future—so one would summarize the principles that governed André Mauric's long career. He began designing in 1930 and stopped in 1985, when Commander Jacques Cousteau's experimental wind ship, one of the ultimate creations of Mauric's office, sailed off for a round-the-world trip via Cape Horn. Expressing his gratitude for the commission, Mauric exclaimed at the time that Commander Cousteau had enabled him to end his career with the great achievement of having designed the vessel *Alcyone*.

Assisted by his future successor, Jean-Charles Nahon, Mauric created a unique hull for *Alcyone*, which had to take into account the requirements of the unique rig and a displacement of 80 tons in 31 meters of length. Having a conventional bow, the hull separates aft into something much like a catamaran in order to give maximum stability while reducing the wetted surface area. Powered by Professor Lucien Malavard's Turbosails, whose principle is drawn from the German Magnus effect, *Alcyone* has ovoid-section, nearly cylindrical sails, but unlike earlier such rigs, the cylinders do not revolve except to orient the sails correctly to the wind. Conceived in 1973, in the midst of the oil crisis, the concept has not seen the success it may have deserved, as energy subsequently became much less expensive. *Alcyone* was an aborted rendezvous with the future, but perhaps the need for environmental preservation might cause us to see more vessels like *Alcyone* sailing the seas.

Mauric began his professional life in 1930 in Charles Baudouin's Massilia shipyard, where highly regarded motorsailers were built. Baudouin, a naval architect and mechanical engineer, designer and builder of navy submarine-hunting launches and minesweepers during World War I, passed on to the young Mauric his expertise. Mauric brought with him a knowledge of mathematics, acquired in Marseille's Sciences University (the Depression obliged him to abandon his studies before receiving his diploma) and enlarged through the technical progress that had taken place between the two wars. His career had not been chosen by chance.

Indeed, Mauric's father Auguste, his uncle, and his brother Edmond were all excellent yachtsmen. A cabinetmaker by trade, Auguste conceived, drew, and built his own yachts, seven in all, and the first regatta won by the Maurics was sailed in July 1898, on *Be-a-ba*. From his early childhood, Mauric crewed on family sailboats and after 1920, he took the helm in regattas. At the end of 1927, at his father's request, he designed the family's next racer, an 8-meter 50 SI (International Series), *Morwark*. Her lines were drawn full scale on the lofting floor and she was built by André's father. As compared to what had previously been done in the 8-meter 50 class, there were several innovations: a rather rounded bow, hull lines and a keel shape that were very soft, a flush deck, and rigging that utilized a mast having three pairs of spreaders, revolutionary for the time. The results were not long in coming: between 1928 and 1929, in twenty-nine starts *Morwark* won twenty-two races.

Orders soon began to flow in. Mauric designed some one-designs, including the MOCAT (Côte d'Azur typical 5-meter one-designs); one 5-Meter International Rule; *Jean Gab*, a very big cruiser designed in 1930 for Jean Gabriel Daragnès (a painter of the Fauvist school); and a 15.6-meter sloop of 24-ton displacement fitted with asymmetrical spinnakers. All these boats were built by Baudouin's Massilia yard. Mauric said, "I am only the successor of my father and Baudouin. My father for sailing boats . . . and Baudouin . . . for motor ships."

As World War II approached, Mauric devoted his time to designing and managing shipyards. His participation in yachting was a sideline: designing the fast cruisers *Lak* and *Ariel*; building Olympic class Star boats; the design of *Cabri*, a 10.5-meter cruising yawl that came out in 1933; *Iroise IV*, designed in 1936; and one 15.4-meter schooner. He became familiar with naval construction, and practically no type of motorboat escaped him: trawlers, small harbor pilot-boats, barges, navy and custom launches, fishing surveillance launches, tugboats, and colonial boats. During the war he took over the management of the arsenal at Toulon, and through his efforts no material was delivered to the enemy by these yards.

After the war, Mauric decided to carry on his career as an independent naval architect.

French yachting had to be rebuilt very quickly. He resumed the rhythm that had been his prewar style and worked primarily with the Estérel yard (Chantiers de l'Estérel). At the end of 1950, a new market for fast coastal surveillance boats appeared. Mauric carved out a reputation for extending frontiers, by deepening his studies of hulls and propellers. He was able to provide the French navy with several 32-meter ships fitted with 4,400-hp engines, and for the Gabon navy a 42-meter missile launcher patrol boat powered by 10,500 hp and able to reach the speed of 40 knots. Besides France, twenty-four nations employ 105 fast patrol boats designed by his office.

These high-powered hulls served as models for Mauric's large motoryachts, the fastest of their type in the world. Examples include *Carinthia IV, Silvercross, Arjuna, Xiphias,* and the latest and most prestigious, *Acajou,* drawn in 1983 in collaboration with Jon Bannenberg. *Acajou* is 42 meters long, powered by 7,000 hp, and reaches 34 knots.

The passion for sail did not abandon Mauric. He designed some big sailboats—*Adventure,* a 22-meter Bermudian cutter (1950); *Chambell II,* a 29-meter ketch (1956); and others—but he had to wait until 1962 for an opportunity to arrive on a larger scale. He designed for his brother a triple-chine hull, for he believed that double chines disturbed the flow of the water at the bow. "I remembered the form of an old dinghy: a widened hull consisting of three developable panels on each side, between which was a central panel." The prototype, *Laurana,* 10.57 meters long, gave birth to the Challenger series, with eighteen boats built in 1963 and 1964. This was followed by the Super Challenger, one of which won the Half-Ton Cup and the Giraglia.

Ten years later, *Impensable* was victorious in the 1973 Half-Ton Cup; she was skippered by Michel Briand (designer Philippe Briand's father). She featured a now-famous aft-raking keel and soon became the Beneteau First 30, of which 1,100 were built. There is also Mauric's One-Tonner *Drac,* of which the Jeanneau yard has built six hundred under the name Melody, and the famous Three-Quarter-Tonner *Tadorne*—the first IOR yacht to be fitted with the fractional rig now adopted on most IOR yachts—which gave birth to the Delph 32 series.

During these years, the Mauric office went on to design large luxury yachts, such as *Aiglon* (1970), a splendid 36-meter aluminum schooner built by Abeking and Rasmussen; *Surama,* a 32-meter ketch built by Cantieri Navali in La Spezia; and the 24.90-meter ULDB sloop *Pioneer,* built by Pouvreau. Nor did Mauric forget the open races. His first significant design of this type was the 17.31-meter aluminum ketch *Raph,* destined for the 1968 English Single-handed Transatlantic Race. She distinguished herself in the 1977–78 Whitbread by winning a leg in the Indian Ocean under the name of *33-Export.*

In 1970 and after long years of research for his friend Baron Marcel Bich, André Mauric became the first French naval architect to design a 12-Meter International Rule yacht for the America's Cup. The opinion of all observers at the time was that France, the French 12-Meter, had an indisputable potential but was put at a disadvantage by bad sails and suffered from a crew that lacked experience. Two years later, he designed *France II* with an eye to the 1974 challenge, but Baron Bich's involvement with Pol Elvström and his bulb-bowed 12-Meter concept (never built) meant that *France II* ended up being built for the 1977 Challenge. And when Mauric saw what had been done to his design,

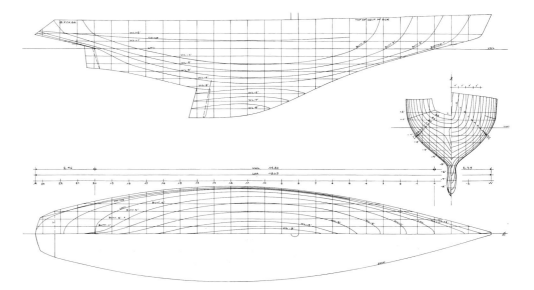

André Mauric: *France.* The 12-Meter *France,* designed for Baron Marcel Bich as an America's Cup challenger in 1970, emphasized minimum wetted surface area. She featured an unusual chine above the waterline aft and extremely blunt waterlines in the forebody of the hull. © *Chevalier & Taglang*

André Mauric: *Pen Duick VI.* Eric Tabarly won the 1976 Observer Singlehanded Transatlantic Race (OSTAR) with his Mauric-designed *Pen Duick VI.* She was launched at Brest in 1973. Still active, the 22.25-meter LOA *Pen Duick VI* has sailed more than 260,000 miles. *Photo courtesy Jacques Taglang*

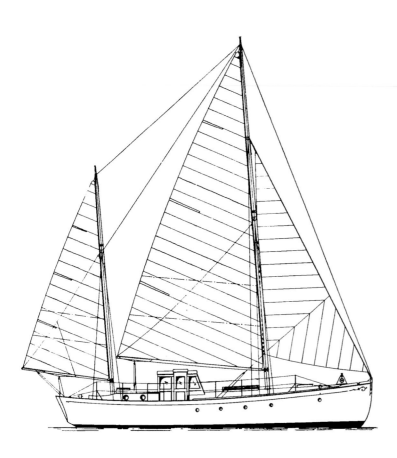

William McBryde: *Glengour.* An early motorsailer, the 39-foot 3-inch LOA *Glengour* was designed to be sailed shorthanded. With twin screws she could turn in her own length in just over 2 minutes, enabling her owners to anchor in very small harbors. © *Tony Dixon*

John McCallum: *Ron of Argyll.* McCallum's work emphasized comfortable accommodations, and while the 50-foot *Ron* is unusually beamy for a British yacht of her day, this seems to contribute to her appealing character. *Photo courtesy* Aussie Adventure Sailing

he barely recognized his child—the old 1970 *France* easily outsailed *France II.*

This period also produced other gratifying projects: *Pen Duick VI*, designed for Eric Tabarly, was launched in 1973 in order to sail the first Whitbread. She was a large flush-decked ketch with a depleted-uranium ballast keel, impressive in her balance and power; however, she suffered two dismastings in the race. Though designed to be sailed with crew, *Pen Duick VI* was skippered to victory by Eric Tabarly in the 1976 Singlehanded Transat Race, overcoming five depressions, of which two were very violent. Mauric also designed *Kriter V*, Michel Malinowski's ULDB, which was beaten by only a few seconds in the first Route du Rhum Race, and *Neptune* for the 1977–78 Whitbread.

Taking advantage of his experience before and during World War II, as a designer and builder, and as a versatile and eclectic inventor, André Mauric was the sole French designer to have exercised his talent in all specialties. To define that talent in a few words, one could remember one of his favorite sentences: "A good boat has to be able to sail without a rudder." To put it in one word, one could say *balance.*   —Jacques Taglang

WILLIAM GRAY McBRYDE

1881–1967 · Scotland

From the 1920's into the mid-1950's, W. G. McBryde flourished as the principal Clyde-based designer of yachts that actually went to sea, as opposed to sailing only in Scotland's sheltered western waters. Despite having a distinguished reputation and an international clientele among the oceangoing set, and having continued to design in semiretirement until his death at age eighty-seven, he seems largely forgotten nowadays; such has been the rapid change in fashion.

McBryde designed proper little ships in the days when that was appreciated: a healthy, seakindly, and comfortable "fifty-fifty" type of yacht of moderately heavy displacement and pleasing appearance. He had the particular knack of drawing a shapely, rounded-off deckhouse that blended well with the rest of the yacht.

McBryde's early career reads like Conrad: an enviable training in deep-sea voyaging with his father, who was a square-rigger captain; chief draftsman at the Hong Kong and Whampoa Dock Company; assistant general manager at Fairfield Shipbuilding Company, Glasgow; a

yacht designer in Vancouver, British Columbia, Canada (in partnership with Frederick C. Brewer) prior to World War I; and recognition as the father of the Scottish fishing boat type of the 1920's to the 1950's, a vessel whose influence is apparent in most of his work.

McBryde eventually settled in Scotland, opening a Glasgow office in about 1920 and subsequently moving down river to Kirn. Immediately before and after World War II he published two volumes of his designs, which stand as a fitting testament to a fascinating life's work.

—Iain McAllister

JOHN A. McCALLUM

1882–1933 · Scotland

John McCallum was one of the earliest designers to satisfy the phenomenal demand for motoryachts that occurred when the internal-combustion engine became a reliable power source a few years into the twentieth century.

Establishing his Glasgow office in 1908, when, as an obituary glibly commented, "steam still held sway and the perfect engine was looked upon with disfavor," McCallum was in the right place at the right time, with the training, a belief in new technology, and the contacts to capitalize on some happily coinciding circumstances.

There were good local engine manufacturers, notably Bergius of Glasgow, whose first Kelvin engine of 1905 immediately gained a reputation for the reliability of its unique ignition system. It featured a low-tension magneto and mechanical "make-and-break" spark within the cylinder ("positively the only system then in use which could be relied upon to start an engine lying unused for a week or so in our damp climate," wrote W. M. Bergius twenty-five years later). There was an extensive local boatbuilding industry famous for its ability to turn out hulls that were lighter and cheaper than those made of steel or teak, which had been required to cope with the heat generated by steam engines. And there was a huge potential client base earning well from the industrial powerhouse of west central Scotland.

Many clients were not from the yachting establishment but would spend their leisure time on the Clyde's superbly sheltered cruising waters. Compared to the steam yacht scene, the rise of "marine motoring" attracted more numerous social groups and introduced new clubs and regattas.

McCallum wasn't unique, but he became the most successful Clyde motoryacht "pioneer" due to the energy he applied to all areas of his chosen profession. He was a founding member of the Clyde Motor Boat Club in 1909, a winner of design competitions, and a regular winner when family cruisers occasionally raced at rallies. He was intimately involved in the construction of his earliest designs.

The ambitious 50-foot LOA, twin-screw motoryacht *Orchid* was McCallum's first commission, ordered in early April 1907 and running trials by July 17. She was the first cruiser-sterned seagoing motoryacht built for the Clyde and the first recorded launching by James A. Silver, who subsequently moved to Rosneath in 1910 to found the yard that still carries his name. McCallum designed much of Silver's early work.

Orchid set a standard for reliability. A reviewer noted, "She has run for 12 hours at a stretch without a hitch occurring." Accommodations were well thought out and spacious, a feature that was to become McCallum's trademark and would help drive the evolution of the motoryacht. Over twenty years later he commented, "One striking feature is that the smaller type of motor cruiser, having the same overall length and beam as the pre-war craft, has about twice as much displacement. This, of course, gives the large roomy accommodation in demand, but it naturally brings in its train heavier building charges and greater horsepower to ensure a reasonable cruising speed."

Orchid's success caused McCallum's workload to steadily increase. Before World War I he drew around eighty-five yachts, and the regular commercial work he attracted increased the number of designs to over a hundred. He recruited an associate, Frank A. Allan, and two apprentices, the cousins W. MacPherson Campbell and Neil A. Campbell (later his successor).

McCallum designs had personality and stood out from the crowd. His early large vessels resembled steam yachts, with buff-colored funnels carrying away the hot exhaust from the accommodation and giving a purposeful appearance, but they also showed the noticeable differences of a cruiser stern and plum stem. By 1910 McCallum had claimed credit for the introduction of the sunk deckhouse, first seen on the far-traveled 60-footer *Kia Ora (II)*. This work set the typical general arrangement of the seagoing motoryacht for a number of years.

Although the annual number of designs never approached the prewar maximum during the 1920's the size of yachts commissioned increased dramatically, reaching a peak between 1925 and 1927, when four vessels, ranging in overall length from 91 to 98 feet and built by Munro of Oban, were merely part of his portfolio. One, the 91-foot *Tiger* (ex-*Waveney II*) was well known in the Caribbean for her striking good looks until she foundered in 2001.

Another interesting survivor illustrates that McCallum did not exclusively design motoryachts. The 50-foot auxiliary gaff ketch *Ron*, now chartering in the Whitsundays as *Ron of Argyll*, was commissioned by Clyde Cruising Club Commodore Colonel Charles L. Spencer in 1928 and built by Robertson of Sandbank. Applying his ideas of commodious accommodation to a sailing yacht resulted in 13 feet of beam, remarkable for the time.

Sadly, the Depression years limited the demand for such vessels. McCallum designed only four more motoryachts between 1928 and 1931, before his sudden death while crewing on a friend's 8-Meter during the 1933 Clyde Fortnight.
—Iain McAllister

JAMES ARRISON McCURDY

1922–August 21, 1994 · United States

As president of McCurdy and Rhodes, James McCurdy only designed sailboats on which he personally would go to sea. His designs—whether for cruising, like the Hinckley Sou'wester 42, 51, 59, and 61 production yachts, or for racing, like *Carina* and *Arcadia*—combined conservatively elegant lines with seaworthy and seakindly forms.

In the mid-1970's, McCurdy eschewed the extreme direction of designs exploiting loop-

Jim McCurdy: Sou'wester 59. The first of the Sou'wester 59's was launched by the Hinckley Company in 1982. A more logical pairing could hardly be imagined. The classic sheerlines, moderately long overhangs, conservative and well-proportioned cabin trunks, and easily handled rigs create the timeless appeal for which both designer and builder are famous. *Photo courtesy the Hinckley Company*

holes in the IOR, the rating rule developed in the late 1960's. Instead, he led committee work in the U.S. Sailing Association and the International Offshore Racing Council to analyze and predict actual sailboat performance, collaborating with such influential sailing-yacht designers of the time as Olin Stephens, Gary Mull, and David Pedrick. The result was the IMS, which eclipsed the IOR in the early 1980's.

McCurdy relished both the intellectual and the artistic challenge of creating yachts that had superior sailing performance, satisfied the eye with the gentle sheers and squared cabin houses he preferred, and met the particular needs of the owners. Often he raced or cruised with his clients, becoming their friends. Ironically, his success in satisfying his clients meant he had little repeat business. Owners kept their boats for years. Forty-three designs were built for custom or production clients, for a total of well over three hundred boats.

Growing up in Philadelphia, McCurdy did not share his family's penchant for golfing and gardening, and decided on his career after discovering sailing at a summer camp. During World War II, poor eyesight thwarted military service. Instead, he graduated with an engineering degree from Yale University and in 1944 went to work for Cox and Stevens in New York City designing vessels for the military.

Following the war, McCurdy joined Philip L. Rhodes, Naval Architects, and headed the sailing yacht design office until 1965, when he left with Philip H. "Bodie" Rhodes, the son of Philip L. Rhodes, to form McCurdy and Rhodes. Their office was established in Cold Spring Harbor, New York, and the partners collaborated until Bodie Rhodes retired in 1982. James's son, Ian McCurdy, joined the firm in 1980 and took over the business after his father's death.

McCurdy and Rhodes's first racing successes were a string of 40- to 50-footers starting with *Carina*. The 48-foot aluminum sloop won the 1970 Newport-Bermuda Race the year after her launching and won the transatlantic race to Spain two years later. Three decades later, she won her class in the 2000 Bermuda Race for her second owner.

The design diversity of the firm is demonstrated by the two 95-foot LOD plank-on-frame schooners *Bill of Rights* and *Harvey Gamage*, designed in the early 1970's, and the 44-foot fiberglass sail training craft for the U.S. Naval Academy, which built twenty identical sloops in the late 1980's and plans twenty-four more by 2005.

To Jim McCurdy, sailing was both his business and his sport. He was active in the CCA and served as commodore in 1986–87.

—Sheila McCurdy

EWING McGRUER JR.
1889–1966
JAMES McGRUER
1906–1988
GEORGE McGRUER
born 1933

Scotland

Along with such yards as Fife's and Nicholson's, the McGruer boatbuilding yard in Glasgow rates as one of the outstanding family businesses in the history of yachting. At one time Ewing McGruer Sr. worked along with his seven sons, each heading a department involved in the running of the yard.

Like many other yards, McGruer's had its own design and drafting office, and from the beginning designed many of the boats it built though it also produced craft using plans by other designers. Alfred Mylne Sr. frequently chose McGruer's to construct from his designs, particularly the smaller craft such as the Clyde 19/24's and the Scottish Islands Class.

Over the years the design office drew plans for a higher and higher percentage of the boats built at the yard, and also produced designs for craft built by other yards. This was a reflection of the skill demonstrated by the three men most responsible for this happy state of affairs.

Ewing Jr. made his name with the development of a new method for making hollow spars. Instead of the usual built-up spars, he rolled laminates of timber around prepared mandrels. The resulting tubes were very light for their strength and stiffness, and came to have many applications besides spars, such as stretcher poles, organ pipes, and even billiard cues. During World War I they were employed as airplane wing-struts and fuselage longerons. Ewing Jr. also designed a number of excellent boats, including the 24-foot Gareloch One-Design.

The McGruer who really made his name as a designer was Ewing Jr.'s younger brother James. By the time he was twenty-one, James had already designed two craft built by the firm. To further his experience, he worked for a time at G. L. Watson and Company in Glasgow, before moving to the United States, where he worked at the Herreshoff Manufacturing Company in Bristol, Rhode Island. On his return in the early 1930's, he was to become more and more involved in design work, benefiting from the experience of his older brother.

James's first racing yacht of note was the 6-Meter *Nike*. She was followed by *Kini,* another 6-Meter for the same owners. Later he produced the excellent 6-Meter *Johan,* which represented Britain in the 1948 Olympics and other important contests.

However, it was in the establishment of the cruiser/racer classes that James really came to prominence—first in drawing up the rules for the cruiser/racers and then in the design of a significant number of the class, many of which were built by the yard. He also designed a wide variety of excellent cruising yachts, prominent among which were a series of yawls, each approximately 17 tons, each slightly different, but all characterized by elegant lines, strong construction, good accommodations, and excellent sailing qualities.

When in 1957 the Royal Yacht Squadron mounted the first post–World War II challenge for the America's Cup in 12-Meter yachts, James McGruer was one of the four architects invited to submit designs—the others were David Boyd, Charles A. Nicholson, and Arthur Robb. In the event, Boyd's design for *Sceptre* was selected.

There is insufficient space to detail all the notable craft that came from James's board. Suffice to say that the excellence of his designs, allied with the outstanding craftsmanship of the yard, produced some truly fine boats. But James McGruer also acquired a reputation for objectivity and integrity. He was a judge on the technical committee of the 1956 Olympics, becoming eventually the chairman of the jury, attending six games.

James's son, George, having obtained his BSc in naval architecture at Glasgow University, joined the firm in 1957 for a year's experience before moving to Hong Kong to work for the government there as a naval architect and ship surveyor.

George returned in 1963 and immediately became immersed in the management of the yard, while his involvement with his father's design work steadily increased. The later cruiser/racers clearly reflect his input, as they have characteristics not associated with his father's work.

In 1969 James McGruer took over as chairman of the company from his elder brother, Willie, and George became managing director. George became increasingly responsible for the firm's designs, and from his board some extraordinarily fine yachts came to life. They had not only the McGruer hallmark but also other qualities that set them apart. Whereas James was a sound, scientific designer, George was that as well as an artist, and his designs have an aesthetic quality largely absent in the earlier boats. Two of the finest yachts of their size, anywhere, are the 55-foot ketches *Cuilaun of Kinsale* and *Talisker Mhor.* He also designed some very pretty cruisers and ocean racers, at a time when aesthetic qualities were largely unknown in such craft.

George McGruer has retired but still consults and designs. The McGruer company, as such, ceased operations in 2000. —David Ryder-Turner

Ewing McGruer Jr.: Gareloch One-Design. Yet another example of the one-design classes that sprang up in post–World War I Britain is the Gareloch of 1924. All sixteen of the class are still in existence and race well on the Clyde. *Photo courtesy David Ryder-Turner*

James McGruer: *Inismara.* As well as being one of the formulators of the Cruiser/Racer Rule of the early 1950's, McGruer designed a number of Cruiser 8's, of which *Inismara* is a good example. © *Benjamin Mendlowitz*

WALTER J. McINNIS

January 11, 1893–January 2, 1985
United States

Walter McInnis was a master of drafting and aesthetics who designed handsome workboats, and yachts that usually retained at least a trace of workboat character. He is known for his superb round-bilged powerboat designs, which included yachts, commercial fishing vessels, and military craft. He also drew plans for chine-hull powerboats and a broad range of cruising sailboats notable for their serious and conservative appearance. He practiced yacht design for seventy years, working most of that time under the business name of Eldredge-McInnis. His partner, Albert E. Eldredge, was not a yacht designer but handled the business and financial details.

McInnis was a fast and accurate designer. His ability to quickly draft a sketch plan that captured its prospective owner's desires within an appealing form obtained for him a great deal of work that might otherwise have slipped away. He then drew highly detailed plans and was able to follow through with a fortunate combination of drive, methodical work habits, mechanical and artistic aptitude, and a renowned ability to cooperate with others.

Because his career spanned practically the whole evolution of internal-combustion engine–powered boats, *traditional* is not a word that describes his powerboat work. Likewise some of his later sailboat designs relate directly to the Gloucester-style fishing schooners he helped design as a young apprentice. So if any of it looks "traditional" to us today, McInnis helped define the term. McInnis was not radical—his thinking progressed by evolution, not revolution. His work was usually modern in the sense of being up-to-date, but it did not push the limits of aesthetics in that direction. At the same time, with a few notable exceptions such as his schooner *Cecelia J* (later *Deliverance*) and a Friendship sloop, *Dottie G*, designed for the same owner, the work is not nostalgic. The designs are clean, sophisticated, polished, and restrained—a type of boat that might go unnoticed by a casual viewer but is simply riveting to the experienced eye.

The design of superstructures—cabin trunks, bridges, windshields, and so on—was one of McInnis's strong points. He helped to define good taste in streamlined forms, knowing just how far he could go with aerodynamic styling without creating a look that would become dated. As a result, his boats are timeless, worthy of construction decades after their creation and impossible to date within a range of twenty or thirty years, a mark of the highest level of talent.

McInnis used to claim that powerboat hulls were not too challenging to design. He once said, "You make the boat as long as you can afford, you build her as light as you can afford, and you give her as much power as you can afford . . . and she'll go like hell." He always used length and fairness of line, rather than excess power alone, to increase performance, and his hull forms emphasized consistency in all conditions, not just speed in smooth water.

Typical McInnis sailboats have a buoyant, beamy, relatively short-ended hull; a long keel; a well-proportioned but snug marconi rig; and often a nicely styled, doghouse-type cabin trunk. They generally retain an air of toughness and workboat-like proportions. His schooners, such as *Cecelia J*, are noted for their strong and

Walter McInnis: Eastward Ho. The 23-foot 5-inch Eastward Ho, drawn in 1957, was one of McInnis's most popular designs. Her shapely, short-ended hull is driven by a modest rig and a powerful auxiliary, while a carefully drawn doghouse provides standing headroom. Providing only two permanent berths frees extra space for the head, cockpit, and galley. © *Mystic Seaport, Ships' Plan Division, Mystic, CT*

appealing sheers and rugged-looking hulls, very unlike the more delicately styled racing schooners of the same period from other designers.

McInnis was also a master in the design of motorsailers, and although he explored much the same combination of workboat and yacht features as did designers William Hand and R. O. Davis, his work is quite distinct. A magnificent example is *Vigilant*, a 100-foot ketch-rigged motorsailer largely based on the sardine-carrier form and built in Nova Scotia in 1939.

In commercial boat design McInnis was widely thought to be the very best, especially in the Eastern-rigged dragger and sardine-carrier types of New England, which he helped to define and of which he created some of the most beautiful, able, and long-lasting examples.

His boats have been extremely popular in the Canadian Maritime Provinces, where government-sponsored programs led to large numbers being built and fished.

Walter McInnis was born in Boston. He graduated from the Mechanics Arts High School in Boston and would have attended MIT had his family not suffered financial reversals that made this impossible. He is said to have regretted his lack of formal training in yacht design for much of his life, but later felt that he may have become a better designer because he learned the trade by immersion in the workaday world and did not acquire preconceived notions.

While a very young man he was an apprentice draftsman for Thomas McManus, a designer famous for his fast and able Gloucester fishing schooners. He had sailed on a Gloucester schooner for a summer during high school. His earliest regular job was with the New England Telephone and Telegraph Company, but he soon talked his way into a job as a draftsman with the George Lawley and Son Corporation, the renowned yacht design and construction yard in Neponset, Massachusetts. He joined them in 1912 and worked there for twelve years, learning the ins and outs of yacht design and drafting and gaining particular experience in powerboat design.

During World War I, Lawley obtained a great many government boatbuilding contracts for subchasers and the like, and McInnis learned not only how valuable these contracts could be but also how to deal with the government as a client. Remarkably, the Lawley yard encouraged its draftsmen to develop their own clientele and to take outside design work. McInnis's first independent design commission was for a 65-foot fast cruiser named *Westerly*, built in 1920.

McInnis left Lawley in 1924 to become the manager of the F. S. Nock boatyard in East Greenwich, Rhode Island. Here he designed the 71-foot *Valia*, a twin-screw express cruiser, along with the first of what would become a long line of high-speed rumrunners. Ironically these boats were so successful that he was later called on by the Coast Guard to design the equally fast 78-foot cutters used to chase the rumrunners. The success of both types brought him broader recognition for his design work.

In 1925 he returned to Lawley, but he and Albert Eldredge soon left to form Eldredge-McInnis, a design and brokerage firm. Shortly thereafter they began a long association with American Car Foundry (ACF), a railroad-car builder in Wilmington, Delaware, that had decided to build yachts on a semi-production-line basis. McInnis designed a whole line of stock cruisers for ACF, ranging from 28 to 68 feet in length. The first was a 30-footer, of which almost 750 were sold. While these boats have a distinctly antique appearance today, they are still considered to be among the best of the type and are much sought after by classic power-boat enthusiasts.

McInnis also did work for ACF's rival Richardson, producing the well-known Cruiseabout model, production of which started in 1929. The firm also built many custom designs, including a number of long and narrow but wholesome fast cruisers such as the 56-foot *Pronto*, 75-foot *Nereus*, and 90-foot *Cyric*, all running about 25 mph with twin screws. Another example was *Marlin*, a 51-foot commuter originally owned by Edsel Ford and used by President John F. Kennedy.

In the late 1920's McInnis designed the first of his famous draggers, beginning an unparalleled run of fishing boat designs from which hundreds have been built in the northeastern United States and eastern Canada. Along with McInnis's sardine carriers, they quickly acquired a reputation for looks, comfort, and safety under offshore conditions. Many are still in service.

The Depression of the 1930's was hard on the yacht design field, but McInnis's ability to acquire and satisfy government contracts provided a steady stream of work, including designing a series for the Coast Guard that continued all the way up to the Korean War.

With the onset of World War II, government contracts began to flood the Eldredge-McInnis office to the point where the staff and facilities were inadequate for the work. In contrast, the rival John G. Alden Company, which had never taken on much of this type of work in the past, didn't have enough for its people to do. The two businesses were combined, and over the next five years they designed $3 billion worth of boats for the war effort, including tugs, salvage ships, minesweepers, and small transports.

After the war the two firms separated again, and Eldredge-McInnis began another active period of designing, including many commercial boats such as the handsome sardine carriers for the William Underwood Company of Portland, Maine, and several large fishing vessels for the Canadian government, which were built in quantity. In 1966 McInnis designed the spectacular 83-foot power yacht *Lion's Whelp* and in 1968 the equally impressive 82-foot *Cassiar*. The latter was such a notable success that a near-duplicate, the 84-foot *Yorel*, was built by Hodgdon Brothers in 1989. Besides a large number of up-to-date custom power yachts, postwar stock power cruisers included 40- and 46-foot Wheelers, and the Marblehead Boat Company's 29- and 32-foot models. A 26-foot sportfisherman originally designed for Brownell Boat Works was so successful that it

Walter McInnis: *Elizabeth Muir*. When McInnis drew cruising schooners, they benefited from his considerable personal experience with the original Gloucester fishing schooners on which they were based. *Elizabeth Muir* is of the knockabout schooner type, designed without a bowsprit, as were her working ancestors, in the interest of safety and ease of handling. © *Benjamin Mendlowitz*

Walter McInnis: *Yorel*. The 84-foot *Yorel* was built by Hodgdon Brothers in 1989. She is a slight modification of McInnis's 1968 design for *Cassiar*, an 82-footer built by Goudy and Stevens. Note how the design of the prominent superstructure creates much of the boat's energetic and competent personality. © *Benjamin Mendlowitz*

is still in production in fiberglass, built by Fortier Boats. Stock sailboat designs included the well-known 23-foot 5-inch Eastward Ho, of which 150 were built; the 30-foot Eastward Ho Senior; the 28-foot Samurai, and the TOR 35.

Designers Wilder B. Harris, Jack Berry, Charles G. MacGregor, and Ralph Winslow all worked in the Eldredge-McInnis office at various times, and marine artist John Leavitt worked there as a broker. When Leavitt left in the mid-1950's, Walter's son Alan McInnis took on that task and began assisting with the design work, which he continued for many years after his father's retirement in 1977. The last Walter McInnis design, No. 590, was a 50-foot fishing vessel. McInnis died at age ninety-two.

The Eldredge-McInnis Collection is at Mystic Seaport Museum in Mystic, CT. Designs after 1950 are in the possession of Alan McInnis.

—Daniel B. MacNaughton with Llewellyn Howland III

DAVID C. "BUD" McINTOSH

1907–1992 · United States

Bud McIntosh was a boatbuilder, designer, yachtsman, and writer. Starting in 1931, he worked in a small shop near his home with just a few helpers. There he built approximately 145 boats, ranging from small skiffs to substantial schooners. He designed about half of the boats he built.

When he wasn't working, McIntosh and his wife Babe, who he often said was a better sailor than he was, were usually off cruising in their sturdy little cutter, *Bufflehead.*

McIntosh's boats stressed simplicity, strength, economy, and beauty of line rather than high finish or high technology. His design work emphasized traditional appearance and ease of construction using traditional methods. His boats were good performers; he once said that if one didn't have to steam the planks to get them to lie on the frames, the boat would probably sail well.

In later years, McIntosh was recognized as an important resource for sound and sensible, historical and technical information about boatbuilding and design. He was eager to share his knowledge with anyone who was interested, and encouraged many would-be designers and builders to enter the trade. He was known for his sense of humor, patience, and great warmth of personality.

As a writer, McIntosh had an easy, friendly style. He communicated the esoterica of boatbuilding with a clarity and readability that most would agree have never been equaled. He is the author of a book titled *How to Build a*

David McIntosh: Advent. The 36-foot schooner *Advent* was designed and built in 1956. While she is small for a schooner, she avoids cuteness, showing the overall simplicity and plain finish of a workboat, with the competence and lack of pretense for which McIntosh yachts are known. © *Benjamin Mendlowitz*

Wooden Boat, published by WoodenBoat Publications of Brooklin, Maine.

McIntosh was born in Dover, New Hampshire, and lived there his whole life. He grew up on a small farm and was introduced to boats when his father bought an island in nearby Great Bay. He graduated from Dartmouth College and later studied English at Harvard.

In 1931 McIntosh set up shop in Sawyer Mills, New Hampshire, moving to a permanent location in Dover Point in 1935. In 1978 he helped to organize the Piscataqua River Gundalow Project, which ultimately resulted in a reproduction of a historic, small local warship. He continued to work and sail until just before his death from a short illness. He was posthumously awarded the W. P. Stephens Award at Mystic Seaport "in recognition of a significant and enduring contribution to the history, preservation, progress, understanding, and appreciation of American yachting and boating."

—Daniel B. MacNaughton

GEORGE MELVILLE "MEL" McLAIN

March 8, 1841–ca. 1930 · United States

Editor's Note: Because the origins of the Friendship sloop are impossible to pinpoint accurately, we have placed our discussion of the type and its many designer/builders under the name of the earliest-known designer. Future

scholars may find an earlier source. Readers looking up other Friendship sloop designers are referred to this entry.

The Friendship sloop is a traditional midcoast Maine working boat that was used in and around the town of Friendship for lobstering and fishing from the late 1800's to the early 1900's. Widely publicized and successful efforts to preserve the type were among the first manifestations of the revival of interest in traditional watercraft that continues to this day. Now used exclusively for pleasure, and with new boats built almost every year, often to new designs, the Friendship sloop has become a genre of yachts, which is why this entry appears in this encyclopedia.

The Friendship sloop's origins are obscure. Current scholarship indicates that the earliest-known building model may have been made by George Melville McLain, born in Bremen, Maine. He was a designer of fishing schooners in Gloucester.

Many other Maine builder/designers of the region are associated with Friendship sloops, including the famous Wilbur Morse, who is often incorrectly credited with originating the type. In actual fact he was merely one of its most prolific builders and perhaps a bit of a self-promoter. Other builders include Wilbur Morse's brothers Charles and Jonah Morse; Abdon Carter; and a number of builders in the Collamore family.

The many builders made their own models and adapted the type, and hence were designers up to a point, but it is notable that the actual range of variations was quite narrow—whoever did the original apparently got it mostly right, as far as they were concerned.

As gasoline-powered boats displaced those that worked under sail on the Maine coast, many sloops were converted into yachts. In recent decades there have also been a good many Friendship sloops designed from scratch as yachts, often with modifications to increase the interior volume (which was always in short supply owing to the type's low freeboard and fine hull lines) and to take advantage of outside ballast (which few, if any, of the originals had). Some were built of fiberglass, and a few are almost-exact wooden replicas of the originals.

It appears that the yachts of the day had a strong influence on the Friendship sloop's original concept. In a time when both yachting and fishing were of necessity conducted under sail, there was much greater kinship between the two camps. Fishermen followed yacht racing with considerable interest. They undoubtedly took pride in a fast boat, and there would have been many races, formal and informal, within the working fleets.

Beginning in the 1880's, designers in the Gloucester, Massachusetts, area were borrowing heavily from yacht designs in an effort to produce safer fishing boats. Yachts had developed deep draft and more "wineglass-like" sections to get their ballast down low, and

the combination produced a much safer boat than the shoal, relatively wide, and flat working types, which were being lost offshore on an alarmingly regular basis.

What we now call a Gloucester schooner was one version of a yacht-inspired fishing boat, and the less well-known Gloucester sloop boat, influenced by the larger Edward Burgess–designed schooner *Fredonia*, was another. With a high clipper bow, deep keel, "schooner"-style oval transom, and sloop rig, these sloop boats strongly resembled a very large Friendship sloop, and since they appeared just a few years earlier and would have been in constant contact with the "Downeast" region, they are probably the immediate ancestor of the much smaller Friendship.

It is also possible that the Friendship sloop simply developed along a parallel course for the same reasons: her immediate predecessors were shoal-draft centerboard Muscongus Bay sloops, which cannot have been very good in a dangerous sea. Applying the same reasoning as the Gloucestermen did, local builders created the Friendship sloop independently.

The new type was well adapted to its purpose. Low-sided amidships and with a large cockpit, she was a good boat from which to haul lobster traps by hand. A high bow and stern added freeboard away from the working area and, combined with great beam and firm bilges for stability, made the boat more seaworthy. The deep keel put the ballast low, improving windward performance and allowing a large

rig for speed. The fine bow and full stern reduced pitching in a bay chop. The rig had most of the sail area in the mainsail, making the vessel easy to stop and start, while the jib on a long bowsprit helped with maneuvering.

In the summer a topsail and flying jib could be carried in light air, while in winter the topmast was removed. The designer/builders put a surprisingly strong emphasis on beauty, when combining these functional elements into a whole. A homely sloop might have done the job as well, but there were very few homely Friendship sloops.

A remarkable number of Friendship sloops survived for decades after they had become obsolete as fishing boats, owing to their good looks and their utility as cruising boats. The design of sailing yachts had long since moved into very different territory when in about 1960 the sloop *Voyager*, owned by Bernard MacKenzie, won a heavy-weather Boston Power Squadron Race, creating renewed interest in the type. MacKenzie was so impressed with *Voyager* that in 1961 he and a number of other sloop owners founded the Friendship Sloop Society.

Since then annual races have been held, first in Friendship and later in Rockland, Maine. Many original sloops have been restored, and scores of new sloops have been built to both original and modified designs, including a number of fiberglass versions. The workboat inspired by a yacht is now a yacht inspired by a workboat, and continues to serve.

—Daniel B. MacNaughton

Essential (Friendship sloop). The Friendship sloop *Essential* displays all the outward characteristics of the original working boats except for a longer cabin trunk, a smaller cockpit, and a higher level of finish. While we have been unable to determine her designer, she is typical of contemporary yacht versions. © *Peter Barlow*

Friendship sloop. This old photograph shows a Friendship sloop converted to a yacht, but probably not long after her working career. Both her house and her counter are longer than average. *Photo courtesy Roger F. Duncan*

Gunnar Mellgren: *Ester.* The extreme scow *Ester* was 18 meters LOD and 10 meters LWL, and featured a bulb keel and spade rudder. Mellgren designed her to defend the Tivoli Cup in 1901, which she did, beating the Estlander-designed *Aldebaran. Photo courtesy Gunnar Johansson*

Gunnar Mellgren: *Garm IV.* The largest of Mellgren's designs was the 60-foot scow *Garm IV,* built in 1902. The strains on a hull of this type and this size were so extreme that it was more practical to build the yacht of steel than wood. She was given to the Swedish navy in 1909. *Photo courtesy Gunnar Johansson*

GUNNAR MELLGREN

1872–March 3, 1929 · Sweden

Gunnar Mellgren began designing yachts as a hobby, despite being a very busy and well-known person in Swedish industry. He started his career as an engineer at Gothenburg Mekaniska Verksted, and later he became head manager at a big match factory.

He was known for his experimental yacht designs, particularly for fin-and-bulb-keel racing boats. *Ester* was built in 1901 in Stockholm and was one of his most famous designs. She was a bulb-keel yacht with a spade rudder

Anton Miglitsch: *Fähnrich 34.* The Fähnrich 34 is a good example of a cruiser/racer that is truly useful for family cruising. Its generous freeboard, made attractive through a strong sheer and relatively long ends, creates plenty of room below, while a narrow cabin trunk provides good room on deck. *Photo courtesy Volker Christmann*

and very low freeboard. Her waterline length of 10 meters and overall length of 18 meters gave *Ester* such speed that she was unbeatable for many years. Another well-known design was the big racer *Garm IV,* built of steel in 1902, which won Kiel Week in Germany and other big events.

At that time, Sweden was attempting to participate in the America's Cup and Mellgren was asked to design a challenger. However, the project was canceled because of business crises in the country in 1907. Gunnar Mellgren did not design many yachts after the America's Cup challenger. —Bent Aarre

ANTON MIGLITSCH

1910–2003 · Austria/Germany

Anton Miglitsch was among the Austrian-born designers and engineers who made a substantial contribution to the Bremen ship and yacht building industry of the twentieth century. His most productive and successful period fell in the twenty-five years after World War II, when he designed boats under the KR Rating formula.

Miglitsch was born in Maribor (formerly Marburg/Drau). After the collapse of the Donau Monarchie (Danube Monarchy), the Miglitsch family moved to Vienna in 1919. There, after finishing school, the young Miglitsch went on to study mechanical and electrical engineering and mechanical drawing. By chance, he came across a book, *Der Junge Schiffbauer* (*The Young Shipbuilder*). Its drawings of ship and yacht plans so fascinated him that he began to draw and build his own, although he regarded this activity at first only as a pastime to satisfy his own interest. He enjoyed his first regatta victory in 1932 with *Satan*, a 15-Square-Meter centerboarder that he designed and had built at a Vienna boatyard.

The year 1936, when he moved permanently to Germany, was decisive for Miglitsch. He won a competition sponsored by the Holland Yacht Association for the design of a 10-meter offshore cruiser, and the subsequent praise of his design by critics and the yachting press brought him to the attention of the German boating world. In that same year he took a position at the Roland Shipyard in Bremen.

After serving at several other yards (among them Maierform and Kröger Shipyard), in 1945 Miglitsch became a freelance designer at Bremer Yachtwerf, owned by Johann de Dood, for whom he designed more than five hundred different centerboarders and other yachts, some of which are still being built. This large body of work makes him one of the leading and most creative German designers of the mid-twentieth century.

Clark Mills: *Siren.* There is no larger class of boat on earth than the Optimist Pram, with over four hundred thousand built, and many are the sailors who got their start in them. Here, Dutch sailor Lisa Westerhof is shown winning the 1996 Optimist World Championship in South Africa. *Photo courtesy Robert Wilkes*

Like most successful yacht designers, Miglitsch adapted the designs of his cruising yachts to the character of the current racing formula, but he never lost the awareness that families need to feel comfortable in them as well. Accordingly, even his successful racing yachts provided appropriate comfort below decks. A Miglitsch design is identifiable as much by the thorough attention to details of layout and construction below deck as by the harmonious classic lines of its hull, for which reason he worked with Germany's most respected boatyards.

Miglitsch was among those who pioneered the use of fiberglass-reinforced building materials in Germany. His *Neptune 22* has been reproduced a thousandfold and must be regarded as one of the most successful production yachts. One of the reasons for its popularity was the unusual feature of a cabin top one could raise to increase comfort below.

With his book, *On Reading Plans* (*Das Lesen von Rissen*), Anton Miglitsch revealed the "secrets" of yacht design and shared his knowledge and experience with the next generation of yacht designers. —Klaus Auf Dem Garten

CLARK W. MILLS

January 28, 1915–December 11, 2001
United States

Clark Mills is best known for the Optimist Dinghy, which he designed in 1947. The largest sailing class in history, with more than four hundred thousand boats built, the Optimist probably has introduced more people to sailing than any other class.

"I guess I was just always headed for the boatyard," Clark Mills wrote of his youth. "Everything that would float in any gutter, ditch, pond, lake, or bog—I had it sailing, you bet, whether it was a match box or a palm frond! Every school book had boats drawn all over it."

When Mills was young, his family moved from Michigan to Clearwater, Florida, where they lived near the water and where he founded a junior sailing club. Steered toward the manual arts by his father, an interior decorator and carpenter, Mills took drafting courses in school and built rowboats for neighbors.

After he learned how to construct a centerboard trunk, he produced small sailboats as well as powerboats in his shop, the Clark Mills Boat Works, in Clearwater. He was a scrappy pragmatist. When a Snipe dinghy that he built failed to fall under the class rules, he and a friend cruised in it for a month along Florida's Gulf Coast. During World War II he was a boatbuilder in the U.S. Navy.

In 1947, the Clearwater chapter of Optimists International, an association of businessmen, hoped to do something for local children that would also publicize its members. The club first planned to sponsor a soap box derby, a competition for children's homemade, engineless vehicles, but when it was pointed out that there were no hills in Clearwater to race down, the Optimists settled on a fleet of sailboats. Mills was commissioned to draw up the plans for a junior boat that would cost less than fifty dollars and be simple enough to be built by children and their parents using commonplace materials and tools. Local businesses would sponsor boats in exchange for advertising displayed on the hull.

Within a few days Mills came up with a blunt-bowed pram, with an overall length of 7 feet 6 inches and a beam of 3 feet 8 inches. Small enough to be built from two sheets of plywood, it had a cat-spritsail rig of 35 square feet. The initial twenty Optimist Prams were destroyed in a fire, but after a local radio station successfully appealed for funds, Mills built fifty new boats that he sold for $42.50 each without paint, hardware, and sails. They were raced singlehanded in regattas that Mills helped manage, and the Optimist became extremely popular in Florida.

In 1958 the skipper of a visiting Danish square-rigged training ship was so impressed by the little pram that he took one home. Within a decade the Optimist Pram—slightly modified and renamed the Optimist Dinghy—became Europe's most popular boat for junior sailing. The "Opti" (as it was nicknamed) spread worldwide, including back in the United States, and by 1999 it was the standard boat for competition between sailors under sixteen years old. Now built in fiberglass, it is sailed in over a hundred countries. More than 250 sailors from fifty-nine countries participated in the class world championship in 2000. Many if not most U.S. yacht clubs use it in their junior programs.

Mills made no royalties off the boat. He modestly credited the dinghy's success to the club's promotional efforts rather than to his design, although observers regard the Optimist as ingenious in its simplicity.

He continued in the boatbuilding business in Clearwater. In the 1950's he designed the Windmill, a fast, two-person racing dinghy, also originally built of plywood. It has long been popular in the eastern part of the United States. After he retired in 1985 owing to a heart attack, Clark Mills wrote, "It does make me happy to know that I have sincerely tried to show those in my reach what deep pleasure and huge joy even a small sailboat can bring one."
—John Rousmaniere

Peter Milne: *Sure Thing*. More than fifteen thousand Fireballs compete in fleets worldwide. Shown is *Sure Thing*, reaching in a moderate breeze in Kenya. Note the scow-like hull form that gives this boat its planing ability and the hard chines that make it easy to build. *Photo courtesy Kenya Fireball Association*

PETER MILNE

Born 1934 · England

Peter Milne is probably best known as the designer of the Fireball in 1960. Measuring 16 feet 2 inches LOA, it somewhat resembles a scow in hull shape, carries a crew of two, and has a class minimum hull weight of 175 pounds. Over fifteen thousand have been built worldwide, and they are known for high speed and planing ability.

After graduating from Saint John's College in Sussex, England, Milne apprenticed in shipbuilding at Vosper Thornycroft. Early in his career Milne was employed as a designer and model maker at the Norris Brothers yard when he designed the Fireball. The yard was perhaps best known for its work on Donald Campbell's record-setting, jet-propelled Bluebird II. While at Norris Brothers, Milne, working with Campbell, designed the Jetstar, one of the early attempts at a commercial, water jet–propelled boat, using an Italian Castoldi jet unit and an existing marine power plant. Jetstar was built as a 13- and 17-foot boat but was not a commercial success, due in part to the death of Campbell in 1951 while he was attempting to break a record on England's Coniston Water.

As well as the Fireball, Milne also designed the 17-foot 7-inch LOA Javelin in 1968 and the 14-foot 6-inch Marauder (originally called the Mirror 14), both high-performance dinghies.

The hard-chine Mirror 14 was the result of a competition by Mirror Newspapers and was designed to be easy to build, using the stitch-and-glue method.

Also in 1968, Milne created the Skipper 12 and the Skipper 14, intended as "family cruising dinghies." They were both gunter-rigged, with all the spars fitting within the boat for ease of transportation. The 12, at 11 feet LOA, was essentially a scaled-down version of its larger, 13-foot sistership, and at 145 pounds was light enough to be carried atop a car, while the 14 could carry four people. In 1972, he designed the Skipper 17, also called the Skipper Mariner, a 17-foot LOA centerboard sloop that came in three versions: one with four berths with seated headroom saloon, an open daysailer, and the Skipper Mate, with two berths.

Milne's boats are distinguished by their small size, speed, and simplicity to sail. Like the Mirror 14, the hard-chined Fireball was designed to be easy to build at home; the Javelin was unique for its period in carrying full buoyancy, as did the Skipper 12 and 14.

Milne is also well known as a yachting journalist. He worked at *Yachts and Yachting*, at which time he designed the Picolo, a lateen-rigged small dinghy designed to be an improvement on the Sunfish. He went on to become the technical editor at *Yachting World* and the editor of *Classic Boat*. —Gregory O. Jones

POUL MOLICH

Born 1918 · Denmark

One of Denmark's top-three wooden boatbuilders following World War II, Poul Molich also has the reputation of being a very fine yacht designer, which is good ballast to have when building boats. He is very well known outside Denmark, especially in the United States, where customers have included Sparkman and Stephens and John G. Alden, who at one time had Molich build forty one-design yawls.

Molich was born in Aalborg and served his apprenticeship in 1941 as a boatbuilder at Nordbjaerg and Wedells yacht yard in Copenhagen. Upon graduation from Helsingor Technical School, he became a ship's engineer.

For a short period Molich worked as boatbuilder for the famous Henry Rasmussen, who had started a yacht yard close to Svendborg after his many successful years in Germany. From him Molich learned all about top-quality construction. In 1943 he became a partner in a fishing vessel yard in the small village of Hundested, about 70 kilometers northwest of Copenhagen. By around 1950 the fishing business had dwindled, and Molich started building yachts in a growing market.

Molich's first big design and build commission came in 1950 for the 75-foot ketch *Sintra*. During the 1950's he designed and built, among

Poul Molich: *Svanen*. This 19.5-meter yawl designed in 1961 was used as a training vessel by the Danish navy. *Photo courtesy Bent Aarre*

others, a 5.5-meter, two Nordiske Krydsere (Nordic Cruisers), an 8-meter cruiser/racer (C/R Rule), and a 10.5-meter cruiser/racer.

In 1960 and 1961 the yard launched two Molich-designed sisterships, the yawls *Svanen* and *Thyra,* as training ships for the Danish navy. The 19.5-meter yawls were very beautiful and still serve the navy. Also during the 1960's the yard launched five sisterships designed to the RORC Rule called the MOD (Molich One-Design) Class along with Molich's own boat, the yawl *Westland.*

In the 1970's and 1980's Molich produced his one-design classes, the Molich 10-Meter and the Molich 12-Meter LWL. Slim, seaworthy, and fast, these boats are still in production upon request.

—Bent Aarre

GEORGE EDWIN "ED" MONK

January 1, 1894–January 21, 1973
United States

Ed Monk was one of the most prominent and influential naval architects on the West Coast of the United States, opening his Seattle office in 1934. His office records show the number of new designs to be over 3,200 at the time of his death in 1973—an extraordinary amount. He is known for his practical and efficient semiplaning cruising powerboat designs, but he also produced fishing boats, tow boats, trawler yachts, planing powerboats, small craft of many types, and sailboats.

Monk felt a strong desire to encourage the amateur builder, and many of his designs were aimed at that clientele. He also wrote two highly regarded books, *Small Boat Building* (1934) and *Modern Boat Building* (1939), intended to facilitate backyard boatbuilding.

Apparently Monk's favorite design work was in sailing yachts, but perhaps due to his location in the Pacific Northwest, where comfortable, all-weather powerboats have always been popular, most of his work was along that line. He had a particular gift for creating modern, graceful craft that were interesting, harmonious, and functional, but he also worked in traditional types.

Most of Monk's powerboats were of single-screw design—and he favored overall simplicity. He once said, "If you don't put it on, it doesn't cost anything, it doesn't weigh anything, it doesn't take up any space, and it won't break down." While he designed a number of heavy trawler yacht types, he favored light displacement in power yachts for lower initial cost, higher speed, and better fuel economy.

Monk's preferred hull forms were of the "monohedron" type developed by naval archi-

George Monk: *Adventure.* The 62-foot power yacht *Adventure* displays her designer's ability to adapt workboat aesthetics for use in cruising yachts. Designed in 1948 for the Pacific Northwest, she puts the emphasis on "indoor" comfort and looks like she would be both able and economical to operate. *Photo courtesy Ed Monk*

tect Lindsay Lord, in a semiplaning form that produced a comfortable, easily handled, all-around boat with moderate speed and moderate power.

Monk's father, grandfather, and great-grandfather were shipbuilders. As a teenager he apprenticed at the yard of Robert Moran, where his father, George Monk, was working on a 135-foot schooner yacht. In 1915 he again went to work with his father in Saint Helens, Oregon, on *The City of Portland,* one of the largest wooden freighters ever built. Monk then worked under his father at the Meacham and Babcock Shipyard, as superintendent of hull construction. At this time he acquired an interest in design, attending night classes and studying his father's books.

George Monk died in 1919, just after Meacham and Babcock shut down. Ed Monk then went on to work at various shipyards and continued his design studies, finding work at the Blanchard Boat Company in 1925. In 1926 he began working for the famous West Coast designer Ted Geary. At the Geary office he worked on a number of the firm's best-known designs.

In 1934, Monk, his first wife, and two daughters moved aboard their 50-foot power cruiser, *Nan,* where Monk set up a drafting table and began his independent practice. *Nan* was followed by nine more motor cruisers that he designed for his own use, but he moved his offices ashore in 1939. Monk always ran his own

office except for several years of partnership in the 1940's with Lorne Garden, brother of designer William Garden.

Monk created designs for the region's custom boatbuilders, first for the Grandy Boat Yard and notably for the stock manufacturer Tollycraft, a long association that Ed Monk's son, Robert Edwin "Ed" Monk, continued. Upon his father's death in 1973, the younger Ed Monk took over his practice and is now teamed up with his son, Dan, within the firm of Tim Nolan Marine Design.

A great many Monk-designed boats—including *Wahoma, Shearwater, Rita,* and *Nonchalant*—are afloat and giving good service in the Pacific Northwest and throughout the world.

—Daniel B. MacNaughton

ROBERT EDWIN "ED" MONK

Born July 27, 1940 · United States

Ed Monk inherited the design tradition established by his late father, George Edwin "Ed" Monk. Mostly by designing large semi-displacement boats built of fiberglass has he departed from his father's boats, which were made of wood. Monk's designs often are primarily for practical, semiplaning motoryachts. Most of them follow conventional modern powerboat aesthetics and include state-of-the-

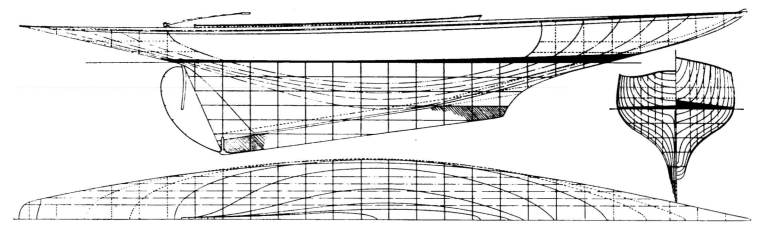

Francis Morgan Giles: *Jonquil.* Designed and built in 1912 for Morgan Giles's own use, the 35-foot LOA *Jonquil* was extremely successful under the 6-Meter rule before the introduction of the Bermudian rig. She was said to be the fastest 6-Meter of 1912, winning forty-four first prizes, eight second prizes, three thirds, and fifty-five prizes out of fifty-seven starts. © *Tony Dixon*

art luxury equipment, though like the elder Monk, he prefers to keep the boats light and simple when possible.

Because Monk is not a fan of the deep-V configuration, most of his work is in the chine-hull semiplaning type known for its good seakeeping ability and its fuel economy when propelled with relatively small horsepower. He feels this is the best combination in the 12- to 14-knot speed range in which most powerboats usually operate.

Monk studied industrial design at the University of Washington, seeking nonmarine work in that line after graduation. He soon found that he preferred to work in yacht design, however, and returned to college for a year to study the necessary engineering, receiving his professional engineer's license in 1970. When his father passed away in 1973, he continued to run the firm of Edwin Monk and Son, turning out modern motoryachts, motorsailers, sailboats, and commercial craft in Seattle. He and his son, Dan, presently work as a team in the naval architecture firm Tim Nolan Marine Design.

—Daniel B. MacNaughton

FRANCIS CHARLES MORGAN GILES

1883–1964 · England

One word sums up this outstanding English yacht designer: *versatile.* Not only did he design beautiful and successful boats, particularly in the 6- and 8-Meter classes, along with a host of popular one-designs, but he also was a first-class builder, seaman, and racing helmsman.

Morgan Giles set up as a boatbuilder in the first decade of the twentieth century at Hammersmith, London, as Morgan Giles and May. Among the products of the yard were several Thorneycroft racing hydroplanes. In about 1912 the firm moved to Hythe, near Southampton,

but the partnership dissolved shortly thereafter. At the outbreak of World War I in 1914, Morgan Giles enlisted in the Royal Naval Volunteer Reserve and served throughout the war in command of coastal motorboats. In 1919, after the end of the war, he purchased a shipyard at Teignmouth in Devon, where he went on to build over a thousand yachts and boats noted for their fine design and construction.

In 1920, Morgan Giles was chairman of the Yacht Racing Association Committee, which wrote the rules for the new National 14-foot dinghy, later to become the International 14. His status as an experienced dinghy designer led to fierce competition with Uffa Fox in the design of dinghies for this class throughout the 1920's, culminating in his winning the Prince of Wales' Cup in 1931. This was, however, his swan song in the class, as Fox became dominant thereafter throughout the 1930's.

Morgan Giles concentrated on the 6- and 8-Meter classes during the interwar period, as designer, builder, and helmsman. In his own 8-Meter *Jonquil*, he won forty-four first prizes in one season. After 1945, he returned to yacht designing and building, concentrating on motor launches, and remained active in the business until his death. It is said of him that it would be hard to decide whether he excelled most as a designer, a builder, or a sailor.

—Brian Smith

GINO MORRELLI

Born March 19, 1957 · United States

A versatile multihull designer from the American West Coast, Gino Morrelli designed what in 2001 became the world's fastest offshore catamaran. He was born in Texas, but his family moved to California when he was twelve years old. He quickly began sailing a Hobie 14

catamaran and, in 1975, built with his father a Lock Crowther–designed Buccaneer 33. This was followed by a series of garage-built, 18-Square-Meter Climax catamarans (18 feet, 1977–81) and the 45-foot, open-bridgedeck racing catamaran *White Knuckler* in 1982.

Morrelli moved to France in 1983, where, still self-taught, he designed and built the successful 60-foot racing catamaran *Region de Picardie.* *The Smyth Team,* a 40-foot racing catamaran, was built in 1985 to his design and went on to become the 1986 Formula 40 world champion. Its success led to the designing and building of several more F 40 catamarans, including *Richmond* (1986) and *Region Nord Pas de Calais* (1986), as well as several 40-foot catamarans for the American ProSail circuit.

Back in the United States, Morrelli became a member of the design team for Dennis Conner's 1988 60-foot America's Cup defending catamaran *Stars & Stripes.* In 1990 he codesigned with Pete Melvin a 25-foot, fixed-wing-sail, Class C catamaran, which became an unsuccessful challenger for the Little America's Cup.

Gino Morrelli: *Alinghi.* Designed for racing on Lake Geneva in Switzerland, the 41-foot daysailing trimaran *Alinghi* was probably the world's fastest trimaran of her size when she was built in 1995. *Photo courtesy Decision Boatbuilders*

Happycalopse (41 feet, 1990) and *Alinghi IV* (41 feet, 1995, codesigned with Pete Melvin) followed. Intended for racing on Lake Geneva in Switzerland, these two trimarans were the world's fastest for their size.

In 1998 Morrelli, who had formed a partnership with Pete Melvin, was given the commission to design a catamaran for The Race, the world's first nonstop multihull regatta around the world. When she was launched in 1999, the 105-foot catamaran *PlayStation* was the world's largest racing catamaran. After a substantial rebuild, which lengthened her to 125 feet, and a lot of teething problems (she had to abandon her circumnavigation), this catamaran finally found her stride in 2001, when, with her designer on board, she crossed the Atlantic in world record time (4 days, 17 hours, 28 minutes, 6 seconds) at an average speed of 25.8 knots. At the same time she set a world record for the fastest twenty-four-hour run when she covered 687.2 nautical miles at an average speed of 28.6 knots. In addition to sailing multihulls, Morrelli and Melvin have designed numerous large power catamarans. Their office is in Newport Beach, California.

—Claas van der Linde

WILBUR MORSE

see George Melville "Mel" McLain

CHARLES DROWN MOWER

October 5, 1875–January 18, 1942
United States

One of America's great designer/editors, C. D. Mower practiced from around 1895 until illness ended his career in late 1939. He designed boats of all types, with special attention to small yachts accessible to average people. In addition, Mower was design editor of *The Rudder* magazine for several years beginning at the close of the nineteenth century, and was a regular contributor to *Motor Boating* magazine beginning in 1926. While he designed many successful racing boats under various handicapping systems, he is today honored primarily for the aesthetic quality of his designs and for his writing and publishing work, which presented many wholesome, home-buildable boats to a broad and receptive audience.

Mower is widely regarded as a superior designer with a highly evolved sense of aesthetics. He had a particular talent for the shapes of bows and sterns, which in general show a bit more "lift" in their profiles than those of other designers. Mower usually retained good curvature in his sheerlines right to their forward

Charles Mower: *Joyette*. *Joyette* was one of Mower's successful Sonder-class yachts. She beat a German crew in the 1909 Kaiser's Cup races, sailed in Marblehead, Massachusetts. *Photo courtesy Hart Nautical Collections, MIT Museum, Cambridge, MA*

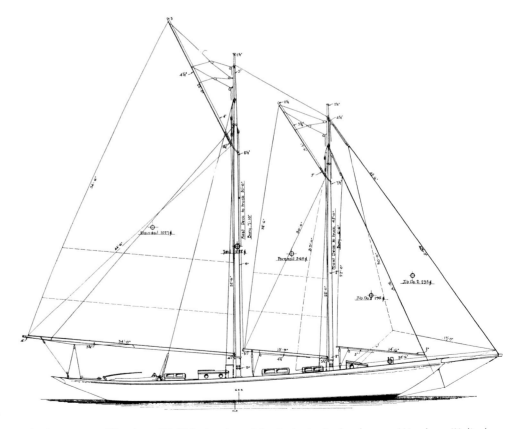

Charles Mower: *Wanderer IX*. This drawing of the 63-foot 5-inch schooner *Wanderer IX* displays Mower's superb draftsmanship as well as his gift for proportions. While the yacht has quite long ends, she also has a strong sheer, conveying a sense of both strength and agility. Note that this big vessel steers with a tiller. *Reproduced from* The Rudder

Charles Mower: *Chantey*. The 42-foot 6-inch ketch *Chantey*, built in 1928, carries a rig that has been altered from that originally drawn, but she shows the kind of confidence-inspiring traditional proportions and details the designer typically utilized in his cruising boats. © *Peter Barlow*

Charles Mower: *Alert IV*. *Alert IV* was designed by Mower and built in 1928 by Henry B. Nevins. The 40-foot 3-inch R-Class yacht seems to capture all that was good in the Universal Rule, a trait the designer is said to have brought to all his work under the various rules of his day. *Photo courtesy Newport Harbor Nautical Museum, Newport Beach, CA*

and aft ends, avoiding the common mistake of letting the line go straight "at the last minute." In general, his sheers tended to be relatively strong, especially in his long-ended designs, to their great benefit.

Born in Lynn, Massachusetts, near the coastal town of Swampscott, Mower did his early sailing in Swampscott dories and other local craft. The Swampscott type was a personal favorite of his, and he drew plans for many such dories over the years. The first boat he built was a 16-footer designed by W. P. Stephens and published in Stephen's 1885 book, *Canoe and Boat Building for Amateurs*.

At age nineteen Mower built a 21-foot centerboard sloop named *Vitesse* in his backyard. Her racing success in and around Massachusetts Bay was one of the factors that got him a job with designer Arthur Binney of Boston; he worked for Binney from 1895 to 1898. In 1898 he took a job with designer B. B. Crowninshield. In the same year Mower received his first independent design commission, for the X-Dory, a 21-foot racing dory for the Swampscott Yacht Club. Like many other Mower-designed ex-

amples of the Swampscott type, the X-Dory remained popular for decades.

Mower moved to New York in 1899 to join the staff at *The Rudder* magazine, ultimately becoming design editor. In his years in that position, Mower continued *The Rudder*'s tradition of how-to-build articles, with an emphasis on small craft. He designed and built several more sailboats and an early houseboat. In 1904 he designed and built his first motorboat, a speed launch that reached about 12 mph, a triumph at the time. He practiced yacht design independently in New York from 1905 until 1910, when he left *The Rudder* and moved to Philadelphia. In 1911 he entered into partnership with designer Thomas D. Bowes, an arrangement that lasted until World War I. During the war Mower served with the Construction Corps of the Naval Reserve as a lieutenant commander, inspecting wooden vessels constructed for the navy.

One-designs drawn by Mower include racing catboats such as the 17-foot Atlantic City Catboat class, plus the popular 28-foot 9-inch Sound Interclub and her derivatives, the Vineyard Interclubs and Great South Bay Inter-

clubs. Among his centerboard boats were a number of 15-foot LWL classes that were popular between 1905 and 1930 in shoal-water parts of North America. Mower also designed several motorsailers and frostbite dinghies.

Among Mower's cruising boats was the 36-foot *Duckling*, launched in 1925, which was awarded the Blue Water Medal of the CCA for a voyage to Iceland. Also well known is the cruising cutter *Crusoe*, launched in 1934 and still sailing out of Port Townsend, Washington. The V-bottom 27-foot yawl *Sea Bird*, codesigned by Mower and Thomas Fleming Day, editor of *The Rudder*, was intended to popularize small vessels for offshore voyaging. Day and two companions sailed her to Europe in 1911. Mower also drew the widely circulated lines of Joshua Slocum's *Spray*, but alas, these were based not on his own observation but on the reports of a boatyard operator. Mower always laughed when anyone spoke of the definitive shape of the *Spray*.

Probably due to Day's influence, *Sea Bird* appears to be the first design Mower drew with a hard chine. She was followed by the similar but larger 34-foot Seagoer and 38-foot Naiad designs. It was in a modified Seagoer named *Islander*, built in 1917, that Harry Pidgeon made his well-publicized singlehanded world circumnavigation. Mower also designed power yachts large and small, including a motor launch whose plans were printed in *The Rudder* magazine in 1901—believed to be the subject of the first "how-to-build" motorboat plan published in the United States. Mower was a crew member on *Ailsa Craig*, winner of the first Bermuda Race for powerboats, held in 1907.

In 1903 Mower was the official measurer for the New York Yacht Club. He measured the America's Cup J-Class boat contenders *Shamrock III* (designed by William Fife III) and *Reliance* (by Nathanael Herreshoff), an experience that included a trip to the top of *Reliance*'s mast, which at 157 feet was then the tallest in the world.

Among Mower's best-known designs were several successful Universal Rule yachts, including the famous R-Class boats *Ardette* (1925) and *Ardelle* (1926), several Q-Class boats, and the big M-Class yacht *Windward* (1929). He designed a number of 6-Meters and 8-Meters under the International Rule, along with the winning Q-Class yacht *Joy* and the Sonder class yacht *Joyette*, which won the Kaiser's Cup in the 1909 series at Marblehead, Massachusetts, against a German crew. Additionally, he produced a number of cruiser/racers such as the centerboard schooner *Windjammer*, launched in 1924, which became well known through competition in ocean races to Bermuda, Havana, and Nassau.

It was W. P. Stephens who said, "Some designers look on a [handicap rating] rule as a challenge, something to be beaten or circumvented. Charley Mower read the rule, interpreted its spirit as well as its wording, and then designed the finest yacht he could embodying that spirit—the kind of yacht the rule was meant to produce."

Mower's work was well represented in *Motor Boating*'s Ideal Series, which started in the 1920's. The concept of the Ideal Series was to provide amateur boatbuilders with a collection of handbooks on the design, construction, and handling of all types of boats. Looking back at the series today shows how well Mower executed the magazine's criteria by the clarity of his instructions and the crispness of his design. In the 1924 volume, *Frances, an 18' Cat Boat* was introduced. The design became the Massachusetts Bay Hustler Class, which by 1954 numbered 88 boats racing, with 177 boats built in all.

Mower designs were also highly regarded by Great Lakes and West Coast boatmen. More than a few of his boats were brought west and achieved success, along with a number that were built in West Coast yards. His 65-foot staysail schooner *Flying Cloud* (ex-*Quicksilver II*, 1940), and the 44-foot cutter *Java Head* (ex-*Jubilee*, 1933), both Maine built, became celebrated Transpac Race standouts, while his R-Class boat *Ace* (1926), built on the West Coast, dominated the class for a number of years. Both *Java Head* and *Ace* still sail and race in classic events.

After World War I, Mower moved back to New York and continued to work as an independent designer, although for a few years in the mid-1920's he was a partner in the firm of Mower and Humphries. Mower and designer John G. Alden were influential in the revival of the Bermuda Race in 1923. Beginning in 1928, he served for a period as chief naval architect at the Henry B. Nevins yard in New York, but he maintained his private practice until he retired.

Mower died in Lynn, Massachusetts, at the age of sixty-six. As William Taylor noted in his tribute to Mower in the May 1942 issue of *Yachting*, "When Charles Mower died the sport of yachting lost one of the men who had given most to it, and hundreds of yachtsmen lost a well-loved friend. An outstanding member of his profession, it was often said that he never designed a slow boat or an ugly one. His boats had a beauty and wholesomeness that made them stand out in a fleet. For years to come yachtsmen who knew his work will recognize some of those yachts, still sailing, as lasting monuments to a great designer's art."

Some of Mower's plans from before about 1920 were donated to Mystic Seaport Museum in the 1950's; most of the later plans were destroyed in a flood.

—Daniel B. MacNaughton

COLIN CRIGHTON MUDIE

Born 1926 · Scotland/England

Few designers have a body of work displaying as much contrast as Colin Mudie's. His designs range from traditionally constructed historic replicas to sophisticated modern power and sailing yachts. He has a particularly recognizable style in his powerboat work, combining strong, tradition-based curves in both hull and superstructure with unmistakably modern arrangements, materials, and details in an appealing mix.

Born in Edinburgh, Mudie was educated in Scotland and England and moved to Hampshire in 1942 to become a design apprentice at the British Power Boat Company at Hythe. Later he spent some years working for Laurent Giles and Partners in Lymington, before moving to London to set up Colin Mudie Naval Architects and Yacht Designers with his wife, Rosemary, in 1958.

Mudie designed the Wing Class, Britain's first production fiberglass boat, and later continued in this series of innovations with his design of the 40-foot catamaran *Rehu Moana*, which in 1968 became the first multihull to circumnavigate the globe. He designed and raced numerous motorboats, including *Avila*, a 62-foot sportfishing boat built in 1964 for King Baudouin of Belgium. He has produced designs for both the Shetland and Hardy series of motorboats. In 1968 he moved to Lymington.

Currently Mudie is best known for his designs of sail-training vessels and a number of replicas. The 76-foot sail-training brig *Royalist* of 1971, the *Brendan*, a 36-foot wood- and leather-hulled curragh of 1975, and the 141-foot barque *Lord Nelson*, built for the Jubilee Sailing Trust in 1986, were followed by the *Matthew*. In 1997, this authentic reproduction of the 68-foot caravel re-enacted John Cabot's voyage of 1497 from Bristol, England, to Newfoundland.

Mudie has been awarded many titles honoring his work in the field of marine architecture, including RDI (Royal Designer for Industry), FRSA (Fellow of the Royal Society of Arts), and FRIN (Fellow of the Royal Institute of Navigation).

Among the many books Mudie has written and illustrated for the yachting press, most cowritten with Rosemary, are *The Story of the Sailing Ship*, *Motor Boats and Boating*, and *The Sailing Ship*.

Colin Mudie: *Sina.* This capable-looking voyaging yacht is the 53-foot yawl *Sina*, one of Mudie's few sailing yacht commissions. © *Tom Zydler*

Colin Mudie's engaging and practical approach to his work has served to promote boating in all its forms to people worldwide. Always trying to remove the mystique from his subject, he brings a deliberate modesty to a field of endeavor that is always in danger of complication through "elegant" solutions.

—Pol Bergius

FRANK MULDER

Born July 5, 1950 · The Netherlands

Frank Mulder's star rose high in the firmament in 1988, when he successfully answered the challenge of a very "driven" American automobile mogul to design the first megayacht to surpass 50 knots. That breakthrough yacht—which was also a handsome, commodious family cruiser at less spectacular speeds—was the 43.46-meter *Octopussy*, a project into which Mulder poured art, science, and not a little naval architecture magic, including careful weight calculations and painstaking tank-testing at the Netherlands Ship Model Basin (MARIN) in Wageningen. *Octopussy* surpassed expectations and attained 53.17 knots in her speed trials, becoming the darling of the yachting press.

But, as is not unusual in this age, Frank Mulder's star didn't rise overnight; it blossomed after years of hard, quiet effort at designing motoryachts of less menacing speed but no less beauty.

Born in Amsterdam, Mulder studied general engineering from 1966 to 1969 at the Hendrik de Keizer School, then entered Haarlem Technical University to specialize in ship design, receiving his naval architect's degree in 1974. Until 1976 Mulder worked at the highly regarded Dutch shipyard Amels, and then for three years

Frank Mulder: *Seashaw.* Although Mulder gained global recognition primarily for the stunning speed and remarkable seakindliness of such yachts as *Octopussy* and *Moonraker*, he fortunately also turned his ingenious naval architecture and technical insight to the design of stately, modern world cruisers such as the nicely balanced 44-meter cruiser *Seashaw*. *Photo courtesy Mulder Yachts*

at the commercial shipyard Damen (which subsequently purchased Amels).

In 1979 Mulder's powerful urge for independence led him to found his own company, Mulder Design, in Gorinchem, 40 kilometers upriver on the Waal (Rhine) from Rotterdam. Using his experience in the shipyards, for the first few years Mulder specialized in designing high-speed commercial vessels.

In 1984 Mulder was commissioned by an American-based entrepreneur to design a private ocean-cruising yacht, the 119-foot *Tropic C*, which began a new and extended phase in Mulder Design's development. The success of *Tropic C*, built in Heesen, Holland, resulted in the formation by the client of a U.S.-based marketing firm, Diaship (Dutch International Association of Shipbuilders). Between 1987 and 1995, Diaship, which built yachts at Heesen, created Mulder's designs for *Extasea* A (37 meters), *Wheels* (32 meters), *Octopussy*, *El Corsario* (40 meters), and *Ladyship* (41 meters). Two fiberglass yachts, *Bonita* and *Teeth* (twin 35-meter, 55-knot yachts for the Royal Household of Johor and Brunei), were started at Norship, but when that yard went bankrupt, the yachts were finished at Heesen.

Octopussy's owner, John Staluppi, then had Mulder draw plans for the 23-meter, 50-knot *Dillinger*. Built at the Derecktor Shipyard in Rhode Island, *Dillinger* won the 1990 Superyacht Society Design Award. For the same client Mulder then designed the 35-meter *Moonraker*, built by Norship in Norway. In 1992 she replaced *Octopussy* as the world's fastest motoryacht when she hit 66.7 knots in her speed trials. *Moonraker* won the 1992 *ShowBoats International* Award for Most Innovative Motoryacht.

Lest one think, however, that Frank Mulder performs only miracles of super-high speed, the record proves satisfyingly otherwise. In the late 1980's Mulder began designing semicustom cruising yachts for two of Holland's most highly regarded builders. For Neptunus, in Aalst, over the next decade Mulder created cruising motoryacht models ranging from 43 to 75 feet long. And over the same period for Moonen, in Den Bosch, Mulder designed semi-custom yachts ranging from 63 to 105 feet LOA. He also designed several motoryacht models up to 125 feet long for Cheoy Lee Shipyards in Hong Kong.

In the late 1990's Mulder's designs included the 43-meter *Lambda Mar*, 32-meter *Blue Velvet*, 44-meter *Seashaw*, and 47-meter *Blowzy*, as well as the Millennium series of motoryachts between 75 and 151 feet long, built at yards in Holland and the United Arab Emirates.

Despite the skilled output of his firm, however, Mulder takes great pride in his small, tal-

ented staff of naval architects and engineers, who together deliver a complete construction-ready package to the builder. And Mulder is among that wise coterie of naval architects totally committed to computer techniques, in particular three-dimensional modeling, which not only helps designers visualize their work but also becomes a valuable tool in demonstrating to clients in an unambiguous, nonverbal fashion what spaces aboard their yacht will be like.

—Jack A. Somer

GARY W. MULL

September 27, 1937–July 14, 1993
United States

Gary Mull was the designer of many popular fiberglass racing and cruising boats produced by such companies as Santana, Schock, Ranger, Newport, and Freedom. He also designed some famous ocean racers, including *Dora*, *Improbable*, *La Forza del Destino*, and *Sorcery*, as well as a host of successful 6-Meters. For the America's Cup Louis Vuitton Challenge in 1987, Mull designed the 12-Meter *U.S.A.* for his lifelong friend, skipper Tom Blackaller.

Mull grew up in San Bruno, California, close to San Francisco Bay. At age twelve he started racing in El Toro prams, and in high school became a member of the Coyote Point Sea Scouts. He raced and cruised extensively as a young man, winning a Northern California Finn championship among others.

Mull graduated from the University of California of Berkeley in 1964. He began his college career with the idea that he would become a poet, but he always considered engineering as an alternative. When (according to Mull) his use of the abbreviation "Eng" for "English" on the form selecting his major led to his being placed in the engineering program instead of the English department, he decided to follow through.

After graduation Mull served briefly in the Coast Guard, and then joined the design firm of Pillsbury and Martignoni, followed by a stint with Sparkman and Stephens. Later he did engineering work for Lockheed and the Pacific Engineering Company, and began designing yachts in his spare time. He opened his own design office in 1969 in Oakland, California.

Mull's very-light-displacement, no-holds-barred racing boats were the foundation of his career, and in his 1971 *Improbable* he introduced the type of ultralight downwind flier that is now popular on the West Coast. He served for many years on technical committees of the IOR handicapping rule, and was a fiercely competitive racing sailor.

Gary Mull: *Aries.* A promoter and developer of the light-displacement type of racing and cruising yacht, Mull also advocated well-engineered construction and helped to create good aesthetic concepts for modern yachts. Here *Aries* is traveling fast with a relaxed-looking crew. © *Peter Barlow*

After a long string of successes, a couple of designs failed to compete successfully on the race course, causing his popularity as a designer to decrease for several years—typical of the fickle nature of the racing boat design profession. However, he continued to work and produced some notable successes later on, such as the maxi yacht *Sorcery*.

A frequent consultant on engineering matters, Mull was of the opinion that far too many boats were built with no more than an educated guess as to their structure, and he was an advocate of careful and detailed engineering specifications. For example, his design for *Sorcery* included thirty-five sheets of drawings and sixty pages of engineering specifications.

Designers Jim Antrim, Chuck Burns, Jim Donovan, Peter Dunsford, Ron Holland, Eva Hollmann, Phil Kaiko, Paul Kotzebu, Carl Schumacher, and Doug Sharp all apprenticed in Gary Mull's office.

Mull helped to create the American Bureau of Shipping's scantlings guide for offshore yachts. He also was actively involved in the 6-Meter class and the IYRU.

—Daniel B. MacNaughton

JOHN MUNFORD

Born July 2, 1947 · England

Originally trained as an antiques restorer and cabinet and furniture designer, John Munford is one of a new breed of designers, working independently and specializing in the design of yacht interiors. Seeming to own the franchise on Edwardian styling in modern megayachts, he might be described as a modest romantic with an unabashed love of mahogany. He says that he views the interior of a yacht like a piece of furniture that is inside out. "You live inside it and use it, but it has a function of its own, creating a controlled environment to suit each particular owner."

Although Munford was raised in the seaside resort city of Bournemouth, yachting was not a part of the family's lifestyle. Academics were not his strong suit, but he quickly developed skills as a woodworker and eventually enrolled at the London College of Furniture. He holds diplomas in fine cabinet making and in advanced furniture design and construction.

Munford soon decided that designing furniture without context was too insular. He took a job designing interior modules for a small production boat manufacturer. Soon he accepted an invitation to visit the Camper and Nicholson shipyard in Gosport, England, where the 212-foot *Shemara*, built in 1938, was in for a refit. Viewing her vast, finely appointed saloon, he felt that a door had opened on another world, and he came away thinking, "That's what I want to do."

In 1970 Munford was hired by Camper and Nicholson as a studio assistant. In one short period he worked on designs for T. O. M. Sopwith's *Philante IV*, with an interior by Eddie Meyers; the Chuck Goodwin–designed *Hedonist* with its round rotating bed; and Jon Bannenberg's *Tiajuana*.

When Camper and Nicholson shifted its focus to small production sailboats, Munford bounced around several architectural firms while freelancing for the shipyard on such projects as the interior of the Nicholson 55.

In 1979 Munford hung out his own shingle. Soon afterward, John Barden, captain of the 174-foot, three-masted schooner *Jessica*, asked Munford to draw deckhouses for the yacht. *Jessica*'s owner then hired him to design the yacht's entire interior. In 1983–84 Munford designed interior refits for *Jessica*, now *Adix*, and for the 156-foot Abeking and Rasmussen–built schooner *Aquarius*, then the two largest sailing yachts in the world.

Munford's favorite project began when he designed the interior refit of the J-Class yacht *Endeavour*. The results have become legendary and led to later commissions to refit the interiors of the other remaining J-Class boats, *Shamrock V* and *Velsheda*. *Endeavour* also led to commissions for a series of Sparkman and Stephens–designed megasailboats, beginning with the 125-foot *Galileo* in 1988.

Munford began designing interiors for motoryachts in the 1990's. His first was at the very apex of the yachting world, a 162-footer named *Aurora* built at Feadship's de Vries yard. Her success lead to commissions for eight more Feadships to date.

Characteristic of Munford's approach is his use of long lines of sight, such that one catches glimpses of other compartments, creating a sense of distance. He often insists on large windows to remind occupants that they are on yachts rather than in apartments. He creates lamps and hardware to match, designs carpets, and selects all the marble and granite for each particular scheme.

Among Munford's favorite commissions is his most challenging, the 147-foot record-breaking ketch *Mari Cha III* designed by Philippe Briand and launched in New Zealand by Sensation Yachts in 1997. With *Mari Cha III*, Munford had to design an Edwardian interior that could be executed in cherry veneers laminated to space-age Nomex coring. His directive was to keep the interior weight to 6.5 tons, roughly one-third of that for a conventional yacht of this length. Furthermore, most of the yacht's interior had to be removable for racing and for such spectacular feats as her successful assault on the transatlantic monohull record in 1998.

To date Munford has received nineteen design awards from the Superyacht Society and *ShowBoats International* magazine. Munford's office is in Southampton.　　—Marilyn Mower

GORDON MUNRO

ca. 1889–October 27, 1967
Scotland/United States

Often called the father of the motorsailer, Gordon Munro did much to develop and popularize the type, starting in 1921. He also drew plans for beautiful sailing yachts and successful development class racers, and innovated plywood and composite construction techniques.

Born in Aberdeen, Scotland, Munro moved with his parents to Massachusetts in the United States when he was five. He attended schools in Weymouth, but dropped out of high school in his freshman year, going to work in a shoe store. He bought his first boat shortly thereafter and became a maker of wooden patterns. In 1910 he went to work at George Lawley and Son in Neponset, where he stayed for six years until he became a draftsman at the Portsmouth Shipyard in New Hampshire. Around 1920 he went into business on his own as a yacht designer.

Between 1912 and 1919 Munro helped to introduce the Sonder development class in his local sailing area on the South Shore of Cape Cod.

Munro (who mysteriously sometimes used an "e" on the end of his name and sometimes didn't) designed his first motorsailer in 1921. By 1929 he felt he had brought the type to a high degree of efficiency. He defined a motorsailer as a yacht that was powerful under both sail and power, capable of sailing or motoring to windward in heavy weather and performing as well as any auxiliary under sail in moderate conditions. His designs did not stress performance in very light air. He probably assumed that most owners would motor under light conditions and took advantage of this to keep the size of his rigs moderate and to avoid the need for reefing except in quite heavy winds. Unfortunately Munro's firm was one of the first casualties of the Great Depression and failed in 1929.

Munro had a good eye. He was able to create charming and harmonious designs for the new motorsailer type despite the lack of aesthetic precedents. He often employed a raised deck forward, to allow for dry, roomy decks and space below, smoothly switching to a side-decks-and-cabin-trunk configuration farther aft, to utilize larger windows in the main cabin for light and visibility.

The designer was involved in tank-testing, starting in the 1930's, and used data from towing models to develop several 6-Meter designs. He also designed at least one of the best American 30-Square-Meters, *Tipler III*, and experimented with hydrofoils.

During the 1930's Munro went back to Lawley's and headed up a new division dedicated to series production of plywood boats, probably the first successful attempt to do so. Production included the famous 110 One-Design, designed by C. Raymond Hunt. Munro helped to run the Lawley yard during World War II and returned to his design practice after the end of the war.

Among Munro's innovations was a patented construction method he called the Duoform hull, featuring wooden planking and a welded-steel backbone and keel. In his correspondence he refers to a newer method combining steel and plastic, but sources provide no further information about this interesting line of thought.

Munro's plans and papers are at the Hart Nautical Collections at the MIT Museum, Cambridge, MA.
　　—Daniel B. MacNaughton

Gordon Munro: *Betty.* One of the earliest motorsailers, *Betty* seems like a clean and practical concept. In this photo she is probably on builder's trials following her launch in about 1922, and does not yet carry her gaff main and mizzen or her club jib. *Photo courtesy Hart Nautical Collections, MIT Museum, Cambridge, MA*

Ralph Munroe: *Presto*. *Presto* was the first of the so-called round-bilged sharpies for which Munroe became famous. Besides her practical success in the shoal waters of Florida, she was also an exceptionally good-looking boat, as seen in this rare, faint photograph. *Photo reproduced from unknown source*

RALPH MIDDLETON "COMMODORE" MUNROE

1851–1933 · United States

One of the first yachtsmen to live and cruise in southern Florida, Ralph Munroe developed *Presto*, a narrow, light, and seaworthy type of shoal-draft cruising boat, to suit the local conditions. His designs in this genre helped to advance the evolution of light-displacement yachts and are closely reinterpreted today whenever their particular combination of virtues is required.

While he began his life and work in New York, it was Munroe's involvement in the then near-wilderness of southern Florida that set the stage for his most important design work. He first sailed to Florida in 1877, camped there in 1881, and moved there in 1882.

In those days Florida was a paradise according to Munroe's taste, with its wonderful climate, fascinating shoreline, and the utter absence of "civilized" development. He lived near the Seminole Indians in a very small community of white people at Coconut Grove on Biscayne Bay, and with his neighbors helped to develop local trade, waterborne transportation, a post office, and eventually a local yacht club. From the first, he perceived a need in the roadless shoreside community for a versatile shoal-draft sailboat that could carry mail and cargo and also serve for recreational use.

Munroe recognized that while most advocates of shoal draft made their boats beamy so as to obtain the stability that would otherwise be provided by ballast on or in a deep keel, the result was speed, not seaworthiness. The beamy skimming dishes of his day were fast, but they had a limited range of stability and if pushed too far were difficult to control and prone to capsize.

From his exposure to the New Haven sharpie type, and by some accounts also the ideas of designer Thomas Clapham, Munroe knew that these narrow shoal-draft types showed a combination of speed and ability that was more favorable to cruising and utilitarian purposes than the skimming dishes. Because the South Florida coastline was more exposed than the sharpie's native waters, and because he wanted to make trips north and south along the coast before the days of the Intracoastal Waterway, Munroe made changes to the sharpie type to improve her rough-water ability and, in particular, her range of stability.

In developing the 41-foot 6-inch ketch *Presto*, launched in 1885, Munroe retained the light and narrow overall form of the sharpie. However, he substituted a round bilge and fine ends to ease motion and avoid pounding; flaring topsides to give a relatively wide range of stability; and deadrise to allow lower placement of the ballast, again for increased stability. The hull allowed better aesthetic options than the older form, and *Presto* was certainly a good-looking boat.

Munroe went on to design numerous variations on the *Presto* theme, including larger and smaller versions, some intended more for offshore cruising and some for inshore gunkholing. Another more economical variation is represented by the well-known *Egret*, a flat-bottomed double-ender with plenty of flare. *Presto* and her relatives became local standards over several decades, and they are frequently reinterpreted today whenever a combination of shoal draft and seaworthiness are sought in an inshore cruising boat. Munroe also designed a number of power craft adapted to local conditions.

As the trappings of the civilization he had left behind began to intrude more and more into the coastal wilderness that he loved, Munroe became an ardent environmentalist. He fought the coming of the railroad, opposed the taming of the shoreline with seawalls and jetties and the draining of the Everglades, and condemned overdevelopment, overfishing, and pollution of the bays. While contemporary accounts don't treat the subject as we would today, it appears that he also defended the rights of the native Seminoles and respected their way of life.

Munroe is said to have been very strong in the defense of his ideals, both nautical and social, but he was held in the greatest affection by almost everyone—indeed one biographer refers to "his genius for friendship." He is called "Commodore" Munroe because of his twenty-three years as founder and commodore of the Biscayne Bay Yacht Club, which began life as a group of similarly minded pioneer

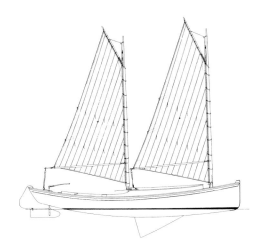

Ralph Munroe: *Egret*. This drawing of Munroe's famous *Egret* was created by Joel White and Dave Dillion based on research by *WoodenBoat* magazine. As with *Presto*, her designer adapted earlier northern sharpies for use in more challenging Florida waters, but in *Egret* he retained the flat bottom and other traditional features. *Drawing courtesy WoodenBoat Publications*

yachtsmen in love with their unique local cruising ground. Late in his life he became a close personal friend of designer Nathanael Herreshoff, who rented a cottage on Munroe's property for several winters. The two designers enjoyed sailing together, building sailing models, and exchanging ideas. L. Francis Herreshoff once said that Ralph Munroe was the only person ever to influence his strong-minded father's design work.

Most of Munroe's drawings and papers were destroyed in a 1926 hurricane, but what was left was passed on to his son, designer Wirth Monroe, and remain with the family. His bungalow, The Barnacle, and his *Presto*-type ketch, *Micco*, are preserved in Coconut Grove.

—Daniel B. MacNaughton

IAIN MURRAY, AM

Born March 14, 1958 · Australia

One of his country's most prominent yachtsmen and designers, Iain Murray epitomizes an Australian approach to sailing. Starting out as a junior racer in Flying Ants, he worked his way up through several local classes—the Cherub, the 12- and the 16-foot Skiff classes—and into the famous Australian 18-foot Skiffs. He won state, national, Interdominion (New Zealand versus Australia), and world titles, often in innovative boats of his own design. Part of his legend is the time he cut up his first 18-foot plywood skiff hull with an electric saw before a championship. The resulting major reduction in beam was a success: he won.

In 1977 he traveled to America to learn the latest composite construction methods from the Californian aircraft industry. In his Australian 18-foot Skiff *Color 7*, a boat built of Nomex core, Kevlar, and epoxy resins (the first of its kind), he won the 1977–78 world championship, as well as the national and state titles of that season. Composite construction quickly became the norm in the class. Along with other skiff sailors, Murray was part of what was arguably the greatest period of development in the class's history.

After his retirement from racing the Australian 18's at age twenty-four, Murray was enlisted to sail aboard the Alan Payne–designed, 12-Meter *Advance*. Though that campaign was a failure, Murray became engrossed in the America's Cup, and after *Australia II* won the event, he oversaw a campaign to defend the Cup with the Kookaburra Syndicate. He designed the Kookaburra 12-Meters together with John Swarbrick. Although they won the right to defend, they were beaten by *Stars & Stripes* in the 1987 Cup series.

In 1992 he led an underfunded campaign to San Diego with the tandem-keel *Spirit of Australia*, which he helped design and manage. The boat was eliminated early on. He played a role once again as a designer in John Bertrand's ill-fated return to the America's Cup scene in 1995, where the main boat sank after splitting in two, owing to structural damage.

Working in partnership with U.S.-born and–trained naval architect Andy Dovell, and computer expert Ian Burns, Murray has had a great success with IMS offshore racing designs, almost all built by Bashford International in Australia. In the partnership of Murray, Burns and Dovell, established in 1989, Dovell now has a principal role in the design team. The office's output ranges from 23- to 110-foot boats and includes a number of production yachts. It has had particular success with a series of production ocean racers for Sydney Yachts. Iain Murray was made a Member of the Order of Australia in 1992 for services to yachting and the community.

—Robert Keeley

Iain Murray: Sydney 40. The Sydney-class ocean racers designed by Murray, Burns and Dovell began with many local Australian successes, but soon made a big impact internationally, led by the Sydney 40, which was exported from Australia and became a well-established class worldwide. *Photo courtesy Bob Ross*

HUGO MYERS

1925–1988 · United States

An engineer and mathematician by profession, Hugo Myers was one of the first to promulgate the use of mathematical formulas to produce hull shapes. Working in California, he pioneered in the design of catamarans. Important catamaran designs include the 43-foot *Dreamer*, in 1956; the 33-foot *Symmetry*, sometime before 1961; the 36-foot *Windsong*, before 1964; the 46-foot *Eunike*, before 1965; and the 44-foot *Sea Bird*, in 1967.   —Claas van der Linde

ALFRED MYLNE THE FIRST

November 20, 1872–1951 · Scotland

Mylne and Company is probably the oldest firm still extant that engages strictly in yacht design. Alfred Mylne the First put up his shingle in 1896. In the ensuing hundred years there have been only three principals. Alfred Mylne was succeeded by his nephew, Alfred Mylne the Second who in 1979 was succeeded by his partner Ian Nicolson, who continues to head the firm.

Alfred Mylne was born in Glasgow to a fairly typical Victorian middle-class family. His father was a blacksmith who prospered and then became an iron-founder. Mylne was educated first at the prestigious Glasgow High School and later at the equally renowned Glasgow Institute of Technology (now Strathclyde University). Concurrent with his studies, he apprenticed as a draftsman to Napier, Shanks and Bell, one of the leading Clyde shipbuilders at the time.

In 1892, at age twenty, Mylne moved to the well-known firm of G. L. Watson. As a draftsman working under the eye of the great designer, he became involved in projects ranging from the largest steam yachts to small raters and daysailers and running the whole gamut of iron, steel, and wooden construction. That Watson approved of Mylne's work is apparent, for he took the young man to New York with him in 1895, when the Watson cutter *Valkyrie III* challenged for the America's Cup, racing against the appropriately named *Defender*, designed by N. G. Herreshoff. Young Mylne's time was fully occupied by drawing up proposals for steam yachts and the like while Watson made his way in the prominent social circles of the yachting establishment.

For reasons not entirely clear, Mylne left Watson the following year and set up his own establishment. That Watson allegedly felt somewhat aggrieved is perhaps understandable, but it does not explain the ill feeling that seems to have persisted over the next half-century.

Hugo Myers: *Dreamer.* This 43-foot catamaran, designed in 1956, is an interesting example of an early large cruising and racing cat. Note how the superstructure, resembling a conning tower, addresses the problem of obtaining headroom between the hulls while, at least apparently, minimizing windage. *Photo courtesy Claas van der Linde*

Working on his own, Mylne prospered during a time of great growth in yacht racing and cruising, particularly on the Clyde, where the effects of the industrial revolution were at their fullest and wealth was accruing at a fast rate. The great ironmasters, shipbuilders, and marine engineers, as well as other captains of industry such as locomotive builders, soon established fine summer homes on the shores of the Clyde estuary, a lovely, sheltered expanse of water well suited to the development of yachting. The urge to succeed in business was mirrored by a similar determination to shine in yachting—to have the largest steam yacht, the swiftest racing yacht. This urge was reflected even in the smaller racing classes, and designers who could meet the demands of these aspiring owners were assured of work. In 1896, the year he parted from Watson, Mylne attracted attention when he won a design competition in *Field*, a widely read magazine that covered a lot of yachting activities.

One of the most fiercely contested classes on the Clyde was the 19/24, a small yacht 19 feet LWL and 24 feet LOA. There was room for plenty of experimentation, and Mylne displayed his ability to extract the most from a rule. His boats, up against those of Fife and others, proved to be highly competitive. Mylne's first racing boat design, *Memsahib*, was built at Rutherglen by Ewing and James McGruer in 1897.

In his first five years on his own, Mylne produced designs for six one-design classes, including the Clyde One-Design, a Twenty-Tonner that was 50 feet long overall, on a waterline of 35 feet. Five yachts were built to this design. These much more substantial boats with scantlings that enabled them to last to the present day were a complete antidote to the Linear Raters of the time. Eventually Mylne designed a total of fifteen one-designs. His Scottish Islands One-Design class sailed on the Clyde from 1929 until the 1960's, and has recently been revived. The newest addition to the class, *Shona*, was launched in 2000.

Along with their functional qualities, Mylne's yachts displayed a beauty of line that led Brooke Heckstall-Smith, a leading yachting writer of the day, to compare them favorably with the sometimes supposedly "ugly" boats of Charles A. Nicholson. Examples of the Dublin Bay 21-footers and the South Coast One-Design boats of 1903, which may still be seen, are evidence of Mylne's eye for fine lines. The beautiful 52-foot Linear Raters (precursors to the 15-Meter class) *Moyana* and *Britomart* were exceedingly successful in their class.

The year 1906 was momentous in yacht-racing circles. Recognizing the dissatisfaction of owners regarding the plethora of rating rules, each of which appeared to be worse than its predecessor, the Yacht Racing Association convened an international meeting—the IYRU in embryo—and such was the eventual degree of agreement that the first International Rule was promulgated in June of that year, to take effect after January 1, 1907. This rule, with amendments and updates over time, has produced some of the loveliest inshore racers of the past century. It is a measure of Mylne's ability and his standing as a designer that he, together with William Fife III and Charles Nicholson, was among the representatives to the 1906 meeting, when he was only thirty-three years old.

The International Rule, unlike its predecessors, guaranteed sound construction by requiring all the new classes to be built to Lloyd's Building and Classification Rules. Ten new classes were agreed upon, ranging from 23 meters down to 5 meters. The most popular were the 6-, 8-, and 12-Meter classes, although the 15-Meter class had a fair following. The 7- and 10-Meters, while they were more popular in Scandinavia and continental Europe, did not pick up a following in the United Kingdom.

Mylne was soon heavily involved with the new rule. In 1908, of the eleven designs from his board, five were International Rule boats—two 12-Meters and one each for the 10-, 7-, and 6-Meter classes. His other boats were cruisers,

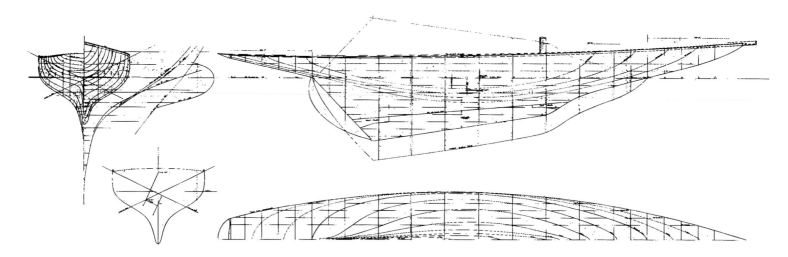

Alfred Mylne the First: *Jenetta*. *Jenetta* was Mylne's last 12-Meter and last class racer. She was up against the later and more successful 12-Meters designed by Charles E. Nicholson. After World War II her rig was reduced and she was shipped to Canada's west coast. *Drawing courtesy Ian Nicolson and the Mitchell Library, Glasgow, Scotland*

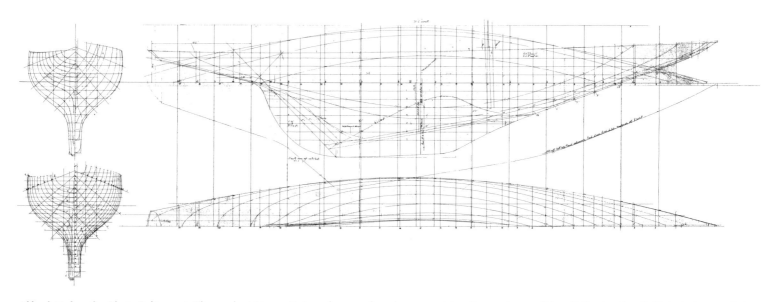

Alfred Mylne the First: *Britomart*. The 52-foot Linear Rating class produced some outstanding racing craft by all the leading British designers. *Britomart* dominated the class in the early 1900's before the Linear Rating Rule was superseded by the International Rule of 1906. Their place was taken by the comparable-sized 15-Meters. *Drawing courtesy Ian Nicolson and the Mitchell Library, Glasgow, Scotland*

including a 60-foot motor cruiser. The following year saw further interest in the meter classes: two 12-Meters, an 8- and a 6-Meter. In 1911 Mylne designed eighteen yachts, the largest of which was the 19-meter *Octavia* for William (later Sir William) Burton, who was to be one of his most enduring patrons and for whom Mylne designed his last yacht, the 12-Meter *Jenetta* in 1938–39.

Scottish designers have long been noted for their ability to produce craft that are both beautiful and puissant, and of light but strong construction. Mylne's boats had all of these characteristics, nowhere more strongly developed than in his International Rule boats, of which he had designed thirty by the time he retired.

In 1911 Alfred's elder brother Charles Mylne returned from South Africa and a banking career. The two brothers went into business to-

gether with the purchase of the boatyard at Port Bannatyne on the Isle of Bute in the Clyde estuary. Renamed the Bute Slip Dock, for the next thirteen years it went from strength to strength and built some of Alfred's finest designs.

Three other persons must be mentioned in connection with Alfred Mylne. The first is William Fife III. Although they were competitors in the field of yacht design, they were also very good friends, and each had a great respect for the professional and personal qualities of the other. Both were unmarried. Fife remained so, but Mylne eventually married Miriam Brown-Constable in 1922, when he was fifty. Fife built four large cruiser/racers to Mylne designs.

The second person was the fascinating Thomas (later Sir Thomas) Glen-Coats, the scion of a wealthy cotton family who came to work in Mylne's office after he had completed his uni-

versity studies, in about 1909. "Tid" Glen-Coats revealed himself to be a very clever young designer who also had the wherewithal to build yachts to his own plans. His 12-Meter *Heatherbell* was the first "twelve" in Britain. Thereafter he continued to design 8- and 6-Meters and other class boats for himself, many being built by the Bute Slip Dock. In a typical arrangement for the time, Glen-Coats's father offered to pay a "premium" to the company for his son's education as a naval architect. Mylne at first refused to accept any money, but they compromised by placing the money into a bank account for "a rainy day."

The third character is a bit of an enigma. Around 1902 John Morton James joined Mylne, but in what capacity is not quite certain. He seems to have been part partner and part office manager. His beautiful copperplate handwriting can still be seen in books and letters.

It would seem that he was responsible for the design of some of the large Mylne cruisers—while the principal concentrated on the racers—but the style of the two men is so alike that it is often impossible to state absolutely who drew what.

These large cruising yachts were some of the finest on the Clyde—big, handsome, and powerful with perfectly balanced rigs: schooners such as *Panda, Panope,* and *Golden Hind* (199, 122, and 144 tons [Thames Measurement], respectively), and ketches such as *Thendara,* 147 tons, and her near-sisters *Fiumara, Albyn, Roska,* and the 109-ton *Vadura.* Apart from *Roska,* which was the largest yacht built at the Bute Slip Dock, the others were built by such shipbuilding yards as Alexander Stephen and Sons on the upper Clyde, and Camper and Nicholson at Southampton.

During World War II, the Bute Slip Dock swung into high gear, turning out launches and other boats at a great rate. But yet another war exhausted the seventy-two-year-old Mylne, and in 1946 he handed over both the design firm and the Bute Slip Dock to his nephew, "young" Alfred, the son of Charles Mylne. Retiring to his wife's home territory of Cheltenham in southern England, they would make the annual pilgrimage north to sail the west coast of Scotland in their Mylne-designed cruiser *Medea.*

"Uncle Alfred" died in 1951 at the age of seventy-eight. Considered a most delightful, sociable, sensitive, and amiable man, he was one of Scotland's greatest designers, with a reputation both high and secure.

—David Ryder-Turner

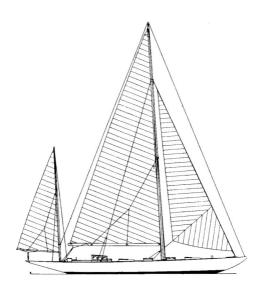

Alfred Mylne the First: *Veronica* After a moderately successful racing career, the 12-Meter *Veronica* was converted to a yawl and cruised extensively, demonstrating the adaptability of International Rule yachts. © *Tony Dixon*

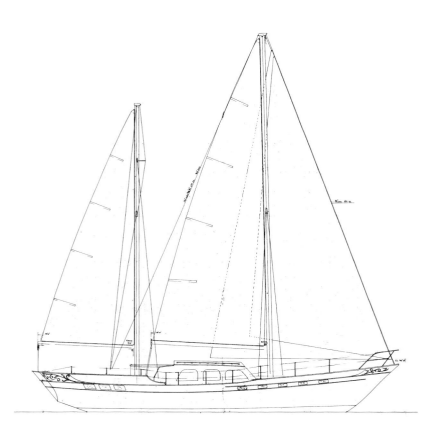

Alfred Mylne the Second: *Glenafton.* Mylne the Second produced some very fine cruising ketches, of which *Glenafton* is an excellent example. Built of wood at Ardmaleish on the Clyde, this yacht is presently owned by Brian Young, in whose yard at Rosneath she is meticulously maintained. *Drawing courtesy Ian Nicolson and the Mitchell Library, Glasgow, Scotland*

ALFRED MYLNE THE SECOND

1918–November 30, 1979 · Scotland

Alfred Mylne the Second was the nephew of Alfred Mylne the first and son of the latter's older brother and business partner, Charles. A remarkable man who suffered a number of difficulties in his life, he not only overcame them, but did so with his sense of humor undepleted and his high standards of work and life unimpaired.

Due to family financial problems Mylne had to leave school at the age of fourteen. He worked as a bank clerk until World War II broke out in 1939, having joined the British Territorial Army in the meantime. During the war he went with his regiment to the Middle East, where he fought in all the early desert campaigns until he was captured at Tobruk in 1942. He remained a prisoner of war until 1945.

After demobilization he joined his uncle in the yacht design business, although *joined* is hardly the appropriate word since his uncle retired a matter of weeks later, leaving young Alfred in charge of the shop. So at age twenty-eight, with no formal training in naval architecture, an incomplete secondary education, and only a limited experience with yachts, he was left to run one of the leading yacht design firms in Britain.

Perhaps it was a more sensible move than it seems. According to his later partner, Ian Nicolson, Alfred Mylne had a wonderful eye for lines and seemed to know instinctively just what would or would not "go." He could call on his uncle for advice, but it was largely precedent that guided him, along with the information contained in the vast body of work in the Mylne files. In his thirty-three years as head of A. Mylne and Company, he turned out very well-regarded sail and motor yachts, all characterized by beautiful lines and efficiency. Perhaps the most successful of his sailing cruiser designs was the 50-foot ketch *Melora III* of 1959, a blending of the beamy but elegant hull typical of the firm's previous work, extensive accommodations, and a subtle but practical deckhouse. The yacht is still based on the Clyde.

In 1959 he was joined by Ian Nicolson, who had rigorous training as a naval architect as well as practical experience in building and sailing.

As he grew older, Mylne suffered a series of heart attacks of increasing frequency. Surmounting each in turn, he "soldiered on," until his final attack in 1979. Nearly all of his yachts are still going strong. Upon his death, the firm was taken over by Ian Nicolson, who continues to design yachts and small commercial vessels and is a prolific writer on yachting subjects.

—David Ryder-Turner

best known for his sportfishing boats. From his office in Fort Lauderdale, Florida, he is presently developing a new line of sportfishing boats for a Florida production builder. These boats will have the "South Florida" look Napier has been developing.   —Daniel B. MacNaughton

BRUCE DAVID NELSON

Born December 8, 1952 · United States

In the 1970's and 1980's a number of young sailor/designers emerged on the Pacific coast of the United States. Of these, Bruce Nelson was arguably the best sailor of the lot. Born in Glen Cove, New York, Nelson spent his boyhood on Long Island Sound and took up sailing as a junior member of the Manhasset Bay Yacht Club. At an early age, he became interested in the science of sailing and was drawn to the work of master designers Nathanael Herreshoff and Starling Burgess; his sailing hero was multiple gold medalist Paul Elvstrom.

While studying at the University of Michigan, Nelson continued to race dinghies with success and was named Intercollegiate All-American over three consecutive seasons, from 1975 to 1978. He graduated in 1978 with a bachelor of science degree in naval architecture and marine engineering.

Although he had always hoped to work in yacht design, Nelson's earliest jobs were with ship design offices in Texas and southern California. His first break came in 1977, when a syndicate of yachtsmen from the San Diego Yacht Club ordered a 25-foot IOR Quarter-Tonner. Named *Blivit*, she departed from the norm in many ways. With her fractional rig, ballasted daggerboard, and relatively light displacement, she was a little tricky and required some practice and tuning to fully optimize. In early racing, the boat showed only bursts of speed, but once fully developed she went on to take the North American Quarter-Ton Championship held in New Orleans the following year.

David Napier: *Moppie.* Bertram Yacht's 54-foot sportfisherman is represented by *Moppie.* This South Florida–style, high-performance production boat has a worldwide reputation as a standard by which high-end sportfishing yachts are judged. *Photo courtesy David Napier*

DAVID LEE NAPIER

Born March 27, 1941 · United States

For most of David Napier's career, he was a staff designer for the Bertram Yacht Company. He is largely responsible for the angular and down-to-earth look of the Bertram powerboats, creating their practical and serious image. He worked on more than forty Bertram designs, from which approximately five thousand boats were built.

Napier was born in Michigan. His early jobs were in boatyards. During the 1960's, while he served in the U.S. Army, he took the Westlawn School of Yacht Design correspondence course. After he left the army, he went to work first as a draftsman, then as division designer for Chris-Craft for five years, which he refers to as his "college" because of the education he received there. He went to work at Bertram in 1969.

After the imposition of the luxury tax and a recession, Bertram was sold in 1991 to Italian owners, and Napier began his independent career. Since then he has continued to design boats for Bertram and many others, always maintaining a tough go-to-sea look. He has also developed an interesting speciality: the lengthening of existing motoryachts, an economical substitute for newly constructed larger boats.

Napier design customers range worldwide and have commissioned a variety of design types, from speed boats to motoryachts, but Napier is

Blivit brought local attention to Nelson's work and led to a commission for the 37-foot One-Tonner *Renegade*. This sloop was fast from the very beginning, and the response to her performance led to the establishment of the Nelson/Marek Yacht Design office with partner Bruce Marek. Although Marek left the practice in the 1980's, the San Diego firm still bears that name.

The boat that brought national attention to Nelson's work was *Rush*, a 36-foot development based on *Renegade* for a Great Lakes client. Built in 1980, *Rush* won every race she entered in her first year and capped the season by winning the One-Ton North American Championship, with her designer as a key player in the afterguard. At the end of the season, *Sailing World* magazine named Nelson Offshore Sailor of the Year. It was the first of many wins for boats of his design on which he also served as skipper, helmsman, or tactician.

In the wake of *Rush*'s success, inquiries and orders poured in from around the country and the firm's reputation blossomed. Early commissions included IOR and MORC racing yachts, ultralight racers, and a few cruising designs.

Yacht racing was perhaps at its most popular in the 1980's, and production racer/cruisers were selling to a large and eager market. Nelson/Marek got their share of this business. Notable among the stock boats developed were the Santana 30–30 class (65 built), the Morgan 36 (150 built), and the Morgan 45 (over 100 built). Perhaps the best of Nelson's production racers was the N/M 41. Eleven of these were built, including *Saeta*, *Brooke Ann*, and *Chimo*. They enjoyed instant and long-term success on ocean races and around triangular courses.

The office continued to prosper and received commissions for larger and larger vessels. Big ultralight racers such as *Drifter* and *Merlin* were grabbing a lot of attention in the Pacific, and Nelson found clients who wanted more refined versions of the same thing. His first ultralights, the 55-foot sisters *Lone Star* and *Strider*, proved extremely able and led to commissions for 68-foot maxi sleds *Saga* (1983), *Swiftsure* (1984), *Drumbeat* (1984), and *Prima* (1985) and the 66-foot *Pandemonium* (1985). These boats dominated the class at the time, and in 1985, *Swiftsure*, *Prima*, and *Saga* swept the Los Angeles to Honolulu Transpacific Yacht Race, finishing first, second, and third, respectively. During this period, the office continued to design numerous IOR boats including several for the extremely competitive 50-Foot class.

The America's Cup races of 1987 saw Nelson working with Dennis Conner's team as co-principal designer of two 12-Meters called

Stars & Stripes (US 54 and US 55). Nelson showed a strong ability to develop fast boats under the constraints of the International Rule. *Stars & Stripes* (US 55) defeated the Swarbrick and Murray–designed Australian defender, *Kookaburra III*, in the final round to return the Cup to American shores. This was the last America's Cup to be sailed in "twelves."

Since then, Nelson has been involved with every running of the America's Cup campaign. He stayed with Conner's team through the catamaran defense of 1988 and codesigned another *Stars & Stripes* (USA 11) for the first series sailed in the new America's Cup Class in 1992. In 1995 he switched teams and designed *Young America* (USA 36) for PACT 95 which Conner borrowed for the Cup finals, ultimately losing to Team New Zealand's *Black Magic*. For the next challenge in New Zealand, Nelson drew the plans for two boats for the America One program headed by Paul Cayard. USA 61 made it to the Louis Vuitton challenger finals but was edged out by the Italian *Prada* team in nine races. For the 2003 Cup challenge, Nelson was a key member of the Laurie Davidson design team for Craig McCaw's OneWorld Challenge.

In 1984, Nelson designed the MORC maxi *Cowboy*, which sailed to victory in the MORC Internationals in 1985, a title Nelson designs were to win an unprecedented six times.

Nelson's enthusiasm for one-design racing continues. His 35-foot "1D35" is perhaps the liveliest boat of its size. Forty-five have been built since they were introduced in 1998. He

has also developed designs for a number of shells and sculls for the builder Vespoli USA. At the Sydney Olympic Games in 2000, eight-oared shells from these designs won the gold and silver medals.

Yacht racing has been in Bruce Nelson's blood since childhood and his skill as a racer has been consistently sharp. There is no doubt that his remarkable sailing ability has added something special to his success as a designer.

The Nelson/Marek office is in San Diego, California.
—J. Scott Rohrer

RICHARD COOPER "DICK" NEWICK

Born May 9, 1926 · United States

In the American and European yachting world, a traditional boat is a ballasted monohull, and in a field as conservative as yacht design typically is, tradition dies hard. Still, thanks in part to Dick Newick, even tradition-minded yachtsmen can understand the appeal of multihulls. Newick has been spreading the multihull word since 1956, extolling the type's advantages of light weight, shallow draft, speed, and minimal heeling. He enjoys making converts.

Newick brought a whole new set of curves to multihull design. Under his influence, the "amas" or outer hulls of trimarans, previously the most aesthetically questionable feature of the type, have acquired springy sheers and efficient shapes that merge cleanly with the structures supporting them. Likewise, the main hulls have

Bruce Nelson: Nelson One-Design 35. A spirited one-design fleet can provide some of the most competitive racing to be found, in boats that retain their value because they are free from the fear of obsolescence. The photo conveys some of the excitement of racing in closely matched yachts. © *Onne van der Wal*

Dick Newick: Limmershin. This example of a 53-foot Limmershin design, moving fast, shows the inclined dagger foil, visible in the ama or outrigger, which provides improved stability and lateral resistance. For increased control, the amas and their supporting structures, or akas, are designed to be temporarily submerged without producing excessive drag. © *Terry Fong, AFA Photography*

a complementary sheer, and cabin structures flow out of the deck in natural-seeming curves. With Newick's designs, few can deny that multihulls can be beautiful.

Newick's work aims for seaworthiness combined with speed, with only as much in the way of light, simple, and practical accommodations as will fit into the boat without impacting its functional aspects.

An innovator in the design of amas, Newick has studied the ideal positions of their centers of buoyancy and lateral area, rocker, and the shape of their sections. The resulting amas are light, allow good maneuverability, provide a strong righting force, and, along with the carefully shaped akas (the outriggers supporting the amas), offer minimum resistance when temporarily submerged. He introduced dagger foils in 1962, which are asymmetrical daggerboards in the amas, angled inward to provide dynamic lift.

Newick grew up in Rutherford, New Jersey, spending summers on the water at the Jersey shore and inland lakes. He began designing and building kayaks at age twelve, which he says gave him a lifelong appreciation of slender, lightweight, easily driven hulls. During World War II the U.S. Navy sent him to the University of Kansas and later the University of Michigan, where he studied naval architecture but did not graduate. He later obtained a degree in business administration from the University of California at Berkeley.

After college Newick helped to revive an ailing boatbuilding concern, which he later leased and operated successfully until the Korean War made it difficult to obtain boatbuilding materials. He then joined the American Friends Service Committee before going to work for a boat distributor in San Francisco for a year.

In 1956, he hopped aboard a freighter bound for Europe, taking a 17-foot kayak he designed and built, and spent two months paddling more than 600 miles of rivers and canals from Belgium to Denmark. In Denmark he bought a cuddy cabin sloop and continued cruising until winter set in, whereupon he earned money by sending used Folkboats home to a friend in California for resale, forming the basis of the still-active San Francisco Bay Folkboat fleet. He then sailed with friends to the Virgin Islands. Newick still has the kayak with which he began this adventure.

Newick lived on Saint Croix in the Virgin Islands for seventeen years, entering the day-charter business with a 40-foot catamaran and then a series of trimarans he had designed and built. Guests liked the boats and spread the word. One Maine boatbuilder built six Newick trimarans after chartering one in Saint Croix.

In 1964 Newick sailed his 36-foot trimaran *Trice* to Newport, Rhode Island, whereupon he very unofficially shadowed the Newport-Bermuda Race to see how the boat would compare with the East Coast's best. She beat all but the famous *Nina* and *Stormvogel*, an accomplishment that opened a few eyes.

Newick's work became more widely recognized after he designed the 40-foot proa *Cheers* for the 1968 Observer Singlehanded Trans-Atlantic Race (OSTAR). Proas sail with either end as the bow, so rig, centerboards, and rudders must be symmetrical forward and aft. *Cheers* was unusual in that her single ama was always kept to leeward, the reverse of the Pacific island proas. A successful transatlantic shakedown cruise satisfied a skeptical British race committee and *Cheers* went on to finish a respectable third in the race.

In 1972, the 46-foot trimaran *Three Cheers* took fifth place in the OSTAR. The 50-foot *Moxie* won it in 1980. Over a dozen of his designs have done well in the OSTAR and its successors.

From the Virgin Islands, Newick and his family moved to Martha's Vineyard in 1973 and then to Kittery Point, Maine, in 1990. He continues to work, with design No. 118 underway at the time of this writing. Almost three hundred boats have been built to his 23-foot *Tremolino* trimaran design alone. Recent work includes the 48-foot trimaran *Traveller*, with one being built in Texas and another in Australia; two Echo II trimarans; a 32-foot power trimaran designed to go 45 knots offshore; and a 24-foot, rough-water commuting trimaran powered by a 50-hp outboard.

Dick Newick now lives in Mexico.

—Daniel B. MacNaughton

BENJAMIN NICHOLSON

1828–1906 · England

While his fame is somewhat eclipsed by that of his son, designer Charles E. Nicholson, it was Benjamin Nicholson who built up the Gosport, England, yard that would send Nicholson-designed yachts all around the world.

Nicholson, the son of an overseer of a prison hulk in Gosport, was apprenticed to yacht builder William Camper at age fourteen. He quickly rose through the ranks at the Camper yard, running the operation by 1859. In 1863, shortly before Camper's death, the operation became a partnership under the name of Camper and Nicholson.

One of Nicholson's most successful yachts was the schooner *Aline*, launched in 1860. This boat reintroduced vertically stepped masts after a period of preference for raking spars influenced by the schooner *America* starting in 1851. She was just the first of a number of Nicholson designs that were specifically built as cruising boats but went on to outperform other yachts intended as racers.

Another example of this phenomenon was the yawl *Florinda*, built as a cruising boat in 1873. Being much faster than anticipated, she was referred to (with tongue in cheek) as "the Gosport mistake." Twenty years after her launch, Nicholson's rival G. L. Watson said she "had been a standing miracle for years." It seems likely that in the case of both *Aline* and *Florinda*, the designer, aiming for comfort and safety, had created more moderate hulls (basically beamier and firmer bilged) than the very deep and narrow yachts that were popular for racing at the time. They would have been stiffer and more powerful and might have pointed the way to a less extreme racing type if enough people had been paying attention.

After *Florinda*, and continuing through the remainder of the 1870's, Camper and Nicholson's primary output was a series of large steam yachts, ranging in size up to the 564-ton *Czarina*. It is not clear to what degree Nicholson himself was involved in their designs, as the firm's steam yacht production dropped

Ben Nicholson: *Amphitrite.* The 161-ton *Amphitrite*, launched in 1887, was Nicholson's last design. Over more than a hundred years, she has had many owners, rigs, and different names, but is afloat today under her original name working as a training ship based in Hamburg, Germany. *Photo courtesy Ian Dear*

Charles A. Nicholson: *Yeoman IX.* This photo shows the 25-foot LWL Jolina-class *Yeoman IX* shortly after her launch in 1960. She was one in a long line of yachts of the same name that Nicholson designed for his friend, Owen Aisher. *Photo by Eileen Ramsay*

off considerably after Camper's nephew, William Camper Storey, left the firm and went on to design many such vessels under his own name. Nicholson's last design was the 161-ton teak schooner *Amphitrite*, launched in 1887 and still in use today.

After 1880 the yard began building more and more yachts not of Nicholson's design, but he remained an active chairman of the firm until a few months before his death. One obituarist remarked that his firm had practically been the pivot from which the huge increase in the popularity of yachting had been directed. He was also very influential in the formation of Lloyd's scantlings rules, which did so much to increase the seaworthiness of yachts.

—Daniel B. MacNaughton

CHARLES ARTHUR NICHOLSON

1906–1993 · England

The nephew of designer Charles E. Nicholson, "Young Charlie," as everyone called him, joined Camper and Nicholson in 1926 after attending Toulouse University. He became a director in 1939, deputy chairman in 1954, and chairman from 1963 to 1969.

Like his uncle, Nicholson learned what he knew from working in the firm; having no formal training in naval architecture did not hinder his ability or creativity. And though what he witnessed aboard *Maitenes II* during the stormy Fastnet Race of 1931 (during which one of the crew was lost overboard) stopped him from ever racing offshore again, his ocean racing designs virtually dominated the 1950's.

His collaboration and friendship with that great patron of postwar British yachting, Owen Aisher, was long and fruitful, and with Nicholson's very first design, *Yeoman*, launched in 1936, they established a long dynasty of successful yachts of that name. After the war he also designed two 5.5-Meters for Aisher, but it was the 35-foot LWL *Yeoman III*, which won the 1951 Fastnet Race, along with her sisterships *Taiseer IV* and *Fedalah* that established his reputation.

However, unlike his uncle's designs, few of Nicholson's boats were built at Camper and Nicholson. For example, in 1952 the Cowes firms of Souter's and Lallow's built, respectively, Adlard Coles's *Cohoe II* and the highly successful Class III *Lothian*. *Lothian* came in second overall in the 1953 Fastnet and spawned a number of near-sisterships, as did the Lallow's-built *Jolina*, a type so popular that fourteen were built and became known as the Jolina class.

When author and naval architect Douglas Phillips-Birt wrote that Nicholson had struck "original and personal lines" with these yachts, he added that the designer now favored the beamy centerboard type of ocean racer so popular in the United States. In fact, Nicholson thought them unsuitable for English conditions, and he disliked the American tendency to produce boats that were fine in the bow and broad in the stern. His designs were noted for their full bows and fine run, a shape with comfortable seagoing characteristics.

All these characteristics were embodied in his most popular and enduring yacht, the 21-foot LWL South Coast One-Design. The SCODs, as they came to be called, were an immediate success, taking the first six places in the 1956 Round the Island Race and winning that year's Boat of the Show Award. Over a hundred were built and many are still racing today.

In 1961 Camper and Nicholson launched the first in a new range of fiberglass boats, the Nicholson 36. A joint project with Nicholson's elder son, Peter, *Janessa* combined the advantages of a fiberglass hull with a wooden deck and an interior built to the owner's requirements. That year she racked up sixteen prizes out of nineteen starts. Next came the all-fiberglass Nicholson 32, another father-son collaboration in which Nicholson drew the hull shape and sections. He was also involved in the Nicholson 26, which first appeared in 1964.

However, Nicholson did not entirely neglect the one-off ocean racer, and in 1961 he and Peter produced *Quiver III* for Ren Clarke. Chosen for that year's British Admiral's Cup team, she came in second overall in the Fastnet Race. By the time Charles A. Nicholson retired in 1969, he had over seventy designs to his credit, not counting the fiberglass boats he codesigned.

—Ian Dear

CHARLES ERNEST NICHOLSON,

OBE 1868–February 27, 1954 · England

In 1954, E. F. Haylock, then editor of the influential British magazine *Yachting World*, wrote, "On February 27th, Charles E. Nicholson, the greatest yacht designer the world has ever known, died at Gosport at the age of 86." Many people, particularly in North America, would challenge the claim of "greatest." But few would deny that Nathanael Herreshoff, Charles E. Nicholson, and George Watson (to list them in alphabetical order)—and, perhaps, William Fife Jr.—stand head and shoulders above the rest.

Whereas Watson was a designer only, both Herreshoff and Nicholson headed very large and important yacht-building yards. It is fair to say that the total output of work by Nicholson is greater than the others; his cruising yachts ranged from Three-Tonners to great schooners

of 700 tons; his racing yachts of all classes and size would constitute a fleet of some magnitude, while his power yachts, mainly diesel driven, were an outstanding feature of the yachting scene of the 1920's and 1930's.

The firm of Camper and Nicholson was probably the outstanding one in Europe, and much of its success must be attributed to the skill of Nicholson as both designer and manager. One of his notable qualities was his ability to choose the right men for the job; he had a very talented drawing office and outstanding craftsmen on the shop floor—a team that was second to none.

The background to Nicholson's career starts in 1782 when Francis Amos established a yard at Gosport, on the south coast of England. Later he took on an apprentice, William Camper,

who bought the business in 1820, developing the yard's interest in yacht building. Camper, in turn, took on Benjamin Nicholson in 1842 as an apprentice. Benjamin Nicholson gradually took on management of the yard. His sons, Charles and his older brother Benjamin Nicholson Jr., joined the firm in 1887, when Charles was nineteen. By the time of Benjamin's death in 1906, Charles Nicholson was well established as the firm's principal designer with a string of successful craft to his name. These were mainly small racing craft, but increasingly larger craft came from his board as his reputation as a successful designer became more widely appreciated. Two of his early designs were in the small rater classes where competition was fierce. The 2½-Rater *Gareth* and the 5-Rater *Dacia* both topped their classes in 1892, the year of their first appearance.

Charles E. Nicholson: *Margherita.* The outstanding racing schooner of the pre–World War I era, *Margherita* was designed and built in 1913. Her steel hull was outfitted and rigged with the spars and equipment from G. Cecil Whitaker's previous schooner, the William Fife III–designed *Waterwitch*, which had failed to meet expectations. *Photo courtesy Ian Dear*

Nicholson had no formal qualifications in naval architecture. This is surprising considering the fact the Scottish yacht designers (at that time preeminent in Europe) placed such importance on the need to have a sound theoretical base to their craft. But Nicholson does not appear to have suffered from the lack of such credentials. The grounding that he got in the yard under the demanding guidance of his father evidently made good any supposed inadequacy. Like the Herreshoff Manufacturing Company, Camper and Nicholson was almost self-sufficient in all departments. Thus, an apprentice received instruction and experience in almost every aspect of yacht design and construction.

For most of Nicholson's first eight years of management, business principally involved repairs and refits rather than new construction. Occasionally there were orders for moderate-sized yachts, or for tenders for yachts being built elsewhere. While most of the work was in wood, the business gradually developed the ability to repair steel craft. This work greatly increased in the early twentieth century, and by the 1920's and 1930's, Camper and Nicholson was designing and building large steel motoryachts.

Nicholson's successful designs were the outcome of a good understanding of the rating rules of the day, and the design ability to make the most of them—and, of course, of having skilled helmsmen to sail the boats. In this last element, Nicholson was very often that helmsman. His skill in that capacity was frequently a major factor in the success of his boats, but was also instrumental in his selection as the designer/builder.

The introduction of the first International Rule in 1906 brought a measure of sanity and rationalization to class racing. It also marked the launching of Nicholson up through the ranks of the preeminent designers. George Watson was dead by the time of the International Rule, so we shall never know what he might have made of it. Fife and Mylne were at the height of their careers and were joined by designers such as Anker, Oertz, Rasmussen, and Estlander. Nicholson almost made his mark with the 23-Meter class *Brynhild II*. She was the largest racer yet built at the yard, and would undoubtedly have been a class leader had she not suffered a mast failure early in 1910, which resulted in the yacht being sunk. So, *White Heather II* and *Shamrock*—both by Fife—dominated big-class racing in the 23-Meters.

In 1911, Nicholson launched the 19-meter *Norada*, joining the other three of the class: *Corona* and *Mariquita* by Fife, and *Octavia* by Mylne. *Norada's* relative lack of success was due more to the quality of the crewing and tacti-

Charles E. Nicholson: *Patricia.* Nicholson frequently designed craft to non-European rules. *Patricia* was designed to the American Universal Rule R-Class. She was built in 1921 in Vancouver, British Columbia, Canada. *Photo courtesy Newport Harbor Nautical Museum, Newport Beach, CA*

cal handling of the boat. When she was helmed by Nicholson, there was every indication that she might well have been the best of the class.

One of the most hotly contested classes prior to World War I was that of the 15-Meters. Again, Fife and Mylne were the stars, but in 1911 Nicholson designed and built a 15-Meter, the incomparable *Istria*. Although something of an ugly duckling, she was an outstanding example of original thinking allied to innovative and skilled use of new materials and methods of construction. Multiskinned planking and a plywood deck, with the obligatory dinghy set into the deck in the form of a cockpit, were but three examples of the originality that went into her design and construction. Not surprisingly, she began to dominate the class—a class that, sadly, did not survive the downgrading of class racing after that war.

World War I also saw the end of the great days of big schooner racing. They were boats with skyscraping rigs, clouds of canvas; they were fast and at times a real handful, as Kaiser Wilhelm's Max Oertz–designed *Meteor IV* was to demonstrate. Fife designed some beauties—*Susanne* is probably the best known—but the outstanding English boat was the 105-foot *Margherita* by Nicholson, which came about in the following way.

Having owned the beautiful and successful Fife-designed *Cicely*, G. Cecil Whitaker ordered a new, steel-hulled schooner from Fife—*Waterwitch*. Right from the start it was apparent that Fife had got it wrong. Whitaker sought Nichol-

son's advice about correcting the problems. In the end they decided to remove all internal fittings, all deck gear, masts, spars, and sails, and scrap the hull. Nicholson designed and built a new hull of steel in time for the 1913 season, which *Margherita* dominated, beating even the much-vaunted N. G. Herreshoff–designed *Westward*.

One other Nicholson-designed racing yacht of the pre–World War I period must be remembered. This was Thomas Lipton's America's Cup challenger of 1914, the fourth *Shamrock*. Approximately 75 feet LWL, she was uncompromisingly a racer. From snubbed bow to sawn-off counter she was the antithesis of the "yacht beautiful." Benefiting from the experience of *Istria*, Nicholson produced a vessel that was generally considered the faster of the two contenders in a series of races that had been postponed by World War I until 1920. That she did not bring back the Cup (in spite of winning two races against the N. G. Herreshoff–designed *Resolute*) was more due to deficiencies in the management and tactical handling of the challenge—deficiencies that dogged British challengers down the years. Lipton was bitterly disappointed, but not with Nicholson, to whom he turned for his last challenger.

While all this racing was going on, cruising yachts of all sizes were flowing off Nicholson's board. Many cruisers had handicap racing in mind as well, and one of his loveliest was the cutter *Merrymaid* of 1903. Although not the outstanding racer that later Nicholson boats were, she fully met her cruising desiderata and

Charles E. Nicholson: *Trivia.* Nicholson's 12-Meters were outstanding and dominated the class in the 1930's (until the Olin Stephens–designed *Vim* came on the scene in 1939) in British coastal waters. *Trivia* (left) is still racing today, a testament to her sound design and construction. *Photo by Douglas Went*

Charles E. Nicholson: *Endeavour.* "The darling jade, she broke my heart," wrote John Scott Hughes of *Endeavour*. Considered by many to be the best looking of all the J-class boats, she may also have been faster than the Starling Burgess–designed *Rainbow*. But in spite of winning the first two races of the 1934 series, she failed to win the America's Cup. © *Mystic Seaport, Rosenfeld Collection, Mystic, CT*

was so well built that she is afloat to this day.

Nicholson did much of his design work at home, where he kept a drawing board, splines, weights, and all the other paraphernalia beloved by those who design boats. He prepared preliminary drawings quickly and clearly, and then took them to the drawing office, where they were discussed with the chief draftsman before being developed into the full and final plans. In this way Nicholson was able to produce a vast volume of work that carried his imprint.

Despite the accent on sailing craft, Nicholson was fully conversant in the development of power craft. In 1908, Camper and Nicholson was commissioned to design and build a 200-foot steam yacht. Not having the steelwork capacity to construct a hull of this size, nor the experience of large steam installations, they contracted part of this work out to the Southampton firm of Day, Summers and Company, after which the yacht, *Sagitta*, was completed by Camper and Nicholson at Gosport.

Recognizing that it was both within the future capacity of Camper and Nicholson and of benefit to the firm to develop their skills in the realm of large powered craft, they took over the yard belonging to the great builders Fay and Company, at Northam, Southampton. This was a prescient move, for the following year, 1913, they were commissioned to design and build a sizable twin-screw motoryacht. Diesel-powered yachts were still a rarity, and the new commission put Nicholson right at the forefront of the development of this type of craft. Not surprisingly, after World War I, when powered craft were smaller than hitherto, and a reduction in crew strength was much desired, the diesel motoryacht became the vogue.

World War I halted all pleasure yachting and placed an increased load on Nicholson's shoulders. The yard had to be geared immediately to the needs of war. Nicholson became interested in aircraft construction and co-founded the Gosport Aircraft Company, which built a number of flying boats for the Royal Naval Air Service. He also designed a large flying boat for service use, but the war came to an end before the project could be developed.

The advent of peace in 1918 was followed by the gradual resumption of yachting. The war had dealt a severe blow to the old economic and social order. Because labor costs were higher, as were the costs of crews, cruising and racing yachts were smaller. As the smaller racing classes prospered, Nicholson came into his own. While Fife still dominated the 6- and 8-Meters, with Mylne snapping at his heels, Nicholson eventually eclipsed both.

Nicholson was a good businessman and an astute negotiator; soon he was able to attract

Charles E. Nicholson: *Norge.* The pinnacle of Nicholson's power-yacht output, *Norge (ex-Philante)* was bought by the Norwegian people after World War II for their King Haakon V. She was built for T. O. M. Sopwith as a tender to his America's Cup challenger *Endeavour II* in 1937, and set a standard of beauty in motoryachts that has seldom been equaled. *Photo courtesy of Ian Dear*

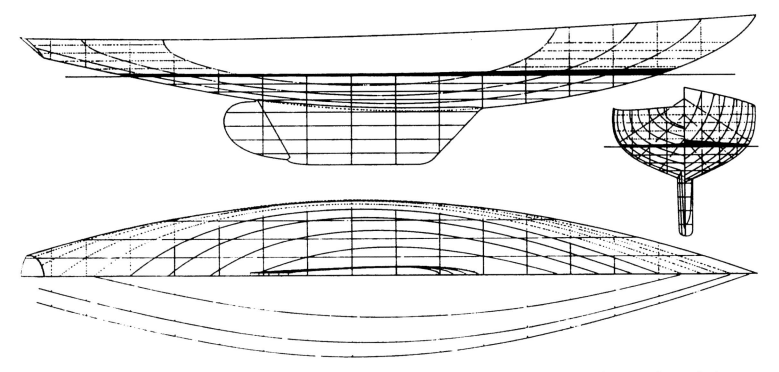

Charles E. Nicholson: Bembridge Redwings. The Bembridge Redwing One-Design class has undergone a series of metamorphoses. The boats are unique in that while the hull is one-design in all aspects, the owner is free to adopt any rig up to the limit of 200 square feet. This is the second series, introduced in 1938. © *Tony Dixon*

prospective yacht owners to the Camper and Nicholson yard. They did not go away empty-handed. His 6- and 8-Meters were more and more successful, and his 12-Meters excellent. *Flica*, *Doris*, *Mouette*, and *Evaine* preceded *Blue Martin*, *Trivia*, and *Tomahawk*, themselves followed by many others, each bettering the earlier, each both beautiful and puissant, each with a glorious future. And then, bright on the western horizon, loomed the formidable and youthful figure of Olin Stephens and the incomparable *Vim*. Another star was rising.

While all this was going on, and the two Camper and Nicholson yards prospered with full order books, America's Cup fever raged. Acceptance by both sides of the Atlantic of the Universal Rule as the basis for future challenges resulted in three challenges to the Americans, and four J-Class racers—all designed by Nicholson—coming from the Gosport yard. The first, *Shamrock V*, for Sir Thomas Lipton's last of five attempts to regain the Cup in 1930, was not successful against the W. Starling Burgess—designed *Enterprise*.

Nicholson's next J-Class boat, *Velsheda* (1933), was a distinct advance. She was not destined to be a Cup challenger, but she paved the way for what proved to be the outstanding J-Class boat of her time: the first *Endeavour*, built for T. O. M. Sopwith in 1934. It is generally conceded that *Endeavour* was a faster boat than the Burgess-designed *Rainbow*. Nevertheless, she failed to lift the Cup, in spite of winning two races. When these two protagonists next met on the water, in 1937, the second *Endeavour* was soundly defeated by the Burgess/Stephens—designed *Ranger*.

Sopwith's second challenger was accompanied to Newport, Rhode Island, by the largest motoryacht to be built in Britain. The 205-foot Nicholson-designed *Philante* was, and is, a superb vessel, representing the pinnacle of Nicholson's virtuosity in power craft design. He designed other smaller, but equally fine-looking motoryachts—*Maid Marion*, *Malahne*, *Argosy*, and *Crusader I* and *II*, to name a few.

It would seem that there was no end to Nicholson's versatility. Further examples are his design of the 3,000-ton training ship *Sebastian de Elcano* for the Spanish government, and the great schooners *Creole* (700 tons built in 1927 of composite construction) and *Ailée* and Sonia (both steel).

The rising sport of ocean racing brought further work to the Camper and Nicholson yards. Nicholson's ocean racers are exemplified by the glorious twins *Foxhound* and *Bloodhound* and their larger sistership *Stiarna*, offshore developments of the 12-Meter rule, and *Firebird*, a later and larger version that remains a magnificent example of the type.

Hedley Nicol: *Wanderer.* *Wanderer* was the cruising version of Nicol's successful 35-foot racing trimaran *Vagabond* of 1964. *Reproduced from an unknown source*

The versatility and agility of Nicholson's mind were endless. Of course, he had a formidable team to develop his thoughts, but his abundance of inspiration and leadership harnessed that force.

Even World War II could not halt his restless spirit, his inquiring mind, and his relentless energy. Camper and Nicholson turned out their own highly successful versions of gunboats, torpedo boats, and blockade runners. Unfortunately, bombing in 1941 destroyed most of the yard along with irreplaceable drawings and records. The yard was rebuilt but the offices never again achieved the opulence of pre–World War II.

After the war, Nicholson produced more fine craft: beautiful and successful ocean racers such as *Saint Barbara*, and, in 1949, the forerunner of the proposed 5.5-Meter class, suitably named *The Deb*. This delightful little boat was sailed by the Nicholson family in Solent events. It was only later that the class developed unsatisfactory characteristics; Nicholson would have shuddered at the strange craft the rule later produced.

And so in his final years this great man retained his interest in, and his profound understanding of, the complexities of yacht design in all its fascinating variety. For many he was the greatest, and the many vessels restored with loving care provide a living testimony to the art and craft of this outstanding designer.

—David Ryder-Turner

HEDLEY NICOL

Died 1966 · Australia

The Australian trimaran pioneer Hedley Nicol became well known for beating all the large Australian yachts in the Brisbane-Gladstone Races in both 1964 and 1965 with his self-designed 35-foot trimaran *Vagabond*. A Queensland policeman with no formal training in yacht design but apparently having a natural feel for trimarans, he subsequently designed several trimarans, among them the *Clipper* (25 feet), *Wanderer* (35 feet, a cruising version of *Vagabond*), and *Voyager* (45 feet).

Equipped with low-aspect-ratio skegs rather than centerboards and suitable for building at home using plywood sheathed with fiberglass, these trimarans were produced in large numbers in Australia as well as the United States. They did much to popularize the trimaran concept in these countries.

Like Arthur Piver, his contemporary trimaran designer from the United States, Hedley Nicol ultimately became a victim of one of his own designs: in 1966 he was lost with two crew en route from Australia to Tahiti with his latest design, the trimaran *Privateer* (37 feet 9 inches).   —Claas van der Linde

KNUD AAGE NIELSEN

January 12, 1904–June 14, 1984
Denmark/United States

The career and marine designs of K. Aage Nielsen exemplify how to become a successful twentieth-century American yacht designer. Nielsen was born in the seacoast town of Faaborg, Denmark, to a family of modest means. His father operated a sawmill and encouraged Aage and his brother Axel to join the lumber business.

With characteristic determination, Nielsen opted instead to pursue marine construction and as a teenager apprenticed for four years with a well-known, local boatbuilder. He built his own sailing dinghy to commute across the harbor to Möller's yard and devoted his free time to fishing and sailing around the island of Fyn, 20 miles from the shipbuilding city of Odense.

Upon completion of his apprenticeship, Nielsen joined the firm of Burmeister and

K. Aage Nielsen: *Sea Flower* (opposite). The 51-foot 1-inch LOA *Sea Flower*, one of many Nielsen designs built in wood by Paul E. Luke, exemplifies graceful lines, efficient rig, comfort below, and success in competition. © *Mystic Seaport, Rosenfeld Collection, Mystic, CT*

K. Aage Nielsen: *Holger Danske.* The 42-foot 6-inch LOA *Holger Danske*, a Nielsen favorite, blends traditional styling, attention to detail, and proven performance in open ocean sailing. She won the Newport-Bermuda Race in 1980. *Drawing courtesy William Peterson*

Wain in Copenhagen as a draftsman, and worked with the naval architect George Berg, one of several key professional associations to strongly influence his career and creativity. Berg had a number of designs that were being marketed in America, including a Danish double-ender named *Nordic*, which helped to convince Nielsen that the best course to success in yacht design was in U.S. waters.

After a brief correspondence with John G. Alden, Nielsen emigrated to Massachusetts in 1925, with a suitcase and a clock in hand, to work for Alden's firm. Thus began his remarkable career, which spanned fifty-five years in the Boston area. During the next six years with Alden and a talented team of designers, he polished his English, his design and engineering talents, and his offshore sailing skills.

When the Depression caused layoffs at Alden's in 1931, Nielsen married Bodil Erichsen (a partnership of fifty-two years) and joined the new firm of Murray G. Peterson in Marblehead, Massachusetts. He worked there for the next five years. The couple lived with Peterson, and their close personal and professional relationship continued after Peterson moved his office to Maine. The Nielsens resided in the Marblehead house throughout their lives, raising two daughters and becoming part of the town's social fabric.

Nielsen joined the growing New York firm of Sparkman and Stephens in 1936 and, with

Emmons Alexander, formed the Boston office of that company. Alexander handled brokerage services while Nielsen was the marine surveyor and yacht designer. Olin J. Stephens and Nielsen had great mutual respect and worked together on designs built in the Northeast until 1941, when Nielsen joined the World War II shipbuilding effort with Simms Brothers and the Samuel Crocker yard in Dorchester, Massachusetts. While at the Simms' yard, Nielsen did design work with William Simms on U.S. naval vessels including high-speed submarine chasers.

In 1944, Nielsen returned to State Street, Boston, designing under his own name custom sail and power yachts built exclusively of wood or aluminum until his retirement in 1980. He also periodically collaborated with Stephens, Peterson, and Fenwick C. Williams. Nielsen became known for semi-shoal-draft, keel and centerboard racing yachts, which proved successful under CCA Rules and won numerous races on both U.S. coasts and to Bermuda. Nielsen created over a hundred custom designs, and he favored two builders—Paul E. Luke of East Boothbay, Maine, and A. Walsted of Thurø, Denmark—for more than forty of his cruising and racing sailboats.

Nielsen had many repeat customers, especially within the membership of the CCA. Bradley Noyes had four *Tiogas*, Clarence Warden had two *Minot's Lights*, and Thor Ramsing two *Solutions*. Other CCA boats included Bill Warden's *Patience*, Bob Stone's *Sea Flower*, Arthur Santry's *Pleione*, Ed Gaynor's *Emily*, and Gardner Barker's *Star Song*. Double-enders included Donald Starr's *Northern Crown*, John Kiley's *Snow Star*, and John Wilson's *Holger Danske*. The latter proved to be a Nielsen favorite in which he often sailed.

K. Aage Nielsen had a rare combination of artistry, skill, and practical experience. A perfectionist, he would not accept shortcuts at the expense of seaworthiness, beauty, or performance, and demanded the best from builders by giving them excellent and detailed drawings from which to work. Behind his wire-rimmed glasses, broad-billed cap, ever-present pipe, and seemingly gruff exterior lay a relentless passion for his craft and the responsibility to provide for his family in a sometimes fickle market. Consequently, Nielsen's designs not only evolved with ever changing opportunities but also influenced that change. They will continue to be admired and imitated for exemplary looks, speed, and comfort.

The Nielsen plans are preserved by the Peabody-Essex Museum of Salem, MA.

—William Peterson

GEORG NISSEN

Born 1944 · Germany

On Germany's northern seaboard, where the Kiel Fjord opens to the Baltic Sea, Georg Nissen, a particularly quiet character, works away. For over two decades this prolific naval architect has designed 220 yachts, and more than six hundred have been built. Among his racing credits are a 1983 world championship in the IOR Mini-ton Class, at the time a hothouse of growing sailboat design talent.

Nissen is well established as a designer of cruising boats, daysailers, and bluewater yachts approaching 80 feet in length. He specializes in the challenging field of shoal- and variable-draft cruisers. He favors the traditional style of centerboard, or a fixed bulb keel with an integral centerboard, rather than the vertically sliding centerboard, because the traditional centerboard can be lifted in case of serious grounding, thus permitting a safe return home.

Nissen is also an early pioneer of deckhouse comfort aboard medium-sized cruising boats. This feature lengthens the sailing season in the chilly waters of northern Europe and has made him popular with the cruising fraternity. In contrast to some rating-optimized designs or "bump-boats," Nissen produces particularly clean designs with straight lines. His Mini-Ton design, for example, was smaller in size and sail area than the average boat in what was then a notably large class.

Popular examples of Nissen's work are the 16- and 20-Square-Meter Jollenkreuzer classes: dinghies that provide accommodation within a prominent superstructure. These daysailers are quite common on shallow lakes in Germany and are actively raced. Nissen's boats in these two classes have won a remarkable string of championships. His designs feature a fine entry, with the boat floating on a slim waterline. Stability is obtained by means of a wide aftersection.

Recently, Nissen collaborated with Juliane Hempel, one of only a few female yacht designers. She is well known for *Spazzo*, an 8-Meter yacht. Together they developed several interpretations of the modern theme, with pleasing traditional lines above the waterline merging into an up-to-date underbody with shallow, U-shaped or hard-chined sections and fairly separated appendages. A typical example is the *Seekreuzer*, a 60-footer providing a comfortable life on the seven seas.

One of the most radical examples of this mixture is a 36-foot, gaff-rigged cutter. The underbody of this yacht is a sport boat with a bulb-ballasted, high-aspect-ratio fin and a free-standing spade rudder of stretched proportions. This configuration delivers a surprising performance at the tiller, is a real shock to other sailors, and is definitely flabbergasting when hoisted high'n' dry. It represents an interesting mix of aesthetics and boatbuilding traditions. The daily business of Nissen's company involves designs of popular compact boats of medium proportions for stock boat builders like Contest in the Netherlands, the Sirius yard in Germany, and Sunbeam in Austria.

Georg Nissen Yacht Design is located in Laboe on the Bay of Kiel, Germany.

—Erdmann Braschos

BERNARD NIVELT

see Michel Joubert

PETER NORLIN

Born 1941 · Sweden

Born into a family of yachting enthusiasts near Stockholm, Peter Norlin trained to become a building engineer, but his love of sailing led him to sailmaking in Upsala. He soon began to develop his own ideas of what a RORC yacht should be. The result was the Half-Ton yacht *Scampi*.

Scampi's astonishing successes in winning the Half-Ton Cup for three consecutive years in 1969, 1970, and 1971 brought Peter Norlin to sudden international prominence and a new career. The Scampi 30 was built of fiberglass and she quickly went into production—about 1,500 would

Peter Norlin: *Raffa*. *Raffa* was the first 22-Square-Meter skerry cruiser made of fiberglass in Sweden. The 12.38-meter sloop was built in Uppsala in 1978 by Peter Carlsson for his own use. © *Per Thelander*

Jacques Normand: *Velox*. The fast 42.27-meter LOA schooner *Velox* was built of wood in Le Havre in 1875. Her design is a compromise between the narrow English cutters and the broad American hull type. *Painting courtesy Jacques Taglang*

be built. Her immediate successors, first the Norlin 34 and then the Quarter-Tonner Accent 26, proved that Norlin would not be a one-boat wonder. There rapidly followed a host of designs for racers, cruisers, and cruiser/racers, most of them intended for series production. Some of the better-known lines are Norlin, Express, Cirrus, Cumulus, Stratos, Nova, Alpha, Omega, Avance, Monark, and Gambler.

However, Norlin did not work exclusively on production boats. Although one-design classes had been steadily gaining in world popularity for decades, in Scandinavia, the older International Rule boats still maintained a substantial following among sailors and yacht designers. Between 1977 and 1989 Norlin designed fifteen 6-Meter boats, from which he developed the somewhat whimsical idea of a "mini 12-meter"—that is, the 2.4-meter singlehander, which has become especially popular among handicapped sailors since it requires minimal mobility in handling.

Currently Norlin is designing the Sweden Yachts line of cruisers in Stenungsund, Sweden.

—Bent Aarre

JACQUES AUGUSTIN NORMAND

1839–1906 · France

In seven generations, the Normand family's shipyards designed only eighteen yachts, while during the same period, from 1728 to 1960, under the stamp "Normand," 577 vessels of other types were launched. Nevertheless, Jacques Au-

gustin Normand made a major, if largely unrecognized, contribution to the development of yacht design.

Born at Le Havre, Normand spent his childhood in his father's shipyard. He didn't go to school but learned his practice from family members. A great capacity for work and an unquenchable thirst for knowledge made him an erudite individual, particularly in his trade as a naval engineer, but also as a mathematician.

When Normand was in charge of the family shipyard in 1871, he designed his first sailboat, *Cours-Après*, which joined the famous pilot-boat fleet of Le Havre. It was followed by another pilot cutter, *Maître-Pierre*, in 1872. The greater part of his time was devoted to creating steamboats for the navy.

Nevertheless, in 1874, the Polish earl Benoît Tyszkiewicz had the audacity to order a large schooner yacht from him. Normand drew a masterpiece, *Zemajteij*, better known under her later name of *Velox*. In her hull design, *Zemajteij* constituted a revolutionary change not recognized or duplicated by other designers for several years. Normand, in the first highly successful "compromise" type, combined the best of the American and British schooners and cutters.

From the American approach Normand retained a relatively wide and flat hull for initial stability, speed, and comfort, but he added a deep hollow keel containing all of the ballast that was not mounted externally, thus duplicating the ultimate stability and power of the British cutters. The resulting low center of gravity allowed a somewhat reduced beam and increased sail area, allowing for greater speed especially in rough conditions, something *Velox* proved many times. Normand was among the first to demonstrate the desirability of characteristics that were developed further and became very popular.

Most surprising is that the superb *Velox* did not inspire more orders from French yachtsmen. He designed and built *Phryné* (1874), a 19-meter LWL steam yacht, and *Goëlo* (1887), a 52-ton cruising yawl. He didn't design another yacht for a decade, but in 1898 he delivered *Gitana II* to Baroness Adolphe de Rothschild. This 36.95-meter LWL, steel-screw yacht was powered by a three-cylinder steam engine of his own design and construction. A sistership, *Aigrette*, was launched in 1906 for the Suez Canal Company.

Thus, *Velox*'s superb reputation for speed, established in informal races from the time of her launching and lasting until the end of her career in 1914—she was never raced in a regatta—hardly influenced yachtsmen, and Normand's abilities in the field of yachting remained virtually unknown. He devoted much of his activity to the French navy, where he built his reputation through the power of his engines and his fast hulls; his torpedo boat *Corsair* reached 31 knots in 1895.

A year after Normand's death, an Englishman delivered an homage to the designer at the Institution of Naval Architects of Great Britain: "None, during the past generation, has done more to credit his country than the late Augustin Normand." —Jacques Taglang

AXEL NYGREN

October 16, 1865–October 20, 1935 · Sweden

Axel Nygren was one of the first people in Sweden who actively worked to get young people out sailing. His designs are notable for their mathematical accuracy and precision. He was educated as an engineer at Chalmers Institute of Technology in Gothenburg, a student of designer Albert Andersson.

In addition to a number of vessels for the Swedish Royal Navy, Nygren designed many yachts. Like most everyone in the 1890's, he was very impressed with Nathanael Herreshoff's *Gloriana*, and drew both small and big yachts with the same cutaway forefoot.

Nygren designed several big yachts during

Axel Nygren: *Galatea*. The design for the 68-foot *Galatea* proved to be an enduring success. Built in 1899 for the royal family of Sweden, she is of composite construction, with wooden planking over steel frames. Originally a cutter, she is sailing today in the Pacific Northwest on her second yawl rig. *Photo courtesy Newport Harbor Nautical Museum, Newport Beach, CA*

Jorma Nyman: *Mischievous.* After building production yachts 30-, 33-, 40-, and 48-feet long, all to his own designs and all in his own yacht-building facility, Jorma Nyman turned in the 1990's to designing and building custom one-offs, most notably this 66-foot IMS racer created for an American sailor who since has garnered much silver with her. *Photo courtesy Jack A. Somer*

the 1890's, including his largest yacht, the 78-ton *Allona*, designed in 1899. Notable were the cruisers *La Gitana* in 1894, *Ariadne* in 1895, *Alca* in 1896, and *Esperanza* in 1897. As the lottery boat for KSSS (Royal Swedish Yacht Club) in 1905, Nygren designed the cruiser *Måsen*.

When the Skerry Cruiser Rule was established in 1908, Nygren began to design for the 30- to 75-Square-Meter classes, among them *Kullan*, winner of an Olympic gold medal in 1920.

To the International Rule Nygren designed eleven 6-Meters as well as some 7-Meters. He designed *Aloha*, Sweden's 6-Meter yacht for the Olympic Games in 1924.

—Bent Aarre with Ulf Lycke

JORMA OLAVI NYMAN

Born January 2, 1940 · Finland

Jorma Nyman was born in Ilmajoki, Finland, where his mother, along with so many other pregnant women, had been sent to escape the bombing of Helsinki during the brutal Finno-Soviet Winter War of 1939–40. In the chaotic aftermath of World War II, Nyman dropped out of school and began messing around with boats. While still in his teens, he bought a small, rotten, wooden sailboat and rebuilt it plank by plank, getting it sailing within a year. As he says, "This was a turning point in my life, leading to

my building wooden boats as a serious hobby."

It remained a hobby while Nyman used his innate artistic and technical gifts to rise swiftly through the ranks of a Finnish advertising agency, becoming an art director in his mid-twenties. With his financial life secure, Nyman taught himself yacht design in his spare time. He then built five mahogany-and-teak sailboats between 30 and 35 feet long, three to his own designs. The boats elicited admiration from others, and as Nyman puts it, "People were willing to pay good money for my boats. So I went into the boatbuilding business."

Nyman set up shop in a rented barn outside Helsinki in the late 1970's and built ten fiberglass sailboats up to 40 feet long to his design, still in his spare time. This was a daring move for a novice, particularly in the homeland of Baltics and Swans. The yachts sold easily. Soon he was able to quit his job and build new facilities in Mantsala, north of Helsinki, introducing a brand he called Jon Yachts (based on his initials). There Nyman designed and built production sailboats 30 and 33 feet long that combined rare architectural beauty with uncompromised seaworthiness.

Hiring skilled workers—many whose families originated in Karelia, the region taken by the U.S.S.R. in the Winter War—Nyman oversaw and worked with them to construct solid vessels of highly refined quality; he also built

some Jon 30's and 33's as incomplete boats, for the do-it-yourself crowd.

In the early 1980's Nyman saw the need to strengthen his company's image and to produce more customized yachts. He sold the rights to the 30 and 33 and established a relationship with an American agent. He also added *meri* (the Finnish word for "sea") to his brand name, making it "Jonmeri."

Nyman displayed his new 40-foot, two-cockpit cruiser/racer at American boat shows, and she served to place Jonmeri firmly on the U.S. map, aided by a favorable exchange rate. The Jonmeri 40 was followed in the late 1980's by the Jonmeri 48, a bluewater cruiser with powerful lines and plush accommodations. In 1988 Nyman sold Jonmeri, but later bought it back. By 1995, when he finally sold the name and facilities, Nyman had built some two hundred fiberglass sailing yachts, plus a few one-offs, all to his design. In the late 1990's he drew plans for a 66-foot IMS racer/cruiser for an American client. It was built of high-tech materials at his old facility. He next designed a 57-foot luxury sailing cruiser.

Though an extremely modest man, Jorma Nyman attributes his success first to an understanding of materials and working methods and second to his insight into a client's desires. Nyman now designs independently and is based in Helsinki.

—Jack A. Somer

O

KURT A. H. OEHLMANN

1909–May 1997 · Germany

As the designer of some twelve hundred sailing craft, more than five hundred engine-powered small ships and yachts, and several hundred merchant ships, barges, tug boats, fishing vessels, and special-purpose craft, Kurt Oehlmann ranks up with the better-known Max Oertz, Henry Rasmussen, and Adolf Harms in the history of German naval architecture. In addition, he was one of the first of his profession in Germany to break new ground by using materials such as concrete, aluminum, and a variety of polyester systems.

Born in Hamburg, Oehlmann gained his first experience at a local shipyard, and then attended courses in shipbuilding at Lubeckertor College in Hamburg. A talented and hard-working student, Oehlmann graduated with honors in 1929. Although the Great Depression frustrated his early efforts to publish designs, during that period he developed a number of ideas that were to be realized in his later work.

In 1936, after several years working in shipyards and in a number of design offices, Oehlmann went to work at Abeking and Rasmussen, probably the most highly regarded yard in Germany prior to World War II. After the war, however, almost no one was able to order pleasure craft, and Oehlmann, by then the father of five children, performed any job that might earn a living.

As early as 1948, though, American customers began to order fine steel and wooden yachts from German yards, and opportunities for both designers and builders began to improve, allowing Oehlmann to return to his chosen profession. Soon he was employed at the Schlichting Yard in Travemunde, where he met Olin and Rod Stephens as well as Philip L. Rhodes.

In 1954 Oehlmann opened his own design office in Travemunde, where he could finally realize his own ideas. Oehlmann's designs ranged from a 15-foot dinghy up to a 350-foot cruise liner. He patented numerous details still used today, and his articles and technological essays appeared in *Yachting World, Boating, Yacht,* and other magazines published around the world.

At age seventy Oehlmann handed over his design office to his oldest son, Herwarth Oehlmann. He then spent another twenty years at the water's edge, sailing the Baltic Sea and gardening, even as he increased his body of work by another two hundred designs. —Michael D. Konig

Kurt Oehlmann: *Islander.* The 39-foot 4-inch yawl *Islander,* designed in 1956, shows the straightforward, balanced design and seaworthy characteristics for which Oehlmann's work was known. She won the 1963 Transpac Race, beating thirty-two other boats, many of them famous ocean racers. *Reproduced from* The Rudder

MAX OERTZ

April 20, 1871–November 24, 1929 · Germany

Max Oertz was born in the year in which the last German states finally united under Prussia to form modern Germany. While he was growing up, the newly formed state also grew into the industrial leader of Europe; when he reached young manhood, his country, urged on by Kaiser Wilhelm II, looked to establish itself as a great cultural power. One of Kaiser Wilhelm II's chief interests was yachting, and accordingly, one of his chief ambitions was to develop a German yachting tradition that might rival that of his uncle, King Edward VII of England. His chose Max Oertz to be his standard bearer.

The son of a sea captain, Oertz was born in Neustadt on the Baltic Sea. He was orphaned while still young and taken by foster parents to live in Berlin. Although the city lies inland, it does have several lakes used for recreational boating, and here the young Oertz nurtured his interest in boats. At age fifteen he designed and built for himself a 5-meter fin-keeler of soldered zinc. Shortly afterward he went to Berlin University, aiming to become a naval architect.

Oertz studied shipbuilding and yacht design, supplementing the university courses with his own studies where the curriculum fell short. Yacht designers of the time worked in a manner Oertz thought amateurish—a combination of experience, intuition, and aesthetics.

A strong academic and scientific influence on his work made Oertz something of a pioneer in yacht design, though few immediately followed his example. Wisely, he combined his theoretical penchant with a solid regimen of practical experience. Following his stay at the university, he spent several years working as an apprentice and then as an employee at shipyards in Bremen. Afterward he traveled to Sweden and Saint Petersburg in Russia to continue his education as an observer.

Max Oertz: *Pesa* (opposite). *Pesa* is the sixteenth and last 10-Meter designed and built by Oertz in the period from 1906 to 1911. She is a sistership to *Feinsliebschen VII* (1910). A winner in various pre–World War I regattas, she was restored in 1995–96 and continues her winning ways in competition. © *Benjamin Mendlowitz*

Max Oertz: *Meteor V*. The 47.61-meter LOA schooner-yacht *Meteor V* of 1914 was designed for Kaiser Wilhelm II and built of steel at the Krupp family's Germania-Werft in Kiel. The outbreak of World War I prevented wider competition by the yacht and her crew, and after her passage through a series of owners, *Meteor V*'s status and whereabouts have been unknown since 1959. *Drawing courtesy Gerard Dijkstra*

At the end of the nineteenth century, prize competitions for sailing yachts were fashionable among yachting nations, and Germany now aspired to be included. In that spirit, Kaiser Wilhelm II offered the "Hohenzollernpreis," to be awarded to the best sailing yacht entirely designed and built in Germany. Oertz, only twenty-three years old, submitted an innovative design specifying aluminum construction, something hitherto untried in Germany. He named the boat *Exempla Trahunt* (May She Be an Example). The design did not win the prize, but when she was built and renamed *Luna*, her marked success brought Oertz to sudden prominence.

In 1896, just two years later, he founded his own shipyard. The Max Oertz Bootswerft in the port of Hamburg quickly gained a national and an international reputation. As early as 1899, he received an order for a 22-foot one-design fleet from the Royal Copenhagen Yacht Club. In 1906, his 10-Meter class yacht *Felca* challenged for and won the Coupe de France.

Particularly important to the growth of Oertz's international reputation were his boats in the Sonderklasse (Sonder class), especially the very successful *Angela* and the various *Wannsee*s. The Sonderklasse was a German open-class development rule that produced deep-keeled scows with sail area limited to 550 square feet.

At Kiel Week, which under Kaiser Wilhelm II's patronage had developed into a premiere showcase for German yachting, there developed an annual challenge series between Germany and the United States that attracted spectators and participants from all over Europe and the United States. Each nation fielded a team of three boats chosen by elimination trials. The ardent participation of Crown Prince Wilhelm and his brother, Prince Henry, lent to this event particular interest and glamour. In 1909, when all three German entries were Max Oertz–designed boats, *Yachting* magazine called him "the only German designer of international repute."

With the launching of *Germania* in 1908, Oertz approached the apex of his career. The 150-foot steel schooner was built for the German steel magnate Dr. Gustav Krupp von Bohlen und Halbach under the motto "German from Keel to Flagpole." Prior to *Germania*, general wisdom said that boats of such splendor and pretension could only be created in countries with long traditions in yachting. Oertz's *Germania* proved them wrong. Her design was entirely original, and her elegance and speed under sail conceded nothing to her foreign competitors. Kaiser Wilhelm, who had campaigned three previous yachts (the G. L. Watson–designed *Meteor I* and *II,* and the A. Cary Smith–designed *Meteor III*), all foreign designed and crewed, was impressed by *Germania*. In 1909 the Kaiser ordered *Meteor IV* from Oertz. She was thus the first of the royal yachts to be designed, built, and sailed in Germany. The Kaiser was so pleased with the result that he returned in 1914 with orders for *Meteor V*. However, this last of the *Meteor* series, which Oertz called his favorite yacht, was never able to prove her capabilities, for World War I intervened and ended an era.

After the war Oertz continued to work in spite of the failing German economy. For the most part he built fishing boats, though there were a few yachts, among them the 125-foot, teak-hulled schooner *Aello* and the 54-foot *Andromeda*, both still active. Altogether, the Max Oertz Bootswerft produced 450 boats of all types, from dinghies, cruisers, and IYRU racers to splendid luxurious yachts.

Max Oertz died in 1929. His Max Oertz Bootswerft counts as the birthplace of German yacht design, and the Akademischer Segler-Verein annually awards the Max Oertz Preis in a regatta for students in the Berlin area, in his honor. —Kristin Lammerting

KATSUNORI OHASHI

Born 1948 · Japan

Having started sailing when he joined the Yacht Club at Nagoya University, Katsunori Ohashi has participated not only in one-design races but also in offshore races, under the influence of his senior colleagues in the Chita Racing Group.

After graduating from Nagoya University, Ohashi worked as an apprentice at the Yokoyama Naval Architecture Office. He worked for the E. G. van de Stadt office in the Netherlands from 1975 to 1977 and established its Japanese branch when he came home. To date, he has designed fifty-six racing and cruising yachts of good performance. The 52-foot sloop *Bengal II*, which Ohashi designed in 1987, participated in the inaugural Melbourne-Osaka Doublehanded Yacht Race and has raced in Japan with a good record. His latest designs include a 68-foot

Katsunori Ohashi: *Bengal II*. The Ohashi 52-foot *Bengal II* is still active and a good example of a sound offshore racer not affected by any rating rule. She entered the Melbourne-Osaka Doublehanded Yacht Race three times and the Transpac Race twice as well as many other East Asia races. *Drawing courtesy Kenosuke Hayashi*

aluminum cruiser for an Australian owner and a 26-foot cruiser for handicapped sailors.

Ohashi served the Nippon Ocean Racing Club (NORC) as the chairman of the Measurement Committee and the Japan Sailing Association (JSAF) as a member of the Technical Committee. —Kennosuke Hayashi

EINAR OHLSSON

Born 1918 · Sweden

In Sweden they always refer to "the Ohlsson Brothers." Einar, the designer, and Karl Erik, the builder, worked as a team all their lives. They were born north of Gothenburg on the island of Orust, famous for its boatbuilders.

They settled in Gothenburg in 1934. Einar was educated as a ship engineer at Gothenburg's Technical Institute, and first became an engineer at Gotaverken and later at the Swedish State's Ship Trial Institute. In 1951, Einar and Karl Erik established their own design firm, Bröderna Ohlsson.

Starting in 1944, Einar began to win local design competitions, but it was while designing according to the International 5.5-Meter class rule that his reputation began to spread beyond Sweden. Over the years, he designed forty 5.5-Meters for over fifteen countries. The boats won gold, silver, and bronze medals in four Olympics and also gold cups four times. The brothers performed tank tests but also used the old idea of starting with a half model of every boat in order to look at the lines.

In the 1960's the Ohlsson name became well known in the United States, as Einar began to design seagoing yachts such as the Ohlsson 35 (lengthened to 36 feet), 38, and 41, and the one-off aluminum yacht Ohlsson 45. When the 38-footer debuted, the first boat won its class in the Bermuda Race. Einar Ohlsson said in 1999 that he liked the 38 best of all the production boats he designed. He also designed smaller production family boats for the northern European market.

The Ohlsson brothers stopped their practice in 1975. —Bent Aarre

Einar Ohlsson: *Saturn*. Ohlsson designed a number of semiproduction yachts for import to the United States. Many were of wooden construction; even the fiberglass boats, like *Saturn*, featured extensive wooden trim. The boats were fast and contemporary in design, and many continue to race successfully in classic yacht regattas. © *Kai Greiser*

GILLES OLLIER

Born February 14, 1948 · France

When his suburban Parisian family decided to register the fourteen-year-old Gilles Ollier in the sailing school near their summer home in Brittany, it was a happy revelation for him. Soon he was a sailing instructor. After completing his secondary schooling, he joined the Ecole Spéciale d'Architecture of Paris, after which he was taken on by the Groupe Finot design firm. He then performed his national service in the Ecole Nationale de Voile (National Sailing School) with such soon-to-be famous skippers as Philippe Poupon, Philippe Facques, Loïc Caradec, and Gilles Le Baud.

When Ollier returned from his service at the Ecole Nationale in 1976, he was determined to strike out on his own. He soon designed a pair of production boats, the Kelt 7.50 and Kelt 8.00. He then designed the 38-foot *Salamandre* for the 1978 Route du Rhum, where she performed honorably. Not only did this yacht become the basis of a series, but also Ollier designed for the same client a 17-meter (56-foot) proa named *Funambule* (later *Sudinox* and then *Lestra Sport*).

This project made Ollier aware that he needed to master the most advanced building techniques in order to design extreme racers.

Thus, for his next flat-out racing project, a 15-meter (49-foot) catamaran named *Jet Services*, Ollier set up the Multiplast yard in Vannes in the Brittany region. He settled on a new concept: having two cigar-shaped hulls connected only by two cylindrical beams reinforced with stays, and a swiveling mast, the whole resembling a giant Class C cat. *Jet Services* won her class in the 1982 La Rochelle to New Orleans Race, despite having to make an emergency stop.

Jet Services perfectly reflected her designer's minimalist philosophy, in which only what is essential is preserved, and optional items, such as a nacelle between the hulls or cabin trunks, are removed. Ollier believes that the problem of creating speed on the water is simple to understand, depending primarily on the ratio of power to weight. This puts a premium on the exploitation of technological advancements. Sandwich construction and carbon fiber have revolutionized multihull design, so that, as French yachtsman Olivier de Kersauson points out, "only boats have doubled their speed in ten years." On *Jet Services*, only the arms connecting the hull were made of carbon fiber. On the Guy Ribadeau Dumas–designed *Crédit Agricole* in 1983, virtually the whole boat was carbon fiber, and was said to fairly leap out of the water.

Jet Services herself went on to break further records, but after 1987, *Jet Services V* became the boat to beat. From 1990 to 2001, she held the Atlantic crossing record of 6 days, 13 hours, and 3 minutes. In 1993, having been lengthened and renamed *Commodore Explorer*, she won the first Jules Verne Trophy by sailing around the world in 79 days, 6 hours, and 15 minutes, and then in 1998, renamed *Explorer*, she established a Pacific crossing record of 14 days, 17 hours, and 22 minutes.

For The Race, the 25,000-plus-mile, nonstop, round-the-world race first held in 2000, Ollier designed three 110-foot sisterships: *Club Med*, *Innovation Explorer*, and *Team Adventure*. *Club Med* came in first, in 62 days, 6 hours, 56 minutes, and 33 seconds, a record still held as this is written in 2003. She was followed by *Innovation Explorer* and *Team Adventure*. *Orange* (ex-*Innovation Explorer*) went on to win the Jules Verne Trophy in 2002, and *Maiden II* (ex-*Club Med*) for the third time beat her own record for distance sailed in twenty-four hours, with 694 miles.

For the 2000 America's Cup, Ollier and his team designed the French challenger *6e Sens* and for the 2002–03 challenge, *Le Défi Areva*. Presently their design for a 120-foot catamaran, the

Gilles Ollier: *Club Med. Club Med* won The Race in 2000–01 (nonstop around the world) in 62 days, 6 hours, 56 minutes, and 33 seconds. Traveling at speeds exceeding 40 knots, she knocked more than nine days off the previous time for a nonstop circumnavigation. She is the sistership of *Innovation Explorer* and *Team Adventure*. © Onne van der Wal

OLLIER

seventh catamaran for Class G, is under construction and expected to participate in The Race in 2004.

Giles Ollier's practice and boatyard are located in Vannes, France. —François Chevalier.

LUIGI ONETO

1842–1923 · Italy

An amateur designer, builder, and yachtsman who from 1866 to 1904 alternated between his nautical career and his soap factory, Luigi Oneto was the first Italian to challenge the supremacy of French and English yacht building in the 1860's. His part-time nautical undertaking earned him the nickname "L'inghreise," meaning "the Englishman" in the Genovese dialect, since like the English, he was building sailboats.

Oneto designed and built his own first boat, a skiff named *Catalano*, in 1866. The English consul in Genoa showed early confidence in Oneto and in 1870 commissioned him to build the cutter *Black Tulip*. Among the Oneto-designed boats that raced in Genoa and on the Riviera was the 25.5-meter schooner *Atalanta*, built in 1876. It was on *Atalanta*, during the races at Nice in March of 1879, that the Regio Yacht Club Italiano, now the Yacht Club Italiano of Genoa, was founded.

A famous cruising boat of Oneto's design was the *Corsaro*, a 25.5-meter yawl built in 1882 by Agostino Briasco in which Captain Enrico Alberto d'Albertis in 1893 retraced the voyage of Christopher Columbus, the Genovese navigator, to the Americas.

Other major yachts were *Sally*, a Ten-Tonner built in 1902 that represented Italy in the Coupe de France in 1904; *Rigoletto*, a 10.85-meter cutter built in 1882; *Fieramosca*, a 14.84-meter yawl built in 1885; *Cristoforo Colombo*, a 14.7-meter cutter built in 1892; and *Los Dos*, his last project, an 8.61-meter cutter built in 1904.

Cristoforo Colombo was the first boat to be designed and built in Italy under the English tonnage formula of Dixon Kemp, adopted by the Royal Italian Yacht Club in 1892. Luigi Oneto designed approximately thirty racing and cruising vessels. —Franco Belloni

IAIN OUGHTRED

Born 1939 · Australia/England

Among those designers whose work combines both modern and traditional elements, one of the best is Iain Oughtred. One of a small number of designers and builders dedicated to the revival of interest in wooden boats in England,

Luigi Oneto: Sally. Little is known of the sloop *Sally*, but she seems like an attractive yacht, particularly in the forward overhang, which has a full and buoyant shape, a strong rise to the sheer, and a pronounced knuckle in the profile. *Photo courtesy Franco Belloni*

Oughtred is breathing life into the field by creating a broad range of designs that are emotionally appealing without being tied down to strictly traditional types, and practical without the coldness and lack of character typical of many modern designs. He frequently combines elements from diverse traditional craft of British, American, and Scandinavian origin in new combinations.

Oughtred is best known for a series of designs appearing in *WoodenBoat* magazine, such as the little cruising sloop *Gray Seal*, and a number of smaller rowing and sailing craft of modern wood construction, such as the Acorn skiffs. Oughtred's designs feature strong sheers and bow and stern profiles, along with cabin trunks that contribute to each design's character in an active and harmonious way, instead of being treated as a hopefully invis-

ible box. Oughtred has even managed to design multihulls with a traditional air about them, making them look like the product of a long-established European maritime culture instead of an engineer's solution to a technical problem.

Born in Australia, Oughtred grew up in Melbourne and Sydney and began sailing high-performance racing dinghies as a teenager. He dropped out of high school in his last year, and is self-educated as a designer.

As a young man, Oughtred was influenced by the designs and writing of L. Francis Herreshoff. His first job was building architectural models, after which he built boats. He specialized in the National Gwen 12-class in which he also raced, at one point winning the national championship. Oughtred emigrated to England in 1964. In his late thirties, he began his current career as a yacht designer, and is currently working in London. Iain Oughtred is the author of *Wooden Boatbuilding in Britain: A Guide to Designers, Builders, and Suppliers*, published by Nautical Books.

—Daniel B. MacNaughton

GEORGE OWEN

May 11, 1871–April 21, 1959 · United States

George Owen was one of the most consistently successful designers of racing sailboats of his time, working largely in the open classes of the Universal Rule handicapping system. While his important work in developing handicapping and scantlings rules was ultimately superceded by that of his friendly rival Nathanael Herreshoff, he was known for his skill with the interpretation of the rating rules and for innovative and well-engineered construction. In his later career he became a professor of naval architecture at MIT, where he helped to develop the curriculum and taught a number of students who went on to become some of the United States' best-known designers.

Owen was born in Cambridge, Massachusetts. He later lived in Providence, Rhode Island, where he attended high school and began his lifelong involvement with racing in boats of all sizes. He attended MIT, studying mechanical engineering and naval architecture, and graduated in 1894.

Following some years of employment in non-marine-related mechanical engineering, he went to work in 1898 at the Herreshoff Manufacturing Company in Bristol, Rhode Island. He worked there for three years as a draftsman and engineer, contributing to several of the yard's most notable large yachts, including the cup defender *Columbia* and cup challenger *Constitution*.

In 1901 Owen moved to Hamilton, Ontario, where he worked as a mechanical engineer and turned out yacht designs in his spare time, when he was not racing on Lake Ontario. His first racing design to be built was *Whirl*, a 20-Rater that he campaigned with great success. She was followed by other successful "Rater" types, along with *Little Rhody*, a successful Universal Rule ocean racer, and many other small boats of both sail and power.

Owen moved to Winthrop, Massachusetts, in 1904 and began a period of intense productivity, becoming a full-time yacht designer in 1908. During this period he designed numerous Universal Rule racing boats for the M, N, R, P, and Q Classes, which were very successful and served to establish him as one of the most prominent designers of the time. He wrote a scantlings rule for wooden yachts that

Iain Oughtred: *Gray Seal*. *Gray Seal*, a 22-foot, trailerable (in the centerboard version shown) gunter-rigged sloop, blends her strong sheer, dramatic end profiles, and great buoyancy into a harmonious whole that is difficult to achieve in such a small cruiser. *Drawing courtesy WoodenBoat Publications*

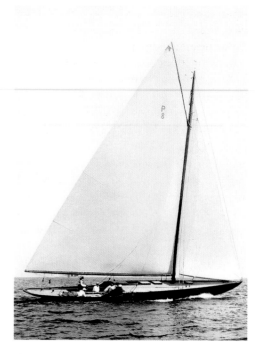

George Owen: *Britomart*. Hodgdon Brothers in Maine built *Britomart*, a 53-foot 9-inch LOD P-Class Universal Rule sloop in 1914. Note her unusual raised-deck configuration. She's moving along well with little fuss either on deck or in the water. *Photograph by Nathaniel Stebbins. Courtesy the Society for the Preservation of New England Antiquities*

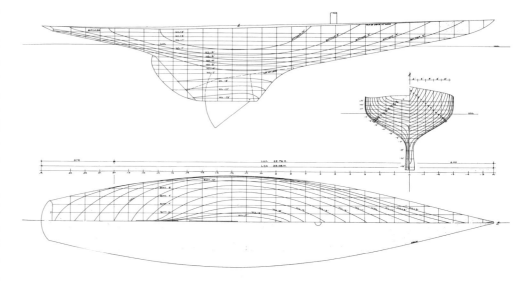

George Owen: *Defiance*. Owen designed the 75-foot LWL sloop *Defiance* in 1914 as an America's Cup contender. Of wood and steel construction, she was lighter and smoother than her rivals and had an improved rig, but mismanagement and ill-advised modifications slowed her down. Modern velocity prediction programs say she should have won. © *Chevalier & Taglang*

was widely used for over twenty years until it was displaced in 1928 by the popular Herreshoff scantlings rule.

As is often the case with yacht designers who are also engineers, much of Owen's success was due to his ability to create strong, rigid hulls that were also very light. This enabled a higher percentage of a boat's overall weight to be concentrated in the ballast, providing a greater ability to carry sail.

In 1913, Owen received a commission to design *Defiance*, a 75-foot LWL sloop that would vie for the right to defend the America's Cup against Sir Thomas Lipton's *Shamrock IV*. She featured a radical rig of a type that had proved successful in Owen's smaller designs: a high-aspect-ratio gaff sloop with a single jib on a short bowsprit, and a main boom that only slightly overhung the transom.

Unlike the other Cup boats of that year, which had all-metal hulls, *Defiance* was double planked in wood, over steel frames and other structural members. As a result her hull was lighter and smoother than her competitors'. Unfortunately her owners did not allow Owen to tune or sail *Defiance*, her rig was twice reduced in size against his objections, and little was done to prepare her for her early racing trials. As a result, while her performance was at times excellent, it was at other times poor, and she was soon withdrawn from racing as the owners attempted to fix the blame on her designer. *Defiance* was Owen's primary disappointment in a long and otherwise successful career.

Recently *Defiance* and her competitors *Resolute* (designed by Nathanael Herreshoff), *Vanitie* (by William Gardner), and *Shamrock IV* (by Charles E. Nicholson) were put through MIT's computerized velocity prediction program, an advanced simulator used to evaluate the performance of yachts under various conditions of wind, course, and sail combinations. With her original rig, *Defiance* was the clear-cut winner by significant margins, under almost all conditions, thus vindicating George Owen's design rather nicely, if unfortunately rather late.

Owen came to MIT in 1915 and taught Wendell Calkins, Spaulding Dunbar, Robert Henry Jr., Bill McNary, Philip L. Rhodes, Henry Scheel, and Winthrop Warner, among others. He also helped to make sailing a college sport at MIT and designed the famous MIT Tech dinghy, first for wood and then, in 1955, for fiberglass construction. He retired from MIT in 1941, but continued to design boats and sail until his death in 1959.

The George Owen Collection of drawings and photographs is at Hart Nautical Collections, MIT Museum, Cambridge, MA.
—Daniel B. MacNaughton

NORMAN G. OWENS

Born May 9, 1912 · United States

The popular, affordable boats of the Owens Yacht Company were designed by Norman Owens, a man with no formal training in naval architecture. He may best be remembered for the Owens cutter, a successful postwar racing class, but most of his work was in the design of production powerboats.

The Owens firm was started by the designer's father, Charles C. Owens, who died in 1933. Norman Owens restarted the business with his brothers Charles J., who handled sales and advertising, and John B., who served as business manager. Having learned the principles of yacht design from his father, Norman took on the roles of designer, chief engineer, and production manager.

In 1936 the brothers moved the company from Annapolis, Maryland, to Baltimore in search of more space and a larger workforce. Owens first specialized in affordable inboard motor cruisers, exhibiting a 30-foot sedan cruiser at the 1937 New York Boat Show. The sedan turned out to be Owens's most popular prewar design, with its round bottom, wide cabin, rear cockpit, and stylized rounded windows and coamings.

During World War II, Owens turned his company's efforts toward wartime production, building more than fifteen hundred 36-foot landing craft, but quickly switched back to inboard cruisers when peace came. In 1946 Owens designed the 40-foot 6-inch Owens cutter, which became one of the most successful racing cruiser designs to emerge from the Chesapeake Bay region. The cutter had graceful overhangs at bow and stern and comparatively high freeboard.

Owens devised a semi-assembly-line method to build the cutter, deck-down instead of keel-down, but customizing cabin arrangements proved costly. After having the first five built by M. M. Davis in Solomons, Maryland, Owens built forty-two cutters. Although Owens cutters won races on the Chesapeake, the Great Lakes, in California, and in New England, they lost money for the company, and the design was sold to the Hinckley Company in 1949. Hinckley built a few in wood with increased ballast and sail area before converting the cutter to fiberglass as the Hinckley 41, with a modified keel, rudder, and sheer. Owens's design reappeared in 1970 as the Allied 39, twenty-four years after the Owens cutter was introduced, this time adding a skeg with an attached rudder.

Owens continued to design power cruisers and runabouts for the family company, briefly using famed industrial designer Raymond Loewy to add styling to the cabins in the mid-1950's. In 1955 he adapted a V-8 Chevrolet engine for use in the company's boats, selecting parts for the marine application, which sold under the Owens Flagship brand.

The brothers sold the company, which had become the second largest boat manufacturer in the world, to the Brunswick Corporation in 1960. Owens retired from the company in 1963 but kept active in boat design from his Kemah, Texas, home. He designed and raced five 5.5-meter boats, which he had built in European yards from 1962 to 1988. He also designed a fiberglass racing cruiser, the Nordstar 25, which he produced in Cambridge, Maryland, though only about ten were built. Although the Owens Yacht Company is long gone, many of Owens's practical motor cruisers are still in use, and a few of his Owens cutters are still sailing.

—Peter Lesher

Norman Owens. This Owens 30-foot sedan cruiser was designed in 1936. It was a model that boosted the reputation of the Owens Yacht Company of Baltimore, Maryland. *Photo by Emery A. Swartz, courtesy Chesapeake Bay Maritime Museum, Saint Michaels, MD*

CHARLES W. "CHUCK" PAINE

Born September 25, 1944 · United States

By combining a thorough understanding of the virtues of modern boat types with sensitivity to tradition, Chuck Paine has become one of the most successful designers of his generation. Versatility is clearly one of his virtues, as his practice has specialized in the design of classic yachts as well as high-speed offshore sailing yachts and a growing line of custom and production powerboats.

Paine achieved early recognition in 1975 with his design for the Frances 26, a 26-foot flush-decked, double-ended sloop. She is what is becoming known as a modern classic, being consistent with the look and feel of older designs but not imitative of them. The term *classic* is not misapplied here, for Frances, with her moderate displacement, modern construction and rig, outboard rudder, and flush deck, reflects a concept that seems to have been missing until her advent.

Much of Paine's work to date has been in a similar vein. His boats are essentially modern in their details but classic in their general themes. Moderation is always evident, no doubt partly because most of the boats are production-built and must appeal to a broad customer base, but also because it would appear that moderation itself and a certain overall wholesomeness are important to the designer.

Paine was born in Long Beach, California, and grew up in Jamestown, Rhode Island. After graduating from Brown University in 1966 with a degree in mechanical engineering, Paine worked for a Boston firm doing computer analysis of navy ship designs. Finding this work unsatisfying, he joined the Peace Corps, teaching in Iran for two years. In 1971 he went to work in the office of designer Dick Carter, where he performed computer work, contributing to a series of very successful racing designs.

In recent years Chuck Paine has earned recognition for a series of highly regarded

Chuck Paine: *Dawnbreaker. Dawnbreaker*, a Kanter 64, working to weather in a moderate breeze and still carrying her reacher, shows the great stiffness that Paine worked into the design. A modern underbody and rig combine with a classic look. *Photo courtesy Chuck Paine*

Chuck Paine: Diverse 75. The Diverse 75 seems smaller and more handy than her 73-foot 6-inch LOA and 80-ton displacement would suggest. Built for comfortable offshore cruising at 18 knots, she has a raised pilothouse, wide side-decks, and generous afterdeck. *Drawing courtesy Chuck Paine*

cruising sailboats drawn for Morris Yachts, combining modern underbodies and contemporary rigs and construction with an overall aesthetic reminiscent of yachts from the CCA rating rule era. As well as many custom designs, Paine has contributed to offshore production cruisers for Cabo Rico, Bowman, Acadia, and others. Some designs, such as the Rockport 30, his interpretation of the gaff-rigged English Falmouth Quay Punt type, lean further toward traditional detailing.

Also receiving a great deal of attention are his range of powerboat designs, which reinterpret older speedboat, picnic launch, and lobsterboat-style cruiser themes in the light of newer power plants, construction techniques, and customer demands. Designs include the Kanter pilothouse motoryachts, the Liberty motoryachts, the Acadia motoryachts, and the Gulf motoryachts.

Paine opened his own office in 1974 and has continued to employ computer programs, some of which he developed himself, as part of his own design work. He practices in Camden, Maine.

—Daniel B. MacNaughton

FRANK CABOT PAINE

July 9, 1890–October 28, 1952 · United States

Few yacht designers have manipulated the Universal and International rating rules to greater advantage than Frank Paine. Although he most likely considered himself a sailor first and a designer second, his body of work produced many very successful racing yachts. Paine is best remembered for designing the J-Class *Yankee* (1929), a contender to defend the America's Cup in 1930; *Highland Light* (1931), long-time holder of the Bermuda Race record; and his 1939 *Gypsy*, a development of his Marblehead 36. Paine's earlier, more prolific work was in the

6- and 8-Meter classes and the Q and R Classes.

Lacking formal training, Paine absorbed yacht design during the year he and L. Francis Herreshoff lived and studied with W. Starling Burgess, and through his own intense yacht racing experience. By his early teens Paine was winning races in the one-design Cataumet Pups designed by Burgess. In 1912 Paine joined Burgess's airplane business in Marblehead, Massachusetts.

The post–World War I years were an important time for yacht design, when the Universal and International Rules had stabilized

Frank Paine: Yankee. Best known for her America's Cup campaigns, *Yankee* (here in 1934) was the only American J-Class yacht to see British waters, successfully competing in the 1935 Big Class series with a modified rig and deck layout. © *Peabody Essex Museum, Salem, MA*

and marconi rigs were introduced. It was natural for a team of aircraft pioneers to exploit this new technology.

In 1921, they founded the firm of Burgess and Paine. L. Francis Herreshoff and Norman L. Skene were draftsmen. Later it became Burgess, Swasey and Paine with the addition of A. Loring Swasey in 1923. The partnership would last until 1925.

Their offices were a meeting place for New England's great yacht designers. Paine mentored C. Raymond Hunt and contributed to his design of the International 110 in the early years

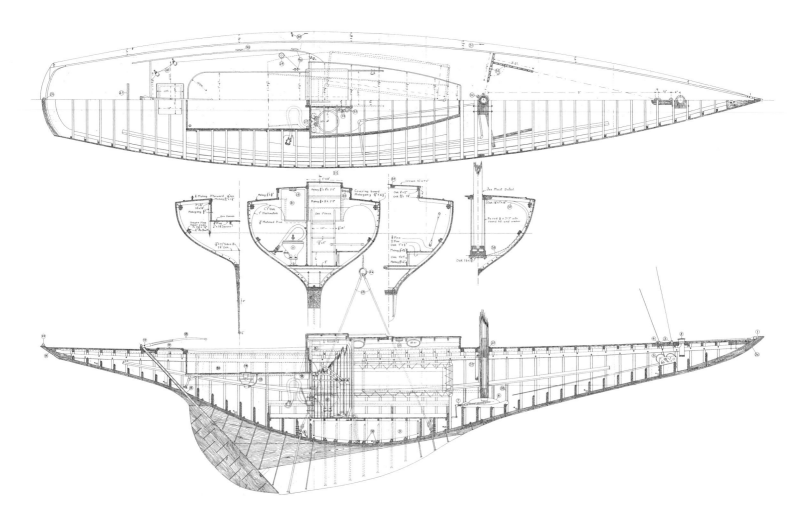

Frank Paine: *Gypsy.* Paine's construction drawing for the R-Class *Gypsy* illustrates several interesting innovations. He employed the drafting talents of L. Francis Herreshoff. *Drawing courtesy Hart Nautical Collections, MIT Museum, Cambridge, MA*

of light-displacement hulls. Francis W. Belknap, Norman L. Skene, and Charles MacGregor also participated in this ongoing exchange of ideas, and the fledgling Concordia Company resided a few doors down the hall.

Paine was associated with the firm of Paine, Belknap and Skene from 1925 to 1932; with the departure of Skene, the firm of Belknap and Paine was in practice from 1932 to 1937. Thereafter, Paine had an independent design office.

As was the pattern throughout his career, Paine designed his first 6-Meter and R-Class boats for himself. The success of these boats while skippered by Paine led to commissions from his racing competitors—wealthy sailors from the Boston area, especially Marblehead's Eastern Yacht Club. During the 1920's Paine also designed a number of successful Q-Class and 8-Meter yachts.

Paine understood and employed actual and sailing waterline length to increase speed, as illustrated by his R-Class *Gypsy* of 1923. At a time when the average waterline length for this class was 23 feet, *Gypsy's* was 25 feet 3 inches. Other successful racing yachts in the 1920's included his Q-Class *Robin,* four-time winner of the Puritan Cup, the annual regatta at Marble-

head's Eastern Yacht Club, and his 8-Meter *Gypsy,* selected in 1929 to defend the Seawanhaka Cup, an international match-race challenge cup for small yachts.

Two of Paine's most recognized vessels, *Yankee* and *Gertrude L Thebaud,* were designed in 1929. The J-Class *Yankee* competed to defend the America's Cup in 1930. *Thebaud* was the last American fishing schooner to vie for the International Fishermen's Cup, an international challenge series for fishing vessels that worked the Grand Banks. Neither vessel achieved its goal that year, although a redesigned *Yankee* nearly won the trials in 1934 and *Thebaud* was the only vessel ever to win a race against her Canadian rival, *Bluenose.* These boats marked a departure for Paine from club to ocean racing designs, and a wider recognition of his talents.

In 1930 Paine acquired a controlling interest in the yacht building concern of the George F. Lawley Corporation, where he served as president until the conclusion of World War II. He continued to maintain a design office, with frequent changes in personnel.

The 50-foot LWL cutter *Highland Light* was designed in 1931. Built to the CCA Rule, her short ends were an aesthetic departure for

Paine. In the final design, an elaborate twin-sparred boomkin replaced the long stern and counter transom of the original sketches, allowing her to carry more than 2,800 square feet of sail. Paine crewed aboard *Highland Light* in 1931–32 and chartered her for the 1932 Bermuda Race. Under Paine's command she set an elapsed time record of 71 hours, 35 minutes, and 43 seconds, which held for twenty-four years.

Paine's redesign of *Yankee* for the 1934 America's Cup campaign saw a much-improved performance. In addition to her updated rig, her bow was sharpened and slightly hollowed. *Yankee* nevertheless lost the trials to *Rainbow* by 1 second. At the request of her skipper, Paine later joined the afterguard of *Rainbow* to oversee downwind sails. Paine brought with him *Yankee's* parachute spinnaker, which he is credited with developing. *Rainbow,* down by two races when Paine came aboard, did not lose another race in Cup competition.

In 1936 Paine designed the Marblehead 36, a one-design cutter, for members of the Eastern Yacht Club. Four boats were built to this 36-foot LWL design. Paine was always more concerned with the racing performance of his boats than with ease of operation. This was certainly the case with his last *Gypsy* of 1939—a flush-decked, double-ended, strip-planked development of the Marblehead 36. Crew members noted her unwieldy rig and dark and cavernous interior, yet she remained competitive into the 1960's.

Aesthetics were also secondary in Paine's designs, but the appearance of his boats did not suffer. His Universal Rule and International Rule designs followed conventional lines with long overhangs and sweet sheers. Some appeared high-sided due to the freeboard credit in these rules.

Paine also designed a few powerboats, but his pure racing boat designs and uncanny ability to extract their performance are the hallmarks of this designer and sailor.

Paine's designs are part of the Hart Nautical Collections, MIT Museum, Cambridge, MA.

—Jonathan E. Rice and Lindsley E. Hand

ALEXANDRE PARIS

ca. 1890–ca. 1961 · France

The 55-foot cutter *Jolie Brise*, one of the legends of European yachting, was designed by Alexandre Paris and built at Le Havre in 1913 by Albert Paumelle. After a short career as a pilot cutter and then as a workboat, she was taken to English waters by Evelyn George Martin in 1923. The legend was born with a superb victory in the first Fastnet Race in 1925, an exploit the cutter repeated in 1929 and 1930.

The son of one of Paumelle's partners, Alexandre Paris had spent much of his youth in the yards of Le Havre, where pilot-boats were frequently under construction. He apprenticed with the builder Emile Galodée. He was also inspired by the work of Colin Archer.

In 1912, Paris was entrusted with the job of designing the pilot-boat H6, *Jolie Brise*. The lines of this gaff-rigged cutter represented the ultimate development of the pilot-boat type, with a lengthened counter, sternpost raked to 45 degrees, great draft, beam a bit larger than usual, and a generalized roundness of shape. However, newer boats, such as the Olin Stephens–designed, marconi-rigged *Dorade*, winner of the 1931 Fastnet Race, were making gaff-rigged racers obsolete, and *Jolie Brise* had to wait many years to become competitive again.

Jolie Brise was acquired by the International Sailing Craft Association together with Dauntsey's School in England in 1977. Used primarily as a training ship, she participates in most Tall Ship races, winning several and becoming the overall winner in the 2000 Tall Ships race out of Southampton, England.   —Jacques Taglang

JAY PARIS

Born 1942 · United States

While Jay Paris has worked as a naval architect, oceanographer, mechanical engineer, writer, technical editor, and house designer, his primary focus has been yacht design and related subjects. His sailboats have evolved from the wineglass midship sections that were the norm when he worked at Sparkman and Stephens in the mid-1960's to hull forms (blended bodies in modern aerospace parlance) with markedly sharp entrances and deep afterbodies fairing into thick rudders, resulting in longitudinal centers of buoyancy further aft and prismatic coefficients higher than the norm. These design characteristics, which serve to reduce drag at higher speeds, are in contrast to today's canoe bodies with fin keels and reflect Paris's research at the Webb Institute and MIT.

Variants on this theme have included the Aeromarine 50, *Questar*, in 1970, one of the first high-aspect-ratio mizzen ketches; *Lone Star*, a 45-foot DWL teak ketch in 1982; and the Freedom 33, a centerboard cat ketch, in 1978.

Paris was born in While Plains, New York. While his family always had powerboats, designing sailboats was his ambition from an early age, and he began amassing his library on yacht design at age twelve. He graduated from the Webb Institute in 1964 with a degree in naval architecture and marine engineering and went on to pursue graduate studies at MIT and Woods Hole Oceanographic Institution. In 1968 he moved to Maine to become vice president of engineering for Aeromarine Corporation, a high-tech start-up company. In an engineer's dream job, Paris was developing winches for America's Cup 12-Meter defenders, the first production three-speed winches, and designing and build-

Alexandre Paris: *Jolie Brise.* The mythic yacht *Jolie Brise* was the penultimate gaff-rigged cutter in pilot service before the changeover from sail to steam. Built in 1913, the 56-footer was converted to a yacht and won the Fastnet Race three times. *Photo courtesy Jacques Taglang*

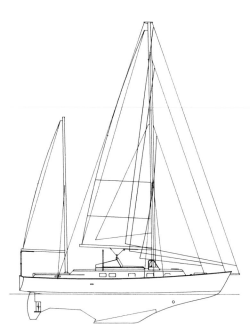

Jay Paris: P-46. The P-46's deep afterbody allows for a full-headroom cabin aft of the center cockpit while maintaining a profile akin to a traditional aft cockpit design. *Drawing courtesy Jay Paris*

ing *Questar*, notable as the first large foam-cored boat built in the United States and for its extensive use of unidirectional fiberglass.

While aspects of his distinctive hull forms are optimized for high speed, frictional drag is reduced by minimizing wetted girth relative to wetted surface area. His nearly straight diagonals forward often induce a slight hollow in the bow reminiscent of N. G. Herreshoff, who often created a similar hollow as he planed his half models.

Paris's arrangements have distinctive features such as transversely gimbaled stoves, for safe cooking offshore, and a centerline aft passageway below a "transmission tunnel" center cockpit that is feet lower than it would otherwise be.

Current projects include derivations of the Petrel 32 trailerable offshore cruising sloop/yawl and the P-46 cutter/ketch designs.

—Lucia del Sol Knight with Jay Paris

REUEL B. PARKER

Born February 19, 1946 · United States

In a field where innovation is often limited to racing boat design and exotic new composites, Reuel Parker has been seeking new combinations of features in his designs for practical cruising, daysailing, and charter boats.

A long-term liveaboard yachtsman, Parker is an advocate of shoal draft, a rarity among today's many deep-fin-keeled stock cruisers. Most of his designs are centerboarders or have

keels shallow enough to allow access to shoal water, where one can seek shelter that is unavailable to others or make an inside passage where others must go offshore to reach the same port. Safety is also a primary concern: when a fin-keeled vessel hits a submerged container or goes on the rocks, it is frequently lost, whereas a centerboard hull can glide over obstacles and even be driven up a beach on its bottom with minimal damage.

Parker's designs often take advantage of plywood and epoxy construction to reduce initial cost, weight, and maintenance, while increasing rigidity and resistance to deterioration. Generally his boats have a pragmatic polyurethane-over-epoxy finish with minimal exterior brightwork and simple but comfortable appointments below. In many cases he takes his departure from traditional types, retaining their aesthetic and functional qualities while adapting them to modern construction.

Rigs are frequently (but not always) traditional, often with gaff sails, bowsprits, and free-standing laminated wooden masts, aimed at making things simple and strong while keeping the sail plan long and low as befits a shoal-draft hull with a smaller range of stability than is found in ballast-bulb fin-keeled racing machines.

Parker favors high form-stability for stiffness and sail-carrying ability, external ballast employing lead-filled steel "flat-iron" box keels, and flaring topsides to provide buoyancy at the deck level. Auxiliary power is often an outboard in a well on smaller vessels, and a diesel under a bridge deck using a Hurth V-Drive in larger vessels. Parker also designs powerboats on the principal of environmental friendliness.

Many of Parker's hulls are modified Sharpies, Chesapeake Bay Bugeyes, and Bateaux, which utilize sheet-plywood planking, double-diagonal planking over stringers ("Quick-Molding"), and his cold-molding technique of double-diagonal planking over tongue-and-groove planking as described in his book *The New Cold-Molded Boatbuilding*. Topsides are often planked with sheet plywood, employing conic-section techniques to save weight, time, and money. These methods allow rapid and economical construction while allowing a great variety of hull shapes.

Parker was born in Denver, Colorado, but grew up from age two on the coast of Maine and the South Shore of Long Island. As a boy he designed and built boat models, and by the time he was twelve had started building and repairing full-sized boats. He attended Colorado State College, State University of New York at Farmingdale, and Columbia University in Manhattan, as well as two schools in California, studying physics, mechanical engineering, music, oceanography, and emergency medicine.

Reuel Parker: *Leopard*. The pilot schooner *Leopard* passing *Western Union* in the March 1998 Wrecker's Race off Key West, Florida. *Photo courtesy Reuel Parker*

Over the years, Parker has designed, built, and restored boats of every common material. He intersperses this work with extensive coastal cruises and offshore voyages. In 1974 he opened Parker Marine Enterprises, a design, construction, and restoration firm. He now concentrates on writing and design, with an occasional construction or restoration project, and continues to live aboard vessels of his own design and construction, ranging seasonally between Nova Scotia and the Caribbean.

—Daniel B. MacNaughton

WILLIAM EVANS PATON

1861–1886 · Scotland

In 1886, W. E. Paton designed *Oona*, the ultimate extreme plank-on-edge cutter, for Mr. Plunket of Belfast. She was built by Harvey and Company at Wivenhoe, and on passage to her home port in May of that year, was lost in a storm in the Irish Sea, drowning her designer, owner, and crew. The demise of *Oona* would contribute to the abolishment of the Tonnage Rule, long considered obsolete and detrimental.

Like G. L. Watson, Paton trained in the drawing office of A. and J. Inglis, the Glasgow shipbuilders, under John Inglis Jr., who was a collaborator with William Froude. He then spent three years as a private student studying naval architecture at the Royal Naval College, Greenwich, graduating in 1881. He subsequently was employed at Armstrong Mitchell and Company in Elswich, the great Victorian shipbuilders.

Between 1879 and 1886 he designed four Five-Tonners to the Tonnage Rule and pursued a policy of increasing length, draft, and displacement while decreasing beam, culminating in *Oona* in 1886. Her sail area of 2,000 square feet was greater than that of many Ten-Tonners and was carried on a hull with an LWL of 34 feet, beam of 5 feet 6 inches, draft of 8 feet, and displacement of 12 tons.

Earlier Paton designs were not so extreme. Generally, they featured a body plan with low bilges joined by virtually straight lines to a wide keel. *Trident*, his own Five-Tonner of 1879, raced very successfully. The Five-Tonner *Olga* of 1883 secured fifteen first places in her first season despite being sunk in collision with a collier. *Currytush*, a Three-Tonner, was also very successful in her class.

In total Paton designed forty boats from Three-Tonners all the way up to a 150-foot torpedo boat. All his yachts were notable for the quality of the engineering that went into them. His career showed glittering promise, but he remains one of the great "What ifs" of Victorian yachting.   —Brian Smith and Martin Black

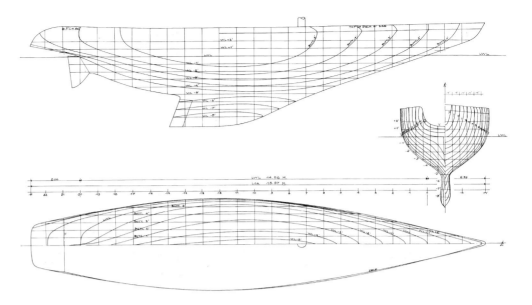

Alan Payne: *Gretel II.* Many say that *Gretel II* had a faster hull than her American rival *Intrepid* in the 1970 America's Cup. She was the pinnacle of Payne's design and engineering career; close attention was paid to structural details and opportunities hidden in the rule. *Drawing courtesy David Payne*

ALAN PAYNE, AM

December 11, 1921–June 20, 1995 · Australia

Alan Payne's name is forever linked to *Gretel* and *Gretel II*, the Australian 12-Meter challengers he designed for the America's Cup races of 1962 and 1970. Although they did not bring the Cup home to Australia, they did mark the beginning of Australia's huge presence in the America's Cup races. As of 1982 his boats had won more Cup races than any challenger since 1958.

Payne was among the first to extensively test new hull forms using models. He is credited with the design of the first fiberglass boat built in Australia. Throughout his career he advocated strong scantlings and sensible design in offshore yachts for both cruising and racing.

The son of a merchant navy captain who moved his family from England to Australia in the late 1920's, Payne lived beside Sydney Harbor during his teenage years, building and racing skiffs whenever possible. Soon the fastest class on the harbor was the Payne Mortlock sailing canoe, designed with Payne's school friend Bryce Mortlock, a class that still races today in South Australia.

Taking up a cadetship in naval architecture during World War II, Payne was rigorously trained in drafting and shipyard operations at the very active government drydock on Cockatoo Island in Sydney. He took night classes in structural and hydrodynamic theory at Sydney Technical College. In addition to relentless drafting and production of ship plans, trainees were exposed to all kinds of shipyard work. Payne was particularly adept in the lines loft. Following his release from Cockatoo Island in

1945, Payne began designing small fishing and harbor sailing craft.

In 1952 the 35-foot *Nocturne*, a sleek and relatively narrow, light-displacement, raised-deck design featuring a spade rudder, became Payne's first entry in the Sydney to Hobart Race. She was by far the lightest-displacement boat in the fleet and in 1953 became the smallest yacht ever to win line honors in this race. Payne and his brother Bill often raced aboard *Nocturne*, and she later set course records in several shorter offshore races.

Payne went on to participate in nine more Sydney-Hobart Races, but never again were his designs as light as *Nocturne*, despite her success. Payne later said that he was unhappy with *Nocturne's* construction (very light plank-on-frame) for offshore use, and that he wished he had had access to glued laminated (cold-molded) or aluminum construction. Today *Nocturne's* proportions reflect those of a more healthy light-displacement hull form than is commonly seen, and it is interesting to speculate how differently Payne's work might have evolved if he had been able to satisfy his concerns over adequate structure in light-displacement types.

After *Nocturne*, Payne's work took full advantage of heavy scantlings allowances in the RORC Rule, and his boats tended toward fairly heavy displacement. Payne designs won prizes in Australian ocean racing throughout the 1960's. A husky, sloop-rigged, 36-foot 4-inch design called the Tasman Seabird has been consistently successful and a good number have been built—they remain popular in Australia today. *Solo*, a 57-footer designed in 1955, was a highly successful, ocean racing sloop built of steel.

The enormous structural strength of steel was favored by Payne in much of his subsequent work. It was his lifelong project to offer affordable, swift, and capable designs to the growing number of people preparing to "sell up and sail." He drew on his heavy-displacement racing successes under the RORC Rule and the favorable characteristics of his earliest offshore designs to create a line of steel bluewater cruisers in the 38- to 45-foot range. By the time of his death, Payne had refined a wholesome, broad multichine hull form with harmonious cabin-trunk lines and modest bulwarks, that has had great appeal to offshore cruisers. Since his death, Payne's family has seen to it that work on this series of designs carries on, and both amateurs and professionals continue to build them worldwide.

Payne began tank-testing hull models early on. Models were towed through swimming pools or self-powered and driven back and forth in the quieter reaches of Sydney Harbour. All the while he would intently study the flow of water, call for an on-the-spot modification, and try again.

America's Cup interest spawned Australia's first towing tank, and Payne was there at all hours riding atop the carriage analyzing his models; even as various institutional tanks became available, however, inadequate project funding often forced Payne back to the shallows with a model and string. For the 12-Meter *Advance,* built in 1982, Payne made two 5-meter manned sailing models, one of which was of the proposed design, modified during the trials, and the other a benchmark model of the American yacht *Freedom.* In many ways this approach was even more accurate than tank-testing. Unfortunately, *Advance,* which was conceived as a light-air-only contender, was not a versatile enough performer and was soon dismantled. Another time, when developing a prototype cruising boat series for Columbia Yachts, Payne had an asymmetrical sailboat built. This little test boat was driven to extremes, analyzing a different form on each tack.

While designing cruising sailboats, Payne strove for a balanced hull form in the interest of seaworthiness. He looked primarily to the comfort and welfare of the crew, producing structurally sound, seakindly craft that had windward ability even in extreme conditions and ran off the wind under good control, with long keels and plenty of buoyancy forward to avoid burying the bow.

Payne participated in IYRU and international design committees and voiced concern over trends in IOR racing hull shapes. Well aware of the wave forms that develop in prolonged bad weather offshore, Payne knew what effects such seas would have on a wide-transomed, high-sided, lightly built contemporary ocean racer. *Sail* magazine published his imaginary devastation of a racing fleet brought on by such a storm, a year before the 1979 Fastnet Race. IMS efforts to address stability and seaworthiness notwithstanding, Payne remained concerned. In a dinner lecture to the Cruising Yacht Club of Australia, he predicted catastrophe if the Sydney-Hobart fleet encountered storm-force conditions, sixteen years before the disastrous 1998 event.

In the 1980's Payne's firm won a commission to design new ferries for Sydney Harbour. Payne and his team addressed the required reduction of wakes with the first catamaran ferries on the harbor—the designs were new in concept but featured a traditional curve in their sheerlines.

Payne was always humble about his achievements and rarely received full financial reward for his long hours, often working alone per-

Alan Payne: *Maris.* Launched in 1959, *Maris* was the first of the Tasman Seabird class. These classic yachts had seaworthy characteristics and robust construction, the minimum qualities Payne felt necessary for ocean racing. *Maris* was still an active participant in 2000. *Photo courtesy David Payne*

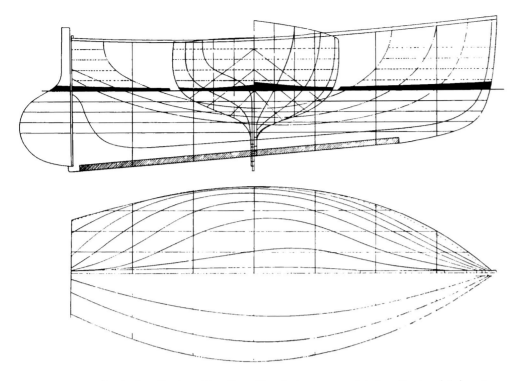

Arthur Payne: *Blue Jacket*. Designed in 1894, *Blue Jacket* was modeled on the local Itchen Ferry fishing boats. These working craft were keenly raced by the fishermen, and both Arthur Payne and his father (also Arthur) designed a number of them. © *Tony Dixon*

fecting designs. Forced to abandon private practice at various stages of his career, he worked on staff or in partnership with firms such as Hawker deHavilland, Burness Corlett, and the Maritime Service Board of New South Wales. For many years he was supported by associate and then partner Howard Peachey.

In 1993 Alan Payne was awarded the Member of the Order of Australia award in recognition of his achievements. —Geoff Payne

ARTHUR EDWARD PAYNE

1858–ca. 1905 · England

Arthur Payne was the second generation of a three-generation dynasty of yacht designers and boatbuilders. He produced many successful designs under the Yacht Racing Association's Length-and-Sail-Area Rule of 1886, particularly in the smaller raters, and his work showed the advantage of larger beam and moderate displacement under the rule.

His father, Alfred R. Payne, was the founder of the family firm and a noted designer of small yachts and Solent fishing vessels. The yard was situated in Belvedere, Southampton, on the Itchen, adjacent to the perhaps more famous yard of Dan Hatcher. On the death of Alfred Payne in 1878, the yard was renamed A. R. Payne and Sons.

Payne served an apprenticeship in his father's yard, designing his first yacht in 1879, the Twenty-Tonner *Louise*. One of the best-known

yachts of his early period was *Foam II*, modeled on the Itchen Ferry fishing boats and built for R. C. Leslie, the author of *A Waterbiography*, in 1884. He designed other yachts of this type throughout his career, as did his father before him, but his real opportunity arrived in 1886 with the introduction of Dixon Kemp's Length-and-Sail-Area Rule, which was in effect for about ten years.

Like many designers, Payne sprang to fame with designs for a particular owner. Saint Julien Arabin commissioned the raters *Dea*, *Minime*, *Gadabout*, *Lollypop*, and *Decime* from Payne during the late 1880's. Payne also produced numerous successful boats in the 1-, 2½, 5-, and 10-Rater classes, including *Lady Nan*, a 2½-Rater. In 1888 he produced his first design with a heavy lead fin keel. Other successful boats in this class were *Hummingbird* (1889), rigged as a lug sloop, and *The Babe* (1890). Both the lead fin and the lug were introduced to the 5-Raters in *Windfall* and *Sevourne* of 1891 and were built by the new firm of Summers and Payne.

In 1890 the Belvedere yards of both A. R. Payne and Sons and Black and Company (formerly Hatcher and Company) were consumed by fire. A Mr. W. Summers bought both yards, took Arthur Payne into partnership, and rebuilt. Payne designed most of the yachts built by the new company, including large raters such as *Corsair*, a 40-Rater, in 1892; small cruisers such as *Ayah*; and large steam yachts. He was a prolific designer; an article in the summer edition of *The Yachtsman* in 1892 reported that he had already

designed seventeen yachts that year, ranging from a Half-Rater to a 100-ton steam yacht.

Payne's early death in 1905 was much lamented, and there was a feeling that, despite his productivity, the best was yet to come. He was succeeded by his son, also Arthur E. Payne, known affectionately as "Little Arthur."

—Brian Smith

DAVID BRUCE PAYNE

Born August 15, 1956 · Australia

One of Australia's most broadly talented yacht designers, David Payne has designed model yachts, kayaks and small dinghies, high-performance racing boats, historic reproductions, and conservative cruising boats of many types, for both sail and power. While he also does work on commission, many of his designs were created as stock plans for the home boatbuilder, meaning that they are expressions of pure concepts straight from the designer's mind, without the compromises necessary to please a client.

Payne grew up cruising and racing with his family, often aboard boats designed by his uncle, the naval architect Alan Payne. Serious racing began with Lasers and 470's before his long involvement as a forward hand on the unrestricted 12-foot skiff class.

A 1979 graduate of Sydney College of the Arts with a bachelor of arts degree in industrial design, Payne is self-taught as a yacht designer. His first designs were drawn in 1983 for the 12-

David Payne: *Paketi*. The 7.2-meter *Paketi* is a single-chine cutter. She combines contemporary construction with a traditional rig and profile. She was built in New Zealand by Payne's brother-in-law, Rob Morton. *Photo courtesy David Payne*

foot skiff class. They were very successful, winning local and Interdominion (Australia versus New Zealand) championships. In 1985 he began working in the office of Alan Payne as a draftsman. Among a range of projects, he worked with his uncle on developing designs for steel yacht stock plans, completing details after Alan's death in 1995. David Payne has continued to assist the family in preserving and documenting the Alan Payne designs.

From 1990 to 1992, Payne worked on a contract basis for Scott Jutson Yacht Design, where the projects included designing cruising and racing yachts and new underwater appendages and rigs for existing yachts. He began his independent career in 1993, creating his range of stock plans and accepting custom designs for cruising vessels, mostly built using wood-epoxy methods and steel.

Besides his regular design work, Payne has used his excellent drafting ability to create display drawings for a number of historic yachts, and to document and preserve the lines and details of historic vessels for the Australian National Maritime Museum in Sydney.

Payne has been one of the voices calling for healthier offshore racing craft in the wake of the Sydney-Hobart Race disaster of 1998, and among other nonyachting activities is working to reestablish native plants and bushland near his home. He has published a catalogue of his designs. David Payne's office is in Sydney, Australia.

—Daniel B. MacNaughton

DAVID PEDRICK

Born January 22, 1948 · United States

Noted for his work in both racing and cruising yachts, David Pedrick is considered one of the leading designers of America's Cup boats. A protégé of famed yacht designer Olin Stephens, Pedrick has been involved in no less than eight America's Cup campaigns.

Pedrick grew up in the Philadelphia, Pennsylvania, area and spent summers on the New Jersey shore. He began sailing at an early age, mostly small boats on Barnegat Bay and later on offshore racers. As a young boy, Pedrick decided he wanted to become a yacht designer. He would say it was a natural use of his abilities in engineering, design, and sailing. Pedrick enrolled in the naval architecture and marine engineering program at the highly competitive Webb Institute in Glen Cove, New York.

An internship at the prestigious firm of Sparkman and Stephens, the foremost America's Cup design firm, led to a full-time job in 1970. Pedrick brought to the team a strong background in engineering research and testing. His

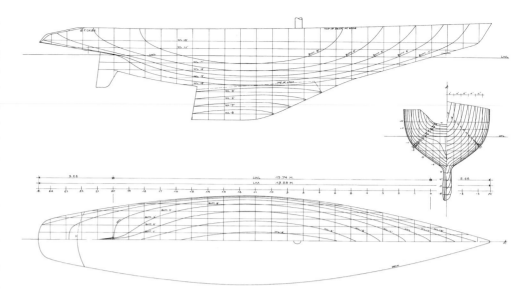

David Pedrick: *Clipper.* Pedrick's entry for the 1980 America's Cup series was *Clipper*, designed for the People to People Sports Committee. She was built of aluminum by Newport Offshore and skippered by Russell Long, but was not chosen to defend the Cup, which was won that year by the Olin Stephens–designed *Freedom.* © *Chevalier & Taglang*

first foray into the America's Cup field was on the design team for *Courageous*, the 1974 winner. *Courageous* would set the standard for future America's Cup yacht designs.

Pedrick later helped design *Stars & Stripes*, the winner in 1987. Other America's Cup yachts he worked on include *Enterprise* (1977), *Clipper* (1980), *Defender* (1983), *Stars & Stripes* (1992, 1995), and a design for the 2000 Virgin Island syndicate that was never built. Pedrick also was instrumental in drafting standards for the International America's Cup Class.

Pedrick left the New York City–based Sparkman and Stephens in late 1976. He opened his own design firm, Pedrick Yacht Designs, in Newport, Rhode Island. In addition to America's Cup boats, Pedrick has developed custom yachts for both racing and cruising that combine technically sophisticated performance with artistic balance and beauty. His produc-

tion work includes designs for Freedom Yachts (the Freedom 35 and Freedom 40) and six designs for the family-owned Cheoy Lee Yachts. He also has been developing high-performance motorsailers using innovative techniques to provide powerful motoryachts with maximum sailing performance.

Pedrick also has an affinity for boat restoration and is a founding member of the International Yacht Restoration School in Newport.

—JoAnn Goddard

CHARLES PEEL

1878–1949 · Australia

One of the earliest Australian-born yacht designers, Charlie Peel was also a boatbuilder, moving between Melbourne, Sydney, and Adelaide over a period beginning around 1905 through to 1947. He was the quintessential, self-taught local designer, creating yachts with an Australian character to suit regional conditions.

Other Australian builders also designed their own craft, but Peel stands out with his significant contributions to Australian sailing history. The 1909 design *Idler* became the basis for the legendary 21-foot Restricted Class, formed after World War I. As the class developed, Peel designed a number of boats for the Forster Cup interstate series. His popular Jubilee class from 1934 was a one-design that expanded into the racing fleets in Victoria when gales destroyed a number of small craft. Both these classes continued to grow around Australia and are still racing in 2003.

Peel's outstanding yachts were *Acrospires III* (1923) and *Acrospires IV* (1929), both over 50 feet

Charles Peel: *Nerana.* The 25-foot 1953 Forster Cup winner *Nerana* surges across the finish line, showing off both the power of these open boats and the hallmark stem profile that adorns many Peel designs. *Photo courtesy Harry Perry Jr.*

long and still active, and the lightweight centerboarder *Thera* (1911) at 36 feet LOA, almost unbeatable on Port Phillip Bay for many seasons. At one stage she was moved up a class and still managed to beat bigger boats on line and handicap times. Considered a freak by disgruntled competitors, the introduction of the Linear Rating Rule finally brought her winning run to an end. *Thera*, too, survives to the present day.

Sturdy, elegant, and fast were typical adjectives applied to Peel's craft. His son, Charlie Jr., and then grandsons Wayne and Barrie have continued boatbuilding in this tradition.

—David Payne

FABIO PERINI

Born September 4, 1940 · Italy

Fabio Perini was not schooled in naval architecture, engineering, or industrial design. In fact, he has no formal advanced education, yet he is unquestionably one of the most influential sailing yacht designers of the era, having personally overseen the conception and creation of more than two-dozen craft of classic style and distinction. Nearly all are ketches measuring between 33 and 58 meters, all are sailing under Perini-designed rigs, and all are equipped with Perini-designed, automated sail-handling equipment.

Perini was born in Villa Basilica, Italy, near Lucca, on the premises of a paper mill where several family members worked. As a child, he became fascinated with the mill's machinery, and when he was eighteen, he built his first device: an automatic felt guide incorporating a Vespa gearbox.

Within a few years the young inventor, filled with instinctive ideas, dared to incorporate his own company, Fabio Perini SpA, to create high-speed machinery for converting bulk paper toweling and toilet tissue into individual rolls and packages. The firm quickly grew to dominate the worldwide market for paper-converting machinery.

An avid sailor, Perini owned several offshore cruising yachts, one of which he sailed from Italy to Africa and Brazil. From his experience at sea, Perini became keenly aware that existing power-assisted devices to control sail set and trim—sheet and halyard winches, headsail and in-mast furlers—were generally inadequate for large yachts.

Accordingly, in Viareggio Perini set up an engineering firm, Perini Navi, to design and manufacture automated sail-handling gear. He installed the prototypes on a custom-built hull of his conception, the 40-meter *Felicita* (now *Aleta*). Perini also introduced into *Felicita* other

features that became standard on all his designs, including the first flying bridge on a sailing yacht. Following the success of *Felicita*, in 1984 Perini decided to move his firm beyond engineering into a complete yacht design and construction firm, in order to develop a luxury sailing yacht line. Perini's idea was to attract the community of wealthy sailors who were buying motoryachts because large sailing yachts had become impossible to sail without very large crews.

Perini's premise was (and still is) that the sailing yacht must offer the convenience, comfort, and romance of the motoryacht, but with stability, long range, low fuel consumption, and a satisfying connection to the environment and the sea. In his own shipyard Perini built the 42.5-meter *Christianne B*, installing improved sail handling gear of his design. The yacht was followed by *Andromeda*, a 40-meter steel and aluminum ketch whose masculine form, twin-screw propulsion, and fully automated sailing systems wrote a new chapter in large yacht design.

Andromeda was followed by a second generation of similar Perini designs, including *Andromeda Ia Dea* (47 meters) and *Marisa* (40 meters). They were succeeded by another "first" for the world—a series of six near-sisterships between 46 and 48 meters long: *Xasteria, Liberty, Corelia, Piropo IV, Morning Glory*, and *Legacy*. To accomplish this, Perini contracted with a Turkish shipyard to fabricate hulls and superstructures; he took over the famed Picchiotti yard in Viareggio to rig and finish the yachts; and he acquired a fine joinery shop to build all furniture.

Perini continued in the 1990's to evolve his concepts, delivering the 58-meter *Taouey* and 53-meter *Independence*. Next Perini Navi delivered the customized 52-meter *Xasteria*, and *Liberty*, the first yacht to have a midships out-

door "lounge." He also began another series, this one of 50-meter near-sisterships, beginning with *Phryne* delivered in 1999.

In another unique practice, Fabio Perini's yachts—designed by in-house naval architects and engineers—nearly all started on speculation; as the twentieth century closed, Perini Navi was building several more pilothouse ketches between 49 and 53 meters long on that basis. In 1999, however, Perini Navi had matured to where it could build the designs of other naval architects.

In the 1990's the world began giving Fabio Perini recognition for his work: by the end of 1999 five Perini yachts had won a total of nine design awards from the International Superyacht Society and *ShowBoats International* magazine. At the time, when most other megayacht shipyards had been family owned for several generations, Perini Navi was not yet twenty years old.

—Jack A. Somer

Fabio Perini: *Liberty*. The 52-meter *Liberty* was built in 1997 at Perini's shipyard, Perini Navi. She is a luxurious staysail ketch built of steel and is active in the charter fleet. She was the first sailing megayacht to have a mid-deck lounge. *Photo courtesy Fabio Perini*.

ROBERT H. PERRY

Born June 25, 1946 · United States

Bob Perry's career has served to illustrate every facet of the performance cruiser concept of sailboat design. Most of Perry's work is in high-speed sailing craft with modern hulls, rigs, and underbodies. However, he also works in a range that includes modern aesthetics as well as deliberately traditional styles involving Danish-type sterns and other details designed to create a classic feel. Even these double-enders are contemporary boats in all their details other than those most casually observed, however. Perry enjoys the sleeper effect, where a fast boat is disguised by traditional details.

The Valiant 40, a moderate-displacement double-ender with a modern underbody, rig, and hull form, was Perry's first big breakthrough. She appeared in 1974, when there was little middle ground between out-and-out heavy-displacement cruising boats of wood or fiberglass, and boats directly influenced by the IOR rating rule, which were beginning to be seen as poor offshore cruising boats. The Valiant 40 fell squarely in between, offering speed and maneuverability without the distortions of hull or rig imposed by the IOR in an aesthetic package dominated by a Danish-style pointed stern.

Few contemporary designers would maintain that a pointed stern is essential to seaworthiness, but at the time the feature was seeing a strong revival in popularity, and combining the pointed stern with an otherwise modern concept was an effective marketing move. It was enough to allow dyed-in-the-wool cruisers, at the time much influenced by more traditional double-enders, such as the Westsail 32, to give the Valiant 40 a second look. She was the right boat at the right time, and she has undoubtedly served as a point of departure for many of Perry's subsequent designs. His plans for the Taiwan-based Tashiba Company are strongly reminiscent of the Valiant 40, but with a great deal more in the way of traditionalist detailing and woodwork.

The immense popularity of Perry's double-enders should not obscure his proficiency in more conventionally modern, flat-out performance cruisers designed without consideration for handicapping rules, many of which range well up into the maxi yacht size range.

Perry was born in Ohio. His family moved first to his mother's native Australia, then to Seattle when he was twelve. After graduating from Seattle University with an engineering degree, he apprenticed under William Garden and later worked for racing boat designer Dick Carter. The Valiant 40, a Perry concept rejected by Carter, launched Perry's independent career. Soon after opening his office in Seattle in 1974, he began a series of designs for the Islander Company. Since then have come a number of additional production designs for Valiant, Hans Christian, Nordic, CT, Tashiba, Tayana, Mirage, Esprit, and Saga.

Current projects include a 57-foot offshore cruising cutter, a 65-foot racer/cruiser, a 30-foot Geezer class sloop, a 21-foot electric launch, a 32-foot plumb-stem cutter, and a 40-foot private submarine.

Perry is probably the most widely read writer on yacht design today. He has been the technical editor of *Sailing* magazine for the last twenty-five years; his reviews have been compiled by *Sailing* into five books called *Sailing Designs*. He is also a regular contributor to *Bluewater Sailing*.　　　—Daniel B. MacNaughton

DOUGLAS BLAIR PETERSON

Born July 25, 1945 · United States

In the 1960's there emerged on the West Coast a number of successful young yacht designers who had little formal training and were unencumbered by orthodoxy. Doug Peterson may be the most notable of these talented individuals.

Peterson grew up in San Diego, where he was active in the San Diego Yacht Club's junior sailing program. He quickly graduated from dinghies to keelboats and raced as crew on the 8-Meters *Cheerio* and *Emily* and the Q-Class *Cotton Blossom IV*. At the same time he was exposed to the light, long-waterline auxiliary racers from the boards of California designers George Kettenburg, Wendell "Skip" Calkins, and William Lapworth, which were proving extremely effective on the long downwind courses of the Pacific Coast.

While they were not Californian in origin, Peterson was to sail on two such types when he crewed aboard the 33-foot, Sparkman and Stephens–designed *Spirit* in the 1964 Bermuda Race and the 73-foot *Stormvogel*, designed by E. G. van de Stadt, in the 1965 Honolulu Race. These boats and their remarkable performances strongly influenced him. During his high school years, Peterson worked part-time in Skip Calkins's San Diego office to gain firsthand exposure to the craft of yacht design.

Peterson's career got off to a good start in 1973 with the launch of the One-Tonner *Ganbare*. Some of her features, such as her relatively small size, squarish bow sections, sharply separate, tapered fin keel, and shallow skeg at the top of a slightly balanced rudder, looked very much out of step with the rest of the fleet at the San Diego One-Ton Championships that year. But she so dominated the event that plans were immediately made to take her to the One-Ton Cup in Sardinia. There her performance was equally good, and only a navigational error on the long-distance race kept her from taking the Cup. The following year the One-Ton Cup regatta at Torquay was dominated by Peterson designs and was won by the Peterson 35 *Gumboots*.

Over the next twenty years Peterson built a worldwide clientele of some of the keenest racing yachtsmen of the time. His boats competed everywhere and at one time or another won every Ton Cup championship except the Quarter-Ton.

In 1975, *Yeoman XX* paced the British team to win the Admiral's Cup, once considered the world championship for national ocean racing teams. From then until the IOR was abandoned, every nation to compete in the event had, at one time, a Peterson boat on their team. The Peterson 42-foot *Moonshine* joined the British team for their repeat win in 1977 and took the title of top inshore boat. In the 1979 event, which included the tragic Fastnet Race, the top individual boat was the 39-foot *Eclipse*.

At the 1978 Clipper Cup, the 37-foot centerboarder *Magic Pudding* (aka *B-195*) grabbed the headlines with an overall first on the grueling Round-the-State Race. In the inaugural Sardinia Cup of 1979, the host Italians upset the favored Americans, primarily owing to the speed of the Peterson Two-Ton twins, *Yena* and *Didaquinta*. The 42-foot *La Pantera's* overall win in the South China Sea Race in the same year seemed to indicate that Peterson's approach could produce winners on any course.

The Peterson Yacht Design office also developed a number of production racer/cruisers based on successful custom racer prototypes. The best known of these are the Islander 40; Baltic 39, 42, 48, and 55; the Serendipity 43; New York 40; and the Sun Legend 40 by Jeanneau (of which nearly six hundred were built). Among cruising sailors, his popular collaboration with Jack Kelly, the mid-cockpit Peter-

Bob Perry: Valiant 40. The Valiant 40 illustrated a new category of cruising-sailboat design when she appeared in 1974. Combining traditional aesthetic elements with contemporary fundamentals, her overall concept was revisited many times by Perry and others, eventually earning her a place in the American Sailboat Hall of Fame for her influence. *Drawing courtesy Robert Perry*

Doug Peterson: *Hi Roler* **(opposite).** *Hi Roler* was an extremely successful 67-foot IOR racer. The fine stern and small mainsails of this era gradually gave way to lighter hulls and fractional rigs in the 1980's. © *Peter Barlow*

Murray Peterson: *Coaster III.* The small schooner designs of Peterson struck a nearly perfect balance between utility and charm. Few designers equaled Peterson in his ability to miniaturize traditional types and create a robust, practical, and appealing yacht with no trace of cuteness. *Photo courtesy William Peterson*

son 44, is widely recognized for her long waterline, roomy interior, and speed under sail.

While so much of Peterson's extant work consists of IOR auxiliaries, he has produced winners and champions under many measurement rules. His 5.5-Meter designs have won more than one Scandinavian Gold Cup. In 1975, his M 50/800 design pond-sailer, *Bingo*, won the Class National Championship, and in 1977, the 6-Meter *Razzle Dazzle* took first at Marstrand Race Week and won the King Olav V Cup in Seattle. In 1979 she won the Sir Thomas Lipton Cup.

During its heyday, the Peterson office in San Diego was a lively place. Peter Wormwood, Bill Tripp, John Reichel, and Jim Pugh all worked there. As they left to form their own offices, Peterson reduced the size of the business, turning to commissions for larger, custom auxiliary cruisers, which he largely developed himself,

such as those built by the Jongert yard in the Netherlands. With the advent of the new International America's Cup Class in 1992, Peterson's instinctive grasp of measurement rules made him a natural for that job, and he was immediately sought out as a designer by several interested syndicates.

First with *America³* in 1992 and again with *Kiwi Magic* in 1995, Peterson played a key role in the design and development of America's Cup winners. In the 2000 America's Cup series in New Zealand, he was at the center of a successful design team with the Prada Challenge *Luna Rossa*, winner of the Louis Vuitton Cup that year. He again worked on the Prada Challenge team for the 2002–03 America's Cup series.

Doug Peterson has split his time between Milan and San Diego for the last several years.

—J. Scott Rohrer

MURRAY GIGNOUX PETERSON

November 23, 1908–February 14, 1974
United States

Among distinguished twentieth-century American naval architects, Murray Peterson stands out as uniquely linked to the state of Maine, in his own roots and in the origin of his marine designs. His reverence for the beauty and capability of Maine's working watercraft was nurtured during his idyllic childhood in Cape Elizabeth, where he was born. He was named for his grandfather, William D. Murray, a distinguished Maine builder of homes, churches, and municipal buildings, and for Judge Frederick E. Gignoux, a close family friend.

The sea was very much a part of Peterson's Danish and Scottish lineage. He grew to love the daily parade of working sail in Casco Bay and was encouraged by his family and a close-knit community to realize his youthful dream of becoming a naval architect. While his young friends were enthralled with automobiles, Peterson devoted much of his after-school time to working and sketching on Portland's bustling waterfront during the waning era of coasting schooners.

Following studies at MIT and employment with his mentor, John G. Alden of Boston, Peterson formed his own office in Marblehead, Massachusetts, in 1931. He weathered the Great Depression, and married Susan B. Reevs. Two of his lifelong friends and fellow naval architects, Fenwick C. Williams and K. Aage Nielsen, joined him during this creative decade of diverse sail and powerboat designs.

Peterson followed Alden's model of building his own designs on speculation and then introducing them to the marine market during the cruising and racing seasons. His famous Coaster yacht designs exemplified this approach and were an exquisite interpretation of Maine coastal schooners. His office became well known for his evolution of other working craft into recreational designs including fishing schooners, Friendship sloops, Pinkies, Norman's Land boats, Cowhorn ketches, and catboats, as well as a series of pilot-boats and double-enders of Scottish and Danish heritages.

Throughout World War II, Peterson worked for John Alden designing naval vessels and support craft, many of which were constructed in the shipyards of Maine. These contracts frequently brought Peterson back to his home state to inspect the construction. At war's end, in 1946, he returned to Maine permanently and opened his office in South Bristol, the location of several fine boatyards and across the Damariscotta River from East Boothbay, where his own designs had frequently been built.

Peterson became a key figure in the transition of Maine shipyards from wartime government contracts, by designing a new generation of draggers, fishing vessels, tugboats, and recreational powerboats. During the 1950's he would have as many as a dozen designs under construction simultaneously in an equal number of Maine yards. He also served as in-house designer to several others converting or restoring vessels for new service.

In addition to creating over a hundred unique marine designs in his own office, Peterson was an accomplished sailor, boatbuilder, musician, and building designer. He was a community leader and, like his grandfather, designed his town's school and re-created for his four children the kind of childhood he had treasured. He balanced his daily activities with the precision and attention to detail that characterized his drafting.

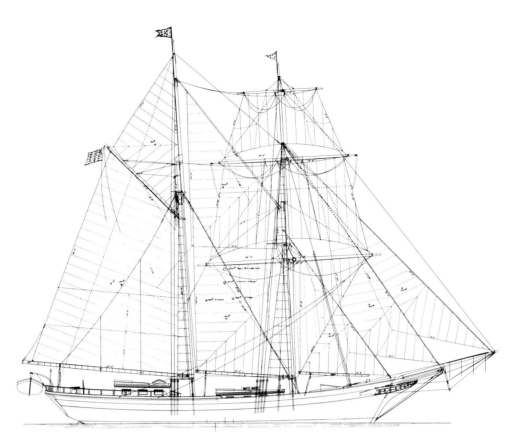

Murray Peterson: *Fritha.* At 57 feet, *Fritha* is one of the smallest hermaphrodite brigs one is likely to see. The beautiful proportions of the hull and rig don't fool us into thinking she is larger; she just looks correct. *Drawing courtesy William Peterson*

Murray Peterson: *Joseph Stuart.* Like much of her designer's work, this able-looking little power yacht takes its inspiration from traditional Maine-coast workboats. Her hull and wheelhouse show the influence of the sardine carrier type, but her spaces are rearranged as befits a much smaller vessel. *Photo courtesy William Peterson*

Peterson was an expert on marine engines, but seldom used them on his sailboats when there was the hint of a breeze on the horizon. During his sailing career, he owned twenty vessels equally divided between his own designs and others that he restored in his own yard. Although Peterson boats were being constructed worldwide, he seldom traveled out of state, as he preferred the Maine way of doing business. His favorite builder was Malcolm H. Brewer of Camden; they collaborated on sixteen of Murray's classic wooden boat designs.

Throughout his career, Peterson was a respected friend to clients and builders alike because of his skills, enthusiasm, and deep appreciation for what each party brought to the boatbuilding process. He chose a profession that never ceased to bring him pleasure, and although he passed away prematurely in 1974, it was not before achieving his boyhood aspirations in full measure and leaving a legacy of traditional designs for generations to come.

Plans are available through Murray G. Peterson Associates—run now by Murray's son Bill—in South Bristol, Maine.

—William Peterson

PELLE PETTERSON

Born 1932 · Sweden

Contemporary 6-Meter design is largely dominated by Pelle Petterson, whose boats have won nearly every World Championship since 1977, with owners from Sweden, England, Switzerland, and Australia. More glamorous but less successful was his 12-Meter *Sverige*, built in 1977 and campaigned for the America's Cup in 1977 and 1980.

Petterson is widely believed to be one of the world's best helmsmen, with World Championship and European Championship victories and a silver medal in the 1972 Olympics to his credit in the Star class. He was *Sverige's* helmsman in her America's Cup bid, and he has a long string of successes in the 6-Meter class as well.

Petterson's father worked as an industrial engineer for the Volvo Company, and originally Petterson trained for the same field, intending to follow in his father's footsteps. He did in fact do a considerable amount of design work for Volvo, including in particular the

Opposite: Pelle Petterson: *Sverige* (opposite). The 12-Meter *Sverige* took part in the America's Cup races in 1977 and 1980 with her designer as a helmsman. She was built in aluminum in 1977 for a syndicate within the Gothenburg Royal Yacht Club. *Photo courtesy Bent Aarre*

Volvo P 1800 sports car, but he did this work on a freelance basis.

Having learned to sail as a child in the waters around Gothenburg, his evident talent and love for sailing led him to try boat design. His early designs included rowboats, small sailboats, and in the 1960's some motorboats for the Monarch Crescent Company. However, the design of International Rule meter boats most engaged his interest, and he soon embarked on this still-active phase of his career.

Ironically, while Petterson is one of Sweden's best racing sailors and racing boat designers, his biggest commercial success has been with the popular Maxi line of family sailing yachts, twenty-nine different models designed with an eye to comfort and economy. Few harbors in Sweden and Denmark are without at least one Maxi. Petterson has also produced a number of successful motoryachts, including the popular Nimbus line.

The Petterson design office is in Kullavik, Sweden.

—Bent Aarre

WALTER PINAUD

1885–1968 · Canada

Walter Pinaud developed an international reputation as a yacht designer and builder through the combination of artistic craftsmanship and aerodynamic principles. A native of Charlottetown, Prince Edward Island, he was a skilled yachtsman and received his early boat design and construction training under his father, Martin Pinaud, and older brother Jack, who had worked at the George F. Lawley and Son yard in Boston.

In 1906 Walter and Jack established a yacht yard in Westmount, Nova Scotia, to serve the needs of club members from the recently founded Royal Cape Breton Yacht Club (RCBYC) (1899), across the harbor in Sydney, Nova Scotia. Pinaud's early design work produced numerous cutters, sloops, ketches, and cutting-edge motoryachts. Most notable was the *Flirt* (1906), a 26-foot motoryacht with a teak deck, two-cycle engine, and a cruising speed of 17 mph that was built for Oscar E. Libbey. She broke a number of maritime speed records. In 1907, Pinaud worked with Commodore George Herrick Duggan to design a series of one-design S-Class boats for the RCBYC's Cibou Cup.

Dr. Alexander Graham Bell consulted with Pinaud in 1913 to remedy a problem with the pontoons for a hydrofoil he was building. As a result, Pinaud was hired to take charge of the boatyard at Bell Laboratories on Beinn Bhreagh, Bell's estate near Baddeck, Nova Scotia. There

Walter Pinaud: *Flirt*. *Flirt* was a 26-foot motoryacht built for Oscar E. Libbey. She was built in 1906 and had teak decks and a two-cycle engine. *Flirt* held many maritime speed records and was the first of many yachts Pinaud would design and build for the same family. *Photo courtesy Bridget Anne Wolfe-Libbey Collection, Neil Libbey*

Walter Pinaud: *Gurnet Light*. This 44-foot cutter, built in 1947, was initially christened *Shenandoah* by Pinaud because she was the boat he dreamed about building. Rechristened *Gurnet Light*, she was a familiar sight in harbors from Buzzards Bay to Baddeck, Cape Breton, for over forty years. *Courtesy Pinaud Collection, Muriel Pinaud and Madeline Pinaud-House*

he had the opportunity to work with some of world's most renowned yacht designers and naval architects, who taught him a more scientific approach to boat design and building. In 1916, Pinaud worked with naval architect George Owen, who at the time was designing the *Elsie* (1917), a 55-foot yawl, using data collected by Dr. Bell about the wave and wind patterns on the Bras d'Or Lakes. Pinaud built the *Elsie*, which was a gift from Dr. Bell to his daughter Elsie and her husband Dr. Gilbert Grosvenor. *Elsie* is still sailing on the Bras d'Or Lakes as of 2002.

After World War I, the HD-4 hydrofoil was completed and on September 9, 1919, it set a world speed record of 114.04 kilometers per hour on Baddeck Bay. It was this early knowledge about aerodynamic design from building the HD-4 hydrofoil and the *Elsie* that culminated in Pinaud's own signature yacht designs.

Throughout its prolific life, Pinaud's Yacht Yard in Baddeck (established in 1926) produced numerous sailing vessels that incorporated Pinaud's developments in yacht design and construction. Most notable was *Gurnet Light* (1947), a 44-foot cutter with an inlaid teak and mahogany deck, built for Charles Bartlett; Pinaud considered it to be his own personal masterpiece. His final work was *Le Chameau* (1966), a motorsailer that had a diesel engine, roller reefing, and a destroyer wheel, yet did not compromise any of the safety and comfort features he created and developed through the years.

—Neil F. Libbey

ARTHUR LINCOLN PIVER

February 12, 1910–March 1968 · United States

Arthur Piver of Mill Valley, California, did more to promote the popularity of trimarans than anybody else in the world during the 1960's and even after his death. A trade-journal publisher and former pilot with no formal training in yacht design, the San Francisco–born Piver had grown up sailing his family's 85-foot schooner, *Eloise*. Only at the age of forty, after having gained experience on a Creger-designed Lear Cat, did he begin experimenting with multihulls. His first design was the 20-foot *Pi-Cat*, which he built of plywood in 1954 with semicircular hulls below the chines.

During the following years, and influenced by the thinking of designer Victor Tchetchet, Piver experimented with different multihull forms and sizes. By 1957 he had built six: two catamarans, a single outrigger, and three trimarans. That year he began to sell plans to amateur boatbuilders. To alleviate their difficulties with building round-bottomed hulls and

centerboard cases, Piver began to offer trimaran designs with easier-to-build, right-angled V-sections and deep-V floats, even though he recognized their inferiority in terms of performance.

In 1960 Piver crossed the Atlantic in the first 30-foot Nimble trimaran from Swansea, Massachusetts, to England via the Azores, making this the first eastward Atlantic crossing by a trimaran in the twentieth century. He was to enter the first Singlehanded Transatlantic Race, but arrived too late to qualify. Nonetheless, the accounts of his Atlantic crossing sparked enormous public interest in multihulls. The following year, in 1961, his 35-foot *Lodestar* became the second trimaran to cross the Pacific.

Public interest continued to increase and by 1964, one thousand Piver-designed trimarans were thought to be sailing. That year, he began to design double-chined hulls, which still were easy to build but gave the advantage of a more rounded shape and represented an improvement over his previous right-angled V-sections. By that time he also had developed a simplified building system—it did away with the need for lofting and allowed even complete novices to build his designs.

Fostered by his eloquent accounts of the advantages of the modern multihull and his superb marketing prowess, sales of Piver's plans to amateurs all over the world took off. Besides the 16-foot daysailer *Frolic*, the Nimble and Lodestar were his most successful designs, and together with *Nugget* (24 feet) and *Victress* (40 feet), hundreds of these cruisers were built by amateurs and professionals all over the

Arthur Piver: *Stiletto*. A particularly elegant 33-foot racing trimaran, *Stiletto* was designed in 1966. *Courtesy the Amateur Yacht Research Society*

world. Other, less well-known designs by Piver were *Trident* (46 feet), *Diadem* (55 feet), and *Empress* (64 feet), as well as *Stiletto* (33 feet), a surprisingly modern trimaran and one of the few outright racing trimarans he designed. In 1966, Piver sailed *Stiletto* from California to New York via the Panama Canal, then participated unofficially in the Bermuda Race for a total of 9,000 nautical miles.

An excellent seaman, Piver accumulated over 35,000 nautical miles on boats of his own design until March 1968, when he vanished off the coast of California while trying to qualify for the 1968 Singlehanded Transatlantic Race. His widow continued selling his plans, and by 1974 it was estimated that some four hundred of his trimarans had completed at least one transoceanic voyage, which made his designs by far the most successful ocean-cruising multihulls of the 1960's and early 1970's.

Much of Piver's success was certainly due to his irresistible writing style. He was not only eloquent and outspoken, but also controversial and a maverick to the yachting establishment. In numerous articles and three books written between 1961 and 1965, he conveyed the excitement of fast multihulls to his ever-increasing group of devotees. Not at all averse to bragging and exaggerations, he relentlessly promoted the strength, safety, and speed of his boats. He even claimed a top speed of 40 knots for his 17-foot *Pi-Cat* (16 to 18 knots would have been more realistic). But he also appealed to his readers' emotions and the dreams to be fulfilled by building their own trimaran and sailing it to unknown countries.

Almost half a century after his death, it is still difficult to pass final judgment on Piver. More so than any other multihull pioneer, Art Piver certainly had a tremendous influence on multihull design and designers. Derek Kelsall's first trimaran was a Piver design, Norm Cross gained his first multihull experience on a multihull designed by Piver, Jim Brown worked together with Piver for some time, and numerous other multihull designers, including Dick Newick, were inspired by Piver's writings when they set out designing their first multihulls. His trimarans have been superseded by faster, safer, and, many will think, more beautiful designs. But this is true for most multihulls of the 1960's.

Piver was the major force behind the rapid increase in the number of trimarans in the 1960's, and many amateurs would not have been able to get on the water without his cheap and easily built designs. By the same token, however, these very same amateurs often violated good boatbuilding practice in order to economize, and this, together with Piver's views, which cheerfully ran against conventional yachting wisdom, may have given the multihull type a bad reputation from which it has taken decades to recover. Whatever the final verdict may be, hundreds of Piver's designs are still afloat and remind us of the early and exciting days of the trimaran.

The Arthur Piver Collection of plans is at the Mariners' Museum, Newport News, VA.

—Claas van der Linde

AUGUST PLYM

March 4, 1856–September 23, 1924 · Sweden

Two characteristics distinguished August Plym: he was enormously accurate and he placed great emphasis on quality.

Very little is known about Plym's early years. He was born in Småland in the south of Sweden. He began work as a gardener. In the early 1880's he started work as a boatbuilder at Kummelnäs shipyard outside of Stockholm under the well-known designer Henning Smith (1850–1923). Sometime during the 1880's and in the beginning of the 1890's, Plym was in England and the United States apprenticing at different shipyards. During this journey he probably met Nathanael Herreshoff.

Back in Sweden in 1893, together with some men of property, Plym started Stockholm's Båtbyggeri (Stockholm Shipyard). After a fire in 1904, the shipyard moved to Neglinge outside Stockholm. Under Plym's rule the shipyard developed new construction methods and very strict quality control. His knowledge and his highly skilled boatbuilders contributed to this. Long after Plym's death, the shipyard continued to build big wooden yachts up until 1963.

In the beginning Plym mostly built yachts designed by Swedish designers Axel Nygren, Albert Andersson, and Hugo Schubert. Early in the 1890's he made his debut as a designer, completely self-taught without theoretical studies. One of his earliest yachts was the fin-keel racer *Trollhättan*, a successful racing boat. He made his name with the *Oberon*, a fin-keel racer camouflaged as a cruiser. It won everything in 1901, the year of its launch, and that led to new and harder rules.

As early as the end of the nineteenth century, Plym designed a one-design class, Plymsnäckan. It was almost 6 meters long, clinker built with a little bulb, and had room for two hammocks below deck. It was built up until World War I.

Plym was one of the first to design to the Skerry Cruiser Rule, including the first 55-Square-Meter, *Nora*, and the first 95-Square-

August Plym: ***Beatrice-Aurore.*** A rare 150-Square-Meter skerry cruiser, *Beatrice-Aurore* was built as *Ebe* at the Neglinge Boatyard by Plym in 1920 for E. Brodin of Torö, Sweden. In the 1990's she was severely damaged when a crane fell on her, but she is now renovated and more beautiful than ever. © *Per Thelander*

Meter, *Irene*, in 1909. That same year he designed one of the earliest 30-Square-Meter yachts, *Lilian*, which was shown at an exhibition in Saint Petersburg, Russia, to generate publicity for Swedish yacht design and building.

Plym created all kinds of skerry cruisers, but he was most successful with the bigger ones. Another publicity triumph was the Viking ship he designed and built for the Olympic Games in Stockholm in 1912. He could watch the races and advertise the shipyard.

In 1914 Plym introduced a yacht with a marconi rig. He used the rig in the design of the 95-Square-Meter *Göta*, and in *Gain* in 1916. Representing the peak of his designing career is the 150-Square-Meter skerry cruiser *Beatrice-Aurore* from 1920. She is still sailing, renovated and more beautiful than ever. In 1918 he created *Miranda*, a yacht 24.5 meters long and with 220 square meters in sailing area. Here

Plym designed a skerry cruiser bigger than the rule prescribed.

After Plym's death, his son, the shipbuilding engineer Carl Plym (1899–1930), took over the management of the shipyard; in 1930 he died in an aircraft accident. During his life Carl Plym designed a few yachts, but mostly he designed motoryachts. Jac M. Iversen was employed as a yacht designer for some time. The yard also built boats from both Swedish and foreign designers.

From 1930, civil engineer Bengt Plym (1906–1966) took over management of the shipyard. His brother Gustav Plym (1911–1993) also took part in the management between 1938 and 1946. During this time the shipyard concentrated on building big, new wooden yachts by such well-known designers as Knud H. Reimers, Tore Holm, and Olin Stephens.

—Ulf Lycke

NICHOLAS SHELDON POTTER

1897–May, 1976 · United States

Nick Potter has been described as "the West Coast's L. Francis Herreshoff." This is probably appropriate, since the two men were lifelong friends and prior to their independent design careers had worked together at both the Herreshoff Manufacturing Company and Burgess, Swasey and Paine.

Potter is best known as the designer of the California 32 sloop, a highly regarded one-design cruiser/racer 46 feet LOA, and the 8-Meter *Angelita* (1930), winner of the 1932 Olympics in Los Angeles. He designed the Dyer 29 powerboat and the Potter Class-B Frostbite dinghy, as well as successful 6- and 8-Meter yachts and the very successful Universal Rule R-Class yacht *Friendship* (1927). Other designs include the 75-foot staysail schooner, *Endymion* (1930), and the 62-foot sloop *Serenade* (1938).

Born in Providence, Rhode Island, Potter grew up sailing on Narragansett Bay. As children, he and L. Francis and A. Sidney deWolf

Nick Potter: Tempest. The California 32 *Tempest* is one of the best-kept 32's still in service. She races and cruises on a regular basis with owner Tom Myers out of Dana Point, California. *Tempest* was built in 1937 by Fellows and Stewart in Wilmington, California. *Photo courtesy Thomas G. Skahill*

Herreshoff became friends. He went to work in the design department at Herreshoff's in Bristol, Rhode Island, from 1918 until 1923. As L. Francis had done earlier, Potter went to work for Burgess, Swasey and Paine in Boston. In 1925, following the closing of the firm, he joined the U.S. Merchant Marine.

While in port in southern California, Potter met designer and builder Hugh Angelman in Wilmington, California. Soon after, Potter joined him in a successful business relationship that allowed Potter to produce some of his most noted work. Family matters caused him to return to Newport, Rhode Island, in 1930, and he went back to work for Herreshoff.

In 1931 Potter and William Strawbridge became partners in a design practice in Greenwich, Connecticut. Together they won a design competition sponsored by *The Rudder* magazine for a new one-design Class-B Frostbite dinghy. This 11-foot 6-inch, clinker-built dinghy became known as the Potter Class-B One-Design Frostbite dinghy and was built of wood for many years around the United States, including at the Herreshoff yard. Ultimately it would be built from fiberglass and continue to race among frostbite aficionados.

Potter returned to California in 1935 and in the following year designed the renowned 46-foot California (Cal) 32's, which was to become his most successful and favorite design. The California 32 gave western yachtsmen a very fast offshore racer with comfortable accommodations for six. *Escapade* won the 1941 Transpacific Race, six San Diego Sir Thomas Lipton Trophy races, and numerous other competitions. A total of seven California 32's were built, five before World War II and two after the war. (An eighth California 32 was a modified version built by Cheoy Lee in Hong Kong in 1965.) Between *Escapade* and the other six, they won virtually every major West Coast race from Seattle to San Diego over the next twenty-seven years.

In the following years came a number of notable designs, including the sleek 8-meter *Yucca* (1937), still racing competitively on San Francisco Bay at the time of this writing (2002) under her owner of the past thirty-eight years, and just before World War II the double-ended sloop *Serenade* (1938) for concert violinist Jascha Heifetz, which was extensively restored in 2000.

During World War II, Potter worked at Douglas Aircraft as head of the design and lofting departments. After the war he went to work for the boatbuilding firm The Anchorage in Warren, Rhode Island, for whom he designed the Dyer 29 in 1955. The Dyer 29 Bass Boat, whose design resembles the traditional New England lobsterboat, is still (in 2002) in continuous

Nick Potter: *Serenade*. The lovely 62-foot N-Class sloop *Serenade* was designed for concert violinist Jascha Heifetz and built by Wilmington Boat Works in 1938. Although seldom raced, she was known to be extremely fast. This boat went east in the early 1970's and has recently been based in Michigan. *Photo courtesy Newport Harbor Nautical Museum, Newport Beach, CA*

production; more than four hundred have been built.

In 1962 Potter moved back to California and continued his independent design work. At his request, his drawings were destroyed upon his death, but both his sail and power yachts continue to be built and rebuilt.

—Daniel B. MacNaughton and Thomas G. Skahill

DOMINIQUE PRESLES

Born August 5, 1939 · France

The man who has largely created formal yacht design training in France describes himself as self-taught. Born in Deauville, Dominique Presles entered the Faculté des Sciences (University of Sciences), but he had a better time helping to deliver yachts from one race to another in the Channel, gaining admiration for the great American designers, especially William Tripp. Between 1964 and 1967, he worked for various shipyards and in several yacht design offices.

In 1966, Presles designed *Emerald*, with a 15-foot IOR rating, which drew attention. Working with designer André Maurie, he designed the 17.37-meter sloop *Raph* for the Singlehanded Transatlantic Race in 1968. In the same year he set up his own office and quickly designed several yachts that marked the 1970's yachting scene. *Saint-Papa, Grand-Louis, Fernande,* and their sisterships large and small were highly successful. Today, Presles makes a speciality of charter yachts, such as the series-built Apaches, ranging up to around 38 meters in length, and also designs commercial vessels.

In 1971, Presles created a naval architecture school within Paris's Ecole des Beaux-Arts (Fine Arts School of Paris); he is associated with the Ecole d'Architecture de la Vilette in Paris (La Vilette Architecture School) and other professional organizations.

Dominique Presles practices in Paris, France.

—François Chevalier.

Dominique Presles: Petrel 42. The roomy Petrel 42 has a versatile double-headsail rig and a short deckhouse, allowing good visibility from below. A deep, narrow, ballasted lifting keel provides minimum wetted surface area and offers the many advantages of shoal draft when raised. *Drawing courtesy Chevalier & Taglang*

ANGUS PRIMROSE

July 4, 1926–October 20, 1980 · England

A *Yachting World* magazine feature called "My Post War Yacht," published at the close of World War II, launched Angus Primrose's career. At school in Gloucestershire, Primrose used his headmaster's type writer and the Easter break to conduct the business of selling to the British journal his first lines, for a 14-foot Sharpie, at the age of fourteen.

His father and grandfather were Clyde yachtsmen, but Primrose did not start sailing until the family moved to Cornwall. He later owned the Dolphin Boatyard on the river Dart, Devon, before moving east to the Solent, first joining designer Reg Freeman and then working as yard manager at Captain John Illingworth's Aero Marine at Emsworth, Chichester.

Illingworth was one of yachting's most influential figures. To Primrose he was "the finest ocean racing skipper in the world of his time." Primrose steered Illingworth away from yacht building to design, the pair forming a "runaway partnership" in the late 1950's that produced a string of famous yachts, including *Blue Charm, Maica, Dambuster, Glenans, Outlaw, Green Highlander,* and *Gypsy Moth IV.*

The partnership was dissolved after eight years in 1968. Primrose's prolific output con-

tinued, with production boat successes in France, Spain, and Taiwan as well as the United Kingdom, where the Moody production yard built more than a thousand of his boats.

Primrose was lost in the Gulf Stream aboard his Moody 33, *Demon of Hamble,* following his participation in the 1980 Observer Singlehanded Transatlantic Race (OSTAR).

—Tim Jeffery

ROLAND PROUT
March 1, 1920–April, 1997
FRANCIS PROUT
Born July 7, 1921

England

Roland and Francis Prout were the British pioneers of the modern catamaran. Based on Canvey Island in the Thames estuary, the Prout brothers built their first catamaran in 1947 by joining together two kayak hulls with a plywood bridgedeck and fitting it with a single lugsail—a natural development given their experience as kayak builders and national canoe champions. They quickly shifted toward production of small, lightweight, affordable beach cats, including the Swift (14 feet 6 inches, 1954) and the Cougar (17 feet 9 inches, before 1959).

Unlike the early American and Australian beach catamarans (which with few exceptions drew on the example set by the double-ended, centerboardless, asymmetrical hulls of Woody Brown's Hawaiian *Manu Kai* from 1947), the Prouts preferred transom-sterned, round-bottomed, symmetrical hulls with centerboards, a shape that ultimately was recognized as superior and adopted worldwide. The first Shearwater catamaran (17 feet 6 inches, later 16 feet 6 inches) was designed in 1954 and made the Prouts world famous. First built from cold-molded wood and later of fiberglass, the Shearwater quickly became the world's largest catamaran class, with more than three thousand units eventually built. It was fast and easy to handle and set a standard for small beach catamarans until the early 1970's.

Always more series production oriented than their more performance-oriented contemporary designer, Roderick MacAlpine-Downie, the Prouts began to augment small catamarans with a line of large cruising catamarans in the early 1960's. *Rehu Moana* (40 feet, a Colin Mudie/Prout codesign) competed in the 1964 Singlehanded Transatlantic Race and then continued to complete a circumnavigation, making her the first catamaran to sail around the world. The 77-foot catamaran *Tsulamaran* was launched in 1965 and for many years was the world's largest.

Roland and Francis Prout: *Snowgoose.* Designed in 1970, the 35-foot *Snowgoose* became the most successful cruising catamaran designed and built by the Prout brothers. *Courtesy the Amateur Yacht Research Society*

The Prouts also engaged in the production of several successful series of rugged cruising catamarans, including the Prout 27 (27 feet 3 inches, 1962) and the Snowgoose 35 (35 feet, 1970), which later became the Snowgoose 37 (37 feet, 1978) and has continued to be one of the most successful cruising catamarans. Other models were the Quest 31 (31 feet, 1976) and the Quasar 50 (50 feet, 1984). In 2000, Prout Catamarans (its original founders having withdrawn from management) was sold to Canadian owners and subsequently went bankrupt. More than four thousand boats had been built by the Prouts to their own designs, almost all of them catamarans.

—Claas van der Linde

EDWARD "NED" PURDY
February 28, 1875–March 13, 1933
JAMES GILBERT "GIL" PURDY JR.
December 5, 1862–March 30, 1946

United States

Brothers Ned and Gil Purdy designed and built some 250 race-winning speedboats, fast commuter yachts, and cruising vessels for a distinguished clientele, including the Vanderbilts, auto tycoon Louis Chevrolet, and international adventurer T. E. Lawrence, also known as Lawrence of Arabia. The Purdy Boat Company was one of the influential builders of the early twentieth century, coinciding with the

Angus Primrose: Moody 33. This Moody 33 cruiser travels under twin running sails in the Solent. © *Alastair Black/PPL*

development of high-speed wooden hulls and increasingly powerful and sophisticated power plants.

The Purdy brothers were the sons of Canadian shipwright James Gilbert Purdy, who settled near New York in the 1880's. After starting out at their father's yard, Ned became foreman at Consolidated Shipbuilding, commuter yacht builders in Morris Heights, New York. Gil worked as chief designer.

In 1915, the two were set up in their own business by real estate developer and entrepreneur Carl Fischer (Indianapolis Speedway). They built their first boat for Fischer in a shop at the newly built Indiana speedway. For the next decade, they worked in Michigan and Florida before settling in Port Washington, New York, in the mid-1920's.

Aphrodite is arguably the Purdys' most famous boat. Built in 1937 for New York Yacht Club member John Jay Whitney and still active today, it is a 74-foot, clipper-bow, barrel-back fast commuter. With its original twin 800-hp Packard engines, the boat could do more than 30 knots. After an active career as a pleasure boat, *Aphrodite* served as a Coast Guard patrol vessel, and once escorted President Franklin Roosevelt's train up the Hudson River to his Hyde Park retreat. *Rascal*, built in 1929, was a 50-foot fast commuter powered by two 600-hp, 12-cylinder Packard engines. Sold to rumrunners, it had a top speed of 50 mph with a full cargo.

Race boats were another Purdy interest. *Imp II* (1929) and *Hotsy Totsy* (1930, 1931) won consecutive Gold Cup speed regattas, and the brothers' *Biscayne Babies* (1924) represented a successful attempt at creating a one-design powerboat expressly for racing. Packing 100-hp, 6-cylinder engines, the 18-footers could hit 40 mph.

Purdy Boat Company also built more than thirty Star-class sailboats during the 1930's. By the time Gil passed away in 1946 (Ned died in 1933), the Purdy yard relied on repairs and storage for its business. The last Purdy Boat Company building contract was for an 18-foot fishing wooden boat, which was delivered in 1950.

—Steve Knauth

Ned and Gil Purdy: *Turtle*. *Turtle*, running at speed, shows the classic Purdy hull-design concept, with a good deal of fullness at the waterline well back from the stem, and a high bow with a lot of flare balanced by the right amount of tumblehome at the transom. © *Peter Barlow*

R

HENRY RASMUSSEN

1877–June 2, 1959 · Denmark/Germany

Americans recognize Henry Rasmussen's name from Abeking and Rasmussen, the German boatyard legendary for the high quality of its work and well known in the United States for producing the Concordia yawl. However, in his own right, Rasmussen counts as one of the most important German yacht designers. His career spanned the whole first half of the twentieth century and his influence helped to direct the course of yachting in Germany.

Born in Denmark to Danish parents, Rasmussen came to boats naturally. His father, Jens Rasmussen, was a yachtsman of some fame, with several circumnavigations of the globe to his credit. His mother, Pouline Poulsen, came from a family that owned and operated the boatbuilding yard in Svendborg where his father and several of his uncles were employed.

As a boy, Rasmussen spent much of his time either working at the Poulsen yard or sailing a succession of small boats designed and built for him by his grandfather. Later in his career, his helmsmanship, which brought him numerous victories in European regattas as well as in the United States, helped him to gain public recognition for his abilities as a designer of fast racing yachts.

It surprised no one when Rasmussen chose boatbuilding as his career, and he started his formal apprenticeship at his grandfather's yard. From the beginning his instruction was not limited to boatbuilding alone as his grandfather included him in conferences with designers, sailmakers, engineers, and all workers in the allied crafts. He also began under his grandfather's tute-

Henry Rasmussen: *Regina* (opposite). The 51-foot sloop *Regina* (ex-*Konigen*), shown flying her big spinnaker on a broad reach, was built by Abeking and Rasmussen in 1954. *Photo courtesy Deutsches—Schiffahrts Museum, and Volker Christmann.*

lage to carve half models and to take their lines.

When the family sold the yard in 1894, Rasmussen continued his education as a boatbuilder, first at the Hansen yard in Odense and then at Burmeister and Wain, a shipyard that specialized in iron shipbuilding. From there he took a leave of absence to study nautical engineering and ship design in Copenhagen, his only academic training in the field. Upon his return to Burmeister and Wain, he was promoted to assistant to the operating director. He moved again in 1900 to the Vulkan yard in Bremen, which commissioned him to establish a subsidiary yard under his own direction. It was while working for Vulkan that he began his favorite employment, designing racing yachts for local businessmen. The success of these early designs quickly brought him local fame.

In 1907, Rasmussen founded his own yard, Abeking and Rasmussen, with Georg Abeking as principal stockholder. Abeking saw Rasmussen's yard merely as a promising investment opportunity and a path toward a comfortable financial independence. He had little interest in yachting or boats and wisely surrendered most of the planning and development of the business into Rasmussen's enterprising hands.

Original plans called for a yard near Kiel, which under the Kaiser's interest and patronage had developed into Germany's most important yachting center, but local opposition made this impossible. The company therefore settled in Lemwerder on the river Weser, near Bremen, where Rasmussen already enjoyed a good local reputation.

The early successes of the yachts designed and built at Abeking and Rasmussen, and a growing respect for their high standards of craftsmanship, kept the yard busy. In the first year, Rasmussen completed sixteen boats. The fifth boat, the 8-Meter *Albert* (built for August Denker of Bremen), with Rasmussen himself at the helm, defeated all its opponents by a ten-minute margin in the Weser Yacht Club regatta.

Other yachts from his drawing board soon confirmed that *Albert* had been no accident. By the third year, the number of completed boats rose to ninety-four, with orders coming from Holland, Austria, Switzerland, and Russia, as well as Germany, as his reputation spread. Almost from the beginning, the company went beyond the limits of typical boatyards, for it also operated as a shipyard accepting orders for steel-built naval and authority ships (customs, police, fireboats, etc.).

Rasmussen's lifelong interest in promoting yachting for a broader spectrum of the population by producing affordable boats led him to develop systems for building wooden boats using molds and jigs, almost on an assembly line. This allowed him to produce large numbers of boats of the same design more economically. His series of eighty Atlantic One-Designs in 1927 was the largest boat production run up to that time.

The reputation of Abeking and Rasmussen for the quality of its work was equaled by Henry Rasmussen's fame as a designer. By 1915, a Berlin Exhibition ranked his work along with that of G. L. Watson, William Fife, and Johann Anker when it chose *Toni IX*, built in 1912, to represent the 8-Meter class. The breadth of his work was astonishing, ranging from 70-foot schooners and yawls to racing yachts in the Meter and the popular Square-Meter classes, to comfortable and seakindly small cruising boats, to 12-foot centerboard dinghies. The number of national and international prizes won by his racing yachts, often meeting their most intense competition in other boats designed by him, was impressive, as were the many testimonials to the seaworthiness and comfort of his cruising boats.

As an important builder and designer he exercised considerable influence on the direction of yachting in Germany. As a member of the Technical Committee of German Sailing, the governing body of German yachting, he took a special interest in the development of smaller and more affordable classes. His encouragement of and contributions to dinghy racing and the popular

Henry Rasmussen: *Starling.* While Rasmussen designed and built many larger yachts, he retained a lifelong interest in making yachting accessible to those of more modest means. Among those efforts was his promotion of the fast, versatile, and relatively economical Square-Meter classes. Here the 30-Square-Meter *Starling*, built in 1933, noses into a sea. *Photo courtesy Peabody Essex Museum, Salem, MA*

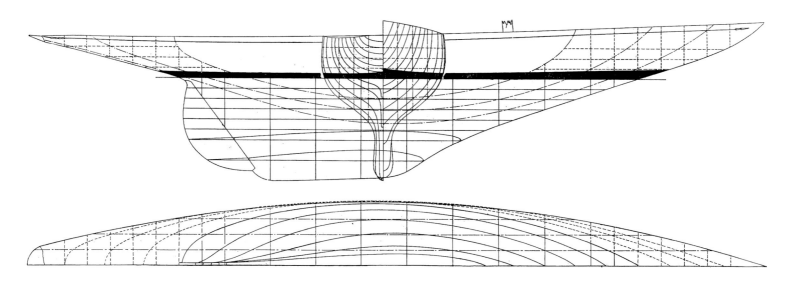

Henry Rasmussen: *Germania III.* The 8-Meter *Germania III* was designed and built by Rasmussen for Alfred Krupp von Bohlen und Halbach in 1935. Like her predecessor *Germania II*, she was a successful competitor throughout Europe and is still sailing today (as are all six of the *Germania*'s). © *Tony Dixon*

Square-Meter classes did much to promote sailing for a rising generation of yachtsmen.

The economic chaos of post–World War I Germany threatened Abeking and Rasmussen. In 1923 Abeking, anticipating a bleak future for yachting in Germany, resigned from the business, and the need to buy him out placed further stresses on the company. Rasmussen responded with an aggressive search for foreign markets, especially in the United States.

By 1925 Rasmussen had sold several R-Class boats in Boston, and in 1926 he undertook a trip to the United States with the guidance and support of W. Starling Burgess. Here he met with the Vanderbilts, the Morgans, and L. Francis Herreshoff. He returned to Germany with orders for fourteen R-Class boats and several W. Starling Burgess–designed Bermuda class boats.

Encouraged by the warm response to these projects, Rasmussen traveled back again the next year, this time bringing with him a prototype of what would become in the United States the Atlantic Class One-Design. This second trip in 1927 met with even greater success, resulting in orders to build six 12-Meters, ten more 8-Meters, several M-Class boats, and eighty orders for Atlantic Class One-Designs, all designed by W. Starling Burgess, from yacht clubs in New York, Boston, and Marblehead.

This profitable connection with the United States continued well into the 1950's, when Rasmussen was offered the plans and a verbal contract by Waldo Howland's Concordia Company for building the Concordia yawls. He produced these for the next fifteen years. At first he delivered the boats fully equipped, but later—for both economic reasons and because of the growing superiority of American

technology—motors, electrical equipment, rig, and sails were fitted in the United States.

On the strength of these lucrative connections and new contracts spurred by a reviving German economy, Rasmussen expanded in 1939 by purchasing another yard that had become available in Denmark. However, the vagaries of history made this a brief and costly venue. Much to Rasmussen's lasting indignation, Denmark seized the yard without any compensation in 1945 as part of the war reparations Germany owed the Allied Powers.

Probably the best known of Rasmussen's boats were *Germania II* (1934) and *III* (1935), both 8-Meter yachts designed and built for Alfred Krupp von Bohlen und Halbach. Surely a part of their fame derived from the importance of the client, but the success of these boats in European regattas enhanced his recognition for designing and building first-class yachts. In all, there were six *Germania*'s; the last, from a Sparkman and Stephens design, was the first welded aluminum yacht built in Germany. All six are still sailing and in good condition.

Henry Rasmussen died in a car crash at the age of eighty-three. —Gerhard Schön

MICHAEL E. RATSEY

1830–1915 · England

A prominent British designer and builder of the 1860's and 1870's, Michael Ratsey designed the first and second yachts to challenge for the America's Cup.

Michael Ratsey's grandfather, Lynn Ratsey, opened the family boatbuilding yard at Cowes in 1807. The business soon grew to include sail-

making, an activity that has continued under the Ratsey and Lapthorne name through today.

Ratsey's design work came to the fore soon after the famous victory of the George Steers–designed schooner *America* against a number of British yachts in 1851, including the cutter *Aurora*, designed by the Ratsey yard in 1838. Ratsey designed *Julia*, a cutter that beat Steers's sloop *Sylvie* in 1853, and went on to design a number of schooners that performed well against all comers.

Most notable among these schooners was the 120-foot LWL *Cambria*, built in 1868, which made the first challenge for the America's Cup in 1870. Under the early rules for challengers she had to sail against a fleet of American yachts, and was unsuccessful.

Cambria was quickly followed by the 264-ton schooner *Livonia*, which in 1871 became the first yacht designed and built especially for an America's Cup challenge. While she did not win the Cup, she did win one race against the Joseph B. van Deusen–modeled schooner *Columbia*, the defender, something no other challenger was to do until the 1920 match.

Ratsey went on to design numerous yachts, many of which were built in his yard, though some were built elsewhere, including in the United States. —Daniel B. MacNaughton

WALTER REEKS

1861–1925 · Australia

Walter Reeks was the most influential yacht designer in late-nineteenth-century Australia. The twenty-four-year-old, English-born naval architect arrived in Sydney in 1885, in search of a warmer climate. From then until the economic recession of 1893, he changed and dominated colonial yacht racing, designing most of the champion yachts on Sydney Harbour.

In England, Reeks had served an apprenticeship with the naval architect Alexander Richardson and with the shipbuilder George Inman and Son. In Australia, he entered a yachting scene in which most of the racing yachts were designed and built by rule of thumb. A few imports were designed by William Fife, George Watson, and Dixon Kemp, but no one working locally had Reeks's formal training.

Reeks's first commissions were to rebuild the older yachts *Assegai* (4 tons) and *Waitangi* (21 tons). Their renewed champion performance quickly led to commissions for the construction of larger yachts. Between 1885 and 1889, Sydney's boatyards were busy building Reeks's designs.

It was a time of rapid change in yacht design as clubs grappled with rating rules, and in this environment Reeks excelled. His new yachts of

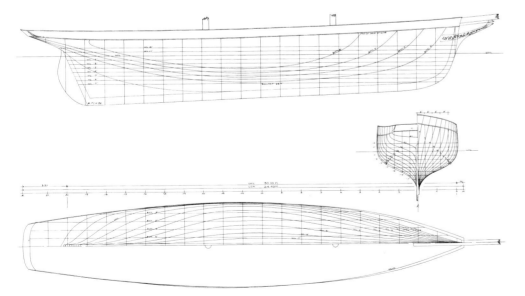

Michael Ratsey: *Cambria.* Designed and built by Ratsey in 1868, *Cambria* was the first boat to challenge for the America's Cup, in 1870. Although *Cambria* won a race across the Atlantic to come to the challenge, she was unsuccessful against the Richard Faning Loper–designed *Magic.* © *Chevalier & Taglang*

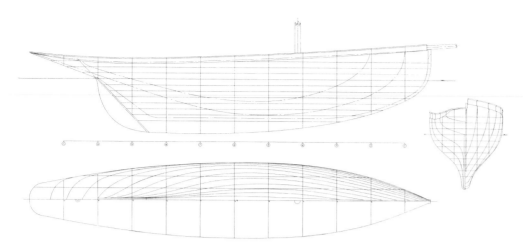

Walter Reeks: *Era.* At 70-foot LOD *Era* was Reeks's largest racing design, and the first yacht designed to the Sail-Area-and-Waterline-Length Rule. She was launched in 1887. These lines were recreated based on a half model and published dimensions. *Original drawing by David Payne*

Walter Reeks: *Isea.* Pictured reaching down Sydney Harbour in a typical nor'east breeze, *Isea* was the second-ever design to the new Sail-Area-and-Waterline-Length Rule. She was designed in 1888 and was 42 feet LOA. *Photo from the Hall Collection, courtesy Australian National Maritime Museum*

1888—the 40-Rater *Era* and the 10-ton *Isea*—were possibly the earliest yachts built to new international rating rules, which took sail area into account for the first time. The new Length-and-Sail-Area Rule calculated the rating as a relationship between waterline length and sail area only. Beginning with *Era,* the "plank-on-edge" hulls favored by the previous rule began to disappear. Eighteen months later, his design for *Thelma* had generous beam and a lovely rounded shape at the turn of the bilge.

Era, with a waterline length of 58 feet, was at that time the biggest sailing yacht built in Australia. She had a rating of 41 under the Length-and-Sail-Area Rule and incorporated Reeks's views about successful yacht design. In an article entitled "Yachting and Sailing" in the *Illustrated Sydney News* on May 31, 1888, Reeks judged that yachts should have "a small skin, big displacement relatively, and perfectly gradual approach and delivery" and "[proper] distribution of weights, balance of canvas to hull, position of centers of buoyancy [relative] to gravity—and good copper."

Reeks also designed the 33-Rater *Volunteer* later in 1888, with a waterline length of 53 feet. At the 1888 Melbourne Intercolonial Centennial Regatta, *Era* and *Volunteer* came in first and second in the first-class yacht race, confirming Reeks's dominance. The smaller 15-Rater *Thelma,* built in 1889, was seen by Reeks as "the flower of his flock." It won in the 5- to 20-Rating class for over twenty years.

In 1888 a Sydney syndicate sent Reeks to the United States and England to inspect champion yachts for the preparation of an Australian challenge for the America's Cup. Unfortunately the project collapsed from lack of financial support.

Yacht racing suffered from the economic depression of the 1890's and Reeks diversified his practice into the more lucrative area of ferry design. His ferries included the first of the double-ended, screw-propelled ferries on Sydney Harbour.

When yacht racing recovered around 1900, it was dominated by the Logan Brothers, designer/builders from New Zealand. Nevertheless, Walter Reeks remained a force on the harbor, designing racing and cruising yachts and centerboard craft. Three of his auxiliary craft are afloat on Sydney Harbour today: the 100-foot steam yacht *Ena* (built in 1901), the Vice-Regal steam launch *Lady Hopetoun* (built 1902), and the 70-foot auxiliary schooner *Boomerang* (built in 1903 as *Bona*). Reeks remained an active sailor, and was vice commodore of the Royal Sydney Yacht Squadron from 1906 to 1910. He was its official measurer until his death in 1925.   —Daina Fletcher

Knud Reimers: *Debutante.* One of the acknowledged masters of the Square-Meter classes, Reimers drew many examples, including in 1937 the 43-foot 11-inch, 30-Square-Meter *Debutante.* The photo seems to capture the ease with which these beautiful wooden arrows make their swift and wakeless way. *Photo courtesy Newport Harbor Nautical Museum, Newport Beach, CA*

KNUD H. REIMERS

1906–1987 · Denmark/Sweden

Knud Reimers's early career reads like a Horatio Alger novel. Reimers, the most international Scandinavian designer between 1930 and the fiberglass age, would have become a typographer like his father had he followed the path laid out for him. When, therefore, the son stated his desire to become a ship engineer instead, all his father could offer him was 1,000 Danish Kröner (approximately $140) with the assurance "that he could spend no more toward his son's education." With this meager inheritance, Reimers left his native Aarhus in Denmark to seek work and experience in Germany.

Reimers found the work, first at Krupps-Germania Shipyard in 1926 and then at Abeking and Rasmussen in Lemwerder in their design department. Concurrently he began a course of study at the nearby Bremen Technical High School. In 1930, he left the school penniless but with a degree in ship engineer-

ing and a confidence in his own abilities, having achieved the highest marks in all subjects. He found, however, that Europe had entered a catastrophic depression, especially severe in Germany, under which the whole yachting industry threatened to founder, and that no one had need of his newly acquired talents.

By good fortune, Reimers learned that Gustaf Estlander, one of Sweden's most distinguished designers and yachtsmen, happened to be in Germany for recreation. Reimers, by way of recommendation, approached him with a portfolio of his own designs. After he surveyed the drawings, Estlander, so says the story, announced, "Mr. Reimers, you may start with me the first of August (1930) in Stockholm." Only a few months later Estlander died prematurely, and Reimers, in January of the following year, succeeded to his place in the drawing office. Later, in 1937, now well established, Reimers received Swedish citizenship.

When Reimers started, the skerry cruiser Square-Meter classes were very popular in the Stockholm area, and his first design for that

class, the 30-Square-Meter *Skjold VIII*, won Kiel Week in 1933. That success suddenly thrust his name before the world, and soon he began to receive orders from all over Europe and even places as distant as the United States, Australia, Shanghai, and Annam (now Vietnam).

Reimers drew Square-Meter yachts in all sizes from 15 to 75 square meters, of which the 30-Square-Meter *Moose* (United States, 1936) was perhaps the most remarkable. These boats characteristically carried a little higher freeboard and a shorter length overall than was common for skerrie cruisers, and thus moderated the type somewhat. Two of his 30-Square-Meter designs later provided patterns for fiberglass production.

Playing only a small part in the general development of International Rule boats, Reimers designed only five of the most common, the 6-Meter. Still, his interest in the smaller and less well-known 5-Meter class, very popular at that time in France, introduced the class to Scandinavia, and so successful were his designs that a large and highly competitive fleet developed, in which the boats of many designers were represented. Once again, Reimers's success led to foreign orders for 5-Meters from France, Switzerland, Argentina, and Brazil.

Unlike Estlander, Reimers did not specialize only in development class racers, for he designed motoryachts and a variety of cruisers, cruiser/racers, and other types. Of these, the slim one-design double-ender *Tumlare* (1934) deserves special mention. More than six hundred of these boats were built (about half of them pirated copies) and there were active fleets in twenty-four countries. Before World War II, Reimers also introduced the doghouse and the deck-stepped mast to Swedish sailors.

During the war years (1939–1945), Reimers turned from yachts to designing fast motorboats and minesweepers in the service of his adopted country, but after the war he returned again to yachting, working now at the top of his powers. He designed a large number of cruiser/racers for important offshore races, including the Transatlantic, the Fastnet, and the Bermuda Races. Two of his boats, *Tre Sang* and *Cohoe*, were the best boats in RORC Class III over two years.

He also drew plans for family boats, such as the very popular short-ended *Swell*, a roomy

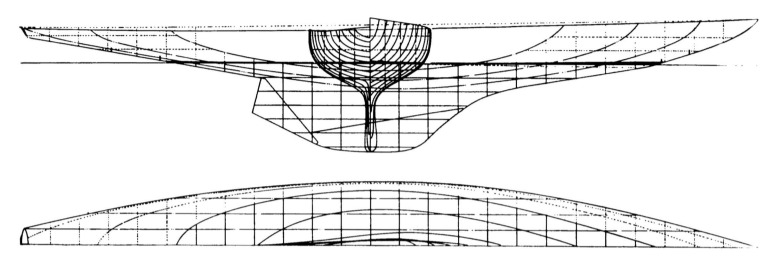

Knud Reimers: *Darling IV.* Reimers designed the 30-Square-Meter *Darling IV* from diagonals, saying that "water-lines and buttocks are of little use in fairing and building a vessel." Uffa Fox shows the resulting waterlines and buttocks here, to demonstrate that this method produces a complete set of lines that are "remarkably sweet and fair and as near perfection as it is possible to get in this imperfect world." © *Tony Dixon*

Knud Reimers: *Taifun.* The 12.84-meter *Taifun*, a 30-Square-Meter skerry cruiser, was built at the Strängnäs Boatyard in 1948 as *Shangri La* for B. Wallin of Stockholm, Sweden. © *Per Thelander*

and seaworthy cruising yacht, and *Fingal*, a small family boat that became popular with Swedish sailors, designed in 1962 and intended for fiberglass construction.

Reimers continued to work until his death at the age of eighty. In his long career some 1,500 boats were built from his drawings, including 32 for his own use, and not counting the hundreds that were built without authorization. The scope of his work embraced the whole spectrum of yacht design, from pure racing boats to seaworthy and comfortable family boats, from small one-design boats to large oceangoing yachts, from sailboats to motoryachts. All his boats, racers, and cruisers alike shared the common characteristic of his designs—a slender and graceful hull form.   —Bent Aarre

KURT REINKE

1933–February 2000 · Germany

Known since 1971 as a productive designer with consistent sales of his double-chined, bilge-keeled, raised-deck, steel and aluminum designs in the 7.5- to 20-meter range, Reinke found his niche in the do-it-yourself building scene. According to his records, his 52-foot, Hydra twin-screw motorsailer has been built more than a hundred times.

It is not surprising that "Reinkes" are a common sight all over the world, particularly in remote and difficult cruising areas. Simplicity of construction and general rigidity and strength appeal to a clientele not only ready to drop out, but also ready to weld together their own sailing home before going.

Reinke's bilge-keel configuration reduces draft, and asymmetrical foils improve upwind performance. Taking the ground in tidal waters or drying out on hard land for maintenance purposes is simple and safe. The use of multiple chines makes plating the hull and raised deck with steel or aluminum relatively simple.

After an education as a shipwright at the Abeking and Rasmussen yard, which specializes in metal construction of military, special-purpose, and large luxury vessels, Reinke gained knowledge in naval architecture working at Sparkman and Stephens in New York City and with Britton Chance Jr. on Long Island.

Back in northern Germany in 1970, Reinke coordinated pleasure boat construction as foreman at Abeking and Rasmussen in the village of Lemwerder on the west bank of the river Weser opposite Bremen. After 1987 Reinke devoted his time solely to designing his range of eighteen different models, all meant to offer their owners good value for their investment.

—Erdmann Braschos

PHILIP LEONARD RHODES

January 15, 1895–August 29, 1974
United States

Philip Rhodes was one of the world's most productive and versatile yacht designers. His body of work includes as many as fifty one-design classes; motorsailers and motoryachts of all sizes; military craft; cargo vessels; and utility boats for many purposes. Rhodes is, however, best known for his sailing yachts, many of which were highly successful ocean racers in the CCA handicapping rule era and are considered to be among the most beautiful yachts designed to that rule. Indeed, Rhodes helped to develop the rule and served for many years on the CCA Measurement Rule Committee.

A typical Rhodes sailboat would be a keel/centerboard sloop or yawl with a strongly curving sheer and balanced, moderate-to-long overhangs with plenty of shape to them. Doghouses were handsome and quite streamlined.

Most of Rhodes's designs were moderate in all respects except for their beauty and performance, and if the racing boats were eventually made obsolete by changing handicapping rules and the evolution of design, they remained universally good cruising and voyaging yachts. Most are still sailing today as a result of this broad-based appeal. Rhodes did not do a great deal of sailing, but he did sail in a number of Bermuda Races and was said to be

Kurt Reinke: Scheffner-segel. Reinke was among the few designers creating larger boats aimed specifically at do-it-yourself builders. His multichine designs were optimized for steel and aluminum construction, and many featured twin-bilge keels for upright grounding. *Photo courtesy Peter Reinke*

a competent tactician, sail trimmer, and helmsman. He owned a 52-foot 3-inch LOA aluminum motoryacht named *Touché Too* of his own design. She was built with a V-bottomed form and hard chines, allowing for quick planing.

Rhodes was born in Raccoon, Ohio. His father built wooden carriages and his stepfather was a master carpenter, which exposed him to the practicalities of fine woodworking, but his was not a nautical background. His first experience of boats was watching working vessels on the Ohio River. Later he acquired first-hand experience at Buckeye Lake, where his family vacationed.

During high school Rhodes developed a strong interest in design. He drew plans for a number of motorboats and had articles published in *Motor Boating* magazine. He attended Denison University for a while, but then transferred to MIT to study naval architecture under Professors George Owen and C. H. Peabody. He became a part-time assistant to Owen in 1917 and graduated from MIT in 1918 as a naval architect and marine engineer.

Like many young designers of the time, Rhodes's primary interest was in the new motorboats, which had been made practical by the development of powerful and relatively lightweight gasoline engines. His first commissioned design was a modification of *Jerry*, a 40-foot motorsailer with which he had won a design competition sponsored by *Motor Boating*'s Ideal Series in 1917.

Rhodes's first sailboat design was a 30-foot auxiliary yawl named *Volante*, with which he again won the *Motor Boating* Ideal Series competition, in 1919. In addition, he had a strong early interest in hydrofoil boats and cooperated on several such projects with Casey Baldwin and his associate, Alexander Graham Bell.

Rhodes served with the army engineers during World War I. After the war he returned to Ohio and became a shipfitter. He later moved to Baltimore, where he did similar work for Union Shipbuilding, and then to New York City in 1920 to design hulls for the same company. He created several cruising sailboats on commission in his spare time, including the 24-foot sloop *West Wind* and the 36-foot schooner *Mary Jeanne II*, the plans for which were published in a 1922 *Motor Boat* magazine, and a 32-foot schooner, published in *Yachting* magazine in 1924. He opened his own design office in 1925, sharing it with designer Weston Farmer.

A friend of Rhodes's, Henry Howard, was the owner of a 52-foot centerboard yawl named *Alice*, designed by Commodore Ralph Munroe, an early advocate of shoal draft. Through this boat Rhodes became interested in centerboarders for offshore use, although he opted for deeper

ballast keels than did Munroe. Rhodes's first design of this keel/centerboard type was *Ayesha*, a beautiful and successful 46-foot yawl that took third place in her class in the Bermuda Race of 1932 and led to a host of other more or less similar designs.

Also around this time, Rhodes drew more than a dozen double-enders, most notably the 32-foot 4-inch *Tidal Wave*, a modified Block Island boat type with a marconi ketch rig that is still sailing, having been beautifully restored. Others were of the Colin Archer type and some had canoe sterns.

During the Great Depression, the number of design commissions fell substantially, as it did for most designers, and in 1932 Rhodes joined the design firm of Cox and Stevens, bringing to their office his talent for relatively small yachts—they had previously designed mostly large luxury yachts. He was given full credit for all of the designs he produced in that office, and in 1935 he was given control over the whole design team.

Among the designers and engineers who worked for Rhodes at Cox and Stevens and in his own firm after World War II were Frederick Bates, Richard Davis, Henry Devereaux, Ralph Jackson, Francis Kinney, Al Mason, James McCurdy, Joseph Reinhardt, Robert Steward, William Tripp, Winthrop Warner, Bob Wallstrom, and Charles Wittholz.

Yachting magazine's editor, William H. Taylor, suggested that Rhodes design an inexpensive frostbite dinghy, and a batten-seamed, gaff-rigged, chine-hull catboat was the result. Unfortunately, she was not particularly popular, and in 1939 the design was revised to accommodate plywood construction and a marconi rig. It became the Penguin class, achieving great popularity and becoming one of the world's largest one-design classes, numbering some ten thousand boats to date.

The 53-foot keel cutter *Kirawan* won the Bermuda Race in 1936, beating one of Olin Stephens's masterpieces, *Stormy Weather*, boat for boat. The keel/centerboarder *Alondra*, better known later as Carleton Mitchell's *Caribbee*, was launched in 1937. She won the SORC twice and made numerous cruises in North America and Scandinavia, which were well publicized

Philip Rhodes: *Tidal Wave* (opposite). *Tidal Wave* is an early Rhodes design for a cruising double-ender with a long keel, from which evolved several other wholesome, attractive, seaworthy double-enders such as *Dog Star*. Measuring 32 feet 4 inches LOD and built by Minnefords Yacht Yard on City Island, New York, *Tidal Wave* is still sailing in Maine. © *Mystic Seaport, Rosenfeld Collection, Mystic, CT*

Philip Rhodes: *Alert*. Launched by the Lester Stone Yard in Alameda, California, in 1949, *Alert* is a 62-foot 3-inch auxiliary ketch that sails on the West Coast. With her clean decks, center cockpit, well-thought-out and easily handled rig, hard dodger, and boom gallows, most would consider her an ideal cruising boat. © *Benjamin Mendlowitz*

Philip Rhodes: *Carina (II)*. Said to be Rhodes's favorite among his designs, *Carina (II)* is one of history's most successful ocean racers, having won two Transatlantic Races, two Fastnet Races, and the Bermuda Race. Designed in 1955, she is also one of the most perfect expressions of the CCA handicapping rule's intended influence, and a happy combination of racing and cruising utility. © *Mystic Seaport, Rosenfeld Collection, Mystic, CT*

in magazine articles. *Escapade*, a maximum-size ocean racer (72 feet) built in 1938, proved that large centerboarders could be both fast and practical. She won many races in the Great Lakes and continued to be competitive for many years in saltwater on both coasts.

In the 46-foot, double-ended, keel/centerboard cutter *Kirawan II*, also built in 1938 and better known later as *Hother*, Rhodes introduced a new and distinctive feature that was also utilized on the well-known 48-foot 9-inch cutter *Thunderhead*, designed in 1959: a "bald" clipper bow with a strong reverse curve to the profile, designed to bring the headstay farther forward without the use of a bowsprit. The structure was executed without any of the tra-

ditional ornamentation typically associated with a clipper bow. Both boats saw considerable success.

In 1937 Rhodes began a series of large designs of about 70 to 100 feet long which featured sleek, relatively long-ended, shoal-draft hulls and full-sized sailing rigs, but with large, well-proportioned deckhouses and powerful engines classifying them as motorsailers. Usually built of steel, these good-looking yachts performed well under both power and sail while providing a high degree of luxury, and served to define a new and popular approach to motorsailer design. The 81-foot *Gray Fox* (ex-*Tamaris*, 1938) is said to have introduced butt-welded steel construction for yacht use, and was also notable

for her five watertight compartments and double bottom. Other examples include the 90-foot *Sea Diamond* (ex-*Bar-L-Rick*, 1956), the 77-foot *Criterion* (1961), the 99-foot *Fei Seen* (1961), and the 83-foot *Sea Prince II* (1954).

Continuing his great output in 1938, Rhodes designed a 39-foot racer/cruiser called the Rhodes 27 and an 18-foot daysailer known as the Rhodes 18, both extremely successful designs that continue to have popular followings. In 1939 he designed the 39-foot Bounty, an early attempt at a boat that could be built less expensively by using premade parts and the newly developed waterproof plywood for many of her interior and deck structures.

During World War II, Cox and Stevens designed minesweepers, patrol craft, salvage vessels, tugs, and subchasers for the navy, and helped to convert ocean liners for use as troop carriers and hospital ships. Rhodes designed fourteen hospital ships from scratch. At one point he had an office aboard the liner *Normandie*, while overseeing her conversion. Cox and Stevens had offices in New Orleans and Montreal, and a staff of 498, producing seven hundred designs in the course of the war.

The busy war years allowed little opportunity to produce yachts, but Rhodes was able to design one; the 46-foot 4-inch centerboard yawl *Carina*, drawn in 1941. His Hurricane class of 1945 ultimately became known as the Rhodes 19 in 1959, and fleets popped up all over the United States.

The big-ship work of Cox and Stevens continued after World War II and represented most of the firm's business until 1947. That year, following Daniel Cox's retirement, the firm became Philip L. Rhodes, Naval Architects and Marine Engineers. After that the firm concentrated more on yachts, although the commercial work continued.

Carina helped to bring publicity to the Rhodes office after her 1952 Bermuda Race victory. In England she came in second in her class in the 1953 Fastnet Race and won several other major races, plus the Bayview-Mackinac, Block Island, Halifax, and Stamford-Vineyard Races in the United States. In 1955 the yawl *Carina II* was designed; she is said to have been Rhodes's favorite. A 53-foot keel/centerboarder, she won two Transatlantic Races, two Fastnet Races, and her class in the Bermuda Race, among other victories.

The Bounty II was introduced in 1956. A modernized and slightly enlarged (40-foot) version of the original Bounty, but built in fiberglass, she was the first fiberglass production boat of significant size.

In 1957 Rhodes designed the 12-Meter *Weatherly*, the only International Rule boat he ever

Philip Rhodes: *Escapade.* One of the largest of Rhodes's keel/centerboard racers, the 72-foot *Escapade* set course records in the Port Huron–Mackinac Race of 1950, the Annapolis-Newport Race of 1965, and the Miami-Nassau Race of 1966, among many other victories. *Photo courtesy Newport Harbor Nautical Museum, Newport Beach, CA*

RHODES

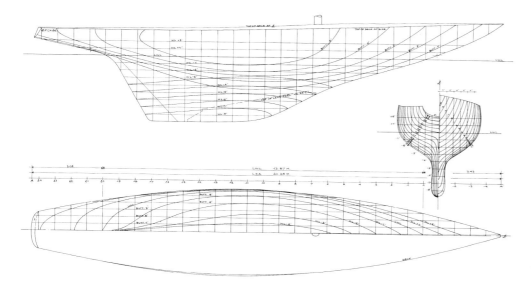

Philip Rhodes: *Weatherly*. The ability to exploit a measurement rule is critical to racing success and usually comes only with long experience. This makes it remarkable that Rhodes was able to create a successful America's Cup defender in *Weatherly*, though she was the only International Rule yacht he ever designed. She defended the Cup in 1962 against the Australian *Gretel*. © *Chevalier & Taglang*

having designed approximately 390 boats during his career. His eldest son Philip H. "Bodie" Rhodes was also a naval architect and worked with him for many years, continuing on after his father died. In 1965 the younger Rhodes teamed up with designer Jim McCurdy to form the design firm of McCurdy and Rhodes. Following the deaths of Jim McCurdy and Bodie Rhodes, Jim's son, Ian McCurdy, has continued the practice in Cold Spring Harbor, New York.

Philip Rhodes's archives are in the Philip L. Rhodes Collection, as well as the Cox and Stevens, Inc. Collection and the Winthrop L. Warner Collection, at Mystic Seaport Museum, Mystic, CT.

—Daniel B. MacNaughton

drew, to defend the America's Cup. The group that commissioned the *Weatherly* design imposed only one condition, which was that Rhodes must personally oversee every detail of her design and construction. She failed to win the defender's trials in that year, but succeeded in 1962, when she went on to beat the Alan Payne–designed *Gretel* from Australia four to one in the best of seven series.

Rhodes began a series of fiberglass designs in 1958 for Seafarer Yachts, including the 33-foot keel/centerboard Swiftsure, the Ranger 28, and the Meridian class. For Cheoy Lee he also de-

signed the Rhodes Reliant, another popular and attractive fiberglass design.

The year 1962 saw the creation of the Pearson Vanguard, said to be Rhodes's most popular fiberglass cruiser. In 1963 he designed the O'Day Tempest and Outlaw. The 1960's saw a number of designs for steel motoryachts over 100 feet in length, many of which had aluminum deckhouses. In 1970 Rhodes designed the 123-foot, three-masted schooner *Sea Star* for Lawrence Rockefeller. One of his last designs was a 170-foot diesel cruiser.

Philip L. Rhodes died at age seventy-nine,

GUY RIBADEAU DUMAS

Born February 21, 1951 · France

Growing up with his family's Johan Anker–designed 10-Meter *Jade*, Guy Ribadeau Dumas has had a lifelong involvement with classic yachts as well as the ultramodern racers for which he is most famous. He is better known for his *Crédit Agricole* (1982) and *Crédit Agricole III* (1986) with which Philippe Jeantot won the first and the second BOC, leading to the Open 60 Class of today.

Ribadeau Dumas enrolled in the Westlawn School of Yacht Design and by the age of twenty was working in the office of designer Georges Auzépy-Brenneur. His first independent sailboat design was the Two-Tonner *Relance*. Her success allowed him to set up his own business and production boats for Jeanneau. Designs range from modern to classic in style. His largest design, the Finnish 34-meter training schooner *Helena*, has quite traditional lines.

Thanks to his brother, Arnaud, a computer engineer, Ribadeau Dumas was working in three-dimensional design programs as early as 1985, using them for *Crédit Agricole III*, and other subsequent designs. The maxi *Charles Jourdan* was among the best in the 1989–90 Whitbread Race. Two times lighter than the other IOR maxis with the first carbon prepreg hull, her new concept convinced the skippers to ask for a new rule. Renamed *Nicorette* by Ludde Ingvall, she later won the Fastnet Race, Gotland Runt, and Chicago Mackinac under IMS and CHS (Channel Handicap System) ratings.

Having a great interest in the history of naval architecture, Ribadeau Dumas has restored a number of classic yachts: the William Fife III–designed *Vanity V* and the Charles E. Nicholson yachts *Wings* and *Firebird*. He has

Guy Ribadeau Dumas: *Crédit Agricole*. *Crédit Agricole* won the first BOC Around Alone Race in 1982, skippered by Philippe Jeantot. The 17-meter design looks conservative today, compared to the Open 60 Class yachts that she helped to inspire. © *Barry Pickthall/PPL*

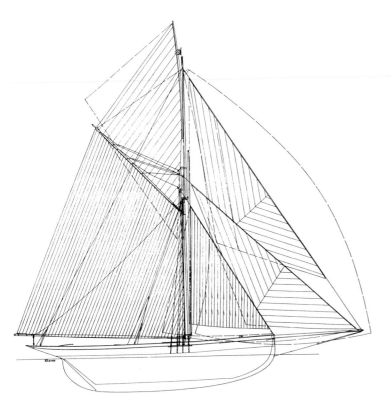

Alexander Richardson: *Irex*. The 64-ton cutter *Irex* was designed in 1884, early in Richardson's career. She was so successful that it was commonly said that she could have won the America's Cup if she had been the 1885 challenger instead of the Beavor-Webb–designed *Genesta*. © *Chevalier & Taglang*

Jacques de Ridder: *Yonder II*. The 19.5-meter *Yonder II* was built of aluminum by Royal Huisman Shipyard in the Netherlands, in 1988. *Photo courtesy Rutger ten Broeke*

even attempted to subtly improve the lines of the *Star* within the tolerances of the class rules. One of his last tasks is the rebuilt of *l'Hermione*, the 200-foot, 60-gun frigate sailed by Lafayette to America in 1780.

Guy Ribadeau Dumas practices in Nantes, France. —François Chevalier

ALEXANDER RICHARDSON

1845–1915 · England

During the 1880's in Great Britain, Alexander Richardson occupied a dominant position in the design of yachts for the big cutter class of over 40 tons or 40-Rating, but the appearance of the George Watson–designed *Britannia* and *Valkyrie II* and the Joseph Soper–designed *Satanita* in the early 1890's brought Richardson's preeminence to an end.

Richardson, the son of a cotton broker, was born at Rock Ferry on the Mersey in western England. While still an amateur, he designed for his father-in-law the Ten-Tonner *Lily* in 1875. She was a successful boat with a heavier lead ballast keel than was usual at that time.

By 1879 Richardson had established himself as a naval architect with an office in Liverpool. Almost immediately he was commissioned by

John Jameson for the design of *Samoena*, 94 tons, built in 1880, a yacht that raced successfully until it was replaced by *Irex*, 64 tons, built to Richardson's design in 1884. Originally a centerboarder, *Irex* was another very successful yacht; at the time it was said that if she had challenged for the America's Cup of 1885 instead of the Beavor-Webb–designed *Genesta*, the outcome would have been different.

There followed a number of yachts, at first to the Tonnage Rule and then to the Length-and-Sail-Area Rule of 1886, some of which were built to extreme dimensions. In 1890, the centerboarder *Iverna*, 119 tons, dominated the class until the appearance of the large cutters *Valkyrie II*, *Britannia*, and *Satanita*, which raced against each other on the Clyde in 1893. During the 1890's, he was reported to be designing some commercial craft, and after the introduction of the International Rule of 1906, he also designed a boat for the 12-Meter class.

Richardson was a private, almost reclusive man who did not give interviews, and as a result, there is little about him in writing. It is notable that in the 1881 census, at a time when women, particularly married ones, did not usually have professions, his wife was assigned the same occupation as her husband.

 —Brian Smith

JACQUES DE RIDDER

Born 1942 · The Netherlands

Like many designers in the Netherlands, Jacques de Ridder learned yacht design primarily from his experiences as a yachtsman and a ship's carpenter, as well as from jobs and apprenticeships under some exemplary teachers.

De Ridder studied naval architecture at the Hendrick de Keyserschool in Amsterdam. In 1963 he was employed at the office of naval architect W. de Vries Lentsch in Amsterdam, where he was introduced to the basics of drawing and design. From 1964 until 1969 he worked as a designer with E. G. van de Stadt in Zaandam, and in 1969 he spent a year working with American designer Britton Chance in Oyster Bay on Long Island in New York.

After de Ridder's return to the Netherlands, he rejoined van de Stadt. It was during this time that van de Stadt, de Ridder, and others embarked on an independent initiative of tank-testing and research with Professor Wiebe Draijer of the University of Delft; it was called the Think Tank.

In 1972 de Ridder went to work for Royal Huisman Shipyard, and later that year he opened his own office in Vollenhove, where he still practices. His first design was the revolutionary Quarter-Tonner *Extension,* which set fabulous race records in 1974, and his next was a 44-foot OSTAR racer, *Bollemaat.* His first production design was *High-Tension,* which placed second in the 1975 One-Ton Cup.

In addition to many one-offs, de Ridder enjoys working on production boats such as the Etap, Friendship, and Spirit series. Characteristic of de Ridder's modesty is that he considers the 12-foot Splash class dinghy, which was adopted as an international class in 1997, to be one of his favorite designs. —Rutger ten Broeke

CARLO RIVA

Born February 24, 1922 · Italy

Carlo Riva was born into a family of boatbuilders in Sarnico on Lake Iseo in the Italian region of Lombardy. Whenever possible, he took time off from technical school to work in the boatyard with his father, Serafino, and to learn the technical secrets of his uncle, Gerolamo Caviglia, former designer at the famous Baglietto Shipyard of Varazze.

The atmosphere that Riva breathed in the yard, at that time specializing in the construction of racing powerboats, was one of great enthusiasm and euphoria. The company's boats had won two hundred first prizes and ten world championships between 1932 and 1937. It was almost enough to make the family forget the yard's continual financial problems, due in part to the time needed for tuning and servicing the racing boats. Even custom-built pleasure craft were not remunerative, as each boat was one of a kind and its cost was difficult to estimate, so in spite of Serafino's great skill and high standards, frequent billing adjustments eroded the profit margins.

In 1939 Serafino suffered a sudden short illness, giving Carlo the opportunity to show his worth. He had learned to design and had willpower and stubbornness combined with enthusiasm, ability, and self-confidence, all gifts that slowly but surely would persuade the most skeptical craftsman to accept his new ideas.

Carlo Riva completely redesigned the racing models, ensuring further success. He also created a series of tunnel-drive inboard motor craft to be used for patrol service in the shallow lakes of East Africa. His objectives for the yard were rationalization and standardization of its output through the construction of boats in series based on a tried-and-tested prototype. He worked to contain to the utmost any unexpected events and defects and to respect quality, cost estimates, and delivery dates.

In the 1940's, the war and a depressed economy put a damper on Riva's projects for a

while. Still, important clients such as Carlo Dusio, the son of Pietro Dusio, the owner of the Cisitalia car factory, and Giuseppe Beretta, owner of the Beretta weapons factory (synonymous with precision and production in series), helped to stimulate in him the idea of a symbiosis of beauty, efficient production, and technical perfection.

Toward the end of the 1940's Riva's projects, which had originally been inspired by the success of American runabouts, began to display a unique character of their own. Prototypes were built for a large number of models that would be produced over the next decade, including the AR, the Corsaro, the AV,

the Scoiattolo, the AU, the BF, the BM, the Ariston, the AT, the BQ, and the twin-engine Tritone. All were runabouts 17 to 27 feet long. In 1950 Carlo became the sole manager of the yard.

In 1952, having obtained exclusive rights to sell reliable American Chris-Craft engines in Italy, Riva was finally able to market models with fittings and engines supplied only by the yard, at a fixed price with a guaranteed delivery date. Alongside the Scoiattolo, the Corsaro, the Ariston, and the Tritone, two family-type models with inboard motors came into production. These were the Sebino and the Florida. In the following year the yard's out-

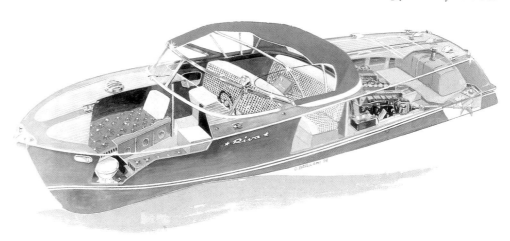

Carlo Riva: Tritone. The twin-engine Tritone runabouts were built between 1950 and 1966. Ranging in length from 7.6 to 8.3 meters, 257 were built. *Drawing courtesy Riva Historical Society, Milan, Italy*

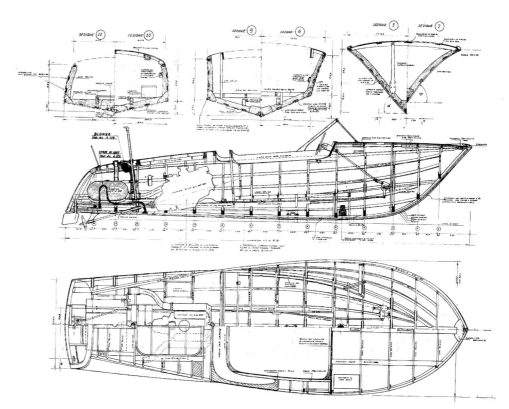

Carlo Riva: Ariston. The single-engine Ariston runabout was produced from 1950 to 1974 in lengths between 6.24 and 6.95 meters. Over a thousand were built. *Drawing courtesy Riva Historical Society, Milan, Italy*

put consisted entirely of pleasure craft, and the construction of racing boats was abandoned.

Soon the Super Florida appeared, which was built especially for water skiing, being broader and longer than the Florida and with a more powerful engine. In 1956, the Ariston also came out in a Cadillac model, with more abundant power in the same hull.

Research continued into the quality and resistance of materials, especially laminated woods made with phenolic resins, which Riva developed along with Remo Lodi. Riva used laminated wood for hull bottoms for the first time in 1955, and after 1957 the hull sides and deck were also laminated wood, preformed with a special system of pneumatic pressing. Research was extended to all particulars and

their execution, so that the design of the boat would be constantly improved and harmonious in all its components.

Riva felt that it was not enough to build, advertise, and sell boats. A network of over forty customer service yards was created near the most fashionable summer yachting centers to provide constant support to the clients. The services included having a team of first-aid technicians on hand for all problems and overhaul and maintenance capabilities for the winter season.

In this way, the boatyard won itself an international clientele of famous names, including aristocrats, actors, singers, and leaders of industry and finance, who formed the best introduction to new markets. Riva succeeded

where no one ever had in the boating field, by making a product that was built strictly to his designs such that not even the most important clients were allowed optional fittings.

In 1962 the most famous of Riva's models, the Aquarama, was first produced. It was a development of the Tritone, which was slowly fading despite some admirers' nostalgia for its pure, vigorous forms. While the Tritone and Ariston were considered Riva's most handsome runabouts, a pleasing design and extra attention to comfort made the Aquarama a cult object around the world. Riva modified the hull over the years, making it smoother and safer and accommodating engines of increasing power. The ultimate Aquarama hull, designed by Riva in 1968, was retained until the last boat, No. 784, was built in 1996.

Riva began an association with the de Vries boatyard in Holland in 1962, so as to build larger yachts that could not be built at Sarnico owing to the difficulty of transporting them to the coast. For production at de Vries he designed the Caravelle series, first 21.8 meters in length and then 22.5 meters; the 26.7-meter Atlantic; and the 35.2-meter Viking.

Smaller models, such as the Scoiattolo, the Sebino, and the Corsaro went out of production in the mid-1950's, and construction of the Florida ceased in 1963. In 1964, Riva acquired a memorable showroom in the heart of New York City, featuring his largest runabout models. A reputation acquired on the Riviera and on the Côte d'Azur had preceded him, and soon Rivas became objects of desire and display in America as well. The Super Aquarama joined the Aquarama, and the Junior and Olympic came out in 1966 and 1969, respectively, to replace the Florida and Super Florida.

In the late 1960's, Riva began to take on the challenge of the new fiberglass construction materials as they became more and more appreciated in the yachting field for their ease of maintenance and greater suitability to series production. Indeed, from his frequent trips to America, and in addition to his impressions of the market trends, Riva brought back some examples of small fiberglass cabin cruisers that he could redesign to European tastes.

In 1969 Italy's general national unrest had reached the Riva yard, and at times even Carlo Riva was unable to get in to work. For the first time he was unable to meet agreed-upon delivery dates, and therefore would have to break his word. Moreover, the season for using wood in series production was drawing to an end, and with it the joy of creation derived from a certain way of working with a natural material. At the peak of success, at age forty-seven, Riva suddenly sold the yard to Whittaker, an

Carlo Riva: Aquarama. This Aquarama is No. 359, built in 1969. These twin-engine runabouts were produced from 1962 to 1971, in lengths from 8.02 to 8.5 meters. Additionally, 278 Aquarama Specials were built between 1972 and 1996 at 8.78 meters in length. *Photo by Maggi & Maggi. Courtesy Riva Historical Society, Milan, Italy*

Carlo Riva: Super Florida. Shown here behind a very appealing small hydroplane is the Super Florida, designed specifically for use in waterskiing. *Photo courtesy Riva Historical Society, Milan, Italy*

American merchant bank that also owned the Bertram boatyard.

Under the sale contract, Riva could not produce small boats under his name and for a certain number of years could not compete with the Riva yard. Therefore, he initially restricted his activity to the design of large yachts, which could be built under his name. Difficulties with the Italian economy proved an obstacle to continued collaboration with the de Vries yard, so in 1970 he had a yacht built in Italy, the first Marco Polo, a 23.8-meter hull in steel. The Marco Polo series was followed by two Vespuccis, the second 100 feet in length.

Riva also undertook the task of building the first private marina in Italy, the Carlo Riva of Rapallo port, and only his stubbornness allowed him to win his battle with the Italian bureaucracy in an up-to-then totally unexplored field. The marina was completed in 1975.

Riva remained at the head of the yard he had sold until July of 1971, assisting with the gradual transfer of the projects and initiating the production of the new fiberglass boats, and then turned command over to his brother-in-law, Gino Gervasoni. From then on he dedicated himself almost exclusively to the management of the Carlo Riva port.

In October of 1998 he contributed to the Riva Historical Society, a nonprofit association founded to preserve the historical heritage of Riva boats, at the request of his biographer, Piero Gibellini, and a group of his admirers. The success of this enterprise has exceeded expectations, and as evidence of the fame of Carlo Riva throughout the world, there are now nine chapters of the organization in as many countries, with almost six hundred members.

—Piero M. Gibellini

ARTHUR CECIL ROBB

1908–1969 · New Zealand/Scotland

A New Zealander who worked in Scotland during much of his career, Arthur Robb designed a wide range of wholesome, moderately proportioned cruising sailboats such as the 34-foot 11-inch LOA Lion class sloops and the 35-foot 6-inch LOA Robb 35 sloops, both built mostly by Cheoy Lee. He also designed small craft, powerboats and motorsailers, and ocean racers influenced by the CCA and RORC handicapping rules. He is perhaps better known in the United States than in Great Britain, as many of the boats built to his designs have been marketed here.

Robb's designs are recognizable by their balanced hull form, being relatively full forward and lean aft compared to American practice,

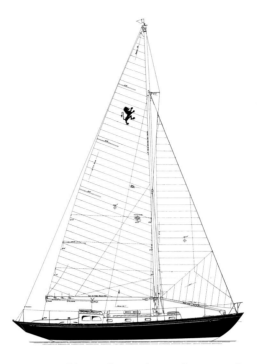

Arthur Robb: *Radiant*. This 34-foot 11-inch Lion class sloop looks longer owing to the diminutive size of her doghouse, which contains a berth and a seat in a sheltered spot with good visibility, close to the cockpit. Her narrow beam, full bow, and dramatic lines make her typical of Robb's work. © *Mystic Seaport, Ships' Plans Division, Mystic, CT*

along with his frequent use of a short doghouse at the aft end of the cabin trunk and a pronounced "toe" and relatively vertical leading edge on the keel. In many of his designs the bottom of the keel slopes up as it approaches the rudder, reducing wetted surface area slightly and offering the rudder some additional protection if grounded. He frequently employed two cabin trunks so as to allow for a strong, flush deck in the way of the mast. Robb's boats have stronger sheers and a beefier look to them than many boats designed in the same time period.

An innovator in his interior designs, one of Robb's favorite tricks was to tuck part of a berth under another interior element such as a countertop or even to put a berth in an adjacent cabin. This fits in more berths and minimized the impact a berth had on a given space. In one extreme example, a 47-foot ketch contains twelve berths in six cabins, one of which is a large saloon, another a roomy owner's stateroom, and another a good-sized sunken deckhouse. It takes considerable study of the drawings to figure out how he did it, but it is clearly a comfortable and workable layout—quite an accomplishment!

Born in Hawkes Bay, New Zealand, Robb grew up in a sailing family and became a well-known local racing helmsman. His design

career dates from his entry in a 1930's *Yachting* magazine design competition. When editor Herbert Stone saw his design, he told Robb, "Whatever you are doing now drop it and design yachts."

Robb moved to Scotland and was employed as manager of the Morris and Lorimers boatbuilding yard. He served as a reserve officer in the Royal Navy during World War II and participated in the design of the airborne lifeboat with Uffa Fox. Robb went into full-time yacht design work after the war and continued to design until shortly before his death in 1969.

The Arthur C. Robb Collection of drawings is at Mystic Seaport Museum, Mystic, CT.

—Daniel B. MacNaughton

FERNANDO ROCA

Born 1943 · Spain

After graduating with a degree in naval architecture at Ferrol, Galicia, Fernando Roca became a Spanish pioneer of yacht design and production in aluminum during the 1970's. The Alcotan 27, Spain's first aluminum production boat, followed his first design, the 7-meter powerboat *Pilar*, of 1974.

During the mid- to late 1970's Roca reorganized the production process at Taylor Española, then considered Spain's best builder, and developed new sailing yachts such as the Somo 20, 23, 27, and 970, and the motorboats Taylor 100 and 800. He returned to aluminum construction from 1981 to 1984 with one-off builder Construcciones Navales Cobo. There Roca supervised the construction of several Ron Holland–designed One-Tonners and 55- to 75-foot motor cruisers, and independently designed the MG 1000 IOR One-Tonner.

In more recent years Roca has concentrated on designs for sportfishermen such as the Fibresport Artaban and Ocre models, the Mundimar 900 design for hand building in Venezuela, and dinghies for sailing schools including a fleet of more than four hundred 5-meter Raqueros. He represented the Offshore Racing Council in Spain from 1980 to 1990 and wrote for yachting magazine *Bitacora* between 1989 and 1992.

—Fernando Roca with John Lynch and Iain McAllister

SIMON MARK ROGERS

Born March 28, 1960 · England

Rogers Yacht Design was founded in 1990, but Simon Rogers's interest in yacht design began long before that. His father, Jeremy Rogers, was one of the United Kingdom's top yacht

Simon Rogers: *Sticky Fingers.* Designed in 1997 for the Mount Gay 30 class, *Sticky Fingers* gets up on a plane and shows her stuff. © *Peter Bentley/PPL Photo Agency*

builders in the 1960's, 1970's, and 1980's, producing the Contessa line of yachts and custom IOR racers until falling victim to the economic downturn in 1981–82, which wiped out three of Britain's principal boatbuilders.

A graduate of the Southampton Institute, Simon Rogers worked in various offices, including that of fellow Lymington designer Rob Humphreys, before placing a plate outside his own premises. His best-known design to date is the 1997 water-ballasted Mount Gay 30 *Sticky Fingers.* Also included in his diverse portfolio are *Alice III*, a 38-foot gaff ketch that looks traditional above the waterline—apart from an unseemly amount of sail—but has an ultramodern underbody; a string of Mini Transat 6.5's, with keels that hinge laterally for upwind sail carrying power and slide aft to ameliorate spinnaker-induced nosedives; the 34-foot *DXB 101*, which was the first modern racing boat built in the United Arab Emirates; and *IFAW 70*, an expedition yacht for the International Fund for Animal Welfare.

—Tim Jeffery

LESTER ROSENBLATT

April 13, 1920–June 13, 2003 · United States

The son of designer Mandell Rosenblatt produced his first of thousands of boat and ship sketches at the age of three. His mother kept that toddler's scribble. He noted that with such a humble beginning, it was easy for his work to improve over time.

Lester Rosenblatt was born in New York City. His career path was largely preordained, as his father was totally immersed in the design of yachts and ships. Prior to his matriculation at the University of Michigan, Rosenblatt assisted his father in the course he taught on naval architecture at the Drake School in New York City.

After graduating from the University of Michigan with a degree in naval architecture and marine engineering in 1942 and attaining membership in the Society of Naval Architects and Marine Engineers, Rosenblatt joined the firm of John H. Wells as a naval architect, working there until 1944, when he entered the U.S.

Navy. He then served in the Design Division of the Pearl Harbor Naval Shipyard in Hawaii with a special billet as naval architect, until his discharge in 1946. He returned for a short time to the John H. Wells firm as head of preliminary design, and in 1947 joined his father as a full partner in founding M. Rosenblatt and Son.

Both father and son had a reputation for producing handsome, seaworthy, and comfortable craft, and both are well known for their attention to detail. Their involvement with the construction of *Rosa II* made them legendary at the Paul E. Luke boatyard in East Boothbay, Maine, where she was built, as they produced seventy-five drawings defining every element of the yacht with remarkable precision. In addition to his yacht work, Lester participated in the design of oceanographic ships, tugs of all sizes, the pilot-boat *New York*, large sealift ships, and the conversion of the hospital ship *Hope*.

In 1979 Rosenblatt was elected president of the international Society of Naval Architects and Marine Engineers. In semiretirement, he continued to be a vital member of the society.

He was involved with the restoration to like-new condition of the 167-foot, twin-screw diesel yacht *Haida*, built in 1947, which his father created and he had worked on while with the John H. Wells firm.

Rosenblatt and *Rosa II* cruised and raced together for many years, amassing an enviable record. Prior to his death, on most weekends Rosenblatt could be found cruising Long Island Sound out of City Island, with an annual cruise to Downeast Maine or Canada. His son, Bruce S. Rosenblatt, born in 1959, now runs the family firm, which continues its large vessel design work. —Bob Wallstrom

MANDELL ROSENBLATT

1891–1966 · United States

Mandell Rosenblatt's extremely diverse career in the field of naval architecture began when he designed and built model yachts as a young lad. He sailed them on Prospect Park Lake in Brooklyn, New York. At age sixteen he entered a yacht design contest sponsored by *Motor Boat* magazine and won—his immaculately drawn design for a 36-foot speedboat was published in the November 1907 issue. He was then hired on as an apprentice draftsman with the New York City naval architecture firm of Whittelsey and Whitaker, specializing in power yacht design.

Over the years Rosenblatt educated himself through home study and frequent attendance at evening courses at Columbia University, New York University, and City College of New York, a practice he continued until the age of fifty. By 1914, he was working for Morris M. Whitaker, who had established his own office. During his stay with this firm he worked on the design of *Aeldgytha*, the second diesel-powered yacht built in the United States.

From 1914 until 1919, Rosenblatt worked variously at the Fore River Shipbuilding Company in Quincy, Massachusetts; Bath Iron Works in Bath, Maine; William Cramp and Sons shipyard in Philadelphia, Pennsylvania; and the Brooklyn Navy Yard. He participated in the design of many large warships and other vessels.

Rosenblatt worked for Consolidated Shipbuilding Corporation of New York City from 1919 to 1924, designing large yachts and other vessels of wood and steel. From 1924 to 1929 he was assistant chief designer for John H. Wells in New York City, creating more large yachts.

From 1929 to 1931 Rosenblatt was chief draftsman for Tams in New York City, and was responsible for the design of several large diesel yachts, including the 148-foot *Alamo*, the 160-foot *Thalia*, the 130-foot *Shogun*, and the 72-foot yawl *Alana* built by the Robert Jacob Yacht Yard.

From 1932 to 1937 he was employed in the structural department of the design division at the Brooklyn Navy Yard.

During the Great Depression, Rosenblatt initiated and taught a course in naval architecture and ship drafting at the Drake School in New York City. He continued in charge of the course until 1943. Hundreds of men (including naval architect Stanley Potter) who contributed directly to the marine design effort of the United States during and after World War II received their training from him.

Rosenblatt was again associated with John H. Wells from 1937 to 1946, this time as chief designer with complete charge of the design of all yachts and other vessels developed by the firm. Among the yachts were the 48-foot commuter *Sandra II*, the 107-foot *Trouper*, the 75-foot express yacht *Seascape*, the 85-foot house yacht *Nambay*, and the 167-foot, twin-screw diesel yacht *Haida*. During World War II, while still with Wells, he did further design work for the U.S. Army and Navy.

Rosenblatt was a member of the Society of Naval Architects and Marine Engineers and the American Society of Naval Engineers.

In 1947 Rosenblatt and his son Lester formed the firm of M. Rosenblatt and Son, Naval Architects and Marine Engineers, as equal partners. From a modest beginning, the firm became one of the largest private naval architectural firms in the world, employing over 950 people at the

Mandell Rosenblatt: *Rhonda III*. One of the largest diesel yachts built in the decade following World War II, the 96-foot *Rhonda III* was built by Ingalls Shipbuilding. Twin 490-hp Superior diesel engines give her a speed of 14.5 knots and a 2,500-mile cruising range. *Photo courtesy Lester Rosenblatt*

time of Mandell Rosenblatt's death. The firm has offices in New York City; San Francisco and San Diego, California; Arlington, Newport News, and Virginia Beach, Virginia; Bremerton, Washington; and Charleston, South Carolina.

Mandell and Lester Rosenblatt loved vessels of all types, but as the firm grew, demand for yacht design diminished and there was less call for commercial design. The firm emphasized service to the U.S. Navy, and both father and son participated in the design of many U.S. naval ships, including large aircraft carriers, submarines, guided-missile cruisers, nuclear cruisers, ammunition ships, guided-missile destroyers, refrigerated-stores ships, submarine tenders, survey ships, cycloidal-propelled oceanographic ships, and training vessels. Perhaps the scope of M. Rosenblatt and Son's design work for the U.S. Navy can best be described by noting that during the second half of the twentieth century, the firm had done the original designs for, or had modified, approximately 90 percent of the ships in the navy, and that almost half of the navy's auxiliary ships were designed by the firm.

The firm also designed nonmilitary oceanographic research vessels, including two unique spar-type oceanographic instrumentation ships. After reaching their destination, these ships were partially flooded, changing their orientation to the water by 90 degrees and floating like a spar buoy.

In addition, the firm created many major yachts, including the 96-foot luxury yacht *Rhonda III*; the 82-foot, twin-screw diesel yacht *Anahita V*; and the 62-foot auxiliary yawl *Gaffer*. But none were of more beauty and personal satisfaction to the Rosenblatts than the 41-foot auxiliary ketch *Rosa II*. Her roots lie in the work of Scottish naval architect George L. Watson, especially his lovely *Thistle*, the America's Cup challenger of 1887, which influenced *Rosa II*'s sheerline, stem, and transom.

The Rosenblatts' philosophy of yacht design was to produce a boat with aesthetic appeal and strong considerations for seaworthiness and cruising comfort. Characteristics that might adversely affect beauty in any way were carefully avoided. In the case of *Rosa II*, the result of their efforts was a design comprising some seventy-five drawings and over ninety-six pages of specifications, modifying letters, checklists, and so forth. *Rosa II* was built by the Paul E. Luke yard of East Boothbay, Maine, and launched on July 3, 1960. At the time of this writing, she was in like-new condition and actively sailed by Lester Rosenblatt on the East Coast of the United States.

—Bob Wallstrom

MURRAY DOUGLAS ROSS

Born March 5, 1950 · New Zealand

Auckland-based designer Murray Ross is known in New Zealand as a talented yacht designer, and also, around the world, as a champion yachtsman. He was born into a sailing family, and his extensive experience includes both cruising and racing; he represented New Zealand in the Flying Dutchman class in 1972 and 1976, was on the winning Quarter-Ton Cup crew in 1975, took part in the entire Whitbread Round the World Race of 1989–90, and sailed legs in the 1993–94 and 1997–98 races.

Ross started out as a sailmaker in 1968 and began an association with designer Paul Whiting in the early 1970's. He worked with Whiting on designs for the IOR Quarter-, Half-, and One-Ton class yachts *Magic Bus*, *Newspaper Taxi*,

Mandell and Lester Rosenblatt: *Rosa II.* The Rosenblatts designed *Rosa II* for their own use, creating a handsome, practical, seakindly, and lively cruising yacht. She was built by Paul E. Luke in 1960. © *Benjamin Mendlowitz*

Murray Ross: Ross 780. The Ross 780 was one of the earliest production classes in New Zealand that delivered the fun of a lightweight racer on a small budget, opening the field up to the wider inshore racing market. *Photo courtesy David Payne*

and *Smackwater Jack*. Paul Whiting was lost at sea late in the 1970's, and soon after Ross began designing professionally by himself. An advocate of light displacement, he has designed boats ranging from 4.9-meter sailing dinghies to 18-meter cruising yachts, and including production cruiser/racers and one-off racing designs. The Ross 780 has been a very popular trailerable sailer. —David Payne

N. D. ROSS, MBE

1882–1967 · South Africa

As an amateur designer, N. D. Ross saw some thirty of his designs built on the Cape of Good Hope during the 1930's to mid-1950's. He became known for producing highly detailed plans for stylish cruising yachts, of which the Grand Banks–style, gaff-rigged schooner *Atlantis* was the best known.

Ross was born in South Africa. He joined the postal service and, by the outbreak of World War II, was the postmaster for Cape Town Harbor, responsible for handling all incoming and outgoing mail. After the war he was awarded the Member of the British Empire (MBE) for his services to wartime troopships.

As a hobby, he started building half models of local yachts, and this quickly led to him producing half models for local yacht builders. From there he soon moved to teaching himself drafting, and adopted Admiral Turner's metacentric shelf theories for achieving good stability and handling as a guide to his designs.

None of Ross's work can be found on the Cape; surviving hulls are found in the United States and the Caribbean. —Tom Roach

WILLIAM JAMES ROUÉ

April 27, 1879–January 14, 1970 · Canada

If he had designed only his most famous schooner, the immortal Grand Banks racing fisherman *Bluenose*, William Roué's reputation would be secure, but there might be some question as to whether or not she was a fluke. Roué was the greatest Nova Scotian designer of the twentieth century. He was also probably the first in his region to work from drawings rather than a half model. He was entirely self-taught, except for

N. D. Ross: *Caprice.* With Ross at the helm, *Caprice* beats into a stiff southeaster on Table Bay, South Africa, in the early 1930's. *Photo courtesy G. D. Ross*

William Roué: *Bluenose*. The *Bluenose*, which has appeared on Canadian coinage since 1937, is Canada's most famous sailing vessel and the best-known design from Roué. Although a fishing schooner, she, like others of the Grand Banks type, was inspired by racing yachts and designed specifically for seaworthiness and speed. © *Mystic Seaport, Rosenfeld Collection, Mystic, CT*

night courses in mechanical drafting at the Victoria School of Art and Design.

In Roué's day, Nova Scotians saw themselves as full participants in the sailing world. Many were designer/builders, with a proud history that remained unbroken until the *Bluenose* was lost off Haiti in 1946. Roué wanted to design boats from boyhood. His first design to be realized was *Babette,* a yawl for Frank Bell, vice commodore at the Royal Nova Scotia Yacht Squadron (RSNYS). It is said that Bell gave Roué's drawings for *Babette* to B. B. Crowninshield and asked him what he thought. Crowninshield asked Bell who had made the drawings. "Oh, a young amateur from home who sails with me." "Well," says Crowninshield, "he won't be an amateur for long. Go ahead and

build. You will never regret it." Bell must have been a mentor as well to the young Roué, for he was the one who gave him a copy of Dixon Kemp's *Yacht Architecture* (1897), which Roué promptly committed to memory.

Though he designed everything from ferryboats to tugs and freighters, Roué's heart was with sailboats. His were always well balanced, easily driven, and equal to the task at hand.

To this day, two of Roué's one-design classes race very competitively in Nova Scotia and elsewhere. One began as the "Star" class, now known as Roué 20's. Originally designed in 1922, they are still being built, though now of fiberglass. They are 28 feet long overall and 20 feet on the waterline. There's a story told of the original fleet. Apparently, all the 20's had claimed a race ex-

cept one. Her owner was sure there was something amiss with the boat. Roué was sure she must be all right, so he took the helm and raced her, and she won. The 20's are able in all conditions, quick and reliable, and just plain beautiful. Few classes have such satisfied owners.

Another class, the Bluenose sloops, continue to thrive, with more than three hundred known to be sailing. Designed at the

---

William Roué: *Eskasoni* (opposite). *Eskasoni,* a serious-looking schooner, is really all about strength, power, and comfort under difficult offshore conditions, but on this day she was taking advantage of her rig's ability to spread easily handled light canvas on an idyllic coastwise race or cruise. © *Peter Barlow*

close of World War II, they are 23 feet long over-all, with a 16-foot waterline and a big open cock-pit. Built of either fiberglass or wood, they offer an interesting comparison between the materials. In Nova Scotia, there is no question in anyone's mind that the wooden Bluenoses are faster, especially the ones whose builders adhered strictly to Roué's exacting specifications. They are great fun to sail and will stand up to a breeze, accelerating in the gusts with an easy helm. The first thing Roué's boats inspire, after affection for their sweet lines, is confidence. His designs seem to respond to the helmsman's thoughts as much as his touch.

Roué's reputation was such that by the 1930's he was offered a partnership at what became Ford, Payne and Roué in City Island, New York. He stayed for two years before the call of home became more than he could resist. It is interesting to note that his design style and philosophy remained perfectly consistent throughout.

Roué went on to design many notable boats. The fishing schooner *Haligonian*, built to beat the *Bluenose*, raced the old champion twice, each boat winning once. The schooner yacht *Malay* won the Bermuda Race twice, once in her class in 1928 and again in 1930 when she was first overall. Also in 1930, his Canada Cup racer *Norseman* became champion of the Great Lakes. His 46-foot schooner *Little Haligonian* won the Saint Petersburg to Havana Race eight times. *Hebridee II*, a schooner of the Bluenose Junior class, won many trophies in the Nova Scotia Schooner Association's annual race week.

Handsome, wholesome, and eye-sweet are Roué's boats. They are powerful to windward. He was no revolutionary, but rather one who preferred to evolve his ideas gently, taking

into account all that had gone before. His boats present themselves as a whole, no part overwhelming the rest. His sheerlines (except perhaps for *Bluenose,* whose sheer was changed by Angus Walters to afford more headroom in the forecastle) are subtle and elegant, his overhangs moderate except where the rules dictated otherwise, and his underbodies shapely.

Roué liked his boats to carry sail and to hold their course with an easy helm. He was very conscious of the wave-form theory, an advance in its day that has since been abandoned. With ballast, be it internal or external, he was a wizard. He made sure he knew exactly what the owners expected from a vessel, and because of the breadth of his experience, ranging from working vessels to the finest yachts, he was able to provide just what was needed. It is often noted that people keep Roué boats for a long time.

—Thomas Gallant

MANUEL "MANOLO" RUIZ DE ELVIRA

Born 1963 · Spain

Manolo Ruiz de Elvira is one of the most experienced designers working within the America's Cup Class Rule, and is a leader in the developing technology of the interface between tank-testing and computer prediction in racing yacht design.

Since graduating with a degree in naval architecture and marine engineering at Madrid's Universidad Politécnica, most of Ruiz de Elvira's career as a yacht designer has been associated with the America's Cup. This has included three Spanish challengers, *España 92 V Centenario* (1992), *Rioja de España* (1995), and *Bravo España*

(2000), and the 2003 Swiss America's Cup winner *Alinghi.* Working with leading designer Rolf Vrolijk, Ruiz de Elvira's principal responsibilities—besides the design itself—were developing, managing, and analyzing the tank-testing and velocity prediction programs.

Other work has included the ILC 30 *Servipack* (third in the 1998 World Championship) and the IMS 42-footer *ONO* (fourth in Class B at the 2001 IMS World Championship). He continues to develop his own "PAP" program: a flexible environment for sailing-yacht performance prediction based on data from different sources—analytical, tank-test, and computational fluid dynamics (CFD)—which is used in IMS and America's Cup projects as well as cruising yacht design.

As if that isn't enough for one very enthusiastic designer, Ruiz de Elvira is also currently writing his Ph.D. thesis "Sailing Yacht Performance Predictions Based Upon CFD and Tank Results," and he succeeded Dave Pedrick as chairman of the International Technical Committee of the Offshore Racing Council in 2003.

—Iain McAllister with assistance from
Manolo Ruiz de Elvira and John Lynch

JOHN SCOTT RUSSELL

1808–June 8, 1882 · Scotland

John Scott Russell apparently designed only one sailing yacht, but his research into the effect of waves on floating bodies, which culminated in his wave-line theory, profoundly influenced all marine design during the mid-nineteenth century. In the late 1870's its practical application was questioned by Colin Archer and John Hyslop, who offered their own, more advanced theories, and it fell out of favor.

The wave-line theory was intended to calculate the line of least resistance for a wave after it meets a vessel's hull. Its most visible result was the long hollow bow, which some earlier yacht builders had chosen through observation and intuition before Scott Russell even began his research. It was an improvement on the "cod's head and mackerel tail" configuration then traditional in Britain.

In 1847 the cutter *Mosquito* (59-foot LWL) was built to Scott Russell's theory, and while she proved highly successful, the long hollow bow did not become popular until the schooner *America,* with the same feature, arrived in English waters in 1851. However, it is not known if *America*'s designer, George Steers, was influenced by Scott Russell's theory or even knew of it.

Born at Parkhead near Glasgow, Scott Russell was a founder in 1860 of what is now the Royal Institute of Naval Architects. He studied

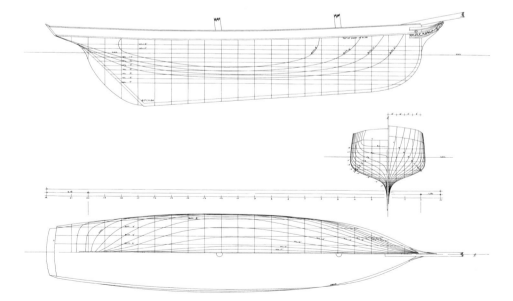

John Scott Russell: *Titania*. The 100-ton schooner *Titania*, the sole sailing yacht designed by Russell, embodies his wave-line theory, which led to her hollow bow. She was soundly defeated by another hollow-bowed yacht, the all-conquering *America*, in a challenge match in 1851. © *Chevalier & Taglang*

at the universities in Edinburgh, Saint Andrews, and Glasgow, graduating from the latter at the early age of sixteen. He gained practical experience in machine workshops, taught science at Edinburgh University, and then returned to the practical side of engineering.

Scott Russell began his experiments on the nature of waves in 1833, after being asked to investigate the possibility of adopting steam navigation on canals, and continued them when he was appointed the manager of a large shipbuilding firm at Greenock. He is said to have performed at least twenty thousand experiments, and he had several vessels built to prove his theory.

In 1844 Scott Russell moved to London and started a shipbuilding business at Millwall. Elected a Fellow of the Royal Society in 1847, he played a leading role in organizing the Great Exhibition, held in London in 1851. This drew the schooner *America* across the Atlantic to exhibit the superiority of American yacht design. When she arrived, her owners issued a challenge to all English yachtsmen for a match. Only Robert Stephenson, the owner of a new schooner designed by Scott Russell, accepted the challenge. However, at 100 tons *Titania* was much smaller than *America*, and when the match took place—after the race in which *America* won her famous cup—she did not sail well and was soundly defeated.

Scott Russell's firm constructed the huge steamship *Great Eastern,* which Isambard Kingdom Brunel had designed to the wave-line theory, but difficulties led to the closure of Scott Russell's business and his financial ruin.

—Ian Dear

JOHN, THOMAS, AND ROBERT (EMIL) RYBOVICH

Various dates · United States

The modern sportfisherman type of yacht had its beginning in 1947 in West Palm Beach, Florida, at the Rybovich and Sons boatyard. From that year until 1975, when the business was sold, seventy-nine meticulously crafted wooden yachts were designed and built. The Rybovich boats influenced countless other designers and builders and earned brothers John, Thomas, and Emil a top-of-the-field reputation and an international following.

In the 1930's the yard made a specialty of modifying power cruisers to sportfishing boats. Ernest Hemingway, one of the most visible sport fishermen in the 1930's, had the firm convert his 38-foot Wheeler. John Rybovich Sr.'s oldest son, John, was a sport fisherman himself, and benefited not only from contact with

David Ryder-Turner. Only a few construction details betray the fact that this shapely 88-foot yawl was designed in the twenty-first century rather than the opening years of the twentieth. Her well-balanced lines, generous sail plan, and graceful elegance are Ryder-Turner hallmarks. *Drawing courtesy David Ryder-Turner*

the owners but also from the experience of renovating cruisers like Chris-Crafts, Elcos, Consolidateds, and Wheelers. Much of the work involved the installation of flying bridges with steering and engine controls.

John began to feel that what was needed was a new type of boat, capable of going offshore and handling the gear and tackle necessary to catch big-game fish such as tuna and marlin. He tinkered with his own boat, experimenting with bamboo outriggers and fighting chairs. But not until after World War II did the opportunity arise to design and build a truly new boat, for established customer Charles Johnson.

Launched in 1947, *Miss Chevy II*, a 34-foot, cedar-planked yacht, was stable and easily maneuverable. She had a generously flared bow, an underbody featuring a deep entry and a flat run, an oversized open cockpit, a high-gloss finish, and expanses of brightwork never before seen on a fishing boat. Her gear included the first set of aluminum outriggers ever built and her fighting chair was so advanced that it has been copied but not improved upon ever since.

As the three brothers took over the yard and steady demand for the innovative Rybovich yachts increased, they began to specialize: Tom designed the boats, John ran the yard and handled sales, and Emil oversaw electrical and mechanical design and service.

In 1951, their eighth boat, *Miss Chevy IV* (again for Johnson), carried a new design detail that became a Rybovich trademark. Departing from the earlier trunk-cabin style of hull and deckhouse, she had a broken sheerline similar to early

Chris-Craft designs, which allowed high freeboard forward for dryness and interior volume and low freeboard aft for fish handling. Her dramatic and appealing profile influenced the design of countless future vessels in the sportfishing community. She also carried the first aluminum tuna tower and the first under coaming tuna door, replacing the earlier gin pole.

Through the years, the Rybovichs continued to experiment and improve their yachts, and changed from plank-on-frame construction to cold-molded construction in the 1960's. They succeeded in designing and building handsome and workable sportfisherman yachts.

Rybovich and Sons was sold in 1975, and then several more times. In 1991 it merged with Spencer to become Rybovich Spencer, located in West Palm Beach, Florida.

—Lucia del Sol Knight

DAVID G. D. RYDER-TURNER

November 21, 1922–September 24, 2004
England/Scotland

Traditional and singularly beautiful, David Ryder-Turner's designs reflect his lifelong familiarity with and close study of the work of the Scottish master William Fife III of Fairlie. He was born in England into a boat-owning family and was educated at Bembridge (Isle of Wight) and Wellington (Somerset). He served as a premium apprentice at Vickers-Supermarine in Southampton in 1939–40 and as a draftsman at British Power Boat Company in Hythe, Southampton, in 1940–42. He joined the British Army in 1942, retiring as captain in 1950.

Ryder-Turner moved to Australia in 1954, where he became a secondary school teacher. He subsequently received bachelor of arts and graduate degrees, serving as a university lecturer in geography in South Australia in the period 1969–83. While in Australia, Ryder-Turner studied yacht design and worked with J. Muir of Battery Point, Hobart. He also designed a number of dinghies and other small boats for his own use and seven keelboats for clients. His drawings from this period, as well as most of his other belongings, were destroyed in a fire.

In 1983 Ryder-Turner returned to Scotland, where he worked with Ian Nicolson at A. Mylne. He designed a number of yachts, including the 23-foot 6-inch, cruising sloop *Amber;* the 24-foot 9-inch, gunter-rigged daysailer *Sonas;* and, for an American client, a 15-meter sloop and a 136-foot ketch.

Ryder-Turner's final design was for a 34-foot daysailing/cruising sloop launched in Camden, Maine, in the fall of 2004.

—Llewellyn Howland III

S

DAVID SADLER

Born 1921 · England

They are among the most aesthetically pleasing and seaworthy yachts of their generation, still sought after and, in the case of the evergreen Contessa 32, still built. David Sadler's Contessa and Sadler designs of the 1960's, 1970's, and 1980's have become British modern classics.

With his Contessa 26 and 32 designs, Sadler's early work is inextricably linked with Lymington-based boatbuilder Jeremy Rogers. In the mid-1960's Sadler was a client for one of Rogers's sought-after, cold-molded Folkboats named *Contessa of Parkstone*, which Sadler optimized for handicap racing with an efficient masthead sloop rig. Their good client-builder relationship developed into a highly successful designer-builder collaboration with the Contessa 26, a fiberglass production Folkboat derivative. Rogers and J. J. Taylor of Canada eventually built around 750 of these popular pocket cruisers between 1966 and 1990. Although the great majority were commissioned and are still cherished as doughty coastal cruisers, some have chalked up circumnavigations and major successes in shorthanded offshore racing.

In 1971 the Contessa 32 was born out of the desire for a bigger sister: to be competitive under the new IOR while still retaining the seaworthy and seakindly values of the 26, and with added comfort. Racing successes for the earliest examples, including class victory at the 1971 Cowes Week followed by the highly coveted Boat of the Show award at the 1972 London Boat Show, cemented a reputation that led to over five hundred 32's being built during the first ten years of production.

In or out of the water, the Contessa 32 is a great beauty, but it may be hard for the untrained eye

to see her as the paragon of seaworthiness in comparatively modern yacht design that she has become. With her relatively petite wineglass form and slim, faired-in fin and skeg configuration, she looks almost delicate. Yet she has superb stability characteristics compared to the modern mass-market production cruiser, exemplified by a Contessa 32 becoming the only Class V finisher in the ill-fated 1979 Fastnet Race.

In 1974 Sadler set up his own production facility, Sadler Yachts, to build his Sadler 25 design, yet another fine, seaworthy vessel. In an era when function seemed to be taking over the importance of form, she bucked trends by sporting a dramatic sheerline, sweeping up to a nicely overhanging bow, which together with the great deal of tumblehome then in vogue created a shapely, stable, and powerful hull. In 1981 the design was extended to become the Sadler 26, and a similar looking 29-footer was also built for a limited period.

By the late 1970's the yacht-buying public's expectations regarding accommodations were becoming influenced by the voluminous hulls developing under the forceful influence of the IOR. Sadler's 1979 answer was to design the spacious Sadler 32 as a direct successor to the Contessa 32. In 1984 David's son, Martin, further developed the lines to the larger Sadler 34.

David Sadler retired in 1981 and spent many years ocean cruising before settling down in New Zealand. —Iain McAllister

H. SAEFKOW

(Dates unknown) · Germany

While few biographical facts are known about H. Saefkow (including his first name), he probably should rank among the famous yacht designers of the 1880's. He was the quintessential "German engineer" in the first hour of German yachting. His is the leading name among designers of the Marine Regatta Association, predecessor of the Kiel Yacht Club, as

well as of the Rhe Sailing Club in Königsberg.

Saefkow drew in equal measure from the traditional forms of English and French coastal workboats and the then-innovative deep and narrow forms of racing yachts, advantageously joining the two schools so that his work represents one of the rare contact points where fast working boats and fast yachts meet. His important and powerful designs equaled those of British designers. *Lolly*, one of the most important racing yachts from the dawn of German yachting, came from his drawing board in 1882, as did *Lust* and *Liebe*, both for the Marine Regatta Association of Kiel.

Saefkow's body of work has yet to be elucidated for the benefit of the history of yachting.

—Eberhard Wetjen

H. Saefkow: *Liebe.* While she is certainly narrow, this 13.7-meter yawl designed in 1882 is not as extreme as other contemporary designs. Described as "a fast cruiser for the coast," she shows the workboat influences for which the designer was known, with firm bilges, a strong sheer, and moderate draft. *Photo courtesy Volker Christmann*

David Sadler: Contessa (opposite). The Contessa's combination of seakeeping ability and good looks has kept her in production for more than thirty years. © *Mark Pepper/PPL Photo Agency*

GEORGES SAHUQUÉ

1862–1906 · France

Georges Sahuqué passed like a meteor over the French yachting landscape. Born into a wealthy family in Bordeaux, he was passionate about drawing boats from a very young age. In 1881, at age nineteen, he became an assiduous contributor to the French magazine *Le Yacht*, creating for this young periodical a series of drawings that are invaluable to French yachting history. Sahuqué spent as much time as possible at the Bassin d'Arcachon on the southern coast of the Bay of Biscay, and through his text and drawings he tells us of the essential role this region played in the development of French yachting.

Sahuqué was a contemporary and friend of designer Joseph Guédon. The two men shared the same ideas on one-design classes and measurement rules, and were members of the various Sociétés Nautiques d'Aquitaine.

In 1889, Sahuqué published his first plans in *Le Yacht*. They showed the 5-ton keel sloop *Véga*, a bateau de promenade or "walk boat" (an early term for a yacht) 8 meters LWL. Elsewhere in 1889, he published the plans for the catboat *Sirius*, appreciably of the same size and drawn the same year. The third yacht he designed that year was the centerboard sloop *Gemma*, which achieved notable victories in that season of races. These three boats probably launched Sahuqué's career as a naval architect.

From 1889 until his early death at age forty-four, Sahuqué designed a multitude of boats of all types, all of which saw success. Indeed, his talent extended to both small and large classes, centerboarders and keelboats, racers and cruisers. He also drew plans for fishing and commercial boats, all designed like yachts. As well, he drew power yachts, such as the steam yachts *Sélika*, 400 tons; *Mouzaffer Eddin*, 379 tons; and *Aimé*, 164 tons.

Sahuqué was associated with Monimeau Brothers in 1896 and set up a well-regarded shipyard. This did not prevent him from designing some boats for other yards such as Bonnin, and Meyney and Son, both from Lormont;

Bossuet in Arcachon; de La Brosse and Fouché in Nantes; Lacour in La Rochelle; and Allégrini in Antibes.

In 1892 Sahuqué drew the Five-Tonners *Etincelle* and *Kelpie*, whose lines plans figured in the series of boats published in a French edition of Dixon Kemp's *Manual of Yacht and Boat Sailing* in 1896. These two boats, especially *Kelpie*, had such success in racing that they continued to be used as a reference even after they were retired. The next year, he designed to very precise specifications the 15-ton cutter *Pourquoi Pas?* and also *Royan*, an original design for the period in France. *Royan* was a pure centerboarder, 9.25 meters LOA with 0.35-meter draft, with 880 kilograms of lead cast in the bottom and a 100-kilogram steel centerboard, adapted to use in the Bassin d'Arcachon. The Cercle de la Voile of Paris awarded him a medal for *Alyette* in 1895. Two years later he received medals from the Union des Yachts Français for his *Malgré Tout* and *Sagitta*.

Georges Sahuqué designed fast boats of all types, and there is no doubt that his talent

Georges Sahuqué: *Etincelle*. Sahuqué drew the Five-Tonner *Etincelle* in 1892. Note the downward steeve of the bowsprit, which seems to emphasize the attractive delicacy of the hull shape. *Drawing courtesy Jacques Taglang*

Eric Salander: *La Liberté.* The 55-Square-Meter skerry cruiser *La Liberté* was built at the Kungsör Boatyard by Oscar Schelin in 1934 for Max Gumpel of Stockholm, Sweden. The 16.3-meter yacht is moving very fast but leaves barely a ripple in her wake. © *Per Thelander*

would have served him well in designing boats for the International Rule, which came out the year he died. After his sudden demise, his friends at *Le Yacht* expressed their regret and admiration in these words: "He paid attention only to kindness, and all appreciated his lively mood and his smiling amiability at the same time as his talent." —Noël Gruet

ERIK SALANDER

October 27, 1883–December 15, 1957 · Sweden

While the turn of the twentieth century saw many wealthy yachtsmen gain much attention racing their palatial oceangoing yachts, along the Scandinavian coasts a growing number of less well-heeled enthusiasts began competing with equal fervor in much smaller and more modest yachts. For the most part, these were the types of boats Erik Salander designed.

Between 1910 and 1940, Salander drew plans for more than three hundred yachts for this new and growing class of sportsmen. As with many successful designers, he was able to create particularly efficient structures as a result of his education. He studied to become a shipbuilder at the Technical School in Dresden, Germany, and at Chalmers Institute of Technology in Gothenburg, Sweden.

Salander designed the first skerry cruiser, the 30-Square-Meter *Älfan,* in 1908. After that he created many yachts in the classes from 15- to 120-Square-Meters. His breakthrough came with the 55-Square-Meter *Eva* in 1915. Up until 1920 he came to design the fastest yachts in the 55- to 95-Square-Meter classes together with Tore Holm and Gustaf Estlander. Among these are the 75-Square-Meter *Ila* from 1917 and *Gun* from 1918, and the 95-Square-Meter *Gerdny I* and *II* from 1918 and 1920. The largest skerry cruiser that Salander designed was the 31-meter 120 S1 *Signe* from 1918.

Salander's best-known boat is the KDY-Juniorboat, a 21-foot keelboat. Originally designed for the Royal Danish Yacht Club in 1926, it became so popular that it was adopted by nearly every club in Denmark to serve as a training boat. He also designed a small keelboat for Swedish youngsters, the Maassun-

gen (Young Gull) class, of which many have been built. In addition to his design work, Salander wrote many articles about boats and sailing, still worth reading today.

—Bent Aarre with Ulf Lycke

CESARE SANGERMANI

1896–1976 · Italy

Born into a boatbuilding family in Ricco, Cesare Sangermani had a passion for racing that soon led him into the boatbuilding business begun by his father. His designs were built in his shipyard under the supervision of his brother Piero, where boats by other major designers, such as Sparkman and Stephens and J. Laurent Giles, were also built.

During Sangermani's tenure, the shipyard launched over two hundred vessels. An early one, built when the Lavagna shipyard was still being set up, was the 5.5-meter *Nibbio II,* a vessel Sangermani never wanted to sell. His first major vessel was *Radiosa Aurora,* a schooner measuring 19.2 meters in length, launched in 1948.

pable of making boats only for money, like those who manufacture bicycles or refrigerators. I build boats with my heart. I dream of them at night. I stroke them. I touch them up like a poet does his verse. To me, every boat is like a work of art. It can't leave my shipyard until it is perfect."
—Franco Belloni

SHIGERU SAWAJI

Born 1949 · Japan

During his days in the Department of Naval Architecture at Tokai University, Shigeru Sawaji designed and built his first sailboat. After graduating from the university, he worked at Chita Company and learned fiberglass boatbuilding. He realized his dream of becoming a yacht designer with the IOR boat *Moa*, a sloop 26 feet long.

In 1981, *Taiyo*, a 37-foot sloop of his design, won the Singlehanded Transpacific Race from San Francisco to Kobe. Sawaji has produced designs for fiberglass production boats such as a 30-foot motorsailer and a 33-foot, center-cockpit cruiser, which have proved popular.

Starting early in his career, Sawaji used computers. He developed previously nonexistent hydrostatic calculation programs and lines output programs for personal computers.

Sawaji is also talented in powerboat design. A 43-foot catamaran for the Arasaki Racing Team won the U.S. Offshore World Champi-

Cesare Sangermani: *Chiar di Luna.* The 10-meter cutter *Chiar di Luna* gained Sangermani an international reputation for his racing boat designs. A Class III RORC racer, she was the first Italian yacht to compete in England at Cowes Week. *Photo courtesy Franco Belloni*

It was, however, *Chiar di Luna*, a Class III RORC cutter designed and built for the Italian navy, that brought recognition to the shipyard and especially to Sangermani as an international designer. She was 10 meters long, 7.7 meters on the waterline, with a sail area of 39 square meters. She achieved success both internationally and nationally.

In 1954 *Chiar di Luna* became the first Italian boat to compete in the Cowes Week races on the Solent. In 1955 and 1957, the boat achieved the best time in her class (Class III) in the Giraglia ocean race (the 208-mile "Saint Tropez–Island of Giraglia–San Remo" route).

Among other boats he designed, Sangermani loved to remember a Class III RORC yawl named *Raggio di Sole*, built in 1956 for Giancarlo Longari. She measured 13.2 meters, with a sail area of 76.3 square meters. Another fondly remembered boat was *Gitana IV*, a yawl built for Baron Edmond de Rothschild measuring 27.57 meters with a sail area of 276 square meters. She is homeported in the Mediterranean and still participates in regattas and rendezvous for classic boats.

Wood was the material used in the construction of almost all of Sangermani's boats. In an interview in 1974 he said, "I am not ca-

Shigeru Sawaji: *Taiyo.* The 37-foot *Taiyo* won the 1981 Singlehanded Transpacific Race in 1981. Sawaji's ultralight design features minimal accommodations concentrating all weight amidships. Her one luxury is an unusually large athwartships chart table under the bridgedeck. *Drawing courtesy Shigeru Sawaji*

onship at Ft. Lauderdale, Florida, in 1993 and also won at Point Peasant, New Jersey, in 1994 and 1998.

To date, Sawaji has designed seventy-seven boats and served as a member of the 1999 Nippon Challenge America's Cup and the JSAF (Japan Sailing Federation) Technical Committee.

The Sawaji design office is located in Yokohama, Japan.　　　—Kennosuke Hayashi

PAOLO SCANU

Born July 2, 1954 · Italy

Paolo Scanu's quintessentially Italian soul won't permit him to take life *too* seriously, even as he designs yachts that are a careful blend of style and science. He grew up in Sardinia, where he gained respect for the sea.

As a youth, Scanu experienced two maritime events that pointed him toward a career in naval architecture: he assembled his first "yacht" from flotsam cork bark, and he took a ride on a motorboat designed by Renato "Sonny" Levi. But Scanu *knew* he would be a yacht designer only when his father, a restaurateur, bought Sir Thomas Lipton's last hurrah for the America's Cup, the 130-foot, J-Class sloop *Shamrock V*. Scanu was fourteen.

Scanu studied naval architecture at Southampton College of Technology in England, apprenticing as a draftsman at nearby Camper and Nicholson. After graduating in 1977 he went briefly into the Italian navy, serving on a minesweeper whose bad motion revealed to him the nature of an ill-conceived vessel. In 1978 he began as a loftsman at the famed Benetti Shipyard in Viareggio and was quickly promoted to do design work.

Though Scanu discovered that his precise Anglo-Saxon training had not prepared him for the endearing Italian practice of drawing a yacht *after* it was built, he also learned from intuitive Tuscan artisans that "before numbers and coefficients, you must use your eyes, your feel, your common sense." Scanu's instinct for New World architecture was honed amid the disorder of an Old World atelier.

When Benetti contracted with Adnan Kashogghi to build his 282-foot motoryacht *Nabila*, Scanu was appointed liaison for the designer, London-based Jon Bannenberg, from whom Scanu gained deep appreciation for a yacht's exterior architecture.

But since his Southampton days, when he had interned at the Wolfson Unit towing tank, Scanu was also obsessed with mastering the flow of water around a hull. He embarked on a serious study of hull forms, enhanced by discussions with yacht masters who knew

the way of a boat. In 1983, he opened Studio Scanu in Viareggio.

Scanu began with contract work for shipyards and designs for fireboats and pilotboats. Then he drew several fast planing hulls, one of which won second place in the 1987 Class II European championship, driven by a contrarotating surface drive of his design. Scanu also managed projects for Brooke Yachts in England, which in 1992 launched his 43-meter *Only You*, with a fast military-style hull and styling by Terence Disdale. He designed boats for yards in Australia, Singapore, and Germany; fast motorboats up to 37 meters long for Italy's CCYD and Cesare Sangermani; a few custom sailing yachts; and fiberglass production motoryachts.

In the 1990's Scanu's designs have included *Pegaso* (49 meters), *Sahab IV* (50 meters), *Pes-*

Paolo Scanu: *Numptia*. It is easy to see why *Numptia* is Scanu's personal favorite among his motoryacht designs. By maximizing the superstructure "footprint," but denying the temptation to add an extra deck, he has drawn a commodious 62-meter thoroughbred that combines comforting mass, appealing trimness, and good speed. *Photo courtesy Paolo Scanu*

tifer (50 meters), and his personal favorite design, *Numptia* (62 meters), built by Italy's CRN, as well as *Georgia* (49 meters), a voluptuous sailing yacht delivered by New Zealand's Alloy Yachts in 2000. Studio Scanu also does hydrodynamic calculations, evaluations of displacement and planing hulls, and consulting for the new Maritime and Coastguard Agency (MCA) safety standards.　　—Jack A. Somer

HENRY A. SCHEEL

December 25, 1911–July 23, 1993
United States

Henry Scheel's work shows a strong evolutionary trend, from his early work in very traditional schooners and motoryachts beginning in 1938, through his innovative high-performance sailing yachts in the 1980's and 1990's. He was not an admirer of traditionalist thinking, but his thorough understanding of traditional aesthetic

notions seems to have enabled him to create an unusually distinctive and pleasing appearance in the most modern of his boats. He patented the Scheel Keel, which concentrates ballast weight low and minimizes cross-flow under the keel. It allows relatively shallow draft without a centerboard and improves speed by reducing the tip vortex of the keel.

Scheel was born in Passaic, New Jersey, but learned about sailing by observing yachts and models during childhood summers on Cape Cod. His first boat was a Wee Scot given to him by his father, and as a young man he crewed in ocean races, including a violent Fastnet Race in 1931 during which the boat he was on, *Maitenes II*, had to be abandoned because of gear failures. One person was lost overboard.

That experience and others caused Scheel to insist on rugged scantlings and strong, seamanlike details in all his boats. He once said, "If you are going to be a designer of boats, you have to use boats, and if you are going to be a good designer, you have to use boats a lot, so that you know what boats have to put up with."

He attended Hamilton College and studied naval architecture at MIT, though he never graduated. His first job was as a spar designer for Sparkman and Stephens, working on the design for the schooner *Brilliant*, and he later apprenticed himself to naval architect Arthur Tiller of Berlin, Germany. During World War II he did some work for Sparkman and Stephens and later worked for the Bureau of Ships.

After the war Scheel entered private practice in New York City and lived in Stonington, Connecticut. He forged a relationship with the Stonington Boat Works and designed a number of boats, including the popular Stonington Motor Sailer series.

During the Korean War, Scheel helped to design *Nautilus*, the first nuclear submarine, at the Electric Boat Company in Groton, Connecticut. He worked in the family textile business for fifteen years, designing yachts on the side and racing a lot. In 1968 he went to work for designer Charley Morgan, in Florida, where he learned about fiberglass construction and oversaw the designs for the boats used at Disney World. Scheel also worked on Morgan's 1970 America's Cup defense contender, *Heritage*.

Scheel then moved to Rockland, Maine, where he and three colleagues set up shop as Scheel Yachts. They built six of the well-regarded, fiberglass, center-cockpit Scheel 45's before the undercapitalized venture went out of business in 1975.

He then returned to his independent design practice and created a wide range of innovative, high-performance yachts built from cold-

Henry Scheel: *Kelso.* *Kelso* is a thoroughly modern, even innovative boat in terms of hull and rig, but she combines that with the sensible conception and traditional overall proportions that characterized Scheel's best work and grew out of his belief that "in yacht design, the client is always the sea." *© David H. Lyman*

molded wood and occasionally aluminum. He designed a number of yachts for the Royal Huisman yard in the Netherlands from the mid-1980's until he died. He drew over 250 designs during his career.

The Henry A. Scheel Collection is at the Mystic Seaport Museum, Mystic, CT.

—Daniel B. MacNaughton

SÉBASTIEN SCHMIDT

Born May 29, 1962 · Switzerland

Who would think that Switzerland, a small, landlocked alpine country in the middle of Europe, could produce so many yachting enthusiasts, famous skippers, high-seas adventurers, builders, and naval architects? It must be due in part to the remarkable Lake Geneva, along with a few other lakes, for as soon as yachting took hold in Europe, some Swiss pioneers were indulging their passion there, first with yachts imported from England and

Sébastien Schmidt. This 14.2-meter racer/cruiser was designed for use on Switzerland's Lake Leman. A massive, retractable, stainless-steel fin keel reduces her draft when desirable, and she features a luxurious wide-open interior layout. *Photo by G. Fauer, courtesy Jacques Taglang*

Edson B. Schock: _Debra._ The 39-foot LOA _Debra_ was Schock's most successful of several R-Class yachts designed to the Universal Rule. Built by master shipwright Herb Matson in 1924, her handsome lines are apparent as she sits in her cradle at Wilmington Boat Works in the 1920's. _Photo courtesy the Newport Harbor Nautical Museum, Newport Beach, CA_

then with yachts designed and built locally.

Sébastien Schmidt belongs to this elite. Designing for the unique local Swiss sailing conditions is a specialized undertaking due to the predominance of flukey air and calm water, which can be abruptly shaken by violent thermal winds and a chop as brutal as it is sudden. This necessitates an approach in which lightweight, reduced wetted surface area, and hydrodynamic appendages must be balanced against strength and ease of control, and where large or extreme sails must be quick and easy to reef. It would seem that if one can design successful boats for Switzerland, one should be able to meet the challenges of more consistent waters.

Schmidt is pursuing his art by mastering this combination of factors. Associated from 1983 to 1993 with Philippe Meier, he established his reputation in a difficult class: the International Rule 5.5-Meter. A fresh approach to the rule, close attention to weight reduction and to minimized angles of heel, and experience gained sailing multihulls on the lakes allowed them to conceive the 5.5-Meter _Chlika-Chlika_ in 1990. She won the European Championship in 1990 and the World Championship in 1991 and 1992.

These victories precipitated a series of orders for 5.5-Meter boats, and more racing successes. The experience allowed Schmidt to refit old 5.5-Meters, as well as 6- and 8-Meters, with optimized masts of carbon fiber and new underwater appendages, to good effect. Schmidt has been successful in designing a number of multihull classes, and also turns out the occasional cruising boat. In recent years Schmidt has achieved success with designs for the lakes, owing in part to his use of velocity prediction programs reflecting the local conditions.

In 1997, Schmidt assisted with the Swiss challenge for the 2000 America's Cup along with Philippe Briand and Peter Van Oossanen, while continuing his work with multihulls, racing yachts for the lakes, and International Rule classes.

Schmidt's design for the 41-foot Lake Geneva racing catamaran _Alinghi V,_ codesigned with Jo Richards in 2000, has dominated the extremely competitive Lake Geneva racing scene. Her success has led to Schmidt's receiving the commission to codesign, with Gilles Ollier, Duncan MacLane, and Mario Caponnetto, the new _Gitana_ trimaran for racing in the French 60 trimaran circuit. _Alenghi V_'s geometry, which fully triangulates the forces coming down from the rig, may well revolutionize catamaran design.

Sébastien Schmidt practices in Geneva, Switzerland.

—Jacques Taglang

EDSON BURR SCHOCK

1871–November 7, 1950 · United States

One of the most versatile and prolific designers on the West Coast of the United States during the first half of the twentieth century was Edson B. Schock. He is known for his sailing yachts of all sizes, one-design and development class boats, power yachts of all sizes, and a wide variety of commercial and military craft. A self-taught designer with no formal education after high school, he had a gift for aesthetics and

Edson B. Schock: *Highlander. Highlander* was built in 1928 at the Long Beach, California, yard of Chalker and Whiting. By 1934 the 61-foot 6-inch staysail schooner had become the flagship of the Transpacific Yacht Club as *Manuiwa*, and proceeded to win that year's race from Los Angeles to Honolulu. After a long career in those islands, she returned to her original home port of San Pedro. *Photo courtesy the Newport Harbor Nautical Museum, Newport Beach, CA*

proportion. He was a scientific designer to the extent that he did many of the basic calculations typically involved in hull design, while relying on a remarkable instinctive grasp of such considerations as engineering and weight calculations. His combination of skills was such that he was even able to design the engine powering one of his boats.

Born in Camden, New Jersey, Schock summered as a young man in Island Heights, where he sailed sneakboxes and catboats. He began designing in 1899 as an apprentice to A. Cary Smith, and just one year later struck off on his own with an office in New York. Business was slow at first, but by 1905 he was, like many designers of the period, designing powerboats to accommodate the new, lighter, and more efficient gasoline engines.

A number of these boats were highly successful cruiser/racers in long, grueling competitions, such as the Philadelphia to Havana Race, a distance of some 1,400 miles. The 40-foot *Irene II*,

for example, is said to have been the most successful racing powerboat of her day.

In 1906 Schock became design editor of *The Rudder* magazine, then headed by Thomas Fleming Day. He held this job for four years and continued to write articles for the rest of his career.

Schock was commissioned in 1910 to oversee the construction of a 58-foot powerboat to his design, and moved his office to Vancouver, British Columbia, to be near her builder. He then moved to Seattle at the beginning of World War I and later back to Vancouver and on to Los Angeles. While in Vancouver, he designed a number of beautiful and seaworthy yachts, and several patrol boats built for the Canadian forestry and fisheries departments. In Los Angeles he designed many cruising boats of rugged and seamanlike appearance. They were often remarkable for their speed, winning more than their share of races. Racing boats included a number of highly suc-

cessful R-Class yachts, some of which, such as the famous *Debra*, won series in both light and heavy air, a notable distinction.

Schock's later cruising and racing boats retained the look of his early designs but tended to have a large sail area ("You can always take it off," he said), lighter scantlings, lower displacement, and less wetted surface area. Presumably experience gave him more confidence, enabling him to press the limits a bit.

Among Schock's cruising sailboats that had considerable success at racing were the 62-foot schooner *Manuiwa*, winner of the 1934 Transpac Race to Honolulu; *Jorie*, a 50-foot cutter that was second only to the famed 56-foot, Sparkman and Stephens–designed cutter *Blitzen* in the 1939 Transpac Race, in a fleet of twenty-six boats; and *Lucky Star*, the 44-foot schooner once owned by Schock himself and still winning Performance Handicap Racing Fleet (PHRF) and classic yacht events today. In March 2000 this boat won, for the second year running, the American Schooner Cup Series at San Diego, over a fleet of schooners designed by Alden, N. G. Herreshoff, Brewer, Sweisguth, and others.

Schock drew many designs intended for amateur construction and is said to have been very generous with his time and advice to amateur builders. During both world wars, he designed various large and small vessels for the U.S. government, including a 270-foot freighter. Even in times of great activity, he seldom worked with draftsmen, but his grandson, Charles Schock, did work for him for a period after World War II. Following his wife's death in 1949, Schock moved to Kingston, Rhode Island, to practice yacht design with his son, Edson I. Schock. He continued to work until his death in 1950.

The Schock, Edson I. and Edson B., Collection of plans is at Mystic Seaport Museum, Mystic, CT.

—Charles D. Schock, Thomas G. Skahill, and Daniel B. MacNaughton

EDSON IRWIN SCHOCK

January 8, 1897–October 24, 1988
United States

As the only child of designer Edson B. Schock, Edson I. Schock came by his interest in yacht design quite naturally. Encouraged by his father to go to MIT (graduating with the class of 1921) to learn the technical side of design, which the elder Schock lacked, he joined his father in his Los Angeles design office in the early 1920's. At that time, however, the design business was quiet, so he sought employment in other fields. After a couple of engineering jobs he entered teaching, and for the rest of his working life he was a professor of mechanical engineering, and also taught a course in yacht design, at the University of Rhode Island (URI).

Schock designed and built over a dozen daysailers and dinghies for use by the family. Several of these designs became classes: the 11-foot Wee Nip sailing dinghies, the Point Jude 15's,

and the 14-foot Sturdee cats. The original Wee Nip was built in 1936, the first Point Jude 15 in 1946, and the earliest catboat in 1938. The latter two classes are still being built.

During World War II Schock was naval architect for the Harris and Parsons Shipyard in East Greenwich, Rhode Island, where 110-foot subchasers were being built. He also taught night classes at the Naval War College in Newport.

Probably Schock's most widely recognized design is the 50-foot hermaphrodite brig *Black Pearl,* owned for several years by the proprietor of the famous Newport watering hole bearing the same name. He also designed powerboats, including several cruisers in the 40-foot range, and sportfishermen ranging up to 50 feet long. Nearly two hundred of Schock's designs have been built, not counting the products of numerous how-to articles, such as those that appeared in *Sports Afield* during the 1950's and 1960's, or racing class boats.

Edson B. Schock: *Jorie.* Designed as a staysail schooner in 1936, *Jorie* was given this cutter rig for the 1939 Transpac Race in which she placed second to the famed 56-foot cutter *Blitzen,* designed by Sparkman and Stephens. Her career was successful but short. She was badly damaged in a storm during World War II and could not be rebuilt due to wartime shortages. *Photo courtesy Thomas G. Skahill*

Edson I. Schock: *Sharon Potts. Sharon Potts* is No. 1 of the first five Point Jude 15's built in 1946 by a group of amateurs. Many of this class were subsequently built of plywood and fiberglass by several boatyards. This boat is now owned and sailed by Charles Schock. *Photo courtesy Charles D. Schock*

Schock pioneered sailing at URI and built two boats that he donated to help get the program launched. The program caught on, and URI sailors continue to do very well in intercollegiate racing. One of the university's research vessels was named for Schock in honor of his contributions to the state and the university. Schock also served a stint at the Mystic Seaport Museum, where he made drawings of many of the museum's historic boats.

In his book, *How To Build Small Boats*, first published in 1952, Schock provides a number of designs and explains his simplified method for building plywood boats. The book radiates his simple, straightforward approach to getting a job done.

Charles D. Schock, the third generation, also came by his interest in yacht design naturally. He worked with his grandfather and in the offices of John Alden and Sparkman and Stephens. Though he designed several boats, most of his career was not in yacht design. He was a marine surveyor for several years and continues to be keenly interested in design.

The Schock, Edson I. and Edson B., Collection of plans is at Mystic Seaport Museum, Mystic, CT.

—Charles D. Schock

WILHELM SCHULZE

1873–1947 · Germany

A silversmith and engraver by trade, Wilhelm Schulze's most important contribution to yacht design was his work in the spidsgatter classes, handsome double-ended cruiser/racers still widely admired today. Working in Oslo under commission by the Kongelige Norsk Seilforening (Royal Norwegian Sailing Association), he established the measurement definitions for the spidsgatter classes: the V Class (40 square meters of sail area), the Q Class (60 square meters), and the J Class (80 square meters). Schulze's work became the almost exclusive basis for these classes, and he continuously experimented with the possibilities they offered.

Another example of Schulze's high standards was his design for the timeless "Junior Boats": 7-meter, open-cockpit canoe racers for young people to sail in the fjords.

In 1920 Schulze resettled in Bremen, his birthplace, where he founded the Bremen Werkstätten für Kunsthandwerkliche Silberarbeiten (Bremen Workshop for Silver Crafts), a shop specializing in fine work, which enjoyed a good name for its regatta trophies. In 1999 Schulze's designs were collected and made part of an exhibition about yacht design.

—Eberhard Wetjen

Edson I. Schock: *Lydia.* Lydia (ex-*Barbarena*) was built in 1957 by C. E. Chapman in Costa Mesa, California. The 40-foot cutter shows how dramatic traditional styling details can be used to create emotional appeal decades after they were typical. *Photo courtesy Charles D. Schock*

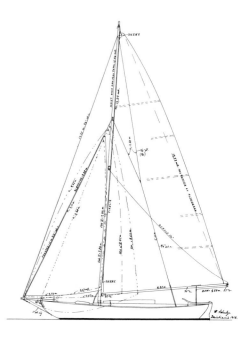

Wilhelm Schulze: *Kvadratmer.* Schulze did a great deal to promote and define the still-popular spidsgatter classes. This example of a 60-Square-Meter spidsgatter has distinctly Norwegian overtones in her bow and stern profiles. Most showed a more rounded Danish-style stern. *Drawing courtesy Volker Christmann*

Carl Schumacher: Alerion Express. The Alerion series of sailboats incorporate classic features in a modern vessel. The hull form of the Alerion 38 evokes reminders of early American yacht designs of similar proportions, but with a more modern underbody and lighter displacement. © *Onne van der Wal*

CARL SHERMAN SCHUMACHER

June 13, 1949–February 5, 2002 · United States

Carl Schumacher grew up in Newport Beach, California, in a sailing family. He began drawing boats at an early age and was encouraged by William Garden, a friend of the family, to take up yacht design. While attracted to the work of Sparkman and Stephens and Nathanael and L. Francis Herreshoff, Schumacher's early work was really more influenced by the lighter designs of William Lapworth. His various auxiliary designs are light, easy-to-sail performers.

Upon graduation from California Polytechnic State University in 1972, Schumacher worked briefly for Jensen Marine, builders of Lapworth's famous Cal 40. By 1973 he had moved to the San Francisco Bay area and was working in the design office of Gary Mull. He opened his own practice in 1977, and within two years, his Quarter-Tonner *Summertime Dream* won the Quarter-Ton North American Championships. No fluke, she repeated in 1980 and competed successfully under both IOR and MORC ratings for some time.

This led to the very successful Express line of sailboats: 27-, 34- and 37-footers. His early designs were primarily built for West Coast clients. Among his boats that have figured prominently in San Francisco Bay racing annals were *Swiftsure II*, *National Biscuit*, and *Recidivist*.

Elsewhere, the Lightwave 395 and 48 (the former a light one-design racer/cruiser and the latter an easily handled performance cruiser) were built in England by Oyster Marine. The Rhode Island–built Alerion Express line of boats (20, 28, and 38 feet long) feature a classic look drawn from the designer's early interest in Herreshoff hollow-bowed designs. These boats (no connection to the earlier Express line) have won numerous design awards.

One of the best known of Schumacher's creations is the light-displacement cruiser *Heart of Gold*. This 50-foot sloop has placed well in several ocean events on the Pacific and, as a shorthanded cruiser, has logged over 50,000 miles and a global circumnavigation. *Heart of Gold* clearly embodied Schumacher's stated goal "to design good-looking boats that sail easily."

At the time of his premature death, nearly six hundred boats had been built to fifty-seven Schumacher designs. —J. Scott Rohrer

FRANCO SCIOMACHEN

Born September 28, 1920

ERNESTO SCIOMACHEN

Born September 10, 1923

ALDO SCIOMACHEN

Born March 23, 1951

Italy

The first Sciomachen design, a 34-foot RORC Class III cutter, dates back to 1951. The Sciomachen office initially dedicated itself to the design of racing and cruising sailboats, and *Arlecchino*, second by a hair at the 1971 Quarter-Ton Cup, *Linda*, winner of the 1983 One-Ton Cup, and *Avant Garde*, winner of the 1984 and 1985 editions of the Centomiglia Race, are testimonials of the racing breed. Many Sciomachen designs were created for production in fiberglass—some directly derived from their racing yachts, others expressly designed for cruising.

The scope of Sciomachen designs has broadened in the last twenty years to encompass planing and displacement powerboats, fast ferries, and fishing vessels. In the powerboats arena, the Sciomachen firm puts particular emphasis on fast hulls, from small production

Ben Seaborn: *Nautilus III.* The first of Seaborn's Swiftsure class, *Nautilus III* is shown here prior to her launching in 1949. Built by Blanchard Boat Company of Seattle, she has a long waterline and easy lines that speak of the speed for which this class is famous. *Photo courtesy Guy Hoppon*

runabouts, some of which are used for racing with speeds over 60 knots, to passenger ferries, the largest of which are capable of speeds over 30 knots with capacities of up to 450 passengers. Functionality and the ability to operate in adverse weather conditions are the leading requirements for fishing vessels, designed with the maximum concern for safety. Sailing is still very much alive in the heart of Sciomachen, with the greatest emphasis on the design of bluewater cruising sailboats.

Sciomachen designs have been built using most construction materials. In the 1950's each boat was one-of-a-kind and built in traditional wooden methods. Later a gradual shift was undertaken to fiberglass and to production boats. Sciomachen was among the first to adopt the new technologies made available by progress in glue and resin research: glued longitudinal planking in the 1960's, cold molding in the

1970's, and advanced carbon and aramid fiber–cored composites in the 1980's. Metals have also been used: steel for large cruising yachts and fishing vessels, aluminum for racing craft and fast ferries.

Design methods have undergone major changes through the years. All large drafting tables, splines, weights, and planimeters have given way to networked three-dimensional, computer-aided-design workstations, each equipped with dual 21-inch, high-resolution monitors. Tools have changed, but each Sciomachen design is still based on creativity, common sense, and the experience of creating more than four hundred designs of boats from about 20 to over 130 feet long.

The Sciomachen family—Franco and his brother Ernesto and Franco's son Aldo—work closely together as a team and would not hear of being listed separately in the *Encyclopedia.*

—Sciomachen family

BEN SEABORN

April 11, 1914–January 31, 1960 · United States

Seattle, Washington, designer Ben Seaborn was one of the first to perceive the advantages of the light-displacement type. His work shows a stunning and rapid transition from his early, graceful, and rather conventional moderate to heavy-displacement sailboats, to a series of light-displacement designs that employed fin keels, separated rudders, reverse sheer, strip planking, and plywood construction in various combinations. Seaborn did some work for the Boeing Aircraft Company and was the first designer to draw keel foil sections using aeronautic plotting methods. His designs for *Sea Fever, Helene,* and *Crusader* are early examples of yachts with trim tabs on the keel's trailing edge.

Seaborn saw considerable racing success at the early age of seventeen, with his design for the 59-foot ocean racing cutter *Circe* for his step-father. She won the 1934 Swiftsure Race and finished just 13 minutes behind the famous Sparkman and Stephens yawl *Dorade* in the 1936 Transpac. His best-known design is the 26-foot, plywood-hulled Thunderbird class, a remarkable boat that is still one of the fastest cruiser/racers of her size. Many were built by both amateurs and professionals, the fulfillment of a lifelong effort on Seaborn's part to produce a boat for "every man" by seeking ease and economy of construction in a versatile, high-performance design.

Self-taught as a designer, Seaborn began to work professionally in the 1930's while he worked for the Blanchard Boat Company, and attended the University of Washington. His early work soon established him as the area's most popular designer of racer/cruisers, and his designs began a long string of victories in the Swiftsure Races. During World War II he worked for Boeing, on loan from Blanchard's, and assisted in setting up the production line for the B-17 bomber. After the war he worked on commercial craft in the employ of George Nickum and Company while maintaining his yacht design office.

By 1948, virtually all of Seaborn's boats were lighter than average. The only exceptions were the yawl *Starbright* and a sistership, both built at Gig Harbor, Washington, in 1949. His thinking was being influenced by such boats as Laurent Giles's *Myth of Malham* and the work of California designers Bill Lapworth and Wendell H. Calkins, which pointed the way toward light-displacement boats and how they might be configured and constructed. In 1948 he produced the 30-foot, 5,300-pound sloop *Twinkle,* with a spade rudder, fin keel, and long, light hull form. She was the first in a line of light-displacement boats including the Seafair, Sierra, and Swiftsure classes, which served to evolve the new type at a rapid pace, indicating the remarkably flexible and capable mind of their designer. The Thunderbird design came out in 1957. All of Seaborn's light-displacement designs were controversial in their day, but time proved virtually all of his thinking to be correct.

The majority of Seaborn-designed boats are still actively sailing and racing, including over a thousand Thunderbirds, some of which are still being built new, each year.

—Daniel B. MacNaughton with J. Scott Rohrer

CHARLES LINCOLN SEABURY

August 4, 1860–April 7, 1922 · United States

Why is it that some designers continue to inspire people's imaginations while others, famous in their lifetime, are forgotten by later generations? Today few people know about Charles Seabury, the man who during the first decade of the twentieth century designed and built some of the world's swiftest steam yachts. His company, ultimately named Consolidated Shipbuilding Corporation, became one of America's largest makers of motorboats.

Seabury was born in Tiverton, Rhode Island. A son of a boatbuilder, he worked for some time in the boiler shop of the Herreshoff Manufacturing Company before he began yacht building in Nyack on the Hudson River, close to New York City, in 1889. By the early 1890's, and profiting from patents on steam engine machinery and safety-tube boilers, he already had made a name for himself. Fast and equipped with innovative machinery, his steam yachts nonetheless were traditional in appearance, with stunning lines, classic clipper bows, and attractive fantail sterns.

Charles Seabury: *Kanawha II.* Designed and built by Seabury in 1899, the famous 227-foot LOA steam yacht *Kanawha II* won the Lysistrata Cup twice, in 1903 and 1904, making her "the world's fastest large steam yacht of her time," according to L. Francis Herreshoff. *Photo courtesy Naval Historical Foundation*

Charles Seabury: *Niagara IV.* Before turning from steam to the internal-combustion engine–powered commuters in the early 1900's, Seabury designed the 111-foot LOA *Niagara IV*. Launched in 1903, she was powered by twin triple-expansion steam engines. © *Mystic Seaport, Rosenfeld Collection, Mystic CT. James Burton, Photographer*

Charles Seabury: *Machigonne.* Photographed here off the coast of California, the 140-foot *Machigonne* was designed and built of steel at the Seabury Company in Morris Heights, New York, in 1909. *Photo courtesy Newport Harbor Nautical Museum, Newport Beach, CA*

In 1896, and possibly as a consequence of the accidental death in 1892 of its former owner, Jabez A. Bostwick, Seabury merged his company, Charles L. Seabury and Company with the Gas Engine and Power Company in Morris Heights, north of Manhattan. This company had been founded in 1885 to capitalize on Frank W. Ofeldt's naphtha engine patent and was famous for small and medium-sized naphtha launches, of which it claimed to have built twenty-five hundred by 1896. However, the fashion for naphtha launches was beginning to subside.

The new organization invested quickly and heavily in the yard at Morris Heights. It built numerous new shops equipped with everything that was needed to build a complete boat with all its component parts at one location, as well as a new marine railway capable of accommodating vessels up to 200 feet in length. Instead of naphtha launches, Morris Heights now became known for large and fast steam yachts.

The newly opened Harlem Ship Canal, which connected the yard with both the Hudson and East River, facilitated this development by providing easy access for large vessels. Eventually all of Seabury's operations were concentrated in Morris Heights. By 1908 the yard was reported to have the world's largest capacity for producing pleasure craft, with buildings, docks, basins, and marine railways occupying practically two hundred city lots.

In 1898, Seabury received the first large order from the U.S. Navy (thereby benefiting from the refusal of the Herreshoffs to meet fastidious navy demands). Launched two years later, *Bailey* achieved 31 knots during her trials, a speed that made her the fastest vessel of her type in the United States for several years.

The experience and reputation gained from *Bailey* and several other torpedo boat destroyers quickly made Seabury a first choice for wealthy customers seeking ultrafast steel and wooden steam yachts. In 1899 the 227-foot *Kanawha II* was launched, and by racing and beating the renowned passenger steamboat *Monmouth* (and twice winning the Lysistrata Cup in later years), she fulfilled her owner's demand for the fastest yacht in New York waters.

The 100-foot steam yacht *Vixen*, built in 1902 and capable of steaming at 22 mph, was widely believed to be the first yacht faster than the Herreshoff flyer *Niagara III* of 1900. In 1903, *Niagara III*'s owner, Howard Gould, came to Seabury for a new and even faster yacht. *Niagara IV*'s speed of 27.75 mph, achieved during her builder's trials, made her the fastest yacht in the United States. In 1905, Seabury designed and built *Vitesse*. Able to steam at 29.75

mph, she became not only the fastest yacht in the United States but also the fastest in the entire world. And the speed increases did not stop here, for six years later Seabury designed and built the 165-foot steam yacht *Sovereign*, whose builder's contract stipulated a speed of 35 mph!

Seabury's large high-speed yachts usually were driven by triple-expansion steam engines, but with the advent of the gasoline engine, he was quick to adopt this new technology and became a pioneer in this field. In 1904, he designed and built the autoboat *Japansky*, a predecessor of today's power speedboats that was equipped with a 41-hp gasoline engine. With maximum speeds of 19.5 knots, it won the first American autoboat contest at the 1904 Manhasset Bay Yacht Club Decoration Day Regatta.

In 1906, the 72-foot *Artful* was built for Payne Whitney and believed to be the fastest cabin motorboat in the world. *Artful* was fitted with two 6-cylinder Speedway gasoline marine engines, which, like most other technologies used in Seabury's boats, were developed and built in-house. Two years later, the 111-foot *Jemina F III* was launched and became the world's largest gasoline-driven yacht.

While the work of the Morris Heights concern continued to focus largely on pleasure

François Sergent: *Varna.* This sketch of *Varna*, built in 1962, shows how designers of the day reached for a new type. The hull remains quite heavy and long-ended, but the underwater appendages have been reduced in area. *Drawing courtesy Jacques Taglang*

yachts and launches, considerable business also involved commercial lines such as passenger boats, tugboats, and lighters, in addition to a great variety of craft for the government. In 1917, at the height of World War I, the company offered its entire resources to the navy, converting pleasure yachts for war service and building numerous small war vessels.

Seabury himself, however, withdrew from the company he had helped to build. During World War I he was a consulting expert with the marine department of the Foundation Company, which operated a shipyard in Kearny, New Jersey, and in 1918 he cofounded the naval construction and marine engineering firm of Seabury and de Zafra. In 1919, the Gas Engine and Power Company and Charles L. Seabury and Company—Consolidated as it had been known since the merger in 1896—was renamed the Consolidated Shipbuilding Corporation. Charles L. Seabury died at the age of sixty-one.

After his death, Consolidated Shipbuilding continued its success. By 1930 the yard had become one of America's largest makers of motorboats. Between the two world wars it turned out six hundred motoryachts, launches, lifeboats, houseboats, schooners, and steam yachts, and during World War II fifty 173-foot patrol chasers, as well as tugs and landing craft. Peacetime, however, found the yard unable to adjust to new demands, and in 1955 Consolidated Shipbuilding closed its plant at Morris Heights. It had operated for sixty-eight years and produced some of the world's speediest yachts.

Three collections of Seabury's drawings are at Mystic Seaport Museum, Mystic, CT: Charles L. Seabury Collection, Consolidated Shipbuilding-Mason Collection, and Consolidated Shipbuilding-Lane Collection.

—Claas van der Linde

FRANÇOIS SERGENT

Born 1911 · France

Along with Eugène Cornu and André Mauric, François Sergent belongs to the small group of French designers who lived during the transitional maritime period beginning in the late 1930's. And if this self-taught designer acknowledges the influence of English designer J. Laurent Giles, his work is also known to have evolved during his career, creating many original concepts.

Sergent spent youthful holidays in Brittany and Vendée, sailing and observing the boatbuilders in the harbors he visited. Voracious reading of *Le Yacht* magazine and accounts by Alain Gerbault, Rudyard Kipling, and Jack London completed his nautical education. At age sixteen, he drew his first sailboat. "I immediately understood how to draw fair hull lines; but above all, I had a sense of volume. When reading lines, I saw them in three dimensions."

After living in England for two years during the depression of the 1930's, Sergent then moved to Paris. He worked as a teacher, devoting his leisure time to the design of sailboats. He sold his first plans, for a 5.5-meter dinghy, in 1935. World War II interrupted his projects, but at the end of 1945 he opened his own design office in Paris. Throughout the country, the yachting fleet had to be rebuilt. For this independent designer, work was not lacking.

In sixty years, Sergent designed more than five hundred yachts, ranging from small dinghies to a 20-meter schooner. He designed many stock boats: the Grondin (codrawn in 1946 with Jean-Jacques Herbulot), with 500 built; plus the first light cruisers in fiberglass, which included the 7-meter Super Mistral, the smaller "630" and larger "1000" at Lanaverre's yard, and the Super Dorade, of which 1,250 were built, along with many others. But he remains primarily a custom designer, working essentially for a French clientele and employing all the materials at his disposal: traditional wooden construction, cold-molded wood, plywood, steel, aluminum, and fiberglass. He was also a sought-after skipper.

Sergent designed his first racer, *Eloise*, in 1949, confirming his reputation when she won the 1950 Plymouth–La Rochelle Race. Others followed: *Aquilon* and *Stemael II* in 1949, *Stemael III* and *Marie Christine II* in 1952, the yawl *Marie Christine III* in 1956, *Eloise II* in 1958, *Varna* in 1962, and particularly *Varna II* in 1964. These boats won prestigious races, such as the Fastnet, Cowes-Dinard, Plymouth–La Rochelle, Plymouth-Santander, Santander–La Trinité, and La Giraglia.

Sergent has never designed International Rule ("Meter") yachts because "that represents too much work for a man working alone–you spend too much time, you can miss new clients." Thus, he has always been able to put his inspiration to work for a clientele that has proved abundant.
—Jacques Taglang

WARD D. SETZER

Born 1960 · United States

One of the most diversely talented naval architects in the United States, Ward Setzer is president of Setzer Design Group in Cary, North Carolina, and works not only in naval architecture, for which he is most noted, but also in the design of marine fittings, sporting goods, and medical product lines, at his sister firm of Paragon Design.

Born in Charlottesville, Virginia, Setzer is a 1984 graduate of North Carolina State University at Raleigh with a BS in environmental design and a major in architecture. He also graduated from the Yacht Design Institute (YDI) of Blue Hill, Maine, in 1984, where he was awarded an ASc in small craft naval architecture technology.

Setzer progressed through the ranks of designers in the traditional manner, putting in his time at drawing boards in the design offices of Robb Ladd and J. B. Hargrave Naval Architects, before joining Hatteras Yachts in High Point, North Carolina, as custom yachts manager, where he led a three-person design team and an eighty-person team of production line workers.

In 1991 Setzer established his Paragon Design office, which later became Setzer Design Group. That firm has since maintained a steady workload of six to eight large megayachts on the design board, with approximately eight vessels usually being built around the world in the finest yacht yards.

Setzer's 150-foot, Trinity-built motoryacht *Bellini* was named ShowBoat of the Year for 2000 by *ShowBoats International* magazine. Setzer has also developed a line called Expedition Yachts. Several, including the motoryacht *Surprise*, were built in New Zealand.

As of this writing his latest yacht to be built in the United States is *Magpie*, a modern high-speed commuter built at Lyman-Morse Boatbuilders in Thomaston, Maine. Setzer's firm has also begun an 83-foot yacht with a new hull form and a classic superstructure.

The latest fleet of vessels—128, 132, and 140 feet in length—is called the Cloud Nine series, and is under construction at Sovereign Yachts in British Columbia, Canada. Setzer Design Group has also built a new mold for a fleet of 130-footers for Northern Marine in Anacortes, Washington. Both these hull forms represent the latest thinking in performance and styling and have been tank-tested. Many parts have been computer-cut by the five-axis routers of Janicki Machine.

Other notable projects have been the 142-foot Christensen *Namoh*, the 88-foot Broward Sportfishing Series, the *Victory Lane* 118- and 150-foot designs, and the 108-foot Intermarine *Lady A*. More recent projects include a growing fleet of world "expedition" yachts, and a new series of New England–styled designs—from jet-drive classic picnic boats to more robust classic weekenders, and the conversion of the former 106-foot Boston Harbor tug *Mars* into an educational vessel, now named *Sea Monster*, in Newport, Rhode Island.
—Bob Wallstrom

WILLIAM SHAW

Born June 9, 1926 · United States

As chief designer at Pearson Yachts, William Shaw helped to define the mainstream of production cruising sailboat design for three decades. His work varied from conservative keel/centerboarders, such as the 30-foot 3-inch Pearson Wanderer of 1966, through much lighter and racier boats, such as the 29-foot 11-inch Pearson Flyer of 1980, and included a host of designs exploring most of the popular variations typical of cruising sailboats of the time.

Shaw got his start working at Sparkman and Stephens in New York City during the 1950's, where among other projects he created the successful MORC racer/cruiser *Trina*. *Trina* spawned the Shaw 24 class, and soon, for the O'Day company, the Dolphin class. Very much in line with the same concept, he and the Sparkman and Stephens office soon produced the very popular Tartan 27. Shaw wrote the MORC Rule with guidance from Olin Stephens.

In August 1964, Shaw went to work at Pearson Yachts in Portsmouth, Rhode Island, as a designer. He became general manager in 1966, and the company enjoyed good success designing and building production boats of broad appeal. He avoided extreme features and emphasized family-oriented comfort and ease of handling, even in the hotter designs. While many companies opted for relatively extreme IOR-influenced cruisers, Shaw's designs largely ignored the pressures of the rule, while at the same time they moved steadily away from the dictates of tradition.

Especially in the design of cabin trunks and deck structures, Shaw and Pearson Yachts did a lot to define a new fiberglass aesthetic. Increasingly over the years, they used the potential of the newer material to create shapes based solely on function and visual appeal, instead of remaining within the narrow range of traditional shapes allowed by wooden construction. Along with his design team, Shaw produced about fifty designs during his thirty years at Pearson. His Pearson 35, another wholesome keel/centerboard cruiser, stayed in production for fourteen years.

Shaw retired in January of 1986, but consulted for Dyer Boats until 2001, designing custom modifications of their popular powerboat, the Dyer 29.
—Daniel B. MacNaughton

Opposite: William Shaw: *Whisker.* One of Pearson Yachts' most popular models, the 30-foot 3-inch *Whisker*, introduced in 1966, was also one of a long line of wholesome keel/centerboarders from her designer. © *Peter Barlow*

Fred Shepherd: *Freelance.* Shepherd was known for handsome and sturdy cruising yachts with particularly well-thought-out accommodations. His 86-foot LOA auxiliary schooner *Freelance* was built in 1907 by W. Chalmers and Company in Rutherglen, Scotland. © *Peter Barlow*

FREDERICK SHEPHERD

(Dates unknown) · England

Many designers draw cruising boats, but it is often through their racing boats that they achieve fame, probably because few cruises are publicized while race results always are. This was particularly true with the large yachts designed before the world wars, for whose owners racing was the usual reason for going yachting. Fred Shepherd, however,

breaks from this pattern as he is best known for his cruising boats, many of them quite large.

Shepherd's designs are noted for their great beauty. Many of them were yawls, with higher bulwarks, sweeter sheers, and more accommodations than was typical of the racing boats of the time. His designs range up to 100 feet in length, but he also drew a number of charming smaller boats including *Selina King,* a 35-foot 6-inch, canoe-sterned cutter for author

Arthur Ransome, and several motoryachts.

Shepherd began his career working in the office of designer Arthur E. Payne in Southampton, where he remained for six years. He worked as a designer for the brokerage firm of Lory and Cornwallis during the 1890's, and established his own office in London in 1899. Beginning in 1926 he and a partner opened a yacht-building business, but he soon returned to his design practice. Shepherd also worked as a yacht broker and surveyor.

While Shepherd's 64-foot cutter *Lexia* was not designed to beat any handicapping rule, she came in ahead of the other British yachts in the 1931 Fastnet Race on corrected time (the race was won by the famous Sparkman and Stephens–designed *Dorade*).

By the time of his retirement in 1939, Shepherd had designed eighty-four yachts, a number that seems small for a career of forty-five years, but he usually supervised the construction of each yacht, thus greatly increasing the time consumed by each design. He came out of retirement in 1946 to design the 50-foot ketch *Glamara*. Shepherd lived to be 101.

—Daniel B. MacNaughton

JOHN SHUTTLEWORTH

Born February 23, 1947 · England

John Shuttleworth belongs to the second generation of post–World War II British multihull designers. Born in South Africa of English parents, he studied engineering and built his first multihull (a 40-foot Kelsall trimaran) in 1974. He began multihull design in 1976 while working for Derek Kelsall, where between 1976 and 1978 he was involved with the design of Kelsall's groundbreaking trimaran *Great Britain IV* as well as the innovative catamaran *V.S.D.*

The first major design under his own name was the 65-foot trimaran *Brittany Ferries GB* in 1980, which won the 1981 Doublehanded Transatlantic Race. An early user of computers, he developed his computerized "Integrated Structure" approach to yacht engineering during these years. Success proved him right, for in the 1984 Singlehanded Transatlantic Race, one of his trimarans set a new race record, while another came third over the line. Four years later, his trimarans won in two classes, setting a new record for Class VI, which still stood in 2002. His 80-foot catamaran *Novanet* was the largest racing catamaran in Great Britain in 1985.

The ensuing publicity and his experience in computers resulted in the 1988 invitation by the New Zealand Challenge to evaluate and advise on their computer performance-prediction and data-gathering methods for the America's Cup. Threatened by the U.S. America's Cup defender, the catamaran *Stars & Stripes*, the team eventually developed the most advanced velocity prediction programs for multihulls. A very analytical design approach, coupled with thorough tank-testing programs, has remained characteristic of Shuttleworth's work.

Building on his experience of six years living afloat on a multihull, he designed a line of fast and efficient cruising catamarans, includ-

John Shuttleworth: Tektron 50. The Tektron 50 is a typically clean and streamlined, 50-foot cruiser/racer catamaran. Underwater, the hulls are narrow for speed, but they flare out above the waterline to provide for a roomy interior. *Photo by Dr. Martin Mai*

ing the little 26-foot *Cheetah*, the fast Spectrum 42 and Tektron 35 and 50, and the big Shuttleworth 70. These cruiser/racers were often much better performers than boats of competing designs, owing to their typical Shuttleworth shape: streamlined, low-windage topsides and rather narrow hulls at the waterline, flaring out to become much wider above the water. This form allowed higher length-beam ratios than was customary in other cruising catamaran hulls.

John Shuttleworth practices in London, England. —Claas van der Linde

CHARLES SIBBICK

1849–1912 · England

The term *Sibbick Rater* was full of meaning at the end of the nineteenth century. It defined exquisitely built, cleverly designed racing yachts of the smaller classes. Owning a yacht designed by Charles Sibbick often meant one owned a successful racer rather than an also-

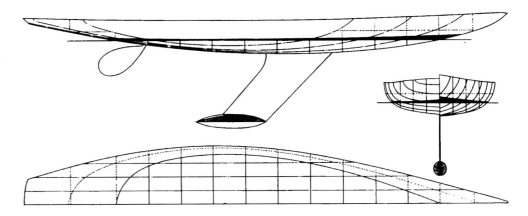

Charles Sibbick: *Unora*. Extreme to our present-day eyes, *Unora* was not atypical of the One-Raters of the 1890's. Capable of great speed off the wind, she is a good example of a Sibbick Rater. Built for Lord Ruthven, it is interesting to note that like others of her type, she had a "fin and bulb" keel, which we regard as a modern innovation. © *Tony Dixon*

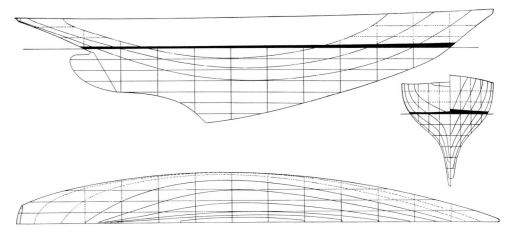

Charles Sibbick: *Beatrix*. In all appearances above the waterline, the 34-foot LOA *Beatrix* is a typical gaff cruising cutter of the 1890's. Yet, below the waterline, she demonstrates the influences of the Raters of that time, with her cutaway keel and deadwood. © *Tony Dixon*

ran. Racing in these classes also indicated wealth and extravagance, for the rater classes were hotly contested and boats were quickly outclassed, to be replaced by a more up-to-date vessel. In this realm, Sibbick was one of the most successful designers of the time.

Starting as a house builder, Sibbick became in time a building contractor's foreman. But sailing small craft and designing yachts had long been an interest and an absorbing hobby for him. In 1888, Sibbick took a chance when he decided to design and build small craft full-time, by purchasing the Albert yard in Cowes, Isle of Wight, off the south coast of England.

Sibbick was particularly interested in creating lightly constructed, light-displacement sailing craft. This was at a time when Dixon Kemp's Length-and-Sail-Area Rule reigned. Nothing could be simpler or more open to exploitation by adventurous designers and owners. Boats built to this rule were divided into discreet classes: Half-, One-, 2½-, Five-, and then less numerous 10-, 20-, and 40-Raters. It was in the first four that Sibbick made his name. His interest in light-displacement, easily driven craft led him to develop the "fin and bulb" keel configuration, with a separate rudder.

Such was the demand for these craft offering exciting racing to those with limited resources, they became a hotbed of competition, among owners and designers both, including the better-known Watson, Fife, Soper, and Payne. In such a galaxy of talent the star of Sibbick shone brightly.

Wealthy owners would often have a new boat each season; some had two or more. This created a lot of work for designers and builders. In 1895 the Duke of York (later King George V) ordered a One-Rater from Sibbick. Built by gangs working back-to-back twenty-four hours a day, *White Rose* was delivered in seven days. She was a successful boat designed in the last year of the Length-and-Sail-Area Rule.

Successive Linear Rating rules produced craft of short-term prominence. In fact, it wasn't until the first International Rule of 1906 that some stability came to racing classes. All this encouraged the growth of the one-design classes that proliferated in the first three decades of the twentieth century.

By this time Sibbick had turned his attention toward cruising yachts. In 1900 he had designed and built the 16-ton yawl *Saunterer*, which was followed in 1906 by her near-sister *Thallassa*. Although Sibbick began construction on *Thallassa*, the firm was encountering a cash-flow problem and she was completed by Fay of Southampton.

Yacht design and building has always had its financial risks. The work is often seasonal,

Alexander Simonis: *Nicorette.* *Nicorette* took line honors and was IRC overall winner in the 2000 Sydney-Hobart Race. This photo was taken in the Bass Strait, with *Nicorette* charging upwind in 35-plus knots of wind and a heavy swell. *Photo courtesy Alexander Simonis*

and at the mercy of owners' whims, changing rating rules, economic trends, and often fashion. Many seemingly buoyant firms have inexplicably suddenly gone to the wall. The circumstances at Sibbick's Yard are not known, but early in February 1912, Charles Sibbick's body was found near the entrance to Cowes harbor. It was assumed he had fallen out of a small boat and drowned.

In his twenty-four years of operation at Cowes, Sibbick had designed and built over three hundred craft, ranging from small Half-Raters to the 60-ton yawl *Ruth*, all of them outstanding of their type and each of them a fitting memorial to a most accomplished designer.

—David Ryder-Turner

ALEXANDER SIMONIS

Born November 27, 1959
The Netherlands/South Africa

When he was eighteen, Alexander Simonis realized that his future lay with the sea. For a young man with this interest, training as a seagoing deck officer was an obvious choice. Born in Holland, Simonis enrolled in the Dutch national Merchant Navy Academy, but quickly found that poor eyesight meant his career was directed to the engineering branch. Lack of ac-

cess to the open air soon dulled his interest in marine engineering, though not his enthusiasm for the sea. He left the academy and earned a degree in naval architecture from the University of Dordrecht, graduating in 1983.

Simonis's first employment as a naval architect was with the South African alloy yacht builders Cenmarine. Gradually, he found himself designing yachts on a part-time basis, but by 1989 he was able to found his own company and leave Cenmarine. In 1991 Simonis hired Maarten Voogd, who became his partner in 1998.

As a designer, Simonis aims to produce yachts that are fast, fun, comfortable, and safe. His early experience in his parents' MacAlpine-Downie–designed Apache class cat, is reflected in his best-known, large cruising multihulls, of which the Moorings and the Voyage series are examples. Most of his work is for European and American buyers, although there is more and more interest from other parts of the world like New Zealand, where he designed the new yacht for Bruno Trouble built by Custom Yachts in Auckland.

Simonis is convinced that his designs benefit from the cross-pollination of multihull with monohull design requirements, advantages, and limitations. His monohull designs, for example, are faster and more comfortable as a result of his extensive experience with multihulls.

Simonis also has a reputation for designing racing monohulls. Recent victories include yachts developed under the IRM rules, such as the 80-foot *Nicorette*, line honor and handicap winner of the 2000 Sydney-Hobart Race. Early in the new millennium, his design for the first Open 85-class yacht will be launched in France. This yacht will be sailed by Pascal Herold, president of the Union Nationale pour la Course au Large (UNCL) and director of the French America's Cup team, in an attempt to break the nonstop, singlehanded, round-the-world record.

The firm of Simonis Voogd Design operates in Cape Town, where Simonis is based, and in Enkuizen, the Netherlands, where Voogd practices. The two travel back and forth.

—Tom Roach

WILLIAM SIMONS II

1821–1902 · Scotland

On the Clyde, the name William Simons and Company is associated with that most functional but necessary of ships, the dredger. For a short period in the mid-nineteenth century Simons also attracted attention with his radically hollow-lined, 45-foot LWL cutter *Tiara*, of 1850.

It is often simplistically stated that prior to *America*'s visit in 1851, the British had never thought of creating fine-lined yachts, or at least hulls with a fine entry. While there is no doubt that the "cod's head, mackerel's tail" type prevailed, a few experiments were made in designing fine hulls; after all, ship's boats had been particularly sleek for many years. *Tiara* followed the trend toward finer bows in yachts begun by the Assheton-Smith–designed *Menai* and the Waterman-designed *Mosquito*, and was influenced by the hydrodynamic findings of John Scott Russell.

Writing in 1881, G. L. Watson said of *Tiara*, "A yacht which was far ahead of anything then afloat in the way of form. . . . I had the pleasure of seeing [her model] the other day, and it is a very beautiful one; her bow was long and hollow, very like *America*'s, while the afterbody was carried sweet and fair, into a long, deep set counter, showing hardly any knuckle at the tuck. She was utterly unlike anything ever launched on the Clyde, and of course was condemned by every old salt that saw her. But *Tiara* came out, and did not sink in the first sea she got into, and was a wonderfully fast and successful boat in all weathers."

Simons didn't produce many more yacht designs, but at a time when no shipyards had test tanks, the experimentation *Tiara* allowed had a bearing on his yard's future success.

—Iain McAllister

DWIGHT SWAIN SIMPSON

1883–1962 · United States

Dwight Simpson became an independent yacht designer only in his "retirement" from John Alden's office in Boston. After graduating from Cornell University with an engineering degree, he worked at a variety of jobs, all connected with yachting, and in 1920 he joined Alden as one of his earliest associates.

Simpson not only became Alden's chief designer of powerboats but also supervised their construction and drafting room operations. He designed a few small boats intended for economical construction by amateurs, and wrote an interesting series of articles in *The Rudder* magazine (1934) in which he traced the design evolution of John Alden's ten *Malabar* schooners. He stayed with Alden through World War II, overseeing the construction of company-designed yachts. During the war he supervised the construction of small naval vessels designed by a collaborative effort between the Alden and Eldredge-McInnis offices.

In 1955, after Simpson formally retired, he opened a small office, Dwight Simpson and Associates. It quickly grew into a highly successful design firm. (The firm later became Potter, McArthur and Gilbert.) He produced a few sailboats, mostly family cruisers with modest racing potential under the CCA Rule, but the great majority of his work was in fishing and commercial vessels. He came to be an acknowledged leading authority especially on power yachts, sportsfishermen, and draggers. Unlike his early designs, which stressed economy and simplicity of construction, these later boats were intended for professional fiberglass manufacture.

—Walter Voigt

KARL EINAR SJÖGREN

September 29, 1871–May 6, 1956 · Sweden

Karl Sjögren is credited for having made the small skerry cruisers a fairly common type of boat. These yachts were perfect for sailing in the flat water around the sheltered skerries, or islands, of which the Swedish coastline has many. He worked as a postmaster but came to be one of Sweden's most prominent amateur yacht designers, creating more than three hundred skerry cruisers. He was also active in introducing the Skerry Cruiser Rule.

Living all his life in Stockholm, Sjögren was active in the Stockholm Yacht Club, for which he designed thirty boats for lotteries between 1901 and 1930. Lotteries were widespread in

Karl Sjögren: *Cobra*. Built as a lottery boat (yacht clubs routinely held lotteries to raise money and the prize was a yacht) in 1925 for the Stockholm Yacht Club, the 12.18-meter *Cobra* was built at the New Boatyard at Gröndal, Sweden. © *Per Thelander*

Sweden from the end of the nineteenth century to the 1950's. They allowed yacht clubs to raise money, offering a yacht as the prize. A further benefit is that people without a lot of money could win a yacht. Sjögren also designed boats for lotteries for sailing associations other than the Stockholm Yacht Club.

Sjögren made his name in 1896 with the yacht *Tjopp*, a fin-keel racer with a sail area of 28.73 square meters that was very successful. From the end of the nineteenth century and some years into the twentieth century he designed several fin-keel boats.

When the Skerry Cruiser Rule was developed in 1908, Sjögren served as one of the delegates. He also took part in the revision of the rule in 1925. During the period up to the 1930's, amateur constructions of Sjögren's skerry cruisers were common. He provided people with inexpensive and simple drawings for cruisers ranging from 15-Square-Meters to 40-Square-Meters.

Sjögren had private commissions as well. These yachts, in the classes 15- to 55-Square-Meters, were modern and intended for racing. The 30-Square-Meter *Lilljojo* won the skerry cruiser trophy in 1920. Another beautiful yacht was *Singva*, a 55-Square-Meter yacht from 1927.

Also a successful sailor, in the Olympic Games in 1908 Sjögren was helmsman for the Swedish 6-Meter yacht. He also won the skerry cruiser trophy in the years 1926 and 1927 with the 30-Square-Meter yachts *Lindagull* and *Solkatten* of his own design. In 1931 the trophy was once again won by one of Sjögren's boats, the 30-Square-Meter *Lillsingva*, but with another helmsman. He himself sailed his 40-Square-Meter *Ingrid* between the years 1918 and 1955. He died from injuries received from a fall from *Ingrid* while he was getting her ready in the springtime.

—Ulf Lycke

A. SLAABY-LARSEN

1912–1988 · Denmark

Born in the small coastal town of Espergaerde, north of Copenhagen, A. Slaaby-Larsen apprenticed at the Helsingør (Elsinore) Shipyard and at the same time studied to be a ship engineer at Helsinør Ship Technical School. In his spare time he sailed and started to design pleasure boats.

Slaaby-Larsen won a design competition in Norway in 1937, but his big break was the design of the International 5-Meter *Indian* in 1943, a very fast boat. However, it was not easy for him to make a living designing yachts. Therefore, he started to design commercial vessels and fishing boats especially suitable for conditions off Greenland. He became his own boss when he took over the firm of another Danish designer, Ferd. G. Hansen, following Hansen's death in 1943.

By the 1950's Slaaby-Larsen knew his heart belonged to yachting. Smaller offshore cruising yachts became his primary interest. Many one-offs and class boats such as the Corsair, Vampire, Larsen, and Danica were built in Danish yards. Many were exported to the United States. His design for the 22-foot LOA Norge 22 was sold by Norge Boats in Connecticut. His yachts had a classic look and were always built of mahogany.

Slaaby-Larsen became known outside Denmark when he placed third in a design competition sponsored by the British magazine *Yachting World*, in 1957. The boat was a well-proportioned 39-foot yawl called *Danica*. The biggest yacht he designed was the clipper schooner *C'est la Vie* for an American owner, made for a scientific expedition around the world.

Slaaby-Larsen's drawings and many objects were donated by his son to the Danish Yachting Museum, Troense, Denmark.

—Bent Aarre

JOHN F. SMALL
1860–ca. 1930
SAMUEL N. SMALL
(Dates unknown)

United States

Around 1901, the brothers John and Sam Small opened a design office called the Small Brothers in Boston. They were well-known local yachtsmen who until then had designed boats only on an amateur basis, aimed at beating the handicapping rules of the day. A J. F. Small cruis-

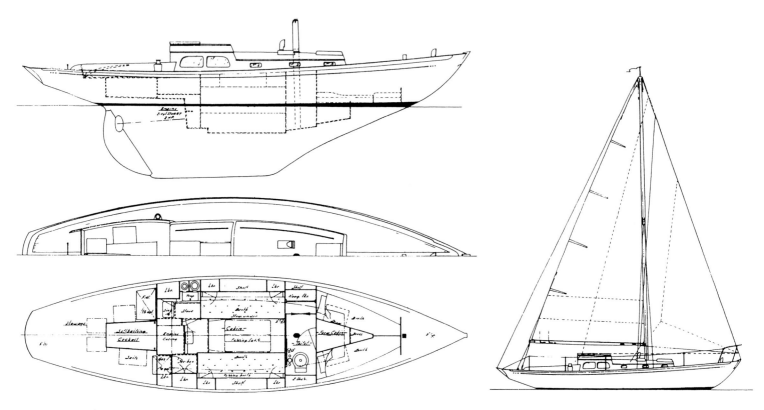

A. Slaaby-Larsen: Vampire. This pretty 32-foot sloop was built in series by one or more Danish yards, probably for export to the United States. This effort may have been hampered by a decision to designate her the Vampire 22 (22 feet LWL). *Drawing courtesy Bent Aarre*

John and Samuel Small: *Ustane*. The sloop *Ustane* was designed by Samuel Small for his own use. Together with their wives, the designers cruised extensively on the East Coast in the early 1900's in boats of this type. *Reproduced from an unknown source*

ing boat design appears in print as early as 1897.

Their sailboats, ranging from small one-designs and development class racers to schooner yachts up to 125 feet long, were often of the keel/centerboard configuration and generally notable for their shallow draft, very flat floors, firm bilges, and long ends. Many of the small designs were particularly appealing, long-ended, gaff-rigged cruising yawls ideally suited for coastwise cruising in the days when auxiliary power was either absent or very feeble in nature.

The Small brothers' powerboats had the typical, canoe-like hull forms of the day, reaching for good speed from the heavy, slow-turning gasoline motors that were just becoming available. After about 1909 their designs appeared in magazines infrequently, mostly under the name of John F. Small.

—Daniel B. MacNaughton

ARCHIBALD CARY SMITH

September 4, 1837–December 8, 1911
United States

By inclination, A. Cary Smith was a marine artist, and he might well have remained in that profession except that he was also one of the most successful and innovative designers in the early period of American yachting and his services were much in demand. Smith was the first American yacht designer to draft his hull lines on paper instead of using a model, and was among the first to substitute scientific calculations for rules of thumb when figuring displacement, stability, and balance.

Smith designed the 1881 America's Cup defender *Mischief*, which in an era of polarization between the extremely shallow and beamy centerboard "skimming-dish" sloops and the equally extreme "plank-on-edge" cutters with their deep, narrow hulls, helped to introduce the successful compromise type he advocated. One of his best-known designs was the radical *Vindex*, one of the first iron-hulled yachts in America. Smith also designed *Ailsa Craig*, winner of the first powerboat race to Bermuda in 1907, and the 161-foot LOA schooner *Meteor III* for German Kaiser Wilhelm II.

Growing up in Chelsea Village, which at Twenty-third Street was then a suburb of New York City, Smith frequently visited nearby boatyards and took an early interest in sailing models. At age fourteen he watched the construction of the schooner *America* at the George Steers yard and later saw her sailing trials. The product of a well-to-do family, he was expected to go to college, but at age eighteen, after taking his entrance examinations, he expressed a desire to learn boatbuilding instead, specifically with nearby boatbuilder Bob Fish. Fish was an uneducated but gifted designer/builder who produced innovative and successful yachts, working mostly by eye.

With his father, a Presbyterian clergyman, paying his board, young Smith went on to learn the art and practice of boatbuilding, along with Fish's design methods. His employer was also a highly successful racing yacht captain, so Smith spent much of his time racing.

Smith's first boatbuilding effort was a 16-footer in which he beat Bob Fish, against all local expectations. Soon after came *Comet*, an 18-footer on which Smith successfully experimented with an improved underbody. At one time he and Fish built two 28-footers with identical hulls, and then match raced them in a series of experiments to judge the merits of various innovations in underbody, ballast, spars, rigging, sails, and sail trim proposed for a larger boat (including fully battened sails and streamlined masts). This may well have been the first such systematic testing in the United States, and the experience probably helped convince Smith of the merits of a scientific approach to design.

During his apprenticeship with Fish, Smith apparently decided that he wanted to learn some things that Fish could not teach him, so he hired a Mr. W. W. Bates to teach him drafting and lofting as they were practiced in the construction of large ships.

Surprisingly, after completing this thorough education in yacht design and construction, Smith turned to marine painting as a profession and began creating some of the finest representations of yachting subjects of the era.

In an effort to explain this professional about-face, it has been theorized that Smith may have run afoul of the peculiar class-consciousness of the day, which held that those who designed, built, and did the work of sailing yachts were a rung or two down on the social ladder from the men who owned them. Smith's upper-class family may have felt that while it was acceptable for

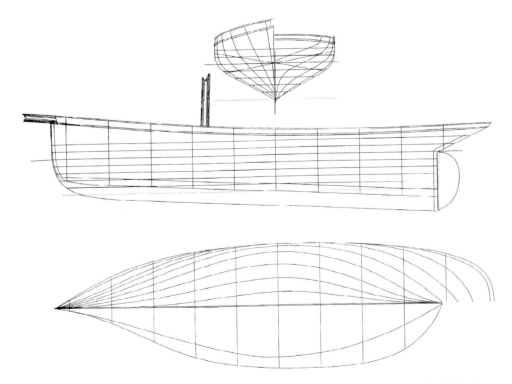

A. Cary Smith: *Vindex*. The 63-foot 3-inch cutter *Vindex* was the first prominent yacht built of iron. Besides being strong and practical, iron construction also meant that her ballast could be stowed lower for increased stability. Her iron bowsprit was 460 pounds lighter than the original wooden one it replaced. *Reproduced from W. P. Stephens's* Traditions and Memories of American Yachting

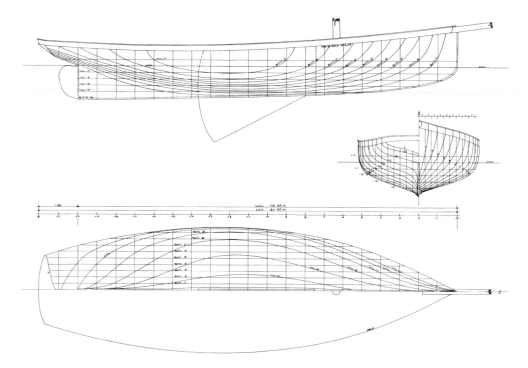

A. Cary Smith: *Mischief.* *Mischief*, a 67-foot centerboarder, defended the America's Cup in 1881 against the Canadian *Atalanta*, designed by Alexander Cuthbert. The first sloop and the first iron yacht to defend the Cup, she was also the first major yacht combining the best features of typical British cutters and American centerboard sloops. © *Chevalier & Taglang*

A. Cary Smith: *Iroquois.* Marine artist and designer A. Cary Smith is thought to have designed some of the most beautiful schooner yachts built in the United States. This is the 80-foot 7-inch centerboarder *Iroquois*, originally *Julia*, built in 1886. © *Mystic Seaport, Rosenfeld Collection, Mystic, CT. James Burton, Photographer*

Smith to dabble in boatbuilding, the experience was best seen as preparation for a more gentlemanly career. There is also some evidence to suggest that Smith simply preferred painting and was more or less dragged back into yacht design by friends and acquaintances. Or it may be that in order to preserve his amateur status for racing purposes, he felt he needed to avoid boatbuilding and design as professions.

Smith had been strictly a marine painter for several years when Robert Center approached him in 1870 for the design of *Vindex*. Center had just spent time in England studying the cutter type, and while there had encountered P. R. Marett's book *Yacht Building*, which proposed abandoning the builder's model and designing yachts entirely on paper, utilizing calculations. Marrett went on to propose a systematic approach by which this might be accomplished. It was an entirely new concept, and we must assume that it captured Smith's imagination, for he was soon persuaded to try. The 63-foot 3-inch LOA cutter *Vindex* was the result. Her iron construction was almost unheard of at the time, and since Smith was strictly self-educated as an engineer, her scantlings must have involved some educated guesswork. Fortunately, Smith was conservative in this regard, and the yacht had a long life.

Vindex was a success as a cruising boat, but Smith called her a "Dr. Jekyll and Mr. Hyde" as a racing boat. She had the peculiar quality of being something of a racing failure in her home waters around Long Island Sound but then doing very well elsewhere. Years later her designer determined that his mistake had been in concentrating her ballast amidships to such an extent that in a certain-size sea (unfortunately typical of her local area) she had a quick motion that slowed her down, while in a larger or smaller sea, she was fine.

In 1873 Smith designed the schooner *Prospero*, with a radical rig inspired by his experience with the cutter *Vindex*. The schooner was given the clean, retractable pole bowsprit of a cutter, as opposed to the heavy, built-in, heavily-stayed bowsprit typical of schooners, and for the first time in such a yacht, a foremast shorter than the main. The innovations received much criticism, and *Prospero* was soon converted to a more conventional configuration, although both features eventually became widely accepted.

Smith returned to painting between design commissions, essentially alternating professions. He designed the centerboard sloop *Madcap* in 1875; she was followed in 1878 by the cruising schooner *Intrepid* and in 1879 by the similar *Norma*. In the fall of 1878 the owner of *Madcap* came to Smith for a new boat, and the result was *Mischief*. Her deep iron hull allowed the lead ballast to be stowed very low, and her tall mast was like a sloop but with the housing topmast and pole bowsprit of a cutter.

Mischief was selected in 1881 to defend the America's Cup. Later that year came another compromise cutter, *Valkyr*, which further served to popularize the emerging compromise type. In 1884 the schooner *Harbinger* introduced Smith's ideas about the schooner rig to Boston waters, and from that point on they were widely accepted, although the young designer Edward Burgess, who had supervised *Harbinger*'s construction, received most of the credit for them when he brought out the similarly rigged *Puritan* the next year.

Interestingly, *Puritan* defeated the Smith-designed *Priscilla* for the right to defend the America's Cup against the Beavor-Webb–designed *Genesta* in 1885, but it is said that Smith labored under so many restrictions imposed by the owner that he was unable to produce a design of which he himself approved.

After *Harbinger*, design commissions came in steadily, and the success of Smith's yachts eventually attracted the attention of Kaiser Wilhelm II of Germany, who had him design the 165-foot schooner *Meteor III*. This big, opulent schooner, built in 1901, apparently became a bone of contention, as she was not successful in her racing career. The designer maintained that he had been commissioned to design a cruising boat, and added that in any event the boat had been improperly handled by men accustomed to cutters, not schooners. Whatever the truth, *Meteor III* was one of the most impressive yachts of her time.

One of the reasons for Smith's success as a designer was his adherence to the theory of John Hyslop, which followed similar efforts by designer Colin Archer, who built on the wave-line theory of John Scott Russell. Hyslop's theory held that the sectional areas (essentially the fore and aft distribution of the underwater volume of a vessel) should follow an ideal curve that its proponents felt would offer the least resistance. Although the theory was eventually found to be inadequate, for a while it appeared to work as it tended to create hulls with greatly improved diagonals, hull lines that were largely ignored at the time in favor of the waterlines and buttock lines but that were later realized to be of critical importance.

For much of his career, Smith's hull designs differed sharply from those of his contemporaries, especially in midships sections, where Smith's hulls had flared topsides, a soft bilge, and very slack sections. In contrast, typical racing yachts of the day had narrow keels faired into a shallow, U-shaped hull with a hard

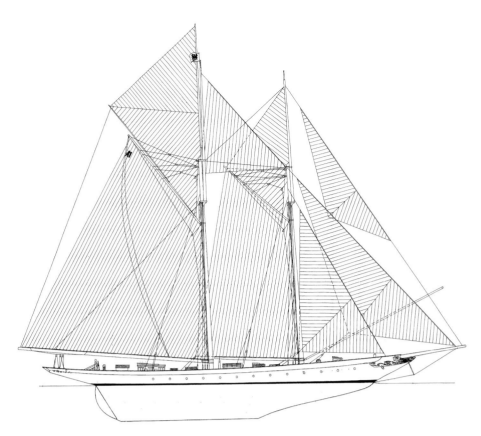

A. Cary Smith: *Meteor III*. A. Cary Smith was known for yachts that did not sacrifice safety, ability, or ease of handling just for speed. Few thought the 165-foot schooner *Meteor III*, designed for German Kaiser Wilhem II, was fast, but she was widely perceived to be the superb cruising boat Smith always said he had been commissioned to design. *Drawing courtesy Gerard Dijkstra*

bilge and little flare. Contemporary writers had a hard time explaining his design's racing successes, and one would have similar questions today if one's observations were confined to the midships section.

The explanation is probably in Smith's long and smooth diagonals, a result of the wave-line theory, and in the minimized wetted surface area inherent in his sections. The sections of the style used by his rivals would not reach their potential until later, when wetted surface area would be lessened by further reduction of the underwater profile. Likewise, while his rivals' designs were becoming wide, flat, and full-ended (basically more scow-like) in search of speed in smooth water, Smith's chosen hull form was inherently superior in rough water, owing to its motion-damping characteristics.

Smith's understanding of hull lines was of great value when in 1889 he was commissioned to design the 300-foot *Richard Peck*, a new passenger steamer for Long Island Sound. In both hull design and construction Smith's efforts were ridiculed while the vessel was being built, but the result was the first in a series of steamers far faster, more fuel efficient, and more free from vibration than anything that had gone before. In 1897 Smith went on to design *New York*, the first successful steam-powered pilot-boat for New York City. Essentially a giant

double-ended lifeboat unlike anything that had preceded it, she was a total success and was able to hold her station at sea in the worst of weather, a feat previously impossible for a powered vessel.

The early 1900's saw a temporary revival in the popularity of big racing schooners. Smith was one of the foremost designers of that type, and some of his are among the most beautiful large yachts ever drawn.

In 1903, Theodore E. Ferris became Smith's partner, bringing with him extensive experience in shipyards. The firm subsequently expanded its scope to include more steamship design, while continuing yacht design.

A member of the New York Yacht Club (NYYC) since 1872, Smith became its measurer from 1874 to 1882. He joined the Seawanhaka Corinthian Yacht Club in 1874 and was its measurer from 1875 to 1883. With John Hyslop and Robert Center, Smith helped to develop the Seawanhaka handicapping rule, which remained in effect until 1900. Because of his building and design work, A. Cary Smith's amateur racing status within the NYYC was questioned repeatedly during his career. At one point in a contentious meeting, a club official is alleged to have declared that yacht design "was no work for a gentleman!"

—Daniel B. MacNaughton

CHRISTOPHER COLUMBUS SMITH

May 20, 1861–September 1939 · United States

Founder of the legendary Chris-Craft motorboat company, Chris Smith began his career in the 1880's with his brother Henry (Hank) as builders of rowing skiffs and duck boats in Algonac on the Saint Clair River north of Detroit, Michigan. It was legendary gunning country, not only for natives like Smith and his brother Hank, but also for sportsmen from throughout the Upper Midwest. The two brothers worked as hunting guides, decoy carvers, market hunters, and trainers of hunting dogs, in addition to being self-taught boat designers and builders.

As a young man Smith worked with his father as a blacksmith, except during duck-hunting season when he worked with his brother. He also crewed on Great Lakes steamers in the summers, working his way up from deckhand to command of the 200-foot passenger vessel *Owana*, which ran between Detroit and Toledo. In the winter he built boats.

In 1896 the boat livery operated by Smith and his brother came into possession of a Sintz engine, the pioneering American gasoline engine for small boats. Clark Sintz had been building these two-cycle power plants to his own patents since 1890. The little one-lung engine was successfully installed in a boat by Chris, Hank, and Chris's eldest son Jay, but "it never ran well until Clark Sintz showed up from Grand Rapids two years later with a gadget called a carburetor," Jay Smith remembered. From that beginning—working first with Sintz and a few years later with Joe Van Blerck, another marine-engine pioneer—the Smith boatshop gained an increasingly widespread reputation for its motorboats.

The design provenance of the later raceboats and speedboats is confused, but there is little doubt that Smith designed the boats he built before 1905, and would have had a lot to say over the next twenty years about the shapes and structures of boats that came along while other designer/builders were working with him. In 1911, C. C. Smith and Company became the Smith-Ryan Boat and Engine Company with the patronage of John J. Ryan. The firm's name was changed again in 1916, when it became Chris Smith and Sons Boat Company.

The partnership with Ryan produced a series of boats named *Reliance* and *Baby Reliance,* which won races all over the Midwest and were offered as stock models for adventurous sportsmen. The most powerful was a $20,000 boat with a guaranteed speed of 50 mph. The *Reliance*s were followed by *Miss Detroit* and

Chris Smith/Chris-Craft: *Baby Reliance II.* The 20-foot *Baby Reliance II* (left) was a single-step hydroplane, and one of the early models of the company that would become Chris-Craft. Racing successfully against boats in the 40-foot class, she and her sisterships traveled at speeds up to 50 mph but were notoriously difficult to control. © *Mystic Seaport, Rosenfeld Collection, Mystic, CT*

Miss Minneapolis, winners, respectively, of the American Power Boat Association's Gold Cup in 1915 and 1916.

Miss Detroit II won the Gold Cup in 1917 and set a speed record of 61.273 mph. The boat was driven by Gar Wood, with Jay Smith as the on-board mechanic. Wood was the new patron of the Smith boatshop, and he proceeded to win the Gold Cup in 1918, 1919, 1920, and 1921 in Smith-built and–designed boats. *Miss America* set a world water speed record of 76.66 mph in 1920, and *Miss America II* took the record to 80.567. Both of these boats were designed by Joseph Napoleon "Nap" Lisee, then a Smith employee.

Gar Wood bought the company's assets in 1922. Smith and his sons reestablished the Chris Smith and Sons Boat Company in the Point du Chene section of Algonac, where they built stock speedboats. They soon dominated the market with the mahogany runabouts they called Chris-Craft. By following Henry Ford's production line model, they were able to build one powerboat and one rowboat a week during their very first season. By the time Chris Smith died in 1939, the company was the largest builder of motorboats in the world.

—Joseph Gribbins

GILBERT MONROE SMITH

1843–1940 · United States

A designer and builder of catboats and other shallow-draft centerboard yachts, Gil Smith worked in Patchogue, Long Island, on New York's shallow Great South Bay. He opened his boatyard in 1876 and continued to model and build boats there for the next sixty-six years. Smith was particularly well known for his many big-rigged racing catboats, competing in Class AA, A, BB, and B.

When the Long Island Rail Road extended its line in the 1870's, tourists and sailors in great numbers flocked to Great South Bay, and the sailors wanted to race. Smith's reputation became well known as he modeled successful racers uniquely suited to these sheltered and shallow waters.

Compared to the beamy, barn door–rudder, Cape Cod catboats most often seen today, Smith's Long Island–style boats were relatively narrow and sleek, with his famously beautiful sweeping sheerlines. *Thetis* (1895) and *Mariam* (1897) were particularly fast. His boats usually had an inboard rudder, rolled-in upper transom edges, and varnished decks. His early boats had plumb stems, but over the years he drew the ends out longer and held the sheerline low.

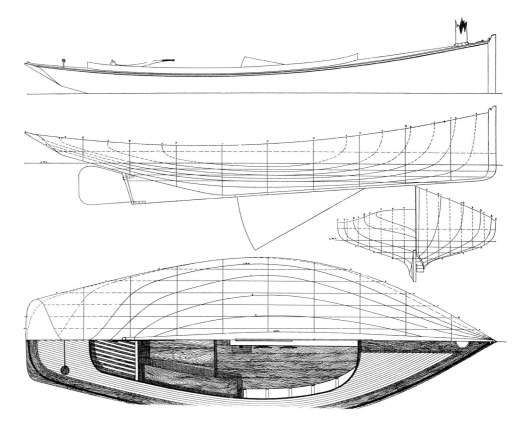

Gilbert Smith: *Lucile*. *Lucile* was a South Bay cat designed and built by Gilbert Smith in 1891. Smith built solely from models, so these lines were taken off the boat in 1896. *Lucile* was considered the "model boat of the bay" but was only raced once and won handily. *Drawing reproduced from* The Rudder

Smith also designed and built sloops for the P and R Classes, and while he seldom produced boats designed by others, he was the builder of C. D. Mower's famous Sonder boat *Joyette*, which won the Kaiser Cup in Marblehead in 1909.

The self-taught Smith kept no records and drew no plans, working entirely from models. It is estimated that Smith modeled and built about four hundred boats. Over the years lines have been taken off a few Smith boats and made into plans.

A collection of twenty-three of Smith's half models is at the Suffolk Historical Society, Riverhead, Long Island, NY.

—Daniel B. MacNaughton

KENNETH L. SMITH

(Dates unknown) · United States

There are cases in yacht design where a prolific yet not well-known designer creates a boat that suddenly captures the public's imagination on a national scale. On such an occasion, the designer becomes defined in the public eye by one or two works, when in fact he has produced scores of successful boats for a devoted coterie.

Connecticut designer Ken Smith is defined by the recreational cruising trawlers he designed for American Marine, a wooden boatbuilder in Hong Kong, in the mid-1960's. Sold under the Grand Banks nameplate, Smith's boats were based on Newfoundland fishing trawlers and set the pattern for the many trawlers and recreational tugs that have followed.

The Grand Banks 32 and 36, introduced in 1965, were the prototypes, with the signature semidisplacement hull, full-length keel, bulwarks, and high bow and sides. Smith designed the boats so that one or two diesel engines would deliver only 6- to 12-knot speeds but impressive range. The teak interior had all the cruising comforts—private stateroom, head, full galley.

The Grand Banks 42 (1966) was a further refinement of the type, "a hefty long-distance cruiser," according to *The Rudder*. With its twin 120-hp diesel engines and more than 600 gallons of fuel, the 42 had a range of some 1,200 miles. More than a thousand were built in a twenty-five-year production run before the boat was redesigned in 1991.

Working from an office in Fairfield, Connecticut, Smith created designs for a wide range of New England customers, and many of his boats were built in Maine. Among his custom designs were a 35-foot fast cruiser for the commodore of the Boston Yacht Club (1958); a 28-foot tugboat for a member of the Pequot Yacht Club in Southport, Connecticut (1958);

Ken Smith: *Excalibur*. *Excalibur*, a Grand Banks 36, is one of more than a thousand Grand Banks cruisers that have been built by American Marine in Hong Kong since 1965. Designed for speeds under 12 knots, they have great range and are famously comfortable cruising boats. © *Peter Barlow*

a 28-foot, flying-bridge power cruiser for a client in the Bahamas (1964); and a 35-foot, ketch-rigged motorsailer designed for a member of the CCA (1965).

Smith also designed sloop- and ketch-rigged motorsailers and at least one 35-foot swordfishing boat that recalls the works of Boston designer William Hand.

Little else is known of Smith, but his work was simple and direct, a reflection of the Canadian and New England fishing boats that shaped his designs. In his notes on *Rocking Chair*, a 35-foot power cruiser, Smith summed up his philosophy: "[to create an] able, sea-kindly, comfortable and easily handled vessel in which the owner and his wife can cruise extensively."

—Steve Knauth

XAVIER SOLER

(Dates unknown) · Spain

Xavier Soler has been an active designer since 1979, specializing first in inshore and offshore racing yachts and later in successful production cruisers. He is also a specialist and author on the technicalities of composites in boatbuilding.

After graduating in science, geodynamics, and hydrology at Barcelona University and Catalonia Polytechnic, Soler earned a diploma from the Westlawn School of Yacht Design in Stamford, Connecticut.

Early significant racing-yacht design projects included an entry for the IOR Mini-Ton Cup in 1979, designed in conjunction with Joaquín

Coello, and the oceangoing racing trimaran *Puerto Principe*, for the 1981 Two-handed Transatlantic Race (and which gained fourth place in that year's Newport-Bermuda Race).

In 1983 Soler's 51-foot potential Whitbread entrant, *Fontvella*, was real-time winner of the first edition of the Round Spain Race and second in the Transmed Race. In 1988 his *Meyba-Fibanc* won her class in Spain's prestigious Copa del Rey Regatta at Palma de Mallorca, and in 1989 she won the Conde de Godó Trophy.

Soler's popular designs for production building include the Puma and Atlas ranges of sailing cruisers and the Fotley sailing catamarans, as well as several fishing boats and other recreational craft.

Recent projects have included the Triana 36, an innovative cruising yacht capable of high speeds and offering spacious interior and cockpit accommodations, and the Cubic 70 for bluewater cruising in comfort. —John Lynch

JOSEPH M. SOPER

1857–June 1938 · England

A versatile designer born and based in Southampton, England, J. M. Soper designed racing yachts of all sizes, rugged cruising yachts, and a number of steam yachts. He is best remembered for the 131-foot LOA cutter *Satanita* of 1893, the largest of the large cutter class containing such yachts such as *Brittania* and *Valkyrie II*, designed by G. L. Watson; *Vigilant*, by N. G. Herreshoff; *Calluna*, by William Fife III; and *Iverna*, by Alexander Richardson. Not a match for some of the other boats in terms of race results, *Satanita* is said by some to have been the fastest cutter ever built, on a reach, but she is also noted for having rammed and sunk *Valkyrie II* on the first day of the class's second season, in 1894, while avoiding a spectator boat.

For their day, Soper's yachts tended toward somewhat greater beam and firmer bilges than other British yachts. He designed a number of fin-and-bulb keel yachts for the smaller classes, and helped to evolve steam yachts in the direction of the modern type, in some cases eliminating vestigial sailing rigs and clipper bows and producing a cleaner and less delicate look. He designed several large cruising boats, often ketch-rigged, that were of striking beauty and highly suited to heavy offshore work, apparently uninfluenced by handicapping rules or racing considerations. Soper was a superb

Joseph Soper: *Vera Mary.* *Vera Mary* is a 61-foot LOD schooner designed in 1932 for G. M. Hamilton-Fletcher. She was later purchased by King George V and given in appreciation to his sailing teacher and friend, Sir Phillip Hunloke.
© *Kai Greiser*

draftsman and showed a remarkable amount of detail in his drawings.

Beginning as second draftsman in the well-known yard J. G. Fay in Southampton (later Camper and Nicholson), Soper was appointed chief designer and manager in 1889. At age thirty-four he was commissioned to design *Satanita* (97 feet 10 inches LWL) under the big cutter class. Another great racer was *Aurora*, launched at the Fay yard in 1896. The 93-foot LWL schooner *Clara* was launched in 1900 for a German yachtsman. Later Soper practiced independently as a designer and surveyor as J. M. Soper and Sons.

Not all of Soper's commissions were huge racers for rich clients. In 1882 he designed the 32-foot LOA *Daisy*, which raced well both in Solent matches and in U.S. waters in 1884. A notable steam yacht of his design was the 135-foot *Adventuress* of 1913. One of his final designs was for the 61-foot LOD schooner *Vera Mary*, designed in 1932 when Soper was seventy-five. Soper and Sons was run by his sons following his death. —Daniel B. MacNaughton

MARK SOVEREL

1949–January 3, 2002 · United States

Specializing in ocean racers for Grand Prix regattas, such as the SORC competition, the MORC championship, and the Admiral's Cup, Mark Soverel was one of the best at wringing possible advantage from the handicapping rules while creating fast boats. Like many designers, he chafed under the restrictions of the rules, which were changed more than once in reaction to his successful designs, in order to make other boats more competitive.

Soverel started sailing with his father in the mid-1950's and by the 1960's was racing boats built by his father's company, Soverel Marine, in regattas around Palm Beach, Florida. After attending Costa Mesa College in California, he taught himself yacht design with the aid of the Westlawn School of Yacht Design correspondence course. *Moody Blue*, his first IOR boat, came out in 1974. She won Class D in the SORC in 1975.

Concentrating on MORC designs for some years after that, Soverel's 26-foot *Stewball* won the 1975 International Regatta, and the 30-foot *JB Express* won it again in 1977. After that he returned to the IOR and had considerable success with boats such as the 43-foot *Locura*, *The Shadow*, and the One-Tonner *Volition*. From 1982 to 1986 he ran the full-service boatbuilding, marina, and brokerage operation started by his father.

Perhaps in response to his frustration with handicapping rules, in 1983 Soverel came out

with the Soverel 33, an ultralight, all-around high-performance boat designed without regard for any rule and intended as an offshore one-design racer. It is said to have been his favorite design. Soverel changed his business emphasis to real estate development in Florida after selling the family business in 1986. He designed a number of fast and efficient powerboats for his own use, in the years prior to his death from cancer at age fifty-two.

—Daniel B. MacNaughton

SPARKMAN AND STEPHENS
see Olin J. Stephens II

MYRON SPAULDING

October 28, 1905–September 11, 2000
United States

Myron Spaulding was a legend on San Francisco Bay and the West Coast; his keen intelligence, precise memory, immense fund of knowledge and experience, and longevity all combined to establish him as the dean of West Coast naval architects. He was known to sailors around the world.

Moving to San Francisco as a boy in 1915, he received his education at Polytechnic High School, where he earned his credential in naval architecture and boatbuilding. As he came from a musical family, he was also required to earn an additional degree in music, playing the violin. Spaulding graduated in 1923 and began a musical career as a violinist. Soon he earned a seat with the San Francisco Symphony (he performed with them until 1957). At the same time, he was racing and winning several class championships in the Bird class, Stars, 6-Meters, and the larger ocean racing classes up to World War II.

In 1936 he was the master and navigator of the historic Sparkman and Stephens–designed, 52-foot yawl *Dorade* when it won the Transpacific Race. He went on to sail five more Transpacs as sailing master and/or navigator, his reputation as a seaman being equal to that of racing sailor.

Spaulding engaged in many facets of marine activity–doing surveys, measuring racing yachts, and creating designs–as was the case with many of his profession. Soon he began designing some significant sailboats up to 56 feet in length for Bay Area yachtsmen.

The first to gain wide recognition was the 38-foot sloop *Nautigal*, built in 1938. Then followed the 50-foot yawl *Suomi*; the 34-foot sloop *Lark III*; and the 37-foot *Buoyant Girl*—all for local owners; the well-remembered Clipper class 20-foot sloops (sixty-three built); and the Spaulding 33 (nine built). A later very successful boat was the 45-foot yawl *Chrysopyle*, which he designed and built at his Sausalito boatyard in 1961. He lofted the lines, steamed the frames, built the spars, and even cast the 12,000-pound lead keel. Spaulding's boats were characterized by a soundness and rationality of design and the best of materials, equipment, and workmanship, whether built by him or other builders.

Yacht measurement was an occupation he inherited from San Francisco naval architect George Wayland in the early 1930's. At the time, the predominant measurement rule was the Universal Rule, followed by the CCA Rule. Early on he was involved in codifying the handicap system for the various open racing classes on the bay. Currently the IOR and IMS systems are in use. Shortly before his death, Spaulding's fellow measurer described his work as "impeccable."

Highly regarded and respected by the current crop of boat designers, Myron Spaulding was a mentor to several of them over the years and a counselor to local and visiting sailors from around the world. He dispensed wisdom, advice, and expertise on a wide range of subjects to all who came.

Myron Spaulding's design collection is at the San Francisco Maritime Museum, San Francisco, CA.

—Thomas G. Skahill

Myron Spaulding: *Suomi.* One of Spaulding's most celebrated designs, *Suomi* was built in 1947. She came in first in the twenty-four-boat Class C and sixth overall in a fleet of thirty-four in the 1947 Transpac Race to Honolulu. Her career was successful but short—she was lost in 1955, run down by a freighter south of San Francisco. *Photo courtesy Thomas G. Skahill*

JOHN ALFRED SPENCER

1931–March 4, 1996 · New Zealand

It has often been said that the common approach toward sailing in New Zealand and Australia today is greatly influenced by John Spencer's "fun" approach to boat design combined with his pioneering hard-chine plywood construction methods. His planing dinghies, the 12-foot Cherub (1952) and 14-foot Javelin (1959), were landmarks in small boat design and opened a new era of high-performance sailing, adopted with enthusiasm by young yachtsmen. He was inspired by Uffa Fox's books to push conventional limits, which he did.

Spencer strongly believed that boating should be available to everyone, and his extensive use of plywood and his simplified designs opened the door to many amateur sailors. He also took the time to provide helpful advice, which he dispensed free of charge, though he did not suffer fools gladly.

Born in Australia, Spencer moved to the Auckland region of New Zealand as a young man. There he began designing and building lightweight powerboats, becoming known as the "Plywood King." By 1964, his reputation gained him an important commission from Sir Tom Clark: the design of the 35-foot keeler *Saracen*.

The following year, Clark commissioned the 62-foot, all-black, hard-chine "rocketship" *Infidel*. She came close to dominating the Auckland racing scene in the late 1960's, but was forbidden to sail in the 1969–70 Sydney-Hobart Race by a rule change that disallowed entries with plywood topsides and a hull thickness such as *Infidel*'s. Sold to the United States in 1970 and renamed *Ragtime*, she continued to win many offshore races, including two Los Angeles–Honolulu Transpac Races.

Again for Clark came the design for *Buccaneer*, a 73-foot maxi built of laminated plywood. She went on to win the 1971 Sydney-Hobart Race. Spencer designed a huge range of successful keeler boats for both cruising and racing, including the mini-schooner *Great Hope* and the 68-foot 4-inch schooner *New World*. His work in larger racing boats did much to advance the cause of light displacement long before the IOR and IMS rule made it almost universal. He was also a popular columnist for *Boating New Zealand* magazine for many years.

After building *Buccaneer* and closing down his Brown's Bay boatshed on Auckland's north shore, Spencer moved to Okiato in the Bay of Islands. There he built a house, where he lived by himself, wrote everything in longhand, and kept no telephone or fax. Only the America's

John Spencer: *Buccaneer*. *Buccaneer* was the biggest of Spencer's chine-hull plywood designs for ocean racing. A follow-up to the iconic *Infidel*, she could not repeat *Infidel*'s domination but still managed to take line honors in many events. *Photo courtesy David Payne*

Cup races in San Diego in 1995 moved him to purchase a television set. Over the last ten years of his life he became interested in radio-controlled model yachting. He was a leading advocate of the sport at the time of his death at the age of sixty-five. —Mark Steele

ERIC W. SPONBERG

Born November 9, 1949 · United States

Hailing from Newport, Rhode Island, Eric Sponberg designs boats that are not just modern in style but push the limits of modern design possibilities. While good aesthetics are one aspect of their design, those aesthetics owe little if anything to what has gone before. Performance, meaning speed and ease of sail control, is number one.

Sponberg's boats usually feature freestanding carbon fiber spars and fully battened sails for aerodynamic efficiency, simplicity of a sort, and ease of reefing and furling. Displacement tends toward the very light side of the spectrum, with some hulls designed to plane as a matter of course. Underbodies are highly abbreviated, with keels and rudders of the most advanced forms.

An early advocate of carbon fiber in spars and other areas of yacht construction, Sponberg did some of the groundwork engineering from which other designers are now benefiting. He earned a degree in naval architecture and marine engineering from the University of Michigan in 1981 and is a licensed professional engineer.

Notable Sponberg designs include *Project Amazon*, an Open 60 Class, aluminum cat-ketch designed for the Around Alone singlehanded round-the-world race; *Corroboree*, a 35-foot wood-epoxy sloop with a freestanding carbon fiber mast, named one of the one hundred greatest sailing yachts of North America by *Sail* magazine in 1993; the Delft 25, a do-it-

Eric Sponberg: *Project Amazon*. *Project Amazon* is an Open 60 Class aluminum cat-ketch with unstayed carbon fiber rotating masts designed for the 1996 Around Alone race. *Photo courtesy Eric Sponberg*

yourself wood-epoxy trailerable sloop; and *Halfling,* a nesting sailing pram for the do-it-yourselfer. The designer continues an active practice in Saint Augustine, Florida, working in both sail and power.

—Daniel B. MacNaughton

PETER SPRONK

1921–1997
The Netherlands/South Africa/West Indies

In the early 1960's the Dutch-born designer Peter Spronk moved from South Africa to Grenada in the Caribbean, where he became that area's most prolific designer of catamarans. Simple in philosophy (the famous Spronk toilet consisted of a comfortable hole well above the waterline), yet extremely fast and powerful, Spronk catamarans were usually built of lapstrake or plywood construction and were frequently staysail schooner-rigged. Their hulls were characterized by very fine bows with flare high up and, for cruising catamarans, unusually high fineness ratios of 16 and higher, making them very easily driven, but also sensitive to overloading.

Though frequently designed for the local Caribbean charter trade, these catamarans nonetheless competed in regattas and were among the world's fastest catamarans designed and built during the 1970's. Among his most notable designs were *Maho* (61 feet, 1975 or before), *Maltese Cross* (50 feet, 1977 or before), *Ppalu* (75 feet, 1978, world's largest sailing catamaran at the time of her launching), *TsjeTsja* (60 feet, 1978), *El Tigre* (60 feet, 1978), and *Shadowfax* (60 feet, probably 1980).

—Claas van der Linde

GEORGE H. STADEL JR.

September 21, 1905–May 16, 1993
United States

Besides being a yacht designer, George H. Stadel Jr. was a noted marine historian, boatbuilder, and surveyor, perhaps the best-possible background for design work. He studied civil engineering at Notre Dame University in Indiana, but was self-taught in naval architecture. His early mentors included A. E. Luders Sr., Al Crouch, and William Atkin.

Launching his design career in 1928, Stadel opened Bluenose Boats and drew plans for yachts built in Nova Scotia by Langelle, Heisler, Robar, and other builders. For some of them he had to make models because they weren't able to read plans. He constructed the interiors of these boats himself.

Peter Spronk: *El Tigre.* The schooner-rigged catamaran *El Tigre* was built in 1978 of lapstrake plywood. Built specifically for charter use in the West Indies, the 60-footer reached speeds of 24 knots on her first voyage. *Photo by Christian Fevrier*

Stadel was the first to record historic Nova Scotian boat types, with lines, photographs, and builder's models. He obtained the last four builder's models of the designer O. B. Hamm, including the only known original one of a Tancook whaler.

In the early 1930's, Stadel began a lifelong friendship with designer and maritime historian Howard I. Chapelle, and later contributed to *American Small Sailing Craft* and *Boat Building,* two of Chapelle's best-known books. He continued to record historic small boats throughout his lifetime.

By the mid-1930's, boats were being built to Stadel's designs and under his supervision in eight or nine yards at a time, from Maryland to Nova Scotia. From about 1932 to 1936 he was a protégé of Thomas F. McManus, noted designer of fishing vessels who was an important influence on Stadel's work. Stadel joined designer Gilbert Dunham in 1938 to form Dunham and Stadel, building boats from 21 to 38 feet long in Stamford, Connecticut.

In 1940 Stadel started Stadel and Jenkins, a yard in Rowayton, Connecticut. A year later, he worked for Sparkman and Stephens on the design of the 497 class of subchaser. He also built lifeboats and did other war work in Essex, Connecticut. Later he became manager of the commercial vessel division of the Milton Point Shipyard, where he headed a crew of eight hundred men, building tugs, barges, and British patrol boats, as well as fishing draggers and trawlers of his own design.

From the 1950's to the 1970's, Stadel continued to have boats built under his super-

vision, but he increasingly concentrated on design. During the same period he also worked as a marine surveyor. In 1978 he started the firm George H. Stadel, Jr. and Sons with his sons George III and William. They designed boats of great diversity, including schooners, replicas of nineteenth-century vessels, modern cruising sailing yachts, motorsailors, several successful ocean racers, cruising powerboats,

George Stadel Jr. This 40-foot cutter shows the aesthetic qualities and balance for which the designer was known. His designs were informed by a lifelong study of the working sailing craft of the United States' East Coast and Nova Scotia. *Drawing courtesy George Stadel III*

sportfishermen, all manner of fishing boats, rowing shells, and many others—over a hundred designs in all.

Some of Stadel's better-known designs included his Pilot series, of which more than fifty were built, ranging from 20 to 41 feet long; the Sound Clipper series, from 21 to 33 feet long, of which more than a hundred were built; and the Egg Harbor 37, of which more than eight hundred were built. He was also designer of the Norwalk Boat Company class of powerboats. Writing about Stadel's schooner designs, marine historian and author John Gardner wrote that they "have rarely been equaled for their beautiful proportions, sea-kindliness and seakeeping abilities."   —Bob Wallstrom

GEORGE H. STADEL III

Born September 16, 1944 · United States

George Stadel III's better-known designs include the Greenwich 24 and Shannon 36, both designed with his father, George H. Stadel Jr. He also designed the Mayflower 48, the Vagabond 42, and the President 41, and with Harwood Ives, the Hans Christian 43. Stadel designs both sail and power boats, mostly in the 30- to 60-foot range, as well as rowing shells and other types. About seventeen hundred boats have been built to his designs.

Stadel worked with his father from about the age of sixteen, and for Sparkman and Stephens

in the late 1960's. He studied mechanical engineering at Bridgeport University and lived in Taiwan from 1972 to 1991, where he worked for several boatbuilders before opening his own office.

George Stadel III now practices yacht design in Stamford, Connecticut.   —Bob Wallstrom

ERICUS GERHARDUS "RICUS" VAN DE STADT

February 4, 1910–September 7, 1999
The Netherlands

More than any yacht designer in the Netherlands, Ricus van de Stadt made his mark as an innovator and an inventor. He was an outstanding designer and boatbuilder who, on the merit of his designs alone, deserves to be named with the best in the world, but it is his completely original mind, enabling him to open new directions in yacht development and design, that in the final analysis put him in a place of his own. His career producing small sailing craft, numerous cruisers, and ocean racers spanned fifty years in the middle of the twentieth century, during the technological revolution that would transform yacht design and building.

The son of a wood merchant in the Zaan, a district north of Amsterdam known for its many waterways, small and large, and for its stubborn and independent population, young Ricus soon focused his attention on boats and boatbuilding. At the age of twelve he built his first canoe.

Others soon followed, and it did not take long before van de Stadt started building sailboats. These early, primitive, hand-chined vessels, built from cheap plywood, formed a starting point for his later innovative career as a boatbuilder and yacht designer.

Van de Stadt's whole career can be seen in the light of purpose, economy, and innovation. He soon found out that plywood sailboats, built over a light wooden skeleton, had many advantages over their traditional plank-on-frame competitors, including increased rigidity, watertightness, and ease of maintenance.

In 1939, family connections in the wood trade were instrumental in obtaining for van de Stadt a design commission from Cornelius Bruynzeel, the Dutch marine plywood magnate—the beginning of a hugely successful relationship. A new, open, 21-foot, one-design class, the Valk (Falcon), was the result, and despite the outbreak of World War II in 1940, she immediately attracted the attention of yachting Holland.

The Valk has been the answer to many yachting and boatbuilding problems; it was a light, fast dinghy. Its large open cockpit made it suitable for daysailing with four people on board. With some minor adaptations and a boom tent, it could also easily sleep the same four, which proved to be an important advantage in the years after the war when money was scarce.

Valken (the Dutch plural) were easy to build and therefore suitable for amateur boatbuilders. They required a minimum of material, making it possible to produce a complete boat at a low price. Yet these boats were elegant and fast—the fastest open dinghies of their time—making them such an attractive class that scores of Valk owners still compete in Dutch national regattas today. With its sharpie hull and iron keel, the Valk showed the way toward the light hulls and abbreviated underbodies that proved basic in later, world-famous designs for ocean racing contenders.

In 1945, immediately after the war, van de Stadt designed and built the 30-foot *Trial,* a new small yacht made of mahogany plywood. She was meant to be a 5-Meter class racer, but when the 5-Meter project faltered, van de Stadt gave the boat a deep iron-ballasted keel and a small cabin and generally modified her to become suitable for deep-sea passages.

On several occasions, van de Stadt crossed the English Channel in this unusual racer to participate in RORC events. Her chine construction offered an unusual appearance, but *Trial* proved to be a serious contender and, in spite of her open cockpit and spartan accommodations, showed her seaworthiness on various occasions. During a force 10 gale between Dover and the Hook of Holland she behaved

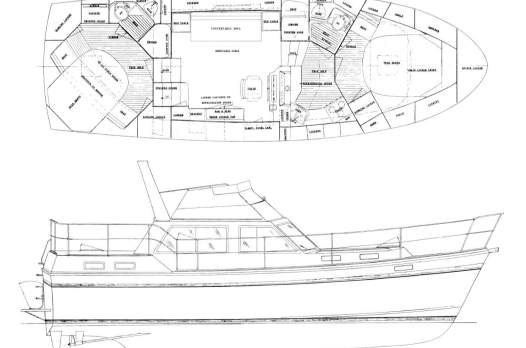

George Stadel III. This small power cruiser shows an unconventional use of space in its interior layouts. By breaking out of the typical long-axis symmetry, he uses the interior volume more effectively and produces more apparent space. *Drawing courtesy George Stadel III*

perfectly under a reefed main and a storm jib. The crew had to pump water constantly because the cockpit was not self-bailing, but she never gave the impression that she was not up to the circumstances.

Trial was a first step in the direction that would eventually make Ricus van de Stadt one of the most celebrated yacht designers in the world. Like the Valk she had an iron fin keel bolted under the hull and a separated rudder, thus reducing wetted surface area and enhancing the boat's surfing ability.

Van de Stadt strongly believed in a proper balance between the amount of sail, the wetted surface area, the depth and weight of the keel, and the amount of freeboard. He was highly skeptical of the IOR, which encouraged underballasting by allowing for "live ballast" on the side decks, resulting in beamy hull designs that would lift the rudder and keel out of the water when strongly heeled, rendering the boats unmanageable.

In 1949 van de Stadt received another commission from Bruynzeel for a larger, more sea-worthy design based on the Valk. The result was *Zeevalk*, a 40-foot plywood, hard-chine racer with 9 feet of beam and 7 feet of draft. In her unusually broad and heavy ballast keel, she held half of her 5 tons of displacement.

In 1951 *Zeevalk* won second place in a Fastnet Race dominated by strong westerly gales. *Zeevalk* was the first active RORC racer with a separate, balanced spade rudder and a trim tab on the aft edge of the keel. With *Zeevalk* van de Stadt initiated a succession of lightweight RORC racers, culminating in the fearsome *Zeeslang* (Sea Snake), the first of two being built in 1956. She was only 30 feet LOA. There was such public outrage about these strange, inexpensive, lightweight boats that the RORC quickly changed the rating system such that, in the opinion of many, they were never allowed to compete fairly. But in strong winds they were unbeatable, sailing against traditional RORC designs.

Willem de Vries Lentsch II, a colleague and close friend of van de Stadt, remembered in 1999 the speed of the boat and her initial technical problems: "Ricus had to re-invent so many details to make such a light boat seaworthy; in her first race she leaked so terribly round her keel construction that we had to pump constantly to keep her afloat. Of course he dealt with that problem later. The Zeeslang still sails as the Royal Cape One-Design Class in South Africa."

Welcoming the transition to fiberglass construction, van de Stadt built the first RORC racer of fiberglass in 1958. *Pioneer* was an immediate success. With a waterline length of 24 feet, she stayed just within the allowable rating, and she was built at a much lower price than conventional wooden competitors. De Vries Lentsch vividly remembered one of the first races in which she participated: "Ricus, after a heavy windward beat, remarked. 'This fiberglass is a lot stronger than I thought,' leaving us crewmembers somewhat puzzled: if he did not actually KNOW how strong it was, then what were we doing here in a gale in the middle of the North Sea?" The new material posed an enormous challenge to any designer/builder. Because there were no established rules on strength and construction, everything had to be built by intuition rather than experience.

Except for her construction material, the *Pioneer*, built in series at van de Stadt's own yard, was a more conventional design than his previous creations. She very soon turned out to be a commercial and racing success. In 1960, a Pioneer named *Zeewijf* (*Sea-Wife*), with the designer at the helm, won the prestigious Queen's Cup. In the Netherlands van de Stadt with his Pioneer won about everything there was to win,

Ericus van de Stadt: Valk (Falcon). When he designed the 21-foot Valk class during World War II, the scarcity of traditional materials forced van de Stadt to turn to economical mahogany plywood, making her one of the first popular plywood boats. The experiment was a success—a Valk can last for over sixty years. *Photo courtesy Rutger ten Broeke*

Ericus van de Stadt: *Zeevalk.* The 12.5-meter *Zeevalk* was a competitive plywood ocean racer. She was extremely light compared to her traditionally constructed competitors, and is said to have been the first planing offshore racer. She frequently beat boats twice her size, boat for boat, without time correction. *Drawing courtesy Rutger ten Broeke*

not only on handicap but also on pure speed. Sailing the smallest contender in 1961, he finished very high overall in a stormy Fastnet, a race that involved mostly windward work. Hundreds of Pioneers have been built and raced successfully, and they have made several Atlantic crossings and circumnavigations.

The Excalibur, a 36-foot version of the Pioneer, was built by Tyler Boat Company and continued the success of the Pioneer while being a far more comfortable cruiser.

After *Zeeslang,* van de Stadt designed yet another sailing speedster, larger than its predecessor and destined for the Observer Singlehanded Transatlantic Race (OSTAR) of 1968. *Voortrekker,* a hot-molded boat with a displacement of 7 tons, was at the time a really futuristic design. In 1983, almost twenty years later, she managed to win the OSTAR against far more recent designs.

Numerous successful one-offs have also come from van de Stadt's drawing board, including the steel 41-footer *Tulla,* a larger version of the Excalibur, which was very successful racing in Holland and England.

Another significant one-off is the 74-foot *Stormvogel,* a forerunner of the later style of maxi boats and Bruynzeel's most spectacular commission for van de Stadt. In 1961, in a unique cooperation with Laurent Giles and Partners, who drew the construction plan, and John Illingworth, who designed the sail plan and rigging, van de Stadt created a 75-foot ultra-lightweight ocean racer that set a new example for deep-

ocean racing. Built in South Africa, *Stormvogel* was the first maxi that could actually surf on a reach. Her racing victories include the 1961 Fastnet Race and line honors in both the Sydney-Hobart Race and Transpac Race of 1967.

In 1973 Dehler Yachts purchased van de Stadt's boatyard, and van de Stadt ceased his boatbuilding activities to concentrate solely on development and design. Van de Stadt and Partners was formed in 1974. A number of young yacht architects started their careers as apprentices at the firm before opening their own offices later. Among them were Dick Zaal, Jacques de Ridder, William Akkerman, and Klaas Kremer. Van de Stadt continued to stay active as a consultant and advisor until his death in 1999. The firm continues to offer design services from their office in Wormerveer, Holland.

—Rutger ten Broeke

LYFORD STANLEY

Born 1924 · United States

Lyford Stanley is best known for the design of lobsterboat-type yachts and working boats, the Stanley 28, 36, 39, and 44. These handsome and traditional boats have been built in Hall Quarry on Mount Desert Island, Maine, by the John M. Williams Company.

The son of a lighthouse keeper, Stanley was born on Mount Desert Island, Maine. During World War II he went to work at Bath Iron

Works in Bath, building Liberty ships. He returned to Mount Desert and went to work for Sim Davis in McKinley (now Bass Harbor) building commercial fishing boats and some pleasure craft. There he learned how to design and build. He then went to work at Henry R. Hinckley and Company. The first boat he built on his own, a 23-foot net tender or "bug boat," was constructed in his bedroom. To get it out he had to cut out one of the walls.

Most of the Stanleys were built for commercial fishermen, but recently most have been finished out as finely appointed pleasure boats.

—Jon Johansen

RALPH W. STANLEY

Born 1929 · United States

Ralph Stanley is a vibrant anachronism at the beginning of the twenty-first century—a builder of wooden boats of his own design that preserve and enhance the traditions of his Maine heritage. He is perhaps more responsible than any other individual for the survival, albeit as a yacht, of the Friendship sloop, the elegant, clipper-bowed gaff-rigger that was once the principal vessel of Maine's lobster fleet.

"I don't go for these complicated boats, these high-tech boats. I think when you go out for a sail you ought to go out and enjoy yourself and not have to worry about how fast you're going, what's on your knot meters, all kinds of stuff."

Ralph Stanley: *Acadia.* The 28-foot Friendship sloop *Acadia* was designed and built by Stanley in 1998. She can be shortened down to just the main and the boomed forestaysail, which was how lobstermen often used these boats. Here, with all five sails flying, you can see the evolution from practical workboat into a fast and beautiful small yacht. © *Benjamin Mendlowitz*

Stanley was born in Bar Harbor and grew up in Southwest Harbor on Mount Desert Island, where his family had settled in the eighteenth century. His father was a lobsterman and both his great-grandfathers were masters on schooners; Ralph was the family's first boat designer and builder.

As a youth, Stanley studied plans published in such magazines as *Motor Boating* and *The Rudder* and observed the activities in Southwest Harbor's many boatyards. He built several small boats during high school and in 1952 launched his first large boat, a 28-foot lobsterboat built for his own use from a half model he carved. He has since built dozens of working lobsterboats (prized by area fishermen), lobsterboat-type yachts, Friendship sloops, and small schooners, each to his design worked out with each owner. "I like to build each boat a little differently because I see something in each one that I would improve in the next." He feels that this interaction between designer and owner has always been an important factor in the development of better boats.

In 1999 Stanley received a National Heritage Fellowship in the Folk and Traditional Arts.

—Stephen Rappaport

WILLIAM STEELE

ca. 1830–ca. 1900 · Scotland

The story of shipbuilding by three generations of Steeles of Greenock is one of the great romances of the Clyde. Their varied output included some of the earliest oceangoing steamships (and one of the first Cunarders), many of the fastest and most famous clippers of the mid-nineteenth century, and—appropriately for the plot of a romance—a major role in what G. L. Watson described as "the poetry of shipbuilding": the designing and building of yachts.

In fact, apart from the Fifes of Fairlie, for most of the nineteenth century Robert Steel and Company (preceded by Steele and Carswell) was the only Clyde yard to recurrently design and build substantial and noteworthy yachts, including the earliest types influenced by excise cutters, and *Wave* of 1834, possibly the first yacht to have a metal keel.

William Steele, grandson of yard founder Robert (I), formally joined the business in 1843, in partnership with his father, Robert (II), and brother, Robert (III). As the yard's designer he took a starring role in crafting some of the earliest compositely constructed yacht hulls: framed in iron (later steel) and wood planked in teak and elm. This mirrored his developments in composite clipper construction: striving to create vessels strong enough to ship vast quan-

tities of ballast in compensation for their towering rigs, and fast and light enough to compete with the Americans on the tea routes.

On the same ways and sometimes alongside the likes of his extreme clippers *Ariel, Taeping, Serica* (which famously raced up the English Channel within sight of each other after 12,000 miles of the 1865 Tea Race), and *Sir Lancelot,* Steele built a succession of fine big cruising and racing yachts, famed in their day. His clippers were once dubbed "veritable cargo-carrying racing yachts." Who wouldn't go to the builder of the finest clippers for the fastest and grandest yacht?

Significantly, Royal Yacht Squadron Commodore Lord Wilton was a client more than once, with his 218-ton iron-composite schooner *Nyanza* of 1867 and 450-ton iron steam yacht *Paladine* of 1870, and the 163-ton cutter *Oimara* (1867) and 98-ton yawl *Garrion* (1871) were among the earliest large Scottish yachts to regularly take part in the "big class" at southern regattas. Other William Steele designs that joined the first great 1860's and 1870's phase of European schooner sailing and racing were *Reverie* (43 tons, 1862), *Aglaia* (45 tons, 1865), *Ferida* (180 tons, 1868), and the all-iron *Selene* (271 tons, 1865). Thirty years after her launching, G. L. Watson eulogized *Selene* as "majes-

tic . . . one of the handsomest schooners afloat."

Typically for shipyard yacht designers at this time, after *Garrion*'s launch Steele concentrated on the more profitable designing and building of steam yachts. His 1878 *Wanderer* was described by Watson as "the finest auxiliary yacht of her day" and the *Sans Peur* of 1880 later became Joseph Pulitzer's *Romola.*

In the final chapter, perhaps inevitably, the last sailing yachts launched by Steele were designed by Watson, representing "the new." The 72-ton, steel-composite cutter *Marjorie* of 1883 was in fact the last ever launched by this famous yard, which had apparently run out of steam by concentrating too much on sail.

—Iain McAllister

GEORGE STEERS

August 19, 1819–September 26, 1856
United States

Best known for the schooner yacht *America,* George Steers was one of the pioneers of yacht design. The yachting historian W. P. Stephens identified him as probably the second American naval architect to devote a considerable proportion of his practice to designing yachts (the first was Louis Winde of Boston). Born in Wash-

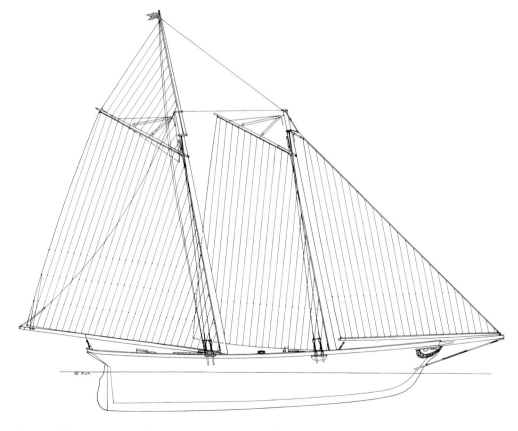

George Steers: *America.* The famous schooner yacht *America,* approximately 100 feet LOD, was the crowning achievement of Steers's all-too-brief career. Her design benefited from experience gained in decades of fierce competition among New York–area pilot schooners, which had to be fast and handy in all weathers—a good foundation for a yacht design. © *Chevalier & Taglang*

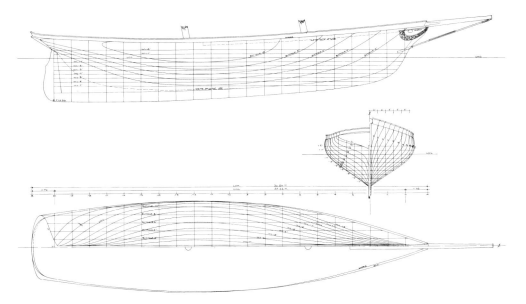

George Steers: *America*. Hulls like that of *America* were quite a departure from the bluff-bowed, lean-quartered designs that came just before, but they set the pattern for yachts to come. Sections would change as outside ballast became the norm, but *America*'s other lines don't look particularly the same and don't look particularly antique, 150 years later. © *Chevalier & Taglang*

ington, D.C., the son of an English shipwright who had come to the United States, Steers was a prodigy who built his first boat at the age of ten and his first successful one at sixteen.

In his early twenties Steers rose to become one of the best naval architects in the country's largest port, New York. Besides designing and supervising the construction of yachts for John Cox Stevens, the founding commodore of the New York Yacht Club, Steers produced a number of pilot-boats—fast, weatherly schooners sailing out from the protection of Sandy Hook to put pilots aboard arriving ships and take them off outward-bound vessels.

Until 1848, like almost all naval architects, Steers produced boats with the combination of bluff bow and fine stern known as "cod's head and mackerel tail." But with the pilot-boats *Mary Taylor* and *Moses H. Grinnell*, built under his supervision at William H. Brown's yard, Steers reversed the order. Each had a fine bow, wide stern, and center of buoyancy located well aft, plus a distinct flare above the hollowed-out bow.

Steers adapted this shape for the yacht *America*, the schooner about 100 feet long on deck (her precise dimensions and lines are still in dispute) that he and Brown built in 1850–51 for a syndicate headed by Stevens. After she was sailed to England for Prince Albert's Great Exhibition, *America* won the race for the Royal Yacht Squadron's 100-Pound Cup, which in time came to be called (in her honor) the America's Cup. This was the first and most influential international sailing trophy.

America's sharp bow was neither a revolutionary element (Howard I. Chapelle, the his-

torian of naval architecture, traced it back to Revolutionary privateers) nor the only decisive one. A yacht that *America* beat badly in England, the John Scott Russell–designed *Titania*, also had a sharp bow. Hers accorded with the highly mathematical "wave-line principle" of her designer, who believed that the hollow in the bow should follow the shape of a sine curve.

Steers undoubtedly knew of Russell's work, but when he spoke of design he tended to be less scientific than artistic. The shape that influenced him most, he once said, was "the well-formed leg of a woman." Proportion likewise ruled *America*. Steers's genius was the ability to balance all the factors—shape, stability, displacement, rig, sail materials—in a neat, beautiful package.

Although *America* may have looked extreme to the English, she was a solid all-round boat, seakindly and fast in most conditions. Her only weakness was a slowness in stays that Steers, nagged by her anxious owner, was unable to correct by making alterations to her underbody.

Sailing off Cowes, on England's south coast, *America* was unbeatable. As one testimonial to her qualities, the commodore of the Royal Yacht Squadron, the earl of Wilton, seriously considered acquiring a sistership. More than a century later, when a model of *America* was tested in the Davidson Laboratory towing tank at the Stevens Institute of Technology, she was found to make only slightly less leeway than a modern-day 12-Meter.

Steers was not aboard *America* in her great race. Owing either to business demands or to hard feelings between him and Stevens, he had gone home to New York, where he and his brother, James, established a shipyard. He later designed and built vessels of all kinds, including fast yachts, a clipper ship, a passenger steamer, and the warship *Niagara*, which helped lay the first transatlantic telegraph cable. A carriage accident in Brooklyn, New York, ended George Steers's brilliant career in his thirty-seventh year.

—John Rousmaniere

GUNNAR L. STENBÄCK

1880–1947 · Finland

One of the early yacht designers in Finland, Gunnar Stenbäck left his native Helsinki for Sweden to study ship engineering at Chalmers Institute in Gothenburg. He returned to Finland after he completed his education and set up as a yacht designer, producing his first boat, the fin-keeler *Mehalla II*, in 1903. Among the many

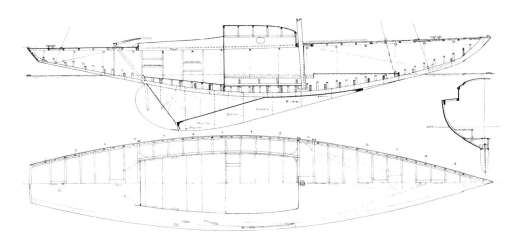

Gunnar Stenbäck: Haj class. The Haj class was designed as a 19-Square-Meter, but became a popular one-design. Still raced in Europe and Scandinavia, and in Camden, Maine, in the United States, the yachts' narrow hull, minimal freeboard, and small wetted surface area render them fast and wet, but they also have useful accommodations. *Drawing courtesy Vaughan and Vera Lee and Ann and David Montgomery*

John Stephen: *Maida II*. Scion of the famous Clyde shipbuilding yard, John Stephen was an innovative amateur yacht designer. Undoubtedly his favorite yachts were 6-Meters; built in 1939, *Maida II* is indicative of his quest to reduce wetted surface area and develop a faster, more lively racing yacht. The underbody anticipates later International Rule yachts, such as 1967's Olin Stephens–designed *Intrepid*. *Photo courtesy Yachting Monthly magazine*

designs to follow were fourteen 6-Meters, numerous skerry cruisers and Sonder boats, and most importantly the Haj class, a 19-Square-Meter one-design boat that is still the most popular keelboat class in Finland. A fleet of these yachts were exported in quantity to Camden, Maine.

Stenbäck's influence extended beyond his work as a designer. He served for twenty-eight years on the board of the Nyländska Jaktklubben (Yacht Club of Nyland), and in that capacity did much to promote the development of yachting in Finland.　　　—Bent Aarre

JOHN G. STEPHEN

1894–1970 · Scotland

During the 1920's and 1930's, when the Clyde's 6-Meter fleet was arguably the strongest in Europe, shipyard owner "Wee" John Stephen became an innovative amateur designer of note. He followed in the footsteps of his equally talented father, Fred J. Stephen, who from 1886 designed his own yachts for construction in the family shipbuilding yard at Linthouse, Glasgow.

Stephen collaborated with his father in the success of three-time Seawanhaka Cup winner *Coila III* of 1922, and his own designs for the balsa-planked, snubbed-bow *Maida* (beaten by Olin Stephens's *Jill* in the 1931 Seawanhaka Cup match) and the highly innovative fin-and-skeg *Maida II* of 1939 were in the vanguard of progress in their time.

During a period when conservatism and commercial sense dictated snail's-pace advances in form and technology in yacht design, Stephen, with friends for clients and without a reputation at stake, was able to boldly experiment both hydrodynamically and aerodynamically. His theories evolved from his experience of racing and experimenting with model yachts, where low wetted surface area and separated keel and rudder forms had been the norm even in the previous century. Formative ideas for *Maida* were tested against a model made from the lines (supplied by her designer) of *Lanai*, the Clinton Crane 6-Meter that finally wrested the Seawanhaka Cup from *Coila III* in 1925.

Stephen initially conducted some of his experiments on a small loch. In one, he attached a bicycle wheel to the stern of a rowing punt to create an axis enabling the slower model of two, tied to opposite extremes of the wheel, to drag the faster one forward. Subsequently he constructed a circular concrete test tank at home, nicknamed the "bull ring," in which he moved the water past the model—a technically imperfect but fascinating development enabling the study of the model from a stationary viewpoint.

His experiments reached a seminal point with his 1935 design for the 6-Meter *Eyra*. She combined an even shorter forward overhang than *Maida*'s with an extreme and almost IOR-type, fin-keel profile and a small rudder with an aft bustle. Such was her total failure that she suffered the unseemly fate of conversion to a motorboat!

But Stephen was on the right track and his development of *Eyra* in the form of the more successful and beautiful *Maida II* of 1939, was the true but understated and misunderstood predecessor of the 1967 Olin Stephens–designed, breakthrough 12-Meter *Intrepid* and her ilk.

After World War II, Stephen continued to test models, especially concentrating on the benefits of rig bending and the problem of hobbyhorsing that allegedly affected the Boyd-designed 12-Meters *Sceptre* and *Sovereign*, but no further full-size yachts were built to his designs.

　　　—Iain McAllister

ROBERT "ROY" STEPHENS
Died 1953
THEODORE "THOD" STEPHENS
Died February 1933

United States

The Stephens brothers were naval architects and boatbuilders who practiced from approximately 1903 until 1945 in Stockton, California. Stephens Marine continues in business today.

Roy and Thod Stephens were primarily known for their motoryacht designs, which spanned most of the early development of the type from the earliest gasoline-powered launches through the streamlined yachts of the postwar period. They also designed working vessels and a number of sailboats, one of the most notable of which was the 38-foot Farallone Clipper, an attractive one-design cruiser/racer class for San Francisco Bay.

The Stephens grew up near the Stockton Channel, where their interest was captured by the commercial vessels that came and went. In 1895 they sailed on San Francisco Bay, and were soon working for their uncle, who owned tugboats and barges. In 1902 they built their first boat, a 33-foot centerboard sloop named *Dorothy*. The boat received favorable word in the local press, and they were soon designing and building professionally, working from a grounded barge on the Stockton Channel.

In 1910 Thod and Roy built a large facility on the land nearby and began designing and building small yachts, barges, and commercial vessels, soon establishing a reputation for quality and productivity. They became particularly well known for the Stephens 26, a popular all-teak speedboat that was raced as a class at the (Lake) Tahoe Power Boat Club. After the 1920's they concentrated on cruising vessels and during the depression placed a higher emphasis on sailboat production. Thod Stephens died in 1933.

After the Depression the emphasis returned to power yachts and then to extensive boat-building efforts for the government during World War II. Roy Stephens retired after the war in 1945, turning operations over to his nephews and sister-in-law.

—Daniel B. MacNaughton

OLIN J. STEPHENS II

Born April 13, 1908 · United States

"I was lucky: I had a goal. As far back as I can remember I wanted to design fast boats." These first two sentences of Olin Stephens's autobiography, *All This and Sailing, Too*, summarize a lifetime's vocation on the part of the most successful and influential designer of the twenti-eth century. He was raised near New York City and, as a boy, was introduced to boats during family vacations on Cape Cod. Along with his father, Roderick, and younger brother, Roderick Jr. (called Rod), he learned to sail in a series of family-owned boats. Fascinated by sailing and its technology, the boys absorbed all they could from yachting magazines and their own experience, and were encouraged and supported by their father.

After graduating from high school, Olin Stephens entered MIT in 1926, only to be forced to drop out during his freshman year because of illness. Throughout his life, although he was a pioneer in scientific yacht design, he would say that he regretted his lack of training in mathematics and engineering. Yet Stephens had aptitudes that suited his calling.

"I started my career with the tools of observation and intuition to which quantitative analysis has been gradually added," he wrote in his autobiography. "Whenever possible I studied lines and tried to see the way shape was coupled to performance."

By 1926 Stephens was sailing regularly at Larchmont Yacht Club in 6-Meters, a restricted-design keelboat about 34-feet LOA and the hot racing class of the day, with top-flight sailor/designers like Clinton Crane and Sherman Hoyt. Six-Meter racing was Olin's laboratory for identifying and analyzing the features that affected a boat's performance—what made a boat of a particular design a little faster upwind or on a reach. By 1928 he was working at a drafting table at home and, with the help of Norman L. Skene's manual *The Elements of Yacht Design*, was teaching himself how to draw plans. His bible was *Yacht Cruising*, by Claud Worth, an English medical doctor, yacht designer, and offshore sailor who favored the idea that sailboats should have balanced lines.

Stephens's on-the-water observations of 6-Meters confirmed the value of that rule of thumb. His first published design, a 6-Meter, appeared in the January 1928 *Yachting* with these comments by the young designer: "In any design the most important factors of speed seem to be long sailing lines and large sail area, with moderate displacement and small wetted surface. Then comes beauty, by which is meant clean, fair, pleasing lines. Though *per se* beauty is not a factor of speed, the easiest boats to look at seem the easiest to drive." To this equation he added stability, owing to considerable external ballast. Worth, like most older designers of offshore boats, placed the lead ballast in the bilge in order to ease the boat's motion through a seaway. Stephens preferred it deep in the keel, where 6-Meters and other modern racing boats had it, in order to provide stability and sail-carrying ability for good upwind performance.

After working as a draftsman for Henry J. Gielow, who specialized in large powerboats, and Philip Rhodes, Stephens in 1929 went into partnership with Drake Sparkman, a successful yacht broker, to form Sparkman and Stephens (S&S). The aggressive Sparkman was the salesman; Stephens, by nature a shy man, ran the design office. Their first project was a 21-foot LOA keelboat for junior sailing on Long Island Sound called the Sound Junior Class, later renamed the Manhasset Bay One-Design (it is still sailing more than seventy years later). Then came a small cruising boat for his father and several 6-Meters, some on referrals from Clinton Crane, an amateur designer who wanted to help the youngster get started on a professional career.

Olin Stephens: *Nancy.* Design No. 17, from 1932, is shown racing for the British-American Cup at Cowes with Stephens at the helm. An early 6-Meter, she was followed by numerous others, with *Goose* of 1938 being the best known. Prior to World War II, Stephens was also designing 8- and 12-Meter yachts to the International Rule. © *Beken of Cowes*

The young designer's greatest ambition was to design a boat for the ocean. In 1928 he had raced to Bermuda with John Alden in *Malabar IX*, and after the finish, the twenty-year-old swam from boat to boat to talk to crews and explore design features, while his back blistered in the sun. After his grandfather sold the family coal business in 1929, his father commissioned S&S design No. 4, the 52-foot yawl *Dorade*. Her concept was much closer to a 6-Meter than a *Malabar*. She had a tall Bermudian rig, balanced ends, narrow beam, lead ballast deep in the keel, and lightweight, sophisticated construction (with steam-bent rather than sawn frames) that closely followed the standards at the old Herreshoff yard in Bristol, Rhode Island. *Dorade* was built at the Minneford yard on City Island, New York, under the supervision of young Rod Stephens, who developed an efficient deck layout and a new type of deck ventilator with a baffle that separated incoming air from spray. Under Olin's command, and with his father and brother in the crew, she did well in the 1930 racing season; then, in 1931, she won the Transatlantic Race to England against many larger boats by 2 days on elapsed time, and also won a rough Fastnet Race.

When they returned to New York, the Stephenses were given a ticker-tape parade up Broadway. Rod Stephens sailed *Dorade* successfully for several years before she was sold to the West Coast in 1935. She promptly won the Honolulu Race. Thinking *Dorade* too narrow and tender, when Stephens had the opportunity to design another ocean racer in 1934 he increased the beam by 2 feet and the result was *Stormy Weather*, which he regarded as the better boat. These two boats transformed the design of offshore sailing yachts.

In the meantime Olin Stephens was playing an important role in the transition of yacht design from an art to a science with artistic disciplines. When the National Academy of Sciences in 1993 awarded him the Gibbs Brothers Medal for outstanding contributions to naval architecture and marine engineering, he said, with characteristic modesty, "I don't consider myself a scientist. I never had good academic training." Yet he acknowledged that "scientific knowledge has contributed a great deal to sailing boat design." Scientific yacht design, using experiments and quantification of performance, came about because of his work with Kenneth S. M. Davidson of the Stevens Institute of Technology, in Hoboken, New Jersey, to develop a method for evaluating a design by towing models in water tanks.

Most early model work involved 6-Meters, but it was soon used to help design an America's Cup winner. Stephens first became involved with the America's Cup in 1934 when he served in the afterguard of the unsuccessful defense candidate *Weetamoe*, designed by Clinton Crane. In 1936 Harold S. Vanderbilt, who had defended the Cup in 1930 and 1934, brought Stephens together with W. Starling Burgess as a design team. Out of a series of tests of models, some of Burgess's design and some of Stephens's, came the great J-Class cutter *Ranger*, which dominated the 1937 America's Cup season. She was one of the most successful racing boats of all time. When the work began, the two designers agreed to keep secret the identity of the one who produced the most successful model. After Burgess's death, Vanderbilt suggested publicly that the credit for *Ranger* should go to Stephens. Stephens corrected him in a letter published in *Yachting*, saying that *Ranger* was largely Burgess's product.

Throughout the 1930's Stephens continued to design 6-Meters, culminating in the very fast *Goose* and her near-sister *Llanoria*, winner of Olympic gold medals in 1948 and 1952. He also designed 12-Meters and many cruiser/racers like the New York 32 class; *Brilliant*, a heavy schooner now owned by the Mystic Seaport Museum; the Dutch *Zeearend*; and the 72-foot yawl *Baruna*, which after World War II enjoyed famously close racing with another S&S-designed 72-footer, *Bolero*, in which Stephens sailed as a watch captain.

When yacht design took a leave during World War II, S&S was occupied with projects for the military, including minesweepers and two projects for the U.S. Army: an amphibious vehicle called the DUKW and a new type of pontoon bridge. The office grew to more than a hundred people. Military work remained a significant part of the firm's work until 1958.

After the war, Stephens's work expanded internationally, and S&S-designed ocean racers with different shapes won in Britain and Europe as in America. The RORC Rule in Britain was encouraging relatively narrow, deep-bodied keelboats. The major championships under this rule, including the Admiral's Cup and One-Ton Cup, were regularly won by S&S boats. In America, the CCA Rule over several years (1955–60) produced beamy centerboarders that also did well in ocean races. While Stephens designed centerboarders, he was not especially enamored of the type because of its relatively low stability. Nevertheless, his name is closely linked with centerboarders because of Carleton Mitchell's 38-foot yawl *Finisterre*, which, beautifully prepared and brilliantly sailed by her owner and his crack crew, won three straight Bermuda Races (1956, 1958, and 1960). In time, the CCA rating rule was adjusted to encourage narrower boats. In the late 1960's Stephens

helped bring about the first international measurement rule, the IOR. He later served as chairman of the rule's International Technical Committee and played an important role in the development of the IMS.

One of Stephens's concerns was the seaworthiness of contemporary boats, many of which he thought too beamy, high sided, light, and unstable. After the 1979 Fastnet Race storm left a trail of capsized boats and fifteen dead, Stephens wrote the shocking statement, "Some modern ocean racers, and the cruising boats derived from them, are dangerous to their crews." In the early 1980's he helped direct a sophisticated study of the causes of capsizes by keelboats that was cosponsored by the United States Yacht Racing Union and the Society of Naval Architects and Marine Engineers. Out of this work came several reports and a book, *Desirable and Undesirable Characteristics of Offshore Yachts*, to which Stephens contributed two articles, one on the development of yacht design in the twentieth century and the other on the importance and measurement of stability.

All this time Stephens was producing successful racing boats, including the winners of eight of the nine America's Cup matches between 1937 and 1980. In 1958 the S&S-designed 12-Meter *Columbia* successfully defended the Cup with her designer in the afterguard, as he had been on *Ranger* in 1937. Other than *Ranger*, the most remarkable of these boats was *Intrepid*, the defender in 1967 and, after alterations by Britton Chance Jr., in 1970. She had a rudder separate from her keel to reduce wetted surface area and improve steering. The separate rudder was not new, but Stephens made it work on a number of increasingly large ocean racers (most notably Thomas Watson's *Palawan*) in the mid-1960's before successfully using it on *Intrepid*.

While designing America's Cup defenders and ocean racers, Stephens also produced a number of powerboats, motorsailers, and cruising boats. S&S-designed cruisers and cruiser/racers built by Tartan in Ohio and Nautor in Finland can be seen in ports almost everywhere. Stephens also was active in the design of day-

---

Olin Stephens: *Stormy Weather* (opposite). Design No. 27 from 1934, *Stormy Weather* came five years after Stephens's groundbreaking *Dorade* and showcased his evolving concept for a flat-out ocean racer. With the same displacement as the earlier boat, *Stormy Weather* was longer on the waterline and, with 22 percent more beam, had the power to carry 18 percent more sail. © *Mystic Seaport, Rosenfeld Collection, Mystic, CT. Image acquired in honor of Franz Schneider*

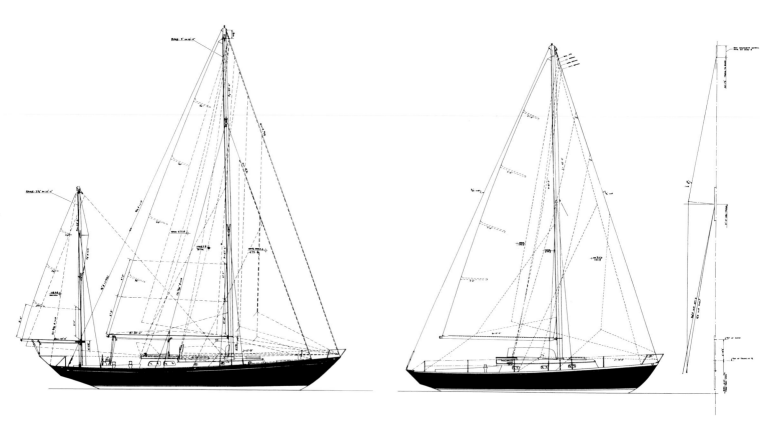

Olin Stephens: *Anitra*. *Anitra* was design No. 1358, and at 48-foot 5-inch LOA was the largest yacht derived from the earlier Pilot designs. With bright topsides, this classic doghouse yawl impeccably constructed by Bengt Plym is considered by many one of the best-looking Sparkman and Stephens designs. Showing speed as well as beauty, she won the 1959 Fastnet Race. *Drawing courtesy Jay Paris*

Olin Stephens: *Hestia*. Design No. 1478, *Hestia* was a modest 34-footer with winning ways that enhanced Sparkman and Stephens's reputation in the United Kingdom and Europe. The most apparent influence of the RORC Rule on her design is a draft of 6 feet on a 25-foot 6-inch DWL. *Drawing courtesy Jay Paris*

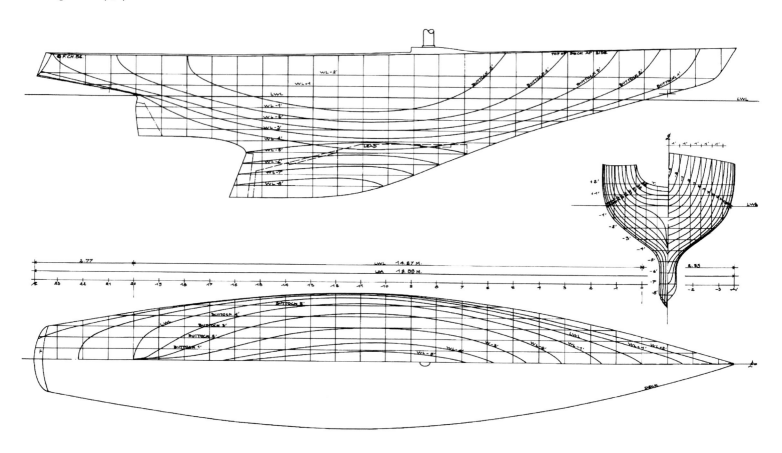

Olin Stephens: *Intrepid*. The 1966 *Intrepid*, design No. 1838, was a milestone in 12-Meter development, having a shortened keel with trim tab and a separate rudder faired into a filled-out afterbody. Other details, including below-deck winches, a lowered boom, and a titanium upper mast, contributed to her victories in the 1967 and 1970 America's Cup series. © *Chevalier & Taglang*

racing boats, the best known of which is the Lightning, a 19-foot, three-person center-boarder designed in 1938 and raced world-wide. Other successful day boats included the 13-foot 6-inch Blue Jay (a small version of the Lightning), the 11-foot 6-inch Interclub Dinghy, and the 30-foot 2-inch Shields keelboat.

After Drake Sparkman's death in 1964, Olin Stephens shouldered the firm's administrative burden. His chief assistants included his brother Rod, who supervised much of the rigging design and construction, and Gil Wyland. Roderick Stephens Sr., who had launched his sons on their careers, handled public relations. Olin often raced in boats he designed and was in regular attendance at Newport during America's Cup summers. Besides his long work on rules committees, he was active in the Society of Naval Architects and Marine Engineers, which awarded him its highest honor, the David W. Taylor medal, in 1959. He also was awarded an honorary degree by the Stevens Institute of Technology.

Sailing was only a part of his life. Beginning in the 1930's, Stephens nurtured a creative, independent life ashore. He studied art and painted, played the piano, and read and traveled widely. He and his wife, Susie, lived in a New York suburb, where they raised two sons. On his retirement in 1978 (after designing or supervising the design of more than two thousand boats or classes), the Stephenses moved to northern New England. Stephens continued his varied life into his nineties. At nearby Dartmouth College he took courses in mathematics and helped teach a course on sailing for engineers. He developed his computer skills, worked with a firm on software for studying aerodynamics, advised America's Cup syndicates, and traveled often and far to technical conferences and meetings of international rating rules committees. He served for many years as a trustee of the Mystic Seaport Museum and advised the Landing School, a boatbuilding and yacht design training institution in Maine. Stephens sailed occasionally and especially enjoyed wooden boats. When *Dorade* was returned to her original form by a dedicated new owner in Italy in 1998, Stephens happily flew over and joined her crew as she won two out of three races.

At the age of ninety, Olin Stephens completed an insightful autobiography whose title, *All This and Sailing, Too*, neatly summarized his view of life. On the last page he wrote, "In all phases of my work I was conscious of the need for balance, and I did my best to find balance in both the long and the short view. Broadly I think I can say that I applied the principles of balance in design, in business, and in the pleasures I enjoyed."

Sparkman and Stephens's plans have been archived at Mystic Seaport Museum, Mystic, CT.

—John Rousmaniere

Olin Stephens: Swan 48. The Swan 48, design No. 2079 of 1971, introduced Nautor's trademark low-profile house with the cabintop fairing into the foredeck. Nautor's reputation as builders of race-oriented cruisers finished to the highest standards was in part due to the significant contributions of Olin Stephens's brother Rod. *Photo courtesy Sparkman and Stephens*

ROBERT W. STEPHENS

Born 1962 · United States

Bob Stephens's career has involved two distinct phases: early self-employment, during which he drew small, easily built boats; and his tenure at Brooklin Boat Yard (Maine), where he designs sophisticated cruising and racing sailboats of contemporary construction but often traditional nature.

Stephens was born in Baltimore, Maryland. Since the age of ten, he has known that he wanted to design boats. After reading Howard Chapelle's books several times, he was hooked. Following a brief apprenticeship at Brooklin Boat Yard, he worked as a lead carpenter for Robinhood Marine Center in Georgetown, Maine. Then the young designer set up on his own in Searsport, Maine, drawing and building small boats: double-paddle canoes, pulling boats, daysailers, beach cruisers, and outboard boats.

The 15-foot 2-inch Ocean Skiff comes from the designer's early independent office. Pushed by a 20- to 40-hp outboard motor, the light plywood-

Robert Stephens: *Lena.* A low, narrow, fast daysailer, *Lena* was launched in 2001. This 46-foot 7-inch, wood-epoxy sloop combines traditional proportions above the water with contemporary underwater lines. © *Elizabeth Coakley*

Rod Stephens. Rod Stephens is shown at the tiller of *Dorade* off Newfoundland on a 1935 cruise to Norway. *Photo courtesy Olin Stephens*

lapstrake utility runs flat and smooth. It banks gently into high-speed turns. In all, it seems the picture of efficiency. As with most of Stephens's early designs, the boat readily can be built in home workshops.

After Stephens returned to Brooklin in 1991, he worked with and learned from Joel White. Bob now is chief designer for the yard. His recent boats have done particularly well in competition. *Lena,* his 46-foot 7-inch, wood-epoxy sloop, won elapsed-time honors in her first major race—against boats that the formulae predicted should outrun her. He drew plans for the sloop in response to a client's request for a "low, narrow, fast daysailer." —Mike O'Brien

RODERICK STEPHENS JR.

August 7, 1909–January 10, 1995 · United States

As a boy Rod was introduced to sailing during family summers at Lake George, New York, and on Cape Cod and Martha's Vineyard. He immediately gravitated toward sail handling and rigging, while also tending an outboard motor. He graduated from Scarsdale High School in 1927 after playing baseball and captaining the football team. He attended Cornell University in the class of 1931, playing freshman football. He sailed the first of his many Bermuda Races in 1928. The family lived in Scarsdale, New York. Our father, who enjoyed sailing and greatly encouraged his two sons in it, often took Rod and me to nearby City Island to visit the Henry B. Nevins yard and other yards in order to observe and photograph boats under construction. The family interest in boats led to a friendship with Mr. Nevins, who offered Rod a job. Rod did not return to Cornell. From 1928 to 1933 he progressed at Nevins under the direction of the superintendent, Rufus Murray.

When the Stephens family decided in 1929 to build the yawl *Dorade* to my design, the Nevins shop was full so she was built by the nearby Minneford yard. Courtesy of both builders, Rod supervised her construction. He sailed on *Dorade* in 1930 in the Bermuda Race and the next year when we won the Transatlantic and Fastnet Races. In 1933 he was her skipper when she cruised to Europe, won the Fastnet, and sailed back to New York. For that 8,000-mile voyage without incident, he was awarded the Blue Water Medal by the CCA. He later won another Transatlantic Race as skipper of *Stormy Weather,* as well as numerous class prizes in the Bermuda Race and other races in his New York 32 *Mustang,* the flagship when he was the CCA's commodore in 1949–50. He sailed in leading 12-Meters and 6-Meters and in several

America's Cup campaigns, serving as deck boss in the successful Cup defenders *Ranger* and *Columbia* in 1937 and 1958, and as navigator in the winning *Constellation* in 1964.

As the yacht design firm of Sparkman and Stephens (S&S) grew, in 1933 Rod joined us and began to apply his expertise in construction. He played an important role in the creation of most of the firm's designs, including the Cup defenders, specializing in rigging, deck fittings, and construction. One of his jobs at S&S was to travel frequently all over the world to inspect new boats and supervise builder's trials. This work made him a good friend of many builders and owners.

Rod brought to his work his invaluable total capability as a seaman, his knowledge of design and construction, and his love of and respect for the ocean. He could handle any boat in any condition, he understood racing and sailhandling, and he knew how to push a boat just far enough to go with safety. Above all, he knew how to put together all the elements of a good boat. Recognizing the need for strength in hull and rig and the importance of identifying the weakest link in order to avoid damage, he developed his own detailed, well-considered rules of thumb for boat construction, rigging, and seamanship. He did not keep this extensive knowledge to himself but with characteristic vigor and unselfishness distributed it widely in letters, magazine articles, lectures, and seminars. He was widely regarded as one of the greatest authorities on boats and their handling.

When he worked on a boat, his concern extended from the top of the mast down into the bilge. Hating to have water below, he knew how to design a tight deck, despite all the necessary hatches and fittings. Because he also loved having fresh air in the same place, he devised a new type of vent for *Dorade* that quickly took her name and became standard equipment in the boating industry. Besides the Dorade vent, he developed many standard designs for cleats, chocks, blocks, and other fittings.

One of his most important assignments came during World War II, when he managed the U.S. Army's amphibian project that created what was called "the truck that goes to sea," the DUKW built by General Motors. Almost one thousand of the half-vehicle/half-trucks were built and many were used as transports at Normandy, Iwo Jima, and other important wartime landings. For this Rod was awarded the Medal of Freedom, the country's highest award to a civilian.

Besides the CCA, he was a member of the New York Yacht Club, the American Yacht Club, the Society of Naval Architects and Marine Engineers, and the Mystic Seaport Museum,

where he was an active and influential volunteer.

Sailing was his life and he continued to go to S&S and inspect new boats until 1991, when he was slowed by a stroke and lost his wife, Marge. He still sailed with friends, spoke at safety seminars, and consulted clients until soon before his death in 1995 at the age of eighty-three.

—Olin J. Stephens II

WILLIAM PICARD STEPHENS

August 5, 1854–May 10, 1946 · United States

W. P. Stephens is universally referred to as the "Dean of American Yachtsmen" and rightly so. Among the first of the United States' great yachtsman/editors, he devoted his entire life to the use of boats and to describing the various ways of enjoying the water. He was an ardent small boat cruiser and did a great deal to bring the sport of canoeing to average Americans. He helped popularize the canoe yawl type, in which the cruising canoe is evolved a few steps toward a seaworthy and affordable coastal cruising sailboat, often large enough to include real cruising accommodations. He was the yachting editor of *Forest and Stream* magazine, one of the earliest popular magazines to cover the sport, and later became the editor of *Lloyd's Register of American Yachts*.

While he is best known for his designs of small sailing yachts, Stephens also designed some of the earliest power yachts, including a few intended for offshore racing. He followed in the footsteps of C. P. Kunhardt, the previous yachting editor of *Forest and Stream*, in the cutter-versus-centerboarder dispute, and was in favor of the cutter type. He was, however, also a dedicated marine historian and wrote about the very un-cutter-like sharpies and other craft with fairness and accuracy.

Stephens was an advocate of Corinthian or amateur yachting, as opposed to racing by professionals, and was widely admired for his

W. P. Stephens: *Ethelwynn.* In 1895 the Seawanhaka Corinthian Yacht Club put up the International Challenge Trophy for the first time. The American entry, *Ethelwynn*, won this first challenge over the British entry, the Brand-designed *Spruce IV*. She had a waterline of 15 feet 8 inches, hollow spars, and was the first yacht with a triangular mainsail to compete in an international match. © Mystic Seaport, Rosenfeld Collection, Mystic, CT. Charles Edwin Bolles, Photographer

good sportsmanship. He was instrumental in the early development of the marconi rig and typically utilized a flaring shape in his outside ballast castings, which to some extent anticipates the "Scheel Keel" developed by designer Henry Scheel many years later. His most important book, *Traditions and Memories of American Yachting*, is a fundamental reference in the yachting history of the nineteenth and early twentieth century.

Self-taught as a designer and builder, Stephens had a good eye for beauty, especially in his lovely small canoe yawls and larger racing sailboats. In some of his small cruising boats and powerboats, the proportions can seem a bit odd to modern eyes, as—like all designers—he struggled to find the right balance between the often-conflicting goals of function and aesthetics. But it must be remembered that he was working in largely uncharted territory. Other examples of his work still seem tremendously appealing and many deserve reproduction today.

Stephens was born in Philadelphia. He studied locomotive design and mechanical engineering at Rutgers University and graduated in 1873. By 1876, he was involved in canoeing, and in 1881 he opened his own boatbuilding shop on Staten Island, producing canoes and small yachts.

In 1883 Stephens became canoeing editor of *Forest and Stream*, and in 1884 took over the yachting department, a post he held for twenty years. In 1903 he began his twenty-nine years as editor of *Lloyd's Register of American Yachts*. After he retired, he continued to write for the yachting press. Stephens was a regular correspondent with British designer Albert Strange, one of the foremost advocates of the canoe yawl type, and they are said to have considerably influenced each other's work.

Traditions and Memories of American Yachting was serialized in *Motor Boating* magazine between 1939 and 1946, and has appeared in book form in four editions, including a handsome fiftieth anniversary edition by WoodenBoat Publications. Stephens also wrote for *Outing* magazine and *The Sportsman*. He wrote *Canoe and Boat Building for Amateurs* (1885), *Supplement to Small Yachts* (1896), and *American Yachting* (1904). He coauthored *The Yacht America*, which appeared in 1925, and wrote *The Seawanhaka Corinthian Yacht Club, Origins and Early History*, published posthumously in 1963.

Stephens designed approximately one hundred boats during his career. His personal boats were *Snarleyow*, a 15-footer he built in 1882, and *Snikersnee*, a 21-foot 9-inch cruising yawl he designed and built during the years 1898 to 1901, and which he used for the rest of his life. His

David Stevens: *Avenger.* The 40-foot schooner *Avenger* is one of four schooners designed and built by Stevens from the same half model. They are all evolutions of the Tancook Island schooners with which he grew up. *Photo courtesy Tom Gallant*

most famous boat was the Half-Rater *Ethel-wynn*, winner of the Seawanhaka Cup of 1895. She defeated two Herreshoff designs in the selection trials and was the first boat to appear with a marconi rig in an international competition.

Along with Nathanael Herreshoff, W. P. Stephens was a founding member of the Society of Naval Architects and Marine Engineers. He lived to be ninety-one.

A substantial collection of many designer's plans are a part of the W. P. Stephens Collection at Mystic Seaport Museum, Mystic, CT.

—Daniel B. MacNaughton

DAVID STEVENS, OC

1907–1989 · Canada

Grandson of Amos Stevens, one of the great Tancook Island designer/builders, David Stevens moved with his family from Tancook to Second Peninsula, also in Nova Scotia. On the death of his father, Stevens, still a teenager, became the man of the house. He was a farmer, a sailor, and, eventually, a boatbuilder. He was a quiet master in the shop and an ardent student at the helm.

His professional career as a designer/builder began with an order for six one-design, 29-foot racing sloops for the Lunenburg Yacht Club in 1946. Made entirely with hand tools in one winter by Stevens and two helpers, they were called S-boats and were an immediate success: fast, easy to handle, and pretty. One wonders what possessed the folks from the yacht club to hire an untried turnip farmer to design and build the boats—David's lineage might have had some bearing.

In his long career, Stevens built over eighty boats, some to lines of other designers, most from his own half models. The workmanship was impeccable and the materials the best available. Most successful were a series of schooners that he built in the 1960's and 1970's, each a thoughtful and purposeful evolution of the Tancook schooners that, as a child, he watched being built. He had a knack for designing wholesome boats with moderate, easily handled rigs, a good turn of speed, and perfect balance.

The author's own boat, *Avenger*, was built from a half model Stevens liked enough to use for four schooners, culminating with *Atlantica*, which he built at Montreal's Expo 1967. These schooners are 47 feet long on deck and are the largest boats he built. They are wonderful cruising boats. Once, *Avenger* sailed from Bermuda to St. Barth's in 5 days and 4 hours, a romp that included 200-plus-mile days.

Stevens's personal favorite was his own *Cathy Anne II*. She won every trophy possible with her designer at the helm. He continued designing and building after he retired because he just couldn't stop, and gave the boats to his children and grandchildren. His swan song, a beautiful 40-foot schooner called *Dorothy Louise*, was sitting in his shop with his caulking tools lying on the deck when he died one afternoon. His grandson, Edward Pyle, owns her now. Stevens never even hung a shingle outside his shop, and yet was given the Order of Canada (OC), one of his homeland's highest civilian honors. He liked to say, "A boat is the nearest thing to a living being a man can make with his hands."   —Tom Gallant

ROBERT MONTANUS STEWARD

November 6, 1913–June 26, 1996
United States

Known reverently to many as the "the Ancient Mariner," Bob Steward had one of the most complete careers in yacht design. Starting as an unpaid apprentice at the Cox and Stevens office, he became a successful author of what probably is the first complete and very readable book on wood small boat construction, *Boatbuilding Manual*, and at the peak of his career, became president of the premier yacht-building firm of Huckins Yacht Corporation.

Steward was born in London, England, but crossed the Atlantic with his parents at the age of three months. Because his father had small fishing boats, Steward became interested in them, and by late grammar school he was sketching them. After learning woodworking, patternmaking, structural design, graphics, and statics at Brooklyn Technical High School, he knocked about fooling with boats until he took a job in a yacht yard as a boatbuilder's helper. During the same period, he also took evening courses in advanced trigonometry, strength of materials, and heat and power at Pratt Institute.

In 1934, Steward sought a job at the New York City naval architecture firm of Cox and Stevens. Dan Cox was sufficiently impressed with him and issued Steward an invitation to hang around the office, at no pay, to see what work he could pick up. He began to work for Phil Rhodes, who had been hired in 1932 to design yachts shorter than 75 feet. Steward's first task was to trace in ink onto the blue linen cloth of the day, drawings Bruno Tornroth, the chief engineer, had made on thick buff paper. He was also called on to make small-scale drawings that brokers could use in advertisements.

Steward considered Rhodes a mentor who taught him much of yacht design. As the Depression waned, Rhodes undertook work that he handed over to Steward, which resulted in the office manager discovering that he was not yet being paid. That was corrected, and with Steward added to the payroll, the Cox and Stevens design staff doubled. Steward's time was spent on many Rhodes designs until early 1940, when he left for better-paying endeavors.

During this time, the foundations for Steward's famous book, *Small Boat Construction* (renamed *Boatbuilding Manual* in the second edition), were being laid. Boris Lauer-Leonardi, publisher of *The Rudder*, and Andy Patterson, editor, called on Steward to write a series of twenty monthly articles and drawings for the magazine; these would eventually become the book, published in 1950. Now in its fourth edition with over eighty-five thousand copies printed, it can be found in boat shops around the world.

In 1940, Steward began work as a traveling salesman for the famous Boston yacht chandlery of Merriman Brothers. By late 1940, with the advent of considerable navy work, he was called back, "or borrowed" by Rhodes at Cox and Stevens. His work then was on the conversion of large vessels into hospital ships in California; the design of refueling systems for vessels refueling at sea; installation of degaussing gear on ships; and a short stint at the Robert Jacob yard at City Island converting yachts into coastal patrol boats. He also worked on the troopship conversion of the famous *Normandie*.

Following the war, Steward worked on the design of the Rhodes 27, and the Rhodes 77-foot motorsailers. Cox and Stevens became Philip L. Rhodes, Naval Architects and Marine Engineers following Dan Cox's retirement in 1947. Steward stayed at Rhodes until late 1956. He left to take a job in California, where he signed on with South Coast Marine in Newport Beach, California, becoming yard superintendent, production manager, and chief designer.

After about a year and a half in California, Steward became disenchanted because of the heavy workload of yard management and design, so when yard management wanted him to design a 50-foot motorsailer in the evening, he "saw the handwriting on the wall," and contacted Ray Teller at Huckins Yacht Corporation in Jacksonville, Florida. Teller invited him to join the firm anytime so Steward soon found his way back East. He was hired by Frank Huckins as a designer under Teller, their chief designer. Steward was quickly recognized by the whole Huckins crew as the "go-to guy." Later, upon Teller's death, Steward became chief designer.

The Frank Huckins–designed Fairform Flyers Quadraconic hulls were fast, and to make them fast, it was Huckins's policy that they carry about half the usual fuel and water capacities than most other designs. He felt you could get where you wanted to go quickly and then fuel up. To carry out the austere weight policy, Huckins decreed even whiskey bottles were to be carried half empty.

In the 1960's Steward began to lead Huckins into the still-young fiberglass boat industry. In 1969, Huckins built the largest sportfishing yacht in United States at that time—the 80-footer *Give Up*, to Steward's design.

In 1976 Steward designed the largest Huckins Quadraconic–hulled motoryacht in the United States, the M/Y *Deep Stuff*, with a sandwich-cored hull that Huckins called their "club sandwich." Even after Steward retired from Huckins as president in September 1981, he continued on as a consultant and worked on the final version of his book. —Bob Wallstrom

EIVIND STILL

Born May 14, 1931 · Finland

The town of Jakobstad in Finland, on the Gulf of Bothnia, has a Swedish cultural tradition dating back to the Middle Ages, and today is home to many of Finland's Swedish-speaking citizens. The area around Pietarsaari, on the other hand, maintains the tradition of the shipbuilder's art, embodied by several superb yachtbuilding companies, including Baltic Yachts and Nautor's Swan. Any map of Finland quickly reveals that "Jakobstad" and "Pietarsaari" are the Swedish and Finnish names of

the same town. Eivind Still has lived there among these dual traditions most of his life. He is one of the Nordic countries' most respected sailboat designers, with some fifteen hundred of his craft floating mostly around local waters to prove it. But, like many naval architects, Still came to the profession indirectly.

In 1950 Still entered Åbo Akademi, the Swedish university in Turku, to study mathematics, physics, and chemistry. He earned a master of science in mathematics in 1956, and for the next two decades taught high school. Since childhood, however, Still had a burning desire to design, build, and race offshore yachts, so he spent every spare moment at the university reading about naval architecture, taking a mathematician's special delight in appreciating rating formulas and complex hydrostatics. In 1963 he took a cautious dip into yacht design by entering a Swedish competition with drawings for a 30-foot sloop; he won second prize. But Still wasn't quite ready to give up his day job.

A dozen years later, however, after perfecting his theoretical approach to design, Still drew a Three-Quarter-Tonner, *Finnfire II*, and built it with his son, Mikael. He then invited Bruce Banks, the U.K. sailmaker, to come aboard as sailing master and helmsman for the 1975 World Championships in Norway, but *Finnfire II* failed to win. However, the next year off Plymouth, England, *Finnfire II* won the World Championship. Now Still confidently resigned from teaching and hung out his naval architect's shingle.

Eivind Still: Maestro 38. The trim, fin-keeled Maestro 38 production cruiser/racer was the queen of the fleet for her Finnish designer, but has since been surpassed by Still's new Maestro 40, with the first hulls launched in 2004. *Photo courtesy Eivind Still*

In the ensuing years Still produced more than seventy designs, mostly cruiser/racers for production by Finnish builders, including the Finn 26 (238 boats built), Finn Flyer 27 (93), Finn Flyer 31 (60), Finn Express 27 (213), Seawind 32 (10), Finnfire 33 (60), Maestro 35 (135), and Maestro 38 (13 boats built). Still is also keenly interested in designing easily handled racing dinghies for adoption by sailing schools and yacht clubs, to encourage kids to get out on the water. Three models of his design, ranging between 12.5 and 17.2 feet long, have resulted in more than seven hundred boats sold.

Still also takes enormous pride in some of the custom one-offs he has drawn, including a 36-footer based on an old Norse seal-hunting hull that could be used on the ice as well as the water: a 52-foot Viking ship: and a replica of the 22-ton sailboat *Eugenia*, which originally carried cargo in the Åland Archipelago and now carries tourists there. But, for Still, his most important project was *Caprice*, a conservatively shaped, 51.5-foot fast cruiser with modern features such as water ballast, self-tacking headsails, carbon fiber spars, and eight single berths. *Caprice* conforms in every way to Eivind Still's well-informed philosophy: to design boats that are elegant, clean, and easy to use.

The first two of Still's latest production model, the Maestro 40, were launched in 2004. Eivind Still practices in Jakobstad, Finland.
—Jack A. Somer

Eivind Still: 380 One-Design. The 380 One-Design, chosen in the late 1980's by the Yacht Racing Association as Finland's official two-man junior training and racing dinghy, is a prime example of Still's concern not only with speed, safety, and practicality, but also with the future of the sport of sailing. *Photo courtesy Eivind Still*

HELMUTH STOEBERL

Born 1930 · Germany

During the two decades following World War II, the German people struggled to rebuild their country. They were successful, and by the 1960's the so-called Wirtschaftswunder (roughly "business wonder") of West Germany's economy offered increased wealth and spare time, making it possible for many Germans to go boating again. The leader among those designing convenient, low-maintenance fiberglass boats with modern lines for the lakes and German seaboard, and for holidays at the nearby Adriatic, was Helmuth Stoeberl.

Stoeberl's Condor 7, a 7.4-meter cruiser that came out in 1962, was the first fiberglass boat to be manufactured in series in Germany. Rollo Gebhard circumnavigated the world in his Condor 7, *Solveig*, between 1967 and 1970, and the voyage illustrated the seagoing virtues of the design, along with the reliability and strength of the relatively new boatbuilding material. Stoeberl designed five more cruising boats in the Condor line ranging from 5.5 to 9 meters in length.

The inventive Bavarian designer is best known for his range of nine different classes of planing open keelboats, the first being the three-person daysailer *Trias* (1967), which clocked 17 knots reaching in a stiff breeze on the Baltic Sea. Five hundred boats have been built to this design. According to Stoeberl, *Trias* was the first medium-sized fiberglass keelboat built without stringers. Instead, he achieved longitudinal stiffness through the use of a double-skin, foam-cored structure.

Stoeberl's 11.50-meter, four-crew inshore racer *Quartas* became a respected competitor in 1970 in long-distance races such as those sailed annually on the lakes of southern Ger-

many, and the Lago di Garda (home of the "Centomiglia," the famous Italian 100-mile race), where the flat-hulled planing boat quickly dominated the local racing scene.

In 1972, Stoeberl developed chemical supplier Bayer Leverkusen's patented four-mold fiberglass construction technique, first utilized for the series production of the 7.15-meter Dyas design, of which 1,650 were built. In this method there was one mold each for the hull surface, hull interior, deck surface, and deck interior. The hollow space in between was filled with polyurethane foam injected under high pressure, creating a rigid structure that was smooth, easy to clean inside and out, and sufficiently buoyant to float if flooded.

Monas (1974), a 7-meter singlehander with an obvious resemblance to the popular Dyas followed; five hundred were built. Keeping the safety and pleasure of his older clientele in mind, Stoeberl equipped this boat with a patented molded seat that swung out of the deck, providing a comfortable place for the helmsman to "hike out."

In all sizes, Stoeberl's keelboats share the same general character: they rely on form stability rather than extensive ballasting, and their U-shaped sections offer generous buoyancy forward, thus helping the hull to climb up on its bow wave in strong downwind conditions. This same shape limits the seakindliness of the boat upwind in a seaway, one of the reasons Stoeberl's attractive and safe open keelboats never became very popular in Scandinavian or British waters, where rough upwind sailing is common. His designs feature a moderately raked stem and a long waterline with little or no overhang aft.

In 1979 Stoeberl developed the Akros, a lightweight and generously canvassed 9.2-meter daysailer featuring a low-profile cabin, rotating mast, and keel fin that can pivot up to 6 de-

grees. The Fighter (1985), the Delphin (1996), and the Twin (1997) share a common 6.23-meter hull along with a bilge-keel configuration and shallow 0.5-meter draft, but they differ in their appeal to the beginner or to the advanced sailor depending on equipment. The Jongleur class, of which thirty were built, was launched in 1975 as an experimental boat with a rotating mast and pivoting lifting keel. Stoeberl's sons Helmuth and Uli serve as test drivers of their father's designs, which have resulted in the construction of over 4,700 boats.

—Erdmann Braschos

LESTER STONE

1892–1975 · United States

Representing the third generation of his famous West Coast boatbuilding family, Lester Stone was the first to concentrate on modern naval architecture. His grandfather, William I. Lidstone, had been a boatbuilder in Dartmouth, England, before moving to San Francisco and changing his name to Stone in 1853. He set up a boatyard upon arrival and over the next forty years built a variety of boats serving local needs, including about two-dozen yachts, apparently to his own design. His son, William F. Stone, took over the yard in 1893, moving it to Tiburon, the first of several moves for the operation.

Lester Stone grew up in the midst of the busy yard, but unlike his father and grandfather, he did not become a woodworker. His decision to pursue modern naval architecture, in which boats were entirely designed on paper, was probably a response to the increasingly technical nature of yacht design and was undoubtedly necessary if the yard was to successfully compete for business.

Stone's first design, built in 1914, was for the 53-foot sloop *Pronto II* (converted to a yawl in 1923), which his father built for him. With Stone at the helm, she won almost every major race in the Bay area. She was followed by the R-Class sloop *Active*, the first of a number of such boats, including *Rascal*, which came out in 1921 and proved almost unbeatable.

Lester Stone took over the yard in 1923 and built boats to his own designs as well as others, and the business experienced extreme ups and downs as the political and economic events of the next twenty-five years unfolded. Yachts such as the 50-foot cutter *Water Witch* (1928), the 61-foot ketch *Marilen* (1930), the 42-foot cutter *Helaine* (1936), and the 43-foot sloop *Vaya* (1955) were very successful under multiple owners on the Bay and in long-distance racing and cruising.

Stone's design work was seldom innovative,

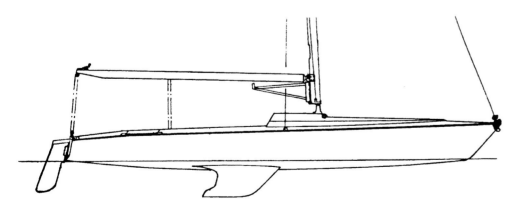

Helmuth Stoeberl: Twin Fighter. Most designers of twin-keel craft have estuary cruising and upright grounding on their minds. Stoeberl, however, has sought performance advantages in the configuration. If sailed with one keel out of the water, this boat enjoys reduced wetted surface area and improved keel orientation. *Drawing courtesy Helmuth Stoeberl*

Lester Stone: *Marilen.* One of Stone's best-known boats, built in 1930, the 61-foot ketch *Marilen* has been raced in most of the principal West Coast events by a number of well-known yachtsmen over the years. *Photo courtesy Newport Harbor Nautical Museum, Newport Beach, CA*

though he was one of the first to utilize the marconi rig on the West Coast. His boats were particularly attractive, with strong sheers and strong character in the shapes of the bows

Lester Stone: *Water Witch* (opposite). The 50-foot cutter *Water Witch* was built in 1928 at the W. F. Stone and Son yard in Oakland, California. Her proportions are particularly graceful, and she proved to be a splendid boat for San Francisco Bay. *Water Witch* performed well in the Transpac Races of 1939, 1955, and 1957. *Photo courtesy Thomas G. Skahill*

and sterns. He believed in especially rugged construction and sometimes adapted the work of other designers to accommodate it. He designed yachts for both power and sail, in a wide variety of types.

In the late 1960's wooden boatbuilding declined, and at age seventy-eight, Stone sold the yard. It subsequently changed hands a few times and is now open again as the Stone Boat Yard, believed to be the oldest continuously operating business on the West Coast. Lester Stone died at age eighty-three.

—Daniel B. MacNaughton

ALBERT STRANGE

July 29, 1855–July 11, 1917 · England

For those who love elegant small yachts combining artistry with practicality, there is no greater treasure than the work of Albert Strange. He designed during a period when most of the yachting world was concerned with big yachts, professional crews, and the mind-boggling luxuries of the very wealthy, but his primary interest was in small boats that were accessible to those of modest means and could be sailed singlehanded.

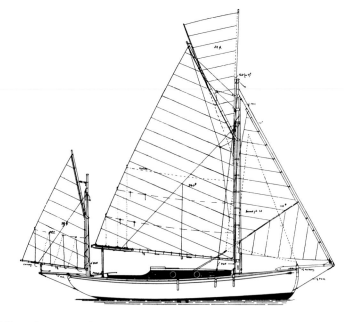

Albert Strange: *Sheila.* Built in 1905 by Robert Groves, the 25-foot LOA canoe yawl *Sheila* was Strange's first full keel design. Her mizzen is 19 percent of the sail plan (here with a reef in) so she will tack closely without the
main. Her owner since 1976, Mike Burn, cruises her extensively; his restorations leave her exactly as she was in 1905. *Photo courtesy Michael Burn*

Albert Strange: *Cherub III.* The 28-foot 6-inch *Cherub III* was the last
yacht that Strange designed and was for his own use. She represents the
culmination of the canoe-sterned Humber yawls for which he was famous.
In the 1911 Humber Yawl Club yearbook, he noted, "She runs very fast
and on all points of sailing her wave making is extremely slight," and her
"bold side and businesslike look were much admired." *Drawing courtesy
Albert Strange Association*

Essentially an amateur yacht designer,
Strange is also well known as an artist, and his
watercolors and sketches of marine subjects are
highly prized. He made his living teaching
art and was headmaster of the Scarborough
School of Art from 1882 to 1916. He also taught
yacht design and drafting to those students who
had an interest.

Born in Gravesend on the Thames estuary,
Strange did his early sailing with the working watermen near his birthplace, and at age
seventeen acquired a converted workboat in
which he began to cruise the local area.
Throughout his life Strange and his friends
made extensive cruises in very small boats,
often for the purpose of sketching and painting the scenes in which they found themselves.
It seems doubtful that they ever felt the smallness of the yachts to be any kind of drawback,
given their joy in natural beauty seen up
close and their willingness to sail alone or with
a single companion.

Perhaps more than anyone else, Strange
founded the uniquely British idea that even a
very small yacht could be taken seriously and
could offer a genteel life aboard, while being
fully capable of handling the worst weather.
Strange's boats were simple but sophisticated
in their functional details both on deck and below, with ease of handling in the rig and economy of space down below being top priorities.
Drawings often show specific storage places for
even the smallest objects.

Strange was a member of the Humber Yawl
Club and, as much as any designer, presided
over the canoe yawl type's remarkable evolution, in an unbroken line, from sailing canoes
to deep-keel yachts around 30 feet long. While
the term *canoe yawl* does not mandate either a
yawl rig or a pointed stern, most boats of that
type did include both characteristics, as did
much of Strange's work. In fact, while absolute
originality is rare in the ancient world of boats,
Strange is often credited with having invented
the canoe stern, in which an overhanging
stern terminates in a graceful, pointed shape.
His canoe sterns were beautiful to look at and
behaved well in a seaway, but they also helped
with the sheeting and staying of the mizzen,
putting as much hull in its vicinity as possible.
It is widely accepted that Strange produced not
only the first but also some of the best canoe
sterns ever drawn.

To keep things confusing, it should be pointed
out that the *yawl* in *canoe yawl* actually refers to
the fact that the yachts were sometimes rowed,
as in "yawl boat." If there is a direct connection
between this term and the name of the rig, it
seems to have been lost. In any case, the Humber Yawl Club and Strange were both so enamored with the easy handling of the yawl rig
that it was sometimes called "the Club Rig."
Strange was instrumental in its refinement over
the years as well as its adaptation to larger boats.

Strange designed about 150 boats during
his lifetime. He wrote numerous, beautifully

illustrated articles on cruising for *Yachting
Monthly,* as well as a series of articles on yacht
design that appeared in 1914 and 1915. His
first canoe yawl design was *Cherub II,* an outside-ballasted 20-footer that is just one step up
from an open boat but brought attention to the
type by making extensive cruises in exposed
waters. Partly owing to the long series of articles written and illustrated with superb pen-
and-ink sketches by her owner, Robert Groves,
Strange is very well known for the 25-foot
canoe yawl *Sheila,* one of several canoe yawls
in this size range in which the type approaches
its peak of development.

Less well known are a number of racing
craft, and some larger yachts, most notably
Claud Worth's *Tern III,* a graceful 43-foot cutter, and *Tally Ho* (originally *Betty*), a 47-foot cutter of more massive appearance. *Tally Ho* won
the stormy 1927 Fastnet Race in which she
was one of only two boats to finish. Strange's
largest designs were around 70 feet in length.

It is said that more than any other designer,
Albert Strange defined the nature of small
British yachts, with his influence lasting to
the present day. An Albert Strange Association
was formed in England in 1972, and interest in
his work is increasing worldwide, with new
boats often under construction.

*Many of Albert Strange's drawings are in the W. P.
Stephens Collection at the Mystic Seaport Museum, Mystic, CT.*

—Daniel B. MacNaughton

TORD SUNDÉN

1909–1999 · Sweden

Growing up in the Gothenburg area among the many skerrie islands, Tord Sundén learned to sail as a boy. He was educated as an engineer and worked until he was pensioned at Eriksberg Mekaniska Vaerk as a ship engineer.

Sundén's free time was spent sailing and designing yachts. His public debut was in 1938, when an International 5-Meter he drew the plans for served as a prize for a lottery sponsored by the GKSS (Gothenburg Royal Sailing Club), a common fund-raising practice in Sweden from the end of the nineteenth century to the 1950's. That boat and many descendents gave him a reputation for being able to design winning 5-Meter racers. The class was big and competitive at that time, especially in Sweden. Sundén also designed some fine 6-Meter boats.

In 1941 a design competition was held among the Scandinavian countries to find an affordable boat class. There were fifty-eight entries. The Dane Knud Olsen and the Swede Jacob Iversen shared second prize, but none of the proposals were nominated by the committee to receive the first prize. Tord Sundén got the job of integrating the best features of the two second-place entries, to create the desired result: the Nordic Folkboat. Sven Salen, the most prominent ship owner in Sweden and a noted yachtsman, supported the Folkboat idea and paid for building the first sixty boats during 1941–42. Just after World War II growth of the class exploded in many countries, including the United States.

From the first, there was a dispute between Sundén and the Scandinavian Sailing Union over recognition of Sundén as the father of the boat, as Sundén design was very close to that of Iversen's. Thus it is hard to determine who should have the credit for this remarkable boat type, but it is acknowledged that Sundén produced the final drawings.

Sundén was again successful in 1967, when he designed a boat very similar to the Folkboat called the IF (International Folkboat) for fiberglass production. More than three thousand have been built. He also designed a popular fiberglass family cruiser called Sunwind, which was built in Finland.   —Bent Aarre

ALBERT LORING SWASEY

1876–1956 · United States

A. Loring Swasey (MIT class of 1896) is best known to yachtsmen as the principal design partner of Swasey, Raymond and Page, a prolific and highly successful firm working in Boston in the first two decades of the twentieth century. Although he designed a variety of sailboats, including the lovely 26-foot Buzzards Bay One-Design, he gained his reputation as one of the foremost designers of power cruisers and launches. At a time when travel over unpaved roads in badly sprung automobiles offered more adventure than convenience, such boats served both as pleasure yachts and as the quickest and most luxurious mode of travel to destinations accessible by water.

Swasey did not produce radical innovations, but in his concern for detail in every facet of yacht design, he frequently developed new and elegant design solutions. He created some of the largest yachts of his day: the auxiliary three-masted schooner *Visitor II* (1904); the 140-foot motoryacht *Paragon* (1929); and the 157-foot,

Tord Sundén: *Loraine.* At first glance a Folkboat might look like little more than a pretty bay cruiser, but in fact these 25-foot 1-inch Scandinavian sloops are famous for their transoceanic voyages and other long-distance cruising. Sundén produced the final drawings, but other designers, notably Jacob Iversen, made their own contributions. © *Benjamin Mendlowitz*

Albert Swasey: *Cigarette*. The 99-ton, 126-foot express commuter *Cigarette* was one of the few steam yachts designed by Swasey, who later pioneered in diesel-powered yachts. She was built in 1905 by George Lawley and was dropped from *Lloyd's Register* in 1930. *Photo courtesy Mariners' Museum, Newport News, VA*

diesel-powered *Aramis* (1916), an important pioneer in the use of diesel power to large yachts. *Visitor II* was renamed *Guinevere* by her owner, Edgar Palmer, for whom Swasey designed the second *Guinevere* in 1919–20, a 195-foot, three-masted schooner.

During both world wars, Swasey became heavily involved with naval service. In World War I he achieved the rank of commander in the Navy's Bureau of Construction. A fleet of 110-foot submarine chasers resulted from one of his designs of that period. More than four hundred of the 110-footers were built, confirming the success and influence of the design. During World War II he served in the Navy Bureau of Ships, ultimately achieving the rank of rear admiral.

Between the two world wars, Swasey was executive vice president for the Herreshoff Manufacturing Company (1917 to 1920), was a partner in the firm of Burgess, Swasey and Paine (from 1923 to 1925), and the Henry J. Gielow Company. As his eyesight failed in later life, he continued to design but left the detailed drawings to others.

—Walter Voigt

FRANCIS SWEISGUTH

1882–June 21, 1970 · United States

A prominent designer of one-designs, cruising and racing catboats, and handsome offshore racers and cruisers, Francis Sweisguth was a superb draftsman and a master of aesthetics. He is most widely known as the designer of the Star-class racing sloop, although the Star was a 1911 product of William Gardner's design office and appears to have been an enlargement of an earlier Gardner design. By this encyclopedia's standards this makes her a Gardner design, although Sweisguth is known to have done the drawings while in the other designer's employ.

Sweisguth also continued to use Star-like features in some of his future work—he drew a number of unusually attractive chine-hull designs. His many one-designs range from sailing prams through handsome keel/centerboard sloops with cuddy cabins. Sweisguth also designed catboats for racing and cruising. Many were highly successful on the race course, including the much-publicized *Scat II* and *Silent Maid*.

Offshore cruising yachts included the 52-foot 11-inch schooner *Savannah* (later known as

Bounding Home), and he also designed a number of comfortable powerboats, all imbued with a particular aesthetic sense that places Sweisguth among the best of his day.

During his career, Sweisguth worked in the design offices of William Gardner, Ford and Payne (later Ford, Payne and Sweisguth), and Henry Gielow, but he was frequently credited by name and did extensive work in his independent practice.

Some of Francis Sweisguth's drawings are in the Sally W. and Donald Malin Collection and in the International Star Class Yacht Racing Association Collection, both at Mystic Seaport Museum, Mystic, CT.

—Daniel B. MacNaughton

Francis Sweisguth: *Bounding Home* (opposite). The 52-foot 11-inch, staysail schooner *Bounding Home*, built in 1933 by Minneford Yacht Yard, is one of many substantial sailing yachts designed by Sweisguth. Accounts of her day emphasize her elegant interior. She was a hot contender on the race course as well as an able and comfortable cruising boat. © *Peter Barlow*

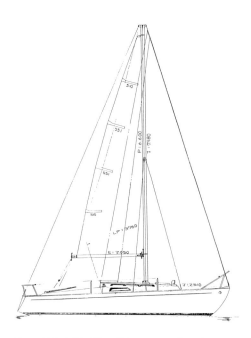

Shun Takeichi: Blue Water 21. The Blue Water 21 was, in 1967, Japan's first production fiberglass sailboat. A popular success, she resulted in several other designs for the same company, and hundreds of boats were built. Note the illusion that causes the yacht's absolutely straight sheer to "read" as a well-drawn reverse sheer. *Drawing courtesy Kennosuke Hayashi*

SHUN TAKEICHI

1934–1992 · Japan

Shun Takeichi could not forget the pleasures of sailing during his youth, and although his first job after graduation from high school was as a car salesman, he soon joined the Yokoyama Naval Architecture Office. While he studied basic yacht designing, he sailed aboard *Sirena*, an outstanding 24-foot, Yokoyama-designed yawl, and distinguished himself in offshore races.

In 1964, Takeichi established Takeichi/ Muramoto Yacht Designers with Nobuo Muramoto. He designed the fiberglass Blue Water 21 in 1967. She proved popular, being the first Japanese fiberglass production keelboat; about three hundred have been built. This success later

resulted in a series of five more Blue Water models. In 1969, he designed the 36-foot *Vago*, and raced in the Sydney to Hobart Race, placing twenty-first overall.

Back in Japan, Takeichi established T&M Marine Engineers and began developing various rig components such as aluminum-alloy masts. The staff members included Taro Takahashi (a designing staff member for the Nippon Challenge America's Cup in 1999) and Osamu Takai (designer of *Tobiume*, winner overall in the Pan Am Clipper Cup of 1982 in Hawaii).

Takeichi was a popular sportsman and an outstanding sailor. He entered the Singlehanded Yacht Race from San Francisco to Okinawa, and delivered a 140-foot, Camper and Nicholson ketch from Italy to Japan and a megayacht from Hong Kong to Italy. During the Japan to Guam Race of 1991–92, he was aboard *Taka*, a 48-foot, Jacques de Ridder design, when it capsized 180 degrees and was abandoned. Takeichi died while he and other crew members were drifting in a life raft waiting for rescue. He designed seventy boats, and his early death was a great loss to the Japanese yachting community.

—Kennosuke Hayashi

JAMES HATHAWAY "JIM" TAYLOR

Born March 1, 1949 · United States

Jim Taylor has made a strong mark with his racing and fast cruising sailboats. In 1974, he signed aboard with Ted Hood's office. Design projects ranged from Canada's Cup Two-Tonners to Transatlantic Race winners.

Born in southern New Jersey, Taylor opened Jim Taylor Yacht Designs in 1979 in Marblehead, Massachusetts, where he continues to practice. The first boat from his drawing table, the 23-foot *Blackjack*, compiled an impressive racing record. Many successful entries followed in the IOR, IMS, and PHRF (Performance Handicap Racing Fleet) arenas. Taylor 40 was a pioneer in IMS Grand Prix racing.

Numbers, Taylor's IMS 50 design, scored overall wins at Key West and the SORC and in the Christchurch Bay races in the Admiral's Cup. Along the way, he found time (1990–95) to work with Bill Koch's *America³*-design team.

Away from the racing circuit, Taylor drew several fast cruising boats for Sabre Yachts including the Sabre 402 and Sabre 452. More than three thousand small production boats have been built to his plans—most of them by Precision Boatworks of Palmetto, Florida.

Taylor now concentrates on applying raceboat technology to cruising boats and daysailers. His current project combines the traditional look of an 8-Meter design above the water with a modern underbody.

—Mike O'Brien

Jim Taylor: *Numbers*. The fast IMS 50 design, *Numbers*, scored impressive wins at Key West, the SORC, and in the Christchurch Bay races in the Admiral's Cup. *Drawing courtesy Jim Taylor*

VICTOR C. TCHETCHET

June 19, 1887–April 1974 · Russia/United States

The Russian-American pioneer designer of multihulls, Victor Tchetchet is best known for his coining of the term *trimaran* and bringing the term *multihull* into widespread use. He built his first catamaran in 1908 in Kiev in his native Russia by joining together two kayak hulls, but began to have an impact only after he emigrated to the United States in 1924.

There, in 1944, he designed and built his first "real" catamaran, a 25-footer he sailed on Long Island Sound. It was quickly followed by several widely publicized trimarans, including the small (22 feet) but influential *Egg Nog* of 1955 and *Flamingo* (26 feet) of 1956, reputedly one of the fastest boats on Long Island Sound.

Tchetchet never formally studied naval design, but was an artist and magazine illustrator who drew much of his inspiration from experiments and a long correspondence of more than twenty years with L. Francis Herreshoff, his mentor.

While Tchetchet's output may have been small in terms of numbers, it cannot be overestimated in terms of the impact it had. In 1946 Tchetchet formed a society called the International Multihull Boat Racing Association, which for the next decade became instrumental in promoting the trimaran concept in the United States and prompted many others, including the trimaran pioneer Arthur Piver, to focus on trimaran design.

—Class van der Linde

MALCOLM TENNANT

Born 1938 · New Zealand

Malcolm Tennant is New Zealand's best-known catamaran designer. His most influential designs stem from the 1970's and early 1980's. Having already built a Rod MacAlpine-Downie catamaran that alerted him to the performance potential of a well-designed catamaran, Tennant's design career started out on a part-time basis in 1966 with the codesign of a Class A catamaran. Its success led to the design of a Class B catamaran and the well-known Paper Tiger and Tiger Cub beach catamaran classes.

Tennant's first large catamaran was *Vorpal Blade,* a 36-footer built for his own use in 1969. The boat's basic lines, including semielliptical hulls with a flat aft run to prevent hobbyhorsing, would become the model not only for many of Tennant's later cruising catamarans but also for those of other designers.

Experience building the Rodney March–designed *Tornado* with the stressed ply con-

Victor Tchetchet: *Egg Nog.* The tiny 22-foot trimaran *Egg Nog* was designed and built in 1955 by Tchetchet, the man who coined the term *trimaran,* and became the progenitor for many modern-era trimarans. *Courtesy the Amateur Yacht Research Society*

Malcolm Tennant: *Afterburner.* *Afterburner,* a 52-foot stretched version of Tennant's *Bladerunner,* was built in 1987. Now based in California, for many years she was considered to be New Zealand's fastest sailboat. © *Terry Fong, AFA Photography*

struction method led to the racer *Bamboo Bomber* (32 feet 2 inches) in 1972, one of the largest stressed (or "tortured") ply vessels that had been built up to that date. Equipped with a wing mast and alloy beams, this catamaran was very advanced for her time.

Tennant's breakthrough design for the first *Great Barrier Express* (27 feet 6 inches) followed in 1972. Basically an enlarged beach catamaran with only minimal accommodations, this boat went on to win numerous coastal races and her success allowed Tennant to become a full-time designer. The 32-foot 7-inch *Turissimo* (1976, later known as *Dakota*) built upon the *Great Barrier Express* but provided better accommodation. The two catamarans became Tennant's most popular boats. In 2001, they represented a quarter of the twenty-three hundred multihulls built to Tennant's design, with each type numbering some three hundred units worldwide.

In the early 1980's, Tennant's design interests developed beyond performance-oriented sailing catamarans. A trimaran, *Wild Thing* (40 feet), was designed in 1983 and became the world's first multihull built with the now-ubiquitous strip-plank composite construction method. More importantly, his first displacement power catamaran was designed that year. Sailing catamarans remained important, but motorsailers and particularly displacement power catamarans have since become the major part of his practice in Auckland, New Zealand.

—Claas van der Linde

J. P. G. THIEBOUT

1873–1941 · The Netherlands

In contrast to design in other countries with a strong nautical tradition, Dutch yacht design experienced a sharp change around 1900. Yachting until then had been a hobby practiced mainly by wealthy ocean trading merchants who were closely connected to skippers of vessels and their builders.

To suit the shallow coastal and inland waters, Dutch boatbuilders had developed a typical sailing craft, with a round, wide hull shape for form stability and leeboards to prevent leeway. These vessels were not suitable for offshore sailing. When Dutch yachtsmen started to commission seagoing yachts, the design confronted boatbuilders with hitherto unknown foreign concepts, since Dutch yacht design had not been based on fast, deep-sea fishing schooners and pilot cutters as had other countries'.

This posed problems that not all yards were willing to solve. A division took place and it still exists at the beginning of the twenty-

J. P. G. Thiebout: *Zerlang.* The charming 23-foot LOA cat-schooner *Zerlang*, built in 1936 and still sailing, is a picture of ease and tranquility. The centerboard design is meant for coastal and estuary cruising. Note the graduated sounding pole in the forerigging, a sure sign that she spends much of her time in shallow water. *Photo courtesy Rutger ten Broeke*

first century. Quite a few yards, like Blom, Piersma and Stofberg, still exclusively produce the traditional types like the Schouw, Lemster Aak, and Schokker (all shallow draft), and they limit developments in building techniques to the parameters dictated by the traditional type of boat.

J. P. G. Thiebout, scion of a wealthy family of bankers and merchants, was a designer and boatbuilder who managed to live and work between historic and contemporary Dutch traditions and actually merged them in a couple of very interesting and beautiful designs.

Little is known about Thiebout's education, although the designer Gait Kroes, who as a

young boy had taken lessons from him in drawing and design, suggested that he must have had some kind of formal education in design.

In 1908 Thiebout, with his friend the boatbuilder H. H. Baay, founded the boatyard Amstel in Amsterdam; it was supported by a board of trustees of wealthy family members and friends. With Thiebout as the designer, the yard specialized in small commercial and pleasure craft for sailing and power, built of wood and of steel. Early on, the designs of Thiebout displayed a freshness and originality that made them different from other contemporary Dutch designs. The partnership with Baay lasted until 1921, after which Baay started a new yard in

Loosdrecht that was successful up until the death of its owner in the 1950's.

Thiebout moved to the town of Zwolle in eastern Netherlands in 1936, where he took a modest job at the railway station. In Zwolle he continued his design activities. Commissions, however, were insufficient to practice full-time, so he entered into a working relationship in nearby Kampen with Gerrit Kroes, boatbuilder and father of designer/builder Gait Kroes. Both father and son were influenced by Thiebout's ideas.

Various yachts designed by Thiebout were built at the Kroes yard prior to World War II and Thiebout's untimely death in 1941. The modest Thiebout seldom published, and not withstanding the fact that many boats of his design are still afloat, little is known about their spiritual father.

In 1946 Thiebout's widow donated his archive to the maritime museum Prins Hendrik in Rotterdam, the Netherlands.

—Rutger ten Broeke

DAVID THOMAS

Born in 1932 · England

David Thomas is the popular designer of some of the most numerous, active, practical, well-mannered, and good-looking production racer/cruiser classes sailing in Europe today, as well as the superbly able, truly sea-tested, 67-foot and 72-foot LOA steel cutters used for the "round the world the wrong way" BT Global Challenge. One of the 67-footers was later sailed singlehanded, nonstop around the world, again "the wrong way," against the wind, breaking a record set in 1971 by Chay Blyth.

Thomas's Hunter and Sigma ranges are best known among mere mortal sailors. Hunter Boats (U.K.) built more than four hundred of the Mini-Ton Rule–influenced, 22-foot LOA National Sonatas from 1975 into the late 1980's. The firm continues to produce his designs for cruisers, racers (including the light-displacement Hunter 707 "sportsboat"), and motorboats. The Sonata still provides excellent club racing and cruising potential at a very affordable price.

Almost four hundred Sigma 33's were built between 1978 and 1991. This class has emerged as the top British Isles club racer, with truly international British Isles and European Championships regularly attracting upwards of sixty boats. The 33 is a particularly fine example of Thomas's ability to create good looks in the modern sense, with the curves seemingly in the right places to avoid a dated appearance. It also perfectly fits the bill as a boat in which one can both cruise and race, with comfortable accommodations and good performance.

Some of Thomas's early work included successful dinghy designs for the restricted Merlin Rocket and National 12 classes, as well as the Unit, which took part in the 1967 IYRU Singlehanded Trials alongside the Bob Miller–designed Contender, and an enduring 1970's classic, the Elizabethan 30 cruiser/racer.

Current work includes a radical, single-handed Open 60 racer featuring a long, shallow bulb keel, twin daggerboards, and movable

David Thomas: Sigma 33. Thomas apparently hit the nail on the head when he drew the Sigma 33. The design remained in continuous production for thirteen years, resulting in almost four hundred yachts, many of which are campaigned as one-design and club racers when they are not engaged in comfortable family cruising. © *Nick Rains/PPL Photo Agency*

ballast and designed for singlehanded racing and the Around Alone race. Its revolutionary but now well-tested freestanding and swinging "Aero Rig" will offer ease of handling and far greater safety from damage or knockdown. Fascinating work from a young-at-heart septuagenarian! —Iain McAllister

HENRI "AMEL" TONET

Born 1912 · France

Like John Brown Herreshoff, the famous builder of Bristol, Rhode Island, Henri Tonet was a talented yachting professional who had lost his eyesight; again, like Herreshoff, he continued to work. Tonet (whose name as a French Resistance fighter was Amel) became a boatbuilder and naval architect in 1946, at Lyon, on his own and self-taught.

There Tonet launched *Suma*, his first sailboat, and then built in series a small wooden centerboard sloop, 5.2 meters long, known as the Mistral class (seventy-one boats were built). In 1951 he discovered fiberglass construction, which became a specialty. In 1953, life dealt him a heavy blow: his eyes, which had been wounded during his time with the resistance during World War II, became infected and rendered him totally blind.

Most other men would have abandoned the trade, but not Tonet. He overcame his handicap and developed a sound sailboat concept, practical and simple, suitable for singlehanded sailing. The type has practical accommodations featuring an absence of bulkheads—the mast is sustained by three girders—and is characterized by an aft cabin, protected center cockpit, powerful engine, and roller-furling gear for the sails.

A dedicated yachtsman, Tonet has several Atlantic and Pacific passages to his credit. After 1957 he settled into a routine of designing only production-built sailboats, each of which is clearly distinguishable from the next. Among his popular designs are the Super Mistral (1957); the Super Mistral Sport (1961); the Euros 39 (1969); the Kirk, an 11.02-meter ketch (1971); the 16-meter Meltem (1974); the 16-meter Super Maramu (1988), still in production; and the 14-meter Santorin (1990). Tonet's boats have proved popular and affordable, democratizing French cruising on both the local and long-distance levels for almost forty years and leaving a distinct mark on European yachting in general.

Located since 1968 in his own yard—Amel's—at La Rochelle, Tonet thought out his sailboats when sailing, imagining new concepts and later describing them to his assistant Jacques Carteau, who would firm them up on the drawing board. In 1997 Tonet gave his boatyard to his partners and retired. —Jacques Taglang

DESMOND THOMAS TOWNSON

Born 1934 · New Zealand

The designer of a number of successful stock boats and one-designs, Des Townson is also a prominent builder of model yachts. He grew up in a sailing family, doing considerable cruising in his father's mullet boat, a traditional local type. The first of Townson's commercially successful designs was the 11-foot Zephyr dinghy,

Des Townson: Townson 32. The Townson 32 and her close sisters were local favorites as cruiser/racers in New Zealand. The classic profile and simple arrangement were trademarks of Townson's design philosophy. *Photo courtesy Leslie Gladwell*

of which 219 were built. The Dart, Mistral, and Starling designs followed, all of them taking their heritage from the earlier Zephyr.

In 1968 he produced *Moonlight*—a cruiser/racer that became the forerunner of the Townson 32 class. *Moonlight* was successfully campaigned in the 1971 One-Ton Cup trials despite not having been designed as a One-Tonner, and this provided great publicity for the designer. In 1974 the first of a hundred Townson 34's was produced. In 1987 Townson started a business building his popular Electron model yacht. Today over six hundred of these almost 3-foot LOA model yachts have been sold, many owned by full-size-boat sailors.

Known to design what he liked, rather than what he felt the public wanted, the quantity of Townson boats still around today is testimony to the wisdom of his ideas. He currently lives in Howick, Auckland.   —Mark Steele

GLENVILLE SINCLAIR TREMAINE

March 5, 1892–March 15, 1986 · United States

Beginning as an apprentice in 1912, Glen Tremaine designed much of the approximately seven-thousand-boat output of the Electric Launch Company, which came to be known as Elco, in Bayonne, New Jersey. Thirty-seven years later, Tremaine was the company's last official employee.

Elco was the United States' first large-scale production builder. Its most popular models were built in lots of fifty, greatly reducing the purchase price and offering a reliable standardized product that made boat ownership affordable for a wider range of people. Tremaine was able to create boats with the broad appeal necessary for this approach, an appeal that is still evident as yachtsmen and collectors cherish their Elco powerboats today.

Tremaine began his career as an apprentice shipfitter at the Bath Iron Works in Maine. He educated himself as a draftsman with the help of correspondence courses, and worked briefly for designers Henry Douglas Bacon and Morris Whitaker. He was hired by Elco on March 4, 1912, one day before his twentieth birthday.

Working initially under designer Irwin Chase, Tremaine was chief draftsman during World War I, when the company built 550 subchasers for the British Admiralty in 488 working days. In 1923 Chase was promoted to general manager and Tremaine became chief designer. In the following years Tremaine, with the help of his assistant, Alfred "Bill" Fleming, designed numerous standardized cruisers ranging up to 56 feet in length, as well as a number of custom yachts, some of them considerably larger. While later models showed some moderate streamlining, many of Elco's most well-known designs are from the pre-streamlining era. Hulls were easily driven displacement types pushed by small engines. The emphasis was on comfort and economy.

With the onset of World War II, the U.S. Navy sought Elco's help in creating the PT boat, and Tremaine became its primary designer. Elco built 399 PT boats during the war, and at one time turned out one of the 80-footers every sixty hours. Elco lost money while it was struggling to downsize in the postwar period and, despite having made a $10 million profit during the war, was shut down by its parent company on the last day of 1949. Glen Tremaine was the man who locked the doors. Among his last duties was the transfer of the Elco drawings and other materials to a nearby building that was said to be fireproof.

Tremaine went on to run a marina in New Jersey and continued to design boats under his own name. He retired in 1957 and moved to Florida. In 1963 the "fireproof" building containing the Elco plans burned down, taking with it most of the existing Elco drawings.

—Daniel B. MacNaughton

WILLIAM H. TRIPP JR.

1920–October 12, 1971 · United States

One of the 1950's and 1960's most innovative and successful designers working in the CCA cruiser/racer type, Bill Tripp is probably best known as the designer of the Hinckley Bermuda 40, which has had the longest production run of any large fiberglass boat.

Tripp's designs have a distinctive look that combines an exciting feel of modernity with clearly evident connections to traditional aesthetics. Almost all have strong conventional sheers with a relatively high bow and low stern. In many cases the ends are quite long, with a strongly curving bow profile and a wide counter terminating in a shapely and nearly vertical transom. Tripp also innovated in a light-displacement hull type, with a large vertical transom and no aft overhang, coupled with a short bow.

Often Tripp employed dramatically higher freeboard than was common in his day, usually combined with a flush deck and a small doghouse. This was partly to simplify construction and to provide the excellent deck space for which his boats are known, but it was also an adaptation to the trend toward light-displacement which, by literally removing volume from the hull below the waterline, meant either that interiors got smaller or freeboard got higher to compensate.

Some designers adopted reverse sheers to increase volume amidships without raising the whole sheer, but Tripp kept a strong sheer and made the topsides higher all around. At the time the effect was shocking to traditionalists (although not as shocking as the reverse-sheer boats), but his designs performed well and were dry and roomy. Today, designers have gone so much further in the same direction that Tripp's designs look quite moderate in character.

The character, seaworthiness, and overall success of Tripp's designs constituted a good recommendation for the CCA Rule under which they were designed, and Tripp fought hard against the IOR when it was proposed as a replacement. After the IOR was introduced, he had no choice but to design boats that accommodated it for a short period near the end of his career.

Growing up in Bayside, Long Island, New York, Tripp began sketching boats as a child and raced in the Star class as a teenager. He was never formally educated in naval architecture, but like many other designers was self-taught and then apprenticed to established design firms. His first such apprenticeship was with Philip L. Rhodes in New York City, with whom he worked for two years.

Tripp joined the Coast Guard during World War II and served in the famous Offshore Patrol, in which yachts were pressed into service to search for enemy submarines off America's East Coast. This gave him an appreciation for the kind of strength and ability a yacht needed to endure actual offshore conditions. After the war he worked for Sparkman and Stephens in New York City.

A centerboard sloop of Tripp's design appeared in 1950 in *Yachting* magazine's design section, and in 1952 he opened his own office. Subsequent designs included *Touché*, a flush-decked, 48-foot keel/centerboard sloop with many innovative features, including a thick, foil-shaped centerboard, unusually full underwater lines, and a unique dual-midships-cockpit deck layout. *Touché* began a long and successful career on the race course and helped to popularize Tripp's work.

One of the earliest designers to utilize fiberglass construction, Tripp's first design for the new material was the well-regarded Block Island 40 in 1958.

In 1959 Tripp designed the Bermuda 40 for Henry R. Hinckley and Company. She is an evolution of the Block Island 40 and had successes in the Transpac Race, the Transatlantic Race, and the Halifax Race, among others.

Bill Tripp Jr.: Bermuda 40. The Hinckley Bermuda 40 has had the longest production run of any fiberglass cruising auxiliary. While superior construction and finish deserve some of the credit, the rest goes to Tripp's design, which combines timeless beauty, moderate proportions, and a simple, practical, and roomy layout both below and on deck. *Photo courtesy the Hinckley Company*

The Bermuda 40 was the first fiberglass boat built by Hinckley.

The success of the 75-foot LOA sloop *Southern Star* in the Miami-Nassau Race led to the commissioning of *Ondine*, a 57-foot aluminum yawl. She became one of the most successful racing yachts in history, taking first in Class A in the 1960 Transatlantic Race and the 1964 Bermuda Race, as well as winning prizes in a majority of the many other races she entered.

In 1964 a Tripp-designed Pearson Invicta named *Burgoo* won the Bermuda Race. At 37 feet she was both the smallest boat and the first fiberglass boat ever to win. In the mid-1960's Tripp began a long association with the Columbia Yacht Corporation, which resulted in a number of designs ranging from 20 to 57 feet in length. He also drew several designs for the Coronado Company.

A new 73-foot *Ondine* was commissioned in the mid-1960's, along with *Blackfin*, another boat built to nearly the same design. Both were dramatic and serious contenders for course records and line honors in every event they entered. They were two of the final superboats built to the CCA Rule.

Bill Tripp was killed in an accident at the age of fifty-one, at the height of his career. His son, William Tripp III, is currently practicing yacht design in East Norwalk, Connecticut.

—Daniel B. MacNaughton

JOHN TRUMPY

January 5, 1879–September 3, 1963
Norway/United States

Working as head designer for the Mathis Yacht Building Company (later John Trumpy and Sons), John Trumpy helped to develop and perfect a type of shoal-draft, luxury power yacht that was referred to as a "houseboat," though it bore little resemblance to the type of boats now commonly identified with that term.

Trumpy houseboat designs show considerable evolution over the years, but from the beginning they were handsome and elegant shoal-draft power yachts. They were only like a house in that they had accommodations not just in the hull, but also in a long deckhouse providing in effect a "second story." This configuration doubled the accommodations compared to a typical cruiser and permitted a larger window area. They often had a partially shaded open deck above the deckhouse for lounging.

Houseboats were popular for long-term living aboard, and were specifically designed for seasonal travel up and down the East Coast of the United States through the sheltered inland passages, which would later be improved and referred to as the Intracoastal Waterway. Early Trumpy houseboats were somewhat blocky in form, but beginning in 1923 he began to design them with a graceful aft overhang and a more shapely overall appearance. They continued to evolve into a faster, better-looking, and more seaworthy type, and Trumpy soon became the most highly regarded designer working in the genre. Both the Mathis and Trumpy boatbuilding yards were known for their very high standards of material and workmanship.

Trumpy was born and raised in Norway. His father and grandfather were shipbuilders and owned a yard in Bradbenken. He was educated at the Bergen Tekniske Skule and Die Technische Hoschschule near Berlin, and apprenticed at a shipyard in Kiel. He moved to the United States in 1902 at the age of twenty-three and took a job as a draftsman at the New York Shipbuilding Company. Born with the first name Johan, he changed it to John after living in the states for a few years. In 1909 he went to work for the John H. Mathis Company, a commercial shipbuilding operation in Camden, New Jersey. By 1910 he had helped conceive and found the Mathis Yacht Building Company,

an offshoot of the larger shipyard. Trumpy's first design for Mathis was for the 70-foot houseboat *Cocopomelo* in 1910. He also drew nonhouseboat power yachts that had lower superstructures and were often deeper and more suitable for offshore use.

Trumpy is not widely known for his sailboat designs, but he did design and build twenty-seven sailboats, including two motorsailers, and five sailing yachts named *Sea Call* for his own use. He personally preferred sail to power, and as often happens this perspective enabled him to imbue his power yachts with an unusually graceful and even "salty" appeal. In 1925 Trumpy designed and Mathis built *Sequoia II* (later simply *Sequoia*) which would become the U.S. presidential yacht, serving nine presidents until she was sold by the government in 1977.

In 1952, John Trumpy turned over day-to-day operations of the yard to his son, John Jr., but continued to do the yard's design work, often with his son's assistance. After his father's death, John Trumpy Jr. continued to operate the yard and to design yachts. The Trumpy yard, then located in Annapolis, Maryland, closed its doors in 1973 rather than convert to fiberglass construction or reduce quality in response to a lack of good materials or skilled labor at prices that seemed reasonable to the management. At that time, John Trumpy Jr. destroyed the plans for the first 206 yachts Mathis-Trumpy produced, saving only the plans which he had drawn himself or with which he had assisted. Approximately ninety-one Trumpy yachts survive, the oldest being the 68-foot *Ibis*, built in 1912, and the newest the 72-foot *Gerifay*, built in 1972. —Daniel B. MacNaughton

John Trumpy: *Treasure IV.* The appeal of large wooden Trumpy yachts is evident in the 67-foot 6-inch LOA yacht *Treasure IV* (ex-*Sereno III*), built in 1955 at John Trumpy and Sons yard in Annapolis, Maryland. © *Peter Barlow*

U–V

HENRY U. "HANK" UHLE

Born 1919 · United States

One of the most versatile and experienced naval architects of his generation, Henry U. Uhle worked at Sparkman and Stephens for over forty-two years and had a major hand in many of their most notable designs.

Uhle began his professional career as an associate of longtime *Motor Boat* editor and West-lawn School of Design head Gerald T. White, and of the Philadelphia yacht designer Frederick C. Geiger. After brief stints with Elco and Philip Rhodes, and wartime service with the Annapolis Yacht Yard, Uhle joined Sparkman and Stephens in New York, working there from the mid-1940's until his retirement in 1987. Although Uhle was involved in a wide range of naval and commercial vessel designs, yachts were always his primary interest.

Among the Sparkman and Stephens designs to which Uhle contributed heavily were the 49-foot yawl *Eroica*, the 114-foot motoryacht *Aurora*, the 73-foot yawl *Baccara*, the 116-foot ketch *Tiziana*, and William Simon's 124-foot ketch *Freedom*. Uhle did most of the research, design, and supervisory work on Rudolph Shaefer's 104-foot replica of the schooner yacht *America*. Now living in Allentown, Pennsylvania, Hank Uhle is still an active design consultant.

—Llewellyn Howland III

AAGE UTZON

1885–1970 · Denmark

It is as a designer of the unique, roomy, and very seaworthy Danish spidsgatters (double-enders) that Utzon is best known. He was born in Hellebaek near Helsingør (Elsinore) and educated as ship engineer and naval architect at Armstrong College, Newcastle, in England.

Utzon was later employed at the Danish shipyards Bermeister and Wain in Copenhagen, the Aalborg Yard, and Helsingør Shipyard. In

Aage Utzon: *Rollo*. The 38-Square-Meter spidsgatter *Rollo* is a typical and apparently perfect example of her class. Initially spidsgatters offered competitive racing in a boat that was unusually seaworthy and commodious. Many examples survive, and most are now carefully maintained and visually stunning cruising boats. *Photo courtesy Bent Aarre*

1928 there were several authorized spidsgatter classes, for 20-, 26-, 30-, 38-, 45-, and 55-square meters of sail area. Utzon designed to all these types, as did his Danish rivals, Georg Berg and M. S. J. Hansen, but he also designed so many custom boats that it is impossible to count them all.

After World War II, Utzon designed for American clients, and many Danish boats were exported to the United States and Canada. Some are still sailing. Many of his boats performed very well in races. For instance, a 30-Square-Meter spidsgatter won the Skaw race and the Around Gotland race in RORC Class IV. In the 1950's and 1960's his sight began to fail, but he continued to draw until he was completely blind.

—Bent Aarre

JOHANNES W. M. VALENTIJN

Born November 28, 1948
The Netherlands/United States

Johannes (Johan) Valentijn is most closely associated with his designs of *five* 12-Meter yachts that competed in *four* America's Cup campaigns under *three* separate flags. But this versatile Dutch-born naval architect has also drawn numerous one-off racing and cruising sailboat designs, and a few motoryachts, each possessing a flair of originality and engineering sophistication that secure his reputation off the America's Cup's course as well.

Born in Ter Aar, the Netherlands, Valentijn entered the Technical University of Haarlem in 1965. While studying, he apprenticed at the de Vries Lentsch shipyard in Amsterdam doing structural design of commercial vessels, at other commercial yards, and at the Netherlands Ship Model Basin (MARIN), in Wageningen, where he gained practical understanding of towing-tank model testing.

Upon graduation in 1969 with a BS in naval architecture and marine engineering, Valentijn joined ARCO, the design firm, where he did structural design and building supervision for motoryachts of 28 meters and 33 meters built by Dutch commercial yards.

In 1971 Valentijn emigrated to the United States to join the preeminent naval architecture firm Sparkman and Stephens in New York City. During the next five years, working under Olin and Rod Stephens, Valentijn designed and engineered some thirty-five racing and cruising sailing yachts between 30 and 90 feet long, including several successful Admiral's Cup competitors. He also designed production yachts for several series builders, including Nautor's Swan in Finland.

Valentijn left Sparkman and Stephens in 1975 to establish his own design, engineering, and project management firm in Newport, Rhode Island. In 1976 he moved temporarily to Australia to join Bob Miller (later Ben Lexcen) in

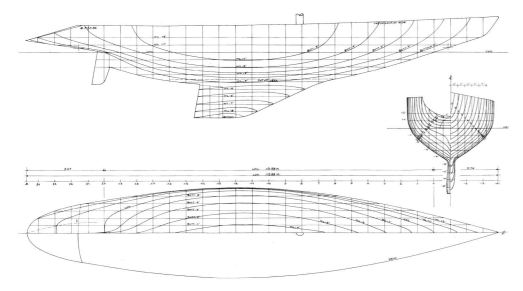

Johan Valentijn: *France III.* Designed for Baron Marcel Bich's third and final America's Cup challenge in 1980, this 65-foot 7-inch 12-Meter is particularly lovely in form. Her design emphasizes ease of handling, partly to compensate for sails that were unlikely to be as good as those of the American defender. © *Chevalier & Taglang*

the design of Alan Bond's America's Cup challenger *Australia*. Conceived particularly for light airs, *Australia* lost to the Sparkman and Stephens-designed *Courageous* with Ted Turner at the helm.

For the 1980 America's Cup campaign, Valentijn moved to France, serving as chief designer and builder for Baron Marcel Bich, in the ballpoint-pen magnate's last of three unsuccessful attempts to wrest Le Coup d'Amérique from the New York Yacht Club. Valentijn designed a handsome 12-Meter, *France III* (with blue, white, and red graphics), and supervised construction of a new boatyard to build the boat.

For the controversial 1983 Cup campaign, Valentijn designed the smallest 12-Meter, *Magic,* for Dennis Connor, while Valentijn's former Sparkman and Stephens colleagues designed *Spirit of America.* Neither proved fast. Connor chose Valentijn to design the burgundy-red *Liberty,* aboard which Conner lost the "Auld Mug" to Ben Lexcen's winged-keel *Australia II.*

Valentijn returned undaunted for the 1987 Cup campaign in blustery Fremantle with *Eagle,* for the Newport Beach, California, syndicate. Although a graphic masterpiece, *Eagle* did not become the American challenger.

Finally shunning the Cup, Valentijn returned to custom design, engineering, and consulting. During the 1980's he designed cruising sailboats 35 and 40 feet long for the French builder Du Four; cruisers 38, 42, and 51 feet long for the American builder Endeavour; and several custom yachts up to 65 feet long. Valentijn next set up a modern American Bureau of Shipping plastic facility to manufacture the multipurpose

"Saroca" (sail-row-canoe), then created a fiberglass facility to revive the dormant "SeaSled" concept.

In 1992 Valentijn's professional life took a different direction when he cofounded Lifesource International, which, in cooperation with UNICEF and the World Bank, developed basic products for the people of developing nations to meet water and sanitation needs, and he patented a family of advanced thermosetting polymers.

Valentijn returned to yachting in 1995 as production manager for the Burger Boat Company

in Manitowoc, Wisconsin, helping the once-bankrupt, hundred-year-old builder return to a much-deserved solid footing. Later Valentijn left Burger to consult on European yacht-building projects.　　　　—Jack A. Somer

JOSEPH B. VAN DEUSEN

1832–November 1875 · United States

Schooner yachts by the American yacht modeler Joseph van Deusen exerted a strong influence on American yachting during the 1860's and 1870's. Born in the Mohawk Valley of upstate New York, van Deusen moved to New York City, where he worked with George Steers and William H. Webb. His first design was *Gipsy* in 1857, followed by *Narragansett.*

Following the end of the Civil War in 1865, van Deusen took advantage of the sudden increase in demand for yachts and established a boatyard in New York City together with his brother. They modeled and built several famous schooners, which soon would leave their mark on American yachting: *Fleetwing* (108 feet), *Fleur de Lys* (108 feet), *Phantom* (101 feet 6 inches), and *Rambler.* Together with *Alarm* (122 feet 6 inches), built also by van Deusen, they all participated in the first defense of the America's Cup in 1870. December 1866 saw the famous race between *Vesta*, *Henrietta*, and *Fleetwing* across the Atlantic. Acting as a judge, van Deusen sailed on *Fleetwing.*

In 1871 van Deusen oversaw the complete rebuild of James Gordon Bennett's famous

Joseph van Deusen: *Mohawk.* *Mohawk* was the 141-foot LOA, 6-foot draft, centerboard schooner whose capsize in 1876 ultimately led American yachting away from the shallow national type toward a deeper and better-ballasted form. *Painting reproduced from a Currier & Ives print*

Dauntless (123 feet 11 inches, formerly *Hirondelle*) from sloop to schooner, as well as the design of the fast schooner *Columbia* (108 feet), defender of that year's America's Cup, before she broke down. A year later he modeled the schooner *Viking* (108 feet 1 inch). He also designed steam yachts (*Ideal*, 1873), as well as several gunboats for the Spanish government in 1869.

Fate probably was merciful to van Deusen, for he did not live to witness the controversy created by his last yacht, *Mohawk*. Launched a few months before his death, the 141-foot *Mohawk* was the biggest centerboard schooner of her time. The following year, in 1876, *Mohawk* made headlines when she capsized in a squall while her anchor was being hoisted; several lives were lost. Barely damaged, the yacht was recovered and acquired by the U.S. government. Her centerboard was converted to a keel, but her capsize triggered a bitter debate on the relative merits of the then-prevalent shallow-centerboard type of which *Mohawk*, with a draft of only 6 feet, had been an extreme exponent. The debate lasted several years and ultimately resulted in the general adoption of a healthier and deeper type of yacht in America.

—Claas van der Linde

CHARLES DOUGLAS "DOUG" VAN PATTEN II

April 1, 1911–February 15, 1990 · United States

Doug Van Patten advanced the development of practical high-speed powerboats with a new type of stepped hydroplane in the 1930's. As chief designer at the Greavette Boat Company, he produced handsome and dramatically styled mahogany runabouts.

A native of Detroit, Michigan, Van Patten's family moved to Pelham, New York, where he began to hang around the boatyards of City Island. He met noted powerboat designer George F. Crouch, who gave him his first job at the Henry B. Nevins yard in the late 1920's. They became lifelong friends. Van Patten started off by working summers on the loft floor and later became a draftsman. When Crouch left Nevins to become dean of the Webb Institute, Van Patten was inspired to return to school. He attended Tri-State College in Indiana and later the College of Science and Engineering at Columbia University in New York, where he earned a degree in mechanical engineering in 1933.

After graduation Van Patten briefly worked for an aeronautical engineering firm, and in 1935 signed on as a designer for the Eddy Marine Corporation in Bay City, Michigan, staying for two years and designing some of their most suc-

cessful powerboats. He soon got into racing powerboat design, inventing the "double concave two-stepped bottom" and "vertex paraboloid hull," a special type of stepped hydroplane.

Van Patten became chief designer of the Greavette Boat Company in Gravenhurst, Ontario, in 1937, where many of the firm's boats were destined for the Muskoka Lake Region. There he designed Greavette's Custom Streamliner and Sheerliner models. In 1939 his *Miss Canada III*, powered with a Miller V-12 engine, won numerous races at speeds up to 122 mph, including the Gold Cup world championship in the 12-liter class.

In 1940 Van Patten moved a few miles north to Bracebridge Falls to work for the Minett-Shields Boat Company, which had been commissioned by the Canadian government to design a boat similar to the United States' PT boat. Van Patten's Motor Torpedo Boat, or MTB, was the same size as an American PT, but it had two-thirds the power, was faster and more fuel efficient, and had a longer range due to the vertex paraboloid hull. Sixteen were built.

After World War II Van Patten did design work for both Greavette and Minett-Shields, creating both racing boats and runabouts until the mid-1950's. In 1946 a repowered and redesigned *Miss Canada III*, with a V-12 Merlin replacing the Miller, set a speed record for Gold Cup racers of 119 mph. Van Patten's designs are seeing renewed public interest with the revival of interest in classic runabouts.

—Daniel B. MacNaughton

MARC VAN PETEGHEM

Born January 9, 1957

VINCENT LAURIOT PRÉVOST

Born August 20, 1955

France

In partnerships between naval architects, usually one partner is doing the creative work, while the other is managing the business or performing calculations. It is unusual to find two creative personalities working to the same pattern, but such is the case with Marc Van Peteghem and Vincent Lauriot Prévost.

Lauriot Prévost was born in Dinard and grew up sailing with his parents in north Brittany. He was soon as enthralled by sailing as they were, devoting his holidays to just about anything that floated. Once he finished his secondary education, he passed the Merchant Navy School test, but decided after several months of internship that he was more interested in yacht design than commercial shipping.

At the time, the only school in Europe for training naval architects was in Southampton, England, at the College of Higher Education, Yacht and Boat Design section. Fifteen days after his arrival in Southampton, Lauriot Prévost met Van Peteghem, who was there for the same purpose. From their common passion, an immediate friendship was born.

Van Peteghem also grew up with yachting parents. Born in Paris, he learned sailing while cruising in the Mediterranean aboard the family yacht. When he was nine, he built

C. Douglas Van Patten. This 30-footer shows the styling that made the Greavette Boat Company famous. Van Patten had the technical know-how to design record-breaking powerboats, plus the ability to create an artistic expression of their speed. Today we associate shapes like this with fiberglass, but these bullet-like speedboats were all varnished mahogany. *Photo courtesy Charles Van Patten III*

a small dinghy and already knew that he was going to design boats. In 1974, he raced a Contessa 35 in the English Channel. He then raced aboard *Variana,* a Dick Carter–designed steel centerboarder, and on *Révolution,* Jean-Marie Finot's famous Admiral's Cup winner. But it was when he encountered the trimaran *Blue Amnesia,* a Dick Newick–designed Val 38, that he knew he had found a pearl. The simplicity of the concept and the construction, linked to the fearsome efficiency of the multihull, captured the imagination of the young naval architect.

In 1983, the two designers opened their own company, Van Peteghem Lauriot Prévost (VPLP) Yacht Design, by designing the advanced 50-foot foil trimaran *Gérard Lambert* for the Observer Singlehanded Transatlantic Race.

Their first years in business were difficult, but 1986 was a good year, with the Formula 40 trimaran *Biscuit Cantreau* and the 75-foot trimaran *Poulain* showing great promise. The next year, *Biscuit Cantreau 2* won the Formula 40 World Championship, *Poulain* arrived second in the Tour of Europe Race, and the Jeanneau yards hired them for the design of their cruising catamaran, the Lagoon 55.

There then followed a number of highly successful racing multihulls, including Formula 40 champions, ORMA 60-foot trimarans, and several offshore racers that set course records in the Round Ireland, Round Isle of Wight, Round Britain, and Round the World races as well as transoceanic records in both the Atlantic and the Pacific. The office has developed ten new Lagoon models for what is now Bénéteau, the largest boatbuilder in the world.

VPLP has also made significant strides into the superyacht market, designing luxury catamarans ranging from 77 to 220 feet in length. In 1994, VPLP worked with Dassault and EADS Company to create *L'Hydroptère,* a 60-footer envisaged by Eric Tabarly that reaches speeds of 40 knots under sail. The design team is proud that they have launched both the largest racing trimaran in the world (the 110-foot *Geronimo* of 2001) and the largest sailing catamaran in the world (*Douce France,* at 138 feet).

The French 60-foot trimaran class has some notable VPLP designs competing with, among others, Nigel Irens and Marc Lombard yachts. The VPLP designs include *Hitachi* (1988), *Pierre 1er II* (1990), *Primagaz* (1990), *Foncia* (1997), and *Sodebo* (2002).

Thus, more than by the number of their designs, the two designers have proved by their results that two talents, working with open and constructive dialogue, can be a formula for success.

The VPLP Yacht Design office is in Paris, France. —François Chevalier.

Marc Van Peteghem and Vincent Lauriot Prévost: *Douce France.* When she was launched in 2002 in France, the 138-foot aluminum *Douce France* was the largest sailing catamaran in the world. *Photo by Yves Ronzier, courtesy VPLP*

Marc Van Peteghem and Vincent Lauriot Prévost: *Geronimo.* Designed for long-distance record-breaking runs, the 110-foot trimaran *Geronimo* was built in France of carbon fiber. *Photo courtesy VPLP*

René van der Velden: *Jules Verne.* The fast commuter *Jules Verne*, built by Vitters Shipyard in the Netherlands, was highly admired and earned van der Velden worldwide recognition. He continues to design production and custom yachts for shipyards in his native land and as far afield as Turkey and Russia. *Photo courtesy René van der Velden*

GILLES VATON

Born 1952 · France

The sailing yacht designs of Gilles Vaton find their elegance in the unique aesthetic concepts of their creator. The distinction of his designs is not simply the result of a group of features (such as the overhangs and the sheer); rather he creates a unified whole that in its overall character is easily identified as a Vaton. Even some well-known superyachts drawn by other designers have been inspired by his style so much that one might think they are Vaton's work.

Born in Quimper, Brittany, Vaton studied in Nantes. He spent his holidays in the Isle Tudy or in La Baule on the Atlantic shore, where he attended sailing schools and joined the Sea Scouts. After high school he began an apprenticeship at the Rouillard research unit in Nantes, which had designed the structure of Eric Tabarly's trimaran *Pen Duick IV*. During this period Vaton was involved in the develop-

Gilles Vaton: *Champagne Charlie* (Opposite). This big sloop has a low and aggressive look that is much in character with her role as a flat-out racer. © *Peter Barlow*

ment of a revolutionary yacht drawn by Rouillard, a One-Tonner fitted with a fork keel, like those that would be seen in San Diego in 1992 on some America's Cup Class yachts.

Vaton spent a year in England at Illingworth and Primrose, and then met Michel Briand, a La Rochelle yachtsman who asked him to sail aboard *Kriter* for the 1973–74 Whitbread. On his return, seduced by *Pen Duick VI*, he joined André Mauric's office in Marseilles.

Vaton designed his first yacht for a contest sponsored by the Beg-Rohu National Yachting School (Ecole Nationale de Voile), and in 1979 he set up his own business at Marseilles. His 1981 maxi, *Charles Heidsieck III*, which won second place in the 1981–82 Whitbread, was a good measure of his success.

In 1984 he designed the big, elegant hydrofoil *Charles Heidsieck IV*, and soon thereafter *Provence*, which have never had their equal. The Gilles Vaton office has produced nearly forty yachts more than 20 meters long, plus the 35-meter *Arrayan II*, and has drawn production sailboats that have been built in the thousands, along with a number of motoryachts and commercial vessels.

Giles Vaton practices in Cannes, France.

—François Chevalier

RENÉ VAN DER VELDEN

Born April 23, 1958 · The Netherlands

René van der Velden's work usually bears an external touch of classicism, although it is modern to the core, which places him squarely in today's "modern classic" revival. But van der Velden does not merely design replicas: like the best of his contemporaries—who came of age with the computer—he merges shapes from the old school into refreshingly new shapes that were unimaginable yesterday.

Van der Velden was born in Zeist, the Netherlands. His early years resemble those of many other naval architects: he was obsessed by boats, idled away many a school hour sketching boats, and couldn't wait to get out on the water. He studied engineering in Utrecht between 1974 and 1978 and majored in naval architecture at the Haarlem Technical School (HTS).

During school years, van der Velden worked summers at a local boatyard. But as part of his curriculum he also apprenticed at Lunstroo Custom Design and worked beside Fritz de Voogt, Feadship's renowned chief designer. Van der Velden also did ship-resistance studies at the Nedlloyd Shipping Company and performed research for Holland's fishery department.

After an interruption for national service on a minesweeper, he graduated from HTS in 1983. Van der Velden then went to work for Pieter Beeldsnijder, handling general arrangements, and construction and lines plans of power and sailing yachts. He assisted with one of Beeldsnijder's masterpieces, the 110-foot schooner *Gloria*. In 1985 he joined Willem de Vries Lentsch, to do similar work for sail and motor yachts up to 200 feet long.

In January 1994 van der Velden established his own office in Amersfoort. Among his outstanding designs are several series of semi-custom motoryachts between 84 and 123 feet long being built by Moonen Shipyards in the Netherlands. In 2000 the Vitters Shipyard launched his voluptuous 61-foot speedster, *Jules Verne*, inspired by American pre–World War II commuters. (*Jules Verne* was nominated for a *ShowBoats International* design award.) Van der Velden has created interiors for the Trintella 42, 47, 55, and 65 sailing yachts, and designs all the handsome long-range Explorer motoryachts between 65 and 125 feet long being built by Peer Gynt Yachts in Antalya, Turkey. He has also designed several custom motoryachts up to 123 feet long.

René van der Velden continues to develop new wrinkles in classicism, having simultaneously mastered the disciplines of naval architecture and interior/exterior design. His office is in Amersfoort, the Netherlands.

—Jack A. Somer

BRUNO VERONESE

1911–1991 · Italy

While he served as an officer in the Italian navy during World War II and for some time after the war worked aboard major Italian liners, Bruno Veronese spent most of his life designing yachts, supervising their construction, and sailing in yachts of all sizes.

In the late 1940's Veronese opened his yacht design practice in Genoa, producing a series of small cruising yachts that would be described as classic nowadays. Heavy, seaworthy yachts of pleasing design, they encompassed Admiral Turner's metacentric theories, as advanced by English designer T. Harrison Butler. These theories attempted to quantify the factors contributing to good helm balance and steering under a wide range of conditions and at varying angles of heel, and resulted in a degree of symmetry between the shapes of a hull's forebody and aft body.

The theory worked, but today's designers usually feel that the degree of symmetry it encouraged conflicts with other important per-

Bruno Veronese: *Selene*. The 12-meter motorsailer *Selene* was launched in 1951 at the Cantieri Costaguta in Genova-Voltri, Italy, for Mario Cucchi. *Photo courtesy Silvia Minas*

Bruno Veronese: *Tyrsa*. The 20-meter ketch *Tyrsa* is shown moored at Portofino, Italy, in May 1960. She was launched in 1958 at the Cantieri di Pisa in Pisa, Italy, for Roberto Bencini. *Photo courtesy Silvia Minas*

formance objectives. The designs represented a turning point in Italian sailing-yacht design at a time when long, narrow, and deep International Rule classes were still dominant in the Mediterranean. Veronese's designs, such as *Flora* in 1962–63, became known abroad after they were published in British sailing magazines as prizewinners in small yacht design competitions.

Veronese's designs of boats under 10 meters in overall length tended to be of relatively heavy displacement and had fine ends with pointed sterns. His larger yachts and motorsailers, such as *Nausicaa* (16 meters LOA), *Val II*

Bruno Veronese: *L'Euridice.* From his most popular Flora design, Veronese built *L'Euridice* for himself. Launched in 1963 at Cantieri Canaletti in La Spezia, Italy, the 9.1-meter sloop continues to reign among beautiful, seaworthy, old wooden boats under sail. *Drawing courtesy Silvia Minas*

(17.20 meters LOA), and *Val III* (21 meters LOA), tended to follow English designer J. Laurent Giles's ideas for large yachts, as displayed in his famous *Leopard* design. They emphasized medium to light displacement, shallow sections, long sailing lines, generous transom, and the ability to be easily propelled to high speeds under either power or sail.

Immediately after the war, Veronese became Italy's pioneer in yachts adapted to the RORC Rule, and helped to popularize the type. He was also an advocate of improved boatbuilding skills in young shipwrights and encouraged a more widespread appreciation of nautical culture.

A brilliant writer, Veronese contributed articles on yacht design, navigation, and cruising to major yachting magazines such as *Yachting World, Yachting Monthly, Voiles et Voiliers, Vela e Motore,* and *Rivista Marittima.*

Under his pen name "Capitano Black," Veronese wrote his book *Yachting,* the first comprehensive modern manual for yachtsmen by an Italian author; it was published in 1948 by Federazione Italiana Vela, Genova, and re-printed in 1962. His book *Yacht—Progetto e Costruzione* (Editrice Incontri Nautici, Roma) was published in 1991 after his death. About thirty yachts were built to Bruno Veronese's designs.

—Silvia Minas

JAVIER VISIERS

Born 1942 · Spain

Javier Visiers is best known internationally as the designer of the Spanish Whitbread Round the World Race entries *Fortuna Lights* (1984–85) and *Fortuna Extra Lights* (1989–90), the latter rebuilt as the wing-mizzen ketch *Fortuna* for the 1993–94 race. During the second leg of the 1989–90 race, the 77-foot LOA maxi *Fortuna Lights* established a record twenty-four hour run of 405 miles.

After finishing engineering studies at Barcelona, Visiers studied yacht design and boatyard management at Southampton College of Technology (to become the Southampton Institute in 1984) in England from 1964 to 1968. He has designed a series of stylish and successful production yachts, including the

Javier Visiers: *Fortuna.* In the second leg of the 1989–90 Whitbread Round the World Race the 77-foot BOC racer *Fortuna* made a record twenty-four-hour run of 405 miles. In this photo she displays the form that makes such a feat seem possible. *Photo courtesy Javier Visiers*

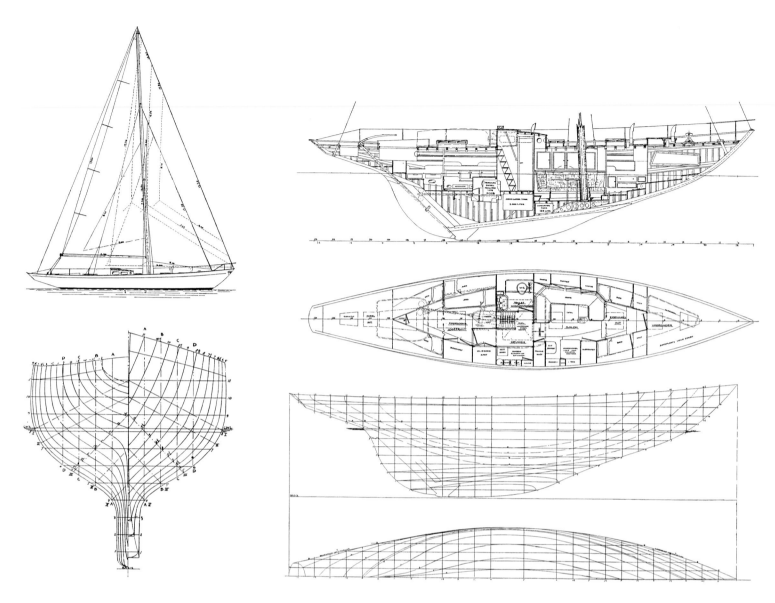

Gerard de Vries Lentsch Jr.: *Olivier van Noort. Olivier van Noort* was de Vries Lentsch's first independent design commission. She was launched in 1938. The 55-foot *Olivier* was a successful ocean racer from the first, and twenty years later was part of the Dutch Admiral's Cup team of 1959, beaten in the Channel Race only by the brand-new *Ramrod* and the famous Rhodes-designed *Carina. Drawing courtesy Rutger ten Broeke*

Spanish Noray series, ranging from 35 to 50 feet; the Danish-built Granada 35 and 38; and Spain's most popular production cruiser/racer, the Fortuna 9, with 280 boats built and counting.

Apart from competing in the 1984–85 Whitbread, *Fortuna Lights* was also winner of the 1983 Transmed Regatta (La Grande Motte–Alexandria–La Grande Motte) and the 1992 Ruta del Descubrimiento Transatlantic Race.

Visiers practices in Gerona, Spain.

—John Lynch with Iain McAllister

GERARD DE VRIES LENTSCH II

1883–July 9, 1973 · The Netherlands

Although one of the younger sons of Gerard de Vries Lentsch I, founder of the de Vries Lentsch boatbuilding dynasty, Gerard II did not automatically start his professional career at his father's famous boatyard "Het Fort" in Nieuwen-

dam. His two brothers, Jan and Willem I, already had important positions at the yard and it did not seem obvious that young Gerard would find a place of his own there.

Instead, Gerard II went to "Ambachtschool" in Amsterdam, a primary vocational educational institute that focused on hands-on technical skills. There he was introduced to engineering and drafting and acquired much practical working knowledge. However, after completing his education he was unable to find employment in the boatbuilding industry, so when the burgeoning use of the bicycle in Holland attracted his attention, he found a place as an apprentice in a small bicycle factory in Amsterdam. There, Gerard operated a small pedal-driven lathe, smoothing the various parts before soldering them together with copper.

After observing seventeen-year-old Gerard's dexterity, his brother Jan finally offered him a job in the family yard, where, with the

help of his brother Willem, he began to develop his skills in design and engineering. His previous training as an engineer at Ambachtschool proved to be a great help, although like so many other well-known designers and builders, Gerard II based his talents largely on a firm, practical knowledge of boatbuilding. Only hand tools were used; wood was delivered by the mill in rough planks and further cut and shaped with handsaws, axes, and adzes at the yard.

In spite of working seventy-two hours a week and more as a carpenter, Gerard II continued to develop his skills as a designer. In a

Opposite: Gerard de Vries Lentsch Jr.: *Brandaris. Brandaris* is a 45-foot 11-inch Lemster Aak, the first sailing vessel type to which the word *yacht* was applied, in the seventeenth century. She was built of steel in 1950. A sistership, built in 1952, is still sailed by the Dutch royal family. © *Peter Barlow*

later interview he spoke about another carpenter who quit his job. When his father asked the carpenter if he did not receive enough pay, the man replied, "I do, but then I don't have time to do anything with the money!"

The family business was running well during this period prior to World War I, and the de Vries Lentsch family established a good name in the Netherlands and abroad. But much to Gerard I's grief, his sons did not get along well. There was a contest of wills between the two older brothers, leaving little space for the younger. Eventually Gerard II separated himself from the family business and started his own yard in Amsterdam, first building dinghies and small working boats. Later, the yard built two yachts he had designed; *Thora*, a 7.3-meter sloop, and *Aemilia*, a 11.3-meter yawl. These first yachts were designed and built with great difficulty, and without help from his elder brothers, for advice was neither asked nor given.

In 1917 Gerard II designed and built a number of yachts to his Regenboog (Rainbow) design, a gaff-rigged, 26-foot boat in the one-design class. Ever since, races in these open daysailers have attracted national attention in the Netherlands, and new boats are built every year, demonstrating the vitality of an almost century-old class and the genius of its designer. Gerard II's choice of names for this class referred to a biblical sign of hope and indeed it was with the building of the Regenboog after World War I that established his name widely in the Dutch sailing community.

His yard, which he called Scheepswerf G. De Vries Lentsch Jr., was located on the "Y" of the open harbor front of Amsterdam, opposite the Central Station. Numerous commercial boats and yachts were launched there in sight of the old waterfront. Among the ships built in Gerard II's boatyard were the motoryacht *Piet Hein*, belonging to the family of Queen Juliana, the mother of Queen Beatrix, and *Zeearend* (Sea Eagle), a 55-foot yawl that was a very successful ocean racer designed by Olin Stephens and commissioned by wood merchant Mr. Cornelius Bruynzeel.

Gerard de Vries Lentsch II achieved international fame with his 6-Meters, of which he designed and built about eight. He also created *Hollandia*, the only 8-Meter designed and built in the Netherlands. In 1927 the yacht *Zonnetij* was the one-thousandth boat built at Scheepswerf G. de Vries Lentsch Jr.

The reputation established by Gerard de Vries Lentsch II's boatyard was on a par with other great builders such as Henry Rasmussen in Germany and Camper and Nicholson in Great Britain. Like those yards, de Vries Lentsch offered complete concepts, including designs, but did not object to building yachts to plans from other yacht designers. Gerard II's designs show a natural elegance and grace, especially in the sailing yachts, stemming from his hands-on knowledge of the material and his lifelong experience in boatbuilding.

Gerard III, born in 1916, joined his father in the late 1930's and took over after World War II, but he established himself more as a builder than as a designer. The boatyard of Gerard de Vries Lentsch II closed down in 1974.

—Rutger ten Broeke

WILLEM DE VRIES LENTSCH II

Born 1919 · The Netherlands

Few designers have had the same degree of influence on the Dutch yacht-design world as Willem de Vries Lentsch II. A scion of a boatbuilding dynasty from the region north of Amsterdam, Willem II was involved in sailing and boatbuilding from a very young age. His father, Willem I, was an enthusiastic regatta sailor, and since the age of seven, Willem II sailed with him whenever a lightweight deckhand was needed. During his secondary education, his elder brother Jan, destined to take over the leadership of the family yard, Het Fort, suddenly died, and Willem II saw himself facing an unexpected (and possibly undesired) future.

It was the time of the Depression, and in order to survive, the yard had had to lay off 125 of its 150 employees. Willem II's school holidays were spent at the yard familiarizing himself with the tools. After college he worked at the yard as a carpenter to learn the boatbuilding trade from the ground up. In spite of working forty-eight hours a week or longer, he still managed to find time for his hobby, making music.

During World War II Willem II expanded his knowledge in boatbuilding and design through self-study. The yard was forced to build a series of transport vessels for the German occupiers. To save the employees from forced labor

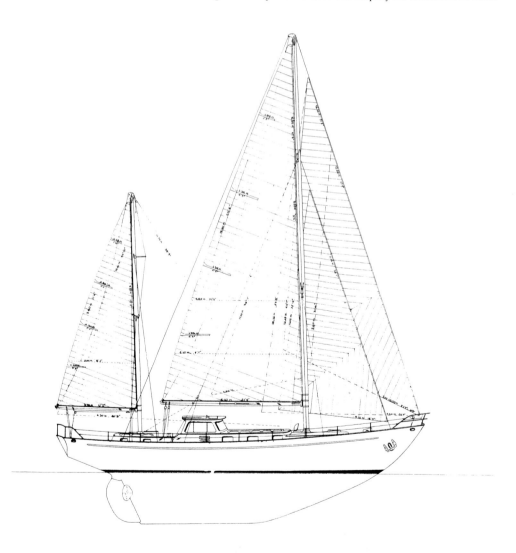

Willem de Vries Lentsch II): *Anna Catharina* The 55-foot *Anna Catharina* was built in steel for offshore cruising. With her doghouse, conservative hull form, and easily handled ketch rig, she is at home in harsh North Sea conditions. Her designer has managed to find a successful aesthetic treatment of the doghouse and center-cockpit configuration. *Drawing courtesy Rutger ten Broeke*

in Germany, the yard started construction, but the work was frequently sabotaged by the management and crew. The first (and last) boat wasn't launched until years later, just before the end of the war. During this time, Willem II, among others, assisted in the design of the Vrijheid (Freedom), a 5.4-meter one-design open dinghy that is still popular in Holland.

After the war, Willem II increased his participation in the yacht racing world. In 1948 he was on the Dutch team selected for the Olympics in Torquay, racing Swallow One-Designs. Lacking experience in sailing against such stiff competition, the Dutch team saw only moderate success in that series and in the 1952 Olympics in Helsinki, where Willem II raced in the 5.5-Meter class.

In 1950, taking advantage of a favorable exchange rate between the Dutch guilder and the U.S. dollar, the yard resumed the design and construction of new yachts. The experience de Vries Lentsch picked up during World War II helped him a great deal in his new position as chief of the design department at Het Fort. Between 1950 and 1960 he and Voogt Designers of Haarlem cooperated in the production of a series of beautiful sailing and motoryachts 26 to 39 meters long for the American market.

Unfortunately the ongoing conflicts between the two leaders of Het Fort, his father Willem I and his cousin Gerard III, were harmful to the business, a situation so serious that in 1960 Willem II started an independent design firm in Amsterdam. This action continued a family tradition, following his uncle Gerard de Vries Lentsch II, who after disagreements with his brothers and Het Fort co-owners started his own very successful yard. Both Willem II's yard and Het Fort became very prestigious and were strongly associated with high quality, but Willem II had to learn that his famous name could be a burden as well as a blessing—clients associated the name de Vries Lentsch with high prices.

Indeed, the start of the young firm was not without difficulties, but after a few hard years and with the help of a favorable economic climate, Willem II expanded his staff with two draftsmen and his son Willem III (born July 3, 1946), who had graduated from the Polytechnicum as an engineer in 1970. Slowly the design offices of Willem de Vries Lentsch II climbed to the top of the design world, and even though sailing remained Willem II's favorite pastime, the firm developed a strong reputation for its motoryachts. After a period of good cooperation, Willem II decided it was time to retire. In 1994 he left his son, who has proved to be a formidable torchbearer for the de Vries Lentsch reputation, in charge.

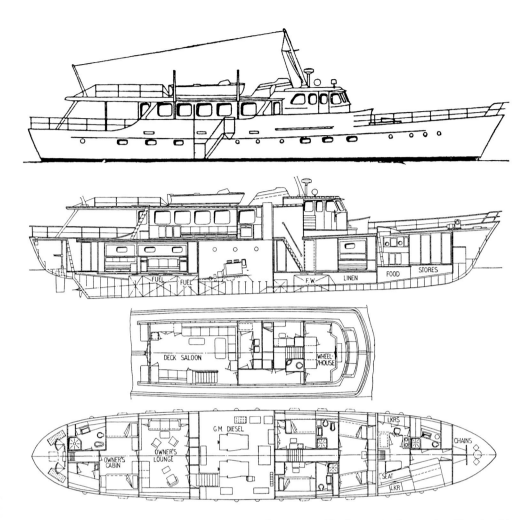

Willem de Vries Lentsch III: *Together IV.* Designed in 1960 and built in 1961, the 100-foot *Together IV* was the committee boat during numerous regattas in the Mediterranean. Her lines reflect the North Sea fishing trawler tradition, with more luxurious appointments. *Drawing courtesy Rutger ten Broeke*

Milestones in the portfolio of Willem de Vries Lentsch's designs are the 200-ton, 106-foot schooner *Eendracht* and two similar vessels for French clients. During the last five years of his design career he drew various sailing yachts between 44 and 114 feet long for the Jongert shipyards in Medemblik. These were meant for series production, and of the Jongert 19M series alone, twenty have been built.

Yet it was not only large yachts that had the attention of the office. In an interview de Vries Lentsch stated that the interior of a small yacht poses a much bigger challenge to the designer than does that of a larger yacht, because in the small yacht one has to be economical and the ergonomic aspects become the paramount factor in the concept. Willem II designed numerous steel and fiberglass motoryachts and motorsailers under 32 feet, of which thousands were built. Many designs were suitable for amateur builders, who could construct a complete boat along the given lines by buying a kit, or they could buy a hull and then fit it with an interior.

From 1952 on, Willem II was drawn to deepwater sailing and participated in many races in the Channel and on the North Sea. He did not own a yacht himself, but crewed extensively with his friends Ricus van de Stadt, Cornelius Bruynzeel, and Simon de Wit, all seasoned and famous ocean racers.

From the beginning of his working life, Willem II has been strongly involved with the promotion of boatbuilding and design in the Netherlands. Currently in his eighties, he is active on many committees and organizations in the field. In 1966 he became a member of the Delft Think Tank, where physical research and experimentation are performed, discussed, and published, to the benefit of boatbuilding and yacht design in general. Since 1967 he has been a member of the board of one of Europe's primary boating exhibitions, the RAI exhibitions in Amsterdam, of which he later became chairman.

Willem de Vries Lentsch II has enjoyed an interesting and rewarding career, in which he made the transition from the highly competitive offspring of a boatbuilding dynasty known for its family arguments to a mild and accessible nurturer of Dutch boatbuilding.

—Rutger ten Broeke

W

ROBERT WALLSTROM

Born 1934 · United States

A multidisciplined marine professional, Bob Wallstrom has worked not only as a designer of yachts and commercial vessels, but also as a marine surveyor, a yacht design school president, a boating writer, and marine historian.

Wallstrom began his design career in the drafting room of Luders Marine Construction Company and continued it in the offices of designers Philip L. Rhodes and John Atkin. In 1969 he moved to Maine, where he went into partnership with designer Edward S. Brewer. The firm, Brewer and Wallstrom and Associates, produced many well-received designs, including the Whitby 42, Cabot 36, Ouyang 28 and 34, and radius-chined designs built by the Huromic Boat Company. In 1979 Wallstrom formed his own firm.

From 1969 until 1978 he and Ted Brewer operated the Yacht Design Institute (YDI), teaching small craft design. Later he was joined by Bob Watkins, a naval architect, and together they developed YDI Schools, a campus program that taught small craft naval architecture and granted an ASc degree in small craft naval architecture, the first such program to have degree status granted by the state of Maine and the first in the nation to offer a degree course in small craft design.

Currently sole proprietor of Delta Marine Small Craft Design and Survey, a design and marine surveying firm, Wallstrom now practices at a more relaxed pace in Brownfield, Maine, where he is writing a definitive history of the Luders Marine Construction Company of Stamford, Connecticut.

—Daniel B. MacNaughton

MATTHEW JOSEPH WALSH

1866–1960 · Canada/United States

An early and important designer/skipper/boatbuilder in southern California, Matt Walsh was born in County Guysborough, Nova Scotia. In 1889 he migrated to Los Angeles and in 1907 he formed an association with financier Frank A. Garbutt to design and sail the 98-foot schooner *Skidbladnir*. Ten years later, these two founded the Garbutt and Walsh Boatyard on Terminal Island in southern California.

Although he had no formal training as a designer, Walsh had learned from his father and could rely on his experience as a skipper and builder to create some very successful boats. He had his own way of doing things, such as lofting, while standing, on the sides of the boatyard sheds. His natural affinity for design

Bob Wallstrom: *Mystic*. A comfortable vessel, *Mystic* was built for extended voyaging in the Pacific for an ideal client who allowed the designer full latitude in creating the design's numerous drawings in fine detail. The 53-foot 11-inch LOA *Mystic* was built by Kato Boat Company of Kurihama, Kanagawa-ken, Japan. *Drawing courtesy Bob Wallstrom*

Matthew Walsh: *Mardo*. When a sailboat designer draws a powerboat for his own use, it is bound to be interesting. This is Walsh's 55-foot express cruiser *Mardo*, clipping along at a good rate. Built in 1930, she is still going strong on the West Coast. *Photo courtesy Bruce Morser*

created some notable performers, including the 53-foot cutter *Otter* (1914, rebuilt and rerigged by Walsh in 1935), the 45-foot *Thorobred* (1928), the 43-foot sloop *Margaret*, the 27-foot Common Sense Class sloop (1933, six built), the 39-foot cutter *Know How* (1950), and his own 55-foot express cruiser *Mardo* (1930). His sailing yachts were typically fine shapes and heavily ballasted with generous sail area.

Probably Walsh's best-known design is the Common Sense. These boats sail much faster than others their size because of the long waterline, big rig, 50 percent ballast ratio, and "champagne glass" midsections. At 27 feet 10 inches LOA, *Common Sense III* will always be the smallest boat to ever sail the Los Angeles–Honolulu (Transpac) Race. Dismasted halfway across, she managed to finish the 1934 contest in 18 days, beating some larger boats on corrected time. Every Honolulu Race since has limited entries to a minimum 30 feet LOA.

Matt Walsh died at age ninety-four at his home on Point Fermin, San Pedro, California.

—J. Scott Rohrer

WINTHROP LORING "WINK" WARNER

1900–1987 · United States

Winthrop Warner is mostly remembered for his cruising sailboat and motorsailer designs, but he also drew plans for many powerboats, sportfishing yachts, commercial draggers, launches, pocket cruisers, daysailers, and dinghies. He has a reputation for precise drafting, and his designs are admired for their strikingly good looks. They typically emphasized strong sheerlines and dramatically shaped ends, with superstructures carefully made to complement these dominant curves.

Born in Middletown, Connecticut, Warner grew up near the Connecticut River. In his early teens he acquired a power launch, which he used on the river. During high school he studied mechanical drawing, and by age seventeen he was working as a draftsman at a boatbuilding yard on Long Island during summer vacations.

Beginning in 1920 Warner spent four years studying for his degree in naval architecture at MIT, and then apprenticed at the Electric Boat Company in New Jersey and the Portland Boat Works in Connecticut. He next worked as a draftsman for designer John G. Alden and then William H. Hand Jr., with a brief stint in the office of Philip Rhodes.

Warner opened his own office in Middletown in 1929. His first commission, from a family friend, was for the 53-foot, gaff-rigged ketch *Felisi*, completed in 1930. A heavy, tough, flush-decked offshore cruiser, she set the tone for

much of his subsequent work. His first power cruiser, the 38-foot 7-inch, raised-deck *Ailenroc II*, designed in 1932, brought him his first high-profile publicity in both *Yachting* and *The Rudder* magazines. Throughout his career, the good opinion of these two magazines would earn him a solid reputation and lead to commissions that enabled him to survive the Great Depression and continue his success in the years following World War II.

Between 1931 and 1941 Warner's office produced thirty designs, from which approximately seventy-five boats were built. Many designs were available as sloops, ketches, or yawls, and some offered either gaff or marconi rigs.

Just before the United States entered World War II, Warner and Henry R. Palmer Jr. joined forces to produce the handsome 55-foot fishing draggers built by Stonington Boat Works, several versions of which were built before the war and drawn out to 57 feet after the war. Four were launched over the next few years. During the war Warner worked with Wilcox, Crittenden and Company, which manufactured hardware for the navy.

The design of yachts picked up again following World War II. The year 1947 was good for Warner, who saw the launching of his own cutter, the 39-foot 10-inch *Mary Loring* (along with the similar *Astral* and *Alarm*) as well as the first of the 28-foot 7-inch stock boats known as Cambridge Cadets, which became one of Warner's most enduring designs.

Warner designed the well-known Warner 33 motorsailers in 1950. As was his custom, he offered owners many options. By the mid-1950's, ten had been built, including two in fiberglass. One of the first built was his own, the final *Mary Loring*, which he owned until 1961. Many custom designs followed.

Unfortunately, many of Warner's yachts were built with such cost-saving measures as galvanized iron fastenings, and were not long lived.

Warner moved from Connecticut to Vero Beach, Florida, in the late 1950's, where he continued to work until retiring in the mid-1980's. He died there at the age of eighty-seven.

All Warner's drawings and files are in the Winthrop L. Warner Collection, Mystic Seaport Museum, Mystic, CT.

—Daniel B. MacNaughton

ALAN BRUCE WARWICK

Born 1934 · New Zealand

As with many designers, Alan Warwick began his career in land-based architecture and later switched to yacht design. Today he heads a design team that is busy creating mostly large sail-

Winthrop Warner: *Typhoon*. While she is one of Warner's smaller designs, *Typhoon* shows all the characteristics that give the designer's yachts strong appeal. A powerful sheer and ample freeboard, a deep keel, and firm sections make a boat that will stand up to her work, while all the lines, including those of the house and rig, are in harmony with the whole. *Drawing courtesy WoodenBoat Publications*

ing and power yachts, often to modern concepts that incorporate traditional proportions.

Warwick was born in Wellington, where he attended school before moving on to Auckland University, graduating in 1958 with a degree in architecture. He became interested in sailing during the 1960's, crewing on racing yachts and eventually becoming a skilled racing skipper in such events as the One-Ton Cup.

During the 1970's Warwick began mixing some small boat design and construction into his architectural practice, and by the end of the decade he committed himself to full-time yacht design. He has made a commitment to New Zealand and encourages his international clients to use New Zealand builders where possible.

Warwick's strong marketing background, attention to detail, and elegant designs maintained a steady flow of work, and today, with a staff of specialists including his wife Gael and son Bruce, Warwick Yacht Design is at the forefront of international yacht design. Using computer-aided design techniques combined with model making and artist's images, his team prepares comprehensive plans for boats to be built with the latest in construction materials. They include mid- to large-sized luxury power and sailing yachts and racing yachts, as well as sportfishing yachts.

Currently more sailboats than powerboats dominate the practice, with recent launch-

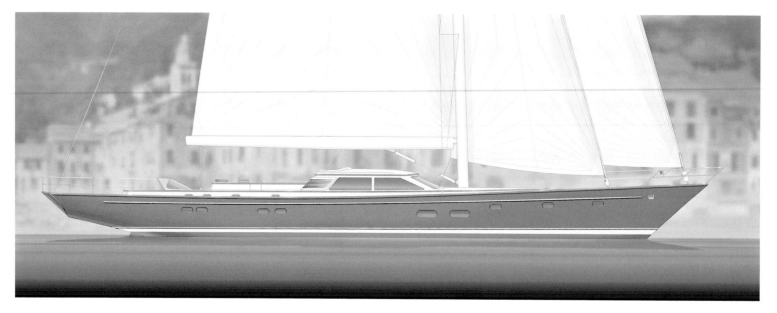

Alan Warwick. Warwick always manages to combine understated but contemporary styling with excellent sailing, motorsailing, and cruising qualities, a blend that makes his yachts popular with discerning owners worldwide. *Drawing courtesy Alan Warwick*

ings including the W55 *Shahtoosh* (the fore-runner of a line of production yachts in Australia ranging from 53 to 66 feet), the W72 Offshore Cruising Yacht in production, plus the Warwick Powercats, which range from 65 to 128 feet.

Warwick Yacht Design is located in Auckland, New Zealand.   —David Payne

SHUJI WATANABE

Born 1919 · Japan

After graduating from the Department of Naval Architecture at Tokyo Imperial University, Shuji Watanabe became a navy technical officer during World War II, designing submarines. After the war, he built the 5-meter, cat-rigged *Miss Dongame*, to his own design. (*Dongame* means a "slow-moving turtle" in Japanese and was a nickname navy personnel used for their submarines.)

Designing yachts is a hobby for Watanabe, but his abilities and personal popularity have contributed to the construction of many boats of his design, coinciding with the development of offshore sailing in Japan. In the 1960's several of his yachts participated successfully in offshore races overseas, such as the China Sea Race from Hong Kong to Manila. One of them was *Contessa II*, a 36-foot sloop that also established a good record at home. In addition, Watanabe designed a 70-foot steel ketch for Hisaya Morishige, a famous Japanese actor.

Throughout the 1950's and 1960's, Watanabe collected many trophies as the designer/owner/skipper of *Dongame II* through *Dongame VII*. He also contributed to the NORC (Nippon Ocean Racing Club) as a founding member, and held various posts including chairman of the Measurement Committee, chairman of the Technical Committee, councilor for the Offshore Racing Council (ORC), and chief measurer of Japan. Watanabe introduced the Rod Johnstone–designed J/24 one-designs to Japan.

Watanabe has designed approximately 180 sailing yachts. *Dongame VIII*, a 36-foot sloop launched in 1986, crewed by his son and a friend, raced in the inaugural Melbourne-Osaka Double-Handed Yacht Race in 1987.

—Kennosuke Hayashi

GEORGE LENNOX WATSON

1851–1904 · Scotland

As Britain's most successful designer during the golden age of yachting, G. L. Watson consistently produced winning racing yachts in both large and small classes, as well as some of the largest, most opulent, and best-looking steam yachts ever built.

Watson designed *Britannia*, one of the most enduringly successful large racing yachts. She helped to prove the superiority of an improved hull form that became the standard configuration of almost all racing and cruising yachts until divided underbodies became dominant many decades later.

Among Watson's early influences was strong exposure to the latest research in hydrodynamics, which gave him an important advantage over his opponents. He claimed to be the first to employ all outside metal ballast on the keel, enabling his boats to be stiffer and faster and to carry more sail. He was a pioneer in steel and composite steel and wood construction, aimed at higher strength-weight ratios.

In his own country Watson's principal rivals were William Fife Sr. (II) and Jr. (III), whose boats were often beaten by Watson's owing to the latter's more scientific approach. But in his America's Cup challengers Watson was unfortunate enough to be matched against the United States' Nathanael Herreshoff. While Watson was on the cutting edge of hydrodynamics, Herreshoff had the edge in engineering skills, and as has often been the case in yachting history, the wins went to the best engineer.

Watson was fortunate to live in an era of prosperity and to have the ongoing support of loyal and wealthy clients, many of whom became personal friends. He enjoyed the friendship and patronage of the Prince of Wales, later King Edward VII, as well as the even more enthusiastic support of Germany's Kaiser Wilhelm II. Other royal patrons included Prince Henry of Prussia, Grand Duke Michael of Russia, and Albert, King of Belgium. One yacht, *Mayflower*, became the U.S. presidential yacht and carried on as such until 1928.

George Lennox Watson was born in Glasgow, Scotland. The family came from Paisley, near Glasgow, where they had been involved in the weaving industry. His father and grandfather were doctors, and his mother was the daughter of an engineer who pioneered in steam locomotion.

Watson's interest in yachting began in his early childhood, after his mother inherited a small villa at Inverkip on the lower reaches of the Clyde estuary.

When Watson was fifteen his father died, causing a reversal in the family fortunes. So instead of going to Glasgow University as had his father and grandfather, Watson had to leave school and pursue employment. In 1867 he became indentured to William Pearce, one of the great names in British shipbuilding and the head of Robert Napier and Sons, the largest Clydeside shipyard and builders of all the great Cunard liners of the period, as well as numerous vessels for British and foreign navies. Most significantly for the young Watson, the yard had a reputation for the high standard of training it gave to its staff. Watson worked in the drawing office, learning the principles of engineering and the fundamentals of design, as well as the nature of wood and iron construction. He supplemented his income working as a yachting correspondent for the *North British Daily Mail* and various other journals.

In 1869, Watson joined A. and J. Inglis, another eminent Clydebank shipyard, where he came under the influence of John Inglis, who with Peter Denny was working closely with William Froude on the development of tank-test theories and a scientific investigation into the laws of hydrodynamics, which up until that time had been dominated by the ideas of Rankine and Scott Russell. What resulted was a radically different approach to hull form. Both Inglis and Froude were amateur yacht designers, but it was Watson who embraced the new order and became its ablest proponent, applying it to the boats he designed when he set up under his own name in 1873. Watson was almost certainly the first yacht designer to have gone through a period of formalized training.

Watson found a ready source of customers among the members of the Royal Clyde Yacht Club (later the Royal Northern and Clyde Yacht Club), which he joined in 1872. At that time it was probably the largest yacht club in the world, in terms of both membership and tonnage.

It was the Five-Tonner *Clotilde*, Watson's third yacht, that in 1875 first brought him broad attention by conclusively beating *Pearl*, the Clyde champion, designed by the great William Fife Sr. (II). From that point on, season after season, Watson turned out a stream of winners in most of the region's major classes.

In 1881 Watson's 38-foot 7-inch LWL, Ten-Tonner *Madge* sailed a series of races in New York Harbor that decisively proved the merits of the cutter hull form over the shallow-draft centerboard sloops typical of the American national type. American yacht designers such as Edward Burgess began to embrace the cutter form. *Shona* followed *Madge* to the United States in 1886 along with other craft designed by William Fife Sr. (II), all of which reinforced the trend toward the cutter type. During the 1881 season, however, *Madge* lost one race and won another against N. G. Herreshoff's *Shadow*, whose design was a compromise be-

tween the two types and proved to be the shape of things to come.

Working under the constraints of the Tonnage Rule, Watson, like other designers, exploited its weak points to produce boats that were fast for their rating. Designers realized that if they sacrificed beam, the rule allowed them to increase the waterline length without a penalty, thus increasing the yacht's potential maximum speed compared to her rating.

This resulted in the plank-on-edge type of hull, in which a yacht of minimal beam carried huge sail areas, counterbalanced by large lead keels. As the type grew more extreme, the yachts sacrificed comfort in the accommodations and ultimately had so little buoyancy that they sailed largely underwater in heavy weather, especially when working to windward. In *Doris*, a Five-Tonner of 1885, Watson pushed the design envelope out to its final extreme, giving her a waterline length of 38 feet 2 inches and a beam of 5 feet 5 inches. The following year a similar boat (the 39-foot 11-inch LWL × 5-foot 6-inch beam *Oona*, designed by W. E. Paton) was lost with all hands on her maiden voyage, and no further boats were built for the class. In 1889 the Tonnage Rule was dropped in favor of the Length-and-Sail-Area Rule.

The 207-foot *Mohican*, one of Watson's first large steam yacht designs, was built in 1885,

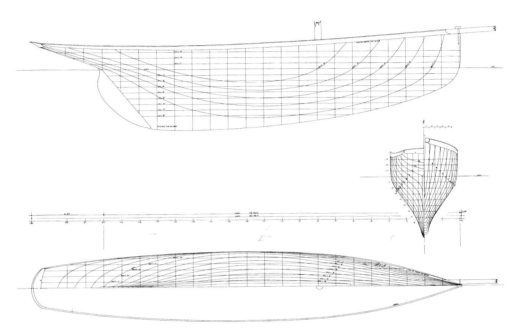

George Watson: *May.* While she is not as extreme as some examples, the 76-foot 10-inch LOA cutter *May* displays the extremely narrow beam and slack bilges typical of yachts built to the Tonnage Rule. © *Chevalier & Taglang*

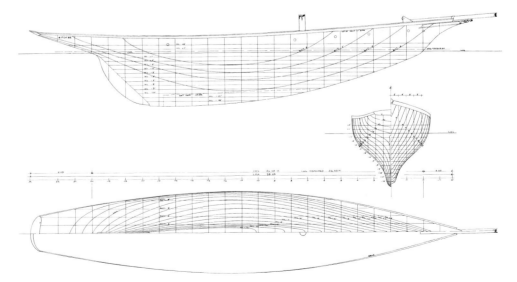

George Watson: *Thistle.* Following the example of Bentall's *Julinar*, Watson adopted a cutaway profile for his 1887 America's Cup challenger *Thistle*. She made too much leeway and was soundly defeated by the Edward Burgess–designed *Volunteer*. Kaiser Wilhelm II purchased *Thistle*, and she became the first of his five *Meteors*. © *Chevalier & Taglang*

and as one of the largest powered yachts of her day, she was a major influence on the emerging steam yacht genre. Watson came to be the foremost designer of the type. Early examples were really motorsailers that—with their handsome clipper bows and functional sailing rigs, often including squaresails on the forward mast—stressed a link with the rapidly fading days of commercial and naval sailing vessels. The designer's cousin Thomas Watson prepared the interior designs for many of the larger yachts in a wide range of styles ranging from Scottish Baronial and Mock Tudor to Louis XIV and Arabic.

Watson's first America's Cup commission came in 1886. Unfortunately the client died before construction commenced. However, because of his preeminence within the United Kingdom, Watson became the designer of choice for every potential challenger for the America's Cup from 1886 until his death in 1904, though he turned down some commissions and some matches did not materialize.

In 1887 Watson designed *Thistle* for a syndicate from the Royal Clyde Yacht Club. An example of the new compromise type, she sported an overhanging clipper bow, as opposed to the plumb stem that had been so typical of the cut-

ter. Watson radically cut away her forefoot in order to reduce wetted surface area, and gave her moderate beam. However, largely due to an overly heavy rig and somewhat too shallow draft, she lost both races against Edward Burgess's *Volunteer*, which also represented a move toward the compromise type.

After she was rerigged, *Thistle* went on to considerable success in the United Kingdom, becoming champion in her class in 1888 and 1890. *Thistle* is still felt to be one of Watson's most beautiful designs. In 1892 she was bought by Germany's Kaiser Wilhelm II, nephew of King Edward VII, who raced her under the name of *Meteor*, the first of his five yachts sailing under that name.

In 1889 Watson designed the cutter *Valkyrie* for Lord Dunraven as an America's Cup challenger. The new Deed of Gift laid down a minimum waterline of 80 feet, but in order to save money and against Watson's advice, Dunraven had him design *Valkyrie* with a 70-foot waterline. Inevitably this led to some acrimonious correspondence with the New York Yacht Club. Although the challenge was ultimately accepted, the Royal Yacht Squadron bowed out. *Valkyrie* did however become the United Kingdom's champion in 1889.

Watson's 85-foot LWL America's Cup challenger of 1893, *Valkyrie II*, also built for Lord Dunraven, introduced a totally new concept. She had greater beam and drastically reduced displacement, and the keel profile was more finlike with a short upper portion, a longer "flat" on the bottom, and a more vertical leading edge, reducing lateral plane and wetted surface area, lowering the center of gravity of the ballast, and using the remaining lateral plane in a more efficient form. The overhanging bow was of the spoon type, with no reverse curve in the profile, and no trailboards or billethead.

In the finals *Valkyrie II* was narrowly beaten by N. G. Herreshoff's *Vigilant*. Newly refitted for an 1894 racing season with the other big cutters on the Clyde, *Valkyrie II* was lost when she was accidentally rammed by her rival, the Soper-designed *Satanita*, during the first start, leaving it to her larger near-sister *Britannia*, also designed by Watson in 1893, to popularize the new type.

The good showing made by *Valkyrie II* encouraged Dunraven to challenge again with *Valkyrie III* in 1895. With her, Watson turned out a broader-beamed yacht than N. G. Herreshoff's *Defender*, as a result of Watson opting for the U.S. model while Herreshoff opted for the

George Watson: *Margarita*. Built in 1900 *Margarita* was one of the most luxurious yachts of her time. She survived until World War II, when she was sunk while in the service of the Royal Navy. *Photo by Nathaniel Stebbins. Courtesy the Society for the Preservation of New England Antiquities*

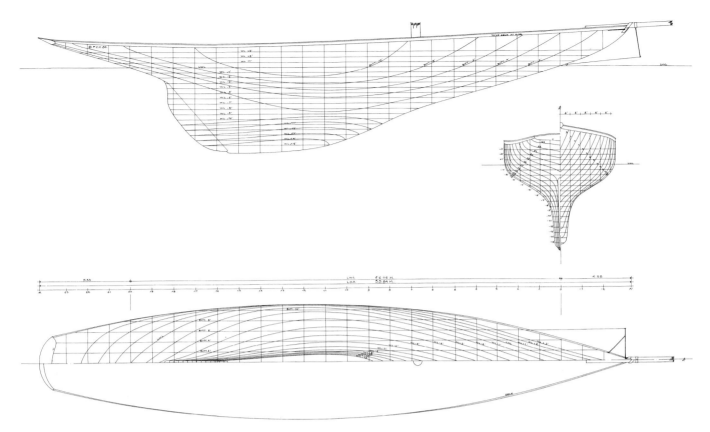

George Watson: *Valkyrie II.* *Valkyrie II*, Britain's 1893 America's Cup challenger, brought into focus a hull shape that would be a standard in yacht designs to come. She narrowly lost to N. G. Herreshoff's *Vigilant*, and was sunk the next year, leaving it to *Britannia*, another Watson design, to prove the new type. © *Chevalier & Taglang*

somewhat narrower British proportions. The match deteriorated into squabbles over sportsmanship, and while *Defender* technically won the series, the final race was not sailed, leaving the contest between designs unsettled.

The cutter *Britannia*, designed in 1893 for Edward, Prince of Wales, is often regarded as Watson's greatest creation. In a racing career that stretched from 1893 to 1935, she earned a place in the *Guinness Book of Records* with the greatest number of prizes of any yacht in racing history: 625 starts and 231 first prizes. It is worth noting that when N. G. Herreshoff's *Navahoe* visited the United Kingdom in 1893, *Britannia* beat her in all but two of their thirteen races, and when *Vigilant* came over in 1894, *Britannia* won all but five of their seventeen races. After King George VI died in 1935, *Britannia* was scuttled.

Such was Watson's authority in the United Kingdom after 1893 that he had an effective monopoly on the design of big class yachts. By the time of Watson's death in 1904, Fife had designed only three big class cutters, only one of which could be counted as a success. Indeed, it was only after Watson's death in 1904 that the careers of men like Charles Nicholson started to gather pace.

With a few exceptions, Watson stopped designing for the small classes in 1896 at the time of the introduction of the Linear Rating Rule. Thereafter, he focused his attention on the

George Watson: *Valkyrie III.* *Valkyrie III* was the vehicle for the Earl of Dunraven's third America's Cup challenge. Typical of the large skimming-dish raters of the late nineteenth century, she was nevertheless beaten by N. G. Herreshoff's *Defender*. She is better known for the controversy surrounding that series, and Dunraven's resignation/expulsion from the New York Yacht Club. *Photo courtesy Hart Nautical Collections, MIT Museum, Cambridge, MA*

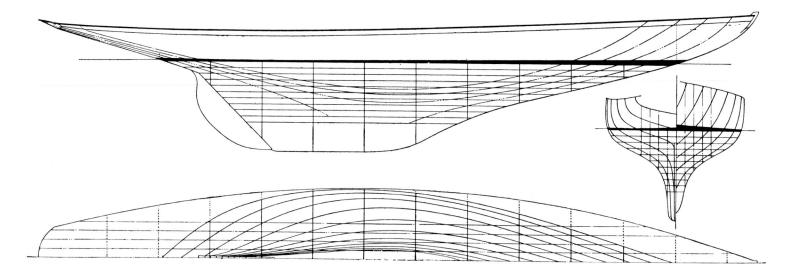

George Watson: *Britannia.* Of all the great cutters, *Britannia* was the most beloved. During the course of a career spanning more than forty years, she was constantly updated to keep her competitive. Built for Edward, Prince of Wales, in 1893, *Britannia* ended her days in the ownership of his son, King George V, who decreed that she be scuttled on his death. © *Tony Dixon*

production of large yachts, including various big class cutters and schooners, as well as palatial steam yachts for the rich and famous in both the United Kingdom and the United States.

In 1896, Kaiser Wilhelm II approached Watson with a request that he should design a yacht specifically to beat *Britannia,* which up until then had been the champion of the big class racing cutters. Watson produced *Meteor II* under the new Linear Rating Rule. It quickly became apparent that *Britannia* could not compete successfully against her. Such was *Meteor II*'s dominance that level racing in the big class ceased, to be replaced by unsatisfactory handicap racing. *Meteor II* was to remain unrivaled until she was vanquished by Watson's *Sybarita* of 1900.

In 1897 Watson designed the 115-foot clipper-bowed schooner *Rainbow,* which set a record for the fastest sustained speed by a nonplaning monohull yacht, traveling 60 miles in 4 hours and twice during that time achieving 16 knots.

When Sir Thomas Lipton made his first America's Cup challenge in 1899, he approached Watson to design *Shamrock.* Watson declined, having decided that involvement with the America's Cup consumed an excessive amount of time and nervous energy. So Lipton went to William Fife Jr. (III), with Watson giving advice and support. After *Shamrock*'s failure, Lipton challenged again in 1901, and this time, by appealing to his patriotic instincts, he persuaded Watson to design *Shamrock II.*

Assisted by Archibald Denny, Watson tank-tested eleven models and sixty modifications over a period of nine months. In *Shamrock II*'s design, Watson turned away from the *Valkyrie III* hull form and back to that of *Britannia. Shamrock II* had a shallow, canoe-like body, steadied by a deep bulb keel, with 95 tons of ballast. She was

102 feet 9 inches LOA and drew 21 feet 9 inches, and the top of her club topsail was 175 feet above the waterline. She was the first Cup boat to be designed and built to truly scientific principles, and as such she represented a considerable improvement over previous challengers. She was, by some estimations, faster than N. G. Herreshoff's *Columbia,* but perhaps due to the skill of the remarkable American skipper Charlie Barr, she lost the closely fought series.

Watson's health collapsed during the 1901 Cup races. When Lipton asked him to design *Shamrock III,* he declined once again and William Fife did the honors. However, Fife was asked to submit his models to Watson for comment, and Watson provided Fife with all his plans and tank-test data. Only a few months before Watson's death, Lipton was trying to persuade him to either design *Shamrock IV* or oversee it while Fife or Alfred Mylne (who had trained in Watson's design office) did the work.

In 1900, Watson designed the big class racing cutter *Kariad,* an out-and-out racer of very light construction featuring yellow-pine planking on steel frames. *Kariad* so completely dominated the yachting scene that no owner was prepared to build a new competitor and the handicap class collapsed. After Watson's death, Charles Nicholson persuaded Sir James Pender to buy *Kariad* and have her broken up, thus opening the doors for new orders to be sent in, principally to Nicholson and Fife. Watson's last design to be built was the 260-foot steam yacht *Honor,* drawn in 1904, the year of his death, and built in 1905.

Following his accession to the throne in 1902, Edward VII offered Watson a knighthood, which he declined. Estimates of the number of yachts he designed range from three to four hundred. In 1899 the total ton-

nage of his yachts was put at approximately 32,000. Overworked and stressed, but wealthy, at the height of his powers, and with his name a household word throughout his country, Watson died at age fifty-three.

Watson's drawings are held in the Mitchell Library, Glasgow, Scotland.

—Martin Black and Daniel B. MacNaughton

JOHN MURRAY WATTS

1879–1951 · United States

If a single word can characterize the work of naval architect J. Murray Watts, it would have to be *varied.* During a career spanning some fifty years, Watts produced more than seven hundred complete designs for power and sailing yachts of every size, both engine- and sail-powered commercial fishing boats, and a diverse collection of other large and small commercial vessels that served in virtually every corner of the world. He was a pioneer in the use of welded steel for yachts and for small commercial vessels.

Watts was born in Philadelphia, Pennsylvania, and received a bachelor of science degree in naval architecture from Yale's Scientific School in 1900. After graduation he toured European shipyards for several months, worked briefly at the William Cramp and Sons shipyard on the Delaware River, and then took a job with the New York Shipbuilding Company in Camden, New Jersey. The next year Watts joined the Philadelphia design office of Swasey, Raymond and Page, remaining for five years. It was there that he got his first chance to design oceangoing sailing and power yachts.

J. Murray Watts: *Emerald.* Launched in 1924 by the W. F. Stone Yard in Oakland, California, *Emerald* is a handsome 50-foot 6-inch LOD yawl and proved ideal for comfortable cruising along the American West Coast. *Photo courtesy Newport Harbor Nautical Museum, Newport Beach, CA*

J. Murray Watts: *Memory.* The 110-foot *Memory* is pretty—a two-stacker—and very comfortable for cruising in style. Note the enclosed aft deck and the handsome launches. Watts designed such oceangoing power yachts for clients all around the world. *Photo courtesy Newport Harbor Nautical Museum, Newport Beach, CA*

George Wayland: *Tamalmar*. The schooner *Tamalmar* is a handsome 57-foot yacht built side by side with her sistership *Alotola* in 1927 at Stephens Brothers in Stockton, California. At first she was seldom raced, but was converted to a sloop in 1949 and began winning many of the major races on Puget Sound in the 1950's. *Photo courtesy Thomas G. Skahill*

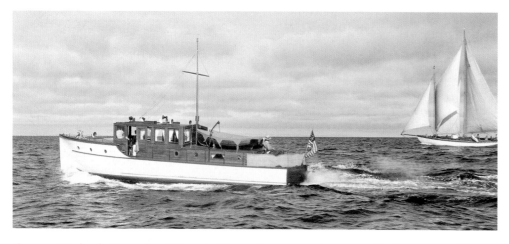

George Wayland: *Marquita*. Although Wayland was better known for his handsome sailboats, his motor cruisers were equally pleasing to the eye. The 50-foot cruiser *Marquita* was built in 1929 by the W. F. Stone and Son yard, Oakland, California. *Photo courtesy Newport Harbor Nautical Museum, Newport Beach, CA*

In 1909, after a short stint in Boston, Watts returned to Philadelphia (where he was to continue to practice naval architecture until his death) and opened a design office with Thomas D. Bowes. Three years later he went out on his own.

Watts became a junior member of the Society of Naval Architects and Marine Engineers (SNAME) in 1909. He held full membership in the organization from 1914 to 1935. During World War I, Watts served with the U.S. Army in France as a captain in the 57th Regiment of Engineers. During World War II, he worked for the Federal Maritime Commission.

Watts's earliest work concentrated on fast, oceangoing powerboats such as the 60-foot *Caliph*, which raced from New York to Havana in 1911. By the time he left for military service in World War I, Watts-designed motoryachts had been built for clients in Finland, Trinidad, the Philippines, and Colombia, as well as in the United States, and several fishing vessels, tugs, and small passenger and freight vessels were in service in Trinidad, Costa Rica, Australia, and on the rivers of Colombia.

Although his clients apparently asked mostly for powerboats, Watts designed many cruising sailboats, from handsome 35-foot auxiliary sloops to a powerful 94-foot auxiliary ketch.

Watts held strong views on the rigging of sailing yachts for offshore cruising. He favored the marconi ketch rig for smaller boats, those 50 to 70 feet LOD. For larger vessels, he preferred the schooner rig, two-masted with a marconi main and gaff foresail or, for yachts longer than 150 feet, three-masted with gaff lowers and topsails worked from the deck. He was no fan of spinnakers on small cruising vessels.

Although many of his plans were destroyed by a fire in his office, nearly 250 of them are now in the J. Murray Watts Collection at Mystic Seaport Museum, Mystic, CT.

—Stephen Rappaport

GEORGE H. WAYLAND

1885–1947 · United States

George Wayland was a contemporary and boyhood friend of L. E. "Ted" Geary. They grew up in Seattle, built several sailboats together, and raced them successfully in the late 1890's and early 1900's prior to their college days.

Educated at the University of Washington, Wayland began his practice in the Seattle area. During World War I he was with the Foundation Company, better known as the Emergency Fleet Corporation, holding important positions as naval architect and marine engineer at their shipyards in Tacoma and Seattle. By war's end, he was assistant superintendent of the Tacoma yard.

In 1920, Wayland joined the firm of Lee and Brinton of Seattle, and thereafter the firm became known as Lee, Brinton and Wayland with offices in Seattle and San Francisco. Fred S. Brinton remained in the Seattle office, while Harold Lee and Wayland opened the San Francisco office.

Wayland decided to go on his own in 1926 and began designing a succession of cruising and racing sailboats that are still remembered on the Bay, up and down the West Coast, and in Hawaii. Although usually designed for San Francisco owners, they later achieved widespread recognition and distinction.

The 56-foot *Alotola* (1927) was converted from her knockabout schooner rig in 1949 and began a very successful career on Puget Sound. Twenty-three years after she was launched and with her new sloop rig, she achieved many honors in ocean racing after being named Boat of the Year on Puget Sound in 1950. Following a 15,000-mile cruise to the Mediterranean, she was sold to a man in Greece who had fallen in love with her.

San Francisco sailors still recall *Volante*, a 43-foot sloop (1936), a perennial winner under several owners, and still on the Bay in 1999. The 57-foot schooner *Tamalmar* (1927) went south to Los Angeles in 1936. *Lady Jo*, a 40-foot staysail schooner (1932), raced in four Transpacs (1936, 1939, 1947, and 1949). Other notable designs include the 48-foot ketch *Altair* (1927); *Rejoice*, a 56-foot schooner (1931); and the 25-foot Golden Gate Class (1930), formerly the Baby Birds, fifteen of which were built and still sailing the Bay in 1999.

Although specializing in sail, Wayland designed some noteworthy motoryachts. The 50-foot *Marquita* (1929), the 47-foot *Skeeter* (1930), and the 57-foot *Graemar* (1940) are fine examples of his work in powerboat design.

As could be expected during the difficult years of the Great Depression, many yacht designers had to pursue commercial work. Wayland was no exception, but having already established himself in this field, he had a solid background, and in the 1930's he designed and supervised the construction of pilot-boats, towboats, fisheries research vessels, auto and passenger ferries. All of his commercial designs display a distinct and handsome style.

A study of Wayland's plans reveal handsome yachts and commercial designs, a thorough familiarity with detail specifications, and meticulous drafting and lettering, as well as a comprehensive knowledge of wood construction methods.

Neat and retiring by nature, Wayland was somewhat of an unsung master during his lifetime. His boats, however, have always spoken for him and thus his name has endured. They have outlived him by many years and remain in high regard by the West Coast maritime community.

Many of Wayland's plans and specifications are in the archives of the Stone Boatyard in Alameda, California, which produced a number of his designs. Others are among the effects of the celebrated San Francisco naval architect Myron Spaulding.

—Thomas G. Skahill

SOPHUS WEBER

1859–1941 · Denmark

When Sophus Weber's first boat hit the water, yachting in Denmark was a well-established tradition. Almost every cove, bay, and estuary had its boatyards where academically trained designers competed on equal terms with traditional-workboat-builders-turned-yachtbuilders to meet the demand of this growing sport. Even amateurs, provided they had the talent and access to a boatyard, made important contributions. Weber was such an amateur.

Weber's inheritance, the largest fruit plantation in Denmark on the south coast of Fyn Island, provided him with the leisure time to pursue his hobby and the wealth to indulge it—that is, to buy a boatyard in the nearby town of Svendborg where he could build what he imagined. There he designed and built boats only for himself and for his friends from Danish yachting society. Free of the restrictions imposed by economic necessity, Weber could afford to experiment by producing a wider range of boats than most yards of similar size.

Beginning in 1892, Weber built the beautiful schooner *Gaea* for himself. There followed boats in all sizes and types, bulb-keeled racers,

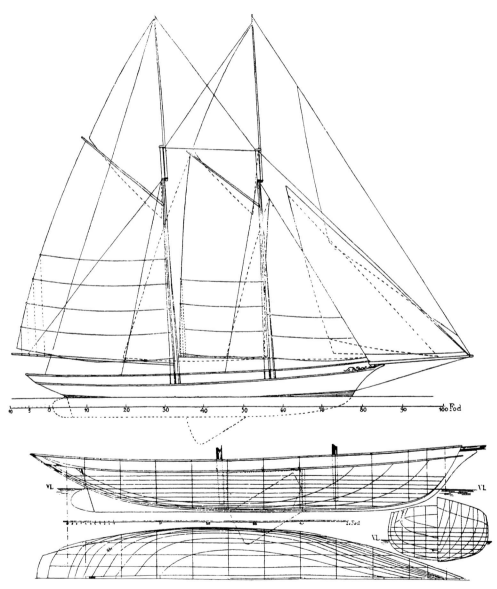

Sophus Weber: *Gaea.* The 28.87-meter schooner *Gaea* was designed by Weber for his own use. She shows considerable Danish character in her sections and afterbody, while the rest of the yacht could be mistaken for a rather extreme shoal-draft schooner from the United States. *Drawing courtesy Bent Aarre*

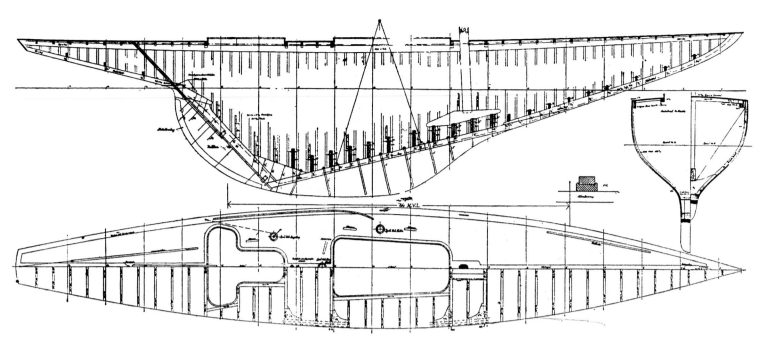

Ernst Wedell-Wedllsborg: *Eva II.* Wedell-Wedellsborg designed at least nine 6-Meters, of which *Eva II* is a handsome example. Highly valued for their good looks, they were seldom very successful on the race course; as in all such cases, the reasons for this were open to debate. *Drawing courtesy Bent Aarre*

John Wells: *Caronia.* A particularly capable-looking luxury cruiser, the 140-foot *Caronia* was designed in 1927 and built of steel by Defoe Boat and Motor Works of Bay City, Michigan. She was powered by twin 300-hp Bessemer diesel engines. A comparably sized yacht built today might well have engines of several thousand horsepower. *Photo courtesy Newport Harbor Nautical Museum, Newport Beach, CA*

centerboarders, even a three-masted schooner. When the International Rule was adopted in 1906, he also made the transition, producing many 6-, 8-, and 10-Meters, and one 15-Meter, *Saharet*. As was common with designers of that era, unless they had been formally trained in naval architecture, Weber did most of his design work by creating wooden models from which he transferred the lines onto paper.

Sophus Weber sold the yard in 1939 to the famous yacht designer and boatbuilder Henry Rasmussen, who returned to Denmark after many years with Abeking and Rasmussen in Germany.

—Bent Aarre

ERNST WEDELL-WEDELLSBORG

1900–1983 · Denmark

Like Gustaf Estlander and Oscar Dahlström, Ernst Wedell-Wedellsborg began his working life as an architect, only to have his love of boats divert him into yacht design. Because he designed few boats, his work is easily overlooked, but the beauty of his 6-Meters and the elegance of his mahogany motoryachts make his work noteworthy.

Every year between 1930 and 1939 Wedell-Wedellsborg designed a 6-Meter for the Royal Danish Yacht Club to enter in the Gold Cup races. It has been said that their sails and handling did not allow them to reach their potential; in many cases their racing record was less than stellar. In 1935 he also designed perhaps the most beautiful one-design class in Denmark, the W-Boat (9.50 meters LOA, 23 square-meter sail area), a slim racing boat with a small cabin. Fifteen of these were built between 1935 and 1939 and raced as a very competitive fleet near Copenhagen.

In 1949, Wedell-Wedellsborg moved from Copenhagen to the island of Thuro, where he joined Aage Walsted's newly established boatyard as its in-house yacht designer. This yard has become well known in the United States for the excellence of its work, and both Aage Nielsen of Boston and Sparkman and Stephens have sent designs to be built there.

—Bent Aarre

JOHN H. WELLS

1879–January 28, 1962 · United States

Working in New York City, John Wells specialized in luxury motoryachts. His work includes examples of virtually the whole range of powerboats that evolved during the years of his career, 1903 to 1960. Early designs included roomy powered houseboats and par-

ticularly beautiful large steam yachts, whereas the middle period involved diesel-powered yachts, some with distinctly "military" styling. Later he produced a series of appealing, exuberantly streamlined yachts of somewhat smaller size. Wells also drew motorsailers and a number of nicely proportioned sailing yachts, many of them large and based on the Gloucester schooner type.

Wells graduated from Cornell University in 1903 with a degree in marine engineering. His first job was with the Mathews Boat Company, for whom he designed a series of fast cruising powerboats. He also worked for Henry J. Gielow of New York and Elco of Bayonne, New Jersey.

During World War I, Wells supervised eleven Midwest shipyards. He opened his own office in 1923, and continued his independent practice until 1956, when his business was joined with that of J. J. Henry of New York. The 168-foot *Haida* (1947) was one of his best-known designs. Wells designed approximately 150 yachts. He retired in 1960 and died in 1962.

Some of Wells' drawings are in the John H. Wells Collection as well as in the Thomas W. Dunn Collection, both at Mystic Seaport Museum, Mystic, CT.

—Daniel B. MacNaughton

KARL ZAKEUS "ZAKE" WESTIN

1886–1938 · Finland

Nowadays, few yards both design and build boats on the same premises, but up until the earlier part of the twentieth century such was the typical pattern. Zake Westin's life and career centered in his father's well-known Abo Boat Yard in Abo (now Turko), Finland, where he worked, learned the craft of boatbuilding, and taught himself how to design yachts.

The Abo Boat Yard found its customers in Finland, Russia, and the smaller states that line the eastern coast of the Baltic Sea. Starting in 1908, Westin concentrated on his Square-Meter boats, which were unusually long and slim, giving them a graceful profile as well as good performance to windward.

When in the 1920's Westin began to design 6-Meters under the International Rule, he maintained a strong aesthetic sense, electing to optimize his boats for beauty and sailing qualities instead of fully exploiting the rule, a unique approach that produced boats of exceptional elegance.

Westin's 6-Meters *Merenneito I* (1927) and *II* (1928) were the best boats from Finland, winning many trophies in Scandinavia. *Merenneito I* won second prize in the Gold Cup in the United States in 1927.

—Bent Aarre

ALFRED WESTMACOTT

1868–1936 · England

The name Alfred Westmacott is synonymous with the growth of one-design classes in the first third of the twentieth century. Dissatisfaction with rating rules led many yachtsmen in all parts of Great Britain to opt for boats built to a one-design class. In the post–World War I period, changed social and economic conditions further encouraged the one-design concept.

Westmacott was the son of Percy Westmacott, founder and managing director of Armstrong, Mitchell and Company, a shipbuilding and engineering firm on the river Tyne in northeastern England. The Westmacotts were a well-to-do family, with a house at Oban on the west coast of Scotland, where they sailed their 99-foot Camper and Nicholson schooner, *Blue Bell*.

In 1886 Westmacott became an apprentice at his father's firm and two years later spent three years studying naval architecture under Harvard Biles at the prestigious Glasgow University. Returning to Armstrong upon the successful completion of his degree, he became the design team's second-in-command.

Deciding to branch out on his own and being interested in small craft, Westmacott moved in 1899 to Saint Helens at the eastern end of the Isle of Wight off the south coast of England. Here he established the firm of Westmacott, Stewart and Company, which designed, built, and serviced yachts and launches and manufactured marine engines.

In 1904, the company acquired the firm of Woodnutt's of Bembridge Harbour on the west end of the Isle of Wight. This was one of the leading yards of the Solent area, with a high reputation for craftsmanship in all aspects of

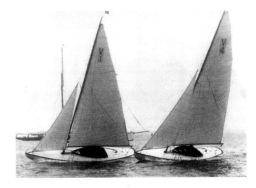

Alfred Westmacott: ***Dainty and Judy.*** Post–World War I social and economic conditions in Britain led to the growth of one-design racing. The Solent Sunbeams are typical of the genre of the time, and still provide exciting and competitive racing. Strict one-designs in all aspects, the name of each boat must end in the letter *y*. Shown here are *Dainty* and *Judy*. *Photo courtesy Andrew Campbell*

their work and a name for the design and building of sound craft. Westmacott's father was in fact responsible for the financial underpinning of the new enterprise, its establishment, and growth. Many of the craft built were for Westmacott Sr.

Much of the design and production work undertaken by Westmacott at the Bembridge yard was for motor launches. Development of the internal-combustion engine and its adaptation to marine use was a feature of the pre–World War I period, and Westmacott was well in the vanguard of that movement. The physical conditions of Bembridge Harbour, a shallow bar with a shallow bay and a relatively sheltered situation, made motor craft and light sailing craft a suitable line to develop. Even so, a 75-foot motoryacht, *Trident*, was built to Westmacott's design at Bembridge.

Westmacott developed the yard to such an extent that it became self-sufficient. As well as the sawmill and building shops, it had its own foundry, blacksmiths, galvanizing tanks, machine shops, and ship's store.

In 1909, Westmacott designed and built the prototype of what was to become one of the largest one-design classes of keelboats in the United Kingdom, the Solent X-boat. Approximately 21 feet LOA with a waterline of 17 feet and a 6-foot beam, these gaff sloop-rigged dayboats were adopted by the Royal Motor Yacht Club in 1912 and quickly spread to the yachting centers on the Solent and adjacent sailing waters. Many of the class were rerigged as Bermudian sloops after World War I, and other yards were approved as builders, in order to meet a demand that has continued to this day. The Cowes Week Regatta frequently sees as many as ninety X-boats coming to the line.

Other one-design classes quickly followed, each developed to suit the specific needs of the particular area where they were based. The best known of these classes include the Victory class based in Portsmouth (and found in other parts of the world where the Royal Navy had bases such as Gibraltar); the Yarmouth One-Designs at the western end of the Isle of Wight; the Seaview One-Designs at Westmacott's homeport; and the Solent and Falmouth Sunbeams. This latter class, somewhat larger than the others, was likely designed by Louis Jacobs, who worked for Westmacott and later became chief draftsman at Camper and Nicholson.

During World War I, Woodnutt's produced small craft for the Admiralty. Westmacott himself was a naval constructor, achieving the rank of captain. After the war, he returned to the Woodnutt yard, designing and building small craft, many of them cruisers.

Small cruising yachts were a growing feature of British yachting during the 1920's because people could no longer afford large craft with a plethora of paid hands. It would be fair to say that the Corinthian ideal reached its greatest height in the period between the wars. Westmacott's response to the demand was to produce some delightful craft of 4 to 5 tons (Thames Measurement), often canoe-sterned, a style that was to find great favor in this period.

At his death, Westmacott left a corpus of work that endures to this day. Woodnutt's, the yard he developed so well, lasted until 1965, when its new owners, who had acquired the premises in 1961, closed it down. In the post–World War II period, the yard built some fine craft, including beautiful 5- and 5.5-Meter racing craft. The quality of the workmanship stands as a testament to the standards set by Alfred Westmacott.　　　　—David Ryder-Turner

JAMES WHARRAM

Born May 15, 1928 · England

In the century following the introduction of the multihull concept to the western world, much of the emphasis has been developing the type's considerable potential for speed. While James Wharram always includes speed among his design's virtues, fulfilling the multihull's potential as a relatively safe, comfortable, and economical cruising boat has been his career's primary focus.

Wharram was inspired by French multihull pioneer Eric de Bisschop and his voyage from Hawaii to France via Cape Town (1937–39) in the 38-foot double canoe *Kaimiloa*, which de Bisschop built on a beach in Hawaii. In the mid-1950's, Wharram, based in England, and Rudi Choy of Hawaii made other transoceanic catamaran voyages. The three designers showed the world that there was a vast untapped potential in multihull sailing yachts.

Wharram grew up in Manchester, England. He attended technical school and after World War II spent some time traveling around Europe. During this period he was exposed to many nontraditional ideas, which led him to become, in terms of lifestyle and philosophy, an early counterculturalist.

Tangaroa, Wharram's first catamaran, was launched in 1954. He sailed her to Trinidad via the Canary Islands. There he and his companions built a larger, improved version that they sailed to New York and then, in 1959, back to Britain, becoming the first catamaran to cross the North Atlantic. After that Wharram began designing catamarans for others and

selling plans, achieving tremendous popularity in the 1970's, when both his "alternative" boats and personal philosophy of life struck a responsive chord in many people.

Wharram believed that catamarans offered global mobility and good liveaboard comfort for a highly affordable price, a notion he has proved beyond all doubt with the sale of over eight thousand sets of plans to date, of which, Wharram estimates, at least 50 percent have resulted in a completed boat.

One of the reasons for the popularity of his designs is their V-shaped sections, developed by Wharram from his personal experiences of ocean sailing and extensive study of the ancient Pacific canoes. The V-shaped hull is not the fastest, but Wharram felt it was best for damping motion and therefore increasing both safety and comfort. In many of his designs it also provides enough lateral resistance to obviate the need for keels or centerboards.

Wharram's hulls generally have strong sheers, generous forward overhangs and flare, plus a moderate freeboard height of 12 to 14 percent of the overall length. The moderate freeboard holds windage to a minimum, the hull shape provides excellent buoyancy, and the dory-like shape is ideal for lifting the hulls over oncoming seas, thus counteracting multihulls' common tendency to bury the lee bow. The two hulls are joined together with flexible connections, allowing some independent movement and dispersal of stress.

While it is desirable to keep any multihull light, Wharram's designs can tolerate heavier loads than other types—an important consideration to the long-distance voyager carrying large amounts of food and water. Wharram catamarans are easily built by amateurs using a simple sheet plywood and epoxy construction method.

In the early years Wharram's catamarans had only open slats and minimal deck structures between the hulls, to keep the center of gravity low and to allow both wind and waves to pass between the hulls without pushing up on the platform and reducing stability. Since the late 1970's Wharram's larger designs have had deck pods and cockpits, giving shelter to the helmsmen and off-watch crew, but he has never allowed the deck structures to dominate the design or to fill the whole area between the hulls, nor has he allowed the overall freeboard to exceed traditional aesthetic values.

Wharram has also searched for close-winded, low center-of-effort rigs to obtain speed without loss of stability. He believes he has achieved this aim in his "Wharram Wingsail Rig." He uses sail area–displacement ratios that put the speed potential of his latest designs in the

James Wharram: *Spirit of Gaia*. *Spirit of Gaia* belongs to Wharram and his family. Launched in 1992, she is 63 feet long and 28 feet wide. Her design is based on the principles of a Pacific voyaging canoe. She was built of plywood, epoxy, and glass by the design team with the help of many volunteers in Cornwall, England. She has since sailed round the world and has been used as a base for research into original canoe-form craft in the Pacific and Indian Oceans. *Photo courtesy James Wharram*

Chris White: *Synergy*. The design for *Synergy*, an Atlantic 55 catamaran, emphasizes excellent performance, a comfortable cruising interior, and ease of shorthanded sailing. *Photo courtesy Chris White.*

performance catamaran range, but due to the low aspect ratio of the rig (most of his larger designs use a two-masted rig) the stability of his designs has always remained high.

The designer's work now falls into three categories: his "Self Build range" of easy-to-build, plywood-epoxy-fiberglass designs; his "Professional range," being built under his supervision in yards in southeastern Asia and England; and his new "Ethnic range" of ancient Pacific double-canoe replicas.

James Wharram and his two partners divide their lives between voyages in their 63-foot double canoe *Spirit of Gaia* and practicing yacht design in Truro, Cornwall, England.

—Daniel B. MacNaughton

CHRIS WHITE

Born 1954 · United States

Chris White is one of the most innovative multihull designers in the United States. Addressing questions of economy and space utilization, he has produced impressive advances. Moreover, in a field where speed and high technology are often thought to be enough, he has created visually appealing boats.

Growing up on Long Island, New York, White's first sailing experience was at age twelve in a Lightning class sloop. Years later, while attending the University of Colorado, he decided that he wanted to build a boat and sail around the world. He worked at odd jobs to make enough money to build a 31-foot, Jim Brown–designed trimaran named *Shadowfax* in his backyard. She was launched in 1974.

In 1978 White met Jim Brown and, along with multihull designer Dick Newick, assisted Brown with the construction of *Sib* (which stands for "small is beautiful"), an experimental trimaran intended to be practical for third world fishermen to construct. In the process he helped to develop the Constant Camber method of construction, in which standardized planks of veneer are arranged on a mold that can be used for multiple purposes, such that panels suitable for hull construction can be quickly and economically laminated.

The 52-foot *Juniper*, constructed in this way and launched in 1980, is a classic example of White's approach to design. Many designers, given the multihull's great beam and initial stability, choose to pile on the deckhouses, creating grand accommodations on small hulls. White, realizing that costs relate more directly to surface area of the whole boat than to hull length alone, in effect took away all the surface area of the deckhouses and put it into the hulls, creat-

Joel White: *Ellisha.* Joel White respected the virtues of small boats and tried to make them perfect in every line. The Bridges Point 24, one of a few of White's designs built of fiberglass, is a pretty, reassuring, easy-to-care-for, and easy-to-handle performer. *Ellisha,* shown here with her designer, was White's own boat. © *Benjamin Mendlowitz*

ing a much bigger boat for about the same cost.

The result, finished off with an unstayed cat-ketch rig, is a profoundly simple boat, economically constructed, with all the improved speed, stability, and motion that a larger boat provides plus a truly impressive interior. She has a beautiful sheer on all the hulls and pleasing shapes to the amas (the arms that connect the outriggers to the hull) and the rig. In another innovation, White has placed the amas very high and made them buoyant, partly so they do not tend to strike passing seas, and partly so that in the event of a capsize they will support the hulls sufficiently high in the water to allow safe occupation of the center hull.

Currently White designs one-offs plus a range of cruising catamarans from 33 to 65 feet long, including the Atlantic series ranging from 40 to 55 feet, the Superior 54, and the Voyager 45 and 48. Cruising trimarans include the Explorer 44 and the Hammerhead 54. He is largely self-taught as a designer, and was among the first to perceive and utilize the advantages of computer design software. White's book, *The*

Cruising Multihull, introduces readers to the many facets of cruising multihull design.

Chris White practices in South Dartmouth, Massachusetts.　　　—Daniel B. MacNaughton

JOEL WHITE

December 21, 1930–December 5, 1997
United States

Joel White's designs embodied staunch integrity, common sense, progressive thinking, and good taste, perfectly reflecting the personality of their creator. His work demonstrated that a blend of modern and traditional features was not only possible but admirable, and he accomplished this blend in a natural-seeming way. White's designs were the product of a highly educated mind familiar with yacht designing history including the most modern innovations, but he was dedicated to the fundamental concepts of beauty, simplicity, efficiency, and long-lived structures.

Probably the best-known of White's designs

is his smallest: the 7-foot Nutshell pram, a good-looking, seaworthy, and practical yacht tender suitable for the home boatbuilder, and arguably the best pram design of its size. His most spectacular design is undoubtedly the W-Class sloop, a 76-foot, cold-molded, wood one-design that combines high speed potential with easy handling and clean, classic good looks.

White designed a number of well-regarded smaller sailing craft such as the Haven 12½, a centerboard adaptation of the popular Herreshoff 12½; the Bridges Point 24, a sleek full-keel sloop produced in fiberglass in several versions; the Sakonnet 23, a canoe-sterned fiberglass keel/centerboard daysailer; and a number of designs drawn, like the Nutshell pram, for *WoodenBoat* magazine. He designed several handsome powerboats based on the Maine lobsterboat type, and numerous classically beautiful cruising sailboats based on his extensive experience in coastal and offshore cruising.

Among the latter is *Dragonera,* a 74-foot, fast cruising ketch launched in 1994. She is a notable example of healthy light-displacement design

Joel White: *Wild Horses* and *White Wings*. The W-76's *Wild Horses* and *White Wings* were built by Brooklin Boat Yard and Rockport Marine, respectively, and launched in 1998. Because he was commissioned to design a classic one-design uninfluenced by any rule, White was free to optimize their appearance, ease of handling, strength, and speed. © *Benjamin Mendlowitz*

drawn without the influence of handicapping rules or racing fads. Long and relatively narrow, with moderate ends, a flush deck with freeboard sufficient for headroom under the deck throughout most of the hull, and an all-inboard ketch rig, she is efficiency personified, and is certainly one of the most practical, large, light-displacement cruising sailboats of the decade.

As a boatbuilder, White combined modern and traditional materials and techniques to produce a steady stream of strong, simple, durable, and appealing sailboats and powerboats of all sizes, working primarily in carvel, strip-planked, and cold-molded wood construction.

White was an early supporter of *WoodenBoat* magazine and later a frequent contributor. His column titled "Designs" analyzed the design, construction, and performance of many different boats and was a "first read" for many *WoodenBoat* subscribers. He was generous with his advice to young boatbuilders, and his steady, warm, direct, and good-humored personality endeared him to people of all ages and from all walks of life. White was a valued advisor to *The Encyclope-*

dia of Yacht Designers, and its first Subscriber.

Joel White was born in New York City, the son of famous author and essayist E. B. White and Katherine Sergeant (Angell) White, fiction editor at *The New Yorker* magazine. The family moved to Brooklin, Maine, in the mid-1930's, where White soon developed a strong interest in the boats he saw sailing around Blue Hill Bay and Eggemoggin Reach. At age ten he and his father built a small scow they called *Flounder*, White's first boatbuilding experience.

As a teenager White acquired *Shadow*, a Herreshoff 12½ that he kept in mint condition for the rest of his life. He attended grade school in Brooklin and then Exeter Academy, graduating in 1947. For two years he attended Cornell University, his father's school, lobstering in the summer months, and then transferred to MIT, from which he graduated in 1953 with a degree in naval architecture.

After graduation White took a job at Newport News Shipbuilding and Drydock, and then was drafted into the army, whereupon he spent two years with the infantry in Germany. Returning

to Maine, he joined designer/builder Arno Day at his boatyard on Center Harbor, later entering into a partnership with Day and then becoming the yard's sole owner in 1960, changing the name to the Brooklin Boat Yard. The yard has become one of Maine's most highly respected facilities for construction, repair, hauling, and storage of boats, mostly wooden.

In 1987 White turned over the day-to-day operation of the yard to his son Joel Steven White, and began concentrating full-time on yacht design. With photographer Benjamin Mendlowitz, he wrote the book *Wood, Water and Light*, a celebration of classic boats. He was on the board of the Mystic Seaport Museum and was chairman of its Ship Committee. He was active in several local organizations. For many years White sailed the 35-foot 6-inch, Aage Nielsen–designed cutter *Northern Crown*, and later enjoyed the first Bridges Point 24, a fiberglass sloop of his design that he named *Ellisha*, for his granddaughter. He could be seen sailing on and around Eggemoggin Reach almost until his death in 1997.   —Daniel B. MacNaughton

Carlton Wilby: *Ionita*. The 50-foot, gasoline-powered *Ionita* was built in 1914. Like much of Wilby's pioneering work, she combines higher speeds made possible by improved engines, with comfortable accommodations seldom seen previously in fast motorboats. These developments would ultimately lead to the commuter yachts of the next decade. *Photo courtesy Naval Historical Foundation*

CARLTON WILBY

July 31, 1881–August, 1966 · United States

Carlton Wilby developed and refined the concept of the express cruiser, forerunner of the commuting cruiser. Surrounded by automobile entrepreneurs in a city that was growing by great leaps and bounds, Wilby found abundant work in Detroit, Michigan, and nationally as his reputation grew through the 1910's. Like his automotive counterparts, he found standardization of design essential for the burgeoning motorboat industry.

Born in Detroit, Wilby received his early training in naval architecture at the boards of Bowdoin B. Crowninshield in Boston. He gained valuable experience subsequently at Bath Iron Works in Maine, the Detroit Shipbuilding Company, and Great Lakes Engineering Works.

In 1907 Wilby established a personal practice in naval architecture in Detroit. That first year he designed two 25-foot hunting cabin cruisers. His sailboat designs, including 65- and 52-foot, schooners, a 50-foot ketch, and a 21-foot sloop, were published in *The Rudder* magazine.

Wilby became interested in standardized design for boats under 50 feet in length and marketed a design for a 31-foot, raised-deck cruiser that could be modified to about anything in the 20- to 40-foot range. "My experience has shown that the average owner of a motorboat under 40 or 50 feet in length has been rather 'up against it' to get a really good design. It is out of the question, of course, to suppose that a naval architect can afford to prepare a special design for a small boat at the same rate, or percentage of the cost, as in the case of a large boat. The same calculations and plans are required, whether the boat is large or small, and consequently the charge for design must be much greater, in proportion, for the latter than for the former," he stated.

Wilby shared his opinion on the lack of sheer on cruisers designed by his contemporaries. "There is hardly anything which makes or mars the appearance of a boat, in the eye of a sailor, as much as the sheer line. Unless this line is 'eye-sweet,' it is impossible to produce a craft of graceful appearance. A reasonably straight sheerline on a speed boat is all right; it gives a racy appearance, cuts down on weight, and is entirely consistent with the use to which the boat is put; namely smooth water work. But to attempt to carry this idea into cruiser design is inconsistent, and ridiculous. The result is a tubby, wall-sided craft, with the 'by-the-head' look that is anything but seaworthy."

Wilby made his most important contributions in express cruisers as they became a popular form of boating by about 1910, foreshadowing the commuter cruisers of the 1920's. Once marine gasoline engines became powerful and reliable enough to withstand long journeys at high speeds, designers quickly did away with the engine room and the attendant engineer, relying instead on the minimal service that the pilot could provide. Improved domestic amenities such as electrical lighting plants, galleys, and larger or better laid-out sleeping accommodations also found their way into the larger boats.

Considered quite fast for their time, Wilby's express cruisers were frequently powered by twin six-cylinder Van Blerck engines, also built locally in Detroit. The cruisers he designed often raced against each other formally and informally, and the series of boats named *Betty M* became well known locally, with orders for similar craft quickly following. Perhaps because of a desire to oversee the design's progress in the constructions stage, Wilby worked extensively with local builders. Occasionally he catered to some of the more outlandish ideas of what buyers thought a yacht should be, once adapting the lines of a tramp steamer into a yacht named *Me Too*.

During World War I, Wilby worked as an assistant naval architect at the Great Lakes Engineering Works in Ecorse, where the firm built Laker-type oceangoing cargo ships. After the war his name seldom appeared in the small craft and yachting press, as his time and talents presumably went toward commercial ships. As his boats disappeared, his work was likewise forgotten.

After 1921, Wilby left Detroit. In 1930 he was working as a marine architect and living in Queens, New York, and later in Oyster Bay. He retired by the early 1960's to Anna Marie, Florida.

Carlton Wilby died at the age of eighty-five in Haddonfield, Camden, New Jersey.

—Scott Peters

RALPH HOUGHTON WILEY

1893–1981 · United States

Ralph Wiley created some of the most distinctive yachts to cruise and race around his adopted waters of the Chesapeake Bay and its tributaries. Although born and raised in Massapequa, New York, Wiley set up a small boatbuilding business in Oxford, Maryland, on the eve of the Great Depression. There he became known for his comfortable motorsailers, as well as yacht adaptations of traditional boats such as Chesapeake Bay bugeyes and Tancook whalers.

Although Wiley experimented with new materials, his innovative and original designs generally relied on local materials and techniques, such as the deadrise V-bottom construction so well known on the Chesapeake. A respected and well-loved personality in yachting circles, Wiley was visited frequently at his yard by cruisers passing though the Chesapeake who enjoyed his storytelling and good humor.

Having graduated from Stevens Institute of Technology in 1915 with a degree in mechanical engineering, Wiley worked at Bethlehem Steel in Bethlehem, Pennsylvania, and the Worthington Pump Company in Hazelton, Pennsylvania. A layoff gave him the determination to seek self-employment as a yacht designer and builder.

In 1929 Wiley launched his first boat, the 41-foot swordfisherman *Alibi*. It incorporated features that made it a forerunner of sportfishing boats, including twin screws with a rudder behind each propeller and multiple steering stations, one of them on a flying bridge. He rented space in a yard to construct this boat, but later in the year acquired land for his own Oxford yard.

Wiley designed and built several motor cruisers in the mid-1930's. However, he began specializing in motorsailers with the 43-foot *Shoemaker's Child* and a slightly enlarged 44-foot version, *Horizon*. He built nine in all, with incrementally larger designs up to 47 feet in length, through the beginning of World War II. He adopted the Chesapeake's characteristic hard-chine for his motorsailers, though on the larger ones the hard-chine is present only amidship, disappearing as it rises above the waterline at both bow and stern.

During the war, Wiley designed life rafts and other equipment for the Maritime Commission, leaving his yard's daily operations and skeletal workforce under the supervision of his wife Mary and son Chuck. Wiley returned on weekends to monitor progress.

In addition to motorsailers, Wiley also designed and built a number of sailing yachts, notably double-enders, beginning with a pair of 40-foot bugeye types. He was inspired by Tancook whalers to turn out *Golden Bough*, a 30-foot yacht adaptation of the traditional type, and *Mocking Bird*, a 31-foot modification. Wiley built two 39-foot Tancook designs, *Fox* (1946) and *Vixen* (1955), the former for himself, which he campaigned successfully in races.

Wiley drew up a one-design class for the local yacht club, a 16-foot hard-chined catboat with a high-peaked gaff. About thirty-five boats were built to this Scrappy cat design. The Scrappy was designed with amateur construction in mind, though several emerged from the Wiley yard. His yard also built several boats with plans from other designers, including the first several of C. Lowndes Johnson's Comet class, as well as yachts designed by Howard I. Chapelle and Fred Geiger.

Respected for stoutly built boats, Wiley could be as innovative with construction methods as with design ideas. He experimented with alternative deck materials and obtained a patent in 1950 for a thwartship method of planking decks that not only required no caulking, but also eliminated the need for deck beams, increasing cabin headroom and lightening deck construction.

Wiley was also an early proponent of glue-strip planking, using this method on his Tancook whaler *Fox*. He tended to eschew brightwork and expensive details in favor of simple, solid construction. The results were boats with lower initial and maintenance costs. During the Depression, Wiley advertised custom-built boats for the price of stock cruisers.

Wiley sold his yard in 1963 to John Case and Edmund Cutts, remaining a consultant to his successor, a business that continued to design and build innovative wooden boats on this site. In 1972 he published an autobiography, *Preacher's Son*, which conveys both his storytelling ability and sense of humor. His reputation is firm as one of the most notable designers to hail from the Chesapeake.

Wiley's design drawings are now in the collections of the Chesapeake Bay Maritime Museum, Saint Michaels, MD.

—Pete Lesher

Ralph Wiley: *Dinghao.* The 46-foot 6-inch *Dinghao*, designed and built in 1939 by Wiley in Oxford, Maryland, was typical of his motor cruisers. *Photo by Fred Thomas, courtesy Chesapeake Bay Maritime Museum, Saint Michaels, MD*

FENWICK CUSHING WILLIAMS

December 22, 1901–August 07, 1992
United States

Fenwick C. Williams, a soft-spoken and unassuming gentleman, had a major impact on American sail and power vessel design for over sixty years, commencing in 1921 with his first employment in the Boston naval architecture firm of John G. Alden. Handicapped by poor eyesight that deteriorated during his early childhood in Lowell, Massachusetts, Williams found solace in pen-and-ink drawings that evolved from nature scenes to boats.

After their parents' divorce, Williams and his younger brother Gordon especially enjoyed the freedom of summers in Sandwich, New Hampshire, and Gloucester, Massachusetts. Fenwick's grandfather, a Lowell engineer, and his mother, an antiques dealer, were his role models. He never married, did not drive a car, and resided in Marblehead with his mother for forty-two years until her passing in 1966.

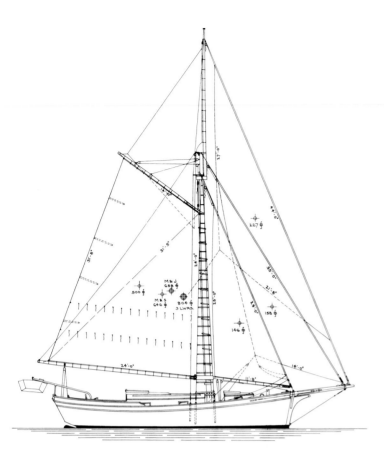

Fenwick Williams: *Champion.* One of the things Williams did best was to create yachts that embodied much of the character and practicality of traditional working boats, without slavishly duplicating the originals. *Champion* somewhat resembles a Friendship sloop, but diverges from that type in many ways, all of which probably make her a better yacht. *Drawing courtesy William Peterson*

Fenwick Williams: *Champion.* The work of great designers often looks better "in the flesh" than on paper. The cutter *Champion* is a good example, as in profile her lines are rather square and blocky. In reality her profile combines with her sections to reveal a design that is lovely in form and staunch in spirit. *Photo courtesy William Peterson*

Fenwick Williams: *Stingray.* While Fenwick Williams is better known for his sailing yacht designs, this fast and efficient-looking power yacht illustrates her designer's versatility. Note that while the yacht is completely free of nostalgic references, the crisply styled hull and superstructure seem to obey traditional notions of proportion. *Photo courtesy William Peterson*

Williams became a Marblehead fixture, leaning forward to see better as he walked or biked the narrow streets and as he rowed in the harbor. He was frugal, industrious, meticulous in drafting, and skilled as an engineer. His warm humor and ability to work with others were also key attributes in achieving a long list of satisfied business partners and clients.

In 1931, when the Great Depression caused large layoffs at Alden's, Williams joined his life-long friend Murray Peterson in the Marblehead firm of Peterson and Williams. For three years, they evolved new lines of traditional workboat designs for recreational and commercial customers. In 1934, Williams returned to Alden's, where he worked until 1945. During World War II, he specialized in the design of navy support craft built in New England, contributing to the massive war effort.

At war's end, Williams joined C. Raymond Hunt to form the firm of Hunt and Williams, creating innovative power and racing sailboat designs. After a number of their designs were built by Concordia, Williams continued as in-house designer for Concordia into the 1970's. Throughout these years and until his retirement in 1985, Williams also created seventy-five custom designs under his own name. Periodically, he designed for fellow Marblehead naval architects, including L. Francis Herreshoff and K. Aage Nielsen.

Two distinct categories of designs characterize Williams's career. One shows a steady evolution in power and sailing yacht designs that began with Alden and ended with his Concordia collaboration. Another was his more traditional style, interpreting workboat designs like the cutter *Champion*, one of three Williams designs for Henry Barkhausen, that reflected his personal preference for simplicity and proven attributes. These gaff-rigged catboats, sloops, cutters, schooners, and ketches were a dramatic contrast to his high-performance, 6- and 12-Meter sloops, ocean racing yawls, and large, high-speed power-boats. During his association with Alden, for example, Williams had full responsibility for dozens of sail and power boat designs in addition to sharing the effort on many of Alden's most representative works.

Alden remarked to a client that "Fenwick is one designer I can give a job knowing that it will result in a design exactly as I would have wished it." This thinking was reflected in the opinions of fellow architects like Aage Nielsen, who described Williams as an "A-1 gentleman from whom I learned greatly during my own early days at Alden." Ray Hunt listed Williams in a *Sports Illustrated* article as the key reason their America's Cup design was a success.

During his association with Hunt, Williams designed and engineered advances in Deep-V hull form with lift strips, like the beautiful *Sunbeam* for George W. W. Brewster, and rule beaters like the sailing ocean racer *Drumbeat* for Lord Beaverbrook. Williams was an early advocate of double planking and multilayered, laminated hull construction. When not designing, he compiled scores of tables of engineering data or comparisons between proven vessels that expedited the laborious work of calculations and scantling or equipment selection. Periodicals on the advances of naval architecture on the East Coast describe him as a "leading engineer of his day."

After his official retirement in the 1970's, Williams became associated with the rebirth of wooden boats for family cruising and amateur construction. His name was synonymous with Cape Cod catboats through his support of the then-fledgling Catboat Association and his design of over a dozen cats of different lengths from 14 to 30 feet.

At the age of seventy in 1970, Williams single-handed his beloved seventy-year-old ketch *Nawadaha* from Marblehead to South Bristol, Maine, as part of his longstanding dream to retire there. With characteristic humor, Williams described this as "the only significant thing I have ever accomplished in my life." By contrast, his immense contribution to marine design is a testament to his exceptional artistry and careful attention to detail.

A collection of Williams's drawings is held by Murray G. Peterson Associates of South Bristol, ME, and selected designs are at the Peabody Essex Museum, Salem, MA.

—William M. Peterson

ANDREW WINCH

Born June 26, 1956 · England

Despite a well-rounded education that extended beyond parochial limits, Andrew Winch acquired his greatest insights into yacht design on the job. Although Winch recalls, with characteristic modesty, that he was hired in 1980 by Jon Bannenberg as a "bottle washer, pencil sharpener, and coffee maker," he clearly took advantage of his five-year apprenticeship at the master's side to hone the strongly individual visions of form, space, and decoration that have become the hallmarks of his work.

By 1986, when he left Bannenberg to start his own studio, Winch had contributed to four important sailing yachts, considered large for their time: *Shirley B* (80 feet), *Starlight* (94 feet), *Garuda* (102 feet, and the first custom yacht ever built by Finland's Nautor), and *Acharné* (112 feet).

He was on his way toward his self-proclaimed goal of achieving "beauty afloat, and a balance of line and form."

Winch was born in London. After studying fine art, art history, general history, and geography at Wellington College from 1969 to 1974, he concentrated on art for one year at Saint Martins in London, then he won a degree in three-dimensional design and interior design from Kingston College of Art/Polytechnic in 1978.

Instead of checking the help-wanted ads immediately after graduation, however, Winch left his academic days behind and embarked on a year's sailing adventure, crossing the Atlantic as paid crew aboard a 52-foot sailboat, then cruising the Caribbean—a liveaboard experience that further sharpened his understanding of what people *do* need and *don't* want aboard a sailing yacht. On his return to London he landed the job with Bannenberg; in 1986 he left Bannenberg to establish Andrew Winch Designs with his wife Jane, in the London suburb of Mortlake.

Winch's first project in his new studio was to design the exterior and interior of Nautor's smallest production sailboat, the Swan 36 (with designer Germán Frers). The outstanding feature Winch gave the Swan was a thwartship "gullwing" coachroof window, conceived generally to enliven a rather conservative line, specifically to open the yacht's interior to the light and realities of the outside world. When the prototype was launched in 1988, it generated much debate, even as it demonstrated that a young designer could try unconventional devices so long as they were ultimately proved sensible, practical, and attractive.

Winch next took a leap into the over-100-foot world of megasailers by collaborating with Ron Holland on three designs: 110-foot *Sensation* (launched by Sensation Yachts, New Zealand, in 1988), and 100-foot *Royal Eagle* (Camper and Nicholson) and 145-foot *Cyclos III* (Royal Huisman Shipyard), both launched in 1989. Each bore the stamp of Winch's individuality; each brought him wider notice and acclaim. When in 1991 Winch's design for Camper and Nicholson's custom-built, 90-foot *Victoria of Strathearn* won the *ShowBoats International* award for Best Sailing Yacht Over 35 Meters, his reputation advanced to a new plateau from which it has never receded.

Through the 1990's Winch designed a variety of production sailing yachts between 48 and 72 feet long, marketed under the brands of Oyster, Wauquiez, Janneau, Feeling, Dynasty, Solaris, and Concepta. And he designed interiors for a number of other important custom yachts, notably *Teel* (a 115-foot Ted Hood design built at Trident Shipworks that won Most Innovative Sailing

Yacht award for 1995), *Hetairos* (a classic 128-foot Bruce King ketch built by Abeking and Rasmussen), *Shaman* (an 80-foot Bill Tripp design built by R. E. Derecktor Shipyards), and *Surama* (a 135-foot ketch designed by Hood and built by Huisman, which won *ShowBoats International's* 1997 award for Best Sailing Yacht Interior).

As with most designers facing the reality of the market, in the mid-1990's Winch recognized the importance of large motoryachts to his *oeuvre*, and he obtained several commissions to create such yachts. Between 1994 and 2000 Winch saw the launch of the Amels-built *Sarafsa* (177 feet) and *Lady Aviva* (203 feet), and the Feadship *Solemates* (170 feet), for which he designed the exterior and interior concepts, as well as the Feadships *Claire* (180 feet), *White Rabbit* (160 feet), and *Cakewalk* (204 feet), for which he designed the interiors. Three of the Feadships won *ShowBoats International* awards. And under way on the boards Winch has, among others, three motoryachts and six large sailing yachts in collaboration with the naval architects Langan Design, Frers, Ted Hood Design, Bill Tripp, Bruce King, and van de Stadt Design.

Perhaps the greatest plum Andrew Winch has plucked out of the megayacht pie is a vessel that is yet to be finished. In 1996 he was asked to design the exterior and interior of a true superyacht—a 160-meter floating city to be built jointly by two German shipyards. Astonishingly, after three years of design and construction, as the hull and superstructure were nearing completion, the project was canceled. Yet, whether finished or not, the sheer size and complexity of the project reflect the confidence that Andrew Winch Design had earned—in less than fifteen years.   —Jack A. Somer

RALPH ELDRIDGE WINSLOW

1886–March 29, 1957 · United States

A quiet and humble man, Ralph Winslow did little to promote himself and designed few racing boats. As a result he is less well known than many of his peers, but he produced a good number of very highly regarded designs for cruising sailboats as well as many handsome and influential powerboat designs. He is known for his impeccable drafting, his gift for proportion and character, and his excellent grasp of engineering, all of which were self-taught.

Most of Winslow's early work, much of which appeared under the name of other designers, was in powerboat design. It reflects both the limitations and the charm of early 1900's gasoline-powered yacht design. He influenced the evolution of the new type by moving away from pointed sterns and amidships engines, substituting instead the transom stern and aft-located engines that became more or less standard from then on. Such innovations aside, Winslow's boats resemble others of the era in their overall character, although his gift for sweet lines and proportions make them stand out.

Winslow's sailboat designs, many of which appeared in *Yachting* and *The Rudder* from the 1930's into the 1950's, seem less dated than the powerboats, as they mostly involve sound traditional forms that, owing to their fundamental virtues, continue to be reinterpreted today. Again, his work stands out for its aesthetic quality as well as the practicality of the boats, most of which were full-keel, moderate- to heavy-displacement cruising and voyaging

boats of contemporary character, although some hark back to earlier eras.

After an apprenticeship in a boatyard in Quincy, Massachusetts, Winslow was hired in 1904 as a draftsman by the Boston design office of the Small Brothers. His first published design, a 33-foot 8-inch power cruiser, appeared in *Motor Boat* in 1906. During this period, Winslow also worked for B. B. Crowninshield and William Hand Jr.

In 1909 Winslow became chief draftsman in the office of Swasey, Raymond and Page, where he stayed until 1917. His 1914 design for a 30-foot double-cabin cruiser differed from other powerboats of the day by placing the engine farther aft, and influenced many other designers. With World War I looming, Winslow's work included designs for handsome military-type express cruisers commissioned by wealthy owners with the intention of donating them to the U.S. Navy should the United States be drawn into the war. From 1917 to 1920 Winslow worked for the Herreshoff Manufacturing Company in Bristol, Rhode Island.

After his stint at Herreshoff's, Winslow began an independent practice that continued until 1928, when he went to work in the office of Eldridge-McInnis for three years before again working for himself. By that time he was primarily designing sailboats. During World War II he was a designer for the U.S. Army. After the war he spent some time in John Alden's Boston office before finally working for himself again, until he died in Quincy, Massachusetts, at the age of seventy-one.

The Ralph E. Winslow Collection is at Mystic Seaport Museum, Mystic, CT.

—Daniel B. MacNaughton

Ralph Winslow: *Allure.* The 50-foot *Allure*, a comfortable-looking cruiser built in 1928, is a good example of early gasoline-powered yacht design. Recently freed from the space and weight restrictions of steam propulsion, designers struggled to determine optimum proportions and arrangements. Winslow helped the new type to evolve in healthy and enduring ways. *Photograph courtesy Peabody Essex Museum, Salem, MA*

Charles Wittholz: *Lizzie Mack*. Drawing from broad experience of many types of designs, Wittholz was able to breathe special life into his catboats. His 25-foot 2-inch design, here represented by *Lizzie Mack*, has an improved layout, somewhat less beam, and other features not exactly like her traditional ancestors. It is comfort and simplicity personified. © *Peter Barlow*

CHARLES W. WITTHOLZ

1918–1993 · United States

Charles Wittholz was a broadly talented individual who designed boats in all building materials and in both power and sail, ranging from small dinghies up to vessels around 90 feet in length. His work included the well-known sloop-of-war replica *Providence*, the brigantine *Young America*, and the schooners *Pegasus* and *Mystic Clipper*.

Among Wittholz's powerboats were practical displacement-hull cruising boats styled after tugboats and trawlers, as well as many designs for trim, tastefully streamlined planing-hull powerboats, which are among the best looking of their type. He was well known for his particularly wholesome and attractive Cape Cod catboat designs.

The majority of Wittholz's work was in custom designs, but his production boats included the Cheoy Lee Midshipman 52 and Wittholz 53, a 17-foot catboat built by the Cape Cod Boat Company, two trawler yacht types built by the Robert Steele Yacht Company, the Windjammer sloop built by Chesapeake Marine, and the ubiquitous SportYak dinghy.

Wittholz became an expert in U.S. Coast Guard regulations for passenger-carrying vessels, and in his later years much of his work was in large vessels built for that purpose. Designed in 1973 for a nonprofit organization in Rhode Island, the 65-foot *Providence* is a fiberglass replica of the United States' first naval vessel, which was also the first command of John Paul Jones.

Wittholz grew up in Buffalo, New York. He came into contact with boats on Lake Erie. As a boy he built two small boats and later studied naval architecture at the University of Michigan. He completed his education through night courses at MIT, afterward becoming an apprentice for designer John Alden. He worked there for two years, and then spent eight years with Philip Rhodes, including the duration of World War II. After opening his own office he produced approximately 250 designs.

The Charles Wittholz Collection (as yet uncatalogued in 2004) is at Mystic Seaport Museum, Mystic, CT.

—Daniel B. MacNaughton

BERT SAMUEL WOOLLACOTT

1878–1964 · England/New Zealand

Because they were largely for the home boatbuilders, who have always contributed a large proportion of the yachts launched in New Zealand, Bert Woollacott designed a full-bodied boat with the ends shortened to provide the most usable vessel for the money. His inspiration was said to be the Falmouth Quay punts. He believed that the most essential quality in a yacht was good balance, and he worked hard on the heeled waterlines to achieve that at all angles of heel. He made sure all his boats were capable of sailing themselves on all points except flat off the wind. His keel yacht designs changed little over the years.

Woollacott was born in Olveston, Somerset, England, and emigrated to New Zealand in 1922. By then he had amassed considerable experience as a boatbuilder and designer, hydroplane designer, and racer in England and the United States. He had worked for Camper and Nicholson in England and Herreshoff Manufacturing Company in Rhode Island (on America's Cup challengers and defenders).

Having settled in Auckland's North Shore suburb of Devonport, Woollacott found plenty of demand for his skills. Over the rest of his life, he produced designs for over fifty yachts, thirty powerboats, and some fishing boat designs, the later designs in association with his son John. A skilled craftsman, he also built thirteen keel yachts for himself. Over three hundred craft were built to his designs

Bert Woollacott: *Ladybird. Ladybird* was designed in 1952 with the help of Woollacott's son, John. Woollacott built her to sail home to England, but sold her after an injury during construction. *Photo courtesy Harold Kidd*

HARRY WUSTRAU

October 15, 1878–March, 1945 · Germany

Harry Wustrau's name is associated with centerboard construction methods and with influential design compromises between cruising and racing yachts which opened yachting to a broader public. He was born to prosperous parents in Berlin, one of the earliest and most important yachting centers in Germany, and home to such important sailing clubs as the Akademische Seglerverein Berlin, the Kiel Yacht Club, and the Flensburg Yacht Club, where his father was among the original member yachtsmen.

After he completed his high school education, Wustrau studied shipbuilding at the Technischen Hochschule in Berlin Charlottenberg. As a student he became an avid reader of *Wassersport* magazine, and inspired by his reading he began to experiment with sailboat design. He received further encouragement from his father, for whom he designed some of the later boats in the series of *Darling* racing yachts.

However, during this time he was frequently summoned from his drawing boards by special assignments for the navy, and the experiences he gathered in the construction of larger ocean-going sailboats influenced his later design work.

Characteristic of his work was the development of new boat types created to allow for savings in construction expenses. His work also reveals his constant quest, regarded as hopeless by his contemporaries, for a viable compromise between comfortable cruising capability and the speed required of a racing yacht, always, of course, to be accomplished at a cost moderate enough to encourage popular participation in yachting.

Wustrau played an important role in the creation of the four national cruising classes, the 35-, 45-, 75-, and 125-Square-Meter classes. He furthermore made decisive contributions in the development of the 12-Square-Meter sharpie one-design and the Olympia dinghy.

But Wustrau most influenced German yachting through his twenty-five-year membership in the German Sailing Association. As the chairman of its Technical Commission, he fought for many years for hull forms of greater beam, freeboard, and displacement, until at last he convinced his colleagues that their fear of "tubby" and "inelegant" boats was misplaced. In the same venue, he championed the principle of maximum and minimum limits in yacht measurements to replace strict measurement formulas. Interestingly, Wustrau typically tested his own design innovations in boats he built for his personal use.

in New Zealand alone. He is said to have had a considerable influence on Arthur C. Robb, the Devonport boy who became an internationally recognized naval architect after he went to England.

The boom that occurred in New Zealand yacht construction after 1945 was largely directed by a thirst for offshore cruising in the Pacific Islands and for ocean racing. Woollacott's designs, frequently rigged as medium-aspect-ratio ketches, were built in dozens of backyards and farmyards all over the country. Woollacott continually traveled to help his amateur clients with advice, inspiration, and considerably deft adze work.

Among Wollacott's famous shortenders were the 34-foot *Ladybird* in 1952, the first Kiwi yacht to win the Trans-Tasman yacht race; *Marco Polo*, the first Kiwi yacht to circumnavigate; and *Ghost, White Squall, Hope, Blue Water, Tanganui,* and *Gesture,* all of which have cruised extensively offshore. Then there were hundreds more that for many years formed a large element of local cruising races.

Woollacott also designed some more conventional large yachts, including *Rambler* (1935) and *West Wind* (1946).

In New Zealand, *Woollacott* is still a byword for sound, practical yachts with exceptional seakeeping qualities.   —Harold Kidd

Wustrau wrote two books, *Vom Kanu zum kleinen Kreuzer* (*From Canoe to Small Cruiser*) in 1917, and *Selbstbau von Scharpiejollen* (*Build Your Own Sharpie Dinghy*) published posthumously in 1947. His articles appeared in *Die Yacht*, until its publication was interrupted in 1943 because of the war. —Volker Christmann

THOMAS H. WYLIE

Born 1946 · United States

Tom Wylie has a reputation for designing fast boats with good habits that have earned their share of yachting history. He was a pioneer in ULDB (ultralight-displacement boat) and cold-molded construction techniques. *Rage* set records for the Transpac Race from San Francisco to Hawaii in 1994 and 1996, *American Express* won the singlehanded Mini-Transatlantic Race of 1979, and *Kropp Duster* won the RORC Commodore's Cup in 1990.

Wylie was born in Salem, Oregon. He started sailing on San Francisco Bay at age sixteen and was soon recognized as having exceptional ability. By age nineteen, he was crewing aboard transpacific racers, and in 1966 he sailed in the Transatlantic Race. He crewed on the 12-Meter *American Eagle* in her 1967 America's Cup campaign. The cold-molded *Nightingale*, Wylie's very first design, won the Hearst Regatta in San Francisco in 1971.

With a degree in industrial design from San Francisco State University, Wylie used his experiences working in boatyards and sail lofts and as a sailor to educate himself in yacht design. He credits designers Myron Spaulding and C. Raymond Hunt as his early influences, citing their innovative approach to design.

Most of Wylie's early work was for racing clients. Designs for *Animal Farm*, winner of the North American Half-Ton Race in 1974, and the Hawkfarm class established him as a competitive talent in the mid-1970's. He earned international acclaim in 1979 when the cold-molded, 21-foot *American Express* won the Mini-

Transatlantic Race from England to the Caribbean, beating the second-place racer by two days. As frequently happens when innovative designs lead to significant advantages in speed, the rule makers limited future water ballast to 50 percent of fixed ballast; *American Express*'s water ballast was 140 percent of fixed ballast. Up to 500 pounds of water could be pumped to the high side, a short-lived advantage.

In 1992 Wylie introduced the Wyliecat 30, a cat-rigged performance cruiser featuring an unstayed carbon fiber mast and wishbone boom. Now with a range from 17 to 48 feet, these boats are easy to sail and fast. He has also drawn heavy-displacement cruising boats including the 65-foot steel yawl *Saga*. In 1998, he designed the ultralight-displacement, narrow-beam (12 feet 6 inches) *Ocean Planet* for the Open 60 class. She was built using the COVE (cored veneer construction) system, as was *Rage* and the 65-foot production series Point Blue.

Tom Wylie practices in Canyon, California. —J. Scott Rohrer

Tom Wylie: Wyliecats. Three Wyliecat 30's and a Wyliecat 39 (aft and to weather) are shown here racing upwind. The simplicity and performance of the Wyliecat 30 attracted enough San Francisco Bay yachtsmen that a one-design class was quickly formed there. Wylie designed a boat light enough and with enough sail to accelerate well in a 10-knot breeze. As the wind increases, the unstayed carbon fiber mast bends and flattens the sail, depowering the rig while increasing upwind performance. *Photo courtesy Thomas Wylie*

AKIRA YOKOYAMA

Born 1915 · Japan

Akira Yokoyama opened his own office in 1959, making him Japan's first professional yacht designer. Many of his yachts were to be built of plywood in the interest of saving money, including the Y-15 (which later became Japan's first fiberglass production boat), the Y-19, the 19-foot Kingfisher Class, and the Y-21. He was also a founding member in 1954 of the Nippon Ocean Racing Club (NORC, now the Japanese Sailing Federation [JSAF]).

Yokoyama was born in Darien, China. He designed a one-design dinghy class for the Olympic Games to be held in Tokyo in 1946, but its production was suspended due to World War II. At the time he said that sailing the boat during its trials was "like listening to swing jazz." During the war, he served the navy by designing various devices for measuring the performance of ships, and conducted experiments using real boats. After the war, he joined the Okamoto and Son

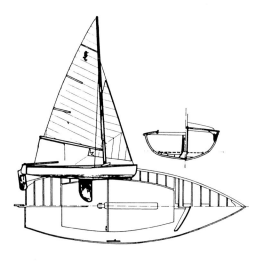

Akira Yokoyama: Seahorse. Japan's first modern sailing dinghy was designed in 1948. A class association was quickly formed and remains active. *Drawing courtesy Kennosuke Hayashi*

Boat Yard in Yokohama as a design engineer.

A number of small wooden sailboats that Yokoyama designed were exported to the United States, including the Bay Lady and Maya classes—light-displacement cruising boats of the type sailed by the United Kingdom's Junior Offshore Group—which were sailed extensively in the San Francisco Bay area. He also redesigned the above-mentioned one-design boat, known as the Seahorse, for his own use. He successfully cruised to islands 40 nautical miles offshore aboard this modern planing dinghy with its excellent course-holding ability. There is a class association for this sailing dinghy and new boats are being built, attracting attention even now.

The first sailing yachts in Japan were those brought by foreigners after 1859 when the Port of Yokohama was opened to foreign vessels. In 1858, Queen Victoria of the United Kingdom gave the 138-foot *Emperor* to the Tokugawa shogunate; however, the time was not favorable for a pleasure boat and the government reconstructed her into a warship. At that time, the history of oceangoing sailing ships in Japan had been suspended for over two hundred years, due to the government's isolation policy and a 1635 law banning the construction of offshore-capable vessels. As part of this restriction, transverse frames and structural bulkheads were not allowed, so wooden vessels for the Japanese coastal trade developed unique design and construction depending on very thick planking and thick, flat keels.

In the 1880's, boat clubs and yacht clubs developed in port cities such as Yokohama and Kobe. Men such as H. Cook, J. Whitfield (a boatbuilder), and A. Auston from the United Kingdom, Dr. G. D. West (a naval architect) from Ireland, K. Ikezawa (a boatbuilder) from Japan, and T. M. Ruffin (who around 1890 moved from Maine to Japan) from the United States were the people most well known to sailing associations in those days. In the early

1900's, Japanese started joining the yachting circle, according to *Yachting History of Japan* by Kentaro Shirasaki (KAZI Company).

In 1932, the Japan Yachting Association (JYA) was formed and a domestic 5-meter class and other classes were developed, only to be completely devastated by the outbreak of World War II. After the war, foreign residents again were the first to start sailing, and in 1948 they founded the Cruising Club of Japan. In 1954 this club was transformed into the NORC.

Yokoyama was the best skipper of the time, and he established the measurement system and safety regulations, taking the RORC Rules as the example. The NORC and JYA were amalgamated into the JSAF in 1999. He has also conducted historical research into Japan's much-interrupted sailing past, looking for original local characteristics that can be incorporated into future work.

To date Yokoyama has designed 492 boats of various types, including 8-foot dinghies, 64-foot offshore cruisers, multihulls, power cruisers, and rowing boats used in the Olympic Games. From his office he has also sent out to the world such yacht designers as Shun Takeichi, Nobuwo Muramoto, Kennosuke Hayashi, and his son, Ichiro Yokoyama.

—Kennosuke Hayashi

ICHIRO YOKOYAMA

Born 1945 · Japan

The eldest son of yacht designer Akira Yokoyama, Ichiro Yokoyama has been involved in sailing since his early years, and closely observed his father's boatbuilding and design work. While studying naval architecture at Tokyo University, he built a plywood Y-15 dinghy of his father's design. After graduation he entered the Marine Division of Yahama Motor Company, but in 1974 and 1975 studied overseas at Groupe Finot, the yacht design

Jim Young: *Extreme*. Realizing that construction methods were leading to very light displacement, Young was one of the first to design a modern yacht with a dinghy shape and great speed potential, qualities exhibited by *Extreme*, a Rocket 31. © *Terry Fong, AFA Photography*

firm in France. He was one of the Yamaha design team that produced *Magician,* a Quarter-Tonner that won the 1978 Worlds, in Japan.

In 1982, Yokoyama left Yamaha and joined his father's office. However, he soon established his own company, Marine Design System (MDS). In this office, he has designed some ninety boats including IOR racers of 30 and 34 feet, built in production at Tsuboi Yachts and proved popular. *Matenrow,* a 39-foot IOR racer built in 1990, participated in the Kenwood Cup in Hawaii, sailed by a New Zealand team, and became the winner overall.

Yokoyama, together with his colleague at MDS, Taro Takahashi, served on the design team of the Nippon Challenge America's Cup from their first attempt in 1992 to the third one in 1999.

—Kennosuke Hayashi

JAMES YOUNG

Born July 7, 1925 · New Zealand

Several of New Zealand yachting's most important innovations are credited to self-taught designer Jim Young. Born in Wellington, Young left school at age fifteen to start a boatbuilding apprenticeship. Following World War II, he built Japan's first yacht, a 13-foot centerboarder with hand-sewn sails made from two-man army tents.

Returning to Auckland, Young went into business as a designer/builder in 1949.

In 1953, Young designed and built *Fiery Cross,* the first glued, laminated, keel yacht in New Zealand, featuring a transversely swinging keel. *Tango,* launched in the same year, was the first New Zealand yacht with a separate spade rudder, inspired by Australian Alan Payne's Nocturne design.

Young pioneered in racing and cruising catamarans. He had a famous victory as part of a New Zealand team in the unrestricted 12-foot skiff class in the 1958 Interdominion Silasec Trophy Race with a catamaran called *Kitty.* Catamarans were banned, as a result of *Kitty's* success, from the next series. There followed the Kitty Restricted Catamaran Class.

One of Young's most successful yachts was designed in 1967, the NZ 37 cruiser/racer. The first launched, *Namu,* won races in Auckland for many years. A number of NZ 37's were exported to the United States. A 1977 foray into the IOR ended in disappointment, and Young opted out of that scene, saying he preferred to design boats that sailed well rather than rated well.

Trailerable sailers have always been popular in New Zealand, and Young was the first to use water ballast in a trailerable sailboat in 1979. In 1980 the spectacular Rocket 31 utilized strip-planked construction, then new to New Zealand, to achieve ultralight displacement, becoming a forerunner to today's planing keelboats. The Rocket 780 became a very potent racer. Young's best-known class yacht is the Young 88, with over two hundred sailing.

Young was also successful with powercraft, designing *Vindex,* an ultralight, all-weather planing powerboat that was then built in various configurations and in large numbers. Jim Young is now retired.

—David Payne

DIRK "DICK" ZAAL

Born January 17, 1939 · The Netherlands

Dick Zaal started his boatbuilding career as a carpenter at the van de Stadt Boatyard in Zaandam, where he also trained himself in the basics of yacht design. Driven by an insatiable curiosity, he took English courses so he could read international literature on sailing and yacht design. His dedication and love for the trade did not go unnoticed, and soon Zaal was promoted to the drafting room. He eventually became one of van de Stadt's associate designers.

In the early 1970's the van de Stadt yard, with its predominantly manual production methods, could no longer compete with the larger production yards and was taken over by the German Dehler Company, which soon closed it

down. The design department merged with Dehler's and the employees lost direct contact with boatbuilding practice. Zaal found another job.

Becoming the main designer at the Conyplex yard, Zaal was responsible for several complete new designs a year, quality control, and test sails with the clients. But working for one yard, where all his designs had to fit into a recognizable line, in the end proved too much of a limitation to his lively mind. In 1980, Zaal established his own office in Hoorn, where he still practices, with Conyplex as a steady client.

Zaal's primary focus is on cruising yachts between 30 and 60 feet long, but he is also an avid ocean racer, experimenting with hydrofoils and outside, removable water ballast contained in a wing profile. For the solo sailor Wytze van der Zee he designed *New Magic Breeze,* an extreme design for high-speed, shorthanded sailing, very much in the old van de Stadt tradition. "NMB" popularized Zaal's name as a designer, but in spite of his interest in speed and experimentation, most of his production designs are more conventional.

Several designs show traditional influences, such as the 47-foot sloop *Peregrine,* which looks like a Danish trader above the waterline, although it has the underbody of a modern

Dick Zaal: *Atlantic 51*. The aluminum Atlantic 51 (54 feet 9 inches LOA) was designed not only for cruising the North Sea and coping with its harsh offshore conditions, but also for retaining access to the shallow northern Dutch islands. Zaal accomplished both goals through a large, ballasted centerboard, giving a minimum draft of 4 feet 1 inch. *Photo courtesy Dick Zaal*

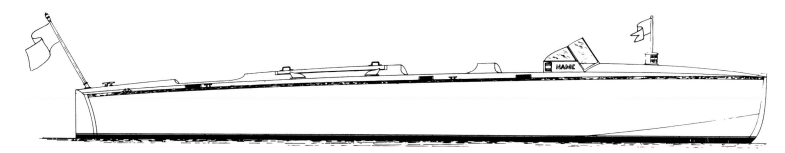

Nelson Zimmer: Bermuda Runabout. The Bermuda Runabout is a waterborne equivalent to the country roadsters of the 1920's—automobiles of moderate power and gentle nature. The 28-foot mahogany hull will run at speeds up to 50 mph. *Drawing courtesy WoodenBoat Publications*

keel/centerboarder, and the 40-foot, full-keeled *Skarpsno*, a double-headsail ketch in the old Scandinavian tradition.

Zaal is a member of the Think Tank, a group of Dutch yacht designers that gets together on a regular basis, guided by Professor Jelle Gerritsma from the University of Delft, to discuss and test developments in yacht design.

—Rutger ten Broeke

NELSON ZIMMER

Born 1914 · United States

Nelson Zimmer has designed boats and small ships professionally and more or less continuously since 1936. Asked for a concise description of his practice, he replies, "Custom designs to 150 feet, sail or power, in wood, aluminum, or steel—no commissions for fiberglass boats will be accepted."

Born in Detroit, Michigan, Zimmer knew from childhood that he wanted to draw boats. As a boy, he taught himself the rudiments of small boat design. In the early 1930's, he enrolled at the University of Michigan to study naval architecture.

His college education complete, Zimmer found work designing yachts at Fisher Boatworks in Detroit. As World War II loomed, he went to Toledo (Ohio) Shipbuilding, where he contributed to the design of large icebreakers. When that shipyard failed during the war, the young naval architect tried to convince the U.S. Navy that it needed his services. As it happened, the government did want him aboard, but not for his professional qualifications. Zimmer spent the final years of the war as a deck officer on a Liberty ship that transported high explosives.

In 1946, noted designer John Hacker, "a very nice man," gave Zimmer space in his Detroit offices. The young fellow marked his return to small boats by drawing a 21-foot gaff sloop. The V-bottomed cruising boat remains popular with amateur builders more than half a century later. After Hacker crossed the bar, Zimmer opened his own design office in 1956. The one-man office remains open for

business at the time of this writing (2002).

Although Zimmer never formally studied with Hacker, the older man's influence is evident in the runabouts that mark Nelson's recent output. He dedicated the 16-foot Gentleman's Runabout to "the creative genius of the late John L. Hacker." Larger, faster 22- and 28-foot designs followed. Intricately detailed, all of the drawings combine the technical and artistic skills that mark Zimmer's work.

Nelson Zimmer practices in Marine City, Michigan.   —Mike O'Brien

DOUGLAS ZURN

Born 1963 · United States

When Doug Zurn was about ten, his father had some large prints of a McCurdy and Rhodes 61-foot boat mounted and framed. This made a lasting impression on the young boy. Born in Erie, Pennsylvania, Zurn grew up boating on Lake Erie aboard the family sailboats and a 17-foot Boston Whaler.

By the age of seventeen Zurn had absorbed Skene's *Elements of Yacht Design*, eventually making his own drawings and boat models in

his high school architecture class. He received his professional degree with honors from the Westlawn School of Yacht Design. Prior to founding Zurn Yacht Design in 1993, he worked in the design offices at Tartan Yachts, Dieter Empacher, and C. W. Paine Yacht Design.

Zurn has a reputation for "a good eye" in drawing pretty boats. Perhaps this talent is most evident in the beautiful Shelter Island 38-foot runabout, built for singer Billy Joel. His attention to detail and excellent draftsmanship are combined with experience in all phases of creating new boats, including conceptualization, job costing, design engineering, and production engineering.

The first 34z to be launched by MJM Yachts is the fiftieth boat of Zurn's designs, varying in length from 20 to 85 feet. His first was the Monomoy 21 sloop in 1996. Others of note include the Vanguard 24 runabout (2003), the Gloucester 20 launch (2002), the 20-knot Marlow Explorer series from 57 to 72 feet long (2001), the Shelter Island 50 (2001), Maine Island 46 (2004), Ocean Bay 30 (2003), Frost Torpedo (2002), and C. W. Hood 50 (2003).

Zurn's office is in Marblehead, Massachusetts.

—Robert Johnstone

Doug Zurn: 34z. The high-tech, Kevlar-epoxy 34z, introduced in 2003 by MJM Yachts, set new speed and fuel efficiency standards. *Photo by Billy Black*

ABOUT THE WRITERS

Bent Aarre is the author of twenty-one books about yachting and cofounded Denmark's Yachting Museum at Valdemar's Castle on the island of Fyn.

Klaus Auf dem Garten realizes his boyhood dreams of seafaring and sailing as a historian, writing books on shipyards such as Abeking and Rasmussen and Burmester.

B. Devereux Barker III grew up sailing in Marblehead, Massachusetts, edited *Yachting* magazine's Design Section from 1962 to 1972, and has chaired America's Cup and Newport-Bermuda race committees.

Franco Belloni is the author of books on the history of sailing, including *150 Years of Sailing in Italy*, and contributes to Italian nautical magazines.

Pol Bergius, sawyer and sailor, credits his forebears and a venerable pilot cutter for kindling his enthusiasm for all maritime traditions and innovation.

Martin Black has not let two Fastnets and crewing on the slowest Etchells in Cowes stop him from researching George L. Watson and his designs.

Erdmann Braschos, born in 1960, familiarized himself with sheet and tiller slightly later, has been publishing maritime since 1987. He favors a 52-foot Knud Reimers design.

Maynard Bray has been intimately involved with boats since childhood—as owner, builder, author, and editor. His books include *Herreshoff of Bristol* (with Carlton Pinheiro).

Rutger ten Broeke sails the Sparkman and Stephens yawl *Laughing Gull* in the Netherlands. He is an editor-journalist for the magazines *Spiegel der Zielvaart, WoodenBoat,* and *Foto.*

François Chevalier is a yacht designer and writer living in Paris. His books include *J Class* and *America's Cup Yacht Designs*, written with Jacques Taglang.

Volker Christmann, after sailing his 51-foot Abeking and Rasmussen yacht through the Mediterranean for ten years, has collected sailing books and magazines that fill a thousand feet of bookshelves.

Dave Cox lives in Durban, South Africa, and wrote the Angelo Lavranos entry for the *EYD*.

Carol Crosby grew up surrounded by Crosby boatbuilders in Osterville, Massachusetts. She spends her spare time working on a book about her family's history.

Penny Cuthbert is the curator of sport and leisure history at the Australian National Maritime Museum in Sydney.

Peter Daniels learned sailing on the Norfolk Broads and has always been fascinated with Linton Hope. He sailed the 2003 Round Britain Experience to celebrate his seventieth birthday.

Ian Dear has written several maritime books. He is the editor of a new edition of *The Oxford Companion to Ships and the Sea.*

Robin Elliott of Auckland, New Zealand, co-owns the 1947 Bob Stewart–designed M-Class *Matana*. He wrote *Emmy, 70 Years of M Class Yachting* in 1994.

Daina Fletcher is senior curator at the Australian National Maritime Museum. She is responsible for the boat collections and is coordinating the Museum's Australian Register of Historic Vessels.

Egmont Friedl sailed to and worked in California, England, and Italy before returning to Germany. He is a professional boatbuilder and yachtmaster, and author of two books.

Dominique Gabirault lives in Paris and wrote the Martin Francis, Richard Hein, and Peter Ibold entries.

Tom Gallant lives in Lunenburg, Nova Scotia, where he sails his David Stevens–designed schooner, *Avenger.*

Piero M. Gibellini, architect and collector of vintage boats, is president of the Riva Historical Society, the Federation of Riva clubs in the world, and is Carlo Riva's biographer.

JoAnn W. Goddard is the senior reporter for *Soundings* magazine, a major source of the nation's boating news. She also has a passion for sailing.

Amadeo González cowrote the Pepin González entry and lives in Spain.

Joseph Gribbins was publications director at Mystic Seaport Museum and the author of *The Wooden Boat, Wooden Boats from Sculls to Yachting,* and *Classic Sail.*

Noël Gruet, a former fisherman, is cofounder and coeditor of *Les Cahiers du Bassin,* a publication dedicated to the maritime life in the Bassin d'Arcachon, France.

Kennosuke Hayashi is a yacht designer and writer about yachting in Japan. He was a chief IOR/IMS measurer in the 1980's.

Rebecca Hayter is editor of *Boating New Zealand* magazine. She owns a 26-foot yacht, has sailed 10,000 offshore miles, and has published two sailing biographies.

Llewellyn Howland III is a writer and antiquarian bookseller specializing in yachting history. He is currently at work on a biography of W. Starling Burgess.

Douglas Hunter is past editor of *Canadian Yachting* magazine and cowrote (with designer Steve Killing) the 1998 book *Yacht Design Explained*.

Tim Jeffery is yachting correspondent of London's *Daily Telegraph*, yacht racing author, magazine writer, and member of the Cape Horners' Association.

Jon B. Johansen is the publisher of *Maine Coastal News* and does extensive ship research. He is also owner of the historic 117-foot tug *Saturn*.

Sir Peter Johnson (1930–2003) wrote fifteen books on sailing and yacht racing handicap systems and records, including *The Encyclopedia of Yachting* and *This is Sailing*.

Robert L. Johnstone III is an accomplished sailor and the marketing wizard behind J-Boat's phenomenal success. He is active on the Down East Maine racing circuit.

Gregory O. Jones, former editorial staffer with *Classic Boat* and *Sailing* and now senior editor with *Blue Water Sailing*, is the author of two sailing history books.

Robert Keeley is past editor of the Australian magazine *Cruising Helmsman* and currently edits Australian *Photography* magazine. He has sailed Cherubs, Moth Class skiffs, and yachts.

Harold Kidd, a New Zealand marine historian, has restored several yachts, including the 1880 Logan-designed *Jessie Logan*. He cowrote *Southern Breeze, A History of New Zealand Yachting*.

Steve Knauth's stepfather took him sailing in a Blue Jay at age eight. He began writing in 1986. He has been honored twice by Boating Writers International.

Lucia del Sol Knight is the creator/coeditor of *The Encyclopedia of Yacht Designers*. She sails her 34-foot John Alden–designed cutter out of Buck's Harbor, Maine.

Michael D. König wrote the Kurt Oehlmann entry and lives in Aichhalden, Germany.

Alfredo Lagos Jr. lives in Spain and cowrote the Joaquín Coello and Iñigo Echenique entries.

Alfredo Lagos Sr. wrote the entry on Fernando Lagos and cowrote the Joaquín Coello and Iñigo Echenique entries, and lives in Spain.

Kristin Lammerting is the author of the 1999 book *Meteor, Die kaiserlichen Segelyachten,* about Kaiser Wilhelm II's five yachts named *Meteor*.

Pete Lesher is curator of the Chesapeake Bay Maritime Museum in St. Michaels, Maryland, and crews on the 1882 Chesapeake sailing log canoe *Island Bird*.

Neil Francis Libbey is a historian and author of *Portside: An Early History of The Royal Cape Breton Yacht Club*. He resides in Sydney, Nova Scotia.

Claas van der Linde has been researching multihull history for many years. His 27-foot all-carbon catamaran tears around Lake Geneva at speeds exceeding 20 knots.

Ulf and Gunilla Lycke from Sweden have been sailing skerry cruisers for a long time. Ulf has written books about the history of Swedish yacht clubs.

John Lynch-Cummins lives in Spain and cruises the Mediterranean in his North Wind 40 designed by Angus Primrose.

Daniel B. MacNaughton of Belfast, Maine, sails the William Atkin–designed ketch *Eric*, a 1924 double-ender. He is chief writer and coeditor of *The Encyclopedia of Yacht Designers*.

Iain McAllister, a native of Scotland, lives in Denmark and travels extensively as a classic yacht consultant. He was formerly captain of William Fife III's *Solway Maid*.

Sheila McCurdy is a freelance nautical writer and daughter of yacht designer Jim McCurdy. She lives in Rhode Island.

Robert McKenna, a former U.S. Coast Guard officer, is a magazine and book editor and author of *The Dictionary of Nautical Literacy*.

Jeffrey Mellefont, variously a wharf laborer, tuna fisherman, yacht skipper, magazine editor, and maritime ethnographer, is publications manager at the Australian National Maritime Museum.

Silvia Minas wrote the entry on Bruno Veronese, who taught her all about sailing and racing as well as his sea stories and history of the seas. She lives in Genoa, Italy.

Marilyn Mower is a twenty-nine-year veteran of the yachting press, including sixteen spent editing *ShowBoats International;* other credits include *The Megayacht Century* and *Caribbean Cuisine: A Culinary Voyage*.

Bette Noble (1944–2002) was an early supporter of the *EYD*, and contributed her extensive research and editing skills to shape the content of the book.

Mike O'Brien, senior editor for *WoodenBoat*, publishes *Boat Design Quarterly* in his spare time. The former boatbuilder/oceanographer now takes his waterborne pleasure aboard sea kayaks.

Juan Olabarri wrote the Juan Allende entry and lives in Spain.

David Pardon was a UK sports journalist and editor of *New Zealand Sea Spray* for eighteen years. He is now a journalism tutor in New Zealand.

David Payne is a self-taught yacht designer with an extensive cruising and racing background. He is establishing a Register of Historic Vessels for the Australian National Maritime Museum.

Geoff Payne welded his own Alan Payne–designed steel cutter, sails it to extreme destinations, and writes and lectures on these award-winning voyages.

Scott M. Peters is collections historian at Michigan Historical Museum in Lansing, Michigan. He studies historical watercraft designed and built in Michigan.

Barry Pickthall is head of PPL Photo Agency in West Sussex, England. He is author of the 2003 book *Germán Frers—A Passion for Design.*

Nannette Poillon has been researching the history of the C & R Poillon shipbuilding company of New York City and is keeper of family records going back to 1670.

Stephen Rappaport edits a marine trade journal and writes frequently for *WoodenBoat.* He sails his 30-foot Bob Perry–designed cutter near Mount Desert Island in Maine.

Jonathan Rice is a great-grandson of designer Frank Paine. He is currently researching a book about the Boston influence on yacht design between the wars.

Lindsley Rice is assistant curator at Chesapeake Bay Maritime Museum in St. Michaels, Maryland. She enjoys building and sailing boats, and ship-smithing whenever possible.

Tom Roach is a Canadian author currently living in India. He is upset he cannot sail the boat he built while living in Cape Town, South Africa!

Fernando Roca lives in Spain and cowrote, together with John Lynch-Cummins and Iain McAllister, his entry.

J. Scott Rohrer collects and writes on West Coast yachting history. He splits his time between his Seattle marine insurance agency, the R-boat *Pirate,* and his beloved golden retrievers.

Mark Rothfield is the editor of the Australian magazine *Modern Boating.* He lives in Alexandria, New South Wales.

John Rousmaniere has written or edited twelve books on yachting history. He serves on the Editorial Advisory Board of *The Encyclopedia of Maritime History.*

Hartmut Rührdanz continued the yacht design practice of Reinhard Drewitz under the name of Drewitz/Rührdanz in Germany.

David Ryder-Turner (1922–2004) was a yacht designer in Helensburgh, Scotland. He belonged to several classic yacht associations and was particularly knowledgeable about the William Fife family.

Charles Schock designed with Alden, Sparkman and Stephens, and Edson I. and Edson B. Schock. He is glad to help anyone seeking information about Schock designs and boats.

Gerhard Schön is an RC-model shipbuilder and sails a Chiemsee-Plätte and model sailing ships on his Bavarian holidays. He is a dentist and father of five children.

Thomas G. Skahill competed successfully in ocean racing and the Star Class for many years. Today maritime history holds his interest and his work is published frequently.

Brian Smith has had a lifelong interest in the design and construction of all kinds of ships and boats. He now sails on the Mersey.

Jack A. Somer, a marine writer since 1970, is former editor-in-chief of *Yachting* magazine and author of ten books about yachts, ships, and marine history.

Mark Steele, of Auckland, New Zealand, is the publishing editor of *Windling World,* an international model sailboat magazine.

Olin J. Stephens II wrote the entry on his brother Rod, who was an integral part of the Sparkman and Stephens design team. Olin remains an active participant in yachting communities worldwide.

Robert Stephens, after an independent career designing small boats of modern wood-epoxy construction, is now chief designer at Brooklin Boat Yard, Brooklin, Maine.

Jacques Taglang has many nautical books to his credit, including *America's Cup Yacht Designs* (with François Chevalier). He frequently sails the classic Mylne-designed *Sindbad* with friends from La Rochelle.

Walter Voigt grew up sailing Lightnings and Dragons. His yellow 16-foot skiff, kept in Deer Isle, Maine, is a frequent visitor to the many nearby islands.

Robert Volmer sailed the Rhine as a youth and continues to be engaged in yachting history. He sails his 1966 34-foot Olle Enderline–designed yacht *Zwerg Nase.*

Bob Wallstrom is a NAMS-CMS, has been a yacht and small craft designer, and is working on the history of Luders Marine Construction Company.

Eberhard Wetjen lives in Germany and wrote the entries on Ferdinand Grünhagen, H. Saefkow, and Wilhelm Schulze.

INDEX

Page numbers in **boldface** refer to entries. Page numbers in *italics* refer to illustrations.

Aalborg Yard, 460
Aas, Bjarne, **1–3,** *2,* 231, 245
Aas, Henrik, 1
Abeking, Georg, 373
Abeking and Rasmussen, *6, 66,* 67, 117, 179, 180, 186–87, 210, 229, 303, 321, 342, 373, *373,* 375, 377, 379, 483, 492
Abo Boat Yard, 483
Abrahamssons and Mobergs Boatyard, 230
Abruzzi, Duke of, 33, 92
Acadia (Lane), 267
Acadia (Paine), 351
Acajou, 30, 303
Acalyouli, 23
Ace, 319
A. C. Gilbert Company, 138
Acharné, 30, 491
Acheron, 200
A. C. Holgate Transport Company, 227
Ackerman Boat Works, 74, 138
Acorn skiffs, 347
Acrospires, 358–59
Active, 445
Acubens, 132
Adams, Charles Francis, III, 64
Adams, George Caspar, 64
Adams, Joe, **3**
Adams 8–meter boats, 3
Adams 10–meter boats, 3, *3*
Adams 40, 3
Adela, 122
Adèle, 224
Adix, 122, 321
Admiral's Cup, 10, 13, 43, 56, 79, 80, 87, 114, 120, 127, 128, 139, 142, 160, 161, 182, 227, 228, 243, 249, 250, 259, 276, 436, 452, 463, *468*
Advance (Burgess), 67
Advance (Paine), 324, 356
Advent, 311
Adventure (Mauric), 303
Adventure (Monk), 315
Adventuress, 425
Aegean Rally, 237

Aeldgytha, 389
Aelling class, 42
Aello, 344
Aemilia, 470
Aero Marine, 243, 370
Aeromarine Corporation, 353
Aeromarine 50, 353
Affinity, 228
Afterburner, 453
Aga Khan IV, 180
Agape, 256
Agawam, 175
Aggressive II, 258
Agir Yacht Club, 269
Aglaia, 432
Agnelli, Gianni, 162
Agnes II, 277
A Group, 207
A. H. Moody and Son, 70
Aiglon, 303
Aigrette, 340
Aikane catamaran, 84
Aikane X5, 85
Ailée, 336
Ailsa, 152
Ailsa, Marquis of, 150, 151
Ailsa Craig, 419
Aimé, 398
Airborne Lifeboats, 156–57
Air Liquide Company, 46
Aisher, Owen, 331, *331*
Aitken, Max, 243
Aje, 230
Akademischer Segler-Verein, 344
Akademische Seglerverein Berlin, 494
Akarana, 281, 282
Akela (Dahlström), 112
Akela (Peterson), 247
Akela 50, 23, *23*
Akesson, A., 36
Akila, 136
Akkerman, William, 431
Akros, 445
Alabama, 212
Alabama, C.S.S., 71
Alagi, 24
Alamo, 389
Alana (Fife), 53
Alana (Rosenblatt), 389
Alaram, 461
Alarm (Fox), 156

Alarm (van Deusen), 473
Alaskan trawler series, 125
Albacore class, 157
Albacore motoryacht series, 243
Alberg, Carl A., **3–4,** *3,* 8
Alberg 30, 4
Alberg 35, 3, 4
Albert, 373
Albert, King of Belgium, 474
Albert shipyard, 416
Albert Strange Association, 448
Albyn, 327
Alca, 341
Alcea, 168
Alcedo, 263
Alcoa, 68, 209
Alcor, 180
Alcotan 27, 387
Alcyon, 23
Alcyone, 302
Aldebaran, 137
Alden, John Gale, 3–4, **5–8,** *5, 6, 8,* 55, 82, 99, 106, 119, 145, 196, 203, 223, 227, 298, 300, 301, 319, 338, 363, 405, 406, 436, 473
Alden, John G. Company, *see* John G. Alden Company
Alden 44, 208
Alden Ocean Shell, 298
Alden O Class, 8
Alejandra, 132, 257, *257*
Alerion, 23
Alerion Express Cat, 236
Alerion Express line, 407
Alerion III, 211
Alert, 75, 381
Alert IV, 318
Aleta, 359
Alexander, Emmons, 338
Alexander Robertson and Sons, 52–53
Alexander Stephen and Sons, 327
Alexandra, 170
Alexandria Bridge, 129
Älfan, 399
Alfard, 160
Alfred Lockhart Ltd., 70
Alfrida, 247
Algeri-Port Mahon (Balearic Islands) Race, 164
Alglas powerboats, 298
Alibaba II, 229
Alibi, 489

Alice III, 388
Alii Kai, 84
Aline, 330
Aline III, 33
Alinghi, 114, 250, *250,* 316, 317
Alinghi IV, 317
Alinghi V, 403
Allan, Frank A., 305
Allègre, André, 9, **9**
Allégrini shipyard, 398
Allende, Juan Manuel Alonso, **9**
Allez-Cat, 84
Alliage 48, 44
Allied 39, 349
Allied Bank, 270
Allied Boat Company, 288
Allied Yachts, *180,* 181
Alligatore, 84
Allona, 341
Allouette, 109
Alloy Yachts, 401
All This and Sailing, Too (Stephens), 435, 439
Allure, 492
Al Mirqab, 207
Aloha (Alden), 227
Aloha (Crane), 94
Aloha (Fellows), 145
Aloha (Nygren), 341
Aloha 28, 54
Aloha 34, 54
Aloha-Oe, 290
Aloma, 271
Alondra, 381
Alone in the Caribbean (Fenger), 147
Alotola, 480, 481
Alouette, 163
Alquati, Gino, 78
Alruda, 279
Altair (Fife), 154
Altair (Wayland), 481
Alter, Hobart L. "Hobie," **9–10,** *10,* 109
Alva, 71
Alyette, 398
Amantha cutter, 99, *100*
Amaryllis, 143, 216, 217
amas, 329–30
Amateur Boat Building (Crosby), 103
Ambachtschool, 468
Amber, 395
Amble, Eivind, **10–11,** *11*
A.M. Dickie and Sons, 29, 76

Amels shipyard, 30, 200, 320, 456, 492

America, 64, 112, 204, 330, 375, 394, 395, 417, 419, *432, 433, 433*, 460

America (replica), 59

America³, 362, 452

American and British Manufacturing Company, 212

American and British Yacht Designs (Chevalier and Taglang), 82

American and English Yachts (Burgess), 63

American Bureau of Shipping, 147, 321

American Car Foundry (ACF), 235, 252, 308–9

American Eagle, 54, 288, 495

American Express, 495

American Fishing Schooners, The (Chapelle), 81

American Geographical Society, 174

American Launch company, 293

American Marine, 74, 125, 147, 423

American Power Boat Association (APBA), *95*, 175, 245

American Power Boat Association Gold Cup, 423

American Promise, 233, *233*

American ProSail, 316

American Sailboat Hall of Fame, 98, 235, 249, 360

American Sailing Craft (Chapelle), 81

American Schooner Cup Series, 404

American Small Sailing Craft (Chapelle), 81, 428

American Society of Naval Engineers, 174

American Yacht Club, 441

American Yachting (Stephens), 442

America's Cup, 13, *13,* 32, 34, 35, 46, *46,* 47–48, 86, 88, 90, 94, 202, 212, 312, 316, 319, 324, 325, 329, 333, 346, 347, 351, 358, 365, *365,* 375, 376, 383, 384, 394, 401, 403, 415, 417, 420, 421, 426–27, 436, 439, 441, 452, 461, *461,* 474, 476, 478, 491, 497
  of 1876, 110
  of 1881, 110, 128
  of 1885, 61, *61,* 63, 205, *205*
  of 1886, 61, *61,* 63, 135
  of 1887, 61, *62,* 63, 64, 151
  of 1893, 219
  of 1895, 219
  of 1899, *150,* 219
  of 1901, *105,* 106, 113, 152, 197, 219
  of 1903, *150,* 153, 219–20
  of 1920, 167, 169, *169,* 219
  of 1930, 97, 186
  of 1934, *67,* 122, 186
  of 1937, 68, *68,* 209
  of 1958, 52, 211, 239, 306
  of 1962, 231, *231,* 301
  of 1964, 52, 288
  of 1967, 219, 233, *233*
  of 1970, 219, 303, *303*
  of 1974, 276
  of 1977, 56, 303–4
  of 1980, 276
  of 1983, *127,* 256, 259, *259,* 276, *276*
  of 1987, 115, 142, 185, 256, 259–60, *259,* 276–77
  of 1988, 237, 250, 256
  of 1992, 132, *160,* 161–62, 182, 206, 256
  of 1995, 114, 115, 250
  of 2000, 114, *115,* 140–42, *162,* 250, 260
  of 2003, 140, 142, *250*
  beginnings of, 204
  books on, 82
  Herreshoff's domination of, 216, 219

America's Cup Class, 51, 97, 132, *160,* 161, 206, 260

America's Cup Hall of Fame, 213

America's Cup Yacht Designs, 1851–1986 (Chevalier and Taglang), 82

America's Teacup Regatta, 259

Amethyst I, 185

Amethyst II, 185

Amorilla, 5

Amorita, 168

Amos, Francis, 332

Amphibi-Con, 194

Amphitrite, 331, *331*

Amstel shipyard, 454

Amsterdam Nautical Academy, 181

Amsterdamse Scheepswerf, 288

Amundsen, Roald, 17, 245

Amundson, Gus, 246

A. Mylne and Company, 39, 325, 327

Anadiomede, 93

Anahita V, 390

Anchorage boatyard, *211*

Anderson Yard, 29

Andersson, Albert, **11–12,** *11,* 277, 367

Andrews, Alan, 12, **12**

Andrieu, Daniel, **12–13,** *13,* 43

Andrillot, 176, *176*

Andromeda (Oertz), 344

Andromeda (Perini), 359

Andromeda la Dea, 359

Anemone II, 83

Anemone III, 83

Angantyr, 202, 295

Ange de Mer powerboat, 250

Angela, 344

Angelita, 208, 368

Angelman, Davis, Ward, 14

Angelman, Eugene, 14

Angelman, Hugh Morgan "Bones," **13–14,** *14,* 257, 301, 383

Angelman and Davis, 14

Angelman and Ward, 14

Animal Farm, 495

Anita, 16

Anitra, 438

Anitra II, 265

Anker, Johan August, 1, **14–16,** *15, 16,* 18, 157, 225, 245, 277, 279, 333, 373, 383

Anker and Jensen, 245

Anna, 277

Anna Catharina, 470

Anna Helen II, 199

Annalokin, 284

Annapolis-Newport Race, 54, 90, *111,* 240

Annapolis Yacht Yard, 460

Annette, 73

Anny, 250

Antares, 227

Anthor, 13

Anticipation, 276

Antigua Race Week, 236

Antiope, 283

Antipodean, 30

Antique and Classic Boat Society, 111

Anti-Submersible Motorboat (MAS), 24

Antonisa, 256

Antrim, Jim, 321

Aorere, 282

Apache (Cox), *94*

Apache (Presles), 369

Apache, Apache catamaran, 293

Apel, Adolf, 245

Aphrodite, 371

Aphrodite 101 class, 260, *260*

Apogee, 181

Apollo, 276

Apollo II, 276

Appalachia, 266

Applause, 207

Apricot, 244

April, 10

Aquanaut line, 51

Aquarama, 386, *386*

Aquarama motorboat, 32

Aquarius, 321

Aquel II, 128

Aquila, 149

Aquilon, 412

Aquitania, S.S., 266

"Arab dhows," 145

Arabin, Saint Julien, 357

Araignée, 73

Aramis, 450

Aramoana, 282

Arasaki Racing Team, 400

Arcachon One-Design class, 188, 189

Arcadia, 305

Archambault boatyard, 249

Archer, Colin, 11, **16–18,** *17, 18,* 22, 77, *77,* 159, 193, 199, 241, 296, 353, 381, 394, 421

Archimedes, 135

Ardelle, 319

Ardette, 319

Arena, Daniel Joseph, Jr., **18**

Arena Craft, 18

Arequipa, 274

Argenteuil boat yard, 83

Argenteuil clippers, 73

Argonaute, 211

Argonaut line, 51

Argosy, 336

Ariadne, 80, 341

Ariel (Logan), 280

Ariel (Mauric), 302

Ariel (Steele), 432

Aries, 312

Ariki, 282

Arion, 211

Ariston, 385, *385*

Arjuna, 303

Arkangel, 270

Arlecchino, 407

Armstrong, Mitchell and Company, 355, 483

Armstrong College (Newcastle), 460

Arneson, Howard, 18

Aronow, Donald, **18**

Around Alone singlehanded race, 154, *155,* 427

Around Gotland Race, 230, 460

A. R. Payne and Sons, 357

Arpège, 267

Arrayan II, 465

Artful, 411

Arthur Binney, 46, **46**

Artica, 93

Artina, 185

A/S Alfred Benzon, 42

Aschanti III, 187

Aschanti IV, 187

Asgard, 17–18

Askadil, 69

Askeladden, 1, 3

Aspanet, 271

Aspect Computing, 291

Aspiration, 207

Assegai, 270, 375

Association of Dutch Naval Architects, 226

Association of Italian Nautical Designers (AS.PRO.NA.DI.), 32

Asso R.B., 24

Astilleros Mefasa boatyard, 132

Astor, Vincent, 93

Astoria Marine Construction Company (AMMCO), 125, 131

Astral, 473

Astral 20, 109

Atalanta (Cuthbert), 110, *420*

Atalanta (Farmer), 138

Atalanta (Oneto), 347

Atalanta dinghy (Fox), 157

Atara, 291, *291*

Athena, 38, *39,* 122

Athene, 219

Atkin, John Davenport, **19–20,** *19, 20, 20,* 22, 22, 40, 472

Atkin, William Wilson, 17, 19, **20–23,** *21, 22,* 98, 156, 428

Atkin and Wheeler, 20

Atkinson, Keith, 228

Atlantic yard, 200

Atlantic (Beavor-Webb), 34

Atlantic (Elsworth), 135

Atlantic (Gardner), *95,* 97, *121,* 167, *168,* 169

Atlantic 51, 497

Atlantica, 443

Atlantic City Catboat class, 318

Atlantic class sloop, 66

Atlantic Class One-Design, 373, 375

Atlantic series catamarans, 486

Atlantic Yacht Club, 134, 174, 205

Atlantis (Harris), 202

Atlantis (Ross), 391

Atlas, 267

Attila, 42

Auckland mullet boat, 27

Auckland Suva race, 133

Audax, 241

Aurora (Lee and Brinton), *273, 274*
Aurora (Munford), 322
Aurora (Ratsey), 375
Aurora (Soper), 425
Aurora (Stephens, Uhle), 460
Australia, 276, 461
Australia II, *127,* 276, *276,* 324, 461
Australia III, 277
Australia IV, 277
Australian Design Award, 110
Australian National Maritime
    Museum, 251, 358
Australian Trailer Yacht Nationals,
    133
autoboats, 145
Auzépy-Brenneur, Georges, 23, **23,**
    383
Avalon, 207
Avant Garde, 407
Avanti, 36
Avatar, 258
Avenger (Fox), 156, *156,* 157
Avenger (Stevens), 442, *443*
Avila, 319
AVR (aviation rescue boat), 282
Aya, 275
Ayah, 357
Ayesha, 381
Azio V, 33
Aztec, *168*
Azteca, 30
Azzurro, 180

Baay, H. H., 454
Babboon, 64
Babe, 357
Babette, 392
Baby Birds, 481
Baby Bootlegger, *104, 104*
Baby Reliance, 422
Baby Reliance II, 422
Baby Reliance III, 279
Baccara, 460
Bacon, Henry Douglas, 457
Badger, 40
Bagages Supérior, 154
Bagatelle (Crowther), 107
Bagatelle (Gruber), 187
Baglietto, Pietro, 24, 26
Baglietto, Vincenzo Vittorio,
    24-26, *24*
Baglietto I, 24
Baglietto Shipyard, 181, *181,* 385
Baglietto XXI, 24
Bailey, 411
Bailey, Charles, Sr., **26-27,** *26*
Bailey, Charles, Jr., **26-27,** *26*
Bailey, Walter, **26-27**
Bailey and Lowe, 27
Bailey family, 280, 282
Bain, John, **27-29,** *27, 28*
Bain stern, 27
Bajazzo prize, 190
Bakker, Nico, 263
Balboa 20, 222
Balboa 26, 222
Baldur, 132
Baldwin, Casey, 379
Ballerina, 135

Ballymena, 218
Baltic model, 360
Baltic Race, 135
Baltic Yachts, 341, 444
Baltimore Clipper, The (Chapelle), 81
Baltimore Polytechnic Institute, 75
Bamba, 181, *181*
Bambetta, 181
Bamboo Bomber, 454
Banco Espirito Santo (Carkeek), 79
Banco Espirito Santo (Judel/Vrolijk),
    250
Bandersnatch, 107
Bandor, 112
Banks, Bruce, 444
Bannenberg, Jon, **29-31,** *29, 30,* 110,
    228, 321, 401, 491
Banque Populaire II, 282
Banque Populaire III, 282
Barbana, 83
Barbara, 48
Barber, Archibald C., *31,* **31**
Barbette, 99
Barcelona, Count of, 77
Barcelona Race, 163
Barcelona University, 424
Barden, John, 321
Bar Harbor, 31, 220
Barilani, Giorgio, **31-32,** *32*
Bark Canoes and Skin Boats of North
    America (Chapelle), 81
Barker, Gardner, 338
Barkhausen, Henry, 491
Barlovento, 186, *186*
Bar-L-Rick, 382
Barnett, James Rennie, **32-33**
Barney, Morgan, *33,* **33,**
Baroda, 189
Barr, Charles, 151, *168,* 169, 478
Barracuda, 182
Barrymore, John, 67
Barter Card, *133*
Bartolone, Vince, 84
Barton, Humphrey, 176
Bas, 83
Bashford International, 324
Basic Naval Architecture (Barnaby),
    13
Bateaux, 354
Bateaux magazine, 13
Bates, Frederick, 381
Bath Iron Works, 68, 74, 89, 93,
    93, 94, 125, 175, 209, 389, 431,
    457, 488
Batitu junior trainer, 160
Båtservice-Gruppen, 277
Baudouin, Charles, 302
Baudouin, King of Belgium, 319
Bava, Antonio, **33**
Bavarian Sailing Association, 274
Bayfield Boat Yard, 183
Bayside Bird class, 169
Bayside-Block Island Race, 99
Bayview-Mackinac Race, 382
Bayview Yacht Club, 256
Bazan shipyard, 88
BBC Challenge, 30
Be-a-ba, 302
Beach, David D., *34,* **34**
Beagle IV, 128

Beal, Adrian, 277
Beal, Clinton, 277
Beal, Riley, 277
Beatrice-Aurore, 367, *367*
Beatrix, 415
Beatrix, Princess of The Netherlands,
    182
Beaupré, 30
Beautemps-Beaupré, 267
Beaverbrook, Lord, 491
Beavor-Webb, John, **34,** *35,* **61,** *63,*
    205, 384, 421
Becker, Harry, **36**
Becker 27, 36
Beckerboats, 36
Bedouin, 205, *205*
Beebe, Jack, 279
Beebe, Martin, 279
Beebe, Robert Park, **36-37,** *37*
Beeldsnijder, Pieter Cornelis
    Johannes, **38-39,** *38,* 122, 466
Beetle, John, 296
Beetle Cat, 296
Beg-Rohu National Yachting School,
    465
Beister, Kurt, **39**
Belfast Fairie, 233, 234
Belisarius, 220-21
Belitz, Georg, 158
Belknap, Francis W., 352
Belknap and Paine, 352
Bell, Alexander Graham, 365-66,
    379
Bell, Frank, 392
Bella class, 41
Bellatrix, 60
Belle Aventure, 153
Belle Isle company, 293
Belleville Marine Yard, 111
Bell Fontaine, 39
Bellini, 412
Belliure boatyard, 242-43
Bélouga, 92
Below the Convergence (Gurney),
    189
Bembridge Redwing One-Design,
    335
Bémol, 43
Benbow, 86-87, *87*
Ben Cope Boat Company, 76
Beneteau Figaro II, 282
Beneteau First 30, 303
Bénéteau shipyard, 44, 142, 154, 463
Bénéton, 282
Benetti shipyard, 30, 401
Benford, Jay R., **39-40,** *39, 40*
Benford 30, 40
Bengal, 30
Bengal II, 344, 345
Benjamin, Nathaniel P., **41**
Bennett, James Gordon, 461
Bentall, *475*
Benzon, Alfred, **41-42,** *42,* 43, 277
Benzon, C. B., 41, 43
Benzon, Eggert C., 41, **42-43,** *42*
Beowulf, 190
Berckemeyer, Oswald, **43**
Beretta, Giuseppe, 385
Berg, Georg, **43,** 338, 460
Bergen Tekniske Skule, 459

Bergius, W. M., 305
Bergius company, 305
Bergstrom, Lars, 228
Berlin Jollyboats Yachtsmen's Racing
    Union, 126
Berlin University, 342
Bermeister shipyard, 460
Bermuda 40, 457, 458, *458*
Bermuda-Cuxhaven Race, 187
Bermuda Race, *5, 6,* 66, 97, *111,*
    159-60, 161, 187, 195, 208, 240,
    241, 255, 267, 268, *268,* 276, 297,
    306, 319, 330, 345, 351, 352, 360,
    366, 378, 381, *381,* 382, 394, 436,
    440, 458
Bermuda Runabout, 498
Berret, Jean, 13, **43-44,** *44,* 154
Berret and Racoupeau, 44
Berry, Jack, 310
Bertelli, Patrizio, 161
Bertram, Dick, 18, 239
Bertram 31, 239
Bertram Yacht Company, 328
Bertrand, John, 324
Bestevaer, 121
Bestevaer cruisers, 122
Best of the Best, The (Kinney and
    Bourne), 258
Best of Uffa (Fox), 186
Bethlehem Shipbuilding Corporation,
    75, 209, 298
Bethlehem Steel Company, 3, 235
Bethwaite, Frank, **44-45** *44*
Bethwaite, Julian, **44-45** *44*
Bettina, 83
Betts Enterprises,
    see James Betts Enterprises
Betts, Jim, 54
Betty, 448
Betty M, 488
Beverly, 295
Beverly Yacht Club, 196
Bianca, 11
Bianca company, 260
Bich, Marcel, Baron, 260-61, 303,
    303, 461, *461*
Biddeford Pool One-Design, 8
Bidou, 125
Biesfarnt, 263
Big Boat Cup, 128
Big Boat Series, 56, 115, 227
Bigoin, Michel, **45-46,** *45,* 131, *131*
Bigoin's Naval Yard of Marseilles, 46
Biles, John Harvard, 136, 212, 235,
    483
Bilitis, 189
Billings boatyard, *172*
Bill of Rights, 306
Billycan, 80
Binker, 186, *186*
Binnenklasse boats, 158
Binney, Arthur, **46,** *46,* 318
Biot yards, 158
Birch, Mike, 244
Bird One-Design class, 55
Birkenhead Ironworks, 71
Birkenhead Model Yacht Club, 71
Biscayne Babies, 371
Biscayne Bay Yacht Club, 323
Biscuit Cantreau, 463

Biscuit Cantreau II, 463
Bissbi II, 229
Bitacora magazine, 387
Black Cat, 123
Black Corsair, 32, *32*
Blackfin, 458
Black Hawk, 196
Blackjack, 452
Black Magic, 56, 115, 329
Black Pearl (Fife), 151
Black Pearl (Schock), 405
Black Tulip, 347
Black Watch series, 231
Bladerunner, 453
Blake, Peter, *244*
Blake, William Maxwell, *47,* **47,** 69
Blanchard, Norman J., 91
Blanchard Boat Company, 166, *171,* 315, 409
Blanchard 36, 91
Blanka, 11
Blauwe Reiger, 263
Blaze, 79
Blerck, Joe Van, 279
Blitzen, 267, 404, *405*
Blitz-Jollenkreuzer class, 48
Blitzkrieg, 114
Blivit, 328–29
Block Island "Cowhorn" boats, 136–37
Block Island 40, 457
Block Island Race, 382
Blohm and Voss Shipyard, 122
Bloodhound (Fife), 150
Bloodhound (Nicholson), 243, 336
Blowzy, 320
Blue Albacore, 38
Blue Amnesia, 463
Blue Arrow, 237
Blue Bell, 483
Bluebill II, 196
Bluebird II, 314
Bluebottle, 157
Blue Charm, 370
Blue Jacket, 38
Blue Jay, 439
Blue Leopard, 179, 467
Blue Martin, 336
Blue Moon, 181
Bluenose, 352, 391, 392, *392, 394*
Bluenose Boats, 428
Blue Peter, 170, *172*
Blue Seas, 285
Blue Swanny, 235
Blue Trout, 112
Blue Velvet, 320
Blue Water, 494
Blue Water Cruising Medal, 77, *77*
Blue Water Medal, 440
Bluewater Sailing magazine, 360
Blue Water 21, 452
Blyth, Chay, 87, 237, 455
Bn-417, *80*
Boardman, Edwin Augustus, **47–48,** *48,* 169
Boatbuilding (Chapelle), 81, 428
Boatbuilding Manual (Steward), 443
Boat House Press, 139
Boating magazine, 342
Boating New Zealand magazine, 426

Boat Journal, 49
Boat magazine, 20
Boats, Oars and Rowing (Culler), 108
Boat Sales International, 142
Boats with an Open Mind (Bolger), 50
BOC, 82, 154, 270
BOC Around Alone Race, 383, *383*
BOC Singlehanded Around the World Race, 3, 270, 383
Boemerang, 263
Bogart, Humphrey, 125
Böhling, Paul, **48**
Bol d'Or, 56, 185
Bolero, 436
Bolger, Philip Cunningham, 20, **48–50,** *49,* 214
Bolkiah, 30
Bollemat, 384
Bona, 24
Bona, 376
Bond, Alan, 276, 461
Bonin shipyard, 398
Bonita, 320
Bonnin's boatyard, 189
Book of Boats (Atkin), 23
Boomerang (Derecktor), 119
Boomerang (Reeks), 376
Boon, Dick, **50–51** *50*
Borkum, 187
Borkumriff II, 289
Borkumriff III, 289, *289*
Borsalino Trois, 127–28
Bossuet shipyard, 398
Boston Power Squadron Race, 311
Boston Whaler, 239
Boston Yacht Club, 270, 423
Boston Yacht Sales, 203
Bostwick, Jabez A., 411
Botín, Marcelino, **51,** 78
Botín and Carkeek, 51, 78
Bouncer, 86
Bounding Home, 450, *450*
Bounty, 382
Bounty II, 382
Bourke, Charles, 258
Bourne, Russell, 258
Bowdoin, 195
Bowes, Thomas David, **51–52,** *51,* 76, 318, 480
Bowes and Mower, 52
Bowes and Watts, 52
Bowler, Russell, 115, 140
Bowman, 351
Box Office, 291
Boyd, David, **52–53,** *52, 53,* 306, 434
Boz, 241
Brand, 15
Brandaris, 468
Brand II, 15
Brand III, 15
Brand IV, 15
Brankiet Class, 112
Brassey, Thomas, 70, 71, 88
Brassey, Thomas, Jr., 71
Bravo, 32
Bravo España, 88, 394
Breeon, 292
Bremen Technical High School, 377

Bremen Technikum, 180, 289
Bremer Yachtwerf, 313
Brendan, 319
Brengle, Lawrence J., Jr., 4
Brett, Peter, **53–54** *53*
Brewer, Edward Samuel "Ted," *54,* **54** 288, 296, 472
Brewer, Frederick C., *55,* **55,** 304
Brewer, Malcolm H., 209, 365, 405
Brewer and McBryde, 55
Brewer and Wallstrom and Associates, 471
"Brewer bite," 54
Brewster, George W. W., 491
Briand, Michel, 56, 303, 465
Briand, Philippe, 13, **55–56,** *56,* 303, 322, 403
Briasco, Agostino, 347
Bridgeport University, 429
Bridges Point 24, 486
Brighton Sailing Club, 234
Brilliant (Brewer), 55
Brilliant (Stephens), 436
Brindabella, 251, *251*
Brinton, Frederick S., **272–74,** *273,* 481
Brisa series, 132
Brisbane-Gladstone Race, 107, 336
Bristol, 130
Bristol Bay gillnet boats, 131
Bristol Channel Cutter, 222
Bristol Yachts, 213
Britannia, 122, 152, 282, 384, 425, 474, 478, *478*
British Admiralty, 457
British Airways, 293
British-American Cup, 258
British Institute for Engineering Technology, 50
British Oxygen, 293
British Power Boat Company, 319, 395
British Steel, 87
Britomart (Mylne), 325, *326*
Britomart (Owen), *348*
Brittany Ferries GB, 415
Britt Brothers, 213
Britt-Marie, 229
Broads One-Design, 233, 234
Bröderna Ohlsson, 345
Brooke, John Balmain "Jack," **56–57,** *57*
Brooke Ann, 329
Brooke Canoe, 56
Brooke Yachts, 401
Brooklin Boat Yard, 439, 487, *487*
Brooklyn Navy Yard, 389
Brooklyn Technical High School, 443
Brook shipyard, 30
Brooks, Jack, 203
Broward shipyard, 207
Broward Sportsfishing Series, 412
Brown, James W., *58,* **58,** 366, 485
Brown, John, 235, 266
Brown, Samuel, 216
Brown Shipyard, *see* William H. Brown Shipyard
Brown, Woodbridge Parker "Woody," 10, 84, 98, 370
Brown-Constable, Miriam, 326

Brown Owl, 27, *28*
Brown Owl class, 27, *28,* 29
Bruce, Ian, 45, 259
Bruce Mines Museum, 147
Bruckmann, Erik, 111, *111*
Bruckmann Manufacturing, 111, 134
Brunel, Isambard Kingdom, 395
Bruno and Stillman, 285
Brunswick Corporation, 349
Bruynzeel, Cornelius, 429, 430, 431, 470, 471
Brynhild, 156
Brynhild II, 333, 153
BT Global Challenge ("round the world the wrong way"), 455
Buccaneer, 426, 427
Buccaneer 33, 316
Buchanan, Alan H., *59,* **59,** 127
Buchanan, Willard, 14
Buck, 291
Buddie II, 20
Buehler, George, **59–60,** *60*
Buenos Aires-Rio Race, 160, 161
Buffalo, 73
Bufflehead, 310
Bug, 82
Bullfrog/Verbatim, 107
Bullimore, Tony, 244
Bullseye (Herreshoff 12½), 220
Bunker, Raymond, 60, *60*
Bunker and Ellis, **60,** *60*
Buoyant Girl, 425
Burger Boat Company, 461
Burger boatyard, 139, 147, 200
Burgess, Caroline "Kitty," 65
Burgess, Charles Paine, 62
Burgess, Edward "Ned," 18, 34, *35,* 46, **61–64,** *61, 62, 63, 64,* 65, 66, 151, 152, 197, 205, 218, 219, 241, *253,* 272, 420, 475, *475*
Burgess, Sidney, 62
Burgess and Donaldson, Megargel and Gruber, 186, *186*
Burgess, Swasey and Paine, 215–16, 351, 368, 450
Burgess, William Starling, 5, 46, 62, 64, **65–68,** *65, 66, 67, 68,* 97, 113, 117, 169, *186,* 209, 215, 328, 334, 336, 351, 436
Burgess and Packard, 65, 66
Burgess and Paine, 215, 351
Burgoo, 458
Burma, 118, *118*
Burmeister and Wain shipyard, 43, 373
Burmester, Ernst, 187
Burmester Shipyard, 186–87, *187*
Burnham Yachtbuilding Company, 112
Burns, Chuck, 321
Burns, Ian, 324
Burton, Sir William, 326
Bussard, 190
Bute Slip Dock, 326
Butler, E. Farnham, 193, 194, *194*
Butler, Thomas Harrison, **69–70,** 69, 466
Butt, 190
Buzzards Bay 15, 25, 220
Buzzards Bay One-Design, 449

Bylgia I, 261
Bylgia II, 261
Byrne, Andrew, 70
Byrne, St. Clare J., **70–71,** *71*, 88

C&C Yachts, 54, 110–11, *111*, 134, 225, 256
C & W Bailey, 27
Cabac, 24
Cabar, 24
Cable & Wireless Adventurer, 245
Cabo Rico, 351
Cabo Rico 34/36, 98
Cabo Rico 38, 98
Cabo Rico 45/47, 98
Cabot 36, 54
Cabot, John, 319
Cabri, 302
Cabrilla, 20
Cadet dinghy, 31
Cadete, 159, *159*
Cagg, 229
Caillebotte, Gustave, *73,* **73,** 82, 83, *83*
Caillebotte, Martial, 73
Caimano, 84
Caique, 164, *165*
Caird, Robert, 82
Cairds of Greenock, 70
Caisse d'Epargne du Pas de Calais, 23
Caixa Galicia, 51
Cakewalk, 492
Cal 20, 268
Cal 24, 268
Cal 28, 268
Cal 30, 268
Cal 40, 267, 268, 269, 407
California, 301
California 32, 368, *368*
Calkins, Wendell H. "Skip," *74,* **74,** 349, 360, 409
Callahan, Constantine, 14, **74–75,** *75*
Callis, Daniel Millard, **75–76** *75*
Calluna, 152, 425
Calvert Marine Museum, 199
Calypso, 6
Camatte, François, *76* **76,**
Cambria (Fife), 153
Cambria (Ratsey), 375
Cambridge Cadets, 473
Camden Shipbuilding Company, 209
Cameli, Filippo, 26
Camellia, 151
Campbell, Donald, 314
Campbell, Jock, 270
Campbell, Neil A., 305
Campbell, William MacPherson, **76–77,** *76,* 304
Camper, William, 330, 332
Camper and Nicholson, 176, 237, 321, 327, 330, 331, 332, 334, 336, 401, 425, 452, 470, 483, 484, 491, 493
Campos, Manuel Maximiliano, *77* **77**
Canada One, 256, 259, *259*
Canada's Cup, 110, 111, 197, *198*, 212, 256, 394, 452
Canada Works, 71, 88
Canadian Yachting Association, 128

Canim, 170, *172*
Canoe and Boat Building for Amateurs (Stephens), 318, 442
Cantieri Navali, 303
Canvasback, 41
Cap Corse, 211
Cape Cod Boat Company, 493
Cape Cod catboat, 101, *101*, 491
Cape Cod Maritime Museum, 90
Cape Cod Senior Knockabout, 130
Cape Cod Shipbuilding Company, 130
Cape Dory 28, 4
Cape Dory Yachts, 3, 4
Cape North 43, 54
Cape Town to Rio race, 77
Cap Horn, 211
"Capitano Black," 467
Caponnetto, Mario, 403
Caprice (Hein), 207
Caprice (Ross), 391
Caprice (Still), 444
Caprice of Huon, 87
Capsicum, 235
Captain Bligh, 107
Captain Nat Herreshoff, the Wizard of Bristol (Herreshoff), 216
Caradec, Loïc, 346
Carcano, Giulio Cesare, **77–78,** *78*
Careel 22, 3
Caribbee, 381
Carina (McCurdy), 305, 306
Carina (Rhodes), 240, 382, *468*
Carina (II), 381, 382
Carinthia, 30
Carinthia IV, 303
Carinthia VI, 30
Carita, 38, 87
Carkeek, Shaun, 51, **78–79**
Carmen, 189
Carnegie, 175
Carnegie Institution, 175
Carol, 199
Carola, 117
Caroler, 90
Caroline, 42
Caroly, 26
Caronia, 482
Carroll Marine 60, 141
Carsaca series, 261
Carteau, Jacques, 456
Carter, Richard Eliot, **79–80,** *79,* 179, 360, 463
Carter 30, 80
Carter 37, 80
Carter 39, 80
Carter 42, 80
Carter Offshore, 80
Carver company, 200
Case, John, 489
Cassandra, 151
Cassian, George, 110
Cassiar (Dobson), *123,* 125
Cassiar (McInnis), *309,* 309
Cassie, 61
Castro, Tony (Antonio de Lancastre de Mello e Castro), *80,* **80,** 228
Catabout, 130
Catalano, 347
Catalina (Allègre), 9

Catalina (Bava), 33
Catalonia Polytechnic, 424
catamarans, 9–10, 13, 80, 84, 98–99, *98,* 108–9, 143–45, *143,* 203, 216, 217, 253, 293, 316–17, 325, 346–47, 366, 370, 403, 428, 453, 463, 484
Catana 40, 108
Cataumet 14–foot class, 65
Catboat Association, 297, 491
catboats, 100–101, *101,* 133, 134, 155, 296–97, 363
Cathy Anne II, 443
Cattaneo, Guido, 24
Cattaneo, Guistino, 24
Cattaneo, Ippolito, 92
Catuamet Pups, 351
CATUG tug-and-barge system, 200
Catus, Jules de, **80–81**
Cavalier 37, 115
Cavalier 45, 115
Cayard, Paul, 329
CCA (Cruising Club of America), 8, 77, 79, 80, 90, 97, 194, 301, 306, 318, 351, 353, 379, 381, 387, 426, 436, 440, 441, 457, 458
CCA Rule, 97, 220, 268
C. C. Hanley boatyard, 116
C. C. Smith and Company, 422
C. C. Smith and Sons Boat Company, 293
see also Chris-Craft
CCYD, 401
Cecelia J, 308
Cecilia, 71
Cedar Sea II, 30
Ceil V, 127
Celina, 154
Celli-Pirelli boatyard, 84
Centennial Races, 247
Center, Robert, 420, 421
Centomiglia Race, 407, 445
Centre Nautique des Glénans (CNG), 201, 211
Cercle de la Voile de Paris (CVP) Yacht Club, 45, 73, *73,* 83, 398
Cercle de Modèles, 91
C. E. Ryder Corporation, 288
C'est la Vie, 418
Chaje II, 239
Chalker and Whiting, 404
Challenge 12, 276
Challenge France, 13, *13*
Challenger, 94
Challenger series, 303
Challenger trimaran, 293
Chalmers Institute of Technology, 3, 12, 135, 230, 265, 269, 277, 340, 399, 433
Chambell II, 303
Champagne Charlie, 465
Champion, 490, 491
Chance, Britton, Jr., 229, 379, 384, 436
Channel Handicap System (CHS), 383
Channel Race, 53, 154, 179
Chantey (Crocker), 99
Chantey (Dole), 125
Chantey (Mower), *318*

Catalina (Bava), 33
Chapelle, Howard Irving, 8, 47, **81–82,** *81,* 125, 428, 433, 439, 489
Chapman, Carl, 268
Charente-Maritime, 250
Charisma, 119
Charles Heidsieck III, 465
Charles Heidsieck IV, 465
Charles Jourdan, 383
Charleston Shipyard, 4
Charming, 80
Charming Polly, 290
Chase, Irwin, **82,** 457
Chatham catboat, 101
Cheerio, 360
Cheers, 330
Cheetah, 415
Chenus, Gérard, 154
Cheoy Lee, 38, 320, 358, 368, 383, 387, 493
Cherub (Holmes), 230
Cherub (Murray), 324
Cherub (Spencer), 426
Cherub II, 488
Cherub III, 448
Chesapeake Bay Bugeyes, 354, 488, 489
Chesapeake Bay Maritime Museum, 210
Chesapeake Marine, 493
Cheshire Yacht Club, 88
Cheta, 181
Chevalier, François, 13, *82,* **82**
Chevreux, C. Maurice, 73, **82–83,** *83*
Chevrolet, Louis, 370
Chewink II, 65
Chiar di luna, 400, *400*
Chicago-Mackinac Race, 12, 90, *111,* 383
Chichester, Francis, 38, 47, 87, 243
Chiggiato, Artù, **83–84** *83*
Chika-Chika, 403
Childers, Erskine, 17–18
Childers, Molly, 17
Chimo, 329
China Sea Race, 474
Chinese lug rig, 89, *89*
Chinook, 221
Chiquita, 57
Chita Company, 400
Chita Racing Group, 244
Choy, Barry, 85
Choy, Rudy, 10, **84–85,** *84,* 484
Choydesign, 85
"C.H.P. rule," 10
Chris-Craft, 1, 279, 293, 294, *294,* 328, 385, 422, *422,* 423
Chris-Craft Catalina, 294
Chris-Craft Cobra, 294
Chrismi II, 158
Chris Smith and Sons Boat Company, 422
Christiane B, 359
Christiania, 17
Christina, 289
Christmas, 68
Christoffel's Lighthouse, 122
Chrysler, 213
Chrysler Buccaneer, 293

Chrysler Mutineer, 293
Chrysler North Atlantic Challenge,
    250
Chrysopyle, 426
Chutzpah, 274
Cibou, 129
Cibou Cup, 365
Cicely, 333
Cigale, 80
Cigarette, 450
Cigarette Boats, 18
Cigarette Racing Team, 18
Cigogne, 91
Cigogne II, 91
Cigogne III, 91
Cigogne IV, 91
Cigogne V, 91
Cinderella, 149
Cindy-Lou, 36, 36
Circe, 52, 409
Cisne Branco, 122
City Island Yacht Club, 301
City of Portland, 315
Claire, 492
Clapham, Thomas, 85–86, 85, 264,
    322
Clara (Fife), 151
Clara (Soper), 425
Clarion of Wight, 228
Clark, James, 39, 162, 213
Clark, Montgomery, 235
Clark, Robert, 38, 86–87, 86, 87, 292
Clark, Sir Tom, 426
Clark Mills Boat Works, 313
Class D scow, 247
Class E scow, 246, 247
Classic 44, 43
Classic Boat, 314
Class II European Championship,
    401
Class National Championship, 362
Class X scow (Cub), 247
Class Y scow, 247
Clayton, Ashley, 88
Clayton, Charles Pole, 88 88
Clearwater, 194
Cleopatra's Barge, 104
Clifton Flasher, 244
Climax catamaran, 316
Clio, 150, 151
Clipper (Beeldsnijder), 38
Clipper (Nicol), 336
Clipper (Pedrick), 358, 358
Clipper Class (Buchanan), 59
Clipper Class (Spaulding), 425
Clipper Cup, 115, 360
Clipper Marine, 98
Clotilde, 243, 475
Cloud of Islands (Crealock), 98
Club Med, 346, 346
Club-Méditerranée, 45, 46
Club Náutico San Isidro, 160
Club Nautique Cup, 33
Club Yacht de France, 80
Clyde 19/24's, 306
Clyde 30–Foot class, 150
Clyde Cruising Club, 305
Clyde Motor Boat Club, 305
Clyde One-Design class, 325
CNAM shipyard, 267

CNB shipyard, 44
Coast Catamaran, 10
Coaster, 363
Coastwise Cruiser, 8
Cobber, 284
Coble, Paul, 288
Cobra, 417
Cochrane, Alexander, 169
Cockatoo Island Dockyard, 233
Cock Robin, 8
Coco Class, 201
Cocopomelo, 459
Codd, E. J., 174
Coello, Joaquín, 88
Cohoe, 378
Cohoe II, 331
Coila III, 434
Coin Collection yachts, 296
Colas, Alain, 45, 46
Coles, Adlard, 331
Colin Archer and the Seaworthy
    Double-Ender (Leather), 18
Collamore family, 310
Colleen (Barber), 31
Colleen (Dobson), 125
Colleen Class, 59
College of Higher Education,
    Yacht and Boat Design (South-
    hampton), 462
Collemer, Elmer, 209
Collibri II, 137
Collier Trophy, 66
Collins, Dwight, 260
Color 7, 324
Colorbond, 251
Columbia (Burgess), 67
Columbia (Herreshoff), 105, 152, 219,
    348, 478
Columbia (Stephens), 52, 202, 211,
    213, 436, 441
Columbia (van Deusen), 110, 375,
    462
Columbia class, 179
Columbia River One-Design, 131
Columbia River Yachting Association,
    131
Columbia 21, 98
Columbia 28, 98
Columbia University, 462
Columbia Yacht Corporation, 458
Columbia Yachts, 356
Columbine, 62
Colvic Craft, 242
Colvin, Thomas Edwin, 89 89
Comanche catamaran, 293
Comet (Fellows), 145
Comet (Fife), 147
Comet (Smith), 419
Comet class, 489
Comforter, 65
Commodore Explorer, 346
Commodore's Cup, 142, 495
Common Sense Class sloop, 473
Common Sense III, 473
Common Sense of Yacht Design, The
    (Herreshoff), 216
Commonwealth Scientific and
    Industrial Research Organization,
    45
Compagnia della Vela, 83

Compass (Gurney), 189
Compleat Cruiser, The (Herreshoff),
    216
"compromise type" racing yacht, 61,
    62–63
computational fluid dynamics (CFD),
    394
Computer Design Marine, 109, 110
Concepta, 491
Concert, 284
Concordia Company, 41, 108, 203,
    238, 238, 240, 352, 375, 491
Concordia series (Harris), 203
Concordia yawl (Hunt), 203, 238,
    238, 240, 373
Conde de Godó Trophy, 424
Condon, Albert E., 89
Condon, Rufus, 89
Condor, 228
Condor cruisers, 445
Conejo, 117, 117
Conidaw, 29
Conner, Dennis, 115, 140, 316, 329,
    461
Conq, Pascal, 154–55, 155
Conquistador, 268
Conradi, Torsten, 250–51
Consolidated Shipbuilding
    Corporation, 19, 136, 175, 371,
    389, 409
constant camber cold-molding
    method, 58
Constellation (Burgess), 63
Constellation (Hein), 207, 207
Constellation (Stephens), 52, 441
Constitution, 348
Constitution, U.S.S., 119
Construcctiones Naval Cobo, 387
Construction pratique des bateaux de
    plaisance et yachts (Practical
    Building of Pleasure Boats and
    Yachts) (de Catus), 81
Container, 250
Contender class, 276
Contessa, 388
Contessa II, 474
Contessa of Parkstone, 397
Contessa 32, 397, 397
Contest, 339
Controversy series, 193, 194
Conyplex shipyard, 497
Cook, William Ewald, 90, 90
Cookson, Charles, 14, 74
Cookson and Callahan, 14, 74
Cookson boatbuilders, 142
Coolidge, Hart and Brinck, 91
Coolidge, Leigh Hill, 40, 90–91, 90,
    91, 145, 199
Coolidge Propeller Company, 91
Cooper Union, 245, 293
Coot, 265
Copa de España, 182
Copa del Rey, 51, 78, 182
Copa del Ray Regatta, 424
Copenhagen Rule (Sejllaengde Rule),
    15, 41, 277
Copponex, Henry, 91–92, 92
Corali, 70
Coral Island, 30
Cordelia, 243

Corelia, 359
Corinne III, 3
Corinthian, 66
Corinthian One-Design, 52
Corinthian Yacht Club, 52
Cork 1720 class, 80
Corliss Steam Engine Company, 217
Cornell University, 272, 417, 483,
    487
Cornithian yachting, 441, 484
Cornu, Eugène, 23, 92, 411
Cornubia, 234
Corona, 333
Coronado Company, 458
Coronation Cup, 34, 35
Coronation Regatta, 15
Corrida 36, 43
Corroboree, 427
Corsair (Beavor-Webb), 34
Corsair (Dunbar), 130
Corsair (Harlé), 201
Corsair (Normand), 340
Corsair (Payne), 357
Corsaire, 211
Corsaro (Barilani), 32
Corsaro (Oneto), 347
Corsaro (Riva), 385
Corster V, 270
Corum, 56
Corzo, 189
Cosak, 42–43
Costaguta, Attilio, 92–93 92
Costaguta, Ugo A., 92–93 92
Costaguta shipyard, 33, 93
Cote, 182
Cote d'Azur, 76
Côte d'Or, 250
"cotre des Glénans," 211
Cotton Blossom IV, 154, 360
Couach, Guy group,
    see Guy Couach group
Cougar, 370
Countess, 195, 195
Countess of Dufferin, 110
Coupe de France, 83, 189, 275
Coupe du Cercle de la Voile de Paris,
    164
    see also Cercle de la Voile de Paris;
    One-Ton Cup
Courageous, 213, 276, 358, 461
Cours-Après, 339
Cours de Navigation des Glénans
    (Course of Navigation of the
    Glénans) (Harlé and Viannay), 201
Cousteau, Jacques, 302
COVE (cored veneer construction),
    495
Cowboy, 329
Cowes-Dinard competition, 154
Cowes-Dinard Race, 412
Cowes Maritime Museum, 156
Cowes Week, 157, 240, 292
Cowes Week Regatta, 397, 400, 400,
    484
Cowhorn ketches, 363
Cowslip, 157
Cox, Daniel H., 93–94, 93, 94, 382,
    443
Cox, Dave, 270
Cox, Irving, 93

Cox and Stevens, *94, 97,* 186, 306, 381, 382, 443

Coyote Point Sea Scouts, 320

Cozzani shipyard, 202

Craig Shipbuilding Company, 137, 172

Cramp, William and Sons, *see* William Cramp and Sons

Crane, Clinton Hoadley, 66, **94–97,** *95, 96, 97,* 113, 129, 145, 169, 212, 235, 288, 434, 435, 436

C. Raymond Hunt Associates, 134, 240

CR (Cruiser/Racer) Rule, 1, 53, 92, *307*

Crealock, William Ion Belton, 17, 22, *98,* **98**

Crealock 34, 98

Crealock 37, 98, *98*

Crédit Agricole, 83, 383

Crédit Agricole III, 383

Creger, Francis H. "Skip," 84, **98–99,** *98,* 366

Creger 32, 98

Creole, 336

Criquet, 73

Cristoforo Colombo, 347

Criterion, 382

Critical Path, 291

CRN, 401

Croce, Beppe, 78

Crocker, Samuel Sturgis, 8, 55, **99–100,** *99,* 100

Croisière, 82

Crosby, Andrew, 100

Crosby, Charles, 101

Crosby, C. Worthington, 100, 101

Crosby, Daniel, 100, 101

Crosby, E. M. Boat Works, *see* E. M. Crosby Boat Works

Crosby, Herbert F., 101, *101*

Crosby, H. Manley, *33,* 100, 101, 103

Crosby, Horace, 100, 101

Crosby, Jesse, 100

Crosby, Jesse, Jr., 100

Crosby, Joseph, 101

Crosby, Nathan, 100

Crosby, Ralph, 103

Crosby, Tirzah, 100

Crosby, William Flower, 103, *103*

Crosby, Wilton, 101

Crosby family, **100–103,** *101, 103*

Crosby Yacht Building and Storage Company, 103, 202

Cross, Norman A., *103,* **103** 366

Cross, Walter, 203

Cross 18, 103

Cross 24, 103

Cross 26, 103

Cross 30, 103

Cross 32R, 103

Cross 36, 103, *103*

Cross 37, 103

Cross 42, 103

Cross 52R, 103

Crossbow, 293, 293

Crossbow II, 293

Cross Trimarans, 103

Crouch, Albert, 103, 428

Crouch, George F., **103–4,** *104,* 118, 288, 462

Crowninshield, Bowdoin Bradlee, 5, 46, **104–6,** *105, 106,* 118, 136, 169, 197, 318, 392, 488, 492

Crown Jewel, 296

Crowther, Brett, 108

Crowther, Lock, **107–8,** *107,* 316

Cruinneag III, 76, 77

Cruise of the Diablesse (Fenger), 147

Cruiser Carrier, 267

Cruiser/Racer (CR) Rule, 1, 53, 92, *307*

Cruising as a Way of Life (Colvin), 89

Cruising Club of Japan, 496

Cruising Houseboat, 267

Cruising Multihull, The (White), 486

Cruising World Design Competition, 122

Cruising World magazine, 123

Cruising Yacht Club of Australia, 356

Cruising Yacht Design (Brewer), 54

Cruising Yachts: Design and Performance (Butler), 69

Crusader (Cross), 103

Crusader (Seaborn), 408

Crusader I, 336

Crusader II, 336

Crusoe, 318

C/S/K Catamarans, 84–85

C-Star race, 250

CT, 360

Cube Rule, 12

Cuckoo's Nest, 291

Cuilaun of Kinsale, 306

Culebra, 125

Culler, Robert D. "Pete," *108,* **108**

Culzean Ship Building and Engineering, 151

Cunningham, Briggs, 66

Cunningham, Charles, 84, **108–9**

Cunningham, Lindsay, 84, **108–9,** *109*

Cupidon III, 189

Curran, Philip Edward, **109–10**

Currytush, 355

Curtiss, Glenn L., 66, 199

Curtiss Aircraft, 199, 293

Custom Streamliner, 463

Custom Yachts (Auckland), 416

Cuthbert, Alexander, **110,** 128, 420

Cuthbertson, George, 54, **110–11,** *110, 111*

Cuthbertson and Cassian, 110–11

Cutts, Edmund, 489

C. W. Hood 50, 498

C. W. Hood Yachts, 1

C. W. Paine Yacht Design, 498

Cyclos II, 39

Cyclos III, 491

Cyfraline, 13

Cyfraline 3, 13

Cygnet Cup, 240

Cymba, 149

Cyprus, 151

Cyrano de Bergerac, 237

Cyric, 309

Cythera, 148, 149

Czarina (Garden), 165

Czarina (Nicholson), 330

Dacia, 332

Daffodil, 112

Dagless Fleur de Lys, 243

Dahlström, Oscar Wilhelm, **112**

Dahut, 73

Dai-Dai III, 164

Dai-Dai IV, 164

Daila, 83

Daila II, 83

Daimler, Gottlieb, 289, 290

Dainty, 483

Daisy, 425

Dakota, 454

d'Albertis, Enrico Alberto, 347

Dalgra, 33

Dallimore, Norman Edward, **112**

Dallimore Owners Association, 112

Dall'Orso, Mario, 93

Dalrymple-Smith, Butch, 228

Dambuster, 370

Dame des Tropiques, 23

Damen shipyard, 320

Dame Pattie, 233, 233

Damien II, 249

Dana series, 98

Danica, 418

Daphne, 27

Daragnès, Jean Gabriel, 302

Darina, 156

Dark Harbor 12½, 104, 106

Dark Harbor 17½, 104, 106, *106*

Dark Harbor class, 94, 104, 106, *106*

Darling racing yachts, 494

Dart, 457

Dartmouth College, 439

Dash 39, 43

Dauntless, 462

Dauntsey's School, 353

Davidson, Kenneth S. M., 68, **112–14,** *113,* 436

Davidson, Laurie, **114–15,** *114, 115,* 140, 329

Davidson 35, 115

Davidson Laboratory, 433

Davis, C. H., 33

Davis, Charles Gerard, 14, **115–16,** *116*

Davis, Merle J., **117–18,** *117,* 145, 267

Davis, M. M., 349

Davis, Richard Ordway, *118,* **118,** 196, 308, 318

Dawnbreaker, 350

Day, Arno, 487

Day, Sumers and Company, 334

Day, Thomas Fleming, 115, 129, 301, 318, 404

Daytona company, 200

Dea, 357

Deb, 339

Deben Four-Tonner, *47, 47*

Deben Six-Tonner, 47

de Bisschop, Eric, 484

Deborah, 34

Debra, 404

Decime, 357

de Dood, Johann, 313

Dee 25, 53

Deep Stuff, 444

Deep-V hull, 18, 239, *240,* 283, 298

Deepwater 28, 109

Defender (Herreshoff), 219, 277, 325, 476

Defender (Pedrick), 358

DeFever, Arthur, *118* **118**

DeFever 50, 119

Defiance, 348, *348,* 349

Defoe Boat and Motor Works, 483

De Groene Draeck, 182

Deguello, 107, 108

Dehler Yachts, 431, 497

de Kersauson-Olivier, 346

de La Brosse shipyard, 398

Delannoy, A., 189

Delaware River Iron Works, 167

Delaware River Marathon, 245

Delfin Class sloop, 265

Delft 25, 427

Delft Denk Tank, *see* Delft Think Tank

Delft Laboratories, 126

Delft Polytechnicum, 226

Delft Think Tank (The Think Tank), 126, 226, 394, 471, 497

Delft University, 126

Delight, 135

Deliverance, 308

Delphine (Gielow), 173

Delphine (Hoyt), 235

Delphines, 104

Delta Marine Small Craft Design and Survey, 472

De Marini, 33

Demi, 73

Demon of Hamble, 370

Dencho Marine, 12

Denker, August, 373

Denny, Archibald, 478

Denny, Peter, 475

Denny's shipyard, 212, 235

Den Swarten Arent, 262

Dent, Clive, 80

De Quincey, Roger, *156,* 157

Derecktor, Robert, **119–20,** *120,* 147, 179, 202

Derecktor shipyard, 320, 492

Der Junge Schiffbauer (The Young Shipbuilder), 313

Dervish, 97

Derwent class, 31

Design Systems, 256

Desirable and Undesirable Characteristics of Offshore Yachts (Society of Naval Architects and Marine Engineers), 436

Despujol's shipyards, 76

Destiny, 75

Destiny Yachts, 297

Details, 12

Detroit, 301

Detroit-Mackinac Race, 99, *111*

Detroit Shipbuilding Company, 488

Deutscher Segler Verband (German Sailing Federation), 190

Deutsche Werft shipyard, 209

Deva, 158

Devereaux, Henry, 381

Devlin, Elizabeth, 120

Devlin, Samuel, **120,** *120*

Devlin's Boat Building, How to Build Any Boat the Stitch-and-Glue Way (Devlin), 120
Devon class, 169
de Voogt, Fritz, 465
de Wit, Simon, 471
D Flawless, 107
Diablesse, 145
Diadem, 366
Diam 40, 267, *267*
Diamond W., 94
Diaship (Dutch International Association of Shipbuilders), 320
Dickie, A. M. and Sons, *see* A. M. Dickie and Sons
Dickie, Peter, 76
Dickie of Tarbert boatyard, 76, 77
Dickson, Chris, 140
Didaquinto, 360
Didi 38, 123
Diesel Duck 48, *60*
Die Technische Hoschschule (Berlin), 459
Die Yacht magazine, 225
Different Boats (Bolger), 49
Dijkstra, Gerard, 39, **121–22,** *121, 122,* 126
Dilemma, 33, 80, 219
Dillinger, 320
Dillion, Dave, 323
Dina series, 132
Dinghao, 489
Dinklage, Ludwig, **122**
Dione, 135
Discovery Yachts, 228
Disdale, Terence, 401
Diva, 249
Diverse 75, *351*
Dix, Dudley, **122–23,** *123*
Dixie, 94
Dixie II, 94, *95*
Dixie IV, 94
Dixon, Tony, 157
Djezyrelys, 275
D. J. Lawlor, 272
DK Yachts, 142
DML Shipyard, *30*
Dobbs, Fred, 91
Dobson, Benjamin T., **123–25** *123*
Dodge, Horace E., 175
Dodge, Mrs. Horace E., 173
Dodge Boat and Plane Company, 104
Doge, 33
Doggersbank motoryachts, *50,* 51
Dog Star, 381
Dole, Wilfred Heinrich "Heinie," II, 125, **125**
Dolphin, 445
Dolphin, 75
Dolphin Boatyard, 370
Dominion, 129
Dominion Bridge Company, 128, 129
Dominion Physical Laboratory, 57
Donald, A. B., 26
Donaldson, Boyd, 68
Dongame, 206
Dongame series, 474
Donnerwetter, 289–90, *290*
Donovan, Jim, 321

Donzi Marine, 18
Dooley's Basin and Drydock, 34
Dora, 320
Dorade, 154, 353, 409, 415, 425, 436, 440, *440,* 441
Dorbyl boatyard, 207
Dordrecht, University of, 416
Doreste, Luis, 51
Doris (Nicolson), 336
Doris (Watson), 475
Doritis, 164
Dorothy, 434
Dorothy Louise, 443
Dorothy May, 65
Dorris, Robert Stayton, **125**
Dottie G, 308
Doublehanded Transatlantic Race, 415
Double Heaven, 207
Douce France, 463
Douglas Aircraft, 74
Douglass, Gordon K. "Sandy," **126,** 258
Dovell, Andy, 324
Dover-Heligoland Race, 254
Dover-Kristiansand Race, *87*
Drac, 303
Drafin, 92
Dragon (Archer), 17
Dragon (Fife), 152
Dragonera, 486
Dragon One-Design Class, 15–16, *16,* 225, 277, *279*
Draijer, Nel, 126
Draijer, Wiebe, *126,* **126,** 226
Draijertje, 126
Drake School, 388, 389
Dreamer, 325
Dream Ships (Griffiths), 184
Dresden Technical School, 399
Drewitz, Reinhard, **126–27**
Drewitz/Rührdanz, 127
Driac, 274
Drifter, 329
Driscoll Boat Works, 74
Droxford, William and Son, *see* William Droxford and Son
Drumbeat, 240, 329, 491
Dublin Bay 21–footers, 325
Dubois, Edward George, **127–28** *127*
Duckling, 318
Dudley Dix Yacht Design, 123
Duende, 213
Duesselboot, 250
Dufour, 54, 202
Dufour cruisers, 461
Dufour shipyard, 44
Dufour Wing sailboards, 23
Duggan, George Herrick, 94, **128–29,** *128, 129,* 365
DUKW, 436, 441
Dulli, 229
Dumas, Vito, 77
Dunbar, Francis Spaulding, **129–31,** *130,* 349
Dunham, Gilbert, 428
Dunham and Stadel, 428
Dunraven, Earl of, 152, 476, *477*
Dunsmuir Cup, 170
Duoform hull, 322

DuPont, 218
Durand, W. F., 272
Durham University (England), 176
Dusio, Carlo, 385
Dutch Built virtual boatyard, 225
Dutch Society of Yacht Architects, 289
Duvergie, Daniel, 46, *131,* **131**
DXB 101, 388
Dyarchy, 176
Dyas, 445
Dyer, Joseph Melville, 125, *131,* **131**
Dyer 29, 368, 412
Dyer Boats, 412
Dynamic Company, 250, 260
Dynasty, 491

Ea (Baglietto), 26
Ea (Giovanelli), 181
Eagle, 461
East and West championship, 65
East Anglian, 156, *157*
East Anglian Class, 59
Easterner, 238
Eastern Sea Skiffs, 298
Eastern Shipbuilding, 234
Eastern Yacht Agency, 62
Eastern Yacht Club, 62, 63, 169, 197, 205, 272, 352
Eastern Yacht Club One-Design, 47
Easter Spi Ouest regatta, 237
Eastward Ho, 308, 310
Ebb Tide, 125
Ebe, 367
Ebella, 280
Echenique, Iñigo, **132**
Echenique 470, 132
Echo, 43
Echo II, 330
Eclipse (Harris), 203
Eclipse (Peterson), 360
Eco, 158, *158*
Ecole d'Application du Génie Maritime, 83
Ecole des Beaux-Arts, 369
Ecole Nationale de Voile (National Sailing School), 346, 465
Ecume de Mer, 154
Eddy Marine Corporation, 462
Edel-Cat 33, 267
Edey and Duff, 99, *100*
Edge I, 109
Edge II, 109
Edge III, 109
Edison Boatbuilding School, 166
Edward VII, King of England, 342, *474,* 477, 478, *478,* 175
Eel, 230, *230*
Eendracht, 471
Effect of the Universal Rule in Recent Yachts, The (Erismann), 138
Effort, 175
Egg Harbor Boat Company, 298
Egg Nog, 453, *453*
Egremont Sailing Club, 55
Egret, 323, *323*
Egythene, 228
Eichler, Curt Walter, **132**
8-Meter class, 53, 153

82–foot Catamaran class, 44
Eileen, 154
Einheits-Revierklasse (Inland Water One-Design Class), 39
EJP, 13
Ekasoni, 392
Elaine, 88
Elco (Electric Launch Company), 82, 116, 130, 138, 235, 288, 293, 457, 460, 483
Elco Cruisette, 82
Elcoplane, 82
El Corsario, 320
Elderyacht, 194
Eldredge, Albert J., 308
Eldridge, George, 82
Eldridge-McInnis, 8, 163, 203, 271, 308, 310, 417, 492
Electra (Alberg), 4
Electra (Geary), 170, 172
Electric Boat Company, 34, 82, 401, 473
Elements of Boat Strength, The (Gerr), 173
Elements of Yacht Design (Skene), 116, 258, 498
Elf, 271
Elf Aquitaine, 13
Elf Aquitaine I, 267
Elf Aquitaine II, 56
El Heirie, 129
Elizabethan 30, 455
Elizabeth II, Queen of England, 157
Elizabeth Muir, 309
Elizabeth Silsbee, 66
Elizabeth V, 1
Elk, 33
El Legarto, 191
Ellen, 66
Elliott, Greg, 55, **132–33,** *133*
Elliott 96, 133
Elliott 770, 133
Ellis, Don, 60
Ellis, Mark, **133–34** *133,*
Ellis, Ralph, *60*
Ellis 36, 60
Ellisha, 486, *487*
Elly, 280
El Machuca, 189
Eloise (Piver), 366
Eloise (Sergent), 412
Eloise II, 412
Elsinore Institute of Naval Architecture, 208
Elsworth, Joe, 134, 135
Elsworth, Philip R. "Phip," **134–35** *134*
El Tigre, 428
El Toro prams, 320
Elvström, Paul, 260–61, 303, 328
Elvström and Kjaerulff Yacht Design, 260, *260*
Elvström-Coronet 38, 261
Elvström Yacht Design, 261
E. M. Crosby Boat Works, 103
Emerald (Presles), 369
Emerald (Watts), 479
Emergency Fleet Corporation, 199, 480
Emily (Nielsen), 338

Emily (Peterson), 360
Emma Hamilton, 293
Empacher, Dieter, 498
Emperor, 496
Empress, 366
Encarnita, 189
Endeavour, 47, 67, 121, 122, 321, 334
Endeavour II, 335, 68
Endeavour cruisers, 461
Enderlein, Olle, **135–36** 135
Endurance 35, 242, 242
Endymion (Crane), 95, 97
Endymion (Potter), 301, 368
Energy 48, 298, 298
English Electric company, 234
English Falmouth Quay Punt, 351
English Singlehanded Transatlantic Race, 303
Enia, 189
Enigma (Bava), 33
Enigma (Dubois), 128
Enschede Polytechnicum, 126
Enten-Eller, 42
Enterprise (Burgess), 67, 97, 186, 336
Enterprise (Stephens), 358
Entre Nous, 100
Enza, 244, 244
Era, 376, 376
Eric, 17, 22, 22
Erichsen, Bodil, 338
Ericson 35, 258
Ericson Cruising 36, 258
Ericson Yachts, 258
Eriksberg Mekaniska Vaerk, 449
Erin, 27
Erismann, Martin Coryell, **136–37**, 136, 137
Erivale, 86, 87
Erl King, 243
Eroica, 460
Escapade (Potter), 368
Escapade (Rhodes), 382, 382
Escapade II, 5
Escuela Tecnica Superior de Ingenieros Navales, 9, 88, 132
Espace stackaway RIB (Rigid Inflatable Boat), 237
Espadon, 80
España 92 Quinto Centenario, 132
España 92 V Centenario, 394
Esperanza, 341
Esprit, 360
Essential, 311
Este 24, 163
Estelle, 217
Ester, 312, 312
Estérel Shipyard (Chantiers de l'Estérel), 30, 303
Estlander, Gustaf Adolf, 137, **137**, 190, 231, 333, 377, 399
Etain, 176
Etap 38, 202
Eternal Laughter, The (Burgess), 65
Ethelwynn, 441, 443
Etincelle, 398
Etiveaud, Jean-François d', 55
Eugenia, 444
Eugenio, Duke of Ancon, 24
Eulalie, 255

Europe 1 Star competition, 23
European Championship (5.5 meter), 403
European (Soling Class) Championship, 260
European International Rule, 15
European KR Rule, 48
European Week, 15
Euros, 126
Eva, 399
Eva II, 482
Evaine, 211, 336
Evening Star, 131
Even Keel Marine, 284, 285
Eventide 24, 184
Eventide 26, 184
Evergreen, 256
Everyday Engineering magazine, 138
E. W. Scripps, 273, 274
Excalibur (Crealock), 98
Excalibur (Stadt), 431
Excalibur (Smith), 424
Exempla Trahunt, 344
Expedition Yachts, 412
Explorer catamarans, 485
Explorer concept yacht, 50
Explorer motoryachts, 466
Expo 1967 (Montreal), 443
Extension, 385
Extrasea A, 320
Extreme, 497
Eyra, 434

F-100, 180
Facques, Phillippe, 346
Fähnrich 34, 312
Fairey Aviation, 234
Fairey Duckling, 157
Fairey Fox, 157
Fairey Marine, 157
Fairfield Shipbuilding Company, 304
Fairform Flyer, 236, 236
Fairlie Yacht Slip Company, 154
Fairmile company, 77
"Fairmile" gunboats, 29
Fair Rover, 53
Faith, 125
Falco I, 180
Falco II, 180
Falmouth Cutter, 222
Falmouth Quay punt, 181
Falmouth Quay punts, 493
Fancy, 60
Fandango, 179
Fantasia class, 202
Fantasy Two, 229
Farallone Clipper, 434
Farmer, Earle Weston "Westy," 116, **138–39**, 138, 139, 379
Farmer, Mary Murray "Bylo," 138
Farr, Bruce K., 114, 115, **139–42**, 140, 141, 182, 227, 250
Farr 38, 140
Farr 40, 140, 142
Farrier, Ian, **142–43**
Fast 2000, 250
Fast Cat, 103

Fastnet Race, 56, 66, 79, 87, 122, 127, 154, 179, 187, 226, 235, 240, 243, 331, 332, 353, 356, 360, 378, 381, 382, 383, 397, 400, 401, 412, 415, 431, 436, 440, 448
Fast Yacht design system, 256
Fatty Knees dinghy, 222
Fauroux, Jacques, 154
Fauvette, 73
Favona, 87
Fawcett Publishing Company, 138
Fay, Michael, 115
Fay and Company, 334, 425
FD-12 design, 229
Feadship, 30, 30, 207, 301, 322, 465, 492
Fearon, Thomas, **143–45** 143
Fedalah, 331
Federal Maritime Commission, 480
Federazione Italiana Vela, 467
Feeling, 491
Feeling 1090, 201
Feinsliebschen VII, 342
Fei Seen, 382
Felicia, 274
Felicita, 359
Felicita West, 228
Felipe, Prince of Spain, 13
Felisi, 473
Fellows, Joseph, 144, **145**
Fellows, Joseph "Rusty," Jr., **145**
Fellows and Stewart, 117, 138, 145, 253
Fellowscraft Thirty-Two, 144
Femfemman, 265
Fenger, Frederic A. "Frits," **145–47**, 146
Ferida, 432
Fernande, 369
Ferris, Theodore D., 93, 421
Fexas, Thomas Eli, 147 **147**
F. F. Pendleton Yard, 186, 186
Fiat, 162, 164
Fiat X, 164, 164
Fibresport Artaban, 387
Fidji, 250
Field magazine, 62, 325
Fieramosca, 347
Fiery Cross, 497
Fife, Alexander, 148
Fife, Allan, 148
Fife, James, 148
Fife, Janet Jamieson, 148
Fife, Robert Balderston, 154
Fife, William, 52, 64, 70, **147–48**
Fife, William, II (Sr.), **148–50**, 148, 149, 150, 243, 280
Fife, William, III (Jr.), 52, 53, 149, **150–54**, 150, 151, 152, 153, 167, 168, 170, 175, 187, 212, 245, 319, 325, 326, 373, 332, 333, 375, 383, 395, 425, 474, 475, 477, 478
Fife Regatta, 153
Fife shipyard, 147–54, 306
Fifty Fathom Trawler, 266
Figaro IV, 119
Fighter, 445
Fila, 154, 155
Fingal, 379
Finisterre, 125, 300, 436

Finn 26, 444
Finn Express 27, 444
Finnfire 33, 444
Finnfire II, 444
Finn Flyer 27, 444
Finn Flyer 31, 444
Finnsailor 30, 185
Finnsailor 34, 185
Finot, Jean-Marie, **154–55**, 155, 463
Fiona, 149
Fireball, 314, 314
Firebird, 336, 383
Firecrest, 254
Firefly, 157
First Class One-Design, 154
Fischer, Carl, 371
Fish, Robert "Captain Bob," **155**, 419
Fish class, 220
Fisher, Dick, 239
Fisher Boatworks, 498
Fishers Island 31, 211, 221
Fishers Island sloop, 288
Fiumara, 327
505 boats, 45, 82
510 One-Design series, 238
Five-Ton Class, 243
Fix, 42, 42
Fjord, 159
Fjord Boats, 10
Fjord III, 160
Fjordling, 277
Fjord V, 160
Fjord VI, 160
Flamenca 25, 43
Flamingo (Becker), 36
Flamingo (Estlander), 137
Flamingo (Tchetchet), 453
Flamingo 40, 36
Flapper, 245
Flash, 237
Flattie class, 172
Fleetwing (Herreshoff), 214
Fleetwing (van Deusen), 461
Fleming, Arthur "Bill," 457
Flensburg Yacht Club, 494
Fleur de Lys, 461
Fleurtje, 38
Fleury Michon IX, 244
Fleury Michon VIII, 244
Flica, 336
Flica II, 177
Flicka, 98
Flight of the Firecrest (Gerbault), 189
Flirt (de Catus), 80
Flirt (Pinaud), 365, 365
Flora, 466
Florida Bay Coaster, 40
Florinda, 330
Flyer, 121
Flying 10, 157
Flying 12, 157
Flying Ants, 324
Flying Cloud (Mower), 319
Flying Cloud (Schock), 117
Flying Cloud III, 196
Flying Dutchman class, 275, 390
Flying Fifteen, 157
"Flying Footpath," 3
Flying Forty, 46
Flying Scot, 126

Flying Scotchman, 267
Foam II, 357
Föhrjolle, 274
Folatre, 253
Folding Schooner, The (Bolger), 49
Folkboat, 245, *245,* 263, 265, 301, 329, 397, 449
Follenfant, Pierre, 250
Folly II, 253
Foncia, 463
Fontvella, 424
Forbes, Alexander, 145
Forbes, J. Malcolm, 30, 62
Ford, Edsel, 191
Ford, Henry, 175, 191
Ford, Payne and Roué, 394
Ford, Payne and Sweisguth, 450
Fore An' Aft magazine, 23
Fore River Shipbuilding Company, 136, *136,* 389
Forest and Stream magazine, 85, 136, 265, 441, 442
Forest and Stream Publishing Company, 116
Forges et Chantiers de la Mediterranée, 83
Forgia, Pierre, 154
Formula 40 class, 251, 282
Formula 40 World Championship, 316, 463
Formula Boat Company, 18
Formula TAG, 244
Forrest and Son's Shipyard, 47
Forster Cup, 358
Fortier Boats, 310
Fortuna (Campos), 77
Fortuna (Smith), 135
Fortuna (Visiers), 467
Fortuna Extra Lights, 467
Fortuna Lights, 467
Fortuna 9 cruiser/racer, 468
Fortune magazine, 98
40–Foot class, *62,* 64
46–Foot class, *62,* 64
49er skiff, 44–45
Foss Tug Company, 40
Foster, Dan, 18
Foster, Norman, 157, 180
Foto, 283
Fouché shipyard, 398
Foundation Company, 411, 480
Fountaine-Pajot shipyard, 44, 250
410 One-Design series, 238
Fox (Benzon), 42
Fox (Wiley), 489
Fox, Uffa, 21, 86, *97,* 126, **155–57,** *156, 157,* 160, 187–88, 258, 316, 387, 426
Foxhound, 336
Fram, 15, 16–17
Fram VIII, 11
France, 303, *303,* 304
France 2, 56
France 3, 56
France II, 303, 304
France III, 461, *461*
Frances, (Mower), 319
Frances 26, 350
Francis, Martin, **157–58,** *158*
Franck, Vic, 166

Francke, Paul, **158**
Franco, Francisco, 266
Frank L. Sample and Son Shipyard, 118
Frea, 154
Freda (Beavor-Webb), 34
Freda (Kemp), 254
Frederikstad Museum, 3
Fredette, Frank, **158**
Fredette, Irene, 158
Fredonia, 311
Freedom, 213, 356, 460
Freedom 33, 353
Freedom 40, *235,* 236
Freedom Yachts, 236, 320, 358
Freelance, 414
Freeman, Reg, 370
Freeman Cup, 110, *110,* 111
Freesia, 51
Free Zone France championship, 211
Freja, 12
French Cup, 24, 26, 78, 93, 347
French Kiss, 56
French Naval Museum, *131*
French Open 60 circuit, 282
French Rule, *73*
Frers, Germán, 39, 140, **160–62,** *160, 161, 162, 162,* 180, 491
Frers, Germán, Sr., 17, **159–60,** *159*
Frers, Germán, Jr., **162–63,** *162, 163*
Frers, Pepe, 160
Frers, Susana, 161
Freya, 193, *193*
Fricaud, Joseph, 261
Fried Krupp shipyard, 93
Friedrich Lürssen Werft, 30, 289
Friendship, 368
Friendship sloop, 310–11, *311,* 363, *431, 431,* 432, 490
Friendship Sloop Society, 311
Fritha, 363
Frolic, 366
From My Old Boat Shop, One Lung Engines, Fantail Launches, & Other Marine Delights (Farmer), 138, 139
Frost, William "Pappy," **163,** 182, 284
Frost Torpedo, 498
Froude, William, 88, 112–13, *355,* 475
FT, 253
Ftot, 267
Fujicolor II, 244
Fuller, Avard, 119–20
Fuller, Buckminster, 120
Fullerton and Company Shipbuilders, 151
Fulton Marine Construction, *75*
Fun, 114
Funambule, 346
Furama, 32
Furnham's Yacht Agency, 203
Future Shock, 133

G37, 183
G41, 183
G44, 183
G54, 183

Gadabout, 357
Gaea, 481, *481*
Gaffer, 390
Gain, 367
Galatea (Beavor-Webb), 34, *35,* 61, 63
Galatea (Matthews), *302*
Galatea (Nygren), 340
Galaxy, 125
Galea Class, 9
Galicia Calidade, 132
Galileo, 321
Galletto motorcycle, 78
Gallinari, Egidio, *164,* **164**
Galodée, Emile, 353
Gambling, 277
Gamela fishing boats, 132
Gamleby Boatyard, *11*
Ganbare, 360
Ganley, Denise, 164
Ganley, Denis Harcourt, **164**
Ganley, Philomena, 164
Gann, Ernest K., *40*
Gannon, Ross, 41
Gannon and Benjamin Marine Railway, 41
Garbutt, Frank A., 472
Garbutt and Walsh Shipyard, 472
Garden, Lorne, 315
Garden, William, 40, 145, **164–67,** *166, 167,* 264, 315, 360, 407
Garden Island Dockyard, 233
Gardner, William, 34, 67, 82, 94, *95, 97,* 115, 117, 129, **167–70,** *168, 169,* 197, 205, 219, 235, 349, 450
Gardner and Cox, 93
Gardner, Ford and Paine, 450
Gareloch One-Design, *309*
Gareth, 332
Garm IV, *312*
Garrion, 432
Gartside, Paul, *170,* **170**
Garuda, 228, 491
Gar Wood company, 279
Gas Engine and Power-Charles Seabury Company, 136, 411
Gatewood and Bowles, 167
Gaubert's shipyard, 45–46
Gaucho (Campos), *77, 77*
Gaucho (Farr), 140
Gauloises IV, 183
Gaynor, Ed, 338
Gazell, 229
Gazelle, 89, *89*
GBR Challenge, 237
Geary, Leslie Edward "Ted," **170–72,** *171, 172,* 199
Geary 18, 172
Gebhard, Rollo, 445
Geiger, Frederick C., **172–73,** *173,* 460, 489
Gemma, 398
General Dynamics, 147, 249
General Motors, 441
Genesee, 197, *198*
Genesta, 34, *61, 63,* 205, 384, 421
Genie, 67
Genoa jib, 93
Gentleman's Runabout, 498
Geodis, 154

George Inman and Son, 375
George Lawley and Son, 3, *5,* 33, 46, *47,* 62, 89, 90, 99, 136–37, *195,* 212, 245, *253,* **270–72,** 308, 322, 365
George Nickum and Company, 409
George Steers yard, 419
George V, King of England, 416, *425,* 477
George Washington University, 283
Georgia, 401
Gérard Lambert, 463
Gerbault, Alain, 189, 254
Gerdny I, 399
Gerdny II, 399
Gerifay, 459
German-American championship, 66
German Emperor's Cup, 254
Germania (Heidtmann), 206
Germania (Oertz), 153, 344
Germania II, 375
Germania III, *374,* 375
Germania-Werft, 344
German Sailing Association, 48, 494
German Yachtsman's Association, 127
Geronimo, 463
Gerr, David, *173* **173**
Gerritsma, Jelle, 126, 226
Gertrude L Thebaud, 352
Gervasoni, Gino, 387
Gherardesca, Gaddo della, 93
Ghost (Clayton), *88*
Ghost (Woolacott), 494
Giaguaro, 84
Gianduia, 33
Gian-Maria, 33
Gibbs, Dick, 293
Gibbs and Cox, 301
Gibbs Brothers, 94
Gibbs Gas Engine Company, 103, 138
Gibellini, Pieri, 386, 387
Gib Sea 414, 237
Gib Sea Master 48, 237
Gib Sea shipyard, 237, 249
Gielow, Henry J., **173–75,** *174, 175,* 235, 435, 450, 483
Gielow, Henry Company, *see* Henry J. Gielow Company
Gielow and Orr, 235
Gilbert, A. C. Company, *see* A. C. Gilbert Company
Giles, Jack Laurent, 86, **176–79,** *176, 177, 179,* 189, 243, 267, 292, 296, 399, 401, 411, 467
Giles, Laurent and Partners, *see* Laurent Giles and Partners
Gilgenast, Gerhard, **179–180,** *179*
Gill, George R., 176
Gillmer, Thomas Charles, **180–81,** *180, 181*
Gimcrack, 113
Gin-Fizz, 249
Gingko, 276
Giovanelli, Francesco, **181**
Giovanelli, Guido, 26
Gipon, Jacob Klaas, **181–82,** *182*
Gipsy, 461
Gipsy Moth II, 47

Gipsy Moth III, 38, 87, 243
Gipsy Moth IV, 243
Gipsy Moth V, 87
Giraglia Cup, 303
Giralda, 77
Giraglia Cup, 303
Giralda, 77
Gitana, 272
Gitana II, 340
Gitana IV, 400
Gitana 43, 43
Gitana 54, 43
Give Up, 444
GKSS (Gothenburg Royal Yacht
 Club), 11, 12, 277, 365, 499
Glad Tidings, 81–82
Glafki III, 237
Glamara, 415
Glasgow, Earl of, 147
Glasgow, University of, 24, 32,
 80, 94, 98, 136, 212, 235, 285,
 306, 483
Glass Slipper II, 84
Gleam (Brooke), 57
Gleam (Crane), 97, *97*
Gleam (Fife), 148
Gleam (Holland), 228
Glenafton, 327
Glenans, 370
Glénans Nautical Center (CNG), 154
Glencairn, 128, 129
Glen-Coats, Sir Thomas, 326
Glen Daisy cruisers, 122
Glengour, 304
Global Challenge race, 237
Gloria (Beeldsnijder), 38
Gloria (van der Velden), 466
Gloriana, 12, 42, 43, 63, 64, 218–19,
 219, 340
Gloucester 20, 498
Gloucester fishing schooner, 5, 106,
 308, *309*
Gloucester Light Dory (Gloucester
 Gull), 48
G. L. Watson and Company, 32–33,
 258, 306
Goderich 35, 54
Godinet, 73
Godinet's Rule, 80
Goeller, Fred, 216
Go for the Gold (Hoyt), 236
Gold Challenge Cup, *95*
Gold Cup (12–liter class), 462
Gold Cup, 1, 18, 78, 104, *104,* 137,
 191, 229, 231, 265, *265,* 279
Gold Cup speed regatta, 371
Golden Apple, 228
Golden Bough, 489
Golden Eye, 297
Golden Gain, 199
Golden Gate Class, 481
Golden Hind (Angelman), 14
Golden Hind (Mylne), 327
Golden Hind 31 (Griffiths), 184,
 184, 185
Golden Shadow, 158
González, Amadeo, 182
González, Pepín, **182**
Goodwill, 175
Goodwin, 126

Goodwin, Chuck, 321
Goose, 52, 436
Gordano Goose, 244
Gosling (Alden), 8
Gosling (Lawley), 271
Gosport Aircraft Company, 334
Gossoon, 64, 152
Göta, 367
Gothenburg International Regatta, 17
Gothenburg Mekaniska Verkstad
 (Gothenburg Technical Institute),
 312, 345
Gothenburg Royal Yacht Club
 (GKSS), 11, 12, 277, *365,* 499
Gotland Runt, 383
Goudy and Stevens, 59, 309
Gould, Harold, 411
Gouwzee series boats, 38
Gower, Harold, **182**
Gozzard, Hedley "Ted," *183,* **183**
Gozzard, Jan, 183
Gozzard, Michael, 183
Gozzard, Wesley, 183
Gozzard 31, 183
Gozzard 44, 183, *183*
Gracie, 101
Graemar, 481
Graf Zeppelin, 159
Granada company, 260
Granada series, 468
Grand Alaskan, 119
Grand Banks company, 266
Grand Banks cruisers, 423, *423*
Grand Banks type, 391, *392*
Grand-Louis, 369
Grand Manan 45, 236
Grand Soleil 44, 250
Grandy Boat Yard, 315
Graves Yacht Yard, 240
Gray Boats, 89
Gray Fox, 382
Gray Goose, 119
Grayling, 135
Gray Seal, 347
Grazia, 181
Great Barrier Express, 454
Great Britain II, 189
Great Britain III, 253
Great Britain IV, 415, 253
Great Eastern, 395
Great Exhibition, 433
Great Fun, 115
Great Harbor 26, 90
Great Hope, 426
Great Lakes Engineering Works,
 488
Great South Bay Interclub, 318
Greavette Boat Company, 462, *462*
Greene, Walter, **183–84**
Green Highlander, 370
Greenwich 24, 429
Gregory, Ed, 293
Grenander, Sven, 12
Grenier, Gaston, 82
Gretchen, 190–91
Gretel, 231, 233, 301, 383
Grey Gull II, 99
Greylag, 53
Griffiths, Maurice, **184–85,** *184,* 222
Griggs, C. Milton, 247

Grimalkin, 296
Grobety, Jean, **185**
Groene Draeck, 38
Grondin, 412
Groop, Hans, *185,* **185**
Groupe Finot, 154, 155, 496
Groupe Sceta, 154
Groves, Robert, 448
Gruber, Heinrich A. "Henry," 39,
 186–88, *186, 187*
Gruber Yachts, 186
Grumete, 159
Grumman Aircraft Corporation, 202
Grünhagen, Ferdinand, *188,* **188**
Gudingen, 135
Gudmundsen's boatyard, 245
Gudrum IV, 88
Guédon, Joseph, 188–89, *188,* 398
Guide to the Davis-Hand Collection,
 The (Hasselbalch), 196
Guinevere, 189, 450
Guinness Book of Records, 477
Gulf motoryachts, 351
Gulfstar 40, 233
Gulfsteamer, 183
Gulfweed, 198, *199*
Gulvain, 177, 179
Gumboots, 360
Gumple, Max, 399
Gun, 399
Gurnet Light, 365, 366
Gurney, Alan P., 110, *189* **189**
Guy Couach group, 207
Guyoni, 189
Guyoni II, 189
Guzzi Motors, 78
Guzzino motorcycle, 78
Gypsy (Hunt), 240
Gypsy (Paine), 351, *352,* 353
Gypsy Moth IV, 370
Gyptis, 80

H-23 class, 211
H-28 class, 215
H35, 185
Haakon VII, King of Norway, 15
Haarlem Technical School (HTS),
 320, 465, 466
Hacht, Willi von, *190,* **190**
Hacker, John Ludwig, **190–91,** *191,*
 498
Hacker Boat Company, 191, 285, 293
Haffenreffer family, 211, 221
Hafling, 428
Haida, 389, 483
Haj class, *433,* 434
Hakvoort Shipyard, 38
Half-Ton Cup, 43, 114, 228, 237, 260,
 303, 339
Half-Tonner World Championship,
 13, 56, 249
Halifax Race, 382, 457
Haligonian, 394
Hallali, 92
Hallberg-Rassy 35, 135
Hallberg-Rassy Yachtyard, 135–36,
 161
Hallowe'en, 154
Halmatic company, 200

Halvorsen, Harold, **191–93,** *193*
Halvorsen, Harvey, 193
Halvorsen, Lars, **191–93,** *193*
Halvorsen, Magnus, **191–93,** *193*
Halvorsen, Trygve, **191–93,** *193*
Hamble Bay, 156
Hambo, 135
Hamburg School of Engineering, 132
Hamburg VI, 187
Hamilton-Fletcher, G. M., 425
Hamlin, Cyrus, **193–94,** *194*
Hamm, O. B., 428
Hammerhead catamarans, 485
Hammill, David, 118
Hand, William H., Jr., 82, 106, 118,
 123, **195–96,** *195, 196,* 308, 424,
 473, 492
handicapping rule, 167, 168
Handy Boat, 183, 184
Hanley, C. C. boatyard,
 see C. C. Hanley boatyard
Hanley, Charles C. "CC," **196–98,**
 197, 198
Hanley, Deborah Stevens, 196
Hanley Construction Company,
 197–98
Hanna, John G. "Jack," 116, *138,* 139
Hans Christian, 360
Hans Christian 43, 429
Hanse Yachts, 250
Hansen, Birger, 246
Hansen, Ferd G., 418
Hansen, Knud E.,
 see Knud E. Hansen design office
Hansen, M. S. J., 460
Hansen shipyard, 373
Hansen, Werner, **199**
Hanson, Harold Cornelius, 91, 166,
 199–200, *200*
Happycalopse, 317
Happy Joss, 39
Harald, Crown Prince of Norway, 11
Harbinger (Hanley), *197, 197*
Harbinger (Smith), 421
Harbor Boat Building Company,
 75, 283
Harco 40, 282
Hardy series, 319
Hargrave, Jack Bertrand, **200–201,**
 201
Hargrave Naval Architects, 412
Harlan and Hollingsworth Shipyard,
 235
Harlé, Philippe, 154, **201–2,** *201,*
 206, 282
Harlequin, 122
Harms, Adolf, **202,** 342
Harmsworth Trophy, 212, 234, 279
Harold, Pascal, 417
Harpoon, 64
Harrauer, Franco, *202* **202**
Harrier, 240
Harris, David, 134
Harris, Frank, 173
Harris, Robert B., 84, **202–3,** *203,*
 295
Harris, Wilder Braley "Bill," **203,**
 238, 310
Harris and Ellis Yachts, 134
Harris company, 285

Harrison Butler Association, 70

Harris and Parsons Shipyard, 405

Hartley, Richard, **203–4**, *204*

Hartley 16, 203, *204*

Hartley 18, 203

Hart Nautical Collections, MIT Museum, 48, 68, 118, 196, 221, 272

Harvey, John, **204–5**, *204*, *205*

Harvey and Company, 355

Harvey and Pryer boatyard, 205

Harvey Gamage, 306

Harvey Yachts, 78

Hasselbalch, Kurt, 196

Hatcher, Dan, 34, 357

Hatteras 41, 200

Hatteras 65 Sail Yacht, 233

Hatteras motoryachts, 200

Hatteras Yacht Company, 297

Hatteras Yachts, 412

Hauoli, 174, *175*

Haven 12½, 486

Havsornen (Holm), 230

Havsörnen series (Enderlein), 136

Hawaii-Okinawa Race, 206

Hawkeye, 258

Hawkins, Cathy, 108

Hayashi, Kennosuke "Ken," *206*, **206**, 496

Haylock, E. E., 332

Hayman, Bernard, 87, *87*

Haywire, 138

Haze, 234

H-Boat, 185, *185*

HD-4 hydrofoil, 366

Hearst Regatta, 495

Heart of Gold, 407

Heartsease, 26

Heatherbell, 326

Heath shipyard, 199

Hebrides II, 394

Heckstall-Smith, Brooke, 325

Hedonist, 321

Heidtmann, Heinrich, *206*, **206**

Heifetz, Jascha, 368

Heike, 187

Hein, Richard, *207*, **207**

Heintüüt series, 274

Helaine, 445

Helene (Binney), 46

Helene (Seaborn), 408

Helgoland, 187

Hellcat II, 293

Helleberg, Niels Christian, 8, **208**

Helsal, 3

Helsingor Shipyard, 418, 460

Helsingor Technical School, 314, 418

Hemingway, Ernest, 395

Hempel, Juliane, *208*, **208**, 338

Hendel, Geerd Nilz, 68, **209–10** *209*

Hendrick de Keyserschool, 384

Henrietta, 461

Henri Wauquiez boatyard, 128

Henry, J. J., 483

Henry, Prince of Prussia, 474

Henry, Robert Goldsborough, Jr., *210*, **210**, 349

Henry B. Nevins shipyard, 104, 118, 319, 440, 462

Henry J. Gielow Company, 235, 450

Henry R. Hinckley boatyard, 194, 223–25, 431, 457

Hensen, Werner, *199*, **199**

Herbulot, Hélène, 211

Herbulot, Jean-Jacques, 131, **210–11**, 412

Heritage, 401

Herman, Sydney R., 152

Hermana, 75

hermaphrodite brig, 363, 405

Hermione, 12

Heron, 106

Herreshoff, Algernon Sidney DeWolf, **211–12**, *211*, 213, 217, 221, 368

Herreshoff, Charles Frederick, *212*, **212**

Herreshoff, Clara DeWolf, 217

Herreshoff, Halsey C., 212, **213**, *235*, 236

Herreshoff, John Brown, 211, 217, 221, 456

Herreshoff, Lewis Francis, 6, 48, 67, 97, 189, 211, **213–16**, *213*, *214*, *215*, 217, 256, 257, 324, 347, 351, 368, 375, 407, 409, 450

Herreshoff, Nathanael G., 12, 42, 43, *46*, 61, 63, *63*, 64, 65, 80, 94, *105*, 129, 143, 145, 150, 152–53, 169, *169*, 197, 211, 213, **216–21**, *216*, *217*, *218*, *219*, *220*, 221, 231, 235, 247, 319, 324, 325, 328, 332, 333, 341, 348, 354, 367, 405, 407, 425, 443, 474, 475, 476, *477*, *478*, 491

Herreshoff, Rebecca Crane, 212

Herreshoff Manufacturing Company, 186, 211, 212, 213, 215, 217–18, 221, 288, 306, 332, 348, 368, 409, 436, 450, 492, 493

Herreshoff 12½ (Bullseye), 220

Herreshoff Marine Museum, 212, 213, 221

Herreshoff Motor Company, 212

Hervé boatyard, 131

Hesper, 272

Hess, Lyle, **221–23**, *222*, 223

Hestia, 438

Hetairos (Beeldsnijder), 39

Hetairos (King), 256, 492

"Het Fort," 468, 471

Hewson, Roger, 259

Hickman Sea Sled, 239

Higgins Boat Company, 34

Higginson, Rosamund Tudor, 65, 66, 67

Higher Technical Institute, 209

Highlander (Bannenberg), 30

Highlander (Douglass), 126, 258

Highlander (Schock), *404*

Highland Light, 351

High Performance Sailing (Bethwaite), 45

High-Tension, 395

Hilda, 243, *244*

Hinckley, Henry R., 194, **223–25**, *223*

Hinckley, Henry R. boatyard, see Henry R. Hinckley boatyard

Hinckley 41, 349

Hinckley 43, 233

Hinckley 70, 258

Hinckley Company, 257, 349, 457

Hindenberg, Edmund, **225**

Hinterhoeller, George, 111

Hinterhoeller Ltd., 111

Hinterhoeller Yachts, 134

Hi Roler, 360

Hirondells, 462

Hiscock, Eric, 176

Hiscock, Susan, 176

History of the American Sailing Navy (Chapelle), 81

History of American Sailing Ships (Chapelle), 81

History of Working Watercraft of the Western World, A (Gillmer), 181

Hitachi, 463

H. M. Iversen and Son boatyard, 245

Hobie Alter Cup, 10

Hobie Cats, 10, 84

Hobie 14, 10, *10*, 316

Hobie 16, 10

Hobie Skiff, 10

Hodgdon Brothers, 195, *196*, *309*, *309*

Hodgdon Yachts, 258

Hoek, Andre, 126, *224*, **225**

Hoek, Ineke, 225

Höevell, G. W. W. C. van, 126, **225–27**, *226*

Highland Light, 352

Holgate, Arthur, 122, **227**

Holger Danske, 338, *338*

Holiday, 118

Holgate, A. C. Transport Company, see A. C. Holgate Transport Company

Holland, Ronald John, 30, 39, 80, 114, 115, 142, 182, **227–28**, *227*, *228*, 256, 267, 321, 387

Hollandia, 470

Hollandia (replica), 208

Holland Jachtbouw, 225

Holland Yacht Association, 313

Hollmann, Eva-Maria, **228–29**, 321

Holm, Knut, *11*

Holm, Tore, **229–30**, *229*, 367, 399

Holm, Yngve, 229

Holman, Kim, 189

Holman and Pye, 189, 237

Holmes, George F., *230*, **230**

Holmström, Carl, **230–31** *230*

Holm's Yacht Yard, 229

Honeymoon, 83

Hong Kong and Whampoa Dock Company, 304

Honolulu Race, *see* Transpacific Race

Honor, 478

Hood, C. W. Yachts, see C. W. Hood Yachts

Hood, Frederick Emmart "Ted," 183, **231–33**, *231*, *233*, 240, 292, 452, 491, 492

Hood, Warwick John, *233*, **233**

Hood 23, 233

Hood sail lofts, 231

Hood Yacht Systems, 231

Hope (Rosenblatt), 388

Hope (Woolacott), 494

Hope, Linton Chorley, **233–34** *233*

Horie, Kenichi, 206, *206*

Horizon, 489

Horten Technical School, 1

Hotfoot, 189

Hotsy Totsy, 371

Howard, Henry, 379

Howland, Llewelyn, III, *176*, 238, 240

Howland, Waldo, 108, 203, 238, 240, 375

How to Build a Launch from Plans (Davis), 116

How to Build Small Boats (Schock), 406

How to Build 20 Boats (editors of *Mechanix Illustrated*), 199

How to Build a Wooden Boat (McIntosh), 310

How to Design a Yacht (Davis), 116

Hoyle, Fred, 9

Hoyt, Charles Sherman, 186–87, **234–35** *234*

Hoyt, Garry, 213, **235–36** *235*

Hoyt and Clark, 235

Huaso, 39

Hubbard, Walton, Jr., 55, *55*

Hubert Johnson company, 298

Huckins, Frank Pembroke, 103, *236*, **236**, 443

Huckins Yacht Corporation, 236, 443

Hudson River Marathon, 245

Hudson River sloops, 194

Hull Yacht Club, 197

Humbert Ironworks, 71

Humber Yawl Club (HYC), 230, 448

Hummingbird, 357

Humphreys, Byrne and Pearson, 71

Humphreys, Robert David "Rob," *237*, **237**, 388

Hunloke, Sir Phillip, 425

Hunt, Anthony, 157

Hunt, Charles Raymond, 18, 78, 203, **238–40**, *238*, *239*, 240, 283, 298, 322, 351, 491, 495

Hunter, Douglas, 256

Hunter 23, *240*

Hunter Boats, 455

"Huntform" hull, 238

Huntform powerboats, 239

Huntington, Lawrence D., Jr., **240–41**, *241*

Huntington, L. D. Shipyard, see L. D. Huntington Shipyard

Huntington Yacht Club, 283

Hunt and Williams, 491

Huromic Boat Company, 472

Hurricane, 203

Hurricane class, 382

Huttetu, 3

Hutton, E. F., 93

Hydra, 379

Hyperion (Beeldsnijder), 39

Hyperion (Frers), 162

Hyperion (Huntington), 240

Hyslop, John, *241*, **241**, 394, 421

IAG Nautica, 202

IAG V5, 202

Ibis, 459

Ibold, Peter A., **242–43,** *242*
Ichiban, 267
Ichiro, Yokayama, **496–97**
ICOMIA, 11
Idea, 33
Idea Jackpot, 138
Ideal, 462
Ideal 18, 260
Idler, 358
Idol, 231
If, 1
IFAN (French Institution of Naval
    Architects), 267
IFAW 70, 388
Ila, 399
iLAN Voyager, 245
ILC 30, 394
Ilderim, 229
Ildico III, 33
Ileen, 205
Illingworth, John, 160, 177, *177,* 179,
    243, **243,** 370, 431
Illingworth and Associates, 243
Illingworth and Primrose, 243
Illusion, 84
Illustrated Sydney News, 376
Il Moro, 140
Il Moro de Venezia V, 160, 161
I. L. Snow boatyard, 89
Ilva, 33
Imi Loa, 84, 84
Imp, 227, 228
Imp II, 371
Impensable, 303
Improbable, 228, 320
Impulse 21, 90
Impulse 26, 90
IMS Rule, 78, 140, 206, 268, 324,
    383, 436
IMS World Championship, 51, 78,
    163, 394
IMX 40, 246
IMX 45, 246
Independence (Crowninshield), *105,*
    106, 197
Independence (Hood), 231
Independence (Perini), 359
Independence, S.S., 147
Independence Seaport Museum, 52
Indian, 418
Indian Achiever, 207
Indian Class/Nantucket One-Design,
    8
Indulgence V, 13
Indulgence VI, 13
Indulgence VII, 13
Industry, 148
Infidel, 426
Inga Lill I, 265
Inga Lill XXVI, 265
Inga Lill XXVIII, 265
Inga Lill XXXXIV, 265
Ingalls Shipbuilding Corporation, 294
Inglis, A. and J., 355, 475
Inglis, John, **243–44,** 475
Inglis, John, Jr., 355
Inglis, P. M., 212
Ingrid, 418
Ingvalle, Ludde, 383
Inishfree, 110

Inismara, 307, 309
Inland Lake Yachting Association
    (ILYA), 247
Inman, George and Son,
    see George Inman and Son
Innovation Explorer, 346
Innovision, 250
Inschallah, 48
Institute of Marine Engineers, 110
Integrity, 108
International Folkboat, 449
Interclub Dinghy, 439
Interdominion Silasec Trophy Race,
    497
Interkeel system, 208
Interlake Regatta, 247
International Amateur Boat Building
    Society (IABBS), 242
International America's Cup Class,
    362
International America's Cup Class
    Rule, 206
International Canoe Championship,
    156, *157*
International Catamaran Challenge
    Trophy (Little America's Cup), 109,
    109, 293
International C-Class, 109
International Club 18–Meter class, 90
International 800, 210
International 5–Meter Trophy, 265
International 5.5.-Meter class rule,
    345
International 500, 210
International Fisherman's Cup, 352
International 14, 258
International 14 One-Design
    Championship, 267
International Harmsworth Trophy, *95*
International Marine Publishing
    Company, 139, 173
International Multihull Boat Racing
    Association, 453
International Offshore Racing
    Council (IORC), 306
International One-Design Class,
    1–3, *2*
International One-Design World
    Class Association, 1
International 110, 351
International Rule, 1, *1, 6, 12,* 33,
    41–42, 80, *97, 152, 153,* 199, 208,
    227, 276, 277, 325, 326, 332, 339,
    351, 353, 365, 382, 384, 483
International Sailing Craft
    Association, 353
International Sailing Federation,
    249
International 600, 210
International Superyacht Design
    Award, 39, 51
International Superyacht Society,
    359
International 25, *245*
International Yacht Design
    Competition, 242
International Yacht Restoration
    School, 271, 358
Intrepid (Beavor-Webb), 34
Intrepid (Smith), 420

Intrepid (Stephen), 434
Intrepid (Stephens), 219, 233, *233,*
    436, 438
Introduction to Yachting, An
    (Herreshoff), 216
Ionita, 488
IOR (International Offshore Rule),
    59, 79–80, 84, 114, 132, 135, 139,
    206, 268, 306, 383, 388, 390, 397,
    430, 436, 457, 497
Iorangi, 282
Iota, 39, 40
Irene, 367
Irene II, 404
Irens, Nigel Anthony, **244–45,** *244*
Irex, 383
Iris catamaran ferries, 13
Irish Cruising Club, 53
Irmi, 202
Iroise IV, 302
Irolita, 175
Iroquois (Lawley), 212
Iroquois (MacAlpine-Downie), 293
Iroquois (Smith), 420
Iroquois catamaran, 293
Irrlicht I, 158
Irrlicht II, 158
Isa, 33
ISAF, 45
Isea, 376, 376
Isis, 73
Island Clipper, *117, 117*
Islander, 342
Islander 40, 360
Islander Company, 360
Islander Yachts, 189, 258
Island Princess, 19, 19
Islip class, 169
Istalena, 214, 216
Istria, 33
IT '82, 244
Italia, 93
Italian Cup, 24, 26, 78, 93
Italian Royal Sailing Federation, 93
Italian Sailing Federation, 83
Italian Technical Society for
    Architecture and Naval Equipment
    (STIAN), 202
Italian Yacht Club of Genoa, 347
Italy Cup, 181, 189
ITC company, 225
Itchen Ferry boats, 357
Iverna, 384, 425
Iversen, H. M. and Son boatyard, *see*
    H. M. Inversen and Son boatyard
Iversen, Jacob M. "Jac," *245,* **245,**
    367, 449
Ives, Harwood, 429
IYRU (International Yacht Racing
    Union), 9, 15, 16, 53, 79, 83, 103,
    276, 279, 321, 325, 344, 356
IYRU Cruiser/Racer Rule, 1, 53, 92,
    307
Izanami, 180

J/24, 247–49, *247*
Jabberwock (Clayton), 88
Jabberwock (Crowther), 107
Jackson, Ralph, 381

Jacob, Rob, 228
Jacob, Robert boatyard, *136,* 175,
    389, 443
Jacobs, Louis, 484
Jacoby, Emile, 245
Jacoby, Fred "Pop," Sr., **245**
Jacoby, Fred, Jr., 245
Jacoby Flyaway Hydroplane, 245
Jacques Borel, 9
Jada, 252, 253
Jade, 237
James, John Morton, 326
James A. Silver boatyard, 27, 305
James Betts Enterprises, 142
James N. Miller and Sons, 29
Jameson, John, 384
Janessa, 332
Janichon, Gérard, 249
Janie, 125
Janneau, 491
Japan Lifeboat Company, 264
Japan Sailing Federation (JSAF), 206,
    345, 401, 496
Japansky, 411
Japan to Guam Race, 452
Japan Yachting Association (JYA),
    496
Jardine-Brown, Joan, 70
Jarvis Newman company, *284,* 285
Jason 35, 54
Java Head, 319
Javelin (Fox), 157
Javelin (Milne), 314
Javelin (Spencer), 426
J/Boats Incorporated, 249
J-Class boats, 46, *68,* 249, *249*
J-Class (Chevalier and Taglang), 82
JC company, 285
Jean Gab, 302
Jeanneau Company, 13, 228, 249,
    250, 303, 360, 383, 463
Jeantot, Philippe, 383
Jeantot-Marine, 282
Jefferson Beach, 38
Jemima F III, 411
Jenetta, 326, 326
Jennifer, 170
Jensen, Christian, 15, **245–46**
Jensen, Jack, 268
Jensen Marine, 407
Jeppesen, Lars, 246
Jeppesen, Niels, *246,* **246**
Jericho, 60
Jersey Sea Skiff, 300
Jessica (Holgate), 227
Jessica (Munford), 321
Jessie, 143
Jessie Logan, 282
Jet Services, 346
Jet Services V, 346
Jetstar, 314
J. G. shipyard, 425
Ji Fung, 57
Jill, 434
Jim-Ken, 298
Joanne of Garth, 29
Jocasta, 87
JOD 24, 13
JOD 35, 13
Joel, Billy, 498

JOG (Junior Offshore Group), 179, 243, 291
Johan, 306
John F. Leavitt, 108
John G. Alden Company, 208, 301, 309, 314, 417, 489, 492, 493
John Gilpin, 216
John M. Williams Company, 431
John N. Robins shipyard, 174
Johns Bay Boat Company, 285
Johnson, Bob, 189
Johnson, Charles, 395
Johnson, C. Lowndes, 489
Johnson, Eads, 137
Johnson, Joel, 301
Johnson, John O., **246–47** *246*
Johnson, Seward, 113, 131
Johnson Boat Works, 246, 247
Johnston, Fraser, *31*
Johnston, Ian, 108
Johnstone, Bob, 249
Johnstone, Rodney S., **247–49,** *247, 249,* 474
John Twigg and Sons, *273*
Johor and Brunei, Royal Household, 320
Jolian, 331
Jolie Brise, 353, 353
Joliette, 87
Jollenkreuzer class, 338
Jolly Boat (Fox), 157
jolly boats, 126–27
jolly cruisers, 126–27
Jon 30, 341
Jon 33, 341
Jones, Greg, 98
Jones, J. Francis, 189
Jonesport-Beals Island lobsterboat, 284
Jonesporter, 163
Jongert shipyard, 80, 362, 471
Jongleur class, 445
Jonmeri 40, 341
Jonmeri 48, 341
Jonquil, 316, 316
Jorie, 117, 405
Joseph Stuart, 363
Joseph W. Russell, 108
Joshua, 261
Joubert, Michel, 13, **249–50**
Jouët shipyard, 92
Jourdain, Roland, 282
Joyce, Michael F., 201
Joyette, 317, 423
Juana, 159
Juan Carlos I, King of Spain, 77, *242,* 250
Jubilee, 319
Jubilee Cup, 12
Jubilee III, 295
Jubilee Sailing Trust, 80, 319
Judel, Friedrich "Fietje," **250–51**
Judel/Vrolijk and Company, **250–51** *250*
Judith, 57
Judy, 483
Jules Verne, 465, 465
Jules Verne Trophy, 244, *244*
Julia, 375, 420
Julinar, 475

Julius Petersen boatyard, 119, *186*
Jullanar, 204
Jumping Jack Flash, 115
Junior Offshore Group (JOG), 179, 243, 291, 496
Juniper, 485
Juno, 41
Jupiter, 263, 263
Justine III, 80
Jutson, Scott, *251,* **251**

K16, 264
K20, 264
K28, 264
K-38, 255
K-40, 255
K-41, 256
K-43, 255
K-50, 255
Kady, Arthur, 264
Kady-Krogen 36 Manatee, 264
Kady-Krogen 42, 264
Kahn, Otto A., 290
Kai, Manu, 98
Kaiko, Phil, 114
Kaimiloa, 484
Kaiser Aluminum, 89
Kaiser's Cup Races, 317, 319, 344, 423
Kaiser's Prize, 158
Kakki M, 166
Kalamoun, 180
Kampen cog, 126
Kanawha II, 409, 411
Kanot pilothouse motoryachts, 351
Karak, 261
Karangi, 57
Karate, 131
Karenita, 8
Kariad, 478
Kasemier, Eelco, 261
Katamarino, 200, 201
Katedna, 172
Kathleen (Davis), 116
Kathleen (Gardner), 168
Katie Ford, 125, 125
Kato Boat Company, 472
Katoura, 67, 218
Katrina (Fellows), 145
Katrina (Kyntzell), 265
Kattegat Cup, 15, 16, 42, 229, 277
Katuna, 4
Kaufman, Ted, 276
KDY-Juniorboat, 399
Kearsarge, U.S.S., 71
Kelly, I. Judson, 145, **252–53** *252*
Kelly, Jack, 360
Kelpie, 398
Kelsall, Derek, **253,** 366, 415
Kelso, 402
Kelt 7.50, 346
Kelt 8.00, 346
Kemp, Dixon, 62, 73, 88, 204, 234, **253–54,** *253,* 357, 375, 392, 398, 416
Kemphaan, 262
Kenwood Cup, 142, 497
Ker Cadelac, 267
Ker Kadelac, 282

Kerstin, 277
Kestrel (Fife), 168
Kestrel (Gerr), *173*
Kettenburg, George, Jr., **254–56,** *254, 255,* 274, 360
Kettenburg Boat Works, 255, *255*
KFK (Kriegsfischkutter), 187
Khashoggi, Adnan, 30, 401
Kialoa IV, 228
Kia Ora (II), 305
Kiariki, 57
Kidman's Boat Builders, 31
Kiele VI, 85
Kiel Week, 312, 344
Kiel Yacht Club, 169, 397, 494
Kiley, John, 338
Killing, Steven, *256,* **256**
Kilt, 73
Kim, 225
King Alfonso Cup, 24
King, Bruce P., 132, 223, **256–58,** *256, 257,* 492
King, C. F., 86
Kingfisher, 131
Kingfisher class, 496
King, John, 277
King Olav V Cup, 362
King's Cup, 175
Kings of Burnham, 112
Kingston College of Art/Polytechnic, 491
Kini, 306
Kinney, Francis Sherwood, **258,** *258,* 381
Kirawan, 381, 382
Kirawan II, 382
Kirby, Bruce, 90, 256, **258–60,** *259*
Kirby, David, 110
Kirby, Margo, 259
Kirby Mark II, 258
Kirby Mark III, 258
Kirby Mark IV, 258
Kirsten, Friedrich, 190
Kiskaddon, George, 228
Kismet (Clayton), 88
Kismet (Hope), 234
Kito Rani, 9
Kitten, 204
Kittiwake, 189
Kitty, 497
Kitty Hawk II, 190
Kitty Restricted Catamaran Class, 497
Kiwi Magic, 140, 362
Kiyi, 40, 91, *91*
Kjaerulff, Jan, **260–61** *260*
Klippan's shipyard, 265
Knocker, Jean, *261,* **261**
Knud E. Hansen design office, 260
Koch, William, 452
Kogakuin University, 264
Kokomo, 128
Kolutoo, 65
Komutu, 282
Konigen, 373
Konkret, 231
Kontrapunkt, 208
*Kookaburra 12-Meters, 324
Kookaburra III, 329
Kookaburra Syndicate, 324

Koopmans, Dirk, Sr., 126, 226, 227, **261–62** *261*
Koopmans, Dirk, Jr., **261–62**
Koopmans, Elly, 261–62
Kormoran, 48
Korsar, 274
Kortjakje, 226
Kraaier, Jaap, *262,* **262**
Kraken 25, 107
Kraken 40, 107
Kremer, Klaas, 431
KR handicap system, 187
Kristiania Technical School, 245
Kriter, 23, 465
Kriter V, 304
Kriter VI, 121
Kroes, Gait, 126, **262–64,** *263,* 454, 455
Kroes, Gerrit, 262, 455
Kroes, Siem, 262–64
Krogen, James, **264**
Krogen, Kurt, 264
Krogen 38 Cutter, 264
Krogen 54 motorsailer, 264
Kröger Shipyard, 313
Kromholz, Louis L., **264**
Kropp Duster, 495
KR Rating, 312
Krupp, von Bohlen und Halbach, Alfred, 374
Krupp, von Bohlen und Halbach, Dr. Gustav, 344
Krupps-Germania Shipyard, *30,* 377
KSSS (Royal Swedish Yacht Club), 12, 137, 277
K'Thanga, 273, *274*
Kullan, 341
Kumalae, Alfred G., 84
Kumazawa, Tokihiro, **264**
Kumazawa Boat Research Laboratory, 264
K'ung Fu-Tse, 89
Kungsör Boatyard, 229, 399
Kungsviken Boatyard, 135
Kunhardt, Charles P., 85–86, **264–65**
Kunhardt, C. P., 441
Kvadratmer, 406
Kyle, S. Clyde, 252
Kyntzell, Gustav Julius "Gösta," 265, **265,** 277

L-24, 288
L26 One-Design, 270
L-27, 288
L34 One-Design, 270
L 36 class, 267
La Baroness, 147
La Baule-Dakar Race, 282
LAC1, 119
LAC2, 119
Lacombe, Jean, 211
La Concorde, 158
Lacour shipyard, 398
Lacustre Class, 91, *92*
Ladd, Robb, 412
Lady A., 412
Lady Anne, 153
Lady Aviva, 492
Ladybird, 494, 494

Lady Ellen, 31
Lady Ghislaine, 30
Lady Helmsman, 293
Lady Hopetoun, 376
Lady Jo, 481
Lady Mary, 138
Lady Maryland, 181
Lady Nan, 357
Lady Rhody, 348
Lady's, 207
Ladyship, 320
Lady Van, 170
Laerning, 277
La Forza del Destino, 320
Lagerwall, J., *11*
La Giraglia Race, 400, 412
La Gitana, 341
Lagoon 55, 463
Lagoon Navigation Firm, 83
Lagos, Fernando, **266**
Lagos 7.5, 266
Laguna cruiser series, 125
Laidier, M. Le, 82
L'Aiglon, 51
Laird Brothers, 71
Lak, 302
Lake Ontario International, *110*, 111
Lake Union Dreamboat, 91, 172
Lake Union Dry Dock Company,
  91, 172
Lake Yacht Racing Association, 128
La Liberté, 399
Lallow's shipyard, 331
Lambda Mar, 320
Lambie and Mabry, 301
Lamlash, 147–48
Lamu, 250
Lanai, 94, 434
Landfall, 214
Landing School, The, 439
Landing School of Boatbuilding and
  Design, 194, 251
Lands End, 125
Landsort, 132
Lane, Carl, **266–67** *266*
Lane, Marie, 267
Lane, Robert, **266–67** *266*,
Langan Design, 492
Langevin, Sylvestre, 267, **267**
Lani Kai, 84, *84*
Lanzerota, 26
La Pantera, 360
La Perrière boatyard, 131
Lapwing, 62, 253
Lapworth, Charles William "Bill,"
  117–18, 189, **267–69**, *268, 269,*
  274, 360, 407, 409
Lapworth, Peggy, 269
L'Aquasition, 180
Lara, 86, 87
Larchmont-Interclub class, 169
Larchmont O-Boat class, 169
Larchmont Yacht Club, 241, 435
Lariano Royal Racing Club, 93, 164
Lark, 116
Lark III, 425
La Rochelle competition, 56
La Rochelle to New Orleans Race,
  346
Laser, 259, *259*

L.A. Shipbuilding and Dry Dock, 74
Latifa, 187
Latona, 150
Lauer-Leonardi, Boris, 216, 443
Laurana, 303
Laurent Giles and Partners, 176, 319,
  431
Lauriana, 31
Laurin, Arvid, *269*, **269**
La Volpe, 14
Lavranos, Angelo, **269–70**, *270*
Law, Robert, *286*
Lawhill, 227
Lawley, Frederic D., **270–72**, *271*
Lawley Boat Owners Association, 271
Lawley, George, 270, 271, *450*
Lawley, George F., Jr., **270–72**, *271*
Lawley, George and Son,
  see George Lawley and Son
Lawlor, Dennison J., **272**
Lawrence, T. E., 370
Laws, Gilbert U., 112
Lawson, Thomas, 34
Lawson, Thomas W., 34, 106, 197
Lazy Days Houseboat Company, 200
Lazy Jack, 121
Lazyjack 32, 54
LCM (landing craft, medium), 210
L. D. Huntington Shipyard, 116
Lea, 235
Leading Wind, 47
Lear Cat, 98–99, 366
Leather, John, 18
Leavitt, John, 310
Le Baud, Gilles, 346
Lebrun, Jacques, 92
Le Chameau, 366
Le Clerq and Garden, 166
Leda, 93
Le Défi Areva, 13, 346
Lee, Brinton and Wayland, 274, 481
Lee, Cheoy, 38, 147
Lee, Harold, **272–74**, *273*, 481
Lee, William Shields, Jr., **274**
Lee and Brinton, 272, 480
Leek, John, 298
Legacy, 359
Legacy 34, 134
Legacy 40, 134
Legacy 40 Express, 134
Legend, 74, *74*
Lehfeld, Ernst, **274**
Lehg II, 77
Leilani, 271
Lejaby, 282
Lelanta II, 8
Le Lézard, 73, *73*
Lello, Bryan, **274–75**
Lello 34 class, 275
Lemanic One-Design class, 91
Le Marchand, Abel, **275**, *275*
Lemster Aak, 468
Lemster Aak type, *182, 182*, 225
Lena, 440
Length-and-Sail-Area Rule, 12,
  83, 88, *88*, 220, 253, 279, 384,
  416, 475
Leonard W, 163
Leopard, 354
Leslie, R. C., 357

Lester E. Jones, 200
Lestra Sport, 346
L'Euridice, 467
Levi, Renato "Sonny," 202, 401
Levriero, 84
Lewella, 200
Lexcen, Ben, 127, *127*, **275–77**, *276*
Lexia, 415
Le Yacht, Journal de la Marine,
  73, 189
Le Yacht magazine, 398, 411
L. Francis Herreshoff Reader, The
  (Herreshoff), 216
l'Hermione, 384
L'Hydroptère, 463
Lia III, 24
Libbey, Oscar E., 365
Libby, Ernest, Jr., **277**
Libelle, 187
Liberty (Barnett), 33
Liberty (Benjamin), 41
Liberty (King), 257
Liberty (Paine), 351
Liberty (Perini), 359
Liberty (Valentijn), 213, 461
Liberty ships, 431, 498
Licor 43, 88
Lidstone, William I., 445
Liebe, 397, *397*
Lightning Class, 439
Lightning, 218
Lightwave cruisers, 407
Lilian, 367
Lilith, 87
Liljegren, Carl O., 12, **277**
Lillian, 253
Lill Inga, 265
Lilljojo, 418
Lily, 384
Limestone series, 134
Limitless, 30
Limmershin, 329
Linda, 407
Lindagull, 418
Linear Raters, 325
Linear Rating Rule, 88, 359, 477,
  478
Linge, Jan Herman, **277–79**, *279*
Linsingva, 418
Lion's Whelp, 309
Lipton, Sir Thomas, 152, 153, 169,
  171, 333, 336, 348, 401, 478
Lipton Cup, 270
Liris, 168
Lisee, Joseph Napoleon "Nap," *279*,
  423
Listers engine company, 164
Little America's Cup, 316
Little Dipper, 131
Little Haligonian, 394
Little Harbor Boatyard, 231
Little Harbor series, 231–33
Little Haste, 65
Little Jim, 282
Little Nell, 195
Little Ships and Shoal Waters
  (Griffiths), 184
Live Yankee, 213, 216
Livingston, Charles, *279*, **279**
Livonia, 375

Liz of Hanko, 10
Lizzie Mack, 493
Ljungström, Fredrik, **279–80**, *280*
Llanoria, 436
Llewellyn, *174, 175*
Lloyd's Building and Classification
  Rules, 325
Lloyd's of London, 140, 142, 167
Lloyd's Register, 23
Lloyd's Register of American Yachts,
  441
Lloyd's Register of Shipping, 204
Lloyd's Register of Yachts, 23, 189,
  205, 234, 253, 254
Lockhart, Alfred Ltd.,
  see Alfred Lockhart Ltd.
Lodestar, 366
Lodi, Remo, 386
Löfmark, Gustav, 231
Logan, Arch, 114, 280, 282
Logan, Jack, 282
Logan, John, 280, 282
Logan, Robert, 26, 27, **280–82**, *281*
Logan, Robert, Jr., 280, 282
Logan, William, 280
Logan Brothers, 280, 282, 376
Lohi-Joemarin, 185
Lolly, 397
Lollypop, 357
Lombard, Marc, *282*, **282**
Lombardo, Guy, 34
l'Onda, 217
London Boat Show, 30, 397
London College of Furniture, 321
London Conference (1906), 15
Lone Gull, 164
Lone Star, 329, 353
Long, Dair N., 145, **282–83**, *283*
Longari, Giancarlo, 400
Long Beach Naval Yard, 74
Long Beach Yacht Club, 76
Long Distance Night Race (Fleet A),
  133
Loomis, Alfred, 159
Loon, 294
Loraine, 449
Lord, Frederick Kissan, **283**
Lord, Lindsay A., 239, **283–84** *283*
Lord Nelson, 319
Loredan, Count, 83
Lorraine, 227
Lory and Cornwallis, 414
Los-Angeles-Honolulu Transpac
  Race, *see* Transpacific Race
Los Baat design, 199, 200
Los Dios, 347
Lothian, 331
lottery boats, *3*, 11–12, 277, 341, 417,
  449
Lotus, 274
Louise, 357
Louisiane, 250
Louis Vuitton Challenge Cup, 56,
  115, 140, 161, 320, 362
Lowe, Peter, 277
Lowell, Carroll, **284–85** *284*
Lowell, Riley, 284
Lowell, Royal, **284–85** *284*
Lowell, Wilhelmina, 163
Lowery, Raymond, 349

L.S. Lauchland Engineering Award, 256
Lubeckertor College, 342
"LUCAN" Bottom Tension Oil Spill Control Boom, 285
Lucander, Nils Karl Johan, *285*, **285**
Luce Boat Yard, 73, 83
Lucerne, 174
Lucifer, 80
Lucile, 423
Luciolle, 275, *275*
Luciolle II, 275
Lucky Star, 404
Lucy, 130
Luders, Alfred Edward, Sr., 82, 94, 145, **285–88**, *286*, 428
Luders, Alfred Edward "Bill," Jr., 54, 113, **285–88**, *286*
Luders 16, *286*, 288
Luders 33, 288
Luders Epoxy Bronze, 288
Luders Marine Construction Company, 20, 54, 235, 285, 288, 472
Luisamar, 38
Luna, 344
Luna Rossa, 161, *162*, 362
Lunenburg Yacht Club, 443
Lunstroo, Henk, **288–89**, *289*
Lunstroo Custom Design, 465
Lürssen, Friedrich, 289, *290*
Lürssen, Otto, **289–90**, *290*
Lürssen Werft shipyard, 30, 180, 289
Lust, 397
Lustkutter und dicke Damper, Seemannsdeutch und Seemannslatein (Dinklage), 122
Lutine, 177
Lutra Design Group, 122
Lux, 42
Luxus Cruise Lines, 297
Lydia, 33
Lyman, Bernard E., 290
Lyman, William E., **290–91**, *291*
Lyman Boat Works, 290, 291
Lyman-Morse Boatbuilders, 90, 412
Lynch, Pat, 228
Lyons, David, *291*, **291**
Lysistrata Cup, 41, *409*, 411

Maage class, 42
Maas, Frans, 79, 126, **292–93** *292*
Maassungen (Young Gull) Class, 399
MacAlpine-Downie, James Roderick "Rod," *253*, *293*, **293**, 370, 453
MacAlpine-Downie/Gibbs, 293
Macaroni, 66
MacArthur, Ellen, 237
Maccoboy III, 167
MacGregor, Charles G., 8, 310, 352
MacGregor, John, 230
Machigonne, 410
MacKenzie, Bernard, 311
MacKerer, Arnold William, **293–94**, *294*
MacLane, Duncan, 403
MacLear, Frank Reynolds, 202, **294–95**, *295*
MacLear and Harris, 173, 202–3, 295

MacNaughton, Nannette, 296
MacNaughton, Thomas Andrew, **295–96**, *296*
Madcap, 4200
Madden, J. H., 273
Madden and Lewis, 55
Maddie Joe, 267
Madeira do Mar (Wood of the Sea) (Echenique), 132
Madeleine, 38
Madeline O, 145
Madge, 475
Maebelle, 271
Maène, 181
Maestro cruiser/racer, *444*, **444**
Magda, 154
Magda IX, 15
Maggie, 17
Maggie Sullivan, 46
Magic, 274, 461
Magic Bus, 390
Magician, 497
Magic of the Swatchways (Griffiths), 184
Magic Pudding, 360
Magnum, 18
Magpie, 412
Mahdee, 100
Maho, 428
Maïa, *188*, 189
Maica, 243, 370
Maida, 434
Maida II, *434*, **434**
Maid Marion, 336
Maid of Arden, 70
Maid of Endor, *19*, 20
Maid of Malham, 86, 177, 179, 243
Maierform, 313
Maine, U.S.S., 64
Maine Coast Fisherman magazine, 200
Maine et l'Ancien boatyard, 267
Maine Island 46, 498
Maine Maritime Museum, 175
Maitenes II, *331*, 401
Maître-Pierre, 339
Major Casey, 203
Malabar I, 6
Malabar II, 6
Malabar IV, *5*, 6
Malabar IX, 436
Malabar Junior, 8, *8*, 99
Malabar schooners, 417
Malabar series, 5–6, 8, 436
Malabar VII, *5*, 6
Malabar X, *5*, 6
Malabar XI, 6
Malabar XII, 6
Malabar XIII, 6, 8
Malahne, 336
Malavard, Lucien, 302
Malay (Hunt), 240
Malay (Roué), 394
Malgré Tout, 398
Malibu, 171
Malinowski, Michael, 304
Mällar 22 class, 137
Mallurca, 182
Maltese Cross, 428
Mammoth, 139

Manana II, 253
Manchester 17½, *106*
Manchester Yacht Club, 48
Mandoo II, 8
Manhasset Bay One-Design, 435
Manhasset Bay Yacht Club, 328, 411
Manhattan Yacht Club, 241
Mania, 57
Manitou, 111
Manola, 27
Manual of Yacht and Boat Sailing, The (Kemp), 234, 254, 398
Manuela, 78
Manuiwa, 404, *404*
Manu Kai, 84, 370
Manureva, 9
Manxman, 67
Manzanita, 228
Maple Leaf, 27
Maple Leaf class, 27
Mapuna, 75
Maquinna, 158
Maramel, 195
Marauder, 314
Marblehead 36, 353
Marblehead Boat Company, 309
Marblehead-Halifax Race, *111*
Marco Polo (Riva), 386
Marco Polo (Herreshoff), 215
Marco Polo (Wollacott), 494
Mardo, 472, 473
Marek, Bruce, 329
Marett, P. R., 420
Margaret, 473
Margarita, 476
Margaux Rose, 179, *180*
Margherita, 153, 332
Maria-Augusta, 290
Maria Delores, 175
Mariam, 423
Mari Cha III, 55–56, *56*, 322
Mari Cha IV, 55, 56
Mariebel, 208
Marie Christine II, 412
Marie Christine III, 412
Marietta, 174
Marilen, 445, *447*
Marine, 120
Marine Construction and Dry Dock Company, 136, 272
Marine Design System, 497
Marine High School, 74
Marine Regatta Association (Kiel), 397
Mariner (Burgess), 67
Mariner (Lyman), 291
Marine Research Society, 116
Mariners' Museum, 116, 191
Marine Trader company, 266
Mari-Pepa, 189
Mariquita, 333
Maris, 356
Marisa, 359
Maritime and Coastguard Agency (MCA), 401
Maritime Commission, 489
Maritime Promotion Service (MPS), 180
Marjorie, 432
Mark Ellis Designs, 134
Marlow Explorer, 498

Marmac, 223
Marola, 266
Marples, John, 58
Marquita, *480*, 481
Mars, 412
Marshall, Breckenridge, **296–97**, *297*
Marshall, Evan Keith, *297*, **297**
Marshall, Roger, **297–98** *297*
Marshall 22, 296
Marshall Marine Corporation, 296, 297
Marstrand Race Week, 362
Martin, Arthur E., 240, *298*, **298**
Martin, David P., **298–300** *298*
Martin, George Martin, 353
Martin, John, 270
Martin, Josef, 208
Mary G Powers, 46
Mary Jeanne II, 379
Maryland Steel Company, 75, 136
Mary Loring, 473
Marymack, 131
Marymount, 274
Mary Taylor, 433
MAS (Anti-Submersible Motorboat), 24
Masconomo, 99
Mascot, 112
Masen, 341
Mason, Alvin "Al," 8, 202, **300–301**, *300*, *301*, 381
Mason, Anita, 301
Mason 31, 301
Massachusetts Bay Hustler Class, 319
Massachusetts Bay Knockabout class, 46
Massachusetts Bay Yacht Racing Association (MYRA), 197
Massachusetts Institute of Technology (MIT), 33, 48, 68, 74, 99, 103, 112, 118, 130, 170, 196, 210, 213, 217, 221, 271, 272, 283, 349, 353, 363, 379, 401, 405, 435, 473, 487, 493
Massilia shipyard, 302
Matador², 90
Matangi, 282
Matara, 282
Matenrow, 497
Matheu, José, 182
Mathews Boat Company, 483
Mathis Yacht Building Company, 458, 459
Matrero, 161
Mattapoisett 15-foot class, 65
Matthew, 319
Matthews, Scott J., **301–2**, *302*
Matthews 38, 301
Matthews Company, 293, 301–2
Matthews Owners Association, 302
Matthiesen and Paulsen, 48
Maud, 245
Mauric, André, **302–4**, *303*, 369, 411, 465
Mauric, Auguste, 302
Mauric, Edmond, 302
Mauritius to Durban Race, 270
Maxim, Hudson, 33
Maximus Austriaticus, 158
Maxi World Cup, 88, 90, 161
May, 475

Maybach Zeppelin motors, 290
May Be, 137
May Be II, 229
May Be III, 229
May Be IV, 229
May Be VI, 229
May Be VIII, 229
May Be IX, 229
Maycraft company, 298
Mayflower (Burgess), 34, *35,* 46, 61, *61, 63, 67, 90*
Mayflower (Watson), 474
Mayflower 48, 429
M-Class (Metric-Class), 114, 131
McBryde, William Gray, *304,* **304**
McCallum, John A., 76, **304–5** *304*
McCaw, Craig, 329
McCurdy, Ian, 306, 383
McCurdy, James Arrison, **305–6,** *305,* 381, 383
McCurdy and Rhodes, 223, 306, 383
McDell Marine, 142
McGraw-Hill, 173
McGruer, Ewing, Sr., 306, 325
McGruer, Ewing, Jr., **306,** *307,* 309
McGruer, George, **306**
McGruer, James, *307,* **306,** 325
McGruer, Willie, 306
McInnis, Alan, 310
McInnis, Walter J., 82, **308–10,** *308, 309*
McIntosh, David C. "Bud," 99, *310,* **310**
McLain, George Melville "Mel," **310–11**
McLaughlin, Damian, *211*
McManus, Thomas F., 105, 428
McNary, William, 8, 349
Meacham and Babcock Shipyard, 315
Meadow Lark, 215
Mebi, 181
Meccarillos, 267
Mechanix Illustrated, 34
Medea, 327
Medicine Man, 12
Megargel and Gruber, 186
Megayacht Award, 39
Mehalla II, 433
Meier, Philippe, 403
Meit, 12
Melbourne Intercolonial Centennial Regatta, 376
Melbourne-Osaka Doublehanded Yacht Race, 3, *344, 345,* 474
Melee, 269
Melisenda, 93
Mellgren, Gunnar, 277, *312,* **312**
Mellon, Richard K., 125
Melody, 303
Melora III, 327
Melvin, Pete, 316, 317
Memory, 479
Memsahib, 325
Menai, 417
Mendlowitz, Benjamin, 487
Mercedes, 66
Mercedes III, 276
Mercedes USA, 66
Mercury, 99–100

Merenneito I, 483
Merenneito II, 483
Merganser, 163, 284
Merlin (Lee), 274
Merlin (Nelson), 329
Merlin Rocket, 455
Mermaid III, 206, *206*
Merrill Stevens Engineering Company, 174
Merrimac, 131
Merriman Brothers, 443
Merry Conceit, 53
Merrydown, 269
Merrymaid, 333
Messing About in Boats magazine, 50
Meta (Benjamin), 41
Meta (Byrne), 71
metacentric theory, 23, 47, 69–70, *70,* 466
Meteor (Bailey yard), 27
Météor (Chevreux), 83
Meteor (Fish), 155
Meteor I (Watson), 344, 475, 476
Meteor II (Watson), 344, 478
Meteor III (Smith), 344, 419, 421, *421*
Meteor IV (Oertz), 153, 333
Meteor V (Oertz), *344*
Methisto, 206
Metolius, 39
Me Too, 488
Meyba-Fibanc, 424
Meyer, Elizabeth, 122
Meyers, Eddie, 321
Meyney and Son shipyard, 398
MFV (Motor Fishing Vessel), 177
MG 100 IOR One-Tonner, 387
Miami-Nassau Race, 18, 90, 269, 458
Micco, 324
Michael, Grand Duke of Russia, 474
Michigan, University of, 40, 138, 145, 282, 294, 388, 427
Michl V, 190
Micro-Cup regatta, 154
Middle Sea Race, 161
Midget Ocean Racing Club (MORC), 12, 179, 274, 329, 407, 412, 425
Midjet, 23
Midnight Lace, 147, *147*
Midnight Special, 237
Midnight Sun, 297
Midshipman 52, 493
Miglitsch, Anton, **312–13** *312*
Mignon, 73, *73*
Mignonne, 189
Mikado, 165
Miki-class tug, 91
Mikimiki, 91
Milan Nautical Exposition, 83–84
Milicete, 136
Milky Way, 100
Millennium Cup, 162
Millennium series motoryachts, 320
Miller, Gordon, *57*
Miller, James N. and Sons, *see* James N. Miller and Son
Miller, Richards T., 210
Miller, Robert Clyde *see* Lexcen, Ben
Miller, Walter, 200
Miller and Whitworth, 127, 128

Mill Pond Boat Yard, 130
Mills, Clark W., *313,* **313**
Millwall Ironworks, 88
Milne, Peter, **314,** *314*
Milton Point Shipyard, 428
Minerva (Andersson), 11
Minerva (Fellows), 145
Minerva (Fife), 64, 151–52, 168
Minett-Shields Boat Company, 462
Mini America's Cup Class, 131
Minime, 357
Mini-Ton class, 13, 338
Mini-Ton Cup, 43, 424
Mini Transat 6.5, 388
Mini-Transatlantic Race, 201, 495
Minneford shipyard, 119, 179, 180, 436, 440, 450
Minnezitka, 247
Minotaur, 239
Minot's Lights, 338
Mirabella IV, 228, *228*
Mirabella V, 228
Mirage (Perry), 360
Mirage (Frers), 160
Miramar II, 31
Miranda, 204, 367
Miranda II, 93
Miranda IV, 179
Mirror 14, 314
Mischief (Fellows), 145
Mischief (Kirby), 110
Mischief (Smith), 419, 420, 421
Mischievous, 341
Misil, 136
Miss America, 423
Miss America series, 279
Missawit, 274
Miss Canada III, 462
Miss Chevy II, 395
Miss Chevy IV, 395
Miss Columbia, 104
Miss Detroit, 422
Miss Detroit II, 423
Miss Dongame, 474
Miss Minneapolis, 423
Miss Syndicate, 104
Mistral (Enderlein), 136
Mistral (Townson), 457
Mistral class (Tonet), 456
Mistress, 234, *235*
Mistress 32, 135
Misty, 138, *139*
Mitchell, Carleton, 125, 381, 436
Mitena, 216
Miura 31, 43
Miura 32 Mk2, 43
MJM Yachts, 498, *498*
Moa, 400
Moana, 282
MoBay Race, 189
Mobjack, 8
Moby Dick, 274
MOCAT class, 76
Moccasin, 49
Mocking Bird, 489
Model Club (Cercle de Modèles), 91
Modern Boat Building (Monk), 315
Modern Boating magazine, 110
Modern Mechanics and Inventions Magazine, 138

Modern Sailing Catamarans (Harris), 202
Modern Yacht, The (Burgess), 65
Modesti, 28
Modwen, 279
Moecca, 30
Mohawk (Clayton), 88
Mohawk (van Deusen), *461, 462*
Mohican, 475
Moiena, 29
Moije Bris, 187
Moira, 243
Moitessier, Bernard, 261
Molich, Paul, 208
Molich, Poul, **314–15** *314*
Molich One-Design, 315
Molita, 279
Mollihawk II, 234
Monarch Crescent Company, 365
Mongoose, 104
Monimeau Brothers, 398
Monk, Dan, 315
Monk, George Edwin "Ed," 166, 315, *315,* **315**
Monk, Robert Edwin "Ed," 264, **315–16**
Monmouth, 411
monohedron hull, 283
Monomoy 21, 498
Mon Reve, 200
Monroe, Wirth, 324
Monsoon, 47
Monsun 31, 136
Montauk, 134, *134,* 135
Monterey Bay race series, 274
Montessinos, Dominique, 282
Moody, 179
Moody, A. H. and Son, *see* A. H. Moody and Son
Moody 33, 370, *370*
Moonbeam, 152, *153*
Moonen shipyard, 320, 465
Moonlight (Griffiths), *184*
Moonlight (Townson), 457
Moonlight III, 297
Moonraker (Gilgenast), 179, *180*
Moonraker (Mulder), 320
Moonshine, 360
Moose, 377
Moppie (Hunt), 239
Moppie (Napier), *328*
Morales, Pedro, 88
Morch, Ian, 111
MORC International Championships, *see* Midget Ocean Racing Club
Morgan, Bill, 191
Morgan, Charlie, 228, 401
Morgan, Dodge, 233, *233*
Morgan, E. D., 63
Morgan, Jasper, 67
Morgan, John Pierpont, Jr., 375
Morgan, J. P., 34
Morgan 36, 329
Morgan 38, 54
Morgan 45, 329
Morgan Cup, 154
Morgan Giles, Francis Charles, *316,* **316**
Morgan Giles and May, 315

Morishige, Hisaya, 474
Morning Glory, 359
Morrelli, Gino, **316–17** *316*
Morris Yachts, 351
Morse, Charles A., 89, 203, 310
Morse, Jonah, 310
Morse, Wilbur, 310
Mortain, Alain, 201
Morton, Rob, 35, 357
Morwak, 76
Morwark, 302
Mosbacher, Robert "Bus," 66
Moses H. Grinnell, 433
Mosquito (Russell), 394
Mosquito (Waterman), 417
Mother Goose, 119
Moth restricted class, 139
Motor Boating & Sailing "Ideal"
    series, 20, 319
Motor Boating magazine, 20, 23, 136,
    136, 173, 236, 294, 317, 319, 379,
    431, 442
Motor Boat magazine, 20, 103, 104,
    116, 156, 199, 379, 389, 460, 492
Motor Boats (Atkin), 23
Motor Boats and Boating (Mudie),
    319
Motor Torpedo Boat (MTB), 462
Mottle 33, 3
Moucheron, 73
Mouette, 336
Mount Desert Yacht Yard, 193, 194
Mount Gay 30, *88*, 388
Mouquette, 83
Mouse of Malham, 243
Mouzaffer Eddin, 398
Mower, Charles Drown, 46, 52, 82,
    317–19, *317*, *318*, 423
Mower and Humphries, 319
Moxie, 183, 330
Moya, 62
Moyana, 325
MSO (minesweepers, ocean class),
    288
Mucilage, 196
Mudie, Colin Crighton, **319–20,** *319*,
    370
Muimai, 57
Muir, J., 395
Mulder, Frank, 180, **320,** *320*
Mull, Gary W., 180, 228, 229, 306,
    320–21, *321*, 407
Multihull Bermuda Race, 203
multihull yachts, 56, 58, 80, 84,
    98–99, 103, 107–109, 143–145,
    148, 173, 183–184, 202–203, *203*,
    244–245, 253, 282, 293, 329, 453,
    484
    see also catamarans; trimarans
Multiplast shipyard, 346
Mundimar 900, 387
Munford, John, *56*, **321–22**
Munro, Gordon, 130, 322, **322**
Munro shipyard, 305
Munroe, Ralph Middleton
    "Commodore," 86, 260, 323,
    323, 379
Muramoto, Nobuo, 206, 452, 496
Muritai, 282
Murray, Burns and Dovell, 324

Murray, Ian, *324*, **324,** 329
Murray, Rufus, 440
Murray and Tregurtha, 99
Muscadet, 201
Muscadet class, *201*
Museum of Yachting, 98, 154, 235
Mussolini, Benito, 31
Must, 158
Mustang, 440
Myers, Hugo, *325*, **325**
Myers, Tom, 368
My Gail III, 30
Mylin IV, 38
Mylne, Alfred, I, 154, 306, **325–27,**
    326, *327*, 333, 334, 478
Mylne, Alfred, II, *327*, **327**
Mylne, Charles, 326
Mylne and Company,
    see A. Mylne and Company
My Sin, 1, 18
Mystery II, 86
Mystic, 54, 472
Mystic Clipper, 493
Mystic Seaport Museum, 33, 34, 37,
    68, 89, 90, 94, 103, 104, 116, 125,
    147, 167, 173, 175, 194, 216, 241,
    264, 272, 279, 283, 288, 297, 319,
    406, 436, 439, 441, 487
Mystique, 30
Myth (Clapham), 86
Myth (Davidson), 114
Myth (Fellows), 145
Myth of Malham, 177–79, *177*, 243,
    409

Nabila, 30
Nabile, 401
Nabob II, 131
NACA (National Advisory Committee
    on Aeronautics), 80
Nada, 164
Nagaôna, 76
Nagoya University Yacht Club, 344
Nahlin, 33
Nahon, Jean-Charles, 302
Naiad (Byrne), 71
Naiad (Mower), 318
Naima, 12
Naini Tal Yacht Club, 234
Najad boatyard, 136
Nalu II, 267, 268
Nambay, 389
Namoh, 412
Namu, 497
Nan, 315
Nancy, 435
Nancy Rose, 77
Nansen, Fridtjof, 17
Nantucket 38 class, 189
Napier, David Lee, *328*, **328**
Napier, Shanks and Bell, 325
Napier I, 234
Naragansett, 461
Narranda, 233
National 12 class, 455
National Academy of Sciences, 436
National Advisory Committee on
    Aeronautics (NACA), 80
National Biscuit, 407

National Fisherman magazine, 139,
    200
National Gwen 12–class
National Heritage Fellowship, 432
National Inland yawl, 128
National Marine Manufacturers
    Association (NMMI), 34
National Maritime Museum, 82
National One-Design centerboard
    sloop, 103
National Research Council (NRC),
    256
National Steel and Shipbuilding
    Corporation, 74
Nature of Boats, The (Gerr), 173
Nausicaa, 466
Nauta Yachts, 142
Nautical Quarterly, 20
Nautical Watercraft Collection, The
    (Chapelle), 81
Nautigal, 425
Nautilus (Gallinari), 164
Nautilus (Scheel), 401
Nautilus III, 408
Nautor, 436, *439*, 444, 491
Nautor, 161, 228
Nautor's Swan, 185, 341, 444
Navahoe, 219, 477
Naval Academy, U.S., 180-81, 265,
    288, 295, 301, 306
Naval Academy Yawl, 288
Naval Architecture (Steel), 148
Naval Architect's Handbook, The
    (Martin), 300
Naval Architecture of Planing Hulls
    (Lord), 283
Naval Ship Engineering Center, 301
Naval War College, 37
Nawadaha, 491
NBSC (National Boating Safety
    Council) class, 88
NC-4 flying boat, 99
Nederlandse Vereeniging van
    Kustzeilers (Dutch Association of
    Coastal Yachtsmen), 226
Nedlloyd Shipping Company, 465
Nefertiti, 231, *231*
Nele, 181
Nelinge Boatyard, 254, *367*
Nella, 33, 92
Nelson, Bruce David, 114, **328–29,**
    329
Nelson/Marek Yacht Design, 329
Nelson One-Design 35, 329, *329*
Neola, 168, 175
Neptune, 304
Neptune 22, 313
Neptunus, 320
Nerana, 358
Nereia, 215
Nereus, 309
Nesea IV, 23
Netherlands Ship Model Basin
    (MARIN), 276, 320
Neva, 149
Nevada, 212
Never Say Never, 110
Nevins, Henry, shipyard,
    see Henry B. Nevins shipyard
New Bedford Race Week, 99

New Bedford Whaling Museum, 125
New Bedford Yacht Club, 33
New Boatyard (Gröndal), *417*
New Brighton Sailing Club, 88
New Channel class, 179
New Cold-Molded Boatbuilding, The
    (Parker), 354
New Haven sharpie, 82
Newick, Richard Cooper "Dick," 58,
    244, 279, **329–30,** *330*, 366, 463,
    485
New Jersey Yacht Club, 283
New London-Marblehead Race, 240
New Magic Breeze, 497
Newman 46, *284*
Newman, Jarvis company,
    see Jarvis Newman company
Newman, R. A., 29
Newpaper Taxi, 390
Newport, 320
Newport 29, 211, 220
Newport 30, 220
Newport-Bermuda Race, 107, 306,
    338, 424
Newport-Marstand Transatlantic
    Race, 48
Newport News Shipbuilding and
    Dry Dock Company, 89, 138, 487
Newport to Ensenada race, 12, 222
Newsboy, 239
News Boy, 272
New Shop (Atkin and Wheeler),
    2, 20
Newton, Robert, 125
New World, 228
New York (Rosenblatt), 388
New York (Smith), 421
New York 30, 220
New York 36, 90
New York 40, 220, *221*, 360
New York 50, 220
New York 65, 220
New York 70, 220
New York Athletic Club Race, 195
New York Boat Show, 349
New York Herald, 212
New York-Poughkeepsie Race, 212
New York Shipbuilding Company,
    459, 478
New York Times, 173
New York Yacht Club, 52, 63, 90,
    136, 140, 153, 174, 175, 197, 205,
    208, 235, 241, 272, 276, 319, 371,
    421, 433, 441, 461, 476
New Zealand 780 class
    championship, 115
New Zealand Challenge, 415
New Zealand Challenge (NZL-20),
    140
New Zealand Half-Ton
    Championship, 114
New Zealand (KZ-1), 250
Niagara, 433
Niagara III, 411
Niagara IV, *410*, 411
Niagra 35, 134
Niagra 42, 134
Niagara Boat Company, 293
Nibbio II, 399
Niccol, George, 280

Nicholson, Benjamin, **330–31,** *331,*
  332
Nicholson, Charles Arthur, 325,
  331–32 *331*
Nicholson, Charles Ernest, 31, *67, 68,*
  121, 122, 153, 154, 158, *169,* 176,
  306, **332–36,** *332, 333, 334, 335,*
  349, 383, 477, 478
Nicholson, Peter, 332
Nicholson 26, 332
Nicholson 32, 332
Nicholson 36, 332
Nicholson 55, 321
Nicol, Hedley, *336,* **336**
Nicolson, Ian, 325, 327, 395
Nicorette (Ribadeau Dumas), 55, 383
Nicorette (Simonis), 417
Nielsen, Knud Aage, 8, 43, 216,
  336–38, *336,* 338, 363, 483, 491
Nightingale, 495
Nightwind 35, 259
Nihon Yusen Kaisha Company
  (NYK Line), 264
Nike, 306
Nikkels, Thijs, 121
Nila II, 33
Nimble 20, 54
Nimble 24, 54
Nimble 30, 54
Nimble trimaran, 366
Nina (Burgess), *66, 67,* 186
Nina (Kyntzell), 265
Nina (Newick), 330
Ninon, 275
Nippon Challenge, 410, 452, 497
Nippon Ocean Racing Club (NORC),
  206, 345, 474, 496
Nissen, Georg, **338–39**
Nivelt, Bernard, **249–50**
Nixon, Lewis, *168*
Nixon Shipyard, 285
N/M 41, 329
NMMI (National Marine
  Manufacturers Association), 34
Noah, 126
Nock, F. S., 308
Nocturne, 355, 497
Nokomis, 136
Nokomis I, 175
Nokomis II, 175
Nolex 30, 140
Noma, 95
Nonpareil sharpie, *85,* 86
Nonsuch catboats, 133, 134
Nora, 367
Norada, 333
Noray series, 467
Nordbjaerg and Wedells, 314
Norderney, 187
Nordic (Nielsen), 338
Nordic builders, 360
Nordic Folkboat (Iversen), 245
Nordic Folkboat (Kyntzell), 265
Nordic Folkboat (Sunden), 449
Nordic 22-Square-Meter class
  (Estlander), 137
Nordic 22-Square-Meter class
  (Jensen), 245
Nordic 22-Square-Meter class
  (Kyntzell), 265

Nordiska Veritas, 12
Nordiske Krydsere (Nordic Cruiser),
  315
Nord Quest, 168
Nordship company, 260
Nordstar 25, 349
Nordwind, 187
Nor'easter, 196
Nor'Easter V, 216
Noreg III, 52
Noreine, 16
Norfolk navy yard, 295
Norge, 335
Norge Boats, 301, 418
Norlin, Peter, *339,* **339**
Norlin 34, 339
Norman Court, 243
Normand, Benjamin, 83
Normand, Jacques Augustin, 83, 94,
  339–40 *339*
Normandie, 382, 443
Normand shipyard, 275
Norman's Land boats, 363
Norna, 15
Norris Brothers, 314
Norrköping Yacht Club (NSS), 277
Nor'sea 27, 222
Norselander, 11
Norseman, 394
Norship, 320
North, John Ringling, 175
North American 40, 80
North American Championship,
  56, 228
North American Half-Ton Race,
  495
North American Quarter-Ton
  Championship, 328, 407
North American Yacht Racing Union,
  97, 128
Northbridge Junior, 45
Northbridge Sailing Club, 45
North Castle Marine/Gozzard Yachts,
  183
Northeast Harbor 30 class, 211
Northeast Harbor A Class, *47, 48*
Northern California Finn
  Championship, 320
Northern Crown, 338, 487
Northern Marine, 412
North Island Restricted Moth
  Championships, 139
North Pacific Shipbuilding
  Corporation, 166
Northwest troller, 199
Norwalk Boat Company, 429
Norwegian Hunting and Fishing
  Association, 16
Norwegian Society for the Rescue of
  the Shipwrecked, 16
Notika-Tecknic, 282
Notre Dame, 18
Nougatine, 189
Nourmahal, 93
Novanet, 415
Nova Scotia Schooner Association,
  394
Noyes, Bradley, 338
NRC (National Research Council),
  256

NS14 restricted development class,
  45
NSW Grand Prix, 291
Nugget, 366
Numbers, 452, *452*
Numptia, 401, *401*
Nurdig I, 199
Nurdig II, 199, *199*
Nurdig III, 199
Nurdig IV, 199
Nutshell pram, 486
Nutting, William, 20–21, 156
Nyanza, 432
Nydia, 174
Nygren, Axel, 12, 277, **340–41,** *340,*
  367
Nyland Yacht Club (Nyändska
  Jajthlubben), 12, 434
Nyman, Jorma Olavi, *341,* **341**
NZ 37 cruiser/racer, 497
NZL 61, 115

Oakley, John, 127
Oberon, 367
Oberti, Max E., 26
Oceana, 30
Ocean Bay 30, 498
Oceanco, 207, *207*
Ocean Cruising 52, 90
Oceanfast Marine, 29, 30, 110
Oceania, 110
Oceania company, 301
Ocean Pearl, 131
Ocean Planet, 495
Ocean Research Corporation, 194
Ocean Sailing Development
  Holland BV, 121
Ocean Skiff, 439
Oceanus, 165, *166*
Ocean Voyager, 297, *297*
Ocean Yachts company, 298
Ocelot, 203
Ocre sportsfisherman, 387
Octavia, 326, 333
Octopussy, *179,* 180, 320, *320*
O'Day Company, 189, 412
O'Day Daysailer, 157
O'Day Outlaw, 383
O'Day Tempest, 383
Odyssea, 40
Odyssey (Alberg), 4
Odyssey (Camatte), 76
Odyssey (Kelly), *252,* 253
Oehlmann, Herwarth, 342
Oehlmann, Kurt A. H., *342,* **342**
Oertz, Max, 245, 333, **342–44,** *342,*
  344
OE series, 135
Oesophage Boogie, 43
Ofeldt, Frank W., 411
Offshore 52, 119
Offshore 90, 51
Offshore Cruiser (DeFever), 119
Offshore Cruiser (Lane), 267
Offshore Cruising Society, 119
Offshore Patrol, 457
Offshore Racing Council (ORC), 11,
  140, 237, 387, 474

Of Yachts and Men (Atkin), 23
O'Hanlon, Rory, 53
Ohashi, Katsunori, **344–45,** *345*
Oheka II, 290, *290*
Ohlsson, Einar, 78, *345,* **345**
Ohlsson, Karl Erik, 345
Oimara, 432
Okamoto and Sons Boat Yard, 264,
  496
Olabarri, Juan, 9
Olav, Crown Prince of Norway,
  1, 15, 16
Olav V, King of Norway, 277
Old Glory, 271
*Old Ironsides: The Rise, Decline,
  and Resurrection of the USS
  Constitution* (Gillmer), 181
Olga, 355
Oliver, Clay, 55
Olivier van Noort, 468
Ollier, Gilles, **346–47,** *346,* 403
Olsen, Knud, 245, 449
Olympia Jolle, 274
Olympic Adventure 37, 54
Olympic Games, 1, 9, 15, 16, *16,* 45,
  259, *259,* 265
of 1900, 234
of 1912, *199,* 277
of 1920, 229
of 1932, 210
of 1936, 92, 93, 159, 208, 210, 262,
  269
of 1948, 53, 91, 210, 306
of 1952, 91
of 1956, 210, 258, 306
of 1960, 92, 239, 265
of 1964, 258
of 1968, 78, 236, 258
of 1972, 277, 279
of 1996, 132
Olympic yacht races, 1, 9, 15, 16, *16,*
  45, 329, 341, 345, 365, 367, 471,
  496
Om, 249
Onatru, 180
Onda III, 66
Ondina, 93
Ondine, 189, 458
103 Sailing Rigs (Bolger), 49
One-Design Yachtsman magazine,
  259
1D35, 329
100 Guinea Cup, 204
110 One-Design series, 238
One-of-a-Kind Regatta, 10, 189,
  202
Oneto, Luigi, *347,* **347**
One-Ton Cup, 1, 53, 73, 80, 114,
  126, 135, 139, 164, 190, 228, 229,
  237, 250, 265, 277, 360, 385, 407,
  436, 457, 473
One-Ton North American
  Championship, 90, 329
One-Ton World Championship, 56
OneWorld Challenge, 114, 329
Onion Patch races, 160, 161
Only You, 401
ONO, 394
Onontio, 174
On Reading Plans (Miglitsch), 313

Ontario Provincial Police, 134
Oona, 355, 475
Oossanen, Peter Van, 56, 276
Opal C, 30
Open 50–foot class, 44
Open 60–foot class, 44, 270, 383
Open Ville de Cherbourg, 250
Opium 39, 282
Optimist Dinghy, 313
Optimist Pram, 313, *313*
Optimist World Championship,
   313
Opus, 297
Oracle BMW, 142
Orange, 346
Oranjebloesem, 226, *226*
Orca, 199
Orchid, 305
Oregon Wolff II, 91
Orestes, 66
Oriva, 204, 205
ORMA, 463
Ormidale, 29
Ormidale class, *28*, 29
Orr, Alec, 235
Ortac, 86
Oryx, 243
Oskar II, King of Sweden and
   Norway, 12
Osprey, 284
OSTAR (Observer Singlehanded
   Transatlantic Race), *9*, 23, 46, 80,
   82, 121, 183, *303*, 304, 330, 370,
   431, 463
Ostkust, 301, *301*
Ostwind, 187
Otter, 473
Oughtred, Iain, **347–48,** *348*
Our Way, 51
Outboard High Point Trophy, 245
Outboard Marine Corporation, 34
Outing Magazine, 442
Outlaw, 243, 370
Outlook, 65, *65*, 66
outrigger canoes, 148
outriggers, 395
Outsider, 132
Outward Bound, 115
Outward Bound, 57
Outward Bound pulling boats, 194
Oviatt Marine, 119
Ovington, 142
Owen, Charles J., 349
Owen, George, 99, 235, 258,
   348–49, *349*, 366, 379
Owens, Charles C., 349
Owens, John B., 349
Owens, Norman G., *349*, **349**
Owens cutter, 349
Owens Shipyard, 119
Owens Yacht Company, 34, *349*
Oxford Boatyard, 210
Oxford 400, 210, *210*
Oxford Sailer, 210
Oyster, 491
Oyster 53, 237
Oyster 56, 237
Oyster 62, 237
Oyster 66, 237, *237*
Oyster Marine, 407

*Ozean-Wettfahrten, 70 Jahren
   Transatlantik-Regatten (Ocean
   Races, 70 Years of Transatlantic
   Regattas)* (Dinklage), 122

Pabst-Werft yacht yard, 137, *137*
Pacane, 23
Pacemaker 40, 164
Pacemaker Company, 298–300, *298*
Pacemaker powerboats, 298, *298*
Pacific American Fisheries Company,
   199
Pacific Asian Enterprises, 301
Pacific Coast Yachting magazine, 76
Pacific Motor Boat magazine, 75, 76,
   91, 125, 200
Pacific Seacraft 37, 98, *98*
Packard, A. A., 65, 66
Packard, J. W., 191
PACT 95, 329
Paine, Belknap and Skene, 352
Paine, Charles W. "Chuck," 80,
   350–51, *350, 351*
Paine, C. W. Yacht Design,
   see C. W. Paine Yacht Design
Paine, Frank Cabot, 67, 97, 240,
   351–53, *351, 353*
Pajara, 253
Pajot, Marc, 267
Paketi, 357
Paladine, 432
Palawan, 436
Palmer Boat Company, 247
Palmer Johnson shipyard, 51
Palmer Scott boatyard, 99, 125
Pampero II, 76
Panama Canal Commission, 235
Pan Am Clipper Cup, 452
Panda, 327
Pandemonium, 329
Panope, 327
Papoose, 62, 64
Paquerette, 275
parachute spinnaker, 352
Paradox, 42
Paragon, 449
Paraiso, 30
Pardey, Larry and Lin, 221–22, 223,
   223
Paris, 83
Paris, Alexandre, 353, **353**
Paris, Jay, **353–54,** *354*
Paris Automotive Exhibition, 275
Paris School of Sail, 282
Parker, George, 148
Parker, Reul B., **354–55** *354*
Parts VI, 30
Party Pro, 132–33
Passagemaker, 37, *37*
Passagemaker Offshore Yachts, 203
Passat, 202
Passion, 56
Pastime, 71
Patience, 338
Patiki M-Class, 282
Patolita, 117
Paton, William Evan, **355,** 475
Patricia, 333
Patronilla, 125

Patterson, Andy, 443
Pattinson, Geoff, 87
Patton, George S., *8*
Pattycat II, 84
Paul E. Luke Shipyard, *336*, 338, 388,
   390, *390*
Paumelle, Albert, 353
Paumonok, 235
Pavillon d'Or, 29
Payne, Alan, 31, 231, 233, 301, 324,
   355–56, *356*, 358, 383, 497
Payne, Alfred R., 357
Payne, Arthur Edward, *357,* **357**, 414
Payne, A. R. and Sons,
   see A. R. Payne and Sons
Payne, David Bruce, **357–58** *357*
Payne Mortlock sailing canoe, 355
Payson, Harold "Dynamite," 48
PB Design, 38
P.C.C. (Pacific Cruising Class), 255,
   255
P-Class boats, 66
P.C. (Pacific Coast) class, *254*, 255
Peabody, C. H., 379
Peabody Essex Museum, 4, 100, 106
Peachey, Howard, 357
Pearl, 243, 475
Pearl Harbor Naval Shipyard, 388
Pearson, Everett, 4, 249
Pearson Ensign, 4
Pearson Invicta, 458
Pearson Vanguard, 383
Pearson Yachts, 4
Pedrick, David, 306, *358*, **358**
Peel, Charles, **358–59** *358*
Peel, Charles, Jr., 359
Peer Gynt Yachts, 466
Pegaso, 401
Pegasus (Fox), 157
Pegasus (Bannenberg), 30
Pegasus (Wittholz), 493
Peggy, 65
Peg Woffington, 243
pelagic sealing skiffs, 158
Pellegrina, 53, 65
Penbo cruising powerboats, 266–67,
   266
Penchant, 266, 267
Pender, James, 478
Pendleton, F. F., *8*
Pendleton, F. F. Yard,
   see F. F. Pendleton Yard
Pendragon, 114, 115
Pen Duick IV, *9*, 9, 23, 465
Pen Duick V, 46, *46*, 131, *131*
Pen Duick VI, 465, *303*, 304
Penguin class, 381
Penn Jersey Shipbuilding, 52
Penobscot Boat Works, 266, *266*
Pequot Yacht Club, 423
Peregrine, 497
Performance Handicap Racing Fleet
   (PHRF), 404
Peridot, 88
Perini, Fabio, *359*, **359**
Perini Navi, 359
Perky, 38
Perry, Robert H., 80, **359–60,** *360*
Persephone, 216
Perseu, 202

Pesifer, 401
Peter Duck, 179
Peter Duck class, 179
Peter Pan, 261
Peter Pan IV, 103
Peterson, Douglas Blair, 12, 74, 115,
   161, *162*, 228, **360–62** *360*
Peterson, Murray Gignoux, 8, 338,
   363–64, *363*, 491
Peterson and Williams, 491
Peterson 35, 360
Peterson 44, 360
*Petit traité de la construction et du
   gréement des modèles de bateaux*
   (de Catus), 80–81
Petra, 181
Pétrel (de Catus), 80
Petrel (Hyslop), 241, *241*
Petrel 32, 354
Petrel 42, 369
Petterson, Pelle, 56, *365*, **365**
P-14 sloop, 74
P-46, 354
Phantom, 272
Phénix, 43
Phffft, 103
Philadelphia Naval Shipyard, 173
Philadelphia to Havana Race, 404
Philante, 335, *336*
Philante IV, 321
Philip, Prince of England, 157
Philip L. Rhodes, Naval Architects
   and Marine Engineers, 94, 301,
   306, 443, 472
Philippe Briand Yacht Architecture
   (PBYA), 56
Phillipot, Jacques, 13
Phillips-Birt, Douglas, 65, 86, 179,
   331
Phi-Phi, 189
Phocéa, 45, 46
Phryne, 359
Pi-Cat, 366
Picnic Boat, 257
Picolo, 314
PIC (Pacific Interclub) sloops, 117
Pidgeon, Harry, 319
Piepgrass, Henry, *204*, 205
Pierce, Bob, 239
Pierce and Kilburn boatyard, 89
Pierre Ier Ier, 463
Pierre Louis, 261
Piet Hein, 470
Pilar, 387
Pilgrim, 46, *46*
Pilgrim 40, 183
Pilila, 189
Pinaud, Jack, 365
Pinaud, Martin, 365
Pinaud, Walter, **365–66** *365*,
Pinkies, 363
Pinky schooner, 82
Pinor Major, 249
Pinta, 250
Pinta Smeralda, 250
Pioche, 83
Pioneer (Mauric), 303
Pioneer (van de Stadt), 430
Pipe Dream, 258
Piper class, 53

Pirate, 170

Piropo IV, 359

Piscataqua River Gundalow Project, 310

Piskie, 244

Pitusa, 189

Piver, Arthur Lincoln, 103, *103*, 336, **366–67,** *366*, 453

Planante Progettato, 202

PlayStation, 317

Pleione, 338

Pluto, 247

Plym, Bengt, 367, 438

Plym, Carl, 245, 367

Plym, August, **367,** *367*

Plym, Gustav, 367

Plymouth-La Rochelle Race, 80, 412

Plymouth-Santander Race, 412

Plymsnäckan, 367

Pocket Cruisers and Tabloid Yachts (Benford), 40

Pocket Cruisers for the Backyard Builder (Gerr), 173

Poillon, C., 134

Poillon, R., 134

Pointhouse boatyard, 243

Point Jude 15, 405

Police Car, 127, 128

Polly, 218

Polynesian Concept, 84, *84*

Polytechnic High School (San Francisco), 425

Polytechnicum Haarlem, 225, 261

Poncet, Jérôme, 249

Ponchette, 189

Pontiac, 66

Porter, 218

Port Huron-Mackinac Race, 161

Portland Boat Works, 473

Portland Speed Trials, 244

Portola, 75, *75*

Portsmouth Naval Shipyard, 89, 322

Posillipo, 297

Post, Marjorie Merriweather, 93–94

Post, Russell, 298

Pot o' Gold, 271

Potter, McArthur and Gilbert, 417

Potter, Nicholas Sheldon, 145, 301, **368–69,** *368, 369*

Potter, Stanley, 288, 389

Potter Class-B Frostbite dinghy, 368

Poulain, 463

Poulsen, Pouline, 373

Poupon, Phillippe, 346

Pour Médecins du Monde, 250

Pourquoi Pas?, 398

Pouvreau company, 303

Ppalu, 428

Practical Small Boat Designs (Atkin), 20

Prada, 115, 329

Prada Challenge, 362

Prague, John G., 134

Prairie company, 200

Pratt Institute, 443

Preacher's Son (Wiley), 489

Precision Boatworks, 452

Precision 40, 110

Precision Marine, 110

Predicted Log Races, 76

Preliminary Design of Boats and Ships (Hamlin), 194

President 41, 429

Presles, Dominique, *369,* **369**

Prestige, 67

Presto, 323, *323*

Presto sharpie, 86

Preve, Riccardo, 26

Prévost, Vincent Lauriot, **462–63,** *463*

Pride of Baltimore, 181

Pride of Baltimore: The Story of the Baltimore Clippers 1800–1990 (Gillmer), 181

Pridie, Mark, 244

Prilla, 66

Prima, 329

Primagaz, 463

Primrose, 33

Primrose, Angus, 243, *243,* 270, *370,* **370**

Prince Philip Duke of Edinburgh design award, 110

Prince of Wales Club, 155

Prince of Wales Cup, 111, *156,* 316

Princess, 231

Principality of Monaco Exposition, 93

Principe Alfonso, 189

Principia, 170, 172

Prisca, 277

Priscilla, 63, 420

Privateer, *81*

Privileges series, 282

Prix de la Ville de Nice, 272

Project Amazon, 427

Promenade, 244

Pronto, 309

Pronto II, 445

Propeller Handbook (Gerr), 173

Prospector, 203

Prosperi, Carlo Alberto Connelli de, 93

Prospero, 420

Prototype, 158

Prout, Francis, 98, 253, 293, 370, **370**

Prout, Roland, 98, 253, 293, 370, **370**

Prout 27, 370

Provence, 465

Providence, 493

Pryné, 340

PSC-31, 98

Psea, 342

PT boats, 82, 103, 104, 130, 138, 236, 282, 283, 288, 457

Puck, 277

Puerto Principe, 424

Puget Sound Maritime Historical Society, 91

Pugh, Jim, 274, 362

Pulitzer, Joseph, 432

Punch, 83

Punch 850, 201

Purdon, John R., 104

Purdy, Edward "Ned," 293, **370–71,** *371*

Purdy, James "Gil" Jr., 293, **370–71,** *371*

Puritan, 8, 34, 46, 61, *61,* 63, 67, 90, 205, 420

Puritan Cup, 352

Pusey and Jones Shipyard, 125, 175

Pyewacket, 274

Pyle, Edward, 443

Pym, 87

Q-Class boats, 66

Quadriga, 250

Quaeso, 38

Quartas, 445

Quarter-Ton Cup, 139, 154, 206, 228, 390, 407, 497

Quarter-Tonner Accent 26, 339

Quarter-Ton World Championship, 56, 182, 270

Queen Elizabeth 2, 30

Queen Mab (Bolger), 49

Queen Mab (Erismann), 136, *136*

Queen's Cup, 88, 234

Queen's Cup (Netherlands), 430

Quest 31, 370

Quest (Angelman), 14

Quest (Frers), 160

Questa, 216

Questar, 353, 354

Quest II, 109

Quest III, 109

Question, 240

Quick Cat, 109

Quicksilver II, 319

Quickstep 24, 54

Quill II, 105, 106

Quilter, Cuthbert, 88

Quimby Veneer Company, 130

Quincy Cup, 65, *65*

Quisetta, 168

Quiver III, 332

Qusar 50, 370

Rabbit, 79

Rabbit II, 79

Rabe, 206

Raccoon, 64

Race to the White Continent, The (Gurney), 189

Racing, Cruising and Design (Fox), 157, 187–88

Racing and Cruising Trimarans (Harris), 203

Racing and Its Rules (Giovanelli), 181

Racoupeau, Olivier, 44

Radiant, 387

Radiosa Aurora, 399

radius-bilge hull form, 54, *54*

Rage, 495

Raggio di Sole, 400

Ragna, 112

Ragtime (Johnstone), 249

Ragtime (Spencer), 426

RAI, 471

Rainbow (Burgess), 67, 68, 175, 186, 334, 336

Rainbow (Callahan), 75

Rainbow (Logan), 282

Rainbow (Watson), 478

Ramaley Boatworks, 138

Ramble, 461

Rambler (Bunker), 60

Rambler (van Deusen), 461

Rambler (Woolacott), 494

Ramrod, 468

Ramsing, Thor, 338

Ranger Class, 320

Ranger, 68, *68,* 113, 186, 209, 436, 441

Rani, 31

Ranita, 189

Rankin and Richard, *195*

Rankine, Macquorn, 243, 475

Ransome, Arthur, 414

Raph (Mauric), 303

Raph (Presles), 369

Rapid, 36

Rascal (Purdy), 371

Rascal (Stone), 445

Rasmussen, Henry, 190, 208, 333, 342, **373–75,** *374,* 470, 481

Rasmussen, Jens, 373

Rassy, Christoffer, *135*

Ratsey, Lynn, 375

Ratsey, Michael E., *375,* **375**

Ratsey and Lapthorn, 121

Ravanello, 24

Rawhiti, 282

"razorcase" type boats, 163, 284

Razzle Dazzle, 362

R-Class, 6, 319, 333

Ready About (Hoyt), 236

Real Club Nautico de Vigo, 266

Real Federacion Española de Clubs Nauticos, 9

Real Sporting Club, 9

Rebecca, 41

Rebel, 154

Recidivist, 407

Recluta, 161

Red, Red Wine, 163

Red Bank Yacht Club One-Design, 212

Red Boat Shop, 20

Red Jacket (Cuthbertson), 110–11, *110*

Red Jacket (Geary), *171,* 172

Redningskoites, 16–17, *17, 18,* 21–22

Red Pirate, 27, 29

Red Rooster, 79

Redwing (Fox), 157

Redwing (Luders), 288

Reed, Bertie, 270

Reeks, Walter, 31, **375–76,** *376*

Reevs, Susan B., 363

Regatta Paint Company, 288

Regenboog (Rainbow) class, 468

Regina, 373

Region de Picardie, 316

Region Nord Pas de Calais, 316

Rehu Moana, 319, 370

Reiach, Herbert, 71

Reichel, John, 274, 362

Reid and Jenkins, 167

Reimers, Knud H., 367, **377–79,** *377, 378*

Reinhardt, Joseph, 381

Reinke, Kurt, **379,** *379*

Rejoice, 481

Relance, 383

Reliance (Herreshoff), 153, 220, *220*, 319
Reliance (Smith), 279, 422
Renegade (Hess), 222, *222*
Renegade (Nelson), 329
Requero, 387
Resolute (Angelman), 14
Resolute (Herreshoff), 169, *169*, 219, *333, 349*
Resolution, 139
Revere, 125
Reverie, 432
Revista Marittima magazine, 467
Révolution, 154, 463
RFR, 158
Rhe Sailing Club (Königsberg), 397
Rhode Island, University of, 405, 406
Rhodes, Philip H. "Bodie," 383
Rhodes, Philip Leonard, 17, 38, 39, 94, 118, 119, 125, 134, 138, 180, 240, 258, 288, 300, 342, 349, **379–83,** *381, 382,* 443, 457, 465, 473, 493
Rhodes 18, 382
Rhodes 19, 382
Rhodes 27, 443
Rhodes 37, 382
Rhodes 77, 443
Rhodes Reliant, 383, 435
Rhonda III, 390
Ribadeau Dumas, Arnaud, 383, *383*
Ribadeau Dumas, Guy, **383–84** *383*
Rice Brothers Corporation, 209
Richard Peck, 421
Richards, Jo, 403
Richardson, Alexander, 71, 88, 375, *384,* **384,** 425
Richardson Company, 309
Richmond, 316
Ridder, Jacques de, 126, 226, *383*, **384–85,** *384,* 431, 452
Riddle of the Sands, The (Childers), 17
Rigg, Lincoln K., 67
Right Royal, 87
Rigoletto, 347
Rigolo, 245
Rioja de España, 88, 394
Ripple, 31
Rita, 27
Riva, Carlo, 31–32, **385–87,** *385, 386*
Riva Historical Society, 386
Rival 41, *53*
Rival production yachts, 54
Riva runabouts, 385–86
Riva 2000 class, 32, *32*
Riverside Yacht Club, 175
Riviera, 217
RM 10.50, 282
RNLI (Royal National Lifeboat Institution), 33
RNSA 24, 179
Roach, John, 167
Roaring Bessie, 137
Roas II, 388
Roastbeef, 73
Robador, 286
Robb, Arthur Cecil, 306, *387,* **387,** 494

Robert Jacob Yacht Yard, *51,* 175, 389, 443
Robert Napier and Sons, 475
Robertson, Bob, 291
Robertson 950, 291
Robertson, Alexander and Sons, *see* Alexander Robertson and Sons
Robertson's Boatyard, 47, 305
Robert Steele and Company, 280, *432,* 493
Robin (Hood), 231
Robin (Paine), 352
Robinhood Marine Center, 439
Robins, John N. Shipyard, *see* John N. Rogers Shipyard
Robinson Shipyard, *see* William Robinson Shipyard
Robob, 111
Rob Roy 23, 54
Roca, Fernando, **387**
Rochester Boat Works, 294
Rochester Yacht Club, 212
Rockefeller, Lawrence, 383
Rocket 31, 497, *497*
Rocket 780, 497
Rocking Chair, 424
Rockport 30, 351
Rockport Marine, 487
Rodéo, 261
Rödesund Boatyard, 36, *36*
Rodman 42, 250
Roger & Gallet, 267
Rogers, H. H., 290
Rogers, Jeremy, 387, 397
Rogers, Simon Mark, 237, **387–88,** *388*
Rogue's Roost, 90
Roland Shipyard, 313
Roland von Bremen, 186–87, *187*
Roland von Bremen II, 187
Roller Coaster 4, 237
Rollo (Anker), *15,* 16
Rollo (Utzon), 460
Romily series, 244
Romola, 432
Ron, 305
Rondina, 62, *253*
Rondinella, 53
Ron of Argyll, 304, 305
RORC (Royal Ocean Racing Club), 53, 79–80, 84, 86, 87, 128, 135, 154, 160, 177, 227, 243, 292, 496
RORC Channel Race, 9, 206, 378
RORC Class I championship, 87
RORC Class III championship, 87
RORC Class I ocean racers, 86, *86, 87*
RORC Commodore's Cup, 495
RORC Rule, 315, 355, 356, 387, 436, *438,* 467
Rorqual, 23
Rosa II, 389, 390, *390*
Rose, H.M.S., 49
Rosenblatt, Lester, **388–89,** *390, 390*
Rosenblatt, Mandell, **389–90,** *389, 390*
Rosenfeld, Morris, 283
Rosenfeld, Stanley, 283
Rose of Devon, 204
Rose of York, 179
Rosette, 71

Roska, 327
Roslyn sharpie, *85,* 86
Ross, Archie, 284
Ross, Murray Douglas, **390–91,** *391*
Ross, N. D., *391,* **391**
Ross, Phil, 8
Ross 780, 391, 391
Rothmans, 237
Rothschild, Edmond de, Baron, 400
Rothschild, Adolphe de, Baroness, 340
Rothschild, Edouard de, Baron, 83
Rothschild, Philippe de, Baron, 189
Roué 20, 392
Roué, William James, **391–93,** *392*
Rouillard research unit, 465
Round Australia shorthanded race, 108
Round Britain Race, 23, 244, 293, 463
Round Europe Race, 244
Round Ireland Race, 463
Round Spain Race, 424
Round the Island Race, 332
Round the Isle of Wight Race, 53, 463
Round-the-State Race, 360
Round the World Race, 463
Rousmaniere, John, 256
Rouss, Peter, 93
Route du Rhum Race, 23, 56, 88, 155, 183, 244, 282, 304, 346
Roxane, 277
Roxanne series, 244
Royal Burnham Yacht Club, 112
Royal Canadian Mounted Police, 134
Royal Canadian Yacht Club (RCYC), 110, 128, 195, 212
Royal Cape Breton Yacht Club, 129, *129,* 365
Royal Cape One-Design Class, 430
Royal Cape Yacht Club, 234
Royal Clyde Yacht Club, 147, 475, 476
Royal Copenhagen Yacht Club, 344
Royal Cork Yacht Club, 228
Royal Cruising Club Trophy, 90
Royal Danish Yacht Club, 42, 43, 399, 483
Royal Designers for Industry, 31
Royal Eagle, 491
Royal Eagle II, 228
Royal Flush, 270
Royal Gothenburg Yacht Club, 15
Royal Hamilton Yacht Club, 256
Royal Huisman Shipyard, 30, 38, *38,* 39, 122, 228, 289, 384, *384,* 401, 491
Royal Institute of Naval Architects, 59, 110, 394
Royal Institute of Yacht Designers, 170
Royalist, 319
Royal Italian Yacht Club, 347
Royal Motor Yacht Club, 484
Royal National Lifeboat Institution (RNLI), 33
Royal Naval Air Service, 334
Royal Naval College, 167, 355
Royal Naval Sailing Association, 179

Royal New Zealand Air Force, 45
Royal New Zealand Yacht Squadron, 57
Royal Northern and Clyde Yacht Club, 147, 475
Royal Northern Yacht Club, 147
Royal Norwegian Sailing Association, 406
Royal Norwegian Yacht Club, 15, 16
Royal Nova Scotia Yacht Squadron, 392
Royal Ocean Racing Club, *see* RORC
Royal Saint Lawrence Yacht Club, 128–29
Royal Swedish Yacht Club (KSSS), 12, 137, 277, 341
Royal Sydney Yacht Squadron, 376
Royal Technical College, 52, 266
Royal Thames, 53
Royal Yacht Club, 70
Royal Yachting Association, 243
Royal Yacht Squadron, *35,* 70, 88, 306, 432, 433, 476
Royan, 398
Royono, 8
Rozinante design, 214–15, *215*
Rubin, 250
Ruby II, 200
Ruby Queen, 148
Rudder, The, 4, 20, 34, 37, 52, 65, 93, 101, 103, 115–16, 129, 136, 165, 195, 199, 215, 216, 272, 288, 301, 318, 319, 368, 404, 417, 432, 443, 473, 488, 492
Rudder Ocean Race, 281
Ruddock's boatyard, 293
Rudy, 32
Ruiz De Elvira, Manuel "Manolo," **394**
Rumpus, 123
Run 50, 282
Runabout, 185
Runaway, 259
Runaway company, 285
Rush, 174, 329
Ruskin, John, 137
Russell, John Scott, 71, 137, 241, **394–95,** *394,* 417, 421, 433, 475
Rutgers University, 441
Ruth (Geiger), *173*
Ruth (Sibbick), 416
Ruth E, 131
Ryan, John J., 422
Rybovich, John, **395**
Rybovich, Robert (Emil), **395**
Rybovich, Thomas, **395**
Rybovich and Sons, 200, 395
Rybovich Spencer, 395
Ryder, C. E. Corporation, *see* C. E. Ryder Corporation
Ryder-Turner, David G. D., *395,* **395**
Rydin, A., 229

S130, 164
Sabine, 292
Sabre Cat, 98–99
Sabre Yachts, 259, 452
Sadler, David, *397,* **397**
Sadler, Martin, 397

Sadler Yachts, 397
Saefkow, H., *397*, **397**
Saeta, 329
Saetta, 175
Saga, 360
Saga (Aas), 1, 2
Saga (Andersson), 12
Saga (Nelson), 329
Saga (Wylie), 495
Sagaling, 277
Sagitta (Bannenberg), 29
Sagitta (Nicholson), 334
Sagitta (Sahuqué), 398
Sahab V, 401
Saharet, 483
Sahuqué, Georges, **398–99** *398*
SAI Ambrosini, 202
Sail magazine, 427
Sail and Sweep magazine, 65
Sail-Area-and-Waterline-Length Rule, 376, *376*
Sailboats and Launches in Metal (Langevin), 267
Sailboats Go by Their Sails (Giovanelli), 181
Sail Craft Boat Yard, 293
Sailing magazine, 360
Sailing, Seamanship and Yacht Construction (Fox), 157
Sailing Designs (Perry), 360
Sailing Ship, The (Mudie), 319
Sailing World magazine, 259, 274, 329
Sailing Yacht Design (Henry and Miller), 210
Sail Training Association (STA), 122
Saint Barbara, 335
Saint Francis Yacht Club, 227, 274
Saint Johns River Shipbuilding Company, 104
Saint Lawrence Bridge, 129
Saint-Papa, 369
Saint Petersburg to Havana Race, 394
Saint Tropez motorboat, 32
Sainty, John Philip, 204
Sako, Masato, 264
Sakonnet, 8
Sakonnet 23, 486
Salamandre, 346
Salamar, 209
Salander, Erik, *399*, **399**
Saleema, 235
Salen, Sven, 449
Sally, 347, *347*
Sally II, 65
Sally VI, 272
Sally VII (Burgess), 66
Sally VII (Lawley), 272
Salty, 267
Salty Goose, 120
Salty Tiger, 119
Samarang, 55
Samasan, 115
Samba Si, 158
Samoa, 9
Samoa Cup, 190
Samoena, 384
Samona II, 170
Samouraï class, 131

Samuel Crocker shipyard, 338
Sample shipyard, *see* Frank L. Sample and Son shipyard
Samurai, 310
Sanderling series, 296
Sandgate Sailing Club, 234
San Diego One-Ton Championship, 360
San Diego to Acapulco race, 117
San Diego Yacht Club, *254*, *255*, 328, 360
Sandpiper, 296
Sandra II, 389
San Francisco Challenge Cup, 66
Sangermani, Cesare, **399–400,** *400*, 410
Sangria class, 201, 202
San Juan 24, 259
San Pedro-Honolulu Transpac Race, *see* Transpacific Race
Sans Peur, 432
Santa Cruz Yachts, 173, 274
Santa Maria, 292
Santana, 125
Santana 30–30 class, 329
Santander-La Trinité Race, 412
Santry, Arthur, 338
Sapphire (Barnett), 33
Sapphire (Grobety), 185
Sappho, 155
Saracen, 425
Sarafsa, 492
Sarah Pryor, 272
Sara Moraea, 135
Saratoga, U.S.S., 37
Sardijn, 263
Sardinia Cup, 142, 161, 250, 360
Särklass A, 230, 277
Särklass B, 230, 277
Saroca (sail-row-canoe), 461
Sartrouville Yacht Club, 131
SAS (South African Shipyards), 207
Satan, 313
Satana, 231
Satanita, 152, 384, 425, *425*, 476
Saturn, 345
Saudad, 250
Saunders, S. E., 156
Saunders Roe, 77
Saunterer, 416
Saurer motors, 290
Sauterelle, 73
Savannah, 450
Sawaji, Shigeru, **400–401** *400*
S. A. Yachting magazine, 275
Sayula, 202
Scamp, 234
Scampi, 16, 339
Scampi 30, 339
Scandinavian Gold Cup, 26, 362
Scandinavian Sailing Association, 16
Scandinavian Yacht Union, 245
Scanu, Paolo, *401*, **401**
Scaramouche, 161
Scarlet, 267
Scat II, 450
Sceptre, 52, 211, 306, 434
Sceptre d'Isle, 208
Sceta Calberson, 154

Schäerenkruezers, 202
Scheel, Henry A., 39, 349, **401–2,** *402*, 442
"Scheel Keel," 401, 441, 442
Scheffner-segal, 379
Scheherazade, 258
Scheldejager, 292, *292*
Schelin, Oscar, 229, 399
Schichau Shipbuilding, 132
Schlichting Yard, 342
Schmidt, Michael, 250
Schmidt, Sébastien, 56, **402–3** *402*
Schnackenberg, Tom, 115
Schock, D. Charles, 8, 405, 406
Schock, Edson Burr, 117, **403–4,** *404*, *405*
Schock, Edson Irwin, 405, **405–6,** *405, 406*
Schock 41, 90
Schubert, Hugo, 12, 277, 367
Schubert's Cup, 229
Schulze, Wilhelm, 406, **406**
Schumacher, Carl Sherman, 321, *407*, **407**
Schweers Yard, 158
Sciomachen, Aldo, **407–8**
Sciomachen, Ernesto, **407–8**
Sciomachen, Franco, **407–8**
Scotia, 234
Scottish Islands One-Design Class, 306, 325
Scott Russell, John, *see* Russell, John Scott
Scripps Institute of Oceanography, 274
Scyth class, 263
Sea Belle, 204
Sea Bird, 145, 318
Seaborn, Ben, **408–9** *408*
Seabright Skiff, 22
Seabury, Charles Lincoln, **409–11,** *409, 410*
Seabury and de Zafra, 411
Sea Call, 196, 459
Sea Cloud, 93
Sea Cloud II, 132
Sea Crest, 29
Sea Diamond, 382
Sea Falcon, 293
Sea Fever, 408
Sea Flower, 336, 338
Seagoer, 318, 319
Sea Goose, 130–31
Seagull, 152
Sea Horse, 225
Seahorse Maxi Series, 56
Seahorse One-Design, 496
Sea Islander, 118
Sea Lion, 4
Sea magazine, 117, 118
Seaman, Warren, 84
Sea Monster, 412
Sea Nymph trailer sailer, 140
Sea-O-Ramic runabout, 266
Sea Prince II, 383
Sea Queen, 60
Search for Speed Under Sail, The (Chapelle), 81

Sea Rover, 14
Sears Cup, 239
Searunner catamarans, 58
Searunner trimarans, 58
Seascape, 389
Sea Scribe, *284*, 285
Seashaw, 320
SeaSled, 461
Seasmoke, 84, *84*
Sea Star, 383
Sea Swallow, 156
Seattle Museum of History and Industry, 91
Seattle Spirit, 91
Seattle Yacht Club, 114, 115
Seaview One-Design, 484
Seawanhaka Corinthian Yacht Club, 129, 205, 241, 253, 421
Seawanhaka Corinthian Yacht Club, Origins and Early History, The (Stephens), 442
Seawanhaka Cup (Seawanhaka International Trophy for Small Yachts), 47, 52, 53, 65, 94, 97, 129, 240, 434, 443
Seawanhaka rating rule, 220
Seaway, 77
Seawind, 181
Sea Witch, 13–14, *14*
Sebago, 184
Sebastian de Elcano, 336
SECMI shipyard, 267
Second International Regatta, 143
Seekreuzer, 338
Seer, 118
Seeschwalbe (Sea Swallow), 39
Segelclub RHE, 132
Seglarbladet magazine, 15
Sejllaengde Rule (Copenhagen Rule), 41
Selbsbau von Scharpiejollen (*Build Your Own Sharpie Dinghy*, Wustrau), 495
Seldén, J. H., 11
Selene (Steel), 432
Selene (Veronese), 466
Sélika, 398
Selina King, 414
Seminol, 271
Sens, 13
Sensation, 491
Sensation Yachts, 297, 322, 491
Sensible Cruising Designs (Herreshoff), 215, 216
Sepoy, 66
Sequoia, 549
Sequoia II, 459
Seraffyn, 222, 223
Serena, 5
Serenade, 368, 369
Serendipity 43, 360
Sereno III, 459
Sergean, François, 267
Sergent, François, 131, **411–12** *411*
Serica, 432
Servipack, 394
Settimana delle Bocche, 161
Setzer, Ward D., **412**
747 One-Design, 132
Seven Seas, 200

Sevourne, 357
Sfinge, 164
Sgarbh, 77
Shadow (Fellows), 145
Shadow (Herreshoff), 64, 475, 487
Shadow (Soverel), 425
Shadowfax (Brown), 485
Shadowfax (Spronk), 428
Shaefer, Rudolph, 460
Shaman, 492
Shamrock, 150, 152, 333, 478
Shamrock II, 32, 113, 152, 212, 478
Shamrock III, 150, 152–53, 319, 478
Shamrock IV, 348, 349, 478, 169, 169
Shamrock V, 321, 336, 401, 121, 122
Shamrock 23–Meter, 153
Shanakee, 39
Shannon 26, 429
Shannon Boats, 297
Shark-B-class series, 293
Sharon Potts, 405
Sharp, Gary, 321
sharpies, 82, 85–86, 260, 354
Sharp-shooter sloop, 74
Shatoosh, 474
Shaw, William, 412, **412**
Shawnee II, 203
Shearwater (Cunningham), 109
Shearwater (Prout), 370
Shearwater 39, 123
Shearwater 45, 123
Shearwood, F. P., 129
Sheerliner, 462
Sheffield Scientific School, 272
Sheila (Burgess), 67
Sheila (Inglis), 243
Sheila (Strange), 448, 448
Shelter Island 50, 498
Shemara, 321
Shenandoah, 365
Shepard's Boatworks, 138
Shepherd, Frederick, **414–15** 414
Shergar, 180
Sherman, William Tecumseh, 234
Sherman Hoyt's Memoirs (Hoyt), 235
Shetland series, 319
Shields, Cornelius, Jr., 1, 66
Shields keelboat, 439
Shining, 163
Shipbuilding Institute, 12
Shipman 28, 136
Shiptechnical School (Elsinore), 246
Shirley B, 491
Shockwave, 114, 115
Shoemaker's Child, 489
Shogun, 389
Shona (Mylne), 325
Shona (Watson), 475
Shotover, 107
ShowBoats International magazine, 39, 51, 110, 237, 320, 322, 359, 412
Shrewsbury class, 169
Shrine Regatta, 245
Shuttleworth, John, 253, 415, **415**
Sialia, 175
Sib, 485
Sibbick, Charles, 415, **415–16**
Sibbick Rater, 415

SIB trimaran prototype, 58
Sicli, 23
Sidewinder, 253
Sieburguer, Julio, 159
Siele, 125
Siemens motors, 290
Sif, 229
Sigma, 455, 455
Signe (King), 256
Signe (Salander), 399
Signor Rizzoli, 111
Sigrun, 274
Sil Enterprise, 282
Silent Maid, 450
Silja, 229
Silva Bay Shipyard School, 54
Silver Cloud II, 193
Silvercross, 303
Silverette class, 27
Silver Fern class, 114, 282
Silver Fox, 29
Silver Gull series, 295
Silver, James A. boatyard,
    see James A. Silver boatyard
Silver Leaf class, 27
Silver Shamrock, 228
Simba, 274
Simbad, 91
Sim Davis Company, 431
Simms, William, 338
Simms Brothers, 100, 338
Simon, William, 460
Simonis, Alexander, **416–17**
Simonis Voogd Design, 417
Simons, William, II, **417**
Simpson, Dwight Swain, 8, **417**
Sina, 319
Sindbad, 91
Sinding, G. A., 245
Sinebrychoff Trophy, 12
Sinergia 40, 51, 78
Singlan, 112
Singlehanded Mini-Transatlantic
    Race, 495
Singlehanded Race to Hawaii, 54
Singlehanded Transatlantic Race,
    87, 211, 244, 253, 366, 369, 370,
    400, 400, 415
Singlehanded Yacht Race,
    San Francisco to Okinawa,
    452
Singoalla, 137
Sing-Sing, 249
Singva, 418
Sintesi, 83–84
Sintra, 314
Sintz, Clark, 422
Sioux II, 36
Sira, 16
Siran, 30
Sirdhana, 93
Siren, 313
Sirena, 452
Sirio, 77
Sirius, 339
Sirius (Crocker), 100
Sirius (Sahuqué), 398
Sirius III, 182
Sir Lancelot, 432
Sir Thomas Lipton, 87

Sir Thomas Lipton Cup, 362, 368
Sir Tom, 170, 171
Sister Syn, 104
Sisu company, 285
Siwash, 75, 75
6e Sens, 346
6–Meter class, 52–53, 153, 154
Sixaern, 126
60 Years a Yacht Designer (Griffiths),
    184
Sjögren, Karl Einar, **417–18** 417
Sjöhistoriska Museet, 136
Skagerak, 277
Skaggerak, 50
Skandia, 269
Skarpsno, 498
Skaw Race, 460
Skeeter, 481
Skene, Norman L., 67, 116, 216, 240,
    258, 351
Skene's Elements of Yacht Design
    (Skene and Kinney), 258
Skerry Cruiser Rule, 12, 230, 277,
    341, 367, 399, 417, 418
Skerry Cruisers Trophy, 36, 230
Skidbladnir, 472
Skiff classes, 324
Skiffs and Schooners (Culler), 108
"skimming dish" sloops, 61, 62–63
Skipper 12, 314
Skipper 14, 314
Skipper 17, 314
Skipper magazine, 210
Skipper Mariner, 314
Skipper Mate, 314
Skylark, 260
Slaaby-Larsen, A., 418, **418**
"sleeping beauty" submersible canoe,
    177
Sloan shipyard, 199
Slocum, Joshua, 108, 318
Sloof, Joop, 276
Smackwater Jack, 391
Small, John F., **418–19**, 419
Small, Samuel N., **418–19**, 419
Small Boat Building (Monk), 315
Small Boat Construction (Steward),
    443
Small Boat Journal, 49
Small Boat Racing (Crosby), 103
Small Boats (Bolger), 49
Small Brothers, 492
Small Craft Medal, 59
Small Craft Plans (Benford), 40
Small Point One-Design, 68
Small Ships (Benford), 40
Small Yacht, Its Management and
    Handling for Racing and Sailing,
    The (Boardman), 48
Small Yacht Racing (Boardman), 48
Small Yachts, Their Design and
    Construction (Kunhardt), 264, 265
Smith, Archibald Cary, 18, 62, 63,
    94, 135, 155, 168, 219, 241, 404,
    419–21, 419, 421
Smith, Carl, 11
Smith, Christopher Columbus, 279,
    293, 422, **422**
    see also Chris-Craft
Smith, F. M., 175

Smith, Gilbert Monroe, 423, **423**
Smith, Harry C., 112
Smith, Henning, 366
Smith, Henry (Hank), 422
Smith, James, 148
Smith, Jay, 423
Smith, Kenneth L., **423–24**, 424
Smith Shipyard,
    see William B. Smith Shipyard
Smith, Thomas Assheton, 70
Smith, Tom, 14
Smith-Ryan Boat and Engine
    Company, 422
Smithsonian Institution, 82, 103
Smyth Team, The, 316
SNAME (Society of Naval Architects
    and Marine Engineers), 76, 110,
    114, 125, 137, 210, 283, 285, 388,
    436, 439, 441, 443, 480
Snarleyow, 442
Snikersnee, 442
Snipe One-Design, 103, 103
Snipper, 230
Snowbird, 164
Snowgoose (Lavranos), 270
Snowgoose (Prout), 370
Snow, I. L. Boatyard,
    see I. L. Snow Boatyard
Snow Star, 338
Snow White, 114
SNS (Société Nautique Suisse Class),
    91–92
Sobre Las Olas, 75
Société Marseillaise, 46
Société Nautique de Genève (SNG),
    80, 92
Société Nautique de Marseilles, 13
Société Nautique Suisse Class (SNS),
    91–92
Sociétés Nautiques d'Aquitaine, 398
Sodebo, 463
Solaris, 491
Soldini, Giovanni, 155
Solemates, 492
Solent Points Championship, 128
Solent Sunbeams, 483
Solent X-Boat, 484
Soler, Xavier, 88, **424–25**
Soling class, 277, 279
Solkaten, 418
Solo, 355
Sol Quest, 121
Solution, 338
Solway Maid, 152, 154
"Some Experimental Studies of
    Sailing Yachts" (Davidson), 113
Somo yachts, 387
Sonas, 395
Sonder boats (Sonderklasse), 66, 83,
    127, 158, 169, 190, 317, 344
Sonia, 336
Sonja III, 245
Soper, Joseph M., 152, 384, 425, **425,**
    475
Sophia Christina, 54
Sophie, 256
Sopra Consulting, 282
Sopranino, 179
Sopwith, T. O. M., 47, 122, 321, 335,
    336

Sorcery, 111, 320, 321
SORC (Southern Ocean Racing
    Conference), 12, 54, 90, 110, 111,
    111, 120, 160, 161, 189, 227, 250,
    268, 269, 381, 452
Sotto Voce, 250
Sound Cup, 42
Soundings magazine, 249, 298
Sound Interclub, 318
Sound of Pacific, 30
Souter's boatyard, 331
South African Shipyards (SAS), 207
Southampton, University of, 282
Southampton class, 169
Southampton Institute
    (ex-Southampton College
    of Technology), 78, 127, 162,
    163, 170, 244, 297, 401, 467
South Coast Company, 14
South Coast Marine, 443
South Coast One-Design, 325, 332
Southern Circuit Race, 255
Southern Cross, 276
Southern Cross company, 147
Southern Cross Cup, 142
Southern Cross II, 77
Southern Cross III, 30
Southern Cross Race, 13
Southern Star, 458
Southern Wind Shipyard, 142
South Pacific Half-Ton Trophy, 139
Southport class, 169
Sou'wester 59, 305, 305
Sou'wester series, 305
Sovereign (Boyd), 52, 434
Sovereign (Seabury), 411
Sovereign Yachts, 412
Soverel, Mark, 425
Soya, 66
Spalding, Eliot, 284
Spanish-American championship,
    66
Spark, 279
Sparkman, Drake, 113, 435, 439
Sparkman and Stephens, 119, 125,
    127, 135, 160, 180, 186, 202, 203,
    209, 210, 223, 225, 228, 258, 260,
    267, 270, 276, 295, 297, 298, 300,
    301, 314, 321, 338, 353, 358, 360,
    379, 399, 401, 404, 405, 406,
    407, 409, 412, 415, 425, 428, 429,
    435, 441, 457, 460, 461, 483
Spaulding, Myron, 425–26, 426, 495
Spaulding 33, 426
Spazzo, 338
Special motorboat, 32
Speedwell, 158
Speedwell class, 275
Speedwell of Good Hope, 275
Speedy Gonzales, 158
Speltz, Robert, 190
Spencer, Charles L., 305
Spencer, John Alfred, 227, 228,
    426–27, 427
Spice Race, 121
Spicy Isles, 194
spidsgatters, 43, 43, 406, 460
Spinlock, 80
Spirit, 170, 360
Spirit of Adventure, 57

Spirit of America, 461
Spirit of Australia, 324
Spirit of Gaia, 485, 485
Spirit of Tradition races, 121
Sponberg, Eric W., 427–28 427
Sports Afield Boatbuilding Annual,
    34
Sports Afield magazine, 405
Sports Illustrated, 491
Sportsman magazine, 442
SportYak dinghy, 493
Spray, 108, 318
Spray: Building and Sailing a Replica
    of Joshua Slocum's Famous Vessel
    (Culler), 108
Sponk, Peter, 428, 428
SQN, 128
Square-Meter-Rule, 137
Squke, 195
Stad Amsterdam, 121, 121, 122
Stadel, George, III, 428, 429, 429
Stadel, George H., Jr., 428–29
    428
Stadel, William, 428
Stadel and Jenkins, 428
Stadt, Ericus van de, 344, 384,
    429–31
Stage Harbor Yacht Club, 130
Staghound, 4
Staluppi, John, 320
Stamford-Vineyard Race, 382
Standfast 43, 293
Stanley, Lyford, 431
Stanley, Ralph W., 431–32 431
Star, 4, 42
Starbright, 409
Star class, 169, 450
Stark, Philippe, 44
Starlet, 255
Starlight (Hunt), 238
Starlight (Winch), 491
Starling (Rasmussen), 374
Starling (Townson), 457
Starling, 457
Starlite, 207
Starr, Donald, 338
Stars & Stripes, 120, 140, 250, 316,
    324, 329, 358, 415
Star Song, 338
State of Washington Maritime
    Heritage Award, 167
State University of New York
    Maritime College, 147
Statimer boatyard, 242
Stealth, 162
Steam Yachts and Launches
    (Kunhardt), 264
Stebbings boatyard, 112
Steel, David, 148
Steel Award for Excellence, 164
Steel Boatbuilding (Colvin), 89
Steelcraft company, 301
Steele, Robert and Company,
    see Robert Steele and Company
Steele, William, 432
Steers, George, 375, 394, 432–33,
    433, 461
Stefaren, 30
Steinlager 2, 140
Stella, 149

Stemael II, 412
Stemael III, 412
Stenbäck, Gunnar L., 433–34 433
Stephanie, 88
Stephen, Alexander and Sons,
    see Alexander Stephen and Sons
Stephen, Fred J., 434
Stephen, John G., 434, 434
Stephens, Barre, 253
Stephens, Dick, 253
Stephens, Olin J., II, 38, 39, 52,
    68, 68, 113, 119, 154, 160, 179,
    187, 211, 233, 249, 292, 306, 334,
    336, 338, 342, 353, 358, 367, 381,
    412, 434, 435–39, 435, 436, 438,
    439, 470
Stephens, Robert "Roy," 253, 411,
    434–35
Stephens, Robert W., 439–40, 440
Stephens, Roderick, Sr., 435, 439
Stephens, Roderick, Jr. "Rod,"
    113, 160, 259, 342, 439, 439,
    440–41 440
Stephens, Theodore "Thod," 253,
    434–35
Stephens, William Picard, 66, 204,
    254, 265, 318, 319, 432, 441–43,
    441, 442
Stephens Brothers, 252, 253, 434,
    480
Stephens 26, 434
Stephenson, Robert, 395
Sterling shipyard, 30
Sterns yacht yard,
    see William B. Sterns yacht yard
Stevens, Amos, 443
Stevens, David, 442, 443
Stevens, Edwin A., 93, 112
Stevens, George Cox, 433
Stevens Institute of Technology,
    68, 90, 93, 112–14, 113, 177, 194,
    277, 433, 436, 439, 488
Steward, Robert Montanus, 381,
    443–44
Stewart, Victor B., 145
Stewart and Binney, 46
STIAN (Italian Technical Society for
    Architecture and Naval
    Equipment), 202
Stiarna, 336
Sticky Fingers, 388, 388
Stiletto (Herreshoff), 145, 217
Stiletto (Piver), 366, 366
Still, Eivind, 444, 444
Still More Good Boats (Taylor),
    186
Still 380 One-design, 444
Stingray, 490
stitch-and-glue construction, 120
Stockholm Shipyard, 367
Stockholm Yacht Club, 417
Stoeberl, Helmuth, 445, 445
Stoeberl, Helmuth, Jr., 445
Stoeberl, Uli, 445
Stone, Bob, 338
Stone, Lester, 445–47, 447
Stone, William F., 445
Stone Boat Yard, 169, 381, 447,
    479, 480
Stone Horse, 99, 100

Stonington Boat Works, 401, 473
Stonington draggers, 267
Storebro Works, 135
Storey, W. C., 122
Storm (Liljegren), 277
Storm (Luders), 54, 286, 288
Storm VI, 38
Stormbird, 31
Stormrider, 115
Stormsvala, 145, 147
Storm Trysail Club, 301
Stormvogel (Kroes), 263
Stormvogel (van de Stadt), 330,
    360, 431
Stormy Petrel, 55, 55
Stormy Weather, 187, 381, 436,
    436, 440
Story of the Sailing Ship, The
    (Mudie), 319
Stove, Rick, 13
Strange, Albert, 17, 69, 230, 442,
    447–48, 448
Stranger (Byrne), 70
Stranger (Geary), 172
Strängnäs Boatyard, 378
Strathclyde University, 80
Strawbridge, William, 368
Striana, 92
Strider, 329
Striker (Netherlands), 38
Striker USA, 38
Striper, 103
Strumpet, 40
Studio Scanu, 401
Sturdee, 405
Styx (Draijer), 126
Styx (Hood), 233
Subversion, 249
Sud-Aviation, 267
Sudinex, 346
Suez Canal Company, 340
Sullivant, Caroline Louisa, 62
Suma, 456
Summers and Payne, 357
Summertime Dream, 407
Summerwind, 200
Sunbeam (Nissen), 339
Sunbeam (Byrne), 70, 71, 71
Sunbeam (Williams), 491
Sunbeam II, 33
Sunbird centerboard class, 57
Sunburst, 53
Sun Dance, 139
Sundén, Tord, 245, 449, 449
Sundsor Shipyard, 135
Sun Fast, 56
Sun Legend 40, 360
Sun Light 30, 13
Sünnschein, 48
Sunrise (Benford), 40
Sunrise (Hein), 207
Sunset Boulevard, 229
Sunshine, 153
Sunwind, 449
Suomi, 425, 426
Super America, 32
Super Challenger series, 303
Super Dorade, 412
Super Florida, 386, 386
Superior catamarans, 485

Supermarine company, 234
Super Mistral, 412
Superyacht Society Design Award, 39, 56, 320, 322
Supplement to Small Yachts (Stephens), 442
Surama, 303, 492
Sure Thing, 314
Surf, 205
Surf Scoter 24, 120
Surprise (Setzer), 412
Surprise (Joubert and Nivelt), 249
Surprise II, 170
Surprise 45 (Beeldsnijder), 38
Surprise 58 (Beeldsnijder), 38
Surprise Owners' Association, 249
Susanne, 151, 333
Susan R. Stone, 272
Suva, 172
Suzette (Guédon), 189
Suzette (Le Marchand), 275
Svanen (Benzon), 43
Svanen (Molich), 314, 315
Sverdrup, Otto, 17
Sverige, 56, 365, 365
Swagman, 158
Swaine, Clifford, 8
Swallow, 215
Swallow and Amazons, 41
Swampscott Yacht Club, 318
Swan, 112, 161
Swan 48, 439
Swan yachts, 161, 185, 341, 444
Swarbrick, John, 324, 329
Swasey, Albert Loring, 67, 235, 351, **449–50,** *450*
Swatchways and Little Ships (Griffiths), 184
Swaysey, Raymond and Page, 449, 478, 492
Sweden Yachts, 3, 339
Swedish Cruising Club, *3,* 135
Swedish Royal Navy, 340
Sweet Pea, 270
Sweisguth, Francis, 170, 405, 450, **450**
Swell, 378
Swift, 370
Swiftsure (Herreshoff), 94
Swiftsure (Nelson), 329
Swiftsure II, 407
Swiftsure Race, 255, 409
Swordfish, 157
Sybarita, 478
Syce, 168
Sydney-40, 324
Sydney-Hobart Race, 3, 31, 59, 107, 193, *193,* 243, 355, 356, 358, 417, 426, 431, 452
Sydney Olympic Games, 329
Sydney Technical College, 233, 355
Sydney Yachts, 324
Sykes, Francis, 155
Sylvania Company, 274
Sylvester Whaler, 272
Sylvia, 229
Sylvie, 375
Symra, 15
Synergy, 485

T & M Marine Engineers, 452
T6Y3T9T3I, 38
Taanganui, 494
Tabarly, Eric, 9, *9,* 46, 131, *131,* 250, *303,* 304, 463, 465
Tabasco, 272
Tabur dinghies, 23
Tadorne, 303
Taeping (Buchanan), 59
Taeping (Logan), 280
Taeping (Steele) 432
Taglang, Jacques, 82
Tahitiana, *138,* 139
Tahiti ketch (Hanna), *138,* 139, *198, 199*
Tahiti passagemaker (Boardman), 48
Tahoe Power Boat Club, 434
Taifun, 378
Taipan, 275
Taiseer IV, 331
Taiyo, 400
Taka, 452
Takahashi, Taro, 452
Takai, Osamu, 452
Takeichi, Shun, *452,* **452,** 496
Takeichi/Muramoto Yacht Designers, 452
Talayha, 219
Taleisin, 222
Talisker Mhor, 306
Talitha G, 30
Tall Ship races, 353
Tally Ho, 449
Tamalmar, 480, 481
Tamaris, 382
Tamerlane, 240, 241
Tam O'Shanter, 284
Tams, 389
Tams, Lemoine and Crane, 94, 104, 288
Tams and King, 116
Tams and Lemoine, 94
Tancook schooner, 443
Tancook whaler, 428, 488, 489
Tang, 101
Tangaroa, 484
Tango, 497
Tanton, Yves Marie, 80
Taouey, 359
Tapie, Bernard, 46
Tara, 164
Tarabocchia, Mario, 297
Tarantella, 217
Targa, 185
Tärnor design, 230
Tartan Boat Company, 436
Tartan Black Watch 37, 233
Tartan 27, 412
Tartan Yachts, 498
Tarua, 282
Tarzan, 245
Tasar, 45
Tashiba Company, 360
Tasman Seabird, 355, *356*
Tassara, Constantino, 93
Tayana/Vancouver 460, 203
Tayana Yachts, 38, 360
Taylor, James Hathaway "Jim," *452,* **452**
Taylor, Roger C., 186

Taylor, William H., 381
Taylor motorboats, 387
TBS-Charente-Maritime, 250
Tchetchet, Victor C., 84, 366, *453,* **453**
Team Adventure, 346
Team New Zealand, 162, 250, 329
Tea Race, 432
Technical Committee of German Sailing, 373
Technical University of Trondheim, 10
Technischen Hochschule (Berlin Charlottenberg), 494
Ted Brewer Explains Sailboat Design (Brewer), 54
Ted Hood Design Group, 231, 492
Teel, 491
Teeth, 320
Te Kana, 282
Tektron catamarans, 415, *415*
Telepizza-Pepsi, 51, 78
Teller, Ray, 443
Temeraire, 212
Tempest, 225
Tempo V, 34
10PF, 163
Tennant, Malcom, **453–54** *453*
Ten-Ton class, 71
Terlain, Jean-Yves, 250
Tern, 241
Terne class, 42
Tern III, 448
Terrorist, 258
Tetera, 279
Teva, 65
Thai series, 293
Thalassa, 33
Thalassi, 228
Thalia, 389
Thallassa, 416
Thames Yacht Building Company, 234
Thaôs, 80
The Anchorage, 368
Thelma (Logan), 282
Thelma (Reeks), 376
Theme, 189
Thendara, 327
Thera, 359
The Race, 317, 346, *346,* 347
Theseus, 38
Thetis, 423
Thiebout, J. P. G., 262, **454–55,** *454*
Think Tank, The (Delft), 394, 471, 497
30-foot class, 64
30 Old Boats (Bolger), 49
30-Square-Meter class, 73, *73,* 83
30-Square-Meter Cup, 73
33-Export, 303
Thistle (Atkin), 17, 98
Thistle (Douglass), 126, 258
Thistle (Watson), 32, 63, 151, 390, *475, 476*
Thomas, 73, 83, *83*
Thomas, David, **455–56** *455*
Thomas W. Lawson, 106
Thompson, Robert, 158
Thomson, William, First Baron Kelvin, 243

Thora, 470
Thorella II, 129
Thorello, 65
Thornycroft on the Thames, 152, 316
Thorobred, 473
Thorsen, S., 230
Thoughts on Yachts and Yachting (Fox), 157
Three Cheers, 330
Three Legs of Man, 253
Three Little Cruising Yachts (Atkin), 23
Three-Quarter-Ton Cup, 114, 132, 139
Three-Quarter-Tonner World Championship, 13, 182, 246
3615 Met, 202
Thriller, 158
Thunder (Bannenberg), 30
Thunder (Fox), 156
Thunder & Lightning, 156
Thunderbird (Hacker), 191
Thunderbird (Seaborn), 409
Thunderhead, 382
Thyra, 315
Tiajuana, 321
Tich, 227
Ticonderoga, 189, 214, 215, 216, 256
Tidal Wave, 381, *381*
Tiempo 2, 119
Tiger, 305
Tiger Cat, 202
Tiger Shark, 202
Tiller, Arthur, 401
Tiller Publishing, 40
Tilly, 190
Tilsag, 228
TI-M-AI ships, 52
Timber, 285
Time, 147
Timeless, 23
Tim Nolan Boat Design, 315, 316
Timoneer, 128
Tina, 79, *79*
Tina V, 289
Tinavette, 68
Tinker, 191
Tioga (Herreshoff), 214, 256
Tioga (Nielsen), 338
Tioga Too, 4
Tipler III, 322
Tirán, 132
Tishé, 91
Titania, 394, 395, 433
Titave, 189
Titia, 53
Tit Tit, 42
Titus Canby, 139
Tiziana, 460
Tjaldur, 53
Tjerne, 1
Tjopp, 418
Tjorns Yacht Service, 1
Tlingit, 165
TM Blue One, 180
Toadstool, 166–67
Tobiume, 452
Todd Shipyard, 74, 75
Together IV, 471
Toja, 230
Tokai University, 400

Tokugawa Shogunate, 496
Tokyo Imperial University, 474, 496
Toledo (Ohio) Shipbuilding, 498
Tollycraft, 315
Tomahawk, 336
Tomalin, Paule G., 288
Tomkins, Warwick "Commodore," 228
Tom Tom, 131
Tonet, Henri "Amel," **456**
Tonga, 38
Toni IX, 373
Tonnage Rule, 355, 384, 475
Tonnere, 122
Tonnerre de Breskens, 292, *292*
TOR 35, 310
Toria, 253
Tornado, 453
Tornroth, Bruno, 94, 443
Toronto Yacht Club, 128
Tosi, Gian Franco, 93
Totem, 288
Touché, 457
Touché-Too, 379
Tour de France à la Voile race, 250
Toureau, Pierre, 131
Touring Club of France, 43
Tour of Europe Race, 463
Tou Ta Ra, 189
towing tank dynamometer, *113*
Townsend, William, 155
Townson, Desmond, **456–57,** *456*
Townson 32, *456*
Townson 34, 457
TPI Composites, 249
Trade Wind, 8
Traditional Small Craft Association, 108
Traditions and Memories of American Yachting (Stephens), 442
Trainera seagoing rowing boat, 132
Traité de la Construction des Yachts à Voiles (Chevreux), 82
Tramp, 114
Transactions of the Society of Naval Architects and Marine Engineers, 113
Transatlantic Race, 34, 154, 160, 235, 306, *381*, 436, 440, 457, 458, 495
Transmed Race, 424
Transpacific Race (Transpac), 4, 5, 12, 13, *14*, 46, 54, 74, *74*, 108, 125, 131, *131*, 161, 175, 187, 189, *195*, 206, 219, 229, 255, 267, 268, *268*, 274, 319, 329, *345*, 360, 368, 404, *404*, *405*, 409, 425, 426, 431, 436, *457*, 473, 495
Transpacific Yacht Club, *404*
Trans-Tasman Race, 108, 494
Traveller, 330
Traveller III, 54
Traylor Shipbuilding Company, 116
Treasure IV, 459
Tree of Life, 54
Trehard, Christian, 158
Trekka, 179
Tremaine, Glenville Sinclair, **457**
Tremolino, 330
Tre Sang (Becker), 36
Tre Sang (Reimers), 378
Trevithick, J. G., 26

Triagoz 25, 267
Trial, 429
Triangle, 8
Trias, 445
Trice, 329
Trident (Duggan), 129
Trident (Paton), 355
Trident (Piver), 366
Trident (Westmacott), 484
Trident Shipworks, 491
Trifle, 253
trimarans, 9, 58, *58*, 103, *103*, 107, 203, 253, 282, 293, *316*, 317, 329–30, 336, 366, *366*, 453
Trina, 412
Trintella boatyard, 228
Trintella, 466
Triple Threat, 66
Tripp, William H., Jr., 180, 189, 223, 288, 362, 369, 381, **457–58,** *458*, 492
Tripp, William, III, 458
Trumpy, John, 172, 173, **458–59,** *459*
Trumpy, John, Jr., 459
Trumpy company, 200
TsjeTsja, 428
Tsulamaran, 370
Tulla, 431
Tumlare, 378
Tumleren, 43
Tuna, 103
Turbosails, 302
Turissimo, 454
Turmoil, 51
Turner, Admiral, 23, 466
Turnroth, Bruno, 443
Turtle, 371
Tuskar Class, 59, *59*
Tweed, Charles, 151
12–Meter class, 15, 94, 97, 140, 153
29er class, 44
Twigg, John and Sons, see John Twigg and Sons
Twin, 445
Twin Fighter, *445*
Twinkle, 409
Twins, 24, 26
Twins VI, 26
Twins VII, 26
Twin Wing, *280*
210 One-Design series, 238, 239

Two-Handed Transatlantic Race, 424
Two-Ton Cup, 161
Tyler Boat Company, 431
Typhoon (Alberg), 4
Typhoon (Atkin), 20–21
Typhoon (Fox), 156
Typhoon (Warner), *473*
Tyra, 16
Tyrrell of Arklow, 53
Tyrsa, *467*
Tyszkiewicz, Benoît, 339

UAP, 250
UCA, 250
UCINA (Union of Italian nautical builders), 32
Uddevalla, 269
Uffa Fox's Second Book (Fox), 157, 186
Uhle, Henry U. "Hank," **460**
ULDB (ultralight-displacement boat), 274, 495
Ultimate, 207
Una, 155
Understanding Boat Design (Brewer), 54
Underwood Company, see William Underwood Company
Unicorn (Davidson), 114
Unicorn (King), 257, 258
Union Bank of Finland, 250
Union des Yachts Français, 73, 398
Union Nationale pour la Course au Large (UNCL), 417
Union of French Nautical Societies, 76
Union of Italian Sailing Societies, 83
Union Shipbuilding, 379
United Engineers Shipyard, 47
United Nations Food and Agricultural Organization, 34
United States, S.S., 94
United States Power Squadron, 236, 284
United States Sailing Association, 128, 306
United States Yacht Racing Union, 10, 436
Universal Rule, 6, 15, 65, 66, *105*, 137, 153, 168, *213*, 216, 277, 336, 348, 351, 353, 426
Universidad Politécnia, 394
Unora, 415
Urgent, 154
U.S.A., 320
USA II, 120
USA 36, 329
USA 61, 329
U.S. Coast and Geodetic Survey, 200
U.S. Merchant Marine Academy, 202
U.S. Offshore World Championship, 400
U.S. One-Design, 8
Usonia III design studio, 297
Ustane, 419
Utowana, 34, 35
Utzon, Aage, 43, *460*, **460**

Vadura, 327
Vagabond 42, 429
Vagabond, 336
Vagabonde, 135
Vagabonding Under Sail (Crealock), 98
Vagabundo, 55
Vago, 452
Vagrant, 151
Vaitses, Allan, 183
Val II, 466
Val III, 466
Valent, Ron, 262
Valentijn, Johannes W. M., 276, **460–61,** *461*
Valia, 308
Valiant, 360
Valiant (Byrne), 70
Valiant (Derecktor), 119, 120
Valiant (Fox), 156, *157*
Valiant (Stephens), 276
Valiant 40, 359–60, *360*
Valk (Falson) sailing dinghy, 429, *430*
Valkyr, 421
Valkyrie, 476
Valkyrie II, 32, 384, 425, 476, *477*, *32*, 152
Valkyrie III, 32, 325, 476, *477*, *478*, *32*
Valletta, *83*
Valsheda, 321
Valtair, 291
Vamoose, 119
Vampa, 78
Vampire, *418*
Vanadis, 33, 97
Van Blerck, Joe, 422
Vancouver series, 203
Van Den Heede, Jean-Luc, 202
Vanderbilt, Frederick William, 370, 375
Vanderbilt, Harold "Mike," *67*, 68, 113, 436
Vanderbilt, W. K., 70, 71
van der Zee, Wytze, 497
van Deusen, Joseph, 110, 375, **461–62** *461*
Vanguard (Dubois), 128
Vanguard (Lyons), 291
Vanguard 24, 498
Vanite, 349
Vanitie, 67, 167, 169, *169*
Vanity V, 383
Vanja, 277
Van Lent shipyard, 30
Van Oossanen, Peter, 403
Van Patten, Charles Gordon "Doug," *462*, **462**
Van Peteghem, Marc, **462–63,** *463*
Van Peteghem Luriot Prévost (VPLP) Yacht Design, 463
Varna, 411, 412
Varna II, 412
Varunna II, 277
Vasco da Gama Race, 270
Vaton, Gilles, *465*, **465**
Vaurien dinghy, 201, 211
Vaya, 445
Véga (Lawley), 271

Véga (Sahuqué), 398
Vega II, 93
Vela e Motore magazine, 83, 467
Velden, René van der, **465–66,** 465
Velox, 339, *339*
Velsheda, 122, 336
Vendée Globe Challenge, 154, *155,* 202, 250
Vendredi 13, 23
Vendredi Treize, 80
Venezia 42, 250
Venire, 65
Venom, 275
Ventnor Boat Works, 34
Vento Perso, 83
Venture, 271
Venture II, 110
Venus, 145
Vera Mary, 425, *425*
Verbano Royal Yacht Club, 164
Verdier, Guillaume, 154
VERITAS, 11
Veritas, 174
Veronese, Bruno, **466–67,** *466, 467*
Veronica, 327
VersilCraft, 207
Verteidigen, 290
Vertue class, 176, *176,* 177
Vespoli USA, 329
Vespucci, 387
Vesta, 461
Vett, William, 1
Viannay, Philippe, 201
Vickers-Armstrong, 176
Vickers-Supermarine, 395
Victoire 22, 261
Victoria 150, 109
Victoria, Queen of England, 496
Victoria School of Art and Design, 392
Victory 82, 127
Victory class, 169
Victory Lane, 412
Victress, 366
Vienna Model Basin, 180
Vigilant (Fox), 156
Vigilant (Herreshoff), 46, *46,* 219, 425, 476, *477*
Vigilant (McInnis), 308
Vigor, 76
Viking (Frers), 159
Viking (van Deusen), 462
Viking class (Long), 282
Viking class (Riva), 386
Vikingen, 12
Viky II, 24
Ville de Paris, 56
Vim (Gardner), 169
Vim (Herreshoff), *212*
Vim (Stephens), *334,* 336
Vindex (Smith), 419, *419,* 420
Vindex (Young), 497
Vindilis, 69, *70*
Vineyard Interclub, 318
Vingen, 279–80
Vingt-et-Un, 94, 145
Vingt-et-Un II, 94
Vinnia, 245
Viola (Bava), 33
Viola (Fife), *153*

Viola (Inglis), 243
Violetta V, 78
Visiers, Javier, **467–68**
Vision (Byrne), 71
Vision (Herreshoff), 212
Visitor II, 449, *450*
Vistona, 77
Vite, 144
Vitesse (Mower), 318
Vitesse (Seabury), 411
Vitters shipyard, 465
Vixen (Seabury), 411
Vixen (Wiley), 489
Voante, 379
Voile et Voiliers magazine, 467
Volador, 39
Volante (Harvey), 204
Volante (Rhodes), 379
Volante (Wayland), 481
Volpina, 78, *78*
Volpina VI, 78
Voltri, 93
Volunteer (Burgess), 46, 61, 62, 63, 64, 151, 475
Volunteer (Reeks), 376
Volunteer (Ellis), *133,* 134
Volvo Ocean 70, 141
Vom Bug zum Heck (Eichler), 132
Vom Kanu zum kleinen Kreuzer (From Canoe to Small Cruiser, Wustrau), 495
Voogd, Maarten, 416
Voogt Designers, 471
Voortrekker, 431
Voortrekker II, 270
Vorant III, 33
Vorpal Blade, 453
Vosper Thornycroft, 314
Vosper Victory PT boats, 138
Voyager, 311
Voyager catamarans, 485
Voyaging Under Power (Beebe), 36
Vries Lentsch, Gerard de, I, 468, 470
Vries Lentsch, Gerard de, II, 38, 126, 182, 288, 384, **468–70,** *468,* 471
Vries Lentsch, Gerard de, III, 471
Vries Lentsch, Willem de, I, 471
Vries Lentsch, Willem de, II, 226, 430, 465, **470–71,** *470, 471*
Vries Lentsch, Willem de, III, 471, *471*
de Vries shipyard, 30, 386, 470
Vrijheid dinghy, 471
Vril, 150
Vripack Yachting, 51
Vrolijk, Rolf, **250–51,** 394
V.S.D., 253, 415
Vulcan, 200

W72 Offshore Cruising Yacht, 474
Waikiki Surf, 84
Wain shipyard, 460
Wairakei, 29
Wairakei II, 29
Waitangi (Logan), *281,* 282
Waitangi (Reeks), 375
Wakatere Boating Club, 56

Wakatere Canoe Club, 56
Wakaya, 57
Walker, G., 13
Wallstrom, Robert, 54, 288, 296, 381, *472,* **472**
Wally Yachts, 142
Walsh, Matthew Joseph, **472–73** *472*
Walsted, Aage, 338, 483
Walters, Angus, 394
Wanda, 80
Wanderer (Nicol), 336, *336*
Wanderer (Steele), 432
Wanderer II, 176
Wanderer IX, 317
Wannsee, 344
Wapipi, 176
Warden, Bill, 338
Warden, Clarence, 338
Warner, Winthrop L., "Wink,"8, 349, 381, *473,* **473**
Wartsila shipyard, 185
Warwick, Alan Bruce, **473–74,** *474*
Warwick Powercats, 474
Wasp, 80, 219
Wassersport magazine, 494
Watanabe, Shuji, 206, **474**
Waterbed, 60
Waterkampioen magazine, 262
Waterwitch (Fife), 153, 333
Water Witch (Stone), 445, *447*
Waterwitch 30 (Griffiths), 184
Watkins, Bob, 472
Watson, George Lennox, 32–33, 63, 71, 113, 122, 129, 150, 151, 152, 167, 205, 212, 218, 280, 282, 325, 330, 332, 333, 355, 373, 375, 384, 390, 417, 425, 432, *467,* **474–78,** *475, 476, 477, 478*
Watson, G. L. and Company, *see* G. L. Watson and Company
Watson, Thomas, 436, 476
Watts, John Murray, 52, **478–80,** *479*
Waupi, 258
Wauquiez, 491
Wave, 432
wave-form theory, 18, 241
wave-line theory, 241, 394, 395
Waveney II, 305
Waverider, 114
Wayfarer, 55
Wayland, George H., 145, 274, 426, **480–81** *480,*
Ways of the Sea (Davis), 115
W-Boat, 483
Weatherly, 54, 288, 301, 382, *383*
Weaver Associates, 68
Webb, William H., 461
Webber's Cove Boat Yard, 285
Webb Institute (ex-Webb Academy), 82, 104, 136, 213, 285, 288, 301, 353, 358, 462
Weber, Sophus, **481–82** *481*
Wedell-Wedellsborg, Ernst, *482,* **483**
Weekender, 259
Wee Nip, 405
Weenonah II, 265
Weetamoe (Crane), 94, 97, *97,* 436
Weetamoe (Gardner), 168, 175

Welcome, 271
Weld, Phil, 58, 183
Wellington, Duke of, 155
Wells, John H., 388, *483,* **483**
Wells, Theodore, 209
Wenonah, 205, 279
We're Away, 204
Werft, Lürssen, 30
Weser-Jolle boats, 188, *188*
Weser kayaks, 188
Weser Yacht Club, 373
Wesling, 277
Westerly, 308
Westerly Centaur, 179
Westerly Yachts, 128, 179
Western Fairliner, 282
Westin, Karl Zakeus "Zake," 231, **483**
Westland, 315
Westlawn School of Yacht Design, 34, 54, 82, 90, 122, 125, 147, 173, 183, 201, 203, 249, 257, 284, 298, 328, 383, 424, 460, 498
Westmacott, Alfred, **483–84,** *483*
Westmacott, Percy, 483
Westmacott, Stewart and Company, 483
Westsail 32, 17, 22, 98, 360
Westsail 42, 98
Westsail 43, 98
Westward (Herreshoff), 333
Westward (Gardner), 117, *169*
Westwind (Bain), 27
West Wind (Rhodes), 379
West Wind (Woollacott), 494
Westwind class, *27,* 29
Wetona, 14
Wharram, James, **484–85,** *485*
Wharram Wingsail Rig, 484
Whatcom Museum, 200
Wheeler, Cottrell, 20
Wheels, 320
W. Hellman's Memorial Prize, 229
When and If, 8
Whim Wham, 174
Whirl, 348
Whirlpool-Europe 2, 282
Whirlwind (Burgess), 97
Whirlwind (Gilgenast), 180
Whirlwind (Herreshoff), 214, *214,* 216
Whirlwind XII, 228
Whisker, 412
Whisper II, 16
WhisperJet 33, 233
WhisperJet 40, 233
Whisstock's Boatyard, 47
Whistler (Dunbar), 130
Whistler (Hess), 209
Whistle Wing, 74
Whitaker, G. Cecil, 333
Whitaker, Morris M., 389, 457
Whitbread Race, 23, 383, 390, 424, 465
Whitbread Round the World Race, 23, 56, 88, 115, 121, 140, 161, 189, 202, 237, 250, 303, 304, 467
Whitbread/Volvo race, 140
Whitby 42, 54
Whitby 55, 54

Whitby Boat Works, 4
White, Chris, **485–86,** *485*
White, Gerald Taylor, 293, 460
White, Joel, 323, **486–87,** *486, 487*
White, Joel Steven, 487
White, J. S. boatyard, 150
White, Reg, 293
White Bear Lake Yacht Club, 247
White Eel, 49
Whitefin, 256
Whitehawk, 256, 258
White Heather II, 153, 333
White Knuckler, 316
White Orchid, 29
White Rabbit (Carter), 80
White Rabbit (Winch), 492
White Rose, 416
White Squall, 494
White Wings, 487
Whiting, Paul, 227, 390
Whitmore and Holbrook shipbuilders, 272
Whitney, John Jay, 371
Whitney, Payne, 411
Whittelsey and Whitaker, 389
Whitworth, Craig, 127, 275
Whizzbang, 90
Whooper, 176
Wianno Junior, 103
Wianno Senior, 101–3
Wianno Yacht Club, 103
Wierdling, 247
Wilby, Carlton, *488,* **488**
Wilcox, Crittenden and Company, 473
Wild Duck, 64
Wild Horses, 487
Wild Rockett, 23
Wild Thing (Brewer), 54
Wild Thing (Tennant), 454
Wild Venture, 29
Wiley, Ralph Houghton, **488–89,** *489*
Wilhelm II, Kaiser of Germany, 149, 169, 333, 342, 373, 419, 421, 474, 475, 476, 478
William B. Smith Shipyard, 90
William B. Sterns yacht yard, 136
William Cramp and Sons, 389, 478
William Cramp and Sons Ship and Engine Building Company, 34, 94, 104, 265
William Droxford and Son, 32
William H. Brown shipyard, 433
William Robinson Shipyard, 209
Williams, David Alan, 115
Williams, Fenwick Cushing, 8, 216, 240, 363, **489–91,** *489*
Williams, Geoffrey, 87
William Saurin, 253
Williams Company,
  see John M. Williams Company
William Underwood Company, 309
Willing, 277
Wilmington Boat Works (Wilbo), 14, *14,* 117, 301, 369
Wilson, Dorcas, 20
Wilson, John, 338
Wilson, Jon, 108
Wilton, Commodore Lord, 432, 442

Winch, Andrew, 297, **491**
Winchester, 93, *93*
Winde, Louis, 432
Windfall, 357
Windjammer, 319
WindRider trimaran, 58
Windrose, 121, *121*
Windspiels, 190
Windward, 319
Windward Passage, 110, 189, *189*
Windwill, 313
Wings, 383
Winslow, Ralph Eldridge, 8, 310, *492,* **492**
Winsome, 75
Winter Harbor 21–foot class, 66
Wintringham, H. C., 33
Wire, 265
Witchie, 10
Witte Raaf, 226, *226*
Witte Raaf II, 226
Wittholz, Charles W., 8, 381, *493,* **493**
Wittholz 53, 493
Wizard, 270
Wizard of Paget, 160
Wizard Yachts, 274
Woge, 190
Wolf, 66
Wolfson Unit towing tank, 401
Wolverine, 189
Wood, Gar, 423
Wood, Water and Light (Mendlowitz and White), 487
Woodell, Debbie, 237
Woodell, Larry, 237
Wooden Boatbuilding in Britain: A Guide to Designers, Builders, and Suppliers (Oughtred), 348
WoodenBoat magazine, 108, 186, 258, 260, 323, 347, 486
WoodenBoat Publications, 442
WoodenBoat School, 58
Woodnutt's of Bembridge Harbour, 483, 484
Woodpecker, 176
Woods Hole Oceanographic Society, 202
Woodside Graving Dock, 88
Woollacott, Bert Samuel, **493–94,** *494*
World Cat, 84
World Championship (5.5 meter), 403
World Championships, 13, 140, 239, 444
Wormwood, Peter, 362
Worth, Claud, 435, 448
W. P. Stephens Award, 167
Wrecker's Race, 354
Wright, Alan, 270
Wright, Howard, 75
Writings of L. Francis Herreshoff (Herreshoff), 216
Wustrau, Harry, **494–95**
Wyland, G. Gilbert, 68, 288, 301, 439
Wylie, Thomas H., *495,* **495**
Wylie, Tom, 228
Wyliecats, 495, *495*

X-73, 246
X-79, 246
X-99, 246
X-102, 246
Xacobeo, 132
Xargo VI, 132
Xargo VII, 132
Xasteria, 350
X-Dory, 318
Xiphias, 303
XL2, 107
X.Y.16, 109
X-Yachts, 246, *246*

Y-15, 496
Y-19, 496
Y-21, 496
Yacht America, The (Stephens), 442
Yacht Architects, Brokers and Surveyors Association, 76
Yacht Architecture (Kemp), 73, 254, 392
Yacht Building (Marett), 420
Yacht Club de Cannes, 250
Yacht Design Explained (Killing and Hunter), 256
Yacht Designing (Kemp), 73, 254
Yacht Designing and Planning (Chapelle), 81
Yacht Design Institute (YDI), 54, 296, 297, 412, 472
Yacht Designs (Garden), 167
Yacht Designs II (Garden), 167
Yachting (Veronese), 467
Yachting magazine, 4, 10, 20, 37, 47, 82, 104, 159, 161, 189, 202, 258, 264, 301, 319, 344, 370, 379, 381, 435, 436, 457, 473, 492
Yachting History of Japan (Shirasaki), 496
Yachting Memories (Crane), 129
Yachting Monthly magazine, 47, 70, 71, 86, 112, 184, 185, 225, 448, 467
Yachting One-of-a-Kind Regatta, 295
Yachting on a Small Income (Griffiths), 184
Yachting World Light Crest, 159
Yachting World magazine, 53, 83, 87, 135, 189, 225, 314, 332, 342, 418, 467
Yacht magazine, 274, 342
Yacht-Progetto e Costruzione (Veronese), 467
Yacht Racing Association (YRA), 88, 234, 253, 316, 325, 357
Yacht Sales and Service, 173
Yachtsman and Associated Sportsman magazine, 301
Yachts and Yachting magazine, 127, 314
Yachtsman magazine, 70, 262, 357
Yachtsman's Holidays, A (Inglis), 244
Yacht-und Bootsbau (Eichler), 132
Yahama Motor Company, 496
Yah Man, 163
Yakaboo, 147

Yale Scientific School, 478
Yale University, 90, 175, 272
Yamaha, 128
Yampl, 233
Yankee (Herreshoff), 216
Yankee (Paine), 97, 240, 351, *351*
Yankee Girl II, 196
Yankee One-Design, 68
Yarmouth One-Design, 484
Yarrows, 77
Y-Class, 57
Ydra, 80
Yellow Pages Edge, 109
Yellow Pages Endeavour, 108, 109
Yena, 360
Yeoman Class, 59
Yeoman III, 331
Yeoman IX, 331
Yeoman XX, 360
YMS class minesweepers, 104
Yngling class, 277–79
Yokoyama, Akira, *496,* **496**
Yokoyama, Ichiro, **496–97**
Yokohama Boat, 264
Yokoyama Naval Architecture Office, 206, 344, 452
Yonder II, 384
Yorel, 309, *309*
You Are First (Kinney), 258
Young 88, 497
Young, Brian, 327
Young, James, 139, 227, *497,* **497**
Young, Marjorie, 68
Young America, 115, 140, 329, 493
Young Brothers (Maine), 277
Young Brothers Towing Company (Hawaii), 91
YP-66 patrol boat, 288
YP 131, 75
Yucca, 368
Yvonne (Cunningham), 108–9
Yvonne (Logan), *281*

Z-4–Tonner, 70
Zaal, Dirk "Dick," 126, 226, 431, **497–98,** *497*
Zabell, Theresa, 132
Zaida, 8
Zalophus, 175
Zarapico, 145
Zeearend, 436, 470
Zeeschouw, 182
Zeeslang (Sea Snake), 430
Zeevalk (Seahawk), 430, *431*
Zeewijf (Sea-Wife), 430
Zemajteij, 339
Zenith, 152
Zephyr dinghy, 456
Zigeuner, 52, *53*
Zimmer, Nelson, *498,* **498**
Zinnia, 244
Zonnetij, 470
Zoraida, 254
Zorn, Anders, 12
Zugvogel, 274
Zurich, 51, 78
Zurn, Douglas, *498,* **498**
Zurrah, 271
Zyklon, 70